T5-BQA-679

Geschichte – Tradition – Reflexion

Festschrift für Martin Hengel
zum 70. Geburtstag

I

Geschichte – Tradition – Reflexion

Festschrift für Martin Hengel
zum 70. Geburtstag

herausgegeben von

Hubert Cancik
Hermann Lichtenberger
Peter Schäfer

Band I

Judentum

herausgegeben von

Peter Schäfer

J. C. B. Mohr (Paul Siebeck) Tübingen 1996

Die Deutsche Bibliothek – CIP-Einheitsaufnahme

Geschichte – Tradition – Reflexion: Festschrift für Martin Hengel zum 70. Geburtstag / hrsg. von Hubert Cancik ... [Mitarb.-Verz. Alexander, Philip S. ...]. – Tübingen: Mohr.
ISBN 3-16-146401-X
NE: Cancik, Hubert [Hrsg.]; Hengel, Martin: Festschrift

Bd. 1. Judentum / hrsg. von Peter Schäfer. – 1996
ISBN 3-16-146675-6
NE: Schäfer, Peter [Hrsg.]

Der Band wurde von Gulde-Druck in Tübingen aus der Times gesetzt, auf alterungsbeständiges Werkdruckpapier der Papierfabrik Weissenstein in Pforzheim gedruckt und von der Großbuchbinderei Heinr. Koch in Tübingen gebunden.

Vorwort

Diese Festschrift möchten die Herausgeber, Autorinnen und Autoren Martin Hengel in freundschaftlicher Verbundenheit anläßlich der Feier seines siebzigsten Geburtstages am 14. Dezember 1996 widmen.

Martin Hengel wurde an der Grenze des *Imperium Romanum*, in der Provinz *Raetia*, die einst direkt an die *Transpadana* (Italien) grenzte, geboren. Sein Elternhaus stand in Aalen, wo noch in der Spätantike aus den Steinen des Tempels des Jupiter Dolichenus die St. Johannis-Kirche gebaut wurde. Hier wuchs er auf, in einer Welt, in der man „von Kind auf die Heilige Schrift kennt" (2 Tim 3,15), wohlgemerkt, die Schrift des Alten und Neuen Testaments.

Die im Titel der Festschrift genannten Begriffe – Geschichte, Tradition, Reflexion – erschließen, auf je verschiedene Weise, Teile der antiken Religionen: ihren Verlauf, ihre Wirkung und die Theorien, die in und seit der Antike über Religion entwickelt worden sind.

Eine dreibändige Festschrift ist gewiß nicht alltäglich; noch bemerkenswerter ist indes der Umstand, daß diese Bände Beiträge aus drei verschiedenen Fachrichtungen – Judentum, Altertumswissenschaft, Neues Testament – enthalten. Sie sind damit ein Spiegel der Forschungs- und Lehrtätigkeit des Jubilars, der es stets verstanden hat, fächerübergreifend zu arbeiten und zu lehren.

Dies zeigt sich in den großen Werken Martin Hengels, von seiner Dissertation „Die Zeloten" aus dem Jahre 1961 über sein 1969 erstmals erschienenes und auch für künftige Forschergenerationen grundlegendes Werk „Judentum und Hellenismus" bis hin zu dem 1976 veröffentlichten Band „Juden, Griechen und Barbaren". In diesem Zusammenhang seien auch seine Unterstützung des „Lexicon Iconographicum" (LIMC), des „Griechischen Lehrgangs" des Graecisten Günther Zuntz (1983), die Hilfe bei der Ausstattung der „Bibliotheca Classica Petropolitana" und nicht zuletzt die Errichtung der „Philipp-Melanchthon-Stiftung" (1992) als Beispiele seiner weit ausgreifenden wissenschaftlichen und fördernden Tätigkeit genannt.

Bei all den großen Leistungen, die er auf dem Gebiet der Judaistik und der Klassischen Antike erbracht hat, hat er sich immer als Neutestamentler verstanden, dem es darum ging, das Neue im Alten zu entdecken. Es ist darum nicht von ungefähr, daß seine erste Publikation eine neutestamentliche war („Über die Heilungen Jesu", 1959) und er gegenwärtig mit dem zentralen Thema des „vorchristlichen Paulus" beschäftigt ist. Im Zusammenhang mit früheren Paulusstudien erhielt auch die Gestalt des Petrus klarere Konturen, ohne daß Martin Hengel dabei seine Sympathie für den Herrenbruder Jakobus verloren hätte. Im Mittelpunkt der Auseinandersetzung der letzten Jahre steht sein Lösungsversuch der „johanneischen Frage" (1993).

Nicht weniger wichtig sind die von ihm in Zusammenarbeit mit Kollegen verschiedener Fachrichtungen herausgegebenen Reihen, die „Texte und Studien zum antiken Judentum", die „Übersetzung des Talmud Yerushalmi", die „Arbeiten zur Geschichte des antiken Judentums und des Urchristentums" und die „Wissenschaftlichen Untersuchungen zum Neuen Testament", Reihen, die schon längst zu den bedeutendsten auf ihrem Gebiet geworden sind.

In allen genannten Bereichen förderte Martin Hengel den Kontakt mit Wissenschaftlern und Forschungseinrichtungen innerhalb und außerhalb Deutschlands, vor allem auch in Israel, und hat damit Wege für eine künftige Zusammenarbeit eröffnet. Seine besondere Gabe des Ratens ist anderen auf ihren beruflichen und persönlichen Wegen stets zugute gekommen. Bei all seinen wissenschaftlichen Arbeiten und Funktionen ist er immer auch Begleiter und Seelsorger gewesen und ist es bis heute geblieben.

Unter den vielen Mitarbeitern und Mitarbeiterinnen, die diese drei Bände redigiert haben, seien für den ersten Band Dr. Hans-Jürgen Becker, Dr. Klaus Herrmann, Dr. Dr. Catherine Hezser, Dr. Martin Jacobs, Sabine Kößling und Gerold Necker (Berlin) erwähnt. Für Hilfe bei der Redaktion des zweiten Bandes ist Christine Baatz (Tübingen) besonders zu danken. Am dritten Band sind Dr. Drs. Gerbern S. Oegema sowie Monika Merkle (Tübingen) maßgeblich beteiligt gewesen. Ilse König und Matthias Spitzner vom Verlag Mohr-Siebeck sei für Mühe und Sorgfalt bei der Herstellung der Bände gedankt. Georg Siebeck hat als Verleger diesem Projekt jede Unterstützung zuteil werden lassen.

Schließlich ist diese Festschrift vor allem ein Zeichen des Dankes verbunden mit dem Wunsch, daß es Martin Hengel und seiner Frau weiterhin wohl ergehen möge.

Tübingen und Berlin im Oktober 1996

Hubert Cancik   Hermann Lichtenberger   Peter Schäfer

Table of Contents

Preface V

List of Contributors XV

I. Bible Interpretation and Archaeology

James H. Charlesworth
Archaeological Research and Biblical Theology 3

Rudolf Smend
Israelitische und Jüdische Geschichte. Zur Entstehung
von Julius Wellhausens Buch 35

Hans-Jürgen Hermisson
Gottesknecht und Gottes Knechte. Zur ältesten Deutung
eines deuterojesajanischen Themas 43

Hartmut Gese
Zur Komposition des Koheletbuches 69

Alan F. Segal
The Akedah: Some Reconsiderations 99

II. Jewish People in the Graeco-Roman World

Leo Mildenberg
yĕhūd und *šmryn*. Über das Geld der persischen Provinzen Juda
und Samaria im 4. Jahrhundert 119

Aryeh Kasher
Hecataeus of Abdera on Mosollamus the Jewish Mounted Archer
(Contra Apionem, I, 200–204) 147

Carl R. Holladay
The Textual Tradition of Pseudo-Orpheus: Walter or Riedweg? 159

ROBERT HANHART
Zur Vorgeschichte von Israels status confessionis in hellenistischer Zeit 181

ALBERT I. BAUMGARTEN
Invented Traditions of the Maccabean Era 197

SHAYE J. D. COHEN
Ioudaios: „Judaean“ and „Jew“ in Susanna, First Maccabees, and Second Maccabees 211

TAL ILAN
Josephus and Nicolaus on Women 221

DANIEL R. SCHWARTZ
God, Gentiles, and Jewish Law: On Acts 15 and Josephus' Adiabene Narrative 263

WILLIAM HORBURY
The Beginnings of the Jewish Revolt under Trajan 283

TESSA RAJAK
Benefactors in the Greco-Jewish Diaspora 305

III. Qumran and New Testament

SHEMARYAHU TALMON
The Essential 'Community of the Renewed Covenant': How should Qumran Studies Proceed? 323

EMANUEL TOV
The Socio-Religious Background of the Paleo-Hebrew Biblical Texts Found at Qumran 353

GEZA VERMES
The Leadership of the Qumran Community: Sons of Zadok – Priests – Congregation 375

PHILIP S. ALEXANDER
Physiognonomy, Initiation, and Rank in the Qumran Community 385

DAVID FLUSSER
Die Gesetzeswerke in Qumran und bei Paulus 395

CHRISTOPHER ROWLAND
Apocalyptic, Mysticism, and the New Testament 405

DORON MENDELS
Pagan or Jewish? The Presentation of Paul's Mission
in the Book of Acts 431

STEFAN SCHREINER
Ibn Kammûnas Verteidigung des historischen Jesus
gegen den paulinischen Christus 453

IV. Rabbinic Judaism, Early Jewish Mysticism and Gnosticism

AHARON OPPENHEIMER
Tannaitic Benei Beraq: A Peripheral Centre of Learning 483

MARTIN GOODMAN
The Function of Minim in Early Rabbinic Judaism 501

GÜNTER STEMBERGER
Die innerrabinische Überlieferung von Mischna Abot 511

JARL FOSSUM
The Adorable Adam of the Mystics and the Rebuttals of the Rabbis . . 529

PETER SCHÄFER
Jewish Liturgy and Magic 541

JOSEPH DAN
Yaldabaoth and the Language of the Gnostics 557

SCHALOM BEN-CHORIN
Leib und Leiblichkeit im Judentum 565

Index of Sources 573

Index of Subjects 595

Greek Terms 600

Hebrew Terms 601

Index of Modern Authors 603

Contents of Volumes II and III

Volume II
Griechische und Römische Religion

I. Geschichte der antiken Religionen

WALTER BURKERT
„Mein Gott?“ Persönliche Frömmigkeit und unverfügbare Götter

ERIKA SIMON
Philoktetes – ein kranker Heros

WOLFGANG FAUTH
Salutatio Solis orientis. Zu einer Form der Heliolatrie bei Pythagoreern, Manichäern, Therapeuten und Essenern

KLAUS THRAEDE
Merkwürdiger Janus. Mit einem Beitrag von Dieter Steinbauer

HILDEGARD CANCIK-LINDEMAIER
Der Diskurs Religion im Senatsbeschluß über die Bacchanalia von 186 v. Chr. und bei Livius (B. XXXIX)

FRANK KOLB
Antiochia in der frühen Kaiserzeit

HANS DIETER BETZ
Heroenverehrung und Christusglaube. Religionsgeschichtliche Beobachtungen zu Philostrats *Heroicus*

WOLFGANG SPEYER
Die Vorzeichen im Bibelgedicht des Dracontius

CARSTEN COLPE
Die Barbarisierung der Weisheit. Eindeutige Belebung von Begriffen – Konstruktion mehrdeutiger Sexualität – Vieldeutige theopoietische Fiktionen

II. Antike Reflexion auf Religion

ALBRECHT DIHLE
Die Theologia tripertita bei Augustin

ALEXANDER ZAJCEV
Aischylos und die monotheistischen Gedanken bei den Griechen

ALEXANDER GAVRILOV
Sizilische Katastrophe und Euripideische Götter

HERMANN STEINTHAL
Platons anthropologische Theologie – aus der Ferne betrachtet

THOMAS ALEXANDER SZLEZÁK
‚Menschliche' und ‚göttliche' Darlegung. Zum ‚theologischen' Aspekt des Redens und Schreibens bei Platon

JÖRG RÜPKE
Innovationsmechanismen kultischer Religionen. Sakralrecht im Rom der Republik

ERNST A. SCHMIDT
Römische Theologie in der Odusia des Livius Andronicus

HUBERT CANCIK
„Nicht blieb übrig für die Verehrung der Götter." Historische Reflexion über Herrscherverehrung bei Tacitus

PIETER W. VAN DER HORST
Maximus of Tyre on Prayer. An Annotated Translation of Εἰ δεῖ εὔχεσθαι *(Dissertatio 5)*

GUY G. STROUMSA
Philosophy of the Barbarians. On Early Christian Ethnological Representations

III. Tradition und Wissenschaftsgeschichte

JÜRGEN MALITZ
Mommsen, Caesar und die Juden

WOLFGANG SCHULLER
Dennoch die Schwerter halten. Der κατέχων Carl Schmitts

Volume III
Frühes Christentum

I. Das Neue Testament und seine Umwelt

Otto Betz
Jesus und Jesaja 53

Helmut Merklein
Ägyptische Einflüsse auf die messianische Sohn-Gottes-Aussage des Neuen Testaments

Petr Pokorný
Antigone und Jesus (Opfer und Hoffnung)

Hans-Josef Klauck
Die kleinasiatischen Beichtinschriften und das Neue Testament

Marc Philonenko
Les paroles de Jésus contre »cette génération« et la tradition quomrânienne

James D. G. Dunn
Two Covenants or One? The Interdependence of Jewish and Christian Identity

II. Evangelien und Apostelgeschichte

Frans Neirynck
The Sayings Source Q and the Gospel of Mark

Lars Hartman
Das Markusevangelium, „für die lectio sollemnis im Gottesdienst abgefaßt"?

Max Wilcox
On the Ransom-Saying in Mark 10:45c, Matt 20:28c

David E. Aune
Luke 20:34–36: A „Gnosticized" Logion of Jesus?

Christian Dietzfelbinger
Aspekte des Alten Testaments im Johannesevangelium

Michael Theobald
Der Jünger, den Jesus liebte. Beobachtungen zum narrativen Konzept der johanneischen Redaktion

Etienne Trocmé
L'arrière-plan du récit johannique de l'Expulsion des marchands du Temple (Jean 2,13–22)

Marinus de Jonge
Jesus' Rôle in the Final Breakthrough of God's Kingdom

JOHN J. COLLINS
Jesus and the Messiahs of Israel

ALEXANDER J. M. WEDDERBURN
Zur Frage der Gattung der Apostelgeschichte

GERD THEISSEN
Hellenisten und Hebräer (Apg. 6,1 ff.). Gab es eine Spaltung der Urgemeinde?

III. Paulus (und Deuteropaulinen)

HARALD RIESENFELD
Die transzendente Dimension des neutestamentlichen Kirchenbegriffs

ERNST BAASLAND
ἀνάγκη bei Paulus im Lichte eines stoischen Paradoxes

KLAUS HAACKER
Der „Antinomismus" des Paulus im Kontext antiker Gesetzestheorie

CHRISTOPH BURCHARD
Nicht aus Werken des Gesetzes gerecht, sondern aus Glauben an Jesus Christus – seit wann?

FRIEDRICH LANG
Paulus und seine Gegner in Korinth und in Galatien

MORNA D. HOOKER
1 Thessalonians 1.9–10: a Nutshell – but What Kind of Nnut?

HOWARD MARSHALL
Salvation in the Pastoral Epistles

IV. Johannesoffenbarung

OTTO BÖCHER
Hellenistisches in der Apokalypse des Johannes

PEDER BORGEN
Emperor Worship and Persecution in Philo's *In Flaccum* and *De Legatione ad Gaium* and the Revelation of John

OTFRIED HOFIUS
Das Zeugnis der Johannesoffenbarung von der Gottheit Jesu Christi

PETER STUHLMACHER
Das Lamm Gottes – eine Skizze

V. Alte Kirche

CHARLES KINGSLEY BARRETT
The End of Acts

SIR HENRY CHADWICK
Disagreement and the Ancient Church

JOHANNES PANAGOPOULOS
Sache und Energie. Zur theologischen Grundlegung der biblischen Hermeneutik bei den griechischen Kirchenvätern

OSKAR SKARSAUNE
Judaism and Hellenism in Justin Martyr, Elucidated From His Portrait of Socrates

PIERRE PRIGENT
Les premières représentations de Dieu dans l'iconographie chrétienne

FRANÇOIS BOVON
Ces chrétiens qui rêvent. L'autorité du rêve dans les premiers siècles du christianisme

VI. Forschungsgeschichtliches

BIRGER GERHARDSSON
Anton Fridrichsen, Rudolf Bultmann, Form Criticism and Hermeneutics

ERICH GRÄSSER
„Die ethische Denk-Religion". Albert Schweitzers Ablehnung einer doppelten Wahrheit

Schriftenverzeichnis Martin Hengel

List of Contributors

ALEXANDER, Philip S., University of Manchester, Great Britain, *1:385*

AUNE, David, Loyola University, Chicago, Illinois, USA, *3:187*

BAASLAND, Ernst, Det Teologiske Menighetsfakultet, Oslo, Norway, *3:357*

BARRETT, Charles Kingsley, University of Durham, Great Britain, *3:545*

BAUMGARTEN, Albert I., Bar Ilan University, Ramat Gan, Israel, *1:197*

BEN-CHORIN, Schalom, Jerusalem, Israel, *1:565*

BETZ, Hans Dieter, University of Chicago, Illinois, USA, *2:119*

BETZ, Otto, Universität Tübingen, Germany, *3:3*

BÖCHER, Otto, Universität Mainz, Germany, *3:473*

BORGEN, Peder, University of Trondheim, Norway, *3:493*

BOVON, François, Université de Genève, Switzerland, and Harvard University, Cambridge, Massachusetts, USA, *3:631*

BURCHARD, Christian, Universität Heidelberg, Germany, *3:405*

BURKERT, Walter, Universität Zürich, Switzerland, *2:3*

CANCIK, Hubert, Universität Tübingen, Germany, *2:305*

CANCIK-LINDEMAIER, Hildegard, Tübingen, Germany, *2:77*

CHADWICK, Sir Henry, The University of Oxford, Great Britain, *3:557*

CHARLESWORTH, James H., Princeton Theological Seminary, New York, New York, USA, *1:3*

COHEN, Shaye J. D., Brown University, Providence, Rhode Island, USA, *1:211*

COLLINS, John J., University of Chicago, USA, *3:287*

COLPE, Carsten, Freie Universität Berlin, Germany, *2:155*

DAN, Joseph, The Hebrew University, Jerusalem, Israel, and Freie Universität Berlin, Germany, *1:557*

DE JONGE, Marinus, Rijks-Universiteit Leiden, Netherlands, *3:265*

DIETZFELBINGER, Christian, Universität Tübingen, Germany, *3:203*

DIHLE, Albrecht, Universität Heidelberg, Germany, *2:183*

DUNN, James D. G., University of Durham, Great Britain, *3:97*

FAUTH, Wolfgang, Universität Göttingen, Germany, *2:41*

FLUSSER, David, The Hebrew University, Jerusalem, Israel, *1:395*

FOSSUM, Jarl, University of Michigan, Ann Arbor, Michigan, USA, *1:529*

GAVRILOV, Alexander, Akademie der Wissenschaften, St. Petersburg, Russia, *2:213*

GERHARDSSON, Birger, Lunds Universitet, Sweden, *3:657*

GESE, Hartmut, Universität Tübingen, Germany, *1:69*

GOODMAN, Martin, The University of Oxford, Great Britain, *1:501*

GRÄSSER, Erich, Universität Bonn, Germany, *3:677*

HAACKER, Klaus, Kirchliche Hochschule Wuppertal, Germany, *3:387*

HANHART, Robert, Universität Göttingen, Germany, *1:181*

HARTMAN, Lars, Uppsala Universitet, Sweden, *3:147*

HERMISSON, Hans-Jürgen, Universität Tübingen, Germany, *1:43*

HOFIUS, Otfried, Universität Tübingen, Germany, *3:511*

HOLLADAY, Carl R., Emory University, Atlanta, Georgia, USA, *1:159*

HOOKER, Morna D., University of Cambridge, Great Britain, *3:435*

HORBURY, William, The Corpus Christi College, Cambridge, Great Britain, *1:283*

ILAN, Tal, The Hebrew University, Jerusalem, Israel, *1:221*

KASHER, Aryeh, Tel-Aviv University, Tel-Aviv, Israel, *1:147*

KLAUCK, Hans-Josef, Universität Würzburg, Germany, *3:63*

KOLB, Frank, Universität Tübingen, Germany, *2:97*

LANG, Friedrich, Universität Tübingen, Germany, *3:417*

MALITZ, Jürgen, Katholische Universität Eichstätt, Germany, *2:371*

MARSHALL, Howard L., University of Aberdeen, Great Britain, *3:449*

MENDELS, Doron, The Hebrew University, Jerusalem, Israel, *1:431*

MERKLEIN, Helmut, Universität Bonn, Germany, *3:21*

MILDENBERG, Leo, Zürich, Switzerland, *1:119*

NEIRYNCK, Frans, Katholieke Universiteit Leuven, Belgium, *3:125*

OPPENHEIMER, Aharon, Tel-Aviv University, Tel-Aviv, Israel, *1:483*

PANAGOPOULOS, Johannes, University of Athens, Greece, *3:567*

PHILONENKO, Marc, Université des Sciences Humaines de Strasbourg, France, *3:89*

POKORNÝ, Petr, Karls-Universität Prag, Czech Republic, *3:49*

PRIGENT, Pierre, Université des Sciences Humaines de Strasbourg, France, *3:613*

RAJAK, Tessa, University of Reading, Whiteknights, Great Britain, *1:305*

RIESENFELD, Harald, Uppsala Universitet, Sweden, *3:347*

ROWLAND, Christopher, The University of Oxford, Great Britain, *1:405*

RÜPKE, Jörg, Universität Potsdam, Germany, *2:265*

SCHÄFER, Peter, Freie Universität Berlin, Germany, *1:541*

SCHMIDT, Ernst A., Universität Tübingen, Germany, *2:287*

SCHREINER, Stefan, Universität Tübingen, Germany, *1:453*

SCHULLER, Wolfgang, Universität Konstanz, Germany, *2:389*

SCHWARTZ, Daniel R., The Hebrew University, Jerusalem, Israel, *1:263*

SEGAL, Alan F., Barnard College, Columbia University, New York City, USA, *1:99*

SIMON, Erika, Universität Würzburg, Germany, *2:15*

SKARSAUNE, Oskar, Det Teologiske Menighetsfakultet, Oslo, Norway, *3:585*

SMEND, Rudolf, Universität Göttingen, Germany, *1:35*

SPEYER, Wolfgang, Universität Salzburg, Austria, *2:141*

STEINTHAL, Hermann, Universität Tübingen, Germany, *2:233*

STEMBERGER, Günter, Universität Wien, Austria, *1:511*

STROUMSA, Guy G., The Hebrew University, Jerusalem, Israel, *2:339*

STUHLMACHER, Peter, Universität Tübingen, Germany, *3:529*

SZLEZÁK, Thomas, Universität Tübingen, Germany, *2:251*

TALMON, Shemaryahu, The Hebrew University, Jerusalem, Israel, *1:323*

THEISSEN, Gerd, Universität Heidelberg, Germany, *3:323*

THEOBALD, Michael, Universität Tübingen, Germany, *3:219*

THRAEDE, Klaus, Universität Regensburg, Germany, *2:55*

TOV, Emanuel, The Hebrew University, Jerusalem, Israel, *1:353*

TROCMÉ, Etienne, Université des Sciences Humaines de Strasbourg, France, *3:257*

VAN DER HORST, Pieter W., Universiteit Utrecht, Netherlands, *2:323*

VERMES, Geza, The University of Oxford, Great Britain, *1:375*

WEDDERBURN, Alexander J. M., Universität München, Germany, *3:303*

WILCOX, Max, Cammeray, Australien, *3:173*

ZAJCEV, Alexander, Universität St. Petersburg, Russia, *2:203*

I. Bible Interpretation and Archaeology

Archaeological Research and Biblical Theology

by

James H. Charlesworth

For decades historians, biblical scholars, and theologians have pondered how – if at all – archaeology may be important for their work. Questions have proliferated, including the following that are significant for readers of the Hengel Festschrift[1]: Are the patriarchal narratives "a glorified mirage," as J. Wellhausen concluded,[2] replete with "facts" as conservative critics claim, or much later accounts that intermittently preserve very ancient traditions? Is there any truth to the biblical story of the "conquest" of the Land under Joshua? Do the Dead Sea Scrolls indicate that Jesus' life can be explained in light of these documents? Do most aspects of Jesus derive from Christian apologetics and polemics? Is there any archaeological evidence that might add credence to the earliest extended narrative in the New Testament, the so-called passion narrative? Are archaeological discoveries in the "Holy Land" irrelevant for seminary and university professors and students and also for graduates of such institutions of higher learning,[3] or are they necessary to "shore up" the Bible – as some journalists claim?

---

[1] It is an honor to be invited to contribute to Martin Hengel's Festschrift. He has been a confidant and mentor for decades, and he has helped revolutionize the study of the New Testament and Christian Origins in the aftermath of Bultmann's overemphasis on the existential portrayal of New Testament Theology and pejorative denigration of acquiring historical knowledge of Jesus. Against the great scholar Bultmann, I have long sided with Hengel in perceiving Jesus as a Jew who was an eschatologically charismatic prophet and teacher who begins and grounds New Testament thought, and is not the presupposition of the theologies in the New Testament. Hengel's interest in archaeology and the social dimensions of the Palestinian Jesus Movement, as well as his insistence that Jesus Research is profitable and essential, is evident in his numerous books, notably in his The Charismatic Leader and His Followers, trans. J.C.G. Greig (Edinburgh 1981), and in his Zur urchristlichen Geschichtsschreibung (Stuttgart 1984 [2nd ed.]).

[2] J. Wellhausen, Prolegomena zur Geschichte Israels, 6th ed. (Berlin 1927) p. 316. ET = Prolegomena to the History of Ancient Israel (New York 1957) pp. 318–19; also see H. Gunkel, The Legends of Genesis, trans. W.H. Carruth (New York 1964 [original in 1901]).

[3] I shall be using intermittently the term "Holy Land," although it is anathema in some academic communities in which I frequent, because this article is focused on reviewing The New Encyclopedia of Archaeological Excavations in the Holy Land. While the term is loaded for some scholars it is appropriate for this article, since I am also seeking to discern how

Recognizing that the last question especially poses false alternatives, let us explore some of the questions forced upon us by such interesting, and perhaps challenging perspectives as these:

- Acknowledging the theological importance of the Exodus-Wandering-Conquest, it is a challenge to theologians to learn that Jericho was no longer a walled city during the Late Bronze Age (c. 1550–1200 B.C.E.) when Joshua successfully led the Hebrews into the land promised to Abraham and his descendants.[4]
- Indeed, archaeologists have shown that there is no coherent pattern of conquest as in the biblical traditions.
- Nothing remains of Solomon's Temple except one tiny (4.3 cm. high) extremely valuable ivory pomegranate.
- The Dead Sea Scrolls, on the one hand help prove the accurate transmission of Isaiah, but on the other hand indicate that the Hebrew texts of Jeremiah and I and II Samuel found in the Qumran caves challenge the choice of basing our translations only on the Massoretic Text.[5]
- While artifacts and ruins have been found in Bethlehem, Nazareth, and Cana nothing has been found there that can be traced back to the first-century accounts of Jesus' life.
- First-century synagogues have been found in the Land but none of them are ones in which Jesus taught according to the New Testament.[6]

It is obvious that the failure to discover evidence must not be confused with the

---

archaeology may be significant for the theological study of both the Old and the New Testaments.

[4] Jericho was not abandoned and unoccupied in the 14th century (Late Bronze Age), but it ceased to be fortified with walls. See T. A. HOLLAND, "Jericho," The Anchor Bible Dictionary (1992) 3.723–37.

[5] See F.M. CROSS, The Ancient Library of Qumran & Modern Biblical Studies (Grand Rapids, Michigan: Baker Book House, 1961 [revised edition]), pp. 179, 186–87. See the new edition of this work (Minneapolis 1995), and Cross' contributions to the recent volumes of DJD. Also helpful is H. SCANLIN's The Dead Sea Scrolls & Modern Translations of the Old Testament (Wheaton, Illinois 1993). Authoritative, including the wider range of manuscripts available for discerning the "Old Testament," is J. A. SANDERS, "Understanding the Development of the Biblical Text," in The Dead Sea Scrolls After Forty Years, ed. H. Shanks (Washington, D.C.: Biblical Archaeology Society, 1991) pp. 56–73. Also essential for research are the contributions to The Community of the Renewed Covenant: The Notre Dame Symposium on the Dead Sea Scrolls, ed. E. ULRICH and J. VANDERKAM (Notre Dame 1994) esp. see the publications by Ulrich and E. Tov.

[6] See Y. TSAFRIR, "The Synagogue at Meroth, the Synagogue at Capernaum, and the Dating of the Galilean Synagogues: A Reconsideration," Eretz Israel 20 (1989) 337–44 [in Hebrew], and A. Kasher, A. Oppenheimer, U. Rappaport, eds., Synagogues in Antiquity (Jerusalem 1987 [in Hebrew]). In the latter L. I. Levine argues, *inter alia*, that the synagogue became a place for "regular communal" prayer only after the destruction of the Temple. S. SAFRAI considers the effect of the Temple on the synagogue, reflecting why after 70 C.E. the fundamental elements of Temple worship and the power of the priests were never transferred to the synagogue.

assumption that no evidences ever existed. As K. A. Kitchen states, thinking about the absence of the patriarchs' names in extra-biblical sources, "Absence of evidence is *not* evidence of absence."[7] Archaeologists have methodologies for assessing only what can be seen, touched, or imaginatively reconstructed when guided by ruins, artifacts, or mere shadows and outlines from the past. In evaluating "biblical archaeology" we must be alert not to succumb to passions to recreate the past out of presuppositions that may be whimsical imaginings, and we must also keep in mind the different methodologies and agendas of archaeology and theology.[8]

The science of "biblical archaeology" is severely criticized as a discipline in many centers of higher learning.[9] This fact along with the recognition that we are blest by phenomenal archaeological discoveries that may be related in some way with the Bible indicate that now is a propitious time to evaluate such discoveries and reflect on their relevance, if any, for a reassessment of the theologies in the Bible. Our thoughts will be focused and stimulated by the publication of the major encyclopedia on the subject: *The New Encyclopedia of Archaeological Excavations in the Holy Land* (NEAEH).[10] The timeliness of this evaluation became even more apparent while I was completing this review article in honor of Hengel; the cover of *U. S. News & World Report* of April 17, 1995, contained a picture of the Bible, a rolled map, a pick, and these highlighted words: "Solving the Mysteries of the Bible – Archaeology's Amazing Finds in the Holy Land."

---

7 K. A. Kitchen, "The Patriarchal Age: Myth or History?" Biblical Archaeology Review 21.2 (1995) 50.

8 See especially the comments by B. W. Anderson, J. Aviram, C. Epstein, I. Finkelstein, P. J. King, H. Koester, M. Mansoor, A. Mazar, Y. Meshorer, K. N. Schoville, P. Wapnish, D. Ussishkin, B. G. Wood, and E. Yamauchi in "Scholars Speak Out," Biblical Archaeology Review 21.3 (1995) 24–35.

9 A presupposition of The New Encyclopedia of Archaeological Excavations in the Holy Land is that one should be allowed to talk about *biblical theology*. In the "Introduction to the English Edition," N. A. Silberman reports that among the "intellectual rationales" for archaeological excavations in the Holy Land is "the search for biblical sites and monuments as a material reaffirmation of biblical belief" (1.x).

10 Ephraim Stern, ed., Ayelet Lewinson-Gilboa, assistant ed., and Joseph Aviram, editorial director, The New Encyclopedia of Archaeological Excavations in the Holy Land, 4 vols (New York 1993) pp. xxii + 1,552. $375. The four volumes are numbered consecutively: vol. 1, pp. 1–383, vol. 2, pp. 385(*sic*)–804, vol. 3, pp. 805–1180, vol. 4, pp. 1181–1552. I will cite these volumes as 1.383 which denotes vol. 1, p. 383. Recognizing Hengel's skill in drawing attention to major publications in notes that guide the reader to avenues for more intensive research, I have added some notes that will draw attention to publications that postdate the NEAEH. Archaeological research advances so rapidly that it is never possible to publish the *status quaestionis*. Only in Jerusalem in academic or confidential discussions shared *viva voce* are the latest discoveries evaluated; that is one reason I find it necessary to be in Jerusalem about three times a year. A helpful guide to the publications in Biblical Archaeology Review is H. Shanks, ed., 20 Year Index: 1975–1994: Title, Author and Subject (Washington, D.C.: Biblical Archaeology Society, 1995).

I shall review these four volumes enlightened by the limits and non-theological methods and concerns of the new archaeology. We thus should ponder such widely held conclusions as these: The correlation the Albright School expected to find between archaeological excavations and the biblical accounts has been a disappointment to many biblical theologians. Early Israelite pottery is singularly inferior artistically to that produced by the Philistines, Canaanites, and especially Edomites. The infancy gospels of Matthew and Luke introduce us not to scientific historiography but to kerygmatic christology. The garden tomb cannot be the place in which Jesus was buried. While the archaeological discoveries from circa 1,000 B.C.E. to 135 C.E. prove the successive incursions into the "Holy Land" from Egypt, Assyria,[11] Babylonia, Persia, Greece, Rome, and elsewhere, I am persuaded the emphasis remains on the indigenous nature of Israelites and Jews; otherwise we could not understand the catalyst for the numerous wars and revolts,[12] and in ancient Palestine the preponderance of Hebrew inscriptions, letters, and scrolls.

In the four volumes of the NEAEH one will be introduced to the stunning and exciting discoveries in a land revered as sacred by Jews, Christians, and Muslims. There are historical *realia* dating from at least circa 8,000 B.C.E. (the Pre-pottery Neolithic Tower in Jericho [see the photograph in 2.676], one of the oldest cities in the world) until at least the Arab rulers' or Pashas' 18th century C.E. walls, mosque, and bath at Acco (1.17, 31). Of course, if one is interested in pre-history in the Levant there is evidence, such as an elephant's skull and intricate cave drawings that can be traced back virtually 1.77 million years, specifically at the Acheulean site of Gesher Benot Ya^{c}aqov and the Geulah Cave on Mt. Carmel.[13] The wealth of information provided in these four volumes is invaluable and clear.

The work includes not only archaeological sites in Israel but also some in

[11] Thus, for example, the name of the prophet Habakkuk is an Akkadian loanword for a garden plant (*ḫabbaququ*), thereby indicating, as J.J.M. Roberts states, "Assyria's domination of Palestine since the late eighth century" (p.86). ROBERTS, Nahum, Habakkuk, and Zephaniah: A Commentary (The Old Testament Library; Louisville 1991).

[12] The reasons for revolting were numerous, and probably never crystal clear to the revolutionaries. Some revolted because they liked action, others because they were excited by some Roman soldiers' activity, others because of subjugation and the spirit of freedom in Judaism, others because friends were involved, and for various other obvious reasons. HENGEL points out that the most impressive aspect of the "attempts made in Palestine to achieve freedom since the end of the Hasmonean dynasty was that they were fragmented and lacked unity." The Zealots, trans. D. Smith (Edinburgh 1989), p.329.

[13] See also the discussions of the following: the Kebara Cave on the western slope of the Carmel Ridge (which revealed human occupation dating back to 64,000 B.C.), the El-Wad Cave, the largest of the Carmel caves which contained layers of human life back to circa 45,000 B.C., and the Tabum Cave twelve miles south of Haifa, which preserved evidence of human habitation from about 500,000 B.C. to roughly 50,000 B.C., which makes it "one of the longest archaeological sequences known at any site" (4.1433).

Egypt (in the Sinai and the Negev)[14] and those in Jordan.[15] The majestic monuments at Jerash, which rival Pompeii, are impressively discussed (2.470–79). The beautiful mosaic in the church at Medeba (Madaba) is attractively presented and illustrated (3.992–1001). Pella receives a masterful examination, and Eusebius' report (*HE* 5.2–3) that "Christians" fled there in 70 C.E. is endorsed (3.1175). Petra is given ample coverage (4.1181–93),[16] but it is disappointing to observe that while numerous universities and seminaries are credited elsewhere in the volumes the excavation of the theater at Petra is discussed without acknowledging that it was sponsored by Princeton Theological Seminary.[17] Rabbath Ammon (=Amman) is presented so that the archaeological remains help us understand the background of many biblical narratives (4.1243–52).

The Old Testament

In NEAEH the reader will find data to help comprehend how and in what ways the biblical account of the Exodus and Conquest should be understood. Excavations of Jericho, Ai, Lachish, and other tells do not provide evidence of a conquest as that described in the Pentateuch.[18] They rather stimulate reflections on how Israelite and Judean authors recorded the way those who felt chosen celebrated their experience of the God with whom they had covenanted and recited, often liturgically, how the patriarchs had walked on earth in history (see the concluding portion of this article).

---

[14] The discussion of St. Catherine's Monastery is inadequate. For sophisticated discussions see K. A. Manafis, ed., Sinai: Treasures of the Monastery of Saint Catherine (Athens 1990). In addition to my monograph of the 1975 discoveries in St. Catherine's Monastery see the two official publications: J. E. Meimaris, with His Eminence Archbishop Damianos, Catalogue of the Newly Discovered Arabic Manuscripts in St. Catherine's Monastery at Mount Sinai (Athens 1985) and I. C. Tarnanidis, The Slavonic Manuscripts Discovered in 1975 at St Catherine's Monastery on Mount Sinai (Thessaloniki 1988). I wish to express my gratitude to His Eminence Archbishop Damianos for the gift of these two books, and for his confiding in me regarding the manuscripts and portions of manuscripts that were found in 1975.

[15] For bibliographical assistance to Jordan archaeology, see D. Homès-Fredericq and J. B. Hennessy, with F. Zayadine, Archaeology of Jordan (Akkadica Suppl 3; Leuven 1986).

[16] See also the spectacularly illustrated *Petra*, written and photographed by Jane Taylor, with a Foreword by H. M. King Hussein (London 1993).

[17] Contrast The Archaeological Encyclopedia of the Holy Land, 3rd ed., ed. A. Negev (New York 1986, 1990): "In 1962–3 the Roman theater was excavated by the Theological Seminary of Princeton under the direction of P. Hammond Jr." (p. 293). W. O. Harris, Head of Archives and Special Collections at Princeton Theological Seminary, informs me that P. C. Hammond was an Assistant Professor of Old Testament at Princeton Theological Seminary from 1961–1966; that is during the time of the excavation of Petra's theater.

[18] Here I tend to side with Y. Aharoni against Y. Yadin; yet, I am not convinced that we can talk about a peaceful settlement without some qualifications.

Jerusalem is discussed with depth and impressively illustrated, especially the history of over three thousand years, from before King David to the present.[19] This city, before David called it "the City of David," has been called "Rushalimum," "Urusalim," "Urusilimmu," and "Jebus." *Yrw* plus *šlm*, we are told, means "Foundation of (the God) Shalem." In Ugarit Shalem denotes one of the alleged beautiful and gracious gods. That is, Shaleim, "Twilight"; the other one is called Shaḥar, "Dawn." There is no reason, however, to imagine some link between the phenomenon that gave rise to the concept "Shaḥar" and the not yet published "Sons of the Dawn" (*bny šḥr*) text among the Dead Sea Scrolls.[20]

While Israel was separated from the East by a vast desert that was tedious to cross, it was connected with the West and Egypt by efficient maritime routes over the Great Sea (the Mediterranean), long before Augustus' defeat of the pirates. Thus, it is informative to learn that in 1985 an ancient boat was found twenty-two miles south of Haifa at Maᶜagan Mikha'el just off the Mediterranean coast (3.918–19). It dates from the end of the fifth century B.C.E. and possessed a loading capacity of 13 tons. Among the artifacts found with it is the shipwright's tool kit and its contents.

Ancient Israel frequently had to endure but also sporadically enjoyed extensive relations with other countries and peoples, especially the Greeks, Hittites, Assyrians, Babylonians, and Egyptians. We hear about such liaisons from the Bible, especially during the time of Solomon; now in the NEAEH we see artifacts from many ancient near eastern cultures unearthed in the Land. For example, at Tell Keisan, which witnesses to a long history from the Neolithic to the Hellenistic Period, objects were recovered from the West and East; that is specifically, Mycenean and Cypriot pottery along with stamped handles of Rhodian and Ionian wine amphorae and also Neo-Syrian pottery and a stamp seal. At Lachish a Mycenean pyxis and kylix, and Egyptian scarabs were unearthed; still visible are the remains of the Assyrian siege ramp (which is reminiscent of the Roman ramp at Masada).

In connection with a perception of foreign influences upon the culture and religion of Israel it is appropriate to report what has surprisingly not – or at least not yet – been found as far as I am informed. Before the destruction of Jerusalem in 70 C.E. no evidence of the mystery religions have been discovered. The mithraeum in Caesarea Maritima dates from the end of the first

[19] See now the volumes edited by D.T. Ariel, et al., titled Excavations at the City of David: 1978–1984 Directed by Yigal Shiloh and published in Qedem (Jerusalem), and D. Ussishkin, The Village of Silwan: The Necropolis from the Period of the Judean Kingdom (Jerusalem 1993) and especially H. Shanks, *Jerusalem: An Archaeological Biography* (New York 1995).

[20] I am grateful to Joe Zias and the authorities of the Rockefeller Museum for permission to study this fragment and to Stephen J. Pfann for insights regarding the interpretation of the document.

century A.D. (1.284).[21] Most importantly for insights of influences from India, it is remarkable that no archaeological evidence of Indian culture, of Hinduism, or of Buddhism has been recovered. This fact seems startling, because caravans brought spices, incense, and jewels like rubies from India to Jerusalem for centuries before the destruction of 70 C.E.,[22] because ideological influences from India have been seen in some biblical books,[23] and because an ivory statute has been found in Pompeii which may well have been brought there before 70 C.E. through ancient Palestine.[24] In exploring the ancient trade routes which connected Israel with cultures to the East we move into complex, even unknown, areas of historical research and confront perplexing issues; for example, it is easier to reconstruct the caravan routes from India to the West than to ascertain the relation between the flow of commodities and the trafficking of concepts, terms, and religious dimensions of different cultures.[25]

Jericho is famous because of the biblical accounts of conquest and the well-known hymns that celebrate at Jericho the victory of good over evil. This city also witnesses to an earlier epoch-making evolution in human history. Jericho (2.674–97) and the Jordan Valley (3.811–14) preserve some of the earliest evidence of the beginning of the agricultural revolution and the commencement of urbanization. At Jericho, thousands of years before Abraham, humans began to develop some control over the production of food and experiment for the first time with complex and stratified societies.[26]

---

[21] For a more detailed discussion of this date with color photographs of the mithraeum see K.G. Holum, R.L. Hohlfelder, R.J. Bull, and A. Raban (who contributed the article on Caesarea Maritima in the NEAEH), King Herod's Dream: Caesare on the Sea (New York, London 1988) pp. 148–53. For more on Caesarea Maritima, see L.I. Levine, E. Netzer, Excavations at Caesarea Maritima: 1975, 1976, 1979 –Final Report (Qedem 21; Jerusalem: The Hebrew University of Jerusalem, 1986).

[22] M. Dayagi-Mendels discusses how spices and perfume plants were brought to ancient Israel from Ceylon, China, India, Nepal, the Himalayas, South Arabia, and North Somalia. See her Perfumes and Cosmetics in the Ancient World (Jerusalem 1989), esp. p. 116.

[23] See notably the following: A.J. Edwards, Buddhist Texts Quoted as Scripture by the Gospel of John (Philadelphia, London 1911). J.E. Burns, The Christian Buddhism of St. John (New York 1971). While there are some valuable insights in these books, I personally find them misleading.

[24] See A. Maiuri, "Statuetta eburnea di arte indiana a Pompeii," Le Arte 1.2 (1939), 111–15. For a general overview and additional bibliographical data see V. Begley and R.D. De Puma, eds. Rome and India: The Ancient Sea Trade (Madison, Wisconsin 1991), pp. 3–7.

[25] Also unknown are the history and script of Troy, the origin and fate of the so-called Sea People, and the indecipherable language of, e.g., the Discos of Phaistos found in 1908. See the popular article by W. Zangger titled "Who Were the Sea People?" in Aramco World 46.3 (1995), 20–31.

[26] See also the authoritative and clear presentation by A. Mazar, Archaeology of the Land of the Bible 10,000–586 B.C.E. (Anchor Bible Reference Library; New York 1990), pp. 38–44.

Early Judaism and Second Temple Judaism

The recent excavations at Hasmonean and Herodian Jericho have significantly altered previous reconstructions. Now we are informed that the "city's houses extended throughout the entire valley of Jericho" (2.683), and that the magnificent palaces built north and south of the Wadi Qelt were constructed by the Hasmoneans and the Herods. Still unanswered is the question of why so many and different mikvahs (ritual baths for purification) were constructed to the west of the twin pools in Herodian Jericho (see the drawing in 2.684, no. 9). Surely the variety and abundance attests to both the obsession for ritual purity during the time of Hillel and Jesus and the factionalism among at least 20 groups and sub-groups of Jews in ancient Palestine before the destruction of 70 C.E.. I also wonder what is the relation – if any – between the pools at Hasmonean Jericho and Bethesda; both were rectangular and double pools placed on a somewhat north-south axis and framed by stoa.

The reader hears clearly, from a Roman Catholic and an Israeli Jew, that Qumran was not a fort but a "monastery" in which Jews copied the Dead Sea Scrolls. That position is the dominant one among scholars today, and it is imperative to add that Qumran was first an Israelite fort, secondly a religious center for exiled priests then other Jews (from c. 150 B.C.E. to A.D. 68), and finally an outpost by Roman Soldiers. These scholars also (rightly in my opinion) endorse the almost certain identification of Qumranites as Essenes,[27] which was first suggested by E.L. Sukenik.[28] These are only some of the enlightening clarifications that may help remove the chaos caused by the news media and experts in other fields wandering into a complex period of Jewish history.

Synagogues dating from the time of Hillel and Jesus have finally been found in what is now the State of Israel. It has become clear that we should abandon the Byzantine concept of a rectangular building designed and constructed as a synagogue in light of the realization that the earliest synagogues were usually converted buildings or designated sections of homes, that do not need to be accompanied by art work or architectural structures such as those found in the fifth-and-sixth century synagogues. Contributors, consequently, rightly stress, despite some hesitant voices or bold disclaimers elsewhere, that the buildings surmised to be synagogues at Gamla (Gamala),[29] the Herodian, and Masada

27 Hengel, along with most experts of Early Judaism, continues to affirm the position that the Qumranites were Essenes. See, e.g., HENGEL, Judaism and Hellenism, 2 vols, trans. J. Bowden (Philadelphia 1974) vol. 1, p. 47, *et passim*.

28 Y. Yadin, who inherited Sukenik's (his father) diary, wrote: "Sukenik was the first who suggested the identification of the sect with the Essenes." YADIN, The Message of the Scrolls, ed. Charlesworth (Christian Origins Library; New York 1992 [original is of 1957]), p. 176.

29 In addition to the publications cited under "Gamala" (2.463), which is by S. GUTMAN, see S. Gutman, Gamla ("Israel": Hakibbutz Hameuchad, 1981 [in Hebrew]).

are, in fact, synagogues – and that the Theodotus inscription is not only authentic but archaeological proof of a synagogal building in Jerusalem before 70 or at least before the end of the first century C. E.[30] Thus, E. Netzer correctly concludes "that it can be stated with certainty" that the building on Masada alleged to be a synagogue is in fact a synagogue (3.981).[31] Not only is the building facing Jerusalem, but an ostracon with the words "priest's tithe" (*ma^caser kohen*) and deliberately buried scrolls of Deuteronomy and Ezekiel were recovered in it (3.981). L. I. Levine astutely calls the earliest synagogues "a center for all communal needs" (4.1421). Although some specialists claim that there were separate places for women in the early synagogues (2.567), Levine, who has published several books on the early synagogues,[32] labels such a claim a "myth"; women and men met in one hall together (4.1423). The growing evidence of synagogues in the area covered by Israel is truly impressive; yet, the earliest building that is identified as a synagogue is not at Gamala but on the island of Delos, which may be so early as the second century B. C. E. Such discoveries help us in reconstructing the setting of Jesus (the gospels) and Paul (Acts).

The Babata Archives are evaluated (3.830–31). They are the largest collection of documents found in the Cave of the Letters. From these 35 legal documents – in Aramaic, Nabatean, and Greek – dating from 93 to 123 C. E. we learn about a wealthy woman's rights in ancient Palestine. Her name is the unprecedented "Babata" (or Babatha [בבתא, βαβαθα]) daughter of Simeon (βαβαθας [sic] Σίμωνος; בבתא ברת שמעון),[33], and among her personal documents is her marriage certificate, and some legal suits concerning her property and family affairs.

The New Testament

Jerusalem during the time of Hillel and Jesus was exceptionally attractive and impressive. The gospels depict Jesus' disciples marveling over the massive stones (Mk 13:1–2). The Alexandrian Jew Philo called the Holy City "the metropolis not only of Judea but of many other countries" (*LegGaium* 281).

[30] Hengel also argues that the Theodotus Synagogue in Jerusalem may "go back to Herodian times." HENGEL, The 'Hellenization' of Judaea in the First Century After Christ, with C. Markschies, trans. J. Bowden (London/Philadelphia 1989), p. 13.

[31] See also E.Netzer, Masada III: The Yigael Yadin Excavations 1963–1965 – Final Reports (Jerusalem 1991), pp. 402–22.

[32] See esp. his Ancient Synagogues Revealed (Jerusalem 1981) and his The Galilee in Late Antiquity (New York/Jerusalem 1992).

[33] See N. Lewis, ed., The Documents From the Bar Kokhba Period in the Cave of Letters: Greek Papyri (Jerusalem 1989), pp. 60 and 113 (for the Greek), p. 95 (for the Aramaic), and p. 98 (for the Nabatean).

The Roman Pliny celebrated it as "the most illustrious city in the East" (*NH* 6.70). The Palestinian Jew Josephus,[34] who did tend to exaggerate, was not as hyperbolic as we once judged when he described Herodian Jerusalem, since, *inter alia*, a stone weighing approximately 600 tons has been found in the lower course of the western wall of the Temple.[35] The ossuary which ostensibly once held the bones of Caiaphas (2.756) is given due prominence, and the map of Jerusalem during the first century C. E. is singularly important (2.718), showing clearly the putative locations of the Third Wall, the Essene Gate, and the Pool of Bethesda; but it certainly should have indicated, as does the model at the Holy Land Hotel, the probable site of Golgotha, just west of the "Second Wall" near the Gennath Gate.[36]

The Galilean boat that dates from the time of Peter, James, and John has been unfortunately called in some publications "the Jesus boat" and judged to have been sunk during a sea battle described by Josephus. In these volumes science is more readily apparent than romantic imaginings. The boat was worn out, stripped, and pushed out into the Sea of Galilee to sink beside a boat repair center near Magdala (2.520). A New Testament scholar would have added that its shallow draft (8.2 × 2.3 meters but only 1.2 meters deep) would have made it a precarious boat during the sudden storms that frequent the Sea of Galilee (see Mark 4:37, "And a great, windy storm arose [καὶ γίνεται λαῖλαψ μεγάλη ἀνέμου]; and the waves beat into the boat so that the boat was already filling [with water]").

The date of the Sepphoris theater has been heatedly debated by archaeologists. Does it date from the second century C. E. or earlier? To rabbinic scholars who yearn to know about the city in which Rabbi Judah Ha-Nasi completed the Mishnah (one of the truly great works of Judaism) this may seem an insignificant issue, but for New Testament experts it is not so irrelevant. Z. Weiss concludes that it was constructed by Herod Antipas (4 B. C. E. – 39 C. E.). Thus, Jesus may well have known about the works performed there and the urban pro-Greek and Roman culture which supported such an impressive theater.

At Bethlehem were recovered remains of Constantine's Church beneath the extant church which dates back to Justinian (1.203–10). Fourth-century remains have been found in the "Shepherd's Field" in Bethlehem (4.1362–63). At Nazareth archaeological evidence jumps from the Middle Bronze Age (a

---

[34] It is noticeable how often topographical and archaeological research prove the credibility of Josephus.

[35] I have not found a discussion of this stone in the NEAEH. Earlier in Jesus Within Judaism (New York 1988) I reported that the stone weighs 415 tons (p. 119). The estimated weight has been revised.

[36] It is unfortunate that no credit is given to W. F. Stinespring, who suffered greatly sliding through the sewers beneath Jerusalem until he rediscovered Wilson's Arch. See his reports, not cited (p. 719), in BA 29 (1966), p. 27–36 and in BA 30 (1967), p. 27–31.

scarab) to the Byzantine Period (shards [3.1103–1106]). The absence of first-century archaeological data from these sites should caution us against unsupported or too impressionistic reconstructions; rather we should contemplate the christological and kerygmatic intentions of the infancy gospels in Matthew and Luke. They function narratively in a way analogous to the Logos Hymn that begins the Gospel of John.

Extremely important for Christian readers of this Festschrift is the year 30 C.E. and the place on which Jesus was most likely crucified, namely Golgotha or the rock to the right just inside the Church of the Holy Sepulchre. Moreover, east of this rock, in inaccessible subterranean areas of the Church protected by the Armenians and on a wall beneath the Chapel of Saint Helena (the so-called Chapel of Saint Vartan) is an outline of a boat, carved surely before the fourth century by Christians who inscribed the words *Domine ivimus*, "O Lord, we shall go" (2.780). This drawing and inscription are virtually unknown to scholars.[37] I am persuaded that *Domine ivimus* does not mean "O Lord, we shall go"; *ivimus* seems to be the perfect of *eo*, "to go, to make a voyage." The inscription would thus mean "O Lord, we have made (the) voyage." Does this translation not better represent the setting: probably the celebrated thanks of Christians who have arrived at the place of Jesus' crucifixion from the West, perhaps Rome?

Weaknesses

Major reference works can always be improved. Here are some suggestions that would have made these volumes even more valuable.

The earliest extant passage found in the Bible is preserved on two silver amulets found by archaeologists just to the east of the Scottish Church on the western shoulder of the Hinnom Valley. They preserve in palaeo-Hebrew the Aaronic prayer (Num 6:24–26) and should have been given more prominence than they receive (2.715); and one at least should have been presented in color. I could not find a discussion and a photograph of the only evidence from Solomon's Temple: the tiny (4.3 cm.) ivory pomegranate with an eighth-century Hebrew inscription (containing in Palaeo-Hebrew the ineffable tetragrammaton, יהוה) whose provenience is unknown because it was smuggled out of the country; it is now beautifully displayed in the Israel Museum. The recently discovered Aramaic inscription at Tel Dan, which is the earliest reference to "the House of David" and to the nation "Israel" needs to be included, as well as a discussion of the not-yet-published Christian scrolls found in the church in Petra.[38]

---

37 Specialists in the field of Christian Origins will be surprised to read (1.292) the claim that *Minim* denoted "the followers of Jesus" (at least in Capernaum in the second century).

38 I am grateful to the American Center for Oriental Research in Amman and especially to Professor Jaakko Frösén of the Universitatis Helsingiensis for the permission and opportunity

The so-called tomb of Herod's family near the King David Hotel is attributed to this famous family; however, it may have belonged to any wealthy family of the first century. Unfortunately, the prefects are confused with the later procurators, continuing the anachronism that derives from Josephus; hence, Pontius Pilate was not a "procurator" (2.719). He was a prefect as the inscription found in Caesarea proves (see the photograph in 1.273). Even though both terms mean "governor" the shift from "prefect" to "procurator" in A.D. 44 was not merely a minor shift in terminology. The appearance of a Syriac inscription in the so-called Nestorian Hermitage two miles east of Jericho hardly suffices as proof that the hermitage was Nestorian (3.1068).

The NEAEH, although it concludes with thoughtful chronological tables and a glossary,[39] is not user friendly for the average reader for whom it is intended. For example, one looking for the Sea of Galilee will need to be guided to "Kinneret," and one seeking to read about Bethlehem will need to know to consult also the entry under "Shepherd"s Field" (4.1362–63). It is a pity there are virtually no cross references as in most exhaustive encyclopedias and biblical reference works. Those interested in studying Abraham, Moses, and David traditions will easily find respectively "Mamre," "Mount Nebo," and "Bethlehem" (as well as "Shepherd's Field"), but someone seeking to learn about the Church of the Holy Sepulchre will need considerable help. I remember studying the Hebrew version of this work with Bishop Kapikion of the Armenian Convent in Jerusalem. It took me considerable time, but I eventually found it in the English translation under "Jerusalem" (2.779–81).[40] It would have been rather simple to seek the help of an assistant living in Jerusalem to see that such entries as the Church of the Holy Sepulchre would have appeared in the "Index to Places." A chronological table on two facing pages linking all the major discoveries would also have been attractive.

The beautiful color photographs are often far removed from the article they illustrate and there are no references to them. For example, the discussion of Tuleilat El-Ghassul (2.510–11) should refer to the spectacular Chalcolithic

---

to examine and study the charred scroll that has been unrolled and pieced together. See Charlesworth, "The Discovery of Scrolls in Petra," *Explorations* 9.2 (1995) p. 3–4 [with two photographs] and G.L. Peterman, "The Petra Scrolls," *ACOR Newsletter* 5 (1993) p. 1–3 [with four photographs].

[39] Under "Judean Desert Caves" Babata is discussed, and the reader is told about her "ketubah" (3.831). Although Israelis and Jews are familiar with the word, the glossary should have included this Hebrew noun which means "wedding certificate."

[40] V.C. Corbo's and C. Coüasnon's work on the Church of the Holy Sepulchre are mentioned but no bibliographical note is provided for the reader. See the following: C. Coüasnon, The Church of the Holy Sepulchre Jerusalem, trans. J.-P.B. and C. Ross (Schweich Lectures; Oxford 1974), V.C. Corbo, Il Santo Sepolcro di Gerusalemme, 3 vols. (Studium Biblicum Franciscanum 29; Jerusalem: Franciscan Printing Press, 1981). Also see the valuable comments by P. Benoit, "Il Santo Sepolcro di Gerusalemme," [correcting the cover of the RB] Revue biblique (April 1984), p. 281–87.

wall paintings in color (opposite 2.441). The presentations of the Burnt House and the Palatial Mansion should draw attention to the colored illustrations opposite page 712 in volume 2 (also see the map 2.731). The discussion of the boat found at Ma^cagan Mikha'el should have been cross referenced to "Marine Archaeology" (3.957–65).[41]

The authors show impressive familiarity with the Old Testament, the Old Testament Apocrypha, Near Eastern Texts from Ugarit, Babylonia, and Egypt, Josephus, and some acquaintance with Philo as well as some of the Dead Sea Scrolls; but, generally, they are unaware of the sociological, historical, and ideological importance of the abundance of documents in the Old Testament Pseudepigrapha. In these 65 writings, dating primarily from the third century B.C.E. to 200 C.E., we hear – for example – about the rejoicing of Jerusalemites similar to the Pharisees over the demise of the "insolent one" who is Pompey (Psalms of Solomon 2), the claim that Vesuvius irrupted in 79 C.E. because God was punishing the Romans for their destruction of Jerusalem in 70 in "the great land of the Jews with its broad roads" (Sibylline Oracles 4.127), that is, "the blameless tribe of the pious" (Sibylline Oracles 4.136).[42]

While de Vaux correctly claimed that ʿEin Feshkha is certainly linked with Qumran (4.1240), where the sectarian Dead Sea Scrolls were composed and copied, some discussion should have been offered regarding other possible Essene settlements.[43] ʿEin Ghweir has been alleged to be also an Essene establishment. This is possible, because pottery contemporaneous with Qumran was recovered, and most importantly the graves excavated are similar to those at Qumran which are unusual.[44] Also, at Khirbet Mazin there is evidence of life contemporaneous with Qumran; perhaps it was here that some Essenes obtained minerals from the Dead Sea to sustain the needs of other Essenes and to prepare skins for writing.[45] Does Pliny mean that Essenes lived not only at Qumran, but also in other locales west of the Dead Sea between Qumran and

---

41 There is a cross reference in "Marine Archaeology," which began in 1960, to this fifth century B.C.E. boat; but no reference to the color plates opposite vol. 3,1020.

42 See the contributions to The Old Testament Pseudepigrapha, 2 vols., ed. J.H. Charlesworth (Garden City, New York, 1983, 1985).

43 For bibliographical information and comments see S.J. PFANN, "Sites in the Judean Desert Where Texts Have Been Found" in The Dead Sea Scrolls on Microfiche: Companion Volume, ed. E. Tov with S.J. Pfann (Leiden 1993), pp. 109–19. The title of this article is misleading in the sense that it wisely includes sites ostensibly linked with Qumran but where no "texts" have been found (notably in Cave 10, and at Khirbet Mazin, Ein Feshkha, Ein Ghweir, and Ein Gedi).

44 See P. BAR ADON, RB 77 (1970) 398–400; BAR ADON, Eretz Israel 10 (1971), p. 72–89 [in Hebrew].

45 I learned much from S.J. Pfann studying this site and pondering with him the purposes of the impressive installations. While the dozens of "anchor-like" weights were most likely used to lift "water" from the Dead Sea into pools for evaporation, the designated use of the deep and carefully plastered adjoining twin pools cannot now be discerned.

ʿEin Gedi? All these sites need to be discussed in a comprehensive reference work on biblical archaeology. The reader should now be informed that a sundial was found at Qumran and has been lying since the fifties in the Rockefeller undetected until the past year, although it is catalogued in R. de Vaux's notes. Moreover, the recent research by scientists which conclusively proves the antiquity of the scrolls through carbon dating, and the evidence that the jars found in the caves were fired at Qumran (thanks to the remains found in the kiln) need to be included in updated editions. This encyclopedia is a landmark event, but like all summaries of archaeological work the rapid advance of the discipline and the repeated explosion of unexpected discoveries indicate such criticisms or suggestions for improvement as noted above do not detract from its high standards for digesting thousands of years of evidence relating to the time and place of biblical events and also for the sophisticated presentation of biblical archaeology.

Features

As already stressed this is a major reference work. Giants stride through these pages; here you hear the words of luminaries like W.F. Albright,[46] P. Benoit,[47] J.A. Callaway,[48] N. Glueck,[49] K.M. Kenyon,[50] B. Mazar,[51] R. de Vaux,[52] and Y. Yadin.[53] The topography covered by these volumes is impressive, from

46 Albright is the dean of American archaeologists; he refined pottery chronology, and trained such international experts as J. Bright, F.M. Cross, N. Glueck, D. Hillers, and G.E. Wright. Two of Albright's influential and popular books are From the Stone Age to Christianity: Monotheism and the Historical Process (Baltimore 1940 [2nd ed. by Doubleday in 1957]), and Archaeology and the Religion of Israel (Baltimore 1942).

47 Perhaps the most accessible of Benoit's archaeological publications are in Jesus and the Gospel, 2 vols., trans. B. Weatherhead (New York 1973, 1974).

48 See the references to him in the following discussion.

49 Glueck, a naturally charismatic person, was as good a teller of stories as he was a gifted, engaging author. His explorations of the desert, on both sides of the Jordan, were pioneering and remain exemplary. See his The Other Side of the Jordan (Cambridge: Mass. 1970 [from the earlier edition of 1940), and his Rivers in the Desert: A History of the Negev (New York 1959, 1968).

50 See her The Bible and Recent Archaeology, with P.R.S. Moorey (Atlanta 1987).

51 See esp. B. MAZAR, The Mountain of the Lord: Excavating in Jerusalem (Garden City, New York 1975).

52 Archaeology is essential for reconstructing and perceiving the social and political setting of the Pentateuch and the Prophets; the most attractive endeavor is by R. DE VAUX, Ancient Israel: Its Life and Institutions, trans. J. McHugh (London 1965 [2nd. ed.]).

53 I was fortunate to have known all of them. The evenings I spent with Albright, Benoit, Callaway, Glueck, Mazar, and de Vaux – sometimes with snow blowing against the windowpanes of what is now called the Albright Institute – were sprinkled with the laughter and joy of those who enjoy each other and the intermittent thrill of victory over the darkness of ignorance.

Mount Hermon (the highest peak of the ante-Lebanon range) to Qumran (near the lowest spot on our globe). The volumes even contain accounts of documents not yet published officially, as for example the Samaritan papyri found in the Wadi ed-Daliyeh (1.320–23). There is even an undeciphered Aramaic inscription (2.544).

Especially appealing for philologians will be the abundant inscriptions or documents in Hebrew, Aramaic, Greek, Latin, and even in Palaeo-Hebrew, Proto-Canaanite, hieratic, hieroglyphics, Nabatean, and Samaritan. The *lmlk* ("belonging to the King") seals are frequent (see e.g. 1.251, 1.165, 2.413, 2.608, 3.909). Challenging the notion that the destruction of 70 C.E. was an absolute break in culture are the discoveries at Sipphoris, Tiberias, Caesarea Maritima, and elsewhere. The elaborate bath at En-Gedi dating from the period between the two great Roman Revolts (i.e. 74–132 C.E.) demonstrates some continuity in Palestine.

Church historians will benefit from the discussions of archaeological discoveries pertaining to the times of Constantine and Justinian, because of the massive building projects they sponsored and which are now exposed for reflection and a reassessment of ancient, patristic, medieval, and even modern history. Caravanserai and evidence of caravan routes from China and India challenge any myth that ancient Palestine was isolated from its neighbors to the East. Remains of churches are almost everywhere, especially from the time of Constantine to the Arab Conquest, or from the fourth to the seventh centuries.[54]

Scholars of human cultures and art historians will be most likely impressed by the variety of ancient art. Surprisingly, some of the most intricate and "advanced" art work is Chacolithic. Of course, those who have studied the evolution of pottery will be pleased with the numerous examples of Phonecian, Canaanite, and refined Nabatean ware.

Archaeology and Theology

Far too frequently biblical theologians ignore archaeology. In *Old Testament Theology: Its History & Development* J. H. Hayes and F. C. Prussner discuss the features of the biblical theology movement in America and Europe from approximately 1945 to 1960.[55] Regarding this movement which helped initiate such new periodicals as *Theology Today* and *Interpretation* they offer these judicious words:

[54] Of course, earthquakes have also devastated churches, especially in the sixth century at Petra and in 741 at Kursi. Also, see Y. Tsafrir, ed., Ancient Churches Revealed (Jerusalem/Washington, D.C. 1993).

[55] See the succinct review of the biblical theology movement by J. Baar in The Interpreter's Dictionary of the Bible, Supplementary Volume (1976), 104–11.

> What was new in the so-called biblical theology period was the close association between archaeological and theological interests and the desire to see archaeological work as supportive of the biblical portrayal of Israelite history and thus, at least indirectly, supportive of the contentions that God acts and is revealed in historical events. German scholarship was certainly interested and engaged in archaeological research but on the German scene there never developed as close an allegiance between archaeology and theology as in American scholarship.[56]

G. von Rad and W. Eichrodt,[57] for example, in their major volumes on Old Testament Theology acknowledged the importance of Form Criticism and historical research, but they tended to write as if archaeologists, namely F. Petrie and W.F. Albright, had not pioneered a revolutionary new approach to the historical study of the Bible in light of which the contextuality of biblical theology is understood.[58] The exception to this tendency is G.E. Wright, obviously of the Albright School, who included archaeology in his *The Old Testament and Theology*.[59]

One searing thought alone may now be taken from Wright's insights into the significance of archaeology for theology. Biblical theology, as practiced by Christians, assumes an evolution from the earliest to the latest writings; thus, the "primitive" Israelite theology builds up to Second Isaiah (Isa 40–55) and then evolves with revelatory spark into Pauline and Johannine theology. As is evident in NEAEH, some of the most "advanced" art work and ornamented pottery appears early. As Wright correctly observed, "many phenomena are at their finest degree of development when first encountered."[60] This "fact" indicates to me that, on the one hand, the allegedly "primitive" theological core must not be jettisoned as only anticipatory, and, on the other hand, that biblical history and theology do not evolve in a coherent trajectory,[61] because to a great

[56] J.H. Hayes and F.C. Prussner, Old Testament Theology: Its History & Development (Atlanta 1985), pp. 217–18 [with a corrected typographical error].

[57] G. von Rad attempted to examine the various expressions of Israel's faith-centered recitals of her special historical relation with God – *without* attempting to relate these with what can be learned from archaeology or from any historical facts. W. Eichrodt was critical of von Rad at this point (vol. 1, p. 34), but he only briefly enriched his presentation with insights obtained from archaeology (notably in his discussion of Phoenician art in vol. 2, p. 202 and in an examination of the etymology of *š^{e}ʾōl* in vol. 2, p. 210). See G. von Rad, Old Testament Theology, 2 vols., trans. D. M. G. Stalker (New York 1962, 1965) and W. Eichrodt, Theology of the Old Testament, 2 vols., trans. J. A. Baker (Philadelphia 1961, 1967).

[58] The School of Alt and Noth, of course, resisted the Albrightian approach. For an authoritative and lucid survey of the Albright School, the Alt-Noth School, and the Mendenhall-Gottwald School, see M. Weinfeld, The Promise of the Land: The Inheritance of the Land of Canaan by the Israelites (Berkeley, Oxford 1993), pp. 99–120.

[59] Wright, The Old Testament and Theology (New York 1969), see esp. pp. 84–86.

[60] Wright, The Old Testament and Theology, p. 84.

[61] I use this word selectively; I am alarmed by the frequent use of this word "trajectory" to indicate the linear development from New Testament Theology to later forms of Christian Theologies. Such was not the intention, I am convinced, of Professors Koester and Robinson.

extent "history is chaos."[62] As Hengel has shown, some of the greatest theological insights were achieved at the outset.[63] These four volumes of the NEAEH reveal that some of the least attractive artifacts are from the time of Isaiah and some of the most attractive are the Chalcolithic copper horns, standards, and heads from the Cave of Treasures (3.824–25) and the Chalcolithic intricately designed wall paintings at Tuleilat el-Ghassul (2.441 [opposite this page and in color]).

One can perceive an evolution, but that results from one's own commitment and faith. Wright's words from the past are words on target for our time:

> If there is a creative providence of God in history, it can only be observed in faith. It cannot be predicted as so regular and dependable that faith and commitment, so often working in the dark, can simply be dispensed with. Yet faith is more than 'whistling in the dark'; it is commitment to what appears to be reasonable and to positive goals of action derived there from ....[64]

What has archaeology then to do with us? The answer involves personal values and commitments, the warning of evolutions towards decay, and the paraenetic dimension in Ozymandias' words, "Look on my works, ye Mighty, and despair".

Wright's insights elevate us above the weaknesses of the post-war years' biblical theology movement (c. 1945–1960). It correctly saw that Israel from the earliest Psalms (if not before) until the thorough-going Jewishness of the Logos Hymn sang the praises of the God who had encountered her in history (*Heilsgeschichte*). But, it too often sought to prove the accuracy of Israel's memory within a paradigm that allowed scholars unperceptively to speak about an objectification of the historic. Now, we need to heed the perspicacity of B. S. Child's insight that

> God has revealed himself in the real events of human life which are found in the Bible. The theologian who seeks this knowledge of God must therefore study history. Since archaeology is the best tool for the study of ancient history, biblical theology and biblical archaeology belong together.[65]

One reason the biblical theology movement proved unattractive was the focus upon only some aspects of the Bible in the attempt to defend a center to it or to develop a systematic presentation of the theology or theologies in it. The recognition that to focus myopically on something or to ignore anything is

---

The German *Entwicklungslinie* is preferable so long as it is understood to denote "line of development."

[62] WRIGHT, The Old Testament and Theology, p. 85.

[63] See esp. HENGEL, Between Jesus and Paul, trans. J. Bowden (London 1983) and HENGEL, The Pre-Christian Paul, trans. J. Bowden (London 1991).

[64] WRIGHT, The Old Testament and Theology, p. 85.

[65] B.S. CHILDS, Biblical Theology in Crisis (Philadelphia 1970), p. 42 [I am grateful to Hayes for drawing my attention to this apt quotation].

unacceptable should be heeded, and that warning ushers in the recognition of the significance of archaeological discoveries from the Land and time in which the biblical accounts were lived out phenomenologically.[66] Not only biblical theology but exegesis itself is enriched and often corrected by a study of the archaeological evidence that is related directly or indirectly to the book or pericope presently under scrutiny.[67]

Archaeological excavations do provide artifacts, but these are not to be, as it were instantaneously, categorized as facts. Indeed even if we scholars have talked about *bruta facta* such a construct is simply an oxymoron, facts unperceived or uninterpreted do not exist in a human world.[68] "Facts" are surely devoid of meaning until they are interpreted; and they always come to us within a context and with perceptions that are formed by personal knowledge and a complex array of presuppositions.[69] Let us observe that it is not by looking at a Tell like Ai or Jericho that we can grasp what transpired there thousands of years ago. We must interiorize and identify ourselves with a valid reconstruction. As Michael Polanyi states in *The Tacit Dimension*, "it is not by looking at things, but by dwelling in them, that we understand their joint meaning."[70] Thus Yadin – by indwelling the flow of the topography and knowing where the water tunnel would have been placed – directed machinery to precisely the correct spot at Hatzor.[71] It was not random guessing; it was the intuitive leap of an ingenious archaeologist who had been living the Tell.

---

66 For a marvelous demonstration of a way to perceive tradition, apologetics, and politics in a liturgy (notably Ps 132) see C.L. Seow, Myth, Drama, and the Politics of David's Dance (Harvard Semitic Monographs 44; Atlanta 1989).

67 See especially the methods and models for exegesis in Archaeology and Biblical Interpretation: Essays in Memory of D. Glenn Rose, ed. L.G. Perdue, *et al.* (Atlanta 1982).

68 As W.H. Poteat pointed out to me on various occasions, we scientific examiners, i.e. archaeologists, are not sealed away in one world peering out so as to examine "objects". In the process of understanding an artifact or a ruin we are in the world with it and in a relationship with it in the attempt to comprehend what it – as subject – has to tell us. On the one hand the barrier created by the Cartesian subject-object dichotomy must be overcome, and on the other hand the full phenomenology to which it partially is witness must be imaginatively re-lived and then reconstructed according to our powers to indwell that perceived world. See W.H. Poteat, Polanyian Meditations: In Search of a Post-Critical Logic (Durham 1985) see esp. pp. 13–14. Hence, I will always remember standing with Benoit within the ruins being excavated just south of the Temple Mount listening to Mazar and Glueck before us forged together in a personal world by their heated debate over the meaning of shards they were holding.

69 I am indebted here to M. Polanyi's Personal Knowledge (Chicago 1958, 1964) and M. Merleau-Ponty's Phenomenology of Perception, trans. C. Smith (London/New York 1962, 1965).

70 M. Polanyi, The Tacit Dimension (Garden City, New York 1966), p. 18. Equally poignant is Polanyi's illustration of X-ray pictures; to an untrained eye "experts seem to be romancing about figments of their imagination; ..." As professors our task is to help students see what is the meaning of odd shapes meaningfully arranged in ancient texts. Polanyi, Personal Knowledge (New York 1958, 1964), p. 101.

71 Y. Yadin, Hazor (New York 1975).

It is evident that the biblical idea that the first human lived only approximately 2,000 years before Abraham, which situates "Adam" around 4000 B.C.E., is inaccurate. The NEAEH shows undeniable evidence of human occupation in the Levant dating back at least one million years (and, of course, in Africa "human" remains seem now to be dated back about 4 million years). It is also certain that the biblical account of the flood is myth, a well-known account of creation that is found in many ancient cultures contiguous with ancient Israel.

While some scholars conclude that Abraham, Isaac, and Joseph are only mythical figures,[72] it is now clear that the partriarchal narratives do preserve striking facts. The consensus among scholars tends to indicate that the oral traditions are ancient, but were shaped by three stages of writing (the three strata are 10th to 6th cent., sometime before 587, and sometime after 538).[73] Most impressive is the evidence that the cost of slaves was 20 silver shekels only in the period when Joseph was sold into slavery for exactly that amount (Gen 37:28); that is, in approximately 1700 B.C.E. In about 2200 B.C.E. the amount was only 10 silver shekels, in 500 B.C.E. it had risen to approximately 120 silver shekels.[74] Hence, if the Joseph story originated only after the Babylonian exile the amount expected in the biblical narrative would be at least 90 silver shekels. Hence, at least portions of the Joseph traditions seem to derive from the time setting of the biblical story – sometime in the early and middle second millennium B.C.E. It has always seemed easy to imagine how an Asiatic like Joseph could find upward advancement among the kindred Hyksos, who indeed had their capital in the eastern Delta during the period when Joseph was a "ruler" among these conquerors of the Pharaohs (Gen 45–47). These facts do not prove anything about the trustworthiness of the Abraham narrative nor indicate the Joseph story to be historically accurate; they do, however, dismiss the conclusion that the Joseph story is purely fabricated. Again, it is methodologically impossible to distinguish between verisimilitude and an accurate record of an historical event. It is certain that the reconstructions of the prehistory of Israel must proceed with utmost caution and realize that the records in the Bible fundamentally serve theological needs.[75]

Let us finally focus on a subject of fascination for all interested in the Bible and archaeology: the conquest of the Land. We know that archaeological

[72] See esp. J. Van Seters, Abraham in History and Tradition (New Haven 1975).

[73] See P.K. McCarter, "The Patriarchal Age: Abraham, Isaac and Jacob," in Ancient Israel, ed. H. Shanks (Washington, D.C. 1988), pp. 1–29, esp. p. 3.

[74] See Kitchen, Ancient Orient and Old Testament (Chicago 1966), pp. 52–53; Kitchen, "Founding Fathers in Canaan and Egypt," The Bible in its World: The Bible and Archaeology Today (Exeter 1977), pp. 56–74 (esp. p. 74). Also see Kitchen, Biblical Archaeology Review 21.2 (1995), 52–53.

[75] As McCarter states, most scholars "remain convinced that the stories about Abraham, Isaac and Jacob contain a kernel of authentic history"; he also points out that "the patriarchal narratives are ideology, not history." Ancient Israel, pp. 16–17.

discoveries neither can disprove nor are necessary to "prove" the Bible true; but how do they help us understand the biblical account of the conquest?

J. A. Callaway of Southern Baptist Seminary contributed the article on Ai to *The New Encyclopedia of Archaeological Excavations in the Holy Land* (1.39–45). As the chief archaeologist, he admits in *Archaeology and Biblical Interpretation* going to Ai entertaining the "notions of bridging the widening gulf between the biblical accounts in Joshua 7–8 and the actual evidence of the ruin itself" (p. 90). After nine seasons of excavations he was forced to admit that the "evidence does not support at any point the account of the conquest of Ai in Joshua 7–8" (p. 97). This is a remarkable statement by a Southern Baptist, who reports in NEAEH that Ai was abandoned from 2400 to 1220 B.C. (1.44).[76]

If the Conquest occurred between 1280 and 1220 B.C.E. then there was nothing at Ai to conquer. What about the even more famous Jericho? Is it not possible – or at least conceivable – that the walls destroyed by Joshua were once visible but now have eroded away? The erosion at Jericho is extensive and readily seen by all, even visitors who have seen no other Tell. And the walls, as all the others extant, would most likely have been composed of *mud* bricks. Should we not ponder or even accept the probability that the walls that collapsed according to Joshua 6 are beneath our feet as formless clay, as we stand on the Tell?

That is the position advocated by the National Geographic Society's "Roots of The City: Jericho and Çatal Hüyük." The author of the article, L. De La Habba, advocates the mud-eroded wall hypothesis:

> ... at a spring near the Mount of Temptation ... rises a dusty, oval mound. In Arabic it is called Tell es Sultan, and it is the site of ancient Jericho. Near the top of the mound, long since eroded by wind and rain, once stood walls that, according to the Old Testament, fell to Joshua's trumpets some time around 1250 B.C.[77]

Leaping over the fact that putative walls are no longer present to study, let us recognize that if the latest remains are centuries before 1250 then what might have been walls when Joshua and his band entered Canaan might have been washed away.

The key question concerns the date of the latest remains at Jericho. They are in fact hundreds of years later than Joshua's time. Archaeologists have found a hut from the Early Arab Period, some Roman graves, and most importantly on the flanks of the Tell evidence of "extensive occupation" in the seventh century

---

[76] A handy succinct account of the discontinuity between archaeology and the biblical account of the conquest is available in G. Báez-Camargo, Archaeological Commentary on the Bible (Garden City, New York 1984).

[77] L. De La Habba, "Roots of The City: Jericho and Çhatal Hüyük", Mysteries of the Ancient World (Washington, D.C. 1979, 1985), p. 32.

B.C.E., and on the eastern slope a "massive building from this period." Thus, Kenyon concluded, "The archaeological evidence shows that occupation on the ancient site came to an end at the time of the Babylonian Exile" (2.674). While a fundamentalist can still state that the walls would not be on the flanks or slopes of Jericho but on the top of the Tell which is eroded, yet the open-minded scholar is surely impressed not only by the lack of data supporting a thirteenth-century conquest of Jericho but also by the pervasive impossibility of "facts" to prove or disprove a position to those dedicated to other sets of proofs.

The biblical account of the conquest of Jericho is not a tape recorded account of Joshua's conquest of – better first visit to – Jericho. In Judges we hear not about Joshua's military exploits; rather we listen to a recital of how Israel acknowledged the Land as *God's gift*. Archaeology has disclosed that there was a Jericho precisely where it should be, and that it had once been a majestic city. Many generations after Joshua an anonymous writer recorded how his fathers and forefathers, for generations, celebrated God's victory over the inhabitants of the Land; certainly he did not intend to give us an objective history (as if such is not a human construct). He begins the fall of Jericho by celebrating the Lord: "The Lord said to Joshua, 'See, *I have handed Jericho over to you...*'" (Jos 6:2 [NRSV, italics mine]). Christians like P.D. Miller and W. Brueggemann and Jews like M. Weinfeld and L.H. Feldman, after studying both archaeology and theology, stress that Israel is a people called by God to receive *the gift of the Promised Land.*[78] As the book of Joshua may be divided into an account of conquest (1–12) and of settlement (13–24) so the archaeological data in the Land should be separated into similar categories. It seems apparent that different cities were captured by different groups, and that conquest should be distinguished from occupation.[79] That is, "new settlement" in the Land of Canaan is obvious about the time discerned as the period of the Conquest. The archaeological evidence is abundant for settlement during the twelfth century in the hill countries of Benjamin especially at Bethel (1.194), and in Manasseh especially at Shechem (4.1346–52). D.N. Freedman and M. Weinfeld judge

---

[78] P.D. Miller, "The Gift of God," Interpretation 23 (1969), p. 451–65. Miller rightly states, the gift of the Land and its blessings "all of this is not the result of Israel's arduous labors but is the gift of God." Miller, Deuteronomy (Interpretation; Louisville 1990) pp. 105–106. W. Brueggemann, The Land (Overtures to Biblical Theology; Philadelphia 1977), pp. 47–53. M. Weinfeld, The Promise of the Land (Berkeley 1993), p. 105. L.H. Feldman, Jew & Gentile in the Ancient World (Princeton 1993), pp. 232, 288. Feldman points out that Josephus' Joshua exhorts piety (Ant 5.116).

[79] See D.N. Freedman's comments in Biblical Archaeology Today: Proceedings of the International Congress on Biblical Archaeology (Jerusalem, April 1984), ed. J. Amitai (Jerusalem: Israel Exploration Society, 1985), pp. 31–95.

that it seems clear that these sites as well as others represent and reflect the *Israelite settlement* in the "Holy Land."[80]

We consequently arrive at three positions. First, the conquest account according to a literal reading of Joshua is not supported by archaeological discoveries.[81] Biblical theologians, however, illustrate that the Bible itself does not present a picture of a violent full scale conquest of the Land; for example, it presents lists of unconquered cities (Josh 13–17 and Judg 1–3). Second, archaeology does support certain aspects of a conquest so that some conquest is conceivable. There is evidence of a conquest in the massive conflagration at Hazor; Y. Yadin is convinced it "is doubtless to be ascribed to the Israelite tribes, as related in the Book of Joshua" (2.603).[82] Third, archaeological evidence of new settlements in the Land parallels some of the accounts in the Pentateuch.[83]

As we have come to learn over the last part of this century archaeological work may often be essential for understanding the world of the Bible and for any theology based upon it. These volumes are focused not on the Bible but upon the science of the archaeology of the Land. Attempts to assess the importance of archaeology for an improved presentation of the theologies in the Bible need to remember that archaeology is an intellectual inquiry into past human lives and cultures,[84] and also that a personal theology needs nothing from archaeology to substantiate it. "Faith seeking understanding" and attempts to purify the reforming church are not threatened but enlivened and clarified by scientific or archaeological discoveries.[85] Yet, we should always try to be cognizant that faith in no way is dependent upon the accumulation of any *realia*, including archaeological *facts*.

---

[80] Freedman, Biblical Archaeology Today, p. 31 [capitals his]). Weinfeld, The Promise of the Land, esp. p. 105.

[81] At Shechem there is evidence of massive conflagration in about 1350–1300 and again circa 1100, but not as expected from the biblical account in the thirteenth century (4.1352).

[82] See the similar hypothesis of R. de Vaux in The Early History of Israel to the Period of the Judges, trans. D. Smith (London, 1971).

[83] See in particular I. Finkelstein, The Archaeology of the Israelite Settlement (Jerusalem, 1988). I am grateful to M. Weinfeld for this reference.

[84] See the comments by W. G. Dever in "Archaeology, Syro-Palestinian and Biblical," The Anchor Bible Dictionary, 1.354–67. Dever rightly stresses that the real question is not "*whether* to use the Bible, but *how*"; see his "Yigael Yadin: Prototypical Biblical Archaeologist," Eretz-Israel 20 (1989), pp. 44*–51*.

[85] W. Harrelson, within many other poignant insights, calls us to contemplate the ancient Israelite who at times praises God and at other times condemns God. Harrelson rightly bewails, "We cannot take seriously the story of his love and redemption and we therefore can neither praise nor blaspheme." See Harrelson's "Blunt Honesty with God," in From Fertility Cult to Worship: A Reassessment of the Worship of Ancient Israel (Garden City, New York 1970), pp. 90–92.

Among the sensational archaeological discoveries and their possible importance for biblical theology – that is, those that have impressed me[86] – I would single out the following:

- the name "David" in a ninth-century Aramaic inscription (which refers to the defeat of "the House of David") found at Tel Dan, proving that despite his legendary exploits he was a real historical person;[87]
- the title "[Pref]ectus" with the name "[Pon]tius Pilate," found in Roman Caesarea Maritima, clarifying that he was not a procurator as most scholars incorrectly assume but a "prefect";
- the name of "Caiaphas" on an ossuary found in a tomb between Jerusalem and Bethlehem, it most likely once contained the bones of the high priest mentioned in the Passion Narratives;
- the ivory pomegranate from Solomon's Temple, evoking the possibility that it once was held by a Levite who directed the singing of Davidic Psalms on the Temple steps;
- the two silver amulets that antedate the Babylonian Exile, containing in Palaeo-Hebrew a text almost identical to the biblical Aaronic Blessing (Num 6:24–26) recited today in synagogues and churches around the world;[88]
- the proof that Golgotha is in the Church of the Holy Sepulcher and that the rock had been rejected because of a crack by ancient builders (see Ps 118:22, Mk 12:10 and par.);[89]
- the remains of a crucified man from the time of Jesus and just north of Jerusalem;[90]
- remains of both the Canaanite city fortress and of the Jebusite town that

[86] Any such list is obviously arbitrary and subjective. See the similar confession and discussion by M.D. COOGAN in "10 Great Finds," Biblical Archaeology Review 21.3 (1995), p. 36–47.

[87] This was found in 1993 and so is too recent to be included in the NEAEH. For a color photograph see U.S. News & World Report (April 17, 1995), p. 66. P.R. Davies thinks that *bytdwd* should not be divided into *byt dwd*, "the house of David." I agree with D.N. Freedman and J.C. Geoghegan that it can (*scriptua continua* is common, esp. in inscriptions). See P.R. DAVIES, "'House of David' Built on Sand," Biblical Archaeology Review 20 (1994); also see DAVIES, In Search of Ancient Israel (Sheffield, England 1992). Consult FREEDMAN and GEOGHEGAN, "'House of David' is There!," Biblical Archaeology Review 21 (1995), p. 78–79.

[88] See CHARLESWORTH, "An Astounding Archaeological Discovery: Two Silver Scrolls Containing the Oldest Biblical Text," Explorations 5.1 (1991), p. 1, 4.

[89] See my discussion in Jesus Within Judaism: New Light from Exciting Archaeological Discoveries (Anchor Bible Reference Library; New York 1988), pp. 123–27.

[90] See the drawings and discussion by CHARLESWORTH and J. ZIAS in Jesus and the Dead Sea Scrolls, by Charlesworth with internationally renowned experts (Anchor Bible Reference Library; New York 1995), pp. 273–89, see the drawing opposite p. 185 and the photograph on the following page.

antedate David's City (2.702–703),[91] and the early Israelite homes – even the House of Ahiel – with structures inside on the east of Ophel (see the photograph in 2.708);
- the undeniable grandeur of the Second Temple and the discovery of a massive stone on the lower coarse of the western retaining wall of the Temple placed there by Herod's engineers, it weighs around 600 tons;
- the abundant evidence of Herod's building projects from Dan in the north to Massada and the Herodium in the south, and especially the aqueduct that shoots straight as an arrow from the Carmel range to Caesarea;[92]
- the inelegance and lack of decoration on Israelite pottery, proving perhaps the power of the first two commandments;
- the recovery of letters from Bar Kokhba's time,[93] with his real name "Simeon Ben Kosiba" (שמעון בן כוסבה [3.834]), and the Babata deeds and documents;
- and, of course, the recovery of the Dead Sea Scrolls which puts in our hands writings formerly held in ancient Palestine by Jews who lived prior to 70 C.E.

Those who wondered why I, a New Testament scholar, was living in Jerusalem in the sixties and interested in archaeology as well as biblical theology would have been astounded by the evidence from the time of Hillel, Jesus, and the evangelists that has been unearthed in the past thirty years.

The specialists working on the Dead Sea Scrolls have been pulled into explaining the limits of historiography, and even into apologetics and polemics. Through the international media, especially in the United States, Germany, and Israel, the charge has been aired that Christians and Jews have not published the Dead Sea Scrolls, even though they were first discovered in 1947, because they know the ideas found in them will endanger, even disprove, the hallmarks of Jewish or Christian faith. Dead Sea Scrolls experts have been forced into an apologetic mode, explaining that all the extensive Dead Sea Scrolls have been published, by Jews and Christians,[94] and that what has not yet

---

[91] N.B. that the editors caution the reader about Shiloh's dating of the terrace system. These represent stratum 15 which dates from Iron Age I or the eleventh century.

[92] See the aerial color photograph in King Herod's Dream: Caesarea on the Sea, by K.G. Holum, et al. (New York 1988), p. 126.

[93] Also see N. Lewis, Y. Yadin, and J.C. Greenfield, eds., The Documents from the Bar Kokhba Period in the Cave of Letters (Jerusalem 1989).

[94] For scholarly publications on the Dead Sea Scrolls see especially the following: M.O. Wise, et al., eds., Methods of Investigation of the Dead Sea Scrolls and the Khirbet Qumran Site: Present Realities and Future Prospects (Annals of the New York Academy of Sciences 722; New York 1994), D. Dimant, and U. Rappaport, eds., The Dead Sea Scrolls: Forty Years of Research (Leiden, New York, Jerusalem 1992), J.T. Barrera, and L.V. Montaner, eds., 2 vols., The Madrid Qumran Congress (Studies on the Texts of the Desert of Judah 11.1; Leiden, New York 1992), the Dead Sea Discoveries: A Journal of Current Research on the Scrolls and Related Literature, Revue Qumran, Revue biblique, and the Journal for the Study of the Pseudepigrapha and Related Literature (esp. issue 10 which is devoted to the DSS).

been published are approximately 100,000 fragments to well over 300 documents.[95] When people hear that 90% of the pieces are now missing and that there is no guide to what any of the documents looked like, or contained, they readily imagine the virtually insurmountable problems involved in putting together hundreds of "jig-saw puzzles."[96]

They are also forced into polemics.[97] That has resulted especially because of the polemic charge that Jesus cannot be the Son of God; he was instead an Essene or deeply involved with them, and did not die on the cross. This view is surely not new; it dates back to K.F. Bahrdt and K.H. Venturini over two hundred years ago. A. Schweitzer labeled such literature "The Earliest Fictitious Lives of Jesus."[98] What is new is the distorted, idiosyncratic, polemical approach to Christian Origins based on an eisegesis of the Dead Sea Scrolls, especially the Pesharim, by B. Thiering. She claims to be able to discover – from reading the New Testament in light of her interpretation of the Dead Sea Scrolls – that Jesus was married, divorced, and remarried. Her precision is astounding: Jesus was betrothed to Mary Magdalene at Ain Feshka (= Cana) at 6:00 p.m. on Tuesday, June 6, 30 C.E. They were married at that place on Saturday at 6:00 p.m., September 23, 30 C.E. Mary Magdalene decided to divorce Jesus in March 44, after "the birth of Jesus' third child."[99] This reconstruction is imaginative eisegesis. Readers of this Festschirft need no demonstrations that Thiering has offended the science of historiography, which at best can approximate probabilities.

The Dead Sea Scrolls do help us understand the time of Jesus, but they do not refer even obliquely to Jesus of Nazareth. These documents help us understand that much of the story of Jesus derives from pneumatic exegesis of passages in scripture (the Old Testament or Hebrew Scriptures),[100] and offer an example of such contemporary biblical interpretation, as well as providing us with syntax

---

[95] Thanks to the support of Hengel the Dead Sea Scrolls – all of the fragments and full scrolls that are not merely a passage of the Hebrew Bible – are being published in ten volumes, with succinct introductions, followed by Hebrew critical texts (sometimes with an apparatus criticus) printed opposite literal English translations. See Charlesworth, ed., Rule of the Community and Related Documents (The Dead Sea Scrolls: Hebrew, Aramaic, and Greek Texts with English Translations Volume 1; Tübingen, Louisville 1994).

[96] A helpful bibliographical guide is J. A. Fitzmyer's The Dead Sea Scrolls: Major Publications and Tools for Study (SBL Resources for Biblical Study 20; Atlanta 1990).

[97] See the helpful book by O. Betz and R. Riesner titled Jesus, Qumran and the Vatican: Clarifications, trans. J. Bowden (New York 1994 [original = Jesus, Qumran und der Vatikan: Klarstellungen, 1993).

[98] A. Schweitzer, The Quest of the Historical Jesus, trans. W. Montgomery (London 1931 [2nd English edition]), pp. 38–47.

[99] B. Thiering, Jesus & the Riddle of the Dead Sea Scrolls: Unlocking the Secrets of his Life Story (San Francisco 1992), pp. 222, 146.

[100] Among the many publications on this subject I am impressed especially by D. Juel's Messianic Exegesis: Christological Interpretation of the Old Testament in Early Christianity (Philadelphia 1988).

and meaning for many words which within the Palestinian Jesus Movement became christological and ecclesiological terms, such as "Son of God," "the Messiah," "Planting," "the Poor,"[101] and "the Way."[102] Jesus was certainly not an Essene, but he was both positively and negatively influenced by some of the Essene's unique theological ideas.[103] The Dead Sea Scrolls, along with other early Jewish documents, such as the Old Testament Pseudepigrapha, help us avoid the greatest danger in Christian theology: Docetism, and the tendency to remove earthly humanness from Jesus. They also transport us from modern western parochial christologies into pre-70 middle-eastern Jewish theologies.[104]

In my judgment the book in the Bible whose interpretation has been most altered by archaeological discoveries is the Gospel According to John. In the nineteenth century the GosJn was read paradigmatically differently than today. The main reason is the phenomenal archaeological discoveries in the Land that date from circa 250 B.C.E. to 135 C.E. (or from the date of the earliest document in the Books of Enoch to the defeat of Bar Kokhba). Exegetes overlooked the mention of stone jars in the desire to discuss the theological importance of Jesus' turning water into wine, dismissed the description of a building with five porticoes as indicative of the "fact" that the author had never been in Jerusalem and evidently knew nothing about that city, and tended to conclude that the Logos Hymn linked the gospel with Heraclitus and the Stoics. The work was thus judged to be a second-century composition heavily shaped by Greek philosophy.

Thanks to revealing and revolutionary archaeological discoveries the GosJn is evaluated to be a first-century writing profoundly shaped by Jewish theology and customs. For example, only in the GosJn, among the gospels, do we read about "stone jars" (ἦσαν δὲ ἐκεῖ λίθιναι ὑδρίαι ἕξ) and they are said to be set aside for the Jewish rights of purification (κατὰ τὸν καθαρισμὸν τῶν Ἰουδαίων κείμεναι, [GosJn 2:6]). Both these asides, often missed by commentators, fit perfectly within the world of pre-70 Judaism. In the Upper City of Jerusalem archaeologists have recovered large *stone jars* which were constructed to fulfill

---

101 Especially attractive is N. LOHFINK's Lobgesänge der Armen (Stuttgarter Bibelstudien 143; Stuttgart 1990).

102 See the contributions in Charlesworth, ed., The Messiah: Developments in Earliest Judaism and Christianity (Minneapolis 1992). The latest volume devoted to Qumran messianic thought is J.J. COLLINS, The Scepter and the Star: The Messiahs of the Dead Sea Scrolls and Other Ancient Literature (Anchor Bible Reference Library; New York 1995).

103 See especially the articles in Charlesworth, with internationally renowned scholars, Jesus and the Dead Sea Scrolls (Anchor Bible Reference Library; New York 1992).

104 One of the best reliable introductions to the Dead Sea Scrolls has been written by J.C. VANDERKAM; it is his The Dead Sea Scrolls Today (Grand Rapids, Michigan 1994). Also popular yet authoritative are the contributions in Understanding the Dead Sea Scrolls, ed. H. Shanks (New York 1992). Extremely focused and reliable is J.A. FITZMYER's Responses to 101 Questions on the Dead Sea Scrolls (New York/Mahwah, N.J. 1992).

the Jewish rites of purification (2.708, 731). These all are dated within the century before the burning of the Temple in 70 C. E. The Dead Sea Scrolls – surely one of the greatest of all archaeological discoveries[105] – contain rules for purification and warn about the dangers of impurity with clay vessels (see esp. the Temple Scroll col. 50). Now the exegesis and theological meaning of the GosJn 2:1–11 is markedly altered; for example, we no longer rush past what once seemed irrelevant details, but contemplate the Johannine use of symbolism and perception of Jewish customs, and perhaps even marvel at a concept of purity that ties the GosJn and apparently Jesus more with the Prophets than with their contemporary Jews. The five-porticoed pool of Bethesda is not a creation out of the world of Johannine symbolism; it has been unearthed and precisely just north of the Temple Mount as the evangelist described it; and, moreover, it witnesses to a temple of Aesclepius and even medical facilities (2.758).[106] Now our exegesis of the GosJn does not meander into the quicksands of juxtaposing Johannine theology with the Pentateuch as if the five porticoes represent the Torah being replaced by Jesus, rather we see Jesus being portrayed as supporting the Torah and being contrasted with Aesclepius whose cult remains are evident there. Hence, the GosJn 5:1–18 may symbolically be conveying the thought that Jesus and not the Greek god of healing is the one who enables one to arise and walk correctly and who alone is accompanied by signs that reveal he reflects the glory of God.

Most importantly, the archaeological evidence called the Dead Sea Scrolls have revolutionized our understanding of Johannine Theology.[107] We now have pre-70 evidence for Johannine terms within Palestinian Judaism itself. Many of the Johannine terms and even some concepts seem to most scholars to derive directly or indirectly from Qumran (Essene) theologies.[108] These minor jottings on archaeology and New Testament Theology indicate that it may be justifiable for books on New Testament Archaeology to ignore theology, but surely it is unwise to continue the practice of writing a New Testament Theology from a purely literary point of view and in ignorance of archaeology.[109] It is

---

105 Most of them were not discovered by archaeologists.

106 Betseda, Bethsaida, or Bethzatha needs to be more adequately discussed in the next edition of the NEAEH. For a photograph of the archaeological evidence see p. 21 of CHARLESWORTH, "Reinterpreting John: How the Dead Sea Scrolls Have Revolutionized Our Understanding of the Gospel of John," Bible Review (February 1993), 19–25, 54.

107 See esp. the contributions in John and the Dead Sea Scrolls, ed. Charlesworth (Christian Origins Library; New York 1991).

108 Regarding Qumran theologies see CHARLESWORTH, "The Theologies in the Dead Sea Scrolls," in The Faith of Qumran: Theology of the Dead Sea Scrolls, by H. Ringgren (Christian Origins Library; New York 1995) pp. xv–xxi. Also very helpful is D. FLUSSER's The Spiritual History of the Dead Sea Sect, trans. C. Glucker (Tel Aviv 1989).

109 As have R. Bultmann, H. Conzelmann, W. G. Kümmel, L. Goppelt, and even J. Jeremias (quite surprisingly in light of his other publications that are heavily influenced by archaeology).

disappointing to report that no present or planned book on New Testament Theology includes the insights and stimulants derived from the incredible mass of data that is Hasmonean Herodian. In G. Hasel's *New Testament Theology: Basic Issues in the Current Debate* we are rightly told the following:

> The history of early Christianity is studied in the context of the history of antiquity with special emphasis on the surrounding cultures from which we have many texts and where archaeology has been invaluable in providing the historical, cultural, and social setting for the Bible.[110]

Since the seventies, when Hasel compiled his assessment, the archaeological discoveries from the first century C.E. in the Land, especially in Jerusalem have been simply sensational, as can be seen in N. Avigad's *Discovering Jerusalem*[111] and especially in the NEAEH. Surely archaeology and an attempt to indwell the communities that have bequeathed us the documents in the New Testament will help protect us from the perennial constructs of a docetic Christology and from a philosophical Christianity that ignores the cries of biblical men and women and the scandalous nature of the kerygma from the viewpoint of Hellenic and Hellenistic Philosophy. Perhaps reviewing the remnants of former lives, whether heard in mute stones jars or in the echoes of credal formulae, will help us grasp the biblical vision of an unfinished story.[112] R. Niebuhr's insight should not be forgotten; the New Testament authors envision that "history remains open to all possibilities of good and evil until the end."[113] In light of the biblical promise of a better day, and ultimately the belief in a resurrection, the reader of NEAEH may be stimulated to think about the meaning of life by the grim reminders of death, burials, and such ubiquitous inscriptions as ΘΑΡΣΙ ΟΥΔΕΙΣ ΑΘΑΝΑΤΟΣ, "take heart for no one does not die."

I am convinced that the information epitomized in these volumes is invaluable for a refined presentation of the diverse theologies in the Old and New Testaments. The archaeological information from the times and places of some of the biblical authors should, to use Eichrodt's words, "afford us some hope of guarding ourselves against pale and abstract theorizing ...".[114] An example

---

110 G. Hasel, New Testament Theology: Basic Issues in the Current Debate (Grand Rapids, Michigan, 1978), p. 214.

111 N. Avigad's Discovering Jerusalem (Nashville 1983).

112 B. W. Anderson emphasizes the paradigmatic concept of "story" in biblical theology; see his "The Bible as the Shared Story of a People" in The Old and the New Testaments, ed. by Charlesworth and W. Weaver (Faith & Scholarship Colloquies; Valley Forge, Pa. 1993), pp. 19–37.

113 R. Niebuhr, Faith and History: A Comparison of Christian and Modern Views of History (New York 1949) p. 235.

114 Eichrodt, Theology of the Old Testament, vol. 1, p. 35. Eichrodt was primarily referring not to archaeology (although he cites with approval Albright's "comprehensive archaeological study" in the preceding lengthy footnote) but to the necessity of avoiding the

from the fifties has been given to us by Th. C. Vriezen who argued that Israel developed her concept of God "by the comparison with the Canaanite-Phoenician conception of the being of God".[115] In contrast to Baal, who dies only to rise again, Israel's God transcends both life and death and is experienced as the Living God. H. Ringgren points to the well accepted fact (meaning that it is endorsed by most scholars) that Israelite theology of covenant and kingship were shaped by the mythology of the countries with her, an insight grounded in numerous archaeological discoveries, especially texts.[116] If foreign ideas, even in redacted form, significantly shaped Israelite theology then what is left with the Jewish and Christian concept of revealed religion? Ringgren astutely answers that there is evidence God influenced the destinies of other nations (Amos 9:7) and thus revelation to other nations may be a possible source of some foreign ideas.[117] Finally, F.M. Cross has shown, *inter alia*, how archaeology helps to correct the Wellhausen dating, assessment of historical reliability, and theological interpretation of the patriarchal period according to the priestly source.[118] Obviously, archaeology cannot provide some dimension lacking in theology. No scientific research is intended to produce theology or any theological faith. As I have endeavored to demonstrate elsewhere,[119] *archaeology cannot form faith but it does inform faith*.

Conclusion

It is abundantly clear that "the Holy Land" covers more territory than the borders of modern Israel. With the optimism felt in many circles by the so-called Peace Accord just maybe some of the political problems that have undermined or hindered biblical archaeology will be removed. My own work-

schemes of Christian dogmatics and plotting "our course as best we can along the lines of the OT's own dialect" (vol. 1, p. 33).

[115] Th. C. Vriezen, An Outline of Old Testament Theology, trans. S. Neuijen (Boston 1958), p. 182.

[116] H. Ringgren, "The Impact of the Ancient Near East on Israelite Tradition," in Tradition and Theology in the Old Testament, ed. D. A. Knight (Philadelphia 1977) pp. 31–46; esp. pp. 36–37.

[117] We need to recognize both that Amos does not indicate God spoke to these other nations or that he revealed himself to them, and that we have no means of detecting where revelation by God outside Israel may be detected. Furthermore, the injunction to destroy other nations and the concept of unique election must be included in the search for answers to this perplexing question.

[118] F. M. Cross, "The Priestly Tabernacle," in Old Testament Issues, ed. S. Sandmel (New York 1968), pp. 39–67.

[119] What has Archaeology to do with Faith?, ed. Charlesworth and W. P. Weaver (Faith & Scholarship Colloquies; Philadelphia: Trinity Press International, 1992).

ing relations with Egypt, Jordan, and Israel are wonderful; but then there is Iran, Iraq, Syria and the echo of G. Ernest Wright's lament over what he labeled the "major inhibiting factor." He called it "the Near Eastern Iron Curtain."[120] Obviously, readers of the daily newspapers and viewers of television news are constantly reminded of the international importance but intermittent unrest in these lands.

Theology is enriched by archaeology. Biblical research, exegesis, and theology – indeed any systematic theology related ultimately to scripture – is moved from subjective idealistic speculation when it is stimulated by biblical archaeology to move beyond our parochialism in a western world to enter cultures over there and back then where the sacred events in history unfolded and our texts were created and edited. Archaeology helps provide stepping stones over the running rivers of time.

Only after 1827 and 1846, when Hieroglyphics and Akkadian were respectively deciphered, was it possible to read Egyptian, Assyrian, and Babylonian literature, and to discern how ancient Israel's poetry and wisdom literature were related, indeed shaped, by the cultures contiguous with "the Holy Land." The unabated flow of archaeological discoveries provide us with "facts," which, as J. A. Fitzmyer states, "a modern reader of the Bible cannot ignore, for they have radically affected our understanding of the written Word of God and of how it has to be interpreted today."[121]

The NEAEH is an encyclopedic and monumental work. It contains 64 pages of full color and an abundance of illustrations (frequently with three on a page). It is an authoritative reference work.[122] It should be in every major library, including those of large churches. An exegesis of biblical passages and the development of Biblical Theology – and not only the essential significance of biblical archaeology for reconstructing biblical history – will be on a firmer foundation by consulting archaeological works, especially the NEAEH.[123] This cornucopia provides authoritative assessments of archaeological data from ancient Israel and Early Judaism, as well as the early history of the Church in

---

120 G. E. Wright, "The Phenomenon of American Archaeology in the Near East," in Near Eastern Archaeology in the Twentieth Century: Essays in Honor of Nelson Glueck, ed. J. A. Sanders (Garden City, New York 1970), p. 35.

121 J. A. Fitzmyer, Scripture, the Soul of Theology (New York/Mahwah, N. J. 1994), p. 14.

122 For a helpful guide to articles on archaeological sites and subjects see the 20 Year Index (1975–1994): Title, Author and Subject, ed. H. Shanks (Washington, DC: Biblical Archaeology Society, 1995). This index to Biblical Archaeology Review and Bible Review includes such theological concepts as baptism, the interpretation of the Bible, canon, circumcision (as a separate entry and under "Christianity"), commandments, conquest, covenant, creation, curses, ecology, eschatology, eucharist, etc.

123 The entries end with a guide to major publications upon which each summary is based; hence, intensive research can continue into areas requiring or inviting additional study.

ancient Palestine; these help us heed the following insight and indeed exhortation:

> Faith itself provides the stimulus towards acquiring a better understanding and therefore sets in motion historical investigation, which must always be critical. To alter Anselm's famous remark slightly, we might say that this is *fides quaerens veritatem historicam.*[124]

124 HENGEL, The Atonement, trans. J. Bowden (Philadelphia 1981), p. xii.

Israelitische und jüdische Geschichte

Zur Entstehung von Julius Wellhausens Buch

von

RUDOLF SMEND

1878 erschien der epochemachende erste Band einer „Geschichte Israels" von Julius Wellhausen. Er enthielt die Kritik der Quellen, der auf bald angekündigte zweite Band sollte die Geschichte selbst darstellen. Der erste Band wurde seit seiner zweiten Auflage (1883) „Prolegomena zur Geschichte Israels" betitelt, ein zweiter Band oder eine selbständig ausgeführte „Geschichte Israels" ist nie gefolgt, stattdessen verhältnismäßig spät, nämlich 1894, die „Israelitische und jüdische Geschichte". Wir fragen, ohne uns hier auf eine tiefergehende Interpretation und Würdigung des Werkes einlassen zu können, nach den Gründen für die Verzögerung und für den Wechsel des Titels. Zwischen beidem besteht ein Zusammenhang.

Was die Verzögerung angeht, so gab es bald ein wenig vornehmes Gerücht, das uns ausgerechnet in einer vornehmen englischen Zeitschrift greifbar wird: Wellhausen habe „a significant intimation" erhalten, es sei „better for him to publish nothing more of that sort"[1]. Wellhausen dementierte das entschieden: „Weder die preußische Staatsregierung noch das preußische Kirchenregiment haben mir abgerathen den 2. Band zu schreiben; auch nicht in der allermildesten Weise hat man versucht eine Pression auf mich auszuüben, sondern mich einfach ignorirt, d.h. mir vollkommene Freiheit gelassen."[2]

Ein anderes Motiv konstruierten konservative Fachgenossen. „Ich höre", schrieb Wellhausen Ende 1879 an seinen Verleger, „daß meine Freunde, die Herren Riesen Dillmann und Genossen, mit Genugthuung die Mähre verbreiten, der zweite Band würde nie erscheinen, und dadurch würde der Beweis geliefert, daß auf der Grundlage meiner Kritik ein positiver Aufbau der israel. Geschichte nicht möglich sei. Aber wenn ich am Leben bleibe, wird diesen guten Menschen und schlechten Musikanten der zweite Band doch noch mal auf den Weihnachtstisch gelegt werden, wenn sies am mindsten

---

[1] Ath. 27. 5. 1881, 683.

[2] Brief an W. R. Smith, 27. 6. 1881 (Univ. Bibl. Cambridge ADD 7449/D 762).

glauben. Ich habe die bestimmte Absicht, ihn zu schreiben, und das Material liegt längst fertig bereit."[3]

Die „bestimmte Absicht" ist evident. Wellhausen hat immer wieder betont, daß er die Analyse um der Synthese willen, die Kritik als „Substruction zu einem positiven Aufbau"[4] betrieb; eine Analyse ohne dieses Ziel (und so übrigens auch fast die ganze auf seiner eigenen Arbeit fußende Pentateuchkritik in den letzten beiden Jahrzehnten des 19. Jahrhunderts) langweilte ihn. Es drängte ihn also zur Fortsetzung, und sogleich nach der Rückkehr von der ersten größeren Reise seines Lebens (zu Abraham Kuenen in Leiden), mit der er sich für den Abschluß des ersten Bandes belohnt hatte, schrieb er im Oktober 1878 an den Verleger: „Den zweiten Band werde ich diesen Winter schreiben, so Gott will. Er wird weit weniger Anstrengung kosten als der erste."[5]

Soll man sagen: Gott wollte nicht? Schon bald nach der eben zitierten frohgemuten Äußerung geriet Wellhausen in einen wenig produktiven Krisenzustand, zu dem außer Tod und Krankheit in der Familie vor allem sein immer negativeres Verhältnis zu den Aufgaben eines Theologieprofessors beitrug. Von ihm machte er im Februar 1879 dem Ministerium Mitteilung, 1882 wurde er nach langem Warten auf eine Entscheidung als Extraordinarius für semitische Philologie nach Halle versetzt. In dieser Übergangszeit fühlte er sich „flügellahm" und, wie er dem Verleger entschuldigend schrieb, zwar imstande „zu wurzeln und gelehrtes Zeug zu machen, aber nicht, von der Leber weg zu schreiben"[6]. Dazu kam, daß er sich ja nun als Semitist qualifizieren mußte. „Ich studire [...] Arabische Poeten und nicht Geschichte Israels", bekam im Sommer 1880, kaum zu seiner Freude, der Verleger zu lesen[7].

Doch bald ergab sich unverhofft die Gelegenheit, wenigstens ein vorläufiges Surrogat herzustellen. Wellhausen verdankte sie seinem schottischen Freund William Robertson Smith, der sich damals in einer ähnlichen Übergangssituation befand wie er selbst. Ihm machte er von Zeit zu Zeit briefliche Mitteilungen über den Stand seiner Arbeit, aus denen wir immerhin wissen, daß er sie nicht völlig aus den Augen verlor. So im Juni 1879: „Mit dem 2. Bande geht es recht schleppend vorwärts; Moses verursacht mir natürlich viel unfruchtbares Kopfzerbrechen, nach der Melodie: ‚so macht' ich's wenn ich Moses wär.' Auf Beweis muß ich vielfach verzichten, ich kann nur meine Anschauung von der Sache geben und die kritischen Zähne dann daran nagen lassen so viel sie

---

[3] Brief an Georg Reimer 30. 11. 1879 (im Besitz des Verlags Walter de Gruyter & Co., Berlin).

[4] Prolegomena zur Geschichte Israels, Berlin ^{2}1883, III.

[5] An Reimer 11. 10. 1878.

[6] An Reimer 30. 11. 1879; vgl. auch schon den Brief vom 14. 2. 1879.

[7] Brief an Reimer, 23. 6. 1880.

mögen."[8] Und genau ein Jahr später, Juni 1880: „Mit dem 2. Theile meiner Geschichte warte ich noch; vieles ist schon geschrieben, so das ganze erste Drittel, Mose, die Richter, die drei ersten Könige; ebenso das 6. Kap: der Untergang Samariens und die Prophetie."[9]

„Warte ich noch" – das klingt nach einstweiligem Liegenlassen dieser „schleppend" hergestellten Fragmente. Hier nun griff Robertson Smith ein. Gerade im Juni 1880 Mitherausgeber der Encyclopaedia Britannica geworden[10], veranlaßte er, daß Wellhausen der Artikel „Jewish History" (später „Israel" genannt) angeboten wurde. Wellhausen reagierte erfreut: „Die Sache ist mir sehr erwünscht; ich habe keine Lust meinen 2. Band bald herauszugeben, da ich weiß daß mehrere Herren darauf lauern ihn abzuschreiben[11]; aber um so lieber mache ich eine kurze Skizze seines Inhalts für eine nicht deutsche Encyclopaedie, die bei uns wenig verbreitet ist."[12]

Der Artikel, deutsch zwischen Oktober 1880 und Januar 1881 niedergeschrieben, umfaßt gedruckt 72 Lexikonspalten[13]. Er gliedert sich in 17 Kapitel: 1. The beginnings of the nation. 2. The settlement in Palestine. 3. The foundation of the kingdom, and the first three kings. 4. From Jeroboam I. to Jeroboam II. 5. God, the world, and the life of men in Old Israel. 6. The fall of Samaria. 7. The deliverance of Judah. 8. The prophetic reformation. 9. Jeremiah and the destruction of Jerusalem. 10./11. The captivity and the restauration. 11. The Hellenistic period. 12./13. The Hasmonaeans. 14./15. Herod and the Romans. 16. The Rabbins. 17. The Jewish Dispersion[14].

Zur Erleichterung der Arbeit des Übersetzers und als Weihnachtsgeschenk für seine Freunde ließ Wellhausen die deutsche Vorlage der ersten neun Kapitel unter dem Titel „Geschichte Israels" in etwa zwanzig Exemplaren mit sehr breitem Rand als Manuskript drucken[15]. Dieser Text bietet zweifellos das Schema und weithin auch schon den Wortlaut des geplanten zweiten Bandes der Geschichte Israels. Ich erinnere an die Aussage vom Juni 1880, „das ganze erste Drittel, Mose, die Richter, die drei ersten Könige" sei schon geschrieben – das entspricht genau den ersten drei der neuen Kapitel des Privatdrucks von Weihnachten 1880, so daß der Schluß unabweisbar ist: weiter als bis zur Zerstörung Jerusalems 586 v. Chr. sollte das Buch damals nicht reichen. Mit

---

8 6. 6. 1879, aaO. D 748.

9 3. 6. 1880, aaO. D 751.

10 Vgl. J. S. Black/G. Chrystal, The Life of William Robertson Smith, 1912, 453ff.

11 Ein uns noch nicht begegnetes Motiv für sein Zögern!

12 An W. R. Smith 14. 8. 1880, aaO. D 754.

13 EBrit [9]XIII, 369–431.

14 Ich gebe die Überschriften, die in der EBrit noch fehlen, nach dem Neudruck in der englischen Ausgabe der Prolegomena.

15 Neudruck in: J. Wellhausen, Grundrisse zum Alten Testament, hg. v. R. Smend, TB 27, München 1965, 13–64.

dem breiten Rand wollte Wellhausen also nicht nur dem Übersetzer die Arbeit erleichtern, sondern auch sich selbst – bei der Herstellung des umfangreicheren, aber nicht über 586 hinaus zu verlängernden deutschen Buches.

Der Tatbestand überrascht, wenn man von der späteren „Israelitischen und jüdischen Geschichte" herkommt. Er könnte aber auch nach flüchtiger Lektüre des ersten Bandes von 1878 bzw. der „Prolegomena" überraschen. Dort trägt der resümierende Schlußteil die Überschrift „Israel und das Judentum" – ist dann nicht eine „Geschichte Israels und Judas" oder eine „Israelitische und jüdische Geschichte" die natürliche Fortsetzung? Doch das wäre ein Mißverständnis. Israel und Judentum bedeuten nämlich in jener Überschrift nicht Größen gleicher Art und gleichen Ranges, sondern ein Gegensatzpaar. Die Kritik hatte sich die Aufgabe gestellt, durch die späteren Entstellungen hindurch zum vorexilischen und vorgesetzlichen alten Israel vorzudringen, dem Wellhausens eigentliches Interesse, um nicht zu sagen: seine Liebe galt. Über die „Geschichte der Tradition" innerhalb des ersten Bandes setzte er das Hesiod-Zitat (Erga 40): Πλέον ἥμισυ παντός, die Hälfte ist mehr als das Ganze, d. h. die israelitische Hälfte des Alten Testaments ist mehr als das durch jüdische Hände hergestellte Ganze. So sollte denn auch die Hälfte und nicht das Ganze der Gegenstand des zweiten Bandes sein: die Geschichte Israels bis zum Beginn des Babylonischen Exils.

Dem entspricht, daß die Kapitel 10–17 in der Encyclopaedia Britannica, um die Jahreswende 1880/81 niedergeschrieben, viel stärker als das Vorangehende den Charakter einer Improvisation tragen. Das gilt am meisten von den Kapiteln 16 und 17, die zeitlich noch über die spätere Israelitische und jüdische Geschichte hinausreichen. Den Schluß der Geschichte Israels von 1880 und die Zäsur innerhalb des Artikels in der Encyclopaedia Britannica bilden die Sätze:

> Die geistigen Zerstörer des alten Israel waren die Propheten. Sonst war die Nation das realisirte Ideal gewesen, sie setzten der Nation das Ideal entgegen. Der Zwiespalt sollte dann dadurch wieder ausgeglichen werden, daß das abgelöste Ideal zum Gesetz gemacht und das Volk ihm conformirt wurde. Der Versuch hatte sehr wichtige Folgen, indem Jahve, nachdem er aus dem Volk gewichen war, als Gesetz weiter lebte, aber der Absicht der Propheten entsprach das nicht. Worauf sie ohne es zu wissen hinarbeiteten, war der religiöse Individualismus, der in dem Verfall der Nation seine geschichtliche Quelle hatte und auch außerhalb der prophetischen Sphäre zu Tage trat. Mit Männern wie Amos und Hosea brach die auf innere Überzeugung gegründete moralische Persönlichkeit durch die Schranken des Volksthums; ein Irrthum war es, daß sie ihre Gesinnung zur Basis des Volksthums machen zu können glaubten. Jeremia sah den Irrthum ein, das wahre Israel schrumpfte auf ihn selber zusammen. An der Wahrheit seiner Überzeugung zweifelte er darum keinen Augenblick; er wußte, daß Jahve auf seiner Seite war, daß an ihm die Zukunft und die Ewigkeit hing. Aber statt des Volkes machte er zum Subject der Religion das Herz und die Gesinnung des Einzelnen. Auf den Trümmern Jerusalems blickte er freudiger Hoffnung voll in die Zukunft, dessen gewiß, daß Jahve die Schuld dermaleinst vergeben und das abgebrochene Verhältnis erneuern werde – jedoch auf Grund eines anderen Bundes als des deuteronomischen. „Ich will meine Thora in ihr

Inneres legen und auf ihr Herz schreiben; es soll keiner dem andern die Kenntnis Jahves beibringen, sondern sie alle werden sie inne haben."[16]

Dieser Schluß, mag er gerade als Schluß wirkungsvoll sein, weist doch voraus. Er enthält bereits die Quintessenz von allem, was später noch kommen sollte, bis hin zum Kapitel über das Evangelium in der Israelitischen und jüdischen Geschichte. Wellhausen formulierte später: „Die Prophetie kann vom Gesetz, von der jüdischen Frömmigkeit, und vom Christentum nicht getrennt werden; sie selber bildet schon den Übergang von der israelitischen zur jüdischen Geschichte."[17] Diese Einsicht hatte er schrittweise gewonnen und historiographisch realisiert.

1884 veröffentlichte er eine Neufassung des Textes von 1880, aber nun schon unter dem Titel „Geschichte Israels und Juda's im Umriß"[18]. Das Neue wird in den späteren Kapiteln immer breiter und betrifft besonders die Prophetie. Dem Kapitel über die prophetische Reformation ist eine ausführliche Erörterung des Deuteronomiums einverleibt, die den Satz enthält, hier zeige sich, „daß Propheten und Gesetz kein Gegensatz, sondern identisch sind und im Verhältnis von Ursache und Wirkung stehen"[19]. Nun hat das Gesetz aber nicht nur (in der Gestalt des Deuteronomiums) der vorexilischen Reformation des Josia, sondern auch (in der Gestalt des Priesterkodex) der nachexilischen Restauration des Esra zugrundegelegen. So überrascht es kaum, daß im „Umriß" ein neues, zehntes Kapitel hinzutritt, „Das Exil und die Restauration". Ganz neu ist dieses Kapitel allerdings nicht; es stand schon in der Encyclopaedia, aber als Anfang des „jüdischen" Teils. Für den „Umriß" wurde es in den Ausgang der Geschichte Israels umgewandelt und dafür mit den Schlußsätzen versehen:

Die Grundlagen des Judentums waren nun ein für alle mal gelegt. Über die weitere Geschichte desselben, bis zu seinem Kampfe gegen den Hellenismus, erfahren wir beinah nichts; über die nächsten Jahrhunderte schlägt das Dunkel zusammen. So bildet die Einführung des Gesetzes durch Ezra, das Endresultat der Geschichte Israels, auch äußerlich einen notgedrungenen Abschluß.[20]

Einen notgedrungenen Abschluß auch dieses „Umrisses", so denkt man, und so war es vermutlich zunächst bei der Niederschrift gemeint. Aber unverhofft kommt noch ein elftes Kapitel, und es ist das mit Abstand längste überhaupt: „Das Judentum und das Christentum". Hier findet das, worauf der Schluß der

16 Privatdruck 76; Grundrisse 63f.; EBrit 417.

17 Israelitische und jüdische Geschichte, Berlin [1]1894, V.

18 J. WELLHAUSEN, Skizzen und Vorarbeiten I, Berlin 1884 (Neudruck 1985), 3–102. Auf dem Titelblatt eine wohl jüngere Fassung der Überschrift: „Abriß der Geschichte Israels und Juda's".

19 AaO. 69.

20 AaO. 86.

„Geschichte Israels“ von 1880 andeutend vorausgeblickt hat, in einer gedrängten Skizze (wir befinden uns in den „Skizzen und Vorarbeiten“!) seine Darstellung: zunächst das Judentum in seiner doppelten Prägung durch das Gesetz und die individuelle Frömmigkeit, dann das Evangelium, von dem gilt: es „entwikkelt verborgene Triebe des Alten Testaments, aber es protestiert gegen die herrschende Richtung des Judentums“[21]. Der Schluß des Ganzen hat geradezu den Charakter eines Bekenntnisses:

> Das wahre Salz der Erde bleibt doch für alle Zeit der religiöse Individualismus des Evangeliums. Die Gewißheit, daß weder Tod noch Leben uns von der Gemeinschaft Gottes scheiden kann, treibt die Furcht aus, die der Liebe entgegensteht; ein völlig überirdischer Glaube gibt den Mut auch zu erfolgloser Aufopferung und zu resigniertem Gehorsam auf Erden. Es muß uns doch gelingen: aufwärts die Herzen![22]

Hermann Gunkel hat den „Umriß“ die „genialste Schrift“ Wellhausens genannt[23] und dabei gewiß nicht zuletzt an das Schlußkapitel gedacht. Etwas anders urteilte der Autor: „Das 11 Kapitel ist vollkommen mislungen, eine vollgestopfte Wurst, lauter Fleisch, ohne die natürliche Gliederung, da die Knochen fortgelassen sind. Außerdem ist es großentheils unverständlich, ich muß viel ausführlicher reden, um klar zu sein. Für richtig halte ich natürlich, was ich gesagt habe; und wenn ich es klarer und ausführlicher sage, wird es Wilamowitz noch viel weniger gefallen.“[24]

Ob es boshafte Absicht war oder nicht (es war wohl eher eine Art freundschaftlicher Nebenabsicht): Wilamowitz mußte sich zehn Jahre später gefallen lassen, daß gerade ihm die Israelitische und jüdische Geschichte gewidmet wurde, in der Wellhausen das im „Umriß“ Gesagte im historischen Zusammenhang (also mit den „Knochen“) „viel ausführlicher“ neu sagte. Bevor er das tat, erschien das elfte Kapitel, die „vollgestopfte Wurst“, noch zweimal auf englisch, nämlich in zwei Neudrucken des Artikels „Israel“ aus der Encyclopaedia Britannica. Schon 1883 hatte Wellhausen den Abschied vom Konzept der Geschichte Israels in zwei Bänden auch dadurch vollzogen, daß er den ersten Band bei Gelegenheit der zweiten Auflage in „Prolegomena zur Geschichte Israels“ umbenannte. Als „Prolegomena to the History of Israel“ erschien er 1885 auch in englischer Übersetzung und mit Hinzufügung des Artikels „Israel“, wobei hinter Kapitel 10 „The captivity and the restauration“ jetzt als Kapitel 11 „Judaism and Christianity“ erscheint – wie im deutschen „Umriß“ von 1884, nur daß sich an das „Sursum corda“ noch die ganze jüdische Geschichte anschließt. Diese unglückliche Disposition beseitigte Wellhausen in dem 1891 separat erschienenen „Sketch of the History of Israel and Judah“, der

---

21 AaO. 98.

22 AaO. 102.

23 In: Vierzig Jahre „Christliche Welt“. Festgabe für Martin Rade, hg. v. H. Mulert, Gotha 1927, 152.

24 Brief vom 20. 10. 1884 an seine Schwiegermutter (im Besitz der Familie Bewer in Berlin).

den Artikel aus der Encyclopaedia Britannica fast unverändert wiedergibt und „Judaism and Christianity" als ein Stück eigener Art in Form eines „Appendix" deutlich abgesetzt an den Schluß stellt.

Dies alles konnte nicht befriedigen, und so fragte Wellhausen 1887 nach dem Abschluß seines ersten Hauptwerks zur Arabistik, der „Reste arabischen Heidentumes", den Verleger, wie es mit dem Absatz des ersten Heftes der „Skizzen und Vorarbeiten" stünde, die den „Umriß" von 1884 enthielten; er habe Lust, „eine selbständige, etwas erweiterte Ausgabe" des „Umrisses" zu machen[25]. Der Verleger antwortete enttäuschend: es werde noch 5–6 Jahre gehen. Folglich machte sich Wellhausen 1892 an die Arbeit, 1894 erschien das Buch. In ihm hat sich das bisherige elfte Kapitel zu vier umfangreichen selbständigen Kapiteln ausgewachsen, die jeweils an ihrer Stelle in den Geschichtsverlauf eingegliedert sind: Das Gesetz (Kap. 13), Die jüdische Frömmigkeit (15), Die Ausbildung des Judaismus (19), Das Evangelium (23). Diesmal beanstandete Gunkel die Disposition[26], und Wellhausen ließ sie auf die Dauer auch nicht ganz unverändert, indem er in der dritten Auflage (1897) das Kapitel über das Evangelium an den Schluß versetzte, wodurch wieder ein Bekenntnis ans Ende des Ganzen zu stehen kam. Der „jüdische" Teil hat 1894 den anderthalbfachen Umfang des „israelitischen" gewonnen, und mag daran auch beteiligt sein, daß hier keine „Prolegomena" vorausgesetzt werden konnten und also vielerlei kritische Noten geliefert werden mußten, so erklärte Wellhausen doch ausdrücklich diese Proportion für „innerlich berechtigt"[27]. Das hätte er zwanzig oder auch zehn Jahre vorher schwerlich getan. Als er nach weiteren zwanzig Jahren aus Anlaß der 7. Auflage einen Dankesbrief von Theodor Nöldeke erhalten hatte, antwortete er ihm:

> Ich bin erfreut und stolz, daß Sie mein Buch noch einmal gelesen haben, und danke Ihnen herzlich dafür. Die alten wilden Israeliten haben mir früher auch vorzugsweise am Herzen gelegen, wobei der Reiz der allerdings vereinzelten schönen alten Erzählungen aus der Richter- und älteren Königszeit mit wirkte. Aber die weltgeschichtliche Bedeutung des Judentums als Grundlage des Christentums hat schließlich mein Hauptinteresse auf sich gezogen.[28]

Als Wellhausen sein Buch der Öffentlichkeit übergab, bekannte er, er habe sich „manchmal auf Gebiete begeben müssen", wo er „nicht zu Hause" sei. Das Judentum, bei aller Originalität „doch im Mittelpunkt der des Altertum ab-

---

[25] An Reimer 19. 9. 1887.

[26] Rezension von Trochs-Lund, Himmelsbild und Weltanschauung im Wandel der Zeiten, CW 14 (1900), 58–61, hier 60.

[27] AaO. (Anm. 17) V.

[28] Brief vom 24. 1. 1914 (Universitätsbibliothek Tübingen, Nachlaß Nöldeke). – Übrigens nennt Wellhausen das Buch, als die erste Auflage im Druck ist, „eine jüdische Geschichte" (Brief an F. Justi, 2. 6. 1894, in meinem Besitz). Es hat auch seinen Sinn, daß auf dem Titelblatt in sämtlichen von WELLHAUSEN selbst besorgten Auflagen „jüdische Geschichte" mit größeren Buchstaben gesetzt ist als „Israelitische und".

schließenden Culturmischung", stelle der Forschung „die schwierigsten Aufgaben, zu deren Lösung sich die Theologie mit der Philologie oder die Philologie mit der Theologie, viel enger verbünden" müsse, „als es bisher geschehen" sei[29]. Zuweilen wird dieses Bündnis auf die engste mögliche Weise, nämlich in einer einzigen Person, Wirklichkeit – heute in keiner Person eindrücklicher und fruchtbarer als in Martin Hengel.

---

[29] AaO. (Anm. 17) V. Während der Vorbereitung der 4. Auflage, bei der er sich „vielleicht genöthigt" sieht, „die spätere jüdische Geschichte noch stärker als bisher umzuarbeiten", äußert WELLHAUSEN: „Leider ist dabei die Schwierigkeit, daß ich vom Hellenismus nichts rechtes verstehe". (An S. Taylor, Univ. Bibl. Cambridge Add 6260 (156).

Gottesknecht und Gottes Knechte

Zur ältesten Deutung eines deuterojesajanischen Themas

von

Hans-Jürgen Hermisson

Gottes Knecht oder Gottes Knechte – das scheint ein Thema zu sein, um das die Exegeten sich bis zum Jüngsten Tage streiten sollen. Die Frage dürfte schon *die* Schriftgelehrten beschäftigt haben, die noch im Kanon selbst zu Wort kamen, vollends ihre Nachfahren; ob man sich aber über die individuelle oder kollektive Deutung schon *gestritten* hat, das ist für die Frühzeit nicht so deutlich und vor der Festsetzung eines kanonischen Textes auch nicht nötig. Immerhin war bekanntlich die kollektive Auffassung des Knechts zwar die vorherrschende, aber nicht die einzige. Das lehrt für Jes 53 das Targum oder jene berühmte Frage des äthiopischen Kämmerers in Acta 8, der gar nicht auf die Idee kommt, daß auch ein Kollektiv gemeint sein könnte. Man wüßte gerne, auf welcher exegetischen Tradition seine Vermutung, es könne sich um den Propheten selber handeln, beruht, hat aber dafür wenig Anhalt. Vielleicht muß man bis ins Jesaja-Buch selbst zurückgehen und auf die prophetische Deutung des Knechts in Jes 61 verweisen – obwohl gerade Jes 53 darin kaum oder nur verborgen anklingt. Wir müssen am Ende auf diesen Text zurückkommen.

Die folgenden Überlegungen betreffen nur einen schmalen Sektor der antiken Deutung der Gottesknechtslieder. Es sind Auslegungen, die diesen Texten im Jesajabuch gegeben werden, somit die ältesten Interpretationen, die durch Texte belegt sind. Dabei ist vorausgesetzt, daß diese Texte im Unterschied zu den drei ersten Gottesknechtsliedern nicht von Deuterojesaja selbst stammen. Stellt sich somit die Frage, ob oder wieweit die ältesten Interpretationen den ursprünglichen Sinn treffen, so muß dieser ursprüngliche Sinn wenigstens in aller Kürze skizziert werden. Das eigentliche Interesse gilt dann aber den interpretierenden Sekundärtexten, vor allem im Deuterojesaja-Buch.

1. Zum Verständnis der Gottesknechtslieder Deuterojesajas[1]

Auch der ursprüngliche Sinn der Gottesknechtslieder ist ein kontextualer Sinn. Ihr Kontext ist aber nicht sogleich ein Buch, sondern die dem Exilspropheten aufgetragene Verkündigung. Deren Grundgedanken lassen sich in wenigen Strichen zeichnen: Jahwe wird Israel durch Kyros aus dem babylonischen Exil befreien und wird es unter Zeichen und Wundern durch eine verwandelte Wüste heimführen zum Zion, den er verherrlicht. Israel wird darüber in Jubel und Lobpreis ausbrechen, und die Völker werden das wunderbare Geschehen sehen und sich – überwältigt von dem einzigen rettenden Gott – diesem Gott anschließen: so kommt die ganze Welt ins Heil.

So einfach könnte es sein, und dafür brauchte es keinen Gottesknecht, oder höchstens *einen*: den Knecht Israel, der das alles an sich geschehen läßt und im Lobpreis Jahwes darauf reagiert, der auf dem Heimzug und in Jerusalem Hymnen singt, wie das eigentlich gar nicht anders möglich ist. Aber die Wirklichkeit ist komplizierter. Israel ist ein verzagtes und kleingläubiges Volk, man muß es erst um Jahwe versammeln, damit der Weg durch die blühende Wüste zum verherrlichten Zion beginnen kann. Dazu kommt ein Zweites. Wenn die Welt überzeugt werden soll, daß *Jahwe* der eine und einzige rettende Gott ist, dann genügt dafür nicht die Anschauung einer sich wunderbar wandelnden Welt – dafür könnten sie auch Marduk oder den Gott des siegreichen Persers verantwortlich machen; nein – man muß es ihnen beweisen. Der Weissagungsbeweis beruht darauf, daß Jahwe sein schöpferisches Wort zuvor, hörbar, artikuliert in die Welt gebracht hat und seine Wirkung tun läßt.

Dazu also braucht Jahwe den zweiten Knecht, den Propheten. Es ist noch immer ein einfaches Modell: Die Aufgabe des Gottesknechts Israel ist gar nicht durchführbar ohne diese Zweiteilung der Rollen. Denn Israel ist als Jahwes Knecht geschaffen, um Jahwes *Zeuge* vor der Welt zu sein. Es ist Zeuge im Welt-Prozeß dafür, daß das schöpferische und rettende Wort Jahwes sich an ihm realisiert und so die Welt einlädt, sich retten zu lassen. Aber Israel muß auf den Weg gebracht, und, vor allem, dieses schöpferische und rettende Wort Jahwes muß durch den Propheten *zuvor* verkündet werden. *Der* Knecht Jahwes also ist notwendig differenziert: Der eine, der Prophet, und die vielen, Israel.[2]

---

[1] Zur Begründung vgl. vorerst H.-J. Hermisson, Israel und der Gottesknecht bei Dtjes, ZThK 79 (1982) 1–24.; ders., Der Lohn des Knechts: Die Botschaft und die Boten, FS H. W. Wolff (1981) 269–287.

[2] Mit großer Raffinesse ist das in Jes 43,8–13 gestaltet: Israel wird als der *blinde* Zeuge für Jahwe im Welt-Prozeß Jahwes aufgerufen, und dieses unmögliche Unterfangen bekäme dadurch Sinn, daß Jahwe Israel befreit und seinen Weg durch die Wüste verherrlicht und Israel somit mehr Beweisstück als Zeuge ist (oder, wie man gern gesagt hat, der „passive Zeuge"). Dazu muß man es *herausführen* (V. 8): sicher kein spezifischer Terminus der Gerichtsszenerie, sondern eine Exodus-Vokabel – und schon dafür könnte der prophetische

Die Gottesknechtslieder spiegeln diesen komplexen Sachverhalt. Sie reden von der prophetischen Knechtsrolle in einem weltweiten und daher königlichen Amt, aber sie reden von dem weltweiten Effekt dieses Amtes selbstverständlich so, daß nur Israel und der Prophet gemeinsam, in der Korrelation ihrer Anteile am Knechtsamt, ihn bewirken können. Sie reden von dem prophetischen Knecht, der das leistet, was Israel verweigert; der das ideale Israel und ein Vorbild Israels ist, indem er Jahwe vertraut. Der prophetische Knecht der Lieder „ist" Israel oder vielmehr: Er repräsentiert Israel, vor Jahwe und vor der Welt, aber bei dieser Repräsentation Israels ohne Israel im ganzen kann es selbstverständlich nicht bleiben, wenn Jahwes Werk zum Ziel kommen soll. Andererseits muß nicht das ganze Israel zum Propheten werden; es genügt der eine, dem das prophetische Amt in Israel jetzt übertragen ist. Aber wieder reden die Texte von ihm und seinem prophetischen Amt, indem sie ihn in die Kette seiner Vorgänger einreihen und in dem einen Propheten *die* Prophetie erscheinen lassen. Jetzt freilich ist *er* der Prophet: der eine, namenlose im Exil.

Mit alledem wird der Versuch gemacht, die zahlreichen und doch wieder in wenige Grundmuster einzureihenden modernen Deutungen zu sammeln und in einer bestimmten Perspektive zu konzentrieren. Vorausgesetzt ist allerdings, daß der prophetische Gottesknecht keine literarische Fiktion ist, ebenso wenig wie das Israel, zu dem er gesandt wird. Die Gottesknechtstexte sind „Reflexionen" über ein Amt, das Amt eines Propheten, „heute", da Jahwe zu seinem endgültigen Heilswerk aufbricht.

2. Deutungen im Deuterojesaja-Buch

Es gibt eine Reihe von Texten im Deuterojesaja-Buch, die den Gottesknecht anders verstanden haben. Daß sie dem Grundbestand deuterojesajanischer Texte angehörten, scheint aus verschiedenen Gründen ausgeschlossen[3]. Da ist

---

Knecht als Mittler gefragt sein. Vollends ist er das in V. 10, und m. E. ist er dort auch ausdrücklich erwähnt: „ihr seid meine Zeugen . . ., und mein Knecht (ist mein Zeuge), damit ihr erkennt und mir glaubt und einseht, daß ich *er* bin: Vor mir wurde kein Gott gebildet, und nach mir wird keiner sein". Der oft beanstandete szenische Knick, da doch eigentlich die Völker erkennen und glauben sollten, ist bewußt gesetzt, weil der blinde Zeuge nicht blind bleiben darf, sondern nun seinerseits im Hymnus auf die Rettungstat antworten muß. Wenn man aber daraus des öfteren gefolgert hat, es gehe in den Gerichtsreden gegen die fremden Völker und ihre Götter gar nicht um die Völker, sondern nur um Israel (so zuletzt J. VAN OORSCHOT, Von Babel zum Zion. Eine literarkritische und redaktionsgeschichtliche Untersuchung: BZAW 206, 1993, 34.37), so ist das m. E. zu kurz geschlossen und wird dem szenischen Aufgebot der Völker in der Gerichtsversammlung nicht gerecht: Zwar muß Israel zuerst glauben, um sein Zeugenamt voll ausfüllen zu können, aber sein erwünschtes Zeugnis für Jahwe zielt noch immer auf die Völker und deren Einsicht.

[3] Vgl. dazu H.-J. HERMISSON, Einheit und Komplexität Deuterojesajas. Probleme der Redaktionsgeschichte von Jes 40–55: The Book of Isaiah/Le livre de Isaïe, ed. J. VERMEYLEN,

einmal ein Unterschied der sprachlichen Gestaltung: Erst hier findet sich der Einfluß des deuteronomistischen Jeremia-Buches, manchmal auch der des Ezechiel-Erbes. Nur hier werden deuterojesajanische Wendungen in Variationen und in Kombination mit anderem Propheten-Erbe zu neuen Texten verarbeitet, so daß manche Texte sich wie Florilegien aus Deuterojesaja lesen. Zu diesem Unterschied in der Sprachgestalt kommt zweitens eine veränderte Sicht der heilsgeschichtlichen Situation Israels. Wenn bei Deuterojesaja das Heil schon da war und alle Hindernisse von Jahwe selbst beseitigt wurden, wenn Israels Schuld bezahlt und getilgt war, so taucht jetzt die Frage auf, warum das Heil noch immer nicht eingetroffen sei. Die Antwort ist doppelter Art: Es liegt an Israels Sünde, Israels Umkehr würde das Heil ermöglichen. Umkehr – das heißt einerseits zwar noch immer: Israels Glaube, aber daneben Israels Gebotsgehorsam (48,17–19; 55,5–7). Neben der Bedingtheit des Heils durch Erfüllung der Tora (was bei Deuterojesaja noch undenkbar gewesen wäre) steht das mahnende und einschärfende Wort vom *nahen* Heil, so daß man beides fast neutestamentlich zusammenfassen könnte:

Tut Buße, denn das Himmelreich ist nahe! (Matth 3,2; 4,17)

Oder mit einem dieser Texte:

Suchet Jahwe, da er sich finden läßt,
ruft ihn an, da er *nahe* ist;
der Frevler verlasse seinen Weg
und der Unheilstäter seine Planungen,
und kehre um zu Jahwe, daß er sich seiner erbarme,
und zu unserem Gott, denn reichlich vergibt er! (Jes 55,6–7).

„Nahe", קָרוֹב, das ist geradezu ein Leitmotiv dieser Schicht. Dieses Motiv aber ist keine neuerfundene Predigtdevise, sondern stammt aus dem dritten Gottesknechtslied. Dort bekennt der Gottesknecht, indem er sein Geschick in einer forensischen Szene zur Sprache bringt:

8 Nahe ist, der mich rechtfertigt,
wer will mit mir streiten?
Laß uns zusammen auftreten!
Wer ist mein Rechtsgegner?
Er nahe sich mir!
9 Siehe, der Herr Jahwe hilft mir,
wer will mich schuldig sprechen?
Siehe, sie alle vergehen wie ein Kleid,
die Motte wird sie fressen. (50,8–9)

BEThL (1989), sowie zu einzelnen Texten DERS., BKAT XI, 7–9 (1987ff.). Mit einer „Naherwartungsschicht" rechnet ebenfalls J. VAN OORSCHOT aaO. 197–242. Vgl. R.G. KRATZ, Kyros im Deuterojesaja-Buch: FAT 1 (1991) 206–216; er weist einen beträchtlichen Teil dieser Texte der von ihm so genannten „Ebed-Israel-Schicht" zu.

Als nächste Parallele zu dem Eingangssatz sei hier nur erst ein interpretierender Satz aus dem Gedicht in 51,1–8* genannt, nun in der Jahwerede:

5 Nahe ist mein Heil, meine Hilfe geht aus ...

Hebräisch ist das noch deutlicher: Dem קָרוֹב מַצְדִּיקִי des Gottesknechtslieds entspricht das קָרוֹב צִדְקִי in der Jahwerede des deutenden und aktualisierenden Textes.

Ehe wir uns näher auf diese Textschicht und ihren Umgang mit den Gottesknechtsliedern einlassen, ist zu überlegen, wem, welchen Kreisen, welcher Zeit wir solche Texte verdanken – da sie doch schwerlich vom Propheten oder höchstens von einem gründlich veränderten und somit auch wieder einem anderen stammen könnten.

Der Umgang mit der Überlieferung, die Mischung aus Respekt vor dem offenbarten Jahwewort und dem Bewußtsein, zu eigener deutend-aktualisierender Neugestaltung legitimiert zu sein, scheint bezeichnend für Prophetenschülerkreise zu sein. Es ist noch nicht der Typus des späteren Schriftgelehrten, der die heiligen Schriften alle – als Schriften – kennt und auslegt; es ist auch noch keine ausdrückliche Kommentierung, aber diese Art der „Textherstellung“ (oder auch Dichtung – mehr oder weniger) setzt den Umgang mit festformulierten und schriftlich oder mündlich überlieferten Texten voraus. Der Befund ist insofern mehrdeutig, als man Texte antrifft, die im geistigen Kontext der deuterojesajanischen Botschaft auch selbständig formuliert worden sein können, und andere, die nur im Zusammenhang des Buches einen Sinn geben: Mit schriftlich-redaktioneller Wirksamkeit dieser Kreise ist zu rechnen, aber es ist schwer zu glauben, daß ihre Tätigkeit sich auf den Umgang mit Tinte und „Papier“ beschränkte. Wir wissen wenig über solche Schülerkreise, weil unsere Paradebeispiele – die Elisa-Schüler und die Qumran-Sekte – beide gleichermaßen weit entfernt liegen; man muß aber solche Modelle suchen, weil der in den Prophetenbüchern dokumentierte Umgang mit der Überlieferung sich nicht als die Summe von Mißgriffen und literarischen Schandtaten von Schreibtischgelehrten erklären läßt, sondern voraussetzt, daß theologische Fragen und Probleme zu bewältigen waren, die Israel angingen und deren Bearbeitung daher auch eine Öffentlichkeit und mündliche Verkündigung (und sei es Verlesung) brauchte.

Schwieriger ist eine Erwägung über die *Zeit*, in der *diese* Schülertexte formuliert wurden. Man darf m.E. nicht zu weit von Deuterojesaja abrücken: Die proklamierte, erneut eingeschärfte Naherwartung und die darin vorausgesetzte enttäuschte oder resignierte Ungeduld bedingt ja, daß man die Botschaft des Propheten noch im Ohr hatte und mit dem Ablauf der Jahre nicht in Einklang brachte. Zu solchen Erwägungen allgemeiner Art treten Indizien einer begrenzten Verwandtschaft mit tritojesajanischen Texten hinzu, die hier nicht auszubreiten sind, die aber auch nicht einfach Identität (von „Tritojesaja“ und diesem „Redaktor") zulassen.[4] Kurz: Die Texte scheinen sich am besten aus der frühnachexilischen Zeit zu erklären, den Jahren zwischen der Eroberung Babylons im Jahre 539 und der ersten größeren Heimkehr von Exulanten um 520.[5] Kyros war gekommen, aber das Heil nicht, die babylonische Herrschaft war gestürzt, aber ihre Götter nicht – so etwa könnte man die Dissonanz zwischen Erwartung und Realität umschreiben. Warum ist das so – und was muß man im Gefolge Deuterojesajas auf solche Einstellung antworten?

Die Grundantwort ist schon genannt: Es liegt an Israel selbst und an seinem Verhalten; Israels Besserung bringt die umstürzende Besserung der Verhältnisse. In diesem Zusammenhang werden auch die Gottesknechtslieder erneut geltend gemacht. Der deutende Umgang der Schüler einer zweiten oder dritten Generation nach Deuterojesaja mit diesen Texten, soweit er sich im Jesaja-Buch niedergeschlagen hat, soll im folgenden an einigen Beispielen gezeigt werden.

2.1 Jesaja 51,4–8

4 Hört auf mich, mein Volk,
und meine Nation, lauscht mir,
denn Weisung geht von mir aus,
und mein Recht laß ich eilen[6] zum Licht der Völker.
5 Nahe ist mein Heil, meine Rettung geht hinaus,
und meine Arme richten die Völker.
Auf mich hoffen die Inseln
und harren auf meinen Arm.
6 Erhebt zu den Himmeln eure Augen
und blickt zur Erde drunten,
denn die Himmel zerflattern wie Rauch,
und die Erde zerfällt wie ein Gewand,
und ihre Bewohner sterben wie Mücken,
aber mein Heil besteht für immer,
und meine Gerechtigkeit zerbricht nicht[7].

---

[4] Jes 56,1 zitiert bereits die קָרוֹב-Schicht.

[5] Bei R. G. Kratz ist die „Ebed-Israel-Schicht" die letzte durchgehende Bearbeitung des Deuterojesaja-Buches, aber er setzt sie nicht viel später an, nämlich in die Anfangsjahre des Xerxes um 480 (aaO. 215). J. van Oorschot denkt an die Wende vom 6. zum 5. Jh. (aaO. 242).

[6] Oder mit W. A. M. Beuken, Jesaja deel II^{B}: POT (1983), z.St. „setz ich in Bewegung". Mit HAL ist das Verb hier wohl als Denominativ von רֶגַע aufzufassen; ob man zwei verschiedene Wurzeln רגע unterscheiden muß, ist fraglich. Unnötig ist die übliche Konjektur, in der das Verb vor allem aus metrischen Gründen mit V. 5 verbunden wird (z. B. in BHK und BHS). V. 4b hat im überlieferten Text einen guten Parallelismus (vgl. W. A. M. Beuken), und die Metrik in V. 5a wird durch den Eingriff erst zerstört, weil dann יצא ישעי keinen Platz mehr hat oder ein anderer Versteil gestrichen werden muß. Tatsächlich sind die beiden Verszeilen V. 4b.5a durch das unregelmäßige Metrum 3+4 und 4+3 aus dem Kontext herausgehoben.

[7] BHS erwägt Ableitung von נחת, was dann etwa „untergehen" bedeuten müßte, aber

7 Hört auf mich, die ihr Gerechtigkeit[8] kennt,
Volk, das meine Tora in ihrem Herzen hat,
fürchtet nicht die Schmach von Menschen,
und vor ihren Schmähungen erschreckt nicht,
8 denn wie ein Gewand frißt sie die Kleidermotte,
und wie Wolle die Motte,
aber meine Gerechtigkeit besteht für immer,
und mein Heil von Geschlecht zu Geschlecht.

Am Anfang steht der Text[9], der seinen deutenden Bezug auf die Gottesknechtslieder am augenfälligsten zu erkennen gibt und deshalb schon oft in diesem Zusammenhang gesehen wurde.[10] Jes 51,4–8 nimmt mit fast jedem seiner Sätze Wendungen aus den drei ersten Gottesknechtsliedern auf, daneben gibt es einzelne Bezugnahmen auf andere Deuterojesaja-Texte. Darüber hinaus klingt wenigstens in der letzten Anrede, „Volk, das meine Tora im Herzen hat" (V. 7), die jeremianische Heilstradition vom neuen Bund (Jer 31,31–34) an.

Der Text beginnt mit einem auffällig formulierten Aufruf zum Hören:

Lauscht mir, mein Volk, und meine Nation, hört auf mich!

תְּחִתּוּ V. 7 kann nur von חתת abgeleitet werden und dürfte wortspielartig die gleiche Wurzel mit unterschiedlicher Nuance gebrauchen.

[8] Wie in tritojesajanischen Texten (vgl. dazu K. Elliger, Deuterojesaja in seinem Verhältnis zu Tritojesaja: BWANT 63, 1933, 184) findet sich auch in dieser Schicht die doppelte Bedeutung von צדק(ה) als „Rechtschaffenheit, Gerechtigkeit" (des Menschen) und als „Heil, Heilserweis" (Jahwes), wobei beides zusammenhängt; vgl. 46,12f. und 48,17–19. Der jeweils vorherrschende Aspekt ergibt sich mit dem Kontext.

[9] Die Verse 1–2, die als eine erste „Strophe" zum gleichen Text und wohl auch zur gleichen Schicht gehören, müssen hier außer Betracht bleiben.

[10] B. Duhm, der den Text für deuterojesajanisch hält, folgert daraus, daß die Gottesknechtslieder nicht von Deuterojesaja stammen können. O. H. Steck hat in einer Reihe von Aufsätzen (Zur literarischen Schichtung in Jes 51 [1988]; Zions Tröstung. Beobachtungen und Fragen zu Jesaja 51,1–11 [1990]; Beobachtungen zu den Ziontexten in Jes 51–54 [1989]; jetzt zusammengestellt in ders., Gottesknecht und Zion: FAT 4, 1992, 60–124 [danach wird hier zitiert]) eine beeindruckende umfassende Analyse von Jes 51 vorgelegt, in der auch die hier besprochenen Texte noch einmal auf verschiedene Redaktionsschichten verteilt werden. Das betrifft im folgenden besonders die Verse 51,6a.8a, die ob ihrer globalen Vernichtungsaussagen nicht in den Horizont des Heilswortes zu passen scheinen (79ff.), sowie 51,16, bereits zur großjesajanischen Redaktion gehörig und auf den Propheten „Jesaja" in der Sicht dieser Redaktion zu deuten (70–72). Außerdem gehören nach Steck auch die Verse 4f.* und 12–15 verschiedenen Sekundärschichten an (vgl. bes. Gottesknecht 69f.). Da eine erneute Analyse von Jes 51 erst bei der Auslegung des ganzen Kapitels möglich ist, muß ich mich im folgenden auf Anfragen zur Beurteilung einzelner Aussagen beschränken; selbst wenn man mit Steck allein innerhalb von Jes 51 mit sechs Fortschreibungs-Schichten zu rechnen hat (vgl. das 9-Schichten-Schema auf S. 125), bleibt ja auch für ihn die Frage nach dem entstandenen Sinnganzen – dazu wird hier eine z. T. abweichende Antwort versucht. Da eine Einigung der Exegeten über die letzten Feinheiten der Schichtung nicht zu erwarten ist (man vgl. nur die beiden Arbeiten von Kratz und van Oorschot [Anm. 2 und 3]), beschränkt sich diese Untersuchung auf die deutlichen Schicht-Differenzen.

Die Anrede ist oft textkritisch korrigiert worden, schon wegen des merkwürdigen לְאֻמִּי „meine Nation" und auch, weil es im folgenden um die Völker geht: „ihr Völker", „ihr Nationen"; man las also das übliche עַמִּים und vor allem לְאֻמִּים. Aber dazu besteht kein Grund, wenn man sieht, daß hier ein vorgegebener Text bewußt abgewandelt wird. Die Vorlage ist Jes 49,1:

Hört auf mich, ihr Inseln, und lauscht, ihr Nationen in der Ferne!

– das ist offenbar eine Adresse, die jetzt nicht mehr oder doch nicht mehr in gleichem Maße aktuell ist und deshalb auf das eigene Volk und die eigene Nation umgemünzt wird. – Der Autor fährt fort:

denn Tora geht von mir aus, und mein Recht laß ich eilen zum Licht der Völker,

und bezieht sich damit auf 42,1.4[11] und 49,6[12] – vielleicht auch auf 42,6[13], falls der Satz dort nicht erst eingetragen ist, also auf das erste und dritte Gottesknechtslied sowie gegebenenfalls auf den Kyrostext 42,5–8, der dann auch schon als Gottesknechtstext verstanden wäre. Daß daneben mit der „Eile" ein eigenes Interesse dieser Schicht namhaft gemacht wird, zeigt sogleich der nächste Vers, V. 5, mit dem Stichwort von der *Nähe* des Heils, dessen Beziehung zum dritten Gottesknechtslied schon genannt wurde; die „harrenden" Inseln in V. 5b stammen wieder aus dem ersten Gottesknechtslied (42,4). Die Aufforderung in V. 6 „Erhebt eure Augen zum Himmel etc." knüpft mehr formal an eine deuterojesajanische Wendung in 40,26 an, was nur deswegen bemerkenswert ist, weil am Schluß des Verses noch einmal der gleiche Kontext anzuklingen scheint: „ihre Bewohner sterben wie Mücken" erinnert an 40,22 „ihre Bewohner wie Heuschrecken", wobei in 40,23f. immerhin vom Untergang von Herrschern und Würdenträgern die Rede ist; endlich könnte man auch auf die Metapher von Jahwes Arm in 40,10f. hinweisen. Ist darin nur ein lockerer Bezug erkennbar, so stammt das Bildwort „zerfallen wie ein Gewand" aus 50,9, dem dritten Gottesknechtslied, nur daß hier auf die Erde bezogen ist, was dort von den Feinden des Gottesknechts gesagt war. Nun wäre die Wiederholung einer Metapher in anderem Zusammenhang alleine noch kein Indiz für einen anderen Autor und auch nicht für den deutenden Umgang mit einem vorgegebenen Text, wenn nicht in Vers 7 und 8 wieder auf das dritte Gottesknechtslied Bezug genommen wäre, sprachlich am engsten in V. 8 „wie ein Gewand frißt sie die Motte etc." (50,9 in zerdehnter Gestalt), in der Sache aber mit den Schmähungen der Menschen auch in V. 7. Schließlich dürfte der Autor mit dem Stichwort יְשׁוּעָתִי, „mein Heil", in V. 6.8 an einen Vers des zweiten

[11] 42,1: „מִשְׁפָּט läßt er zu den Völkern ausgehen (יוֹצִיא)"; 42,4: „. . . bis er auf Erden den מִשְׁפָּט aufrichtet, und auf seine Tora harren die Inseln".

[12] „. . . ich mache dich zum Licht der Völker".

[13] „. . . ich bilde dich und mache dich . . . zum Licht der Völker".

Gottesknechtslieds, Jes 49,6, anknüpfen[14], und לְעוֹלָם mag durch vergleichbare Wendungen in 40,8 und 40,28 angeregt sein.

Überblickt man diese Zusammenstellung, so fällt die massierte Bezugnahme auf die Gottesknechtslieder auf: Das setzt doch wohl voraus, daß man sie noch als eine Größe sui generis kannte.

Nun hat W. A. M. Beuken gerade diesen Text als ein Beispiel für die Entbehrlichkeit literarkritischer Eingriffe genommen, wenn man ihn nur als ein Glied in der fortschreitenden Entwicklung des Deuterojesaja-Buches läse[15]. Dann muß man als Urheber des dramatischen Konzepts wohl einen einheitlichen Autor annehmen, weil ein Redaktor mit dem ihm vorgegebenen Material alsbald in unüberwindliche Schwierigkeiten geraten wäre. Aber ähnliche Schwierigkeiten ergeben sich bei der Annahme eines einheitlichen Autors. Denkt man an den Propheten und seine Verkündigung, die sich doch immerhin in diesem Buche niedergeschlagen haben müßte, so könnte man zwar eine naheliegende biographische Entwicklung des Propheten unterstellen, die ihn am Ende zu ganz anderen Aussagen nötigte als am Anfang, also Phasenmodelle, wie sie schon Joachim Begrich entwickelte. Aber die Frage nach einem einheitlichen Verkündigungskonzept wäre nicht beantwortet, sondern nur von verschiedenen Personen auf verschiedene Lebensphasen des Propheten verschoben, so daß man wieder unterscheiden müßte. Wir gehen also – gleichviel wer immer diesen Text verfaßte – von den Unterschieden aus und versuchen sie zu verstehen, ohne sie sogleich mit anderen Aussagen des Buches in Einklang bringen zu müssen.

Was hat sich gegenüber den Gottesknechtsliedern verändert? Eine Differenz ist vielfach erkannt und auf unterschiedliche Weise gedeutet worden: An die Stelle der Aktivität des Gottesknechtes tritt Jahwes Aktivität, wie man sogleich in V. 4 und 5 sieht: „Tora geht von mir aus ... auf mich warten die Inseln, und auf meinen Arm harren sie“ – das ist ja die Variante zu 42,1.4: „... Recht läßt er hinausgehen zu den Völkern ... auf seine Tora warten die Inseln“. Indes besagt die in dieser Weise festgestellte Variante noch gar nichts. Sie notiert nur eine Banalität prophetischen Sprachgebrauchs: Ob der Prophet verkündet, daß Jahwe selbst zu Gericht oder Rettung erscheint und die Geschichte gestaltet, oder ob er davon redet, daß Jahwe durch den Assyrer oder Kyros oder seinen Knecht – kurz, durch einen Beauftragten wirksam ist, das ist zunächst eine Frage der Form prophetischer Verkündigung und ganz und gar kein Widerspruch. Denn die Tora des Knechtes Jahwes in unserem Beispiel ist natürlich keine andere als Jahwes Tora, und daß Gott durch Menschen wirkt, ist eine biblische Selbstverständlichkeit. Insoweit wäre es also nur eine Scheindifferenz. Aber sie steht in einem Zusammenhang, der diesen Unterschied nun doch zur Geltung bringt. Der Knecht bleibt ja nicht einfach unerwähnt, so daß er in konkretisierender Formulierung an derselben Stelle wieder eingesetzt werden könnte, sondern er ist in den Angeredeten, denen die Botschaft gilt,

---

14 יְשׁוּעָה bei Deuterojesaja sonst nur 49,8 sek. und 52,7.10; ישׁע noch 45,8 und hier 51,5.

15 W. A. M. Beuken, Jesaja II^{B} 107–120, bes. 119 (zu Jes 51,1–8).

präsent. Das heißt, präsent ist *die* Rolle des Knechtes, wie sie im zweiten Teil des dritten Gottesknechtslieds erscheint: des Knechtes, der von Jahwe gegen alle Angriffe geschützt und gegenüber der Anklage gerechtfertigt wird. Und zur Verdeutlichung sei ausdrücklich hinzugefügt: Nicht der Knecht, der zu den Müden zu reden weiß, nicht der, dem Jahwe Morgen für Morgen das Ohr weckt, der eine gelehrte Zunge hat – nicht dieser Knecht wird hier geltend gemacht, sondern allein der passive, schutzbedürftige und schutzempfangende. Dieser Knecht aber ist „mein Volk", „meine Nation", „Volk, das meine Tora im Herzen hat" – aber nicht ein Knecht, der Tora und *mišpāṭ* zu den Inseln hinausgehen läßt: Dafür ist jetzt allein Jahwe zuständig, und in dieser Konstellation erlangt die zuerst genannte Differenz zu den Gottesknechtsliedern doch Gewicht. Der Knecht ist jetzt Israel, damit hängt das zusammen, oder genauer: Er ist *nur* Israel, nicht Prophet. Denn jene Angewiesenheit auf Jahwes Schutz und Rechtfertigung hatten ja die beiden Knechte bei Deuterojesaja gemeinsam. So darf man die zweite Differenz nicht einfach auf die Formel bringen, hier träte die kollektive an die Stelle der individuellen Deutung, sondern muß präzisieren: Hier werden die kollektiven Züge der Gottesknechtslieder isoliert und allein geltend gemacht. Kein scharfer Bruch zwischen diesem und dem ursprünglichen Sinn, sondern durchaus ein Moment der Kontinuität und eine unter neuen Bedingungen legitime Auslegung der Texte: Das scheint aus diesem neuformulierten und deutenden Gottesknechtstext zu sprechen.

Das ist aber noch nicht alles. Man müßte ja fragen, was das Israel nach 539, also nach der Befreiung durch Kyros, eigentlich noch zu fürchten hatte, daß es eines solchen neuen Zuspruchs bedurfte. Die Antwort kann mangels geeigneter Quellen nur hypothetisch gegeben werden, aber sie liegt sehr nahe. Es ist nur zu wahrscheinlich, daß die Israeliten weiter den Anfeindungen der Babylonier ausgesetzt waren, und man muß nur die Aufstandsbewegung der zwanziger Jahre in Erinnerung rufen, um die Furcht zu verstehen, zwischen solchen Aufständen zerrieben zu werden. Der Sieg des Kyros war glänzend, aber nicht gleichermaßen glanzvoll war der Effekt des Sieges für die Exulanten – obwohl der Chronist sich das viel später so vorstellt. Auf diesem Hintergrund kann man eine dritte, nicht ganz so auffällige Differenz verstehen, zunächst nicht zu den Gottesknechtsliedern, sondern zu einem programmatischen Text Deuterojesajas. Wenn in Jes 40,6–8 der proklamierten Herrlichkeitserscheinung Jahwes vor allem Fleisch der prophetische Widerspruch begegnet, daß doch alles Fleisch vergänglich sei, so ist damit m.E. nicht die Vergänglichkeit der altorientalischen Großreiche gemeint (wie man immer wieder gedeutet hat[16]), sondern die theologische und anthropologische Unmöglichkeit des göttlichen Vorhabens: Wie kann göttliche Herrlichkeit vor allem Fleisch erscheinen, ohne daß

---

16 Auch K. ELLIGERS Deutung läuft darauf hinaus, wenn er meint, daß bei der vergänglichen „Kraft" allen Fleisches „in erster Linie an Babylon gedacht" sei (BK XI/1, 24f.).

alles Fleisch zugrunde geht?! Die Antwort auf jenen prophetischen Widerspruch ist dort noch verschlüsselt, nicht expliziert, ein bloßes „doch": „das Wort unseres Gottes besteht, setzt sich durch, für immer". Unser Text ist dagegen viel massiver. „Mein Heil, meine Rettung besteht für immer" – das ist der Vergänglichkeit der Menschen, ja von Himmel und Erde entgegengesetzt. Man mag das, was Himmel und Erde betrifft, für eine rhetorische Figur halten oder auch neue Töne darin anklingen hören, die später im Modell eines neuen Himmels und einer neuen Erde voll zur Geltung kommen – jedenfalls müssen mit den vergehenden Menschen, vor deren Schmähungen sich Israel als Gottesknecht nicht zu fürchten braucht, nun in der Tat die Israel feindlichen Mächte seiner Umwelt gemeint sein – ob Babylonier, Perser, Meder oder Elamiter –, denn das Exil war durch Kyros gewiß kein Paradies geworden.

Das Heil für Israel, während die feindlichen Mächte aus den Völkern vergehen – damit sind wir bei der Frage nach einer möglichen letzten Differenz. Wie steht es jetzt, in dieser Auslegung der Gottesknechtslieder, mit den Völkern? Die Frage ist nicht ganz einfach zu beantworten, wie ein kurzer Seitenblick in die Forschungsgeschichte zeigt: Man hat ob des Widerspruchs von Völkerheil in V. 4f. und Weltuntergang in V. 6 den Vers 6 für eine noch spätere Zufügung gehalten, oder man hat V. 4f. anders interpretiert und allen Nachdruck auf das Gericht über die Völker gelegt.[17] Lassen wir die literarkritische Frage einmal außer Betracht, weil man gleichwohl nach dem Sinn fragen müßte. Die Negativdeutung von V. 4f. kommt jedenfalls nicht in Frage, weil man die Metapher vom „Licht der Völker" und das Wort vom Hoffen und Harren der Inseln schon gewaltsam uminterpretieren müßte. Von Jahwes heilsamer Machtentfaltung in der Welt ist also die Rede, wie zum Beispiel in den Jahwe-Königs-Psalmen, und man mag als weitere Sachparallele auch Jes 2,2–4 danebenstellen, jenes berühmte Wort vom Völkerfrieden, gestiftet durch die Tora, die von Zion ausgeht. Das aufrichtende, wiederherstellende Gericht Jahwes ist hier wie in den Psalmen gemeint, aber dazu gehört hier wie dort fast selbstverständlich, daß die Durchsetzung der צְדָקָה eine Kehrseite hat: Wo das Heil kommt, müssen die Mächte des Unheils weichen. Insofern müßte das alles Deuterojesaja nicht fremd sein – der Siegeszug des Kyros zur Durchsetzung des göttlichen Heilsplans hat auch bei ihm als die Kehrseite Unterwerfung und Vernichtung von Völkern. Das Wort vom Untergang von Himmel und Erde und von der Vergänglichkeit der Menschen in V. 6 ist in diesem Kontext nur als ein scharfer Kontrast zur Unvergänglichkeit des Heils zu verstehen, ähnlich wie in der ersten Strophe von Ps 46. Aber etwas anderes hat sich geändert. Die Völker

[17] Bei STECK findet sich beides: der Widerspruch, der zur Literarkritik nötigt (Gottesknecht 79–81), und die Erklärung, warum die letzte Redaktion V. 4f. negativ verstehen konnte (88 mit Anm. 43). Das ist redaktionsgeschichtlich konsequent, weil man davon ausgehen muß, daß die späteren Redaktionen den vorgegebenen Text sinnvoll einbeziehen wollten. Aber eine Negativdeutung von V. 4bβ und von V. 5b ist schwer denkbar.

sind nicht mehr, wie im zweiten Gottesknechtslied oder in Jes 45,18ff., die Adresse einer solchen Botschaft. Darum wird die Adresse von Jes 49,1 mit dem sprachlich merkwürdigen לְאֻמִּי abgewandelt. Darum wird auch Jes 49,6 umformuliert: nicht mehr לִהְיוֹת יְשׁוּעָתִי עַד־קְצֵה הָאָרֶץ (49,6), sondern וִישׁוּעָתִי לְעוֹלָם תִּהְיֶה (51,6; ähnlich 51,8). Es geht nicht mehr um den weltweiten Effekt der Rettung Israels in der Rettung der Völker als das Ziel aller Pläne Jahwes, sondern fast umgekehrt um die Sicherung der Rettung Israels durch den Weltfrieden[18]. Man muß sich nicht fürchten, denn auch die Inseln warten auf Jahwes Machterweis, und er wird sich weltweit durchsetzen. Das ist gewiß alles andere als Partikularismus, aber es ist eine Nuance, die der veränderten Verkündigungssituation entspricht.

2.2 *Jesaja 51,12–16*

Andere Texte dieser Schicht lassen ähnliche Konturen erkennen. Ein eigentümlicher Text ist 51,12–16, gedichtet zur Ergänzung von 51,9–10.(11?) als göttliche Antwort auf die Klage, also von vornherein als ein literarischer Text. Er knüpft in seinem Eingang zugleich eng an die Thematik von V. 7 und 8 an und mahnt wie dort zur Furchtlosigkeit vor dem doch sterblichen Menschen; dabei klingt erneut Jes 40,6–8 mit dem Motiv „alles Fleisch ist Gras" an. Er malt wiederum eine Situation der Bedrückung, die sich sehr wohl den „Nachkriegsverhältnissen" Babyloniens zwischen 539 und 520 einzeichnen ließe[19].

12 Ich, ich bin's, der euch (masc. pl.) tröstet,
wer bist du (fem. sg.), daß du dich fürchtest,
vor dem Menschen, der stirbt,
und dem Menschenkind,
das als Gras dahingegeben wird?
13 Und vergißt (masc. sg.) Jahwe, deinen Schöpfer,
der den Himmel ausspannt
und die Erde gründet,
und zitterst beständig den ganzen Tag

---

[18] W. A. M. Beukens schöner Gedanke, in V. 4 und 5 seien gewissermaßen die Namen vertauscht, Israel als Nation (לְאֹם), die Völker als עַם angesprochen (Jesaja II^{B}, 114), trifft m. E. die Meinung des Autors nicht. עַם steht für die Menschheit schon 42,5, עַמִּים für die Völker in 49,22 (mit dem Gedanken der Völkerwallfahrt); die Bezeichnung ist also bei Deuterojesaja nicht exklusiv.

[19] Für die schwierige Deutung der Situationsangaben in V. 13 und 14 muß hier auf die überzeugende Erörterung von Beuken z. St. verwiesen werden. Man kann dann die Aussage von dem Bedrücker, der zu verderben „gründet" (כונן viell. mit Anspielung auf die „Gegengründung" der Erde durch den Schöpfer in 13a, dort mit יסד, s. Beuken), im Rahmen allgemeiner Feindklagen verstehen; man kann aber auch fragen, ob denn die Babylonier vor 539 wirklich darauf aus waren, ihre Gefangenen zu vernichten, und ob nicht eher eine Situation späterer, unruhigerer Zeiten gespiegelt ist. Aber wie dem auch sei: Es ist im ganzen die Situation der Klage, auf die das Heilsorakel sich einläßt.

vor dem Grimm des Bedrückers,
da er sich anschickt[20] zu verderben.
Aber wo ist der Grimm des Bedrückers?
14 Eilends wird der Gefesselte gelöst,
daß er nicht stirbt zur Grube
und daß nicht mangelt seine Nahrung.
15 Ich aber bin Jahwe, dein Gott!
Der das Meer aufschreckt, daß seine Wellen tosen:
Jahwe Zebaot ist sein Name.
16 Und ich lege meine Worte in deinen Mund,
und im Schatten meiner Hand verberge ich dich,
um den Himmel zu pflanzen/,auszuspannen'(?)[21]
und die Erde zu gründen
und zu Zion zu sagen: „Mein Volk bist du"

Der Text hat im Hauptteil nur einen allgemeinen Bezug auf das dritte Gottesknechtslied, sofern auch hier eine Streitsituation und die göttliche Hilfe zur Sprache kommt. Bemerkenswert ist eine sprachlich-syntaktische Eigenart, die in einem frei formulierten Text unmöglich wäre, aber in diesem konstruierenden und kombinierenden Text nicht textkritisch beseitigt werden darf. Die pluralische Anrede am Anfang ist in der Komposition von Kap. 51 nur die konsequente Fortsetzung der Anreden in V. 1–8, und in der *Komposition* ist auch V. 9f. gewiß als Volksklage verstanden.[22] Die Fortsetzung im femininen Singular – im gleichen Atemzug! – ist in lebendiger Rede allerdings ungehörig, aber hier wohlbegründet, weil damit eine theologische Identifikation vollzogen wird: Israel ist angesprochen und getröstet in der Zion-Gestalt, die in den umliegenden Texten eine so große Rolle spielt. Dadurch wird auch die Brücke zum unmittelbar folgenden Text 51,17ff. geschlagen, in dem (ursprünglich als direkte Antwort auf die Klage von V. 9f.) *Zion* aufgerufen wird. Am Schluß von 51,12–16 wird die Gleichung von Zion und Israel ausdrücklich hergestellt, indem Jahwe zu *Zion* sagt *„mein Volk* bist du". Da hier am Ende das maskuline Genus in der Anrede an Zion erscheint, ist nicht sicher, ob der schon in V. 13 vollzogene schnelle Wechsel vom Femininum zum Maskulinum einen tieferen Sinn hat; angesichts der singularischen Aussage von V. 14 („der Krummgeschlossene") bietet es sich vielleicht an, hierin die andere Repräsentationsgestalt Israels, den Erzvater Jakob, angesprochen zu sehen.[23]

20 Oder: „zielt"? Vgl. HAL s. v. pol. Nr. 3.

21 Mit *S* דמתחת könnte man das geläufige לִנְטֹת lesen, aber möglicherweise ist der seltsame Ausdruck „zu pflanzen" beabsichtigt, s. u.

22 Ob auch ursprünglich, kann hier auf sich beruhen.

23 Vgl. 42,18–25 (V. 22.24) in der gleichen Schicht. STECK, Gottesknecht 66, erklärt den Anredewechsel mit Bezugnahmen auf unterschiedliche Texte des Deuterojesaja-Buchs, neben der auch hier vertretenen Zion-Beziehung in V. 12b vor allem mit dem stilistischen Bezug von V. 12a auf 43,25a (und auf 50,1b mit der 2. P. pl. masc. „eure Sünden" etc.), der nach ihm auch ein sachlicher Bezug wäre: „Trösten" bedeutete dann hier vor allem Sündenvergebung.

Wichtig ist für uns der Schluß, weil er wieder einen deutenden Bezug auf die Gottesknechtslieder bringt und scheinbar nachträgt, was wir in 51,4–8 vermißten: das Wortamt des Knechtes. Dabei bleibt außer Betracht, daß die ursprüngliche Zugehörigkeit der beiden Verse[24] zu dieser Schicht nicht ganz sicher ist; jedenfalls sind sie in diesem Zusammenhang zu verstehen. Aber das machen sie nicht ganz leicht. Das erste Problem stellt sich mit der Frage, wer eigentlich das hier angeredete „Du" ist. Nach der Schlußwendung könnte man an eine prophetische Gestalt denken, die Zion das tröstende „mein Volk bist du" zu sagen hätte.[25] Aber die Reihe der Infinitive in V. 16b macht diese Annahme schwierig: Die Gründung von Himmel und Erde ist ja Jahwes Geschäft und wohl nicht als durch einen Propheten vermittelte (Neu-)Schöpfung zu verstehen; dann ist auch mit dem letzten Infinitiv kein prophetisches Wortamt gemeint. Dazu kommt, daß ein Wechsel der Adressaten in V. 15f. oder 16 durch nichts angedeutet wird; man muß also bei Israel-Zion-(Jakob) bleiben. Was aber ist dann gemeint?

Man kann beobachten, daß neben dem (variierten) Zitat aus dem dritten Gottesknechtslied („im Schatten meiner Hand deckte ich dich", vgl. 49,2a) schon in V. 15 ein Satz aus dem Jeremia-Buch aufgenommen ist (Jer 31,35b[26]), und ebenso scheint der Anfang von V. 16 aus der Jeremia-Überlieferung zu stammen: „Ich legte meine Worte in deinen Mund" – das entspricht am ehesten dem Satz aus dem Berufungsbericht Jeremias, Jer 1,9: „Siehe, ich gebe meine Worte in deinen Mund"[27]. Vielleicht ist sogar das höchst merkwürdige לִנְטֹעַ „(den Himmel) *pflanzen*" dort hergeleitet (Jer 1,10 „zu bauen und zu pflanzen") und nicht zu korrigieren, obwohl man in dieser Verbindung das übliche לִנְטוֹת „auszubreiten" erwartet[28]. Der „Mund" des Knechts ist auch Jes 49,2 genannt, aber der Satz wird nun „jeremianisch" interpretiert, das heißt aus dem Kontext von Jer 1,9. Dort legt Jahwe dem Propheten seine Worte in seinen Mund und setzt ihn ein „über Völker und Königreiche", und gerade das ist die Stellung, die schon in 49,22f. Zion-Israel zukommt[29]; das Wort im Munde Zion-Israels wäre dann vor allem das *herrscherliche* Wort. Diese Deutung wird nicht dadurch verhindert, daß hier ein Maskulinum angeredet ist, denn man

Doch spricht der unmittelbare Textzusammenhang nirgends von Israels Sünde, sondern nur von der grundlosen Furcht und der in Jahwes Schöpfermacht fest gegründeten Erwartung der Befreiung.

[24] Oder nach STECK des V. 16.

[25] So STECK 71 mit Verweis auf Jer 1.

[26] Falls nicht umgekehrt Jer 31,35b dort zugefügt ist.

[27] Vgl. Dtn 18,18, aber wohl abhängig von Jer 1; außerdem Jes 59,21, abhängig von dieser und anderen Stellen. STECK 71f. schließt u.a. wegen des Zusammenhangs von 51,16 mit 51,6 und der Wiederaufnahme der Wendung in 59,21 auf eine großjesajanische Redaktion.

[28] Vgl. Anm. 21 und STECK 71. Zum Sinn der Wendung kann man Dan 11,45 vergleichen: ein Zelt „pflanzen", d.h. Zeltpflöcke einschlagen (s. Ges-Buhl s.v.); die Zeltmetapher für den Himmel – ebenso bei נטה שמים – wäre dann hier schon vorausgesetzt.

[29] Vgl. auch noch 55,1–5.

muß von *Israel* in der Zion-Perspektive reden – wie es der Schluß ja auch ausdrücklich sagt.

Daß die Fortsetzung der Zeile dann wieder den Schutzaspekt von 49,2 hervorkehrt, ist evident, wird aber besonders gewichtig, wenn es dabei um die Neugründung der nach V. 6 vergehenden Himmel und Erde geht[30]: In diesem Umsturz ist Israel in Jahwes Hand geborgen. Im übrigen mag ein Blick auf Hag 2,6f.; 3,21f. zeigen, daß Vorstellungen von einer bevorstehenden Erschütterung von Himmel und Erde der frühnachexilischen Zeit nicht fremd waren.

2.3 Jes 49,7

7 So spricht Jahwe,
der Schöpfer Israels, sein Heiliger,
zu dem, dessen Leben ‚verachtet'[31],
zum ‚Verabscheuten' des Volks,
zum Knecht der Herrschenden:
Könige werden sehen und sich erheben,
Fürsten, und werden niederfallen,
um Jahwes willen, der treu ist,
des Heiligen Israels, der dich erwählt hat.

Die Zionperspektive in der Auslegung der Gottesknechtslieder tritt auf andere Weise in Jes 49,7 in Erscheinung. LELAND E. WILSHIRE[32] sieht im Gottesknecht der Gottesknechtslieder eine Metapher für (die Frau) Zion, aber er geht zu leicht über den Genuswechsel hinweg: Auf die theologische Konstruktion von 51,12ff. darf er sich schwerlich berufen, und in 52,1 ist keine maskuline Anrede Zions zu finden.[33] Tatsächlich ist seine Idee erst die einer sekundären Deutung im Deuterojesaja-Buch, und sie braucht ein *tertium*, nämlich Israel, als Bindeglied: Dieses Israel in der Zionperspektive wird hier zum Knecht der Lieder. In 49,7 bleibt es also bei der Rede vom Knecht als einer männlichen Gestalt. Das (passive) בזה[34] verweist zwingend auf Jes 53,3, und das nur hier bei Deuterojesaja belegte תעב meint den gleichen Zusammenhang: die Schilderung des tief verachteten Gottesknechts. Der „Knecht" wird in 49,7 sogleich genannt, aber wenn er nun „Knecht von Herrschenden" heißt, kann schwerlich ein einzelner gemeint sein; auch hier ist die Israel-Deutung die wahrscheinlichste. Auf das

---

30 Vgl. STECK 71.

31 L. mit Q^a u.a. לִבְזוּי oder einfacher לִנְבְזֶה (vgl. Ges-Buhl s.v.). Für die passive Lesung der beiden ersten Verben vgl. die vorbildliche Erörterung bei BEUKEN z. St.

32 L. E. WILSHIRE, The Servant-City: A New Interpretation of the „Servant of the Lord" in the Servant Songs of Deutero-Isaiah: JBL 94 (1975) 356–367.

33 Gegen WILSHIRE aaO. 358.

34 Nur bei בזה ist auch die aktive Lesung von *M* erwägenswert, da hier das Passiv durch einen Eingriff in den Konsonantenbestand herzustellen ist; man müßte dann 53,12 (הערה למות נפשו), entfernt auch 50,5f. vergleichen. Aber da das Verb bei Deuterojesaja nur noch 53,3 und dort im Passiv (nif.) vorkommt, ist solche Umdeutung eher unwahrscheinlich.

vierte Gottesknechtslied weist schließlich die folgende Wendung von den Königen als Zuschauern, offensichtlich einer wunderbaren Wende (cf. Jes 52,15). Hier wäre also das vierte Gottesknechtslied erstmals eindeutig in die deutende Interpretation der Gottesknechtslieder einbezogen. Aber wieso ist damit von Israel-Zion die Rede? Das zeigt die Fortsetzung derselben Verszeile, die im Parallelismus membrorum als eine Ganzheit verstanden werden will: „Könige sehen und erheben sich, Fürsten und fallen (huldigend) nieder" – man soll sich das doch wohl plastisch vorstellen: Die Herrscher erheben sich von ihren Thronen und fallen dann huldigend vor dem Knecht nieder. Das geht über das vierte Gottesknechtslied hinaus und verweist auf Jes 49,23 (dort מלכים neben שׂרות), wo Könige „mit der Nase zur Erde" vor Zion niederfallen und den „Staub ihrer Füße lecken". Für Israel in der Zionperspektive kann man noch den letzten Satz geltend machen, der an 55,5 angelehnt ist – auch dort ist es ja Zion-Israel, das „ein Volk" (wieder גוֹי in kollektivem Sinn) herbeiruft „um Jahwes, deines Gottes, und des Heiligen Israels willen, denn er verherrlicht dich". Schließlich ist das Stichwort נֶאֱמָן dem Text 55,1–5 entnommen: Jahwes Treue ist es, die dort den Gnadenbund mit David in der Verherrlichung Zion-Israels als zuverlässig erweist.

Jes 49,7 ist mit alledem auch eine Auslegung der Schlußwendung des vorangehenden Gottesknechtsliedes: „... ich mache dich zum Licht der Völker, daß mein Heil reiche bis an die Enden der Erde" und knüpft mit seiner neuen Deutung konsequent daran an. Der folgende Text, 49,8–12, zeigt die Verbannten auf dem Heimweg, zumindest in V. 12 aus dem Blickwinkel des die Heimkehrer erwartenden Zion („kommen von ferne ..., von Norden ..., vom Meer ..."), und von diesem wartenden Zion ist gleich darauf in 49,14–23 die Rede: von dem Zion, das erst mit seinen heimgekehrten Kindern wieder Zion, Gottesstadt im vollen Sinn wird (vgl. bes. V. 18).

Es ist an diesem Text mit seinen vielfältigen Bezügen vor allem zu nachfolgenden Texten mit Händen zu greifen, daß es sich um ein kompositionelles und redaktionelles Stück handelt – darüber herrscht kein Streit. Zu bezweifeln ist nur, daß der Vers ein Baustein einer ursprünglichen und das ganze Buch beherrschenden Komposition ist und daß er vom Gottesknecht in dem gleichen Sinn redet, wie das in 49,1–6 oder 52,13–53,12 ursprünglich gemeint war. Soweit das nur den unaufhörlichen Streit über „kollektiv" oder „individuell" betrifft, ist hier noch nicht darauf einzugehen, aber die Zionperspektive spielt in den ursprünglichen Gottesknechtsliedern nirgends eine Rolle[35]. Zuerst ist ein weiterer Text dieser Schicht heranzuziehen, in dem wieder eine ähnliche Deutung der Gottesknechtstexte erscheint.

---

[35] Trotz Wilshire aaO., dessen Vergleiche zwischen Zion- und Knechtsaussagen alle nur den deutlichen Unterschied zeigen.

2.4 Jes 54,11–17

11 Du Elende, Verwehte, Ungetröstete:
Siehe, ich belege/ich lagere(?)[36]
mit/in ‚Malachit'[37] (?) deine Steine[38]
und gründe dich in Lapislazuli,
12 Mache deine Zinnen (?) aus Rubinen (?),
deine Tore aus Beryll,
deinen Wall ganz aus Edelsteinen.
13 Und alle deine ‚Erbauer'[39] sind von Jahwe gelehrt,
und groß ist das Heil deiner Söhne.
14 In Gerechtigkeit/Heil wirst du gegründet,
fern ‚bist' du[40] von Drangsal, daß du dich nicht fürchten mußt,
und von Schrecken, denn er naht dir nicht.
15 Wenn man dich angreift, so ist's nicht ‚von mir'[41],
wer dich angreift[42], kommt an dir zu Fall.
16 Siehe, ich habe den Schmied geschaffen,
der bläst an das Feuer der Glühkohlen
und bringt die Waffe hervor zu ihrem Zweck;
ich habe auch den Verderber geschaffen zu vernichten:
17 Jede Waffe, die gebildet gegen dich, hat keinen Erfolg
und jede Zunge, die mit dir zum Gericht aufsteht, wirst du ins Unrecht setzen.
Dies ist das Erbteil der Knechte Jahwes
und ihre Gerechtigkeit von mir, Spruch Jahwes.

Ein Ziontext ist 54,11–17 ohne Frage; die durchgehend feminine Anrede, die Beschreibung des künftigen Baus, die Rede von den Söhnen der Angesprochenen zeigt das zur Genüge. Aber es fällt schon vom sachlichen Gehalt her schwer, ihn zu den ursprünglichen Deuterojesaja-Texten zu rechnen. Wenn nämlich in V. 14–17 über das sichere Scheitern künftiger Angreifer Jerusalems reflektiert wird, so fragt man sich, wo denn der Prophet solche zukünftigen

---

[36] Vgl. den Parallelismus und die wörtliche Übersetzung von רבץ hi. „lagern lassen". Auch wenn man in V. 11bβ mit *Q*[a] *G* וִיסֹּדֹתַיִךְ zu punktieren hätte (so BHS), kann man so übersetzen, vgl. Anm. 38.

[37] L.? בַּנֹּפֶךְ (Ex 28,18; Hes 28,13 …; KBL: Grüner Halbedelstein: Türkis? Malachit?; HAL notiert als Möglichkeiten noch Granat oder farbloser Stein) vgl. *G* ἄνθρακα. – *M* פּוּךְ heißt in der Regel „Augenschminke"; „Hartmörtel" in KBL ist eine Verlegenheitslösung, die nicht in den Zusammenhang paßt (Hartmörtel neben Lapislazuli!). Vgl. noch אַבְנֵי פוּךְ 1Chron 29,2 (*G* λίθους πολυτελεῖς), auch da kommt unter lauter Edelsteinen „Hartmörtel" gar nicht in Betracht.

[38] C. C. Torrey prp. אֲדָנַיִךְ „deine Fundamente"; das paßt gut zur Lesung von *Q*[a] im par. Stichos. Auch dann ist פּוּךְ (oder was immer) aber noch nicht als Beleg zu verstehen, sondern „ich lege deine Fundamente mit פּוּךְ-Steinen" (בְּ „nennt d. **Stoff**, aus dem etwas besteht" HAL 101 s.v. Nr. 18).

[39] Wahrscheinlich ist *hier* בֹּנַיִךְ zu lesen; *Q*[a] hat das für בניך[2] (ו supra additum).

[40] L. תִּרְחֲקִי.

[41] L. מֵאִתִּי.

[42] Wegen der Beziehung zu Jes 50,8 מִי יָרִיב אִתִּי muß *M* wohl bleiben.

Feinde des neuen Jerusalems noch hernehmen wollte, wenn doch unumstößlich gewiß ist, daß jedes Knie sich Jahwe beugt und jede Zunge ihm schwört (45,23). Es ist also auch hier die kleinräumigere Perspektive, nicht geradezu partikularistisch, aber doch ohne Gedanken an ein weltumspannendes und *alle* Völker einschließendes Heil: Die Herrlichkeit Jerusalems ist Selbstzweck, ist Erbteil der Knechte Jahwes, nicht der Völker.

Daß dieser Text wiederum an das dritte, zum Teil wohl auch an das vierte Gottesknechtslied anknüpft und es „zionistisch" auslegt, zeigt sich an einer ganzen Reihe von Beziehungen. Da sind die Söhne Jerusalems Jahwes Schüler, לִמּוּדִים (50,4) – vielleicht als die Baumeister der Stadt (ein Wortspiel in V. 13[43]), aber vielleicht auch, weil sie jede Zunge, die zum Rechtsstreit gegen Jerusalem antreten will, Lügen strafen können (vgl. לְשׁוֹן לִמּוּדִים 50,4 und כָּל־לָשׁוֹן 54,17); beides muß sich nicht ausschließen. Zu „Bedrückung" und „Schrecken", die Jerusalem fortan fernbleiben werden, könnte man in der Sache, wenn auch nicht terminologisch, die Schilderung des Geschicks des Gottesknechts in 50,6 vergleichen, ebenso 53,7ff. Vor allem wird die Gerichtssituation wiederholt, auch terminologisch bezeichnend; man vergleiche מִי־הוּא יַרְשִׁיעֵנִי 50,9 mit תַּרְשִׁיעִי 54,17 einerseits und מִי־יָרִיב אִתִּי 50,8 mit מִי־גָר אִתָּךְ 54,15 andererseits. Es ist nur natürlich, daß die forensische Szene von 50,4–9 auf potentielle Anfechtungen einer Stadt ausgedehnt und mit den Möglichkeiten von Belagerung und Angriff konkretisiert wird. Man kann danach sogar vermuten, aber natürlich nicht beweisen, daß die kostbaren Bausteine des künftigen Jerusalem ein Gegenstück zu jenem Kieselstein sind, dem der Gottesknecht sein Angesicht gleichen ließ (54,11 f./50,7).

Der Text unterscheidet sich (wie schon 49,7) in der Auslegung des dritten Gottesknechtsliedes insofern von 51,4–8 und 51,12–16, als er allein die zukünftige Sicherheit und Geborgenheit der Stadt in Anknüpfung an 50,4–9 zur Sprache bringt, aber darin liegt kein Widerspruch, weil eine Textauslegung, wie sie hier unternommen wird, den Text nicht auf einen eng begrenzten Sinn festlegen will. Auffällig sind vielmehr die Übereinstimmungen: die Beschränkung auf die Binnenperspektive, die besondere Betonung der passiven Rolle des Knechts als Schutzempfänger, die Aufnahme aktiver Elemente nur im eigenen Interesse, dazu wenigstens in den drei letzten Texten die Israel-Zion-Perspektive. Wenn der letzte Text am Ende alle Herrlichkeit und Sicherheit Zions als das Erbteil der Knechte Jahwes herausstellt (54,17), so ist damit dieser Auffassung der Gottesknechtstexte eine konsequente abschließende Formulierung gegeben: Der Knecht – das sind die Knechte, die Söhne Zions. Man kann dafür eine Beziehung zum vierten Gottesknechtslied erwägen, aber terminologisch nicht sichern: Es wäre denkbar, daß mit dem *Erbteil* der *Anteil*

---

[43] Vgl. Q^a בוניכי. Auch 49,17 (text. em. vgl. Q^a) hat implizit das Wortspiel „Söhne"/ „Erbauer".

des Knechts nach 53,12 aufgenommen wäre und daß die Knechte zu verstehen sein sollen als der „Same“, den der Knecht nach 53,10 sehen soll.

2.5 „Kollektive“ und „individuelle“ Deutung

Neben den vorgeführten Texte explizieren auch 49,8–12 und 42,18–25 den Gottesknechtsgedanken. 42,18–25 kommt zu einer ähnlichen Sicht, und die abweichende Position von 49,8–12 fügt sich am Ende auch in die Zion-Israel-Perspektive der umgebenden Texte[44]. Das kann hier nicht mehr verfolgt werden; wir sind jedoch mit dem Schluß von 54,11–17 noch einmal bei der Frage nach „kollektiver“ oder „individueller“ Deutung, auf die ich etwas näher eingehen muß.

Die Wissenschaft liebt klare Alternativen, und so sind wir denn in der Regel auch mit dem Gottesknechtsproblem verfahren; wer einen Mittelweg suchte, war schnell als Kompromißler verdächtig. Getreu solcher Alternative müßten wir also konstatieren: Waren die Gottesknechtslieder einmal individuell gemeint, so sind sie hier kollektiv umgedeutet worden.

Aber die Dinge gehen in solcher einfachen Alternative nicht auf. Auch die Deutung der Gottesknechtslieder auf den Propheten, die mir unumgänglich erscheint, solange man die drei klassischen Texte nicht als sekundäre Hinzufügung erweisen kann, ist ja keine „autobiographische“ Deutung, und es ist nur terminologische Bequemlichkeit, sie so zu bezeichnen. Sie ist auch nicht einfach individuell. Vielmehr zeigen gerade die mannigfachen Bezüge zwischen dem Knecht der Lieder und dem Knecht Israel, daß der prophetische Knecht eine stellvertretende und repräsentative Rolle für Israel einnimmt. Und das ist ganz und gar nicht ungewöhnlich und neu, weil eine solche Rolle längst vom Propheten praktiziert wird: bei der Fastenfeier nämlich, bei der der Prophet Israels Klage vor Jahwe bringt und Israel vor Jahwe vertritt. Die Jeremia-Tradition hat davon – in mannigfacher Brechung – eine Menge Spuren erhalten.

Damit sind wir bei einem zweiten „kollektiven“ Gehalt der Gottesknechtstexte. Der prophetische Gottesknecht steht nicht für sich allein, sondern repräsentiert in seinem Amt alle Propheten vor ihm. Das heißt, er macht sich in der Amtsbeschreibung des jetzt wahrzunehmenden prophetischen Amtes die wesentlichen Erfahrungen seiner prophetischen Vorgänger zu eigen (das ist das Wahrheitsmoment der Deutungen auf vergangene Propheten).

Das ist jetzt nicht weiter auszuführen und nur deshalb zu nennen, weil es für die Verhältnisbestimmung zwischen ursprünglichem Sinn der Gottesknechtslieder und ihrer Deutung in der „Naherwartungsschicht“ wichtig ist. Da besteht kein scharfer Bruch zwischen diesem und jenem Sinn; die Sekundärdeutung

[44] S.o. S. 58.

kann vielmehr an die kollektiven Züge der Gottesknechtslieder anknüpfen und sie verstärkt und als den jetzt gültigen Sinn herausstellen. Wahrscheinlich ist auch das berühmt-berüchtigte „Israel“ in Jes 49,3 jetzt hinzugefügt worden, aber nicht deswegen, weil es zum ursprünglichen Sinn gar nicht paßte – der Knecht vertritt ja Israel –, sondern weil es stilistisch zu plump ist oder auch weil es erst jetzt nötig war, wo es um Eindeutigkeit ging. Gewiß ist dabei vorausgesetzt, daß der ursprüngliche Repräsentant Israels, der Prophet, nicht mehr am Leben war. Aber das schließt nicht einmal aus, daß erneut einer oder eine Gruppe jene stellvertretend-repräsentative Rolle übernehmen und mit den Gottesknechtsliedern geltend machen konnte. Ob sich das innerhalb des Jesaja-Buches bestätigt, soll jetzt noch ein kurzer Blick auf einen tritojesajanischen Text zeigen.

2.6 Jes 61[45]

1 Der Geist des Herrn Jahwe ist auf mir,
weil Jahwe mich gesalbt hat,
zu verkünden den Gebeugten hat er mich geschickt,
zu verbinden die mit zerbrochenen Herzen,
den Weggeführten die Freilassung auszurufen,
den Gefesselten Entfesselung,
2 auszurufen ein Jahr des Wohlgefallens Jahwes
und einen Rachetag unseres Gottes.
Zu trösten alle Trauernden,
3 [zu setzen für die Trauernden Zions,]
ihnen Schmuck statt Asche zu geben,
Freudenöl statt Trauer,
Lobpreis-Gewand[46] statt zerbrochenen Geist,
und man wird sie nennen Eichen der Gerechtigkeit,
Pflanzung Jahwes zur Verherrlichung.
4 Und sie werden bauen uralte Trümmer,
Wüsteneien der Vorfahren wieder aufrichten,
und sie werden erneuern verwüstete Städte,
Wüsteneien von Geschlecht zu Geschlecht.
[5 Und Fremde werden dastehen und euer Kleinvieh weiden,

[45] Vgl. zur Auslegung des Textes O.H. Steck, Der Rachetag in Jes 61,2. Ein Kapitel redaktionsgeschichtlicher Kleinarbeit: VT 36 (1986) 323–338, wieder abgedr. in: ders., Studien zu Tritojesaja: BZAW 203 (1991) 106–118; ders., Zu jüngsten Untersuchungen von Jes 60–62: ebd. S. 119–139; K. Koenen, Ethik und Eschatologie im Tritojesajabuch. Eine literarkritische und redaktionsgeschichtliche Studie: WMANT 62 (1990) 103–122; schließlich für die Fragestellung dieses Beitrags besonders W. A. M. Beuken, Servant and Herald of Good Tidings. Isaiah 61 as an Interpretation of Isaiah 40–55: The Book of Isaiah/Le Livre d'Isaïe, hg. J. Vermeylen, BEThL 81 (1989) 411–442 (hier werden weitere Bezüge zu Deuterojesaja benannt).

[46] Zwar scheint es naheliegend, mit Oort, Duhm u.a. מַעֲטֵה vor אֵבֶל zu stellen, doch ist *M* metrisch besser (Doppelvierer).

und fremde Söhne sind eure Bauern und Weingärtner.
6 Ihr aber werdet Priester Jahwes gerufen werden,
Diener unseres Gottes werdet ihr genannt werden.
Den Reichtum der Völker werdet ihr essen,
und ihr Vermögen werdet ihr für euch eintauschen (?) 7 statt eurer Schande.]
...ein Doppeltes...,
und Schmach ‚und Speichel' (?)[47] ihr Anteil (?)[48],
darum werden sie in ihrem Land ein Doppeltes erben,
ewige Freude wird ihnen zuteil.
8 Denn ich bin Jahwe, der das Recht liebt,
der haßt Raub ‚mit Frevel'[49],
und ich gebe ihren Lohn wahrhaftig,
und einen ewigen Bund schließe ich ihnen,
9 und bekannt ist ihr Same unter den Nationen,
und ihre Nachkommenschaft inmitten der Völker,
alle, die sie sehen, werden sie erkennen,
daß sie der Same sind, den Jahwe gesegnet hat.
10 Freuen, ja freuen will ich mich in Jahwe,
meine Seele soll jubeln in meinem Gott,
denn er hat mich bekleidet mit Kleidern des Heils,
mit einem Gerechtigkeitsgewand ‚mich angetan'[50],
wie ein Bräutigam, der den Kopfbund anlegt[51],
und wie eine Braut, die sich schmückt mit ihren Schmucksachen.
11 Denn wie die Erde, die hervorbringt ihr Gesproß
und wie ein Garten, der seine Aussaaten sprossen läßt,
so läßt der Herr Jahwe Gerechtigkeit sprossen
und Lobpreis vor allen Nationen.

Die Hauptschwierigkeiten des Textes liegen bei den Fragen nach seiner Einheitlichkeit und nach dem am Anfang und wieder am Ende redenden „Ich". Was die Einheit betrifft, so scheinen jedenfalls die Verse 5–6 mit ihrer unmotivierten und ganz aus dem Zusammenhang fallenden Anrede der Hörer ein Nachtrag zu sein[52], der auch in V. 7aα seine Spuren hinterlassen hat. Es fällt überdies auf, daß die zahlreichen Beziehungen von Jes 61 zu Deuterojesaja

---

47 *M* : „werden sie jubeln". Erwägenswert ist jedoch die Konjektur וָרֹק in Anlehnung an das dritte Gottesknechtslied (Jes 50,6).

48 V. 7a ist insgesamt gestört; wahrscheinlich muß man mit Duhm תחת בשתכם noch zum vorherigen Vers nehmen und im verbleibenden Text die Reste eines Vergleichssatzes sehen, der sein Gegenstück in V. 7b hat.

49 L. בְּעַוְתָה; *M* punktiert anscheinend in Gedanken an Verhältnisse, wie sie Mal 3,8ff. tadelt, oder an Jes 58 (Beuken, Servant 430). Aber eine implizite Kritik Israels paßt nicht gut in den Zusammenhang.

50 Die Masora will anscheinend von einem sonst nicht belegten יעט ableiten; besser ist יַעֲטֵנִי (impf. hif. von עטה) zu lesen.

51 L. יָכִין oder mit Duhm יְכוֹנֵן, vgl. *G* περιέθηκε (aber mit Subj. Jahwe: „wie einem Bräutigam..." etc.). *M* יְכַהֵן „priesterartig umwindet" ist wahrscheinlich unter dem Einfluß von V. 6 entstanden.

52 Anders Steck aaO. 106–108.

gerade in diesen beiden Versen fehlen; dagegen ist der späte Text Ex 19,6 zu vergleichen. Ob der verbleibende Rest in einem Zuge geschrieben wurde, mag hier dahingestellt bleiben. Die Probleme setzen schon bei V. 4 ein, dann erneut beim unvermittelten Wechsel zur Jahwerede in V. 8.[53] Aber die Frage stellt sich bei solchen literarischen und auslegend auf andere Texte bezogenen Stükken anders als bei einem frei komponierten Text. Man mag also das Kapitel – zunächst ohne V. 5f. – als eine kompositorische Einheit verstehen.

Wichtiger ist in unserem Zusammenhang die Frage nach dem jeweiligen Sprecher und nach dem Bezug zu den Gottesknechtsliedern Deuterojesajas. Dieser Bezug ist häufig notiert worden; man hat Jes 61 sogar für ein weiteres (ursprüngliches) Gottesknechtslied gehalten, aber das kommt aus vielen Gründen nicht in Betracht. Vielmehr hat der, der zumindest in V. 1–3 redet, wesentliche Züge aus der Amtsbeschreibung des Gottesknechtes für sich beansprucht. Das wichtigste übernommene Element steht am Anfang: die Geistbegabung des Gottesknechts nach 42,1. Dazu kommen als Stilelemente des zweiten und dritten Gottesknechtslieds die Ich-Rede und aus dem dritten Gottesknechtslied die dort vierfach gebrauchte Wendung „der Herr Jahwe". Aber dann wird sogleich der jetzige *Kontext* der Gottesknechtslieder in Anspruch genommen: die Freilassung der Gefangenen nach Jes 42,7 oder 49,9, das „Gnadenjahr" in Anlehnung an 49,8, der Trost für die Gebeugten nach 49,13, die Kundgabe der guten Nachricht (בַּשֵּׂר) wohl aus 41,27.

Diese Zusammenstellung zeigt, daß die Gottesknechtslieder für den Autor unseres Textes wie für viele moderne Exegeten bereits weitgehend in ihren Kontext eingeebnet waren, jedoch nicht ganz, da er ja mit ihnen ein besonderes Amt geltend machen kann. Aber wer ist das „Ich", das uns mit diesem Anspruch entgegentritt? Zunächst kann kein Zweifel sein, daß dieses „Ich" ein prophetisches Amt innehat, denn Jahwe hat den, der sich hier vorstellt, gesandt (שׁלח), um eine Botschaft zu überbringen. Es muß nicht auffallen, daß daneben königliche Züge begegnen, weil das bereits seit Jeremia (1,4–10) und Deuterojesaja zur prophetischen Tradition gehört. Der Prophet also hat auch ein königlich-messianisches Amt, wie neben der Salbung insbesondere die Verkündigung der Amnestie für die Gefangenen zeigt. Aber wer ist dieser Prophet? Nach Odil Hannes Steck[54] wäre es das in Jes 60 angesprochene Zion, wofür dann auch die „Freudenverkünderin" Zion aus 40,9 geltend zu machen wäre. Man kann dagegen schon fragen, ob Zion wirklich „gesandt" werden könnte – es kann im Staub sitzen, aufstehen, Licht werden (60,1), gar auf einen hohen Berg steigen (nämlich seinen eigenen 40,9) und von dort aus mächtig die Stimme erheben (im Unterschied zum Gottesknecht in 42,2), aber Zion kann nicht seinen Ort verändern und als Bote Adressaten einer Botschaft aufsuchen.

53 Vgl. zur Analyse K. Koenen aaO.
54 Studien 107 Anm. 4; 16f. Anm. 29.

Vor allem ist in diesem Text zwischen Verkünder und Empfänger der frohen Botschaft zu unterscheiden, und Zion gehört auf die Empfängerseite. Das spricht auch beim Danklied in V. 10 und 11 für die konventionelle Auslegung, die *hier*, in der Antwort auf das empfangene Heil, Zion als Sprecherin sieht. Wer „der Prophet“ ist – ein einzelner oder ein Prophetenkollektiv –, das läßt sich, wenn überhaupt, nur im Blick auf das ganze Tritojesaja-Buch beantworten, jedenfalls ist es nicht Israel. Daß „seine“ Prophetie schriftgelehrte Züge trägt und vielleicht überhaupt nur Schriftgestalt hatte, zeigt wohl schon unser Text mit seiner Einbindung in den Zusammenhang. Aber das hier redende „Ich“ mit seinem prophetischen Anspruch ist m.E. wieder eine konkrete Gestalt und keine Fiktion.

Aber wie immer dem sein möge – wichtig ist in unserem Zusammenhang etwas anderes. Der Dualismus zwischen dem am Anfang und dem am Ende redenden „Ich“ – das letztere mit den „Sie“ zusammen, denen die Botschaft gilt – wird in gewisser Weise dadurch aufgehoben, daß beide, prophetischer Bote und „zionistischer“ Heilsempfänger, in den Kategorien des Gottesknechtes beschrieben werden. Für den Propheten wurde das schon gezeigt; für die Empfänger aber ist zunächst auf V. 7 und V. 8 zu verweisen. Da ist zuerst von erlittener Schmach und Schande die Rede – vielleicht ursprünglich in wörtlicher Anlehnung an das dritte Gottesknechtslied, dann aber von מִשְׁפָּט und פְּעֻלָּה, Recht und Lohn des Knechts wie in 49,4, dem zweiten Gottesknechtslied. Auch ein Bezug zum vierten Gottesknechtslied ist zu erwägen: Schmach und Schande des Knechts sind ja dort in aller Breite dargestellt, und dem steht in 53,12 sein *Anteil* unter den vielen gegenüber.

Wieder stehen daneben andere Deuterojesajabezüge, die hier nicht einzeln aufzuführen sind – insbesondere spielen Anfang (40,2) und Ende (55) des Deuterojesaja-Buches eine Rolle. Die Gottesknechtslieder aber werden für die Heilsempfänger mit ihren „passiven“ Elementen eingebracht, während der aktive Teil vom prophetischen Sprecher übernommen wird.

Noch etwas anders ist die Rollenverteilung in V. 3. Mit dem „glimmenden“ oder „verlöschenden“ Geist ist ja gewiß auf das erste Gottesknechtslied angespielt. Wenn dort gesagt war, daß der Knecht den glimmenden Docht nicht auslöschen werde, so war das nach dem Zusammenhang eine allgemeine und die Völker einschließende Aussage. Hier sind es Israels Freigelassene, die statt des verlöschenden Geistes ein „Lobpreis-Gewand“ bekommen, und als Lobpreisende betätigen sie sich am Ende – vor allen Völkern. Das war Israels Aufgabe auch bei Deuterojesaja, nur daß hier der Effekt einer solchen Demonstration wohl anders gedacht ist als dort. Aber das ist wieder eine Frage nach der Deutung des größeren Zusammenhangs.

Worum es hier ging: Die Gottesknechtslieder sind in dieser Wiederaufnahme nicht mehr eindeutig kollektiv gedeutet, sondern dieser Autor bringt *neben* den kollektiven Zügen die ursprünglichen prophetischen Züge kräftig zur

Geltung. Er hat auf seine Weise verstanden, daß Israel und der Gottesknecht zusammengehören, und er geht selbstverständlich davon aus, daß es in dieser übergeordneten Einheit eine Rollenverteilung geben muß – auch wenn der Zweck jetzt nicht mehr der Einzigkeitserweis des Gottes Israels vor der Welt ist, sondern die Sonderrolle Zion-Israels: *Sie* sind ja der Same, den Jahwe gesegnet hat (V. 9).

3. Ergebnis

Was läßt sich am Ende zusammenfassend sagen? Hier sollen erstens einige Beobachtungen zum exegetischen Verfahren dieser frühen Schriftgelehrten gesammelt und zweitens die wichtigsten Züge ihrer Neuinterpretation des Gottesknechts genannt werden.

3.1 Man kann fragen, ob denn Begriffe wie „Exegese", „Auslegung", „Deutung" nicht allzu sehr vergröbern, was uns hier als Bezugnahme auf die Gottesknechtslieder begegnete. Allerdings hat jene Deutung mit unserer modernen Exegese nichts zu tun, schon deshalb nicht, weil die neuen Texte nicht am historischen Sinn ihrer Vorlagen interessiert sind. Darüber hinaus stehen sie ihnen nicht einmal als Deutung *gegenüber*; das Verfahren der *P^{e}šarim* ist also ein ganz anderes: Die Denkbewegung, die in dem „das ist seine Deutung" steckt, ist unseren Texten noch fremd. Vielleicht kann man solche Texte am besten als „Fortsetzungen" verstehen, aber indem sie sich so dem alten Textbestand anfügen, geben sie ihm zwanglos und von selbst eine Deutung, ziehen ihn in einen neuen Sinnhorizont.

Der deutende Umgang mit den vorgegebenen Texten ist da am sichersten zu greifen, wo bezeichnende Stichwörter und Wendungen der Gottesknechtslieder aufgegriffen werden, „Zitate" also, die durchaus nicht in unserem Sinne exakt sein müssen. Wenn „man", d.h. der mit den Deuterojesaja-Texten Vertraute, nur die jeweiligen Bezugnahmen erkennen kann, ist das genug. Wenn die Beziehung zu einem anderen Text auf diese Weise gesichert ist, darf man auch weitere, den vorgegebenen Text in eigenen Worten umschreibende Passagen in den Vergleich einbeziehen, obwohl solche Vergleiche weniger sicher sind.

Neben der Bezugnahme durch „Zitate" kann der Zusammenhang mit einem vorgegebenen Text allein durch die Position angezeigt werden. Nur ist unsere Möglichkeit, eine solche Bezugnahme zu sichern, wesentlich beschränkter, jedenfalls dann, wenn es sich bei der positionellen Hinzufügung um einen selbständig existenzfähigen Text handelt. Dafür rasch zwei Beispiele: Jes 54,1–10 soll *jetzt* wahrscheinlich als Fortsetzung des vierten Gottesknechtslieds gelesen werden, aber der Text wurde dafür nicht gedichtet; der Redaktor nutzte nur das gemeinsame Motiv der Nachkommenschaft und des Erbanteils, um den zweiten Text als Fortsetzung und implizite Deutung des ersten erscheinen zu lassen. Ganz anders Jes 49,7: Der Text besteht aus lauter Anspielungen auf umliegende Texte, aber auffälligerweise hat er überhaupt keine bezeichnenden terminologischen Beziehungen zum vorhergehenden Gottesknechtslied. Offenbar hat dem Autor von 49,7 für diesen Bezug die Position genügt, während er fernerliegende Bezugnahmen durch terminologische Anspielungen verdeutlichen mußte. Dieser Text ist – im Unterschied zu 54,1ff. – gewiß von vornherein für seine jetzige Stelle im Buch verfaßt.

Die „Zitate" haben freilich nicht nur technische Gründe – nämlich den Bezug zu fernerliegenden Texten zu sichern, sondern sie bezeugen auch den Respekt vor dem Prophetenwort, das man in einer neuen Situation sprechen läßt. Bemerkenswert ist, daß man sich dafür nicht auf die Deutung beschränkt, sondern Neues hinzufügt, teils aus anderer prophetischer Tradition, teils wohl aus Eigenem. Der vorgegebene Text erlaubt also diesen schriftgelehrten Tradenten eine große Freiheit im Umgang mit der Tradition, dann offenbar auch unterschiedliche deutende Bezugnahmen: die Einlinigkeit eines einzigen ursprünglichen und verbindlichen Sinns der Texte war den Tradenten offenbar fremd. Aber damit kommen wir schon zu unserem zweiten Punkt.

3.2 Der abgeleitete Sinn sekundärer Texte läßt sich nur im Verhältnis zu ihren Vorlagen bestimmen. Aber die Gottesknechtslieder als Vorlagen sind, obwohl einheitlich und eindeutig, doch in ihrem Sinn komplexe Gebilde, nicht einfach mit den gängigen Kategorien „kollektiv" oder „individuell" zu beschreiben. Wenn die Originale, wie ich meine, den prophetischen Anteil an der Rolle Israels zum Inhalt haben, wenn sie kollektive und individuelle Züge in dem Propheten als Repräsentanten Israels versammeln, so ist für die Sekundärschicht bezeichnend, daß sie – zumindest vorrangig – nur noch von Israel, nicht mehr von seiner prophetischen Repräsentation reden. Sie machen für die Knechtsgestalt vor allem die Züge der Gottesknechtslieder geltend, die von Schutz und Bewahrung und Lohn des Gottesknechts reden. Aktivität des Gottesknechts und Außenwirkung auf die Völker – ursprünglich Jahwes Werk durch die beiden Knechte – fällt nun nicht mehr in die Kompetenz des Knechts, oder sie wird – in der Perspektive Israels als „Königin Zion" – als Herrschaft zur Sprache gebracht, ohne daß doch die Einladung an die Völker zur Partizipation am Heil erneuert wird. Wie beweglich die Möglichkeiten des Bezugs auf die Gottesknechtslieder sind, das zeigt schließlich ein Text wie Jes 61, in dem die prophetisch-„individuelle" und die kollektive Seite, verteilt auf prophetischen Sprecher und Israel als Empfänger, *zugleich* mit Anspielungen auf die Gottesknechtslieder zur Sprache kommen.[55] Solche Beweglichkeit gewinnen die Gottesknechtslieder da, wo sie sich von ihrem ursprünglichen Bezug gelöst haben, das heißt konkret: wo nicht mehr das Amt des Propheten in Gottes Weltplan in

---

[55] Vgl. das ähnliche Ergebnis bei BEUKEN, Servant, bes. 438f.

den Texten reflektiert wird. Wie man als praktischer Ausleger und Prediger heute mit den Gottesknechtsliedern umgehen soll, das müßte freilich zuerst an ihrem ursprünglichen Sinn gemessen werden – auch wenn kein Prediger den Tod des Propheten Deuterojesaja zu verkünden hat, sondern ihm in den Texten Modelle der Wahrnehmung göttlichen Handelns angeboten sind, die ihre Erfüllung zu einer anderen Stunde gefunden haben.

Zur Komposition des Koheletbuches

von

Hartmut Gese

Kompositionsuntersuchungen spielen in der Exegese eine zweitrangige Rolle. In der Einzelexegese fällt die inhaltliche interpretatorische Entscheidung, und man mag danach auch noch die Komposition, die doch nur eine rein formale Bedeutung zu haben scheint, klären. Es können in der Exegese aber auch interpretatorische Schwierigkeiten grundsätzlicher Art auftreten, die es geraten sein lassen, von der Komposition her den Text zu betrachten, um mit den dort gewonnenen Einsichten dann in der Einzelexegese auf festerem Boden zu stehen.

In der neueren Exegese Kohelets herrscht gern die Tendenz, das inhaltlich Negative immer mehr zu betonen, so daß der Verfasser als ein radikaler Theologe erscheint, der kaum noch in die Formen alttestamentlicher Frömmigkeit hineinpaßt und bei dem es zum Problem werden müßte, wie seine Lehre sogar kanonische Geltung erlangen konnte. Von einer extremen Interpretation gewisser Einzelaussagen ausgehend, verfolgt man diese Linie konsequent, indem man dem Widersprechendes als traditionelles Gut neutralisiert oder als sekundäres ausscheidet. Ja es begegnet sogar die Methode, im Text Zitate der von Kohelet *bekämpften* Lehre auszumachen; aber wenn die Zitatform sich nicht zweifelsfrei nachweisen läßt, kommt diese Methode einer Umkehrung der Textintention gleich. Auffällig ist dagegen, wie wenig Kompositionsbetrachtungen in der Exegese Kohelets eine Rolle spielen. Gewiß muß hier die Einzelexegese praktisch vorausgesetzt werden, und doch kann eigentlich nur bei dieser Berücksichtigung des Textganzen ein sicheres inhaltliches Urteil gewonnen werden, wobei auch die für Kohelet abgewiesenen Aussagen sich herausschälen müßten. Es soll daher versucht werden, einen Gesamtaufbau des Koheletbuches nachzuzeichnen, wenn auch der festgesetzte Rahmen dieses Aufsatzes nicht gestattet, in eine Auseinandersetzung über die Bedeutung von Einzelaussagen einzutreten und eine thetische Darlegung ausnahmsweise genügen muß.

Nach der redaktionellen Überschrift 1,1[1] beginnt der Text des Buches mit dem als Kernsatz der Lehre Kohelets mottoartig zu Beginn vorangestellten Vers 1,2, alles sei הֶבֶל. Der Satz findet sich leicht variiert am Ende 12,8 wiederholt – es folgt lediglich noch der doppelte Kolophon 12,9–11.12–14 –, und mit solcher Inclusio wird natürlich die Abgeschlossenheit und Wohlkomponiertheit des Buches unterstrichen[2]. 1,2 verhält sich zu der anschließenden Frage 1,3, was denn für einen Vorzug und Vorteil der Mensch „unter der Sonne" habe, die geradezu das Thema der philosophischen Untersuchung bezeichnet, wie eine negative Antwort, die eben als Ergebnis thesenartig vorweggestellt ist. Auf jeden Fall bezieht sich die הֶבֶל-Aussage auf alles menschliche Tun und Erfahren im Leben, und so durchzieht sie das ganze Buch als Urteil (1,14; 2,1.11.15.17.19.21.23.26 usw.). Die הֶבֶל-Aussage begegnet im Alten Testament in diesem Sinn in der weisheitlich geprägten *Frömmigkeits*sprache (Ps 39,6.12; 62,10; 94,11; 144,4, auch in weisheitlichen Texten, vgl. Spr 31,30; Hi 7,16 u. a.); geradezu formelhaft scheint אַךְ הֶבֶל כָּל־אָדָם zu sein (Ps 39,6.12, ähnlich Ps 62,10), in dem die intensive und extensive Steigerung, die sich dann in Koh 1,2 in הֲבֵל הֲבָלִים und in הַכֹּל findet, schon einen Vorläufer hat[3].

Die an den Kernsatz 1,2 sich anschließende Frage 1,3 (man vgl. die Nebeneinanderstellung 2,11) darf nicht von vornherein als eine rhetorische verstanden werden[4]. Sie formuliert das thematische Grundproblem der Untersuchung, und sie kann gelegentlich auch positiv beantwortet werden (2,13; 5,8; 7,12, wobei dann allerdings zusätzliche Einschränkungen zu beachten sind, die in der Textumgebung auch zur Sprache gebracht werden). Auffällig bei der Frageformulierung ist die ausdrückliche Begrenzung תַּחַת הַשָּׁמֶשׁ „unter der Sonne", ein Begriff, der präzise gefaßt werden muß. Er bedeutet nicht „allüberall" – das meint das bei Kohelet auch vorkommende תַּחַת הַשָּׁמַיִם (1,13; 2,3; 3,1), von dem es deutlich zu unterscheiden ist[5] –, sondern bezeichnet die immanente

[1] Wobei die aufgrund von 1,12–2,26 erfolgte Bestimmung Kohelets als eines davidischen Königs in Jerusalem sekundär sein mag.

[2] Es ist darum die Wiederholung am Ende am ehesten auch auf den, der das Buch zusammengestellt hat, zurückzuführen. Die textliche Variation am Ende mag darauf beruhen, daß hier angesichts des Todes und der Trauerriten (12,5b.7) der qinaartige Fünfer angebracht schien, während 1,2 mit V. 3 (und V. 4) die Grundform des Sechsers zeigt (אָמַר קֹהֶלֶת und הַכֹּל הָבֶל 1,2 sind wohl einhebig zu lesen). Die in 12,8 auftretende etymologisierende Namensform mit Artikel ist am Ende gut verständlich, wo sich die Berechtigung dieses Ehrennamens erwiesen hat.

[3] Es ist daher unnötig, traditionsgeschichtlich auf die τῦφος-Aussage, die in der kynisch-philosophischen Tradition auftaucht (Diogenes Laert. VI 26 und 82f.), zu verweisen, zumal die Metaphorik unterschieden ist; הֶבֶל ist nicht Rauch und Qualm, sondern Windhauch. Auch verbindet sich mit dem τῦφος-Begriff die positive Verblendung. 3 Makk 3,18 z. B. könnte nicht einem הֶבֶל entsprechen.

[4] Auch die מַה יִּתְרוֹן-Frage 3,9 und 5,15 findet im folgenden 3,10f. bzw. 5,16 eine Antwort.

[5] 1,13 kann eben nicht תַּחַת הַשָּׁמֶשׁ gebraucht werden, denn es handelt sich um die *vergangene* menschliche Geschichte, ebensowenig in 3,1, wenn von Leben *und Tod* gesprochen wird. In 2,3 steht es neben „die Zahl ihrer Lebenstage", und das würde genau תַּחַת הַשָּׁמֶשׁ entsprechen,

Lebenswelt im Gegensatz zu der transzendenten Welt des Todes und selbstverständlich der göttlichen Transzendenz[6]. Da der Ausdruck bei Kohelet immer wieder erscheint (29mal!), stehen wir vor einer eigenartigen Betonung der ausschließlichen Diesseitigkeit seiner Beobachtungen und Feststellungen. Von vornherein geht es um rein diesseitig gültige Erkenntnisse, und konsequenterweise wird dann später der Ausschluß einer darüber hinausgehenden menschlichen Erkenntnismöglichkeit thematisiert.

An die thematische Frage reiht sich als erster Abschnitt 1,4–11 an, sich gliedernd in eine die kosmische Gesetzmäßigkeit beschreibende Aufzählung V. 4–7 und, daran unmittelbar anschließend, eine Darlegung der sich daraus für den Menschen ergebenden Konsequenzen V. 8–11. Dieser ersten Lehre, einer physischen Ontologie in Form einer Bewegungslehre der vier Elemente, entspricht eine zweite, eine Kairoslehre der Lebenswirklichkeit, in 3,1ff., wobei wiederum der Text in Aufzählung V. 1–8 und daraus sich ergebende Konsequenzen V. 9–15 geteilt ist. In 1,4–7 werden als Repräsentanten der physischen Weltelemente Erde, Sonne, Wind und Wasserströme aufgezählt in Hinsicht auf ihre unterschiedlichen Bewegungsarten: der Stillstand der Erde, sozusagen die Null-Bewegung, die regelmäßige Bewegung der Sonne (die ja als Grundlage des Jahreskalenders Gegenstand der menschlichen Berechnungen von Anfang an gewesen ist), die völlig unregelmäßige Bewegung des Windes (wie sie der sprichwörtlichen Unberechenbarkeit des Wetters entspricht, vgl. 11,5aα; Joh 3,8) und schließlich die intermittierende Bewegung des Wasserkreislaufs (als Mysterium des Baal-Zeus von besonderer religionsgeschichtlicher Bedeutung in Syrien, vgl. den Hymnus Hi 36,26ff., besonders V. 27f.). In all diesem, also der Gesamtnatur, bildet sich eine Geschlossenheit der Bewegung ab, der „*alle* Dinge nachkommen" (V. 8aα), während für den Menschen in seiner Geschichte (vgl. V. 4aα) die Welt offen ist: der Mensch vermag die Vielfalt aller sich verändernden Dinge nicht zu beschreiben, ja kommt mit Sehen und Hören nicht ans Ende (V. 8aβb). Neues kann es aber nach diesem

---

und so wird dieser Text hier auch von 𝔊 (𝔖) vorausgesetzt, was aber deswegen gerade als lectio facilior zu beurteilen ist; vielmehr bezieht sich „Salomos" Experiment auf das Beste im menschlichen Leben überhaupt und soll eben auch historisch von niemandem übertroffen werden.

[6] Vgl. Hi 8,16 לִפְנֵי שָׁמֶשׁ; sehr schön sind die genauen Parallelen in den phönizischen Sarginschriften KAI 13,7 und 14,12, wo von den Lebenden unter der Sonne (תחת שמש) im Gegensatz zu den Toten die Rede ist. Natürlich ist hier kein sprachlicher Einfluß anzunehmen, man vgl. etwa aus der altbabylonischen Version der 3. Tafel des Gilgameschepos (ANET S. 79): „Wer, mein Freund, ist vom Tode frei ?/ Nur die Götter leben immer unter der Sonne; / aber die Menschen: gezählt sind ihre Tage, / was immer sie erreichen, ist nur Wind". Griechischer Spracheinfluß (ὑφ' ἡλίῳ), den man für Kohelet postuliert hat, kommt auch nicht in Frage, da hier neben der bei Kohelet vorliegenden Bedeutung (sehr schön z. B., Euripides, Alkestis 393ff., der Sohn nach dem Tod der Alkestis: „O weh, mein Geschick ! Mama ist eben hinabgegangen; sie ist nicht mehr, o Vater, unter der Sonne !") sich auch die geographische häufig findet (z. B. Demosthenes, Kranzrede 18,270).

physischen Grundgesetz gar nicht geben, und wird etwas vom Menschen dafür gehalten, so ist es illusionär, weil das menschliche Gedächtnis so begrenzt ist (V. 9–11[7]).

Expressis verbis wird die Frage nach dem Vorteil für den Menschen (1,3) nicht beantwortet, aber indirekt ist deutlich, daß er etwas „Außerordentliches" nicht erwarten kann, denn er unterliegt einer gleichbleibenden physischen Gesetzmäßigkeit, die zwar für ihn im einzelnen undurchschaubar ist, jedoch eine feste Grenze darstellt. Aber ergibt sich nun eine positive Antwort auf die Frage von einem Standpunkt höchster menschlicher Möglichkeiten her? Zur Durchführung dieser Untersuchung nimmt die Lehre Kohelets in 1,12–2,26 künstlich die Position Salomos, des größten Weisen Israels, ein (1,12). Der zusammenhängende Text teilt sich formal A) in eine erste Hälfte dreier kurzer Abschnitte I) die Geschichte 1,13–15, II) die Weisheit V. 16–18, III) den materiellen Lebensgenuß 2,1f. betreffend, jeweils untergliedert in 1) Fragestellung 1,13.16–17a; 2,1a, 2) negatives Ergebnis in formelhafter Sprache 1,14.17b; 2,1b, 3) Begründung in sprichwortähnlichem Weisheitswort und daher etwas dunkler, hintergründiger Formulierung (Maschalform) 1,15.18; 2,2, und B) in längere Beschreibungen eines in Salomos Leben durchgeführten Experiments I) den materiellen Lebensgenuß (≙ A III) 2,4–11, II) die Weisheit (≙ A II) 2,12–17, III) die Zukunft der weisheitlich erworbenen Güter (≙ gegensätzlich A I) 2,18–23 betreffend[8]. Eine Folgerung von der allein möglichen Wahrnehmung des präsenten Heils als von Gott gegeben, die Lehre von der „Heilspräsenz", beschließt die Untersuchung 2,24–26.

Gehen wir in aller Kürze die Argumentation durch! AI. Eine Durchforschung aller Geschichte ergibt: alles geschichtliche Geschehen ist הֶבֶל und ein Trachten nach Wind, denn es ist irreversibel und fragmentarisch (Anspielung auf das Altwerden). II. Auch alles Weisheitsstudium (ist zwar *nicht* הֶבֶל, aber) heißt dem Wind nachdenken, denn es steigert nur Empfindlichkeit und leidvolle Wahrnehmung (Anspielung auf die pädagogische Zucht). III. Der praktische Lebensgenuß ist auch הֶבֶל, denn er ist Selbsttäuschung (Anspielung auf den Rausch). Die etwas dunklen Begründungen werden in der zweiten Hälfte B durch längere Explikationen ersetzt, die gleich beim letzten Thema einsetzen. I. Salomo verschafft sich alle Güter der Welt, paradiesische Gärten (Anspielung auf Gen 2,8ff.), Dienerschaften und Viehbesitz, private und öffentliche Schätze bis hin zum äußersten höfischen Luxus mit Musikanten und Kurtisanen – aber ohne die kritische Nüchternheit um der rechten Beurteilung willen zu verlieren. Das Ergebnis ist abgesehen von der augenblicklichen Freude selbst

[7] Das sing. הָיָה in V. 10bβ muß sich auf עֹלָמִים beziehen: entweder ein Textfehler oder eine sich abzeichnende neutrische Auflösung der Numeruskongruenz bei היה, wofür auch die Numerusverwechslung bei היה in 2,7 spricht.

[8] Man beachte die in diesen längeren Abschnitten besondere Abtrennungsmarkierung durch die Wiederaufnahme: וּפָנִיתִי V. 11 und V. 12, וְשָׂנֵאתִי V. 17 und V. 18.

(V. 10b), daß „alles הֶבֶל ist, ein Trachten nach Wind, einen Vorteil gibt es nicht unter der Sonne" (V. 11). II. Wohl erkennt ein Salomo den „Vorteil" der Weisheit vor der Torheit[9] (wie den des Lichts vor der Finsternis), aber ebenso deutlich ist die Begrenztheit dieses Vorteils der weisen Existenz angesichts des Todes; weder macht das Geschick zwischen Weisen und Toren einen Unterschied, noch gibt es ein bleibendes ehrendes Angedenken an den Weisen. So gilt letztlich hier ebenso das הֶבֶל-Urteil. III. Was die Zukunft des weisheitlich erworbenen Gutes angeht[10], so gibt es keine Möglichkeit, es als Erbe für die Zukunft gesichert zu erhalten[11].

Die ganze wohlkomponierte Untersuchung über die menschliche Möglichkeit eines wirklichen Vorteils und Gewinns schließt 2,24ff. mit dem positiven Ergebnis der Heilserfahrung als eines gnädigen Gottesgeschenks an den, der „gut vor Ihm" (V. 26), dem anderen bleibt nur das Geschäft des Sammelns und Aufhäufens von Gütern. Die bei Kohelet immer wieder konsequent auftretende Lehre von der durch Gott geschenkten „Heilspräsenz" (neben 2,24–26: 3,12f.; 5,17–19; 8,15; 9,7–10; in gewisser Hinsicht auch 11,7ff.), unterliegt nur allzu leicht einem hedonistischen Mißverständnis, das darin begründet ist, daß hier insbesondere vom Essen (und Trinken) die Rede ist. Es kommt hier aber philosophisch darauf an, die tatsächliche *Aneignung* des Guten als einer Gottes*gabe* sprachlich zum Ausdruck zu bringen, wozu sich das Urphänomen des Freudenmahls in seinem symbolischen Rang geradezu anbietet. Hier „höhere" Güter aufzuführen, bringt leicht das Mißverständnis mit sich, sie würden letztlich vom Menschen selbst erzeugt und hervorgebracht oder unterlägen außerhalb des Heilskairos der Fragwürdigkeit des dem Menschen unverfügbaren Geschehensablaufs. Immerhin kann die freudige Erfahrung des Heilskairos zur Arbeits*möglichkeit*, zur Möglichkeit, im Leben Gutes zu tun, ausgezogen werden (3,12; 9,10). Wie grundsätzlich das „Essen" verstanden wird, zeigt gerade diese erste Stelle der „Heilspräsenzlehre" in 2,25 durch den Gottesspruch(!): „Wer kann essen oder muß sich Sorgen machen ohne mich?".

Dem Lehrstück von den räumlichen Bewegungen in der physischen Welt in 1,4ff. steht in 3,1ff. ein solches von dem zeitlichen Wechsel in der Lebenswelt gegenüber, und es teilt sich auch wie in 1,4–6.7–11 in eine Aufzählung 3,1–8 und die daraus zu ziehende Lehre V. 9–15. Die die alte Form der Listenwissenschaft imitierende Aufzählung all der verschiedenen Kairoi erfolgt in Gegensatzpaaren, wobei sich eine Strukturierung auf die Weise kenntlich macht, daß

---

9 V. 12b mag sekundär den Gedanken einfügen, wie wenig es gelingt, weisheitliche Erfahrung weiterzugeben.

10 Das חכם-Motiv wird ausdrücklich in V. 19 und V. 21 aufgenommen, so daß sowohl auf I wie auf II Bezug genommen wird.

11 Der Abschnitt 2,18-23 ist zur Markierung des Abschlusses der ganzen Gedankenreihe als Duplik gestaltet, V. 18f. und V. 20ff., wobei letzteres gesteigert sich wieder in V. 20f. und V. 22f. doppelt.

der positive Begriff von seiner Anfangsposition in V. 2a.b in die Endposition V. 3a.b rückt, von dieser Endposition auch in V. 4a.b wieder in die Anfangsposition in V. 5a.b, von dieser Anfangsposition auch in V. 6a.b wieder in die Endposition V. 7a.b, während der Übergang zu V. 8a und V. 8b jedesmal mit einem chiastischen Positionswechsel einhergeht. Nun hebt sich V. 8b dadurch ab, daß hier am Ende nicht mehr Verben, sondern Substantive, „Krieg“ und „Frieden“, zu עֵת treten, aber auch in V. 8a kann es sich ursprünglich nicht um Verben gehandelt haben, wie man aus der defektiven Schreibung des *o* ersieht, wo doch dieser Vokal des Qal-Infinitivs stets[12] plene geschrieben wird, d.h. hier sind die Adjektive אָהֵב und שָׂנֵא vorauszusetzen: „eine Zeit für den, der liebt, und eine Zeit für den, der haßt“[13]. V. 8a und V. 8b sind also zwei Schlußglieder, die in Hinsicht auf die Person und den Zustand die Reihung zusammenfassen und sich durch jeweils chiastische Anordnung abheben. Das Korpus der Aufzählung mit עֵת und Infinitiven besteht, wie nun der Chiasmus im Übergang zu V. 3, V. 5 und V. 7 zeigt, aus drei Viererblöcken V. 2f., V. 4f., V. 6f., deren Mitte jeweils durch besagte Inversion des negativen Begriffs spiegelbildlich gekennzeichnet ist. Der erste Viererblock hat es mit dem Sein selbst zu tun. Die Grundaussage von Geburt und Tod (V. 2a) wird kausal gesteigert im vegetativen Bereich (V. 2b), die Steigerung geht zum animalischen Bereich über (V. 3a), und am Ende steht die sachliche Verallgemeinerung (V. 3b). Der zweite Block bezieht sich auf die seelische Bewegung: Weinen und Lachen (V. 4a) wird zum Rituellen der Totenklage und des (Hochzeits-)Tanzes gesteigert (V. 4b), die Steigerung zum Liebesvollzug[14] weitergeführt (V. 5a), und am Ende ist verallgemeinernd vom Eros überhaupt die Rede (V. 5b). Der dritte und letzte Block hat das sachliche Verhältnis, die Beziehungswelt zum Thema: Suchen und Verlorengeben (V. 6a) wird zur Dauerkategorie, Bewahren und Wegwerfen, gesteigert (V. 6b), dies weiter zum aktiven Zerstören und Reparieren intensiviert (V. 7a), und am Ende erreicht die Aufzählung als Umfassendstes den Logosbereich: Schweigen und Reden (V. 7b). Es geht in dieser Aufzählung der Kairospaare ja um die Nachzeichnung von Ordnung, und die Komposition vermittelt den Eindruck einer universalen Ordnungswelt, einen Eindruck, der sich dem an die Strukturgesetze hebräischer Poesie geschulten Ohr unschwer erschließt.

Wie in dem Gegenstück 1,4ff. schließt sich in 3,1ff. an die die Ordnung abbildende Aufzählung, dort 1,8–11, hier 3,9–15 die sich aus dieser Ordnung ergebende Lehre für die menschliche Existenz an. War in 1,3 die Frage nach

---

[12] Die einzige scheinbare Ausnahme לִרְחֹק in V. 5b läßt auf ein ursprüngliches Piel לְרַחֵק schließen („eine Zeit des Sich-Fernhaltens von Umarmung“), und diese Lesung wird durch 𝔊 tatsächlich belegt.

[13] 𝔅 bestätigt dies, indem nicht mehr wie vorher Gerundien gebraucht werden.

[14] Die Deutung des אֲבָנִים-Werfens durch den Midrasch (KohR 3,7 z.St.) ist noch immer die überzeugendste (d.h. Annahme einer künstlichen Umschreibung: א׳ von בָּנִים).

dem „Vorteil“ für den Menschen vor die Aufzählung gestellt, so erscheint sie jetzt danach (3,9), und, gegliedert in eine grundsätzliche Erfahrung (רָאִיתִי V. 10f.) und zwei Konsequenzen (יָדַעְתִּי V. 12f. und V. 14f.), wird ausgeführt, daß alles zu seiner Zeit „schön“ (יָפֶה), d.h. angemessen, passend ist[15], aber in den Menschen ist als Geistwesen der Drang gelegt, das Ganze, den ʿOlam, zu erkennen und zu bedenken, jedoch ist und bleibt das von Gott durchgeführte Gesamtgeschehen dem Menschen grundsätzlich verborgen (V. 10f.). Das heißt, dem Menschen (V. 12f.) ist nur die Wahrnehmung der „Heilspräsenz“ als Gottesgeschenk gegeben, während Gottes Werk (V. 14f.) auf den verborgenen ʿOlam ausgerichtet ist, und diese grundsätzliche Einschränkung der menschlichen Erkenntnis hat ihren Sinn in der damit begründeten Gottesfurcht[16]. Dieser für die religiöse Weisheit prinzipielle Begriff kommt bei Kohelet zu besonderer Bedeutung, wie sich kompositionell jeweils in Endstellung hier und nach den kultischen Sentenzen 5,6b und sachlich in dem Ersatz des Gerechtigkeitsbegriffes durch den der Gottesfurcht in 7,18 ergibt. Die Summa der Koheletschule in 12,13 ist also ganz im Recht und nicht eine mildernde Uminterpretation. Wir finden am Ende in 3,15 auch inclusiohaft die Bewegungslehre 1,4ff. aufgenommen, womit sich nicht nur unsere Kompositionsbeobachtung bestätigt, sondern auch die zeitliche Kairoslehre und die räumliche Bewegungslehre als zwei Seiten des von Kohelet beschriebenen Weltvorgangs erscheinen.

Zum Stil Kohelets gehört der Abschluß mit einem sprichwortähnlichen, hintergründig formulierten Maschal, und so wird die Inclusio V. 15a jetzt in V. 15b weitergeführt: „Die Gottheit sucht das Verfolgte“. בִּקֵּשׁ hat gern einen rechtlichen Nebenton, „einfordern“, hier jedenfalls dem Vermißten nachgehen, um so Recht und Ordnung wiederherzustellen (man vergleiche dazu auch den herrlichen Schlußsatz von Ps 119 und die Bedeutung des auf das Verlorene gerichteten göttlichen Suchens in den neutestamentlichen Gleichnissen). Das נִרְדָּף kann sich nur auf den (positiven) vom negativen עֵת verdrängten Kairos beziehen. Sir 5,3 zitiert dieStelle und deutet sie gleich personal auf die Verfolgten. Auf jeden Fall wird hier am Ende doch angedeutet, daß Gottes ʿOlam-Werk in der dem Menschen so uneinsichtigen, unverständlichen Kairosabfolge Heilshandeln ist. Um so bedeutender muß der Anschluß des nun Folgenden wirken.

Das 3,1–15 entsprechende ontologische Lehrstück 1,4–11 führte zu der historischen Darstellung umfassendster positiver menschlicher, sozusagen „salomonischer“ Lebenserfahrung, um von hier aus die Ontologie aus dem Gesichtspunkt menschlicher Erfahrung zu ergänzen. Auch im Anschluß an

---

[15] Es wird nicht טוֹב gebraucht, denn Tod, Zerstörung, Krieg usw. sind nicht „gut“. Ein Einfluß des griechischen καλός-Begriffes liegt also nicht vor; man vgl. die Rolle des traditionellen טוֹב-Begriffes in 6,11 mit der Ausführung in 7,1-14.

[16] Man vgl. die Entstehung der Gottesfurcht aus dem Essen vom Erkenntnisbaum Gen 3,10.

3,1–15 kommt es zur Ergänzung aus dem Gesichtspunkt menschlicher Erfahrung, aber nun unter dem negativsten, unglücklichsten Aspekt: 3,16–4,3. Es handelt sich um zwei sich entsprechende Erfahrungslehren (vgl. וְעוֹד רָאִיתִי 3,16 und וְשַׁבְתִּי אֲנִי וָאֶרְאֶה 4,1) 3,16f. und 4,1–3, die jeweils aus einer mit auffälligen Epiphora stilisierten Beobachtung (שָׁמָּה הָרֶשַׁע 3,16 bzw. וְאֵין לָהֶם מְנַחֵם 4,1) und der unmittelbaren Reaktion (3,17 bzw. 4,2f.) bestehen und die ein größeres reflektierendes Mittelstück 3,18–22 umfassen. Zunächst zu den beiden Erfahrungen: 1) (3,16f.) Am Gerichtsort, wo Recht stattfinden sollte, geschieht (gemäß der Kairosabfolge; vgl. V. 17b[17]) Unrecht. Kohelet reagiert darauf mit dem Postulat eines *göttlichen* Gerichtes, offensichtlich als Totengericht gedacht (V. 17). 2) (4,1–3) Kohelet nimmt alle Bedrückung wahr, die Leidenstränen der Bedrückten, und daß gerade durch die Unrechtsgewalt der Bedrücker[18] ihre unüberwindliche Macht entsteht, ohne daß die Bedrückten einen Helfer und Tröster haben. Deutlich ist die Steigerung dieser Erfahrung gegenüber 3,16f., und so kommt es zur emphatischen Reaktion eines Preises der Toten, ja der noch nicht Geborenen (V. 2f.).

Während man diesen Preis derer, die nicht mehr oder noch nicht „unter der Sonne" sind, als typisch für Kohelet ansieht, möchte man gern 3,17 für sekundär halten. Aber das verbietet 8,12f. und 11,9b, was man dann gleichfalls tilgen müßte, und wir sehen, daß auch die Komposition die Echtheit verlangt. Zudem knüpft nun das Mittelstück 3,18ff. daran an: Die Zulassung des Unrechts dient Gott dazu, die Menschen zu sichten und zu sondern – eine ohne den Gerichtsgedanken sinnlose Aussage. Zu dieser Sichtung und Prüfung des Menschen gehört aber ebenso als Voraussetzung, daß die Menschen „sehen, daß sie (nur) Vieh sind für sich" (V. 18b), also aus ihrer Perspektive einer ihnen völlig verschlossenen Transzendenz wie die Tiere ohne Transzendenzbezug sind. V. 19–21 begründet dieses mit dem den Tieren entsprechenden Todesgeschick und dem Staubsein von Mensch und Tier unter Anspielung auf Gen 2,7.19; 3,19. Eine Lehre, daß die Lebensruach beim Menschen im Gegensatz zum Tier „nach oben" steigt[19], entzieht sich nach Kohelet menschlichem Wissen. Konsequent schließt dieser Mittelabschnitt mit dem Hinweis auf die Lehre von der Heilspräsenz V. 22.

---

[17] Die Punktation שָׁם V. 17 scheint sich an dem doppelten שָׁמָּה V. 16 zu orientieren: „denn einen Kairos gibt es für jedes Vorhaben, und für jedes Geschehen ist dort (ein Ort)"; aber der Wechsel von לְ und עַל und der Rückgriff auf V. 16 mit zu ergänzendem מָקוֹם ist problematisch. Liest man שָׂם, ist ein befriedigender Zusammenhang mit V. 17a hergestellt: „denn einen Kairos gibt es für jedes Vorhaben, aber auf jede Tat achtet er" (zu שִׂים ohne לֵב vgl. GesB s.v. שִׂים Qal 4c).

[18] Man beachte die feine Aufeinanderfolge der Formen der Wurzel עשק: Abstraktplural, pass. Partizip, akt. Partizip.

[19] Selbstverständlich sind in V. 21 wie üblich statt der jetzt punktierten Artikel in הָעֹלָה und הַיֹּרֶדֶת die Fragepronomina הַ bzw. הֲ zu lesen. MT will angesichts des Gegensatzes zu 12,7 die Frage entschärfen.

Die Auffassung der menschlichen Vergänglichkeit widerspricht gerade nicht einer Lehre vom Totengericht. Nach uralter Tradition ist bei Kohelet selbstverständlich an eine Totenexistenz in der Scheol gedacht (vgl. auch 9,5f.10b neben 4,2f.), und an eine solche Zukunft des Menschen zu erinnern, gehört auch zur späteren Weisheit (Sir 7,17, fast identisch mit Aboth 4,4). Totengerichtsvorstellungen setzen an und für sich keine Auferstehung voraus, sondern nur verschiedene Hadesorte (vgl. Luk 16,19ff. neben den viel bezeugten antiken Hadesvorstellungen). Aber entscheidend wichtig ist für Kohelet, daß dem Menschen die Transzendenz jenseits der Todesgrenze absolut verborgen ist, damit auch das Totengericht. Gerade dadurch prüft Gott den Menschen (V. 18a), und ein Gutsein an sich kann nur unter der völligen Ungewißheit einer Vergeltung (V. 18b und V. 19ff.) geprüft werden. Sehr interessant sind dabei die zurückhaltenden Formulierungen: Die Menschen erfahren ihre die Tierheit nicht übersteigende Existenz nur לָהֶם, also aus ihrer menschlichen Perspektive (V. 18b). Und das Nichtunterschiedensein vom Tier nach dem Tod kann nur als Möglichkeit formuliert werden, ja noch vorsichtiger: niemand weiß, ob es eine prinzipielle Unterschiedenheit hinsichtlich der Transzendenz zwischen Mensch und Tier gibt. Kohelet verkündet also keine Transzendenzlosigkeit des Menschen, sondern ausdrücklich nur ein diesbezügliches Nicht-Wissen-Können, das den Menschen in die „Versuchung" stellt. So ist der Mensch von sich aus in ein Diesseits eingeschlossen, in dem der Kairos des Unrechts und der Bedrückung das Leben unwert machen kann, und sein Anteil am Guten besteht nur in der niemals einzufordernden oder auch nur bestimmt zu erwartenden „Heilspräsenz" (V. 22). Stärker kann der Prüfungsgedanke nicht gefaßt werden: es wird vom Menschen gefordert, daß er *an sich* gut sein soll[20].

Wir überblicken jetzt den ersten großen Komplex des Koheletbuches 1,4–4,3 in seinem symmetrischen Aufbau. Ein Anhang von drei kleinen Lehrstücken 4,4–6.7–12.13–16 schließt sich daran an, der dadurch veranlaßt ist, daß mit den in 1,4–4,3 dargestellten Erkenntnissen die Grundlehre der alten Weisheit vom Tun-Ergehen-Zusammenhang völlig überwunden ist, so daß noch drei weitere mit dem menschlichen Tun verbundene prinzipielle Erscheinungen aufgeführt werden können, die eine unmittelbare Inbezugsetzung von Tun und Ergehen ad absurdum führen. 4,4–6 führt aus, daß mit jedem gelingenden Werk auch schon als Negativum Neid und Eifersucht entsteht, was dem Tun-Ergehen-Zusammenhang grundsätzlich widerspricht. Sprichwortartig wird deswegen gefordert, ohne faul und träge zu sein (V. 5), nicht übermäßig nach Erfolg zu trachten (V. 6). Ist die Perspektive des Tun-Ergehen-Zusammenhangs auf das Verhalten des Einzelnen gerichtet, so beweist 4,7–12, daß zwei, die sich unterstützen, *mehr* als das Doppelte erreichen – auch hier wieder

[20] Ein seit Hiob (1,9; 2,4f.) grundlegender „sokratischer" Gedanke; vgl. „Die Frage nach dem Lebenssinn: Hiob und die Folgen" (ZThK 79, 1982, 161–179 = H. Gese, Alttestamentliche Studien, 1991, 170–188) S. 172f. bzw. 163f.

ein grundsätzlicher Widerspruch. Schließlich stellt in 4,13–16 die mit einer Sentenz (V. 13) eingeleitete Lehrerzählung (V. 14f.) von der Thronusurpation eines armen, aber klugen Untergebenen dar – und der Kommentar V. 16 erweitert den Blick auf die spätere Zeit des Thronfolgers –, daß nicht der gegenwärtige Zustand ein gültiges Urteil erlaubt, weil die in ihm verborgen enthaltene und unter Umständen ganz gegensätzliche Zukunft berücksichtigt werden müßte. Alle drei Lehrstücke weisen auf eine Komplexität menschlicher Handlungen hin (hinsichtlich des sozialen Umfelds, hinsichtlich der Subjektzahl und hinsichtlich der unbestimmten Dauerhaftigkeit), die von den Grundsätzen traditioneller Weisheit ebensowenig erfaßt wurde wie die in dem Kairos zutage tretende Eigengesetzlichkeit des Geschehens.

Wie wir sehen werden, erscheint im hinteren Teil des Koheletbuches 7,15–10,3 eine jeweils doppelt aufgebaute zweiteilige Komposition, die in einer ethischen Betrachtungsweise über Gerechtigkeit und Retribution handelt zusammen mit drei kurzen Anhängen, und dieser gesamte Komplex bildet zu unserem ersten Komplex 1,4–4,16 mit seiner ontologischen Betrachtungsweise ein Gegenstück. Dazwischen finden sich drei Themen behandelt: 1) die kultische Frömmigkeit 4,17–5,6 (mit einem Anhang in 5,7f.) 2) die Besitzgier, eine streng symmetrische doppelte Rahmenkomposition in 5,9–6,9, und 3) die Frage nach dem für den Menschen Guten (mit einer Einleitung in 6,10f.) 6,10–7,14. Diese Themen, religiöser Kultus, äußerer Besitz und die allgemeine Frage des Guten, bilden, jeweils klar abgegrenzt, nach der ontologischen Betrachtung des ersten Hauptteils 1,4–4,16 also den Mittelteil des Buches.

Daß 4,17–5,6 den Tempelkult zum Gegenstand hat, ist unbestritten. Der Text gliedert sich in vier Sentenzen betreffend a) den Tempelbesuch überhaupt 4,17, b) das Gebet, insbesondere das Bittgebet, also das sog. Klagelied des Einzelnen, 5,1f., c) das Gelübde, mit dem ja das Klagelied des Einzelnen üblicherweise schließt, 5,3f., d) die Sünde mit dem Wort und das entsprechende Sündopfer 5,5–6a, während die allgemeine Mahnung zur Gottesfurcht den ganzen Abschnitt in 5,6b zusammenfassend beschließt. Traditionell für die Weisheit ist die Unterordnung des Opfergottesdienstes unter das Ethos (Spr 15,8; 21,3.27). Die Weisheit Kohelets kommt darüber hinaus zu einem positiven Verhältnis zur kultischen Frömmigkeit, die also in gewisser Weise weisheitlich vertieft wird. In der ersten Mahnung 4,17 wird die religiöse Verantwortlichkeit beim Tempelbesuch angemahnt, und zu der traditionell weisheitlichen Einschränkung einer *äußerlichen Opferfrömmigkeit* tritt die Mahnung zu dem (sicherlich deuteronomisch verstandenen; vgl. Dt 6,4) lernenden „Hören“, aus dem sich dann auch, wie 4,17b indirekt andeutet, das Wissen um Gut und Böse ergibt. Aber auch die *Gebetsfrömmigkeit* kann sich veräußerlichen in der πολυλογία (vgl. Matth. 6,7f.), und so wird hier ebenso ehrfürchtige Verantwortlichkeit angemahnt (5,1f.). Hatte diese Mahnung besonders das Bittgebet im Auge, so schließt sich daran die entsprechende verantwortliche Zurückhaltung im Gelübde folgerichtig an (5,3f.), wobei Kohelet Dt 23,22 zitiert; und daß die Mahnung zur Zurückhaltung nicht einer der kultischen Frömmigkeit skeptisch gegenüberstehenden Weisheit entspringt, sondern eben der Tora, zeigt die inhaltliche Aufnahme von Dt 23,23. Bei der letzten Sentenz 5,5–6a könnte man konkret an eine Warnung vor Flüchen denken, aber man muß hier eine viel allgemeinere Bedeutung ins Auge fassen. Wie V. 5aβ zeigt, ist an das חַטָּאת-Ritual gedacht, bei dem Vergehen vor dem Priester[21] als שְׁגָגָה (bereutes Versehen) erklärt werden, so daß eine Entsühnung möglich ist (vgl. Num 14,22ff., besonders einen Einzelnen betreffend V. 27ff.). Natürlicherweise sind solche Entsühnungen in erster Linie für Toraübertretungen gedacht, die in klar zutage liegenden *Handlungen* bestehen. Hier wird das nun auf *Wort*sünden bezogen, und bedenkt man den für die biblische Tradition mit dem Wort aufs engste zusammengesehenen Bereich des Denkens[22], so wird die Tendenz Kohelets deutlich, das Verantwortungsbewußtsein zu steigern[23] und die Verantwortlichkeit auch für das geistige Verhalten, das sich im Wort äußert, zu wecken[24]. Sehen wir auf das Ganze von 4,17–5,6, so können wir alles auf den Logosbereich beziehen, dessen grundlegende Bedeutung für Religion und Kultus herausgestellt wird, und Kohelet setzt damit eine im Deuteronomismus gegebene Tradition in den weisheitlichen Bereich hinein fort[25]. Der zusammenfassende Aufruf zur Gottesfurcht am Ende in V. 6b entspricht der Bedeutung dieses für die weisheitliche Frömmigkeit grundlegenden Begriffes bei Kohelet in 3,14; 7,18.

Das Einzelwort 5,7f. könnte angesichts der in sich geschlossenen Kompositionen von 5,9–6,9 und 6,10–7,14 nur als Anhang zu dem Komplex über die kultische Frömmigkeit 4,17–5,6 verstanden werden. Aber welcher (natürlich sekundäre) Zusammenhang könnte hier bestehen? 5,7 beschreibt die durch eine Beamtenhierarchie in spätpersischer und hellenistischer Staatswelt fast notwendig entstehende Unterdrückung und Unrechtsherrschaft. Angesichts dieser Verwaltungshierarchie und -bürokratie sieht er in dem ursprünglichen Königtum für ein bäuerlich bestelltes Land die einzig mögliche Staats- und Kulturform, die für das Land ein Gewinn ist[26]. Bei dem Königtum ist natürlich

---

[21] Man beachte die Mal 2,7 entsprechende ehrfürchtige und höchste Autorität zuerkennende Priesterbezeichnung הַמַּלְאָךְ!

[22] Man unterscheidet für gewöhnlich eben nur λόγος und ἔργον und nicht „*Gedanken*, Worte und Werke".

[23] Bezeichnend ist im Maschal 5,2.6a der Hinweis auf die im Traum liegende Unverantwortlichkeit (an letzterer Stelle scheint וַהֲבָלִים וּדְבָרִים ein Hendiadyoin zu sein).

[24] Eine gewisse Analogie finden wir in der Torafrömmigkeit, wie Ps 50,19f. zeigt; auch hier ergeben sich wieder Beziehungen zur Bergpredigt.

[25] Die Beziehungen zumindest des späteren Deuteronomismus zur Weisheit liegen andererseits auf der Hand; vgl. Dt 4,6.

[26] Die Zusammenhänge des sakralen idealen Königtums mit dem Landbau brauchen hier nicht ausgeführt zu werden; für das Alte Testament sei auf die stereotypen Beschreibungen des sog. Königsheils verwiesen (Ps 144,12-15; Ps 72,3.16; Ez 34,23-27; vgl. auch den Bildge-

an kein anderes als an das davidische zu denken. Kohelet ist als Weiser kein Apokalyptiker und kann keiner messianischen Hoffnung Ausdruck geben, aber daß die Frage nach dem „Vorteil" für das Land in einer solchen Weise zu beantworten wäre, wenigstens das darf er sagen. Machen wir uns klar, ein wie enger Zusammenhang zwischen dem Zionskult und dem Davidismus besteht, ja daß es eigentlich zwei Seiten *einer* Sache sind, so können wir auch die Anhangsstellung von 5,7f. im Verhältnis zu 4,17–5,6 verstehen.

Das zweite Stück des mittleren Hauptteils des Koheletbuches (und damit die kompositorische Mitte dieses Textes) liegt in der Komposition über den Besitz und die Besitzgier 5,9–6,9 vor. Es ist eine symmetrisch aufgebaute doppelte Rahmenkomposition[27], d.h. ein erster Rahmen (A) wird 1) von drei Maximen über den Besitz in 5,9–11 und 2) von drei weiteren Maximen desselben Themas in 6,7–9 dargestellt, ein zweiter Rahmen (B) von der lehrmäßigen Behandlung des Paradigmas über ungenutzt verlorenen Reichtum (eingeleitet jeweils mit יֵשׁ רָעָה ... רָאִיתִי תַּחַת הַשָּׁמֶשׁ) 1) in 5,12–16 und 2) in 6,1–6; und in der Mitte steht die daraus gefolgerte Lehre der „Heilspräsenz" (הִנֵּה אֲשֶׁר רָאִיתִי אָנִי) 5,1–19.

Die einführenden drei Maximen (A 1) betreffen a) das Unbefriedigtsein vom Reichtum, die mit der Besitzliebe verbundene Unersättlichkeit (V. 9), b) die fehlende Eigennutzung bei größerem Besitz (V. 10), c) als argumentum e contrario das ungesunde Leben des Reichen. Die abschließenden drei Maximen (A2) 6,7–9 behandeln a) wieder die Unersättlichkeit der Besitzbegierde (V. 7), b) die weisheitliche Enthaltsamkeit (V. 8): „Welchen Vorteil hat denn der Weise vor dem Toren? Welchen der Arme (הֶעָנִי) hat, der dem Leben gegenüber zu wandeln weiß", c) die Bescheidung mit dem Verfügbaren (V. 9a): „Besser, was vor Augen ist, als das Leben mit Gier". Am Ende (V. 9b) steht die bekannte Abschlußformel גַּם זֶה הֶבֶל וּרְעוּת רוּחַ, die sich auf das in dem Abschnitt A 2 doppelt vorkommende נֶפֶשׁ „Gier" bezieht. Diese abschließenden drei Maximen übertreffen die drei einleitenden insofern, als hier auf die Wurzel der Erscheinung in der habsüchtigen נֶפֶשׁ hingewiesen und dagegen das positive Ideal des enthaltsamen Weisen als eines „Armen" aufgestellt wird.

Bei der so künstlich aufgebauten Rahmenkomposition ist besonders auffällig, daß der als Paradigma aufgestellte Fall in B 1 (5,12–16) prinzipiell der gleiche ist wie der in B 2 (6,1–6): Ein Reicher verliert seinen schwer erworbenen, aber ungenutzten Reichtum unglücklicherweise während seines Lebens, endet also so arm, wie er geboren, und auch seinem Sohn kann er nichts

brauch 2 Sam 23,4; Ps 72,6). Und gerade im Zusammenhang mit dem natürlichen Gedeihen des Landes wird dann auf die königliche Begründung des rechtlichen und sozialen Heilszustandes hingewiesen, wie der „salomonische" Ps 72 hinreichend zeigt.

27 Vgl. dazu „Die Krisis der Weisheit bei Koheleth" (Les Sagesses du Proches-Orient ancien, 1963, 139–151 = H. Gese, Vom Sinai zum Zion, 1974, 168–179) S. 171 bzw. 142 Anm. 9.

hinterlassen. Der Fall in B2 erscheint nur in der Formulierung gesteigert: *Gott* hat ihm den Reichtum zukommen lassen, und *Gott* hat ihm die Möglichkeit der Nutznießung nicht gegeben. Das Vermögen wird als besonders groß bezeichnet; es ist auch von Ansehen die Rede. Es wird betont, daß das Vermögen einem Fremden, Ausländer zufällt. Es wird andererseits von hundert Söhnen gesprochen und ungeheuer langem Leben: Alles ist ohne Nutznießung unnütz; hyperbolisch hat der Verarmte schließlich noch nicht einmal den Nutzen eines Begräbnisses. Deutlich sind in dieser äußerst emphatischen Steigerung der Beschreibung des im Prinzip gleichen Falles wie in B1 ironische Töne zu hören. Und wenn die Beurteilung des Falles in B2 dann noch mit dem Vergleich mit einer Fehlgeburt schließt (6,3b–6), so ist auch dies nur um der Emphase willen von Bedeutung. Wir erkennen also in der Komposition hier nicht das Interesse an sachlicher Kasuistik, sondern die künstlerische, sozusagen poetische Absicht, die eine und grundsätzliche philosophische Erkenntnis mit allem Nachdruck auszusagen und einzuschärfen.

Der Kern der doppelten Rahmenkomposition, die Lehre von der Heilspräsenz 5,17–19, wirkt einheitlich, läßt aber doch eine gewisse Doppelung im Ausdruck verspüren. Gegenüber der einfachen Formulierung in V. 17 wiederholt V. 18f. die Lehre in verstärktem Maße, so daß hier im Positiven die negative Entsprechung, die zwischen B1 und B2 besteht, ein Gegenstück findet. Dazu paßt die Rede von הָאֱלֹהִים, von עֹשֶׁר וּנְכָסִים, von שׁלט Hi. in V. 18, was man alles in 6,2 aufgenommen sieht. So stehen wir in diesem Komplex 5,9–6,9 über den Wahn der Habsucht vor einer poetisch durchgeformten und rhetorisch meisterhaften Komposition, deren Höhepunkt auch die Souveränität des ironischen Tons verspüren läßt.

Mit 6,10ff. kommen wir zum dritten Lehrstück des mittleren Hauptteils des Koheletbuches. 6,10–12 ist eine in sich geschlossene Texteinheit von der Determiniertheit des Geschehens und damit insbesondere des menschlichen Lebens. Die Determiniertheit, die sich selbstverständlich aus der Kairoslehre ergibt, wird dabei nicht ausdrücklich begründet, sondern es wird die Folgerung gezogen, daß es für den Menschen sinnlos ist, mit Gott, dem, „der stärker ist als er", zu rechten (V. 10b) und mit vielen Worten über sein Schicksal zu hadern (V. 11), weiß doch der Mensch garnicht, was für ihn gut ist, fehlt ihm doch jegliche absolute Beurteilungsmöglichkeit, da er die Zukunft über sich hinaus nicht kennen kann (V. 12).

Die hier als entscheidend auftauchende Frage nach dem, was gut für den Menschen sei, wird von Kohelet in einer eigenen Komposition von Weisheitsworten in 7,1–14 behandelt, die hier nun unmittelbar auf 6,10–12 folgt, so daß in der Buchkomposition 6,10–12 zum Einführungsstück von 7,1–14 wird, und 6,10–7,14 bildet damit einen Komplex, der als drittes Lehrstück im mittleren Buchhauptteil erscheint.

Um 7,1–14, das aus einer Reihe von weisheitlichen Lehrsätzen der beliebten

Form... מִן... טוֹב „besser x als y“ besteht, zu denen aber zunehmend andere Formulierungen treten, im Sinne der Zusammenstellung richtig zu analysieren, ist es geraten, streng auf das Auftreten des Ṭob-Prädikates zu achten. Der erste Satz liegt zweifellos in V. 1 vor mit der für die tiefe Weisheit Kohelets typischen Lehre, daß das Ende des Lebens besser als sein Anfang ist[28], der zweite Satz in V. 2aαβ mit der Lehre vom Vorzug des Trauerhauses, wozu aber nun eine Begründung in V. 2aγb tritt. Die in Weisheitsspruchsammlungen geradezu übliche Aneinanderreihung zweier inhaltlich entsprechender Sprüche in Analogie zum Parallelismus – selten auch dreier Sprüche in Analogie zum Tristich – ist eine bekannte, wenn auch zu wenig beachtete Erscheinung (z.B. in Spr 10: V. 2 und V. 3, V. 4 und V. 5, V. 6 und V. 7, V. 8 und V. 9 usw.)[29]. Auch hier liegt ein inhaltlicher Zusammenhang der beiden Sprüche V. 1f., *Lebensende* und *Totentrauer*, also der Tod des Menschen, auf der Hand.

Der dritte Ṭob-Min-Spruch liegt in V. 3 vor (schon innerhalb des Parallelismus in V. 3b mit der Erkenntnisbeförderung begründet, um die provozierende Aussage, Ärger sei besser als Lachen, überhaupt verständlich zu machen). V. 4 ist wiederum Begründung zu V. 3: „ist doch das Herz der Weisen im Trauerhaus...“. Der vierte Spruch ist als reine Ṭob-Min-Formulierung in V. 5 gegeben, wozu aber als maschalartige Begründung – man beachte die Paronomasie הַסִּירִים, הַסִּיר, הַכְּסִיל, die die in שִׁיר כְּסִילִים liegende fortsetzt – V. 6 tritt. Auch V. 7 ordnet sich dem noch als Begründungssatz zu; denn geht es in V. 5f. um den Vorzug der Rüge vor dem törichten Loblied, so liegt nach der Gefahr des Schmeichelns die in V. 7 angesprochene Gefährdung negativ durch Nötigung und positiv durch Bestechung nahe. Auch beim dritten und vierten Ṭob-Min-Wort über den Vorzug des *Verdrusses* und der *Rüge* ist ein näherer Zusammenhang, nämlich das jetzt im seelischen Bereich auftretende Unangenehme, das in einem selbst oder durch andere entsteht, klar zu erkennen.

V. 8 enthält gleich zwei Ṭob-Min-Formulierungen, und doch kann das nur als Einheit gemeint sein. Da im einfachen Parallelismus die zweite Hälfte das gesteigerte Gewicht trägt, hier außerdem die erste Hälfte inhaltlich nichts anderes ausdrückt als V. 1 aufs Sachliche übertragen, ist das logische Verhältnis von V. 8a zu V. 8b nur so zu fassen, daß die eigentliche Aussage V. 8b ist, die aus V. 8a entwickelt wird, also die Lehre, daß Langmut besser als Hochmut sei. Die dazu parallel laufende Warnung vor Ungeduld in V. 9a mit Begründung V. 9b ist nichts anderes als eine Explikation.

---

[28] Die Weisheitssprüche sind poetisch selbstverständlich im Parallelismus membrorum formuliert, und so läuft V. 1a parallel zu V. 1b, hier in der Weise, daß die eine offensichtlich sprichwörtliche Rede aufnehmende Formulierung V. 1a in V. 1b interpretiert wird, שֵׁם, „Name“, ist das aus dem gelebten Leben sich ergebende Ansehen, das dem שֶׁמֶן טוֹב, dem „Parfüm“, gegenübergestellt wird (man beachte die Paronomasie).

[29] Vgl. „Wisdom Literature in the Persian Period“ (The Cambridge History of Judaism, Bd. 1, 1984, 189–218) S. 202.

Auffällig ist nun die mit V. 9 völlig übereinstimmende Struktur von V. 10 (... כִּי ... אַל), während inhaltlich zu V. 9 nur noch eine abgeschwächte Verbindung besteht (*Unmut* über die Gegenwart), aber ein neuer, auf die *Weisheit* bezogener Aussageskopus wird sichtbar, von der dann ein großer Ṭob-Satz in V. 11f. handelt. Wir müssen daraus schließen, daß V. 10 unter formaler Anknüpfung an V. 9 die Überleitung zum neuen und letzten Ṭob-Wort V. 11f. darstellt. Wenn hier am Ende der ganzen Komposition im Preis der Weisheit selbst nicht mehr die Vergleichsform „besser... als...“, sondern die reine Ṭob-Aussage erscheint, so ist das eine höchst passende Steigerung und nicht als Formabbruch zu sehen. V. 11f. ist sehr kunstvoll: die Ṭob-Aussage selbst in V. 11, in der die Kraft der Weisheit mit Erbbesitz gleichgesetzt wird, wird in V. 12 wieder aufgenommen[30] und überboten, insofern Geld nicht Leben zu retten vermag. Doppelt findet in V. 11f. die Frage nach dem „Vorzug“ eine positive Antwort[31]. Was aber ist die Lehre dieser „guten“ Weisheit? Das führt dann V. 13f. aus. Es ist im Grunde die Lehre der „Heilspräsenz“, die von Gott geschenkte Gegenwart anzunehmen (der Einsatz in V. 10 bestätigt sich!), am Guten sich zu freuen und am bösen Tag der aus der Kairoslehre sich ergebenden göttlichen und für den Menschen uneinsichtigen Geschehensleitung zu gedenken[32].

Schließlich noch die Frage der Zuordnung des letzten, sechsten Wortes der Reihung 7,1–14, V. 10–14, zu ihrem fünften von der Langmut, V. 8f.: Aufzählungen haben gern am Ende das verallgemeinernde Glied. Darüber hinaus verweist die inhaltliche Explikation der V. 10–14 gepriesenen Weisheit in V. 13f.[33] – und dem entspricht ja auch der Einsatz in V. 10 – auf das rechte Verhältnis des Menschen zu seiner Gegenwart. Das Thema der *Langmut* (man beachte auch den Gegensatz zum Hochmut) von V. 8f. schließt sich mit dem der weisen *Annahme der von Gott gegebenen Lebensgegenwart* als des Prinzips weisen Verhaltens also ganz offensichtlich zusammen: es geht um die in der alten Weisheit schon so grundsätzlich geforderte demütige Geisteshaltung des Weisen[34]; nur – wie sehr ist dies bei Kohelet vertieft erfaßt!

7,1–14 besteht somit aus einer Reihe von drei Paaren von sich umfänglich steigernden Ṭob-Bestimmungen, die im Preis der Gottes Zeitenwerk annehmenden Weisheit gipfeln. 7,1–14 ist Kohelets Lehre von dem, was für den Menschen gut ist, und in ihr wird positiv überwunden, was in 6,10–12 verwehrt wird, das Hadern des Menschen mit seinem Lebensschicksal. In der Zusammenstellung mit 7,1–14 wird 6,10–12 zum einführenden Text, und der Hin-

---

30 Man beachte das Spiel mit „Sonne“ und „Schatten“.

31 יֹתֵר und יִתְרוֹן, vgl. auch 2,13.

32 Vgl. das doppelte רְאֵה V. 13 Anfang und V. 14a Ende.

33 Man beachte den determinierenden Artikel vor חָכְמָה in V. 12b (siehe auch unten zu 7,19): in der folgenden Ausführung wird das Wesen der Weisheit gesehen.

34 Vgl. H. Gese, Lehre und Wirklichkeit in der alten Weisheit, 1958, S. 40f.

weis auf die dem Menschen verschlossene Zeitgrenze אַחֲרָיו am Ende (7,14bβ) bildet eine Inclusio mit 6,12b und bestätigt die kompositorische Zusammenstellung von 6,10–12 mit 7,1–14.

Mit 7,15 beginnt ein völlig neuer Abschnitt. Er behandelt das Thema der eigenen Gerechtigkeit. Ein צַדִּיק zu sein, ist in der alten Weisheit geradezu die inhaltliche Füllung des Begriffes des Weisen[35]. Ausgehend von der Beobachtung einer mit dem Gerecht-Sein nicht zusammenstimmenden Wirklichkeit (V. 15), gibt Kohelet den provokanten doppelten[36] Rat, nicht zu sehr ein „Gerechter" zu sein, sich nicht übermäßig als weise zu zeigen, bzw. nicht zu ungerecht zu handeln und ein Tor zu sein (V. 16f.). Der empfohlene Kompromiß, das sprichwörtliche „eines tun und das andere nicht lassen" (V. 18a), meint aber nun nicht einfach ein mittelmäßiges Recht- und Unrechtsein, denn die Formulierungen in V. 16f. sind charakteristisch verschieden – V. 16 beschreibt ein äußerliches Gerechtsein[37] –, sondern weist auf eine andere Instanz, die die problematischen Wertmaßstäbe äußerlichen Ansehens transzendiert, die Gottesfurcht (V. 18b); d.h. Kohelet begründet die Ethik im religiösen Gewissen. Diesen entscheidenden Durchbruch in der Weisheitslehre unterstreicht er mit dem sprichwörtlichen Weisheitspreis V. 19[38] und begründet philosophisch sein Urteil mit der grundlegend wichtigen Erkenntnis, daß es einen völlig Gerechten auf Erden garnicht gibt (V. 20), woraus wiederum in Erinnerung an eigenes Fluchen die Mahnung folgt, Gerede und heimliche Verwünschung, selbst des eigenen Knechtes, vergebungsbereit zu überhören (V. 21f.).

7,15–22 stellt einen Höhepunkt im Entwicklungsgang der alttestamentlichen Weisheitslehre dar. Hier wird eine entscheidende Vertiefung der Erkenntnis erreicht, und es ist daher durchaus verständlich, daß der Verfasser diesen bedeutsamen Abschnitt mit V. 23f. schließt. In V. 23a bekennt er, daß all diese Erkenntnis[39] das Ergebnis seiner philosophischen Untersuchung ist; aber demütig fährt er fort, daß die Weisheit sein Erkenntnisvermögen weit übersteigt (V. 23b), ja daß grundsätzlich „das, was geworden ist (also das Seiende[40], die Wirklichkeit) fern ist und tief, tief – wer kann es herausfinden?"

[35] Z.B. können in Spr 10 von den 32 Versen 14 vom „Gerechten" handeln.

[36] Inhaltlich entgegengesetzte Mahnungen, die natürlich cum grano salis zu verstehen sind, gibt es schon in der älteren Weisheit, vgl. Spr 26,4f.

[37] Kohelet sagt *nicht*, wie es V. 17aβ entsprechen würde: sei kein Weiser, sondern *zeige* dich nicht *übermäßig* weise, und sagt nicht, wie es V. 17aα entsprechen würde: handle nicht zu gerecht, sondern *sei* nicht zu sehr ein צַדִּיק; es ist also auf die Erscheinung als צַדִּיק abgehoben.

[38] Der Artikel determiniert „diese" Weisheit im Sinne des Kontextes.

[39] זֹה kann sich nur auf das Vorhergehende beziehen, da V. 25 eine neue Einleitung zu V. 26ff. darstellt.

[40] Ein Partizip von היה ist ungebräuchlich, so muß ein Perfekt praes. an die Stelle treten. Zu מַה vgl. 6,8b. Wichtig ist die durch 𝔊 ὑπὲρ ὃ ἦν bezeugte Lesart מִשֶּׁהָיָה, d.h. die Aussage, die Weisheit transzendiere das Seiende. Und diese Transzendenzlehre von der Weisheit ist ja in Hi 28 und Spr 1-9 bezeugt. Für MT spricht aber das Mask. רָחוֹק, und es ist für Kohelet wohl typisch, die Transzendenzgrenze erkenntnistheoretisch a priori zu respektieren und zurück-

(V. 24). Angesichts von V. 24 sollte man nicht von Kohelets Verzweiflung sprechen; die Aussage von Unergründlichkeit und Verborgenheit hat einen das Schöpfungssein preisenden Charakter.

Thematisch eng verbunden mit diesem fundamentalen Lehrstück über die eigene „Gerechtigkeit“ 7,15–24 ist die in 7,25 nun eingeleitete Untersuchung über weises Verhalten angesichts von רֶשַׁע, also der „Ungerechtigkeit“ in der persönlichen Umwelt. Sie gliedert sich in zwei Abschnitte: 7,26–8,1 bezieht sich auf den Bereich der Liebe (Freundschaft) und 8,2–8 auf den Bereich der (staatlichen) Macht; 8,9 bildet den zusammenfassenden Schlußsatz (mit einer ähnlichen Eingangsformulierung wie 7,23): es gibt – bei entsprechendem Kairos – die Möglichkeit, daß ein Mensch über den anderen „ihm zum Bösen“ herrscht. 7,15–8,9 muß also als zusammenhängender Komplex über das ethische Grundthema der Gerechtigkeit und der Verführung zur Ungerechtigkeit angesehen werden.

Der erste Teil dieser zweiten Hälfte 7,25–8,9 über die „Ungerechtigkeit“ in der persönlichen Umgebung nimmt in 7,26ff. das sexualethische Thema auf, das uns in Spr 1–9, nämlich 2,16–19; 5; 6,20–7,27; 9,13ff. besonders betont entgegentritt, die Warnung vor der „fremden Frau“, was dann zur weisheitlichen Begründung der Monogamie führt. Bei Kohelet wird sehr kurz die „Todesgefahr“ der Verführung in V. 26a dichterisch geschildert und in V. 26b demgegenüber die grundsätzlich bestehende menschliche Schwäche zugegeben, um in V. 27 abschließend unter Betonung der Autorität des Weisheitslehrers[41] diese negative Beurteilung als immer wieder bestätigt zu bezeichnen. V. 28f. führt zwar dieses Verführungsthema noch weiter, bezieht aber jetzt die Enttäuschung auf dem Gebiet der Freundschaft unter Männern mit ein und kommt zu dem Urteil einer grundsätzlichen Schlechtigkeit des Menschen, der, von Gott wohl recht erschaffen, durch die vielen egoistischen „Künste“ verdorben ist. In Anbetracht dessen wird abschließend 8,1 die Erziehungsfunktion der Weisheit bestimmt, die diesen menschlichen Charakter diagnostizieren[42] und durch Selbsterkenntnis wenigstens den „dickköpfigen“ Trotz, das Bestehen auf Willensdurchsetzung[43], ändern[44], also den Menschen lernfähig machen kann.

Nach dem Bereich der Liebe (und Freundschaft) kommt der zweite Teil 8,2–8 auf den der Macht zu sprechen und stellt hier die Verführung zur

---

haltender schon von der Unergründlichkeit der (diesseitigen) Wirklichkeit zu sprechen, wie es ja auch seine Kairoslehre 3,11 (und auch 1,8ff.) lehrt.

[41] Nach 12,8 ist natürlich אָמַר הַקֹּהֶלֶת zu lesen; der MT denkt spitzfindig an ein Urteil der ganzen Schule.

[42] Zu פֵּשֶׁר vgl. Sir 38,14.

[43] Zur „Angesichtshärte“ vgl. Spr 7,13; 21,29.

[44] Das אֲנִי zu Beginn von 8,2 ist korrupt, die nota acc. אֵת ist zu erwarten, und die Verlesung könnte über ein יְשַׁנֶּאנּוּ am Ende von 8,1 entstanden sein: „(und seine Angesichtshärte) er (der Mensch) ändert sie“.

Ungerechtigkeit fest. Eingesetzt wird in 8,2 mit dem Grundsatz: Dem Königsbefehl soll man gehorchen, „und zwar wegen des Gotteseides", also nicht wegen der von der alten Weisheit vertretenen Lehre vom göttlichen Königtum – man denke z. B. an Spr 16,10–15 –, sondern in dieser Zeit des Fremdherrschertums wegen der eidlichen Untertanenverpflichtung, die unter Gott steht[45]. Damit ist auch schon die Grenze des Gehorsams im Sinne von Apg 4,19; 5,29 angedeutet, die von Kohelet in 8,3f. wegen der scheinbar unumschränkten Verfügungsgewalt des Königs angemahnt wird: ohne sich einer königlichen Forderung übereilt zu entziehen, soll man doch keinesfalls sich auf eine böse Sache einlassen (Audienz-Bild). Die Bewahrung (שׁמר) des königlichen Befehls ist also der Bewahrung (שׁמר) des göttlichen Gebotes untergeordnet (V. 5a), und der Weise erkennt den Gerichtskairos (V. 5b), über den in V. 6–7aβ gelehrt wird, daß er, je größer das Unrecht, um so sicherer eintreten wird, ohne daß man seinen Zeitpunkt und seine Gestalt berechnen und ihn menschlicherseits beherrschen und verhindern kann (Wind-Bild). Ist der Zeitpunkt da – so endet der Abschnitt in V. 8aγδb –, dann gilt: „Es gibt keine Herrschaft über den Todestag und keine Entlassung im Kriege", und רֶשַׁע, die „Ungerechtigkeit", kann den, der damit umgeht, nicht retten.

8,9 blickt als Abschlußsatz auf die gesamte Ausführung zur „Ungerechtigkeit" im persönlichen Umfeld, wie wir sahen, zurück, so daß nun der Gesamtkomplex von I) der eigenen Gerechtigkeit 7,15–24 und II) der Ungerechtigkeitsverführung 7,25–8,9 mit den Teilen a) Liebe-Freundschaft 7,26–8,1 und b) staatliche Macht 8,2–8 abgeschlossen zu sein scheint. Um so auffälliger ist die Einführung eines neuen Themas, das der Retribution, im unmittelbaren syntaktsichen Anschluß וּבְכֵן, „und dabei...". Nun ist weisheitlich die Frage von Lohn und Vergeltung mit der des gerechten Handelns so eng verbunden, daß beides sogar eine höhere Einheit bildet und die Grundlage der ethischen Erkenntnis darstellt, zumal in der alten Weisheit im Denken des sog. Tun-Ergehen-Zusammenhangs Gutes (Böses) tun und erfahren a priori wesensmäßig eines ist, sozusagen die zwei Seiten einer Sache. Mit diesem engen Anschluß in 8,10 soll also die Behandlung der von der (Un-)Gerechtigkeit nicht wegzudenkenden Frage des „Lohnes" – nach der theologischen Umbildung des Denkens im Tun-Ergehen-Zusammenhang zu dem Grundgedanken der göttlichen Vergeltung: diese Frage der göttlichen Retribution – als unmittelbar dazugehörig eingeführt werden[46].

Dieser an die Behandlung des Themas der (Un-)Gerechtigkeit 7,15–8,9

[45] Eine Deutung des Gotteseides im Sinne eines gen.subj. oder im technischen Sinne im Prozeßverfahren gibt der einfache Zusammenhang nicht her.

[46] Wir finden dieselbe Kompositionsmethode im Anschluß von 11,7ff. an 11,1-6: die Lebensfreude als unmittelbare Folge des rechten Tuns – diese enge Verbindung wird durch die einfache Kopula zum Ausdruck gebracht („und" im Sinne von „so", „dann", vgl. GesB s. v. ְו 2e).

unmittelbar angehängte Komplex über die göttliche Reaktion des „Lohnes“ stellt sich in einer doppelten Durchführung dar: (I) 8,10–17 behandelt die Frage der Retribution und endet (8,10ff.) mit der Lehre von der Heilspräsenz verbunden mit der von der Nichtnachweisbarkeit eines retributiven Lebensgeschehens, und (II) 9,1–10 behandelt nach einer Neueinführung der Untersuchung (9,1aα[47]) die parallele, aber gesteigerte, spiritualisierte Frage der Erkennbarkeit des göttlichen Wohlgefallens am gerechten Tun und endet (9,7–10) wieder mit der Lehre von der Heilspräsenz, die jetzt aber entsprechend stärker formuliert und einerseits mit der Zusage des göttlichen Wohlgefallens und andererseits mit der Aufforderung zum Tätigsein verbunden ist.

Im einzelnen können wir uns kurz fassen. Schon gleich im Einsatz der ersten Durchführung 8,10 ist vom Ausbleiben der Retribution im konkreten Fall die Rede (ehrenvolles Begräbnis des angesehenen Ungerechten, während die Rechten vertrieben und vergessen sind), und dieser Mangel an Erkennbarkeit des göttlichen Vergeltungsspruchs[48] verführt den Menschen zum Bösen (V. 11–12a). Als Lehre stellt Kohelet in feierlicher Formulierung das Postulat der göttlichen Retribution auf (V. 12b–13), verbindet dies aber mit der Feststellung der Möglichkeit eines der Retribution völlig widersprechenden „Geschehens auf der Erde“ (V. 14). Es ergibt sich daraus wieder die Lehre der Heilspräsenz als eines gnädigen Gottesgeschenks (V. 15), während das „Geschehen auf der Erde“ und „unter der Sonne“ auch bei größter Anstrengung (sprichwörtlich V. 16b) weisheitlicher Forschung unerklärbar bleibt (V. 16f.), ja diese Unerklärbarkeit wird bis zum Prinzipiellen ausgezogen (V. 17b).

Man beachte, daß in dem dargestellten Zusammenhang die betonte Formulierung des Retributions-„Dogmas“ V. 12b–13 kein sekundärer Texteinschub sein kann; denn gerade aus dem Gegensatz des Postulats (!יוֹדֵעַ אֲנִי) zur Wirklichkeitserfahrung V. 14 ergibt sich ja die Lehre von der Undurchschaubarkeit des irdischen Geschehens V. 16f. Außerdem ist die Formulierung des Retributionspostulats ganz gemäß 7,18b nicht mit dem Begriff der Gerechtigkeit, sondern mit dem Begriff der Gottesfurcht betont (dreimal!) vorgenommen worden, also ganz Kohelets Weisheitslehre entsprechend.

Der zweite Durchgang 9,1ff. verschiebt die Ebene der „auf der Erde“ sichtbaren Retribution auf die spirituelle Ebene der Wahrnehmbarkeit des auf die gute Tat reagierenden göttlichen Wohlgefallens in der Gottesverbundenheit des Menschen[49]. Der Text setzt nach der Einführung (V. 1aα) mit der

---

47 Nach 𝔊 καὶ καρδία μου εἶδε ist וְלִבִּי רָאָה für ולבור את zu lesen (die BHS-Angabe ist fehlerhaft).

48 Da V. 11 פִּתְגָם mask. ist, ist auch vorher נעשׂה mask. zu punktieren.

49 Das „Lieben“ und „Nichtlieben“ in 9,1b wird statt auf das göttliche Subjekt gern auf den Menschen als Subjekt bezogen, was sich durch V. 1aβ, als Aussage allgemein menschlicher Determiniertheit verstanden, nahezulegen scheint (so auch fälschlich a. Anm. 27 a.O. S. 173 bzw. 144). Der Zusammenhang mit V. 2f. macht das aber ganz unwahrscheinlich. Zum „Lieben“ und „Hassen“ Gottes dem menschlichen Täter gegenüber vgl. Ps 11,5.7; Spr 15,9.

Aussage ein, daß die Gerechten und Weisen samt ihren (guten) Taten in der Hand Gottes sind (V. 1aβ), womit nicht eine allgemeine Determiniertheit zum Ausdruck gebracht werden soll – denn dann wäre von *allen* die Rede –, sondern die Gottesnähe, wobei darauf hingewiesen wird, daß der Mensch jedoch seinerseits die göttliche Liebe oder Nichtliebe nicht erkennen kann (V. 1bαβ). „Beides steht vor ihnen, beides wie bei jedem" (V. 1bγ-2aα), und *ein* Geschick haben alle trotz ihrer so gegensätzlichen Stellung zu Gott (V.2aβ-3a). Wieder erscheint eine Liste von Gegensatzpaaren bei Kohelet, um die Vollständigkeit in ihrer Ordnung nachzuzeichnen: zwei Paare zeigen die allgemein ethischen Begriffe gerecht-ungerecht und gut-böse[50], zwei die kultischen Begriffe rein-unrein und opfernd-nichtopfernd und zwei die Frömmigkeitsbegriffe Braver-Sünder, Gelobender-Nichtgelobender[51]. Wie die mangelnde Erkenntnis einer Retribution in 8,11-12a so führt diese „Gleichgültigkeit" hinsichtlich des Geschickes bei völlig entgegengesetzter Gottesbeziehung zum Anwachsen der Bosheit (9,3b), während vom Zustand des Toten aus (wo Kohelet offenbar entsprechend der Totengerichtsvorstellung, vgl. 3,17a, die „Gültigkeit" der fundamentalen Unterscheidung im Gottesverhältnis voraussetzt) jegliche Beziehung zur Welt „unter der Sonne" definitiv abgebrochen und nichts zu ändern oder besser zu machen ist (V. 4-6). Wie schon ausgeführt, ist die parallel zu 8,15ff. am Ende erscheinende Lehre der Heilspräsenz 9,7-10 hier nach dem zweiten Durchgang besonders kräftig formuliert und um die theologisch bedeutsame Zusage des göttlichen Wohlgefallens zu Beginn (V. 7b) und um die Aufforderung, im Leben zu wirken, solange es Tag ist, am Ende (V. 10) vermehrt.

Wir hatten schon vorwegnehmend den Gesamtkomplex 7,15-9,10 als die grundlegend ethische Betrachtung im hinteren Teil des Buches mit der grundlegend ontologischen Betrachtung des ersten Gesamtkomplexes 1,4-4,16 im vorderen Teil des Buches verglichen. Dieser erste Komplex hatte drei kurze Anhangsstücke, die sich auf den Widerspruch der Weisheit Kohelets gegen die das einzelne Subjekt und das Einzelgeschehen isolierende Betrachtungsweise der alten Weisheit bezogen, in 4,4-6.7-12.13-16. Auch der ethisch grundlegende Komplex 7,15-9,10 hat gegenüber altem Denken einen neuen Charakter entwickelt, nämlich ein vertieftes Bewußtsein von der Unergründlichkeit der menschlichen Wirklichkeit und damit der engen Begrenztheit der menschlichen Weisheit; vgl. 7,23f.; 8,16f. Natürlich ist diese Begrenztheit für die Weisheit Kohelets schon in seinen Lehrstücken von Anfang an typisch, aber angesichts der ethischen Grundfragen und der Verborgenheit Gottes im Lebensschicksal samt dem Wissen um die grundsätzliche Fragwürdigkeit des Menschen (vgl. 7,22.29; 8,11-12a; 9,3b) gewinnt diese Erkenntniseinschrän-

[50] Mit 𝔊 ist וְלָרַע nach לַטּוֹב einzufügen.

[51] Man beachte, daß die Zusammenfassung in jeweils zwei Paare sich in kleinen formalen Differenzen niederschlägt (wobei mit 𝔊 כַּנִּשְׁבָּע zu lesen ist).

kung und Begrenzung der menschlichen Weisheit noch eine neue Dimension gegenüber dem alten Denken. Und so finden wir in 9,11f.; 9,13-16; 9,17-10,3 drei Anhangsstücke, die sich inhaltlich diesem Gesichtspunkt zuordnen.

Mit dem Vorangehenden ist am engsten 9,11f. verbunden (vgl. die Einführung שַׁבְתִּי וְרָאֹה). Es wird der Charakter der Zufälligkeit und Plötzlichkeit beim Todeskairos, eben seine Unberechenbarkeit herausgestellt, was allen Fähigkeiten und Künsten, die menschliche Weisheit ausbilden mag (die Weisen erscheinen in dreifach mit וְגַם herausgehobener Bezeichnung neben den Kriegern, deren Vortrefflichkeit in der Schlacht nichts nützt), ein Ende setzt und sie bedeutungslos macht; und darum kann das Todesgeschehen mit den die absolute Überlegenheit zum Ausdruck bringenden Jagdbildern gemalt werden. Das Stück hat zwar inhaltlich mit dem Hinweis auf das allgemeine Todesgeschick einen Bezug zu 7,15-9,10 (besonders 9,3), aber dort geht es nicht um die Schreckensgewalt des Todes, um seine absolute Macht, sondern um die Nichtaufweisbarkeit eines dem gerechten Tun entsprechenden Lebensglückes und deswegen um die Unterschiedslosigkeit des Todes. Somit läßt sich 9,11f. schwerlich *primär* dem Komplex 7,15-9,10 kompositionell zuordnen, vielmehr muß man das Stück als eine *Ergänzung* ansehen, die am Todesgeschehen das Zunichtewerden aller Weisheit demonstriert und sich dann sehr gut an 7,15-9,10 anfügt, aber eben den Ton auf das Thema der so wesentlichen Begrenztheit aller menschlichen Weisheit legt.

In einer Beispielerzählung wird dieses Thema in 9,13-16 dergestalt behandelt, daß sogar eine die Katastrophe einer Lebensgemeinschaft (Stadt) abwendende Weisheit nur wirken und nützen kann, wenn sie, also der sie kennende und vertretende Weise, auch gehört wird. Das der alten Weisheit fremde Phänomen des unbekannten, eben verachteten Weisen wird bei Kohelet in seiner späten und komplexen geschichtlichen Situation voll erkannt.

Kohelet vertieft dies weiter zu der Frage der eingeschränkten Selbstevidenz der Weisheit. War für das alte Denken die Selbstevidenz der Weisheit unumstritten, so sieht er die Möglichkeit, diese Weisheitswirkung zu behindern, die Weisheit zu unterdrücken, und dafür genügt schon ein wenig Torheit. Mit 9,17f. wird übergeleitet zu der Lehre von der im Gegensatz zur Weisheit vollen Wirkungskraft der Torheit. Über sie wird gehandelt in dem gleichnishaften Sprichwort von dem durch tote Fliegen verdorbenen kostbaren Parfüm (10,1a), in der weisheitlichen Rätselantwort „Teurer als Weisheit, (ja) als Ansehen? – *Wenig* Torheit" (10,1b) und in dem Lehrbeispiel von dem Toren, der wegen seiner Torheit jeden, der ihm begegnet, für töricht halten muß (10,2f.). Mit dieser gattungsmäßig so vielseitigen Zusammenstellung wird das Thema in 10,1-3 nicht ohne Ironie behandelt. So bilden also wie in 4,4-6.7-12.13-16 als Anhang zu 1,4-4,3 auch hier in 9,11f.; 9,13-16; 9,17-10,3 drei kleine Lehrstücke einen thematisch zusammenhängenden Anhang zum letzten Komplex 7,15-9,10.

Die Form der weisheitlichen Lehre Kohelets ist die der thematisch entwikkelten Darstellung, und man muß davon ausgehen, daß in sich geschlossene Zusammenhänge wie 1,4-11; 1,12-2,26; 3,1-15; 3,16-4,3 usw. schon primäre Kompositionen sind und nicht erst für die Sammlung im Buch zusammengestellt wurden. Es ist bezeichnend, daß dann auch die sekundäre Sammlungskomposition im Buch den Charakter der thematischen Entwicklung beibehält. Die spätere Weisheit in Spr 1-9 und die späteren Weisheitsbücher zeigen ähnlich die thematische Anordnung. Die ältere Weisheit begnügt sich dagegen mit der Zusammenstellung kurzer Sprüche, wie die alten Sammlungen in Spr 10ff. zeigen, wobei sich in der Regel nur die inhaltliche Zusammengehörigkeit von zwei (bisweilen drei) Sprüchen beobachten läßt[52]. Diese ältere Form einfacher, wenn auch bedacht komponierter Zusammenstellung von Einzelsprüchen muß auch Kohelet noch geübt haben, wie man an einer Reihung wie 7,1-14 ablesen kann, wenngleich die poetisch-rhetorische Gestaltung um der Steigerung willen weit über die einfache Reihung hinausgeht. Nun findet sich aber auch in 10,4ff. eine einfache Reihe von Weisheitssprüchen verschiedensten Inhalts, und diese Form entspricht also der alten Tradition. Wenn sie im Koheletbuch am Ende erscheint – 11,1-12,8 ist ja nur noch das (allerdings inhaltlich einen Höhepunkt darstellende) Finale –, so eben aus dem Grund, daß diese Form bei Kohelet ungewöhnlich ist und sich wegen der Verschiedenartigkeit des Inhalts garnicht in die thematisch angeordnete Buchkomposition einordnen läßt; 10,4-20 gibt sich also als Anhang oder Zusatz in der alten Form einfacher Spruchsammlung. Gewiß sind nun auch inhaltlich die meisten Worte in 10,4ff. traditionell in ihrem Grundcharakter, man stößt aber immer wieder auf die Diktion und den Geist Kohelets, ja unter der Hand wächst sich die einfache Spruchform des Mahn- und Aussageworts zur ausgeführten Lehre aus, so daß man keinen Grund sehen kann, 10,4ff. Kohelet etwa abzusprechen.

Aber kann man Teile herausnehmen? Dagegen spricht nun entschieden die Geschlossenheit der Form. Es handelt sich um zehn Weisheitsworte, von denen wieder je zwei eine thematische Zusammengehörigkeit zeigen. Es liegt also eine dem Dekalog vergleichbare Kompositionsform vor[53]. Daß diese dekalogartige Komposition von fünf Paaren in der Weisheit geübt wurde, zeigt z.B. die Beschreibung der zehn der Menschenwelt feindlichen oder doch fremden Tiere in Hi 38,39-39,30, die in fünf Paaren angeordnet sind[54].

Das erste Wort 10,4 mahnt zur Gelassenheit angesichts des Zorns des Vorgesetzten, des Herrschers. Auch das zweite Wort V. 5-7 hat es mit der Abhängigkeit gegenüber den Mächtigen zu tun; es beschreibt in für Kohelet typischer

---

[52] Siehe dazu oben S. 82 und Anm. 29.

[53] Vgl. dazu „Der Dekalog als Ganzheit betrachtet“ (ZThK 64, 1967, 121–138 = H. Gese, Vom Sinai zum Zion, 1974, 63–80) S. 73ff. bzw. 131ff.

[54] Zur Analyse vgl. „Die Frage nach dem Lebenssinn: Hiob und die Folgen“ (ZThK 79, 1982, 161–179 = H. Gese, Alttestamentliche Studien, 1991, 170–188) S. 179ff. bzw. 170f.

Diktion die ungerechte Zufälligkeit der Ehrung durch die Machthaber. Das nächste Wortpaar führt uns in die Arbeitswelt. V. 8f. lehrt, daß jede Arbeit die ihr eigene Gefahr in sich birgt, während V. 10f. zeigt, daß mühselige Schwierigkeiten bei der Arbeit wenigstens zur Einsicht, was man falsch gemacht hat, führen. Kohelet fügt aber die Lehre in Maschalform (beißende Schlange) hinzu, daß diese Einsicht zu spät kommen kann. Das dritte Paar hat es mit dem Toren zu tun. V. 12-14a bezieht sich auf sein ausgiebiges Reden, das immer törichter wird. V. 14b-15, auf das Interesse des Toren bezogen, ist für Kohelets Weisheit bezeichnend: „Der Mensch weiß nicht, was sein wird, und wer könnte ihm sagen, was nach ihm sein wird: (das ist) die Bemühung der Toren; es ermüdet ihn aber, wenn man nicht weiß, wie man zur Stadt kommt“. Der Zukunftsspekulation hingegeben, versagt der Tor in der konkreten einfachen Frage, wo es lang geht. Das vierte Wortpaar hat die Liederlichkeit zum Thema. V. 16f. wendet sich in Wehe- und Wohl-Ruf gegen die Prasserei, V. 18 gegen die Faulheit. Schließlich das fünfte Paar: V. 19 beschreibt das fröhliche Mahl, weist aber darauf hin, daß Geld seine verborgene Voraussetzung ist; V. 20 warnt vor dem Fluchen gegen den Machthaber oder Reichen auch in der intimsten Umgebung[55], weil das nicht geheim bleiben wird. Selbst hier ist eine Zuordnung gegeben: es geht um die verborgene Macht, derer man (positiv) bedarf (Geld), oder vor der man (negativ) sich vorsehen muß (der Mächtige). Zehn selbstverständlich an und für sich bestehende Weisheitsworte werden also in dieser künstlichen Komposition so in Paaren zusammengestellt, daß fünf Bereiche sich ordnungsgemäß aneinanderreihen, die jeweils einen doppelten Aspekt bieten.

Man könnte sich zunächst fragen, ob die Reihe der Weisheitsworte in 10,4ff. nicht in 11,1ff. fortgesetzt wird: 11,1 und 11,2 erscheinen ja wieder als ein Paar; aber man erkennt sofort, daß die folgenden Ausführungen, die zwei Beispiele in V. 3, die Entsprechungen von V. 4f. und parallel dazu von V. 6 eine viel kompliziertere Struktur verraten. So muß nun der folgende zur rechten Tätigkeit mahnende Abschnitt 11,1-6 zunächst für sich betrachtet werden. Leider besteht Unklarheit über die Bedeutung der parallelen und auch im Aufbau (imperativischer Satz mit *ki*-Satz) gleichen Mahnworte 11,1f., insbesondere über V. 1, der traditionell, schon im Targum, als Mahnung zum Almosengeben verstanden wird, so wie Goethe darauf anspielt: „Was willst du untersuchen, wohin die Milde fließt? Ins Wasser wirf deine Kuchen – wer weiß, wer sie genießt!“. Moderner ist die Tendenz, in V. 1f. statt einer Mahnung nur tiefste Skepsis ausgedrückt zu finden: Tu etwas völlig Sinnloses, und doch nimmt es ein gutes Ende; sei übervorsichtig, und doch kann dich das Schlimmste treffen. Angesichts so waghalsiger Interpretationen ist es schon besser, beim wörtlichen Verständnis vom „Fortschicken des Brotes (also nicht nur des Überflüssigen)

55 Man punktiere בְּמֹדָעֲךָ „bei deinem Vertrauten“ (vgl. Spr 7,4).

auf die Oberfläche des Wassers“ zu bleiben und an den bekanntermaßen risikoreichen Seehandel zu denken, woran die gegensätzliche[56] Mahnung, Anteil an sieben oder sogar acht Unternehmungen zur Risikoverteilung zu haben, bestens komplementär anschließt. Und auf diese beiden sich entsprechenden Mahnungen zum Tätigsein beziehen sich die analogen V. 4f. und V. 6[57], angesichts einer unbekannten Zukunft nicht zu vorsichtig, aber mit Fleiß besonders vorsorglich zu sein. Beziehen sich die Mahnungen zu Beginn in V. 1f. auf das Kaufmannsleben, so die ausführlicher formulierten[58] am Ende in V. 4f. und V. 6 auf die traditionelle Welt des Bauern[59]. Zwischen die beiden Teile V. 1f. und V. 4-6 schiebt sich in Form zweier naturgesetzlicher Beispiele die Lehre von der unüberschreitbaren Grenze menschlicher Einflußnahme auf das naturgesetzlich bestimmte Geschehen[60]. Um dieser Begrenztheit alles menschlichen Tuns willen muß diese doppelte Mahnung zu einem entschlossenen, nicht zu vorsichtigen, aber durchaus vorsorglichen Handeln aufgestellt werden.

Am Ende des Koheletbuches wird in 11,1-6 also dieser doppelte Rat als maßgebend für ein richtiges Handeln im menschlichen Leben gegeben, und die Grundsätzlichkeit und Allgemeinheit dieses Doppelrats ist für eine Stellung am Buchende, wo alles auf eine bedeutsame Zusammenfassung hinausläuft, durchaus passend. Ebenso erwartet man nun auch, und zwar auf das engste damit verbunden, eine Aussage von Freude und Heilserfahrung im Leben, die diesem angemahnten richtigen Tun entspricht. Ein solcher Abschnitt schließt in 11,7ff. auch unmittelbar an, indem mit einem וְ im Sinn von „und so“ ähnlich wie in 8,10 bei der Retributionslehre[61] eins ins andere übergeht. Nach allem, was Kohelet lehrt, kann aber nun nicht von der „Heilspräsenz“ als aus dem menschlichen Tun hervorgehend die Rede sein, denn das ist Gottes unerrechenbares gnädiges Geschenk, aber ist von der nun einmal mit dem Leben gegebenen Lebensmöglichkeit, dem Lebensgeschenk die Rede, „die Sonne zu sehen“, so wird angesichts dessen, daß sich das nicht von selbst versteht, sondern von der Finsternis des Todes umgrenzt ist, von der *Freude* gesprochen, ja Kohelets Wunsch, der Mensch möge sich daran alltäglich freuen (V. 8), wird

---

56 Siehe oben S. 84 zu 7,16f. und Anm. 36.

57 Man beachte die mit כַּאֲשֶׁר / כִּי אֵינְךָ יוֹדֵעַ mit nachfolgendem Fragesatz V. 5 und V. 6b auch formal ausgedrückte Parallelität.

58 Man beachte auch die positive inhaltliche Ausrichtung der Begründungen in V. 5 und V. 6b, das Geheimnis des göttlichen Heilsschaffens V. 5 (mit MSS und 𝔗 ist בָּעֲצָמִים vorzuziehen, weil MT die Aussage V. 5aα in Bezug auf 1,6; 8,8 isoliert betrachtet sehen will) und die besonders positive Begründung zum Abschluß V. 6bβ.

59 Diese Komposition läßt nach dem Prinzip des Achtergewichts auch etwas von einer verschiedenen Bewertung verspüren; vgl. dazu das zu 5,8 Gesagte.

60 Ein doppeltes Beispiel, sozusagen ein Parallelismus, wird wegen der in der Doppelheit liegenden Vollständigkeit gegeben. Die alles antike Reden und Denken beherrschende Duplik bestimmt als Prinzip, wie wir immer wieder sahen, die Komposition des Koheletbuches im Großen wie im Kleinen.

61 Siehe oben S. 86 Anm. 46 zu 11,7.

zum Imperativ (V. 9) und das dann noch durch das negative Verbot (V. 10) logisch bis zum letzten gesteigert.

Wir stehen vor einer dreifachen Komposition von der Lebensfreude in 11,7ff. als Konsequenz von 11,1-6: a) 11,7f., b) 11,9 und c) 11,10-12,1. In a) entspricht dem Jussiv von שׂמח der von זכר, um durch das Gedenken an den Tod der Lebensfreude den rechten Grund zu geben. In b) erscheint der Imperativ von שׂמח als Steigerung, die auch in der Anrede an den jungen Menschen und inhaltlich in der Explikation des mit Herz und Sinnen gelebten Lebens vollzogen ist. Dem זכר entsprechend erscheint gesteigert der Imperativ von ידע, und aus dem Todesgedenken wird als inhaltliche Steigerung das Wissen um das Totengericht Gottes. In c) wird die Steigerung vollendet durch die inhaltlich negativen Imperative, die die Nicht-Freude abwehrend verbieten. Und als Gegenpart erscheint der Imperativ von זכר, nun aber nicht wie in b) auf das göttliche Totengericht, sondern auf den Schöpfer bezogen. Unmöglich ist es, in dieser großartig dreifach aufgebauten Struktur von 11,7-12,1 ein wesentliches Stück wie die Aussage vom göttlichen Gericht zu streichen, zumal sie in 3,17 ebenso fest kompositionell verankert ist.

Aber wir sind noch nicht am Ende. Auch der wichtige Gegenpart des Gedenkens ist in 12,1 abschließend zu vollem Ernst gesteigert, wenn in V. 1b in einem mit עַד אֲשֶׁר לֹא, „ehe denn", „bevor", eingeleiteten Satz auf die zu Ende gehende Lebenszeit hingewiesen wird. Die dreifache Aufforderung zur Lebensfreude, die auf dem Grund des Wissens um den Tod aufgebaut sein muß, wird nun von dem Weisheitsdichter, der wie kein anderer weiß, daß das Ende bedeutender ist als der Anfang (7,1), mit einer dreifachen Beschreibung des Lebensendes ausgeleitet. Klar gekennzeichnet durch die dreifache Anapher עַד אֲשֶׁר לֹא tritt zu c) 1) die einfache sachliche Beschreibung in 12,1b, 2) die ausgearbeitete Altersallegorie in 12,2-5a mit der Auflösung in eigentlicher Rede in V. 5b und 3) eine geradezu symbolische Beschreibung des Todesgeschehens in 12,6 mit der Auflösung in eigentlicher Rede in V. 7.

Zum Verständnis der Altersallegorie ist zunächst zu beachten, daß V. 2 von V. 3ff. sowohl als Tristich (3+3+3 gegenüber den folgenden Sechsern) als auch durch die das עַד אֲשֶׁר לֹא aufnehmende Zeitbestimmung בַּיּוֹם שֶׁ· zu Beginn von V. 3 abgesetzt ist: handelt V. 2 von der „Verdunkelung" des Geistes, so V. 3ff. von den Gebrechen des Körpers. V. 3a spricht von Dienern, V. 3b von Dienerinnen; daß Arme und Beine, Zähne und Augen[62] gemeint sind, dürfte ohne weiteres deutlich sein. Nach diesen beiden Versen V. 3a und V. 3b vom „Dienstbereich" kommen wir in V. 4a und V. 4b zum „Sprachbereich". V. 4a handelt von den abstumpfenden Ohren bei gleichzeitig leiser Rede und V. 4b von der zirpenden Stimme und den gedämpften Gesangstönen. In den beiden

---

[62] Zu Augen und Zähnen als *den* Kopforganen vgl. Spr 10,26.

poetischen Versen von V. 5a[63] kommen wir schließlich – man beachte die Endstellung des Tristichs – zum dritten den Körper betreffenden Bereich, dem der zwischenmenschlichen Begegnung. Die bekannte Metapher von dem nach draußen führenden Lebens*weg* aufnehmend, ist im ersten Vers V. 5aα von der Furcht, die man vor den Lebensschwierigkeiten draußen hat, die Rede: die Steigungen, die man da bewältigen muß, ja schon auf dem normalen Lebensweg liegen hintereinander Schrecken[64]. Der zweite Vers V. 5aβγ spricht innerhalb des zwischenmenschlichen Bereichs nun am Ende von der geschlechtlichen Liebe. Nichts scheint im tieferen Sinn deutlicher zu machen, daß der Mensch sich von der Macht des Lebens abwendet (vgl. 1 Kön 1,1-4). Der erste Teil des Tristichs vom Schema A B1 B2, V. 5aβ1, drückt mehr die seelische Seite des Geschlechtlichen aus: der „erwachende“ Frühling wird verschmäht[65]. Der im frühesten Frühling aus dem Holzstamm unmittelbar die Blüten treibende „Erwach-Baum“ wird alttestamentlich immer als Hinweis auf die wunderbar hier hervorbrechende, „erwachende“ Schöpfungskraft verstanden (Num 17,23; Jer 1,12). Für die innere Parallele B1 (V. 5aβ2) und B2 (V. 5aγ) können wir uns auf Talmud[66] und Midrasch[67] berufen, wenn wir in חָגָב die kryptische Bezeichnung für das membrum virile (=עגב) erkennen und in der אֲבִיּוֹנָה, der „Vaterschaftlichen“ (Kaper), das Aphrodisiacum, dessen Kraft nun am Ende auch nichts mehr nützt. Klar setzt sich in seiner eigentlichen Redeweise V. 5b von der Allegorie ab (auch metrisch mit seinem 4+3). Wir finden hier die „Auflösung“, die Aussage, auf die diese kunstvolle allegorische Darstellung hinausläuft: Der Mensch geht zu seinem ewigen Haus, es vollzieht sich sein Leichenbegängnis.

Meisterhaft ist diese Altersallegorie komponiert, und deutlich ist das Bedürfnis des Weisheitslehrers bei all der Betonung der Lebensfreude in 11,7ff. eindrücklich die menschliche Begrenztheit ins Bewußtsein zu rufen, das für alles Menschenwesen so wesentliche הֶבֶל; Lebensfreude ohne dieses Bewußtsein wäre nur Torheit und Wahn (vgl. 2,1f.3-11). Aber wir müssen in der Altersallegorie auch den ironischen Ton verspüren, den unser Dichter ja auch

---

63 In V. 5a ist die Akzentuierung ganz unglücklich. Es handelt sich um zwei poetische Verse: V. 5aα1//α2 (ab וְחַתְחַתִּים) und V. 5aβγ als Tristich (2+2+2 unter Beibehaltung des Sechsers), nämlich V. 5aβ1//β2 (ab וְיִסְתַּבֵּל)//γ.

64 Es wäre verkehrt, in V. 5aα plötzlich eigentliche Redeweise vorauszusetzen (Bergbesteigung bei Herzschwäche), wenn doch nicht nur vorher, sondern auch im nächsten poetischen Vers Bildgebrauch vorliegt, zumal דֶּרֶךְ als Metapher geradezu gängig ist.

65 Das Ktib וְיָנֵאץ ist grundsätzlich *vor* einem Qre als Möglichkeit zu erwägen, zumal hinter der Rede vom Erblühen der Mandel die jüdisch-traditionelle Auslegung auf die leibliche Auferstehung steht, die sich aus dem unvergänglichen mandelförmigen Os coccygis (Steißbein) heraus „blühend“ vollziehen soll.

66 bSchab 152a.

67 KohR 12,5; wenn hinsichtlich des חָגָב von „Knöcheln“ gesprochen wird, so unterscheidet sich das nicht von der talmudischen Interpretation, da hinter diesem Begriff wieder die sexuelle Auffassung von רֶגֶל steht.

anderswo gezeigt hat. In diesem Ton drückt sich geistige Souveränität, eine innere Freiheit und Überlegenheit aus, die auf mehr gründet als auf das, was „unter der Sonne“ ist. Und das kommt nun deutlicher in V. 6f. zur Sprache.

Noch ein drittes Mal setzt in V. 6 die עַד אֲשֶׁר לֹא-Bestimmung ein. Was kann denn nun noch weiter in der Darstellung vertieft werden, und die dritte Ausführung zu streichen, ist bei der ab 11,7 herrschenden Dreierstruktur völlig verfehlt[68]? Auch hier haben wir in V. 6 zuerst Bildersprache, dann in V. 7 die „Auflösung“. Die Bilder gehen stärker in den symbolischen Bereich über als vorher. Es ist von der goldenen Schale die Rede, die zerbricht, wenn die silberne Schnur, an der sie hängt, entfernt[69] wird. Entsprechend Sach 4,2 haben wir an einen goldenen Leuchter zu denken, der mit den silbernen Kettchen natürlich oben aufgehängt ist. Entgegengesetzt das zweite Bild: der Wasserkrug zerbricht unten an der Quelle im Brunnengrund, während das Schöpfrad zerbrechend in den Brunnen stürzt. Also ein Doppelbild, Feuerlicht und Wasser aus der Tiefe, und ein chiastischer Aufbau – גֻּלָּה am Ende, כַּד am Anfang des Verses – bindet beides in eins. Der Bedeutung des Lichtes als Symbolon des Geistes brauchen wir nicht weiter nachzugehen[70], aber worauf weist das aus der Tiefe geschöpfte Wasser? Wir können hinweisen auf die allgemeine und eben auch alttestamentlich bezeugte Vorstellung der Herkunft des Menschen aus der Erdentiefe (Ps 139,15), in die er wieder zurückkehrt (Hi 1,21). Besonders eindrücklich ist die im Zionspsalm Ps 87 belegte Parallele, daß bei der Feier des Neujahrfestes im nachexilischen Israel, wenn die „Geburtsregister“ von Gott geführt werden, die geistliche Geburt auf dem Zion tanzend mit dem Lied gefeiert wird „Alle meine Quellen sind in dir (Zion)“ (V. 7). In diesem Schöpfrad von Koh 12,6 haben wir wohl auch den Vorläufer des τρόχος τῆς γενέσεως des weisheitlichen Briefes Jak 3,6 zu sehen, nur daß dort die Möglichkeit hinzukommt, daß in Entgegensetzung zum Lebenswasser der Tiefe die Zunge mit dem Höllenfeuer das Rad des physischen Lebens entzündet. Jedenfalls werden wir nicht fehlgehen, wenn wir im Bild von Koh 12,6 die Bindung von Geist und Physis an den Menschen beim Todesgeschehen aufgelöst sehen. Und so sagt es dann die „Auflösung“ in V. 7: Unter Aufnahme von Gen 2,7; 3,19 heißt es, daß die Physis als Staub zur Erde zurückkehrt (vgl. Ps 90,3), aber der Geist zu Gott, der ihn gegeben.

Der Schlußsatz Kohelets – ein Widerspruch zu 3,21? Es ist nur ein scheinbarer. Wenn Kohelet hier in seiner Aussage über 3,21 hinausgeht, so kann er das, weil er in seinem Satz nicht weisheitlich argumentiert, sondern ein Geheimnis

---

[68] A. Anm. 27 a.O. S. 175 bzw. 146 Anm. 17 habe ich unter dem Eindruck des Widerspruchs von 12,7 zu 3,21 und der communis opinio in diesem Punkt diesen Fehler auch gemacht.

[69] Man kann es beim Ktib lassen, nach dem Qre „zerreißt“ die Schnur (יֵרָתֵק).

[70] Vgl. z.B. H. Gese, Zur biblischen Theologie, 1977, S. 190ff.

enthüllt. Es fiel doch schon 3,18b auf, daß für das menschliche Existenzverständnis die Wahrnehmung notwendig ist – aber eben לָהֶם, also vom Menschen aus betrachtet –, daß hinsichtlich des physischen Todes der Mensch sich nicht vom Tier unterscheidet (3,19f.). Nur so vollzieht sich die Prüfung des menschlichen Lebens durch Gott (3,18a), d.h. nur so handelt der Mensch *an sich* gut oder böse. Wenn in 3,21 ein *Wissen* über das transzendente Telos des Menschen nur im Fragesatz formuliert wird, so zeigt sich darin noch einmal eine auffällige Zurückhaltung in der Aussage. Am Ende aber spricht Kohelet es nun offen aus, was eben keine „selbstverständliche" Erkenntnis ist, sondern ein Geheimnis bleiben muß. Die erkenntnismäßige Verschlossenheit der Transzendenz ist für die Weisheit Kohelets grundlegend; sie gehört zum menschlichen Wesen „unter der Sonne". Aber wie Kohelet mit seinen Postulaten des göttlichen Totengerichts (3,17; 11,9) und der Vergeltung der Gottesfurcht (8,12b-13) über die Grenze hinausweist – sie aber nicht überschreitet! –, so weist er auch im letzten Satz seines Buches auf das hin, was der fromme Weise mit menschlicher Weisheit nicht traktieren kann. Für diese ist vielmehr nichts so nötig wie die Erkenntnis dessen, was in 12,8 steht und den Rahmen des ganzen Buches, 1,2 und 12,8, bildet. Aber es wird doch wohl deutlich, woher Kohelet über die auffällige Souveränität seiner feinen, eben „wissenden" Ironie verfügt, die sich so meisterhaft in 12,2-5 ausspricht, während in dem nun sehr kurzen letzten Abschnitt 12,6f. der Lehrer an der Grenze aller Weisheit steht und eher in priesterlichem Ernste spricht.

Wir stehen am Ende der Kompositionsanalyse. Sie hat ergeben, daß keinerlei Abtrennung sekundären Materials nötig war[71], ja daß solche Ausscheidungen garnicht vorgenommen werden konnten, ohne den Aufbau zu beeinträchtigen. Gerade die oft umstrittenen „positiven" Sätze waren als inhaltlich gewichtig auch in kompositionell markanten Positionen anzutreffen, und ihre Entfernung würde die klar zutage liegende Komposition zerstören.

Von dieser Kompositionsbetrachtung her ergibt sich nun ein anderes Bild für Kohelet als das des radikalen Skeptikers, zerfallen mit der religiösen Tradition, auch der der Weisheit. Er steht vielmehr vor uns als einer, der in einer Krise weisheitlichen Denkens die neu gesehenen Probleme in umfassender Weise aufnimmt, um sie in einem neuen theologisch-weisheitlichen Denken zu durchdringen und zu klären. Ausgehend von dem schon einer weisheitlichen Frömmigkeitstradition entstammenden Urteil, daß alles Menschliche הֶבֶל sei, gelingt es ihm, durch eine Intensivierung und Extensivierung dieses Urteils die Begrenztheit, die Fragwürdigkeit und Hinfälligkeit alles Menschlichen zu definieren. Es gelingt ihm, zur Einsicht in die prinzipielle Begrenztheit der menschlichen *Erkenntnis* und damit menschlicher Urteils- und Erklärungsfähigkeit zu kommen: Angesichts der kosmischen Ordnung in der Geschlossenheit der

[71] Von einer Kleinigkeit wie 2,12b können wir absehen.

Bewegungsabläufe der Weltelemente ist menschliche Wahrnehmung immer aufs Einzelne gerichtet und auf einen engen Ausschnitt bezogen, so daß nicht vom Ganzen her geurteilt werden kann; und im Ablauf der Kairosfolgen, der die dem Menschen verschlossene Ewigkeitssicht des ʿOlam voraussetzt, kann die göttliche Teleologie des Geschehens nicht erkannt werden. Deswegen ist jede Theodizeefrage des Menschen sinnlos. Gleichermaßen richtet Kohelet den Blick auf den Menschen selbst und erkennt die menschliche Illusion der Gerechtigkeit, das menschliche Nichtgerechtsein in seinem Innern ebenso wie in den privaten und öffentlichen Lebenszusammenhängen mit ihrer Verführung zum Bösen, ja er entdeckt die Macht der Torheit gegenüber der Weisheit.

All dieses radikale Durchdringen der Probleme bleibt aber nicht stecken in der Negation überwundener Ordnungsvorstellungen und in der Aporie der Sinnlosigkeit. Kohelet sieht positiv in der prinzipiellen Begrenztheit des menschlichen Erkennens die wesentliche Begründung der Furcht Gottes, und dieser primär religiöse Begriff wird ihm zum Schlüssel für das menschliche Gewissen, das den in der Gerechtigkeit irrenden Menschen leitet. Kohelet sieht in der prinzipiellen menschlichen Begrenztheit im Wahrnehmen der göttlichen Geschehensleitung und Wirklichkeitsordnung, eben der göttlichen Gerechtigkeit und Liebe, die Prüfung des menschlichen Wesens und Handelns. Nur in dieser Dunkelheit seines Seins zeigt sich das Gutsein des Menschen an sich. Neben der Furcht Gottes wird das Postulat des göttlichen Gerichts über das gelebte Leben, der Gedanke der menschlichen Bewährung, zur Grundlage seiner Weisheit. Ist aber das Leben jeglicher menschlicher Berechenbarkeit entnommen, so wird alle Heilserfahrung zum gnädigen persönlichen Geschenk Gottes. Es entsteht bei Kohelet eine neue innere Freiheit in einem in der Gottesfurcht verantworteten freudigen Lebensvollzug: Mögen in der Welt Übel, Bosheit und Willkür mächtig ihre Häupter erheben, all das vergeht mit seinem Kairos und geht dem Gericht zu – wie der Mensch in seiner Physis. Das Wissen um die Grenze ermöglicht die Freudigkeit.

Das Buch Kohelet wurde jüdisch voll kanonisiert, es war nicht nur auf dem Wege dazu wie Sirach und, in geringerem Maß, Sapientia. Daran kann nicht nur das wohlwollende „Mißverständnis" der Salomofiktion von 1,12-2,26 als Hinweis auf den salomonischen Verfasser Schuld sein, sondern es wird seinen Grund in schon längst erfolgter Anerkennung weiter Kreise haben. Denn wenn die Tradition das Buch zum herbstfestlichen Studientext der weisen Frommen macht, dann nicht, weil es nun einmal unter den Megilloth steht, sondern umgekehrt, weil das alter Brauch gewesen sein muß. Darauf weist der Name Kohelet, der immer noch am besten als „(Weisheits-)Versammlungsleiter" erklärt wird. Es ergibt sich auch aus dem erstaunlich echt[72] klingenden ersten

[72] Man beachte die typische Diktion Kohelets, besonders den Gebrauch der Maschalform am Ende (V. 11). Damit wäre aber auch die Abfassung des Buches und die hier vorliegende Sammlung der Worte und Wortkomplexe durch Kohelet selbst voraussetzen. Das ja immerhin

Kolophon 12,9-11, wo als erstes in V. 9bα Kohelets an größere Kreise sich richtende Lehrtätigkeit bezeugt wird. Daß diese Weisheit, die auch den schwersten und bedrückendsten Fragen nicht aus dem Weg geht und dabei positiv zu einer weisheitlichen Vertiefung der Frömmigkeit hilft, schon zu Kohelets Lebzeiten zur Bildung größerer Studienkreise führte, ist gut zu verstehen.

Man verstand Kohelet also nicht als negativen Skeptiker, sondern mit vollem Recht als den Lehrer einer tieferen weisheitlichen Frömmigkeit, und dafür ist der zweite Kolophon 12,12-14 Zeuge. Denn wenn jetzt als Summe seiner Lehre hinsichtlich des Menschen die Gottesfurcht mit der praktischen Folge der Gebotsbewahrung erscheint[73] (V. 13) und hinsichtlich Gottes das Gericht[74], so ist das die Bestätigung dafür, daß seine Schüler und Tradenten präzis erkannt und verstanden haben, was er lehrte. Hier von einer „orthodoxen Milderung" zu sprechen, besteht nach allem, was wir erkannt und festgestellt haben, nicht der geringste Anlaß.

---

erstaunliche Phänomen, nicht *einen* wirklich sekundären Vers im Buch zu finden, kann am besten mit der Autorität Kohelets als des Verfassers der gesamten Komposition erklärt werden. Und wie sehr er übrigens auf Komposition Wert legte, mag aus der Bezeichnung בַּעֲלֵי אֲסֻפּוֹת für die Weisheitsworte (V. 11) hervorgehen, die also immer einen (inhaltlich entscheidenden) festen Platz in ihrem kompositorischen Kontext haben. Schließlich spricht auch die Existenz eines natürlich sekundären zweiten Kolophons für die Echtheit des ersten.

[73] Vgl. 3,14; 5,6; 7,18; 8,12b-13, und zum zweiten speziell 8,5.

[74] 3,17; 11,9, vgl. auch 8,12b-13.

The Akedah: Some Reconsiderations

by

ALAN F. SEGAL

It is a pleasure to contribute this paper to a jubilee volume for Martin Hengel, who has devoted his scholarly life to New Testament study and, in particular, to the study of early Christianity in its Jewish milieu. Nothing could be more appropriate in his honor than turning to the issue of the sacrifice of Isaac, which has important implications in both Judaism and Christianity.

The sacrifice of Isaac in Genesis 22, or as it is normally called in Jewish sources – עקידת יצחק, "the binding of Isaac" – is clearly one of the most powerful and terrifying stories in all Western literature. Both the church and the synagogue used it to discuss the notion of resurrection and martyrdom. I discussed this tradition in an earlier paper on the subject, but in the intervening years a number of important new studies have appeared and the time now feels right to return to the subject.[1] In particular, there is the new and very important study by Jon D. Levenson, *The Death and Resurrection of the Beloved Son: the Transformation of Child Sacrifice in Judaism and Christianity*,[2] which innovates in studying the relationship between the Genesis account and various other biblical texts which suggest that ritual or narrative may serve as a substitution for the sacrifice of the firstborn.

We must begin by looking at Genesis 22. There are innumerable peculiarities in the narrative itself, which have given commentators interesting topics of speculation throughout the centuries. The usual understanding of the story is that at its roots is the rejection of human sacrifice and the substitution of an animal in its place. However, there are several obvious difficulties with this theory. As N. Sarna has put the question: "We cannot evade the fact that the

---

[1] See my "He Who Did Not Spare His Only Son ...' (Romans 8:32): Jesus, Paul, and the Sacrifice of Isaac," in From Jesus to Paul (ed. Peter Richardson and John C. Hurd) (Waterloo, Ontario: Wilfried Luarier University Press, 1984) 169–184 reprinted as "The Sacrifice of Isaac in Early Judaism and Christianity," in The Other Judaisms of Late Antiquity (BJS 127) (Atlanta: Scholars Press, 1987), 109–130. Some of the arguments I stated there are reiterated here. See, especially M. HENGEL The Atonement: The Origins of the Doctrine in the New Testament trans John Bowden Philadelphia: Fortress, 1981.

[2] New Haven: Yale, 1993.

core of the narrative actually seems to demand a human sacrifice."[3] In his more recent commentary on Genesis, Sarna is even more decidedly against the human sacrifice theory:

> It has often been claimed that the story of the Akedah is a polemic against human sacrifice and thus constitutes a turning point in the history of religion, marking the transition from the ritual killing of human beings to animal substitution. Such an understanding of the narrative cannot be supported either by history or by biblical tradition. The story of Cain and Abel in Genesis 4:3f., the first incidence of sacrifice in the Bible, belies it, for it regards an animal or the products of the soil as the natural constituents of an offering. Similarly, on emerging from the ark, Noah sacrifices animals and birds, as related in 8:20.[4]

Professor Sarna's opinions are always to be taken seriously, even now, when I need to take a stand against them. But his articulation of the problem sums up the moral quandary: How could a story that purports to be about the extinction of human sacrifice actually make as its premise the demand to take such a sacrifice. Furthermore, there is the historical problem that during the patriarchal period in Mesopotamia, there is no real evidence of human sacrifice.

The answer to this problem is to be found in a significant conceptual move. We must see the story of the Akedah, not within the supposed period of the patriarchal wandering but in the context of the settled life in Canaan. Although it is a radical move, it is a well understood one within biblical scholarship for we know that writers of later periods in Israelite history constantly reunderstood or even recreated the stories of the patriarchal period in terms that made sense to them. Certainly the issue of human sacrifice was so important to the monarchy that Jeremiah risks direct contradiction with Genesis in his prophecy descrying it in chapter 19:

בנו את במות לבעל לשׂרף את בניהם באש עלות לבעל
אשר לא צויתי ולא דברתי ולא עלתה על לבי.

[They] ... built altars to Ba'al to burn their children in fire as a whole offering to Ba"al, which I never commanded and I never spoke about and which never entered my mind. (Jeremiah 19:5)

Jeremiah here records that Israelites were sacrificing their children to Ba'al and even suggests that this might have been misunderstood as an appropriate honor to YHWH, the Lord of the Israelites. To remove that possible implication, Jeremiah states clearly that God never commanded such horrifying sacrifices. He conveniently ignores the important story of Isaac's binding. But the temptation to think that God might ask for human sacrifices was clear and important in the book of Deuteronomy as well:

---

[3] Nahum Sarna Understanding Genesis (New York: Schocken Press, 1970), *ad loc.*

[4] See Nahum Sarna, "Excursus 17: The Meaning of The Akedah" *Genesis* בראשית, The JPS Torah Commentary (Philadelphia: JPS, 1989), pp. 392–3.

Take heed that you not be ensnared to follow them after they have been destroyed before you, and that you do not inquire about their gods, saying: "How did these nations serve their gods? that I may do likewise. You shall not do so to the Lord Your God, for every abominable thing which the Lord hates they have done for their gods for they even burn their sons and daughters in the fire as whole offerings to their gods. (Deuteronomy 12:31 See also Deut. 18:9f).

Furthermore Exodus 22:28 says explicitly that the firstborn of everything is dedicated to the Lord: "You shall give me the firstborn of your sons. You shall do the same for your cattle and flocks; seven days it shall remain with its mother, on the eighth day you shall give it to me."

Sarna to the contrary, when put in this context, scholars had clearly understood that the background of these passages is a polemic against infant sacrifice, as practiced by the Canaanites contemporary with First Temple times and, unfortunately for the prophets, apparently sometimes imitated by the Israelites. The YHWH adherents of monarchic times saw human sacrifice as horrible sinning and represented that God demanded not the actual sacrifice, though that might have been miscomprehended in the Exodus laws, but the dedication of the Levites or the redemption of the firstborn: "All the firstborn of your sons you shall redeem" (Exodus 34:20) or "but I have taken the Levites in place of all the firstborn among the Israelites" (Numbers 8:18). This is the basis of the rabbinic practice of the פדיון הבן or "Redemption of the firstborn," in which male firstborn are ransomed by a donation to the priesthood.

Now it is not in every way clear how or when the Canaanite peoples indulged in these sacrifices. Scholars debate as to how common the practice was, even though the practice is noted by outside sources down to the Roman period, when the Carthaginians, a Canaanite people, are described as indulging in this particular savagery. What is clear is that when it was practiced, even the Israelites felt that some terrible power adhered to it, as Elisha's campaign against Mesha, king of Moab, shows:

When the King of Moab saw that the battle was going against him, he took with him seven hundred swordsmen to break through, opposite the king of Edom; but they could not. Then he took his eldest son who was to reign in his stead, and offered him up for a burnt offering upon the wall. And there came great wrath upon Israel; and they withdrew from him and returned to their own land. (2 Kings 3:26–27)

This story shows the power which adhered to human sacrifice during the divided monarchy. In the Akedah story part of the blessing given to Abraham because he was willing to sacrifice his son is precisely the victory that Mesha received, presumably from his performance of the sacrifice. The Israelites tell the story so that it is possible to understand the victory as merely due to the fear of the Israelites, for the term "great wrath" (קצף גדול) is somewhat ambiguous. In any event, the sacrifice was believed to have some important effects. This is probably the reason why YHWH promises Abraham's progeny victory for not having performed the sacrifice:

I swear by myself, declared the Lord, that because you have acted thus, and did not withold your beloved son from me, I will therefore bestow my blessing upon you and make your offspring as numerous as the stars in heaven and the sands of the seashore; and *your descendants shall take over the gates of their enemies*. All the nations of the earth shall bless themselves by your descendants, all because you obeyed my command. (Genesis 22)

I see no reason to doubt the notion that the binding of Isaac was meant to serve the same stead as the sacrifice of Mesha's son. It was the obedience of Abraham which gave this surrogate blessing to Israel, without requiring the actual sacrifice. Even without sacrifice, the people of Israel will be victorious over the gates of their enemies, as the blessing explicitly states.

If so, we realize that we are dealing with a highly mythologized piece of writing, which deeply polemicizes against the practices of the evil Canaanite or tribal societies which surrounded Israel and, at the same time, promises the same benefits to Israel as the god Chemosh has given to Moab. This is essentially the answer to the question of how a story which purports to be about the end of child sacrifice could actually seem to request it. The Israelites wanted the power and divine grace that adhered to their neighbors' performance of the rite. This story, which almost requires the actual child sacrifice, then gives the blessing to the offspring of Abraham, for an act which is almost but not quite the same as performing it. It changes the power from the sacrifice itself to the obedience or faithfulness of Abraham.

In this highly mythological context, it is easy to see how Edmond Leach's investigation of the structural similarities between the sacrifice of Isaac and the story of Jephthah's daughter in Judges 11 is valid. His analysis sees in Abraham the positive example in whom the promise continues and in Jephthah's daughter the negative example in whom the promise ends, ostensibly because of Jephthah's rash vow and half-breed status.[5] Even more important is the recognition that these legendary tales contain within them important mythologems which have specific meanings to Israelite culture of First Temple times and do not necessarily recommend themselves to us as moral lessons without the requisite process of demythologization.

Furthermore, although mythological structures do not have to be expressible in polar opposites, Israelite mythologems often are. To take but another example, the stories of special births in the Hebrew Bible often begin with the polar opposite–namely, the barrenness of the matriarch. This has the effect of emphasizing God's special purpose in his unlocking the wombs of many Israelite women–Sarah, Rachel, Hannah, Sampson's mother. It may even explain

[5] EDMOND LEACH, "The Legitimacy of Solomon," *Genesis as Myth* (London: Cape, 1969).

the language which Jeremiah uses in describing God's foreknowledge of his existence while he was still in his mother's womb. One emphasizes the one by starting with the opposite. So in the case of the commanded sacrifice of Isaac, the point for us may be that Isaac is not sacrificed but the point of the ancient world may have been that Isaac was as good as sacrificed; thus the blessings of devotion adhere to Israel as well as its neighbors.

In his extremely erudite and complete study of the the sacrifice of Isaac, Jon Levenson also points out a number of other ways in which Israel partakes of the power of the sacrifice without actually performing it. A number of different customs or institutions in Israelite society are linked to the notion of sacrifice. The blood of the rite of circumcision (Exodus 4:21–26), the Passover lamb (Exodus 12:21–23), sacrifice of the firstling (Deut. 15:15–17), the selection of the Levites and redemption of the firstborn (as above), the nazirite vow (1 Samuel 1:11), and even the ordinances of the law (Ezekiel 20:25–29) are meant as substitutions for human sacrifice. Deuteronomy 14:1–2 among others assumes that all Israel is holy to God; thus, by extension, what later is known as the special laws of Judaism seem to function as substitution for human sacrifice, especially in hellenistic times.

This is a major step forward in out attempt to understand this puzzling tradition. But in spite of Levenson's great erudition, is he correct in his most extravagant claims that Israel must still sacrifice the firstborn; it only has received methods for substitutions? I doubt it. I don't think that the story was ever meant to suggest it, since it was a polemic written long after the events described in it. Levenson's conclusion seems to ignore the development of Israelite culture in favor of a kind of metaphysical preservation of ancient notions intact. Although his book is both fascinating and erudite, the central hypothesis of the book seems to me to be highly unlikely and, in fact, antihistorical. It does some injustice to summarize his argument so succinctly, when his chapters are so interestingly detailed by specific texts; but it is the grand scheme, not primarily the individual exegeses, which is most in need of historicization.

Levenson essentially claims that God never did actually rescind the commandment, only provided for several different substitutions. Thus, by disallowing the Law, Christianity, in effect, made the sacrifice necessary again:

> The survival and elaboration of so many ritual sublimations gives the lie to the charge that the sacrifice of the first-born son was eradicated in Israel. If child sacrifice had been utterly and universally repugnant in ancient Israel then it would have made no sense to ground these rituals in that very practice. To do so would have been to give them the kiss of death. What these etiologies actually suggest is the opposite, that the impulse to sacrifice the first-born son remained potent long after the literal practice had become odious and fallen into desuetude. The further question can be asked as to whether all the sublimations were of a ritual character. (p. 52)

> For Paul, then participation in the Christ is the equivalent of conversion to Judaism, but more than that: it is also the *only* means of conversion to Judaism, for the Jewish means – acceptance of the Torah and its commandments, symbolized in men by circumcision – have, in Paul's mind, ceased to be efficacious. For reasons that remain unclear, Paul insists that the two modes of conversion to the status of children of Abraham must not be combined: contrary to the Gospel of his opponents, Paul demands that a Gentile who comes into the Christ must not become circumcised and practice the Torah. To do so is to forfeit the precious status of the promised son – Isaac – and to fall into the carnality and subjugation of the offspring of Abraham whom Isaac displaced and superseded – Ishmael, son of Hagar the Egyptian slave-woman. (pp. 216–217)

> John's statement in 3:16 that God gave his only begotten son in order to secure life for the believers thus almost certainly found rich resonance in the religiously syncretistic world of Greco-Roman antiquity. For it not only drew upon the classic Jewish elaboration of the theme of the beloved son but also recalled the ancient but persistent Canaanite story of the deity who sacrificed his only begotten son in order to eliminate a lethal menace. (p. 225)

Essentially, Levenson claims, by means of elaborate textual equivalences, that when Christianity gave up observance of the law, with its specified substitutions, it was faced with the literal sacrifice of the only begotten son again. It would seem chronologically closer to me to argue the other way around – that once Christianity perceived the death of the messiah as the death of God's son, it could do away with the specified substitutions at law which were provided in the Bible. And, of course, circumcision was one of the laws which Christianity forfeited first. But there is no evidence that this was the sort of logic which Christianity actually followed. Indeed, there were many varieties of Christianity, each taking its own path through these difficult problems.

In the end, neither formulation seems to me to be adequate. First of all, the whole argument has a suspiciously theological and metaphorical quality, even though it is deliciously teased out of midrashic and typological treatments of the Genesis 22 passages, as if Israelite tradition continuously understood its legal provisions as temporary substitutions for the death of the first-born. But no such belief is present in the Bible. Nor did the cultural assumptions of The First Temple period necessarily continue into the Second Temple period. Does this theological exposition at all describe the way in which Jews and Christians used the story of the sacrifice of Isaac? Certainly not at the beginning. By the time of the church fathers, a consistent and full typology had emerged but there is no evidence of all of it in New Testament texts. In fact, the church was interested in the story of Isaac, as was Judaism, because, as an example of Abraham's steadfast obedience to God, it could also be understood as a story of martyrdom–the death of the innocent to fulfill the will of God. Furthermore, and this is the most important part of the tradition, when Jews interpreted part of the tradition, they did not necessarily assume all of the rest of the tradition. Jewish literature is a communal enterprise; different interpreters were interested in different notions as each interpreted the texts. One cannot assume that all possible interpretations are present when an interpreter exposes some of them as important.

There has already been a good deal of criticism on the topic, which both he and I have cited in more detail than is necessary here. Rather I want to stress that one has to be exacting about what is evidenced in the tradition if one really wants to recover the pre-Christian Jewish traditions about the question of martyrdom and find out what the Christian transformation(s) actually were. Of course, to the completely uninitiated, the story of the sacrifice of Isaac will seem of dubious importance to Christianity. But those who know a little Jewish tradition will know that occasionally Isaac was viewed by the rabbis as being sacrificed and his ashes used to atone for Israel's sins.[6] The later rabbis even suggested, seemingly originally in competition with the Christian typological interpretation, that Isaac had been resurrected by God from the ashes on the altar.

Though there have been dozens of studies of the Akedah, the major methodological steps can be summed up by mentioning a few major studies of the material. Shalom Spiegel was the first important scholar to draw attention to it in recent times.[7] The fact that Spiegel turned his attention to it when he did was surely influenced by the growing recognition of the horror of the European holocaust. The theme of the sacrifice of Isaac has continued to draw artistic attention when the problem of theodicy must be raised – from Britten's *Requiem* to Kierkegaard's concept of the "leap of faith" to Segal's memorial statue to the fallen at Kent State. Apparently the frequency of the model in discussions of theodicy points to its deep symbolic effect upon our sensibilities.

Geza Vermes must also be mentioned as having suggested that the sacrifice of Isaac is a major model for the New Testament's understanding of Jesus. His arguments are based upon a bold thesis: the Palestinian Targum tradition contains a core of first century tradition which can be self-consciously isolated, besides containing the material which has entered the text much later. Vermes' conclusion, based on this hypothesis and his supporting evidence, is that the account of the sacrifice of Isaac and not the suffering servant of Isaiah 53 may be the most important model of the early church in its understanding of Jesus'

---

[6] See Mekhilta de Rabbi Ishmael H-R p. 24–25,38–39 for examples.

[7] See The Sacrifice of Isaac: Studies in the Development of a Literary Tradition ed. Eli Yassif (Jerusalem: Makor, 1978), p. 34f in the Hebrew section. The most important early book is Shalom Spiegel, מאגדות העקידה. Alexander Marx Jubilee Volume (אלקסנדר מארקס ספר היובל לכבוד) Hebrew Section (New York: 1950), p. 519. The English translation is: The Last Trial, tr. Judah Goldin (New York: Random House, 1967). After this work was published the following publications should be of interest: P. R. Davies and B. D. Chilton, "The Akedah: A Revised Tradition History," *CBQ*, 40, (1978) The fullest treatment to date is James Swetnam, Jesus and Isaac: A Study of the Epistle to the Hebrews in the Light of the Akedah (Rome: BIP, 1981).

passion, for, according to Vermes, the Jewish community had already begun to use the death and resurrection of Isaac as the model for the reward of the martyrs and hence naturally became the paradigm for the suffering of Jesus.

At the outset, the hypothesis seems rash, for there are only a very few references to Isaac in the N. T. But scholars[8] have consistently reminded us that in spite of the common assumption, Isaiah 53 is rarely quoted in the N.T. and rarer yet is any use of it to show vicarious atonement. Since one of the central aspects of the Isaac story in the midrash is vicarious atonement or *zekuth aboth* (זכות אבות) as the rabbis put it, the story of the sacrifice of Isaac may well give us a source for vicarious atonement in Christianity.

Now, Vermes' hypothesis of the early date of the Palestinian Targum (in its present shape) may one day be proved. We know that targumim were in use in the first century. But it has so far been almost impossible to develop consistent criteria for isolating the first century traditions in the targumim. In such a case, though we may appreciate the creativity of the targum and must come to some understanding of its method, we must bracket the targumic evidence of Vermes to bring the historical problem to the fore again: Just what can be established as the commonly understood text of Genesis 22 in the first century?

For the time being, we must look for other pre-rabbinic and pre-Christian uses of the tradition. The book of Jubilees does contain an explicit connection between the sacrifice of Isaac (or "Akedah," loosely speaking) and the Passover.[9] The fact that Jubilees also connects other events in the lives of the patriarchs with other holidays does not override the obvious fact that a significant connection between passover and the sacrifice of Isaac has been made.

The passage is clearly the subject of much popular hermeneutical activity before Jesus. We have fragments of Philo the Elder (see Eusebius, *Praeparatio Evangelica* 9.20.1, Mras 506f.), Demetrius, and Alexander Polyhistor (Eusebius, same passage) as well as a passage from Sirach 44:19–21, which is devoted to the subject (see *Swetnam*, p. 29f.). The fragment from Philo the Elder, though puzzling in many respects, is a reference to the sacrificial scene. Polyhistor's reference is clearer but he follows the biblical story without major alteration. The Book of Judith 8:25–27 certainly links the sacrifice of Isaac with the trials which the Jewish community is facing, since it uses the same word (πειραζειν) as does the LXX in describing the testing of Abraham. But it is quite true that the focus of the event is Abraham's steadfastness rather than Isaac's. The testing of Isaac to which the text refers may be a reference to Rebecca's barrenness in Gen. 25:21 (See *Swetnam*, p. 35). However, the Greek

---

[8] M. D. Hooker, Jesus and the Servant (London: SPCK, 1959).

[9] See Jubilees 17:15–18:19. The heavenly discussion takes place on the twelfth of Nisan. Three days later (Gen. 22:4) would bring us to Passover for the sacrifice itself. Jubilees also connects Noah's ark, Abraham at Shechem and Jacob at Bethel. The sacrifice of Isaac is related to the liberation from Egypt and all future liberations as well.

version of the text singles out Isaac as having been the object of God's testing, thus implying the martyrological analogy.

Philo does not give us many discussions of the sacrifice of Isaac. It is missing from his *seriatim* interpretation of the Pentateuch. However, he does give us some interesting traditions about the sacrifice of Isaac in *de Abrahamo*. There, the emphasis is on Abraham as priest officiating at a sacrifice (even though the sacrifice does not take place). The sacrifice which Philo has in mind must be the *tamid* (תמיד) offering: "Perhaps too, following the law of burnt offering, he would have dismembered his son and offered him limb by limb." He also clearly understands the concept of giving one's life for others' benefit (*de Abrahamo* 198).

Josephus' version of the sacrifice of Isaac appears in *Antiquities* 1.130.1–4 (222–236, see also 20.12, 1.267), a work probably completed in 94 C. E. For the most part, Josephus follows the biblical story closely. As with Philo, Josephus is interested in Abraham, rather than Isaac, and he takes special pains to show that Abraham's piety (θϱεσκεια) is tested, his piety rewarded. Josephus has Isaac greet the news of his impending sacrifice with great joy, rushing in anticipation to the altar. He is twenty-four or five when the event takes place, apparently an interpretation of *na'ar* (נער), paralleled in the story of Jephthah's daughter, and designed to show that the victim was not a minor, rather a willing adult. This is a major aspect of martyrological tradition.

Resurrection was still a new idea within Judaism in Hellenistic times. It appears to enter the Bible in the Book of Daniel (c. 165 B. C. E.) although there may be hints in the difficult to date parts of Isaiah and Ezekiel. Resurrection in Daniel and 2 Maccabees is closely associated with the notion of marytrdom. The problem of the martyrdom, the person who dies a painful death precisely in staying true to the commands of God, is a Hebrew expression of a broad ethical and moral question which was being debated actively in the Hellenistic world. While the themes of martyrdom and resurrection are clearly connected and developed by the book of Daniel and 2 Maccabees and especially by the addition of the story of Hannah and her seven sons to the text of 2 Maccabees 7, the motif of Isaac's sacrifice as the example *par excellence* of martyrdom does not appear until the first century, pre-eminently in the book of 4 Maccabees dated to the early 30's but devoid of Christian influence. This, not the targumim and not Jubilees, seems to me the best evidence supporting Vermes' general observations that some pre-existent Jewish tradition formed the basis of the Christian view of Jesus as a type for Isaac.

More interesting still is the occurrence of the concept of vicarious atonement in this book. Eleazar prays that his death may serve not only to atone for his own sins but also for the sins of the people as a whole:

Thou knowest God that though I might have saved myself, I die in fiery torment for the sake of the Law. Be merciful to thy people and let my punishment be sufficient for their sake. Make my blood an expiation for them and take my life as a ransom for theirs. (4 Maccabees 6:27f.)

Isaac's sacrifice is brought in later on as a paradigm of martyrdom. This work seems to me evidence of extraordinary importance, especially when one notes the absence of Isaiah 53 as a significant part of martyrological discussion in the pre-Christian era. Instead, there are discussions of the paradigmatic value of the innocent sufferer, of which many could be adduced.[10]

Even in the Greek paraenesis of 4 Maccabees, Isaac's sacrifice itself is never directly linked with vicarious atonement. Martyrdom is associated with vicarious atonement while Isaac is pre-eminent among the martyrs. 4 Maccabees may even imply that Isaac actually underwent martyrdom: ῾υπομενη, the word used at that point, may mean to suffer or undergo or await. This is in line with the editor's desire to use Isaac's example as a type for martyrdom, while yet preserving the biblical story intact. Jewish tradition required that for atonement to be effected, sacrificial blood must be spilt. We find that the midrashic spirit is not present in Fourth Maccabees. Since the editor evidently wanted to preserve the original story, he could not link Isaac's sacrifice with vicarious atonement directly. All the ideas clearly come together in this work, but the explicit relationship between the themes depends on the scriptural passage under consideration. Since the exegete will not contradict the text, 4 Maccabees could not mention Isaac's death and subsequent resurrection, which is the most important part of the story from the Christian perspective.

From the early Jewish exegesis of the Akedah, several conclusions are possible. First, the Akedah was heavily used in Jewish exegesis and had already gained a firm grip on Jewish sensibilities by the time of Jesus. Like all exegetical *cruces*, it could be used in many ways, but this particular passage was used especially to clarify the meaning of martyrdom and encourage Jews in persecution. Associated concepts of death and resurrection are clearly present in 4 Maccabees but they are not attracted to the Genesis 22 passage because of the biblical text itself. Although there are occasional references to the righteous character of the sufferer, the focus of the story is still on the trial of Abraham and his obedience. Finally, and this is the most important part, the story is nowhere used as a prototype of messianic suffering.

How different is the Christian material! Here, one finds that the identification of the martyred figure as the messiah is absolutely central to the typology. Paul's use of the scripture immediately shows this distinction. Like the exegetes before him, Paul does not subject these traditions to systematic comparison. At

---

[10] See Ideal Figures in Ancient Judaism: Profiles and Paradigms ed. John J. Collins and G. W. E. Nickelsburg (Chico, California: Scholars Press, 1980).

most, one can say that he is using the Isaac story with considerable exegetical functionalism. Possible references to Isaac come up only twice and only in indirect ways in Paul: "He who did not spare his son but gave him up for us all" (Rom. 8:32) clearly sounds the note of vicarious atonement but it neither mentions Isaiah 53 nor the temple service nor the passover sacrifice nor blood.[11] Rather it appears to make a kind of implicit analogy between God's action and the action of Abraham in sacrificing his son. Like Abraham, God compensated mankind in a kind of "measure for measure" (כנגד מידה מידה) argument that is elsewhere found in rabbinic midrash. Of course, the understanding that Christ died for sins is not really in need of proof for Paul. It can be found in I Cor. 15:3b and frequently elsewhere. But only here in 1 Corinthians does he say that this saving death is in accordance with scripture. He does not explicitly tell us that Is. 53 is the scripture he has in mind and there is nothing specific in this text to suggest Isaiah 53. Almost all scholars agree that he is using traditions which were taught to him by the community which he joined and which therefore antedate his entrance into Christianity.[12]

Note that in Romans 8:32, in discussing the sacrifice of Isaac, the focus of the passage is Abraham, not Isaac, just as in the earlier Jewish interpretations. The "us" in Romans is left unspecified. But by means of Galatians 3:13–14 the reference can be further clarified. "That the blessing of Abraham might come upon the Gentiles" is a paraphrase of Gen. 22:18 "and in your offspring shall all the nations of the earth be blessed," although the expression "blessing of Abraham" may have been taken from Gen. 28:4 where it occurs explicitly. In any case "in Christ Jesus" has been substituted for the original "in your offspring."[13]

Dt. 21:23 curses a man hanged upon a tree. But Paul, who applies the reference to Jesus, says that the curse has been turned into a blessing. He may thus be playing upon the Genesis story of the lamb caught in the thicket.[14] However, in this case, the analogy would be between the ram and Jesus, since both are seen as the sacrifice provided by God.

---

[11] It is possible that the language of this passage implies a direct relationship with Isaiah 53, as both MARTIN HENGEL, The Atonement and before him E. LOHSE, Maertyrer und Gottesknecht have implied. The evidence for this is the use of the terms *paradidonai* and *peri*. It appears to me that literary evidence based on this general use of language is very suspect. The general idea of vicarious atonement, however, is not rare; nor is this language particularly rare in Hellenistic Jewish contexts. In any case, I would be prepared to concede some use of Isaiah 53, although it would be much less explicit even than the figure of the sacrifice of Isaac, which itself is very allusive!

[12] See M. HENGEL, The Atonement, p. 36f.

[13] This is the argument of N.A. DAHL, The Crucified Messiah (Augsburg: 1974) p. 153, which is very persuasive.

[14] These themes are actually fairly common in the Ancient Near East. See T.W. DOANE, Bible Myths and their Parallels in other Religions (New York: 1948) 94f; E.O. JAMES,

The novel aspect for Paul is a story of a crucified messiah, the obvious aspect of the story missing from the pre-Christian Jewish exegesis, where Isaac is never understood as a type of the messiah. Paul takes the crucified Jesus to be messiah and son of God because of his faith commitment, not because of a pre-existing development of the midrash. Only because of his prior faith can he say that as Abraham had offered up his son, so too God offered up his son for Isaac's children so that all the families of man would be blessed. It is a new idea totally absent from Jewish exegesis, even when Jewish exegesis stresses the vicariousness of the sacrifice. The received Jewish midrash, which certainly post-dated Paul, does not use the scripture for that particular purpose. Again, the most probable explanation for this event is Paul's own personal experience and exegetical freedom which that experience placed upon him. He was more interested in the consequences of this passage for a gentile mission than had any Jew been previously.

It is difficult to tell for sure which is earlier, Paul or Hebrews. One must wonder, however, why, if Hebrews is earlier, Paul did not reproduce the argument, which would have suited him fine. Rather Paul does not seem to know Hebrews and this argues that although it is possibly earlier than the gospels, it is probably later than and certainly independent of Paul.

The Hebrews reference to Isaac is particularly full:

Πίστει προσενήνοχεν Ἀβραὰμ τὸν Ἰσαὰκ πειραζόμενος καὶ τὸν μονογενῆ προσέφερεν, ὁ τὰς ἐπαγγελίας ἀναδεξάμενος,
πρὸς ὃν ἐλαλήθη ὅτι Ἐν Ἰσαὰκ κληθήσεταί σοι σπέρμα,
λογισάμενος ὅτι καὶ ἐκ νεκρῶν ἐγείρειν δυνατὸς ὁ θεός, ὅθεν αὐτὸν καὶ ἐν παραβολῇ ἐκομίσατο.
Πίστει καὶ περὶ μελλόντων εὐλόγησεν Ἰσαὰκ τὸν Ἰακὼβ καὶ τὸν Ἠσαῦ.

By faith Abraham, when put to the test, offered up Isaac. He who had received the promises was ready to offer up his only son,
of whom he had been told, it is through Isaac that descendants shall be named for you.
He considered the fact that God is able even to raise someone from the dead–and figuratively speaking, he did receive him back. (Hebrew 11:17–19)

As before, the analogy is between God and Abraham. Here, however, the figure of God's raising Isaac is explicitly mentioned and Isaac's role in the blessing is explicitly mentioned. It occurs only in a figure but it is a significant advance, no doubt brought on by analogy with Jesus and not the other way around, because the author of Hebrews is careful to express the relationship as a parable.

In fact, if one looks at the fragments of Melitto of Sardis,[15] one sees that even in the second century, one of the important points that the church fathers made

---

Sacrifice and Sacrament (London: 1962) 68–73; GRAVES AND PATAI, The Myths of the Hebrews in Hebr. (Ramat Gan: 1967) 166–169.

[15] See M.J. ROUTH, Reliquiae sacrae, J.C.TH. OTTO and A. v. HARNACK, Geschichte der

about this passage was that Jesus actually suffered while Isaac did not. We see here the converse use of the very Jewish tradition which made for conservatism in 4 Maccabees – that blood must be spilled to effect atonement. In this case, it is the reality of the Christian sacrifice, not the mercy of God in the Genesis account, which is explicitly discussed.

But, we also learn that it was unlikely that Melitto and the other fathers following his point had heard any Jewish tradition that Isaac actually underwent martyrdom. Rather, as is clear from the frequency of the reference, they knew only the Jewish tradition linking Isaac with martyrdom. From the Christian perspective the typology was even more appealing when applied to Jesus. Yet there is no evidence of an explicit Jewish tradition about Isaac's death and resurrection which was known to those fathers who stressed that Jesus' sacrifice was greater on account of his actual suffering. This suspicion, arising from the Christian evidence, is entirely confirmed by the Jewish material which we have already surveyed. There is no good evidence for a lost *pre-Christian* Jewish tradition of Isaac's resurrection.

At this point it seems that Levenson's error is a literary one. It is entirely inappropriate to assume that, because many of the motifs which dominate Christian exegesis are present in Jewish exegesis, Christianity merely took them all over, effecting a simple transformation in the traditions as it employed them. Levenson, unlike previous interpreters, does assume that the Christian interpretation is a transformation, but he does not allow that every understanding of the tradition is partial and imperfect at particular moments. It does not happen all at once.

For him, the basic transformation takes place not really in Christianity but already in Hellenistic Judaism, suspiciously lawless itself, where the Akedah becomes a foundational act (pp. 174–177). (Actually I would maintain that the Akedah is already a foundation act as early as the Bible, as Genesis 22 suggests that Israel gets the rewards of the human sacrifice when God forbears and in 2 Chronicles 3:1 where Moriah is identified with Zion.)

For Levenson, it is Jubilees that explicitly links the sacrifice of Isaac with the Paschal sacrifice. But this shows his occasional attempt to homogenize the tradition. It may be that Jubilees does accept this identification, because it certainly places the sacrifice and Passover together. But it also says that Passover is seven days long because of the total journey of Abraham, both coming and going, which took seven days. This chronology might put the sacrifice too late to be the Passover sacrifice. Even if it means to identify the two, it by no means explicitly exegetes it. Such identification would have to wait for the Christian interpretation after all.

---

altchristlichen Literatur and see the discussion of DAVID LERCH in Isaaks Opferung, christlich gedeutet (Tuebingen: Mohr, 1950), p. 29f.

Rather, Christian exegesis was founded on various Jewish exegeses but the method was carried out with an entirely new understanding of what exegesis was meant to demonstrate. In other words, the method of Jewish midrash was adopted when necessary into the new Christian community but brought to an entirely new purpose in Paul and Hebrews, the purpose of exposing the actual victory of an ostensibly failed messianic candidate.

In spite of Levenson's great erudition, he has homogenized the text in quite a novel, theological way. The missing terms in the pre-Christian interpretation are just as important as the attested ones because they underline the thought processes of the Jewish interpreters before Jesus as well as emphasize the central aspect of the new Christian interpretation. I have tried to show in my previous writing that the midrash is not a single text but an anthology made up of different interpretations of individual commentators. Not all interpretations assume knowledge of the others. Each single interpretation takes on some but not all the themes of later Christianity, while none interprets the Isaac passage messianically. Christianity takes themes of (1) death, (2) resurrection, (3) martyrology, (4) vicarious atonement and (5) messiahship from Judaism, but it does not find any of them ready-made or united in one place in Jewish tradition. Instead it hunts for what it needs and applies it to the events which it is seeking to explain. Thus we cannot define a single idea which gives us the complete sum of past experiences as Vermes does, even though his use of Jewish tradition is to be commended. Midrash records a complex mixture of past traditions being re-interpreted in light of new events.

In other words, as we would expect from Jewish tradition, we can find many contexts which link some parts of this tradition together in Jewish thought. However, if one wants an explicit reference to the messiah or to Isaac's resurrection, one does not find it until later Christianity. The reason, it seems to me, is to be found not in exegetical tradition but in the events surrounding Jesus' life. It makes no sense to begin the discussion of Christian exegesis in any other place than in the Easter event accepted as fact by Christians, that Jesus, who was manifestly crucified as a messianic pretender by the Romans ("King of the Jews,")[16] and taunted by that title in his execution, was believed to have merited the title ironically when his followers experienced what they took to be his resurrection. That experience, which is predictable if not normal on the part of a Jewish community of the First Century most often in the case of martyr-dom, justified the earliest Christian community in thinking for the first time in Judaism that there could be such a thing as a crucified messiah. From this oxymoron everything else derives and, of course, all of it is post-resurrection in formulation.

There is no historical evidence for an expectation of a crucified or suffering

---

[16] See N. A. Dahl, the title essay in The Crucified Messiah (Minneapolis: Augsburg, 1974).

messiah until the events of Jesus' life proved to the early church that this was the true and secret meaning of scripture. All discussions of suffering in the Bible thereafter take on a new meaning, as prophecies of Jesus' suffering. But no Jew would have seen them in this way before Jesus' crucifixion. Rather, like a magnet, everything dealing with "sonship" or "messiah" or "suffering" or "servant" is attracted to Jesus.[17] When applied to Jesus all traditions collapse into a single figure, in order to show how prophecy was fulfilled in the person of Jesus. One can see this at work in Paul's writing. Although his Christian commitment is evident, the strands of Jewish tradition are still intact. Paul talks about vicarious atonement and suffering but normally uses no scriptural references to demonstrate his point. The fact that he does not need them for vicarious atonement is a widely accepted understanding of the significance of the suffering of the martyrs. When he brings in the sacrifice of Isaac, it is to prove Jesus' sonship. He also knows why a crucified messiah is a stumbling block to the Jews, folly to the Gentiles, in a way that would be incomprehensible only a few generations later, for instance, to the readers of Acts.

Of course, Paul's use of the material represents only the beginning of the tradition. John's use of the Akedah in 3:16 provides another allusive reference to reinforce the concept of sonship. So do James and Hebrews, but they each develop the theme in new and interesting ways. In the church's later interpretation, the elaborate typologies comparing the three day journey with the Easter event, the wood for the sacrifice with the cross, one need not look for any further influences than the New Testament.

A word should also be said about the later Jewish material, although it too has been often reviewed in detail. On the Jewish side, in the first century, it is easy to see that the discussion of the Akedah was greatly elaborated after the destruction of the Temple. The placing of the *Akedah* at Rosh Hashanah, rather than Passover, the motif of the *shofar* as the horn of the ram caught in the thicket, the reading of Genesis 22 on the second day of Rosh Hashanah, with the first day being reserved for the biblical passage describing the sin-offering, all of these motifs make sense if one sees the Jewish community trying to

---

[17] Strangely however, Isaiah 53 is brought in relatively late, as Hooker has shown us. Even then, it is brought in to show that Jesus must suffer, not that the suffering was vicarious, which was apparently in no need of proof to those that accepted it. See MARTIN HENGEL, The Atonement: The Origins of the Doctrine in the New Testament Tr. John Bowden (Philadelphia: Fortress Press, 1981). Hengel first notes the widespread Hellenistic notion that dying for others is heroic. The context is fairly often one of sacrificial death to appease the gods, as well. So one must not get the idea that vicarious atonement was entirely a semitic idea. Hengel himself feels that the particularly Hebrew aspect of the notion can be seen in Isaiah 53, which is, in turn, used by the church (and even Jesus in his estimation) to understand Jesus' sacrificial death. Thus, the Pauline use of the notion of vicarious atonement only reflects the pre-Pauline idea, which in turn, goes back to the earliest notions in Christianity. While I have my own ideas about the value of Isaiah 53 to the early church, I think it safe to say, on the basis of Hengel and others, that the notion of vicarious atonement is quite widespread.

understand the destruction of the temple by means of an Isaac martyrology and anything else at its disposal. The process starts as early as Yohanan ben Zakkai with the *takkanah* about the blowing of the Shofar in the synagogue. This simple action of moving a temple ritual to the synagogue is in many ways the ritual and symbolic equivalent of the Christian community's understanding of the crucifixion. Seemingly impossible events must be understood within the context of meaning available to the community. A new understanding of history had to be found on account of an anomalous event. Therefore, the scripture was re-read in new eyes until the event could be appropriated into a new web of meaning.

Rabbinic exegesis followed entirely different directions from Christianity as the tradition about Isaac emphasizes. But this tradition-history also shows that they operated by very similar methods. From a methodological perspective, it is Christianity with its known history which serves as a model for the unknown but reconstructable rabbinic tradition-history. From my perspective, Isaac's relationship with the new year festival of Rosh Hashanah is most appropriately dated to post 70 C.E. Judaism, when a substitution, as it were, for temple service had to be found. It is then, after the temple is destroyed and sacrifice is only possible in a symbolic way, that the connection between Isaac and the word "Akedah" through the agency of the *tamid* sacrifice is most likely to have been developed, though again, it is theoretically possible for the connection to have been formulated even earlier. It is beyond dispute that the midrashim stressing explicit sacrificial typologies developed more strongly at this time.

But, it is also reasonable to expect that the Passover tradition of Isaac's martyrdom in rabbinic midrash received further development at this time. Rabbinic exegesis, being a compilation of individual homiletics, need not be entirely consistent even when it is compiled into a single midrashic work, as we all know. There is no reason why rabbis should not have continued to discuss Isaac's relationship to the Passover holiday. Furthermore, it is not out of the question that rabbis continued to discuss this connection in competition with the Church-fathers' use of Isaac as a *typos* for Christ. The amoraic traditions of the death and ashes of Isaac and his subsequent resurrection can be reasonably understood as an attempt to enrich Judaism with a figure that was as colorful as the one known to Christian exegesis. This rather astounding possibility, that the rabbis learned from Christian exegesis, must be investigated further. Considering the sure rabbinic knowledge of the central aspect of Christian doctrine, one does not even need to posit very much cultural contact between the two communities to allow for such a development. Indeed, it is the Christian material itself which provides the best evidence that any tradition later found in rabbinic Judaism was already present in the Jewish world of the first century. Ironically, it is Christianity that often demonstrates first century Jewish traditions, rather than the other way around, as is the normal method in New Testament studies. But using Christian documents to demonstrate Jewish traditions may only be attempted when the specific motivations and goals of Christian exegesis are carefully outlined.

In sum then, we can outline two different routes taken by the two developing communities, in line with the events which shaped those communities. Both in some ways one may use the Akedah tradition to explain the founding events of the community. Both the Christian and the rabbinic exegesis of Isaac's sacrifice is based upon the pre-Christian, Jewish exegetical tradition, which stressed martyrdom. But each community makes its own significance of the tradition from its own experience and also listens to what the other community is saying to an extent. The pattern is simple enough but, in order to see it, one must give up the idea of traditions of hypothetical figures circulating in Judaism (as they did in later times among the Church fathers). Instead one is left with an appreciation of how the Jewish community sought the meaning of its scriptures through hermeneutical reinterpretation. We have also come to the position of appreciating much more strongly the *Sitz-im-Leben* of each tradition that we have traced. These traditions did not develop under the pressure of literary transmission alone. They are the result of the response of exegetes to specific events within their community.

Bibliography

COLLINS, J. J., ed. Ideal Figures in Ancient Judaism: Profiles and Paradigms. Chico, CA: Scholars, 1980.

DAHL, NILS A., The Crucified Messiah. Minneapolis: Augsburg, 1974.

DAVIES, P. R. and B. D. CHILTON. "The Akedah: A Revised Tradition History." *CBQ* 40 (1978).

DOANE, T. W., Bible Myths and Their Parallels in Other Religions. New York, 1948.

EPSTEIN, I., Midrash Rabbah. 3rd ed. New York: Soncino, 1983. 10 vols.

HENGEL, MARTIN, The Atonement: The Origins of the Doctrine in the New Testament. Trans. John Bowden. Philadelphia: Fortress, 1981.

HOOKER, MORNA D., Jesus and the Servant. London: SPCK, 1959.

JAMES, E. O., Sacrifice and Sacrament. London, 1962.

LEACH, EDMUND RONALD, Genesis as Myth, and Other Essays by Edmund Leach. London: Cape, 1969.

LERCH, DAVID, Isaaks Opferung, christlich gedeutet. Tübingen: Mohr, 1950.

LEVENSON, JON D, The Death and Resurrection of the Beloved Son: The Transformation of Child Sacrifice in Judaism and Christianity. New Haven: Yale UP, 1993.

SARNA, NAHUM, Understanding Genesis. New York: Schocken, 1970.

SEGAL, ALAN F., "'He Who Did not Spare His Only Son ...' (Romans 8:32): Jesus, Paul and the Sacrifice of Isaac," ed. Peter Richardson and John Hurd. From Jesus to Paul. Waterloo, Ontario: Wilfred Laurier UP, 1984. 169–84. reprinted as "The Sacrifice of

Isaac in Early Judaism and Christianity in Alan F. Segal, The Other Judaisms of Late Antiquity (BJS 127) (Atlanta: Scholars Press, 1987).

SPIEGEL, SHALOM, The Last Trial. Translation of מאגדות מעקידה Alexander Marx Jubilee Volume Hebrew Section (New York, 1950). trans. Judah Goldin. New York: Random House, 1967.

SWETNAM, JAMES, Jesus and Isaac: A Study of the Epistle to the Hebrews in the Light of the Akedah. BIP. Rome: BIP, 1981.

YASSIF, ELI, ed. The Sacrifice of Isaac: Studies in the Development of a Literary Tradition. Jerusalem: Makor, 1978.

II. Jewish People in the Graeco-Roman World

yĕhūd und *šmryn*
Über das Geld der persischen Provinzen Juda und Samaria im 4. Jahrhundert[1]

von

LEO MILDENBERG

Im Spätherbst 1993 habe ich im Oberseminar Martin Hengels über die Silber-Kleinmünzen Judas und Samarias gesprochen. Der Vortrag fand in seiner einzigartigen Bibliothek statt. Nun, *verba volant – scripta manent*. Der verdiente Forscher, dem diese Festschrift gewidmet ist, möge es erlauben, daß ich auf mein mündliches Referat hier in schriftlicher Form zurückkomme.

1. Begriffliches

Das Kleingeld der persischen Provinz *yhd* (*yĕhūd* – Juda), erst bekannt geworden in der letzten Zeit, wird allgemein zu den jüdischen Münzen gerechnet[2]. Wirklich „jüdisch" sind aber nur die souveränen Prägungen im Bellum Iudaicum und im Bar Kokhba-Krieg[3]. Der Schreibende hat außerdem mehrfach betont, daß die Silber-Kleinmünzen von *yhd* und *šmryn* (*šamerayn* – Samaria)

---

[1] Juda steht hier vor Samaria, nicht weil die judäischen Kleinmünzen lange vor denen Samarias bekannt waren und nicht weil *ydh* andernorts viel häufiger belegt ist als *šmryn*. Vielmehr ist die Reihenfolge durch das Vorliegen aller Elemente der numismatischen Evidenz (hierzu MILDENBERG 1987) bedingt, die nur in Juda (gesicherte Namen der Provinz und von zwei Gouverneuren sowie deren Titel, kein Fremdmaterial im Fundgut) anzutreffen sind.

[2] So MESHORER AJC und SNG ANS Palestine sowie die Kataloge STERNBERG und BROMBERG I–II.

[3] Der Verf. hat im April 1949 festgehalten, daß die Münzen des Bar Kokhba Krieges souveräne Prägungen der judäischen staatlichen Organisation darstellen, also noch vor der Entdeckung der Qumran-Dokumente und der Bar Kokhba-Briefe („The Eleazar Coins of the Bar Kochba Rebellion", Historia Judaica, New York, vol. XI, No. 1, 99–100). – Die Münzhoheit für die Silber-Kleinmünzen liegt bei den von der achämenidischen Verwaltung bestellten Provinzgouverneuren, für die Bronzemünzen der Hasmonäer letztlich bei den Seleukiden und denen für die Herodianer bei Rom.

Provinzialgeld[4] sind und in das Münzwesen der Achämeniden gehören[5]. Sie sind ein wichtiges Bindeglied zwischen dem einheitlichen Reichsgeld und den vielfältigen Lokalprägungen. Ferner muß hier klargestellt werden, daß das für die beiden Provinzen im zentralen Hinterland Palästinas[6] geschaffene Kleingeld nichts mit den Philisto-Arabischen Münzen zu tun hat[7]. Die letzteren gehören in den Süden und sind von den hier besprochenen Provinzialprägungen grundlegend verschieden[8]. Schließlich ist festzuhalten, daß der Name *yhd* für die Provinz Juda innerhalb der riesigen Haupt-Verwaltungseinheit Transeuphratesien (aram.: ʿbar naharā, hebr.: ʿeber ha-nāhār) durch die numismatische und archäologische Evidenz gesichert ist, und der Name *šmryn* für die Provinz Samaria ebenfalls feststeht. *šmryn*, voll ausgeschrieben und in Abkürzungen, ist aber ebenso der Name der Stadt wie der Provinz Samaria. Nur die letztere Bedeutung ist in unserem Zusammenhang gemeint, also die *mdynt'*, die Provinz, und nicht die *yrt'*, die Stadt, gemäß eines Textes aus dem Wădī-ed Dălyeh.[9] Von entscheidender Wichtigkeit ist das Erscheinen des Titels *hpḥh*, der Gouverneur oder Stadthalter, in hebräischer Sprache und palaeo-hebräischer Schrift, auf den Münzen von Juda, nicht aber auf denen von Samaria. Das hebräische *hpḥh* und aramäische *phw'* bezeichnet eindeutig den zweithöchsten Funktionär, der unter dem persischen Granden, dem Herrn über Transeuphratesien, eine Provinz verwaltet. Zudem steht der Name des Gouverneurs neben seinem Titel; in Verbindung mit *yhd* und Varianten in aramäischer Sprache und in palaeo-hebräischer Schrift oder mit hebräisch *yhdh* ist schließlich auch noch die Provinz angezeigt, der er vorsteht. All dies ist eine vollständige und sonst so nirgends festzustellende Evidenz – was nicht genug betont werden kann, auch wenn dies bisher kaum beachtet worden ist.

---

4 Mildenberg 1979, erstmals mit der Bezeichnung „Provincial Coinage" im Titel; idem 1988, 726 („Die Münzhoheit").

5 Mildenberg 1993, 60–61 („Das Provinzialgeld").

6 Dieser auf Herodot II 104,3 zurückgehende Begriff bezeichnet für den Verf. den Südwesten der großen persischen Satrapie Transeuphratesien, bestimmt durch die südliche Grenze Phöniziens im Norden, den Jordan und das Tote Meer im Osten, das Mittelmeer im Westen und den Besor-Flußlauf im Süden.

7 Machinist 1994, 367 rechnet die achämenidische Gruppe der *yhd*-Münzen zu den „so called ‚Philisto-Arabian' issues of the fourth century B.C.", was der numismatischen Evidenz widerspricht.

8 Die Münzherren der philisto-arabischen Prägungen sind die autonomen Städte an der südwestlichen Küste und die Autoritäten in den anschließenden Wüstengebieten. Namen von den Gouverneuren und Provinzen finden sich nicht und dürfen auch nicht erwartet werden. Hauptnominal ist die Drachme und nicht deren Sechstel, der Obol, wie beim *yhd*- und *šmryn*-Geld. Die Münzbilder sind verschieden.

9 F. M. Cross, Samaria Papyrus 1: An Aramaic Slave Conveyance of 335 B.C.E., Naḥman Avigad Volume, Eretz Israel, vol. 18, 9–13, besonders 8–9 und 11 mit Anm. 10 (qryt' und byrt' für die Stadt).

2. Der Stand der Forschung

Über die 200jährige Geschichte der Yĕhūd-Münzen liegen heute neuere, ausführliche Darstellungen vor.[10] Hier seien deshalb nur die wichtigsten Wegmarken und Erkenntnisse vermerkt. Die einzige Drachme gelangte wohl in den ersten Jahrzehnten des 19. Jahrhunderts ins Britische Museum (Abb. 1) und ist bis heute ein Unikum geblieben[11]. Dies ist schon ein Hinweis auf die anderen wesentlichen Unterschiede zwischen dieser großen Denomination und den Kleinmünzen. Die heute klar als *yhd* erkannte Legende zeigt eindeutig aramäische Schrift, und die Bilder kommen nur auf der Drachme vor. Es müssen – nach unserem heutigen Wissensstand – andere Voraussetzungen für die Prägung des Unikums als für die Produktion des Kleingeldes angenommen und ein deutlicher, zeitlicher Abstand zwischen beiden zugestanden werden. Endgültig festlegen[12] sollte man sich aber hier nur für die Zuordnung der Drachme zu der judäischen Provinzialprägung aufgrund der Legende.

In den letzten zwei Jahrzehnten ist die Erforschung der *yhd*-Kleinmünzen durch gezielte Einzeluntersuchungen[13] maßgeblich gefördert worden. Gleichzeitig tauchten immer wieder Einzelstücke und Münzgruppen auf. Eine Gesamtdarstellung, die auch dieses neue Material in öffentlichen und privaten Sammlungen, im Handel und insbesondere in Auktionskatalogen[14] erfassen würde, wäre zwar eine mühsame, aber doch sehr lohnende Aufgabe.

Daß im 5. und 4. Jahrhundert das Gebiet nördlich der persischen Provinz Juda in der persischen Provinz Samaria organisiert war, ist durch Sachquellen erwiesen. Wenn in Juda im 4. Jahrhundert die Notwendigkeit einer Provinzial-Münzprägung bestand, und alle Voraussetzungen dafür gegeben waren, hätte man das Gleiche oder etwas Ähnliches zur selben Zeit auch in der nördlichen Provinz Samaria erwarten können. Überraschend war dennoch das Auftau-

---

[10] Mildenberg 1979, 183–188; Rappaport 1984, 27–29; Meshorer AJC I, 21–26; Mildenberg 1988, 721–728; Machinist 1994, 365–366.

[11] Das Unikum wurde zum ersten Mal – nur kursorisch – beschrieben: Taylor Combe, Veterum populorum et regum numi qui in Museo Britannico adservantur, London 1814 (Mitteilung U. Wartenberg). – Siehe G. F. Hill, BMC Palestine, 181 mit Nr. 29 und LXXXVI–LXXXVII mit älterer Literatur. Für eine neuere Deutung siehe Mildenberg 1979, 183–184 und idem 1993, 61.

[12] Das Bar Kokhba Corpus des Verf. von 1984 war nach der seit Jahrhunderten feststehenden Stückelung gestaltet, bis eine bisher völlig unbekannte Denomination, eine Didrachme, auftauchte, die der Verf. dann selbst beschrieb („A Bar Kokhba Didrachm", *INJ* 8, 1984–1985, 33–36).

[13] Siehe insbesondere Kindler 1974, Jeselsohn 1974, Spaer 1977, Meshorer 1981, Spaer 1986–1987 und Barag 1986–1987.

[14] Eine Gruppe von 28(!) *yhd*-Kleinmünzen der ptolemäischen Zeit ist im Auktionskatalog 5 des Schweizerischen Bankvereins Zürich vom 16. 10. 1979, Lot 281 angezeigt. Einzelstücke finden sich in den Kat. Sternberg und Bromberg I–II.

chen gänzlich neuer Prägungen aus den Funden von Nablus und Samaria.[15] Es erwies sich nun, daß ähnliche Geldverhältnisse zur gleichen Zeit in den beiden zentralen Provinzen im palästinensischen Bergland herrschten. Zwar ist das ganze Fundmaterial von Nablus noch nicht veröffentlicht, aber große Teile sind heute schon greifbar. Der Depot-Fund von Samaria und dortige Streufunde sind in einer wertvollen Publikation festgehalten[16]. Diese wurde ergänzt durch größere neue Gruppen der nördlichen Kleinmünzen. Eine solche wurde in einem Auktionskatalog veröffentlicht[17]. Weiteres Material ist in verschiedenen anderen Versteigerungen angeboten worden. Eine Darstellung dieses neuesten Materials dürfte nicht lange auf sich warten lassen.[18]

3. Die Funde

Die Fundumstände der neuen *yhd*-Materialien liegen immer noch im Dunkeln. Es steht nur fest, daß sie im Jahre 1966 erstmals zum Vorschein kamen und aus der näheren Umgebung von Jerusalem stammen. Es handelt sich um Kleingeld, um Obole und deren Halb- und Viertelstücke, immer von derselben Machart und ähnlicher Patinierung. Dazu fanden sich bisher nur zwei *yhd*-Halbdrachmen (Abb. 23–24).[19] Fremdmaterialien wurden gleichzeitig nicht angeboten, was darauf hinweist, daß das gesamte, neue Ensemble aus wenigen Depot- oder Streufunden stammt. Für diesen Befund spricht auch das Auftauchen zusätzlicher Einzelstücke bis in die jüngste Zeit. Es liegt auf der Hand, daß aus diesen Fundumständen allein keine verläßlichen Angaben über Vergrabungszeit und Chronologie gewonnen werden können.

Ganz andere Voraussetzungen für die Forschung ergeben sich aus den nördlichen Horten von Nablus und von Samaria. Diese sind Depotfunde: Samaria-Kleinmünzen gemeinsam mit phönizischen und kilikischen Prägungen und lokalen Athen-Kopien[20], jeweils in verschiedenen Stückelungen. Diese sind

---

15 IGCH 1504: Nablus Region. – Für Samaria siehe M-Q, 45–63 (106 an Samaria gegebene Prägungen) sowie M-Q, 71–80 (334 unter SH registrierte Stücke aus dem „Samaria Hoard").

16 Die Sammlung, Sichtung und Präsentierung des neuen Materials wurde von Y. Meshorer und S. Qedar in vorbildlicher Weise geleistet. Erst dadurch wurde die Möglichkeit zu Deutungen gegeben, die begreiflicherweise auch von denen der beiden Autoren abweichen können.

17 Sotheby Zürich, 27. 10. 1993, Lots 900–909 mit nicht weniger als 160 Fundstücken.

18 Mitteilung S. Qedars an den Verf. vom 18. 6. 1995.

19 Meshorer AJC, Addendum auf S. 184.

20 Der in den letzten Jahren des Peloponnesischen Krieges völlig versiegende Import von athenischen Tetradrachmen ins Perserreich führte zu einer Massenproduktion von Nachahmungen dieser großen Stücke in der Levante im 4. Jahrhundert. Noch umfangreicher ist die dortige, lokale Herstellung von Obolen und deren Teilwerten mit den Bildern der Tetradrachmen. Siehe dazu Mildenberg 1993, 62–63. – Der wichtigen Aufgabe, fast einer Sisyphus-Arbeit, dieses Material zu ordnen und zu bestimmen, hat sich bisher noch niemand unterzogen. Schon vorbereitende Einzelstudien würden weiterhelfen.

von großer Bedeutung für die chronologische Einordnung der eigentlichen Samaria-Münzen, weil sie bisweilen datierbar sind. Sie geben weiterhin wichtige Hinweise auf das Münzwesen, die Wirtschaftsentwicklung und die kulturelle Vielfalt in der Küstenregion mit seinem Hinterland in der Zeitspanne von drei Jahrzehnten vor dem Alexander-Sturm. Wichtig ist, daß die meisten Fundmaterialien miteinander vereinbar sind; es gibt jedoch auch Einzelstücke, die zwar Samaria zugeschrieben wurden, deren Herkunft aber nicht eindeutig feststeht.[21]

4. Die zeitliche Zuordnung

a) Juda

Über das Unikum im Britischen Museum (Abb. 1) hat sich der Schreibende ausführlich geäußert[22] und ist kürzlich darauf mit der Feststellung zurückgekommen, es sei „ungefähr zur Zeit entstanden, als der Großkönig den Antalkidas-Frieden von 387 v. Chr. diktierte".[23] Hier ist nochmals zu betonen, daß die Drachme der jüdäischen Provinzialprägung zuzurechnen ist. Daß sie in den Beginn der Explosion des Geldwesens im Perserreich des 4. Jahrhunderts gehört, die ihren Höhepunkt um 350 v. Chr. hatte, ist ebenso offensichtlich. Wieso es aber zu der Prägung einer solch frühen, großen Silbermünze in Juda kam, nicht aber – nach unserem heutigen Wissensstand – zu etwas Ähnlichem in Samaria, bleibt uns noch verborgen. Die oben erwähnte große Lücke könnte nur durch neue Funde geschlossen werden.

Der äußere Rahmen von ca. 360 bis 331 für die achämenidische Gruppe der judäischen Kleinmünzen dürfte feststehen[24]. Auch bei der Zeitbestimmung für die ptolemäische Serie von 300 bis 282 sollte man bleiben. Sie Ptolemaios II und III zuzuschreiben, geht schon deshalb nicht, weil unter ihnen das Kleingeld aus Bronze hergestellt wurde, und die rege königliche Prägetätigkeit von Alexandria und in der Levante keinen Raum mehr für das Kleinsilber von Juda ließ.[25] Die im Jahr 1979 getroffene Zuschreibung einer kleinen Gruppe an die make-

---

21 Siehe unten Abschnitt 8.

22 Mildenberg 1979, 183–185.

23 Mildenberg 1993, 61.

24 Mildenberg 1979, 191.

25 Siehe Barag 1986–1987, 7 mit Anm. 20. – Eine wichtige Tatsache hat der Empfänger dieser Festschrift selbst festgehalten, nämlich die Aussage der palästinensischen Münzfunde, in denen die Prägungen von Ptolemaios II alle anderen im 4. und 3. Jahrhundert um ein Vielfaches übertreffen (Hengel 1973, 85 mit Anm. 331 und 573 mit Anlage II). Wenn in der Zeit von Ptolemaios II soviel Geld in Palästina vorhanden war, gab es unter ihm keinen Grund für eine *yhd*-Kleinmünzenproduktion. – Auf die Bedeutung, ja Einzigartigkeit, des ptolemäischen *yhd*-Geldes haben – außer dem Verf. – nur Mørkholm, 70 und Machinist, 379 hingewiesen.

donische Zeit mit der Folge einer im Wesentlichen lückenlosen Juda-Prägung von 360 bis 282 erfuhr jüngst eine starke Stütze. Überzeugend wurde darauf hingewiesen, daß die achämenidische Gruppe mit Gouverneur-Titel (Abb. 15–18) und die makedonische ohne Titel (Abb. 19–20) gänzlich verschiedene Bilder für Vorder- und Rückseite zeigen.[26]

b) Samaria

Für die Chronologie der Silber-Kleinmünzen von Samaria gibt das Fremdmaterial wichtige Hinweise. Es steht fest, daß der Nablus-Fund um 338 vergraben wurde. Von den tyrischen Stateren sind volle 21 im Jahr 10 (339–338) datiert, dem letzten Jahr im Fund[27], und alle sind frisch erhalten. – Das Samaria-Fundgut kam schon um die Mitte des Jahrhunderts in die Erde, wohl um 345; denn – im Gegensatz zum Nablus-Hort – findet sich in dem von Samaria kein einziges Stück mit dem Namen des persischen Granden Mazday-Mazaeus, der im Jahre 344/343 zu Kilikien auch noch die Verwaltung von Transeuphratesien übernahm[28]. Obwohl eine negative numismatische Evidenz nie endgültig sein kann[29], ist die Amtsübernahme Mazdays als *terminus ante quem* mit großer Wahrscheinlichkeit anzunehmen. Alle Münzen im Fund von Samaria sind so vor 345 geprägt worden. Für die Bestimmung des *terminus post quem*, also des Zeitpunktes, von dem an das Provinzgeld von Samaria geprägt wurde, ist der Vergleich der nachgeahmten dortigen Stücke mit den früheren Vorbildern geeignet. Diese Münzen sind in unserem Fall jedoch nur ungefähr datierbar: die Tarsos Originale mit dem sitzenden Baal wurden von etwa 375 an laufend produziert. Für die sidonische Galeere in der entwickelten Bauart darf ein ähnlicher Ansatz angenommen werden, ebenso für den weiblichen, von vorne dargestellten Kopf in der Art des Kimon von Syrakus, der Samaria über Tarsos erreichte. Der Schluß dürfte wohl erlaubt sein, daß es sich um eine kompakte Zweckprägung handelt, die ungefähr um 360 begonnen und dann etwa 20 Jahre lang fortgeführt wurde, womit sie zur Blütezeit des Geldwesens im Reich der Achämeniden um 350 gehört.

Während bei dem Kleingeld von Juda eine Gruppierung und ungefähre Abfolge der Prägung festgestellt werden konnte, war dies bisher für Samaria nur beschränkt möglich. Auch hier mögen neue Funde weiterhelfen. Bis dahin wäre eine weitere Sammlung und Sichtung des weit zerstreuten Materials nützlich.

---

[26] Machinist, 370–371.

[27] Diese wichtige Mitteilung wird A. Spaer verdankt, der auch darauf hinweist, daß sich im Fund keine Münze aus der Zeit von Darius III fand, dagegen eine Datierung des 20. und letzten Jahres von Artaxerxes III. Der Ansatz Mildenberg 1993, 74 mit Anm. 124 „Vergrabung um 332" ist daher zu korrigieren.

[28] Siehe hierzu Mildenberg 1990–1991, 9, 18, 20 sowie ‚legend 5'.

[29] Mildenberg 1987, 393–395.

5. Zur Herstellung

a) Stückelung

Die Juda-Münzen sind Kleingeld, Obole und deren Teilstücke. Am Anfang steht jedoch die Drachme im Britischen Museum[30] und gegen Ende[31] die zwei bisher bekannt gewordenen Halbdrachmen. Erst jüngst wurde die Auffindung von zwei Athen-Nachahmungen im Drachmengewicht mit dem Provinznamen von Juda als *yhd* (Abb. 3) und *yhdh* gemeldet. Auch die Stückelung des Provinzialgeldes von Samaria ist nach der Ansicht des Schreibenden einheitlich. Alle bisher bekannt gewordenen und der nördlichen Provinz Samaria zuzuschreibenden Münzen sind Obole und deren Teilstücke[32]. Dieses Bild mag sich durch neue Funde sehr wohl noch ändern. Es dürfte jedoch unwahrscheinlich sein, daß um die Mitte des Jahrhunderts größeres Geld in Samaria geschaffen wurde. Wie die bisherigen Funde zeigen, zirkulierten damals ausschließlich fremde, größere Sorten. Für die kleinen bestand aber Nachfrage, welche von der Provinzialverwaltung befriedigt wurde.

b) Stempelschnitt

In Juda steht die frühe Drachme des Britischen Museums unter griechischem Einfluß. Die Gestaltung ist sehr ansprechend. Vorder- und Rückseite dürften von der gleichen Hand stammen. Ob der Stempelschneider ein Fremder oder Einheimischer war, steht dahin. Von den beiden veröffentlichten, späten Halbdrachmen[33] zeigt die eine ein bemerkenswert stark profiliertes Porträt (Abb. 23) des ersten Ptolemäers, während die Darstellung auf der zweiten etwas abfällt (Abb. 24). Die Stempelschneider der Kleinmünzen sind lokale Handwerker. Ihr Griffel ist ungelenk. Nur die Stempelkoppelungen mit Lilie-Falke (Abb. 8) und die Rückseiten mit dem geflügelten Katzentier (Abb. 19–20) sind geglückte Darstellungen.

Die Arbeit bei den meisten, eindeutig zu Samaria gehörenden Kleinmünzen ist unsorgfältig, insbesondere bei den aus dem Samaria-Fund stammenden Stücken. Dort wird der rohe, aber nicht kraftlos geschnittene bärtige Kopf in

---

[30] Siehe oben Anm. 11.

[31] Vorerst nicht möglich dürfte eine genauere zeitliche Einordnung der zwei Halbdrachmen innerhalb der ptolemäischen *yhd*-Gruppe sein. Ähnliches gilt für die zeitliche Stellung der beiden Stücke zueinander. Der krasse Qualitätsunterschied im Stempelschnitt weist das mindere Stück noch nicht zwangsläufig in eine spätere Prägeperiode.

[32] Der samt dem Gefäß vollständig geborgene „Samaria Hoard" ist ein Kleinmünzenfund. Für den Verf. bleiben die Samaria zugeschriebenen Drachmen vorerst Incerta, was unten in Kapitel 8 begründet wird.

[33] Vgl. oben Anmerkungen 19 und 21.

der persischen Tiara durch die schlechte Prägung stark verzerrt (Abb. 37). Auffällig ist die bessere Arbeit bei den Stempeln mit dem Großkönig aus dem Nablus-Hort und aus Streufunden (Abb. 42–45). Die ähnliche Darstellung aus dem Samaria-Hort wirkt dagegen wie eine majestätsbeleidigende Karikatur. Offensichtlich kommt das Samaria-Material des Nablus-Fundes aus einer ruhigeren Zeit und einem besser arbeitenden Atelier.

c) *Prägung*

Während im Westen im Laufe des 4. Jahrhunderts beim Kleingeld das Silber durch Bronze verdrängt wurde, blieb es in der Levante beim Alten. Die Kleinmünzenprägung im persischen Kilikien ist ebenso umfangreich wie vielseitig und ansprechend. Ähnliches gilt für die autonomen Silber-Kleinmünzen der Küstenstädte von Arados bis Gaza. Der Produktion des Provinzialgeldes von Juda und Samaria mangelt es jedoch an Zeit, technischem Können und Kunstverstand. Die Vorbereitung der kleinen Schrötlinge und deren Ausprägung zeugt nicht gerade von Sorgfalt und guter Technik, wie die oft schlechte Zentrierung, die Flanrisse und flaue Stellen zeigen (Abb. 37–38). Wesentlich ist, daß nicht jedes der kleinen Stücke gewogen wurde. Die Gewichte sind deshalb sehr verschieden, die Bestimmung der Denomination läßt sich nur ungefähr ermitteln. Daher bleiben auch die sonst so wichtigen Gewichtstabellen wenig aussagekräftig.

6. Die Namen in Sprache und Schrift

a) *Juda*

Auch hier hebt sich die frühe Drachme von den späten Kleinmünzen ab. Sprache und Schrift sind aramäisch. Entsprechendes gilt für die beiden späten Halbdrachmen: Sprache und Schrift sind hier hebräisch. Der Befund bei den zeitlich dazwischen liegenden Kleinmünzen ist dagegen alles andere als einheitlich. Der wichtigste Name *yhd* ist aramäisch, dagegen sind die Personennamen *yḥzqyh* und *ywḥnn* hebräisch, ebenso die Titel *hpḥh* und *hkwhn*. – Die Schrift der Kleinmünzen ist durchweg paleohebräisch. Auffallend ist der markante Unterschied in den einzelnen Legenden. Die Qualität geht von den makellosen, eleganten Buchstaben der *yḥzqyh*-Legende neben dem Katzentier (Abb. 19) über die flüchtigen Buchstabenformen desselben Namens links und rechts der Eule (Abb. 15–16) bis zu der ungelenken, ja verballhornten Schrift von *ywḥnn hkwhn* (Abb. 17) sowie *yhd* neben dem Greifvogel (Abb. 12–13). In die oben betonte Zeitlücke zwischen der *yhd*-Drachme und den *yhd* Kleinmünzen könnte ein einzelner, schwerer Obol[34] eingefügt werden, der im südlichen Juda gefunden wurde (Abb. 2). Nach den Bildern gehört er in die riesige Kleinmünzengruppe der Levante des 4. Jahrhunderts, welche die athenischen Vorbilder nachahmte[35]. Die Inschrift jedoch hebt ihn heraus. Als Lesung wurde *ydw*ʿ in aramäischer Schrift vorgeschlagen. Der erste Buchstabe *yod* hätte allerdings eine ganz ungewöhnliche Form[36]. Wenn man den Fundort und das tiefe deutliche *quadratum incusum* als maßgeblich betrachtet, käme man zu einer Zuschreibung an Juda um 370/360.

b) Samaria

Der Name *šmryn* der Provinz ist aramäisch. Neben der vollen Legende finden sich Abkürzungen. Retrograde Schrift ist häufig, sowohl im ganzen Namen wie bei einzelnen Buchstaben. Dazu sind die Formen der fünf Buchstaben auch noch sehr verschieden. Der allgemeine Eindruck des Namenszuges mag paleo-aramäisch sein, aber das *yod* kommt auch in der palaeo-hebräischen Form vor. Ähnlich ist der Befund beim *mem*. Schon die Schreibung des Provinznamens ist eine Misch-Schrift[37], die dazu noch von ungeübter Hand geschnitten wurde. Dies ist besonders störend bei den Legenden der Stücke mit dem Provinznamen aus dem Samaria-Hort, während die Schrift bei dem Nablus-Material etwas besser ist. – Ein anderer wichtiger Name ist Mazday[38], der ausschließlich in der Abkürzung mit den zwei ersten Buchstaben vorkommt, und zwar nur in dem Nablus-Fund. Das *mem* ist wie bei den meisten *šmryn*-Legenden geformt. Das *zayin* jedoch ist sehr ungewöhnlich. Es ähnelt etwas unserer Zahl „3" und erinnert an die frühe lapidare Form. Auf Mazdays Münzen von Tarsos, Sidon und Babylon sieht das aramäische *zayin* ganz anders aus. Die Stempelschneider der Samaria-Kleinmünzen haben also keinesfalls die sidonische Legende kopiert, sondern wußten, was sie zu schreiben hatten, nämlich den Namen des Granden, der um 340 Transeuphratesien regierte, was der ihm unterstellte Gouverneur sehr wohl zu beachten hatte[39].

Ein im Nablus-Fund vielfach vertretenes Stempelpaar mit *mem zayin* für Mazday neben einer Ahuramazda-Darstellung und den klaren aramäischen Buchstaben *šin* und *nun* neben dem sitzenden Großkönig darf an Samaria

---

[34] Spaer 1986–1987, 1–3.

[35] Vgl. oben Anm. 20.

[36] Der Aufstrich ist rechtwinklig mit einer gebogenen Linie verbunden. Eine *yod*-ähnliche Form ergibt sich nur, wenn man allein diesen ersten Buchstaben von oben betrachtet und nicht die ganze Legende.

[37] So auch M-Q 11.

[38] Zu diesem bedeutenden persischen Granden, der von 361 bis 328 (!) die höchsten Ämter bekleidete, siehe jüngst Mildenberg 1990–1991, 9–17 und idem 1993, 60.

[39] Betont von Mildenberg 1990–1991, 15.

gegeben werden (Abb. 42). Dafür sprechen nicht nur die Bilder und die Sonderform des *zayin*, sondern auch die Tatsache, daß eine solche Prägung für Mazday andernorts bisher nicht festzustellen ist. Das *šin-nun* wäre dann eine Abkürzung für *šmryn* durch den ersten und letzten Buchstaben des aramäischen Namens der Provinz Samaria.

Schwierigkeiten macht dem Schreibenden ein anderer Obol, dessen Legenden *šmryn* und *mbyg* gelesen wurden (Abb. 31); denn der als *yod* gedeutete Buchstaben hat beide Male eine unverständliche Form. Das in der Samaria übliche Bild des sitzenden Großkönigs macht die Lesung *šmryn* trotzdem wahrscheinlich. Die Deutung von *mbyg* auf Hierapolis-Bambyke ist hingegen kaum nachvollziehbar. Ein ähnliches Münzbild der Tierkampfszene, das aus der fernen Stadt am Euphrat stammt und in die Alexander-Zeit datiert, zeigt ebenfalls nicht die Legende *mbyg*.[40]

Es gibt eine weitere große Gruppe, für die ein und dieselbe Legende *yrb'm* feststeht[41], wobei die Schrift gemischt ist. Sowohl das offene aramäische, wie das geschlossene hebräische *ayin* erscheinen. Die Fundorte in Samaria machen eine Zuschreibung an die nördliche Provinzialprägung möglich, wenn nicht gar wahrscheinlich. Die faszinierende Bilderwelt dieser Gruppe ist allerdings eine *res sui generis*, die noch der Deutung harrt (Abb. 46–49).

7. Die Bilder

a) Juda

Wie hier mehrfach betont, gehört die Drachme im Britischen Museum zur jüdischen Provinzialprägung und datiert um 380. Wieso es aber im palästinensischen Hinterland so früh zu einer großen Denomination mit zwar eindeutig griechisch beeinflußten, aber doch ungewöhnlichen Bildern kam[42], ist keinesfalls geklärt. Wer das Stück selbst, und nicht eine Abbildung, vor Augen hat, erkennt bald, daß der bärtige Kopf wirklich in Dreiviertel-Ansicht gestaltet ist und dennoch von den von vorne dargestellten Köpfen des ersten Viertels des 4. Jahrhunderts angeregt wurde. Daß „Der Gott auf dem Flügelrad“[43] uns

---

[40] Vgl. SEYRIG 1971, Münze Nr. 12 (Prägungen mit dem Namen Alexanders: Nummern 8–13). – Zwei Ortsnamen auf einer Münze kommen in diesem Gebiet und Zeitraum nicht vor. Sie wären auch nur bei Nachbarorten möglich.

[41] SPAER 1979 und idem 1980.

[42] Vgl. oben Anm. 12. – Es ist schon erstaunlich, daß die nach rechts sitzende Gestalt mit dem nackten Oberkörper noch am ehesten an ein anderes, früheres Unikum erinnert, nämlich den sitzenden Zeus von Aitna auf Sizilien, wie W. Fischer-Bossert beobachtete. (FRANKE-HIRMER, Die griechische Münze, München ²1972, Nr. 33).

[43] Titel von KIENLE 1975.

heutzutage als eine synkretistische Gottesdarstellung erscheint[44], mag einleuchten. Ob der damalige Betrachter es aber so auffaßte, steht dahin.

In der Ikonographie des *yhd*-Kleingeldes sind die Nachahmungen der Athener Tetradrachmen mit Pallas und Eule am Anfang der Prägung noch stark vertreten, kommen aber später nicht mehr vor. Dafür erscheint die erstaunliche Koppelung der Eule mit dem weiblichen[45] Kopf ganz von vorn (Abb. 14–18), einer zeitlich später und räumlich weit entfernten Nachahmung der Arethusa des Kimon von Syrakus. Auch für den sitzenden Raubvogel in dieser Gestaltung dürfte es keine nahe Parallele geben (Abb. 12–13). Der Großkönig, ein häufiges und beziehungsreiches Münzbild des Samaria-Kleingeldes, kommt in Juda nur in einer Bilderkoppelung und auch nur in Verbindung mit dem Falken vor (Abb. 10). Juda war eben noch weiter weg von Susa als Samaria. Näher lag es bei Alexandria, weswegen die ptolemäischen Juda-Kleinmünzen das Portrait des Königs und der Königin sowie den Zeus-Adler auf dem Blitz zeigen. Aus den Porträts von Ptolemaios I auf dem Kleingeld heben sich zwei Stempel durch ihre nicht alltägliche Qualität ab (Abb. 22, 27). Sie erinnern an das oben besprochene markante Porträt des Königs auf einer der beiden bisher bekannt gewordenen Halbdrachmen (Abb. 23). Bemerkenswert ist die gute Arbeit bei den Stempelpaaren mit der Lilie und dem Falken.

b) Samaria

Bei den eindeutig in die Provinzialprägung von Samaria gehörenden Kleinmünzen sind die beidseitigen Athener Nachahmungen viel seltener als in Juda. Dagegen war in der nördlichen Provinz der Einfluß der persischen Hoheitssymbole eher größer als selbst in Sidon, das diese Bilder nach Samaria weiter gab. Die große Prägung von Tyros, wie Sidon eine autonome Stadt, fand in Samaria kaum Beachtung, wohl weil die Tyrer ihre eigenen städtischen Bilder beibehielten und auf die achämenidischen verzichteten, die aber für die persische Provinz Samaria wichtig waren. Die vorherrschenden sidonischen Bilder sind hier neben der Galeere die Darstellung des achämenidischen Herrschers im Wagen und als Herrn der Tiere im Kampf mit dem Löwen. In Samaria kommen noch dazu die lokalen Bilder des Großkönigs im Kampf mit dem geflügelten Stier und seine Gestalt im Knielaufschritt ganz in der Art des Reichsgeldes (Abb. 29, 41). Ebenso verblüffend wie kennzeichnend dabei ist die Verwandlung des sitzenden kilikischen Baal von Tarsos mit dem Zepter in den Großkö-

---

[44] So Mildenberg 1979, 184.

[45] Man hat in dieser Darstellung ein männliches Gesicht sehen wollen (Barag 1986–1987, 9 mit Anm. 35). Man könnte allerdings an Vorbilder in Karien und Lykien denken. Aber Tarsos mit dem eindeutig weiblichen Kopf in Kimons Manier und gewiß Samaria liegen näher. Ferner sprechen Umrahmung, Haartracht und das Fehlen des Chlamys-Knotens unter dem Kinn für einen weiblichen Kopf und das ferne Echo der Erfindung des Kimon aus Syrakus.

nig durch die Hinzufügung der achämenidischen Zackenkrone (Abb. 31, 42). Der schwer zu deutende, mehrfach im Nablus-Fund vertretene Obol mit der Beischrift Zeus neben diesem Bild (Abb. 45) sowie dem dahersprengenden persischen Reiter mit aramäischer Legende auf der Rückseite[46] wäre dann ein Wink, daß ursprünglich der höchste Gott mit der Darstellung gemeint war und nicht der höchste weltliche Herrscher. Jedenfalls müßte man vorausgesetzt haben, daß im Umlaufgebiet dieser Münze Aramäisch und Griechisch verstanden wurde. Ein Zeichen für die Weltoffenheit des Münzherrn ist die Prägung gewiß.

8. Mögliche und unsichere Zuschreibungen

Mit dem Namen *yhd* und *šmryn* wurde dokumentiert, daß Provinzialgeld zirkulierte. Die Zuschreibung ist auch gesichert, wenn der Name eines Gouverneurs mit oder ohne Titel erscheint oder eine nur für die Provinz feststehende Besonderheit vorliegt[47]. Die unbestreitbare Herkunft von Prägungen aus Funden von Nablus und Samaria ist gewiß wesentlich, insbesondere wenn eine größere Anzahl mit gleichen Vorder- und Rückseitenbildern[48] oder gar aus dem gleichen Stempelpaar vorhanden ist. Aber die Fundevidenz darf nicht überstrapaziert werden; denn die genannten Horte enthielten viel Fremdmaterial. Wenn einzelne Stempelkopplungen nur hier auftauchen und solche oder ähnliche bisher weder in den nördlichen noch in den südlichen Gebieten Samarias zu lokalisieren sind, so ist dies noch keine unumstößliche Evidenz, da ja neues Material uns eines Besseren belehren kann.[49] Auch die Beobachtung, daß auf dem Markt von Jerusalem bisher in den Funden aus dem Norden kein Material aus dem Süden vorkommt und umgekehrt, muß relativiert werden; denn im Fund von Nablus war nachweisbar ein Exemplar aus dem Süden (Abb. 16), nämlich ein judäischer Obol mit der vollen Legende *yḥzkyh hpḥh*.

In den Horten von Samaria finden sich nicht wenige Kleinmünzen mit Namen, wohl von Personen, ausgeschrieben und abgekürzt. Selbst eine Bilin-

---

[46] Vgl. zu diesem wichtigen achämenidischen Münzbild Mildenberg 1993, 70–72.

[47] Bei den judäischen Münzen ist die Sachlage eindeutig. Die nicht wenigen Personennamen auf dem Kleingeld von Samaria mögen Gouverneure oder andere Provinzbeamten bezeichnen, auch wenn sie sonst nicht bekannt sind. Gewißheit besteht hier jedoch nicht. Die Abkürzung *samekh-nun* dürfte für den vielfach bezeugten Gouverneursnamen Sanbalat stehen, zumal diese beiden Buchstaben samt einem *šin*, dem ersten Buchstaben von Samaria, auf einem Stempelpaar vorkommen, dessen Bilder in das dortige Repertoire gehören. – Solche Bilder schmücken auch eine lokale Kleinmünze mit der ersten Hälfte des semitischen Alphabets – ein einmaliger und zugleich rätselhafter Fund. Siehe hier Abb. 52.

[48] Wenn für einen Fund diese Voraussetzungen zutreffen, wird die Annahme einer Münzstätte wahrscheinlich, die nahe beim Fundort liegt. Dies gilt nicht für importierte Münzen, die aus der Münzstätte von Athen oder anderen fernen Ateliers stammen.

[49] Siehe oben Anmerkungen 12 und 42.

gue kommt vor. Daß diese Namen Funktionäre der persischen Verwaltung bezeichnen und damit Provinzialprägungen bekunden, kann man als wahrscheinlich annehmen, zumal die Bilder großenteils nicht aus dem Rahmen fallen. Weiter sollte man aber in der Deutung nicht gehen.

Daß die Provinzialverwaltung von Samaria in der doch wohl kurzen Prägeperiode von 15, höchstens 20 Jahren Drachmen prägen ließ, ist nicht anzunehmen. Große Geldstücke wurden für den täglichen, lokalen Gebrauch kaum benötigt. Wenn dies bisweilen doch der Fall war, gab es genügend fremdes Geld, wie die Depotfunde zeigen. Einige Kleinmünzen mit den vollen Legenden *bdyḥbl* (Abb. 50), *yhwʿnh* (Abb. 45) sowie der Bilingue *bt* – βαγαβατας (Abb. 44) wurden wegen der Herkunft aus dem Nablus-Hort an die Provinzialprägung von Samaria gegeben. Die vollen Legenden sind Personennamen und können wohl ebenfalls persische Funktionäre bezeichnen. Die Bilder, welche diese Namen begleiten, passen in den ikonographischen Rahmen, ebenso Vorder- und Rückseite des Obols mit der Bilingue. Die Drachme hingegen, welche nur die beiden Buchstaben *bt* zeigt, hat ganz andere Bilder, nämlich den üblichen Pallas-Athene Kopf und die Eule in deutlich nahöstlichen Formen. Dazu kommt, daß sie keine gesicherte Fundevidenz aufweist[50]. Die überraschende Zuschreibung der faszinierenden Drachme mit dem Leierspieler und dem Kampf von Mann und Tier (Abb. 55) an Samaria kam deshalb zustande, weil man eine entsprechende Darstellung des Leierspielers auf einem Obol (Abb. 43) aus dem Nablus-Fund sehen wollte. Den dreieckigen Gegenstand auf dem Obol könnte man durchaus als eine Art Leier deuten. Nur zeigt das Fehlen der Saiten, daß der Stempelschneider das Münzbild nicht verstanden hat, womit sich die Darstellung auf dem Obol als eine Imitation erweist. Die ungeschickt gestaltete Darstellung auf der Kleinmünze ist also von der feinen Drachme beeinflußt und nicht umgekehrt. Über die Herkunft und Zeitstellung des Leierbildes auf der Drachme ist damit noch nichts ausgesagt. Die Vorderseite zeigt ein allgemein vorderasiatisches Motiv. Wo immer die Leierdrachme hingehören mag, sie bleibt vorerst eine Prägung aus einer unbestimmten Münzstätte. Es ist besser, eine solche Münze als Incertum zu bezeichnen als eine Fehlzuschreibung zu riskieren.

9. Der Aufschwung des Münzwesens unter Artaxerxes III

Mit dem Abschluß des Königsfriedens von 387 setzt eine starke Münzproduktion ein, die sich unter Artaxerxes III Ochos zu einer regelrechten Münzexplosion in weiten Gebieten des Reiches und an seinen Grenzen[51] steigerte. Die

---

50 M-Q 34. Die Drachme stammt aus einer Auktion von 1974.

51 So entstand u. A. die Hauptgruppe der Prägung von Goldstateren in Pantikapaion auf

Mitte des 4. Jahrhunderts sah eine Massenproduktion großer Geldstücke. Nur die wichtigsten seien hier genannt: in Gold das Reichsgeld der Dareiken und das Lokalgeld der Lampsakos-Statere; in Elektron das zweihundertjährige Konventionalgeld der Statere von Kyzikos und in Silber die großen Emissionen von Maussollos und seinen Nachfolgern in Karien, der Herrscher auf Zypern, der Inseln Chios, Kos und Rhodos[52] sowie der Städte[53] Kyzikos, Klazomenai, Ephesos, Milet, Knidos, Aspendos, Nagidos, Tarsos, Arados, Byblos und Tyros. Dazu kommen die noch immer umlaufenden persischen Sigloi[54] sowie das reich strukturierte Silber-Kleingeld[55] insbesondere der großen Hafenstädte Tarsos und Sidon. Gleichzeitig begann die Bronzeprägung für den lokalen Gebrauch sich durchzusetzen, und dies auch im Inneren Kleinasiens. All dies spricht für einen stark gesteigerten und weitgefächerten wirtschaftlichen Aufschwung im Reich. Gewiß sind die meisten der zuletzt genannten Orte griechische Städte und ihr geprägtes Geld griechischer Art, aber die Herrschaft von Artaxerxes II und III war dort unbestritten. Wir haben es hier und damals mit dem Geld des Perserreiches zu tun, und nicht mit den Emissionen souveräner griechischer Stadtstaaten, ob man nun diese Münzen zur griechischen Numismatik rechnet oder nicht.[56]

In unserem Zusammenhang ist festzuhalten, daß die Provinzialprägungen von Juda und Samaria eben auch ein integraler Bestandteil gerade dieser Geldexpansion unter Artaxerxes III sind. Wir Heutigen sehen in der Vergrößerung des Geldumlaufes das untrügliche Zeichen eines Inflationsschubes. Voraussetzung eines solchen Vorganges ist, daß der Wert des Geldes sinkt und der

der Krim um die Mitte des 4. Jahrhunderts. Das Gleiche gilt auch für die Drachmen und Obole der an Juda südlich angrenzenden Gebiete, also die philisto-arabischen Prägungen.

52 Erst durch Maussollos und seine Nachfolger in ihrer Funktion als karische Satrapen wurde das persische Großreich auch auf Rhodos maßgebend. Da dies um 350 geschah, gehört die entsprechende ausgezeichnete Prägung zur Geldfülle unter Artaxerxes III. Der „rhodische" Standard mit der etwas leichteren Tetradrachme von etwa 15 g, gegenüber der attischen von etwa 17 g, hatte sich bereits vorher in Kleinasien weitgehend durchgesetzt.

53 Starr I, 85 hat 73 Städte gezählt, die in Kleinasien im 4. Jahrhundert Münzen prägten gegenüber nur 31 im 5. Jahrhundert. – Es kann nicht genug betont werden, daß die häufigen Münzfunde aus dieser Zeit großes Silbergeld in beträchtlichen Mengen enthielten. – Zu Münzfunden als Indiz für den wirtschaftlichen Aufschwung siehe Hengel 1973, 84. Münzen kamen eben nicht nur zu Kriegszeiten unter die Erde.

54 Nach Carradice 1987, 93 fällt die Produktion der Sigloi in der 1. Hälfte des 4. Jahrhunderts stark ab. Dieses handliche persische Silbergeld ist aber, wie das Aussehen vieler der erhaltenen Stücke zeigt, äußerst langlebig und ergänzt deshalb immer noch den Geldumlauf um die Mitte des Jahrhunderts. Die Administration ließ Reichsgeld nur produzieren, wenn sie es brauchte. Also verzichtete sie um 350 auf die Neuproduktion ihrer kleinasiatischen Sigloi, weil anderes hochwertiges Geld reichlich vorhanden war.

55 Die umfangreiche und vielfältige Prägung von Silberkleinmünzen in Kilikien diente der allgemeinen Geldversorgung und nicht als Soldzahlungen. Die Schönheit und der Reichtum ihrer Bilder zeugt für Impulse aus Ost und West. Siehe hier unten Abschnitt 10.

56 Die Forschung rechnet noch immer die Münzprägung Kleinasiens, der Levante und Nordafrikas zur griechischen Numismatik. Siehe hierzu Mildenberg 1993, 63.

Wert der Ware steigt. Die antike Wirtschaft kennt sehr wohl Geldentwertungen. Es kann jedoch keine Rede davon sein, daß die Edelmetallprägungen um 350 nur noch entwertetes Geld sind. Man neigt ferner dazu, die Aufstände der Satrapen und der phönizischen Städte als wichtige Ereignisse anzusehen, vergißt allerdings dabei, daß sie nur in Teilgebieten des Westens und nicht etwa des Ostens und nur während eines begrenzten Zeitraumes stattfanden und ihre Wirkung überhaupt erst noch bewiesen werden muß.[57] Schließlich erklärt man die gesteigerte Geldproduktion mit der Notwendigkeit, Söldner zu bezahlen. Gewiß brauchte man im Westen Münzen für diesen Zweck, aber doch nur große Stücke und nicht Kleingeld.[58] Der Söldner gab einen Teil des Geldes wieder aus. Wenn große Mengen Tetradrachmen aus einer Münzstätte wie Ephesos und Milet auf einmal gefunden werden, müßte es sich nach der Söldnerthese um eine Kriegskasse handeln. Da es mehrere dieser Funde gibt, müßte man auch mehrere solcher Kassen annehmen, was für eine Zeit der Konsolidierung des Reiches unter Artaxerxes III eher unwahrscheinlich ist. Prägten Maussollos[59], der nur zögernd am „Satrapenaufstand" teilnahm, und insbesondere seine Nachfolger ihre vielen Tetradrachmen nicht eher für ihr sich ausweitendes und prosperierendes Gebiet? Die lykischen Dynasten Mithrapata und Perikles[60] haben ihre Statere doch wohl nicht für Zahlungen an Söldner schlagen lassen, die sie gar nicht brauchten.

Die Forschung hat mit der Aufarbeitung dieser Massenprägung erst begonnen[61], wobei die Tatsache als solche bisher kaum gewürdigt wurde[62], und die

---

[57] Zum „Großen Satrapenaufstand" gegen Artaxerxes II siehe neuerdings R. A. Moysey „Diodorus, the Satraps and the Decline of the Persian Empire," Ancient History Bulletin, 5. 4. 1991, 111–120 und insbesondere M. Weiskopf, The so called ‚Great Satrap's Revolt' 366–360, Stuttgart 1989. In den Titeln spiegeln sich bereits die gegensätzlichen Positionen. Für den Verf. spricht allein die Stärke des Reichs unter Artaxerxes III dafür, daß der Satrapenaufstand keinesfalls der Anfang vom Ende sein konnte. Daß die letzten Jahre von Artaxerxes II eine unruhige Zeit waren, muß dabei nicht geleugnet werden. – Die Erhebung der phönizischen Städte unter Tennes von Sidon war zeitlich und lokal begrenzt, hat wohl aber die Rückeroberung Ägyptens etwas verzögert. Die Münzprägung von Juda und Samaria wurde davon jedoch nicht berührt.

[58] J. Wiesehöfer, Das Antike Persien, Zürich 1993, 134–135 betont, daß der Söldner „nach Xenophon Kost und Logis und einen Monatslohn von 1 Golddareike erhielt". Kleingeld kam nicht in Betracht. Das viele Geld kann also von Soldzahlungen nicht aufgesogen worden sein.

[59] Vergleiche S. Hornblower, Mausolus, Oxford 1982, 155.

[60] Zur breitgefächerten Literatur Mildenberg 1993, 64 mit Anm. 55.

[61] In den Auktionskatalogen der letzten Jahrzehnte finden sich viele Stücke aus großen Funden, die teilweise in IGCH und CH genannt sind. Für die Tetradrachmen-Prägungen der Städte gibt es einige wenige Einzeluntersuchungen; S. Hurter, „42 Tetradrachmen von Klazomenai" SNR 45, 1966, 26–35; B. Deppert-Lippitz, Die Münzprägung Milets vom 4.–1. Jahrhundert v. Chr., Typos V, 1984, Taf. 1–2; D. Berend, „Les tétradrachms de Rhodes de la première période I", SNR 51, 5–39.

[62] Siehe jetzt die aufschlußreiche Wertung in Starr I, 93–99; dazu Briant 322, n. 130.

Ursache überhaupt noch nicht überzeugend erklärt werden konnte[63]. Die hinsichtlich der Qualität und Quantität erstaunliche Geldschöpfung spricht für eine Blütezeit der Verwaltung, Wirtschaft und Kultur im Vielvölkerreich der Achämeniden. Sie setzt unter Artaxerxes II ein und fand ihren Höhepunkt in der Regierungszeit des mächtigen Großkönigs Artaxerxes III[64], dessen Ermordung am Anfang des Jahres 338[65] erst den Weg ebnete für Alexanders Eroberungen.

10. Ost und West

Eine aufschlußreiche Betrachtung des sich im 4. Jahrhundert stark entwickelten kleinasiatischen Münzwesens erwies eine fruchtbare Durchdringung von Elementen aus Ost und West.[66] Nun macht diese Entwicklung nicht halt an der kilikischen Pforte, sondern war gleichermaßen wirksam in Phönizien, Juda und Samaria, den südlichen Küstenstädten Ashdod, Askalon und Gaza sowie sogar in der angrenzenden, südlichen Grenzregion.[67] Es ist offensichtlich, daß die Anstöße aus dem Westen mit der Erfindung der Münze, dem Import griechischen Silbergeldes in den Osten, der Vorherrschaft der „Athener Eulen" im 5. Jahrhundert und der Faszination der griechischen Münzbilder des 4. Jahrhunderts große Wirkung zeitigten. Aber der Beitrag des Ostens zeigt sich schon bei der Erfindung der Münze und später bei der Gestaltung der lydischen Doppelmetall-Währung, der einheitlichen, prägnanten Erscheinung des persischen Reichsgeldes und den Bildern des weitverzweigten Lokalgeldes von der Aegeis bis an den Euphrat, nicht zuletzt in Juda und Samaria.

Die Produktion und Wertschätzung der graeco-persischen Gemmen[68] ergab sich aus der wechselseitigen Erfahrung der Künstler von Ost und West sowie aus dem reichen, sich gegenseitig befruchtenden Bilderschatz. Es waren nun

63 Vorläufige Feststellung bei Mildenberg 1993, 65 und 74.

64 Zur Bedeutung von Artaxerxes III vgl. E. Badian, CHI 2, 421; G. Wirth in Arrian, Tusculum Reihe, München und Zürich 1985, 816 mit Erläuterung 123; E. Bresciani, CHI 2, 526.

65 Weder der Beginn der Regierungszeit dieses bedeutenden Herrschers steht fest (359 oder 358), noch weiß man genau, wann Bagoas ihn vergiftete. Zu dieser folgenschweren Tat siehe die treffende Wertung durch Badian (oben Anm. 64): „It was at this point that court intrigues impenetrable to us assured the destruction of the Persian empire."

66 Starr I, 75–76 und 104–109.

67 Von etwa 360 bis 332 prägten die Herrscher der Gebiete südlich und südöstlich von Gaza Silbermünzen, Drachmen und deren Teilwerte, die griechisch sowie nahöstlich beeinflußte Motive sowie eigene lokale Bilder zeigen. Gründe dafür sind ihre Verbindung zum Mittelmeer über die Weihrauchstraße und die Produktion ihres Geldes in der Münzstätte Gaza. Zu ihrer Vorliebe für groteske Kompositionen siehe den nachfolgenden Text.

68 Vgl. insbesondere J. Boardman, BMC Tharros, ed. R. D. Barnett and C. Mendleson London 1987, plates 53–63 and idem, Escarabeos de piedra procedentes de Ibiza, nos 96–111.

nicht mehr zwei Welten, die sich gegenüberstanden, sondern eine Welt, in der verschiedene Lebensweisen Platz fanden. Gemmen- und Stempelschnitt sind nahe verwandt. Beeinflussungen sind wahrscheinlich. So finden sich die auf den Gemmen häufigen Flügelwesen aus dem Osten in ganz ähnlicher Gestaltung auf dem Kleingeld von Samaria. Ganz verblüffend ist, daß sich die kunstvoll zusammengesetzten Gebilde von Mensch und Tier auf den Gemmen in grünem Jaspis um 400[69] aus dem Westen auch noch auf vielen Bildern der philisto-arabischen Münzen in der südlichen Wüstenregion wiederfinden. Auch die Samaria-Funde haben in ihrer wohl unübertroffenen Vielfalt der Bilder gezeigt, wie weit eine kleine, innerpalästinensische Provinz in der Perserzeit gegenüber Einflüssen aus vielen Richtungen offen stand. Uralte östliche Tierkampfbilder und Fabelwesen sowie achämenidische Hoheitszeichen gesellen sich zu den Athener Eulen sowie den männlichen und weiblichen Köpfen des 4. Jahrhunderts aus dem Westen. Selbst die sidonische Galeere war, wie der Provinzname zeigt, in Samaria heimisch geworden. Auch der Baal von Tarsos macht hier seine Aufwartung. Der weibliche Kopf von vorn, mit Sicherheit aus Sizilien stammend über mehrere Durchgangsorte dann auch nach Juda gewandert, vereinigt dort durch die Verbindung mit der Eule die griechischen Zentren Syrakus und Athen am fernen Ort und in später Zeit. Aus dem Gegeneinander von Griechen und Persern ist im 4. Jahrhundert in vielen Bereichen, gewiß im Münzwesen, ein Miteinander geworden, ein Zusammenfließen gleichwertiger Ströme, wie es so nach Alexander nicht mehr bestand. Auch das Kleingeld von Samaria gab es nicht mehr, nur das von Juda überdauerte – ein überraschender Sonderfall – die Makedonen und noch den ersten Ptolemäer. Man versteht den Betrachter, wenn er sinnend fragt[70]: „What, that is, would have happened to this fruitful interpenetration, if the brutal sword of Alexander had not slashed accross the Near and Middle East?“

Abkürzungen

AJC	Siehe hier unten unter Meshorer AJC
AMI	Archaeologische Mitteilungen aus Iran
ANS	American Numismatic Society
Barag 1986–1987	D. „A silver Coin of Yoḥanan the High Priest and the Coinage of Judea in the Fourth Century B.C.,“ *INJ* 9, 4–21
BASOR	Bulletin of the American Schools of Oriental Research
BMC	British Museum Catalogues of Greek Coins
Briant 1982	P. Rois, Tributs et Païsans, Paris

[69] „The Graeco-Persian phenomenon was actually a positive two-way encounter“ (M. C. Root, „Lifting the Veil,“ Achaemenid History VIII, 1990/1994, 16).

[70] Starr I, 108). – Vgl. R. A. Stucky „Il Sanctuario di Eshmun a Sidone e gli inizi dell'Ellenizzazione di Fenicia“, *Scienze del Antichità* 5, 1991/1994, 461–482.

BROMBERG I–II The Abraham Bromberg Collection of Jewish Coins, Part I, Superior, New York 1991; Part II 1992

CH Coin Hoards, The British Museum London

CHI Cambridge History of Iran IV^2, Cambridge England 1992

CHJ Cambridge History of Judaism I, ed. W. D. DAVIES and Louis FINKELSTEIN, Cambridge England 1984

CARRADICE 1987 I. „The Regal Coinage of the Persian Empire,“ BAR International Series 343, Oxford, 73–95

DEUTSCH 1990–1991 R. „Six Unrecorded ‚Yehud‘ Silver Coins,“ *IEJ* 11, 4–6

HdA Handbuch der Archäologie, München

HSCP Harvard Studies of Classical Philology, Cambridge Mass.

HENGEL 1973 M. Judentum und $Hellenismus^2$, *WUNT* 10

IEJ Israel Exploration Journal, Jerusalem

IGCH Inventory of Greek Coin Hoards, ed. M. THOMPSON – O. MØRKHOLM – C. M. KRAAY, ANS, New York 1973

INJ Israel Numismatic Journal, Jerusalem

JESELSOHN 1974 D. „A New Coin Type with Hebrew Inscription,“ *IEJ* 24, 27–28

KIENLE 1975 H. K. Der Gott auf dem Flügelrad, *Göttinger Orientforschungen* VI, 7, Wiesbaden

KINDLER 1974 A. „Silver Coins Bearing the Name of Judea from the Early Hellenistic Period,“ *IEJ* 24, 73–76

MACHINIST 1994 P. „The first Coins of Judah and Samaria: Numismatics and History in the Achaemenid and Early Hellenistic Periods,“ *Achaemenid History* VIII, Leiden, 365–380

M-Q Y. MESHORER and S. QEDAR, The Coinage of Samaria in the Fourth Century BCE, Los Angeles-Jerusalem 1991

MESHORER 1966 Y. „A New Type of YHD Coin,“ *IEJ* 16, 217–219

MESHORER 1981 Y. „New Types of Judean Silver Coins,“ *INJ* 5,4

MESHORER AJC Y. Ancient Jewish Coinage, Volume I, Dix Hills NY 1982

MESHORER 1990–1991 Y. „Ancient Jewish Coinage-Addendum I,“ *INJ* 11, 104–131 (YHD Coins 104–106)

MILDENBERG 1979 L. „Yehud: A Preliminary Study of the Provincial Coinage of Judaea,“ FS Thompson, Wetteren, 183–196

MILDENBERG 1987 L. „Numismatic Evidence,“ *HSCP* Volume 91, 381–395

MILDENBERG 1988 L. „Über das Kleingeld in der Persischen Provinz Judäa,“ HdA II, Bd. I Anhang, 721–728

MILDENBERG 1990–1991 L. „Notes on the Coin Issues of Mazday,“ *INJ* 11, 9–23

MILDENBERG 1993 L. „Über das Münzwesen im Reich der Achämeniden“, *AMI* 26, 55–79

MØRKHOLM 1991 O. Early Hellenistic Coinage, ed. P. GRIERSON and U. WESTERMARK, Cambridge England

RAPPAPORT 1984 U. „Numismatics“, CHJ I, 25–29

RN Revue Numismatique, Paris

SEYRIG 1971 H. „Le monnayage de Hiérapolis de Syrie à l'époque d'Alexandre,“ RN 13, 11–21

SNR Schweizerische Numismatische Rundschau, Bern

SPAER 1977 A. „Some More ‚Yehud‘ Coins,“ *IEJ* 27, 200–203

SPAER 1979 A. „A Coin of Jeroboam,“ *IEJ* 29, 218

SPAER 1980	A. „More about Jeroboam," *INJ* 4, 2–3
SPAER 1986–1987	A. „Jaddua the High Priest?" *INJ* 9, 1–3
STARR I–II	C. G. „Greek and Persians in the Fourth Century B.C.," part I, *Iranica Antiqua* vol. XI, 39–99 and part II, *Iranica Antiqua* vol. XII, 49–115
STERNBERG	F. Auktionskataloge Frank Sternberg, Zürich
WUNT	Wissenschaftliche Untersuchungen zum Neuen Testament

Abbildungen

Vergrößerung: 3 ×, wenn nicht anders vermerkt. Abkürzungen gemäß Verzeichnis. Dazu: NF für Nablus-Fund, SH für „Samaria Hoard", Me für Meshorer 1990–1991, Mi für Mildenberg 1988 und T für Tafel. Stempelstellungen, soweit bekannt, mit Pfeilen. Einzelne Zahlen hier Nummern. Nur Silber.

JUDA
Persische Zeit 380–332

Frühe Prägungen

1 Drachme um 380. *yhd* in Palaeo-Aramäisch. Bärtiger, behelmter Kopf in Dreiviertel-Ansicht/Bärtige Gestalt, Oberkörper nackt, mit Falken auf Flügelrad nach r. in Perlkreis. Davor r. unten Beskopf n. l. 3,29 g. ↑ Unikum. London, BMC Palestine pl. 19, 29.

2 Obol um 365. Kopf der Pallas Athene n. r. *ydw*ʿ–Yaddua (Lesung und Transkription Spaer 1986–1987) neben AΘE. Eule n. r., daneben Wedel. 0,85 g. ↘

3 Drachme um 360–350. Bilder wie vorher. Legende *yhd* spiegelverkehrt. Deutsch 1986–1987, 1,2,70 g. ↗

Kleinsilber 4–18 (ca. 350–332), Legende yhd

4 Obol. Bilder und Schrift wie 3. Mi T. 22,3. 0,65 g.

5 Obol. Kopf n. r. über Bogen/Eule wie vorher. Sternberg 25, 125. 0,45 g.

6 Viertelobol. Lilie/Eule. Mi T. 22,8. 0,13 g. ↙

7 Halbobol. Lilie/Falke, Kopf n. l. Me 8. 0,39 g.

8 Halbobol. Lilie/Falke, Kopf n. r. Mildenberg 1993, 31 aus Sternberg 26, 131. 0,29 g.

9 Obol. Persische Mütze/Falke. Me 7. 0,58 g.

10 Halbobol. Kopf des Großkönigs in der Zackenkrone/Falke wie vorher. Mildenberg 1993, 32 aus Sternberg 26, 133. 0,35 g.

11 Halbobol. Tierkopf n. r./Falke wie vorher. Sternberg 26, 137. 0,33 g.

12 Obol. Tierkopf n. r. wie vorher/Greifvogel n. r. Kopf nach rückwärts. Große, unübliche Buchstaben. Sternberg 25, 198. 0,43 g. ca. 8 mm.

13 Halbobol. Lilie, stilisiert/Greifvogel wie vorher. Deutsch 1990–1991, 3. 0,32 g. 7 mm.

14 Halbobol. Kopf von vorn, verwildert, in Rahmen/Eule. Legenden *yhd* und (!) *yhwdh*. Me 4 und S. 105 (dort *yhd* für Jerusalem vermutet; plausibel der Vorschlag ebendort, *yhwdh* als Personennamen aufzufassen). 0,21 g. ca. 6 mm.

15 Halbobol. Weiblicher Kopf von vorn/yḥzkyh hpḥh. Mi T. 23, 2. ca. 0,20 g. 7,5 mm.

16 Halbobol. Wie vorher. Aus dem Fund von Nablus (!). Unveröffentlicht. 0,20 g. ↑ ca. 7 mm.

17 Viertelobol. Bilder wie vorher. Legende ywḥn[n] *hkhn*. Yoḥanan der Priester. Barag 1986–1987, 7–8, 0,17 g. 8 mm.

18 Viertelobol. Wie vorher, aber verwilderte Bilder und Legenden. Mi T 23,5. 0,14 g. ↓

Makedonische Zeit 332–312

19 Halbobol. Jugendlicher, männlicher Kopf n. l. (Portrait?)/*yḥzqyh* in makelloser, palaeohebräischer Schrift. Geflügeltes und gehörntes Katzentier. Sternberg 25, 194. 0,23 g.

20 Halbobol. Männerkopf mit deutlichen Porträtzügen n. r./Katzentier wie vorher (gleicher Stempel?). Sternberg 25, 196. 0,23 g.

Ptolemäische Zeit 300–283/282

21 Viertelobol. Kleiner, jugendlicher Kopf eines Mannes n. l./*yhd* Ptolemäischer Adler n. l. Spaer 1977, 4. Mi T. 23,8. 0,12 g.

22 Viertelobol. Veristisches Porträt von Ptolemaios I mit der Königsbinde n. r./*yhdh* Adler wie vorher. Mi T. 23, 11. 0,18 g. 7 mm.

23 Halbdrachme. Bilder und Legenden wie vorher. Hervorragendes Porträt und gute palaeohebräische Schrift. AJC Addendum 184, 2. 1,75 g. ↑

24 Halbdrachme. Wie vorher, nur BA (für ΒΑΣΙΑΕΥΣ) l. neben Adler. AJC Addendum, 184, 1. 1,55 g. ↑

25 Hemiobol. Jugendlicher, männlicher Kopf n. r./Adler wie vorher. *yhd* l. Me 11. 0,30 g.

26 Viertelobol. Idealisiertes Bildnis von Ptolemaios I in der Königsbinde n. r./Wohl *yhd[h]* Kopf von Berenike I nach r. Sternberg 26, 140. 0,19 g. ca. 6 mm.

27 Viertelobol. Gutes, veristisches Porträt von Ptolemaios I/Gutes Porträt von Berenike I n. r. Spaer 1979, 5 a. Mi T. 23,13. 0,16 g. 6 mm.

28 Halbobol. Kopf von Ptolemaios I in der Königsbinde n. r./Ausdrucksvolles Bildnis der Berenike I n. l. Legende unklar. Me 13. 0,20 g. ca. 6,5 mm.

JUDA

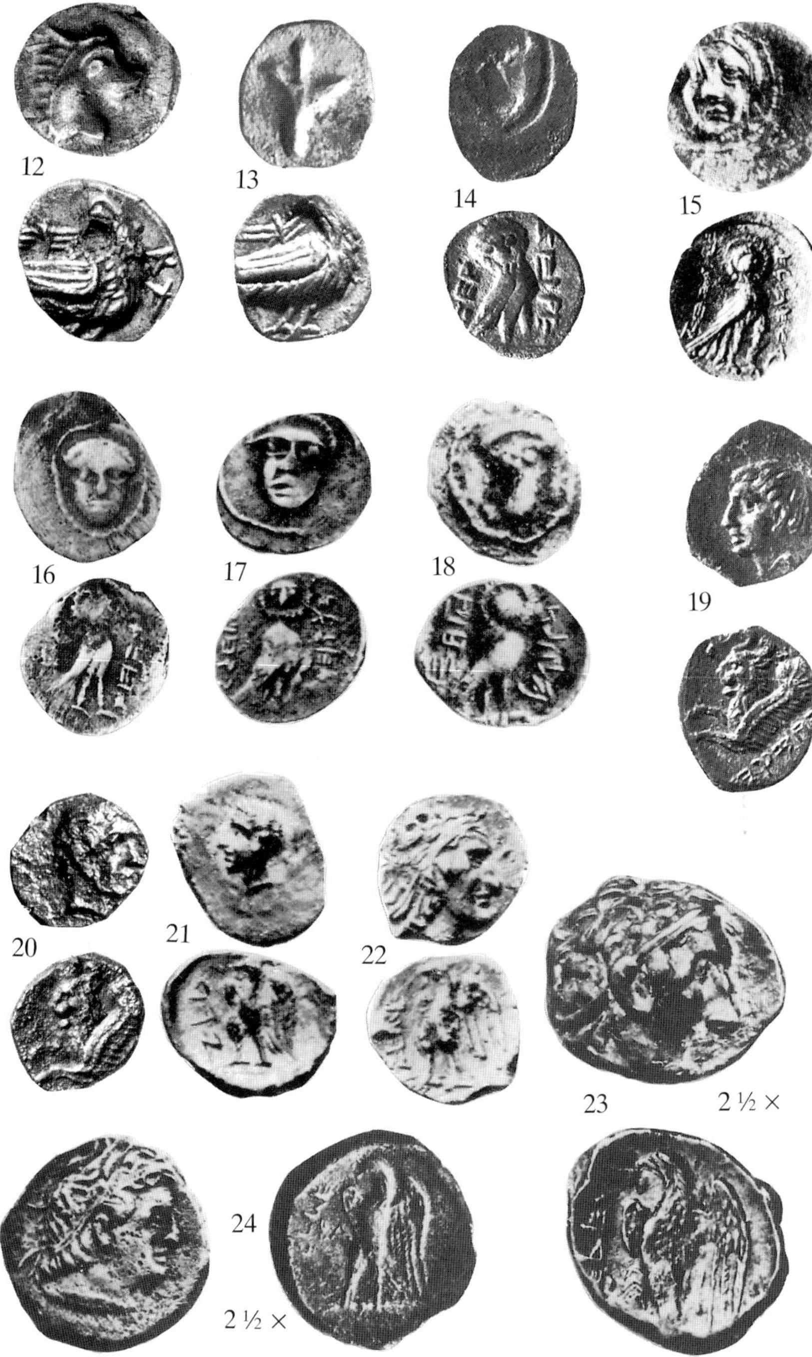
12
13
14
15
16
17
18
19
20
21
22
23
2 ½ ×
24
2 ½ ×

25
26
27
28
4 ×
SAMARIA
29
30
31
32
33
34
35
36

48
49
50 4 ×
51
52
56
53
54
55 2 ×

SAMARIA ca. 360–338/337

Provinzial-Kleingeld 29–42

29 Halbobol. *šmryn* Sidonische Galeere über Wellen n. l./Großkönig mit Speer und Bogen, ganz in der Art der Hauptgruppe, „3. Typ", des Reichsgeldes. Sammlung Sofaer. M-Q 17. Vgl. Mildenberg 1993, 30. 0,28 g. ca. 8 mm.

30 Obol. Wie vorher, *mz* für Mazday. Großkönig im Kampf mit Löwen - nach sidonischem Vorbild. Sammlung Sofaer. M-Q 16. 0,63 g. ←

31 Obol. *šmryn* Großkönig in der Zackenkrone mit Zepter n. r. thronend - in der Art des Baal von Tarsos. Löwe über Hirsch n. r. *mbyg* (Lesung M-Q 18). 0,64 g. 9 mm.

32 Obol. Löwenprotome n. r., Kopf nach vorn./Bärtiger Kopf n. l., dahinter *šmryn* Sternberg 27, 200. 0,65 g.

33 Obol. Kopf eines Persers in der Tiara n. l. *šmryn* Großkönig im Kampf mit Stier. SH 4, 0,3 g. ↓

34 Obol. Kopf eines Persers n. r./*šmryn* Pferdeprotome n. r. M-Q 1 = SH 1. 0,85 g. →

35 Obol. Kopf der Pallas Athene. Lokale Arbeit/Löwe über Hirsch, darüber *šmryn*. SH 43, 0,66 g ↖

36 Obol. Kopf von vorn/*šmry[n]* retrograd. Eule. Privatsammlung Los Angeles. M-Q Addendum S. 83, 1. 0,70 g. ca. 9 mm. ↑

37 Obol. Wie vorher/Behelmter, bärtiger Kopf. Vertieftes Quadrat. SH 74. 0,69 g. ↗

38 Obol. Weiblicher Kopf n. r./*šmr* wie vorher. Schnitt und Prägung sorglos. SH 157. 0,52 g. ↖

39 Obol. Thronende Gestalt mit Adler n. r./*šmr* undeutlich. Großkönig mit Zackenkrone und Dolch bekämpft Stier. Sternberg 24, 141 = M-Q 19,5.

40 Viertelobol. Weiblicher Kopf von vorn in der Art der Arethusa des Kimon von Syrakus/*šmr* retrograd. Pferd im Galopp n. l. SH 145. 0,13 g. ca. 5 mm. ↖

41 Halbobol, schwer. Löwe mit menschlichem Gesicht n. r., darüber *šn*. Großkönig wie oben Nr. 29. Aus NF, unpubliziert. Vgl. M-Q 22. 0,41 g. ca. 6,5 mm.

42 Obol. Großkönig wie oben Nr. 31. Dahinter *šn*/Großkönig mit Zackenkrone als Ahuramazda, Oxford aus NF. M-Q 21. 0,78 g. ca. 8,5 mm; Legende *mz* (Mazday), ca. 344 zu datieren.

Zuschreibungen 43–52

43 Obol ca. 345. Sitzender Perser mit dreieckigem Gegenstand, dahinter Datum (14. Jahr von Artaxerxes III). Unten Bogen/Großkönig bekämpft Stier. In der Mitte Kugel im Kreis. Oxford aus NF = M-Q 32. 0,62 g. ca. 8 mm. ↓

44 Obol ca. 345. Sitzender Perser mit Pfeil n. r. Unten r. Bogen. Oben *bt*, links Datum 14 wie oben/Großkönig in der Zackenkrone mit Dolch bekämpft Stier. In der Mitte Kugel im Kreis. Rundum ΒΑΓΑΒΑΤΑC (Lesung M-Q 31,2). Oxford aus NF. 0,55 g. ca. 8 mm.

45 Obol. ΙΕΥΣ Großkönig mit Blume thronend/*yhwʿnh* Perser nach r. reitend, Oxford aus NF = M-Q 38. 0,77 g. 1 cm.

46 Obol. *yrb'm*, verwischt. Gestalt mit langem Stab und übergeschlagenen Beinen n. r. sitzend/Zwei menschliche Gestalten, einander gegenüber, in Gebäude stehend. Sternberg 24, 145 = M-Q 26,4. 0,53 g. ca. 9 mm.

47 Obol. Kopf r./*yrb'[m]* Pferd. Vgl. Spaer 1980, S. 2, 1. M-Q 24. 0,77 g. ca. 8 mm.

48 Obol. Volle Legende *yrb'm* Bärtiger Kopf l./Reiter nach r. Aus NF, unpubliziert. Vgl. Sternberg 24, 142 = M-Q 23,3 (stempelgleich) und Spaer 1979, S. 218, T. 25 A–B. 0,67 g.

49 Obol. Kopf r./Nackte und bekleidete männliche Gestalt einander gegenüber, dazwischen *yrb'm*. Nahe Kopie des Staters von Tarsos unter Datames (Mildenberg 1993, Nr. 93). Sternberg 24, 143 = M-Q 25,2. 0,74 g. ca. 8 mm.

50 Obol. Großkönig in Biga n. l. nach sidonischem Vorbild/*bdyḥbl* Perser reitet im Galopp n. l. Aus NF. Vgl. M-Q 35. 0,64 g. ca. 8,5 mm. ↗

51 Obol. Großer Kopf n. l./Männliche Gestalt thronend n. r., dahinter *ḥnnyh* (Lesung M-Q 29,2). Sammlung Sofaer. 0,52 g. ca. 9 mm.

52 Obol. Sidonische Galeere n. l. Darunter in zwei Linien die ersten 12 Buchstaben des aramäischen Alphabets/Zwei Perser mit Dolch einander gegenüber. Dazwischen sitzender Löwe n. r. M-Q 54. 0,78 g.

Incerta

53 Halbobol. Sitzende Gestalt mit großem Bogen (undeutlich)/Weiblicher Kopf von vorn mit großen Ohrringen. Sternberg 24, 155 = M-Q 78. 0,34 g. ca. 7 mm.

54 Obol. Großkönig in der Art des Reichsgeldes, „3. Typ", um 400/Ebenso, aber *dalet* l. im Feld l. oben (Fehlprägung mit zwei gleichen Bildern?). Sammlung Sofaer, M-Q 52. 0,70 g. ca. 1 cm. →

55 Drachme. Männliche Gestalt und Pferd, beide aufgerichtet, einander gegenüber/Sitzender, bärtiger Mann mit großer Leier auf den Knien. Unten r. Bes-Maske. Privatsammlung Los Angeles = M-Q 58,2. 3,60 g. 1,5 cm. Incertum um 370.

Zum Vergleich

56 Tyros. Stater 339–338. Reiter auf Hippokamp. n. r./Eule mit Flegel. Im Feld r. Zahlzeichen für Jahr 10 und *ayin*. Aus dem Fund von Nablus; letztes, datiertes Stück.

Zürich im Juli 1995

Hecataeus of Abdera on Mosollamus the Jewish Mounted Archer (*Contra Apionem*, I, 200–204)

by

ARYEH KASHER

In his treatise *Contra Apionem* (I, 200–204), Josephus cited in the name of Hecataeus of Abdera an illustrative story with a philosophical and religious instructive lesson. The hero of the story is a Jewish mounted archer called Mosollamus, who apparently served Alexander the Great in one of his campaigns near the Red Sea. For the purpose of discussing the authenticity of the story, the English translation of the source by Thackeray[1] is offered here as follows:

200. The author (i.e. Hecataeus) further attests the share which the Jews took in the campaigns both of King Alexander and of his successors. One incident on the march, in which a Jewish soldier was concerned, he states that he witnessed himself. I will give the story in his own words:

201. "When I was on the march towards the Red Sea, among the escort of Jewish cavalry which accompanied us was one named Mosollamus, a very intelligent man, robust, and by common consent, the very best of bowmen, whether Greek or barbarian. **202.** This man, observing that a number of men were going to and fro on the route and that the whole force was being held up by a seer who was taking the auspices, inquired why they are halting. **203.** The seer pointed out to him the bird he was observing, and told him that if it stayed in that spot it was expedient for them all to halt; if it stirred and flew forward, to advance; if backward, then to retire. The Jew, without saying a word, drew his bow, shot and struck the bird, and killed it. **204.** The seer and some others were indignant, and heaped curses upon him. 'Why so mad, you poor wretches?' he reported; and then, taking the bird in his hands, continued, 'Pray, how could any sound information about our march be given by this creature, which could not provide for its own safety? Had it been gifted with divination, it would not have come to this spot, for fear of being killed by an arrow of Mosollamus the Jew'".

Like all other citations ascribed by Josephus to Hecataeus of Abdera, this too has driven not a few scholars to raise grave doubts concerning the historical authenticity of the evidence. The skeptics have tended to relate the story to a Jewish Hellenistic writer from Alexandria, who preferred, out of purely prop-

---

[1] H. ST. THACKERAY, Josephus, Vol. I, Cambridge Mass., 1926, p. 245.

agandic motives, to have recourse to pseudonymity in order to peg his own ideas onto the great authority of Hecataeus; those scholars, however, were divided among themselves with reference to the date of writing.[2] Walter was the first to raise the view that the Pseudo-Hecataeus in question was actually not one writer but two.[3] Wacholder initially follwed Walter, but after some time he changed his mind, stating that there were, in fact, three writers and not two. However, with regard to the contents of the above citation, he took an intermediate position, according to which he believed most of its details to be basically authentic (even if anecdotal in nature), but to have been written, as stated, by the author whom he terms "Pseudo-Hecataeus I".[4] He thought this

---

[2] For detail see. H. WILLRICH, Juden und Griechen vor der makkabäischen Erhebung, Göttingen 1895, pp. 20ff., 48ff.; idem, Judaica. Forschungen zur hellenistisch-jüdischen Geschichte und Literatur, Göttingen 1900, pp. 86–104; TH. REINACH, Textes d'auteurs grecs et romains relatifs au Judaïsme, Paris 1895 (reprint 1963), pp. 227ff. (cf. TH. REINACH und L. BLUM, Flavius Josèphe contre Apion, Texte établi et annoté, Paris 1930, pp. xxxi–xxxii); J. GEFFCKEN, Zwei griechische Apologeten, Leipzig-Berlin 1907, pp. x–xvi; E. SCHÜRER, Geschichte des jüdischen Volkes im Zeitalter Jesu Christi[4], III, Leipzig 1909 (Darmstadt 1964), pp. 605–608. (cf. idem, The History of The Jewish People in the Age of Jesus Christ [eds. G. Vermers, F. Millar *et al.*]. III.1, Edinburgh 1986, pp. 671–677); F. JACOBY, Die Fragmente der Griechischen Historiker, III A, pp. 46–52, 61–74; idem, s. v. 'Hekataios aus Abdera (4)', in: Realencyclopädie der klassischen Altertumswissenschaft (eds. A. Pauly, G. Wissowa *et al.*), VII (1912), cols. 2766–2767; W. BOUSSET, H. GRESSMANN, Die Religion des Judentums im späthellenistischen Zeitalter[3], Tübingen 1926 (1966[4]), pp. 26ff.; V. TCHERIKOVER, Hellenistic Civilization and the Jews, Tel-Aviv 1931 (Hebrew), pp. 278–279 (later, in the 1963 edition of his book, he changed and accepted the authenticity of Hecataeus cited by Josephus; M. STEIN, 'Pseudo-Hecataeus, his Time and the Purpose of his Book on the Jews and Their Land', *Zion* Collection - 1934 (Hebrew), pp. 1ff.; J. EPHRON, The Hasmonean Kingdom and Simeon Ben Shatah (–), The Hebrew University, Jerusalem 1962, p. 11; P. DALBERT, Die Theologie der hellenistisch-jüdischen Missionsliteratur unter Ausschluss von Philo und Josephus, Hamburg 1954, pp. 65–67; B. SCHALLER, 'Hekataios von Abdera über die Juden. Zur Frage der Echtheit und der Datierung', Zeitschrift für die neutestamentliche Wissenschaft, 54 (1963), pp. 15–31 (esp. 16–17, nn. 12–13), 20ff.; M. HENGEL, 'Anonymität, Pseuepigraphie und "Literaraische Fälschung" in der jüdisch-hellenistischen Literatur', in: K. von Fritz (ed.), Pseudepigrapha, I (Entretiens sur l'Antiquité Classique, XVIII), Geneva 1972, pp. 301–303; P. M. FRASER, Ptolemaic Alexandria, Oxford 1972, II, n. 115, pp. 968–969; cf. C. R. HOLLADAY, Fragments from Hellenistic Jewish Authors, I: Historians, Chico 1983, pp. 277–335, esp. 279–290; and recently L. H. FELDMAN, Jew and Gentile in the Ancient World, Princeton 1993, p. 8.

[3] See N. WALTER, Der Thoraausleger Aristobulus. Untersuchungen zu seinen Fragmenten und zu pseudepigraphischen Resten der jüdisch-hellenistischen Literatur, Berlin 1964, pp. 187–200; idem, 'Pseudo-Hekataios I and II', in: Fragmente jüdisch-hellenistischer Historiker. Jüdische Schriften aus hellenistischer und römischer Zeit (ed. W. G. Kümmel), Gütersloh 1976, pp. 144–146; cf. also W. SPOERRI, s. v. 'Hekataios (4)', Der Kleine Pauly, II, pp. 981–982; idem, 'Hekataios von Abdera', Reallexikon für Antike und Christentum, 14 (1987), cols. 291–298.

[4] B. Z. WACHOLDER, 'Hecataeus of Abdera', Encyclopaedia Judaica, VIII (1971), pp. 236–237; idem, Eupolemus: A Study of Judaeo-Greek Literature, Cincinnati-New York-Jerusalem 1974, pp. 263ff. He maintains that Pseudo-Hecataeus I is connected with Contra Apionem, I, 183–205, 213ff.; II, 44–47, and Letter of Aristeas, 83–120.

Jewish writer to have been a priest closely associated with the High Priest in Jerusalem, who left his position and became friendly with another Jew (namely Mosollamus), who was in military service under Alexander the Great. He held that the source was written some time around the battle of Gaza (312 BCE)[5]. Moreover, in his eyes, the information on the Persian era, which is given in close connection,[6] was still fresh, and therefore could confirm this chronological conclusion. The lack of any linguistic affinity to the Septuagint with regard to the description of the Temple[7] can, as he sees it, corroborate an additional conclusion: that the source was written before the completion of the Septuagint. Wacholder's grounds for both the date and the historical authenticity of the testimony (despite the several anecdotes included therein) are acceptable to me; however, his conclusion that the work was not written by Hecataeus himself, is not. In support of his view about the content, it is important to note here that not all the skeptic scholars were determined in their suspicions about the substance of the testimony related to Hecataeus, nor did they all rule out the possibility that at least part of it was true and reliable from historical point of view.[8] In this article, I shall try to encourage this direction of research, at least with respect to the Mosollamus story.

As stated above, there were those determined skeptical scholars who tended to judge the story as no more than a literary anecdote. Rappaport, for example, cast doubt on the reliability of its information, claiming that the story is obviously legendary, fictional, moralizing, and utterly unrelated to any real historical event.[9] As he would have it, the expression "on the march" (κατὰ τὴν στρατείαν) is an obscure phrase indicating nothing; accordingly, the story is devoid of any real historical or factual background. However, in utter contrast to his opinion, it should be mentioned that the opening words of § I, 200 clearly denotes that this was an incident which took place under Alexander or under one of his immediate successors. In my view, the fact that the story does not include an exact chronological identification need not constitute grounds for its classification as imaginary or historically unfounded, since the purpose of writing in this case was by no means a historiographic one, but rather a philosophical one, as we shall see below. As the author did not intend to

---

5 It is mentioned in Contra Apionem, I, 184ff.

6 It is referred in Contra Apionem, I, 193.

7 Contra Apionem, I, 198ff.

8 See e.g. REINACH 1895 (n. 1 above), p. 227; W. SCHMID and O. STÄHLIN, Geschichte der griechischen Literatur[6], München 1920, p. 619; HOLLADAY 1983 (note 2 above), pp. 281–283; D. MENDELES, 'Hecataeus of Abdera and a Jewish "patrios politeia" of the Persian Period (Diodorus Siculus XL, 3)', Zeitschrift für die neutestamentliche Wissenschaft, 95 (1983), pp. 96ff.; WACHOLDER 1974 (n. 4 above), pp. 263ff.

9 U. RAPPAPORT, Jewish Religious Propaganda and Proselytism in the Period of the second Commonwealth (Dissertation), The Hebrew University, Jerusalem 1965 (Hebrew), p. 142 and n. 16.

describe a historic event, but rather to draw a philososophical lesson from an amusing story, we should judge him as a writer who made a statement in ignorance of its historical bearing. It is not necessary, therefore, to evaluate the authenticity of story by means of pure historiographic criteria.

As mentioned above, by contrast with the skeptic group of scholars, not a few researchers have accepted the story which Josephus ascribed to Hecataeus as basically authentic, at least as far as the historical content is concerns.[10] To my satisfaction, this view has recently become even more widely accepted in the modern-day scholastic community.[11] An entirely different question is whether Josephus quoted the real Hecataeus directly from the original work, or from a second-hand source. The latter possibility, in my opinion, is quite attractive, although not definitely proven; perhaps, in this respect, my opinion may somehow resemble that of Wacholder, if we assume that the second-hand

---

[10] See A. ELTER, De Gnomologiorum Graecarum historia atque origene commentatio, Bonner Universitätsprogramm Teil IX, Bonn 1893–5; A. SCHLATTER, Zur Topographie und Geschichte Palästinas, Stuttgart 1893, pp. 333 ff.; P. WENDLAND, '(Rezension über Willrichs Judaica)', Berliner philologische Wochenschrift, 20 (1900), pp. 1199–1202; M. ENGERS, 'De Hecataei Abderitae Fragments', Mnemosyne, NS, 51 (1923), pp. 232–233; H. LEWY (Levy), 'Hekataios von Abdera περί Ἰουδαίων', Zeitschrift für die neutestamentliche Wissenschaft, 31 (1932), pp. 117–132; idem, Studies in In Jewish Hellenism, Jerusalem 1960 (Hebrew), pp. 44 ff.; F. DORNSEIFF, Echtheitsfragen antik-griechischer Literatur. Rettungen des Theognis, Phokylides, Hekataios, Choirilos, Berlin 1939, pp. 52–65; THACKERAY 1926 (note 1 above), pp. 236–237 (n. b); Y. GUTMAN, The Beginnings of the Jewish-Hellenistic Literature, Jerusalem 1958, I, pp. 39 ff.; V. TCHERIKOVER, Hellenistic Civilization and the Jews (Engl. trans. by S. Applebaum), Philadelphia 1959, pp. 56–57, 272–273, 300, 425–427 (nn. 46, 49); J. G. GAGER, 'Pseudo-Hecataeus Again', Zeitschrift für die neutestamentliche Wissenschaft, 60 (1969), pp. 130–139; M. HENGEL, Judaism and Hellenism. Studies in their Encounter in Palestine during the Early Hellenistic Period (trans. by J. Bowden), I–II, London 1974, II, p. 11, n. 84; idem, Jews, Greeks and Barbarians. Aspects of the Hellenization of Judaism in the pre-Christian Period, Philadelphia 1980, pp. 85–86; cf. idem, 'The Political and Social History of Palestine from Alexander to Antiochus III (333–187 B.C.E.)', in: Cambridge History of Judaism II (1989), p. 40; M. STERN, Greek and Latin Authors on Jews and Judaism, Jerusalem 1974, I, pp. 20–25; J.-D. GAUGER, 'Zitate in der jüdischen Apologetik und die Authentizität der Hekataios-Passagen bei Flavius Josephus und im Ps. Aristeas-Brief', Journal of the Study of Judaism in the Persian, Hellenistic and Roman Period, 13 (1982), esp. pp. 28–35; J. J. COLLINS, Between Athens and Jerusalem. Jewish Identity in the Hellenistic Diaspora, New York 1983, pp. 137–141; E. GABBA, 'La Palestina e gli ebrei negli storici classici fra il V e il III sec. a. C.', Rivista Biblica, 34 (1986), p. 137; idem, 'The Growth on anti-Judaism or the Greek attitude towards Jews', The Cambridge History of Judaism, II (1989), pp. 626 ff.; R. WILK, Jews in Seleucis Syria (Dissertation), Tel-Aviv University, Tel-Aviv 1986 (Hebrew), pp. 27, 169–170; G. E. STERLING, Historiography and Self-Definition. Josephus, Luke-Acts and Apologetic Historiography, Leiden-New York-Köln 1992, p. 90; FELDMAN 1993 (n. 2 above), pp. 11, 48.

[11] See e.g. the studies P. BORGEN s.v. 'Judaism (Egypt)', Anchor Bible Dictionary, III (1992), p. 1063; STERLING 1992 (n. 10 above), pp. 78–91; M. PUCCI BEN-ZE'EV, 'The Reliability of Josephus Flavius: The Case of Hecataeus' and Manetho's Accounts of Jews and Judaism: Fifteen Years of Contemporary Research (1974–1990)', Journal of the Study of Judaism in the Persian, Hellenistic and Roman Period, 24/2 (1993), pp. 215–234.

source was a Jewish author.[12] At the same time, however, we must not reject the basic authenticity of the testimony ascribed to Hecataeus with regard to its historical contents; at most, some matters included therein should be ascribed to the editing and emendation performed by the second-hand source. Even Josephus may have allowed himself to decorate Hecataeus' testimony here and there; after all, this would have been neither the first nor the last time that he did so. As I cannot cope here with all those important questions for reasons of space, I shall content myself with a partial analysis limited to the Mosollamus story, in which I join those who maintain the authenticity of the citations ascribed to Hecataeus.[13]

It is worth noting, even here at the outset of my discussion, that several scholars have had basic difficulty accepting the possibility that Jews might have served in Alexander's army, as it is told in the Mosollamus story.[14] Those scholars were apparently guided by a tendency to detract from the military skill of the Jews, based on modern-day prejudices, according to which the Jews were depicted as a people incapable of waging war or productive work, and suited only to trade, peddling, money-lending and shady dealings. I think that an opinion of that kind is obviously inappropriate: not only is it based on prejudice, which is reprehensible in itself; it is actually founded on the projection of a false view which historically arose much later, in a distant and foreign environment. This was also the reason for the scholarly rejection of the information on the establishment of the Jewish military settlement in Phrygia and Lydia under Antiochus III; however, the reliability of that information has since been shown to withstand the test of historical criticism and has been verified by epigraphic findings as well.[15] The enlistment of soldiers from conquered countries into the armies of the Hellenistic kingdoms has been proven beyond all doubt. Philip of Macedonia, father of Alexander the Great, is known to have recruited "barbarians" into his army; Alexander not only granted his foreign recruits rights

---

[12] Cf. STERN 1974 (n. 10 above), p. 24; MENDELES 1983 (n. 8 above), p. 97; HOLLADAY 1983 (n. 2 above), p. 283; STERLING 1992 (n. 10 above), p. 91.

[13] These question will be discussed at length in my forthcoming commentary to Contra Apionem.

[14] This is also true in regard to I, 192; II, 35, 42; Bell. Jud., II, 487–488; Ant. Jud., XI, 339; see e. g. TCHERIKOVER 1959 (n. 10 above), pp. 277 ff.; 320 ff.

[15] See Ant. Jud., XII, 147–153. The opinions of those rejecting that testimony have been reviewed in detail by MARCUS, Josephus, VII 1943, Appendix D, pp. 743–766; for the contrasting views, see E. BICKERMANN, 'La charte Séleucide des Séleucides', Revue des études juives, 100 (1935), pp. 4–35; A. SCHALIT, 'The Letter of Antiochus III to Zeuxis regarding the Establishment of Jewish Military Colonies in Phrygia and Lydia', Jewish Quarterly Review, 50 (1959/60), pp. 289–318, including all relevant information. Similarly, some scholars unjustly doubted the authenticity of Josephus' testimony (*Ant. Jud.*, XI, 345) with regard to Alexander having taken the troops of Sanballat the Samaritan with him into Egypt, settled them in the vicinity of Thebes, and assigned them the duty of guarding that region; see A. KASHER, The Jews in Hellenistic and Roman Egypt: The Struggle for Equal Rights, Tübingen 1985, p. 159, 188.

equal to those of his Greek troops, but sometimes even preferred them to his Hellenistic mercenaries.[16] The same is to be said of later Hellenistic rulers; it was not therefore so much of an extraordinary phenomenon. Those rulers were simply in need of the services offered by non-Greeks, whether for tactical reasons or due to a lack of fighting manpower. As stated above, Alexander himself was known to have enlisted such units into his army – whether on a voluntary or a compulsory basis.[17] This was a well-known phenomenon in both the Ptolemaic and the Seleucid armies from the very beginning of the Hellenistic period. We know for sure that Jews served in both of those armies as well, and even in independent Jewish detachments commanded by Jews.[18] Rappaport, although aware of the plethora of evidence attesting to the service of Jews in the armies of Persia and the Hellenistic empires, expressed reservations with respect to the credibility of this story – precisely due to its mention of a Jewish cavalry unit.[19] According to him, aside from Tobias' army on the east bank of the Jordan River during the Hellenistic era (mentioned in the Zenon papyri), no Jewish cavalry has been mentioned anywhere, and all the sources which discuss Jewish military service speak of infantrymen and garrison forces only. In reply, I would say that this reservation actually cuts both ways: the very existence of cavalry units in Tobias' army and under his command – even if most of their soldiers were not Jewish – may constitute a basis for precisely the opposite conclusion. Furthermore, Jewish cavalrymen were known to have existed in Ptolemaic Egypt starting in the mid-third century BCE, and especially since the second century BCE; some of them even banded together in their own units, under Jewish command.[20] In short, the mention of a Jewish cavalryman cannot in itself support the opinion that the story is no more than a work of fiction.

Another, more current matter, which cast doubts on the credibility of this information with regard to Jews having served in Alexander's army, is related to the civic status question of the Jews of Alexandria.[21] We may state with some certainty that Tcherikover, more than any other scholar, vehemently expressed

---

16 See e.g. J. Lesquier, Les institutions militaires de l'Égypte sous les Lagides, Paris 1911, p. 137. For more details seel below in the commentary to § 1, 201 below.

17 See Arrian, IV, 4; VI, 1, 6, 8, 10–11, 23, 29; cf. Plutarch, Alexander, 45, 47, 71; cf. Kasher, *op. cit.*, p. 188.

18 The whole issue will not be discussed here for reasons of space, but see Schalit 1959/60, pp. 289–318; V. Tcherikover, The Jews in Egypt in the Hellenistic-Roman Age in the Light of the Papyri, Jerusalem 1963, pp. 30ff. (Hebrew); Stern 1974 (n. 10 above), I, p. 43; Kasher, *op. cit.*, pp. 38ff.; B. Bar-Kochva, Judas Maccabaeus. The Jewish Struggle against the Seleucids, Cambridge 1989, pp. 85, 500–507.

19 Rappaport 1965 (n. 9 above), pp. 142–143.

20 See CPJ (= Corpus Papyrorum Judaicarum, ed. V. Tcherikover *et al.*), I, nos. 18, 24; P. Tebt. (= The Tebtunis Papyri, eds. A. S. Hunt, J. G. Smyly *et al.*), no. 79 (b); cf. P. Gurob (= Greek Papyri from Gurob, ed. L. G. Smyly), No. 26; Kasher, *op. cit.*, pp. 47f., 53–55.

21 Bell. Jud., II, 487–488; see also II, 35, 37, 42.

his reservations in this context.[22] In his opinion, the testimony to that effect is tainted with Jewish apologia, and can therefore not be accepted as reliable, having been written at a later date and unfounded on any exact historical sources. According to Tcherikover and other scholars after him, the supposed Jewish forger ("Pseudo-Hecataeus"), or possibly Josephus himself, sought to cite an impressive precedent (Alexander the Great) in corroboration of the argument related to the source of rights conceded to the Jews of Alexandria and their demand for equal civic status.[23] In my opinion, this argument is based on the erroneous assumption that the Jews of Alexandria really craved citizenship in the Alexandrian polis.[24] Once the foundations have been knocked out from under the "house of cards" built by those scholars on the basis of that premise, the testimony ascribed to Hecataeus could certainly be accepted as more reliable.

Let us refer at the outset to the style of writing. As the story of Mosollamus is written in the first person,[25] J.H. Levy (after F. Jacoby) rightly believed it to have been taken from a travel diary, in which Hecataeus recorded his experiences and memoirs, and whose style was well in line with the spirit of his times.[26] It should also be noted, in this context, that Levy has convincingly proved that even the pathetic literary characteristics of the tale are well in line with the commonly accepted norms of Greek literature, and therefore give it considerable reliability. This is especially true with reference to the "hypomnematic" and intentionally simplistic style as Levy puts it so appropriate to the travel stories written during and following Alexander's time. The same is to be said of the description of Mosollamus as "a very intelligent man and robust" (ἄνθρωπος ἱκανὸς κατὰ ψυχήν, εὔρωστος); these, as we know, were the basic traits for which the Greeks appreciated their heroes: a combination of mental and physical prowess. Moreover, the mention of the seemingly insignificant detail that the Mosollamus incident was associated with a march to the Red Sea adds credibility to the tale, at least by making it difficult to deny the impression that this was based on a real incident. Quite a similar conclusion can be reached with regard to the Hebrew name of the hero, Mosollamus (Μοσόλλαμος). This is undoubtedly a garbled Greek transcription of the Hebrew name Meshullam (משלם), which is mentioned 23 times in the Bible.[27] It appears in the Septuagint in several variations – Μεσουλαμ, Μεσολλαμ, Μοσολλαμ, Μασσαλημ, Μοσολλαμος – one of which is the same as that given in *Contra*

[22] Tcherikover 1959 (n. 10), pp. 272–273, 320ff.

[23] *Op. cit.*, pp. 254ff.

[24] For more details, see Kasher, *op. cit., passim*.

[25] See e.g. § I, 201: ἐμοῦ γοῦν etc.

[26] J. H. Levy, Studies in Jewish Hellenism, Jerusalem 1960 (Hebrew), p. 57.

[27] See S. Mandelkern, Veteris Testamenti Concordantiae Hebraicae atque Chaldaicae, Tel Aviv 1959, II, s. v. משלם, p. 1481; M. Kennedy, s. v. 'Meshulam', Anchor Bible Dictionary, IV (1992), pp. 712–714.

Apionem.[28] Josephus cites the name one other time, but in a slightly different spelling – Μεσσάλαμος, Μεσσαλόμος.[29] It also figures in the Elephantine papyri,[30] as well as in Rabbinic sources (the *Mishnah* and the *Tosephta*).[31] In my opinion, the mention of Mosollamus by name is intended to give this description the reliability of an actual event which Hecataeus himself witnessed. This is also true with regard to another story, ascribed to Hecataeus, on the emigration to Egypt of the "chief priest" Ezechias and his men after the battle of Gaza in 312 BCE, which is quoted by Josephus in close connection (I, 184–189).

In the introductory words to the story at hand Josephus says that Hecataeus "attests the share which the Jews took in the campaigns both of King Alexander and of his successors" (§ I, 200). Unfortunately, he did not specify who were those successors (i.e. Diadochi). It appears, however, that by attributing the information to Hecataeus, he was first of all making indirect reference to Ptolemy I, in whose days the aforementioned Ezechias the "chief priest" and his men emigrated to Egypt and probably founded a military settlement there.[32] But as he noted "successors" in the plural, we must take into account at least one more king. Regrettably, there is not enough information to confirm such a conclusion. On another occasion, however, Josephus spoke of similar Jewish military service under Seleucus I Nicator,[33] but without giving details on the source of his information. This, I feel, could scarcely have been Hecataeus, as he was well known for his service and affinity to the Ptolemies.

To return to the matter at hand: Hecataeus' story indicates that the military unit in which Mosollamus served was a "barbarian" one – that is, a non-Greek one. Although there is no clear indication whether or not it was a Jewish unit by origin, it is quite reasonable to assume that Mosollamus was not the only Jew to have served in it. The existence of ethnically mixed units in a Hellenistic army is well known from Ptolemaic Egypt, and this is no less true as far as Jewish soldiers are concerned.[34] As for the case at hand, many scholars have been aware of the excellence of Eastern peoples at archery in war.[35] Jews were no

---

28 See that appearing in I Chronicles 3:19.

29 Ant. Jud., XIII, 75.

30 See e.G. E.G. Kraeling, The Brooklyn Museum Aramaic Papyri, Yale University, New Haven 1953, Nos. 2, 5, 7.

31 mTerumoth IV:7; tDemai III:1 (M. S. Zuckermandel ed., p. 49); for more details, see R. Zadok, The Pre-Hellenistic Israelite Anthroponymy and Prosopography, Leuven 1988, p. 125 (cf. Alphabetical List [s. v.], pp. 435–436).

32 This is mentioned in close connection with the Mosollamus story; see Contra Apionem, I, 186–189; Kasher 1985 (n. 15 above), p. 188. On the first Jewish military units to serve under the Ptolemies, see also A. Kasher, 'First Jewish Military Units in Ptolemaic Egypt', Journal of the Study of Judaism in the Persian, Hellenistic and Roman Period, 9 (1978), pp. 57–67.

33 Ant. Jud., XII, 119.

34 Kasher 1985 (n. 15), pp. 38ff.

35 As there is no reason to list all of them here, I would refer the readers first to the Bible

exception to this; indeed, no small number of Biblical quotations indicate the excellence of Jewish archers, starting in rather ancient times; the most outstanding of these appear to have been members of the tribe of Benjamin.[36] Josephus, too, appears to have been well aware of Jews' skillful use of the sling and the bow from earliest times; see e.g. his description of Moses' war against the Amorite King Sihon, which, in this matter, does not correspond to the Biblical account.[37] In any event, Mosollamus' skill as a mounted archer is in line with the later information concerning a certain Zamaris and the soldiers under his command, who were Jewish mounted archers from Babylonia in the service of King Herod.[38] The combination of cavalrymen and archers was often an obvious tactical conclusion in order to meet the requirements of great mobility, speed and effective "fire".[39] It is, of course, important to emphasize that Jews were renowned professionally as archers and slingshooters in early Hasmonaean times, as have already been proved by B. Bar-Kochva.[40] Problematically, however, Bar-Kochva has also stated the opinion that there were no Jewish mounted archers before the time of Pseudo-Hecataeus, or as he has put it, not before the first years of Alexander Jannaeus' rule.[41] This obviously conflicts with his own position, because he himself admitted the existence of Jewish cavalry units (not just individual cavalrymen) as early as the times of Judas Maccabaeus, as may be plainly seen from his excellent analysis of the battles of Marisa and Elasa.[42]

My discussion so far has been dedicated to the question of historiographic authenticity proper. In my opinion, however, not only can the information ascribed to Hecataeus be defined as authentic on purely historiographic grounds; it is precisely the philosophical justifications which may convincingly

---

which states for example that Ishmael "dwelt in the wilderness and became a bowman" (Genesis 21:2), and that Esau was also an accomplished archer (Genesis 27:3). A scholarly work on this Eastern art of war, see e.g. Y. Yadin, Torat ha-Milhamah be-Artzot ha-Mikra, Ramat-Gan 1963, esp. pp. 18ff., 94ff., 295ff.; indem, s.v. נשק (weapons), Encyclopaedia Biblica, V, cols. 949ff., 970ff. (Hebrew).

[36] See: Genesis 49:23-24; Iudges, 20:16; I Samuel 2:4; 18:4; 31:3; II Samuel 1:18,22; 22:35; II Kings 6:22; 9:24; 13:15-18; Hosea 1:5; Amos 2:15; Zechariah 9:10,13; 10:4; I Chronicles 5:18; 8:40; 10:3; 12:2; II Chronicles 14:7; 17:17; 26:14-15; Nehemiah 4:7; 10; cf. H. Raviv, s.v. צבא (army), Encyclopaedia Biblica, VI (1972), cols. 651ff. (Hebrew).

[37] cf. Ant. Jud. IV, 91–92. the duel between David and Goliath may also illustrate this; cf. Ant. Jud., VI, 185, 189.

[38] See Antiquities, XVII, 23–27; S. Applebaum, 'The Troops of Zamaris', Studies in the History of the Land of Israel, I (1970), pp. 79–88 (Hebrew); G. M. Cohen, 'The Hellenistic Military Colony: A Herodian Example, TAPA, CIII (1972), pp. 83–95.

[39] For a detailed account of the important role played by archers and mounted archers in, for example, the Seleucid army, see B. Bar-Kochva, Judas Maccabaeus. The Jewish Struggle against the Seleucids, Cambridge 1989, *passim*.

[40] Cf. I Maccabees 10:73,80; see also Bar-Kochva, *op. cit.*, 68, 72, 74 etc.

[41] See Bar Kochva, *op. cit.*, p. 74, n. 19.

[42] Bar-Kochva, *op. cit.*, pp. 69–71, 77–78, 82, 393, 395, 398.

link that information to him. This link, I feel, has been admirably formulated by two scholars: J.H. Levy and Y. Gutman,[43] whose viewpoint I shall therefore adopt in my discussion below. In other words, I am inclined to think that the historiographic arguments are not so much decisive in this case as the philosophical ones.

The Mosollamus story states that, while the army (probably of Alexander) was on the march, "the whole force was being held up by a seer who was taking the auspices" (§ I, 202). The taking of auspices is known in the Greek world as early as Homer.[44] A special body of priests called augures, whose function was to observe the flight of birds (*auspicium* = *avis-spicium*) and use it to interpret the position of the gods vis-à-vis certain actions and decisions in matters of state, is known to have existed in ancient Rome.[45] Also worthy of notice is the fascinating testimony given by Celsus in the third century CE (!), which made mention of the common pagan belief in the ability of various animals, especially birds, to foretell the future.[46] But this phenomenon was not only well known in Rome, it was actively controlled and limited by the Emperors altogether.[47] The phenomenon of seers watching the flight of birds appears to have been common among pagan Eastern peoples as well, and one may even go so far as to show that portents related to encounters with birds (ravens), a significant number of which are mentioned in literature, are frequently cited in contexts involving large groups of people such as armies, as in the case at hand.[48] Anyone studying the history of Alexander the Great will find that various visionaries, prophets, soothsayers and seers were closely involved in his world.[49] This very fact adds to the reliability of the testimony before us, as we shall see below. The instructions of the seer – that "if it [the bird] stayed in that spot it was expedient for them all to halt; if it stirred and flew forward, to advance; if backward, then to retire" (§ I, 203) – are very picturesque and recall the abovementioned reference from Homer.[50] Moreover, it appears that the various histories of Alexander include

[43] J. H. Levy 1960 (n. 27 above), pp. 56ff.; Y. Gutman 1958 (n. 10 above), I, pp. 66ff.

[44] Iliad, I, 69–72; cf. II, 358; VIII, 241–251; XV, 160ff.; Odyssey, II, 146ff. On the antiquity of Greek literary traditions with regard to auspices of this kind, see J. G. Müller, Des Flavius Josephus Schrift Gegen den Apion, Text und Erklärung aus dem Nachlass, Basel 1877, p. 178; N. Spiegel, Homer, Jerusalem 1989, pp. 240–241, 313–314 (Hebrew); cf. Stern 1974 (n. 10 above), I, p. 44.

[45] See M. Gil, 'Augures, Soothsayrs etc.', Commentationes Ad Antiquitatem Classicam Eiusque Hereditatem Pertinentes, Docto Viro Emerito Shalom Perlman, Tel Aviv 1989, pp. 74ff. (Hebrew), including considerable information and bibliographical references.

[46] Celsus, The True Doctrine, IV, 86, 88.

[47] See R. MacMullen, Enemies of the Roman Order: Treason, Unrest, and Alienation in the Empire, Cambridge Mass. 1966, pp. 147–148.

[48] See Y. Avishur, Phoenician Inscriptions and the Bible, Jersualem 1979, pp. 25ff.

[49] See Arrian, I, 11; II, 18, 26–27; III, 2–3, 7, 16; IV; 4, 13; V, 2; VI, 3, 19; VII 1, 11, 16, 18; Plutarch, Alexander, 2–3, 14, 24–27, 31, 33, 37, 50, 52, 57, 73–75.

[50] Iliad, XII, 237–240.

a number of cases involving quite similar motifs. This may (and, I believe, should) increase the credibility of the testimony ascribed to Hecataeus. Thus for example, on one occasion, we find the story of Aristander, Alexander's favorite seer, which mentions an eagle whose flight directed the marching army toward the Persian enemy.[51] The literary *topos* of that story, as well as that of Mosollamus, are undoubtedly derived from Homer's epic poetry,[52] a fact which once more enhances the credibility of the story. Another, similar incident happened to Alexander in Egypt (!), during his desert march toward Amon's temple at the oasis of Siwah. Having lost his way, he believed that the divine gifts of two serpents would be able to show him the right way to go. In fact, the story on this incident is told in two versions; according to the second one, which was preferred by Arrian, Alexander was guided, not by serpents, but by two ravens, which flew before his army as guides.[53]

The Mosollamus story goes to state that "the Jew, without saying a word, drew his bow, shot and struck the bird, and killed it" (§ I, 203). There can be no doubt that, in this action, he was fulfilling the Biblical precept with regard to seers, diviners, magicians, witches and wizards.[54] But as one may rightly cast doubts on the possibility that Hecataeus was familiar with this Biblical law, it is logical to think that he could have in mind some Greek tradition which denounces the taking of auspices. It is illustrative, and therefore worth emphasizing here, that already Homer expressed sarcastic scepticism with reference to this practice.[55] Indeed, Mosollamus, according to the story, did not content himself with the act of killing the bird, but also mocked the seer. More than that, Levy has shown that his philosophical derision is in line with similar motifs in the writings of Greek philosophers dating from Hecataeus' day (!), and that the Jew's position, superior to that of any magician, corresponded with that of the enlightened Greeks of his time.[56] As stated above, the Stoic concept held that the birds themselves were not capable of prophecy or divination; rather, it was the gods who conveyed knowledge of the future through them. In my opinion, this subtle distinction provides reasonable grounds for understanding Mosollamus' (or rather Hecataeus') derision;[57] after all, anyone capable of ascribing the gift of foretelling to birds (rather than to the gods) must have been an utter

---

51 See PLUTARCH, Alexander, 33.

52 Cf. also Odyssey, XII, 201, 218–219.

53 ARRIAN, III, 3; cf. also PLUTARCH, Alexander, 27.

54 See Leviticus 20:6; Numbers 23:23; Deuteronomy 18:10-14; cf. Numbers 20:6ff; Joshua 13:22; I Samuel 28:3ff.

55 See e.g. Iliad, XII, 237–240; cf. Odyssey, II, 157ff.

56 J.H. LEVY 1960 (n. 27), p. 56; cf. also E.S. GRUEN, 'Response', in: E. Gabba, Greek Knowledge of Jews up to Hecataeus of Abdera (Berkely: Center for Hermeneutical Studies), 1981, pp. 15–18.

57 On Josephus' own derision with regard to seers and soothsayers, see Contra Apionem, I, 259.

fool. Feldman, who followed Levy in this matter, believed the tale to be very reminiscent of that stated by Diogenes Laertius (6, 24) with reference to the opinion of Diogenes the Cynic on fortune-tellers, and therefore claimed that the story had a typically authentic Hellenistic air.[58] In addition to these convincing arguments, let us note the interesting fact that, even among the events involving Alexander himself, we find evidence of similar philosophical derision, uttered by the renowned Indian gymnosophist Calanus;[59] this, in my opinion, adds even more credibility to the tale. It may also provide a response to the difficulty which Rappaport had in accepting the idea that Hecataeus presented the Macedonian army as a pack of fools, by contrast to Mosollamus the wise Jew.[60] At first glance, it might seem possible to argue that the real Hecataeus could not have permitted himself such a belittling attitude with regard to the prophetic characteristics of birds, as this would appear to contradict his own words on the swans dedicated to Apollo in the temple of the Hyperboreans. Such an argument may be countered by stating that, in fact, Hecataeus did not credit the swans themselves with prophecy; rather, he believed that only the god knew what the future held, and that it was he, through the swans, who passed that information on to humanity. As this is a typical Stoic viewpoint, it certainly does not contradict with the expression of derision with reference to the belief that birds could tell the future. In any event, the examples discussed above speak for themselves, and give the story ascribed to Hecataeus a more comprehensible character.

Josephus seems to have been using the story as a proud presentation of the Jewish faith, whose norms in this matter dated back to antiquity. He could have expected that Roman reservations with regard to augury, especially in his time (see above), might cherish sympathy to Judaism through the story and its philosophical messages, at least in the hearts of his educated Roman readers. It sounds no less reasonable that he desired to phrase his criticism of fortune-telling indirectly through Hecataeus, but in accordance with the norms acceptable to the Roman authorities of his day. I personally feel that the story also constitutes a sort of indirect propagandist response (by Josephus) to the libel that the Jews were given to "*barbara superstitio*".

---

[58] Feldman 1993 (n. 2 above), p. 464, n. 24.

[59] Cf. § I, 179. Calanus is the name of a famous Indian gymnosophist and ascetic, who impressed Alexander the Great and his army with his asceticism and willingness to die for his ideals; in the end, he actually did die for them (at the stake). Strabo (Geographica, XVI, 1, 4; 64) referred to him by the Greek term "sophist" and assigned him to a group known as "the philosophers of India" (*op. cit.*, 68). Philo of Alexandria (Quod Omnis Probus Liber Sit, 92–96) praised him as a man whose philosophical behavior proved him to be the type whose free will was in control of his body; see also Arrian, VII, 3; 18; Plutarch, Alexander, 64–65; 69; for additional details on Calanus, see W. Kroll, s. v. 'Kalanos', Realencyclopädie der klassischen Altertumswissenschaft (eds. A. Pauly, G. Wissowa *et al.*), X (1919), cols. 1544 ff.

[60] Rappaport 1965 (n. 9 above), p. 143.

The Textual Tradition of Pseudo-Orpheus: Walter or Riedweg?

by

CARL R. HOLLADAY

Among the many intriguing questions relating to the study of the Jewish pseudepigraphical text Pseudo-Orpheus, none is more pressing than the history of its textual tradition. It is perhaps the most pressing question, since it directly affects so many other interpretive "cruxes" in this fascinating text. With the appearance in 1993 of Christoph Riedweg's *Jüdisch-hellenistische Imitation eines orphischen Hieros Logos*, the whole question is re-opened.[1] Because this monograph offers a fresh interpretation that challenges many previously held positions, it deserves a close look.

Summary of Riedweg's Interpretation

Before evaluating Riedweg's textual theory, we should note the main features of his overall interpretation. This can most easily be done with reference to his stemma (p. 177), which is provided here as Appendix 1.

After listing the relevant textual witnesses and briefly characterizing them (pp. 6–8), Riedweg examines their distinctive textual features, on the basis of which he determines their interrelationship (pp. 9–23). In evaluating the textual witnesses, one of his most important decisions is to accept, at face value, Eusebius' testimony in *P. E.* 13.12.5 that the long version of the poem was quoted by Aristobulus. Accordingly, this version of the poem (which I designate EusA) is dated ca. 150 B. C. E., after which it was transmitted unchanged to Eusebius and later used by both Theodoret (= Thdrt) and Theosophia Tubingensis (which I designate TTu). This gives EusA pride of place as the earliest witness to the poem.

[1] C. RIEDWEG, Jüdisch-hellenistische Imitation eines orphischen Hieros Logos. Beobachtungen zu OF 245 und 247 (sog. Testament des Orpheus). Classica Monacensia. Münchener Studien zur Klassischen Philologie. Münchener Universitätsschriften. Philosophische Fakultät. Bd. 7. Tübingen 1993.

A second crucial decision is made by Riedweg in determining the relationship between Pseudo-Justin *De Monarchia* (= *Mon.*) and *Cohortatio ad Graecos* (which I here designate *Coh.*, although Riedweg prefers the title *Ad Graecos de vera religione)*.[2] He thinks that *Mon.* was a Jewish composition written in either the first century B.C.E. or the first century C.E, thus the earliest witness that preserves the shorter version of the poem.[3] Even though Theophilus *Ad Autolycum* 3.2 does not constitute a witness in the sense that it preserves verses of the poem, Riedweg thinks its brief reference to Orpheus reflects dependence on *Mon.* Because of its derivative character, its testimony is secondary. (This becomes an important consideration in his discussion of the the genre of the work, pp. 44–55.) For *Coh.*, Riedweg accepts the more conventional view that it was an early fourth century Christian work that preserves *Mon.*'s shorter version of the poem, more or less unchanged.[4] (Riedweg explains *Mon.*'s omission of the two opening lines found in *Coh.* as historical accident, and thus inconsequential for determining their relationship to each other.) A direct line is then drawn from *Coh.* to Cyril, thereby accounting for the unusually large number of distinctive readings that these two witnesses have in common.

Thus, what emerges are two separate streams of tradition that transmit the longer and shorter version of the poem – the Aristobulus-Eusebius-Theodoret tradition, on the one side, and the Pseudo-Justin – Theophilus – Cyril tradition, on the other.

Riedweg thinks both streams of tradition stem ultimately from a single version of the poem – the "Urfassung" (designated "A" in the stemma). As reconstructed by Riedweg, "A" comprises some twenty-six hexameters, about five more than occur in the shorter Ps.-Justin version (reconstructed "Urfassung" text, translation, and critical notes, pp. 26–31).[5] Riedweg's analysis of

---

[2] See C. Riedweg, Ps.-Justin (Markell von Ankyra?), Ad Graecos de vera religione (bisher 'Cohortatio ad Graecos'). Einleitung und Kommentar. Schweizerische Beiträge zur Altertumswissenschaft, Bd. 25. Basel/Berlin 1995.

[3] This early dating for *Mon.* is worked out by Riedweg in his Ps.-Justin (see n. 2). A third century C.E. dating is accepted by M. Marcovich, Pseudo-Iustinus, Cohortatio ad Graecos, De Monarchia, Oratio ad Graecos. Patristische Texte und Studien, 32. Berlin/New York 1990, 82.

[4] More specifically, he dates *Coh.* around the time of the composition of Eusebius *P.E.*, i.e., between 312–322 C.E. See Imitation, 7.

[5] No uniform system of numbering the verses has been developed. In this paper, I use the numbering scheme from my edition of Pseudo-Orpheus in Fragments from Hellenistic Jewish Authors, vol. 4 (= FHJA 4), forthcoming in the Society of Biblical Literature Texts and Translations (Pseudepigrapha) Series, Atlanta 1996. My numbering system corresponds to that used in A.-M. Denis, Fragmenta pseudepigraphorum quae supersunt Graeca ... Leiden 1970; also, N. Walter, "Pseudepigraphische jüdisch-hellenistische Dichtung: Pseudo-Phokylides, Pseudo-Orpheus, Gefälschte Verse auf Namen griechischer Dichter," in: W.G. Kümmel, et al., eds., Jüdische Schriften aus hellenistisch-römischer Zeit, Bd. 4, "Poetische Schriften", Lfg. 3, Gütersloh 1983, 173–278, esp. 217–43. To facilitate referring to Riedweg, when appropriate I have enclosed his equivalent verse numbers in parentheses. Since he numbers

this "Urfassung" convinces him that it is a sophisticated poetic composition reflecting intimate familiarity with the Greek epic tradition (pp. 64–69) and a pervasively Stoic outlook (pp. 62–64). Rather than classifying the poem as a "testament" given by Orpheus to his son Musaeus, Riedweg thinks it is best understood as an imitation of an earlier Orphic ἱερὸς λόγος with a formal structure reflecting the cultic setting of Hellenistic mystery initiation rites (pp. 44–55). Although based on an earlier pagan model, the "Urfassung" was composed by a Jewish author sometime around the end of the third century B. C. E. (pp. 55–62).

The "Urfassung" then moves in two directions. First, it undergoes extensive revision and expansion by a Jewish author/redactor, and what results is the "Aristobulische Überarbeitung", a poem consisting of forty-one hexameters (reconstructed text, translation, critical commentary, pp. 32–43). In its revised form the poem retains many of the epic features of the "Urfassung", but the quality of the poetry reflected in the redactional changes is not as high (pp. 69–73). More philosopher than poet, the author makes redactional changes that reflect a shift from a Stoic to a Platonic-Aristotelian point of view (pp. 79–95). Such heavy philosophical overlay, among other things, convinces Riedweg that the author is Aristobulus himself – a proposal that gives greater credibility to the persistent ancient tradition identifying Aristobulus as a Peripatetic philosopher (pp. 95–101).

In the second stream of tradition, the "Urfassung" retains its shorter form and undergoes less change. Between the time of its composition in the third century B. C. E. and its first citation in *Mon.*, Riedweg envisions a middle step – the composition of "α", an early copy of the "Urfassung." This hypothetical version retains several "better readings" of the "Urfassung", which are transmitted to Clement, but which disappear in *Mon.*-*Coh.*-Cyril (p. 18, esp. n. 61).

A third critical decision involves Riedweg's construal of Clement's testimony (pp. 14–18). As other scholars have long recognized, Clement's scattered quotations of the poem tend to fall into two groups: those in *Strom.* 5.14.123.2–124.1 that tend to align with EusA, and those in *Protr.* 7.74.4–5; *Strom.* 5.78.4–5; 5.14.123.1; 126.5; 127.2 and 133.2 that tend to align with the shorter version of the poem in Pseudo-Justin.[6] But whereas other scholars, such

---

the verses of the "Urfassung" and the Aristobulus version consecutively, the same verse might have a different number in each version. For example, his v. 13 in the "Urfassung" (p. 26) becomes v. 16 (p. 32) in the Aristobulus version. In referring to RIEDWEG, I distinguish the "Urfassung" from the Aristobulus revision, which I designate as "AR". Thus, his v. 13 is (R v. 13) and (R AR v. 16) respectively.

[6] No scholarly consensus has been reached as to which Clement passages constitute the second group, but in his stemma on p. 24 Riedweg places the second group in a mediating position between "α" and Clement. In his classification of the Clement quotations, he basically follows DENIS and M. LAFARGUE, "Orphica", in: J. H. CHARLESWORTH, ed., The Old Testament Pseudepigrapha, 2 vols.; Garden City, N. Y. 1983–85, 2. 795–801, esp. p. 795. See

as Abel, Kern, and Walter, construe the Clement quotations as evidence for a separate recension, Riedweg does not.[7] Instead, he is only willing to use the Clement quotations as *indirect evidence* for establishing both the "Urfassung" and EusA (see p. 103). For him this is a critically important distinction, since he thinks that all of the verses (and consequently all the readings) found in Clement can be traced, in one way or another, either to EusA or to the "Urfassung". To be sure, Riedweg insists that Clement knew both EusA and the "Urfassung" – the former directly, and the latter indirectly through "α" (see pp. 18, 103).

One of the most important consequences of this construal of Clement is Riedweg's contention that Clement knew the longer version of the poem found in EusA. But, as scholars have long noticed, several verses that appear in EusA – most notably the verses referring to Moses (esp. vv. 41–42, but also vv. 2, 25–26, and possibly v. 9 = R AR vv. 37–38, 2, 21–22, and 9) – are nowhere quoted by Clement.[8] Quite naturally, Clement's omission of these verses requires some explanation, especially since one of his chief purposes in *Strom.* 5.14 is to demonstrate that Greeks derived their wisdom from Moses. But Riedweg is convinced that previous scholars, from Lobeck onward,[9] have overestimated the significance of Clement's omissions, while at the same time underestimating the importance of EusA as the earliest witness to the poem.

For the later stages of the textual history, Riedweg accepts the earlier scholarly consensus. The thirteen lines of the poem that occur in Theodoret show the closest correspondence with EusA, although there is also evidence of dependence on Clement. As is commonly agreed, TTu draws on virtually all of the previous witnesses in compiling its conflationary version of the poem.

Alternative Construals of The Textual History

In developing his theory of textual transmission, Riedweg rejects the notion of separate recensions.[10] Throughout his analysis he consistently avoids using

---

Denis, Fragmenta, 164; also, idem, Introduction pseudépigraphes grecs d'ancien testament, Leiden 1970, 232–33.

[7] See E. Abel, Orphica, Leipzig/Prague 1885, 144–148 (Frgs. 4–7); O. Kern, Orphicorum Fragmenta, Berlin 1922; Reprint 1963) 255–66 (Frgs. 245–47); N. Walter, Der Thoraausleger Aristobulos (TU, 86. Berlin 1964) 202–61; also idem, JSHRZ 4(3).217–43.

Riedweg, Imitation, 14 n. 49, notes that Kern, unlike Abel, gave up on the idea of trying to reconstruct a separate "Clement" recension.

[8] See Imitation, 4, where Riedweg notes the earlier observations of Lobeck, Elter, and Walter.

[9] C. A. Lobeck, Aglaophamus, Königsberg 1829; Reprint. Darmstadt 1961, 447.

[10] In his summary (Imitation, 102), Riedberg characterizes the current dominant view as one envisioning two independent recensions ("zwei eigenständige Rezensionen"), which are finally synthesized by TTu. Yet those who propose two or more different recensions ordinarily

"recension" terminology, preferring instead to speak of an "Urfassung" (presumably best understood as an early version) and the "Aristobulische Überarbeitung" (presumably best rendered as the Aristobulus revision, which I designate AR). While critical of a number of earlier proposals, he challenges in particular Walter's four-stage recensional history because of its far-reaching influence in shaping recent scholarly opinion concerning the textual history.[11]

Since Riedweg intends for his proposal to serve as an alternative to the more widely accepted model, especially as articulated by Walter, that envisions two or more recensions, these two alternative ways of construing the textual history invite comparison.

As noted earlier, the critically important element in the comparison is Clement's testimony. To facilitate the discussion, I have prepared the table in Appendix 3 where the witnesses are aligned in order to highlight Clement's "middle position". On the left side I have placed the testimony from Pseudo-Justin in the chronological order proposed by Riedweg. Clement's *Protr.* precedes *Strom.* since it was composed earlier. I have placed EusA in the next column to represent the other stream of tradition – the left side of Riedweg's stemma. The final two columns – Cyril and Theodoret – are contemporaries, although Riedweg dates *Graecarum affectionum curatio* before 431 C.E. and *Contra Julianum* before 441/42 C.E. But since the readings in Cyril are more directly relevant to this comparison, I have placed them next, followed by Theodoret. I have not included TTu in this table, since its readings, as a rule, are not germane to this comparison.

The variants listed in the table are those most relevant for this comparison. Riedweg discusses most of them, often at some length, which tends to confirm that they are the decisive pool of variants that must be taken into account by anyone attempting to address this problem.

As an alternative to Riedweg's theory, I propose a modified version of Walter's four-stage recensional scheme, which is represented in the stemma in Appendix 2. Essentially, I accept Walter's basic construal of the recensional history – an evolutionary development of the poem, each stage of which is seen as a separate recension. But I disagree with Walter in the following respects: (1) I am not convinced that it is necessary to posit a separate Stoicizing recension – Walter's Recension X – between Recensions A & B. There are clearly Stoicizing features in Recension B not found in Recension A, but I attribute these to

see them as having gone through redactional stages; e.g., DENIS, Inroduction, 233–35. Even though LAFARGUE, OTP, 2.795–96, conceives of the recensional history quite differently as one in which the longer version was shortened for theological reasons, he does not envision independent recensions.

[11] WALTER's four-stage model was originally worked out in Thoraausleger, 202–261, but refined in JSHRZ 4(3).217–43, where separate translations of Recensions A, B, and C are given, with extensive annotations documenting the redactional changes at each stage.

the author/redactor of Recension B. (2) Nor am I convinced, as Walter is (following Elter), that it is necessary to date Recension C between the time of Clement and Eusebius.[12] I think it is possible to date Recension C as early as 150 B.C.E., and see it as directly transmitted to Eusebius. (3) Naturally this means that I also disagree with Walter's dating of Recension B. Whereas he allows a first-, perhaps second-, century C.E. dating, probably prior to the time of Trajan, I would date it prior to 150 B.C.E. (4) Similarly, whereas Walter dates Recension A in the mid- to late first century B.C.E., I think it can be dated between the late third century and early second century B.C.E.

I do agree, however, with Walter's classification of the Clement material, at least in the modified form that appears in JSHRZ. The passages that reflect Clement's use of the shorter recension (Recension A) are: *Strom.* 5.12.78.4 (the version reading τέτυκται); 5.14.126.5, 127.2, and 133.2. (These he designates "A'".) The passages that reflect Clement's use of Recension B are: *Protr.* 7.74.4–5; *Strom.* 5.12.78.4 (the version with πέφυκεν); 5.12.78.5; 5.14.123.1–2 and 124.1. (These he designates "B".)

Thus I accept the widely held view that Clement had before him at least two, possibly more, recensions of the poem. Moreover, I agree with Walter that these two recensions are basically represented in Recensions A and B.

Thus, in certain respects, I tend to agree more with Riedweg's stemma, namely, in dating the original composition of the poem, and its editorial expansion(s), in the Hellenistic period. In this sense, my Recension A roughly corresponds to his "Urfassung" "A", and my Recension C would roughly correspond to his "Aristobulische Überarbeitung". But I am not convinced that Recension C was composed by Aristobulus himself. Forced to choose, I would be inclined to argue that Recension B is the version originally quoted by Aristobulus; that it underwent another stage of revision shortly thereafter, and that this revision was transmitted to Eusebius. This refinement would be required by the indisputable fact that Clement not only knows Aristobulus but quotes him extensively.[13] I simply find it incredible that Clement knew the longer version that now appears in EusA and omitted, for whatever reason, the Moses verses. The reasons for this I will indicate below.

But, in one sense, the dating of the various recensions can be separated from the question of the recensional model itself. The essential question I wish to pursue here is which of the two models better explains the textual history. Is it

---

[12] Denis, Introduction, 233, agrees with Walter that Recension C, or what he designates the "Aristobulus-Eusebius-*Theosophia*", postdates Clement.

[13] Clement's testimonia for Aristobulus include Strom. 1.15.72.4; 1.22.150.1; 5.14.97.7; 6.3.32.5. He quotes portions of Aristobulus in Strom. 1.22.150.1–3 (Frg. 3.1) and 6.3.32.5–33.1 (Frg. 2.14–15). The following passages also reflect Clement's dependence on Aristobulus: Strom. 5.14.99.3 (Frg. 4.4); 5.14.107.1–4 (Frg. 5.13–16); 6.16.137.4–138.4 (Frg. 5.9–11); 6.16.141.7b–142.1 (Frg. 5.11); 6.16.142.4b (Frg. 5.13); also, probably 5.14.101.4b (Frg. 4.7) and Protr. 7.73.2a (Frg. 4.7). See Walter, Thoraausleger, 107–8.

more convincing to construe the Clement material as evidence pointing to a separate recension, that represents, in some sense, a middle stage of development between a shorter version of the poem that appears in Pseudo-Justin (Recension A; or Riedweg's "Urfassung") and the longer version, including the Moses sections, that appears in Eusebius (Recension C; or Riedweg's "Aristobulische Überarbeitung")? (Since the version of the poem in TTu is not directly germane to this discussion, I will refer hereafter to this first model as the three-recension model.) Or, is Riedweg's model, which uses Clement only as *indirect evidence* for reconstructing either the "Urfassung" or the "Aristobulische Überarbeitung" more convincing?[14]

We can begin by examining several features of Riedweg's reconstruction of the "Urfassung".

(1) In v. 7 (R v. 6) he adopts the reading εὖ δ' ἐπίβαινε, which is read by Clement in both *Protr.* 7.74.4 and *Strom.* 5.14.123.1, as well as EusA, whereas the MS tradition for Ps.-Justin reads εὖ τ' ἐπίβαινε. By proposing that εὖ δ' ἐπίβαινε was originally read in "α" (and, by extension, in "A" as well), and that it passed from there to Clement, one must explain what accounts for its change to εὖ τ' ἐπίβαινε in *Mon.*, and its retention by *Coh.* Moreover, εὖ δ' ἐπίβαινε appears in Cyril as an undisputed reading. Since Cyril is directly dependent on *Coh.*, how does one account for the change back to the earlier form? Presumably not on the basis of Cyril's knowledge of Clement, since the stemma shows no connection between Clement and Cyril. Riedweg (following Walter and Marcovich) suggests that this is a case where Cyril probably preserves the better reading, which originally stood in the "Urfassung", and that both *Mon.* and *Coh.* should be emended accordingly (cf. p. 28). Even if this is the case, one must still explain how εὖ δ' ἐπίβαινε is originally read in the "Urfassung" (and "α"), is then changed to εὖ τ' ἐπίβαινε, and then changed back in Cyril.

In my stemma, this variant would be tracked as follows: εὖ τ' ἐπίβαινε first occurs in *Mon.* and *Coh.*, is modified by the redactor of Recension B (which Clement uses in both *Protr.* 7.74.4 and *Strom.* 5.14.123.1), and is retained in Recension C. As with Riedweg's model, accounting for Cyril's reading poses a difficulty. If it is not to be explained as owing to the interchangeability of δ' and τ', this may be a case suggesting Cyril's knowledge of either Clement or Eusebius.

(2) In v. 9 (R v. 7a) Riedweg includes ἀθάνατον as part of the "Urfassung",

---

[14] Although eschewing the notion of two separate recensions, and preferring to speak instead of versions or "Fassungen", RIEDWEG's textual theory does not appear to be that different in its fundamental conception from other two-recension models. Like LAFARGUE, for example, he still works with the notion of a "shorter" and "longer" form of the poem. And quite clearly, since the Aristobulus revision is understood as a reworked expansion of the "Urfassung", they are genetically connected. In this respect, therefore, his model does not differ radically from that of many of his predecessors.

even though it is not attested in the MS tradition of Ps.-Justin. Moreover, he supplies the rest of the verse as a conjectural addition drawn from EusA.

This decision to include ἀθάνατον, which is absent in both *Mon.* and *Coh.*, and occurs as the only word quoted from this verse in *Protr.* 7.74.4 and *Strom.* 5.14.123.1, once again, is explained on the basis that it, along with the rest of the verse, belonged to the "Urfassung", as well as to "α". From there it was transmitted to Clement in its partial form, and to Aristobulus in its full form, although in Aristobulus there is a word change from ἄνακτα to τυπωτήν in the immediately preceding verse. Assuming that it was present in "α", it then drops out in *Mon.*, which would explain its absence in both *Coh.* and Cyril. This is one of those instances noted by Riedweg where Pseudo-Justin does not preserve the full version of the "Urfassung", although there is no explanation as to why this particular verse might have been omitted.

It is worth noting that the section of the poem cited by Clement in *Protr.* 7.74.4 consists of the first seven verses that correspond to the first seven verses in *Coh.*, and that the quotation in *Strom.* 5.123.1 consists of the last three verses of this same section; in both cases, the section concludes with ἀθάνατον, the first word of a verse that does not appear in *Coh.* (or *Mon.*). Clement's decision to quote only the first word of the next line requires no special explanation. In such cases, it is quite appropriate to break off a quotation in the middle of a line, especially when it is the last word of a sentence, as is the case here.

But the absence of the entire verse in *Mon.* (and subsequently *Coh.*) does require explanation, precisely for the same reason. If v. 9 (R v. 7a) were present in the "Urfassung" (and subsequently in "α"), for the author of *Mon.* to omit the entire verse, it was necessary to interrupt the sentence, breaking it off after ἄνακτα. I find it easier to believe that the author's inclination would have been to complete the sentence, thus adding ἀθάνατον; and, if παλαιὸς δὲ λόγος περὶ τοῦδε φαείνει constituted the remainder of the verse, to include it, if for no other reason because it would give added authority to the following statements about the one, inscrutable God. Pitifully little would be required to include an additional verse within a nineteen-verse quotation, especially if it occurs in the middle of the quotation. By contrast, it would be much easier to omit the verse if it were at the beginning or the end of the quotation, as would be the case with vv. 41, 43, 46 (R vv. 21a, 21b, 21c), which Riedweg includes in the "Urfassung".

Alternatively, on the three-recension model, ἀθάνατον (and the remainder of v. 9) is absent in Recension A, which accounts for its absence in *Mon.* and *Coh.*, and subsequently in Cyril. Without ἀθάνατον, v. 8 forms a complete, meaningful sentence. But the editor of Recension B then adds v. 9, and does so by supplying ἀθάνατον as a suitable ending to the sentence begun in v. 8. The motivation for adding the sentence would be to enhance the claim in the following verses with an introductory reference to an "ancient saying". The entire verse then passes unaltered to Recension C.

(3) In v. 11 (R v. 9) Riedweg reads περινίσσεται, which is found in Clement *Protr.* 7.74.5, and also EusA, whereas the uncontested MS tradition for Pseudo-Justin reads περιγίνεται. He proposes that περινίσσεται was the original reading in the "Urfassung", that it was transmitted to "α" (from which Clement *Protr.* 7.74.5 derives it); that it was then changed to περιγίνεται in *Mon.*, then transmitted to *Coh.*, and finally to Cyril.

Quite obviously, Riedweg's decision to read περινίσσεται (along with his emendation of v. 24 [R v. 16]) contributes significantly to his interpretation of the "Urfassung" as a pervasively Stoic composition.

But some explanation is required for why περινίσσεται is changed to περιγίνεται in *Mon.* To account for the change, Riedweg suggests that it might have been an attempt, influenced by Heraclitus 22 B 114 D.-K., to stress God's transcendent, exalted position over the cosmos as a way of correcting the Stoic stress on immanence in the "Urfassung" (p. 29). To be sure, it would have this effect. But if a Jewish author of *Mon.*, who is presumably transmitting a version of the poem that is otherwise pervasively Stoic, and does so approvingly, felt the need to change περινίσσεται to περιγίνεται to protect God's transcendent status, presumably Aristobulus himself, who was consciously modifying the "Urfassung" from a Stoic to a more thoroughgoing Platonic/Aristotelian viewpoint, might have felt the same urge to do so. And yet, περινίσσεται is retained in Riedweg's Aristobulus version.

Using the three-recension model, this reading would be tracked as follows: περιγίνεται occurs in the earliest recension, and fits the context, which stresses the inscrutability, as well as the transcendent character of God. As the poem moves through the tradition, its change to περινίσσεται in Recension B reflects a Stoicizing tendency that is also present in other ways, e.g., the portrait of Abraham as one who comes to know God through natural revelation. This reading is retained in Recension C. Cyril's reading of περιγίνεται would still be explained as owing to his direct dependence on Ps.-Justin.[15]

(4) Riedweg's decision to read εἰνὶ in v. 34 (R v. 18) obviously provides a metrically suitable form in the "Urfassung", and would naturally account for its presence in the Aristobulus version. That some witnesses saw the need to supply this form is seen by its presence in *Mon.* MS q, EusA, and Cyril. Elsewhere, ἐνὶ is read: *Coh.* and Clement *Strom.* 5.14.124.1.

But the question is whether the correct form was in the "Urfassung" from the outset, and was later misread by various copyists, or whether it was absent initially and tended to be corrected later. One difficulty with Riedweg's propos-

[15] RIEDWEG, Imitation, 13 n. 43, notes the fluctuation within the Cyril MS tradition: περιγί(γ) νεται MN(?) C VB F[2]: περινίσσεται EP F. RIEDWEG suggests that TTu might have written περινίσσεται into his Cyril MS, thereby introducing this reading into the Cyril MS tradition. But the variations within the Cyril MS tradition might simply reflect awareness of differences within the two streams of the tradition.

al to read it in the "Urfassung", and presumably in "α", is how one explains its subsequent history through Pseudo-Justin and Cyril. Both forms are present in the *Mon.* tradition: ἐνὶ in s and εἰνὶ in q; but the form that is passed on to *Coh.* is ἐνὶ, which would presumably then pass to Cyril. But Cyril reads εἰνὶ, which would presumably require that he altered the reading he received from *Coh.* in order to supply the metrically correct form.

Given the MS evidence as it stands, instead of the improved readings suggested by subsequent editors, this variant would be more easily explained using the three-recension model: the metrically incorrect form ἐνί occurs in Recension A and is transmitted unchanged to Recension B. Noting the problem, the editor of Recension C supplies the metrically suitable form. Cyril makes a similar change.

These four cases, it seems to me, pose difficulties for Riedweg's theory of textual history. For one thing, they raise questions about "α" – his hypothetical early translation of the "Urfassung" – what might be termed a proto-*Mon.* version of the poem. While his positing such a document allows him to explain how some of the "better readings" that originally existed in the "Urfassung" show up in Clement, it also requires him to explain why these better readings become altered in *Mon.*, as well as why the entirety of v. 9 is omitted. The question here is whether positing such a hypothetical document creates more problems than it solves. I think it does.

What all four of these cases have in common, of course, is that they all, with the possible exception of #3, are instances where Clement and EusA tend to agree over against Pseudo-Justin. Another large group of readings are those where Pseudo-Justin and Clement tend to agree over against EusA. Here, there is less controversy about which model is more convincing, because, in a sense, both tend to explain the evidence the same way, namely, that these readings occurring in Pseudo-Justin are either confirmed in Clement (Riedweg) or are transmitted from Recension A to Recension B unchanged (the three-recension model), and then become modified in EusA. These can be rehearsed briefly.

(1) In v. 3, πάντες ὁμῶς, which occurs in *Coh.*, is retained in Clement *Protr.* 7.74.4 (and thus, in my view, Recension B), since the verse is unchanged. But the addition of verse 2 in EusA, which introduces the motif of God's having given the "ordinances of the just", requires that the beginning of v. 3 be changed to πᾶσιν ὁμοῦ.

(2) In v. 4, the future form ἐξερέω, which occurs in both *Mon.* and *Coh.*, is retained in Clement *Protr.* 7.74.4, but changed to the present form ἐξενέπω in EusA. It is a metrically suitable substitute, and there is no apparent reason for the change.

(3) The occurrence of ἰθύνων in v. 7 is a little different, because it is a case where Pseudo-Justin and EusA agree against Clement. It is probably best

explained as an instance where Clement, in both *Protr.* and *Strom.*, preserves a corrupt reading, and where EusA assists in confirming the correctness of the reading in Pseudo-Justin (so Riedweg, p. 16 n. 54).

(4) In v. 8, EusA's alteration of ἄνακτα to τυπωτήν is not easily explained, but no real explanation is required. Since the version of the poem in EusA introduces Moses as lawgiver, the shift in image from God as master to creator of the universe may be influenced by the biblical account of creation; or, as Riedweg suggests, it may just as easily be influenced by the Greek philosophical tradition (p. 82).

(5) V. 10 is a more complicated case, primarily because of the configuration of the evidence in Clement. For the most part, the pattern is the same as the other readings in this group: Pseudo-Justin and Clement agreeing over against EusA. But there are several questions, the first of which is the occurrence of αὐτοτελής in *Strom.* 5.12.78.4. Since αὐτογενής is read in *Protr.* 7.74.5, both Riedweg and Walter think that the same form should be read in *Strom.* 5.12.78.4, and that it is subsequently changed to αὐτοτελής in EusA. But I think it is plausible that Clement had αὐτογενής in his shorter recension (Recension A) and αὐτοτελής in his longer recension (Recension B), and that Recension C retained this form from Recension B.

Another question involves the well-known occurrence of πέφυκεν in *Strom.* 5.12.78.4, which Clement himself introduces as a variant reading of τέτυκται. As can be seen from the table, it occurs nowhere else. This may suggest that Clement had yet another recension before him; or, at least knew another recension. But another explanation is that πέφυκεν, along with αὐτοτελής, were read in Recension B, and that Recension C supplies τελεῖται as the metaphorically appropriate verb to go with αὐτοτελής.

(6) V. 12, in both the Pseudo-Justin and Clement quotations, retains the idea that God, though invisible, sees all. Whether Riedweg is right in seeing this as a motif present in the "Urfassung", that is confirmed in Clement, or, as I think, a motif present in Recension A that is retained in Recension B, clearly it undergoes significant change in EusA. Not reflected in the table is the variant involving ψυχήν, which is read by MS I, whereas ψυχῶν is read by MSS ON (this verse occurs in a section omitted by B). Mras adopts the former reading, suggesting that it be understood as an adverbial accusative, in which case, two modes of seeing God are being contrasted: "with the soul (ψυχή)", which is impossible, and "with the mind (νοῦς)", which is possible.[16] Riedweg rightly sees the change as influenced by the Greek philosophical tradition (pp. 83–84).

(7) V. 14 is instructive both in terms of its form and content. In the Pseudo-Justin MS tradition, the δ' following οὗτος is absent in *Coh.*, but read in MS q of

[16] K. Mras, Die Praeparatio Evangelica. Bd. 8, Eusebius Werke. GCS, 43. 2 vols. Berlin 1954–56. 2.192.

Mon. (the verse is omitted by MS s). Without the form, the line is metrically deficient, which may explain the change to αὐτὸς δὲ in Clement. This is almost another case that belongs to the previous category, where EusA and Clement agree over against Pseudo-Justin. Yet, since the only extant MS of *Mon.* that preserves the line reads οὗτος δ', it is a less clearcut case. One could then argue, on Riedweg's model, that δ' simply drops out in *Coh.* as a scribal mistake. Since the verse does not occur in Cyril, the error ends there.

In terms of its content, the verse, at least in some sense, portrays God as giving evil to mortals. According to Riedweg's explanation, this verse belongs to the "Urfassung", which is confirmed by its presence in *Strom.* 5.14.126.5, but is altered for theological, but primarily philosophical, reasons in EusA. Alternatively, I would argue that it was present in Recension A, altered slightly in Recension B (οὗτος or οὗτος δ' is changed to αὐτὸς δὲ, and δίδωσι is altered to φυτεύει), then altered substantially in Recension C.

Even though we will consider below the difficulties entailed in the claim that Clement knows EusA, it is worth noting that a similar problem exists here. When Clement cites this verse in *Strom.* 5.14.126.5, he does so with specific reference to Deut 32:39, where God is described as the one who kills and makes alive, smites and heals. In keeping with the pattern throughout this section of *Strom.*, Clement is showing how the biblical tradition is echoed in various Greek authors, in this case Orpheus. Presumably, had he known EusA, whose version of v. 14 vitiates this claim, this might have given him some pause in making such an unqualified comparison here.

(8) In v. 16 κρυόεντα καὶ, which occurs in both *Mon.* and *Coh.*, and also in Clement *Strom.* 5.14.126.5, is altered in EusA to accommodate the introduction of v. 15. Riedweg would see this as Aristobulus' expansion of the "Urfassung", whereas on the three-recension model it would be seen as Recension C's expansion, and corresponding modification, of Recension B.

(9) Similarly, in v. 17, in spite of the disparity within the readings of Pseudo-Justin, a similar pattern occurs. However one construes these variants, clearly Clement in *Strom.* 5.14.133.2 retains μεγάλου βασιλῆος, whereas the poem undergoes significant change in EusA, primarily to accommodate the introduction of new verses in vv. 18–20.

In yet a third category are the readings in vv. 33–36, primarily because in them Clement, in most cases, provides two separate versions of the readings in *Strom.* 5.14.124.1 and 5.14.127.2. As the table shows, in vv. 34–36, the readings in 5.14.124.1 tend to align with EusA, while those in 5.14.127.2 tend to align with Pseudo-Justin. For this reason, the readings in 5.14.127.2 are classified in the special cluster of Clement readings, designated by Walter as A' and by Denis and LaFargue as C^1, and are understood, on Riedweg's model, to confirm the readings of the "Urfassung", or, in the three-recension model, as present in Recension A, and thus known directly to Clement, or also present in

Recension B, and similarly known to Clement from this second source. Similarly, the readings in 5.14.124.1 are assigned to another group, designated "B" by Walter and C^2 by Denis and LaFargue.

What this doubtless means is that, at least for this later section of the poem, Clement has before him two recensions. According to Riedweg's model, the one set derives from the "Urfassung" via "α", the other set from EusA. According to the three-recension model, the one set Clement gets from Recension A, the other set from Recension B, the latter of which are transmitted, more or less unchanged, to Recension C.

Did Clement Know the Longer Version in EusA?

One of the most important features of Riedweg's theory of textual transmission is his claim that Clement knew the longer Aristobulus version of the poem. This would naturally explain why the "Abraham" section, which occurs in the Aristobulus version (vv. 27–31; R AR vv. 23–27), is found in Clement. But, as scholars have long noted, the "Moses" portions, which occur in the Aristobulus version (esp. vv. 41–42, but also vv. 2, 25–26, and perhaps v. 9; = R AR vv. 37–38, 2, 21–22, and v. 9), are not quoted by Clement.

Riedweg's explanation for the absence of these "Moses" verses in Clement has several elements (see esp. pp. 75–76, also p. 4). Riedweg frequently emphasizes that neither Clement nor Pseudo-Justin quote the poem in its entirety, and that Clement's pattern of quoting the poem is to do so in snippets – to quote lines here and there, sometimes one verse, sometimes a section of several verses, depending on the point he is trying to illustrate (see p. 18, n. 58; p. 103). Since Clement nowhere expressly says that he intends to quote the entire poem, nor even leaves the impression of intending to do so, as Eusebius does when he cites Aristobulus, Riedweg insists that Clement was under no obligation to quote every verse from the poem (p. 4). Moreover, to draw hard conclusions from such omissions has all the tenuousness associated with arguments from silence. In one instance, however, Riedweg does venture an explanation that was earlier proposed by Valckenaer: that Clement might have omitted vv. 41–42 (R AR vv. 36–37) because he found the reference to Moses too audacious in what they claimed (see p. 17, esp. n. 56).[17]

Riedweg is certainly correct to point to Clement's pattern of citing verses here and there from the poem. Were that the case uniformly, it would be easier to account for the "Moses" omissions as random occurrences. But if we closely examine Clement's pattern of quoting the poem, we discover that, other than those cases where he quotes a line or two (e.g. *Strom.* 5.14.126.5; 5.14.127.2; or

[17] L. C. VALCKENAER, Diatribe de Aristobulo Judaeo, Leiden 1806, 14.

5.14.133.2), he tends to quote complete sections. Thus in *Protr.* 7.74.5 he quotes vv. 10–12 (R vv. 8–10). Or, when, in *Strom.* 5.12.78.4, he quotes these same verses, he only interrupts to note the textual variant πέφυκεν. Then, in *Strom.* 5.12.78.5, he quotes vv. 21–23 (R vv. 14–15a). In the longer section of *Strom.*, running from 5.14.122.4 through 5.14.126.5, in 5.14.123.1 he first quotes vv. 6–9a (R vv. 5–7a); in 5.14.123.2, he quotes vv. 27–31 (R AR vv. 23–27). In each of these cases, he quotes sections of continuous lines. The only exception is *Strom.* 5.14.123.1, where he quotes only the first word of v. 9 (R v. 7a).

But in the other two cases where he quotes lengthy sections, the omitted lines occur in the middle of the quotation. The first instance is *Protr.* 7.74.4, where he quotes seven complete lines, followed by the first word of v. 9 (vv. 1, 3–9a = R vv. 1, 2–7a). Omitted, of course, is v. 2 (R AR v. 2), which is omitted in both Pseudo-Justin *Mon.* and *Coh.* The standard explanation here is that Clement omits v. 2 here because for the first part of the poem he is using the "short version" from Pseudo-Justin.

The second instance is *Strom.* 5.14.124.1, where he quotes vv. 33–36, 38–40, and vv. 43–44 (R AR vv. 29–32, 33–35, 38–39). The absence of v. 37 poses no problem since it is absent in EusA. But the absence of vv. 41–42 (R AR vv. 36–37), the "Moses verses", is especially significant because this omission occurs in the middle of this nine-verse section. In none of the other Clement quotations do we find this occurring. At the end of this section, when Clement wants to indicate that he is breaking off the quotation, he does so by noting, "and so forth" (καὶ τὰ ἐπὶ τούτοις, *Strom.* 5.14.124.2) – his clue to the reader that there are more lines that he chooses not to quote. This makes it clear that he had before him a version with v. 44b, and possibly vv. 45–46 (R AR vv. 39b, 40–41).

He makes use of similar transitional devices as he moves from one quotation to the next. In *Protr.* 7.74.4, after citing the section of seven-plus verses, he notes, "then proceeding, he clearly adds" (εἶτα ὑποβὰς διαρρήδην ἐπιφέρει), by which he suggests that the lines from the next quotation (vv. 10–12 = R vv. 8–9) immediately follow the previous quotation, which, of course, is the case. In *Strom.* 5.12.78.4, after introducing v. 10 (R v. 8), he notes the textual variant πέφυκεν, then resumes, noting, "he adds" (ἐπιφέρει), which is then followed by the last part of v. 11 and all of v. 12 (R vv. 9, 10). In this instance, his omission of the first part of v. 11 (R v. 9) is understandable, since the point he wishes to illustrate is God's inscrutability; accordingly, vv. 11b–12 (R vv. 9b–10) are all he needs to quote. The next quotation (vv. 21–23 = R vv. 14–15a), which is cited to illustrate the same point, he introduces with the phrase, "and he adds more clearly" (σαφέστερον δὲ ἐπιλέγει). As Riedweg himself observes (pp. 16–17), in the two cases where he cites successive sections, he indicates this by introducing the second section with εἶτα (*Protr.*

7.74.5; *Strom.* 5.14.124.1; cf. 5.14.126.1). But when he cites a section that does not immediately follow, he uses αὖθίς τε (*Strom.* 5.14.123.2).

Although they are not guaranteed indications in every case, these various examples suggest that Clement gives appropriate indications when he is quoting partially, or when he is quoting successive sections. Yet none of these devices is employed in relation to the "Moses verses" (vv. 2, 25–26, 41–42; R vv. 2, 21–22, 36–37), and this is what previous scholars have been hard pressed to answer. To be sure, in at least two instances he quotes partial lines (*Protr.* 7.74.4 || *Strom.* 5.14.123.1), and in one case the order of the verses is scrambled (*Strom.* 5.14.127.2). But if we set aside v. 2 (R AR v. 2), and concede that its omission was owing to his dependence on a shorter version of the poem at that point, we are still left with the other two cases. The omission of vv. 25–26 (R AR vv. 21–22) just before the "Abraham" quotation in *Strom.* 5.14.123.2 might be accounted for by saying that his intent, at this point, is to speak about Abraham, and that verses relating to Moses would be irrelevant to his purpose.

But the other case is more difficult to account for – and this is the special force of the argument from silence in this case. One of Clement's overarching concerns in *Strom.* 5.14 is to demonstrate that Greeks stole their wisdom from the Jews. He cites repeated examples where he attempts to show that Greek philosophers, poets, and other distinguished thinkers derived their wisdom specifically from Moses. In *Strom.* 5.14.122.4–126.5 he proceeds to give quotations from Orpheus that are in some way resonant with the biblical tradition. Typically he cites an Orphic passage, then correlates it with biblical passages of similar import. His object, of course, is to show by repeated examples that what was being expressed, in this case, by Orpheus, had already been expressed – even better – by biblical writers. In the quotation in *Strom.* 5.14.123.2, Clement is quite explicit in claiming that the reference to the "offspring of the Chaldean race" to whom Orpheus referred was none other than Abraham, although he concedes that it might refer to Isaac. Nothing prevents him from making such a bold claim. For Clement, Orpheus bears clear testimony that God was inscrutable, except to the Chaldean Abraham (or Isaac) whose knowledge of God was derived from his astronomical expertise.

The following passage (vv. 33–36, 38–40, 43–44; R AR vv. 29–32, 33–34, 38–39) is cited to illustrate God's heavenly enthronement, most notably as expressed in Isa 61:1, but also Isa 64:1–2 and Isa 40:12, which speak of the dramatic power that emanates from the enthroned God. The lines cited from Orpheus, as one would expect, are those depicting God's heavenly enthronement, his cosmic reign, and the effects of his overpowering strength on the natural order – all of which is conveniently expressed in the three – part formula claiming that God is Beginning, Middle, and End. It is at this point in the Aristobulus version that vv. 41–42 (R AR vv. 36–37) occur: "As a word of the ancients, as one born in the undergrowth proclaimed, having received God's teaching in statements on the two-tablet law." These lines have the force of underscoring that the source of the divine revelation concerning God's cosmic strength and power is the Mosaic law. And this is precisely the point Clement has repeatedly made, and presumably would have made again, had these lines been before him: that Orpheus himself testifies not only to God's heavenly enthronement and awful power, but to Moses as the one who had received such revelation from God.

When Riedweg takes up Valckenaer's suggestion that Clement might have regarded these verses as too bold an assertion of Moses' status (p. 17, n. 56), presumably as a recipient of divine revelation, he recognizes how strong a claim it is.[18] But so is the claim about Abraham in the previous section. Surely it required no less confidence for Clement to assert that Orpheus' reference to the Chaldean who was privy to the heavenly secrets was none other than Abraham or Isaac. Moreover, what was it precisely about these verses that would have prompted Clement to omit them?

For these reasons, I find it difficult to believe that Clement knew the longer version of the poem found in EusA. Accordingly, whatever stemma is devised must provide some plausible explanation of the omission of the "Moses" verses in Clement. On the other hand, as noted earlier, I do not think this requires a late dating for EusA, as Walter does. I think it is defensible to argue that Clement has before him Recension B, or something close to it, which contained the Abraham sections, but not the Moses sections; that shortly thereafter Recension B underwent a further stage of redaction, which added, among other things, the Moses portions; and, that this is the recension transmitted to Eusebius.

Riedweg's Interpretation of the Urfassung and the Aristobulus Version

Because of the problematic character of Riedweg's reconstruction of the "Urfassung", his interpretation of the poem at this early stage as a pervasively Stoic document is equally problematic. This makes it more difficult to argue that the Aristobulus expansion reflects a distinct philosophical shift to a more explicit Platonic-Aristotelian viewpoint. Nevertheless, Riedweg's insistence that many features of the poem, in both its versions, suggest sophisticated levels of philosophical reflection is convincing. Moreover, his thorough analysis of the poem, especially the "Urfassung", in light of the Greek epic tradition is quite

[18] VALCKENAER, Aristobulo, 13–14.

illuminating for our understanding of its poetic quality. If he is correct that the "Urfassung" is a Jewish composition, then this would constitute a remarkable achievement at such an early period.[19]

Riedweg also makes a convincing case for re-thinking the question of literary genre. As earlier scholars noted, in none of its forms does the poem really resemble a "testament", at least as this genre is represented in the Jewish tradition. But the evidence of the tradition is not as clearcut as it might be. To be sure, the poem is called a "testament" first in *Mon.*, and subsequently in Theophilus *Ad Autolycum*, whose testimony is admittedly derivative. But arguing that it is best understood as a ἱερὸς λόγος, because of the testimony of Aristobulus, as confirmed by Clement, does not constitute a compelling counter argument, since Clement is also obviously dependent on Aristobulus.

The case can be better made from the internal structure of the poem, and here Riedweg's argument that the overall structure, as well as other internal indicators, suggest some connection with Hellenistic mystery initiation rites has merit.[20] Quite obviously, the poem draws on mystery language, especially in the opening verses, and highlights throughout the esoteric quality of the terrifying knowledge of God. The fact that a composition with such explicit emphasis on the esoteric nature of divine revelation is both adopted and adapted by Jewish redactors places it well within established Jewish traditions where hidden, esoteric wisdom about God is both revered and fostered. It is obviously

---

[19] The authorship of the "Urfassung", or Recension A, is a separate question in its own right. The problematic verse 14 (R v. 11) that portrays God as responsible, in some sense, for sending evil to mortals does not, according to Riedweg, speak against Jewish authorship, since similar claims can be found in the Jewish Scriptures (he adduces ample evidence, pp. 8–10, esp. p. 56, n. 158). Nor does v. 24 (R v. 16), which, in various versions, mentions "Zeus the ruler of all things", since RIEDWEG, following a suggestion by BURKERT, emends the line to read διὰ πάντων τὸν μεδέοντα (pp. 30–31, 60). As is commonly recognized, the mere mention of Zeus in a writing does not speak against its Jewish authorship (e.g., Ep. Arist. 16). The most telling clue for Jewish authorship RIEDWEG finds in v. 17 (R v. 13): οὐδέ τις ἔσθ' ἕτερος χωρὶς μεγάλου βασιλῆος (pp. 61–62). Noting especially LXX Exod 20:3; Deut 32:29; Isa 44:6, Riedweg places this claim directly within the biblical tradition of radical monotheism, and finds it inconceivable that a pagan author could have penned the line.

[20] According to RIEDWEG's formal analysis, the opening lines (vv. 1 & 3; R vv. 1–2), which employ formulaic language used in mystery settings to address initiates, constitute a formal address (πρόρρησις), which has the effect of excluding the uninitiated from the initiation rite. The next section (vv. 3–9; R vv. 2–7a) asks the initiate to abandon old ways of thinking and seek true guidance from the divine Logos. Since ridding the mind of erroneous thoughts serves as a form of purification, RIEDWEG sees this section as a καθαρμός. Then follows the transmission of the tradition (παράδοσις, vv. 10–12, 14, 16–17, 21–24, 33–37, 41, 43, 46; R vv. 8–21), where the initiate receives instruction in the "holy word" (ἱερὸς λόγος). The instruction consists of two parts: learning about the character of the one, inscrutable God (vv. 10–12, 14, 16–17, 21–24; R vv. 8–16), and being given a picture of his universal sovereignty (vv. 33–37; R vv. 17–21). As Riedweg reconstructs the "Urfassung", a concluding section (vv. 41, 43, 46; R vv. 21a–c) underscores the gravity and secrecy of what has been transmitted.

a tradition elevated to an art form by Philo of Alexandria, but one that takes many other forms of expression as well, both in Palestine and the Diaspora. Riedweg's thorough examination of Pseudo-Orpheus opens up many fresh avenues of approach through which these connections can be more fruitfully explored.

Bibliography

ABEL, E., Orphica. Leipzig/Prague, 1885.

DENIS, A.-M., Introduction aux pseudépigraphes grecs d'ancien testament. SVTP, 1. Leiden, 1970.

–, Fragmenta pseudepigraphorum quae supersunt Graeca una cum historicorum et auctorum Judaeorum hellenistarum fragmentis (published with M. Black, Apocalypsis Henochi Graece). Leiden, 1970.

HOLLADAY, C.R., Fragments from Hellenistic Jewish Authors. Volume IV: Orphica. SBL Texts and Translations Pseudepigrapha Series. Atlanta, 1996. Forthcoming.

KERN, O., Orphicorum Fragmenta. Berlin, 1922; Reprint 1963.

LAFARGUE, M., "Orphica", in J.H. Charlesworth, ed. Old Testament Pseudepigrapha. 2 vols. Garden City, N.Y., 1983–5. 2.795–801.

LOBECK, C.A., Aglaophamus. Königsberg: Bornträger Fratres, 1829. Reprint Darmstadt, 1961.

MARCOVICH, M., Pseudo-Iustinus, Cohortatio ad Graecos, De Monarchia, Oratio ad Graecos. Patristische Texte und Studien, 32. Berlin/New York, 1990.

MRAS, K., Die Praeparatio Evangelica. Bd. 8, Eusebius Werke. GCS, 43. 2 vols. Berlin, 1954–56.

RIEDWEG, C., Jüdisch-hellenistische Imitation eines orphischen Hieros Logos. Beobachtungen zu OF 245 and 247 (sog. Testament des Orpheus). Classica Monacensia. Münchener Studien zur Klassischen Philologie. Münchener Universitätsschriften. Philosophische Fakultät. Bd. 7. Tübingen, 1993.

–, Mysterienterminologie bei Platon, Philon und Klemens von Alexandrien. Untersuchungen zur antiken Literatur und Geschichte, 26. Berlin/New York, 1987.

–, Ps.-Justin (Markell von Ankyra?), Ad Graecos de vera religione (bisher 'Cohortatio ad Graecos'). Einleitung und Kommentar. Schweizerische Beiträge zur Altertumswissenschaft, Bd. 25. Basel/Berlin, 1995.

VALCKENAER, L.C., Diatribe de Aristobulo Judaeo. Leiden, 1806.

WALTER, N., "Pseudepigraphische jüdisch-hellenistische Dichtung: Pseudo-Phokylides, Pseudo-Orpheus, Gefälschte Verse auf Namen griechischer Dichter", in W.G. Kümmel, et al., eds., Jüdische Schriften aus hellenistisch-römischer Zeit, Bd. 4, "Poetische Schriften", Lfg. 3 (Gütersloh, 1983) 173–278.

–, Der Thoraausleger Aristobulos. TU, 86. Berlin, 1964.

Appendix 1: Riedweg Stemma

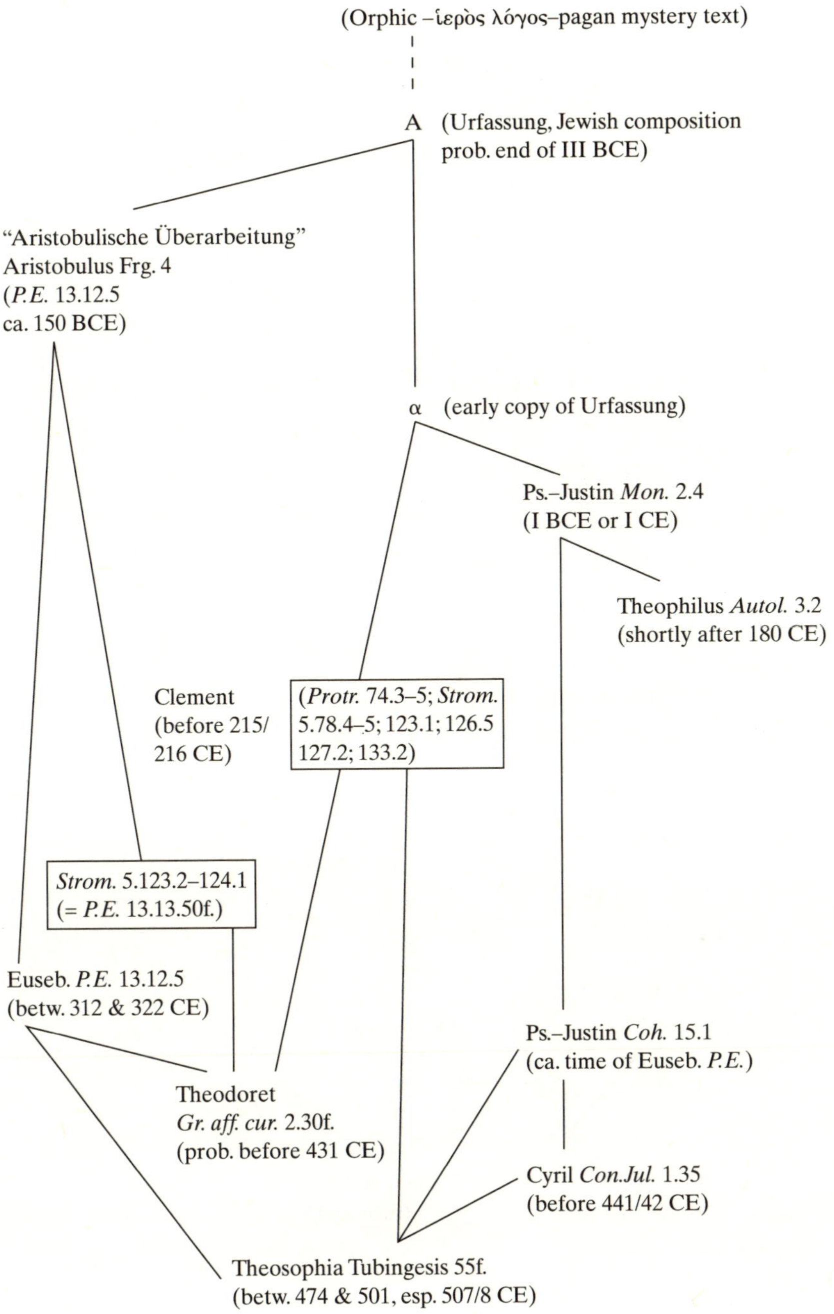
(Orphic –ἱερὸς λόγος–pagan mystery text)
A (Urfassung, Jewish composition prob. end of III BCE)
"Aristobulische Überarbeitung" Aristobulus Frg. 4 (P.E. 13.12.5 ca. 150 BCE)
α (early copy of Urfassung)
Ps.–Justin Mon. 2.4 (I BCE or I CE)
Theophilus Autol. 3.2 (shortly after 180 CE)
Clement (before 215/216 CE)
(Protr. 74.3–5; Strom. 5.78.4–5; 123.1; 126.5 127.2; 133.2)
Strom. 5.123.2–124.1 (= P.E. 13.13.50f.)
Euseb. P.E. 13.12.5 (betw. 312 & 322 CE)
Ps.–Justin Coh. 15.1 (ca. time of Euseb. P.E.)
Theodoret Gr. aff. cur. 2.30f. (prob. before 431 CE)
Cyril Con.Jul. 1.35 (before 441/42 CE)
Theosophia Tubingesis 55f. (betw. 474 & 501, esp. 507/8 CE)

Appendix 2: Holladay Stemma

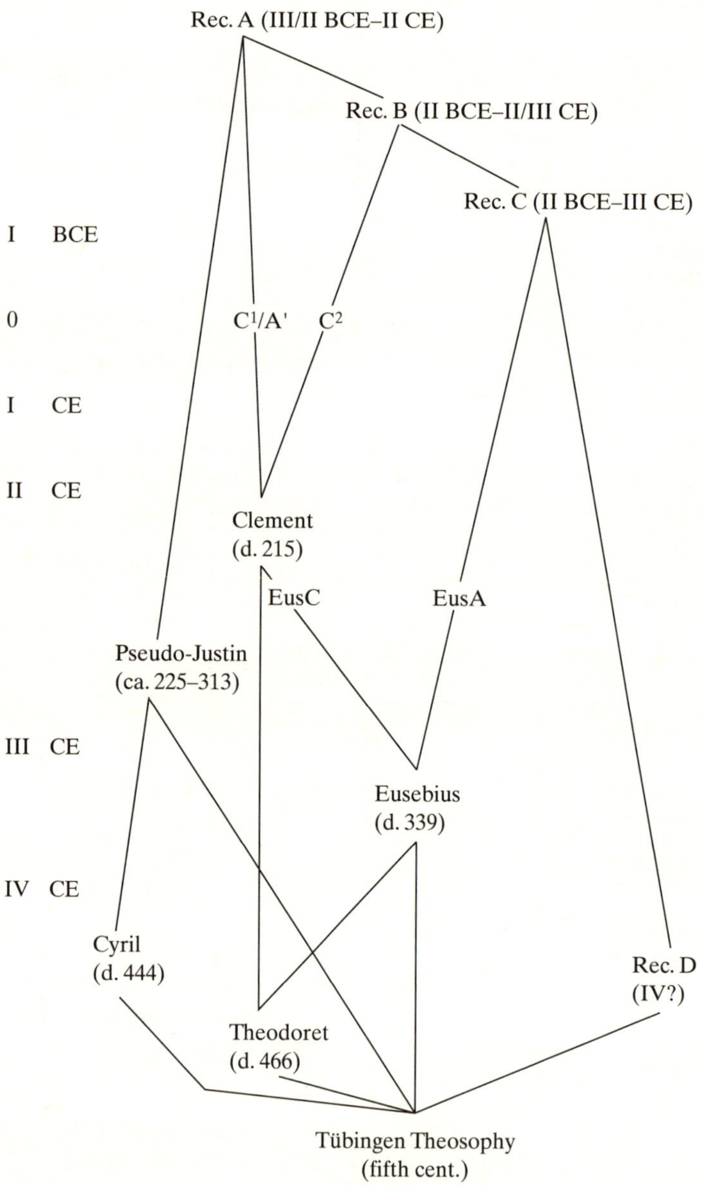

Appendix 3:
Textual Variants: Pseudo-Justin, Clement, Eusebius-Aristobulus, Cyril, Theodoret

Verse	P-J Monarchia	P-J Cohortatio	Clement Protrepticus	Clement Stromata	Euseb.-Aristobulus	Cyril	Thdrt
3	–	πάντες ὁμῶς	7.74.4 πάντες ὁμῶς	–	πᾶσιν ὁμοῦ	πάντες ὅμως	–
4	μουσαῖε (q) μουσαῖ (s)	μουσαῖε (A^{pc}) μουσαῖ (sg) μούσαις (A^{ac})	7.74.4 μουσαῖε (P^{pc}) μούσαις (P^{ac})	–	μουσαῖε	μουσαῖ	
4	ἐξερέω	ἐξερέω	7.74.4 ἐξερέω	–	ἐξεν(ν)έπω	ἐξερέω	–
7	ἰθύνων	ἰθύνων	7.74.4 εἰθύνων (P^{ac}) εὐθύνων (P^{pc})	5.14.123.1 εὐθύνων	ἰθύνων	ἰθύνων	–
7	εὖ τ' ἐπίβαινε	εὖ τ' ἐπίβαινε	7.74.4 εὖ δ' ἐπίβαινε	5.14.123.1 εὖ δ' ἐπίβαινε	εὖ δ' ἐπίβαινε	εὖ δ' ἐπίβαινε	–
8	κόσμοιο ἄνακτα	κόσμοιο ἄνακτα	7.74.4 κόσμοιο ἄνακτα	5.14.123.1 κόσμοιο ἄνακτα	κόσμοιο τυπωτήν	κόσμοιο ἄνακτα	–
9	–	–	7.74.4 ἀθάνατον	5.14.123.1 ἀθάνατον	ἀθάνατον + v. 9	–	–
10	αὐτογενής	αὐτογενής	7.74.5 αὐτογενής	5.12.78.4 αὐτοτελής	αὐτοτελής	αὐτογενής	αὐτοτελής
10	τέτυκται (s) τέτεκται (q)	τέτυκται	7.74.5 τέτυκται	5.12.78.4 τέτυκται 5.12.78.4 πέφυκεν (v.l.)	τελεῖται	τέτυκται	τελεῖται
11	περιγίνεται	περιγίνεται	7.74.5 περινίσσεται	–	περινίσσεται	περιγίνεται	περινίσσεται
12	αὐτὸς δέ γε πάντας ὁρᾶται	αὐτὸς δέ γε πάντας ὁρᾶται	7.74.5 αὐτὸς δέ γε πάντας ὁρᾶται	5.12.78.4 αὐτὸς δέ γε πάντας ὁρᾶται	ψυχὴν . . . νόῳ δ' εἰσοράαται	αὐτὸς δέ γε πάντας ὁρᾶται	αὐτὸς δέ γε πάντας ὁρᾶται

Appendix 3 (Cont.): Textual Variants: Pseudo-Justin, Clement, Eusebius-Aristobulus, Cyril, Theodoret

Verse	P-J Monarchia	P-J Cohortatio	Clement Protrepticus	Clement Stromata		Euseb.-Aristobulus	Cyril	Thdrt
14	οὗτος δ' ἐξ ἀγαθοῖο κακὸν θνητοῖσι δίδωσι	οὗτος ἐξ ἀγαθοῖο κακὸν θνητοῖσι δίδωσι	–	5.14.126.5	αὐτὸς δὲ ἐξ ἀγαθοῖο κακὸν θνητοῖσι φυτεύει	αὐτὸς δὲ ἐξ ἀγαθῶν θνητοῖς κακὸν οὐκ ἐπιτέλλει	–	–
16	κρυόεντα καὶ	κρυόεντα καὶ	–	5.14.126.5	κρυόεντα καὶ	καὶ λοιμὸν ἰδ'	–	–
17	βασιλῆος μεγάλοιο (s) μεγάλοιο ἄνακτος (q)	μεγάλου βασιλῆος (s) μεγάλοιο ἄνακτος (q)	–	5.14.133.2	μεγάλου βασιλῆος	σὺ δέ κεν ῥέα πάντ' ἐσορήσω	–	–
22	πᾶσι (q) πᾶσιν (s)	πᾶσι (A pqg) πᾶσιν (rs)	–	5.12.78.5	πᾶσι	–	–	πᾶσι
33	οὗτος γὰρ χάλκειον ἐπ' οὐρανὸν	οὗτος γὰρ χάλκειον ἐς οὐρανὸν	–	5.14.124.1	αὐτὸς δ' αὖ μέγαν αὖτις ἐς οὐρανὸν	αὐτὸς δὴ μέγαν αὖθις ἐπ' οὐρανὸν	αὐτὸς γὰρ χάλκειον ἐς οὐρανὸν	αὐτὸς δ' αὖ μέγαν αὖτις ἐπ' οὐρανὸν
34	ἐνὶ (s) εἰνὶ (q)	ἐνὶ	–	5.14.124.1 5.14.127.2	ἐνὶ –	εἰνὶ	εἰνὶ	ἐνὶ
34	γαίης δ' ἐπὶ ποσσὶ	γαίης δ' ἐπὶ ποσσὶ	–	5.14.124.1 5.14.127.2	γαίη τε ὑπὸ ποσὶ γαίη δ' ἐπὶ ποσὶ	γαίη δ' ὑπὸ ποσσὶ	γαίῃ δ' ἐπὶ ποσσὶ	γαίη δ' ὑπὸ ποσσὶ
35	χεῖρά τε	χεῖρά τε	–	5.14.124.1 5.14.127.2	χεῖρα χεῖρα δὲ	χεῖρα δὲ	χεῖρά τε	χεῖρα δὲ
35	ἐπὶ τέρματος	ἐπὶ τέρματος	–	5.14.124.1 5.14.127.2	περὶ τέρμασιν ἐπὶ τέρματος	ἐπὶ τέρμασιν	ἐπὶ τέρματα	περὶ τέρμασιν
36	πάντοθεν ἐκτέτακεν	πάντοθεν ἐκτέτακεν	–	5.14.124.1 5.14.127.2	ἐκτέτακεν ὀρέων πάντοθεν ἐκτέτακεν	ἐκτέτακεν ὀρέων	πάντοθεν ἐκτέτακεν	ἐκτέτακεν ὀρέων

Zur Vorgeschichte von Israels status confessionis in hellenistischer Zeit

von

Robert Hanhart

Daß die religionspolitischen Maßnahmen Antiochos' IV. Epiphanes sich für das Volk Israel in der Gestalt der jerusalemischen Glaubensgemeinschaft in der Weise auswirkten, daß Israels Reaktion ihrem Wesen nach mit Recht als „status confessionis" bestimmt werden muß, war immer und ist auch heute unumstritten. Umstritten – in einem bestimmten Grade auch zwischen dem Jubilar und dem Gratulanten – ist nur die Frage, wie sich in diesem Phänomen tiefere Ursache und äußerer Anlaß – polybianisch gesprochen αἰτία und πρόφασις[1] –: die Ursache des oberherrlichen Eingriffs in Israels legitimiertes Recht der Bewahrung seines Glaubens zum Anlaß innerisraelitischer Zwistigkeit, die diesen Eingriff für den Oberherrn opportun erscheinen ließen, zueinander verhalten.

Es geht uns hier nicht um die Frage nach dem Verhältnis zwischen Ursache und Anlaß, nicht um die Frage, in welchem Maß die inner-israelitische Konfrontation zwischen traditioneller Orthodoxie und hellenisierender Heterodoxie für den oberherrlichen Eingriff mitbestimmend waren; es geht uns unter Voraussetzung einer nicht näher bestimmbaren Wechselwirkung zwischen oberherrlicher Machtdemonstration und untertaner Veranlassung um die Frage, ob sich innerhalb des Zeitraums oberherrlich legalisierter Freiheit einer untertanen Kultgemeinschaft, des Zeitraums, den wir im danielischen Sinn als die Herrschaft des persischen und des makedonisch-hellenistischen Weltreiches bezeichnen, vorbereitende Konfrontationen erkennen lassen, die zu diesem letzten und endgültigen Machteingriff führten und die durch ihren vorläufigen Charakter auch die Grenze aufzeigen, jenseits derer der Bruch zwischen Oberherr und Untertan notwendig war.

Es ist nicht nur in theologischer Hinsicht, im Blick auf das, was innerhalb der innerisraelitischen Parteiung als die „traditionelle Orthodoxie" zu bezeichnen wäre, sondern auch in historischer Hinsicht, im Blick darauf, wie Israel die Faktizität der Geschichte dieses Zeitraums erlebte, berechtigt und notwendig,

---

[1] Vgl. P. Pédech, La méthode historique de Polybe, CEA, 1964, S. 75–98. 166–177.

der Untersuchung die apokalyptisch verhüllte Schau des Buches Daniel zu Grunde zu legen; denn aus dieser Schau wird aus dem Blickwinkel von Israels status confessionis, innerhalb von Israels Zeugnissen aus hellenistischer Zeit, am deutlichsten erkennbar, wie sich Israels Glaube und Bekenntnis zur Erkenntnis seiner Geschichte verhält: als fides quaerens intellectum.

Denn der Glaube an den Gott Israels als Urheber der hier verhüllt dargestellten Geschichte ist es allein, der den Apokalyptiker nach der Bedeutung der ihm in letzte Einzelheiten bekannten Geschichte des vierten Weltreiches – mit Walter Baumgartner zu sprechen „Satz um Satz, und Zug um Zug: bei Daniel die Weissagung, in der aus griechischen und jüdischen Historikern genau bekannten Geschichte der Diadochenzeit die Erfüllung“[2] – zu fragen und nach dem verborgenen Ratschluß zu suchen zwingt, der in dieser Vorgeschichte den Grund der Leiden der Gegenwart, der Religionsverfolgungen, offenbart.

Die ganze Zeit der irdischen Daseinsform Israels als untertane Glaubensgemeinschaft, die Zeit des persischen und des makedonisch-hellenistischen Weltreiches, ist nach dieser Schau eine „Zeit der Bedrängnis“. Sie hebt nach der Deutung der jeremianischen 70 Jahre der babylonischen Verbannung auf die 70 Jahrwochen nach den 7 Jahrwochen des Exils mit dem Auftreten eines „gesalbten Führers“, משיח נגיד, des ersten Hohenpriesters, Josua, an und endet in der letzten Jahrwoche in der Religionsverfolgung, die mit der Beseitigung des rechtmäßigen „Gesalbten“, משיח, des Hohenpriesters Onias, einsetzt. Die 62 Jahrwochen der Zwischenzeit, innerhalb derer sich der Übergang von der persischen zur makedonischen Herrschaft ereignet, ist als ganze die Zeit, in der „Platz und Graben“, der untertane jerusalemische Tempelstaat, „wieder aufgebaut sind“, תשוב ונבנתה רחוב וחרוץ; aber dieser Wiederaufbau steht „unter der Bedrängnis der Zeit“, בצוק העתים (Dan 9,24-26a).

Die Zeit „der Bedrängnis“ ist auf diese Weise als Vorgeschichte wesenhaft unterschieden von jener letzten Zeit der Verfolgung, deren Wahrzeichen der im jerusalemischen Heiligtum aufgerichtete „Greuel der Verwüstung“ ist, שקוצים משמם, über den sich zuletzt selbst „Vernichtung und Gericht ergiessen wird“, ועד־כלה ונחרצה תתך על־שמם (V.26b–27).

Worin besteht dieser wesenhafte Unterschied? Worin unterscheidet sich die Vorgeschichte der „Bedrängnis“ von der Geschichte der „Vernichtung“? Die Antwort kann nur in der großen Audition des letzten Gesichtes (Dan 11,1-12,13) gesucht werden, in welcher der Geschichte der Religionsverfolgung unter Antiochos IV. Epiphanes (11,21-45) in apokalyptischer Verhüllung die Vorgeschichte des Übergangs des persischen Weltreichs auf das makedonische und der ptolemäisch-seleukidischen Diadochenkämpfe, der Kriege des „Königs des Südens“, מלך הנגב, mit dem „König des Nordens“, מלך הצפון, vorgeordnet ist: V.2-20.

---

[2] W. Baumgartner, Das Buch Daniel, AWR. AT 1, 1926, S. 11.

Die „Bedrängnis der Zeit", deren Interpretation dieser Teil der Apokalypse Daniels darstellt, scheint zunächst nichts anderes zu sein als Profangeschichte, in der die Geschichte Israels, die es in dieser Zeit erleidet, kaum zur Sprache kommt und die darum auch über die Intention des berichtenden Zeugen, der diese Geschehnisse in apokalyptische Chiffren verhüllt darstellt, nicht mehr erkennen läßt, als „daß man" – um mit Martin Hengel zu sprechen – „die Auseinandersetzungen zwischen dem „König des Südens und des Nordens" auch in Jerusalem aufmerksam verfolgt hat"[3].

Aber das aufmerksame Hören dieses Zeugen muß dem Hörer, der aufmerksam auf ihn hört, als ein Hören offenbar werden, das gerade darin, daß es Geschichte scheinbar unabhängig von der Geschichte seines Volkes aufmerksam verfolgt, sagt, was die Existenz Israels als irdisches Volk für die Geschichte der Schöpfung in ihrem letzten Stadium des vierten Weltreiches bedeutet.

Denn es ist gerade der Verzicht auf eine Aussage über die Bedeutung, die Israel als Volk Jahwes innerhalb dieser weltgeschichtlichen Ereignisse hat, der das Wesen Israels in dieser Zeit bestimmt: Es ist nicht mehr wie in vorexilischer Zeit die im Kräftespiel der es umgebenden Großreiche hin und her gerissene Nation – „einen Bund mit Assur schließen sie, Öl wird nach Ägypten getragen" (Hos 12,2b) –; es ist das Volk, das diesen beiden Mächten in der Gestalt der Diadochenreiche, des ptolemäischen „Königs des Südens" und des seleukidischen „Königs des Nordens", als untertane Glaubensgemeinschaft unterworfen ist, diese Unterwerfung als den Willen seines Gottes anerkennt und sich nur dann berechtigt weiß, sich gegen sie zu erheben, wenn das ihm in der Unterwerfung garantierte Recht angetastet würde.

Darum muß die Frage an die danielische Darstellung dieser Periode der Geschichte lauten: Lassen sich in ihr Aussagen erkennen, nach welchen dieser Rechtsgrund von Israels Existenz in hellenistischer Zeit gefährdet erscheint?

Der Rechtsgrund als solcher wird an einer Stelle der diese Periode darstellenden Geschichte verhüllt, aber eindeutig ausgesprochen: Dieses Volk, das kein Königreich mehr ist, das im Kampf der Diadochenreiche um den Besitz des von ihm mitbewohnten geographischen Bereiches eine politische Bedeutung hätte, ist nach der Schau des Apokalyptikers „die Herrlichkeit des Königtums": הדר מלכות (Dan 11,20); das kann nur bedeuten – und von dieser Bedeutung her ist auch der Ausdruck „Land der Zierde", ארץ הצבי (V.16.41; vgl. 8,9), zu erklären –, daß diese untertane Gemeinschaft darum, weil ihr Gott der Herr „des Königtums", des sie beherrschenden Weltreiches, ist, dadurch, daß ihr Rechtsanspruch gewährt bleibt, die Existenz der oberherrlichen Macht garantiert, daß mit dieser Gewährung das Daseinsrecht des Oberherrn steht und fällt.

Diese irdische Daseinsform Israels als untertane Glaubensgemeinschaft, die

[3] M. Hengel, Judentum und Hellenismus, Studien zu ihrer Begegnung unter besonderer Berücksichtigung Palästinas bis zur Mitte des 2. Jh. v. Chr., WUNT 10, 1969 (2. durchgesehene und ergänzte Auflage 1973), S. 11.

als solche das Daseinsrecht ihres politischen Oberherrn garantiert, erscheint nach der apokalyptischen Schau Daniels unverändert realisiert seit der Herrschaft des persischen Weltreiches über den Wechsel von der persischen zur makedonischen Macht (Dan 11,2-4) bis auf die Oberherrschaft der beiden Diadochenstaaten, des ptolemäischen (V.5-12) und des seuleukidischen (V.13-20). Diese politischen Umbrüche werden als solche nirgends als Ursache oder äußerer Anlaß der Zerstörung der zwischen Israel und seinem Oberherrn vereinbarten Rechtsgrundlage bestimmt.

Aber es erscheinen in dieser Darstellung drei Aussagen, die nicht anders erklärt werden können, denn als Hinweis auf Ereignisse, die die Gefahr in sich bergen, daß diese Rechtsgrundlage zerstört wird. Es ist hinsichtlich der historia profana der Weltmächte der Übergang der Herrschaft über den von Israel mitbewohnten Bereich Kölesyrien von den Ptolemäern auf die Seleukiden, und es ist hinsichtlich der historia sacra der jerusalemischen Kultgemeinde die Reaktion einer ihr zugehörenden Gemeinschaft auf diesen Übergang:

Es ist in profangeschichtlicher Hinsicht die Aussage über die im Kampf der Diadochenherrscher um diesen Herrschaftsbereich erwachende Selbstüberhebung, beim Ptolemäer als letztes, vergebliches sich Aufbäumen nach seinem letzten Sieg: **ירום לבבו והפיל רבאות ולא יעוז** (V.12), beim Seleukiden als Trachten nach der Wiedererlangung der Weltherrschaft, **וישם פניו לבוא בתקף כל־מלכותו** (V.17), das schließlich zu seinem Untergang führt: **ונכשל ונפל ולא ימצא** (V.19). Es ist hinsichtlich der historia sacra die Parteinahme von „Gewalttätigen" aus Daniels Volk, **פריצי עמך**, für den Seleukiden, die an dem Plan, „eine Weissagung zu erfüllen", scheitern: **ינשאו להעמיד חזון ונכשלו** (V.14).

Die profangeschichtlichen Ereignisse sind – „bei Daniel die Weissagung, bei Polybios, Diodor und Livius die Erfüllung" – „genau bekannt"[4]. Aber an der Stelle, an der innerhalb der Profangeschichte das Volk Jahwes zur Sprache kommt, ist über das hinter der apokalyptisch verhüllten Aussage stehende Faktum weder aus jüdischer noch aus außerjüdischer Geschichtstradition ein sicherer Aufschluß zu gewinnen.

Die Selbstüberhebung des Königs des Südens ist die Selbsttäuschung Ptolemaios' IV. Philopator nach seinem letzten Sieg über den Seleukiden bei Raphia 217 v. Chr., die ihn die wahre politische Lage, den trotz dieser Niederlage unaufhaltsamen Aufstieg der seleukidischen Macht, verkennen läßt. Polybios führt sein Verhalten auf „den ihm angeborenen Leichtsinn und die Verworfenheit seines Charakters" – ἑλκόμενος ὑπὸ τῆς συνήθους ἐν τῷ βίῳ ῥᾳθυμίας καὶ καχεξίας (Historiae V.87,3) – zurück. Die Selbstüberhebung des Königs des Nordens, Antiochos' III. Magnus – Polybios schreibt seinem Charakter in seiner frühen Zeit „Angriffslust, Kühnheit und Entschlußkraft" zu: 'Αντίοχος ὁ βασιλεὺς ἐδόκει κατὰ μὲν τὰς ἀρχὰς γεγονέναι μεγαλεπίβολος καὶ τολμηρὸς

---

[4] Vgl. Anm. 2.

καὶ τοῦ προτεθέντος ἐξεργαστικός (XV 37,1) – ist sein Plan, nach der endlichen Eroberung Kölesyriens durch den Sieg über den Ptolemäer Ptolemaios V. Epiphanes 198 v. Chr. in der Schlacht bei Paneas gegen den ägyptischen Feldherrn Skopas (V.15-16; Polybios XVI 39,1-5.XXVIII 1,1–4) vermittels der Vermählung seiner Tochter Kleopatra mit dem besiegten Ptolemäerkönig (Polybios XXVIII 20,9; Livius XXXIII 40,1-3) die Alleinherrschaft über das in die Diadochenstaaten auseinandergebrochene Weltreich Alexanders des Großen zu erreichen, ein im Willen zur Vernichtung gleichgestellter politischer Mächte gründendes Unterfangen, בת הנשים יתן־לו להשחיתה (V.17), das zum Gegenschlag der hier zum ersten Mal in Erscheinung tretenden römischen Großmacht, zur Niederlage durch den römischen Konsul L. Corn. Scipio Asiaticus 190 v. Chr. bei Magnesia (V.18; Livius XXXVII 37,1-45,21; Polybios XXI 16–17), und zuletzt zur Selbstzerstörung, der Tötung durch die eine Tempelplünderung in der Elymais rächenden Glieder seines eigenen Volkes führt (V.19; Diodor XXVIII 3; XXIX 15).

Hochmut und Fall des Ptolemäers, Selbstüberhebung und Selbstzerstörung des Seleukiden haben nach der danielischen Darstellung nichts zu tun mit dem Geschick, das das Volk Jahwes durch den Machtwechsel in dem von ihm bewohnten Bereich erleidet: In den Aussagen über den Ptolemäer wird seiner gar nicht gedacht, in den Aussagen über den an seine Stelle tretenden seleukidischen Oberherrn nicht wertend im Kontext der Darstellung seiner Machtgier, sondern nur berichtend in der Erzählung des Herrschaftswechsels: „Keiner wird vor ihm standhalten, er wird eintreten in das Land der Zierde und es fällt gänzlich in seine Hand“ – ויעמד בארץ־הצבי וכלה בידו (V.16b) –; was über das Volk Jahwes in diesem Zusammenhang gesagt wird, ist lediglich das Urteil über ein innerisraelitisches Geschehen: die Verurteilung der Parteinahme (V.14b).

Das sind die drei Aussagen über Israel, die im Zusammenhang der Weltgeschichte stehen, in der es als untertane Glaubensgemeinschaft so bedeutungslos ist, daß es kaum mehr zur Sprache kommt: (1) Als Volk Jahwes ist es der Rechtsgrund für die Existenz der oberherrlichen Macht (V.20). (2) Es bewahrt diese Bedeutung auch im Wechsel der einen oberherrlichen Macht zur anderen, sofern ihm sein Existenzrecht gewährt bleibt (V.16). (3) Es würde diese Bedeutung verlieren, wenn es sich selbst die Macht anmaßte, über die ihm bestimmte oberherrliche Macht zu entscheiden (V.14).

Von hier aus stellt sich nun aber die Frage, ob sich aus der danielischen Charakterisierung der Selbstüberhebung der beiden Könige nicht bereits jene Züge herauslesen lassen, die im danielischen Sprachgebrauch die Auflehnung gegen den Gott Israels kennzeichnen, so daß die Gefahr eines oberherrlichen Eingriffs in das garantierte Recht der jerusalemischen Glaubensgemeinschaft nach der apokalyptischen Intention schon in dieser Zeit nur noch dadurch gebannt wäre, daß die Religionspolitik dieser beiden Herrscher den jerusalemischen Tempelstaat noch nicht erreicht hatte.

Für diese Deutung spricht, daß die hier den Charakter der Könige bezeichnenden Begriffe, רום für Ptolemaios IV., תקף für Antiochos III., auch die Begriffe sind, mit welchen beim ersten Herrscher der danielischen Weltreichlehre, Nebukadnezar, die Überhebung über den Gott Israels dargestellt wird: 4,19 (vgl. V.27) als Begründung seines Falls in den Wahnsinn und 5,18–23 als Reminiszenz an diesen Fall gegenüber Belsazer, mit der sein eigener Fall begründet wird, und daß in analoger Formulierung zuletzt das Handeln des letzten widergöttlichen Widersachers, Antiochos' IV., dargestellt wird, das den Widerstand Israels, den status confessionis, hervorruft: „Er überhebt sich über jede Gottheit und wider den Gott der Götter redet er Lästerung", ויתרומם ויתגדל על־כל־אל ועל אל אלים ידבר נפלאות (11,36).

Die Analogie in der Charakterisierung der Machthaber weist auf die Gefährdung der jerusalemischen Glaubensgemeinschaft. Die – der Historie entsprechende – unterschiedliche Darstellung des geschichtlichen Verlaufs aber zeigt die vorläufige Bewahrung vor jener Konfrontation an, die den status confessionis Israels hervorrufen mußte.

Für beide Aspekte, für die Bewahrung der alten Rechtsstruktur und für ihre Gefährdung durch die ptolemäisch-seleukidischen Rivalen in diesem Machtbereich, liegen in den jüdischen und in den außerjüdischen Dokumenten über diese Zeit Traditionen vor, die das Verhältnis beider Phänomene zueinander erhellen. Die Bewahrung der Rechtsstruktur ist dokumentiert in den von Josephus überlieferten Erlassen Antiochos' III., in welchen den Juden die „innere Autonomie" (Hengel[5]), die Gewährung der Einhaltung ihrer Gesetze (Ant XII 138–144) und das Verbot ihrer Mißachtung durch Fremde, des Betretens des Heiligtums, der Einführung verbotener Speisen in die Stadt (145–146), garantiert wird. Die Gefährdung kündet sich an beim letzten ptolemäischen Oberherrn in einer legendär im 3. Makkabäerbuch, historisch im Raphiadekret sichtbar werdenden Religionspolitik, die die Grenze der zuvor gewährten Religionsfreiheit zu überschreiten droht, beim ersten seleukidischen Oberherrn in dem bei Polybios und Livius öfter angedeuteten Machtstreben, das vor allem angesichts der neu aufstehenden Weltmacht Rom auf die Aufrichtung einer östlichen Gegenmacht tendiert, in der das in die Diadochenreiche auseinandergebrochene Weltreich Alexanders des Großen wiederhergestellt wäre.

Dieses Machtstreben aber bedeutet für die apokalyptische Schau des Buches Daniel, in der das makedonische Weltreich als das vierte und letzte vor dem Anbruch der Endzeit erscheint, die letzte Erhebung der widergöttlichen Macht, deren Ziel in der Vernichtung der jerusalemischen Glaubensgemeinschaft besteht. Das zerbrochene vierte Weltreich, die Diadochenherrschaft,

---

[5] Judentum S. 16, vgl. 493f.

war der κατέχων, seine Wiederherstellung das Zeichen des Endes. Was jetzt noch geschehen konnte, stand für Israel unter diesem Zeichen[6].

Das Nebeneinanderbestehen der Bewahrung und der Gefährdung von Israels Existenzrecht als Volk Jahwes ist die Zeit des κατέχων, der oberherrliche Widerruf der Bewahrung ist der Beginn der Zeit des Endes. Wie nahe die Gefährdung in der Zeit der Bewahrung während der *ptolemäischen* Herrschaft schon dem Widerruf stand, zeigt die im 3. Makkabäerbuch überlieferte Legende – und das ist ihr „historischer Kern" – über die Judenverfolgung unter Ptolemaios IV. Ein historisch glaubwürdiger Aspekt über das „historisch gute Material" hinaus, das ihm der beste Kenner dieser Zeit zugesteht[7], dürfte gerade auch in der legendenhaften Intention bestehen, die Maßnahmen des Ptolemäers im Licht der realisierten seleukidischen Religionsverfolgung zu sehen – der unmittelbare Anlaß ist der oberherrliche Bruch von Israels Gesetz, der Wille des Königs, das Allerheiligste zu betreten, die Verfolgung selbst besteht in der Antastung von Israels Bekenntnis, dem Zwang zur Ausübung

---

[6] Daß die Schau der sich ablösenden Weltreiche in der danielischen Apokalypse endzeitlich ausgerichtet ist, das vierte Weltreich, das makedonische, als das letzte mit seinem eigenen Ende in Israel die letzten Leiden der Endzeit hervorruft, die in der Bedrängnis seiner Existenz als Glaubensgemeinschaft bestehen, erweist sich zuerst durch den Aufbau der ganzen Apokalypse, nach dem die Folge der vier Weltreiche auf dieses Ziel hin drängt; es erweist sich hier, wo es zum ersten Mal um das Weltmachtstreben des seleukidischen Diadochenstaates geht, darin, daß hier apokalyptisch verhüllt die Macht in Erscheinung tritt, die das makedonische Weltreich, bevor es aus seiner Zerspaltung in die Diadochenreiche wiederhergestellt werden kann, ablösen wird, Rom in der Gestalt des römischen Feldherrn, der dem Seleukiden seinen Machtwillen mit dem gleichen Willen vergilt: in der Vorgeschichte das Vorspiel der Vergeltung, die in der Geschichte dem letzten Bedränger durch die römische Macht in der Gestalt der „chittäischen Schiffe" endgültig zuteil werden wird (11,30; vgl. S. 189f.). Es ist zu beachten, daß das Weltreich, das in der historiographischen Tradition dieser Lehre das makedonische ablösen wird, in der danielischen Apokalypse nicht in der Gestalt eines Weltreiches, aber doch – als die einzige Macht, die in dieser Schau nicht das Königreich „des Südens" oder „des Nordens" ist – als politische Macht in Erscheinung tritt: Gerade auf diese verborgene Weise erscheint es als das Zeichen des Endes, weil es für Israel kein Weltreich mehr ist (vgl. Vf., Kriterien geschichtlicher Wahrheit in der Makkabäerzeit, Zur geschichtlichen Bedeutung der danielischen Weltreichlehre, in: Drei Studien zum Judentum, TEH 140, 1967, S. 7–22; hier S. 10f.); auf diese Weise zeigt es sowohl die Gemeinsamkeit als auch die restlose Andersheit gegenüber der Tradition, die für die apokalyptische Weissagung Schritt für Schritt die historische Verifizierung darstellt: Polybios, dessen Geschichtswerk in der Klage seines Freundes Scipio im Angesicht der Trümmer von Karthago über die Vergänglichkeit der Weltreiche, zuletzt auch des römischen, gipfelt (XXXVIII 22,1–3): Es ist die säkulare Gestalt der danielischen Schau, entsprechend der psychologischen polybianischen Charakterisierung der Oberherren Israels gegenüber dem Erscheinungsbild, das Daniel von ihnen im Angesicht von Israels Gott zeichnet (vgl. S. 184f. und 189f.), der völkerpsychologischen der untertanen Anwohner dieses Bereiches gegenüber dem, was für Daniel die Parteinahme für den einen der oberherrlichen Rivalen durch eine innerjudäische Abspaltung bedeutet (11,14; vgl. S. 192f.). In dieser Weise, als säkulare Gestalt, wäre dann auch die Konzeption der rächenden Gottheit bei Diodor in ihrem Verhältnis zur danielischen Vergeltungslehre zu bestimmen (vgl. S. 191 mit Anm. 12).

[7] M. Hengel, Judentum S. 480 mit Anm. 43.

des Dionysoskultes –, und das Raphiadekret bestätigt durch die Darstellung der Art und Weise, wie Ptolemaios IV. nach dem Sieg von Raphia die religiöse Huldigung der neu eroberten Gebiete fordert, daß, wäre solches in Jerusalem geschehen – ob er die Stadt betrat, läßt die kurze Notiz des Polybios, „daß er sich drei Monate ἐν τοῖς κατὰ Συρίαν καὶ Φοινίκην τόποις aufhielt und die Ordnung in den Städten wiederherstellte, καταστησάμενος τὰς πόλεις" (V87,5), nicht erkennen –, der religiöse Widerstand der Juden hätte erwachen müssen[8].

---

[8] Ob die Gefährdung zur Konfrontation führte, entscheidet sich nicht daran, ob der König auch nach Jerusalem kam, sondern daran – und hier versagt sowohl die legendäre als auch die historische Überlieferung –, ob er die religiöse Huldigung, die er von den anderen Kultstätten entgegennahm und die sowohl mit Polytheismus als auch mit Selbstvergottung verbunden waren – Polybios spricht von „übertriebener Liebedienerei", ὑπερβολὴ ἀρεσκείας, in Darbringung von Kränzen und Opfern und Errichtung von Altären zu Ehren des Ptolemaios (V 86,11), das Raphiadekret in bezug auf die ägyptischen Heiligtümer darüber hinaus von der Errichtung einer Statue für ihn (Zeile 17), der Verleihung göttlicher Ehren „dem König Ptolemaios, dem ewig lebenden, von Isis geliebten und seiner Schwester, der Königin Arsinoe, den vaterliebenden Göttern, Θεῶν Φιλοπατόρων" (31) –, auch von der jerusalemischen Kultgemeinde gefordert hätte, oder ob er entsprechend der seit der Perserzeit geübten Religionspolitik Kulte ihm untertaner Völker, die er als solche bestehen ließ, als unterschiedliche Formen der Verehrung der einen Reichsgottheit anerkannte. Die in der hieroglyphisch-demotisch-griechischen Trilingue nur demotisch bruchstückhaft überlieferten Aussagen von Zeile 23–25, in welchen die ersten Herausgeber H. Gauthier und H. Sottas (Un décret trilingue en l'honneur de Ptolémée IV., Service des antiquités de l'Égypte, Cairo 1925) den zum Schluß auf eine Begegnung führenden Namen Eleazaros vermuteten, sind heute, nachdem schon W. Otto, Zu dem dreisprachigen Priesterdekret von Memphis aus dem sechsten Jahre Ptolemaios' IV., Beiträge zur Seleukidengeschichte des 3. Jahrhunderts v. Chr., IV, ABAW.PP, XXXIV. Band, 1. Abhandlung, 1928, S. 80–87, aufgrund der Lesung von W. Spiegelberg begründete Bedenken gegen diese Deutung angemeldet hatte (S. 81, Anm. 4, vgl. M. Hengel, Judentum S. 13, Anm. 18; H.-J. Thissen, Studien zum Raphiadekret, BKP 23, 1966, erwähnt sie gar nicht mehr), nur noch hinsichtlich des im vorliegenden Zusammenhang irrelevanten Problems umstritten, ob die hier nach einer Aktion des Ptolemaios auf syrischem Gebiet angesetzte Vereinbarung mit Antiochos mit dem von Polybios (V 87,1–4) berichteten Waffenstillstand, σπονδαὶ ἐνιαύσιοι identisch sei (so A. Momigliano, Il decreto trilingue in onore di Tolomeo Filopatore, Aeg. 10, 1929, S. 180–189, dem sich H.-J. Thissen anschließt), oder mit dem endgültigen Friedensschluß (Polybios XV 25,13), so daß die Aktion des Ptolemäers einen Bruch des Waffenstillstandes darstellte (so W. Otto). Seither gefundene Fragmente des Dekrets, die J. Schwartz und M. Malinine, Pierres d'Égypte (RAr 1, 1960, S. 77–90; hier S. 81–82 (griechisch, ed. J. Schwartz) und S. 87–90 (demotisch, ed. M. Malinine)) veröffentlicht haben, geben keinen weiteren Aufschluß. Vgl. noch F. Daumas, Les moyens d'expression du Grec et de l'Égyptien comparés dans les décrets de Canope et de Memphis (Supplément aux annales du service des antiquités de l'Égypte, Cahier 16, Le Caire 1952, Appendice S. 253–274) und Ders., Les textes bilingues ou trilingues, in: Textes et langages de l'Égypte Pharaonique, cent cinquante années de recherches 1822–1972, hommage à J.-F. Champollion, Le Caire 1974, S. 41–45. Das Verhältnis der historia: der Geschichte Israels in dieser Zeit – „vermutlich" – oder vielleicht? – „werden sie (sc der siegreiche Philopator und seine Schwester Arsinoe) auch Jerusalem besucht haben" (M. Hengel S. 13) –, zu ihrer interpretatio Graeca, einer denkbaren Identifizierung des jüdischen Monotheismus mit dem monotheistisch ausgerichteten Dionysoskult – „die vielleicht schon in der Religionspolitik des Ptolemaios IV. Philopator gegenüber den Juden nach seinem Sieg bei Raphia

Wie nahe die Gefährdung in der Zeit der Bewahrung während der *seleukidischen* Herrschaft schon dem Widerruf stand, zeigt in der danielischen Formulierung die Parallelisierung des Geschickes Antiochos' III. mit demjenigen des wider den Gott Israels sich erhebenden Nachfolgers Antiochos IV., die, abgesehen davon, daß sich sein Wille zur Macht über den politischen Herrschaftswechsel hinaus noch nicht auf den jerusalemischen Tempelstaat auswirkt, wie eine Vorwegnahme der göttlichen Rache formuliert ist, die den Widersacher des Gottesvolkes, Antiochos IV., treffen wird: Sein Machtwille ist, wie der Wille des ersten Herrschers des vierten Weltreichs (11,3) und wie der Wille des letzten Bedrängers (V.36), Willkür: כרצונו... ויעש (V.16); sein Versuch, die beiden Diadochenreiche zu vereinigen, entspringt nicht dem Willen zur Versöhnung, sondern, wie die Maßnahmen Antiochos' IV. in seinem eigenen Herrschaftsgebiet (V.24), dem Willen zur Zerstörung: להשחיתה (V.17)[9]; als

217 v. Chr. eine gewisse Rolle spielte" (M. Hengel S. 480) –, wie „monotheistisch" diese Politik auch immer bestimmt sein mochte – „Philopator... arriva presque certainement à une conception monothéiste concernant l'assimilation en un seul culte des éléments disparates de son peuple" (F. Jesi, Notes sur l'édit dionysiaque de Ptolémée IV Philopator, JNES 15, 1956, S. 236–240; hier S. 238) –, wird sich aus dem Grund nicht mit Sicherheit definieren lassen, weil es historisch ungeklärt bleibt, ob es eine Berührung zwischen beiden überhaupt gab, ob es nicht lediglich bei einer „interpretatio Graeca" der ägyptischen Religion blieb; das Verhältnis wird aber, wenn es diese Berührung gab, wenn nicht den seiner Form nach eindeutig legendären, von den makkabäischen Traditionen über Heliodor und Antiochos Epiphanes beeinflussten Teilen des 3. Makkabäerbuches ein „historischer Kern" zugestanden wird – hierzu vgl. Vf., Zum Text des 2. und 3. Makkabäerbuches, NAWG.PH 13, 1961, S. 427–486; hier S. 485 f. (= MSU VII, 1961, S. 63 f.); das Problem des historischen Hintergrundes von Mac III, seiner Quellen und seiner Abhängigkeit von Überlieferungen, die spätere Ereignisse von Seleukos IV. und Heliodor bis in die römische Zeit zum Gegenstand haben, Argumente und Gegenargumente gedrängt bei H. Conzelmann, Heiden–Juden–Christen, BHTh 62, 1981, S. 135–137 –, im Blick auf Israel nur so bestimmt werden können, daß die interpretatio der ptolemäischen Religionspolitik hinsichtlich ihrer Anerkennung durch die jerusalemische Glaubensgemeinschaft höchstens im Zugeständnis einer neuen Form der überlieferten Vereinbarung zwischen Oberherrn und untertanem Tempelstaat bestand, die sich ihrem Wesen nach von der seit der Perserzeit getroffenen in nichts unterschied: Der Oberherr anerkennt Kult und Gesetz Israels als Form der Anbetung der Reichsgottheit.

[9] להשחיתה: Das nächstliegende Bezugswort zum Pronominalsuffix fem. sing. wäre בת הנשים, „Tochter der Frauen" in der Bedeutung „eine der Frauen". Dieser Bezug könnte, wie der Bezug auf das vorangehende Feminium מלכותו, „um *es* (sc sein eigenes Reich) zu vernichten", nur so verstanden werden, daß er durch seinen Machtwillen unwillentlich seine eigene Tochter bzw. sein eigenes Reich ins Verderben treibt. Von den Übersetzungen läßt die jüngere griechische („ϑ'") mit dem Pronomen αὐτήν, das sich sowohl auf τῆς βασιλείας αὐτοῦ als auch auf ϑυγατέρα γυναικῶν beziehen läßt, die Erklärung offen, während die Vulgata mit illud auf das Königreich, regnum eius, bezieht und die beiden hexaplarischen Zeugen der älteren griechischen Übersetzung („o'"), 88-Syh, da מלכות mit ἔργον (für מללאכה; Syh liest עבדא) wiedergegeben ist, mit dem Femininum αὐτήν – Syh unterscheidet das Suffix ה an dieser Stelle durch darüber gesetzten Punkt als Femininum von der gleichlautenden maskulinen Form – als allein mögliches Bezugswort θυγατέρα voraussetzen. Aber der J. Ziegler an dieser Stelle für seine Edition in der Göttinger Septuaginta (XVI 2, 1954) noch nicht zugängliche Chester Beatty-Papyrus 967 (Der Septuaginta-Text des Buches Daniel 5-12, sowie Esther 1-2,15, hrsg. von A. Geissen, PTA 5, 1968, S. 254), der hexaplarisch noch unbeeinflußt ist,

Instanz, die seiner Selbstüberhebung Einhalt gebietet, erscheint, wie bei Antiochos IV. das Heer der „chittäischen Schiffe" (V.30), die neu erstehende Weltmacht Rom als göttlicher Arm ausgleichender Gerechtigkeit: „Ein Feldherr treibt ihm seinen Hochmut aus; ja er läßt seinen Hochmut über ihn selbst kommen", והשבית קצין חרפתו לו בלתי חרפתו ישיב לו (V.18); sein Fall ist, wie der erst prophetisch erschaute Fall Antiochos' IV. – „er kommt zu seinem Ende, und keiner hilft ihm mehr" (V.45) –, die selbstverschuldete und selbst nicht erkannte Selbstzerstörung: „Er wird gefällt, fällt; man findet ihn nicht mehr", ונכשל ונפל ולא ימצא (V.19). Die zum schmachvollen Tod hintreibende Selbstüberhebung, die im Grund ein Versagen ist – abgeschwächt klingt die danielische Charakterisierung im Urteil des Polybios[10] über die spätere Lebenszeit dieses Königs nach: προβαίνων δὲ κατὰ τὴν ἡλικίαν ἐφάνη πολὺ καταδεέστερος αὑτοῦ καὶ τῆς τῶν ἐκτὸς προσδοκίας (XV 37,2): Selbsttäuschung, die die Enttäuschung seiner Untertanen hervorruft –, wird denn auch, entsprechend der Bedeutung, die der römische Antipode in der danielischen Schau gewinnt, bei Polybios und Livius darin sichtbar, daß im Angesicht seiner Niederlage gegen Rom sein eigener Machtanspruch von Anfang an gefährdet und seine Einschätzung dieses Feindes zwischen Furcht und Trotz schwankend erscheint: Die nach der anfänglichen Festigung seines Reiches aufscheinende Hoffnung, daß er „würdig der Königsherrschaft nicht nur über Asien, sondern auch über Europa erschien" (Polybios XI 34,16), wandelt sich, sobald der römische Antipode in seinem Machtbereich erscheint, in die furchtsame Klage über die Römer, die „kämen, um alle Königreiche zu beseitigen, daß es nirgends mehr eine Herrschaft außer der der Römer gebe", venire eos ad omnia regna tollenda, ut nullum usquam terrarum nisi Romanum imperium esset (Livius XXXVII 25,5), um dann vor der endgültigen Niederlage bei Magnesia angesichts der Antwort Scipios auf seine Friedensbedingungen – das ist „der Hohn" gegen den Römer, den dieser „auf sein eigenes Haupt zurückfallen" läßt (Dan 11,18): quod in praesentia dare possim, fidele consilium est: abi, nuntia meis verbis,

deutet mit αὐτόν, „um ihn zu vernichten", auf die – willentliche – Vernichtung des ptolemäischen Rivalen. Unabhängig von der Frage nach dem richtigen Bezugswort ist sicher, daß der Ausdruck להשחיתה nur die durch den Willen zur Erreichung der Macht verursachte Vernichtung „des Reiches", d.h. des erstrebten, aber nicht verwirklichten Reiches der wiedervereinigten Diadochenstaaten, meinen kann, und diese Aussage ist es, die das politische Ziel Antiochos' III. als „Willen zur Vernichtung" von der gleichgerichteten Wiedervereinigungspolitik durch Heirat unter Ptolemaios II. Philadelphos und Antiochos II. Theos wesenhaft unterscheidet, die zwar auch im Unheil – der Rache der verstossenen Laodike an der ptolemäischen Königstochter Berenike und dem dadurch hervorgerufenen Λαοδίκειος πόλεμος – endet, von der aber nicht gesagt ist, daß sie mit der Absicht להשחיתה initiiert wurde (V.6): ein Zeichen des fortschreitenden Niedergangs innerhalb der Geschichte des letzten Weltreichs schon in der Periode der Vorgeschichte bis zu jener Zäsur, in der die Geschichte der Religionsverfolgung einsetzt.

[10] Vgl. S. 184f.

bello absistat, pacis condicionem nullam recuset! (Livius XXXVII 36,7–8) – in die Selbstüberhebung des Siegers zurückzufallen: nihil ea moverunt regem, tutam fore belli aleam ratum quando perinde ac victo iam sibi leges dicerentur (9).

Vergebliches Streben nach der Weltmacht mit dem Ziel der Vernichtung des Antipoden (Dan 11,17), mit dem Hohn der Gegenmacht vergoltener Hohn (V.18), Bedrängnis des eigenen Reiches – „er, der die Festungen anderer bedrängt hatte (V.10.15, cf 18), muß sich – so heißt es ironisch – jetzt... an der Eroberung seiner eigenen genügen lassen“ (A. Bentzen[11]) –, die zum Untergang durch die Untertanen seines eigenen Reiches führt (V.19), sind Formen jener Aktualisierung ausgleichender Gerechtigkeit, die nach der Vergeltungslehre Israels in hellenistischer Zeit als geschichtliches, nicht als endzeitliches Gericht, an den Bedrängern vollzogen wird, die Israels Rechtsgrundlage als untertane Glaubensgemeinschaft gefährden[12].

Was aber die Gefährdung durch die Politik und Religionspolitik der Oberherren noch in der Zeit der Bewahrung der alten Rechtsgrundlage im Blick auf die Existenz der jerusalemischen Tempelgemeinde *wesenhaft* von jener Gefährdung unterscheidet, die nach danielischer Schau aufgrund der Maßnahmen Antiochos' IV. den religiösen und politischen Widerstand, den status confessionis, hervorrief, das muß zuerst aus dem Ereignis erschlossen werden, das als einziges während dieser Periode als eine Aktion berichtet ist, die aus Angehörigen des Tempelstaates hervorging: die Parteinahme von „Gewalttätigen“ aus Daniels Volk, בני פריצי עמך, für den Seleukiden (V.14b).

Im profangeschichtlichen Kontext des ptolemäisch-seleukidischen Machtkampfes um Kölesyrien ist nur gesagt, daß diese Aktion im Zusammenhang von Bewegungen steht, die auch außerhalb Judäas in den umkämpften Gebieten erwachten: ובעתים ההם רבים יעמדו על־מלך הנגב (14a). Das läßt, da gleichgerichtete religiöse Tendenzen innerhalb dieser verschiedenen Volksgruppen unwahrscheinlich sind, auf eine rein politisch motivierte Bewegung schließen, die mit möglichen Unterschieden zwischen der ptolemäischen und der seleukidischen Religionspolitik nichts zu tun hat.

Aber – und das ist der entscheidende Punkt – die „Söhne der Gewalttätigen

---

[11] A. BENTZEN, Daniel, HAT 1. Reihe 19, 1937, S. 49; 2. Auflage, 1952, S. 81.

[12] Vgl. Zum Text des 2. und 3. Makkabäerbuches (wie Anm. 8) S. 18f. mit Anm. 4 und Zur Zeitrechnung des I. und II. Makkabäerbuches, BZAW 88, 1964, S. 49–96; hier S. 74, Anm. 33. Diodors Charakterisierung von Antiochos' III. Geschick (Vgl. S. 184f.), nach welcher der von den Göttern herbeigeführte Untergang seines Reiches als Zeichen seiner eigenen Taten erscheint – ὥσπερ ἀπὸ παραγραφῆς τῶν ἰδίων πράξεων ἐπὶ τὸ χεῖρον ἑώρων τὰς αὑτῶν βασιλείας ὑπὸ τοῦ δαιμονίου προαγομένας (XXVIII 3) –, dürfte wiederum als hellenistisch geschichtsphilosophische Verifizierung des jüdisch apokalyptischen vaticinium ex eventu bestimmt werden (vgl. Anm. 6): jüdisch-apokalyptische interpretatio Graeca hellenistischer oder griechisch-hellenistische interpretatio Graeca jüdischer Tradition?

aus Daniels Volk" selbst verstehen diese Aktion „religionspolitisch" als „Erfüllung eines Gesichtes", einer Weissagung – להעמיד חזון –, und dieses Verständnis ist es, das der Apokalyptiker als Abfall verurteilt, der sich als solcher durch ihren Fall offenbart: ונכשלו. Das kann als apokalyptische Offenbarung nur bedeuten, daß das Verständnis der Parteinahme zwischen den um die Herrschaft über den jerusalemischen Tempelstaat kämpfenden Mächten und der Teilnahme an der politischen Realisierung dieser Gesinnung als „Gesicht", als göttlicher Auftrag, ein Akt des Ungehorsams gegen den Gott Israels ist.

Daß das Widergöttliche des Unternehmens der „Söhne der Gewalttätigen" nach danielischer Schau nicht in einer „falschen Politik", der Parteinahme für den nach göttlicher Vorsehung nicht als Herrscher über Israel bestimmten König, besteht, sondern im Verständnis der politischen Parteinahme als göttlicher Auftrag, das wird darin offenbar, daß die Parteinahme für den Seleukiden und die als Erfüllung einer Weissagung verstandene Aktion, die letztlich zum Fall ihrer Urheber führt, ein Unternehmen ist, das dem vorgesehenen Verlauf der Geschichte nicht widerstrebt, sondern ihm dient: das Eintreten für die Macht, die Israels Oberherr werden wird, eine noch vergebliche Aktion – ein Opfertod? –, die seinen Sieg vorbereitet. Da diese Aktion einer innerisraelitischen Abspaltung aber noch in die Zeit fällt, in welcher der Kampf lediglich um die Herrschaft über Kölesyrien geht, noch nicht um jenes von Daniel als בוא כתקף כל־מלכותו bezeichnete Trachten nach der Wiederherstellung des makedonischen Weltreiches (V.17), die für Israel das Zeichen des Anbruchs der Endzeit bedeutet, wird zu schließen sein, daß es sich bei den „Söhnen der Gewalttätigen aus Daniels Volk" nicht um eine endzeitlich bestimmte Abspaltung handelt, sondern um eine politisch diesseitig bestimmte, die die Ablösung der ptolemäischen Oberherrschaft durch die seleukidische als göttlichen Beschluß versteht, zu dessen Ausführung beizutragen sie sich vom Gott Israels berufen glaubt.

Eine weiter gehende historische Ausdeutung der apokalyptisch verhüllten Aussage ist auch von außerdanielischen Quellen her kaum möglich. Daß in den Völkerschaften der ptolemäisch-seleukidisch umkämpften Gebiete politische Parteiungen entstanden, zeigt der Bericht des Polybios – seine völkerpsychologische Betrachtung nach dem ptolemäischen Sieg von Raphia, nach der die Begrüßung des Ptolemäers nicht nur im politischen Opportunismus – ἁρμόζεσθαί πως ἀεὶ πρὸς τὸ παρόν –, sondern auch in der größeren Zuneigung zur ptolemäischen Herrschaft – τῆς εὐνοίας προκαθηγουμένης πρὸς τοὺς ἀπὸ τῆς Ἀλεξανδρείας βασιλεῖς – begründet ist (V 86,9–10), spräche hinsichtlich der „Gewalttätigen" eher für eine Gegenbewegung gegen die allgemeine Tendenz –; aber um diese Alternative geht es dem Apokalyptiker nicht. Die in sich widersprüchliche Überlieferung des Josephus über die „Tobiaden" und ihr Verhältnis zur hohepriesterlichen Familie des Onias gibt über die Feststellung hinaus, daß es innerhalb der Judenschaft ptolemäisch und seleukidisch gesinnte

Kreise gab, über diese Frage keinen weiteren Aufschluß[13] –; aber für die Frage, um die es uns geht – inwieweit unterscheiden sich die hier dargestellten Ereignisse nach danielischer Schau von denen der seleukidischen Religionsverfolgung unter Antiochos IV. Epiphanes? –, ist nicht das Besondere des historischen Faktums, sondern allein die Art und Weise, wie der Apokalyptiker es sieht und beurteilt, von Bedeutung.

Es geht hier um nichts anderes als darum, daß eine Schar Menschen aus der jerusalemischen Gemeinde wähnt, durch ein ihr zuteil gewordenes Gesicht den Herrschaftswechsel mitentscheiden zu können. Für die Machtdemonstration des seleukidischen Prätendenten ist die Aktion bedeutungslos. Der jerusalemischen Gemeinde, so wie sie im Zeugen Daniel personifiziert ist, erscheint sie als Häresie von Gewalttätigen, בני פריצים, die politisch ebenso erfolglos ist, wie analoge Bewegungen in anderen Gebieten des umkämpften Bereichs von

[13] Vgl. M. Hengel, Judentum S. 486–503. Was man mit der hier vorsichtig interpretierten Überlieferung unvorsichtig durch spekulative Ergänzung fehlender Zwischenglieder alles machen kann, zeigt z. B. A. Schlatter, Die B^{e}ne pariṣim bei Daniel 11,14 (ZAW 14, 1894, S. 145–149), dessen Deutung der Stelle auf „die" Tobiaden, deren gewaltsames Geschick von Hyrkan bis Menelaos mit dem Ausdruck ונכשלו ausgesagt wäre, schon daran scheitert, daß die danielischen Aussagen in der großen Audition von Kap. 11 verhüllt chronologisch aufeinander folgende Ereignisse berichten und nie Voraussagen enthalten, die dem kontinuierlich historischen Bericht vorgreifen. Von dem bei Polybios (XVI 39,1), auf ihm fußend Josephus (Ant XII 135) und dem Porphyrios tradierenden Hieronymus (in Danielem zur Stelle) überlieferten Verlauf der seleukidisch-ptolemäischen Kämpfe während dieser Zeit bleibt die von M. Hengel (S. 14) mitvertretene historische Deutung die wahrscheinlichste, daß es sich bei dem „Fall" der „Söhne der Gewalttätigen" um die Bestrafung einer proseleukidischen judäischen Bewegung durch den ptolemäischen Feldherrn Skopas in der Zeit jener ersten militärischen Erfolge handelt, die er vor seiner Niederlage bei Paneas noch zu erringen vermochte. Gesteht man der danielischen Aussage die größte Geschichtsnähe und, was die Geschichte Judäas anbetrifft, beste Geschichtskenntnis zu, dann wäre die außerdanielische Überlieferung, nach der es sich nicht um die Bestrafung einer proseleukidischen Partei, die Hieronymus als der ptolemäischen ebenbürtig darstellt – Iudaea ... in contraria studia scindebatur, aliis Antiocho aliis Ptolomaeo faventibus –, sondern aufgrund der proseleukidischen Unternehmung um eine Unterwerfung ganz Judäas handelt – ὁ δὲ τοῦ Πτολεμαίου στρατηγὸς Σκόπας ὁρμήσας εἰς τοὺς ἄνω τόπους κατεστρέψατο ἐν τῷ χειμῶνι τὸ Ἰουδαίων ἔθνος (Polybios nach Zitat des Josephus), Scopas ..., dux Ptolomaei partium, adversum Antiochum fortiter dimicavit cepitque Iudaeam (Hieronymus auf der Grundlage des Porphyrios) –, als monumentale Ausgestaltung eines historisch geringfügigen Ereignisses zu erklären. Daß die verhüllte Geschichtsaussage Daniels früh historische Deutungen hervorrief, zeigt die ältere, dem Original zeitlich nahe stehende, aber freiere und teilweise auf anderer hebräischer bzw. aramäischer Vorlage beruhende der beiden griechischen Übersetzungen, nach der aufgrund der Lesung ובנה פרצים nach Am 9,11 für בני פריצי: καὶ ἀνοικοδομήσει τὰ πεπτωκότα τοῦ ἔθνους σου – auch die Übersetzung ist aus der Amos-LXX übernommen –, die Erfüllung der Weissagung vom Wiederaufbau der zerfallenen Hütte Davids aus Am 9,11-12 durch den ptolemäischen König, durch dessen Werk – so wird der Kontext zu verstehen sein – seine Widersacher zu Fall kommen, προσκόψουσιν, aus der danielischen Aussage herausgelesen wird, eine historische Deutung, die Hieronymus, ohne daß er die Quelle nennt, dazu verführt haben dürfte, in diesem Ereignis den Bau des Tempels von Leontopolis durch den geflohenen Hohenpriester Onias nach der Prophetie von Is 19,18-21 zu sehen.

Kölesyrien (V.14a). Sie sind – und das unterscheidet sie von den Bewegungen innerhalb Israels während der Zeit jenes „Verachteten, dem die Königsherrschaft nicht zukommt" (V.21a) – nicht in die Machenschaften des Herrschers verstrickt. Sie sind – und das unterscheidet sie gleicherweise von den Verwirrungen jener Zeit – innerhalb der jerusalemischen Glaubensgemeinschaft nicht zwischen „Rechtgläubigkeit und Ketzerei" umkämpft; sie sind nur „Abgespaltene"[14]. Sie sind nicht – und darum geht es zuerst – hineingenommen in jene oberherrliche religionspolitische Machtdemonstration einer Erhebung „über alles was Gott ist" (V.36–39), in deren Angesicht Daniel auch in der letzten Zeit der Bedrängnis nicht mehr von einer Verstrickung judäischer Bewegungen zu sagen weiß: Sie sind nicht eine innerjudäische Bewegung, die daran mitschuldig wird, daß der נגיד ברית durch die Maßnahmen des Oberherrn beseitigt werden kann (V.22). Sie sind nicht die, die „den heiligen Bund verlassen", auf die darum der Widersacher „sein Auge richten" kann, so daß durch ihre Mitschuld die Schändung des Heiligtums eintritt (V.30–32).

Und darum „fallen sie" – ונכשלו – in anderer Weise als jene „Weisen des Volkes", die im geistigen Widerstand gegen die „Frevler am Bund", מרשיעי ברית fallen (V.32–35) –; denn sie sind nicht משׂכילי עם, sondern פריצי עם –: nicht „zur Reinigung auf die Zeit des Endes hin" (V.35), sondern als solche, die in dieser Zeit "gewalttätig" ein Gesicht, das nicht von Jahwe kam, „erfüllen" wollten.

Und darum darf für ihr Ziel und ihre Aktion nicht jener Bruch in der oberherrlichen Religionspolitik als Ursache, αἰτία, vorausgesetzt werden, der nach der Schau Daniels, und wie es – nach meinem Urteil – der Historie entspricht, Israels Augapfel, das Jahwebekenntnis, antastet (Sach 2,12).

---

[14] Dem Begriff פריץ eignet an allen Stellen, an denen er im Alten Testament vorkommt, die Bedeutung des Gewaltsamen im widergöttlichen Sinn. Wenn er an dieser Stelle, was bei apokalyptischer Formulierung wahrscheinlich ist, von vorgegebener Tradition her geprägt ist, kommt an erster Stelle der ezechielische Ausdruck für den gottlosen Sohn (18,10) in Frage – nur hier liegt auch die Konstruktusverbindung mit בן vor, und die Übersetzung der jüngeren Daniel-LXX („ϑ'") bestätigt den Bezug mit der Übernahme des im ursprünglichen Übersetzungstext der LXX nur an diesen beiden Stellen überlieferten Äquivalents (υἱὸς) λοιμός, das aber als genuines Übersetzungswort Theodotions auch in Ez 7,22 und Is 35,9 nachgewiesen und als altüberliefertes Äquivalent für בליעל (Reg I 1,16; 2,12; 10,27; 25,17.25; vgl. 29,10; 30,22) als Inbegriff des Frevlers in der Septuagintasprache verankert ist –; als vorgeprägte Tradition für die danielische Bedeutung der בני פריצי עמך erscheint bei Ezechiel neben dem gottlosen Sohn noch der Schänder des Heiligtums (7,22), bei Jeremia der Übertreter des Gesetzes, der durch seinen Kultdienst das Haus Gottes zur „Räuberhöhle", מערת פרצים, macht (7,11), im Psalter der Gottlose, vor dessen Wegen der Jahwe Zugekehrte bewahrt wird (17,4), aufgrund ihrer Zuordnung zum Gott Israels, seinem Gesetz und seinem Haus denkbar. Für die danielische Prägung des Begriffs dürfte aber, da es um das Werk von Abtrünnigen geht, die sich die Erfüllung eines Gesichtes anmassen, auch die Grundbedeutung des Stammes פרץ, das „Einreissen" im Sinne der Abspaltung, mitbestimmend sein, die in LXX beim Verbum und der Nominalbildung פרץ durch die bestbezeugte Äquivalenz διακόπτειν bzw. διακοπή bewahrt ist.

Von der Politik und Religionspolitik des Seleukiden Antiochos III. aus gesehen dürfte dann jener Bruch in seiner Königsherrschaft, den Polybios mit seinem Aufstand gegen Rom verwirklicht sieht – die αἰτία der Zorn der Aitoler gegen die Römer, der im Seleukiden das Machtstreben gegen Westen weckt, die πρόφασις die so begründete Befreiung Griechenlands, die ἀρχή sein Zug nach Demetrias (III 7)[15] –, im Blick auf den jerusalemischen Tempelstaat als die dem politischen Großmachtstreben entsprechende religionspolitische Aufhebung jener bei Josephus überlieferten Zugeständnisse freier Religionsausübung[16] zu postulieren sein, die nur aus dem Grund noch nicht widerrufen waren, weil die seleukidische Macht außenpolitisch voll in Anspruch genommen war, die aber Daniel „diese Auseinandersetzungen aufmerksam verfolgend" bereits gefährdet sah: die αἰτία das Weltmachtstreben, die πρόφασις die innere Gefährdung seines Reiches, die ἀρχή, die an Israel noch vorbeiging, der Aufstand gegen die „Festungen seines eigenen Reiches", der zu seinem Tod führt (V.19).

An diesem Punkt, bei der Frage, wie sich die in der Vorgeschichte der seleukidischen Religionsverfolgung für Israel noch nicht realisierte αἰτία der Wandlung oberherrlicher Religionspolitik zur πρόφασις der für sie günstigen innerisraelitischen Zwistigkeiten verhält, dürfte dann wieder, teilweise von verschiedenen Positionen her, das freundschaftliche Gespräch – bis hin zur unterschiedlich beantworteten Frage, wie lange Zeit ein Kamel benötigt, bis es die Nachricht vom Tod des Antiochos Epiphanes von der medischen Grenze nach Jerusalem getragen hat[17] – zwischen dem Jubilar und dem Gratulanten einsetzen.

Bibliographie

W. Baumgartner, Das Buch Daniel, AWR. AT 1, 1926.

A. Bentzen, Daniel, HAT 1. Reihe 19, 1937; 2. Auflage 1952.

H. Conzelmann, Heiden–Juden–Christen, BHTh 62, 1981.

F. Daumas, Les moyens d'expression du Grec et de l'Égyptien comparés dans les décrets de Canope et de Memphis, Supplément aux annales du service des antiquités de l'Égypte, Cahier 16, le Caire 1952, Appendice S. 253–274.

–, Les textes bilingues ou trilingues, in: Textes et langages de l'Égypte Pharaonique, cent cinquante années de recherches 1822–1972, hommage à J.-F. Champollion, Le Caire 1974.

H. Gauthier et H. Sottas, Un décret trilingue en l'honneur de Ptolémée IV., Service des antiquités de l'Égypte, Cairo 1925.

A. Geissen (ed.), Der Septuaginta-Text des Buches Daniel 5-12, sowie Esther 1-2,15, PTA 5, 1968.

---

[15] Vgl. S. 181 mit Anm. 1.

[16] Vgl. S. 186.

[17] M. Hengel, Judentum S. 178 mit Anm. 299 und 300.

R. Hanhart, Zum Text des 2. und 3. Makkabäerbuches, NAWG.PH 13, 1961, S. 427–486 (= MSU VII, 1961).

–, Kriterien geschichtlicher Wahrheit in der Makkabäerzeit, Zur geschichtlichen Bedeutung der danielischen Weltreichlehre, in: Drei Studien zum Judentum, TEH 140, 1967, S. 7–22.

–, Zur Zeitrechnung des I. und II. Makkabäerbuches, BZAW 88, 1964, S. 49–96.

M. Hengel, Judentum und Hellenismus, Studien zu ihrer Begegung unter besonderer Berücksichtigung Palästinas bis zur Mitte des 2. Jh. v. Chr., WUNT 10, 1969 (2. durchgesehene und ergänzte Auflage 1973).

F. Jesi, Notes sur l'édit dionysiaque de Ptolémée IV Philopator, JNES 15, 1956, S. 236–240.

A. Momigliano, Il decreto trilingue in onore di Tolomeo Filopatore, Aeg. 10, 1929, S. 180–189.

W. Otto, Zu dem dreisprachigen Priesterdekret von Memphis aus dem sechsten Jahre Ptolemaios' IV., Beiträge zur Seleukidengeschichte des 3. Jahrhunderts v. Chr., IV, ABAW.PP, XXXIV. Band, 1. Abhandlung, 1928, S. 80–87.

P. Pédech, La méthode historique de Polybe, CEA, 1964.

A. Schlatter, Die B^{e}ne pariṣim bei Daniel 11,14, ZAW 14, 1894, S. 145–149.

J. Schwartz et M. Malinine, Pierres d'Égypte, RAr 1, 1960, S. 77–90.

H. J. Thissen, Studien zum Raphiadekret, BKP 23, 1966.

J. Ziegler, (ed.), Susanna, Daniel, Bel et Draco, Septuaginta, Vetus Testamentum Graecum, Auct. Soc. Litt. Gottingensis ed., vol. XVI, pars 2, 1954.

Invented Traditions of the Maccabean Era

by

Albert I. Baumgarten

The collection of essays edited by E. Hobsbawm and T. Ranger, published in 1983 as *The Invention of Tradition*,[1] introduced the notion of invented traditions. These are defined by the authors as a set of repeated practices, which regularly seek to inculcate certain values and norms, and are intended to establish a continuity with the past. Insofar as these practices refer to a historic past, that past is often factitious, hence these traditions are "invented." These are then "responses to novel situations, which take the form of reference to old situations,"[2] which proliferate particularly at times of rapid change. Their objectives fall into three overlapping categories: (1) establishing or symbolizing cohesion or membership in groups; (2) establishing or legitimizing institutions, status or relations of authority; (3) socialization, the inculcation of beliefs or of behavior.[3]

The notion of invented tradition has implications and applications well beyond the chronological and geographic limits of the studies in the Hobsbawm/Ranger volume: the idea that certain circumstances favor the invention of traditions – as a means of closing the gap between the old and the new, of giving a certain aura of legitimacy to a changed cultural context – has the ability to illuminate examples not restricted to Britain or Europe of the past few hundred years, the focus of the papers in the Hobsbawm/Ranger collection.

The contribution of the Hobsbawm/Ranger volume is highlighted by considering it from another perspective. The ways in which societies invent a new past to serve changing needs in the present and then institutionalize these structures in conventions and practices, as analyzed in the essays in *The Invention of Tradition*, were known to historians before 1983.[4] The merit of its editors and contributors is therefore not in having discovered these ways, rather it is in

---

1 Hobsbawm/Ranger, Invention. Indicative of its status, this book was then reprinted seven times – in 1984, 1985, 1986, 1987, 1988, 1989, and 1992.

2 E. Hobsbawm, "Introduction," in Hobsbawm/Ranger, Invention, 2.

3 Ibid., 9.

4 To mention one classic example see B. Lewis, History, Remembered, Recovered, Invented (Princeton, 1975).

having thematized the understanding of a technique by which societies cope with rapidly changing circumstances. Calling attention to the phenomenon, giving it a name, can help historians more readily recognize its presence and significance in other times and locations.

It is therefore not surprising that analysis of invented traditions has found a place in recent scholarship on Jewish history.[5] This paper will be devoted to identifying and analyzing two invented traditions of the Maccabean Era: the half sheqel Temple tax and the recitation of the *Shema*.

I

The second century BCE was a time of rapid change, whose elements included: (1) the encounter with Hellenism; (2) the persecutions of Antiochus IV, altering the terms of close to four hundred years of control of Jews and Judaism by different world empires;[6] (3) the cooperation of at least some of the traditional leaders with those persecutions; (4) the successful revolt against Antiochus IV and his decrees; (5) the achievement of independence under the leadership of the Maccabees – the last four events on this list having taken place over a quarter of a century.

A poignant indication of the breakdown of the old order is suggested by comparison of Ben Sira 50:24, according to the Hebrew version, with the Greek translation of the same verse. The Hebrew reads:

> May His love abide upon Simon, and may He keep in him the covenant of Phinehas; may one never be cut off from him; and as for his offspring, (may it be) as (enduring as) the days of heaven.

Ben Sira, who wrote in the first quarter of the second century BCE, represented traditional values in the attitudes displayed here. He regarded Jewish life as it existed under the reign of his hero, the High Priest Simon son of Onias, as the virtually complete embodiment of the nation's highest aspirations, as the flowering of all God's works in creation during human history.[7] He put his trust in the hands of the descendants of Simon, praying for their loyalty and continued rule as priests. Yet, within a few decades after his death, some of the

---

[5] See M. Silber, "The Emergence of Ultra-Orthodoxy: The Invention of a Tradition," in J. Wertheimer (Ed.), The Uses of Tradition (New York/Jerusalem, 1992), 23–84; Y. Zerubavel, Recovered Roots: Collective Memory and the Making of Israeli National Tradition (Chicago, 1995).

[6] The terms go back to the Persian Empire and were copied virtually without change by Alexander the Great and his successors. For an example of the old arrangement see Ezra Chapter 7.

[7] For a full discussion of this aspect of Ben Sira see Mack, Wisdom and the Hebrew Epic.

progeny of Simon collaborated, at the very least,[8] with the decrees of Antiochus IV; others of his offspring were to leave Jerusalem and found the "House of Onias," in service of the Ptolemies, at Leontopolis in Egypt.[9] The priests in charge in Jerusalem were to be the Maccabees. One indication of the gap between Ben Sira's expectations and the reality which ensued has been noted by Segal:[10] when Ben Sira's grandson translated his ancestor's work into Greek he changed the meaning of 50:24, rendering it "May He entrust to us His mercy, and let Him deliver us in our days." The grandson did this, Segal suggests, so as to avoid embarrassing his grandfather in the eyes of later readers. Had the original been translated without alteration, later readers would have been aware of the painful contrast between the author's hopes as expressed in the Hebrew original and events as they had unfolded. It seemed better to the grandson to conceal this awkward situation by modifying the translation. So great had been the changes in the two generations which separated author from translator! This time period between grandfather and grandson, however, is precisely the era under consideration here, the middle years of the second century BCE.

Under those circumstances, with such momentous changes having taken place, how was a new elite such as the Maccabees to respond? It is in moments such as these, when the new seems to threaten to overwhelm, that the spirit of the past is often invoked. In that sense, to paraphrase a comment of Karl Marx, the revolutionary thus becomes the most eager consumer of precedents, whether real or imaginary.[11] The stage is set for the invention of tradition, to be recorded as history, reinforced as liturgy and ceremony, celebrated as ritual.

II

To appreciate the background of the half sheqel Temple tax, the first of the invented traditions to be discussed in this paper, we must begin at the time of Nehemiah. One of the planks of Nehemiah's reforms in Jerusalem was his intention to create an egalitarian Jewish society, in which the ties which bound one Jew to the other were to be more important than the connections between

---

[8] As is well known, according to some scholars – most notably E.J. BICKERMAN and the honoree of this volume – these Oniads had a large share in initiating the persecutions.

[9] The history of this house is discussed several times by Josephus. See War 7. 421ff.; Ant. 12. 387f.; 13. 62ff.; 20. 236.

[10] M. SEGAL, Sefer Ben Sira Hashalem (Jerusalem, 1972), 348. A number of other scholars have also adopted this interpretation. See MACK, Wisdom and the Hebrew Epic, 180; A. DI LELLA and P. SKEHAN, The Wisdom of Ben Sira (New York, 1987), 554.

[11] See the discussion in H. DESROCHES, The Sociology of Hope (London/Boston, 1979), 157.

Jews and outsiders.[12] Among the steps taken to achieve this goal was his support for redistribution of land and cancellation of debts, in an attempt to cope with the dislocations which had resulted in the concentration of wealth in the hands of the rich. Nehemiah supported the lesser clergy, the Levites, against the higher clergy, the priests. As yet another aspect of this strategy, Nehemiah instituted a one-third sheqel poll tax to support the Temple and pay for its public offerings, from the shewbread and the daily sacrifices, to the sacrifices on holidays and the public sin offerings (10:32–33). As a logical continuation of these steps, the responsibility for the wood offering for the Temple was to be allocated by lot (10:34). We cannot be certain what alternative means of funding sacrifices and supplying wood these steps were intended to replace, but it seems likely that, prior to Nehemiah, these obligations had been assumed by wealthy individuals or families (note the way in which Nehemiah funded the building of sections of his wall, Chapter 3). As such, these wealthy families would have enjoyed a sense of special connection with the worship of God in His Temple. Nehemiah's policy, by contrast, was intended to impose an equality of obligation and feeling of participation on all Jews, yet one more aspect of the egalitarianism which he intended to promote among Jews.

Nehemiah may have been able to invoke scriptural authority for some of his actions, such as cancellation of debts and redistribution of land, understanding them as application of sabbatical year and Jubilee legislation in the Torah. The scriptural basis for a poll tax of one-third sheqel, and its use to support the Temple, is beyond our knowledge.[13] Equally beyond our information is the fate of these reforms after Nehemiah left Jerusalem. In all likelihood, however, they did not long endure. Nehemiah himself discovered how short-lived his actions had been when he returned for a second time (13:6–31). One generation after Nehemiah the sons of his enemy Sanballat were consulting together with the priests in Jerusalem in response to the petition of the Jews of Elephantine (P. Cowley 30). I therefore believe it likely that the old methods of funding the Temple, favorable to the aristocracy and its preeminence, were restored sometime (soon?) after Nehemiah's departure.

---

[12] In this discussion of Nehemiah my debt to the insightful analysis of M. SMITH, Palestinian Parties and Politics that Shaped the Old Testament (New York, 1971), 126–145, cannot be overstated. When Nehemiah's policy is considered as a whole, both the egalitarian side and his insistence on increasing the distance between Jews and the surrounding nations, it appears as a classic case of enclave culture. On the nature of enclave cultures see M. DOUGLAS, In the Wilderness (Sheffield, 1993), 42–62. See also A.I. BAUMGARTEN, "Finding Oneself in a Sectarian Context," in J. ASSMANN, A. BAUMGARTEN and G. Stroumsa (Eds.), Self, Soul and Body in Religious Experience, forthcoming.

[13] According to 2 Kings 12:4–16; 22:4 there was a box where money was collected for repair of the Temple. The money deposited in the box was not a poll tax. At the Jewish garrison of Elephantine, in the fifth century BCE, an (annual?) assessment of two sheqels per person was collected (P. Cowley 22).

The Maccabees, as new high priestly rulers in the aftermath of the tumultuous events of the second century BCE summarized above, also needed ways to reinforce the legitimacy of their rule. This was especially true in light of the restriction, albeit much more theoretical than practically meaningful, placed on their rule by the special assembly that ratified their status (1 Macc. 14:41): that they should be "leaders and high priests forever, until a true prophet should arise." Among the various means employed by the Maccabees to promote their acceptance as rulers of the Jews was their encouragement of observance of the holiday of Hanukkah (see the two letters at the beginning of 2 Macc.). Anyone who celebrated that holiday was acknowledging that the hand of God had foiled the evil plans of Antiochus IV and placed the rule over the newly purified Temple in the hands of the Maccabees.

A second method to achieve that same objective was the imposition of the half sheqel Temple tax.[14] As Bickerman has shown on numismatic grounds, the half sheqel Temple tax was instituted sometime between 125 and 88 BCE. Much more successful than Nehemiah, the authorities of the Maccabean era managed to connect their tax with Exod. 30:12. The latter verse speaks of a one-time ransom, levied to purify the people at a time of census, and employed to pay for the construction of the Tabernacle. This verse has now become the justification for an annual tax to be used to support the Hasmonean Temple of Jerusalem.[15] This interpretation of the verse was to be so secure that Philo did not doubt the Mosaic origin of the Temple tax (*Spec. Leg* 1.76–78). In other words, an invented tradition has been created.[16]

Appropriate to the role played by such invented traditions, the half sheqel Temple tax served to bolster loyalty to the Temple in Jerusalem and its Maccabean priesthood. It was to be so successful that it became a marker of being Jewish. According to the Rabbis, it was imposed on adult males, accepted from females, slaves or minors, but declined if paid by a gentile (*mSheq* 1:5). As in the days of Nehemiah, the money was used to fund public sacrifices, reinforcing the sense of participation of all Jews who paid the tax in every public offering on the altar.

---

[14] On the history of this tax see E. J. Bickerman, "La Charte Seleucide de Jerusalem," Studies in Jewish and Christian History, Part Two (Leiden, 1980), 75–81; D. Flusser, "Matthew XVII, 24–27 and the Dead Sea Sect," Tarbiz 31 (5722) 150–156 [in Hebrew]; J. Liver, "The Half Shekel Offering in Biblical and Post-Biblical Literature," HTR 56 (1963), 172–198; Y. Sussmann, "Research on the History of the Halacha and the Scrolls of the Judean Desert," Tarbiz 59 (5750), 32 n. 91 [in Hebrew]. E. & H. Eshel, "4Q471 Fragment 1 and Ma amadot in the War Scroll," in J. Barrera and L. Montaner (Eds.), The Madrid Qumran Congress: Proceedings of the International Congress on the Dead Sea Scrolls Madrid 18–21 March, 1991 (Leiden, 1992), 2. 619–620.

[15] As one way-station in the trajectory from original context in Exod. to final meaning at the time of the Maccabees compare 2 Chron. 24:6.

[16] For an analysis of the extent to which Jews worldwide paid this tax see S. Mandell, "Who Paid the Temple Tax when the Jews were under Roman Rule?" HTR 77 (1984), 223–232.

Approval of the new tax was not, however, unanimous. The Qumran sectarians, who had qualms either about the legitimacy of the tax and/or of the way the Temple was being run by those who collected it, refused to pay it.[17] Those at Qumran agreed that a ransom to God should be paid (Exod. 30:12), but insisted that it need be done only once in a lifetime. Who received their money on behalf of God is a very interesting question beyond our ability to answer.[18]

This debate over the Temple tax and its use had one further consequence. The Mishnah (*mSheq* 3:3) informs us that those who supported the Temple establishment would pay their tax demonstratively. Furthermore, when the time came to gather up the money which had been collected and apply it for the purposes of supporting the Temple, that too was done demonstratively. This behavior was necessary because the issue was controversial, because there were those who dissented. Those endorsing the symbolic structure reinforced by the invented tradition of the half sheqel tax, who shared the identity it established, felt the need to make their agreement with these objectives evident by their actions.[19]

III

The recitation of the *Shema*,[20] the anthology of Biblical passages said twice daily – Dt. 6:4–9; 11:13–21; Num. 15:37–41, to which the Ten Commandments were originally added – is the second major topic of this paper. The history of the recitation of these passages is shrouded in obscurity. Just when did it become a regular feature of practice in the Temple? The difficulty of answering this question is such that in many recent discussions, such as that in the new Schürer, the question of date of origin is not even posed.[21] Thus, no context is proposed in which the recitation of the *Shema* was supposedly

[17] The attitude of the Qumran community towards the Maccabean family is no longer perceived to be as simple an issue as once believed. See my summary of the matter in A. I. Baumgarten, "Crisis in the Scrollery: A Dying Consensus," Judaism, 44 (1995), 399–413.

[18] See 4Q159, 6–7, published in J. M. Allegro, Discoveries in the Judean Desert V (Oxford, 1968), 47.

[19] On these passages see also M. Broshi, "Anti-Qumranic Polemics in the Talmud," Madrid Qumran Congress Volume 2, 593.

[20] Note, formally speaking the Shema is not a prayer: it is an affirmation of faith. Hence it is "recited." According to one Rabbinic account, SifreD 53, the use of the Shema as an affirmation of faith goes back to the sons of Jacob, assuring their father in his last living moments on earth that they will remain loyal to the best part of the family tradition. This story thus understands the declaration "Hear O Israel," as having then been addressed to Israel = Jacob.

[21] See Schürer, History, 2. 454–455. The same situation prevails in J. Heinemann and J. Petuchowski, The Literature of the Synagogue (New York, 1975), 15–28. See also E. Fleischer, "On the Beginnings of Obligatory Jewish Prayer," Tarbiz 59 (5750), 417- 418 [in

introduced. The same situation prevails in Kimelman's studies of the *Shema*.[22] In their agnosticism, scholars of our times are implicitly rejecting the conclusions of an earlier generation of scholars, who argued that the *Shema* had been introduced by the "Men of the Great Assembly," in the pre-Maccabean era.[23] Given the haziness of the portrayal of the "Men of the Great Assembly" in Rabbinic sources, the scepticism of contemporary scholars is well justified. In addition, the Talmudic sources which connect the "Men of the Great Assembly" with the institution of prayer never explicitly mention the *Shema* as one of their contributions.[24] In fact, Rabbinic sources simply assume the recitation of the *Shema*, and make no claim whatsoever attributing its establishment to any particular authority.[25] Caution is therefore necessary. Nevertheless, awareness of the existence of invented traditions encourages greater daring.[26]

Ben Sira reports on the splendor of daily worship in the Temple under the aegis of his hero Simon son of Onias (Chapter 50).[27] This account begins with a description of the sacrificial ritual in almost loving detail (50:1–15). Trumpets were then sounded, and the people fell prostrate on their faces (50:16–17). Songs (Psalms) were sung and prayer recited (50:18–19). Simon then blessed the people, who responded by bowing down in worship a second time (50:20–21). The recitation of the *Shema* simply does not appear in this account. Given the detail in which the proceedings were described, it seems best to conclude that the recitation of the *Shema* was not part of the service in Ben Sira's day, in the first quarter of the second century BCE.

The absence of the *Shema* is also notable in another text from this period.[28] Abraham and Isaac, in Jubilees, bless their children prior to their deaths (Ch.

Hebrew] who concedes that the Shema was said in the Temple prior to 70 CE but does not suggest a date for its origins.

[22] See R. KIMELMAN, "The Sema and its Blessings," in L. LEVINE (Ed.), The Synagogue in Late Antiquity (Philadelphia, 1987), 73–86; IDEM, "The Shema and its Rhetoric: The Case for the Shema being more than Creation, Revelation and Redemption," JJTP 2 (1992), 111–156.

[23] See L. ZUNZ, Die gottesdienstlichen Vorträge der Juden (Hildesheim, 1966 Reprint), 379; H. STEINTHAL, Über Juden und Judentum (Berlin, 1910^2), 254; I. ELBOGEN, "Studies in Jewish Liturgy," JQR 19 (1907), 230. One exception among studies of that era is BLAU, "Origine et Histoire," 180 who admits that the date of the introduction of this practice is beyond our knowledge.

[24] See, for example, the tradition attributed to R. Yohanan, bBer. 33a.

[25] This is the basis of BLAU's unwillingness to propose a date for the introduction of the practice of recitation of the Shema (see n. 23).

[26] The discussion of the history of the Shema below owes much to suggestions I heard in class, many years ago, from the late Gerson D. COHEN. As COHEN never published these ideas, responsibility for the contents of the argument below is solely mine. Nevertheless, I would not conceal COHEN's role in sparking my thinking on this subject. Recognition of the existence and function of invented traditions encouraged me to persist and formulate the conclusions, as presented below.

[27] My interpretation of this chapter of Ben Sira follows F. O'FEARGHAIL, "Sir. 50:5–21: Yom Kippur or the Daily Whole Offering?" Biblica 59 (1978), 301–316.

[28] I owe this discussion of Jubilees to a suggestion of Professor J. KUGEL.

20 & 36). Both commence their blessings with encouraging their children to follow the commandments of God. In each case, these begin with versions of Lev. 19:18, loving one's neighbor as oneself (Jub. 20:2; 36:4; see also CD vi, 20–21). The significance of this blessing is apparent when one compares the discussion in the gospels, reflecting a situation towards the end of the Second Temple era. Jesus was asked concerning the "Great Commandment," Mk. 12:28–34, Mt. 22:34–40, Lk. 10:25–28. Answering the question what is the first (i.e. most important) commandment (in Mt. and Mk.), or what must one do to inherit eternal life (Lk.), Jesus responds, according to Mk. 12: 29–31:

The first is, 'Hear O Israel: The Lord our God, the Lord is One. And you shall love the Lord your God with all your heart and with all your soul, and with all your mind, and with all your strength.' The second is this, 'You shall love your neighbor as yourself.' There is no other commandment greater than these.

In Mt. 22: 37–40 the response is:

'You shall love the Lord your God with all your heart and with all your soul, and with all your might.' This is the great and first commandment. And a second is like it. 'You shall love your neighbor as yourself.' On these two commandments depend all the law and all the prophets.

In Lk. 10:26–27 Jesus replies by way of a question:

What is written in the Law? How do you read? And he answered 'You shall love the Lord your God with all your heart, and with all your soul, and with all your mind: and your neighbor as yourself.'

Analyzing these passages, one sees that the response in Mk. is Dt. 6:4–5, while in Mt. and Lk. it is Dt. 6:5 alone. Furthermore, in all of these versions another biblical verse is also cited – to love one's neighbor as oneself (Lev. 19:18) – at times as the second most important commandment (Mt. and Mk.), at times conflated with the citation from Dt. (Lk.).

The contrast between Jubilees and the gospels is impressive. A verse not even cited in Jubilees takes precedence in the gospels, while the verse occupying the central place of the discussion in Jubilees is explicitly relegated to secondary status in two of the three gospel accounts. The best explanation for this, I propose, is that at the time of Jubilees, sometime in the mid-second century BCE,[29] the recitation of the *Shema* was not a fixed part of practice, hence its opening verse had not yet achieved prominence. By the

---

[29] I treat Jubilees, as many scholars do, as proto-sectarian, dating from a period in the second century BCE, just prior to the rise of full-blown sectarianism, and sharing a number of crucial concerns with the Qumran community, the calendar in particular. For one recent summary of scholarship on Jubilees see the introduction by O. WINTERMUTE, "Jubilees," in J. CHARLESWORTH (Ed.), OTP, 2. 35–50.

time of Jesus and the gospels, however, circumstances had changed and the *Shema* seemed the most celebrated verses of all.

That innovation may already be reflected in *Ep. Arist.* 160, which refers to the twice daily meditation upon the law, in a context in which *tefillin* and *mezuzot* have just been mentioned, indicating that the author has the practical application of the verses from Dt. 6 in mind. Nevertheless, the date and provenance of *Ep. Arist.* are very problematic, opinions varying from the third century BCE to the first century CE,[30] hence this indication is not of much use.[31]

The change which took place by the end of the Second Temple period can, however, be dated more precisely on the basis of Qumran evidence. The Manual of Discipline seems aware of the existence of the practice of reciting the *Shema*. Thus we learn that the sectarian proclaims:

> with the entry of day and night I will enter the covenant of God, and at the exit of evening and morning I will speak of His laws (1QS x, 10).[32]

Taking place twice a day, at morning and evening, and characterized by expressions such as "enter the covenant of God," and "speak of His laws," both significant themes of the *Shema*, it seems evident that the Manual of Discipline is alluding here to the recitation of the *Shema*.[33] This conclusion is reinforced by another line of the text, a bit further down (1QS x, 14): "I will praise Him before I go out or enter, or sit or rise, and while I lie on the couch of my bed." Here too the expressions evoke themes to be found in the *Shema*, specifically in this case Dt. 6:7.[34]

Josephus, summarizing the laws of Moses, with "all written as he left it: nothing have we added for the sake of embellishment, nothing which has not been bequeathed by Moses (*Ant.* 4. 196)," included among these laws:

---

30 For a summary of views on the date and provenance of Ep. Arist. see R. J. SHUTT, "Letter of Aristeas," in J. CHARLESWORTH (Ed.), OTP 2, 8–9. SHUTT guesses that the author was an Alexandrian, who lived ca. 170 BCE. If one follows the opinion which SHUTT concedes to be the majority view, the date of composition of Ep. Arist. would be sometime during the second half of the second century BCE, which would accord well with the argument proposed below. For a forceful presentation of the majority view, see further E. J. BICKERMAN, "Zur Datierung des Pseudo Aristeas," Studies in Jewish and Christian History, Part One (Leiden, 1976), 109–136.

31 Note that the description of the Temple cult in Ps. Arist. 92–95 consists of nothing but animal sacrifice.

32 The Shema, as noted above, was part of the Temple service. The Qumran sectarian, in the opinion of many scholars, conceived his life in the community as a replacement for the life of the Temple. Hence it was entirely appropriate for someone at Qumran to recite the Shema.

33 My analysis follows the discussion in L. SCHIFFMAN, Reclaiming the Dead Sea Scrolls – The History of Judaism, the Background of Christianity, the Lost Library of Qumran (Philadelphia, 1994), 293.

34 See the discussion in J. LICHT, The Rule Scroll (Jerusalem, 1965), 217 [in Hebrew]. On the Shema at Qumran see further ESHEL, "4QDeut^{n}," 151–152, esp. 152, n. 114.

twice each day, at the dawn thereof and when the hour comes for repose, let all acknowledge before God the bounties which He has bestowed on them through their deliverance from the land of Egypt (*Ant.* 4. 212).

Josephus refers here to the twice daily recitation of the *Shema*, and the anthology recited includes either the Ten Commandments or the section from Numbers, or more likely both, as only these passages make explicit reference to the Exodus.[35] For Josephus, this practice is written in the law of Moses, even if we might find it impossible to find the requirement specifically formulated in scripture. What has happened in this case is analogous to the instance of the Temple tax above. The Torah does mention that one should talk about the belief in one God and its consequences, as well as about the law and its observance, in the very verses recited as part of the *Shema*. Nowhere, however, is this a fixed obligation to recite a specific text on some particular occasion(s) (Cf. Dt. 21:7–8; 26:3, 5–10, 13–15).[36] By Josephus's day, however, the vague requirement has become institutionalized in a twice daily obligation to recite the *Shema*, all based on what is understood to be explicitly written in the law of Moses.[37]

The Mishnah informs us that the *Shema* was recited in the Temple (*mTamid* 4:3). This practice, however, was not a simple act, affording us confirmation that we are dealing with an innovation. According to the Mishnah (*mTamid* 4:3), the priests first completed the offering of the daily sacrifice, then "betook themselves to the Chamber of Hewn Stone to recite the *Shema*." Why was it necessary to leave the sacrificial area to recite the *Shema*? I suggest that this practice reflected the awareness that introducing the *Shema* into the Temple service was an innovation. The old sacrificial ritual – the essence of the service of God in the Second Temple period – continued to be accomplished without change. To recite the *Shema* in the same place as the sacrifice had been offered would have been an intolerable intrusion of the new in the realm of the old. In order to mark off the new from the old, the new ritual was performed in a different place. In the highly conservative environment of the Temple, innovation was allowable only if acknowledged in some way as such.

Just when after the time of Ben Sira this innovation was instituted is difficult to determine.[38] The allusion to the recitation of the *Shema* in the Manual of

---

[35] For this analysis of Josephus see SCHÜRER, History, 2. 455, n. 153.

[36] According to the Rabbis, because of the specific words to be recited enjoined by the Torah, many of the items on this list may only be said in Hebrew. The Shema, by contrast, may be recited in any language; see *mSot*. 7:1–2, and the subsequent discussion in the Mishnah.

[37] On this point see further BLAU, "Origine et Histoire," 181.

[38] The Nash papyrus, once thought to have been prepared for the daily recitation of the Shema, will not help establish a date for the institution of the practice. Recent scholarship has noted the fact that the text was folded a number of times, and hence argued that the Nash papyrus was probably part of a set of tefillin or a mezuza. For the older view of the purpose of the Nash papyrus see M. GREENBERG, "Nash Papyrus," EJ 12. 833. For more recent interpreta-

Discipline indicates that the step was taken before the end of the second century BCE. Both on palaeographic and radiocarbon grounds, the conclusion that the Manual of Discipline "goes back as far as ca. 100 BCE is now beyond reasonable doubt."[39] The institution of the recitation of the *Shema* should therefore be dated sometime between Ben Sira and 100 BCE. As the age of the persecutions of Antiochus IV seems an unlikely time for such actions, with the Temple under control of the reformers and more practical preoccupations such as waging a guerilla war uppermost on people's minds, I suggest that the most likely time for this step would be the first generations of Maccabean rule. Sometime after the Temple was restored to its traditional rite under Maccabean priesthood the practice of saying the *Shema* was introduced. If so, the goal of this innovation was probably to regularize recitation of an anthology which would remind all Jews, beginning with priests serving in the Temple, of the essentials of their faith, from belief in one God, to reward and punishment, culminating in the deliverance from Egypt in the past (and perhaps thus alluding to the hope of future salvation). The Ten Commandments would then add specific instances of the requirements of life under the covenant, examples of what was permitted and forbidden. All this would make excellent sense in the aftermath of the reforms of Antiochus IV, supported, at the very least, by some members of the priestly aristocracy. In the minds of those who instituted this practice, anyone who recited the *Shema* would realize himself that the hellenizing Judaism of the reformers was a perversion of the divine truth. Skilful interpretation gave this innovation a pedigree, perhaps even going back to Moses himself, as we have seen from Josephus. This construction, unlike the half sheqel Temple tax discussed above, was so successful that it was also adopted by the Qumran sectarians.[40] They too shared the conviction of the merit of twice daily reminders of certain fundamental biblical concepts.

The recitation of the *Shema*, I propose, fits well into the category of invented tradition: it was an action attributed to Moses, to be repeated twice daily, serving the objective of inculcation of beliefs and behavior, among the regular goals of such traditions. As such the conclusion proposed above for the date of the introduction of this practice illuminates its background. It was intended to reinforce an identity which had been challenged at the time of the reforms, while reminding Jerusalem priests in particular, of what their new rulers saw as the essentials of their faith.

---

tions see C. Sirrat, Les Papyrus en caractères Hébraïques trouvés en Egypt (Paris, 1985), 25–29; E. Fleischer, Eretz-Israel Prayers and Prayer Rituals as Portrayed in the Geniza Documents (Jerusalem, 1988), 259, n. 1 [in Hebrew]; Eshel, "4QDeut^{n}," 123, n. 36.

[39] G. Vermes, "Preliminary Remarks on Unpublished Fragments of the Community Rule from Qumran Cave 4," JJS 42 (1991), 250.

[40] On the attitude of the Qumran community towards the Maccabean rulers see above n. 17.

IV

The first of the invented traditions under consideration in this article, the half sheqel Temple tax, dates from either the second or third generation of Hasmonean rulers, sometime in the reign of John Hyrcanus or his sons. The second invented tradition, the recitation of the *Shema*, may be earlier, either from the first generation (Jonathan or Simon) or the second. If the analysis above is correct, we can see these rulers taking forceful steps to strengthen the faith for which they had fought. This conclusion needs to be brought into focus with other evidence which demonstrates that the Maccabean dynasty became rapidly hellenized. How can the data above be harmonized with the double Greek-Hebrew names of the Maccabean rulers from the era of John Hyrcanus and thereafter? Will anything but intellectual or cultural schizophrenia explain how Judah Aristobulus I could have been a ruler of the Jews from the family which took these steps to reinforce traditional faith, yet had also taken the nickname *philhellen*?[41] This difficulty was particularly acute for scholars of the previous generation, who insisted that the attitude of the Maccabees towards their tradition and the surrounding culture had to be consistent, virtually without exception.[42] It is far less serious for scholars of the current generation, who expect reality to be intellectually "messier" and less congruous with ideals.[43] From this perspective the invented traditions of the Maccabean era provide an additional corrective to the picture of uncontrolled Maccabean hellenization sometimes drawn. They remind us of the steps taken by that dynasty to bolster traditional faith. They show that it is unfair to accuse the rulers of that family of having simply betrayed the revolution which brought them to power.[44]

V

Writing with the benefit of hindsight, the successes of the Maccabean dynasty, as well as its eventual fall, have a certain sense of inevitability in our eyes. For us, the Maccabees represent "Judaism," plain and simple. The invented traditions of that era, calling attention to points which seemed in need of additional

---

41 Josephus, Ant. 13. 318.

42 Compare the two classic studies by E. J. Bickerman, "Genesis and Character of Maccabean Hellenism," From Ezra to the Last of the Maccabees (New York, 1962), 153–165 and V. Tcherikover, Hellenistic Civilization and the Jews (Philadelphia, 1959), 235–268.

43 See U. Rappaport, "On the Hellenization of the Hasmoneans," Tarbiz 60 (5751), 447–503 [in Hebrew], and from a slightly different perspective, T. Rajak, "The Hasmoneans and the Uses of Hellenism," in P. R. Davies and R. White (Eds.), A Tribute to Geza Vermes (Sheffield, 1990), 261–280.

44 See further my discussion of these issues in A. I. Baumgarten, "The Hellenization of the Hasmonean State," in H. Eshel and D. Amit (Eds.), The History of the Hasmonean House, (Jerusalem, 1995), 77–84 [in Hebrew].

support at a time of transition, can serve as a correction for the distortion produced by hindsight. They take us back to an era when biblical faith as understood by the Maccabees was still precarious and far from obvious, when the challenge posed by other interpretations of the faith such as that of the Hellenists was real, and when loyalty to the Temple in Jerusalem under its new leadership needed to be bolstered. They provide additional examples of the complex relationship between the new dynasty and the members of the Qumran community, reminding us of just how complicated reality usually is. They also supply further evidence of the nuanced relationship between members of the Hasmonean dynasty and their ancestral faith, in whose name they had come to rule.

Bibliography

J.M. Allergo, Discoveries in the Judean Desert V (Oxford, 1968).

A.I. Baumgarten, "Crisis in the Scrollery: A Dying Consensus," Judaism, 44 (1995), 399–413.

–, "Finding Oneself in a Sectarian Context," in J. Assmann, A. Baumgarten and G. Stroumsa (Eds.), Self, Soul and Body in Religious Experience, forthcoming.

–, "The Hellenization of the Hasmonean State," in H. Eshel and D. Amit (Eds.), The History of the Hasmonean House, (Jerusalem, 1995), 77–84 [in Hebrew].

M. Beer, "The Sects and the Half Sheqel," Tarbiz 31 (5722) 298–299 [in Hebrew].

E.J. Bickerman, "Genesis and Character of Maccabean Hellenism," From Ezra to the Last of the Maccabees (New York, 1962), 153–165.

–, "La Charte Seleucide de Jerusalem," Studies in Jewish and Christian History, Part Two (Leiden, 1980), 44–85.

–, "Zur Datierung des Pseudo Aristeas," Studies in Jewish and Christian History, Part One (Leiden, 1976), 109–136.

L. Blau, "Origine et Histoire de la Lecture du Schema," REJ 31 (1895), 179–201.

M. Broshi, "Anti-Qumranic Polemics in the Talmud, in J. Barrera and L. Montaner (Eds.), The Madrid Qumran Congress: Proceedings of the International Congress on the Dead Sea Scrolls Madrid 18–21 March, 1991 (Leiden, 1992), 2. 589–600.

H. Desroches, The Sociology of Hope (London/Boston, 1979).

A. Di Lella and P. Skehan, The Wisdom of Ben Sira (New York, 1987).

M. Douglas, In the Wilderness (Sheffield, 1993).

I. Elbogen, "Studies in Jewish Liturgy," JQR 19 (1907), 589–599.

E. Eshel, "4QDeut^{n} – A Text that has Undergone Harmonistic Editing," HUCA 62 (1991), 117–154.

E. & H. Eshel, "4Q471 Fragment 1 and Ma amadot in the War Scroll," in J. Barrera and L. Montaner (Eds.), The Madrid Qumran Congress: Proceedings of the International Congress on the Dead Sea Scrolls Madrid 18–21 March, 1991 (Leiden, 1992), 2. 611–620.

E. Fleischer, Eretz-Israel Prayers and Prayer Rituals as Portrayed in the Geniza Documents (Jerusalem, 1988) [in Hebrew].

E. Fleischer, "On the Beginnings of Obligatory Jewish Prayer," Tarbiz 59 (5750), 397–441 [in Hebrew].
D. Flusser, "Matthew XVII, 24–27 and the Dead Sea Sect," Tarbiz 31 (5722) 150–156 [in Hebrew].
M. Greenberg, "Nash Papyrus," EJ 12. 833.
J. Heinemann and J. Petuchowski, The Literature of the Synagogue (New York, 1975).
E. Hobsbawm, "Introduction," in Hobsbawm/Ranger, Invention, 1–14.
E. Hobsbawm and T. Ranger, The Invention of Tradition (Cambridge, 1983).
R. Kimelman, "The Sema and its Blessings," in L. Levine (Ed.), The Synagogue in Late Antiquity (Philadelphia, 1987), 73–86.
–, "The Shema and its Rhetoric: The Case for the Shema being more than Creation, Revelation and Redemption," JJTP 2 (1992), 111–156.
B. Lewis, History, Remembered, Recovered, Invented (Princeton, 1975).
J. Licht, The Rule Scroll (Jerusalem, 1965) [in Hebrew].
J. Liver, "The Half Shekel Offering in Biblical and Post-Biblical Literature," HTR 56 (1963), 172–198.
B. Mack, Wisdom and the Hebrew Epic (Chicago/London, 1985).
S. Mandell, "Who Paid the Temple Tax when the Jews were under Roman Rule?" HTR 77 (1984), 223–232.
F. O'Fearghail, "Sir. 50:5–21: Yom Kippur or the Daily Whole Offering?" Biblica 59 (1978), 301–316.
T. Rajak, "The Hasmoneans and the Uses of Hellenism," in P. R. Davies and R. White (Eds.), A Tribute to Geza Vermes (Sheffield, 1990), 261–280.
U. Rappaport, "On the Hellenization of the Hasmoneans," Tarbiz 60 (5751), 447–503 [in Hebrew].
L. Schiffman, Reclaiming the Dead Sea Scrolls – The History of Judaism, the Background of Christianity, the Lost Library of Qumran (Philadelphia, 1994).
E. Schürer, G. Vermes, F. Millar and M. Black, The History of the Jewish People in the Age of Jesus Christ (Edinburgh, 1979), 2.
M. Segal, Sefer Ben Sira Hashalem (Jerusalem, 1972).
R. J. Shutt, "Letter of Aristeas," in J. Charlesworth (Ed.), OTP 2. 7–34.
M. Silber, "The Emergence of Ultra-Orthodoxy: The Invention of a Tradition," in J. Wertheimer (Ed.), The Uses of Tradition (New York/Jerusalem, 1992), 23–84.
C. Sirrat, Les Papyrus en caractères Hébraïques trouvés en Egypt (Paris, 1985).
M. Smith, Palestinian Parties and Politics that Shaped the Old Testament (New York, 1971).
H. Steinthal, Über Juden und Judentum (Berlin, 1910[2]).
Y. Sussmann, "Research on the History of the Halacha and the Scrolls of the Judean Desert," Tarbiz 59 (5750), 11–76 [in Hebrew].
V. Tcherikover, Hellenistic Civilization and the Jews (Philadelphia, 1959).
G. Vermes, "Preliminary Remarks on Unpublished Fragments of the Community Rule from Qumran Cave 4," JJS 42 (1991), 250–255.
O. Wintermute, "Jubilees," in J. Charlesworth (Ed.), OTP, 2. 34–142.
Y. Zerubavel, Recovered Roots: Collective Memory and the Making of Israeli National Tradition (Chicago, 1995).
L. Zunz, Die gottesdienstlichen Vorträge der Juden (Hildesheim, 1966 Reprint).

Ioudaios: "Judaean" and "Jew" in Susanna, First Maccabees, and Second Maccabees

by

SHAYE J. D. COHEN

Greek *Ioudaios* and Latin *Iudaeus* (or *Iudeus*) are usually translated "Jew." Indeed, the English word "Jew" (like the German "Jude," French "Juif," etc.) ultimately derives from the Greek via the Latin. Behind the Greek word lies the Hebrew *Yehudi*, also usually translated "Jew." These translations, however, are sometimes misleading, because in contemporary speech the English word "Jew" has a range of meanings different from that of its ancient forerunners. English "Jew" is primarily a "religious" term: a Jew is someone who believes in (or is supposed to believe), and practices (or is supposed to practice), Judaism, as opposed to a Catholic, Lutheran, Episcopalian, Hindu, Muslim, etc. etc. In some contexts the designation "Jew" may also have "ethnic" overtones, although it never has a geographic meaning and, outside of the state of Israel, seldom has a political one. In contrast Greek *Ioudaios*, Latin *Iudaeus*, and Hebrew *Yehudi* are originally, and in antiquity primarily, ethnic-geographic terms, designating the eponymous inhabitants of the land of *Ioudaia/Yehudah*. Like Egyptians, Moabites, Edomites, Syrians, Lydians, etc. *Ioudaioi* constitute an *ethnos* living on its ancestral land. It does not much matter that the limits of *Ioudaia/Yehudah* in antiquity (as in modern times!) could be defined either narrowly or broadly. Well into the Hellenistic period, *Ioudaia/Yehudah* (or *Yehud* in Aramaic) designated the land of Judah, the district surrounding Jerusalem, in contrast with other districts like Samaria, Galilee, Idumaea, the plain, the coast, the trans-Jordan, etc. In Roman times Judaea retained this narrow, technical meaning, but also became the common designation for the entire country. In any case, when referring to the ethnic inhabitants of Judaea and their descendants, even if not living in Judaea, the term *Ioudaioi* should be translated not "Jews," a religious designation, but "Judaeans," an ethnic-geographical designation.

Elsewhere I hope to study these meanings in some detail.[1] My thesis is that all

[1] Two of my studies of this topic have already appeared: "Religion, Ethnicity, and 'Hellenism' in the Emergence of Jewish Identity in Maccabean Palestine," Religion and Religious

occurrences of the terms *Ioudaios* and *Yehudi* before the end of the second century BCE mean not "Jew" but "Judaean." After the end of the second century BCE these terms may mean either "Jew" or "Judaean," depending on the context. Behind this semantic shift lies a significant development in the history of Judaism. It was only in the Maccabean period that the "ethnic" or "national" self-definition was supplemented by a "cultural" or "religious" self-definition. "Judaeans," the citizens of Judaea, gradually become "Jews," the followers of a certain way of life or "religion." In this modest essay, I shall illustrate this development by studying three exemplary passages, one each from Susanna, First Maccabees, and Second Maccabees.

Susanna

The original language and date of composition of the book of Susanna, one of the additions to the book of Daniel in the Greek version, are most obscure. The book is extant in two versions, the "Septuagint" (LXX) and "Theodotion"; the former is shorter, less polished, and less dramatic, than the latter. I accept the view that the Septuagint version is a product of (the second half of) the second century BCE and that the version of Theodotion is a revision of the Septuagint's. Whether the original language of composition was Greek, Hebrew, or Aramaic, does not much matter for my purposes here.[2]

Two wicked elders are inflamed with lust for Susanna, the beautiful and virtuous heroine. The elders try to have their way with her, but Susanna resists. Verses 22–23 run as follows in the LXX version (trans. MOORE):[3]

> The Jewess said to them, "I know if I do this thing, it'll be my death, and if I don't do it, I'll not escape your hands. But it's better for me not to do it and so fall into your hands than sin in the Lord's sight.

What is the meaning of *Ioudaia* here? Moore translates "Jewess," but why should Susanna be identified as a Jewess – her attackers are no less "Jewish" than she is. We may presume that Theodotion was puzzled by this question

---

Practice in the Seleucid Kingdom, ed. Per Bilde et al. (Aarhus University Press, 1990) 204–223, and "*Ioudaios to genos* and Related Expressions in Josephus," Josephus and the History of the Greco-Roman Period: Essays in Memory of Morton Smith, ed. Fausto Parente and Joseph Sievers (Leiden: Brill, 1994) 23–38.

[2] It is possible, if not likely, that the story circulated for a long time before being redacted in Greek, but of this pre-Septuagint (Hebrew? Aramaic?) version not a trace is extant. No fragment of Susanna has (yet) been discovered among the Qumran scrolls. For a discussion of the origins of the book of Susanna, see MOORE, Daniel, Esther, and Jeremiah 28–29 and 77–92; ENGEL, Susanna-Erzählung.

[3] MOORE, Daniel, Esther and Jeremiah 99.

and therefore omitted the word "Jewess" (*Ioudaia*), substituting "Susanna." The key to the passage is provided by verses 56–57 (trans. MOORE).[4]

And he [Daniel] said to him [one of the wicked elders], "Why was your progeny corrupted like Sidon and not like Judah? Beauty has beguiled you – petty lust! And this is how you have been treating the daughters of Israel; and being afraid of you, they had relations with you two. But this daughter of Judah would not tolerate your villainous sickness."

The elder's behavior indicates that he is of the seed of Sidon more than he is of the seed of Judah (*sperma ... Iouda*). In contrast Susanna has behaved as a true daughter of Judah (*thugathêr Iouda*); daughters of Israel have succumbed to the elders' threats, but not Susanna. The contrast between "Israel" and "Judah" is stark and somewhat puzzling, but what is clear is that a son or daughter of Judah behaves virtuously, even in the face of temptation (unlike the elders) or compulsion (like Susanna).[5] Surely this explains why Susanna is called a *Ioudaia* in vs. 22. In her resistance to the elders, she shows that she is a *Ioudaia*. The word should be translated not "Jewess" but "daughter of Judah," or, perhaps, "Judaean."[6]

First Maccabees

First Maccabees uses the plural *Ioudaioi* many times, and in all of these occurrences the meaning is "Judaeans." Many official Seleucid and Roman documents in First Maccabees are addressed to the "people" (*dêmos*) or "nation" (*ethnos*) or "crowd" (*plêthos*) of the *Ioudaioi*, that is, the Judaeans. The documents concern Judaeans, either in Judaea or outside it.[7] The narrator usually designates the heroes of the book as "Israel" or "those of Israel," but occasionally calls them *Ioudaioi*. In these passages too the meaning seems to be

---

[4] MOORE, Daniel, Esther and Jeremiah 114.

[5] Theodotion here substitutes "Canaan" for "Sidon," but otherwise is rather close to the LXX. On the contrast of "Israel" with "Judah," see ENGEL, Susanna-Erzählung 126–127 and MOORE, Daniel, Esther and Jeremiah 111–112.

[6] ENGEL, Susanna-Erzählung 98–99 and 178–179 suggests that "Susanna the *Ioudaia*" is meant to represent the people of Judaea, the "Jews"; for a sustained reading of the book from this perspective see Amy-Jill LEVINE, "'Hemmed in on Every Side': Jews and Women in the Book of Susanna," Reading from this Place: I: Social Location and Biblical Interpretation in the United States, ed. F.F. Segovia and M.A. Tolbert (Minneapolis: Fortress, 1995) 175–190. This allegorical (or typological) reading does not convince me. In any case, at least Engel too saw the connection between *Ioudaia* and Judaea. If Susanna had a Hebrew original it would have read *ha-yehudiyah* (thus D. HELLER apud KAHANA, Hasefarim hahitzonim 1.566), a word that is not attested in the Tanak (1 Chron 4:18 is corrupt).

[7] Documents in 1 Maccabees referring to Ioudaioi: 8:20 (plêthos), 23, 27 (ethnos), 29 (dêmos), 31; 10:23, 25 (ethnos), 29, 33, 34, 36; 11:30, 33 (ethnos); 12:3 (ethnos), 6 (dêmos), 21; 13:36 (ethnos), 42; 14:20 (dêmos), 22; 15:1, 2 (ethnos), 17 (dêmos).

"Judaeans" consistently.[8] Where the Greek has *Ioudaioi*, the Hebrew original will have been *(ha)Yehudim* which everywhere and always in the Tanak means "Judaeans," either the men of Judaea living in Judaea (2 Kings 16:6 and 25:25) or the men of Judaea living in exile (for example, the books of Esther and Daniel, passim).

In one passage, however, *Ioudaios* appears in the singular. First Maccabees 2:15–25 (with some omissions) runs as follows in the New Revised Standard Version:[9]

(15) The king's officers who were enforcing the apostasy came to the town of Modein to make them offer sacrifice. (16) Many from Israel came to them; and Mattathias and his sons were assembled. (17) Then the king's officers spoke to Mattathias as follows: "You are a leader, honored and great in this town, and supported by sons and brothers. (18) Now be the first to come and do what the king commands, as all the gentiles and the people of Judah and those that are left in Jerusalem have done. Then you and your sons will be numbered among the friends of the king ..." (19) But Mattathias answered and said in a loud voice: "... (22) We will not obey the king's words by turning aside from our religion to the right hand or to the left." (23) When he had finished speaking these words, a Jew came forward in the sight of all to offer sacrifice on the altar in Modein, according to the king's command. (24) When Mattathias saw it, he burned with zeal and his heart was stirred. He gave vent to righteous anger; he ran and killed him on the altar. (25) At the same time he killed the king's officer who was forcing them to sacrifice, and he tore down the altar.

Like numerous other versions the NRSV translates *anêr Ioudaios* in verse 23 "a Jew." So do SCHÜRER-VERMES-MILLAR in their standard history of the period; Jonathan GOLDSTEIN in the Anchor Bible edition ("a Jewish man"); Joseph SIEVERS in his recent study of the Maccabean party; and many others.[10] At first glance, the translation seems unobjectionable: the verse describes the dramatic moment when "a Jew" was prepared to sacrifice to a pagan god but was cut down by Mattathias, filled with zeal for the Torah. But since *Ioudaioi* in First Maccabees never means "Jews," it is unlikely that *Ioudaios* should mean "Jew." In 1 Maccabees 2:23 *anêr Ioudaios* should be translated not "a Jew" but "a man of Judah" or "a Judaean."[11] The Hebrew original will have been *ish*

---

[8] Narrative passages in 1 Maccabees with Ioudaioi: 4:2; 11:47–51; 14:33, 34, 37, 40, 41, 47.

[9] The New Oxford Annotated Bible, ed. B. METZGER and R. MURPHY (New York: Oxford University Press, 1991), p. 190 in the Apocrypha.

[10] EMIL SCHÜRER, The History of the Jewish People in the Age of Jesus Christ, rev. G. VERMES, F. MILLAR, et al. (Edinburgh: T. & T. Clark, 1973ff) 1.157; GOLDSTEIN, I Maccabees 230; Joseph SIEVERS, The Hasmoneans and their Supporters (Atlanta: Scholars Press, 1990) 30; Martin HENGEL, Die Zeloten (Leiden: Brill, 1976; 2nd ed.) 156 writes "Als nun in Modein ein *Israelit* [my emphasis – SJDC] dem Aufruf des Königs Folge leisten wollte" – this is German usage. Hugo BEVENOT, Die beiden Makkabäerbücher (Bonn, 1931) 59, translates "einer von den Juden."

[11] In the footnote to 1 Maccabees 2:23 The New Oxford Annotated Bible suggests that Ioudaios "here perhaps means 'Judean'."

Yehudi,[12] a phrase which in Zechariah 8:23 means "a man of Judaea" (cf. the reference to Jerusalem in 8:22) and which in Esther 2:5 means "a man from Judaea" (cf. the reference to Jerusalem in 2:6). In the Greek version Zechariah 8:23 is translated *anêr Ioudaios*, precisely the same as in our passage of Maccabees, and Esther 2:5 is translated similarly, *anthrôpos Ioudaios*.

Modein, the site of the dramatic confrontation, was just outside Judaea (narrowly defined).[13] In verse 18 the king's officer tells Mattathias and the assembled crowd that "the men of Judah" (*hoi andres Iouda*; the Hebrew will have been *anshei Yehudah*) had acceded to the king's orders, and in verse 23 one of these Judaean men, who had accompanied the officer in his foray outside of Judaea, approached the altar in order to set an example for the assembled throng of non-Judaeans. No doubt this man was one of those Judaean "renegades" who had made a covenant with the gentiles and followed the edict of the king, thereby gaining the opprobrium of 1 Maccabees (1:11, 1:43). In Modein this man was an outsider twice over: he was a Judaean, probably from Jerusalem, intruding into the affairs of a village remote from Jerusalem,[14] and he was an advocate of gentile ways in a bastion of country piety. No wonder he was unwelcome in Modein.

Second Maccabees

Ioudaioi occurs even more frequently in 2 Maccabees than in 1 Maccabees, and here too the meaning is "Judaeans." The first verse of the book, the salutation of a letter written in 124/3 BCE, contains greetings "to (our) brethren the *Ioudaioi* in Egypt" from "the brethren the *Ioudaioi* in Jerusalem and in the land of Judaea" (2 Macc 1:1); a second letter has a similar salutation (2 Macc 1:10). The meaning "Judaeans" is clear (cf. 2 Macc 1:7, a reference to "we Judaeans"). These documents are of Judaean provenance, and Seleucid documents continue this usage.[15] The narrator too regularly uses *Ioudaioi* to mean the citizens of Judaea and occasionally uses the term to designate Judaeans living outside Judaea.[16]

---

[12] See the rendering by KAHANA, Hasefarim hahitzonim 2.106.

[13] This is the simple implication of 1 Maccabees 2:6 (I am not convinced by GOLDSTEIN's note ad loc.). If it was in Judaea, it was near its outermost limits.

[14] For a brilliant analysis of the social background to the emergence of the Maccabees, see Seth SCHWARTZ, "A Note on the Social Type and Political Ideology of the Hasmonean Family," Journal of Biblical Literature 112 (1993) 305–309.

[15] 2 Macc 9:19; 11:16,24,27,31,34. The first of these references derives from a document (2 Macc 9:19–27) that in all likelihood is a forgery; see HABICHT, "Royal Documents," 5–7; idem, 2. Makkabäerbuch 246–247; STERN, Documents 22; GOLDSTEIN, II Maccabees 357–359. In contrast 11:22–26 and 27–33 are authentic.

[16] Judaeans in Judaea: 2 Macc 3:32; 4:11,35 (contrast between *Ioudaioi* and "many other

In at least one verse, however, Second Maccabees uses *Ioudaioi* in a manner that clearly anticipates the meaning "Jews." Second Maccabees 6:1–11 (with some omissions) runs as follows in the New Revised Standard Version (I *italicize* all occurrences of the word *Ioudaioi*, translated here "Jews"):[17]

(1) Not long after this, the king sent an Athenian senator to compel the *Jews* to forsake the laws of their ancestors and no longer to live by the laws of God; (2) also to pollute the temple in Jerusalem and to call it the temple of Olympian Zeus, and to call the one in Gerizim the temple of Zeus-the-Friend-of-Strangers ...

(3) Harsh and utterly grievous was the onslaught of evil. (4) For the temple was filled with debauchery and reveling by the Gentiles ... (5) The altar was covered with abominable offerings ... (6) People could neither keep the sabbath, nor observe the festivals of their ancestors, nor so much as confess themselves to be *Jews*.

(7) On the monthly celebration of the king's birthday, they were taken, under bitter constraint, to partake of the sacrifices ... (8) At the suggestion of the people of Ptolemais a decree was issued to the neighboring Greek cities that they should adopt the same policy toward the *Jews* and make them partake of the sacrifices, (9) and should kill those who did not choose to change over to Greek customs ... (10) ... two women were brought in for having circumcised their children. They publicly paraded them around the city, with their babies hanging at their breasts, and then hurled them down headlong from the wall. (11) Others who had assembled in the caves nearby, in order to observe the seventh day secretly, were betrayed to Philip and were all burned together ...

The numerous textual and historical problems raised by these verses are not our concern here. I am interested instead in the meaning of the word *Ioudaioi*, which occurs three times in this passage. In the last of these (verse 8) the word simply means "Judaeans" and refers to Judaeans living in Greek cities outside Judaea, a usage that recurs elsewhere in 2 Maccabees.[18] In the first of these (verse 1) too the word simply means "Judaeans," but here apparently it refers to the inhabitants of Judaea broadly defined, even the people of Samaria who venerate the temple on Mount Gerizim. Similarly, in 5:22–23 the term "the people" (the *genos*) includes not only those of Jerusalem but also those of Gerizim.

The second of our three occurrences (verse 6) is far more intriguing than the other two: "People could ... no[t] so much as confess themselves to be *Jews*" (*oute haplôs Ioudaion homologein einai*). *Ioudaioi* cannot mean "Judaeans" here, because why should Antiochus care if people identify themselves as

---

ethnê"); 5:23,25; 6:1; 8:10–11 (synonymous with *tês Ioudaias genos* in 8:9),32,34,36; 9:4,7, 15,17,18; 10:12,14,15,24,29; 11:2,15,16; 12:1,3,4,8,34,40; 13:9,18,19,23; 14:5,6,14,37,39; 15:2,12. Cf. 2 Macc 13:21 *ioudaikê taxis*, troop of Judeans. Judaeans outside Judaea: 2 Macc 4:36 (in Antioch); 6:8 (Ptolemais and Greek cities); 10:8 (ethnos of Ioudaioi presumably includes those outside Judaea too); 12:17 (in Charax); 12:30 (Scythopolis). 2 Maccabees also uses *Hebraioi* (7:31; 11:13; 15:37) and *Israel* (1:25–26; 9:5; 10:38; 11:6); these terms, in 2 Macc at least, have theological overtones absent from Ioudaioi.

[17] The New Oxford Annotated Bible, p. 239 in the Apocrypha.

[18] See note 16.

Judaeans? Ethnic-geographic identity seems to be irrelevant. Here, in contrast with verses 1 and 8, the translation "Jews" seems right: people could not identify themselves as "Jews."[19] Why not? Are we to understand that the mere name "Jew" aroused the ire of the Seleucid state just as centuries later the mere name "Christian" aroused the ire of the Roman? I assume not.[20] I presume that what is at stake here is the observance of the Jewish laws. "People could not confess themselves to be Jews" means that they could not declare themselves to be practitioners of the ancestral laws, the laws of God (6:1).[21]

What ancestral laws are intended? Perhaps the phrase simply summarizes what has come previously: "to confess oneself to be a Jew" means to observe the laws of temple, Sabbath, and festivals. However, verse 6 can also be understood as foreshadowing what follows. "People could neither keep the sabbath" adumbrates 6:11, which describes how people who gathered in a cave in order to observe the Sabbath were burned to death. People could not "observe the festivals of their ancestors" adumbrates 6:7–9, which describes how people were compelled to observe the king's birthday, a festival of Dionysus, and the festivals of Greek cities. If this is right, then the final phrase, people could not "so much as confess themselves to be Jews," adumbrates 6:10, which describes how two women were executed for having circumcised their sons. Antiochus proscribed circumcision, thus preventing people from "confessing themselves to be Jews."[22]

All ancient peoples, including Egyptians, Syrians, Lydians, Athenians, Corinthians, had ancestral laws and customs, practices and beliefs. The phrase "to live (or conduct public life, *politeuesthai*) in accordance with ancestral laws

[19] Cf. ZEITLIN's comment ad loc., "The term 'Jew' here connotes the meaning of adhering to a particular religion." See Solomon ZEITLIN, The Second Book of Maccabees (NY: Harper and Bros. for Dropsie College, 1954) 152.

[20] In his commentary GRIMM assumes the opposite, "Niemand dürfte sagen: ich bin zwar Jude, habe aber die griechische Religion angenommen; selbst der Name Juden sollte getilgt werden"; see Carl L. W. GRIMM, Das zweite, dritte, und vierte Buch der Maccabäer (Leipzig, 1857) 110. GOLDSTEIN, II Maccabees 276, suggests that the phrase may be hyperbole.

[21] In addition to suggesting that the phrase may be hyperbole (see previous note), GOLDSTEIN, II Maccabees 276, also suggests that the phrase might refer to the recitation of the Shema.

[22] To strengthen this interpretation my friend Jan Willem van Henten brings to my attention Assumption of Moses 8:1, which describes how a king will "hang on the cross those who confess circumcision" (qui confitentes circumcisionem in cruce suspendit). If "to confess circumcision" means "to confess Judaism," it is a close parallel to 2 Macc 6:6; see Johannes TROMP, The Assumption of Moses: A Critical Edition with Commentary (Leiden, 1993) 217. A slight obstacle to this interpretation is the fact that vs. 10 is linked by *gar* to vs. 9 (thus NRSV reads "(9) ... and should kill those who did not choose to change over to Greek customs. One could see, therefore, the misery that had come upon them. (10) For example, two women were brought in for having circumcised their children ..."), but this does not mean that the content of the verse cannot have been adumbrated in vs. 6.

(*patrôi nomoi*)" recurs frequently in Hellenistic diplomacy and politics.[23] The Judaeans were hardly unique, or even unusual, in this regard. What made the Judaeans ("Jews") unique, however, is the essential role that these ancestral laws and beliefs would come to assume in the construction of Judaean identity. This point is evident in the subtle but significant shift in emphasis in the meaning of the word *Ioudaios* between 2 Macc 6:1 and 6:6. In the former passage, the word is to be translated "Judaean"; the Judaeans have ancestral laws by which they live and conduct their public life. In the latter the word is to be translated "Jew"; the essence of "being" a Jew is the observance of the ancestral laws.

"Confessing oneself to be a Jew" involves more than just circumcision and the observance of the other ancestral laws. As 6:1 says, the laws of the *Ioudaioi* are from God. Being a Jew also means believing in the God of the Jews, the one true God, creator of heaven and earth. Near the end of his life, afflicted by God with severe torments, and hoping for divine mercy, Antiochus pledges to grant various boons to the Judaeans: the city of Jerusalem shall be free, the Judaeans shall be the equals of the citizens of Athens, the holy sanctuary shall be adorned with the finest ornaments, and the sacrificial cult shall be maintained at royal expense (2 Macc 9:13–16). "In addition to all this he also would become a Jew (*Ioudaion esesthai*) and would visit every inhabited place to proclaim the power of God" (2 Macc 9:17).[24] We may presume that Antiochus is offering God a theological conversion, not a change in domicile or political affiliation. That is, he promises that he will become a Jew, a worshiper of the true God, but he does not intend to become a Judaean, a member of the house of Israel living on God's holy land. After all, Antiochus is a Macedonian king and intends to remain one. Thus, in both 6:6 and 9:17 *Ioudaios* means "Jew."

In addition to the common usage of an ambiguous word, dramatic irony and a satisfying sense of closure link these two verses. At the beginning of the persecution one could not even declare oneself to be a Jew, but at the end even the arch-enemy pledged to become one. A crucial bridge between these verses is provided by 7:37, the final declaration of the last and youngest of the seven martyrs, "I ... give up body and life for the laws of our ancestors, appealing to God to show mercy soon to our nation and by trials and plagues to make you confess that he alone is God." This prayer, which speaks of "confessing" (*exhomologein*) God, clearly looks back to 6:6, the prohibition

---

23 E. BICKERMAN, "La charte séleucide de Jérusalem," Studies in Jewish and Christian History (Leiden, 1980) 2.44–85.

24 Note that this sentiment is absent from the subsequent document which is a forgery (see note 15). GOLDSTEIN, II Maccabees 356, suggests that the vow to become a Jew was probably inferred from the king's gratitude to "God" (in the singular, 9:20), but surely gratitude to God and becoming a Jew are distinct.

of confessing (*homologein*) oneself to be a Jew, and looks forward to 9:17, Antiochus' promise "to become a Jew."[25]

Second Maccabees 6:6 and 9:17 mark an important turning point in the history of the word *Ioudaios* and, indeed, in the history of Judaism. As is well known, Second Maccabees is the first work to use the word *Ioudaismos* (2:21; 8:1; 14:38), which means "the aggregate of all those characteristics that make Judaeans Judaean (or Jews Jewish)." Among these characteristics, to be sure, are practices and beliefs that we would today call "religious," but 2 Maccabees does not distinguish practices and beliefs that are of a religious nature from those that are not. Thus *Ioudaismos* should be translated not "Judaism" – "religion" is not the focus of the term – but "Jewishness" (Judaeanness?).[26] Its antonym is *allophulismos* (4:13; 6:25), the adoption of foreign ways, and, more particularly, *Hellenismos* (4:13), the adoption of "Greek" ways. Second Maccabees presents the conflict between the Judaeans and their opponents as (inter alia) the attempt by the latter to have the former "go over" to "Greek ways" (4:10, 15; 6:9), a perspective that appears also in an official Seleucid document quoted by the author (11:24).[27] It is a conflict between "Judaism," the ways of the *Ioudaioi*, and the "Hellenism," the ways of the Greeks. 2 Maccabees is the first work to use *Ioudaismos* and the first work to use *Ioudaios* in the sense of "Jew."

In the Maccabean and early Roman periods the ways of the *Ioudaioi* loomed larger and larger in the definition of a *Ioudaios*, while ethnic and geographic factors loomed smaller and smaller. Circumcision, support of the Jerusalem temple, the sabbath, and the food laws emerged as essential boundary markers between "Jews" and "Greeks." Conversion to Judaism, a process by which an ethnic non-Jew somehow becomes a Jew, now became possible. This development led a Jewish author in the first century CE to the logical, if radical, conclusion, "for he is not a real *Ioudaios* who is one outwardly ... [but] he is a

[25] I am indebted to Jan Willem van Henten for pointing out to me the importance of 7:37 in this connection. Antiochus's promise "to become a Jew" is similar to a comment of the Babylonians in Bel and Dragon 28, "The king has become a Jew (*gegonen Ioudaios*); he has destroyed Bel, and killed the dragon, and slaughtered the priests." The difference, of course, is that the former is the promise of the subject himself, while the latter is the comment of outsiders. They mean "the king is behaving like a Ioudaios," and the word can, and probably should, be translated "Judaean." Similarly, an Athenian politician who is excessively devoted to Isis could be mocked as an "Egyptian"; see Ladislaus VIDMANN, Sylloge inscriptionum religionis Isiacae et Sarapiacae (Berlin, 1969) 4, commentary on no. 1. Octavian could say of Mark Antony: "Therefore let no one count him a Roman, but rather a rank Egyptian (*mêt' oun Rômaion einai tis auton nomizetô alla tina Aiguption*), nor call him Antony, but rather a Serapion" (Dio Cassius 50.27.1; I have slightly modified the Loeb translation).

[26] See Yehoshua AMIR, "The Term Ioudaismos, a Study in Jewish-Hellenistic Self-Identification," Immanuel 14 (1982) 34–41. HABICHT translates "die jüdische Sache."

[27] This document is authentic and is to be attributed to Antiochus V: HABICHT, "Royal Documents," 12. The same perspective appears in a document of Antiochus IV quoted by Josephus, Jewish Antiquities 12.263, and in Tacitus, Histories 5.8.2.

Ioudaios who is one inwardly" (Romans 2:28–29). Most Jews, in antiquity at least, were not prepared to go as far as Paul on this trajectory; for them *Ioudaios* never entirely lost its ethnic meaning. In 100 BCE we are near the beginning of this process; Second Maccabees is an important milestone.

Bibliography

Engel, Helmut, Die Susanna-Erzählung. Freiburg (Schweiz): Universtitätsverlag, and Göttingen: Vandenhoeck & Ruprecht, 1985.

Goldstein, Jonathan, I Maccabees. Garden City, NY: Doubleday, 1976.

–, II Maccabees. Garden City, NY: Doubleday, 1983.

Habicht, Christian, "Royal Documents in Maccabees II." Harvard Studies in Classical Philology 80 (1976) 1–18.

–, 2. Makkabäerbuch. in Jüdische Schriften aus hellenistisch-römischer Zeit I (Gütersloh: Mohn, 1976).

Kahana, Avraham, Hasefarim hahitzonim. repr. Jerusalem: Makor, 1978.

Moore, Carey A, Daniel, Esther, and Jeremiah: The Additions. Garden City, NY: Doubleday, 1977.

Stern, Menahem, The Documents on the History of the Hasmonean Revolt. Israel: Hakibbutz Hameuchad, 1965. Hebrew.

Josephus and Nicolaus on Women[1]

by

Tal Ilan

Despite much recent research carried out on the question of Jewish women in Greco-Roman time and sources, the writings of Josephus, the most important historian for this period, have been almost entirely ignored. A case in point would be a collection of articles edited by Amy-Jill Levine and published in 1991[2] that discuss the position of women in practically all Jewish documents preserved in Greek from the Greco-Roman world (Sirach; Philo; Maccabees; Pseudo-Philo; Tobit; Testament of Job; The Conversion of Asenath; Judith; Susanna; even the New Testament). Josephus is conspicuously missing from the list. The little research carried out on Josephus' women has tended to concentrate on his portrayal of biblical women in the Antiquities,[3] with the aim of demonstrating Josephus' attitude to women by comparing his work with the original descriptions of the women in the Hebrew Bible. Feldman stated explicitly that this was his aim: "... we may expect that Josephus' portraits of women may reflect his own personal life."[4] However, it appears that Feldman held some preconceived notions of Josephus' attitude to women, based on data

---

[1] In 1983 my teacher D. R. Schwartz published an article entitled "Josephus and Nicolaus on the Pharisees" (Journal for the Study of Judaism 14, pp. 157–71). His assumption had been that much of the information found in Josephus on the Pharisees should be ascribed to his main source for the Herodian period – Nicolaus of Damascus. In a similar vein I wish to suggest that much of the material found in Josephus on women is taken from the same source. I also wish to thank Prof. Schwartz for reading this paper and making many useful comments.

[2] "Women Like This": New Perspectives on Jewish Women in the Greco-Roman World (Atlante: Scholars Press).

[3] L. H. Feldman, "Josephus' Portrait of Deborah," in A. Caquot, M. Hadas-Lebel and J. Riand (eds.), Hellenica et Judaica: Hommage à Valentin Nikiprowetzky (Louvain: Peeters, 1986), 115–28; J. L. Bailey, "Josephus' Portrayal of the Matriarchs," in L. H. Feldman and G. Hata (edd.), Josephus, Judaism and Christianity (Detroit: Wayne State University Press, 1987), 154–79; Betsy H. Amaru, "Portraits of Biblical Women in Josephus' Antiquities," Journal of Jewish Studies 39 (1988), 143–70; Cheryl-Ann Brown, No Longer be Silent: First-Century Portraits of Biblical Women (Louisville KY: Westminster/John Knox Press, 1992); Eileen Schuller, "Women of the Exodus in Biblical Retellings of the Second Temple Period," in Peggy L. Day (ed.), Gender and Difference in Ancient Israel (Minneapolis: Fortress Press, 1989), 178–94. For Josephus see pp. 186–9.

[4] Feldman, ibid., p. 115.

not derived from biblical women: (1) The sparse information Josephus volunteers about his female relatives: Here Feldman makes comments such as "... one guesses that Josephus must have been difficult to live with, to judge from the fact that he was, it appears, married three times,"[5] a statement that can hardly be corroborated from the little information at our disposal, and, even if true, is certainly not an indication of Josephus' intellectual attitude to women; (2) General negative statements he makes about women as a group: "... in his summary of the commandments, he adds the detail (Ant. 4.219) not found in the Bible, that the testimony of women is inadmissible in Jewish law because of their levity (κουφότητα) and because of the boldness (θράσος) of their sex."[6] But while it is undeniable that Josephus does make this statement and half a dozen others (all of which, according to my inventory, are cited either by Feldman or by Bailey), these proclamations are few and far between, occasionally contradicted by Josephus himself, and can hardly be counted as a major issue which pre-occupied Josephus;[7] (3) Feldman stands in awe at Josephus' negative description of the reign of the Jewish Hasmonean queen Shelamzion Alexandra (76–67 BCE), of whom, he claims, "[t]he Talmudic rabbis poured lavish praise upon her piety ... (while) Josephus disparages her for listening to the Pharisees with too great deference." "This criticism (of Josephus)," Feldman goes on to claim, "is particularly striking in view of the fact that Josephus identifies himself with these selfsame Pharisees."[8]

This last observation of Feldman is to be the topic of this article. Josephus' portrayal of the Hasmonean queen is only the most blatant part of a larger very damaging picture emerging from his description of the royal women in the Hasmonean and Herodian courts. The vehemently negative portrayal of royal women (the queen, her granddaughter Alexandra, Herod's wife Mariamme, Herod's sister Salome, Pheroras' wife), which has no precedent in Josephus' earlier writings, and is not surpassed in his description of later events, leaves an uneasy impression on the reader that the author of these texts believed that behind every calamity lurks a woman, or as the French would have it – *cherchez la femme*. Small wonder that Feldman felt inclined to brand Josephus a misogy-

---

[5] Ibid., p. 116 = Vita 414; 415; 426–7. Actually, Josephus was probably married four times. Feldman has missed the wife Josephus left in Jerusalem, whom he mentions in his speech to the besieged in the city, BJ 5.419.

[6] Ibid., p. 117.

[7] Unlike his counterparts, Ben Sira and Philo, who are often grouped together with Josephus as the prime examples of male Jewish misogyny of the Greco-Roman period. For Ben Sira and women see: C. W. TRENCHARD, Ben Sira's View of Women: A Literary Analysis (Chico CA: Scholars Press); CLAUDIA V. CAMP, "Understanding a Patriarchy: Women in Second Century Jerusalem Through the Eyes of Ben Sira," in Amy-Jill Levine (ed.), above, n. 2, pp. 1–39. On Philo and women see recently: DOROTHY SLY, Philo's Perceptions of Women (Atlanta: Scholars Press, 1990).

[8] FELDMAN, "Deborah," 118–9.

nist. However, in his article about the Pharisees in Josephus, D.R. Schwartz had argued convincingly that Josephus did not originally compose the description of the Pharisees during Shelamzion's reign.[9] It stems from the writings of a non-Jew and a sworn enemy of the Pharisees, whose writings Josephus dutifully followed, often contradicting his own statements elsewhere. The most likely candidate for this role was, in Schwartz's mind, Herod's court historian, Nicolaus of Damascus. Following Schwartz in his assertion, I would like to test the case that not just Shelamzion's Pharisees, but Shelamzion herself, and all the other royal Hasmonean and Herodian women, as portrayed in Josephus, are creatures of Nicolaus' imagination and outlook. The purpose of this claim is not to acquit Josephus and lay the burden of misogynism at someone else's doorstep, but rather, as will become apparent, to demonstrate that this assertion has far-reaching consequences for the question of Josephus as a historian of women, for the history of royal Judaean women during the Second Temple period and for the personal involvement of Nicolaus, as a court-historian, with the heroines/villainesses of his history.

Josephus himself freely admits that he read the *Historiae* of Nicolaus (AJ 1.94; 108; 159; 7.101; 13.250–1; 347; 14.9; 68; 104; 16.183–6 CA 2.84). That he is indebted to them much more than he concedes is a common scholarly assertion. Scholarly debate revolves around the ways he borrowed from Nicolaus. Some scholars claim he copied directly from Nicolaus, seldom checking for internal inconsistencies as a result.[10] Others would have him mold the material he found in his source to fit his own agenda.[11] Some scholars, with no apparent methodology, resort to mentioning Nicolaus occasionally, but totally ignore him elsewhere.[12] Yet others disregard Nicolaus altogether.[13] Many scholars claim that while in BJ Josephus used Nicolaus slavishly, in AJ he had meanwhile come across other sources and rewrote his material independent of Nicolaus.[14] Yet others claim that in AJ he is not less but more dependent on Nicolaus because he wrote in greater detail.[15] In the following lines I will make

---

[9] Above, n. 1, pp. 159; 162.

[10] O. MICHEL, O. BAUERNFEIND, De Bello Judaico, (München: Kösel Verlag, 1959), XXV–XVI.

[11] S.J.D. COHEN, Josephus in Galilee and Rome (Leiden: E.J. Brill, 1979), 232–3.

[12] See e.g. A. SCHALIT, König Herodes: Der Mann und sein Werk (Berlin: Walter de Grutyer, 1969) who mentions Nicolaus, Herod's advisor, often, but only very rarely as Josephus' source, primarily in the story of Mariamme's execution, pp. 566–71.

[13] E.g. S. ZEITLIN, "Herod: A Malevolent Maniac," Jewish Quarterly Review 54 (1963–4), 1–27. On p. 1 Zeitlin mention Nicolaus as source but never refers to him again. And see also his "Queen Salome and King Jannaeus Alexander: A Chapter in the History of the Second Jewish Commonwealth," Jewish Quarterly Review 51 (1960–1), 1–33.

[14] G. HÖLSCHER, Die Quellen des Josephus für die Zeit vom Exil bis zum jüdischen Krieg (Leipzig: B.G. Teubner, 1904).

[15] H. ST JOHN THACKERY, Josephus: The Man and the Historian (New York: Jewish Insti-

the case that the "*cherchez la femme*" syndrome found in Josephus' descriptions of the Hasmoneans and Herodians is typically Nicolean, and Josephus does not resort to it before, or after he exhausts Nicolaus as a source.

I. Josephus on Women

Josephus' attitude to women probably could be inferred from his rewriting of biblical women's roles. The way he reworked their roles, when systematic, could teach us, for example, something about how he reworked the roles of women he found in his lost source – Nicolaus' *Historiae*. However, the results of such an investigation are not straightforward, and interpreting them requires *finesse*. Unfortunately, all work done up to now has not discovered significant trends and attitudes, primarily because the question scholars have posed, namely, whether Josephus is more positive or more negative to women than his source, is not very sophisticated, and most data adduced for this issue could be interpreted either way. Thus, Feldman claimed that Josephus denigrated and belittled Deborah's role,[16] but Bailey, to his own astonishment, found Josephus' description of the matriarchs exceptionally accommodating, and in fact an improvement on the Bible.[17] These contradictory finds show that the criteria "positive" and "negative" are not useful in determining Josephus' attitude to women. In a footnote, however, Feldman points out a useful indicator as to the way Josephus reworked his material on women: "(he) often heightens the romantic element in his retelling of the Biblical narrative."[18] This observation is very interesting, but the two best examples Feldman brings to demonstrate this trait – Josephus' retelling of the story of Joseph and Potiphar's wife (AJ 2.41–58), and his story of Moses' marriage to the Ethiopian princess (2.243–53) – are notoriously famous for being narratives Josephus borrowed from other sources.[19] So while it is true that the romantic atmosphere in some of

tute of Religion Press, 1929), 66; WACHOLDER, Nicolaus of Damascus (Berkeley: University of California Press, 1962), 60–1, 63; COHEN, Josephus, 57–8; M. STERN, Greek and Latin Authors on Jews and Judaism I (Jerusalem: Israel Academy of Sciences and Humanities, 1976), 229.

16 FELDMAN, "Deborah."

17 BAILEY, "Josephus' Matriarchs," 168–76.

18 FELDMAN, "Deborah," 127, n. 28.

19 For Potiphar's wife see M. BRAUN, Griechischer Roman und hellenistische Geschichtsschreibung (Frankfurt: Klostermann, 1934), 17ff.; idem, History and Romance in Graeco-Oriental Literature (Oxford: Blackwell 1938), 92; MAREN NIEHOFF, The Figure of Joseph in Post-Biblical Jewish Literature (Leiden: E.J. Brill, 1992), 105–6. For the Ethiopian princess, see BRAUN, Romance, 98–102; TESSA RAJAK, "Moses in Ethiopia: Legend and Literature," Journal of Jewish Studies 29 (1978), 120–1; A. SHINAN, Moses and the Ethiopian Woman: Sources of a Story in the Chronicles of Moses," in J. HEINEMANN and S. WERSES (eds.), Studies in Hebrew Narrative Art = Scripta Hierosolymitana XXVII (Jerusalem: Magnes, 1978),

Josephus' retellings of the Bible is greater than the original, we should legitimately ask, is this a trait of Josephus' writing, or is he again dependent on his sources? If the latter is correct, perhaps we should test Josephus attitude to women in another way.

I propose that we examine Josephus' texts on women in places where he could use no historiographic or aggadic sources, and where he can be described, so to speak, as his own source – the latter parts of BJ, beginning from the middle of the second book, and his Vita. In composing them he may have used his notes, or notes taken by military and imperial clerks during Vespasian's campaign to Judaea in 67–70 CE, but these can hardly be considered historiographic sources.

The most striking feature of these texts is the almost absolute absence of women in them. Only two women (Queen Berenice, and Mary daughter of Eleazar of the Peraea – BJ 6.201) are mentioned by name, and even then only briefly. All other women mentioned on these pages are nameless, characterless and float out of the text almost as soon as they enter it. One may, justifiably, claim that Josephus does not mention women because he is describing a war, and, as is natural, women are the victims rather than the perpetrators of wars. Josephus pays tribute to their victim position by mentioning numerous cases in which women suffered and died of hunger during siege (BJ 5.430; 433; 513); were captured (4.115), raped (4.560), slaughtered (3.336; 4.81) and sold into slavery (6.384). However, these stereotypical descriptions certainly do not tell the whole story, for women's roles in the war must have been more varied, as Josephus himself occasionally admits. Thus, he mentions that in Japhia women joined men in defending their town against the Roman army (BJ 3.303). Not surprisingly, Josephus relates, beside the fate of the men (they were all killed), also the fate of the women of Japhia (they were all sold into slavery – BJ 3.304). This should be compared with the fate of Gabara for example (BJ 3.133), where Josephus also mentions the slaughter of all the men but says nothing there about the fate of the women. Furthermore, Simon bar Giora is said to have had women followers in his entourage (4.505). These minor notices indicate that there were women who took a greater, more active interest in the war than Josephus cared to explore. However apart from neglecting to mention the general contribution of women to the war, some specific women were too important for the narrative to be completely ignored, and the way they are mentioned may help uncover what Josephus' interest in them was.

69–72; Donna Runnalls, "Moses' Ethiopian Campaign," Journal for the Study of Judaism 14 (1983), 135–56. Wacholder, Nicolaus, 57–8 suggests that for these two accounts Josephus' source is also Nicolaus.

a. *Justus of Tiberias' Sister*

One of Josephus' most worthy literary opponents, and perhaps the man whose attack on Josephus' historical integrity spurred the composition of the Vita, was a certain Justus of Tiberias. Justus' career was, to a certain extent, similar to that of Josephus. They both toyed with the idea of fighting against Rome, but they both, finally, found themselves on the Roman side, Josephus as a direct client of the emperor Vespasian and Justus as a loyal servant of the client king Agrippa II. Thus, Josephus moved in higher circles, and his version of the war received royal sanction. However, Justus, too, eventually published his version of the war, and in it he portrayed Josephus in a less than favorable light. Because of the antagonistic relationship between them in his Vita Josephus volunteers new information not found in BJ about Justus actions during the war in Galilee.

In Vita 186 Josephus relates certain events that took place in Gamla, in which Philip son of Jacimus, another of Agrippa's men, was involved. Josephus recounts a purge carried out by the inhabitants of Gamla on Philip's and Justus' relatives, when the two and their forces were out of town. The inhabitants of Gamla, Josephus relates, executed a certain Chares, one Jesus his kinsman and the sister of Justus. This last victim of the purge is curiously absent from most modern editions of Josephus. For example, in his translation, Thackery writes "the brother(!) of Justus." A glance at the Greek text is just as misleading for it reads "ἀδελφόν," and the only indication that another reading is available is found in a footnote, which states: "Most mss. read ἀδελφήν (i.e. sister)." If this is indeed true, why did the editor choose the version "brother"? Surely the reason is not *lectio difficilior*. While the principle of *lectio difficilior* instructs us not to rely on the quantity of the readings, a reading should not be dismissed *because* it is represented in the majority of manuscripts. The question should rather be: In what direction would we expect a scribe to "correct" his misunderstood, or bizarre manuscript? In the case before us I think the *lectio difficilior* is "sister" for three reasons. First of all the involvement of women in the business of war is unexpected. It is true that the woman here seems to have been a pawn in some political maneuver, but even so, this is the only political assassination of a woman described by Josephus in the entire war. For this reason alone a scribal correction of the text from female to male is more logical than a move in the other direction. Secondly, I believe a general tendency can be detected in the transmission process of ancient texts in which women are gradually eliminated.[20] Thirdly, and most importantly, the copyist who altered "sister" into "brother" did so, in this case, not as a result of a whim, but presumably under the influence of an earlier passage in Vita. For this reason too, modern editors

---

[20] This is a topic I am working on, and my conclusions regarding the manuscript traditions of rabbinic literature will, I hope, be published soon.

and translators have chosen the version "brother." Let us now turn to that other text.

In Vita 177 Josephus tells of the same incident in quite a different context. Sitting at table with Justus, after having tricked, taken prisoner and cordially released him, Josephus urges Justus to realize that he is his natural ally, while the Galileans and inhabitant of Gamla are not. Thus he reminds him that the Galileans had cut off his brother's hands, and that at Gamla, obviously referring to the same incident of AJ 186, associates of Justus were murdered: Chares, Jesus and the husband of Justus' sister.[21] The discrepancies between the two lists are probably irreconcilable.[22] The inhabitants of Gamla killed either Justus' sister, in which case Vita 186 is correct, or his brother-in-law, in which case Vita 177 is correct, or both, in which cases both lists are correct, or neither, in which case neither list is. Thus it remains unclear whether the inhabitants of Gamla killed Justus' sister. However, the correction "brother" is obviously based on Vita 177, where Justus' brother is mentioned, but in another context and with another fate.

On the basis of *lectio difficilior,* I suspect the version "sister" in Vita 186 is, if not the only, at least one of the correct readings. The confusion results, in my opinion, from Josephus' utter lack of interest in the role women *qua* women played in politics. For Josephus politics is a dangerous game in which people could get killed and the gender of the victims was insignificant. Furthermore, by not mentioning the sister in his conversation with Justus, Josephus fails to capitalize on the emotional consequences of the woman's death. He makes it clear to Justus that her death, as also the death of his other associates, spelt danger, but does not suggest that it may have been emotionally more traumatic for him.

---

[21] In the literature about Justus of Tiberias mention of the sister is also missing. For example, TESSA RAJAK, "Josephus and Justus of Tiberias," in L.H. FELDMAN and G. HATA (eds.), Josephus, Judaism and Christianity (Detroit: Wayne State University Press, 1987), 89, mentions only Vita 177, where a brother is mentioned, and totally ignores Vita 186. Y. DAN, "Josephus Flavius and Justus of Tiberias," in U. RAPPAPORT (ed.), Josephus Flavius: Historian of Eretz Israel in the Hellenistic-Roman Period (Jerusalem: Yad Izhak Ben Zvi, 1982), 71–2 (Hebrew), uses Vita 177 as evidence that Justus was a relative of Philip b. Jacimus, and also ignores 186; COHEN, Josephus, 167, does state that Vita 186 mentions a sister, but further down he states: "Josephus even suggests that Justus' brother was harmed before the war, but here V 177 is refuted by V. 186." In other words, Cohen discards the reading "sister" in 186.

[22] For an attempt at reconciliation, see: J.J. PRICE, "The Enigma of Philip ben Jakimos," Historia 40 (1991), 90–2, although Price ignored the reading "sister" altogether.

b. *Simon bar Giora's Wife*

In the factional warfare that gripped Jerusalem in the year of 69 CE between the militias of John of Gischala and Simon bar Giora, the former kidnapped the latter's wife (BJ 4.538–44). This was obviously done in order to blackmail Simon into accepting John's terms, but Simon must have called his opponent's bluff, for he did not capitulate and John's faction finally released the woman unharmed. In this context it is important to note several details which Josephus mentions about this event, and which should suggest to us that the woman played a greater role in the war than as a mere victim of a kidnapping. The wife was captured in an ambush which had obviously been laid for Simon himself. Furthermore, she was captured "with a large number of his attendants." Thus Simon's wife was to be found in the same places and under the same circumstances as her warring husband, suffering the hardships and misfortunes of a brigand band. Simon had not left her at home, either because he was a jealous patriarchal husband, who never let his wife out of his sight, or because she was an important partner in his exploits. In support of the second interpretation one could quote Josephus' statement, that when bringing her prisoner to Jerusalem her captors celebrated "as if their prisoner had been Simon himself" (BJ 4.538). However, from the brief description of the episode both reconstructions are plausible. Josephus himself makes no effort to clarify which is the correct one. He says nothing about Simon's relations with his wife and she disappears from the scene as soon as this unpleasant episode is over. This is certainly not the writing of a historian bent on heightening romance.

c. *Eleazar ben Yair's Wise Relative*

Although some scholars doubt Josephus' description of the dramatic and tragic fate of the defenders of Masada,[23] the story in itself seems credible,[24] and sufficiently supported by the archaeological data.[25] Its one flaw is the disturbing fact that in cases of mass suicide there are usually no survivors to tell the tale. So who told Josephus about the fate of the Sicarii on Masada? Josephus seems to be quite clear on that one. In the wake of the events "... an old woman and another relative of Eleazar, superior in sagacity and training to most of her sex, with five children ..." (BJ 7.399) had hidden themselves in the subterranean

[23] See primarily TRUDE WEISS-ROSEMARINE, "Josephus' 'Eleazar Speech' and Historical Credibility," Proceedings of the Sixth World Congress of Jewish Studies I (Jerusalem: World Union of Jewish Studies, 1973), 417–27.

[24] M. STERN, "Sicarii and Zealots," in M. AVI-YONAH and Z. BARAS (edd.), The World History of the Jewish People, VIII Society and Religion in the Second Temple Period (Jerusalem 1977), 278–81.

[25] See Y. YADIN, Masada: Herod's Fortress and the Zealots' Last Stand (London: Weidenfeld and Nicolson, 1966), 193–201.

water system of Masada. If, as I claim, Josephus is telling the true fate of Masada, his source for the events leading up to the mass suicide, for the life of the defenders during the years from the fall of Jerusalem to the fall of Masada and perhaps even for his surprisingly accurate description of the fortress[26] was the evidence of the younger woman, the relative of Eleazar, for unless she were his source, Josephus would not have praised her superior wisdom, which, because of his apparent prejudice against women, seems to him superior to what he usually expected to find in members of the second sex.[27]

Nevertheless, Josephus' description displays no characteristics even remotely related to a woman's outlook on the events. We do not know whether the wives of the defenders supported the decision to commit suicide. They are found in their traditional role as victims of men's war, and the only emotions described are those of the men: "Like men possessed they went their way ... so ardent the passion that had seized them to slaughter their wives and little ones and themselves ... For while they caressed and embraced their wives and their children in their arms, clinging in tears to those parting kisses, at that instant, as though served by hands other than their own, they accomplished their purpose ... Wretched victims of necessity, to whom to slay with their own hands their own wives and children seemed the lightest of evils!" Furthermore, Josephus nowhere explains the motives behind the actions of Eleazar's relative – when, why and how did she defect. For him she was a source of information but not an actor in events.

d. Queen Berenice

The historical importance of all the women discussed thus far may be inferred only by conjecture. Josephus leaves them as hazy as possible. A completely different case is that of Queen Berenice, Agrippa II's sister, an important historical figure of Josephus' times, who genuinely influenced events in the highest political circles. A biographical sketch of Queen Berenice runs as follows: Daughter of King Agrippa I, as a teenager she was married to and almost immediately widowed by Marcus, the nephew of the philosopher Philo. She earned the title "queen" through her second marriage, to her uncle, Herod king of Chalcis (AJ 19.277). On being widowed a second time, she married and

---

26 It is not clear whether Josephus ever visited Masada. Yadin asserts that his description of the walls is of an external observer, ibid, 141: S. J. D. COHEN, "Masada: Literary Tradition, Archaeological Remains and the Literary Credibility of Josephus," Journal of Jewish Studies 33 (1982), 398, n. 41, claims that Josephus described the fortress from the notes of Romans who surveyed the site after its capture.

27 That the woman was Josephus' source is the opinion of L. H. FELDMAN, Josephus and Modern Scholarship (1937–80) (Berlin: Walter de Grutyer, 1984), 776. TESSA RAJAK, Josephus: The Historian and his Society (London: Duckworth, 1983), 219 maintains that the woman gave this information to the Romans, and not directly to Josephus.

divorced yet another king – Polemo of Cilicia, and then lived single for many years next to her brother, King Agrippa II, causing gossips to brand their relationship incestuous (20.145–6). During the war of 66–70 CE Berenice met the general Titus, son of the emperor Vespasian and became his lover (Tacitus, *Historiae* 2.2.1). She must have harbored hopes of yet another, even greater, royal marriage, but her hopes were dashed (Seutonius, *Titus* 7.1; Cassius Dio, *Historia Romana* 66.150.3–4). Nothing more is known of her.[28]

Although Josephus' writings are certainly the most important and extensive source for the Herodian dynasty, most of this information is absent from BJ, and his later AJ is only slightly more informative. Details about the most important part in Berenice's career, her relationship with the soon-to-be emperor Titus, are available only in the writings of contemporary and later Roman historians. It is not as though Josephus did not know of her. On the contrary, he probably knew her personally.[29] The best explanation for Josephus' total silence on the question of her relationship with Titus is, apparently, his own special relationship with the general. Josephus was a *protégé* and friend of the emperor-designate, and his history of the war, more than being the official Flavian version, was the chronicle of Titus' campaign and victory.[30] It has often been claimed that Josephus deliberately concealed damning information about Titus' conduct. Thus, for example, Josephus acquits Titus of the charge of burning the Temple, although most historians doubt the historical accuracy of such a claim.[31] If the romantic attachment of Titus to the Jewish queen was viewed in Rome as a weakness rather than an asset, it should come as no surprise that the details are totally absent from Josephus' account.

However, Josephus does not totally ignore the existence of Berenice, and her

---

[28] For the historical sources, see: STERN, Greek and Latin Authors, index s. v. Berenice. For epigraphic data see: W. DITTENBERGER, Orientis Graeci Inscriptiones Selectae 1 (Leipzig: S. Hirzel, 1903), 638–9; L'Année Épigraphique (1928), 23, no. 82. On Berenice see also: GRACE H. MACURDY, Vassal Queens and Some Contemporary Women in the Roman Empire (Baltimore: John Hopkins Press, 1937), 84–90; J.A. CROOK, "Titus and Berenice," American Journal of Philology 72 (1951), 162–75; E. MIREAUX, La Reine Berenice (Paris: Albin Michel, 1951); RUTH JORDAN, Berenice (London: Constable, 1974); P.M. ROGERS, "Titus, Berenice and Mucianus," Historia 29 (1980), 86–95; D.C. BRAUD, "Berenice in Rome," Historia 33 (1984), 12–3. An important contribution to the study of Berenice is recently S. SCHWARTZ, Josephus and Judaean Politics (Leiden: E.J. Brill, 1990), 110–69. SCHWARTZ did to Josephus' works what I am trying to do here to Nicolaus', namely search in his writings for a personal motivation. His work, however, has no particular bearing on women.

[29] RAJAK, Josephus, 75; SCHWARTZ, ibid., 156. Schwartz comments and speculates on the absence of Agrippa from Josephus' description of the siege of Jerusalem, but the absence of Berenice, which I find more intriguing, he totally ignores (pp. 132–3).

[30] On the publication of BJ during Titus' reign see: M. STERN, "The Date of the Composition of BJ," in Studies in Jewish History – The Second Temple Period (Jerusalem: Yad ben-Zvi, 1991), 402–7 (Hebrew).

[31] E.g. G. ALON, Jews, Judaism and the Classical World (Jerusalem: Magnes Press, 1977), 252–68.

appearance and disappearance from the scene in BJ is extremely similar to the way other women enter and exit Josephus' account of the war. Berenice is mentioned as present in Jerusalem when hostilities between the Roman governor Florus and the Jerusalem Jews broke out.[32] Josephus incidentally discloses the fact that her presence in Jerusalem was in a private, religious, rather than public, political context. She had made a Nazirite vow and now came to fulfill it. This gives us a glimpse of her physical appearance at the time for Josephus says: "it is customary for those ... (who take this vow) to shave their heads ... and she would come barefoot before the tribunal" (BJ 2.313). Berenice intervened, so we understand, in order to try and stop the massacre and the plunder carried out by the procurator's troops in Jerusalem, but ultimately failed (BJ 2.310–4). She is then mentioned, in the same context, as, on the one hand, writing to the Roman governor of Syria, describing the outrages of the procurator (BJ 2.333) and, on the other hand, attempting, together with her brother, who had now also arrived in Jerusalem, to restrain the Jewish insurgents in their eagerness to fight Rome (BJ 2.344; 402–5). Here she disappears from the scene. Even in the description of the escape of King Agrippa from Jerusalem, which must have included Berenice she is not mentioned (BJ 2.407).[33] Berenice's importance and influence are never followed up in BJ, although Tacitus names her as an ally in her own right of the general Vespasian (Tacitus, *Historiae* 2.81.2), probably indicating that she played a prominent role in the later events of the war, not just as Titus' mistress. Thus, had we known nothing more of Berenice than what Josephus tells in BJ, her role in the events would be only slightly less obscure than that of Simon bar Giora's wife.

However, Josephus wrote other books after BJ, and his personal situation had sufficiently altered by that time (for several reasons, not the least of which was the death of his one-time patron, Titus) to merit a different evaluation of Berenice and her role in history.[34] The detailed information about her marriages comes mainly from AJ. Her marriage to Marcus, Philo's nephew, is mentioned only in AJ (19.276–7).[35] Then, on the death of Agrippa I, Josephus

[32] Berenice is mentioned earlier three times, all in genealogical contexts. In BJ 2.217 as the wife of Herod of Chalcis; in BJ 2.220, as the daughter of king Agrippa I; and in BJ 2.221 as the widow of Herod of Chalcis and mother of his two sons. All these descriptions come from genealogical lists Josephus used in his description of Agrippa's reign, not from a literary account.

[33] Berenice is further mentioned by name together with Agrippa II as the joint-owner of a palace in Jerusalem burnt down by the rebels (BJ 2.426) and as the joint-employer of a certain Ptolemy, who is robbed by some Jewish rebels (BJ 2.595), but these could hardly be counted as events in which she took part. After book 2 of BJ Berenice is never mentioned again.

[34] It is also S. SCHWARTZ's assertion, (Josephus, 151–2), that Josephus portrayal of the Herodians in AJ is a result of a change in personal interests, but he does not single out Berenice.

[35] Berenice is mentioned earlier, in AJ 18 on two occasions: Once in a genealogical list of Agrippa I's children (132), probably the same source Josephus had used in less detail in BJ

relates the outrageous treatment of the statues of Agrippa's daughters by the Cesarean mob (AJ 19.357).[36] AJ further mentions Berenice's marriage to her uncle, King Herod of Chalcis (AJ 19.277; 354; 20.104 – where Berenice's children are mentioned). These are all rather dry, factual details, which add little to the description of Berenice's role in Jewish politics, except insofar as to note that her father used her as a pawn in his political power-games, marrying her off to desirable allies and close relatives. [37]

However, Berenice's last two appearances on the pages of AJ have a completely different function. In AJ 20.143 we are informed that Berenice's jealousy of Drusilla, her sister, made the latter's life impossible, so that, against the ancestral laws of the Jews, she married the Roman procurator, Felix, a strange charge indeed, which can hardly be corroborated, sounds very unconvincing, and is, without doubt, intended to damn Berenice. It contains one of the two stock charges against evil women – jealousy. Finally, Berenice's marriage to King Polemo of Cilicia is described in AJ 20.145–6 with no less malice:

After the death of Herod, who had been her uncle and husband, Berenice lived for a long time as a widow. But when a report gained currency that she had a liaison with her brother, she induced Polemo, king of Cilicia to be circumcised and to take her in marriage; for she thought that she would demonstrate in this way that the reports were false. Polemo was prevailed upon chiefly on account of her wealth. The marriage did not, however, last long, for Berenice, out of licentiousness, according to report, deserted Polemo. And he was relieved simultaneously of his marriage and of further adherence to the Jewish way of life (AJ 20.145).

Licentious sexual behavior mentioned here is the second stock charge against evil women. Berenice is accused both of incest with her brother, and desertion of her husband "out of licentiousness." While the charge of incest may have been a rumor current at the time (see Juvenal, *Saturae* 6.155–8), a negative view of Berenice's wedding to Polemo need not be.

These last two passages on Berenice contradict Josephus' restrained attitude to the woman in all his previous discussions of her. They both put Berenice in a position to influence negatively the flow of events, and makes her capacity to

---

2.220; another time as co-heir with her brother Agrippa II to the services of a certain Thaumastus. Both can hardly be considered accounts of Berenice's role in Jewish history.

[36] Jordan (Berenice, pp. 89–90) suggested that Josephus, for reasons of modesty, is here refraining from relating a shocking tale of how the king's daughters themselves were violated, because in the writings of the ninth-century monk, Photius, the same is told of the daughters themselves, rather than the statues, but the difficulties with Photius are too great to dismiss Josephus' account in favor of his.

[37] In Vita also, Berenice is mentioned only as a co-ruler with Agrippa II. Twice Josephus tells of a letter Their Majesties received from Philip son of Jacimus (Vita 48; 180), and twice Josephus reminds Justus of Tiberias that King Agrippa had planned to put him to death, and it was only at the intercession of the queen that this punishment was averted (Vita 343; 355). Berenice is further mentioned incidentally as the owner of lands in the vicinity of Besara (Vita 119).

cause shame through sexual misconduct a liability on her relatives. The report is so damning for both Berenice and her family, that scholars have surmised that Josephus must have written it after the death of Agrippa II, who according to Josephus' own account, was also his patron (Vita 362–4).[38] However, this suggestion contradicts the dates of both the publication of AJ (93/4 CE), and of Agrippa II's death (100 CE).[39] Therefore, Schwartz has come up with what he terms "a partial solution" to the problem, by suggesting, on the basis of a whole body of evidence, that here too Josephus is not espousing the "*cherchez la femme*" approach, but rather following his source, written by a priest, whose concern seems to have been the preservation of the ancestral Jewish laws,[40] as manifest in the two incidents involving Berenice. If Schwartz is correct in his assumption, and I for one, am convinced he is, than here again it is not Josephus who puts a woman in the center of events, but rather his source.

Thus, to sum up Josephus' account of Queen Berenice, the historian was convinced that her attempt to influence Florus in the summer of 66 CE could, if successful, have had major historical repercussions. It failed however. All other actions taken on Berenice's behalf seemed to him hardly worth mentioning. His lack of interest in her romantic entanglement with Titus may be explained by his need to be discrete when discussing Titus, but that he was not tempted to return to the topic after his patron's death suggests that Josephus did not view the episode as sufficiently important for the historical course of events. Thus, in the words of Grace Macurdy: "Josephus is no Plutarch, and we do not get from him an impression of Berenice's character and charm to equal that of which Plutarch gives of Cleopatra ..."[41]

All these are examples of Josephus' treatment of women's outlook, fate and involvement in Jewish history. The meager and fragmented data demonstrates quite convincingly that Josephus, as a historian, found women to be a topic of little interest. He found it neither necessary to blame them for negatively affecting the course or history, nor did he see sexual misconduct lurking behind every catastrophe. This conclusion tells us nothing about Josephus' personal attitude toward women, and even if he could be branded a misogynist, he certainly did not allow such sentiments to meddle with his analysis of the causes

---

[38] On this problem see: D.R. Schwartz, "KATA TOYTON TON KAIPON: Josephus' Source on Agrippa II," Jewish Quarterly Review 72 (1981–2), 241–3. S. Schwartz, on the other hand (Josephus, 150–7) suggests it was probably oral and perhaps came from a competing line of Herodians – the descendants of Herod of Chalcis. Such a claim ignores the fact that Berenice had at one time been married to Herod of Chalcis and two of his descendants were her sons.

[39] On the date of Agrippa II's death see now: D.R. Schwartz, Studies in the Jewish Background of Christianity (Tübingen: J.C.B. Mohr, 1992), 243–75.

[40] D.R. Schwartz, "Agrippa II," pp. 241–68. On the nature of this source, see particularly pp. 258–9.

[41] Vassal Queens, 90–1.

and developments in political and social life. I am tempted to surmise that Josephus is an even worse source for women's history than has previously been suggested.

However, Josephus' writings are replete with passages that place women precisely in a position to influence political events negatively through their intrigue, cunning, jealousy and capacity to bring shame through sexual misconduct. These texts are curiously concentrated in books 1 and 2 of BJ and between books 13 and 17 in AJ – those same texts that describe the Hasmonean and Herodian Kingdoms, a period for which Josephus is principally dependent on Nicolaus of Damascus.

II. Nicolaus on Women

A short biographical note on Nicolaus is in order here. A native of the city of Damascus, Nicolaus received a formal Greek education and emerged as an important rhetor, dramatist and historian. Antony and Cleopatra hired his services as tutor to their children. After the battle of Actium, in which his patrons were defeated and subsequently committed suicide, Nicolaus found himself unemployed, and was grateful for King Herod's generosity in taking him into his service. Nicolaus served as a companion, mentor, court historian and political advisor to the king. He served him to the king's death, and then retired, apparently to Rome, where he finished writing his World History.[42]

Nicolaus belonged to the Peripatetic school of thought, whose philosophical theory maintained that written history should be dramatic, emotional and entertaining, much like a good play. It is the historian's imperative to add to dry historical data psychological effects and dramatic moments, as well as share with the reader the emotions of the heroes. For this purpose the historian needed no further historical proof. In this vein Nicolaus wrote his *Historiae*.[43] Or in Wacholder's words: "... faced with the conflict between telling a good story and telling the truth[, t]here is no doubt that Nicolaus preferred a good story."[44] The historian Polibius attacked the Peripatetic school for its deceitful methods, and counted himself among the disciples of Thucydides. It is, thus, not surprising that Josephus, who had read Thucydides (CA 1.18; 66), though not mentioning him by name, also considered himself a member of Thucydides' historical school (BJ 1.3; 14), and thus wrote very differently.

[42] On Nicolaus see: Wacholder, Nicolaus; Stern, Greek and Latin Authors I, 227–32.

[43] For a discussion of Nicolaus as a Peripatetic, and a demonstration of his techniques in the description of an event which has no bearing on Herod, see: Schalit, Herodes, 583–4, nn. 38–9; and see also G. Giangrande, "On an Alleged Fragment of Ctesias," Quadesni Urbinati di cultura classica 23 (1976), 38.

[44] Wacholder, Nicolaus, 67. Thackery, Josephus, 66 also stresses Nicolaus the dramatist.

Furthermore, Nicolaus seems also to have had a personal preference for describing the domestic, rather than the political, and for concentrating on peace rather than on war.[45] Such history naturally accords women a greater role in the events, whether real or imagined. Thus it is not surprising that, of the 39 women mentioned by name in the entire corpus of Josephus' writings on the Second Temple Period (AJ 11–20; BJ; Vita), 20 are found in those sections dependent on Nicolaus, and of these only one (Acme – BJ 1.641; AJ 17.134) is not of royal blood. These women are mentioned numerous times, and play a decisive role in the events Nicolaus describes, which include much plotting and court intrigue. Thus, the difference between Josephus' and Nicolaus' attitude to women can be a useful tool for scholars of Josephus, in seeking to differentiate the writings of one from the other.

For example, one debated question is: where does Josephus rely on Nicolaus for his description of the Hasmoneans? M. Stern claims that Josephus relies quite heavily on him, and "(t)his explains the rather strange fact that Josephus, notwithstanding his patriotism and the pride he took in his kinship with the Hasmoneans, presents us with a rather cold picture of the three main figures of the Hasmonean monarchy, namely Aristobulus I, Alexander Jannaeus and Salome-Alexandra."[46] However, Stern says nothing about Josephus' portrayal of John Hyrcanus, presumably because the latter is portrayed much more favorably than the three first mentioned monarchs, and Stern may have suspected that for the description of his reign Josephus had used as a primary source some documents more accommodating than Nicolaus (see 1 Macc. 16.23–4). However, I think we are now in a position to ascribe to Nicolaus the primary description of that reign too.

In his description of the Hasmonean revolt and its aftermath in AJ, Josephus is dependent on 1 Maccabees as his primary source. 1 Maccabees' lack of interest in women surpasses even Josephus' apathy. Women are mentioned only in a matter-of-fact way, as victims of Antiochus' persecutions (1 Macc. 1.60–1; 2.37), and of the hardships of war (1 Macc. 5.13). No female relative of the Hasmonean brothers is ever mentioned, and we only learn that they had a mother because Simon is described as building a monumental tomb for his father, *mother* and brothers (1 Macc. 13.28), that Jonathan and Simon were married, because they had sons (1 Macc. 13.16–20; 16.16) and that Simon had a daughter, because he had a son-in-law (1 Macc. 16.11). It would be instructive if Josephus had found it necessary to mention more women in his narrative than 1 Maccabees, but he did not, not even his own ancestor, the daughter of

---

45 For a discussion and an example unrelated to Herodian history, see: Wacholder, ibid., 57; 80.

46 Greek and Latin Authors I, 230.

Jonathan the Hasmonean (Vita 4). Thus, Josephus was absolutely loyal to his source.[47]

1 Maccabees ends with the death of Simon the Hasmonean. Simon, we are told, was tricked by his son-in-law, who invited him for a banquet, took advantage of his drunken state and murdered him together with his two sons.[48] No woman is mentioned and the final words of the book reassure the reader that one of Simon's sons, John, succeeded in escaping and took power after his father. In Josephus' account, however, both in BJ and in AJ the same story ends with an extensive epilogue on the behavior and fate of the wife of Simon the Hasmonean, who is mentioned here for the first time:

Attacking the fort, (Hyrcanus) proved superior in other ways, but was overcome by his righteous feelings. For Ptolemy, as often as he was hard pressed, brought forward his mother and brothers upon the ramparts and tortured them within full view of Hyrcanus, threatening to hurl them over the battlements, if he did not instantly retire. At this spectacle indignation in the breast of Hyrcanus gave way to pity and terror. His mother, unshaken by her torments or the menace of death, with outstretched hands implored her son not to be moved by her outrageous treatment to spare the monster; to her, death at Ptolemy's hands would be better than immortality, if he paid the penalty for the wrongs which he had done to their house. John (Hyrcanus), as often as he took his mother's unflinching courage to heart and gave ear to her entreaties, was impelled to assault; but when he beheld her beaten and mangled, he was unmanned and quite overcome by emotion. The siege consequently dragged on ... Ptolemy now relieved of the siege, put John's brethren and their mother to death (BJ 1.57–60; cf. AJ 13.230–5).

This is indeed a description coming from the pen of another author. Obviously the entire scene was composed for the purpose of drama and psychology. Since it ends with the death of the mother, her heroic actions add nothing to the course of events, and are thus utterly superfluous. For no other reason than

---

[47] Although it is a scholarly consensus that Josephus is not dependent on 1 Maccabees for his account of the first generation Hasmoneans in BJ (31–54), women do not feature in that narrative either. The assumption is that in BJ Josephus was dependent on the description of Nicolaus of the Hasmonean revolt (e.g. HÖLSCHER, Quellen, 17–8; THACKERY, Josephus, 40–1). Thus, it is surprising that BJ does not mention any women either. A partial solution to the problem would be an investigation into Nicolaus' sources for the revolt. I would submit that Nicolaus himself used 1 Maccabees for his narrative. Josephus account in BJ is thus a shorthand version of Nicolaus, which, in itself, must have been an epitome of his source (1 Maccabees?) leaving little room for elaboration. But note that Josephus' (Nicolaus'?) description of Eleazar's death under the elephant in BJ (1.42–4) is slightly more dramatic than in 1 Maccabees (6.43–47); while the episode is completely absent from 2 Maccabees 13. In L. H. FELDMAN, "Flavius Josephus Revisited," in W. HAASE (ed.) Aufstieg und Niedergang der Römischen Welt 21.2 (Berlin: Walter de Gruyter, 1984), 808, this episode is discussed but the differences between AJ and BJ are shrouded because of a comparison between AJ and 1 Maccabees.

[48] It is not important for the present study, that for most of Simon's reign Josephus did not use 1 Maccabees (see: Destinon, Quellen, 80–6; N. BENTWICH, Josephus, [Philadelphia: JPS, 1914], 181–2), because this does not add any women to the narrative and they appear in AJ (as well as in BJ) exactly where 1 Maccabees ends.

Nicolaus' interest in precisely such elements, and their ever increasing presence as we move from events Nicolaus describes second-hand (the Hasmonean period) to events he was a first-hand witness to (the later years of Herod's reign), I would claim that this drama is the composition of Nicolaus' pen. Nicolaus, then, is Josephus' major source for John Hyrcanus' reign, beginning with his rise to power.

The remaining space will be devoted to Josephus' (i.e., Nicolaus') treatment of three prominent Hasmonean and Herodian women: Queen Shelamzion, Herod's wife – Mariamme the Hasmonean, and Herod's sister – Salome.

a. Queen Shelamzion

Joseph Sievers discussed the women of the Hasmonean court[49] and correctly noted that in the Hasmonean dynasty women played a surprisingly prominent role. All the wives of Hasmonean rulers, beginning with John Hyrcanus', make a brief appearance on the pages of Josephus' two books (in almost identical form) always with relation to the succession, i.e., on the death of one monarch and the ascent of the heir to the throne. (1) John Hyrcanus nominates his wife as successor, but his son, Judas Aristobulus, usurps the throne and starves the woman to death (BJ 1.71; AJ 13.302); (2) Judas Aristobulus' wife plots against and murders his brother Antigonus (BJ 1.76; AJ 13.308) and then (3) nominates his brother Alexander as successor (BJ 1.85; AJ 13.320); (4) finally the wife of Alexander Jannaeus assumes the royal power herself (BJ 1.107; AJ 13.407). Most of this information, which Josephus obviously and studiously copied from Nicolaus, was reworked by the latter from some unknown source on the Hasmoneans, since Nicolaus himself was not a contemporary of these kings, and could not write of them first-hand. One indication for the existence of this source is the absence of names for the women. Nicolaus did not write like this. When we arrive at the Herodian period, all royal women are named.[50] The situation for the earlier period is different. The interest of Nicolaus' source in women seems not to have been great, perhaps in the same tradition as 1 Maccabees. He had to mention women because they evidently played an important historical role. Why else would Hyrcanus nominate his wife to succeed him, unless she had proved a capable co-ruler, whom Hyrcanus trusted to manage the affairs of state better than his sons? Yet the source does not mention her even once during the reign of her husband, indicating what little interest he had in her. Nicolaus, on the other hand, delighted in describing the

---

49 "The Role of Women in the Hasmonean Dynasty," in L.H. FELDMAN and G. HATA (edd.), Josephus, Bible and History (Detroit: Wayne State University Press, 1988), 132–46.

50 Save one, Pheroras' wife. On this unusual woman see TAL ILAN, "The Attraction of Aristocratic Women to Pharisaism During the Second Temple Period," *Harvard Theological Review* 88 (1995), 13–14.

murder of this woman at the hands of her son, as part of the gruesome description of Aristobulus' court.

In the same context, and as part of the same train of events, Aristobulus I's wife is also implicated in the plot to murder Antigonus (BJ 1.76; AJ 13.308). How anybody could have known such a detail is not clear, as the plot was a secret, and Aristobulus himself was tricked by it. Since it was also a successful plot, who could know, and publish, the members of the court responsible for it? At best it could have been a malicious rumor, in which case the historian could have ignored it. At worst it was not even a rumor, but a literary assumption on the part of the author. The historian thus places himself in the position of a novelist, who not only tells the events, but also creates the motivation for them. This, as I shall show presently, is precisely the sort of writing in which Nicolaus was involved in his description of the Herodian court. I would guess that in this case Nicolaus found Aristobulus' widow in his source choosing her husband's successor, but I suspect *he* made her responsible for the murder of Antigonus. This would create a neat pattern. The original plan of succession, laid out by Aristobulus himself, was that his brother Antigonus take his place. The inexplicable execution of the latter frustrated this plan and a new heir was required. The queen chose the heir, so Nicolaus connected her action with Antigonus' murder.[51] What is the root of all evil? *Cherchez la femme!*.

This brings us to the main female heroine of the Hasmonean dynasty – Shelamzion Alexandra. Josephus' two descriptions of her reign in BJ and AJ differ greatly, if not in detail, at least in emphasis. Both narratives contain the following details – Shelamzion succeeded her husband even though she had adult sons (BJ 1.107; AJ 13.407). In her internal policy, she installed the Pharisees in power (BJ 1.110–1; AJ 13.409), and her eldest son, Hyrcanus, in the high priesthood (BJ 1.109; AJ 13.408). The Pharisees carried out reprisals against their former (Sadducee?) enemies (BJ 1.113; AJ 13.410). Shelamzion's foreign policy consisted of recruiting a large force of mercenaries (BJ 1.112; AJ 13.409), sending an abortive expedition to Damascus (BJ 1.115; AJ 13.418) and contracting a peace agreement with Tigranes of Armenia (BJ 1.116; AJ 13.419–21). When she was lying sick on her death bed, her younger son, Aristobulus, attempted to take the reins of power by force (BJ 1.117; AJ 13.422–7). While all these details are described in both accounts, their appraisal is, surprisingly, quite different. In BJ Josephus gives the following evaluation of the queen's reign:

[51] But even he did not marry her with the new King Alexander, although this would have made the story more romantic. This was to become the prerogative of modern scholars; and see my "Queen Salamzion Alexandra and Judas Aristobulus' Widow: Did Jannaeus Alexander Contract a Levirate Marriage?" Journal for the Study of Judaism 24 (1993), 181–90, particularly pp. 189–90. I would guess that Nicolaus could not marry the dowager to the new king because the identity of Yannai's wife was too well-known.

Alexander bequeathed the kingdom to his wife, Alexandra, being convinced that the Jews would bow to her authority as they would to no other, because by her utter lack of brutality and by opposition to his crimes she had won the affection of the populace. Nor was he mistaken in these expectations; for this frail woman firmly held the reins of government, thanks to her reputation for piety. She was indeed the very strictest observer of the national traditions and would deprive of office any offenders against the sacred laws (BJ 1.107–8).

BJ further states that her association with the Pharisees was negative, but says only positive things about the queen. She listened to the Pharisees overmuch because she was "intensely religious," while they took advantage of her "sincerity (ἁπλότητα τῆς ἀνθρώπου)" (BJ 1.111). As opposed to the Pharisees, however, "(s)he proved ... to be a wonderful administrator in larger affairs" (BJ 1.112).

AJ, on the other hand, while adding only one important detail, i.e., that the queen appointed the Pharisees at her husband's advice (AJ 13.399–404),[52] usually views the queen's reign very negatively.[53] In the first place, her ascent to the throne is commented upon as a mistake: "Now although Alexander had left two sons, Hyrcanus and Aristobulus, he had bequeathed the royal power to Alexandra" (AJ 13.407). That this is meant as a negative statement is reinforced later by the author, who portrays Aristobulus and his (Sadducee?) followers in a far more favorable light than in BJ, making their fate the topic of a melodramatic diatribe, which he, however, ends with the words: "But still they themselves were to blame for their misfortunes, in allowing a woman to reign who madly desired it in her unreasonable love for power, and when her sons were in the prime of life." (AJ 13.417). However, the worst publicity accorded to Shelamzion is in the closing lines, but one, of book 13:

She was a woman who showed none of the weakness of her sex; for being one of those inordinately desirous of power to rule, she showed by her deeds the ability to carry out her plans, and at the same time she exposed the folly of those men who continually fail to maintain sovereign power. For she valued the present more than the future, and making everything secondary to absolute rule, she had, on account of this, no consideration for either decency or justice. At least matters turned out so unfortunately for her house that the sovereign power which it had acquired in the face of greatest dangers and difficulties was not long afterward taken from it because of her desire of things unbecoming a woman and because she left the kingdom without anyone who had their interests at heart. And even after her death she caused the palace to be filled with misfortunes and disturbances which arose from the public measures taken during her lifetime (AJ 13.430–2).

---

52 This detail is not taken from Nicolaus, but is rather Josephus' own reworking of a Jewish tradition, see: bSotah 22b, and see now ILAN, "Aristocratic Women," 9–11.

53 For a comparison of the two accounts, see S. MASON, Flavius Josephus on the Pharisees (Leiden: E.J. Brill, 1991), 248–59.

In this text the queen is blamed for all the misfortunes of the Hasmonean household, including the Roman conquest of Palestine, for no specific reason other than the fact that she was a woman, and women should not assume supreme power. Indeed, her very conduct is described as unladylike. This is certainly a typical trait of the *cherchez la femme* attitude, usually absent in Josephus' historical writings, and it is a very strong misogynistic statement. Who made it? The usual reconstruction of the relationship between the description in AJ and BJ is to maintain that in BJ Josephus is slavishly loyal to his source (Nicolaus?) while in AJ he voices his own opinion.[54] This, however, is not the only possible reconstruction. For, as Stern had amply demonstrated: "In his Antiquities ... Josephus continues to draw upon the *Historiae* of Nicolaus,"[55] and elsewhere Josephus makes it quite clear that, in his opinion, the blame for the fall of the Hasmoneans should be laid at someone else's doorstep. In the 14th book of the Antiquities, after describing the dynastic squabble between Hyrcanus and Aristobulus, the sons of Shelamzion, and the conquest of Jerusalem by Pompey, Josephus make the following statement:

For this misfortune which befell Jerusalem Hyrcanus and Aristobulus were responsible, because of their dissension. For we lost our freedom and became subject to the Romans, and the territory which we had gained by our arms and taken from the Syrians we were compelled to give back to them ... and the royal power which had formerly been bestowed on those who were high priests by birth became the privilege of commoners (AJ 14.78).

Josephus is clearly blaming the brothers for the fall of the Hasmonean dynasty. Burdening Shelamzion with the downfall of the Hasmonean dynasty does not necessarily imply that Josephus could not blame further accomplices for the crime, but the different styles of the two paragraphs leaves one in no doubt as to which one Josephus composed. That Josephus is the speaker in the second one is clear from his digression into the first person plural (we, the Jews of Palestine) and from the description of the Hasmoneans as respectable high priests, while branding the Herodians "commoners." Josephus truly voices his opinion of the royal Hasmonean dynasty, the family of his ancestors.[56] On the

[54] For such an assumption in R. LAQUER, Der jüdische Historiker Flavius Josephus (Giessen 1920), 128–34. See however, SIEVERS, "Hasmonean Women," 139, who, while claiming our passage is not by Nicolaus, cannot bring himself to convict Josephus of such bad language; MASON, Pharisees, 257–8, does charge Josephus with this judgment; but see now S. SCHWARTZ, Review of S. MASON, Flavius Josphus on the Pharisees: A Composition-Critical Study," AJS Review 19 (1994), 86–7; and see D. R. SCHWARTZ, "Josephus on Hyrcanus II," in F. PARENTE and J. SIEVERS (edd.), Josephus and the History of the Greco-Roman Period (Leiden: E.J. Brill, 1994), 219–23, who thinks this part was written by Josephus and not copied (The fact that this article is formulated much like mine is mere coincidence. I only saw it after most of this work was already completed).

[55] Greek and Latin Authors I, 229.

[56] And see further on this: SCHWARTZ, "Hyrcanus II," 217–20.

other hand, in the first paragraph the Hasmonean fate is described in a distant, third person, and while the blame is made to fall on the queen, the consequences of the Hasmoneans' demise (Roman and Herodian rule) are not elaborated upon. If indeed Nicolaus is its author, this should come as no surprise. As Herod's servant, Nicolaus took pleasure in gloating over the downfall of the Hasmoneans, while blaming them for what he saw as the greatest incompetence – leaving royal power in the hand of a woman – but he certainly had no intention of denigrating the beneficiaries of this misfortune.

There is also another reason why the summation of Shelamzion's rule should not be assigned to Josephus. In the last line of book 13 the following words are added to the derogatory description of queen's reign: "Nevertheless, in spite of reigning in this manner, she kept the nation in peace" (AJ 13.432), indeed an unexpected assessment. At least two scholars solved this contradiction in the same way. Sievers wrote: "This contradiction ... is hard to explain by any other means than by Josephus' careless juxtaposition of sources."[57] Klausner ventures a bolder suggestion: "This obvious contradiction can only be explained by presuming that the two conflicting statements have their origin in two different sources: a Jewish Pharisee source in defense of Salome (sic) and a Greek source hostile to the Jews."[58] Both authors pursued the issue no further. I myself am of the opinion that, having faithfully copied Nicolaus' summation of Shelamzion's rule, Josephus was suddenly taken aback. After all, he knew, as is shown in his description in BJ, that queen Shelamzion had been exceptionally popular with the people, or at any rate with those associated, like himself, with the Pharisees.[59] So he modified the words of Nicolaus. This last sentence is the voice of Josephus himself.

Shelamzion is thus only the most prominent example of how Nicolaus treated his Hasmonean female subjects. These women (except, perhaps John Hyrcanus' mother) were not the creatures of his imagination. They were mentioned in a source he used, of which we know nothing. Nicolaus only highlighted their role, and, when possible, implicated them in adversely influencing the events. One question, however, remains open. If 1 Maccabees mentions no women, and Nicolaus was not the initial source of the subsequent Hasmonean history, but was using a Hasmonean source similar in character to 1 Maccabees, how did women become prominent in the narrative? I think the answer is obvious. Later Hasmonean sources mentioned women, because they became historically prominent in later Hasmonean history. John Hyrcanus really thought it would be best for Israel if his wife were to succeed him. However, his plans failed. Alexander Jannaeus really thought Shelamzion would be the best queen for

57 "Hasmonean Women," 139.

58 J. Klausner, "Queen Salome Alexandra," in A. Schalit (ed.), The World History of the Jewish People VI The Hellenistic Age (London 1972), 243.

59 For her popularity in rabbinic literature, see: Klausner, ibid., 247–54.

Israel. And she did rule. All sources, save Nicolaus, concur that she did this rather well. Thus, for the Hasmoneans it was not anathema for a woman to rule.[60] This notion had far-reaching consequences in the continued history of Hasmonean women, as the next part of this discussion will show.

b. *Mariamme the Hasmonean*

Herod married the great-granddaughter of Shelamzion Alexandra – Mariamme (BJ 1.344; AJ 14.465). He was married to her from 37 BCE to 27 BCE. They had five children – three boys and two girls (BJ 1.435). Then he executed her (BJ 1.444; AJ 15.231). These details seem beyond dispute. Yet in BJ, and to a far greater extent in AJ, Mariamme dominates large chunks of the narrative. She is described as the subject of Herod's great passion and consuming love; she is portrayed as proud and arrogant:

> For the love which he felt for Mariamme was no less intense than those justly celebrated in story. As for her, she was in most respects prudent and faithful to him, but she had in her nature something that was at once womanly and cruel, and she took full advantage of his enslavement to passion. Since she did not take into account that she was subject to the king and that he was her master, as would have been proper under the circumstances, she frequently treated him with arrogance (AJ 15.218–9).

Furthermore, she is repeatedly portrayed as the subject of Herod's uncontrolled jealousy. Her death, we are told, came about in a storm of terrible jealousy. Herod suspected her of committing adultery with his servant (BJ 1.443; AJ 15.227–8). On this score, however, Josephus feels that he should set the record straight. In one of his rare attacks on Nicolaus' credibility, Josephus makes the following comment:

> ... since (Nicolaus) lived in Herod's realm and was one of his associates, he wrote to please him and to be of service to him, dwelling only on those things that redounded to his glory, and transforming his obviously unjust acts into the opposite or concealing them with the greatest care. For example, in his desire to give a color of respectability to the putting to death of Mariamme and her sons, which had been so cruelly ordered by the king, Nicolaus makes false charges of licentiousness against her and treachery against the youths ... We however, being of a family closely related to the kings descended from Asmonaios ... have considered it unfit to tell any falsehoods about them (AJ 16.183–7).

Indeed, Josephus refrains from charging Mariamme's sons with plotting against their father, and from accusing Mariamme of unfaithfulness. Yet did Nicolaus accuse Mariamme of such a crime, or is Josephus using Nicolaus when he acquits her of the charge? We have no way of knowing this directly, because Nicolaus' description of this event is, alas, lost. Fortunately we do have a text

[60] For the Hellenistic milieu of this notion, see: Macurdy, Vassal Queens, 65–6; Ilan, "Salamzion Alexandra," 189–90.

coming from the pen of Nicolaus, not via Josephus, relating his position on the accusations Herod leveled against his two sons by Mariamme; accusations that resulted in their execution. In an excerpt from his autobiography, preserved in the writings of the tenth-century Byzantine scholar emperor Constantinus Porphyrogenitus, Nicolaus makes the following statement:

At the same time the court of Herod was thrown into confusion since the eldest of his sons *falsely* accused the two next born of plotting against their father. These were indeed younger than he, but were his superiors in rank, because they were children of a queen, whereas his mother was a commoner. Before Nicolaus had returned from Rome, the young men were convicted by the council, and the father, having been much exasperated, was on the point of having them executed. After Nicolaus had sailed home, Herod informed him of what happened and asked his advice. Nicolaus suggested that they should be removed to one of the fortresses, in order to gain time for better consultation, and thus not appear to make a fatal decision concerning his nearest while actuated by anger. Antipater, perceiving this, looked on Nicolaus with suspicion, and, suborning various persons, frightened his father into the belief that he was in danger of being immediately killed by his sons, who had corrupted the whole army ... and that his only safety lay in their quick execution. And Herod, being afraid for his life, took a quick but not a good decision. No more did he communicate about the matter with Nicolaus, but at night he secretly sent the executioners. Thus the sons died ...[61]

Nicolaus is here clearly counseling Herod not to execute his sons, suspecting that they are not guilty of treachery, as charged. If the opinion voiced by Nicolaus in his Vita is the same as the one he made in his *Historiae*, and I see no reason for him to have changed his mind,[62] than Nicolaus' opinion on the execution of Mariamme's sons seems suspiciously similar to the version presented by Josephus in his AJ. So whose version is it? And if Josephus misrepresents Nicolaus' opinion on the execution of Herod's sons, may he not be equally incorrect in his claim that Nicolaus accused Mariamme of adultery? I would thus like to suggest that, notwithstanding Josephus' outburst of indignation in AJ 16, his description of Mariamme's relations with Herod, culminating in her trial and execution in AJ 15, all stem from Nicolaus.

A notoriously difficult problem in the writings of Josephus is the confusion over Herod's command concerning Mariamme in his absence. In BJ we are told that when in 35 or 34 BCE Herod was summoned by Mark Antony, he entrusted Mariamme to the care of his brother-in-law Joseph, ordering him to kill the woman in the event that Antony is displeased with him and has him executed. In his absence Joseph tells Mariamme of the order, in an attempt to persuade her of Herod's love, and when Herod returns and finds out that Mariamme knew of the order, he is convinced that only sexual intimacy would have induced Joseph to reveal the secret, so he executes both partners for

---

[61] STERN, Greek and Latin Authors I, 253; emphasis mine.
[62] For a different view see S. SCHWARTZ, Josephus, 121–3.

adultery (BJ 1.441–3). In AJ the situation is much more complex. First we are told that, indeed in 35–4 BCE, when summoned by Antony, Herod left Mariamme in the charge of the same Joseph, who similarly disclosed the secret to the woman. Curiously, when Herod returned and discovered the breach of faith by his servant, he did indeed suspect the two of misconduct, but executed only Joseph (AJ 15.65–70; 80–7), allowing Mariamme to live on until in 30 BCE Herod was again summoned, this time by the victor of Actium – Octavian. Here Josephus tells a similar tale – Herod left Mariamme in the charge of his servant, Soemus, with a similar order to kill her if Herod fails to return. On his return he discovers that Soemus had also disclosed the order to Mariamme and immediately suspects the two of sexual misconduct. Soemus is executed directly and shortly afterwards Mariamme is brought to trial as well. This tribunal condemns and then executes her.

Which is the preferable version? The problem is extremely complex. If AJ is correct, we have an inexplicable literary doublet, which a historian should reject if possible. If BJ is correct the entire chronology is in jeopardy, for the date of Mariamme's execution after Actium seems imperative if she was to bear Herod five children, and for another reason I will suggest later.[63] Furthermore, the account in BJ is given in a summary description of the Hasmoneans' fate at the hands of Herod and is deliberately concise. If this were Nicolaus' version of Mariamme's death, she did die (whether in 34 BCE or in 27 BCE) on a charge of adultery, but Nicolaus thought the charge was false. However, I am not convinced that this was the entire story found in Nicolaus, or that Nicolaus claimed that these were the charges brought against Mariamme.

In order to disentangle the problem, several other factors should be brought into the debate. (1) In the summary description in BJ that relates the death of Mariamme's brother Jonathan, that of her grandfather Hyrcanus and her own execution, the absence of another Hasmonean execution is quite conspicuous – that of Alexandra, Mariamme's mother, who, according to AJ (15. 247–51), was put to death shortly after her daughter. A closer look at the text in BJ reveals a strange fact not previously noted, namely that Alexandra is totally absent from the entire work.[64] This absence is truly curious. Is it possible that Nicolaus, Josephus' main source for BJ, knew nothing of Alexandra, who plays

---

[63] For a recognition of the difficulty and a bold attempt to solve it, see: W. OTTO, "Herodes," in RE Supplementband II (Stuttgart: J.B. Metzlersche Verlagsbuchhandlung, 1913), 8–9. OTTO, however, was misguided because of his adoption of Destinon's thesis on the anonymous Jewish author who reworked Nicolaus and which Josephus used, a theory that is greatly out of favor these days, see e.g. STERN, Greek and Latin Authors I, 229–30; SCHWARTZ, "Agrippa II," 244–5. Other scholars discussed the problem but offered no solution for it, see: THACKERY, Josephus, 66–7; ZEITLIN, "Herod," 9–16; MICHAEL GRANT, Herod the Great (London: Weidenfeld & Nicolson, 1971) 83.

[64] Even S. SCHWARTZ (Josephus, 119–28), who is on the lookout for differences in the description of the Hasmoneans in BJ and AJ missed this one.

such a prominent part in AJ, and that all the information about her in the latter work derives from another source? Conversely, is it possible that Josephus, who so slavishly followed Nicolaus in BJ, effectively eliminated all traces of the woman? What possible motive could he have had for this? (2) BJ's description of Mariamme's brother's intentional drowning in Jericho in the dead of night is very damning to Herod (BJ 1.437). It has been suggested that in this description Josephus cannot be relying on Nicolaus, because it is so negative about Herod.[65] The description in AJ also assumes that (Jonathan) Aristobulus was drowned intentionally, but the way the story is told, namely that the murder was made to look like an accident (AJ 15.54–6), suggests that someone else could have recorded the story not as murder but as an accident. Perhaps this was Nicolaus' apologetic version, which in AJ Josephus turned on its head. Since Herod obviously never admitted planning or carrying out such an assassination, even we today should be more cautious in our judgment. After all, accidents do happen. (3) In AJ (15.174) Josephus admits that he was using two sources in the description of Hyrcanus' attempted escape, trial and execution. One he describes as Herod's personal *memoirs* (ὑπομνήματα) but scholars doubt very much that Josephus had access to the king's personal archives.[66] Nicolaus, on the other hand, probably did, and it should come as no surprise that, for the period prior to his arrival at court, Nicolaus used Herod's personal notes. Thus, Josephus is probably quoting Herod indirectly, through Nicolaus. Not surprisingly, in the account of Hyrcanus' defection, which Josephus claims is derived from Herod's *memoirs,* Alexandra, Herod's daughter, plays a prominent role. This is in keeping with Nicolaus' style, where behind every evil deed a woman is lurking. In the other description Alexandra plays no part in the plot at all.

This information I think requires the following general conclusions: The source Josephus used in BJ to describe Herod's relations with the Hasmoneans does not seem to have been Nicolaus for two reasons. The first reason is literary-formal. Scholars who claimed that Josephus used Nicolaus for Herodian history puzzled over the question, why all the information in BJ about the elimination of the Hasmoneans by Herod is condensed together, and not placed in correct chronological sequence. The solutions they have come up with are varied,[67] but the most natural solution, namely that Josephus interrupted his main source, obviously Nicolaus, in order to insert information on two topics

---

[65] M. STERN, "Nicolaus of Damascus as a Source of Jewish History in the Time of Herod and the Hasmoneans," in Studies in Jewish History: The Second Temple Period (Jerusalem: Yad Izhak Ben-Zvi, 1991), 453 (Hebrew).

[66] See e.g. R. MARCUS' note to the passage in his translation, p. 83, n. c; THACKERY, Josephus, 66.

[67] On Josephus' arrangement of the material concerning his domestic difficulties and building activity in BJ, see: THACKERY, Josephus, 65; and especially Cohen, Josephus, 52–8.

(Herod's building activities and his relations with the Hasmoneans 1.401–44) from other sources, has not been suggested.[68] The second reason is in the contents. The source was pro-Hasmonean and anti-Herodian, describing the death of the Hasmoneans as a serial killing. This could hardly be a Nicolean description. In answer to the claim that it may be Josephan, one may note that while in AJ Josephus is usually more negative toward Herod, precisely on this topic Josephus becomes more moderate toward him. What was the nature of this source? It seems to have been Jewish, for it uses the Hebrew name of Mariamme's brother – Jonathan. Some information on the Hasmoneans in it is unique to BJ, for example, the story of Antigonus' sister, who held the fortress of Hyrcania and resisted Herod's assault for close to seven years (BJ 1.364); the story of Mariamme's portrait sent to Antony is different from the one in AJ, and does not mention Mariamme's mother (BJ 1.439); as a matter of fact the source seems curiously not to be aware of the significance of Alexandra, the mother of Mariamme. This source may also have referred to the marriage between Pheroras, Herod's brother and another Hasmonean princess, a detail unknown to the source of AJ (BJ 1.483). Finally this source related the story of Herod's journey, his command to Joseph, return and execution of Mariamme as taking place under Antony's reign and made the chronological mistake of placing Mariamme's death in 34 BCE.

In AJ Josephus still used the BJ source, but supplemented it with information that he now found in Nicolaus. Several factors support this conjecture. Mariamme's brother, who is described as dying in an accident, rather than intentionally murdered, is called Aristobulus, rather than Jonathan; the defection of Hyrcanus is told from Herod's point of view; and Alexandra, Mariamme's mother enters the scene. Nicolaus probably also correctly placed Herod's journey, and the instructions he left to kill his wife, were he not to return, after the battle of Actium and its aftermath and Herod's journey to Octavian. Josephus however, faced with the two versions of the story, one about Actium and one about Antony, told them both. If my conclusions are correct, I suggest a very unconventional reconstruction of source relations. For the description of the death of the first three Hasmoneans (Aristobulus III, Hyrcanus II and Mariamme) at the hands of Herod in BJ Josephus was not dependent on Nicolaus, whose influence is only in AJ evident. The only explanation I can suggest for this is that when Josephus was writing BJ, of the 144 *Historiae* books of Nicolaus, he did not have the relevant volumes on this topic; he only later came by them and used the information in them to supplement his material in AJ.

Thus returning to the question of Mariamme's execution: if in BJ, not based on Nicolaus, it is obvious that she was implicated for adultery, in AJ the picture

---

[68] On Josephus' method of writing this way, see SCHWARTZ, "Agrippa II," 248–54 and elsewhere.

is not so clear. For while we are told that Soemus was executed because the king suspected him of seducing his wife (AJ 15.229), Mariamme seems to have been charged with another offense. We read the following in Josephus:

> One noon the king lay down to rest and out of great fondness which he always had for her called for Mariamme. And she came but she did not lie down (with him) in spite of his urging. Instead she expressed contempt for him and bitterly reproached him for having killed both her (grand)father and her brother. And when he showed resentment of her arrogance and was about to do something rash, the king's sister, Salome, who perceived how greatly he was disturbed, sent his butler, who had long before been prepared for this, and ordered him to say that Mariamme had tried to persuade him to help her prepare a love-potion for the king. And (she said) if Herod should be disturbed and ask what it was (he should reply that he did not know), for Mariamme had poured the drug while he had (merely) been requested to serve it ... having given him these instructions in advance, she sent him to speak to Herod on that occasion. And so he went in obediently and with alacrity, saying that Mariamme had ... tried to persuade him to give the love-potion to the king. ... Herod showed great excitement over this and asked what the love potion was[. T]he butler said that it was a drug given him by Mariamme ... On hearing these statements Herod, who was already in an ugly mood, was even more provoked ... (AJ 15.222–6)

The story than goes on to tell of the torture of Mariamme's household slaves and, in the end, when Mariamme was brought to trial, "(Herod) brought an elaborately framed accusation against her concerning the love potions and drugs which she was alleged to prepare" (AJ 15.229). This description obviously shows that Mariamme was not charged with adultery at her trial but with attempted poisoning of the king.[69] If I am right in my conjecture that this text comes from Nicolaus, the historian thought Mariamme was innocent, and had been framed by another woman, who, as we shall presently see, Nicolaus considered the root of all evil – Salome, Herod's sister. Thus, Josephus had misread Nicolaus. Nicolaus neither claimed that Mariamme's sons were guilty of treason nor that Mariamme was guilty of adultery nor, for that matter, of attempted poisoning, for which charge she was brought to trial.[70] But if Nicolaus believed that Mariamme was innocent, would that not make Herod that much more guilty for her death? Not according to Nicolaus' perspective.

In writing the description of Herod's domestic misfortunes, Nicolaus, who knew he could not acquit his master of the elimination of many family members, decided to portray the entire affair as a tragedy. Hereby Nicolaus was thinking in Greek philosophical terms. By definition a tragedy happens when the chief characters suffer greatly, but the cause of their suffering is beyond their control. This is how Nicolaus decided to portray Herod's and Mariamme's relationship. The king had married her not for political profit but out of a great

---

[69] And see on this OTTO, "Herodes," 51; ZEITLIN, "Herod," 18–9.

[70] And see already DESTINON, Quellen, 110–3.

and passionate love. This love is so powerfully described, that historians, beginning with Josephus, have been totally misled by it. Schalit, for example, agreed with Nicolaus that Herod actually had little to gain from marrying the Hasmonean.[71] Most other scholars, even when conceding that Herod had much to gain from a Hasmonean match, nevertheless stress the love element involved in the relationship between the two.[72] Nicolaus further described Mariamme as an ideal tragic heroine. She was beautiful, good, tender, and above all innocent. Her only weakness was her arrogance (ὕβρις – AJ 15.219), a fatal flaw of a tragic hero. This combination of passionate love and *hybris* was deadly. It made both heroes vulnerable, and wicked people soon took advantage of this vulnerability. Court intrigue and sheer wickedness teamed together to devise the downfall of these "star-crossed" lovers.[73] The malicious, scheming individuals, who brought this tragedy about were, as is usually the case in the writings of Nicolaus, two women – on Mariamme's side her mother, Alexandra, and on Herod's side his sister, Salome. A third woman, who seems no less guilty, but remains somewhat in the shadowy background, is none other than that *femme fatale*, Cleopatra.

The figure of Alexandra is, from the outset, that of a ruthless insurgent who will stop at nothing to obtain for her family their rightful patrimony. She first appears on the scene when Herod appoints as high-priest some one other than her son (AJ 15.23), whereupon she immediately enlists in her cause the aid of the most powerful (but evil) woman in the world – Cleopatra (24). Even after her scheme succeeds, and her son is appointed high-priest (41), she does not rest, but plots further with Cleopatra to flee the country with her son (probably in order to return at the head of an army, remove Herod and place her son on his rightful throne – 44–6). The plot is discovered (47–9) and is immediately followed by the death of Aristobulus (53–6), which may have been an accident, but which Alexandra interpreted, once again to her friend Cleopatra, as murder (62–3). Cleopatra urges Antony to summon Herod to a hearing, and Antony, who is totally enslaved by this woman, complies (64–5). At his point in the narrative Josephus inserts the story of Herod's order to his brother-in-law Joseph, but the Nicolean narrative is soon resumed, with the presentation of

---

71 Herodes, 61–6; elsewhere SCHALIT claims that, on the contrary, it was in the Hasmoneans' political interest to form a marriage alliance with the Herodians, p. 564; and see also S. PEROWNE, The Life and Times of Herod the Great (London: Arrow Books, 1960), 81.

72 OTTO, "Herodes," 21; 50; A.H.M. JONES, The Herods of Judaea (Oxford: Clarendon, 1938), 37; 55; ZEITLIN, "Herod," 15–6; 22; GRANT, Herod, 57. Even EDITH MARY SMALLWOOD (The Jews Under Roman Rule: From Pompey to Diocletian, Leiden: E.J. Brill, 1976), who stresses most the political motive (pp. 49; 71), does not doubt the emotional element involved (pp. 71–2).

73 Although I have used a phrase from Shakespeare's Romeo and Juliet, I think a better Shakespearean model for Herod and Mariamme's story is actually Othello; see PEROWNE, Herod, 86.

the scheming Alexandra, now enlisting her daughter to aid her, and for the first time interfering with the relationship of the king and his wife. When a rumor spreads in the town that Antony has executed Herod, Alexandra persuades her guard to flee with her and her daughter to the Roman legions stationed outside the city, so that "they might recover the throne ... which it was proper for those of royal blood to have" (71–73). Herod's safe return, however, frustrated this new conspiracy. For this failed attempt Alexandra, no longer favored by Herod, was put in chains (87). Next we hear of Alexandra plotting with her father his escape to the Arabs, who are, at the time, Herod's bitterest enemies (166–8); this plan also failed (169–73); her execution, which followed close on that of her daughter, was also for a failed conspiracy. When Herod fell into deep depression following his wife's death, and left town, Alexandra, had made a final attempt to seize power (247–5), and when the king heard of it, he "without delay ... gave orders for her to be put to death" (251). Somewhat out of character is her behavior at the execution of her daughter:

> Alexandra considered the situation and having small hope of escaping similar treatment from Herod, changed her attitude in very unseemly fashion to one which was opposite of her former boldness. For in her desire to make plain her ignorance of the things which Mariamme was charged, she sprang up and in the hearing of all the people cried out and reproached her daughter with having been wicked and ungrateful to her husband, and said that she was suffering just punishment for her reckless behavior, for she had not properly requited the benefactor of them all. In so indecently acting a part and even daring to seize Mariamme by the hair she naturally incurred the strong disapproval of the others for her unseemly play-acting. Especially was this clear in the case of the condemned woman herself, for she spoke not a single word nor did she show confusion as she watched her mother's disgusting behavior, but in her greatness of spirit she did make it plain that she was indeed greatly distressed by her offense in behaving in this conspicuously disgraceful behavior (AJ 15.232–5).

This presentation of Alexandra, so out of character with the woman, is included in order to stress the wickedness of the one compared with the magnanimity of the other. Thus, on Mariamme's side, Alexandra, the ever-scheming Hasmonean did all that was in her power to create tension and discord between the lovers, and justly deserved to die for her constant disloyalty. One may even commend Herod for his patience in putting up with her constant disloyalty, and only executing her when all other measures proved ineffective.

Herod's sister, Salome, is of another cloth altogether, but no less wicked than Alexandra. Since I intend to return to her later, I will outline here only her participation in the death of Mariamme. She is portrayed as having a personal grudge against the queen, because she "had shown a proud spirit in their disputes and had reproached Salome's family with their low birth" (AJ 15.81). However, Salome's malice was so effective, and her counsel so trustworthy in the king's eyes, that almost all her accusations ended in the death of her victims.

When blaming Mariamme and her mother for attempting to escape to the Roman camp, she persuades Herod of her husband Joseph's disloyalty, and he is executed (81; 87). Further, Salome is also responsible for framing Mariamme for attempted murder (213; 223–4). Even after the condemnation of Mariamme, when Herod was seriously considering clemency, Salome pressed her brother to carry out the execution (231). Alexandra's treachery together with Salome's loyalty conspired to defeat the tragic and ill-fated love of Herod and Mariamme. Herod, and his perfect wife, Mariamme, were the victims of two evil women. Mariamme died guiltless and Herod was destined to suffer the intolerable grief of the loss of his loved one (AJ 15.240–6).

Because we are on the subject of women, Nicolaus' treatment of Cleopatra is also interesting. It should be remembered that, like Herod, Nicolaus himself had been in the service of Antony and Cleopatra prior to Actium, and if he is apologizing for Herod's conduct at the time, he is, at the same time, apologizing for himself. In a typical Nicolean trait, his line of defense turns out to be laying the blame for all ills at a woman's doorstep. In this case the woman was readily available. Cleopatra was the object of hatred and reproach of many Roman writers. Nicolaus followed suit. Rather than blame his master, Nicolaus brought charges against his mistress. Thus Cleopatra was made out to be not only responsible for Hasmonean plotting against Herod, and for the occasional discord between him and Antony, but she was also blamed for trying to seduce the king (AJ 15.97–9). Sexual danger lurks everywhere. Herod, on the other hand, is portrayed as contemplating the removal of Cleopatra (99–101), and, in his speech before Octavian after Actium, he claims he advised Antony to rid himself of the woman.

Let us now return to Mariamme. The description of her execution, which is undoubtedly Nicolean, fits the reconstruction I have suggested:

> Mariamme herself, at least, went to her death with a wholly calm demeanor and without change of color, and so even in her last moments she made her nobility of descent clear to those who were looking on. Thus died Mariamme, a woman unexcelled in continence and in greatness of soul, though lacking in reasonableness and of too quarrelsome a nature. But in beauty of body and in dignity of bearing in the presence of others she surpassed her contemporaries more greatly than one can say. And this was the chief source of her failure to please the king and to live with him agreeably. For being constantly courted by him because of his love, and expecting no harsh treatment from him, she maintained an excessive freedom of speech. And since she was also distressed by what had happened to her relatives, she saw fit to speak to Herod of all her feelings and finally succeeded in incurring the enmity of the king's mother and sister and his own as well, though he was the one person from whom she had mistakenly expected not to suffer any harm (AJ 15.236–9).

Here all the elements of the tragedy are brought together. The description begins with the disgraceful behavior of one villain – Mariamme's mother – and ends with the malicious actions of the other – Salome. Mariamme comes out unscathed. She had been rightly loved by the king and been indeed worthy of the love. The end of the love is the tragedy which Nicolaus composed.

But is this true? Did Herod indeed love Mariamme? I think that as historians we are not in a position to answer such a question, as even Nicolaus was not. But the more important historical question still remains, why did Herod execute Mariamme? For example, we may suspect that Salome did not send the butler with the poison, but that Mariamme did, in which case the charge against her would have been true. Or we may conjecture that Mariamme had indeed been unfaithful to Herod. After all, she would not be the first woman to have been unfaithful to her husband. However, if we remain within the framework of the information Nicolaus and Josephus wanted us to contemplate, we will be missing the main point. As the BJ neatly put it, Mariamme's death at the hands of Herod was preceded by those of her brother and grandfather, and followed by the execution of (her mother and) two sons. This pattern has attracted attention in the past, beginning with Josephus himself in BJ,[74] but no logical conclusions have been drawn from it. I think, however, that the picture emerging here is quite clear. Herod's attitude to the Hasmoneans had always been one of possible gain or loss. From the very beginning he realized he had no chance of winning the favor of Aristobulus II's house, so he courted Hyrcanus II. When fighting against the Hasmonean pretender Antigonus, Herod felt that he stood a better chance of rising to the purple if he were to come in the name of another Hasmonean pretender, so he became engaged to Mariamme. Although both Antony and Octavian appointed him king, the animosity that arose between them almost immediately made him hang on to his Hasmonean match in the hope that, if one triumvir rejected him, he could return to the throne through the person of his wife. This becomes clear when Nicolaus explains the motives for Soemus revealing to Mariamme Herod's order: "the women (Mariamme and Alexandra) ... it was natural to suppose, would not lose their present rank, but would improve their position either by becoming sovereign themselves or by being close to the sovereign" (AJ 15.206). Before he went to visit Octavian after Actium, Herod rid himself of the most serious Hasmonean contender to the throne, Hyrcanus II, making himself the most eligible candidate, if not because of his past services, than because of his marriage to a Hasmonean. All these measures, however, turned out to be unnecessary, and Herod returned to Judaea to be sole ruler, but with a wife who was no longer an asset. On the contrary, she constituted a constant danger to the stability of his regime. So he executed her and then her mother. For the time being there were no more Hasmoneans left. It is impossible to know whether Mariamme was

74 E.g. ZEITLIN, "Herod," 22; SMALLWOOD, Roman Rule, 64.

charged with adultery or attempted murder. In any case the charges were trumped up.

But was she indeed innocent, as Nicolaus makes us believe? I think Nicolaus himself knew better. Herod executed the male Hasmoneans first because they seemed a more imminent threat to him. In the Hasmonean dynasty, however, there had been a precedent: A woman (Shelamzion) had ruled, and she had done so successfully. The people could hope for a repetition of such a reign. With no male candidates around, Mariamme and her mother Alexandra were themselves legitimate Hasmoneans, worthy of the throne, who could rally popular support. The repeated attempts of Alexandra to dominate centers of power, such as the army, were probably shared by Mariamme. I doubt very much that according to Herod's outlook Mariamme could ever be described as innocent.[75]

c. *Salome Herod's Sister*

Finally, I shall discuss Salome, the sister of Herod. An outline of her life runs as follows: Daughter of Antipater, Hyrcanus II's advisor, early in life she married a certain Joseph, who was, perhaps, her uncle (BJ 1.441; AJ 15.65).[76] After his fall from favor and execution, Salome remarried, this time a certain Costobarus, an Idumean noble. Between her two first husbands Salome had three (or four) children (BJ 1.446; 566; 2.26; AJ 17.9), two of whom we know by name: a son, Antipater who may have been the son of Costobarus (AJ 16.227), and a daughter, Berenice, whose father *was* Costobarus (AJ 18.133). Costobarus was also executed, for the only Idumean attempt during the Second Temple period to revolt against the Jewish establishment that had forcefully converted them (AJ 15.253–66). What Salome's role in his downfall was is unknown, although much is made of it by Nicolaus, as we shall presently see. After Costobarus' death, Salome remained a widow for several years, arousing the interest of gossip-mongers, who claimed that she was infatuated with a certain Arab diplomat – Syllaeus (AJ 16.220–6). Meanwhile her daughter, Berenice, who was by now a grown woman, married one of Herod's sons by Mariamme, Aristobulus. Toward the end of Herod's rule, the king matched Salome with one of his close friends, Alexas (AJ 17.10; BJ 1.566). Apart from these biographical details of marriage and divorce, we may add that Salome was on good terms with the empress Livia, wife of Augustus (*ibid.*). In his will Herod left Salome the revenues of the cities: Jamnia, Azotus, and Phasaelis, as well as his residential palace at Ascalon (BJ 1.646; 2.98; AJ 17.147; 189; 321), and these Salome in turn willed to the empress (AJ 13.81). Salome's final

---

[75] And see also GRANT, Herod, 99.

[76] On the problem of his identity, see R. MARCUS, note d in his translations to AJ, ad loc.

appearance on the scene is in Rome, where she contests Herod's last will, claiming that Judaea should be handed to Herod Antipas rather than to Archelaus (BJ 2.15; 26; AJ 17.220; 224; 230). Presumably she stayed in the capital with her family, because we next hear of her grandson, Agrippa I growing up there (AJ 18.143).

Despite this rather unimpressive record of events, Salome dominates the pages of books 15, 16 and 17 of the Antiquities in an unprecedented sequence. We have already seen Nicolaus' judgment of her involvement in the downfall of her first husband, Joseph, whom she denounced for seducing Mariamme, and in the indictment of Mariamme herself. However, these are hardly the only victims of her intrigue. Further down Nicolaus accuses her of denouncing her second husband, Costobarus, before Herod.[77] This, however, is not portrayed as an act of loyalty on her part. After Herod had appointed Costobarus governor of Idumea (AJ 15.254), Costobarus conspired against Herod, and approached Cleopatra with an offer to defect to her side together with the territories under his charge (256–8). When the conspiracy was discovered, Salome, rather than side with her brother, protected her husband (258). Thus it was not loyalty to Herod but a falling-out with her husband that eventually made her denounce him. Nicolaus reports that Salome sent Costobarus a bill of divorce (259), a statement which Josephus feels he needs to comment upon, saying that it "was not in accordance with Jewish law. For it is the man who is permitted by us to do this, and not even a divorced woman may marry again on her own initiative unless her former husband consents" (AJ 15.259).[78] Whether Josephus' legal statement has any significance here is, at this point, unimportant. What is of significance is that while Costobarus had been plotting against Herod all these years, Salome had disloyally protected him, denouncing him only when she fell out with him on a personal matter. This indicates that Nicolaus is out to rob Salome of her one positive asset, her loyalty to her brother. The end of the story is already set out: Costobarus turns out to be hiding dangerous Jewish oppositionists who had been on Herod's "wanted" list for a long time and Costobarus, together with several accomplices, is executed (260–6).

Salome is also portrayed unkindly in two other personal affairs. The first is

---

[77] In support of my claim that for these years (35–25 BCE) Josephus did not have Nicolaus' account when writing BJ, is the fact that this entire episode, although not connected with the Hasmoneans, is missing in BJ, while Costabarus is mentioned in passing in the descriptions of the events of 10 BCE (BJ 1.486) as though he is familiar to the reader.

[78] Salome's action and Josephus' response have been the subject of much debate. See: e.g. E. Bammel, "Markus 10 11f. und das jüdische Eherecht," Zeitschrift für Neutestamentliche Wissenschaft 61 (1970), 95–101; Bernadette J. Brooten, "Konnten Frauen im alten Judentum die Scheidung betreiben? Überlegungen zu Mk 10, 11–12 und 1Kor 7, 10–11," Evangelische Theologie 42 (1982), 65–80; A. M. Rabello, "Divorce of Jews in the Roman Empire," The Jewish Law Annual 4 (1981), 92–3.

the issue of Syllaeus the Arab. Syllaeus, the Nabatean king's most trusted advisor, is portrayed throughout Josephus' writings as Herod's bitterest enemy (AJ 16.275–85), and the only person who actually succeeds in bringing discord between Herod and Augustus (286–99). He is also accused of collaborating in a plot to assassinate Herod (BJ 1.574–7; AJ 17.54–7), and then to poison him (BJ 1.583, cf. AJ 17.63). His eventual downfall was facilitated through the mediation of Nicolaus of Damascus (336–50). Nicolaus' personal involvement suggests that this absolutely negative portrait is perhaps in need of modification. As is often claimed of Josephus' description of the war against Rome, where he is personally involved with his characters, his description is least trustworthy.[79] It is thus interesting that in his first appearance on the pages of AJ,[80] the description of this man is not so negative, but it does allow for a further denigration of Salome.

The king of Arabia, Obadas, was inactive and sluggish by nature; for the most part his realm was governed by Syllaeus, who was a clever man, still young in years and handsome. Having come to Herod on some business or other, as he was dining with him, he saw Salome and set his heart on having her. And as he knew that she was a widow, he spoke to her about his feeling. Salome ... regarded the young man with anything but indifference [and] was eager to marry him, and during the following days, when many people came together for dinner, there appeared numerous and unmistakable signs of an understanding between these two. These were reported to the king by other women, who derided their lack of discretion. Herod then inquired further about it of Pheroras and asked him to watch them during dinner to see how they felt about each other. Pheroras reported that they both made their passion clear by gestures and looks. Some time after this the Arab left under suspicion but after the lapse of two or three months he came again on the same matter and made proposals to Herod, asking that Salome be given him in marriage. This connection, he said, would not be unprofitable to Herod through his association with the government of Arabia, which was even now virtually in his hands and by rights should be more so. When Herod brought the proposal to his sister and inquired whether she was ready for this marriage, Salome quickly agreed. But when they asked Syllaeus to be initiated into the customs of the Jews before the wedding – otherwise, they said, marriage would be impossible – he would not submit to this but took his departure, saying that if he did submit, he would be stoned to death by the Arabs. Then Pheroras began to accuse Salome of lewd behavior, and even more did the women of the court, who said that she had been intimate with the Arab (AJ 16.220–6).

Without the hindsight of Nicolaus, who knows what trouble Syllaeus eventually caused Herod, this story sounds very simple. An important diplomat proposes to the king's sister but is not prepared to meet the conditions of the marriage.

---

[79] See e.g. Rajak, Josephus, 161.

[80] Again, this episode is missing from BJ, but is alluded to occasionally in flashback: 1.487; 534; 566. The date of the event has been suggested by Otto ("Herodes," 100) to be 25 BCE (and not 14–12 BCE, as would result from the present position of this passage in AJ). This date would help explain its absence in BJ. These are, apparently, still the dates in which Josephus did not use Nicolaus.

Nothing comes out of the affair. Here, however, Nicolaus stresses the indecent behavior of the woman in question, who though not married to the suitor, is rumored to have yielded to his seduction, a common slander, designed to defile the name of any decent women. That it is mere rumor is unimportant. Most of what Nicolaus writes of Salome is in the form of gossip, or rumor. However, when removing the indignant tone of the storyteller from the episode, we discover a serious blunder on Herod's part. Had he given Salome in marriage to the Arab, he might have gained an important ally instead of a dangerous enemy.[81]

In connection with the previous event, Salome's last marriage to Alexas is related:

> And though Salome was eager to be married to the Arab Syllaeus, for whom she felt an erotic desire, Herod forced her to become the wife of Alexas; in this situation Julia (= the empress Livia) co-operated with him, persuading Salome not to refuse the marriage lest open enmity be declared between them, for Herod had sworn that he would not be on good terms with Salome if she did not accept marriage with Alexas. And she took Julia's advice, both because she was the wife of Caesar and because on other occasions she would give her very helpful counsel (AJ 17.10; cf. BJ 1.566).

Instead of simply describing Salome's last marriage, Nicolaus again felt inclined to report Salome's continous infatuation with Herod's deadly enemy. Yet it is evident from this text that Salome, whether against her wish or not, dutifully complied with Herod's demands, and was again used as a pawn in Herod's political alliances.

But, according to Nicolaus, Salome's most wicked and most spectacular "success" was the removal of Mariamme's two sons, Alexander and Aristobulus, from the scene. The space is too short here to treat in any detail both BJ 1 and AJ 16's descriptions of Salome's continuous hunting down of Mariamme's two sons: spying on them by turning her daughter informer against her husband, Aristobulus (AJ 16.201; cf. BJ 1.478), spreading rumor against them (AJ 16.9–10; 69); denouncing them (BJ 1.479; cf. AJ 16.205), accusing them (BJ 1.535; AJ 16.73–4), and finally serving as a witness against them in their trial (BJ 1.538). Here is a sample of some of these statements:

> Salome had taken over hatred for the youths as if it were a legacy, and was trying everything that had succeeded against their mother in a desperate and reckless way so as not to leave alive any of her offspring who would be able to avenge the death of the woman who had been destroyed by her ... Thus there was equal amount of hatred on both sides but the form of their hatred was not the same, for the youths were open in their abuse and rash in their reproaches, believing, in their inexperience, that it was noble to let their anger be unrestrained, while the other ... did not act in the same way but made use of slander in a calculatedly malicious way ... (AJ 16.66; 69; cf. 8–10).

---

[81] And see also Smallwood, Roman Rule, 95–6.

Nicolaus further feels he should demonstrate what a thoroughly wicked woman Salome was, charging her with both jealousy and sexual immorality. The object of her jealousy is her nephew Alexander's wife:

Salome's hostility was aggravated by Glaphyra, Alexander's wife, who boasted of her noble ancestry ... on the other hand, she was constantly taunting with their low birth Herod's sister and his wives ... (BJ 1.476; cf. AJ 16.193).

Sexually, Salome is accused of raping her nephew:

(Salome, Alexander) declared, had one night even forced her way into his chamber and, against his will, had immoral relations with him (BJ 1.498; cf. AJ 16.256).

This story seems no more true than Nicolaus' account of Cleopatra's seduction of Herod, but certainly belongs to the same literary genre that assumes that an evil woman must also be sexually immoral.

The execution of Herod's sons undoubtedly has the makings of another tragedy. The innocent, young and inexperienced orphan princes are pitched against evil itself, personified by Salome. The woman hates the princes with a vengeance and would stop at nothing to bring them to their grave. The other tragic hero of these events is of course Herod himself, whose *naïvité*, blind trust in his sister and suspicious nature Salome exploits to the utmost. The bottom line is, again, the success of the plot. The sons are brought to trial, found guilty on the basis of false evidence, and executed. This took place, according to all indications, in the year 7 BCE.

Salome's ally in these feats is none other than Herod's eldest son, Antipater, who was soon to meet his own death at the hands of his father, in 4 BCE. Salome is often present in the events leading to the latter's execution: She informs on Antipater's plot against his father, as well as on his alliance with Pheroras (BJ 1.269–71; AJ 17.36–40); she reveals to Herod the Pharisees' alliance with Pheroras' family (AJ 17.44) and is eventually herself the victim of a plot by Antipater (BJ 1.641–4; AJ 17.137–41). In his trial, she serves as a witness for the prosecution (AJ 17.93). Surprisingly, even though these actions also lead to the death of a prince at the hands of his father, Salome is not portrayed as negatively as in the previous events. Probably this is due to the fact that at Antipater's trial, Nicolaus, as Herod's advisor, also played a very active role for the prosecution, serving as the accuser and denouncing the son before the father (AJ 17.106–21). Nicolaus' participation at this trial, his access to the evidence and his patent dislike of Antipater, convinced the historian that the king's son had been the main force behind the execution of Mariamme's sons. In his autobiography, as we have seen above, Nicolaus says as much.

Why then, in his *Historiae* did Nicolaus implicate Salome together with Antipater? She did not emerge guilty of crime at the princes' trial, nor at Antipater's trial, or thereafter. Her guilt is mere conjecture. Furthermore, why is Salome portrayed so negatively in all of Nicolaus writings? One possible solution to this puzzle is that Nicolaus portrays Salome as an absolute monster because she was indeed such a woman. This is the unqualified opinion of many scholars who have studied her. Schalit wrote of her "Alles was uns über diese Frau berichtet wird, läßt mit Sicherheit darauf schließen, daß sie ein durch und durch verdorbenes Geschöpf war. Ihre hervorstechenden Charakterzüge sind die Fähigkeit zu abgrundtiefem Haß und das Fehlen aller moralischen Hemmungen bei der Verfolgung ihrer verbrecherischen Absichten."[82] Jones describes her as follows: "... jealous and vindictive, she had pursued Mariamme ... with relentless hatred, and it was to her indefatigable intrigues that Mariamme owed her disgrace and death. She had few scruples and rarely allowed sentimental considerations to stand in her way. She callously sacrifices her first husband ... to her schemes against Mariamme. Her second husband Costobarus she also delivered to the executioner."[83] Somewhat less vehement, but still thoroughly negative is Perowne: "Capable she may have been, and faithful to Herod in her fashion. But as a character she was ... vile ..."[84] Most accommodating, but still indebted to Josephus, is Grant: "Whatever her faults, and they were numerous – including an extremely ready ear for gossip – she was never lacking in what she regarded, often wrongly, as her duty to her royal brother."[85]

However, I suspect that this conclusion is rather naive. While it is true that the only record of Salome outside the writings of Josephus is a very brief note by Strabo on the *good* relations between the woman and Augustus,[86] it would be instructive to inquire whether Josephus himself did not retain some information about her that he derived from a source other than Nicolaus. I think two scraps of this sort can be culled out of Josephus. A study of their attitude to the woman would be very enlightening. The first derives from the fact that Salome outlived

---

82 SCHALIT, Herodes, 571.

83 JONES, Herods, 111.

84 PEROWNE, Herod, 104.

85 GRANT, Herod, 84.

86 Geographica 16.2.46; It has been claimed that Salome is mentioned in one of the papyri designated "Acts of the Alexandrian Martyrs" (see: V. A. TCHERIKOVER and A. FUKS [edd.], Corpus Papyrorum Judaicarum II [Cambridge MA: Harvard University Press, 1960], 80, no. 156d). In this document, in a derogatory diatribe against the emperor Claudius by a citizen of Alexandria, he is accused of being "the outcast son of the Jewess Salome." Scholars have assumed that this Salome is none other than Herod's sister (ibid, 81; SMALLWOOD, Roman Rule, 252, n. 123; STERN, Greek and Latin Authors I, 310). In my opinion, however, there is nothing to warrant such an assumption. The woman in the document is identified as "Jewess," and as such could be any Jewish woman, because, in the eyes of the Alexandrians, being of Jewish blood is derogatory enough. And indeed, they could hardly have chosen a more typical name for a Jewish woman, since Salome was the name borne by practically a quarter of the Jewish women of Palestine at the time, see my: "Notes on thc Distribution of Women's Names in Palestine in the Second Temple and Mishnaic Period," Journal of Jewish Studies 40 (1989), 191–2.

Nicolaus, or if not the man, at least his written source. It is a scholarly consensus that Josephus ceases to use Nicolaus after his description of the outbursts of violence following Herod's death, which Varus, the Roman legate of Syria, crushed (BJ 2.110; AJ 17.339).[87] After the detailed description of these events Josephus' writings become sketchy, and brief. Among the notes Josephus inserts after this date is a mention of Salome's death:

His successor in office was Marcus Ambivulus, during whose administration Salome, the sister of king Herod died. To Julia she bequeathed Jamnia and its territory, together with Phasaelis, which lay on the plain and Archelais where palms are planted in great numbers and the dates are of the highest quality (AJ 18.31; cf. BJ 2.167).

This description is brief indeed. Unlike the end of Shelamzion's reign, or the execution of Mariamme, it is not followed by a summation of her activities. Nicolaus would not have ended Salome's story with so brief a note. Josephus, however, did not feel compelled to conclude the life of this woman with a note, either based on the evidence he brought previously from Nicolaus, or from his own personal repository of historical data. He did feel, however, that she was important enough to merit mention at her death. What his source was for this information is unclear, but it is obvious that wherever he found it, he did not find with it a long diatribe on the faulty character of the woman. Furthermore, this notice, together with some earlier information found in Nicolaus, on the bequest Herod made to Salome of territory and money (BJ 1.646; 2.98; AJ 17.147; 189; 32), show that the king too, on his death, did not consider Salome evil. In this he differed from Nicolaus. This raises the question: Why did the historian dare to go against his master in so serious a matter?

The second detail independent of Nicolaus is the description of Salome's action immediately on the death of Herod. We are told that before Herod died, he assembled all the elders of the Jews at the hippodrome in Jericho giving instructions to his sister to have them executed in the event that he die, so that the mourning of the elders be interpreted as a mourning of the king. However, when he died,

before the death of the king became known, Salome and Alexas dismissed those who had been summoned to the hippodrome and sent them to their own homes, telling them that the king ordered them to go off to their fields and look after their own affairs. And this act of theirs came as the greatest benefaction to the nation (AJ 17.193; cf. BJ 1.666).

The story, although told both in AJ and in BJ, is so anti-Herodian, that it could hardly have come from the pen of Nicolaus.[88] This contention derives further support from the fact that the same story is found also in rabbinic literature, albeit told of King Yannai, and his wife Shelamzion:

---

87 E.g. STERN, Greek and Latin Authors I, 229.

88 Ibid., 230.

They said: when King Yannai fell ill, he seized seventy of the elders of Israel. He put them in chains ordering the prison guard: When I die, kill the elders, so that even as Israel rejoice, they shall mourn their masters. It was said: He had a good wife named Shalminon and when he died, she removed his ring from his finger, presented it to the prison guard and said: Your master released them in a dream. He released them and they went home. Then she said king Yannai was dead (Scholion to Megilat Taanit 2nd Shevat).

Josephus, particularly in AJ, often quotes sources that are also told in one way or another in rabbinic literature. It is usually assumed that these traditions derive from a Jewish source, or sources, rather than Hellenistic or Roman sources.[89] The mistaken identity of the participants in the rabbinic story is easy to explain. The original story had Salome and Herod, but since it is common in rabbinic literature to blame all evil doings of a wicked king on Yannai,[90] and since Yannai had a famous wife with a name quite close to, or actually the same as Salome,[91] the mistake became almost inevitable.[92]

So what does this source tell us? It tells us that other circles, quite far removed from Nicolaus, and probably Jewish, portrayed Salome in a favorable light, as a sort of savior who could counter with wit and courage the evil plans of her brother. I return therefore to my initial claim – evil Salome is the literary creation of Nicolaus.

But why did Nicolaus hate Salome so much? The answer to this question, I think, has to do with the personal relations between the historian and the king's sister. This becomes apparent when we survey the way Nicolaus portrays himself in the pages of his *magnum opus.* He participates in four major episodes in the life of Herod, in each case delivering a blazing speech and carrying the day. Stern, in his *Greek and Latin Authors on Jews and Judaism* refrained from including these speeches in the Josephan excerpts of Nicolaus, on the assumption that, due to Josephus' inclination to write speeches, he could easily have composed them himself.[93] However, while Stern may be right about the contents of the speeches, I suspect that the situation in which Nicolaus is addressing

---

[89] E.g. Hölscher, Quellen, 81–5, who claims that these traditions were Pharisaic and oral; cf. B. Dinur, "Historiographical Fragments in Talmudic Literature and their Investigation," Proceedings of the Fifth World Congress of Jewish Studies II (Jerusalem: World Union of Jewish Studies, 1969), 142–3, who claims, on the contrary, that these are traces of written documents in rabbinic literature. And see also S.J.D. Cohen, "Parallel Historical Traditions in Josephus and Rabbinic Literature," Proceedings of the Ninth World Congress of Jewish Studies 2 (Jerusalem: World Union of Jewish Studies, 1986), 7–14, especially 12–3; but on 9, n. 3 Cohen state explicitly that his conclusions do not extend to the Scholion.

[90] J. Efron, Studies on the Hasmonean Period (Leiden: E.J. Brill, 1987), 143–218.

[91] On the two names see my: "New Ossuary Inscriptions from Jerusalem," Scripta Classica Israelica 11 (1991–2), 156–7.

[92] On the curious fact that Herod comes out unscathed in rabbinic literature, see: D.R. Schwartz, "Herod in Jewish Sources," in M. Naor (ed.), King Herod and his Age = Idan 5 (Jerusalem: Yad Izhak Ben Zvi, 1985), 38–42 (Hebrew).

[93] Greek and Latin Authors I, 231–2.

an audience, and probably also to a great extent the themes found therein, derive directly from Nicolaus. In Josephus' entire description of the Herodian period, one finds only twelve direct speeches, of which, save for one short address by a certain Tiro in Alexander and Aristobulus' trial (AJ 16.346–5), all are delivered by either Herod or his sons or Nicolaus. Moreover, he is the single person with the most numerous speeches and the longest speech recorded in AJ 15–17. This aggrandizement of Nicolaus could hardly be considered the work of Josephus. It would thus be instructive to follow Nicolaus in his speeches. His first speech, before Marcus Vipsanius Agrippa on behalf of the Jews of Asia Minor (AJ 16.31–57), results in impressive legislation in their favor (59–60). His next two speeches, however, are for the prosecution rather than for the defense. In the first he accuses the above-mentioned Syllaeus, before Augustus, of treachery and treason (16.346–50). His accusations are so successful that not only is Herod reconciled with his patron Augustus, but Syllaeus is found guilty and executed (352). Nicolaus wants us to think that his use of language is so effictive, it can be deadly. However, whether this episode is really true is not absolutely clear, both because sometime after it we meet Syllaeus still very much alive, and because elsewhere, Antipater, Herod's son, claims for himself the success of having removed Syllaeus (AJ 17.54 cf. BJ 1.574; AJ 17.81; cf. BJ 1.605; 633). In light of Nicolaus' hate for Antipater, it should come as no surprise that he would credit himself with the positive deeds of his enemy. His third address is his famous prosecution speech in the trail of Antipater, Herod's son (AJ 17.110–20; cf. BJ 1.637). Once again, Nicolaus' eloquence overrides Antipater's passionate appeal to his father (BJ 1.630–5; cf. AJ 17.100–5), and even though Herod himself was fatally ill, and had already executed two of his sons, an action viewed negatively in the Roman empire,[94] Antipater was executed (17.187). Nicolaus thus credits himself with the same characteristics he denigrates in Salome – the ability of his words to secure life or death.

Finally, and this time in indirect speech, Nicolaus is portrayed as defending Archelaus' claim for Herod's throne in Judaea, in accordance with Herod's last will and testimony (BJ 2.34–6; AJ 17.240–7; 315–6). In this episode, Archelaus was contested by his brother, Herod Antipas, who claimed that in an earlier draft of Herod's will, when the king was still of sound mind, he had bequeathed Judaea to him (BJ 2.31; AJ 17.238); and by a delegation of Jews who wished to rid themselves of Herodian rule entirely (AJ 17.299–314). Just as Archelaus had Nicolaus as his counsel, Antipas, too, brought his legal aides and advisors with him. Standing up against Nicolaus at Augustus' court was Antipater, Salome's son (BJ 2.26; AJ 17.230), but Nicolaus makes it quite clear

[94] See Augustus' comment on Herod, recorded by Macrobius, that it is safer to be Herod's pig than to be his son: Stern, Greek and Latin Authors II, 665.

that the real power behind the appeal on behalf of Antipas was Salome herself. Nicolaus describes Salome's actions as follows:

> With (Archelaus) also went Salome, the sister of Herod, who took her family ... ostensibly meant to help Archelaus in his attempt to obtain the throne but in reality meant to work against him and in particularly to protest against the things he had done in the Temple (AJ 17.220; cf. BJ 2.14).

Further down Nicolaus continues:

> At this time Herod's son, Antipas, also sailed to Rome to claim the throne, for he was encouraged by Salome's promises to believe and considered that he would be taking over the government with greater right ... (AJ 17.224; cf. BJ 2.20).

Thus we can see that a real feud developed between Salome and Nicolaus, and Nicolaus in his greater eloquence won. Augustus ruled in favor of Archelaus who became the governor of Judaea, while Herod Antipas had to make do with Galilee and the Peraea (BJ 2.93–5; AJ 17.317–20). Salome, apparently remained in Rome with her family, possibly under the protection of Livia. She is not heard of again until her death. Nicolaus, conceivably did the same, and settled down to complete his *magnum opus* and particularly his detailed description of the end of Herod's reign. His fancy for drama, his belief that behind every calamity lurks a woman, and his personal hatred of Salome made her the target of his deadly pen. His writings could be as venomous as his speech. Salome has come down to later generations as evil, ruthless, cunning, the ultimate *femme fatal* whose mere presence kills. Against such incrimination she had no way of defending herself.

However a final sober note should be made on Salome's political choice in the case of Herod's successor. Because Nicolaus no longer supplied Josephus with material on for events after 4 BCE, we cannot know why Archelaus was so unsuccessful in his reign; but very soon we hear that in the year 6 CE August found his services intolerable and had him removed and exiled (BJ 2.111; AJ 17.344). Thus, perhaps Nicolaus had indeed defended the wrong candidate for Herod's succession. Antipas' rule, however is another matter altogether. He ruled Galilee for 42 years, and survived not only Augustus but also his successor, Tiberius. When he was finally removed in 38 CE, it was by the mad emperor Caligula, on a false charge, and as a childish prank or a mere whim (BJ 2.183; AJ 18.250–3). Interestingly, whoever is our source for Antipas' downfall, also blames it on a woman (BJ 2.182; AJ 18.240–6).[95] Thus, Salome again made a better political judgment. She recommended a person who truly had the administrative capability to rule. One wonders what history

[95] On the source see: D.R. SCHWARTZ, Agrippa I: The Last King of Judaea (Tübingen: J.C.B. Mohr, 1990), 48.

would have looked like if her recommendations had been followed. But this is where the task of the historian ends.

Summary and Conclusions

In this article I have claimed that all powerful women of the Hasmonean and Herodian dynasties who dominate Josephus' writings are the literary creations of Nicolaus of Damascus, who wrote drama and firmly believed that women were the root of all evil. This belief results in women attaining prominent and often demonic roles on the pages of his writings, but whether his historical judgment of their roles can be believed is another matter altogether. We have seen that Nicolaus' personal resentment of his heroines in some of the cases, and dramatic requirements in others, can easily cloud our vision of these women's real roles. One wonders, therefore, whether the situation of a historian like Josephus, who totally ignored women *qua* women, and only wrote about them when they become absolutely essential to his narrative, is not preferable.

Nicolaus of Damascus was not alone in his belief that women, through cunning and craft, dominate all. The idea is well developed in the Jewish apocryphal book Esdras, where Zerubabel proves to king Cyrus that women have more power than kings (4.14–32). Many ancient histories, beginning with Herodotus, accord royal women a major role in influencing events through their counsel, intrigue and sexual irresponsibility. In the historiography of the Herodians, too, Nicolaus was not alone. Schwartz has shown that one of the sources about Agrippa I's rule which Josephus used, described women as forceful actors on the historical stage.[96] A story on the evil character of Herodian women has even entered the New Testament (Matthew 14.3–12; Mark 6.17–28). One wonders whether the morbid impression we have of the Julio-Claudian dynasty and its family intrigues is not the result of the same historical genre. I hope that this study will generate similar criticism of other classical works where the negative portrayal of women has been uncritically accepted.[97]

---

96 Ibid.

97 The best example of this sort of gullibility still remains: GRACE H. MACURDY, Hellenistic Queens (Baltimore: John Hopkins University Press, 1932).

God, Gentiles, and Jewish Law: On Acts 15 and Josephus' Adiabene Narrative*

by

DANIEL R. SCHWARTZ

Luke's account in Acts 15 of the Apostolic Council and the debate which preceded it, and Josephus' report in *Antiquities* 20 of the conversion to Judaism of the royal family of Adiabene, especially its central section (§§ 34–48), are quite similar. Dealing with nearly contemporary events,[1] both address the issue of Gentiles who wish to worship God and the question whether they must observe Jewish law; both term Jewish laws not only *nomoi* but also *ethê* ("customs"); both give special attention to circumcision; and both refer to Jewish law as "the law(s) of Moses". However, while Luke's account is fairly straightforward, Josephus' is somewhat difficult to construe – more difficult than is usually assumed. After a brief review of Luke's report we will turn to Josephus'; after establishing its meaning, in part with the help of the clarification of issues supplied by Luke's account, we will turn to a comparison of the two texts. Finally, the question of a possible Josephan influence upon Luke's narrative will be raised.

I. Acts 15: Gentiles Need not Observe the Jews' *ethê*

Luke's report is, as stated, quite straightforward. In response to the claim urged by Jewish-Christian hardliners, that one cannot be saved if not circumcised according to the custom (*ethos*) of Moses (Acts 15:1), a council was convened.

* This is an expanded version of a paper first given in May 1994 at the Jerusalem symposium on "Jewish Traditions in Christian Contexts" sponsored by Hebrew University's Dept. of Comparative Religions and the Graduate Studies Program of the University's School for Overseas Students. My thanks to Dr. David Satran, the organizer, for the opportunity to present the matter in nuce and to receive helpful comments from the symposium's participants, especially Prof. David Runia.

[1] For the dating of Izates' conversion to the mid-40's, see SCHWARTZ, Studies, pp. 195–196. The Apostolic Council described in Acts 15 is usually placed ca. 48 B.C.E; so, for example, HAENCHEN, Acts, pp. 64–65.

* Here, more fully, and more stridently, the position of the hardliners, now termed Pharisees, is said to be that converts must be circumcised and instructed to keep what they now term the law (*nomos*) of Moses (v. 5). After some debate, James rules that one need not burden those Gentiles who are turning to God (v. 19): since "Moses has from ancient generations had those preaching him in every city, namely, he is read every Sabbath in the synagogues" (v. 20), Gentiles have had plenty of opportunity to accept Mosaic practice and there is no need or point for the Church to attempt to impose it now.[2] Rather, James rules that only a few restrictions are to be imposed upon Gentile converts to Christianity, restrictions which are evidently understood as moral and universal and not especially as part of the Mosaic legislation.[3]

The logic of this chapter, and of James' decision, is clear. Jewish laws are *ethê*, national practices, but since God has now "taken out of the nations a new people for His name" (v. 14), out of "the remainder of mankind, all peoples" (v. 17), one need not be a member of the Jewish people in order to worship Him. Rather, James concludes, it would be contravening God's purpose to encumber those "of the nations" who would worship Him by obliging them to observe the Jews' national customs, which he terms "Moses" (vv. 19–21). That is, Luke portrays a two-tiered world: there is one God, and He is or should be worshipped by individuals among all peoples, but these peoples each have their own national *ethê*, perhaps legislated by such national legislators as the Jews' Moses.[4] There is no need to require members of one people, worshipping the true God, to adopt the national practices of another – any more than an Italian missionary in Africa, for example, would require those he brings to Catholicism to adopt the Italian language and eat pasta.

In short, Luke argues that God is for everyone but Moses and his laws are for the Jews; they are Jewish customs, not God's laws. This argument in Acts 15 reaps the benefits of two Lukan habits in evidence elsewhere in his two-volume work: he frequently links the law to Moses (Luke 2:22, 5:14, 16:19.31, 24.27.41, 26:32; Acts 6:11, 13:28, 15:1.8.21, 21:21, 24:27, 26:32, 28:23), and he frequently terms Jewish laws *ethê* (Luke 1:9, 2:42, 22:39; Acts 6:14, 15:1, 16:21, 21:21, 26:3, 28:17).[5]

---

[2] For this interpretation of vv. 19–21, see my "The Futility of Preaching Moses (Acts 15,21)," Biblica 67 (1986), pp. 276–281.

[3] On the perplexing and oft-debated question, what criteria governed the selection of those few prohibitions imposed on Gentiles according to Acts 15:20, see WILSON, Luke and the Law, pp. 73ff.; SEGAL, "Conversion and Universalism", pp. 181–190.

[4] For the notion of Moses as the Jewish legislator, comparable to those of other peoples, see esp. Diodorus Siculus 1.94 (STERN, GLA I, no. 58), Ps. Aristeas, Philo and Josephus; SCHWARTZ, Studies, p. 18.

[5] On these two Lukan predilections and the question of their Jewish background, see WILSON, Luke and the Law, pp. 1–11. On Moses in Luke-Acts, see also J. M. KASTNER, Moses im Neuen Testament (Diss. München 1967), pp. 172–179, 203–232; on *ethê*, see also SPICQ,

II. Josephus' Izates Narrative

In contrast, Josephus' Adiabene narrative is anything but transparent.[6] According to the usual reconstruction of the story told in *Ant.* 20.34–48, when Izates (son of Monobazus and heir apparent of Adiabene) was staying with King Abennerigus of Charax Spasini, a Jewish merchant named Ananias taught the king's[7] wives to worship God (*ton theon sebein* – § 34) according to the Jewish tradition, and, with their help, Izates too was won over. Around the same time, back in Adiabene, Helene too (Izates' mother) had been won over to Jewish laws (*nomoi* – § 35). When Izates returned to Adiabene and saw how happy his mother was with her Jewish practice, he too resolved to become fully a Jew, viz., by circumcision (§ 35). But Helene and Ananias were afraid that Izates' subjects would not tolerate a circumcised king, so they talked him out of it, Ananias assuring him that if he observed all the rest of Jewish law God would forgive him if he omitted circumcision alone due to his fear of his subjects. However, Izates did not give up his enthusiasm for circumcision (§ 43), and so when one Eleazar, a Galilean hardliner, came along and told Izates that it was wrong to go only halfway, Izates indeed had himself ciricumcised (§ 46).

In the literature, accordingly, we are told time and again that this story depicts Izates' progression from Gentile, to God-fearer who kept all Jewish practices except circumcision, to Jew – the status which Eleazar, and the approving narrator, allowed him only after circumcision.[8] Josephus' Izates narrative is thus thought to illustrate and corroborate, with friendly testimony, the kind of gradual process assumed by Juvenal's famous vicious depiction, in *Satirae* 14.96–106 (STERN, *GLA* II, no. 301), of Gentiles who slide from Sabbath observance to abstention from idolatry and from eating swine, eventually (*mox*) completing the process by circumcision.

This interpretation is more than debatable. Indeed, lately it has been attacked, from two opposing directions. On the one hand, Cohen suggested in a brief

---

Notes – Supplément, pp. 194–201. For Josephus' distinction between universal justice (*to dikaion*) and the *ethê* of individual nations, see Ant. 16.176–177.

6 For recent detailed discussions of this narrative, see SCHIFFMAN, "Conversion of the Royal House"; GILBERT, "The Making of a Jew"; and BROER, "Konversion des Königshauses". For older literature, see L. H. FELDMAN's list in vol. 9 of the Loeb Josephus (1965), p. 586.

7 This seems clearly to refer to Abennerigus, and so I have assumed below. Others have assumed that the reference is to the wives of Monobazus (Izates' father) or Izates himself. The point is immaterial here.

8 For this understanding see, inter alia, H. GRAETZ, History of the Jews, II (Philadelphia 1893), pp. 216–217; SIEGERT, "Gottesfürchtige und Sympathisanten", pp. 128–129; MCELENEY, "Conversion", pp. 323–324; SCHÜRER III/1, p. 165; REYNOLDS and TANNENBAUM, Jews and God-Fearers, p. 50; I. M. GAFNI, The Jews of Babylonia in the Talmudic Era (Jerusalem 1990), pp. 64–66 (in Hebrew); E. WILL & C. ORRIEUX, "Prosélytisme juif"?: Histoire d'une erreur (Paris 1992), pp. 194–195; FELDMAN, Jew and Gentile, p. 329 (in Charax Spasini Ananias "won him over to Jewish practices, though without circumcision").

comment that Josephus held Izates observed no Jewish practices prior to his circumcision.[9] On the other hand, Gilbert argued in a detailed study ("Making of a Jew") that Izates and Ananias, perhaps Eleazar too – although not Josephus – considered Izates a Jew even before he was circumcised, not merely a "God-fearer", viz., a righteous Gentile tending in the direction of Judaism. Both scholars, in other words, have contested the notion that Izates is to be understood as somewhat midway between Gentile and Jewish prior to his conversion: he was either a non-Jew (Cohen) or a Jew (Gilbert). In our opinion, Cohen's position is to be preferred. Gilbert's is weakened not only by the doubtful proposition that we can distinguish between Josephus' notion and that of his characters, but also by a few fine points of Josephus' diction.[10]

Let us begin with the main point: Are we indeed to understand that Izates observed (any, many or most) Jewish practices before he was ciricumcised? The usual affirmative answer is based upon two words in § 35. Namely, after § 34 reports that Abennerigus' wives had been taught by Ananias to fear God after the manner of Jewish tradition, they brought Ananias to Izates' notice too, whom Ananias *homoiôs synanepeisen*; Feldman (Loeb Classical Library) renders "similarly won over with the cooperation of the women". However, as a transitive verb *peithô* is conative, meaning not only "persuade" but also "urge" (i.e., attempt to persuade), and the prefixed *synana-* would not seem to change much. For a nearby example, note *epeithen* in § 69, followed in § 70 by *ou mên epeithen*; Feldman appropriately gives "urged" for the former. Why not in § 34?[11] Note, moreover, that our text says that what Ananias did to Izates was similar (*homoiôs*) to what he did to Abennerigus' wives – but of them we learn only that Ananias taught (*edidasken*) them to worship God the Jewish way, but not that they did so. It is only of Helene, back in Adiabene, that we read not only that she had been similarly (*homoiôs* again) instructed (*didachtheisan*) but that she had actually been brought over to the Jews' laws (*eis tous ekeinôn metakekomisthai nomous* – § 35).[12]

---

[9] S.J.D. COHEN, "Respect for Judaism by Gentiles According to Josephus", Harvard Theological Review 80 (1987), p. 420, n. 34.

[10] See below, nn. 12,15,16.

[11] So too, for example, the imperfect (*epeithon/en*) in Acts 13:43 and 18:4 and the participial *peithōn* in Acts 19:8 and 28:23: HAENCHEN, Acts, inter alia, renders them all with "seek to convince", and the Revised Standard Version translates the first, third and fourth with "urge", "plead" and "try to convince", giving "persuaded" only at 18:4; for more, see W. BAUER, A Greek-English Lexicon of the New Testament (edd. W.F. Arndt and F.W. Gingrich; Chicago 1979^2), p. 639. On Josephus' usage, see SPICQ, Notes – Supplément, pp. 541–542. True, in Ant. 20.35 we have the aorist, not imperfect, and the imperfect is more congenial to "urge" as opposed to "(successfully) persuade"; but it is not clear that this should make a difference. SPICQ (ibid.) emphasizes – although in reference to the New Testament – that transitive *peithô* means "vouloir, s'efforcer de persuader" whether in present, imperfect or aorist.

[12] That Helene is to be seen as a full convert was recognized by MCELENEY, "Conversion", p. 323; indeed, as GILBERT ("Making of a Jew", p. 307) notes, no one contests this. Concerning

Furthermore, if the upshot of §§ 34–35 were that already in Charax Spasini Izates began to worship God the Jewish way apart from circumcision, what would that leave for § 38, where we read of the impression which his mother's satisfaction with Jewish *ethê* made upon Izates?[13] Here we read that after Izates saw that satisfaction he decided "to convert to them"; only afterwards comes the catch, namely, notice of his recognition that in order fully to become a Jew he would have to be ciricumcised. That is, after returning to Adiabene he first decided to undertake life according to Jewish *ethê*, as his mother had. Ergo, he had not lived according to them previously, in Charax Spasini, prior to § 38. Thus, Josephus' account plainly means that Izates' mother's example succeeded where the urging of Ananias, and Abennerigus' wives, had not.

But if this is the case, then what are we to make of the fact that immediately after Izates makes his decision to become a Jew, up to and including circumcision (§ 38), his mother and Ananias argue him out of it? As stated, the usual interpretation has them arguing against circumcision alone, leaving him already observing all the other Jewish practices. But, first of all, Helene's argument (§ 39) says not a word about circumcision: she tells Izates that his subjects will not tolerate him if they should discover that he was devoted (*epithymêseien*) to foreign *ethê*. Next, in § 40, we read that Ananias agreed with Helene's argument, which leads us to expect the same sweeping front. Indeed, in § 41a Ananias expresses his own personal fear for his own fate if the king's subjects discovered that he, Ananias, was responsible for the king's having adopted "improper works" – in the plural. There is no reason to limit the debate to circumcision.

It is the next few lines, § 41b, which supply the main case for the widespread assumption that Ananias told Izates to observe all Jewish practices apart from circumcision.

The king could, he said, fear (*sebein*) the Deity (*to theion*) even without being ciricumcised if indeed he had fully decided to be a devoted adherent of the Jews' national practices (*patria tôn Ioudaiôn*), for this counted more than circumcision.

Abennerigus' wives, however, McEleney once (ibid.) tells us they were only God-fearers and once (p. 327) – that they seem to have been full converts . This uncertainty reflects well the fact that Josephus didn't tell us what came of Ananias' instruction of them, nor – all the more so – what came of their "similar" evangelizing of Izates. Gilbert (loc. cit.) takes the use of *homoiôs* in § 35 to indicate that the women were converts like Helene was – ignoring the additional statement that Helene was brought over to the Jews' laws.

[13] This problem is made especially evident by J. Neusner's paraphrase ("The Conversion of Adiabene to Judaism", Journal of Biblical Literature 83 [1964], pp. 61–62, similar in A History of the Jews in Babylonia, I [Leiden 1969²], p. 63): "During his stay in Charax Spasinu [sic], Izates was converted to Judaism by a Jewish merchant there ...". This leaves nothing more for Izates to do upon his return to Adiabene, and, indeed, there is no mention of the events reported in §§ 38ff.

This translation is based on L. Feldman's in the Loeb Classical Library, but with three changes: for the Greek words brought in parentheses, Feldman gives, respectively, "worship", "God" and "Judaism". My translations are all more literal, and these differences are, I believe, important. First, while "worship" implies activity,[14] "fear" need not;[15] second, correspondingly, "God" is a proper noun and in a Jew's mouth refers to the God of Israel, while "the Deity" (or: "the divine") is abstract and can refer to a universal.[16] Note, especially, that when Ananias taught the women of Abennerigus' court Jewish practices Josephus says they were taught to fear *God* (*ton theon sebein* – § 34), but now, when Ananias urges Izates *not* to observe Jewish practices, Josephus has him tell the king he can fear "the Deity". Third, it is obviously easier to imagine a Gentile adopting "Judaism" (as Feldman) than "the Jews' national practices"; Josephus' use of the latter terminology, in a Jew's address to someone who is not a member of the Jewish nation, rather indicates why those practices are not for the addressee.

Let us now move from translation to interpretation of this crucial passage. As noted above, it is usually assumed that § 41b means that, according to Ananias, Izates could worship God sufficiently by zealously observing all the other

---

14 And FELDMAN properly uses it for *proskynêsai* in § 49.

15 Here I must take issue with GILBERT's argument ("Making of a Jew", pp. 306–308) that since Josephus often refers to the Jews as fearers of God, he or his source could mean Izates was a Jew. After admitting that Gentiles are termed god-fearers in Ant. 14.110, he nevertheless argues: "it is Jews, not Gentile 'god-fearers', who are the ones most often described [by Josephus] as worshippers of God, *sebein ton theon/to theion*, [so] unless the context of a given sentence suggests otherwise, I would argue, we should proceed from the assumption that this phrase refers to Jews" (p. 306). Whatever we are to think of such statistics, it is nevertheless the case that here the context does suggest otherwise: Abennerigus' wives, and Izates, are Gentiles, to begin with, and even by GILBERT's argument it takes more than the terms in question to show they have become Jewish.

16 In Jew and Gentile, p. 351, FELDMAN indeed translates our passage with "the Divine". Similarly, in his paraphrase of Ananias' message M. GOODMAN pointedly uses the lower-case: "Ananias who taught the royal family in Charax Spasinou and Adiabene to revere the god (without converting to Judaism) presumably thought this would be pleasing to God ..." ("Jewish Proselytizing", p. 73). In general, see R. J. H. SHUTT, "The Concept of God in the Works of Flavius Josephus", Journal of Jewish Studies 31 (1980), pp. 173–179, who concludes that "usually *to theion* is used by Josephus to mean 'the Deity', without necessarily referring to the God of Israel" (p. 179). SIEGERT ("Gottesfürchtige und Sympathisanten", p. 129, n. 1) briefly remarked upon Josephus' usage here ("*to theion* = *ho theos*, aber weniger bestimmt und weniger jüdisch. Vgl. Apg. 17,29") but failed to draw any conclusions, locked in, as he was, to the notion that Izates should be viewed as a God-fearer separated from full Jewishness only by circumcision; similarly, GILBERT ("Making of a Jew", p. 306 and p. 313, n. 32) must consider *to theion* to be equivalent to *ho theos* and interchangeable with it. It is true that a Jew could use either of his God. Nevertheless, the fact that one term is used here and another there calls for an explanation. Paul's (Luke's) Areopagus speech, to which Siegert alludes, is in fact a good example of the preference for "Diety" instead of "God" in universalist contexts. The usage is similar to the rabbinic usage of "fearers of Heaven" rather than "of God" for righteous Gentiles; see FELDMAN, Jew and Gentile, pp. 353–356.

Jewish practices; God – Ananias continues in § 42 – would forgive Izates for the necessary omission of the one "act" (*to ergon*), circumcision, due to fear of his subjects' opposition. However, even apart from the above-mentioned consideration that Ananias is said to have agreed with Helene, whose dissuasion related not to circumcision in particular but rather to all the Jewish *ethê*, this interpretation is fraught with difficulties: (a) it takes *ta patria tôn Ioudaiôn* in § 41b as the antecedent of *touton*, but the former is plural while the latter is singular (this difficulty may have been among the reasons why Feldman preferred the singular "Judaism"); (b) it does not explain why Ananias says Izates could revere God if he fully *decided* to follow Jewish practice instead of, more simply, if he fully followed (or: by fully following) Jewish practices – why mention the decision?;[17] (c) it does not explain why the perfect (*kekrine*) is used of Izates' decision;[18] (d) after his conversation with Ananias Izates is in fact not said to have adopted any of the Jewish practices; we read only (§§ 42b-43a) that he did not perform "the act" (circumcision) but did not lose his enthusiasm (*epithymian*) – a term which refers us back to *epithymêseien* in § 39, where it refers to Jewish *ethê* in general;[19] (e) similarly, it is nowhere said, and humanly difficult to imagine, that Izates was enthusiastic about circumcision, but it is said, in § 38, that he was enthusiastic to undertake Jewish *ethê*, as his mother had; (f) after Izates is circumcised, his mother and Ananias are terribly concerned that if Izates' *praxis* were to become known his subjects would rebel against him, since they would not accept a man who was a devotee of foreign *ethê* (§ 47); neither *praxis* nor *ethê* refers specifically to circumcision,[20] and it is likely that such public activity as observance of the Sabbath or dietary laws would become public knowledge much more easily than would the fact of circumcision;[21] and, finally, (g) note the parallel with *Ant.* 16.225, which deals with Syllaeus' refusal to convert to Judaism: neither the narrator (Josephus)

---

17 Note that SCHÜRER (as above, n. 8), who follows the usual position, has Ananias say to Izates "that he could worship God (*to theion sebein*) even without circumcision, provided that he observed the Jewish laws in general; this was more important than circumcision"; no reference to "deciding". So too SCHIFFMAN ("Conversion of the Royal House", p. 303): "Ananias suggested to Izates that he 'worship God' (*to theion sebein*) without circumcision". These paraphrases make sense, but are not what Josephus wrote.

18 A problem avoided by H. CLEMENTZ: "wenn er nur die gottesdienstliche Gebraüche der Juden befolgen wolle" (Des Flavius Josephus Jüdische Altertümer, II [Berlin-Wien 1923], p. 641).

19 As also in § 75. For the comparability of these two parts of the Adiabene narrative, see below, at n. 27. On the common understanding of our text Josephus should have specified in § 43 that Izates did the other "works" and did not lose his enthusiasm for circumcision.

20 Note that in § 76 *praxis* refers to all Jewish practice, circumcision not even being mentioned; see the preceding note.

21 Note that we are discussing an eastern monarch, not a Greek who appears naked in the gymnasium. See S. J. D. COHEN, "'Those Who Say They Are Jews and Are Not': How Do You Know a Jew in Antiquity When You See One?", Diasporas in Antiquity (edd. S. J. D. Cohen and E. S. Frerichs; Atlanta 1993), pp. 20–21.

nor Syllaeus refers to circumcision – indeed, as an Arab, he may already have been circumcised[22] – but Syllaeus expresses the fear that if he adopts Jewish *ethê* his people would stone him. This parallel[23] supports the conclusion that the similar references to Izates' fear, and to his abstention from Jewish *ethê* at this stage of the story, are equally general and not limited to circumcision.

All of these difficulties would be resolved if we understand Ananias' position to have been that Izates could revere God ("the Deity") without circumcision and the other Jewish practices because God accounted the fact that he had fully made the decision to observe these practices as more important than their actual fulfillment. Ananias' point is that God accounted Izates' reverence for Him, a reverence demonstrated by Izates' wholehearted decision to undertake Jewish practice, which includes and begins with circumcision, as more important than such practice itself, so God would pardon Izates if he omitted such practice due to his subjects' objections.[24] Ananias' pointed use of the "the Deity", which alludes to God's universal aspect, and of *patria*, which portrays Jewish law, in contrast, as a matter of Jewish national practice, contributes to his case.

This interpretation resolves or avoids all the difficulties enumerated with regard to the usual one: Izates' decision is mentioned because it is the point and the perfect is used because the decision was completed in the past, *touton* refers to that decision,[25] and Izates' abstinence from all Jewish practice corresponds to what Helene and Ananias had urged; his enthusiasm for Jewish practices remained, however, and Eleazar would eventually lead him to fulfill it.

Thus, our conclusion is that Izates saw only two options. He could either become a Jew, as his mother had, by doing all that Jews do. Since he was a male, that would include circumcision. Or else he could abstain from becoming a Jew, a course suggested by his subjects' expected opposition to having a Jewish king. In that case, Ananias told him, he could revere the Deity.[26] *The only reason*

[22] See COHEN, ibid., p. 19; STERN, GLA II, p. 620.

[23] Recently noted in another context by M. HADAS-LEBEL, "Les mariages mixtes dans la famille d'Hérode ...", Revue des études juives 152 (1993), p. 401.

[24] Recently, it seems, FELDMAN (Jew and Gentile, p. 351) interpreted this story in a very similar way, equally putting the emphasis on Izates' decision. He understands Ananias to mean that while as a rule no male Gentile can be fully (*bebaiôs*) a Jew without circumcision, Izates is exceptional because he "fully" decided to be an adherent of Judaism, "for it was this that counted more than circumcision". If I understand FELDMAN correctly, he is saying that – according to Ananias – the king's wholehearted decision to be fully a Jew, and not his observance of the other Jewish practices, makes up for his omission of this one practice. The difference between FELDMAN's understanding and the one suggested here is only that we have taken Ananias to mean that such a wholehearted decision counts more than Jewish practice altogether.

[25] After the designation of two alternatives, *touton* normally refers to the latter. Here, on our interpretation, we have such a normal case: circumcision is contrasted to the decision to observe Jewish practices.

[26] For a modern echo of the same idea, see J.J. WEINBERG, Responsa Seridei Esh, II

circumcision receives special attention in this narrative is because Izates' case is compared to Helene's: he wants, like her, to convert to Judaism, but for him, as a male, that entailed circumcision. But the basic question remained: would he convert, or would he not? Izates eventually took the former course, at the urging of Eleazar, who viewed Jewish practice as a matter of "the law", not *ethos*, and did not distinguish between God and the Deity; hence, he considered those, even Gentiles, who failed to God's law, to be sinners against Him (§ 44).

This interpretation, which entails the conclusion that Josephus' narrative contemplates no "God-fearers" who observe Jewish law but are not Jews, receives solid support from the continuation of Josephus' Adiabene story, in connection with the conversion of Izates' brother, Monobazus, which opens as follows (*Ant*.20.75):[27]

> Izates' brother Monobazus and his kinsmen, seeing that the king because of his pious worship of God had won the admiration of all men, became eager to abandon their ancestral religion and to adopt[28] the practices of the Jews (trans. Feldman).

As Schiffman has pointed out,[29] there is an interesting shift of terminology here: "The Greek terminology used to express Izates' pious 'worship of God' (*pros ton theon eusebeian*) raises the possibility that Monobazus and his relatives wanted only to be semi-proselytes and not undergo the conversion process according to Jewish law, [but] on the other hand, the words *ethesi chrêsthai tois Ioudaiôn* (XX,75), 'to adopt the practices of the Jews', can mean only that they underwent the process of conversion according to Jewish law." Having raised the question, however, Schiffman leaves it unresolved.[30] The

---

(Jerusalem 1961/62), no. 102 (Hebrew). Here WEINBERG, a prominent Lithuanian rabbi in Berlin, deals with the 1926 case of a man who had fallen in love with a Jewish woman and had undertaken to become Jewish. But after learning Hebrew and otherwise demonstrating his full sincerity (his intention was "for the sake of Heaven"), it was discovered that his medical condition precluded circumcision. While the local rabbi urged the possibilty that the man be allowed to convert without circumcision, WEINBERG ruled that option impossible, leaving only the possibility that the man "observe the seven Noahide laws and be a righteous Gentile" (p. 246). Similarly, GOODMAN ("Jewish Proselytizing", pp. 73–74, now developed in his Mission and Conversion [Oxford 1994]), argues that many first-century Jews held righteous Gentiles were fine in God's eyes and had no reason to convert; see also SEGAL, "Conversion and Universalism", pp. 173–177, and idem, "The Costs of Proselytism and Conversion", Society of Biblical Literature 1988 Seminar Papers (ed. D.J. Lull; Atlanta 1988), pp. 356–357.

[27] Our confidence that we may use § 75 as an aid to interpreting the Izates story is supported by the reappearance of *epithymia* and *ethê*; note also *para pasi zêloton* (§ 49) just as the *zêloton para pasin anthrôpois* (§ 75). The same hand is at work.

[28] "Live according to" would be better than "adopt"; Josephus uses the term frequently with regard to born Jews (e.g. Ant. 11.281, 338; 12.126, 150; 16.47).

[29] SCHIFFMAN, "Conversion of the Royal House", p. 304.

[30] In his n. 39 ad loc. SCHIFFMAN refers us back to his n. 28 – a reference to KLAUSNER which has nothing to do with this issue. Prof. SCHIFFMAN informs me that, unfortunately, he doesn't recall what he meant to refer to.

obvious resolution is that, according to this narrative at least, Schiffman's first alternative was impossible. Rather, people who "revere God" should observe Jewish law. If not, they can revere the Deity. That was our conclusion regarding Josephus' narrative on Izates too. Whether or not this conclusion should lead to a reopening of the "Disappearance of the God-Fearers" debate, which was basically silenced by the publication of the Aphrodisias inscription, I shall leave to others to decide.[31]

III. Luke and Josephus

If we now compare the Izates narrative and Acts 15, we find some interesting similarities. As noted at the outset, the basic issues are the same, and both discuss circumcision alongside of the other laws, rather than as a separate national marker. Circumcision, that is, is just as much of Mosaic or divine legislation as the other practices, and is not treated separately due to its Abrahamic origin. Moreover, we now see that both narratives presume an "all or none" position: no one entertains the possibility that Gentiles should observe some of the Jewish *ethê* but not circumcision. They must either observe none (Luke and Ananias) or all (Eleazar). Eleazar's position, that Gentiles cannot properly worship God without observing Jewish law, is identical with that of the hardliners of Acts 15:1,5; indeed, in v. 5 Luke terms them Pharisees, and Josephus' description of Eleazar as "having a reputation for being very accurate about the ancestral laws" (§ 43) does sound just like several of Josephus' *and Luke's* references to the Pharisees.[32] Ananias' position, on the other hand, is like that of Luke himself: there is a two-tiered world, in which worship of the

---

[31] For the main stages of that debate, see: T. KRAABEL, "The Disappeance of the 'God-Fearers'", Numen 28 (1981), pp. 113–126; L.H. FELDMAN, "The Omnipresence of the God-Fearers", Biblical Archaeology Review 12/5 (Sept.–Oct. 1986), pp. 58–69; and REYNOLDS and TANNENBAUM, Jews and God-Fearers. For a more recent survey of the issue by one of the participants in the debate, see FELDMAN, Jew and Gentile, pp. 342–382.

[32] See War 1.110; 2.162; Ant. 17.41; Vita 191; Acts 26:5 (and 22:3 with 5:34: Gamaliel, Paul's accurate teacher, was a Pharisee). For the suggestion that Josephus' characterization of Eleazar as *akribês* with regard to the *patria* indicates Eleazar was a Pharisee, see K. G. KUHN & H. STEGEMANN, "Proselyten", Paulys Realencyclopädie der classischen Altertumswissenschaft, Supplementband IX (1962), col. 1271; A.I. BAUMGARTEN, "The Name of the Pharisees", Journal of Biblical Literature 102 (1983), pp. 413–417 (esp. 414, n. 10); G. THEISSEN, Lokalkolorit und Zeitgeschichte in den Evangelien (Freiburg - Göttingen 1989), p. 242; and HENGEL, Pre-Christian Paul, p. 30. GOODMAN ("Jewish Proselytizing", p. 76, n. 9) is more cautious, noting that Josephus even has Spartans observing their laws *akribôs* (C. Ap. 2.227). But 1) Eleazar was not a Spartan, and 2) GOODMAN does not relate to the fact that Josephus not only uses *akribês* of Eleazar but also, as for the Pharisees in Vita 191 and War 1.110 and 2.162, says that he was "reputed" (*dokêo*) to be so; on both terms, see S. MASON, Flavius Josephus on the Pharisees (Leiden 1991), pp. 89–110. In any case, whether or not we can be sure that Josephus meant us to view Eleazar as a Pharisee, it is clear that if Luke read

supreme deity is not linked up with Jewish law. The only difference is that Luke, the non-Jew, allows all to worship God and relegates Jewish law to the realm of national practices established by a national legislator (Moses), while Ananias (Josephus), a Jew, has God linked closely to Jewish law but posits a universal Deity (above God? somehow identical with Him?)[33] whom all can worship. Nevertheless, Josephus' Izates narrative repeatedly uses *ethê* of Jewish law and once links it to Moses (§ 44), and it would not take much effort for a reader of Josephus to develop this usage and its potential.

Moreover, we should point out that both narratives share a certain mimetic quality. This is most obvious in Acts. Luke, who by preference speaks of Jewish law as customs,[34] carefully reflects the hardliners' approach in Acts 6:13, where they accuse Stephen of speaking against "the Law", and at Acts 21:28, where Paul is said, by hardliner opponents, to teach men everywhere to violate "the Law". In contrast, only a few verses earlier, the conciliatory leadership of the Jerusalem church is equally mimetically made to tell Paul only of reports that he taught Jews abroad to abandon "Moses, telling them not to circumcise their children nor to walk in the *ethê*" (ibid., v. 21). Another passage illustrative of our point is Acts 18:12, where Jews in Achaia – as those of Acts 6:13 and 21:28 – accuse Paul of teaching men to worship not according to "the Law" but Gallio, the wise proconsul, refuses to deal with the charge since it has to do not with "the Law" but, as he says, with "your law". The adjective "your" knocks the law down to something lower-case and national, not universal.

In Acts 15, in contrast, Luke has the hardliners refer to "custom of Moses" (v. 1) and, even among themselves in Jerusalem, they refer not to "the Law" *simpliciter* but, rather, to "the law of Moses" (v. 5). By doing so Luke prepares the way for the answer given later in that chapter, viz., that one need not impose mere "Moses", i.e. Jewish practices as opposed to divine Law, upon non-Jewish converts. It is, indeed, obviously less necessary to impose the Torah upon non-Jews if it is custom and Mosaic rather than law and divine, for Moses was a Jew while God is universal, just as customs are less binding than law is.[35] Thus, Luke is generally mimetic in his references to the Law, but in Acts 15, where the "Gentiles and the Law" question is addressed head-on, he prefers to adumbrate the decision by making even hardliners use

---

Josephus he could have easily inferred that was the case – as such scholars as KUHN-STEGEMANN, BAUMGARTEN, THEISSEN and HENGEL did.

33 While this might sound gnostic, the issue of the universal God vis à vis the God of Israel need not be removed from its biblical background or overly problemized. See S.E. LOEWENSTAMM, "Nach^{a}lat Hashem", Studies in Bible (Scripta Hierosolymitana 31, ed. S. Japhet; Jerusalem 1986), pp. 155–192.

34 See above, n. 5.

35 Note that even when the rebel-martyrs of Ant. 17.159 refer to Moses as the legislator, they emphasize that what he gave the Jews were received from God and are laws.

some of the liberals' terminology – so while v. 5 does speak of law, v. 1 speaks of custom and vv. 1 and 5 both mention Moses.

Similarly, while Josephus, here and elsewhere, frequently uses *ethê* and *patria* of Jewish law, and these function in the Ananias part of the narrative, when he refers to Helene's full conversion he speaks of *laws* (§ 35) and when he quotes Eleazar in § 45 he refers to "the laws" and says that he who violates them offends against God; he urges Izates to do "that which is commanded (*prostassomena*) by them" – whereupon Izates does indeed perform that which was commanded (*prostachthen* – § 46). Ananias, in contrast, never spoke of commandments, only of national practices, customs. Thus, Josephus varies his diction to reflect the way a a hardliner (Pharisee?) Eleazar would speak about the Law as opposed to the way the liberal Ananias did. The usage is very glaring in Josephus, and any reader could pick it up and apply it.

Finally, what is striking about Josephus' narrative is that it emphasizes in an exemplary manner that becoming Jewish has no relationship to one's national affiliation. Izates was, after all, king of Adiabene (not Judaea!), yet the point of the story is that his people only gained from his conversion, due to God's resultant watchful providence (§§ 48,49[36],72,75,81,85,91). Anyone reading this story comes away with the conclusion that worship of God need not affect one's national status. When combined with the premise that Jewish law is only a matter of national *ethê*, an obvious conclusion is that those who choose to worship God need not become Jews nor, consequently, observe the practices of that people. But that is the point of Acts 15.

IV. Did Luke Read Josephus?

The question, whether or not Luke read Josephus, has often been debated, whether in connection with the dating of Luke-Acts (does Josephus's *Antiquities*, completed in 93/94 C.E. [*Ant.* 20.267], supply a *terminus post quem*?) or in connection with the reconstruction of events alluded to by Luke.[37] Opinions vary (the most quotable being E. Schürer's judgement that Luke either did not read Josephus or, if he did, forgot it all before he began to

[36] FELDMAN renders *tên ek tou theou pronoian* as "the prudence which God gave him"; that is, it is Izates, not God, who exercises forethought. However, there is no verb of "giving" and the parallels cited here support the other alternative, just as at §§ 18,91 FELDMAN indeed renders *theou pronoia* "the providence of God". For God's providence in Antiquities, see H.W. ATTRIDGE, The Interpretation of Biblical History in the Antiquitates Judaicae of Flavius Josephus (Missoula, Montana 1976), pp. 71–107, 154–165. As GILBERT notes ("Making of a Jew", p. 300), the theme is recurrent in the Adiabene narrative and, appearing in §§ 18 and 91, forms an inclusio.

[37] For surveys of this issue, and bibliography, see SCHRECKENBERG, "Flavius Josephus" and MASON, Josephus, pp. 185–229.

write),[38] reflecting the fact that it is difficult to uncover clear evidence for such usage. General similarities might reflect only the general similarity of Luke's Sitz im Leben and Josephus', and references to the same events and individuals might merely flow from independent knowledge of the same events and individuals.[39] What is needed are cases of common errors, but when Josephus and Luke agree on something there are usually no competing sources.

So far, the most impressive evidence for Luke having read Josephus comes at Acts 5:36–37, where Luke wrongly states Judas the Galilean rebelled *after* Theudas did, a mistake which could easily result from a careless reading of *Ant.* 20.97–102, where Judas the Galilean is mentioned after Theudas (although the Josephan context makes it clear their historical order was the opposite). This is, indeed, a persuasive bit of evidence for Lukan use of Josephus, as even some pessimists have always admitted.[40] And the fact that between Josephus' reference to Theudas and that to Judas there appears one to the famine under Claudius (§ 101) lends some further support, for Acts 11:27–30 makes reference to the same episode, using it as a way to explain the sending of Barnabas and Saul back to Jerusalem from Antioch. This passage, which raises some

[38] As SCHRECKENBERG noted ("Flavius Josephus", p. 204), in recent decades few have posited Lukan use of Josephus; MASON (as in preceding note), however, has since come in forcefully in favor of it. For the divided opinions of nineteenth-century scholarship, which included prominent scholars on both sides, see A. VON HARNACK, Neue Untersuchungen zur Apostelgeschichte (Leipzig 1911), p. 80, n. 1; SCHÜRER's view, cited by HARNACK, concludes his "Lucas und Josephus", Zeitschrift für wissenschaftliche Theologie 19 (1876), pp. 574–582. As HARNACK shows, M. KRENKEL's ambitious Josephus und Lukas (Leipzig 1894) brought the whole thesis into disrepute, and it seems to have given the whole topic a kiss of death; for similar cases of scholarly babies being thrown out with the bathwater, cf. SCHWARTZ, Studies, pp. 44, 183, 262.

[39] See B. J. HUBBARD, "Luke, Josephus and Rome: A Comparative Approach to the Lukan Sitz im Leben", Society of Biblical Literature 1979 Seminar Papers, I (ed. P. J. Achtemeier; Missoula, Montana 1979), pp. 59–68. Thus, for example, the fact that instead of mere "scribe", as in Mark 12:28, Luke has Pharisees in Acts 23:6–8 need not be explained by Luke's having discovered, from Josephus, that it is Pharisees who believe in an afterlife; cf. M. J. COOK, Mark's Treatment of the Jewish Leaders (Leiden 1978), p. 27.

[40] On this passage, see SCHRECKENBERG, "Flavius Josephus", pp. 195–198 (he begins by admitting that the assumption that Luke read carelessly here is "auf den ersten Blick bestechend"); MASON, Josephus, pp. 208–213. The alternatives here are clearly stated by H. KOCH, Die Abfassungszeit des lukanischen Geschichtswerkes (Leipzig, 1911), p. 36: "wenn man nicht zu einer falschen Leseerinnerung seitens des Lukas seine Zuflucht nehmen will", then one must assume either that Luke made the error all by himself or that in fact Theudas-Judas is the correct historical order and the error is Josephus'. Koch's preference for one of the latter two options is unargued. A very influential rejection of the case for Lukan dependence upon Josephus here has been an appendix in M. DIBELIUS, Aufsätze zur Apostelgeschichte, Göttingen 1951, pp. 159–160 (= Studies in the Acts of the Apostles [London 1956], pp. 186–187). However, all he shows is that if Luke's error resulted from reading Josephus, it was a bad error. It all comes down to our perceptions as to how badly readers, or listeners, of historical works might err concerning details which hardly interested them. See below, n. 43 (!), and, for my experience with careless readers of Josephus, D. R. SCHWARTZ, Agrippa, p. 215, n. 12.

historical conundrums (reflected in the textual difficulties of 12:25),[41] reminds us of Luke's use of Quirinius' census as a way of bringing Joseph and Mary from Nazareth to Bethlehem (Luke 2:1ff.) – which raises its own, worse, historical conundrums.[42] From our point of view, what is important is that for the famine, as for Quirinius' census, Josephus is our only source apart from Luke-Acts, and we know of none other which could have served Luke. We must emphasize, of course, that *we* know of no others; perhaps there were such. But it must be said that there is less evidence for other writers than has often been thought; the main modern theory of this type is chronologically impossible and is based on careless reading, similar to that which we imputed to Luke.[43].

On the other hand, note also that while Josephus refers only to a census by Quirinius in Judaea, and to a famine in Judaea, Luke in both cases refers to "the whole *oecoumenê*" (Luke 2:1; Acts 11:28). This is a good indication that Luke is not subjugated by his sources, or by the facts; rather, his own universalist program shines through always.[44] Accordingly, in evaluating the probability that Luke has read and used this or that Josephan passage, we should not expect to find him following it *verbatim*.

---

41 See ibid., p. 154, n. 33.

42 The standard discussion of these is SCHÜRER I, pp. 399–427; see also, inter alia, FITZMYER, Luke I, pp. 399–405. For Quirinius' role in the Josephus-Luke debate, see SCHRECKENBERG, "Flavius Josephus", pp. 182–186; MASON, Josephus, pp. 205–208.

43 Namely, as part of his defense of an early date for Acts, A. ERHARDT once suggested ("The Construction and Purpose of the Acts of the Apostles", *Studia Theologica* 12 [1958], pp. 64–65 = IDEM, The Framework of the New Testament Stories [Manchester 1964], pp. 85–86) that Nicolaus of Damascus supplied both Josephus and Luke, independently, the material about Theudas and Judas of Galilee; thus, the date of Josephus' *Antiquities* need not be a *terminus post quem* for Acts. This suggestion is noteworthy because Ehrhardt is *the only* scholar cited in this connection in such central discussions as KÜMMEL's and FITZMYER's, which summarily dismiss the possibility that Luke read Josephus: KÜMMEL, Introduction, p. 186; FITZMYER, Luke I, p. 57. But Nicolaus of Damascus was already about sixty years old in 4 B.C.E.: see JACOBY, Fragmente der griechischen Historiker IIA 90 F136,8 = STERN, GLA I, no. 97 (for Nicolaus' career in general, see STERN, ibid., pp. 227–228). There is no way he could have described events of the forties, when Theudas was active. Erhardt (loc. cit.) claims to have found his suggestion in W. L. KNOX, The Acts of the Apostles (Cambridge 1948), p. 22(–23). But all KNOX says is that he believes Josephus' representation of Judas as the first rebel because – although Josephus is "in general the most unreliable and mendacous of writers" – his dating of Judas derives from Nicolaus. KNOX is evidently referring to the opening of War 2.118 or Ant. 18.4, where Josephus reports Judas' rebellion; KNOX does not suggest that our passage, Ant. 20.97–102, which refers to Theudas and Judas in that order, is based on Nicolaus. If ERHARDT could read KNOX so carelessly, Luke could do the same with Josephus; cf. FITZMYER's comment (Luke I, p. 405) on TARN. – Again, when SCHRECKENBERG ("Flavius Josephus", p. 204) emphasizes that according to the first lines of Josephus' War there were other historians who described the Jewish War, this too hardly resolves the issue, for there is no evidence that they covered events as early as Quirinius' census, which preceded the war by six decades.

44 On Luke's universalism, see S. G. WILSON, The Gentiles and the Gentile Mission in Luke-Acts (Cambridge, 1973); D. R. SCHWARTZ, "The End of the *gê* (Acts 1:8): Beginning or End of the Christian Vision?," Journal of Biblical Literature 105 (1986), pp. 669–676.

The present paper, in honor of a great scholar who devoted much effort to restoring the links between Acts and history,[45] has – apart from attempting to clarify Josephus' Izates' narrative – raised the possibility that Luke read, and was influenced by, Josephus' account of the conversion of the royal house of Adiabene (*Ant.* 20.17–96), which immediately precedes that about Theudas, the famine and Judas the Galilean. In particular, we would suggest that Luke was influenced by the account of Izates' conversion (§§ 34–48), which comes just before the account of Helene's trip to Jerusalem (§§ 49–53), to which Josephus' alludes at § 101: "as stated above". In other words, if Luke indeed read *Ant.* 20.97–102, then, even if he did not read all of *Antiquities*, it is likely he read the Adiabene episode too, or, at least, the central passage on Izates – which, given its central issue (Gentiles and Jewish law), would have interested him greatly. And why, indeed, if it were available, would Luke have abstained from reading the rest of *Ant.* 20, which deals with the very period covered by his Acts?

We of course admit and underline that our case concerning Lukan use of Josephus is not probative. Nevertheless, it may be bolstered by noting that it can explain a certain error in Acts. Namely, it seems that Luke's case in Acts 15 is not as good as it should have been, and a likely explanation is that this happened because Luke was writing under the influence of a similar narrative – Josephus' Adiabene narrative – where another formulation, the one Luke adopted, made perfect sense. Naturally, such a rhetorical error is less compelling evidence for dependence than is a chronological one, such as the one concerning Judas and Theudas, and we cannot claim for it full cogency. Nevertheless, it is worthwhile to consider the matter, whether as an index of Lukan use of Josephus or – in any case – in order to better understand the intricacies of ancient Jewish attitudes toward the interrelationship of Jewish peoplehood and Jewish law to God, on the one hand, and to Gentiles, on the other.

The rhetorical error is, that Acts 15 considers circumcision a Mosaic rite, rather than linking it up with Abraham. In and of itself this is surprising. After all, the Torah itself presents circumcision as Abrahamic, and the rite's connection with Abraham is of no passing importance for Luke's hero, Paul – as for Philo and for Josephus.[46] Moreover, in Acts 7:8 Luke himself portrays circum-

---

[45] See esp. his Acts and the Earliest History of Christianity (Philadelphia, 1979); Between Jesus and Paul: Studies in the Earliest History of Christianity (London-Philadelphia, 1983); and Pre-Christian Paul.

[46] See inter alia Romans 4:9–12 and Galatians 3:6, also Josephus' Ant. 1.191–193 and the first eleven paragraphs of Philo's De specialibus legibus, which, significantly, discuss circumcision before the body of the treatise, which analyzes Mosaic law (§ 13!) under the rubrics provided by the Ten Commandments. For the understanding of that Philonic discussion within the context of Genesis 17, not Moses and Sinai, see R. D. HECHT, "The Exegetical Contexts of Philo's Interpretation of Circumcision", Nourished With Peace: Studies in Hellenistic Judaism

cision as Abrahamic, and the same may be implied by Luke 2:21–22: while these two verses read very parallel one to another, the contrast of the "eight days of circumcision" to the "days of her purification according to the law of Moses" seems to indicate that circumcision is not part of that law.

In particular, however, linkage of circumcision to Abraham would have functioned quite well in Acts 15. For James' argument is that God meant to call out of the nations a new people for His name (v. 14), out of "the remainder of mankind, all peoples" (v. 17) – so one need not be a member of the Jewish people to worship God. Hence, James concludes, it would be contravening God's purpose to encumber those "of the nations" who would worship Him by obliging them to observe the Jews' national customs, which he terms "Moses" (vv. 19–21). Now, that one need not be a member of the Jewish people in order to worship God is a standard Lukan claim. In the present context, especially two cases are apposite: in Acts 10–11 we read of a paradigmatic Gentile, Cornelius, who begins as a God-fearer (Acts 10:2) and brings the Church to realize that "repentance unto life" is given to the Gentiles too (11:18), and in Acts 18:6–7 we see Paul turning from the Jews to the Gentiles (*ethnê*) and yet immediately moving in with a God-fearer.[47]

But we are not dealing with just some isolated texts: the whole two-volume work is "included" between an opening promise that all the nations shall see the salvation of God (Luke 3:6) and the closing report that the evangelist of salvation gave up on the Jewish *people* and turned to the other *peoples*, who will indeed be saved (Acts 28:26–28).[48] What is special about Acts 15, in this respect, is that it offers a special focus upon circumcision – but fails to integrate it into this general perspective. The claim that Gentiles need not become Jewish in order to worship God would have been made best, in this context, by asserting that one need not do something instituted by Abraham, the father of the Jewish people, and practiced by his descendants. But Acts 15 (as Acts 21:21) presents circumcision as a *Mosaic* rite. Why?

We would suggest that Luke took over the *Fragestellung* of the Izates story, although it was somewhat inappropriate for his own context. In the Izates story, considering circumcision another one of the Jewish (Mosaic) *ethê*, as Ananias did, made sense, for the question addressed is, "Must those who worship God observe Jewish law?" The question of Jewish peoplehood is not raised. Izates is and will remain a Gentile, and the only question is, whether he must observe

---

in Memory of Samuel Sandmel (edd. F.E. Greenspahn, E. Hilgert and B.L. Mack; Chico, California 1984), pp. 51–79. In general, see the appendices on "Circumcision and the Abrahamic Covenant" and "Abraham in Jewish Literature" in G.W. Hansen, *Abraham in Galatians: Epistolary and Rhetorical Contexts* (Sheffield 1989), pp. 170–199.

[47] See Reynolds and Tannenbaum, Jews and God-Fearers, p. 51.

[48] On this "Q.E.D." of Luke-Acts, see my "The End of the Line: Paul in the Canonical Book of Acts," Paul and the Legacies of Paul (ed. W.S. Babcock; Dallas 1990), pp. 11–13.

Jewish law. In Acts 15, in contrast, as we have seen, the issue is not simply, "Must Gentiles who worship God observe Jewish law?"; that question has an obvious negative answer, for Jewish law is assumed to be a matter of national *ethê*. Rather, the question is, "Must Gentile converts to Christianity join the Jewish people?", the assumption being that an affirmative answer will entail their obligation to do as Jews do. Given that question, and given the fact that the issue was raised in connection with the salient issue of circumcision, Luke should have had Peter and James respond, inter alia, by pointing out that circumcision is Abrahamic and hence applies to the Jewish people alone; since God has selected a new people, there is no need to impose the old national rite of the Jews. Then he could have preceded to associate all the other Jewish laws with peoplehood – and let them all fall together.

In short, Abraham symbolizes Jewish peoplehood; Moses – Jewish law. But while laws obviously can be undertaken by erstwhile non-Jews, it is not so clear that peoplehood can. Even the rabbis would be hard put to decide whether a convert could refer to the Patriarchs as his fathers.[49] So once the question of circumcision was raised, and linked to the rest of Jewish practice, Luke – who chose to phrase the issue in terms of peoples – should either have linked all Jewish practice at the Abrahamic level and then rejected them or, if he preferred to stand by his usual association of the law with Moses, he should have at least associated circumcision with Abraham and then argued that since Gentiles could not become Abraham's descendants they should not be burdened with the *ethê* Moses imposed upon those descendants. As it is, however, Luke has failed to take the opportunity circumcision offers to prove that the Jews are an *ethnos*, and, by doing so, he has missed the chance of proving, out of the Jews' holiest book, that their practices are only a matter of *ethê*. He asserts it, but cannot prove it.

If Luke, who is very familiar with Genesis and elsewhere takes circumcision as Abrahamic, failed to apply that point here and thereby came up with a weaker argument, it may be that he did so because he was writing under the impact of a story where the basic issues were the same but the setting of circumcision on the same plane a other laws made sense. Josephus' Izates story is the only one we know of.

One troublesome question remains. Even if we assume Luke was influenced by the Izates narrative, is it clear – given the fact that Josephus' Izates narrative is evidently based on one or more written sources, as various criteria indicate[50]

[49] See Mishnah, Bikkurim 1:4. For doubts as to whether ancient Jews, even of the rabbinic variety, saw converts as members of the Jewish people, see S.J.D. Cohen, "Crossing the Boundary and Becoming a Jew", Harvard Theological Review 82 (1989), p. 30; Schwartz, Agrippa, pp. 124–130.

[50] See my "KATA TOYTON TON KAIPON: Josephus' Source on Agrippa II," *Jewish Quarterly Review* 72 (1981/82), p. 251, and Schiffman, "Conversion of the Royal House",

– that Luke found the narrative in Josephus' *Antiquities* and nowhere else? Certainly, it is not absolutely clear.[51] Nonetheless, it seems likely that at least in our crucial passage (§§ 34–48) Josephus was heavily involved in his text. This results not only from the use of typically Josephan diction, but, also, in particular, from the identity of Izates' fear (his subjects will not tolerate his adoption of Jewish *ethê*) and that of Syllaeus in *Ant.* 16.225.[52] Evidently, these passages reflect awareness of popular concern over conversion to Judaism by members of the ruling class – a concern well-justified by circumstances in Josephus' time and place.[53] Josephus' significant involvement in this text leads us to suspect that Lukan similarities to this narrative mean he read it in Josephus. Can anyone really pretend that the criteria commonly taken to date Luke-Acts to the mid-80s are so exact as to preclude him reading a text Josephus published in 93/94?[54]

---

pp. 294–295. E. Täubler suggested that Josephus' narrative is based on a "Missionsschrift": Die Parthernachrichten bei Josephus (Diss. Berlin, 1904), pp. 62–65.

[51] Cf. above, n. 43.

[52] Note also the identity of Josephus' moralizing remarks in § 48 to others elsewhere, e.g. on the demise of the Herodian line – 18.127–128. In general, on Josephus' active involvement in the Adiabene narrative, see Broer, "Konversion des Königshauses", pp. 139–149.

[53] See Stern, GLA II, pp. 382–384. In general, on Jewish success in attracting proselytes and sympathizers in the Greco-Roman period, and on Josephus' defense of Judaism in this context, see Feldman, Jew and Gentile.

[54] Fitzmyer (Luke I, p. 57), for example, places Luke ca. 80–85 C. E., citing others, such as Kümmel (Introduction, p. 186), who prefer to speak of 80–90 and note that 90–100 cannot be excluded; we have already seen (n. 43) the weakness of their exclusion of the Josephan terminus post quem, 93/94 C.E. Similarly, P. Vielhauer (Geschichte der urchristlichen Literatur [Berlin – New York 1975], p. 407) gives 70 C. E. and "etwa 1. Hälfte des 2. Jh.s" as the basic parameters, builds upon Luke's failure to use the Pauline letters as an indication that Luke-Acts was composed before the end of the first century but depends upon Dibelius (above, n. 40) to reject the notion of Lukan dependence on Josephus for Acts 5:36f.; the admittedly speculative result leaves Luke ca. 80 and Acts ca. 90. As for the late first-century terminus ad quem given Luke's failure to use Paul's letters, Kümmel's Introduction, in particular, illustrates how flimsy the case is. At p. 186 he writes that the letters "by all appearances were collected toward the end of the first century (see below, § 35)", but in § 35 (pp. 480–481) that collection is said to be clearly in evidence no earlier than Marcion (ca. 140). True, Kümmel does adduce some inferential evidence from I Clement, Ignatius and II Peter (3:15f.), resulting in the conclusion that there was such a collection "at least by the beginning of the second century". But while the first two witnesses, such as they are, do point us to the early second century, at p. 434 Kümmel places II Peter in the second quarter of the second century. None of this inspires much confidence, and one can well understand how H. Koester (History and Literature of Early Christianity [New York – Berlin 1982], p. 310) could ignore the whole issue and bring Luke-Acts down to 125–135. That, we note, would certainly have allowed Luke enough time to read Josephus.

Bibliography

BROER, "Konversion des Königshauses" – I. BROER, "Die Konversion des Königshauses von Adiabene nach Josephus", in: Nach den Anfängen Fragen (edd. C. Mayer, K. Müller and G. Schmalenberg; Giessen 1994), pp. 133–162.

FELDMAN, Jew and Gentile – L.H. FELDMAN, Jew and Gentile in the Ancient World (Princeton 1993).

FITZMYER, Luke – J.A. FITZMYER, The Gospel According to Luke, I (Anchor Bible; Garden City, N.Y. 1981).

GILBERT, "The Making of a Jew" – G. GILBERT, "The Making of a Jew: 'God-Fearer' or Convert in the Story of Izates", Union Seminary Quarterly Review 44 (1990/91), pp. 299–313.

M. GOODMAN, "Jewish Proselytizing" – M. GOODMAN, "Jewish Proselytizing in the First Century", The Jews Among Pagans and Christians In the Roman Empire [edd. J. Lieu, J. North and T. Rajak; London – New York 1992], pp. 53–78.

HAENCHEN, Acts – E. HAENCHEN, The Acts of the Apostles (Oxford 1971).

HENGEL, Pre-Christian Paul – M. HENGEL, The Pre-Christian Paul (in collaboration with R. Deines; London-Philadelphia, 1991).

KÜMMEL, Introduction – W.G. KÜMMEL, Introduction to the New Testament (Nashville 1975).

MCELENEY, "Conversion" – N.J. MCELENEY, "Conversion, Circumcision and the Law", *New Testament Studies* 20 (1974), pp. 319–341.

MASON, Josephus – S. MASON, Josephus and the New Testament (Peabody, Mass. 1992).

REYNOLDS and TANNENBAUM, Jews and God-Fearers – J. REYNOLDS and R. TANNENBAUM, Jews and God-Fearers at Aphrodisias (Cambridge 1987).

SCHIFFMAN, "Conversion of the Royal House" – L.H. SCHIFFMAN, "The Conversion of the Royal House of Adiabene in Josephus and Rabbinic Sources", in: *Josephus, Judaism, and Christianity* (edd. L.H. Feldman and G. Hata; Detroit 1987), pp. 293–312.

SCHRECKENBERG, "Flavius Josephus" – H. SCHRECKENBERG, "Flavius Josephus und die Lukanischen Schriften", *Wort in der Zeit: Neutestamentliche Studien, Festgabe für Karl Heinrich Rengstorf zum 75. Geburtstag* (edd. W. Haubeck and M. Bachmann; Leiden 1980), pp. 179–209.

SCHÜRER – E. SCHÜRER, The History of the Jewish People in the Age of Jesus Christ (175 B.C. – A.D. 135), I–III, (new English ed. by G. Vermes et al.; Edinburgh 1973–1986).

SCHWARTZ, Agrippa – D.R. SCHWARTZ, Agrippa I (Tübingen 1990).

SCHWARTZ, Studies – D.R. SCHWARTZ, Studies in the Jewish Background of Christianity (Tübingen 1992).

SEGAL, "Conversion and Universalism" – A.F. SEGAL, "Conversion and Universalism: Opposites that Attract", in *Origins and Method: Toward a New Understanding of Judaism and Christianity – Essays in Honour of John C. Hurd* (ed. B.H. McLean; Sheffield 1993), pp. 162–189.

SIEGERT, "Gottesfürchtige und Sympathisanten" – F. SIEGERT, "Gottesfürchtige und Sympathisanten", *Journal for the Study of Judaism* 4 (1973), pp. 109–164.

SPICQ, Notes – Supplément – C. SPICQ, *Notes de lexicographie néo-testamentaire*, Supplément (Göttingen 1982).

Stern, GLA – M. Stern, Greek and Latin Authors on Jews and Judaism, I–III (Jerusalem 1974–1984).
Wilson, Luke and the Law – S. G. Wilson, Luke and the Law (Cambridge 1983).

The Beginnings of the Jewish Revolt under Trajan

by

WILLIAM HORBURY

Eastern and western diaspora populations both took part in a sustained revolt under Trajan. In Mesopotamia, Cyrene, Egypt, and Cyprus its volcanic energy and destructiveness were met by merciless repression, although the eastern diaspora went on to prosper under the Parthians, and in the west the important Jewish communities in Asia Minor, Greece and Italy seem to have suffered no harm. What were the circumstances of this dual uprising? Its outbreak at the time of Trajan's Parthian war (113–17) can hardly be ascribed to chance, and its tenacity and intensity have been among features taken to suggest that it was also influenced by messianism. The importance of messianic hope in the theatres of the western revolt was shown with particular force and detail by M. Hengel; endorsing S. Applebaum's view that the rebels intended to march on Judaea in a return to Zion, he urged that the ruthlessness shown on both sides suits a war of religion, and that the sudden explosive outbreak of the revolt was primarily caused by messianic hope, which was possibly strengthened by the involvement of the Parthians.[1]

The causes were reconsidered, and the importance of messianism in the revolt was questioned, in a reappraisal of the chronology by T. D. Barnes.[2] The heart of his argument was a critique of Eusebius' dating of the outbreak of the revolt in the eighteenth year of Trajan, closely corresponding to 115 (Eusebius, *Ecclesiastical History* iv 2, 2, discussed below). Barnes urged a return to the view that the revolt broke out a year later, in 116. He argued that Cassius Dio indicates the later date; for in Dio's narrative as preserved in epitome (Dio lxviii 32, discussed below) the revolt in the west is said to have been in progress during the siege of Hatra, towards the end of Trajan's Parthian war and not long before the emperor's death in 117. Barnes went on to note that this date would permit a reconstruction of the revolt which places greater emphasis on events in the east. The revolt began, in this view, in Mesopotamia during Trajan's

[1] HENGEL, 'Messianische Hoffnung', endorsing the main contentions of Applebaum, Cyrene, on the objectives of the revolt.
[2] BARNES, 'Trajan and the Jews'.

Parthian war. Here both non-Jews and Jews had risen in the regions just taken by Rome. The western Jewish uprisings in Cyrene, Egypt and Cyprus then immediately ensued. Their prime object would have been to make Trajan's eastern conquests untenable, and so to ensure Jewish prosperity in Babylonia. Messianism was an element in the uprisings, but it has been overrated, Barnes suggests, in explanations of their outbreak; for the revolt had a clear – and successfully achieved – defensive aim. His redating has received recognition, although his verdict on messianism is contested.[3]

Did the revolt break out in 116 rather than 115, and can a messianic element in it properly be identified? These questions will be considered here in turn.[4]

I. Chronology

The revolt is widely but fragmentarily attested in ancient sources. Year-dates are lacking in the papyri which unambiguously refer to it, notably letters from the archive of Apollonius, strategos of the nome of Apollonopolis of the Heptacomia, north of Thebes (*CPJ* ii, nos. 436–9, 442–6).[5] A papyrus (*CPJ* ii, no. 435) from Tebtunis in the Fayum, a place with a Jewish community, dated 13th October in the nineteenth year of an emperor whose name cannot be read with certainty, is concerned with judicial procedures in a 'city', no doubt Alexandria, after 'the battle of the Romans against the Jews'. It can be tentatively dated to 115, if Trajan's name is read (the regnal year in Egypt being taken to begin on 29th August, see n. 24, below); for it suits the period of *stasis* which Eusebius ascribes to the first year of the revolt. Roman troops would then have fought to quell Jewish insurgence in the city in 115, somewhat as when two legions and other troops fought and slaughtered Jews in an insurrection in the Delta quarter of Alexandria in 66 (Josephus, *B. J.* ii 494–8).[6] This dating of the

[3] Frankfurter, 'Egypt's City', nn. 1 and 79; Grabbe, Judaism, 596–9 (there was unrest in Egypt in 115, but the main revolt there broke out in 116). Barnes' article will have appeared too late for comment by Mélèze-Modrzejewski, Les juifs d'Égypte (1991); I have not seen the English translation (Edinburgh, 1995).

[4] What follows includes a revised form of some material from my chapter on 'The Jewish Revolts under Trajan and Hadrian', forthcoming in W.D. Davies & L. Finkelstein (edd.), The Cambridge History of Judaism, iv.

[5] For papyri relevant to the revolt in Egypt, see CPJ ii, nos. 157–8, 435–50 and iii, no. 520, and (listing papyri published after CPJ) J. Mélèze-Modrzejewski, 'ΙΟΥΔΑΙΟΙ ΑΦΗΙΡΗΜΕΝΟΙ. La fin de la communauté juive d'Égypte (115–117 de n.é.)', in G. Thür (ed.), Symposion 1985, Vorträge zur griechischen und hellenistischen Rechtsgeschichte (Akten der Gesellschaft für griechische und hellenistische Rechtsgeschichte, Bd 6, Cologne & Vienna, 1989), 337–61 (341, n. 14).

[6] Barnes, 'Trajan', 153–4 accepts this dating and interpretation, but lays emphasis on the difference between faction and war, and dissociates the 'battle' from the revolt, without noting that Eusebius describes the first year of the revolt as one of faction.

papyrus, however, is materially aided by Eusebius' report. A series of ostraca recording payments of the Jewish tax in Apollonopolis Magna (Edfu), south of Thebes, breaks off with a receipt dated Year 19 of Trajan, Pachon 23 (18th May, 116) (*CPJ* ii, no. 229).[7] This suggests that the revolt spread to the Thebaid about this time, but does not date its outbreak.[8]

Chronology therefore depends on the literary sources. The oldest of these attest the gravity and scope of the revolt, and its repression by Trajan, rather than its precise date. Thus, tantalizingly brief eye-witness references to it as a 'war' (πόλεμος) are preserved from Appian of Alexandria (on the demolition of the Nemeseion near Alexandria by the Jews for the needs of the war 'when Trajan was exterminating the Jewish race in Egypt', and on Appian's own narrow escape from Jewish naval forces near Pelusium) and by Artemidorus of Daldis (on the dream of a Roman camp prefect which signified 'death to the Jews of Cyrene' in 'the Jewish war in Cyrene'); the Suda lexicon (? eleventh century) quotes a sentence from Arrian, which is almost certainly a contemporary reference to the punitive slaughter of Mesopotamian Jews by Lusius Quietus (subsequently made governor of Judaea by Trajan, but recalled and executed under Hadrian); and the Mishnah and Seder Olam probably allude to similar repression in Judaea under the name 'the war [*pôl*ᵉ*môs* = πόλεμος] of Quietus' (M. Sotah ix 14, Seder Olam Rabbah 30).[9]

---

7 SMALLWOOD, Roman Rule, 401–2, noting also a dedication to Trajan in the northern Thebaid in May 116 (OGIS 677); the community attested in these ostraca is discussed by SCHWARTZ, 'Edfu', and a photograph of a receipt of 31st March 116 (CPJ ii, no. 227) is reproduced by MÉLÈZE-MODRZEJEWSKI, Les juifs d'Égypte, 175.

8 BARNES, 'Trajan', 157–8 infers from the normality attested in May 116 by the ostraca and the dedication (see the preceding note) that the Jews of Alexandria and lower Egypt cannot have rebelled in 115, but in view of the distance between lower and upper Egypt this seems questionable; note the mention of Thebes and of the Thebaid separately from 'Egypt' in Josephus, B. J. vii 416 and Eusebius, Chronicle, Trajan xvii, respectively, and the weak hold of Alexandrian government over Thebes under the later Ptolemies (THOMPSON, Memphis, 153–4).

9 For the Greek sources see STERN, Authors, ii, nos. 348, 396, 332a, respectively. Seder Olam R. and the Mishnah (where the name Qitos survives in the Cambridge MS.) both attest the series war of Vespasian, war of Quietus, war of Bar Kokhba; see S. KRAUSS, Griechen und Römer (Monumenta Talmudica v. 1, 1914, reprinted Darmstadt, 1972), nos. 163–4 (texts with translation and comment), and SCHÜRER revised, i, 533–4. Compare Eusebius on Quietus' appointment in Judaea as an acknowledgement of his success in extirpating the eastern Jews (Chronicle, Trajan xviii; History, iv 2, 5) and Historia Augusta, Hadrian v 2, quoted in the text below, on the rebellious spirits produced by Palestine as well as Libya at the beginning of Hadrian's reign. These passages together strongly suggest some upheaval and repression in Palestine, as affirmed by LEPPER, Parthian War, 91 (on Eusebius and Hadrian, only) and (with discussion of further evidence) by HENGEL, 'Hoffnung', 664–5, despite doubts concerning a fully fledged uprising there expressed by P. Schäfer, Geschichte der Juden in der Antike: Die Juden Palästinas von Alexander dem Grossen bis zur arabischen Eroberung (Stuttgart, 1983), 156–7, STEMBERGER, Herrschaft, 77–8, GRABBE, Judaism, 567–9, and F. MILLAR, The Roman Near East 31 B.C.-A.D. 337 (Cambridge, Mass., & London, 1993), 103.

Two narratives in the Talmud Yerushalmi (Sukkah v 1, 55a-b) and parallel texts, in the names of the second-century teachers Judah b. Ilai and Simeon b. Yohai, respectively, deal with repression by Trajan in Egypt, with a hint at the Parthian war and the Cypriot revolt. They ascribe to Trajan the destruction of the Alexandrian basilica-synagogue of which Judah b. Ilai said, 'He who has not seen the double colonnade of Alexandria has never seen the glory of Israel', and (in the second narrative) the slaughter by the legions of Jewish women as well as men in Egypt, until their mingled blood streamed out to Cyprus; Trajan's wife is imagined as having told her husband 'Instead of putting down the barbarians, come and put down the Jews, who have rebelled against you' – a remark well suited to the setting of the revolt in the Parthian war.[10] The process of repression by colonization in Cyrene under Trajan is epigraphically attested.[11] In Cyprus, similarly, the dedication of a statue to Trajan at Soli in his 20th year (reckoned there from September 116) suggests that repression was then in progress.[12] Continuation of the revolt in Cyrene and elsewhere at the beginning of Hadrian's reign is suggested, however, by *Historia Augusta*, Hadrian v 2, on the troubles at the time of his accession in August 117: 'Aegyptus seditionibus urgebatur, Libya denique ac Palaestina rebelles animos efferebant.'[13]

The revolt is therefore set in the last years of Trajan and the beginning of Hadrian's reign. Closer dating can be attempted, however, on the basis of notes of time in the more extended narratives by Cassius Dio in the early third century (as epitomized by Xiphilinus in the eleventh), and by Eusebius, both in the *Chronicle* and in the *Ecclesiastical History*, at the end of the third and the beginning of the fourth century.[14] The colourful account by Orosius, in the

---

[10] For discussion especially of the second of these narratives in the context of the revolt, see LOEWE, 'A Jewish Counterpart to the Acts of the Alexandrians'; STEMBERGER, Herrschaft, 75–6.

[11] The career of a camp prefect, Publius Gavius Fronto, as recorded in a Greek honorific inscription from Attaleia in Pamphylia, includes his having been commissioned by Trajan to lead 3000 veteran legionaries to settle Cyrene; the inscription is reprinted in P.M. FRASER (with a note by S. APPLEBAUM), 'Hadrian and Cyrene', JRS xl (1950), 77–90 (84, n.37), and as SEG 17, 584, and discussed by APPLEBAUM, Cyrene, 270, 287.

[12] SMALLWOOD, Roman Rule, 414, n. 103.

[13] This interpretation is given by W. WEBER, Untersuchungen zur Geschichte des Kaisers Hadrianus (Leipzig, 1907), 50. The Life of Hadrian has 'high factual content', and comes from the section of the Historia Augusta which is indebted to a good Latin source earlier than 250, according to T.D. BARNES, The Sources of the Historia Augusta (Brussels, 1978), 47, 98, 102–7, 125. 'Rebelles animos efferebant' may mean something less than full revolt, as noted by T. LIEBMANN-FRANKFORT, 'Les juifs dans l'Histoire Auguste', Latomus xxxiii (1974), 597–607 (581–2); but it still means something other than quies.

[14] Since the Chronological Canons, the second and major part of Eusebius' Chronicle, are mentioned as already written in his Prophetic Eclogues, soon after 303, the Chronicle is unlikely to be later than c. 303, and will be based on collections made before that (A. HARNACK, Die Chronologie der altchristlichen Litteratur bis Eusebius, ii (Leipzig, 1904),

early fifth century, has repeatedly been cited by historians as if it were independent;[15] but it seems to be wholly drawn from Eusebius, whose *Chronicle* and *History* were known to Orosius in the Latin versions by Jerome and Rufinus.[16]

The relevant annals in Eusebius' *Chronicle* (223rd Olympiad, Trajan xvii–xix) may be rendered as follows, on the basis of Jerome's Latin version.[17]

xvii. The Jews, who were in Libya, fight against their gentile fellow-inhabitants. Similarly in Egypt and in Alexandria, about Cyrene also and the Thebaid, they strive in great sedition; but the gentile party prevails in Alexandria.

xviii. The Jews of Mesopotamia being in revolt, the emperor Trajan orders Lysias [*sic*] Quietus to extirpate them from the province. Quietus, drawing up a force against them, kills countless thousands of them; and for this he is designated procurator of Judaea by the emperor.

xviiii. The Jews overthrow Salamis, a city of Cyprus, slaying the gentiles therein.

The more detailed narrative in Eusebius' *History* may be summarized as follows.

(i) 'When the emperor was already moving into his eighteenth year' factional strife broke out 'in Alexandria, the rest of Egypt, and also about Cyrene'; it developed next year into war, Lupus being governor of all Egypt at the time' (*Ecclesiastical History* iv 2, 2).

111–2.). Books i-vii of the History are mainly based on the same material. The first editions of the Chronicle and the History are dated before 293 and c. 295, respectively, by T. D. Barnes, Constantine and Eusebius (Cambridge, Mass., & London, 1981), 113 & n. 68, 128–9 & nn. 9–10, and (in answer to the view of the composition of the History advanced by R. M. Grant, Eusebius as Church Historian (Oxford, 1980)) 'Some Inconsistencies in Eusebius', JTS N. S. xxxv (1984), 470–5. By contrast, the first edition of the History is placed in 313–4 (the time of the second edition, according to Barnes) by A. Louth, 'The Date of Eusebius' Historia Ecclesiastica', JTS N. S. xli (1990), 111–23; he leaves open the date of the first edition of the Chronicle. With these datings of the History compare Harnack, Chronologie, ii, 112–5 (composition lasting c. 303–312/3), and R. Laqueur, cited by Louth, 113 (303). Whenever the first edition of the History is dated, the passages on the revolt in both Chronicle and History are likely to be based on the material gathered in Eusebius' initial period of work, towards the end of the third century.

[15] Orosius is treated in this way by V. Tcherikover, CPJ i, p. 87; Fuks, 'Aspects', 98–9, 102–3; the revisers of Schürer, i, 530–2, nn. 74, 75, 79, 81, 83 (quotations taken over without reproduction of Schürer's own warning that Orosius is derivative, cited in the following footnote); Applebaum, Cyrene, 270, 291, 296, 336; Smallwood, Roman Rule, 393–4, 396, 401, 411–3, 418–9; Barnes, 'Trajan', 159; Grabbe, Judaism, 560–1, 569, 597.

[16] The individual debts are registered by C. Zangemeister (ed.), Pauli Orosii Historiarum adversus Paganos Libri vii (CSEL v, Vienna, 1882), 467; the general debt to Eusebius' Chronicle was noted by Schürer, Geschichte, i (1901), 661, and to both Eusebius' works by Motta, 'La tradizione', 474, n. 1. The possibility of debt to Eusebius was recognized by Pucci, 'Qualche osservazione', 61 and Rivolta, 55, 73, although she also cites Orosius separately (Rivolta, 41, 49, 138).

[17] R. Helm (ed.), Eusebius Werke, 7: Die Chronik des Hieronymus (GCS xlvii, 2nd ed., Leipzig, 1956), 196–7; on Jerome's mainly reliable witness to the text, see A. A. Mosshammer, The Chronicle of Eusebius and Greek Chronographic Tradition (Lewisburg & London, 1979), 65–7.

(ii) 'In the first battle' the Jews overcame the Greeks, who fled to Alexandria, and captured and killed the Jews in the city. The Jews from Cyrene, deprived of help from the Egyptian Jews, turned to devastating the Egyptian *chora*, 'under the leadership of Lucuas' (iv 2, 3).

(iii) The emperor sent Marcius Turbo, who waged a war with many battles, lasting no little time, against the Cyrenaican Jews in Egypt and against the Egyptian Jews who had joined 'Lucuas, their king' (iv 2, 3–4).

(iv) The emperor, suspecting the Mesopotamian Jews of rebellion, ordered Lusius Quietus to purge the province of them; he slew an immense multitude, and for his success was made governor of Judaea (iv 2, 5).

(v) Greek writers on the events of those times recounted them in the same words (iv 2, 5).

Dio and Eusebius differ widely in emphasis, but rest on complementary and consistent information. Dio (lxviii 32), as mediated by Xiphilinus, gives a brief account of the western revolts after his notice of the siege of Hatra, introducing them as events that were occurring 'meanwhile' (ἐν τούτῳ); he then immediately recounts Trajan's illness and death (117). Barnes follows Dio, urging that the placing of the relevant passage implies that the revolt broke out in 116, and accordingly he rejects Eusebius' date of 115 for the outbreak. It can nonetheless be argued that in chronology also the two historians are consistent.[18] Eusebius includes in the revolt an initial phase of factional strife in 115, which in the next year (116) became war (*History* iv 2, 2); Dio notices the revolt when it had already reached this second stage of war.

This point, noticed further below, calls into question Barnes' rejection of Eusebius in favour of Dio; but comparison of Eusebius and Dio suggests a second point of importance for chronology. The overall outline of the revolt emerging from the relatively full report in Eusebius implies a duration for the revolt which suits 115 better than 116 as the year of outbreak.

The significance of this aspect of Eusebius' report for chronology can best be appreciated when Eusebius and Dio are compared. Their common stock of information should be noticed first. Eusebius made no use of Dio, as also appears from his narrative of the Bar Kokhba revolt. Both historians, however, are indebted to Arrian on repression of rebellion in the newly conquered regions of Mesopotamia by Lusius Quietus, although the Jewish element in this eastern uprising is not specified by Dio. Dio and Eusebius both, however,

---

18 This was maintained, in a way different from that suggested below, by T. MOMMSEN, The History of Rome: the Provinces, from Caesar to Diocletian, ii (E.T. London, 1886), 221–3; he held that the 'eighteenth year' mentioned in Eusebius' History should be understood, in accord with the reckoning of Trajan's years in the Chronicle although against its allotment of events to years, as the penultimate year of Trajan's reign – 116. This solution encounters the difficulty about to be noted, that Eusebius' information on events suggests a longer span than 116–117.

mention Cyrenaica, Egypt and Cyprus as centres of specifically Jewish revolts. They both name a leader of the Cyrenian Jews, Andreas in Cyrene (Dio) and Lucuas in Egypt (Eusebius). These are often taken to be different names for the same leader;[19] but as Cyrene was still disturbed at Hadrian's accession it is natural to envisage one leader there, as Dio says, and another at the head of the Cyrenian Jews in Egypt, as Eusebius says. Dio gives the figure of 220,000 gentile deaths in Cyrenaica. Eusebius adds special references to Alexandria and the Thebaid, but in the *History* (by contrast with the *Chronicle*) he omits Cyprus. The *Chronicle* notice on Cyprus records massacre and destruction *by* Jews at Salamis, complementing Dio, who notes the name of a Jewish leader in outrages in Cyprus (Artemion), the figure of 240,000 gentile deaths, and the subsequent slaughter and expulsion *of* Jews. Here, as in the case of the Cyrenian Jews, the two sources offer differing but consistent information.

Within this common framework, however, Dio and Eusebius differ in topographical focus. Both give fair detail on Cyprus, but otherwise their emphasis is not the same. Dio concentrates on the region about Cyrene, and the atrocities of the revolt there, led by Andreas (here his narrative recalls his account of Boudicca's atrocities, lxii 7).[20] In accord with with the imperial interest which also marks his account of the Bar Kokhba revolt, he specifies that Romans as well as Greeks were attacked. Then 'the revolt in Egypt is dismissed in half a dozen words' (E. M. Smallwood), and Dio adds the fuller notice of Cyprus summarized above.[21] His emphasis on Cyrene recalls the independent importance of 'the Jewish war in Cyrene' in Artemidorus, as cited above. In Eusebius' two narratives, by contrast, Alexandria and Egypt are central, and Greeks in general, without special mention of Romans, are the object of Jewish attack. The Egyptian emphasis appears further in his *History*, where the Cyrenaican Jews are prominent because of their presence in Egypt, Cyrene itself is mentioned only generally in a passing phrase (iv 2, 2 καὶ πρόσετι κατὰ Κυρήνην), and the date is confirmed by Lupus' Egyptian prefecture (iv 2, 2). The *History* includes notices of factional strife and of military engagements in Alexandria and the *chora*, and of the protracted war waged on land and water by Marcius Turbo, πολλαῖς μάχαις οὐκ ὀλίγῳ τε χρόνῳ, against Lucuas of Cyrene and his followers (iv 2, 3–4). In the end, therefore, Eusebius in his two accounts gives a fuller and more detailed picture of the revolt,

---

[19] For example by Tcherikover in CPJ i, 86, 88–90; Stern, Authors, ii, no.437, pp. 386, 388; Mélèze-Modrzejewski, Les juifs d'Égypte, 162; but the possibility that two different men are in question is left open by Applebaum, Cyrene, 259 and Smallwood, Roman Rule, 397, n. 23.

[20] This is noted by Stern, Authors, ii, no. 437, p. 387. There seems no need to ascribe the Cyrenaic atrocity narrative to Xiphilinus rather than Dio, as suggested by Mélèze-Modrzejewski, Les juifs d'Égypte, 165.

[21] Smallwood, Roman Rule, 393–4 (holding that what survives in Xiphilinus is only a short excerpt from a fuller account of the revolt by Dio).

with special reference to Egypt but including its other theatres, than can be gained from Dio.

Eusebius says that he is following the 'very words' of earlier Greek historians in this passage of the *History* (iv 2, 5). Arrian is almost certainly one of these, but the strongly Alexandrian and Egyptian interest evident in Eusebius' material permits the tentative suggestion that another is Appian of Alexandria, cited above. Appian's lost book xxii may well have said more about the Jews.[22] Eusebius would then preserve further important excerpts from an eye-witness source. In any case, however, his narrative rests on earlier historical writing with a special Egyptian interest.

This point suggests that he should be taken seriously in his view (*History* iv 2, 1–2) that a Jewish tumult (κίνησις), constituted by faction (στάσις) against Greeks in Alexandria, the rest of Egypt, and Cyrenaica, escalated in the following year into war (πόλεμος). Eusebius in the *History* dates the first of these two years as the time 'when the emperor was moving into his eighteenth year' (iv 2, 1 τοῦ αὐτοκράτορος εἰς ἐνιαυτὸν ὀκτωκαιδέκατον ἐλαύνοντος). Trajan's eighteenth regnal year would be expected to be reckoned from his accession day at the end of January 115, or from the tribunician New Year on 10th December 114; in either case, it would closely correspond to 115.[23] Eusebius' *Chronicle* gives the *seventeenth* year, but probably indicates the same time, for the *History* specifically notes that it was about the turn of the regnal year, and the *Chronicle* reckons regnal years from the September after the monarch's accession.[24] The *Chronicle* allots the events of the revolt to the seventeenth, eighteenth, and nineteenth years of Trajan (114–15 to 116–17, on the September-based reckoning), but it also suggests an aftermath under Hadrian, in the annals of his first year (he 'takes Jews in revolt a second time') and his fifth (he 'sends colonies to Libya, which had been laid waste by the Jews'). Here of course it agrees with the time-span indicated by the life of Hadrian in *Historia Augusta*, as noted above.

Barnes points out that Eusebius' year-dating may be erroneous, as is widely

22 STERN, Authors, ii, p. 178. Appian has been mentioned as a possible source of Eusebius here (for example by MÉLÈZE-MODRZEJEWSKI, Les juifs d'Égypte, 162), but so far as the present writer is aware the coherence of Eusebius' Alexandrian and Egyptian emphasis with this possibility has not been discussed.

23 SCHÜRER, Geschichte, i, 663, n. 46; E. T. revised, i, 530, n. 73.

24 C.H. TURNER, 'The Early Episcopal Lists: i The Chronicle of Eusebius', JTS i (1900), 181–200 (187–92), followed by SMALLWOOD, Roman Rule, 393–4, n. 11. BARNES, 'Trajan', 154–5 draws attention to the apparent discrepancy between Chronicle and History without mentioning this suggested explanation. MÉLÈZE-MODRZEJEWSKI, Les juifs d'Égypte, 162, accepting that the revolt began in 115, points out that in Egypt the eighteenth year of Trajan would have been reckoned as running from 29th August 114 to 29th August 115, as was also noted by SCHÜRER, Geschichte, i, 663, n. 46 (in a clause not reproduced in the revised English translation, i, 530, n. 73).

accepted.[25] He draws special attention to Eusebius' placing of his annal on the Antiochene earthquake which, as Dio notes, threatened Trajan's life when he was wintering during his Parthian campaign (Dio lxviii 24–5). Eusebius' annal on the earthquake appears in the *Chronicle* immediately before the notices of the revolt, and in the *sixteenth* year of Trajan – corresponding, Barnes says, to 112–3 (should not this be 113–4?). This date implicitly questions the general accuracy of Eusebius' annals, in Barnes' view, because the earthquake occurred in December 115. (This is the date given by the sixth-century Antiochene chronicler John Malalas; it is consistent with Dio's statement that Pedo, who was alive at the beginning of 115, was killed in the earthquake, and was accepted by F. A. Lepper in his reconstruction of the chronology of Trajan's Parthian war.) On the other hand, Barnes suggests, the *sequence* of events in the *Chronicle*, in which the earthquake precedes the Jewish revolt, may well be right; and the *Chronicle* would then converge with Dio to indicate that the revolt broke out in 116.

Yet, this felicitous double exploitation of Eusebius' annal on the earthquake may not lead quite so far. The present writer would certainly not dispute that the assignation of events to years in the *Chronicle* will have been subject to error. The question of the overall length of the revolt, however, seems to receive little or no notice from Barnes. Eusebius' allotment of three years to the revolt, which Barnes implicitly rejects when he opts for an outbreak in 116, coheres with the relatively full account of events which Eusebius derived from his sources, and with the convincing depiction in the *History* of an initial development from factional strife in the first year to war in the second. The intensity of this internecine war, reflected in Appian, Dio, and papyri as well as Eusebius, suggests that a further year should be allowed for repression to be complete. Given the continuation of revolt at the time of Hadrian's accession in August 117, Eusebius' source-derived outline of events would itself suggest a starting date in 115, irrespective of the accuracy of individual annals.

With this point in mind, two comments may be offered which slightly modify Barnes' discussion of Eusebius on the earthquake. First, the dating of the earthquake itself is bound up with the broader problem of the chronology of Trajan's Parthian war, and is not reconsidered here; but it may be noted that Malalas' dating was not regarded as fixed in earlier study. Thus J. B. Lightfoot, against whose reconstruction of the course of the war (followed by R. P. Longden) Lepper argued in detail, viewed the winter mentioned by Dio as that of 114–5 and put the earthquake early in 115, much nearer to Eusebius' September 113–4 dating, and in time for the sequence earthquake-revolt to agree with a date of 115 for the outbreak of the revolt.[26] S. Applebaum was

---

[25] For what follows see BARNES, 'Trajan', 152–5.

[26] J.B. LIGHTFOOT, The Apostolic Fathers, II.ii (2nd ed., London & New York, 1889), 395–8, 413–8; R.P. LONGDEN, 'The Chronology of the Parthian War of Trajan', in S.A.

accordingly ready to envisage early 115 as a possible date for the earthquake.[27] Secondly, the *Chronicle* seems in any case, as already noted, to place the earthquake one year nearer to 115 than Barnes suggested. Thus the error in Eusebius' dating of the earthquake is somehat less grave, and perhaps also less absolutely certain, than might be gathered from Barnes' discussion.

The possibility of an error in this particular year-date in the *Chronicle* remains. This does not, however, detract from the chronological importance of the overall outline of the revolt given by Eusebius. He derived from his sources a fuller picture than Dio of the revolt as a whole, which suits a duration of more than two years. This fuller picture is, nevertheless, wholly consistent with Dio's information. Moreover, Eusebius himself makes 116 the year in which *stasis* became war (*History* iv 2, 2), and there is therefore, as already noted, no significant disagreement between his dating and that implied by the order of Dio's narrative.

115 should therefore be preferred as the date of the outbreak of the revolt. Correspondingly, historical reconstruction should take seriously Eusebius' source-derived picture of earlier faction in 115 escalating into war in 116. 'As though caught up by some terrible spirit of faction, they rushed into civil strife with their Greek neighbours; having greatly increased its scope, in the following year they began a very considerable war' (Eusebius, *Ecclesiastical History*, iv 2, 2). This element of his report falls into the background in Barnes' treatment. Eusebius' description recalls the gradual escalation of the First Revolt against Rome in Judaea from factional strife in Caesarea and the Syrian cities, with the concurrent disturbances in Alexandria already mentioned above as repressed by two legions and reinforcements. Moreover, the regions in which Eusebius sets the earlier unrest in 115 are those which saw the final disturbances of the First Revolt.[28] After describing the fall of Masada Josephus mentions successively the activity of refugee Sicarii in Alexandria, Egypt, and Thebes; the closure of the temple of Onias in the nome of Heliopolis as a suspected centre of Jewish revolution; and the spread of 'the madness of the Sicarii' to the cities about Cyrene, when Jonathan the weaver took refuge there (Josephus, *B.J.* vii 409–19, 420–36, 437–50). Coins of Year II of the First Revolt, discovered at Cyrene and Saqqara, possibly bear independent witness to the presence of

---

COOK, F.E. ADCOCK & M.P. CHARLESWORTH (edd.), The Cambridge Ancient History, xi (1936), 858–9. It should perhaps be added to the praises of LIGHTFOOT that his reconstruction of Trajanic chronology received detailed discussion from F.A. LEPPER more than half a century later; for the importance of LIGHTFOOT's Apostolic Fathers in New Testament study, see M. HENGEL, 'Bishop Lightfoot and the Tübingen School on the Gospel of John and the Second Century', in J.D.G. DUNN (ed.), The Lightfoot Centenary Lectures (= Durham University Journal, Special Number, January, 1992), 23–51.

27 APPLEBAUM, Cyrene, 268.

28 This point was made by C. MERIVALE, History of the Romans under the Empire, v (London, 1865), 166–8, and MOMMSEN, Provinces, ii, 221.

Judaean refugees in both Cyrenaica and Egypt – in the latter case at Memphis, which had a Jewish community and was not far from the temple and district of Onias (as noted by Josephus, *B. J.* vii 426).[29] These narratives in Josephus attest not only urban disturbance (the κινήμα in Alexandria which ended with martyr-like endurance of torture by the Sicarii) but also incipient assembly for revolt in the countryside (expected in the 'land of Onias' round the temple by the Roman authorities), and the leading of the disaffected into the desert (by Jonathan at Cyrene). Alexandria, Egypt, the Thebaid and Cyrenaica are all named again in Eusebius' reports of the inception of the revolt under Trajan, just over forty years after the flight of the Sicarii.

The anti-Roman aspect of factional strife which this comparison suggests for the Trajanic revolt is of course continuous with the broader anti-gentile aspect specified in Eusebius, and best known from the Jewish-Greek conflict in Alexandria; the Acts of the Alexandrians envisage this from the Greek viewpoint as continuing from Gaius to Trajan and Hadrian. In the Acts of Hermaiscus Trajan is imagined as charging the Greeks with committing 'such dreadful acts', τοιαῦτα χαλεπά, against the Jews (*CPJ* ii, no. 157 (P. Oxy. 1242), lines 36–7). This phrase from the vocabulary of *stasis*, in a complaint such as it is imagined the Jews would have made, evokes the spiral of outrage and reprisal which Jewish partisans developed into war.[30]

Faction in Cyrenaica, Egypt and the city of Alexandria then probably antedated the uprising in the east. This may have been the case in Cyprus too, which was formerly under Ptolemaic rule and had close historical links with Egypt and Cyrene (Josephus, *Ant.* xiii 284–7), but was also closely connected with nearby Syria and Antioch, as appears especially from the Acts of the Apostles (xi 19–20 and xiii 1, on the Jews of Cyprus and Antioch, and on Cypriot and Cyrenian Jews at Antioch; xiii 4–6, on emissaries from Antioch in the synagogues of Salamis, and then in Paphos). The importance of Cyprus in the revolt is strongly suggested by these contacts with both Syria and Egypt, viewed together with the presence of detailed reports in both Dio and Eusebius, including Dio's notices of the leader Artemion, 240,000 gentile deaths, and the subsequent banning of Jews from the island. C. Merivale, stressing the proximity of Cyprus to Antioch, conjectured that the island was the arsenal and rallying

[29] J. F. HEALY, 'The Cyrene Half-Shekel', JSS ii (1956), 377–9 (one half-shekel found near a tomb to the north of Cyrene, by the road to Apollonia), registered by LÜDERITZ, Cyrenaika, no. 27; THOMPSON, Memphis, 270 (two coins). Revolt coins have also been found in Cyprus and Dura Europus (PRICE, Jerusalem, 242, suggesting that these and other finds may indicate commerce, or the travels of Roman soldiers).

[30] For χαλεπός and a cognate in the vocabulary of stasis see Thucydides, iii 82, 5 and Plato, Laws, 629; in this debasing Sitz im Leben it could be used with pride as well as criticism, and overtones of pride in Greek ruthlessness can perhaps be detected in the phrase in the Acts of Hermaiscus.

point of the whole revolt.[31] Repression in Cyprus and its region may perhaps be reflected not only in the inscription noted above, but also in the rabbinic tradition that 'Trajan slew Pappus and Lulianus his brother at Laodicaea' on the Syrian coast.[32] In any case, in Cyprus too urban faction, leading to the Jewish overthrow of Salamis, may well have raged in advance of the eastern uprising. This order of events would still allow the revolts in the west as well as the east to be understood as having some connection with Trajan's eastern expedition.

When Eusebius as well as Dio is given weight, therefore, the sources suggest two formative circumstances in the origins of the revolt. First, it swelled into war at the time when Trajan and his forces were committed in the east against the Parthians; the rebels will have taken advantage of this period of weakness, and are not unlikely to have viewed the Parthians as potential deliverers (see below). Comparably, Josephus takes it that the German revolt in 68–9 will have been encouraged especially by the opportune moment (καιρός) of Roman instability after the year of four emperors (*B. J.* vii 78). Secondly, however, the Jewish revolt developed from deep-rooted factional strife against gentiles, operative in the countryside as well as the city, as emerges especially from the Egypt-oriented source reproduced by Eusebius, but is again confirmed by Dio. The anti-Roman as well as anti-Greek aspect of Jewish faction can be seen in Josephus' notices of Alexandria, Egypt and Cyrene at the beginning and end of the First Revolt, cited above.

The connection of the revolt with existing faction invites attention to the outlook which accompanied this long-standing Jewish unrest. In the years leading up to the revolt Jewish detestation of gentile and especially Roman oppression, and hopes for deliverance from it, were characteristically bound up with messianism. During this period there is great plainness of speech on the defeat of Rome in the messianic prophecies of II Baruch, II Esdras and the Fifth Sibylline book, and a comparably anti-Roman Christian attitude appears in the Epistle of Barnabas, probably from Egypt, as well as in the Christian adoption of the Jewish messianic prophecies just mentioned.[33]

---

[31] MERIVALE, History of the Romans under the Empire, viii, 166–7.

[32] Sifra, Emor, pereq ix 5, on Lev. xxii 32, in early MSS. (see for example the facsimile edition by L. FINKELSTEIN, Sifra or Torat Kohanim according to Codex Assemani lxvi (New York, 5717–1956), 442), discussed with Eccl. R. iii 17 and other parallels by ALON, The Jews in their Land, 421–2; that Laodicaea would fit the route of Trajan's return from the east is noted by M. D. HERR, 'Did Galilee take part in the War of Quietus or the Revolt of Ben-Cosebah?', reprinted from Cathedra iv (1977) in ROKEAH, Rebellions, 191–7 (194).

[33] See II Baruch xl (last leader of fourth kingdom executed by messiah on mount Zion; compare the slaying by the Prince of the Congregation, the Branch of David, in the Qumran Rule of War fragment, 4Q 285); II Esdras xi 45, xii 34 (messiah rebukes eagle, executes kings, and saves inhabitants of holy land); Sib. v 403–33 (blessed man burns cities of evil-doers and rebuilds temple); and Barn. iv 3 (the Beloved displaces the Fourth Kingdom), xii 9 (the Son of God will tear up Amalek by the roots at the end), and xvi 4 (Jews acting with Roman sanction are 'servants of the enemy'), discussed by the present writer, 'Jewish-Christian Relations in

Three conclusions reached so far may now be set out as follows.

(*a*) A review of chronology, in the light of Barnes' proposal, has suggested that 115 should be preferred to 116 as the year of the outbreak of revolt. The longer duration seems better suited to the outline of events discernible in Eusebius, who used a source with good knowledge of Egypt, and it remains consistent with information from Dio and other sources.

(*b*) Eusebius' two accounts draw attention to the escalation of the revolt from factional strife with a long prehistory, carried on in the countryside as well as the city. Four localities named by Eusebius – Alexandria, Egypt, the Thebaid and Cyrenaica – had been affected forty to fifty years before by 'the madness of the Sicarii', according to Josephus. In Cyrenaica and Alexandria, and perhaps also in Cyprus, *stasis* in 115 probably antedated the rising in Mesopotamia, although Trajan's Parthian war will still have been a vital factor in encouraging the western insurrections.

(*c*) The outlook which accompanied this long-standing factional strife in the years after the destruction of Jerusalem is likely to have been messianic, for anti-Roman feeling is closely bound up with messianism in prophetic works of this period.

II. Messianism

Yet, can a messianic element properly be identified in the revolt under Trajan? The roots of the revolt in long-standing unrest might lead one to suspect it, despite the silence of the sources, when this unrest is viewed together with the clearer though still disputed significance of messianism in the Judaean revolts which broke out under Nero and Hadrian;[34] the ethos of the First Revolt was influential in Alexandria, Egypt and Cyrene, as just noted, and the uprising of

---

Barnabas and Justin Martyr', in J. D. G. DUNN (ed.), Jews and Christians (Tübingen, 1992), 315–45 (333–4). R. S. MACLENNAN, Early Christian Texts on Jews and Judaism (Atlanta, 1990), sets Barnabas during the revolt itself, but an earlier date, under Nerva, is preferable; see J. N. B. CARLETON PAGET, The Epistle of Barnabas: Outlook and Background (Tübingen, 1994), 9–30. The hostility to Rome implicit in Alexandrian Christian adoption of the Jewish Sibylline books is stressed by R. VAN DEN BROEK, 'Juden und Christen in Alexandrien im 2. und 3. Jahrhundert', in J. VAN AMERSFOORT & J. VAN OORT (edd.), Juden und Christen in der Antike (Kampen, 1990), 101–115.

[34] On the importance of religious as well as political and social motivation in the First Revolt see W. WEBER, Josephus und Vespasian (Stuttgart, 1921), v, 31–40; M. HENGEL, 'Zeloten und Sikarier', in O. BETZ, K. HAACKER & M. HENGEL (edd.), Josephus-Studien: Festschrift für Otto Michel (Tübingen, 1974), 175–96 (181–2). A distinction between insurrectionists, using messianic concepts simply to aid their power struggle in the style of argument described by Thucydides on faction, and believers who held that the messianic events were in train, is drawn by PRICE, Jerusalem, 15–17, 25–7; one should perhaps allow for a considerable range between these two sharply opposed types, in view of the pervasive influence of the ancestral hopes.

Jonathan the weaver was in form closely similar to those led in Judaea, before the outbreak of revolt in 66, by prophetic commanders like Theudas and 'the Egyptian'.[35] The latter name might hint uncertainly at the contemporary importance of messianism in Egypt too, but that is more surely attested by the messianic victory depicted in Philo, *Praem.*, 95 on the basis of Num. xxiv 7 LXX.

Thus in the First Revolt against Rome the coinage displayed the slogans g^{e}'ullah and *ḥerut*, 'redemption' and 'liberation' (the latter occurs on the Cyrene half-shekel). These evoke the biblical hope for deliverance on the pattern of the exodus, a hope which is linked with specifically messianic expectation in the Pentateuch in the oracles of Balaam, uttered during the march to the promised land, and in the prophets, for example at Isa. xi 10–16; this link makes Moses and Joshua into types of the messiah, as appears from the miracles at the Jordan and the walls of Jerusalem expected with Theudas and the Egyptian, respectively, and it contributes to the Qumran expectation of a prince 'over the congregation', like Joshua in Num. xxvii 16–17.[36] Against this background the coin-legends are interpreted by the Seventh and Tenth benedictions of the Amidah ('Look on our affliction and plead our cause and redeem us (g^{e}'alenu) ...'; 'Blow the great horn for our liberation (*ḥerut*) ...'), and by the Passover thanksgiving for the exodus (Mishnah, Pesahim x 5), in which both nouns used on the coins occur.[37] Comparably, the defenders of Jerusalem were encouraged by the specifically messianic hopes for a Jewish world-ruler (Josephus, *B.J.* vi 312–3). Similarly again, in the revolt of Bar Kokhba the slogans of the First Revolt coinage reappear on coins and in documents, and rabbinic texts show that he was widely viewed as a messianic figure (Talmud Yerushalmi, Ta'anith iv 8, 68d; Talmud Babli, Sanhedrin 93b).

---

35 See Josephus, Ant. xx 97–9, 169–72; with the name 'the Egyptian' compare the Greek (transliterated Aramaic) surname Mesraia, 'the Egyptian', attested in a Murabba'at document ('Ιωσήπ Μεσραιᾶ in P. Benoit, J.T. Milik & R. de Vaux, Les grottes de Murabba'at (DJD ii, Oxford, 1961), p. 218, no. 90a, line 6); the use of ὁ Αἰγύπτιος on its own in Josephus and Acts xxi 38 might suggest that in this case the regional indication of the adjective was still strong, and that it had not become simply a surname.

36 The description of Moses and Joshua as 'two prophets', 'pure generals' (προφῆται δύο, καθαροὶ στατηγοί) in Clement of Alexandria, Eclogae Propheticae vi 1–2 recalls the prophetic commanders Theudas and the Egyptian, and perhaps reflects earlier Jewish as well as contemporary Christian piety in Egypt; for purity in the messianic king compare Ps. Sol. xvii 41 καὶ αὐτὸς καθαρὸς ἀπὸ ἁμαρτίας, and Sib. iii 49 ἁγνὸς ἄναξ, cited above. The influence of Num. xxvii 16–17 is also important at Mark vi 34, in a scene which in the Johannine parallel leads to identification of Jesus as prophet and king (John vi 14–15).

37 This thanksgiving is brought into connection with the coins by M. Hengel, Die Zeloten (Leiden, 1961), 124 & n. 6; E.T. (Edinburgh, 1989), 119–20, n. 234; he notes that it is among the texts which suggest the implausibility of attributing a 'political' and 'eschatological' sense to the two nouns, respectively. (The Tenth Benediction of the Amidah, quoted in the text above, points in the same direction.) Price, Jerusalem, 113 follows this debatable distinction between the nouns.

With regard to both Judaean revolts, however, the importance of messianism is widely debated, despite these relatively clear indications of its presence.[38] In some of this questioning perhaps too little is made of the political and this-worldly aspect of messianism, to be further illustrated below. In any case, even such indications as the Judaean revolts provide are lacking for the revolt under Trajan. Signs of a messianic element have indeed been discerned in the apparently sudden outbreak of this revolt,[39] and the encouragement which it probably gained from the Antiochene earthquake;[40] its tenacity, its devastation of land[41] and destruction of buildings[42] (which might suggest that the Jews left Cyrene with no intention of coming back again),[43] its damage to shrines, and its ruthless repression by the Romans; in the description of Lucuas as 'king' in Eusebius, which recalls the 'kings' of rebel bands in Herodian Judaea (Josephus, *Ant.* xvii 285); and in the possibility that the Cyrenian march into Egypt and the operations near Pelusium, and perhaps also in Cyprus, were intended to prepare for a return from exile into Judaea.[44]

Yet all these signs are ambiguous. The explosive outbreak was preceded by a long history of resentment and civil strife, during which the First Revolt in Judaea and its repression had contributed to Alexandrian, Egyptian and Cyrenian disturbances; the slave-revolts of Sicily and southern Italy, which comparably could draw on part only of the population, were also comparably tena-

---

38 See for example, on the First Revolt, PRICE, Jerusalem, 15–17, 25–7; on the Second, L. MILDENBERG, The Coinage of the Bar Kokhba War (Aarau, Frankfurt a.M. & Salzburg, 1984), 44–5, 73–6, 90–91, 102.

39 The case is put cautiously but strongly by HENGEL, 'Hoffnung', 665–8.

40 This would apply whether the earthquake occurred in December 115 or in the preceding January. It has been conjectured that it was the signal for the outbreak of revolt (as by MERIVALE, History, viii, 166–8), but if the revolt was already in progress it would still fit among the generally accepted portents of war, for Jews especially messianic war; see II Esdras ix 3 'motio locorum, populorum turbatio', possibly influenced by Hag. ii 6–7 'Yet a little while, and I will shake the heavens and the earth, ... and I will shake all nations', which is understood as a prophecy of redemption at Sanh. 97b (R. Nathan, ascribing the interpretation to R. Akiba), Exod. R. xviii.12, on xii 42, Deut. R. i 23, on ii 31 and (with a special Christian interpretation) Heb. xii 26–7.

41 'Plundering the chora of Egypt καὶ τοὺς ἐν αὐτῇ νομούς φθείροντες, Eusebius, Ecclesiastical History, iv 2, 3; 'Hadrian sent colonies to Libya, which had been laid waste (vastata) by the Jews', Eusebius, Chronicle, Hadrian v (HELM, p. 198[g]), quoted above. Orosius vii 12, 6, on war per totam Libyam, which interfectis cultoribus desolata est to such a degree that it would have remained depopulated had Hadrian not recolonized, is sometimes quoted as a testimony to the total devastation of Libya (e.g. by APPLEBAUM, Cyrene, 270, 291; BARNES, 'Trajan', 159), but it is simply a rhetorically heightened combination of Eusebius' Chronicle, Trajan xvii (first sentence, translated in the text above), on the Jews in Libya fighting against their fellow-inhabitants, with this later annal (Hadrian v).

42 For Cyrenaic inscriptions noting rebuilding after destruction and burning *tumultu iudaico* in Cyrene see LÜDERITZ, Cyrenaika, especially nos. 17–18 (Caesareum), 21 (temple of Hecate) , 23 (baths cum porticibus et sphaeristeris), 24–5 (port road to Apollonia).

43 FUKS, 'Aspects', 104; APPLEBAUM, Cyrene, 335.

44 APPLEBAUM, Cyrene, 260, 318, 335–7, 339–40, endorsed by HENGEL, 'Hoffnung', 660.

cious, and also produced 'kings';[45] devastation of fields was a regular act of aggressive war, the destruction of buildings was involved in street fighting, and it seems probable in any case, as noted above, that many Jews remained in Cyrene during the revolt. The part played by opposition to idolatry in the destruction of shrines is not always clear (Appian held that the Nemeseion was demolished for the needs of the war); probably there was some patriotically Jewish iconoclasm and destruction in the revolt, but this need not of itself point to messianism. Roman repression of a genocidal character was not unknown in cases of revolt;[46] Lucuas is one of three leaders who are named, as noted above, and to that extent is less clearly a candidate for messianic king than has sometimes been assumed, although leadership by more than one commander is in fact compatible with messianic hope (see below); and the rebel operations may be over-interpreted when they are taken to suggest a concerted return to Zion. (A. Fuks left a question-mark at this point, even though he seemed to expect the answer Yes.[47]) G. Alon noted, as pointing away from messianic interpretation, the silence of Dio on this aspect;[48] but this silence too is ambiguous, for Dio describes the Bar Kokhba revolt in some detail without any mention at all of a Jewish leader, and even Eusebius, who comments on Bar Kokhba's nickname 'star', does not specify that he was regarded as a messianic figure.

Despite these ambiguities in the sources, it remains likely that messianism played a part in the revolt under Trajan, as is suggested by comparison with the two Judaean revolts and by the background of earlier unrest in Egypt. Some characteristics of messianism itself at this period point towards this conclusion. First, it was based on common traditions, not esoteric texts. The hope for return from exile was scripturally founded and central in Jewish prayer, as can be seen in the Seventh and Tenth Benedictions quoted above, and in their antecedents such as the prayers of Ps. cvi 47, Eccles. xxxvi 11 and II Macc. i 27; Moses was held to have prescribed thanksgiving for the exodus in daily morning and evening prayer (Josephus, *Ant.* iv 212, no doubt a reference to the Shema, with thanksgiving corresponding to the accompanying benediction Ge'ullah). The integration of this hope with specifically messianic expectation, as in Ps. Sol. xvii 21–46 and the Amidah, is also biblically grounded, as noted above, in

---

45 On the slave rebellions (139 or 135–132, 104–99, and, in southern Italy under Spartacus, 73–71) see M.I. FINLEY, Ancient Sicily (London, 1979), 137–47. In the first of these the Syrian leader Eunus became 'king Antiochus', with a court on the Seleucid model, and, as with the Jewish revolts, there was a religious element of debated importance; contrast FINLEY, 142 (on the primacy of political features) with W. Speyer, 'Religiöse Betrüger', reprinted in id., Frühes Christentum im antiken Strahlungsfeld (Tübingen, 1989), 440–62 (449–50).

46 The Roman opinion in favour of severity towards rebels is documented, with examples of extirpation in Gaul and Germany, by BRUNT, Themes, 314–6.

47 FUKS, 'Aspects', 104.

48 ALON, The Jews in their Land, 427–8.

Balaam's oracles and the prophetic connection of the return from exile and captivity with the reign of a coming Davidic king (e.g. Isa. xi 10–16, Jer. xxiii 5–8, Ezek. xxxvii 19–28, Amos ix 11–15). These politically significant hopes were a universally familiar part of the ancestral tradition; their influence can be expected irrespective of evidence for the circulation of particular post-biblical prophecies and apocalypses, and their currency is confirmed by.their prominence in ancient biblical translations used in the diaspora, notably the Septuagint. They are similarly prominent in a New Testament work based on diaspora as well as Judaean traditions, Luke-Acts, where Moses is a 'redeemer' (λυτρωτής, Acts vii 35) and Jews await 'the redemption of Jerusalem' (Luke ii 38, compare the coin-legend 'of the redemption of Zion' from the First Revolt).[49]

Secondly, the importance of these hopes among Jews in the period leading up to the revolt is in fact further confirmed by contemporary anti-Roman messianic prophecies, as noted already. Applebaum drew attention especially to II Esdras, II Baruch, the Sibyl and the War Scroll in his interpretation of the western revolts as movements in which social discontent coalesced with a Zealotic messianism, and the *Jubilar* expounded the messianism of the revolts through sources of particular relevance to the western diaspora, the Fifth Sibylline book together with an authoritative work of undoubtedly general influence, the Septuagint rendering of Balaam's oracles in Num. xxiv.[50]

Thirdly, building on this foundation, a little more can be said on the political aspect of messianism, with special reference to the diaspora. The biblical interpretation current in this period attests specifically region-related messianic hopes. Their connection with the eastern and western diaspora in Mesopotamia and Egypt should be reckoned with in reconstruction of the background of the revolt.

'Assyria and Egypt' begin the list of diaspora communities in Isa. xi 11, cited above, and hold the stage elsewhere (Isa. xxvii 13, Hos. xi 11, Zech. x 8–12). The Jews in 'Assyria', beyond the Euphrates, were thought to include the multitudinous Ten Tribes who would return at the last (Josephus, *B.J.* i 5, *Ant.* xi 133; II Esdras xiii 45–6), and under the Flavians this region was imagined as the refuge of Nero (Sib. v 137–49), whose second advent could mingle with expectations of the advance of 'kings from the east' against Rome (Sib. iv 138–9, Rev. xvi 12, cf. I Enoch lvi 5–6). This advance was envisaged at the time of the messiah and the ingathering, with respect either to Judaea (Micah v 4, as interpreted in the name of Simeon b. Yohai in Lam. R. i 13; cf. I Enoch lvi 5–lvii 3) or Egypt (Isa. xix 19–23, LXX and Targum). In the latter case blessing would come upon the Jews of both Assyria and Egypt, according to Isa.

[49] See also Luke ix 31 (discussed below), xix 27 (compare II Baruch xl and other texts cited in n.33, above), xxi 28, and xxiv 21, in the light of Acts i 6.

[50] Applebaum, Cyrene, 251–6, 336–7; Hengel, 'Hoffnung', 665, 668–83.

xix 25 as interpreted in LXX, Peshitta and Targum. Complementarily, a Roman advance against Parthia could initiate the last battle foreseen by the Mesopotamian seer Balaam (LXX Num. xxiii 7), when the 'Kittim' would afflict Assyria and the Hebrews, but themselves would perish (LXX Num. xxiv 24, where the 'ships' are 'legions' in the Peshitta, and the 'Kittim' are Romans in Targum Onkelos).[51] The oracle of Elchasai, predicting the outbreak of war among the angels of impiety in the north three years after Trajan had subdued the Parthians, suggests the significance of these interpretations of prophecy during Trajan's eastern campaign.[52] In this connection non-Jewish speculation on the Roman destiny overlapped with Jewish hopes; Rome's doom was feared from the east, and victory there would be the great confirmation of her divine mission to rule.[53]

Egypt and its Jewish population became comparably important in prophetic interpretation, as has already begun to emerge. In the 'vision of Egypt' in the Septuagint of Isaiah the prayer of Egyptian Jews will be answered by the sending of a deliverer, 'a man who shall save them' (Isa. xix 20 LXX); the solemn ἄνθρωπος here in the Greek (not needed to render the Hebrew) serves to link this saviour with the messianic 'man' of Num. xxiv 7 and 17, LXX.[54] This prophecy of deliverance was linked with the Leontopolis temple service (Josephus, *Ant.* xiii 68) – a point which may ultimately have contributed to the temple's closure, mentioned above. Earlier in Isaiah, in the prophecy of return in xi 11–16 cited already, a highway will be made not, as in the Hebrew text, for the Assyrian Jews, but for 'my people left in Egypt' – a 'thoroughfare' (δίοδος) across the Delta and the 'Egyptian sea', which could help to inspire such visions as are postulated for the rebels in Egypt.[55] The hostile face of Egyptian Jewish hopes appears in the updating of place-names in biblical woes against Egypt, which in the Septuagint threaten Tanis and Memphis (Isa. xix 13), Tanis, Diospolis (Thebes), Sais, Memphis, Syene, Heliopolis, Bubastis, and Taphnas (Daphnae) (Ezek. xxx 13–18). A comparable list in Sib. v 86–8 ends with Alexandria, which in the Targum to the Prophets gains a suitably ill-omened

---

[51] The importance of this verse is shown by HENGEL, 'Hoffnung', 669, n. 54.

[52] His revelation, received in Parthia according to its early third-century advocate Alcibiades (see Hippolytus, Ref. ix 13 and 16), was linked with the revolt by W. H. C. FREND, Martyrdom and Persecution in the Early Church (Oxford, 1965), 223.

[53] For example Horace, Epod. xvi 1–14 and Virgil, Geo. i 509, iv 560–2; on the overlap with Jewish prophecy, WEBER, Josephus und Vespasian, 34–40 and IDEM, Der Prophet und sein Gott (Leipzig, 1925), 55–60, 76–80, developed in connection with the Trajanic revolt by J. GUTMANN, 'Milḥ^{a}môt hayy^{e}hûdîm bîmê Traianus', reprinted from *Sepher Assaf* (1953) in ROKEAH, Rebellions, 33–68 (37–47); HENGEL, 'Hoffnung', 668–74.

[54] Occurrences of ἄνθρωπος in a messianic sense are discussed by the present writer, 'The Messianic Associations of "the Son of Man"', *JTS* N. S. xxxvi (1985), 34–55 (48–52).

[55] The reflection in these two passages of special Egyptian Jewish applications of the hope for national deliverance is noted by I. L. SEELIGMANN, The Septuagint Version of Isaiah (Leiden, 1948), 116–7.

position by identification as No (Targ. Jer. xlvi 25, Ezek. xxx 13–14, Nah. iii 8). These identifications make a threateningly detailed application of the general doom on Egypt (Joel iii 19, Zech. x 11), which – in the case of this as of other gentile nations – could take the imagined form of defeat by the Jews in the war of the last days (Test. Sim. vi 4, 1QM ii 13–14). The Kittim who sail to Egypt in Daniel (xi 30) are 'Romans' in the Old Greek,[56] as in Targum Onkelos on Num. xxiv, cited above; and the same identification is probably assumed in the War Scroll, where the children of light, after their first victory, march on the Kittim in Egypt (1QM i 4). Somewhat comparably, according to Sib. iii 46–60, when Rome reigns over Egypt, the kingdom of the immortal king will appear, a holy lord will rule the world for ever, and Rome will be devastated.

The fate of the diaspora communities was therefore the subject of a complex of biblical interpretation, attested especially but not only in the Septuagint, and correspondingly familiar and influential. Calamities for the Jews dispersed to east and west were viewed as the preliminaries to their return under messianic guidance. The Egyptian diaspora cherished special hopes. Trajan's Parthian war, and Jewish conflict in the west with Greeks and Egyptians as well as Romans, would have fitted readily into this topographically elaborated pattern of expectations.

To move from these expectations back to the Trajanic revolt, this profile of messianism implies that an uprising which will have had its own political and social motivation would nevertheless have been set by Jews within the frame of national hopes for messianic redemption, and that participants would have been pervasively affected by these hopes; indeed, messianism has an important political aspect, exemplified in many of the passages noted above. In a partly comparable way, the Egyptian resistance to the Jews in the *chora*, a fully practical military operation, would have been interpreted by Egyptians against the background of Egyptian anti-Jewish prophecy.[57] Recognition of messianic characteristics in a revolt does not therefore necessarily imply that it must have been an otherwise inexplicable outbreak.

The fanatical violence of the Trajanic revolt was accompanied by a great measure of Jewish military success. Barnes rightly stressed this point, but it has also been fully recognized in interpretations of the revolt as a messianic war.[58] The 'terrible spirit of faction' among the Jews of Cyrene, Egypt and Cyprus will have had, as its positive side, not only the experience and tradition of conflict, but also something of the zeal and solidarity associated with the exodus pattern

---

56 P.M. BOGAERT, 'Relecture et refonte historicisante du livre de Daniel attestées par la première version grecque (Papyrus 967)', in KUNTZMANN & SCHLOSSER, Études, 197–224 (216–7). This text in xi 30 survives in the Chigi MS. of Daniel according to the LXX, followed in the hand-editions of H. B. SWETE and A. RAHLFS.

57 FRANKFURTER, 'Egypt's City'.

58 BARNES, 'Trajan', 161; compare APPLEBAUM, Cyrene, 341; HENGEL, 'HOFFNUNG', 661–3.

just considered; 'they set up the divine law with one consent, that the saints should share alike in good things and in dangers' (Wisd. xviii 9). The insurgents went far to justify the view, which Philo suggests would have worried the legate of Syria under Gaius, that a combination of Jewish diaspora forces would be an 'unbeatable thing', ἄμαχόν τι ... χρῆμα (see Philo, *Leg. ad Gaium* 214–7). The co-ordination of Cyrenaican and Egyptian Jewish forces is clear, their co-operation with Cyprus seems likely especially in view of their naval operations, and at least friendly contact with the Jews of Judaea and Mesopotamia is probable. Yet the immediate diaspora settings of the uprisings will throughout have been of prime importance in any concerted planning there may have been.

This is one of the considerations which make identification of a common strategic aim so speculative. Barnes' proposed aim, the saving of Babylonian Jewry by making it impossible for Trajan's conquests to be retained, seems open to question for other reasons.[59] Thus it has been asked whether Hadrian's withdrawal from the east was really necessitated by the situation, or whether it was not rather a manifestation of his policy of rejecting imperial expansion, by deliberate contrast with Trajan.[60] Irrespective of this point, it is not so clear that the western insurgents would have fought specifically for the sake of the easterners. It seems more likely that the Jews of Cyrene, Egypt and Cyprus would have felt for Judaea and the ruins of Jerusalem, 'most holy to them as it is', in a phrase of the Alexandrian Appian which sounds almost like an echo of 'Jerusalem the holy' on the Jewish revolt coinage (Appian, *Syr.* 1252, cf. *Mithr.* cvi 498). This is strongly suggested by the centrality of Jerusalem in the hope for national redemption considered above. Accordingly, the hope of regaining Judaea would certainly have come into view among the rebels. It is difficult, as Fuks' question-mark implies, to go beyond this point. To the present writer, however, it seems probable that at least the combined Cyrenian and Egyptian forces aimed ultimately at Judaea. This view is favoured by the overlap between the instinctive desire for return illustrated by messianic texts, and the strategic consideration of the defensibility of those southern areas of Judaea which held out at the end of the First Revolt, and were soon to be central in the Second.

Consideration of messianism has shown that strategic considerations such as these were scarcely separable, in public opinion, from hopes for the return of the diaspora under the guidance of a messianic deliverer. Jewish victories in the revolts will already have brought Andreas, Lucuas and Artemion into the aura of these expectations. 'As the seditious lighted upon any of their fellows to head them, he became a king', says Josephus, wearily but not without verisimilitude, speaking of Simon the royal slave, Athrongaeus and other rebel leaders in Judaea after the accession of Archelaus (*Ant.* xvii 285, cited above). The three

---

59 See Barnes, 'Trajan', 161–2.
60 Brunt, Themes, 473–4.

named leaders of the western revolts are likely to have emerged in this way, but the exodus tradition offered more positively presented models for the choices described dismissively by Josephus; so, in Philo's amplified paraphrase of Exod. xxxii 2–9, the Levites are looking for a leader, take Moses for their general, and wipe out the backsliders with a ruthlessness redolent of zeal and revolution (*Mos.* ii 273). The revolt leaders could then hardly have escaped contact with messianic glory. This lustre could extend over more than one; Moses or Elijah, with king messiah, will lead different bodies of exiles back to the land at the end of days (Fragment Targum on Exod. xii 42; Targum Ps.-Jonathan on Deut. xxx 4).[61]

The revolt will then have had a messianic element from the beginning. Jewish insurgents will have been affected by a widespread messianism, which had the strongly diaspora-oriented political aspect noted above. Yet there is also a sense in which the revolt itself will have been taken up into messianism as a whole, as its progress converged more and more with the familiar expectations of the hope for messianic redemption. The questions initially posed on the beginnings of the revolt can then be answered summarily as follows. (*a*) 115 should be preferred to 116 as the year of the outbreak, as argued above. (*b*) The revolt was influenced by messianism from the start, and this influence will have increased with its success; at the same time messianism will have helped to sustain resistance over the relatively long duration, 115–117. Now it is an honour to offer the *Jubilar* this garland from a field which is peculiarly his own; *laurea donandus Apollinari*, he adds to his great learning the imaginative and inspiring insight of the *vates*.

Bibliography

G. Alon, The Jews in their Land in the Talmudic Age (translated and edited by G. Levi, Jerusalem, 1980, 1984; repr. (one vol.), Cambridge, Mass. & London, 1989).

S. Applebaum, Jews and Greeks in Ancient Cyrene (Leiden, 1979).

T. D. Barnes, 'Trajan and the Jews', JJS xl (1989), 145–62.

P. A. Brunt, Roman Imperial Themes (Oxford, 1990).

CPJ = Tcherikover & Fuks, Corpus (see below).

D. Frankfurter, 'Lest Egypt's City be Deserted: Religion and Ideology in the Egyptian Response to the Jewish Revolt (116–117 C. E.)', JJS xliii (1992), 203–220.

A. Fuks, 'Aspects of the Jewish Revolt in A. D. 115–117', JRS li (1961), 98–104.

L. L. Grabbe, Judaism from Cyrus to Hadrian (Minneapolis, 1992, reprinted London, 1994).

---

61 Compare the Lucan narrative of the Transfiguration, in which Moses and Elijah talk of an 'exodus' of Jesus (ix 31), in the context of the redemption passages in Luke-Acts mentioned in n. 49, above. The eastern tribes are led back by the three patriarchs and the twelve minor prophets in '5 Ezra' (II Esdras i 38–9).

M. HENGEL, 'Messianische Hoffnung und politischer "Radikalismus" in der "jüdisch-hellenistischen Diaspora"', in: D. HELLHOLM (ed.), Apocalypticism in theMediterranean World and the Near East (Tübingen, 1983), 655–86.

F. A. LEPPER, Trajan's Parthian War (London, 1948).

R. LOEWE, 'A Jewish Counterpart to the Acts of the Alexandrians', JJS xii (1961), 105–22.

G. LÜDERITZ, Corpus jüdischer Zeugnisse aus der Cyrenaika, mit einem Anhang von-Joyce M. Reynolds (Wiesbaden, 1983).

J. MÉLÈZE-MODRZEJEWSKI, Les juifs d'Égypte de Ramsès II à Hadrien (Paris, 1991).

L. MOTTA, 'La tradizione sulla rivolta ebraica al tempo di Traiano', Aegyptus xxxii (1951), 474–90.

J. J. PRICE, Jerusalem under Siege (Leiden, 1992).

M. PUCCI, La rivolta ebraica al tempo di Traiano (Pisa, 1981).

–, 'Qualche osservazione sulla tradizione letteraria della rivolta ebraica al tempodi Traiano (115–117 d. C.)', RSA ix (1979), 61–7.

D. ROKEAH (ed.), Jewish Rebellions in the Time of Trajan (in Hebrew: Jerusalem, 1978).

E. SCHÜRER, Geschichte des jüdischen Volkes im Zeitalter Jesu Christi (3rd–4th ed., 3 vols., Leipzig, 1901–9, reprinted Hildesheim, 1964); E. T. revised by G. Vermes, F. Millar, M. Black, M. Goodman & P. Vermes (3 vols in 4 parts,Edinburgh, 1973, 1979, 1986, 1987).

J. SCHWARTZ, 'La communauté d'Edfou (Haute-Égypte) jusqu'à la fin du règne de Trajan. Réflexions sur les juifs dans le plat-pays égyptien', in: R. KUNTZMANN & J. SCHLOSSER (edd.), Études sur le judaïsme hellénistique (Paris, 1984), 61–70.

E. M. SMALLWOOD, The Jews under Roman Rule (2nd ed., Leiden, 1981).

G. STEMBERGER, Die römische Herrschaft im Urteil der Juden (Darmstadt, 1983).

M. STERN, Greek and Latin Authors on Jews and Judaism (3 vols, Jerusalem, 1974, 1980, 1984).

V. TCHERIKOVER & A. FUKS, ed., Corpus Papyrorum Judaicarum (3 vols., Cambridge, Mass., 1957, 1960, 1964).

DOROTHY J. THOMPSON, Memphis under the Ptolemies (Princeton, 1988).

Benefactors in the Greco-Jewish Diaspora[1]

by

Tessa Rajak

While Martin Hengel's name will always be linked with Hellenism in Palestine, he has shed light too on the Jewish Diaspora, with his fundamental studies of the Stobi inscription, of the terms for 'synagogue', and, not least, of Paul. This paper touches directly on the first topic; moreover, encompassing as it does ancient expressions of gratitude and praise, it may perhaps seem an appropriate vehicle for the expression of a personal appreciation for a great scholar.

Philo opens his book *On the Decalogue* by asking why Moses gave the laws in the desert rather than in a polis. The answer is concerned with the evils of city-life. "In cities there arises that most insidious of foes, pride (τῦφος), and some people admire it and bow down to empty appearances of distinction and make it important by means of golden crowns and purple robes." He declares that "pride is the creator of many other evils: boastfulness, haughtiness, inequality;[2] and these are the sources of war, both foreign and civil". He also makes the fundamental claim that "pride brings divine things into contempt, although these ought to receive the highest honour (τιμή)" *(de Decal.*1,4–7).

Josephus writes in similar vein in *Against Apion*, belittling the award of crowns and public announcements of honours: "for those who live by our laws, the reward is not silver or gold or a crown of olive or of parsley or any such proclamation." (*CA* II,217–8). The allusion is surely not just to the time-honoured way of treating victors in the Olympic and other great games of Greece, as Thackeray's note suggests[3], but rather to the modes of recognition of the powerful and the munificent in the Greek civic milieu of Josephus' own day and age. The writer is making an ideological point, sharpening a distinction

---

[1] For the data-base and breakdowns on which this paper is based and for other help, I am much indebted to Dr David Noy. Joyce Reynolds was a kind and generous adviser on the material from Berenice. A paper on this subject was read at a conference on the Jewish Diaspora held in the Rosenberg School of Jewish Studies, Tel-Aviv University, in January 1991, and I thank the organizers, Professors B. Isaac and A. Oppenheimer, and also the other participants, for a most congenial forum in which to discuss these ideas.

[2] Or perhaps "impiety", depending on the manuscript reading adopted (Colson prefers ἀνισότητος as in R, to ἀνοσιότητος: see Loeb Philo VII, n.ad.loc.).

[3] Loeb Josephus, I, n.ad.loc.

between Jews and pagans to establish an ethical contrast between two world views. He would not have needed, in this moralizing context, to take account of an awkward case like that of a man from Leontopolis in Egypt, perhaps a near contemporary of the historian. This was the most blessed Abraham, Ἄβραμος ὁ μακαριότατος, who was "not without honour" (ἀγέραστος) in his city but, in the interesting metaphor of his verse epitaph, "wore the wreath of magistracy for the whole people, in his wisdom."[4]

Once more in *Against Apion*, Josephus reminds readers that Jews, unlike Greeks, do not believe in making statues of those they like or admire (*CA* II,74). Here, of course, the second commandment is at least as much a consideration as distrust of honours. And finally, at yet another point in that work, in a discussion of death, it is asserted by Josephus that "the Jewish law does not allow for expensive funerals or the erection of conspicuous monuments." (*CA* II,205). This is another way in which the display values of the late Greek polis are undercut, at least in theory. In fact, we may be inclined to think that the tombs of the high priests in Jerusalem, still visible in the Kidron valley, told another story; but it might then be suggested that, in Jerusalem, Jewish self-differentiation from Greco-Roman values was less necessary. In any case, we need not be wholly surprised to find practice diverging from principle.

Visible abstention from social competition and from its various manifestations was a way of marking out a community from its civic environment and binding it together. This at least partly explains the stress laid upon such ideas by another diaspora Jew, Paul of Tarsus, as he sought to define a place in society for the developing Christian church.[5] The Epistle to the Romans (12.3) offers, appropriately enough, a particularly clear statement: "I say to everyone among you: do not be conceited or think too highly of yourself; but think your way to a sober estimate based on the measure of faith that God has dealt to each of you. For just as in a single human body there are many limbs and organs, all with different functions, so all of us, united with Christ, form one body."

It is instructive, and also ironic, to note that these critiques are expressed in terms indebted to Greek culture itself, even if they are fuelled, ultimately, by a biblical sense of justice. For there is a familiar *topos* favoured by writers of Stoic inclination – though not necessarily of modest lifestyle – which bears a clear resemblance to our theme, especially as Josephus expresses it. Plutarch, a near-contemporary, has this *topos* on occasion. But particularly with Dio Chrysostom, the second- century orator from Prusa, it is a characteristic stance to denounce the pursuit of public popularity. For him the absurdities of honours offer an excellent subject for satire or vituperation. So, Dio describes how cities "led their victims about with a sprig of green, as men lead cattle, or clapped

[4] CPJ III 1530A.

[5] I owe to Professor Halvor Moxnes the suggested connections between this strand in Paul's thought, and civic patronage, made in a paper given in Aarhus University, Denmark.

upon their heads a crown or a ribbon" (*Or.* 66,2). Some men might be equipped with any number of crowns: olive, oak, ivy, myrtle. Yet, he says, the cost of getting a purple mantle from the dyers is less than that of getting it by public award. No nanny-goat would hurl herself over a cliff for the sake of a sprig of wild olive, and no sane person would walk around with his head bound unless he had suffered a fracture (*Or.* 66,4–5). But with Dio, the whole issue is given a Stoic twist which is crucial to his philosophical position: to pursue δόξα, fame, is to be the victim of a passion like any other, and thus to be at the mercy of people and events and so unable to achieve true happiness.[6] This conclusion puts an entirely different complexion on the matter from that in Philo and Josephus.

The various practices from which the two major Jewish-Greek writers distance themselves are ones which, at any rate from the Hellenistic period, were deeply ingrained in the fabric of city life around the Greek world and in areas influenced by it. We need to define it more closely, if we are to understand the Jewish reaction.[7] The bestowal of lavish honours on those who had power, which might be manifested through office-holding, through personal connections, through family prominence, or, most often, through all three, and nearly always with the accompaniment of conspicuous wealth, was one of the most visible features in the life of a city. Those honours were the repayment for an expenditure of a large part of that wealth within the public domain, for supposed benefits, demonstratively conferred on the citizens. And they were a not-too-subtle statement to the donor that he had a reputation which could only be kept up by further benefaction.

So, those who were honoured were honoured not just for what they were or even for what they had achieved, but by way of trade-off for what they had done or given or were going to do or to give, for the enhancement of the city and for the advantage of its gods or its people. In a watered-down form, such phenomena are perfectly familiar today. But in the Greco-Roman world, they made up a tighter structure, with patterns that were more fixed, and they were also more crucial to the working of the cities and to social relations. Paul Veyne regards the unusual combination of apparently contradictory features, a sense of constraint on the one hand, and a measure of spontaneity, as the distinguishing

---

6 On these themes in the speeches of Dio Chrysostom, who still endorsed generosity to one's city, see C. P. JONES, The Roman World of Dio Chrysostom (Cambridge, 1978), 110ff.

7 For an excellent discussion of the system of benefaction in relation to synagogue construction, see L. MICHAEL WHITE, Building God's House in the Roman World: Architectural Adaptation among Pagans, Jews and Christians (Baltimore and London, 1990), chap. 4. M. LEWIS discusses male as well as female benefactors in a Roman context in: Money, Sex and Power. An Examination of the Role of Women as Patrons of the ancient Synagogues." In: P. J. HAAS ed., Recovering the Role of Women. Power and Authority in Rabbinic Jewish Society. South Florida Studies in the History of Judaism 95 (Atlanta 1992), 7–22. Cf. T. RAJAK and D. NOY, "*Archisynagogoi*: Office, Title and Social Status in the Greco-Jewish Synagogue", JRS 83 (1993), 75–93.

mark of Greco-Roman euergetism.[8] Public buildings and works, provisioning, politics and diplomacy, entertainment and festivals, religious life, medicine: all these a city was likely to owe to its benefactors, who were usually prominent citizens, but occasionally interested outsiders. The process was also, as Philo and Josephus well appreciated, an intrinsic part of the moral formation of the pagan elites: benefactors were praised in the highest terms, and the φιλανθρωπία or μεγαλοψυχία which were understood to have motivated their actions were deemed supreme virtues.

It is because the system was both distinctive and central that recent historians have labelled it, evolving the term "euergetism", from the Greek εὐεργέτης, a benefactor.[9] The manifestations of classical euergetism are familiar to us largely through an extensive and increasing epigraphic record.[10] Euergetism, indeed, went hand in hand with the "epigraphic habit", since, in the first place, it was advantageous to donors to put their donations on public record, while, from the other side, honours could be made meaningful by being perpetuated in stone by a grateful recipient community or its representatives. Thus the act of giving could best be made to serve not just the donor but his children and descendants, and the social standing of an entire family could be enhanced.

Honorific decrees are often framed in the most lavish of terms. Moreover, a city council's resolution that decrees should be inscribed on a stele in a prominent place is itself sometimes listed as one of the honours accorded to the honorand. It has been aptly pointed out that there is a careful reciprocation in the transactions, with honours being seen as due payment for services rendered. In fact, honours might well be spoken of as having to be commensurate in quantity and quality with the benefactions, as well as with the importance of the individual in question. Honours ranged from crowns, wreaths, and titles, to front seats at ceremonial occasions (προεδρία), the linking of parts of festivals or of whole festivals to the name of the donor, statues in precious metals, freedom from obligations, further and higher offices, and perpetuation to eternity of some or all of these benefits.

There were evidently local and temporal variations in custom (it would

---

8 Paul Veyne, Bread and Circuses (abridged English translation, London, 1990), 103.

9 Veyne's landmark study appeared in French in 1976: Le pain et le cirque: sociologie historique d'un pluralisme politique (Paris, 1976). Cf. A. R. Hands, Charities and Social Aid in Greece and Rome (London, 1968), chap. 2; P. Gauthier, Les cités grecques et leurs bienfaiteurs (IVe-Ier siècle avant J-C). Bulletin de Correspondence Hellénique Supplément 12 (Athens, 1985). Other important studies tend to focus on individual foundations: recently, and with bibliography, see Guy M. Rogers, "Demosthenes of Oenoanda and Models of Euergetism", JRS 81 (1991), 91–100. See also a collection of translated texts primarily for students of the New Testament: Frederick W. Danker, Benefactor: Epigraphic Study of a Graeco-Roman and New Testament Semantic Field (St Louis, 1982).

10 R. McMullen, "The Epigraphic Habit in the Roman Empire", AJP 103 (1982), 233–46; E. A. Meyer, "Explaining the Epigraphic Habit in the Roman Empire: the Evidence of Epitaphs" JRS 80 (1990), 74–96.

seem that honours became more elaborate as time went on), but on the whole the system surprises us with its uniformity. One typical instance – so typical, indeed, as to be described as "banale" by its editor – will therefore suffice for illustration. In the decree of the city of Kyme now in the J. Paul Getty Museum,[11] which probably dates from the Augustan period and which honours the πρύτανις, Kleanax, it is on record that this man's ancestral nobility of character (ἀμφιθάλεια, εὐγένηα, *sic*) and his goodwill toward the people, aimed εἰς φιλοδοξίαν (love of glory) had made him overlook no opportunity of conferring benefit upon them. This φιλοδοξία combined with εὐσέβεια had ensured extensive subvention of the mysteries of Dionysus, with public banquets and, of course, wine. His education of his son (obviously a future benefactor) merited special comment. The imperial cult had been well served. Altogether, an open and shut case for a gold crown. It is not clear, due to defects in the stone, what other rewards Kleanax received. It is worth pointing out that Kleanax does not appear to have belonged to the very highest social stratum in Kyme.

To get the honours right was vital in order to secure future services, from the donor in question or from others, and sometimes the gifts expected in the future are even spelled out in an inscription. Also, we find a number of formulae in which the donor is described as an example to others; and the actual inscription itself may also be explained as being intended to inspire emulation. Indeed, it is in this light that the various terms of praise for the generosity and the moral qualities of the donor should be seen, especially the stress on the virtues of devotion to honour or to glory – precisely those attributes which Jews professed to disregard.[12]

An additional feature to be observed in certain inscriptions is that there exists an opportunity for self-congratulation even for the givers-of-thanks: to pay due acknowledgement is itself an act within the sphere of public morality.[13]

It is clear that in the civic context and even more widely, on the regional and imperial levels, euergetism played a major economic role, though how far it is right to analyse it ultimately in those terms is a matter of disagreement: Paul Veyne would say rather little, stressing that the self-gratification of the donor, and the accumulation of honour and of power, are basic commodities in this kind of transaction, which needs therefore to be analysed in terms of social relationships and not of economic rationality. I shall not to enter into these

---

[11] The inscription is published by RENÉ HODOT in Journal of the J. Paul Getty Museum 9 (1982), 165–80; I owe my acquaintance with it to an unpublished seminar paper given by Riet van Bremen at the Institute of Classical Studies, London.

[12] On *philotimia* manifested by gods when they are honoured, see the interesting remarks of H. S. VERSNEL, "Religious Mentality in Ancient Prayer", in H. VERSNEL (ed.), Faith, Hope and Worship: Aspects of Religious Mentality in the Ancient World (Leiden, 1981), 51.

[13] A striking example is DANKER no.15, from Iasos.

theoretical questions here. What is more to the point is to notice that the same patterns of language and behaviour operated also on a smaller scale, within the clubs and associations with which the cities proliferated.These too had their patrons, their notables and their benefactors, and they too honoured them in a variety of ways.[14] We recall Polybius' unforgettable remarks about those wealthy families in Boeotia who had distributed the greater part of their fortunes among the clubs, so that many Boeotians had more dinners in the month than there were days in the calendar (XX,6–7). In such a context, we quite often see individuals of moderate means acting out the roles of the good and the great.

Thus two major questions arise, when we come to consider the Jews. First, did they have any role to play in the civic euergetism of their environments, or rather was their reluctance to accept its principles a factor which contributed to marginalizing them? Second, did they take on board any aspect of these practices within their own organizations, and if they did, are there any signs of limits being set to their adoption? The protests of Philo and Josephus offer a background against which to ask these questions.

The foreground, as with the study of pagan euergetism, is necessarily epigraphic. Neither Diaspora Jews, nor in due course those of Palestine, proved immune from the "epigraphic habit" and, as is well known, we have a body of inscriptions concerning benefactions within a Jewish or Judaizing context. Baruch Lifshitz[15] collected the majority of them, a total of 102. His valuable collection with its commentary is the basis for this study and, indeed, a stimulus to it. Those rare cases where the benefaction is not synagogue-related, or ones where the benefactor appears not to be a Jew, as well as those in languages other than Greek, and of course those surfacing since 1967, are not included in the volume. In contrast to Lifshitz, I shall take into account the small number of relevant Latin inscriptions along with the Greek, though it is hard sometimes to avoid the shorthand "Greek inscriptions", because that is what the bulk of them are. Aramaic and Hebrew material will appear here only peripherally.

I have chosen to focus on the Jewish Diaspora. But it has to be recognized that this delimitation introduces a certain arbitrary element when it comes to inscriptions, and, indeed, to Jewish communities, since there is no hard-and-fast distinction between a Diaspora Greek city, a city within Palestine but with a cosmopolitan population, like Caesarea, one on the fringes of Palestine such as Gadara, and one a little further afield but still within the same cultural world, for example, Beirut. One might adopt the Talmudic definitions of what was a Jewish city, but that would not advance matters very far. If we stop for a moment to consider Jerusalem itself, we recall that it is the provenance of one

---

[14] See Hands, op.cit. (n.9), 49–53.

[15] Donateurs et fondateurs dans les synagogues juives (Paris, 1967).

our most important donor inscriptions, the text about the refurbishment by Theodotus son of Vettenus of the synagogue founded by his forbears (Lifshitz 79; *CIJ* II, 1404). We also recall that the apparently Roman name "Vettenus" has encouraged a *communis opinio* that this was a family of returnees from Rome; that, then, is where the father and grandfather will have been *archisynagogoi*. It becomes arbitrary to exclude even the Theodotus inscription. Then again, in terms of cultural patterns, Syria seems to be closer to Palestine sometimes than to what is regarded as the Diaspora. We shall see an example of this later. A further complication is that, when it comes to synagogue building within Palestine, donors are recorded in the Galilean villages of the later Roman empire, and not only in cities and towns, so we are no longer dealing with a civic phenomenon; these inscriptions are more often in Hebrew or Aramaic than in Greek.

These are very real problems and I do not pretend that I can see exactly how they should be dealt with. They affect discussion of the Greco-Roman Diaspora over a wide range of issues, and they suggest that the Diaspora-Palestine distinction may not always be the most useful one with which to operate, in writing the Jewish history of this period. Now, however, I shall keep the subject within limits, restricting the main discussin to texts in Greek or Latin, and directing the focus onto those which technically originate from outside Palestine.

There survive four reasonably extended texts concerning individual benefactions in a Jewish context, apart from the Theodotus inscription. One (from Berenice in Cyrenaica) in fact involves a non-Jewish patron of the Jewish community. The Aphrodisias inscription, which is the longest known Jewish inscription, concerns two groups of contributors to a foundation, including both Jews (among them proselytes) and sympathizers. Significant groups of benefactors are listed in the fourth major text, once again from Berenice. Groups also appear in a series of small inscriptions, as contributors to a mosaic floor in late fourth century Apamea in Syria, and at Sardis where they contribute to the wall-paintings of the synagogue, in much the same period. In the synagogue of Naro (Hammam Lif), the mosaic was also paved collectively.[16] The group at Hammath Tiberias does not concern us.

A few middle-length inscriptions are of enormous interest, especially, perhaps, that concerning a woman called Tation in Phocaea, Ionia – whose Jewishness has also been doubted; that of the refurbishers of Julia Severa's synagogue at Akmonia, Phrygia, where the builder herself had been a pagan priestess; and that of Polycharmus, the *archisynagogos* at Stobi, Macedonia.

Short texts are occasionally of special note, as is the dedication of Publius

[16] See Y. Le Bohec, "Inscriptions juives et judaïsantes de l'Afrique romaine", Antiquités Africaines 17 (1981), 165–70.

Rutilius Ioses (thus disentangled by L. Robert, from the letters PROUTIOSES), an ἀξιολογώτατος ἀρχισυνάγωγος in Teos in Ionia (Lifshitz 16; *CIJ* II,744). Often enough, we are just dealing with scraps, perhaps a name or a couple of names and a formula. All this is, in fact, very far from the verbose world of pagan epigraphic benefaction and honour. It may seem surprising, then, that I should claim the possibility of drawing any conclusions at all about Jews and euergetism. Yet a careful study, in which the dossier is considered as a whole rather than as individual items, throws up some striking possibilities.

For this purpose, a body of 94 inscriptions was studied. This number excludes those from Palestine, which Lifshitz included, but adds to his list several items in the categories already mentioned, including the Aphrodisias inscription, two items from Egypt, one Ptolemaic and one Roman, some short texts from Hammam Lif and Utica in Africa, an inscription from Ostia, and one from Philippopolis (Plovdiv) in Thrace. While not every one of these can receive individual discussion here, my general observations and tentative conclusions are based on this corpus. I have not been able to take into account material from Sardis, beyond what was known to Lifshitz, though when all of this is eventually published, it will obviously be of very great importance. A pair of inscriptions from the Samaritan community on Delos, who, as is well known, describe themselves as Israelites from Shechem, have here to be excluded from the reckoning, though not because they are undeserving of attention.

The overwhelming majority of inscriptions, while giving the names and sometimes the offices of donors, do not describe honours accorded to them. If we compare the non-Jewish epigraphy, this is already a striking fact, even taking into account the accidents of survival. Six post-third century Syrian inscriptions might be deemed an exception in that they confer blessings on the donors or on their memories and in one case on their children too; this pattern is also found in nine late texts from Palestine, but nowhere else.

What of honours proper? Is there evidence that benefactors in the Diaspora Jewish milieu were repaid with visible honours, as was normal in a euergetistic system, but as should have been discouraged, if the principles of Philo and Josephus meant anything?

It does seem to be the case that Jews did not honour one another with statues. There is one possible exception, but it is a very dubious one. This is an Egyptian fragment now in the Hermitage (Lifshitz 98), in which one Artemon son of Nikon, eleven times a προστάτης, is recorded, apparently, as having given something to a synagogue (probably that term is to be taken in the sense of "community"). This inscription in fact derives from a statue base, no doubt belonging to Artemon's honorific statue (a fact seemingly unknown to Lifshitz). However, it seems that we should probably discount altogether any Jewish attachment. A *synagoge* can also be a pagan grouping in Egypt and other places, and there are no other indicators of Jewishness, even if both Artemon and Nikon are names used by Jews. Were this to be taken as a Jewish inscription, it would constitute a striking exception, on existing evidence.[17]

We now need to consider other kinds of honours conferred on benefactors. There are five clear-cut instances, three from Cyrenaica. It is important to note that all five may be described as in some sense marginal. I use the word "marginal" neutrally, without begging any questions, and its implications will emerge in the course of discussion.

One of the inscriptions from Berenice, now in Toulouse[18], is a virtually complete decree made at the *sukkoth* convention (σύλλογος) honouring a certain M. Tittius, son of Sestus, evidently a Roman official (ἔπαρχος), who has been a patron both to the Jewish πολίτευμα and to individual members. He is to receive an olive wreath and a wool fillet at each assembly (σύνοδος) and at each new moon, and the archons are to have the decree itself inscribed on marble in the most prominent position in the amphitheatre. The garlanding may well presuppose the existence of a statue. Tittius himself is described as a man καλὸς καὶ ἀγαθός, but no further praise is offered. Arguably, no more would be expected, however, at so early a date as this: the inscription is perhaps even as early as the first century B.C., but more likely belongs to the first half of the first century A.D.[19] In general terms, we see here a Jewish community honouring a pagan benefactor in the established Greek way. The question arises whether the amphitheatre was that of the city, in which the Jews as a group could conceivably have had a share and perhaps their own patch, or an oval building of their own, as was already proposed by Applebaum[20].

Applebaum's solution would seem to be demanded by the sister inscription, where the amphitheatre of Berenice figures prominently. This decree honours M. Valerius Dionysius, also a Roman citizen, as the *tria nomina* indicate (though no tribe is given) and it is now to be found in Carpentras, of all places.[21] For Dionysius had surfaced the amphitheatre's floor and decorated its walls. His rewards are comparable, with the addition of freedom from liturgies. But since those liturgies can only be understood as those paid to the Jewish *politeuma* (such terminology can be parallelled in pagan epigraphy in the context of

---

[17] For arguments against the Jewishness of this inscription, see W. Horbury and D. Noy, Jewish Inscriptions of Graeco-Roman Egypt (Cambridge, 1992), no.20, where it is now newly edited. Cf.no.26, for an even more dubious case of what may have been a statue connected with a possibly judaizing association.

[18] G. Lüderitz, Corpus jüdischer Zeugnisse aus der Cyrenaika, mit einem Anhang von Joyce M. Reynolds (Beihefte zum Tübinger Atlas des Vorderen Orients Reihe B, 53, Wiesbaden 1983), no.71.

[19] The identification of the dating era remains uncertain. For the early dating, see Martha W. Baldwin Bowsky, "M..Tittius Sex.F.Aem. and the Jews of Berenice (Cyrenaica)", AJPh 108 (1987), 495–510.

[20] Shimon Applebaum, Jews and Greeks in Ancient Cyrene (Leiden, 1979), 164–7.

[21] CJZC 70, with bibliography.

clubs and associations), Dionysius is normally taken as a member of that *politeuma* and therefore as a Jew. I cannot see any way round this conclusion: we otherwise have to go to the lengths of supposing that Dionysius has refurbished the *city's* amphitheatre, that he has been honoured by the city's archons for it (the largely pagan names given for the archons might support this) and that the Jewish *politeuma*, being a constituent part of the city, has joined with the archons in endorsing those honours, as part of the give-and-take process in a highly integrated city[22]. If we do not accept this last, rather strained reconstruction, then we have here a case of a Hellenized and Romanized Jew honoured in Greek style, just possibly even with a statue, though that, it should be stressed, is nowhere mentioned in what survives of the text. The alternative reconstruction would show us the Jews as a community operating freely within the Greek euergetistic pattern, in relation to an outsider and to the affairs of the city. Both scenarios would be remarkable and the Berenice community was indubitably a remarkable community. But we should treat it not as a unique case to be explained away, but as a fortunate surviving instance of what could be possible in certain circumstances.

At Akmonia in Phrygia, an interesting mixed environment of a different kind[23], the three first century restorers of the synagogue earlier established by Julia Severa were honoured by the community for their virtuous benevolence and zeal with a golden shield (Lifshitz 33; *CIJ II,*766). The honour is a familiar one; so too are the virtues; but in the Jewish world they stand out. The donations are explained as having been made ἐκ τῶν ἰδίων, from the individuals' own resources. Of the dedicators, one is a Roman citizen, P. Turronius Cladus; he and Lucius son of Lucius are *archisynagogoi*, the former for life (διὰ βίου),[24] and the third individual is described as an archon. Julia Severa, the foundress, is attested as a pagan priestess on the city's coinage, while the Turronii were a well-known family in pagan Akmonia. The presumption is that this Turronius Cladus, being an *archisynagogos* is attached to the Jewish community (I deliberately put it no more strongly than this). It makes sense that in such circles, the honour system should be firmly rooted. It is noteworthy, on the other hand, that a degree of restraint is observable in its application: there is no statue mentioned, and the praise is modest.

In the old Greek colony of Phocaea, in Ionia, Tation daughter of Straton, who was the son of Empedon, was honoured by the synagogue for favours to

---

22 I am grateful to Joyce Reynolds for discussing this problem with me.

23 On this environment, see A. R. R. SHEPPARD, "Jews, Christians and Heretics in Acmonia and Eumeneia", Anatolian Studies 29 (1979), 169–80; P. TREBILCO, Jewish Communities in Asia Minor (Cambridge, 1991), 58–84. There is much that is still of value in W. M. RAMSAY, The Cities and Bishoprics of Phrygia vol.I, part 2 (Oxford, Clarendon Press, 1897), who perhaps over-estimates actual Jewish involvement in the society.

24 On the significance of this title, see T. RAJAK and D. NOY, "*Archisynagogoi*: Office, Title and Social Status in the Greco-Jewish Synagogue", JRS 83 (1993), 80–98.

the Jews (Lifshitz 13; *CIJ* II,738). Some have taken this formulation to suggest that she herself was not in any real sense Jewish, which is certainly not to be excluded[25]. If this were the case, then the construction of a meeting place (οἶκος) and courtyard for which she was honoured with a gold crown and προεδρία (a front seat) would be another instance of Jewish involvement in the wider honour system of the city. We would be witnessing a mutual exchange of courtesies, with Tation appearing on occasion in the synagogue to take up her front seat. If Tation was Jewish, which is more likely, then the gold crown is something to be remarked on; but so, too, perhaps, is the absence of encomium. It is worth pointing out, however, that Jewish communities appear to have had no difficulty about awarding gold crowns to rulers who were benefactors, and even displaying them in (or perhaps in the entrance to) synagogues.[26]

There are also two honorific decrees of a very fragmentary nature. One from Samos, of which three fragments survive, is apparently a decree by the presbyters of the Jews, and its concern seems to be with honours. We can make out here some of the characteristic language of the conferring of honours. [27] The second is a damaged Latin text from Castel Porziano, south east of Ostia, in which the word "universitas" has been supplemented before "Iudaeorum" and a plot of land is given to a *gerousiarch*, for a family tomb; this is done presumably, though not explicitly, as a recompense for his services (*CIJ* 533).

An interesting and difficult document from Tlos in Lycia (*CIJ* 757) has a citizen called Ptolemaios Leukios setting up a tomb for his family, under public protection, though at his own expense, as a consequence of his having held office – ὑπὲρ ἀρχοντείας τελουμένης. In this formula, the office-holder is conceived of as a *euergetes*, who is owed something by the city.

Now it is a possibility which we have to acknowledge that the donors in the bulk of our inscriptions were simply not big enough people to receive crowns, shields or garlands: had they been wealthy enough to give on a large scale they might, it could be argued, have done so. The lack of awards and eulogies would then tell us more about the economic status of Jewish communities than about their values and beliefs. And indeed many donations seem to be moderate, consisting in portions of a synagogue floor or wall, or perhaps an accoutrement or vessel. Perhaps one third of donors are not specified as title-holders.

---

[25] See Trebilco, op.cit. (n.19), 230, n.34. On Tation, see also Bernadette J. Brooten, Women Leaders in the Ancient Synagogue (Brown Judaic Studies 36 Chico, California,1982), 143–4.

[26] See Philo, Legatio 133, with discussion in E. Mary Smallwood, Philonis Alexandrini Legatio ad Gaium (Leiden, 1961), n.ad.loc., 220–1. To Smallwood's list of Jewish honours to rulers from the Roman period, add Alexander Scheiber, Jewish Inscriptions in Hungary (Budapest, 1983), no.3: a soldier who seems to be an archisynagogos, for the safety of Alexander Severus.

[27] ἐτίμησαν ... πάσης δόξης ... ἀνεθήκαν. For the inscription see B. Lifshitz in CIJ I, ed.2, Prolegomenon, 89 (731f).

Where there are groups of donors, the cost of an operation is split, and separate names or groups of names may be recorded, but that record, as one among many, is the only visible honour conferred. In the case of the Berenice group of AD 56 *(CJZC* 72), where sums of money are, uniquely, given, these range from ten drachmas from each of ten archons of the community, and from one priest, to twenty eight from one individual without office and twenty five from each of two others. Further names are missing. The great new Aphrodisias inscription, which lists those responsible for a mysterious memorial, gives a large number of names, perhaps the entire roster of the equally opaque δε-κάνια, which may or may not have included also the sympathizers on the second face of the stone.[28]

It is tempting to argue that these and other group donations are nothing less than another strategy to minimize the impact of the donor and his or her wealth within the Jewish community, by asserting the act of giving as a communal and equalizing activity, not a field for display, for the exercize of power or the accumulation of privilege. The identity of the sums given by each and every one of the listed Berenice archons might support this case. Office-holding in that society carried its obligations, but was scarcely a route to outshining others. Lists of group donations are not unique to Jewish communities,[29] but they do seem to have taken root in the Jewish environment.

Our last major inscription, a 32-line text known since 1931, suggests another strategy for taking the donor out of the limelight, and that is to link the donation into the sphere of religious obligation. Claudius Tiberius Polycharmus of Stobi in Macedonia could have been no mean donor. This is suggested both by his Roman citizenship, evidently predating A.D. 212 and by what he owned: a property with a courtyard in the city large enough for him to hand over a major part of it, so that its downstairs could serve as a synagogue and a communal facility. He has the respected position of being father of the synagogue. But he makes over the gift εὐχῆς ἕνεκα, in fulfilment of a vow. That being so, self-advertisement might not seem in order, and we do not find any in the text. The detailed record of the donation appears to designed largely to clarify the legal position, enshrining the right of Polycharmus and his heirs to the upper storey of the house, and securing against any change to the arrangements by the imposition of a fine to be paid to the patriarch (presumably a local Jewish official). More recent excavations have established something of an archaeological context for the inscription, though its date remains controversial. Fresco fragments in red on white repeat Polycharmus's name, with the formula Τιβέριος ὁ πατὴρ εὐχήν.

The vow formula is repeated in numerous small inscriptions, to be precise,

---

28 J. Reynolds and R. Tannenbaum, "Jews and Godfearers at Aphrodisias" (Cambridge Philological Society, supplementary volume 12, Cambridge, 1987).

29 See Hands, op.cit.(n.9), 51, for examples of collective donations in the Greek world.

we find it in 42 of them, in one form or another. In inscriptions that can be established as later in date, the formula ὑπὲρ σωτηρίας (*pro salute*) tends to take over, but to have the same implications. So standard are they that it is hard to decide whether a real vow was to be seen as underlying the donation in every case. These votive formulae are perfectly well-known in pagan contexts, where they are normally associated with various smaller or larger thank-offering dedications to deities. But the high correlation of votive formulae with essential building projects seems to be a distinctive feature of the Jewish epigraphy. [30]

Yet another such strategy is what might be called the Sardis formula, where a contribution, instead of being described as coming from the individual's own resources in the customary fashion, is rather specified as the gift of God, or, more often, of the divine *pronoia*. This formula appears in Lifshitz 20, where the editor adduces later Christian material; we now know, from circulated but unpublished texts, that it was widespread in the city. There is one parallel from Aegina (*CIJ* 722). Sardian variants are, ἐκ τῶν τῆς προνοίας δομάτων and ἐκ τῶν δωρεῶν τοῦ παντοκράτορος θεοῦ and, more concisely, just ἐκ τῶν τῆς προνοίας. Kraabel has associated the formula with the cultured neo-Platonist milieu of late Roman Sardis; but the term *pronoia* for the deity is rooted in Greek-Jewish thought, being quite at home in Josephus.[31]

The ultimate strategy comes in a late inscription from Scythopolis (Beth She'an).[32] This might be thought to represent a more extreme self-effacement than anything from the Greco-Roman Diaspora, because here the contributors to a sixth-century mosaic floor are anonymous and we are explicitly informed that their names are known to God. Perhaps those names were not entirely unknown to friends and neighbours either! Such a formula has affiliations, on the one hand, with the Palestinian Aramaic synagogue dedications, with their characteristic Semitic request that the donor be remembered for good: there is obvious mutual influence between the Aramaic and Greek styles in Palestinian dedications, but the directions of influence are not easy to disentangle.[33] On the

[30] On votive formulae, cf. LEA ROTH-GERSON, "Similiarities and Differences in Greek Synagogue Inscriptions of Eretz-Israel and the Diaspora", in Synagogues in Antiquity, eds. A. KASHER, A. OPPENHEIMER, U. RAPPAPORT (Jerusalem, 1987), 133–46; for the pagan context, W. H. D. ROUSE, Greek Votive Offerings (Cambridge, 1902).

[31] On the synagogue inscriptions, see G. M. A. HANFMANN, "The Sixth Campaign at Sardis (1963)", BASOR 174 (1964), 3–58 (30ff., The Synagogue, by D.G. MITTEN; cf. A.T. KRAABEL, "Impact of the Discovery of the Sardis Synagogue", in Sardis from Prehistoric to Roman Times. Results of the Archaeological Exploration of Sardis 1958–75, ed. G.M.A. HANFMANN (Cambridge, Mass., 1983), 178–90.

[32] See LEA ROTH-GERSON, The Greek Inscriptions from the Synagogues in Eretz-Israel (Hebrew) (Jerusalem, 1987), no.9; FROWALD HÜTTENMEISTER and GOTTFRIED REEG, Die antiken Synagogen in Israel, vol.I (Wiesbaden, 1977), 62, no.4.

[33] For discussion of Greek influence on the Hebrew/Aramaic formulae, see ROTH-GERSON, op.cit. (n.30); for another angle on the formulae, GIDEON FOERSTER, "Ancient Synagogue Inscriptions and their Relation to Prayers and Blessings" Kathedra 19 (1981), 12–46. For

other hand, the formula points forward to Christian epigraphy, which takes it up: a little text from Grado in northern Italy, for example, *both* gives us the name of a donor and then solemnly says "cuius nomen deus escit". We might also compare the wording of the Aramaic inscription from the synagogue of Severus at Hammath Tiberias: "may peace be to all those who donated in this holy place and who in the future will donate."[34]

The different strategies I have pointed to will not have been employed with equal enthusiasm in all communities at all times. Local patterns can be dimly discerned. Yet it is not fanciful to detect also a certain consistency of principle, limits beyond which Jewish communities could not allow themselves to go in adopting local modes of giving and of honouring, limits which allow us to suggest that somewhere in this area lay one of the defining marks which were seen by Diaspora Jews as distinguishing them from their neighbours. If this suggestion is right, then they will have been striking an extremely delicate balance, doing things the Greek way up to a point, but stopping short where it mattered to them. It is the setting of that sticking point which constitutes the art of Diaspora living, and perhaps the art of being an ethnic or religious minority of any kind.

We might go further, and suggest that there are some practices of features of life in the host community which will acquire a symbolic value. They are perceived as a danger area, standing for what is alien, controversial, impermissible. This conscious distancing from selected items in a culture is as significant a part of acculturation as the corresponding, and more often remarked on, process of selective appropriation.

Jews in the cities were not outside the framework of euergetism. Indeed, within it they manifested a complex interaction with the society around them. Through its agency, important political gestures were made. A pagan woman might build a synagogue; so might a centurion in Palestine, who sympathized with Judaism (Acts 10–11). A Roman administrator might be honoured in an amphitheatre. There are even possible instances of Jews making contributions to pagan cults: at Iasos, a Jerusalemite called Niketas son of Jason, specified as a metic, μέτοικος, contributed to the Dionysia, and two further donors are described as Iouda (*CIJ* 749). At Smyrna, οἱ πότε 'Ιουδαίοι, participate in honouring Hadrian, appearing in a 45-line list of donors (*CIJ* 742). This last phrase is particularly intriguing.

---

donation in Palestine, A. KINDLER, "Donations and Taxes in the Society of the Jewish Villages in Eretz Israel during the Third to Sixth Centuries C.E.", in Synagogues in Antiquity (see n.25), 55–6; also in R. HACHLILI, ed., Ancient Synagogues in Israel. Third-Seventh Century C.E. (BAR International Series, 499, Oxford, 1989). For Aramaic and Hebrew texts, see J. NAVEH, On Stone and Mosaic (Hebrew) (Tel-Aviv, 1979).

[34] See M. DOTHAN, "The Aramaic Inscription from the Synagogue of Severus at Hamat Tiberias", Eretz Israel 8 (1967), 183–5. (Hebrew); 73–4 (English).

At the same time, it is hard to believe that the absence in the Jewish epigraphy of virtually all the language in which the transactions of euergetism can be conducted can be an accident. To enter the Jewish world, as a sympathizer or proselyte, would have been to learn a new dialect of a familiar language.

For Paul Veyne, Christian society substituted charity for euergetism – to his mind, an entirely different concept,[35] involving a radical redefinition of philanthropy. In the new version, individual self-gratification is no longer the leading motivation, and reward is not precisely measured out in the currency of privilege. Veyne suggests more than once that the changed concept had its roots in Judaism; and in a general sense this must be true. But I am not sure that the sharp dichotomy can deal adequately with a very complex process of change. As far as the Jews of the Greco-Roman Diaspora go, the evidence for charitable foundations is slight indeed. Admittedly, we can now say that if the πάτελλα of the Aphrodisias inscription was indeed a soup kitchen (*tamhui*), as Reynolds and Tannenbaum, its editors, inventively propose[36], then we would have, through that one word, extraordinary epigraphic evidence of a real alternative to civic pride and self-aggrandizement, set in a judaizing context, yet close to the heart of the city, and involving even town councillors of pagan Aphrodisias. We have to confess, however, that uncertainty still reigns over the identification of the Aphrodisias club. Our other epigraphic evidence for Diaspora Jewish arrangements suggests, as we have seen, forms of organization rather closer to, if still distinguished from, those of the city at large.

[35] op.cit.(n.9), 19–34.
[36] op.cit.(n.28), 26–8.

III. Qumran and New Testament

The Essential 'Community of the Renewed Covenant': How Should Qumran Studies Proceed?[1]

by

SHEMARYAHU TALMON

I.

Like in any other field of scholarly enterprise, also in the area of Qumran research, the specific interests and the subjective bent of the student in question will prescribe the course of his investigations. Every scholar has his own agenda, and is fully convinced that only his procedure will eventually lead to an adequate comprehension of what the scrolls are all about. Hence, even to attempt the charting of guidelines along which future Qumran studies should proceed is a mission impossible. I can only suggest some avenues of approach which in my appreciation hold out promise for a better understanding of the Essential 'Community of the Renewed Covenant',[2] יחד הברית החדשה, in short the *yahad*, its singular communal structure and ideational make-up.

In the present framework, it is obviously not feasible to survey and contemplate in depth the numerous weightly problems in the ever growing field of Qumran studies which need to be reviewed. Therefore, I shall address myself to the elucidation of some pivotal phenomena which, I believe, were not given adequate attention in the ongoing discussion, proposing solutions of some problems under scrutiny, which in many respects differ from those put forward by other scholars. My dissenting opinion should add some fuel to the ongoing debate.[3]

Let me first mention two basic premises on which I concur with the communis opinio.

---

[1] This paper was read at a Qumran symposium held in connection with the opening of the *Scrolls of the Dead Sea* exhibition at the Library of Congress, Washington, DC (April 22–23, 1993). I am grateful for permission to publish the paper in the present volume.

[2] I shall yet explain my reasons for thus naming the community. See also: S. TALMON, "The Community of the Renewed Covenant. Between Judaism and Christianity," in: The Community of the Renewed Covenant. The Notre Dame Symposium on the Dead Sea Scrolls, Ed. by E. ULRICH and J. VANDERKAM (Notre Dame, IN 1994) 3–24.

[3] The scholarly apparatus will be restricted to a bare minimum.

1. I subscribe to the widely accepted dating of the Qumran scrolls to the time span between the 2nd century or the middle of the 3rd century BCE, and the 1st century CE. Moreover, since the mss discovered in the caves are not necessarily autographs, it must be presumed that at least some of the works of which copies or fragments were found, were in fact authored before the 3rd century BCE. On the strength of these chronological parameters, the existence of the 'Community of the Renewed Covenant' is firmly set within Judaism of the waning Second Temple period. Concomitantly, all hypotheses are invalidated which seek to identify the *yahad* with the mainstream Jesus-movement or with a subgroup of primitive Christanity, not to mention any dissident community which ensuingly arose in Judaism, such as the Karaites.

2. I fully endorse the linkage of the cave-finds with the extensive ruins discovered on the adjacent site, known by the modern Arabic name 'Qumran'. The written documents from the caves and the material remains at Qumran: public buildings, a large number of earthenware plates, a jar which the heavy rainfalls in the winter of 1991/2 laid bare and which is of exactly the same make as those found in the first cave etc., complement each other.[4] The combination of the mutually supportive evidence must be considered the basis of any endeavor to gauge the importance of the scrolls, and sketch the essential character of the 'Community of the Renewed Covenant' whose members deposited them in the caves.

3. In distinction, I do not subscribe to the definition of the 11 Qumran caves as 'Genizah', nor as 'Library', for the following reasons:

a. In the very first stage of Qumran studies, E. L. Sukenik designated the caves 'Genizah'.[5] This technical term implies that the caves served as storage rooms for tattered scrolls and faulty texts,[6] which were taken out of circulation to prevent their being used by members of the community in a cultic setting.[7] The care taken over the storage of the scrolls in tightly closed jars, discovered in situ in the first cave, militates against this assumption. While the mistaken designation 'Genizah' is occasionally still applied in Qumran studies, on the whole it has lost its lease on life.

In contrast, the designation of the caves as 'The Library of Qumran', first

---

[4] See R. de Vaux, Archaeology and the Dead Sea Scrolls. The Schweich Lectures of the British Academy 1959 (London 1973), rev. translation of the original French survey L'archéologie et les manuscrits de la Mer Morte (London 1961); and int. al. M. Broshi, "Qumran – Die archäologische Erforschung. Ein Überblick," Qumran, Ein Symposion, ed. J. H. Bauer, J. Fink und H. D. Galter, Grazer Theologische Studien 15 (1993) 87–116.

[5] E. L. Sukenik, מגילות גנוזות מתוך גניזה קדומה שנמצאה במדבר יהודה. סקירה שניה (Jerusalem 1950); idem, אוצר המגילות הגנוזות (Jerusalem 1956).

[6] The Cairo Genizah is the classical example of this institution.

[7] Yadin suggested that two covered pits in the floor of the 'synagogue' on Masada served as a genizah. In these hollows fragments of a Deutoronomy and an Ezekiel scroll were discovered. See: Y. Yadin, "Qumran and Masada," BIES 30 (1966) 126 (Hebrew).

proposed by Frank Cross,[8] has won wide acceptance. The appellation 'Library' implies that we are concerned with a purposefully assembled collection of scrolls which presumably served the Covenanters as textbooks in their daily studies, and as manuals by which to regulate the life pattern of the community and the individual member.

N. Golb uses the designation 'library' with a special twist. He proposed to view the manuscript find in the Qumran caves as a comprehensive collection of books which were current at the time, and had been initially assembled in Jerusalem. The diversity of contents, and the conflicting views which characterize the collection of works preserved in the Qumran find, are thus taken to have arisen from its very library-character. Pace Golb, officials transferred that library from Jerusalem to the Judean Desert, in an effort to save the collection of writings from falling into the hands of the Roman soldiers who were about to lay siege on the city.[9]

I beg to sound a caveat against the application of the technical appellation 'library' to the cave finds, whether with the assumption that this library was located from the outset at Qumran or at first in Jerusalem. It is hard to visualize the ancient librarian who set out to assemble in an 'official' collection scores of exemplars of a given work, e.g. of the biblical book of Psalms, much less of writings which give expression to quite variegated, even mutually contradictory views on matters of religious significance. We cannot credit ancient Jewish literati with the professional zest and objectivity which are the hallmark of modern librarians and book-collectors.

In addition to these general considerations, reports and anecdotes preserved in classical sources militate against the assumption that unknown agents had methodically amassed in one locality the surprisingly large number of approximately 800 scrolls. Our sources convey a quite different picture, which shows that in those days only a rather small number of books could be found in any one Palestinian locality, including Jerusalem. Some examples will illustrate the point: rabbinic traditions report that 'three copies of the Pentateuch were kept in the Temple precincts', שלושה ספרים מצאו בעזרה (*Sifre Deut.* 33,27; *y. Ta'an.* 4.68a et al.), which in three instances exhibited variant readings.[10] Other texts speak of one master-copy of the Pentateuch deposited in the Temple-court, ספר

---

[8] F. M. Cross, The Ancient Library of Qumran and Biblical Studies (Garden City, NY, rev. ed. 1961; repr. Grand Rapids, MI 1980).

[9] N. Golb, "Who Hid the Dead Sea Scrolls," BA 48 (1985) 68–82; idem, "The Dead Sea Scrolls: A New Perspective," American Scholar 58 (1989) 177–207; idem, "Die Entdeckungen in der Wüste Judäas – Neue Erklärungsversuche," Qumran, Ein Symposion (above, n. 4).

[10] See my discussion of the pertinent texts in: "The Three Scrolls of the Law That Were Found in the Temple Court," Textus 2 (1962) 14–27.

העזרה (*m. Kelim* 15:6; *b. B. Bat.* 14b), against which Jerusalemite scribes checked and corrected the copies of biblical books which they produced.[11]

Similarly, the Book of Maccabees reports that after having recaptured Jerusalem, Judah the Maccabee collected books which had been dispersed during the war, and commissioned scribes to prepare new copies of the Holy Scriptures.[12] He then supplied an exemplar to every locality and community in the country which informed him that the copy or copies of the biblical books which it had owned were lost in the turbulent war years: "And in like manner Judah also gathered together for us all those writings which had been scattered by reason of the war that befell and they are with us. If therefore ye have need thereof, send some to fetch them unto you" (2 *Macc.* 2:14-15).

These and other such traditions give persuasive evidence to the relative paucity of books which at the time could be found in towns and villages of ancient Palestine, and do not support the presumed existence of comprehensive book collections of the 'library' type, either at Qumran or in Jerusalem. But if we are not concerned with a planned 'library', how can we explain both the original presence in the Qumran caves of the unprecendented large number of 800 scrolls and the exceedingly variegated character of the literary works which they represent?

Before tackling this question, let me draw attention to the discovery of fragments of some 15 Hebrew manuscripts on Masada,[13] approximately 15 miles to the south of Qumran. The *terminus ante quem* of this find is without doubt 73 C.E., the year in which Masada fell to the Romans. It follows that the fragments are roughly contemporary with the latest Qumran items. Now, the composition of the small Masada find is surprisingly similar to that of the incomparably larger collection of manuscripts in the Qumran caves which can be subsumed under four main categories:

a. Copies of books of the Hebrew Bible make up approximately 30%.

b. Manuscripts of known apocryphal writings – such as Jubilees, 1 Enoch, and the Testaments of the Patriarchs, together with previously unknown compositions of a similar genre – e.g. the Genesis Apocryphon (1 QapGen),[14] and

---

[11] T. Sanh. 2.7: ומגיהין אותו מספר העזרה על פי בית דין של שבעים ואחד; y. Šeq. 4.48a: מגיהי ספר העזרה נוטלין שכרן מתרומות הלשכה; b. Ketub. 100b: מגיהי ספרים שבירושלים נוטלים שכרן מתרומות הלשכה. Cp. the episodes related in b. Shab. 115a–b which revolve on single exemplars of a 'tome of prayers' and of an Aramaic Targum of the book of Job.

[12] M. H. Segal, "The Promulgation of the Authoritative Text of the Hebrew Bible," JBL 72 (1953) 35–47.

[13] I refrain from citing a definite number, since I have not yet been able to establish the origin of three unmarked slivers of parchment found in the *Nachlass* of Y. Yadin. I doubt that they stem from Masada or from Qumran. More likely, Yadin acquired them somewhere, but did not record details of the acquisition.

[14] N. Avigad & Y. Yadin, A Genesis Apocryphon: A Scroll From the Wilderness of Judaea. Description and Contents of the Scroll. Facsimiles, Transcription and Translation of Columns II, XIX–XXII (Jerusalem 1956).

the Psalms of Joshua from Cave 4,[15] amount to some 25%. These works do not bear upon them the stamp of the Covenanters' world of ideas.

c. Another 25% are copies of wisdom compositions, prayers and prayer compilations et sim., most of which do not exhibit specific pecularities which tie them to the Convenanters' theology. We may conclude that works which belong into one of the above three categories are parts of the common literary tradition of comtemporary Jewry, and are most probably Jewish *Gemeingut*.

d. Approximately 20% of the fragments stem from scrolls which evidently represent particular literary traditions of the 'Community of the Renewed Covenant'.

The Masada find can be similarly subdivided into four categories:

a. Seven fragments, viz. almost one half of the total, stem from copies of biblical books.[16]

b. Considerable parts of the extra-biblical Proverbs of Ben Sira are preserved.[17] A sliver of parchment with a few partial lines of text stems possibly from a copy of the apocryphal book of Jubilees, or else from a copy of the book of Genesis which contained a variant reading witnessed to by Jubilees.[18] We have further a group of small pieces of an unknown extra-biblical work based on the Joseph story of possibly on the book of Genesis in its entirety. This composition is typologically akin to the Genesis Apocryphon (1QapGen) and to Jubilees. Of the same genre is another, equally unkown, fragmentary text woven on the biblical book of Joshua.[19] It brings to mind the already mentioned 'Psalms of Joshua' from Qumran Cave 4.[20] These four items of the apocryphal genre constitute about 25% of the Masada find.

---

15 C. NEWSOM, "The 'Psalms of Joshua' from Qumran Cave 4 (4QJosh[a,b], 4Q378 and 379)," JJS 39 (1988) 56–73.

16 One each of Genesis, Deuteronomy and Ezekiel; two each of Leviticus and Psalms. I published one item which contains Ps 150 in "Fragments of a Psalms Scroll from Masada, MPs[b] (Masada 1103–1742)," Minḥah le-Naḥum. Biblical and Other Studies Presented to Nahum M. Sarna in Honour of his 70th Birthday, ed. M. BRETTLER and M. FISHBANE. JSOT Suppl. Series 154 (Sheffield 1993) 318–327, and "Fragments of Two Scrolls of the Book of Leviticus," Eretz Israel 24, A. Malamat Volume, ed. S. AHITUV and B. A. LEVINE (Jerusalem 1993) 99–110 (Hebrew). "Fragments of a Scroll of the Book of Ezekiel" (Ezek 35:11-38:14, Masada 1043–2220) will be published in the forthcoming FS M. Greenberg.

17 Y. YADIN, The Ben Sira Scroll From Masada (Jerusalem 1965).

18 S. TALMON, "Fragments of of Scrolls From Masada," Eretz-Israel 20, Y. Yadin Memorial Volume, ed. A. BEN-TOR, J. GREENFIELD & A. MALAMAT (Jerusalem 1989) 281–283 (Hebrew).

19 S. TALMON, "A Masada Fragment of an Apocryphal Composition Based on the Book of Joshua," שי לחיים רבין, Studies on Hebrew and Other Semitic Languages Presented to Professor Chaim Rabin on the Occasion of his Seventy-fifth Birthday, ed. M. GOSHEN-GOTTSTEIN, S. MORAG & S. KOGUT (Jerusalem 1990) 147–157 (Hebrew).

20 C. NEWSOM, 'Psalms of Joshua' (see above, n. 15).

c. Of special interest is a fragment of the 'Songs of the Sabbath Sacrifice'.[21] Substantial parts of this work were discovered at Qumran.[22] In addition, we have fragments of three further compositions which appear to be related to the Covenanters' literature. One fragment mentions the 'prince of evil', שר המשטמה, the heavenly protagonist of all sinful humans. This title is known from the book of Jubilees. It is documented at Qumran, where we also find the synonymous appellation מלאך המשטמה.[23] The noun משטמה, 'evil/hatred', by itself is widely attested in the Covenanters' credal-conceptual vocabulary. The plene spelling לכה preserved in another line of that fragment gives credence to its presumed connection with the Covenanters' literature. The same pertains to one other small piece which exhibits the typical Qumran spelling הואה. I would further tentatively assign to the same category two slivers of one document in which the vocable אלכן turns up three times.[24] It follows that three items, i.e. approximately a sixth part of the Masada find, exhibit evident characteristics of the Covenanters' literary tradition.

Some additional features shared by the Qumran and the Masada finds should be mentioned. The great majority of the Qumran scrolls are of leather. Only a small number of papyrus fragments were found. The documents are mostly written in the Hebrew square alphabet. Some are penned in the ancient Hebrew script. Equally, the Masada fragments are of leather, and the lettering is in square characters, to the exception of one papyrus fragment, which on the obverse and the reverse is inscribed in the ancient Hebrew script by two different hands.[25]

I suggest that the astonishingly similar composition of the large Qumran collection and the incomparably smaller Masada find can be explained by the historical circumstances of their genesis. At Masada, fugitives carried parts of their cherished possessions to the desert stronghold where they sought refuge. At Qumran, the assemblage is composed in part of manuscripts penned there, and to a larger part of scrolls which had been owned by newcomers who hailed from different parts of the country, from various social strata and possibly had previously been members of diverse religious factions. They were brought to Qumran by novices at their joining the 'Community of the Renewed Covenant' or when they entered the 'Commune' at Qumran for a specified period.[26]

---

21 C. NEWSOM & Y. YADIN, "The Masadah Fragment of the Qumran Songs of the Sabbath Sacrifice," IEJ 34 (1984) 77–88.

22 J. STRUGNELL, "The Angelic Liturgy at Qumrân – Serek Širot 'Olat Haššabat'," SupVT 8 (1960) 318–345; C. NEWSOM, Songs of the Sabbath Sacrifice: A Critical Edition (Missoula, MO 1985).

23 E.g. 1QM xiii, 11; CD xvi, 7; cp. 1QS iii, 2; 1QH frg. 4,6; 1QM xiv, 9–10.

24 See TALMON, EI 20 (above, n. 18) 278–280.

25 This item is of Samaritan origin. See TALMON, EI 20 (above n. 18) 283–284.

26 I shall yet explain my use of the discrete terms 'Community' and 'Commune'. The latter

II.

I shall now present a concise summary of the premises which have informed my work on the Scrolls and on the 'Community of the Renewed Covenant' for over forty years, underpinning their validity while I go along. En passant, I shall offer some critical comments concerning procedures in Qumran research which I deem to stand in need of revision.

1. At the outset, an important rule of scholarly method should be highlighted. Although it may sound commonplace, it still needs to be stressed, that the study of the Covenanters' distinct ideonic tenets and the structure of their community must take its departure from the examination of the plethora of scrolls found in the caves. Likewise, the student must always return to those documents for double-checking results obtained in the process of their interpretation. All considerations based on evidence extracted from extraneous sources, or resulting from comparisons with other socio-religious 'philosophies' and movements in Second Temple Judaism, are of secondary importance.[27] In other words, the 'World of Qumran' can be properly elucidated only by an investigation from within.[28]

This is easier said than done. When one comes to assess the Qumran finds in their totality, one is confronted with a perplexing linguistic-textual pluriformity and a provoking heterogeneity of cogitative content. We should, however, keep in mind that this state of affairs is not unique. Other corpora of early Jewish literature pose a similar problem. It will suffice to mention the ideational complexity which baffles the student of the Hebrew Bible. The same may be said of the apocrypha and pseudepigrapha, some of which were authored prior to the works discovered in the Qumran caves, while others stem from approximately the same period. Again, consider the ideational crosscurrents and differing parallel traditions traceable in the Gospels, which in part may be contemporaneous with some of the latest Qumran materials. Not less perplexing is the diversity which marks the corpus of early rabbinic writings. All this seems to imply that the rule of 'non-contradiction', which obtains in the conceptual universe of classical Greece and Rome, does not apply to Judaism at the height of the Second Temple period. The Jewish sages seem to have entertained a diversity of thought patterns with equanimity.

2. The question arises, how can we sift the wheat from the chaff? Which

term designates the group of members of the 'Community' who lived at Qumran for a circumscribed span of time, but were not life-long monks.

27 For a short summary of my views see "The New Covenanters of Qumran," Scientific American 225, 5 (November 1971) 72–81.

28 I have explicated my approach in more detail in "Between the Bible and the Mishnah," The World of Qumran From Within = WQW (Jerusalem 1989) II–52. See also S. Talmon, "Die Bedeutung der Qumranfunde für die jüdische Religionsgeschichte," Qumran. Ein Symposion (above n. 4) 117–172.

components of the bewildering literary mélange that emanated from the caves represent the essence of the Covenanters' world of idea, and which other components do not seem to exhibit evident traits of the Covenanters' specific theology, and therefore presumably belong with the *Gemeingut* of contemporary Judaism? Lastly, we must take into account the possibility that some pieces got into the caves by sheer happenstance.

Scholars have proposed various criteria for the differentiation of particular Covenanters' products from manuscripts and literary compositions which had a wider currency in Judaism of the period. The criteria offered fall in two main categories:

a. Distinctive scribal techniques, linguistic and morphological peculiarities serve as touchstones for the identification of documents which were authored and copied by members of the *yahad*, setting them apart from materials which do not exhibit these peculiarities and therefore are deemed to be non-*yahad*. Editors of biblical manuscripts from Qumran assembled an impressive corpus of scribal identifiers.[29] At first these criteria were applied toward the separation of manuscripts which exhibit characteristics of a particular scribal system and were assumably penned at Qumran, from others which appear to be of a proto-MT variety or exhibit similarities with the Samaritan or the Greek text traditions of the biblical books. Ensuingly, these criteria, and some additional crucibles, were also employed in the endeavor to differentiate non-biblical works of presumed Qumran vintage from non-Qumranic compositions.[30] This approach resembles altogether what in biblical research and other fields of study is known as 'lower criticism'.

b. A more widespread method concentrates on the discernment of specific literary tropes, genres, and peculiar facets of content, predominantly in extra-biblical writings from Qumran. This pursuit can be likened to 'higher criticism' in biblical research.

An intensified and refined application of a combination of these and similar criteria in the analysis of the Qumran corpus of writings can indeed provide important yardsticks for the separation of intrinsic *yahad* works from copies of literary compositions which do not display the Covenanters' particular concepts. However, the above categories of identifiers stand in need of amplification. They must be buttressed by diagnostic considerations, which I consider to be of highest importance. In this context, pride of place should be given to ideational and sociological signifiers which encapsulate the Covenanters' theol-

---

29 See especially E. Tov, "Hebrew Biblical Manuscripts from the Judaean Desert: Their Contribution to Textual Criticism," JJS 38 (1988) 5–37.

30 E. Tov, "The Orthography and Language of the Hebrew Scrolls Found at Qumran and the Origin of these Scrolls," Textus 13 (1986) 31–57; idem, "Scribal Habits Reflected in the Documents from the Judaean Desert and in the Rabbinic Literature – A Comparative Study" (to be published in the forthcoming FS M. Haran, 1995).

ogy and the bases of their communal organization, edge the spiritual profile of the *yahad*, and set it apart from all other known socio-religious streams in Judaism at the turn of the era. Such characteristics are indeed taken into account in the scholarly exploration of the *yahad* phenomenon. But I believe that their decisive importance in the comparison of the 'Community of the Renewed Covenant' with other discrete entities in the contemporary Jewish society is not sufficiently appreciated.

III.

It is my thesis that the 'Community of the Renewed Covenant' should be viewed as an early 2nd or late 3rd ctry. BCE crystallization of a major socio-religious movement which arose in early post-exilic Judaism,[31] was prophetically inspired, and inclined to apocalypticism. It perpetuated a spiritual trend whose origin can be traced to the prophets of the First Temple period – foremost Isaiah, Jeremiah and Ezekiel – and to the post-exilic prophets Haggai and Zechariah.[32] The development of the movement runs parallel to that of the 'rationalist' stream which surfaces in the book of Ezra and especially in the book of Nehemiah, and will ultimately crystallize in rabbinic or 'normative Judaism'.[33]

It follows that the roots of the *yahad*'s prophetically inspired belief-system, as that of the contemporaneous rationalist stream, reach down into the period of the return from the Babylonian Exile, that is to say into the fifth, possibly even the sixth century BCE. At that time, or possibly somewhat later,[34] a bifurcation in the Jewish body politic appears to have set in. Led by rival priestly houses, two major movements emerged, which were divided on a variety of issues pertaining to belief and ritual. In their subsequent development, both movements experienced internal diversifications of their respective interpretations of the biblical tradition. In the flow of time, this differentiating process generated the formation of new schismatic groups, and culminated at the turn of the era in the distinct pluriformity of Judaism, to which the classical sources give witness.

Two main phases in the historical development of the prophetic stream can be discerned:

---

31 Now sometimes referred to as 'Middle Judaism'.

32 Divergencies in the appreciation of the returnees' political situation which show in the oracles of Haggai and Zechariah respectively, seem to be reflected in successive stages of the *yahad*'s redemption hopes. See below.

33 G. F. Moore defined thus mainstream Judaism of early mishnaic times. See his Judaism in the First Century of the Christian Era: The Age of the Tannaim (Oxford 1927) I, 3.

34 For the present, I cannot suggest a more definite date.

The beginnings of the unstructured 'movement' are only sparsely documented. A later phase in which this ideonic-religious stream took on the form of the 'Community of the Renewed Covenant' is abundantly documented in the Qumran writings.

I propose to address my ensuing remarks to highlighting some more significant factors in the confrontation of the prophetically inspired movement with the concomitantly emerging brand which is to culminate in rabbinic Judaism.

1. From its inception, the movement attracted followers in many Palestinian localities on a countrywide scale. In their urban habitations members lived a regular family life, conforming to the exceedingly familistic stance which biblical society put on a pedestal. While we cannot accurately assess the size of the membership, we may assume that it was substantial. The prophetic movement could in fact vie with other groups for supremacy in the Jewish body politic, foremost with the emerging rationalist stream which, as said, underwent a parallel process of progressive consolidation.

2. The 'movement' crystallized gradually in the fourth and third century BCE. In the late third or early second century it emerged as the structured 'Community of the Renewed Covenant'. It follows that in the diverse stages of its development, the life-span of this spiritual-ritual stream in early Judaism extends from some time after the Babylonian conquest of Judah in 586 BCE or from the period of the return of waves of exiles in the sixth and fifth centuries, to the destruction of the Second Temple by the Romans in 70 CE.

3. The sector living at Qumran was the spearhead of the 'Community'. It was constituted as a 'Commune' of exclusively male members for whom Qumran served as a retreat, and who resided there for a specified number of years. These men were organized in para-military divisions, in preparation for the final war of cosmic dimensions, expected to erupt at an uncharted future point in time.[35] During the period of service to the wider community, and only during that circumscribed span of time, 'Commune' members refrained from sexual intercourse and family life. Their temporary abstention from relations with women differs categorically from the lifelong celibacy which Josephus ascribes to the Essenes. Qumran was the site of a permanent settlement with a periodically changing population of not more than 200–250 temporarily celebate males at a time.[36]

4. The Covenanters' theology was stressed between a utopian vision of an

[35] See below.

[36] J. BAUMGARTEN, "The Qumran-Essene Restraints on Marriage," Archaeology and History of the Dead Sea Scrolls, ed. L. H. SCHIFFMAN (Sheffield 1989) 13, underlines "the continuing uncertainty as to whether celibacy was in fact practiced at Qumran," but does not resolve the problem. E. QIMRON distinguishes between a class of non-marrying *yahad* members and other Covenanters who did marry. See his "Celibacy in the Dead Sea Scrolls and the Two Kinds of Sectarians", The Madrid Qumran Congress. Proceedings of the International Congress on the Dead Sea Scrolls, Madrid 18–21 March 1991, ed. J. T. BARRERA & L. V.

imminent restoration of the past historical status of biblical Israel, and the palpably different actuality of Jewish life in the Greco-Roman period. In their literature wishful thinking coalesces indiscriminately with historical reality.[37] No other Jewish faction at the turn of the era, or for that matter nascent Christianity, bears upon itself this stamp of facts welded with fancy, and of a hyper-nomism wedded with a fervent messianism, of which I shall yet speak.

5. The considerable length of time of the movement's existence stands in the way of fully gauging its essential character. The diversity of contents, of ideas and literary genres, which marks the collection of scrolls preserved in the caves, may reflect, as said, diachronous stages of a spiritual development which was shared by all members. But it may also have resulted from a synchronous diversity of opinions concerning theological and organizational issues which arose in the membership over the span of half a millennium.

6. Before this background, the 'Community of the Renewed Covenant' must be viewed as a socio-religious phenomenon *sui generis* which should not be identified with any subdivision of Second Temple Judaism of which the classical sources speak. Similarities of the *yahad*'s communal structure with that of the Essenes,[38] of the Covenanters' ritual laws with Zadokite *halakhah*,[39] of their legalistic outlook with that of the Samaritans, or of a religious vocabulary which at times dover tails with the credal terminology of primitive Christianity, resulted from a common fundus of traditions rooted in the Hebrew Bible, which was the heritage of all or most configurations of Judaism at the turn of the era.[40]

7. We must further keep in mind a general sociological principle. Comparable traits in the posture of discrete religious, or political groups are wont to arise from analogous societal conditions and credal tenets which were operative in the initial stages of their formation. The very confrontation with established religious and/or secular authorities may produce surprising similarities of thought and organization in the conceptual worlds of discrete, often widely divergent, opposition parties, foremost in dissident factions which lay in the same 'historical stream'.

8. It follows, that when we compare various configurations of Judaism at the turn of the era and probe the specific profile of one or another group, divergencies in their disparate interpretations of the common heritage are decisive, not

MONTANER (Leiden/Madrid 1992) I, 287–294. This hypothesis reflects the differentiation between marrying and non-marrying Essenes, proposed in the past.

37 See my remarks in "The New Covenanters" (above, n. 27) 73–77.

38 See below.

39 See publications cited below (n. 59 and 60).

40 I fully concur with J. BAUMGARTEN's assessment in "The Disqualifications of Priests in 4Q Fragments of the 'Damascus Document'," The Madrid Qumran Congress (above, n. 36) 513, that "there is a large, very significant body of halakhah which apparently was not limited to any of the three groups (viz. those singled out by Josephus: Pharisees, Zadokites and Essenes, S.T.), but represents the common traditional law of the Second Temple Period."

analogies.[41] A disregard of discrepancies in the search for similarities produces 'Parallelomania',[42] and obfuscates the individuality of discrete societal entities. By fusing the *yahad* with any other faction in late Second Temple Judaism, one loses sight of the importance of this major socio-religious movement in Jewish history. Viewed as a phenomenon *sui generis*, the 'Community of the Renewed Covenant' significantly enriches the multicolored mosaic in which Judaism presents itself to the historian and the sociologist of religion at the turn of the era.

IV.

It will have become apparent that the premises which underlie my investigative method differ in many respects from basic assumptions which inform the prevalent approach in Qumran research. Qumran experts study the Covenanters' community and their literature almost exclusively in the framework of Judaism at the height of the Second Temple Period. The beginning of the second century BCE, at the best the middle of the third century, is the base line from which practically all investigators take their departure.

This *modus operandi* leads inevitably to a comparison of the 'Community of the Renewed Covenant', whose existence was totally unknown before the late forties of this century, with one or another group in Judaism at the height of the Second Temple period. It further generates diverse attempts to define the *yahad*'s historical milieu by identifying it with a 'sect' or a 'philosophy' in ancient Judaism known from classical sources: reports of Jewish authors of the Hellenistic era, Flavius Josephus and Philo of Alexandria, and the Roman historian Pliny the Elder, or from mentions in the Gospels and in early rabbinic literature.

There is scarcely a group to which these sources refer with whom the Community was not identified. It will suffice to recall here the most conspicuous theories, now mostly passed over in silence or cursorily mentioned in retrospective surveys of the history of Qumran research: The putative connection of the *yahad* with the Samaritans or Dositheans,[43] the identification of the Covenanters with the Hasidim of the Second Temple period[44] with the Boethusians, the Zealots,[45] or their presentation as proto-Pharisees, etc.

---

[41] See my paper "The Comparative Method in Biblical Interpretation: Principles and Problems," SupVT 29, Göttingen Congress Volume 1977, ed. J. A. EMERTON (Leiden 1978) 320–352, repr. in Literary Studies in the Hebrew Bible. Form and Content (Jerusalem 1993) 11–49.

[42] See S. SANDMEL, "Parallelomania," JBL 81 (1962) 1–13.

[43] J. BOWMAN, "Contact Between Samaritan Sects and Qumran?," VT 17 (1957) 184–189.

[44] C. RABIN, Qumran Studies (Oxford 1959).

[45] C. ROTH, "The Zealots in the War of 66–73," JSS 4 (1955) 332–355; idem, The

The same pertains to hypotheses which conceive of the Convenanters' community as a forerunner of factions which grew out of Judaism after the turn of the era. One hardly recalls Zeitlin's presentation of the Qumran scrolls as medieval documents of Karaite origin.[46] Equally unsuccessful were attempts to link the Covenanters with nascent Christianity. Their equation with the Ebionites proposed by J. Teicher soon lost out.[47] We may predict that the same fate will overcome present-day identifications of the main agonistes in the Covenanters' struggle against their adversaries with Jesus' brother James the Just, Paul and other pivotal figures in the Gospel traditions.[48]

The discernment of possible 'connections' of the Covenanters with the mainline Jesus movement, or one of its sub-groups, has a more lasting effect.[49] However, credal similarities and organizational analogies do not necessarily prove a historical continuity between the *yahad* and early Christianity. Rather, as said, such phenomena indicate that both shared in a common body of traditions, and evince comparable socio-religious conditions which were severally operative in the discrete processes of their emergence. Père Benoit's warning "against an imprudent tendency to accept as immediate contacts arising from direct influence what in fact may be no more than independent manifestations of a common trend of the time" has lost nothing of its cogency.[50]

Historical Background of the Dead Sea Scrolls (Oxford 1958); idem, The Dead Sea Scrolls. A New Historical Approach (New York 1965); idem, "The Zealots and Qumran: the Basic Issue," RQ 2 (1959–60) 81–84; G. R. DRIVER, The Judaean Scrolls. The Problem and a Solution (Oxford 1965).

[46] S. ZEITLIN, The Dead Sea Scrolls and Modern Scholarship, JQRMS 3 (Philadelphia 1956), and a series of essays published over the years in JQR; cp. N. WIEDER, The Judaean Scrolls and Karaism (Oxford 1962); N. GOLB, "Literary and Doctrinal Aspects of the Damascus Covenant in Relation to those of the Karaites," JQR 47 (1957) 354–374. We can completely disregard Zeitlin's earlier invalidation of the scrolls as modern forgeries.

[47] K. KOHLER had already suggested this identification on the basis of the Zadokite Documents from the Cairo Genizah. J. TEICHER developed it in a series of detailed studies, published in JJS 2–5 (1950–54).

[48] R. EISENMAN, Maccabees, Zadokites, Christians and Qumran: a New Hypothesis of Qumran Origins (Leiden 1983); R. EISENMAN – M. WISE, The Dead Sea Scrolls Uncovered (Shaftesbury, Dorset/Rockport, MA/Brisbane, Queensland 1992); B. THIERRY, Jesus & the Riddle of the Dead Sea Scrolls: Unlocking the Secrets of his Life Story (San Francisco 1992).

[49] See int. al. J. VANDERKAM's review of "Messianism in the Scrolls and in Early Christianity," The Community of the Renewed Covenant (above, n. 2) 211–234; É. PUECH, "Messianism, Resurrection, Eschatology at Qumran and in the New Testament," ibid., 235–256.

[50] P. BENOIT, O. P., "Qumran and the New Testament," NTS 7 (1960–61) 276–96, repr. in J. M. O'CONNOR and J. H. CHARLESWORTH, eds. Paul and the Dead Sea Scrolls (New York 1990) 1–30. Cp. further the recent overviews in J. H. CHARLESWORTH, "The Dead Sea Scrolls and the Historical Jesus," Jesus and the Dead Sea Scrolls, ed. J. H. CHARLESWORTH (New York/London/Toronto/Sydney/Auckland 1992) 1–74; and P. SACHHI's succinct summary, "Recovering Jesus' Formative Background," ib., 123–139; O. BETZ and R. RIESNER, Jesus, Qumran and the Vatican. Clarifications (London 1994), transl. by J. Bowden from Jesus, Qumran und der Vatikan. Klarstellungen (Giessen/Basel/Freiburg/Wien 1993); H. STEGEMANN, Die Essener, Qumran, Johannes der Täufer und Jesus. Ein Sachbuch (Freiburg/

Of all hypotheses proposed, the identification of the 'Community of the Renewed Covenant' with the Essenes is without doubt most persuasive.[51] It will suffice to recapitulate the most salient analogies on which this hypothesis rests:

a. The geographical proximity of the 'Commune' center and the Essenes' settlement which ancient writers locate some 15 km to the south of Qumran on the shores of the Dead Sea, suggests that these two groups were but one.

b. One seeks to buttress the identification by pointing up parallels of religious tenets and similarities of communal structure: celibacy,[52] a frugal communistic lifestyle, stringent rules of behavior to which members are subjected, and affinities of the socio-religious vocabulary.[53]

c. Josephus identifies three 'philosophies' in Judaism of his days: Pharisees, Sadducees and Essenes.[54] The Pharisees and their theological concepts are abundantly documented in Hellenistic, Jewish and Christian writings. Some rather meager and biased information on the Sadducees derives from the same sources. The enigmatic Essenes are known only from the probably interdependent reports of Josephus,[55] Philo and Pliny. They are never mentioned in rabbinic or early Christian writings. Therefore, it is natural to claim that in the Qumran scrolls "for the first time, the hitherto mysterious Essenes stand revealed to us. The story of their spiritual struggle swells out of the past like a mighty hymn."[56]

Frank Cross, the most forceful proponent of the Covenanters = Essenes hypothesis, summarizes the arguments as follows:

"The scholar who would 'exercise caution' in identifying the sect of Qumran with the Essenes places himself in an astonishing position; he must suggest seriously that two major parties formed communistic religious communities in

---

Basel/Wien, 4. überarbeitete Aufl. 1994); J. C. VANDERKAM, The Dead Sea Scrolls Today (Grand Rapids, MI 1994).

51 See J. H. CHARLESWORTH, "Qumran Scrolls and a Critical Consensus," ib., 6ff. 42, n. 16; 72, and H. STEGEMANN's comprehensive survey in "The Qumran Essenes – Local Members of the Main Jewish Union in Late Second Temple Times," The Madrid Qumran Congress (above, n. 40) 81–166.

52 The presumed analogy does not stand up to scrutiny. A Covenanter's abstention from sexual intercourse during the cinrcumscribed period of his membership in the Qumran 'Commune' differs intrinsically from the lifelong celibacy which ancient reports ascribe to the Essenes. I expect to underscore the difference in a forthcoming study. For the present, see: "The New Covenanters" (above, n. 27) 77–78.

53 Recent summaries of the issue are offered int. al. by STEGEMANN, Die Essener, 194–360 and J. C. VANDERKAM, The Dead Sea Scrolls, 71–91 (above, n. 50).

54 The Zealots are mentioned only en passant.

55 See the recent summary offered by R. BERGMEIER, Die Essener-Berichte des Flavius Josephus. Quellenstudien zu den Essenertexten im Werk des jüdischen Historiographen (Kampen: Kok Pharos, 1993).

56 A. D. TUSHINGHAM, "The Men Who Hid the Dead Sea Scrolls," National Geographic Magazine 94.6 (1958) 785–808.

the same district of the desert of the Dead Sea and lived together in effect for two centuries, holding similar bizarre views, performing similar or rather identical lustrations, ritual meals, and ceremonies. He must suppose that one, carefully described by classical authors, disappeared without leaving building remains or even potsherds behind: the other, systematically ignored by classical authors, left extensive ruins, and indeed a great library. I prefer to be reckless and flatly indentify the men of Qumran with their perennial houseguests, the Essenes."[57]

However, in addition to methodolocigal considerations already mentioned, further weighty arguments militate against the identification of the Covenanters with the Essenes:

a. Geographical proximity, analogous or even identical rites and customs, and a similar community structure, do not necessarily evince the socio-religious identity of two 'secret' and self-centered communities which totally isolated themselves from the outside world.

b. Josephus' picture of a troika of Jewish philosophies cannot be taken at face value. Writing for outsiders, Josephus could not expect his Greek speaking Roman readers to be interested in a more detailed description of the internal diversity of the Jewish people, nor to be able to digest a more subtle portrayal of the various religious groups which were then. Therefore, like biblical authors before him, and like rabbinic and Christian writers of his own time, he availed himself of the 'triad' as the smallest schematic figure which stands for 'many'.[58]

c. The identification of the Covenanters as Zadokites,[59] and of the Essenes as a Sadducean splinter-group, now being proposed again on the basis of the document which its editors entitled *miqṣat ma'aśe/dibre ha-torah* (4QMMT),[60] effectively undermines Josephus' 'troika' image. We are suddenly left with only two philosophies or parties – the Pharisees and the Zadokites – with the Essenes becoming mere Sadducean dissenters.

d. I consider it significant that all comparisons are one-directional: the Qumran evidence is used to enrich the scant information pertaining to the Essenes. In contrast, one does not draw on the ancient reports on the Essenes for

57 F. M. CROSS, Canaanite Myth and Hebrew Epic: Essays in the History of the Religion of Israel (Cambridge, MA 1973) 331–332.

58 The reader will find a more detailed presentation of this matter in TALMON, "Bedeutung" (above, n. 28) 130–133; idem, "The 'Topped Triad': A Biblical Literary Convention and the 'Ascending Numerical Pattern'," Let Your Colleagues Praise You. Studies in Memory of Stanley Gevirtz, ed. by R. J. RATNER, L. M. BARTH, M. LUJKEN GEVIRTZ, B. ZUCKERMAN, Maarav 8 (1992) II, 104–190.

59 See L. H. SCHIFFMAN, The Halakha of Qumran (Leiden 1975); BAUMGARTEN, "Disqualifications" (above, n. 40).

60 E. QIMRON and J. STRUGNELL, Misqṣat Ma'aśe Ha-Torah. Qumran Cave 4. V. DJD X (Oxford 1994). See especially Y. SUSSMANN, "The History of the Halakha and the Dead Sea Scrolls," ib., 179–200, and E. QIMRON, "The Halakah," ib. 123–177.

illuminating unclear issues concerning the Covenanters, nor for solving problems for which the scrolls do not offer a solution.

e. More important. The protagonists of the Convenanters' equation with the Essenes seem to carefully avoid giving attention to the circumstance that not one of the ancient authors ascribes to the Essenes any of the *yahad*'s essential tenets, of which I shall yet speak, foremost:[61]

1. Their self-identification with the biblical world which triggered a particular attitude towards the composition and the text of the Hebrew Bible.

2. Their 'restoration hope', and the expectation of the rise of 'twin-anointed': a laic messiah of the Davidic line, and a priestly messiah of the house of Aaron.

3. The outstanding figure of the מורה (ה)צדק, the 'Legitimate Teacher',[62] and his singular function in the organization of the community.

4. The particular interpretation of the concept 'Covenant', which echoes the bibilical understanding of ברית, but differs significantly from its connotation in the writings of other contemporary groups in Judaism, predominantly in rabbinic literature.

5. The Covenanters' adherence to a solar calendar of 364 days as against the lunar calendar of 354 days by which pharisaic Judaism abided.

6. Their distinctive legal literature.

V.

I propose to present an outline of how Qumran studies shold procede by sketching from 'within' a composite picture of the 'Community of the Renewed Covenant', its societal structure, and its members' world-view. The building stones for this undertaking are won first and foremost from the 'Foundation Documents',[63] which were found well guarded in closed jars in Cave 1: the Community Rule (1QS) together with the Rule of the Congregation, or the Messianic Rule ($1QS^a$), the Habakkuk Pesher (1QpHab), the War Scroll (1QM), (to some extent) the Hodayoth Scroll (1QH), the Temple Scroll (11QMiq), fragments of diverse calendrical rosters, and in conjunction with these the Zadokite Documents (CD). The 'Foundation Documents' address the membership directly, and clearly detail the main tenets of the community. Other writings, as e.g. the polemical document 4QMMT whose author

[61] The glaring omission of 'differences' detracts from the weight of Baumgarten's roster of "characteristics of Essene halakha which Josephus thought worthy of notice", and which are analogous to Covenanters statutes. See his "Disqualifications" (above, n. 40) 503–513.

[62] S. Ivry's translation captures the essence of the Hebrew term better than the prevalent renditions 'Righteous Teacher' or 'Teacher of Righteousness'.

[63] This term was independently suggested by H. C. KEE, "Membership in the Covenant People at Qumran and in the Teaching of Jesus", Jesus and the Dead Sea Scrolls (above, n. 50) 119–121.

enumerates twenty-two legal matters on which he and his adherents differ from the addressee and his followers,[64] pieces of halakhic import, 'Testimonia', 'wisdom writings' etc., do not qualify as 'Foundation Documents'. They can only furnish supplementary information on the *yahad*'s world of ideas.

1. The Covenanters' self-implantation in the History of early Post-exilic Israel.[65]

The Covenanters view their community as the sole legitimate representative of biblical Israel. This self-identification, their *Eigenbegrifflichkeit*,[66] distinguishes them from their rabbinic opponents who conceived of the biblical period as a closed chapter, and of their own times as an intrinsically new phase in the history of Israel. For this reason, the Sages abandoned the use of typical biblical literary *Gattungen* – historiography, psalmody and the prophetic genre, and developed or initiated altogether new literary modes, such as *midrash*. Equally, the legal language of the Mishnah differs perceptibly from biblical Hebrew.

Moreover, the Sages drew a clear line between the corpus of biblical literature, termed תורה שבכתב, 'written law', and their own writings, designated תורה שבעל פה, 'oral law'. Both collections were held 'holy' and 'authoritative'. But their respective 'holiness' and 'authority' were considered to be of a quite distinct quality.[67] A third category consisted of 'extraneous books', ספרים חיצונים, which were not subsumed under either of the categories 'written' or 'oral law.[68] The compositions designated חיצונים were not handed down in the rabbinic tradition, but are preserved in Greek, Latin, and Ethiopic translations in the Old Testament canon of the Church, classified as apocrypha or pseudepigrapha. Hebrew and/or Aramaic originals of several of these works, and also fragments of hitherto unknown writings of this genre, turned up among the Qumran finds – 1 Enoch, Jubilees, Tobit, the Testaments of the Patriarchs, and the Proverbs of Ben Sira.

2. The Covenanters' Living Bible.[69]

a. The *yahad*'s literature conveys a quite different picture. We may assume that, like the Sages, also the Covenanters invested some of their writings with various grades of authority and holiness, and considered others profane and not

[64] See above, n. 60.

[65] I developed this point at some length in the publications cited above, n. 28.

[66] I adopted this term from B. LANDSBERGER, "Die Eigenbegrifflichkeit der babylonischen Welt," Islamica 2 (1926) 355–372.

[67] For a discussion of this issue, see S. TALMON: Oral Tradition and Written Transmission, or the Heard and the Seen Word in Judaism of the Second Temple Period," Jesus and the Oral Gospel Tradition, ed. by H. WANSBOROUGH, JSNTsup 64 (Sheffield 1991) 121–158.

[68] In addition, we find in rabbinic literature scattered references to sundry works which did not belong to any of these three classes. They seemingly did not have a common denominator: translations of biblical books in Aramaic, prayer collections, compositions of a presumably foreign origin, such as the rather nebulous ספרי המירם (m. Yad. 4,6), and possibly also writings of a heretical character.

[69] I developed the following remarks more fully in WQW (above, n. 28) 21–51.

binding. However, to-date no explicit statement has come to light which gives evidence to a clear-cut differentiation between books of the Hebrew Bible, on the one hand, and 'extra-biblical' writings, like Jubilees, or the 'Foundation Documents', on the other hand. Quite to the contrary. As said, the *yahad*-members conceived of their community as an extension of biblical Israel. Living conceptually in the world of the Bible, they did not develop the notion of a closed canon. Rather, they viewed the biblical books as constituent parts of an open-ended, still expandable collection of sanctified writings. In the context of the *yahad*, the very application of the term 'canon', and the pursuance of 'canon research' are anachronisms.

b. Similarly, the exceeding textual variability which shows in the copies of biblical books found in the caves, proves that a fixed text, a *textus receptus*, had not (yet?) crystallized at Qumran. I would suggest that the concept of an unalterable wording of Scriptures took root in Judaism after the destruction of the Second Temple when the recitation of Bible texts became an integral part of the synagogue service. A close reading of the pertinent sources proves that in the Covenanters' assemblies and convocations only prayers were offered. There is no hint at a concomitant reading of biblical texts.[70]

Yahad-authors and scribes appear to have preserved with equanimity copies of biblical books which exhibit varying text-traditions. Like the Chronicler before them and some translators of the ancient VSS, they injected their personalities into the materials which they transmitted, adapting biblical texts to their own needs, rephrasing, expanding and contracting, within the limits of a 'legitimate latitude of variation'. The demarcation of the boundaries of permissible variation in the transmission of the Bible text remains a desideratum. The indispensable basis for such an undertaking are scholarly editions of Qumran bibilical scrolls and fragments, and the collation of variant readings in a reasoned apparatus. But we must realize that it does not suffice to collate variants, and to ensuingly align Qumran manuscripts severally with the MT or a proto-massoretic tradition, the Samaritan version of the Pentateuch, the Septuagint, Theodotion, proto-Theodotion, καιγε, etc. The 'Text and Version' approach which informs modern biblical scholarship, deriving primarily from the study of the ancient versions and medieval Hebrew manuscripts, obfuscates a more fundamental issue. The biblical scrolls from the caves should not be studied only from the angle of the history of text transmission.[71] There is

---

70 See S. TALMON, "The Emergence of Institutionalized Prayer in Israel in the Light of Qumran Literature," WQW (above, n. 28) 200–243.

71 The prevalent method of study is exemplified by E. ULRICH's "The Bible in the Making: The Scriptures at Qumran", The Community of the Renewed Covenant (above, n. 51) 77–94; further: E. TOV, "Biblical Texts as Reworked in Some Qumran Manuscripts with special Attention to 4QRP and 4QPara Gen-Exod," ib., 111–134, and pertinent publications adduced in these essays.

another extension to the issue which requires attention. The manuscripts from the caves have the advantage of affording us a glimpse into late stages of biblical literary creativity, when biblical literature was yet 'in the making', alive and mallable, when tradents, scribes, and even translators still functioned as minor partners of the original authors in the transmission of literary materials.[72]

c. The *yahad* embraced unreservedly the Bible's high appreciation of prophetic teaching and continued to subject the life of the individual and the life of the community to the guidance of personalities who were possessed of the divine spirit, first and foremost the מורה (ה)צדק, the exclusively 'Legitimate Teacher'. Being prophetically inspired, the Teacher's decisions were beyond debate and unconditionally binding. In contrast, the nascent rabbinic faction shelved prophetic inspiration,[73] and progressively developed a rationalist stance: "After the demise of the last (biblical) prophets Haggai, Zechariah and Malachi, the holy spirit (viz. prophetic inspiration) departed from Israel (*t. Sota*, ed. Zuckermandel 318, 21–23; b. Sotah 48b; *b. Sanh.* 11a). From now on incline your ear and listen to the instructions of the Sages"[74] (*S. 'Olam Rab.* 6)[75] *et al.* Majority decisions, arrived at by logical investigation and finely honed interpretation, took the place of prophetically inspired dicta, which are beyond questioning. Rational thought,[76] and expert knowledge replaced pronouncements which drew their legitimization from the unfathomable divine spirit.

3. Millenarian Restoration Hopes.

a. The author of the Zadokite Documents establishes a direct connection between the beginnings of the history of this community and the termination of Israel's pre-exilic past. Like other *yahad* writers, he disregards altogether the 'returners from the exile' of whom the post-exilic biblical books speak.[77] The leading figures of that period: Zerubbabel, Joshua the Highpriest, Ezra and Nehemiah, are passed over in silence in the Covenanters' literature. The writer of the Zadokite Documents presents the founding fathers of the community as the first 'returners to the land' after the deportation of the Judeans in the wake

---

[72] I discussed some of these aspects in "The Textual Study of the Bible – A New Outlook," Qumran and the History of the Biblical Text, ed. by F. M. Cross and S. Talmon (Cambridge, MA 1975) 321–400.

[73] See E. E. Urbach, "When did Prophecy Cease," Tarbiz 17 (1945) 1–11 (Hebrew).

[74] משמתו נביאים אחרונים, חגי, זכריה ומלאכי, ניטלה רוח הקדש מישראל; מעתה הט אזנך ושמע דברי חכמים.

[75] Ed. Ratner, 2.

[76] M. Weber speaks of a "Rationalisierungsprozess" which unfolded already in the biblical era, setting off Israelite religion to advantage vis à vis paganism. I suggest that this process came to full fruition in the world of the rabbinic Sages. See S. Talmon, "The Emergence of Jewish Sectarianism in the Early Second Temple Period," Ancient Israelite Religion: Essays in Honor of F. M. Cross, ed. P. D. Miller Jr., P. D. Hanson and S. D. McBride (Philadelphia 1987) 599–616 = idem, King, Cult and Calendar (Jerusalem 1986) 186–201.

[77] The books of Haggai, Zechariah, Malachi, and Ezra-Nehemiah, are poorly represented at Qumran in comparison with other biblical writings.

of the Babylonian conquest of Jerusalem (CD I, 2–8). Qumran authors show a penchant for biblical 'Exile and Return' terminology and imagery, preferring vocables derived from שוב over constructions with עלה. They claim for their community honorific titles, such as זרע ישראל, 'Israel's' (legitimate) seed', and זרע הקדש, 'holy seed' (4QMMT 79–82), by which the prophet Isaiah had designated the remnant, עֲשִׂרִיה, that God will save from the impending debacle (Isa 6:13), and which the returning exiles had applied to themselves (Neh 9:2; Ezra 9:2).

"For when they were unfaithful and forsook him, he (God) hid his face from Israel and his sanctuary and delivered them up to the sword. But remembering the covenant of the forefathers, he left a remnant for Israel and did not deliver them to (utter) destruction (cp. Jer 5:18; 30:11; 46:28; Neh 9:31 *et sim.*). At the preordained latest period (viz. of the present generation)[78] he caused the root he had planted to sprout (again) from Israel and Aaron to take possession of his land and enjoy the fruits of its soil (CD I, 2–8,[79] cp. Isa 6:11-13; Hag 2:18-19; Zech 3:10; 8:12)".[80]

The repatriated exiles of the early Persian period of whom the Bible speaks, had seen in their return the realization of Jeremiah's prophecy that 70 years after the destruction of the Temple God would restore Israel's fortunes (Jer 25:11-13). The returnees took that figure at face value (Jer 29:10; Zech 1:12; Ezra 1:1; 2 Chr 36:21-22; cp. Dan. 9:2). They maintained that the period of punishment which began in 586 BCE had not yet run its full course in 520, and that accordingly the prophetically announced era of restitution had not yet set in: "the time has not yet come for the rebuilding of the house of God" (Hag 1:2).[81] Haggai rejects his fellowmen's contention. He never tires of proclaiming that from the very day on which the foundations of the Temple were laid, the 24th of the ninth month in the reign of Darius I (520 BCE), from this day on, מן היום הזה ומעלה, God's blessing will again be on his people (Hag 2:15-23).

The Covenanters likewise established an ideational connection between the destruction of the Temple and the founding of their community. Disregarding Jeremiah's prophecy of 70 years, they ascertained the exact onset of the hoped

---

78 I suggest to read ובקץ אחרון instead of ובקץ חרון. In the scrolls, קץ connotes mostly 'predetermined period' or 'juncture in history'. See S. Talmon, TWAT 7 (1990) 84–92, s. v. קץ *qēṣ*.

79 Translation by C. Rabin, The Zadokite Documents 2nd ed. (Oxford 1958), slightly adjusted.

80 I presume that the passage CD 1,2-11 ist paraphrased in 4Q390 I 4 (quoted here, courtesy Prof. D. Dimant): ויעשו גם הם את הרע בעיני ככל אשר עשו ישראל/ בימי ממלכתו הרישונים מלבד העולים רישונה/ מארץ שבים לבנות/ את המקדש ואדברה בהמה/ ואשלח אליהם מצוה ויבינן בכל אשר/ עזבו הם ואבותיהם, "They too did what is evil in my eyes, just as Israel had done in (the days of) its first kingdom (viz. the monarchic period), except for those who first came up from the land of their captivity to build the temple. I addressed them and sent them instructions. And they understood all in which they and their fathers had strayed."

81 לא עת בא עת בית יהוה להבנות.

for era of redemption by attaching a real-historical interpretation to a symbolic act which the prophet Ezekiel had performed when the Babylonians laid siege on Jerusalem. At divine command, Ezekiel lay immobile on one side for 390 days, to thus symbolize a period of woe for Israel which would last for 390 years. Then he lay on his other side for 40 days which represent 40 years of Judah's punishment (Ezek 4:4-6). Relying on 'millenarian numerology' or 'arithmetics',[82] and reading a message of hope into the prophet's oracle of woe, the *yahad*'s founding fathers resolved that exactly 390 years after the fall of Jerusalem, Israel's glorious past would be restored.

b. The members of the 'prophetic movement' initially fostered a quietist millenarianism, and confidently awaited the unfolding of history, immutably established by a prophetically revealed divine fiat.[83] No human initiative was required to ensure the restitution of Israel's good fortunes at the preordained turning point in history. However, when the 'appointed time' passed uneventful, the millenarian numerologists were caught in a dire predicament. The author of CD woefully relates that "for twenty years they were like blind men groping their way" (CD I, 9–10). His complaint appears to echo the equally mournful question which Haggai's contemporary, the prophet Zechariah, quotes from the mouth of the mediator-angel who confronts God in a similar situation: "for how much longer will you not have mercy with Jerusalem and the cities of Judah, against whom you have turned your anger for seventy years" (Zech 1:12).[84]

The Covenanter's despondency was ameliorated when in his mercy God "raised up for them the legitimate teacher, מורה צדק, to guide them in the way of his heart" (CD I, 11).[85] The Teacher was evidently born out of the existential stress which resulted from the unfulfilled restoration hope. He was not a 'founding-prophet',[86] and not an innovator of religious precepts, bur rather an inspired interpreter in the line of the biblical prophets. He complements the "sprout(s) from Aaron and Israel," mentioned previously in the text, who represent the priesthood and the royal house of David. Together, they form the triad of public figures and institutions which had been the pillars of biblical society: kingship, priesthood and prophecy. In the Covenanters view, the combination of the 'Sprouts' with the 'Teacher' was the prerequisite for the reestablishment of biblical Israel's body politic.

However, in the wake of the disappointment which they experienced when their millenarian arithmetics failed them, the Covenanters dared not anymore

---

[82] Believers of the מחשבי קצים variety attach a realistic value to millenarian numerology. Outsiders will view such computations as a mere product of religious phantasy.

[83] Their quietism cannot be construed to prove the Covenanters' intrinsic pacifism.

[84] עד מתי אתה לא תרחם את ירושלים ואת ערי יהודה אשר זעמתה זה שבעים שנה.

[85] Cp. the passage from 4Q390 quoted above n. 80.

[86] In M. Weber's categories.

to rivet the fervently awaited onset of the restoration to a specific date. Now it was expected to occur at an undeterminable future juncture in time.

Their incertitude mirrors Zechariah's resignation when the turn to the better of Israel's fortunes which Haggai had announced (Hag 2:20-23) failed to materialize. Zechariah did not despair of the hope that there will indeed be a restitution. Rather, he defuses Haggai's excessive confidence founded on 'millenarian numerology', by deferring its realization to an uncharted future time. He comforts himself and his contemporaries with the divine promise: "I will return to Jerusalem in mercy, my house will be (re)built in her and the (builder's) measuring rod will be again upon Jerusalem. Announce *yet*, עוד, thus speaks God: my cities will *yet*, עוד, brim over with (all that is) good ... God will *yet*, עוד, comfort Zion and will *yet*, עוד, elect Jerusalem" (Zech 1:13–17; 8:1–17). But in glaring contrast to Haggai's "from this day on," the four times repeated "yet" highlights Zechariah's reluctance to set a precise date for the foreseen restitution of Israel's national sovereignty.

4. From 'Restoration Hope' to 'Messianic Expectation'.

When the fervent hope of an imminent restitution did not materialize, the Covenanters' world of beliefs underwent significant changes. Searching for factors which had prevented the realization of their expectations, they found the causes, on the one hand, in their own shortcomings, ויבינו בעונם וידעו כי אנשים אשימים הם, and on the other hand, in the sinfulness of their opponents, עדת בוגדים, the "gang of backsliders who stray from the (rightful) way," הם סרי דרך (CD I, 12–13). Their erstwhile quietism turned militant millenarialism. Now, the members of the 'Community of the Renewed Covenant' see themselves called upon to overcome the obstacles which stood in the way of the realization of their hopes. Led by the 'Teacher', the founding fathers of the community repaired to the desert of Judah to "prepare a road for YHWH through the wilderness" (Isa 40:3), and subsequently every male member retreated for a season to Qumran to ready himself for the final cosmic battle, portrayed in the War Scroll (1QM), in which the Sons of Light will vanquish all Sons of Darkness.[87]

The non-realization of the hoped for restitution of Israel's political fortunes prompted the infusion of the messianic idea into the Covenanter's restoration hope which initially had been history-oriented without clear discernible messianic overtones, as the above quoted opening passage from the Zadokite

[87] As said, the Covenanters' initial quietism does not evince an intrinsic pacifism. Equally, their utopian militancy does not prove them to be Zealots. This hypothesis, first proposed by Roth and Driver (see above, note 45), was recently revived by EISENMAN (Maccabees, above, n. 48) who opines that the Covenanters were inspired by a "nationalist, and resistance-minded ethos," and that their literature is connected with "the Zealot mentality and movement" (EISENMAN-WISE, above, n. 48) 31, 276 and passim.

Documents (CD I, 5–11) illustrates.[88] The reestablishment of Israel's body politic was now expected to occur in a messianic age.[89] While its onset could not be anymore geared to a determinable juncture in history, it is succinctly described in the 'Rule of the Congregation' (1 QS[a]), which is part of the Community Rule (1 QS), a major 'Foundation Document'.

5. The Concept of Covenant.[90]

The suspended realization of the restoration hope, triggered the fashioning of adequate societal mechanisms which would enable the Covenanters to successfully bridge the hiatus between the 'here and now', and the undeterminable messianic eon. In this context the Moses-like figure of the מורה צדק(ה), the 'Legitimate Teacher', plays a decisive role.[91]

a. The Teacher molded the amorphous prophetic movement into a viable socio-religious order. Under his guidance, the Covenanters established the 'Community of those who entered into the Renewed Covenant', באי הברית החדשה (CD VI,19) or אשר באו בברית החדשה (CD VIII,29),[92] from which are excluded all opponents and backsliders who betray the "covenant and the compact[93] which they had established in the Land of Damascus,[94] which is the renewed covenant" (CD VIII,35; cp. 1 QpHab II,3). Resultingly, "anyone who was not introduced into the (renewed) covenant", [איש] אשר לוא הוב[א ב]ברית, should not be permitted to touch the member's agricultural produce, since he is considered ritually unclean, טמא (4 Q 275 Tohorot[b]).

b. The pregnant term 'Renewed Covenant', which the Covenanters apply to

---

88 Portions of text which presumably preceded the present beginning of the Documents are not preserved in CD.

89 I shall yet give attention to the Covenanters' particular brand of messianism.

90 It must suffice to list here only some items from the rich literature in which ברית, 'covenant' is discussed: G. Quell – J. Behm, "διαθήκη. AT ברית", TWNT II, 106–137; M. Weinfeld, "ברית *b^erith*", TDOT II (Grand Rapids 1972) 253–279; A. Jaubert, La Notion d'Alliance dans le Judaïsme aux abords de l'ère chrétienne (Paris 1963); N. Lohfink, Der niemals gekündigte Bund (Freiburg 1989).

91 The scrolls do not reveal any details concerning the Teacher's origin and his life. A reference to "torments and bodily harm" which were inflicted upon him, gave rise to the baseless assumption that he suffered a martyr's death, which in its turn suggested an equally unproven parallel with Jesus. This train of thought is altogether untenable.

92 R. F. Collins, "The Berith-Notion of the Cairo Damascus Covenant and its Comparison with the New Testament," ETL 39 (1963) 555–594; A. S. Kapelrud, "Der Bund in den Qumranschriften," Bibel und Qumran, Beiträge zur Erforschung der Beziehungen zwischen Bibel- und Qumranwissenschaft. FS H. Bardtke (Berlin 1968) 137–149; N. Ilg, "Überlegungen zum Verständnis von Berît in den Qumrantexten," Qumrân, Sa pieté, sa théologie et son milieu, ed. M. Delcor. BETL XLVI (Paris 1978) 257–264.

93 ומאסו בברית ואמנה אשר קימו בארץ דמשק והיא ברית החדשה. The author of CD used in this context the biblical hap. leg. אמנה, which in the Bible designates Nehemiah's 'compact' (Neh 10:1; 11:23).

94 I subscribe to the interpretation of the expression ארץ דמשק as a topos for the community center at Qumran.

themselves, significantly only in 'Foundation Documents',[95] underscores the intended self-implantation in the world of biblical Israel. Like אמנה, 'compact',[96] the collocation ברית חדשה is a biblical hap. leg. which Jeremiah employed (Jer 31:31) in a pronouncement set in a series of oracles of comfort (Jer 31:1-14; 23-30; 31-34; 35-40).[97] The prophet invokes there the divine promise of a future renewal of YHWH's ancient covenant with the Exodus generation (Jer 31:32), which had been factually suspended in the wake of the destruction of Jerusalem and the ensuing exile (Jer 31:15-22). Biblical historiographers and prophets of the post-exilic period viewed the return from the Babylonian exile as the realization of Jeremiah's prophecy that 70 years after the fall of Jerusalem the Judean kingdom would be reconstituted.

In contrast, the Covenanters evidently ignored Jeremiah's prophecy. They set their hopes upon the above mentioned symbolic act of Ezekiel, and claim for themselves the thereby implied promise of a restoration. They view their community as the youngest link in a chain of sequential reaffirmations of the covenant, to which the Bible gives witness (CD II,14–III,20). God had originally established his covenant with Adam. He renewed it after each critical juncture in the history of the world and of Israel: after the flood, with Noah, the 'second Adam'; then with the patriarchs; again with the entire people at Sinai; with the priestly house of Aaron; and ensuingly, after the introduction of the monarchic system in Israel, with the royal house of David. In their own days, the days of the present generation, בדור אחרון, "he raised for himself" from among all the evildoers "men called by name, that a remnant be left in the land, and that the earth be filled with their offspring" (CD II,11–12). The thread of Israel's historical past, broken when Jerusalem and the temple were destroyed, is retied with the foundation of the *yahad*'s renewed covenant.[98]

c. The intrinsic pertinence of ברית to the *community* comes to the fore in the Covenanters' induction rite of novices, when also the membership of veterans was presumably reaffirmed. This annually repeated ritual is palpably molded upon the Penteuchal tradition of the 'Blessing and Curse' ceremony set in the days of Moses, which preceded Israel's enrootment in the Land of Canaan (Deut. ch. 27-28).[99] That covenant ceremony was reenacted by Joshua to give the *de facto* conquest a *de iure* underpinning (Jos 8:30-35;

---

[95] To the best of my knowledge, ברית (ה)חדשה has not turned up in any other published or unpublished document.

[96] See above.

[97] The term is picked up in the καινὴ διαθήκη of the NT.

[98] See S. Talmon, "Eschatology and History in Biblical Thought," Literary Studies in the Hebrew Bible, Form and Content (Jerusalem 1993) 177–185.

[99] N. Lohfink, "Der Bundesschluss im Lande Moab: Redaktionsgeschichtliches zu Dtn 28,69–32,47," BZ 6 (1962) 32–56.

cp. 23:1-24:27). The *yahad* members interpreted the reenactment of the biblical tradition in their induction ritual as a confirmation of their community's claim to be the only legitimate heir to biblical Israel.

d. The above analysis of the Covenanters' understanding of ברית, points up a fundamental difference between their bible-oriented posture and the non-biblical stance maintained by the rabbinic faction. The *yahad*'s conception of ברית is totally absent from the rabbinic conceptual universe.[100] As already mentioned, the Sages understood their existenial situation to differ fundamentally from that of biblical Israel[101] and did not develop the notion that God renewed his ancient covenant with Israel with their community in their own days. In contrast to the pointed *communal* thrust of the Covenanters' understanding of ברית and ברית חדשה, in the rabbinic vocabulary, the noun ברית, *per se* and in diverse word combinations, connotes exclusively the act of circumcision.[102] On the strength of this rite, every male infant is *individually* accepted into ברית אברהם אבינו, God's covenant with the forefathers, which foreshadowed his later covenant with the people of Israel. The act of circumcision proleptically symbolizes the *individual* child's readiness to abide by the divine law when reaching maturity. This conception of ברית is not imbued with the societal dimension, the *community*-centredness, which attaches to (ה)ברית (ה)חדשה in the Covenanters' ideonic world as reflected in their 'Foundation Documents'.

6. The Development of a Particular Life-style.

The Covenanters developed a socio-religious code and devised a closely-knit communal structure in order to forestall a possible dissolution of the initially rather amorphous prophetic movement in the undeterminable time span between the 'now' and the messianic 'then'. Such societal mechanisms were justifiedly considered a *sine qua non* for ensuring their movement's continuous and semi-independent existence alongside the rabbinic stream which progressively consolidated. Under the Teacher's guidance, the erstwhile anti-establishment millenarians formed an establishment of their own, which soon was to surpass that of their opponents in societal rigidity and legalistic exactitude. The Teacher initiated a canon of norms, rules and statutes, which gave the movement the required structural underpinning for successfully bridging the chasm between the disappointing historical present and the fervently awaited messianic age. It seems logical to date the inception of the Foundation Documents, as well as of the many halakhic-legal texts, including 4QMMT, and diverse

---

[100] For a different view see A. Segal, "Covenant in Rabbinic Writings," The Other Judaisms of Late Antiquity, BJS (Atlanta, GA 1987) 147–165.

[101] See below.

[102] See Ch. J. Kasowski, Thesaurus Talmudis, Concordantiae Verborum Quae in Talmude Babylonico Reperiuntur, vol. 8 (Jerusalem/New York 1960) 812–814; M. D. Gross, אוצר האגדה מהמשנה והתוספתא התלמודים והמדרשים וספרי הזהר (Jerusalem 1942) I, 137–138.

calendrical rosters, to this early stage in the genesis of the Community of the Renewed Covenant.

7. The *yahad*'s Special Calendar.

The Covenanters' adherence to a solar calendar of 364 days,[103] which exceeds the Jewish lunar year of 354 by 10 days per annum, precipitated their final separation from the rabbinic faction. The civil and religious leadership in Jerusalem justifiedly viewed the Covenanters' adherence to a different timetable as an act of open defiance of their authority. Each side accused the other of following an aberrant time table, thereby throwing out of kilter the correct, divinely established flow of the hallowed seasons. The calendar-controversy, to which I drew attention from the very inception of Qumran Research, played a decisive role in the total separation of the Community of the Renewed Covenant from the rabbinic mainstream faction.[104]

By harnessing of the dates of their religious observances to the revolution of the sun the Covenanters were effectively prevented from participating in the sacrificial service at the temple, which was riveted to the lunar calendar by which mainstream Judaism and the Jerusalem priesthood abided. There resulted a void in the Covenanters' religious life which they filled by introducing 'institutionalized prayer' as a substitute for sacrifice. This 'innovation' explains the presence of a substantial amount of standardized prayer texts among the Qumran finds.[105] The novel type of worship may possibly have served as a model for the development of institutionalized prayer in nascent Christianity, and in rabbinc Judaism after the destruction of the Second Temple in 70 C. E.[106].

8. The Covenanters' Distinctive Legal Literature

The particular *yahad* statutes may be viewed as functionally paralleling rabbinic law, codified in the Mishnah. But these two bodies of legal ordinances

---

[103] The authors of 1 Enoch and the Book of Jubilees considered this ephemeris the exclusively legitimate basis for the proper conduct of life.

[104] See S. Talmon, "Yom Hakkippurim in the Habakkuk Scroll," Biblica 32 (1951) 549–563; idem, "The Calendar of the Covenanters of the Judean Desert," Aspects of the Dead Sea Scrolls. Scripta Hierosolymitana 4, ed. C. Rabin and Y. Yadin (Jerusalem 1958) 162–199 = WQW (above, n. 28) 186–199 and 147–185. Since the publication of these papers, the volume of studies of the Qumran calendar increased in leaps and bounds.

[105] See int. al. the already mentioned "Songs of the Sabbath Sacrifice" (above, nn. 21,22), and the "Textes Liturgiques", edited by M. Baillet in Qumrân Grotte 4 III (4Q482–4Q520), DJD VII (Oxford 1982) 73–286. Further: E. M. Schuller, "Prayer, Hymnic and Liturgical Texts from Qumran," The Community of the Renewed Covenant (above, n. 2), 153–173, and pertinent literature cited there. The speedy publication of as yet unpublished prayer texts is certainly a desideratum.

[106] See S. Talmon, "The Emergence of Institutionalized Prayer in Israel in Light of Qumran Literature," Qumrân, Sa pieté etc. (see above, n. 92) 265–284; idem, "The Manual of Benedictions of the Judean Covenanters," RQ 2 (1959–60) 475–500, combined in WQW (above, n. 28) 200–243; idem, "Extra-Canonical Psalms from Qumran – Psalm 151," WQW 244–272.

are marked by intrinsically discrete literary structures. The Mishnah is presented as the record of deliberations in the academy, which are often formulated in a question and answer pattern without a specific address,[107] leading to decisions arrived at on the basis of precedents, tradited rulings, or a majority vote. Learning and expert knowledge are of paramount importance. The correct exploration of the traditional lore is subject to an ever-growing fundus of interpretation-precepts, מידות שבהן התורה נדרשת, the proper application of which can be acquired through diligent study.

Tradition has it that from its very inception the rabbinic world of discourse revolved on pairs of dissenting Sages, זוגות, the first of whom were Josi ben Jo'ezer and Josi ben Joḥanan, Hillel and Shammai. The system was perpetuated in later stages when pairs like Akiba and Ishmael, Rabah and Abayye *et al.* arose. Their respective disciples formed schools, tradited their masters' teachings, and spun out their discussions. Rational debate was the lifeblood of the rabbinic academy. The very structure of the academy, and the aura of discourse which pervaded it, furthered the democratization of learning. These modes filtered down into the wider community, and decisively shaped the contours of public life.[108]

The Sages designedly discarded biblical terminology and literary genres, and cultivated a vocabulary and style which are patently different from their biblical counterparts. They summarized their innovative attitude in the pithy saying: לשון תורה לעצמו לשון חכמים לעצמו, "the language of Torah (viz. of the Bible) is one matter; the language of the (teachings of the) Sages is another matter" (*b. 'Abod. Zar.* 58b; *b. Menah.* 65a).[109]

The Covenanters' world is altogether different. Their Foundation Documents – the Rule of the Community, the Rule of the Congregation, the Zadokite Documents and the Temple Scroll *et al.* – are addressed to a specific audience. The legal pronouncements contained in them are never debated. Being underpinned by inspiration, like biblical ordinances, they are imposed upon the membership, and are irrevocably binding. This *ex cathedra* aura also pervades the repeatedly mentioned fragmentary work entitled by its editors *miqṣat ma*ʿaśe (or *dibre*) *ha-torah* (4QMMT), possibly an epistle addressed to an unnamed recipient. The equally unnamed writer records one after the other a series of his and his followers' ritual practices, resolutely laying down the law, without ever allowing for a discussion or even mentioning a dissenting opin-

---

[107] See J. Neusner, Max Weber Revisited: Religion and Society in Ancient Judaism with Special Reference to the Late First and Second Centuries (Oxford 1981) 3.

[108] See E. E. Urbach, "Class Status and Leadership in the World of the Palestinian Sage," Proceedings of the Israel Academy of Sciences 2 (Jerusalem 1968) 38–74; D. R. Schwartz, "Law and Truth: On Qumran-Sadducean and Rabbinic Views of Law," The Dead Sea Scrolls. Forty Years of Research, ed. D. Dimant and U. Rappaport (Jerusalem/Leiden 1992) 229–240.

[109] See my "Oral Tradition and Written Transmission" (above, n. 67) 139–158.

ion,[110] in glaring contrast to the procedures of the Sages. He exhorts the addressee, presumed to be a Pharisee who evidently abides by different interpretations of the legal issues in question, that only by following "the precepts of the Torah according to our (viz. the writer's) decision ... he will be doing what is righteous and good in His eyes for your (viz. the addressee's) own welfare and the welfare of Israel" (end of composite text).[111]

Furthermore, passages of legal import in Foundation Documents are often couched in a manifestly biblical wording, in contrast to the Sages' above mentioned avoidance of the biblical style and literary genres. This characteristic again evinces the authors' intention of conceptually implanting their community in the historical framework of biblical Israel.[112]

9. A 'Dual Messianism'.

The messianic idea emerges in the Foundation Documents in a characteristic bifurcation.[113] In the expanse of time between the actual present and the envisaged future era of redemption, the Covenanters are admonished to abide strictly by the fundamental precepts, which the Legitimate Teacher had established, and which the first *yahad* members had observed. At the onset of the ideal eon, two figures will simultaneously arise on the historical horizon together with the Prophet: a (priestly) Anointed (of the House) of Aaron, and an Anointed of Israel, associated with the royal house of David.[114] The triad King, Priest, Prophet – the three pillars of biblical society – will be reconstituted in the messianic age, as it had been previously expected to be reestablished in the Period of Restoration.[115]

The doctrine of a priestly anointed and a royal messiah, who together preside over Israel's body politic, is reflected in some strata of the apocryphal literature. This wider currency proves that the concept is not the Covenanters' exclusive legacy. Rather it is rooted in a common Jewish tradition. However, in no other known context was it accorded the significant role which it plays in *yahad* theology.[116]

Also in this instance comes to the fore the Covenanters' conceptual self-implantation in biblical Israel, and their self-identification as the first returners

---

110 Some experts of *halakhah* conclude that the author of 4QMMT propagates Sadducean rulings. See above, n. 59 and 60.

111 See Qimron-Strugnell, 4QMMT (above n. 60) 62–63.

112 See S. Talmon, "Between the Bible and the Mishnah," WQW (above, n. 28) 32–37.

113 See S. Talmon, "Waiting for the Messiah: The Conceptual Universe of the Qumran Covenanters," Judaisms and their Messiahs, ed. J. Neusner, W. S. Green & E. Frerichs, (New York/Cambridge 1988) 111–137 = WQW (above, n. 28) 273–300.

114 ונשפטו במשפטים הרשונים אשר החלו אנשי היחד לתיסר בם עד בוא נביא ומשיחי אהרון וישראל (1QS IX,10–11).

115 See above, pp. 341–344.

116 See int. al. A. S. van der Woude, Die messianischen Vorstellungen der Gemeinde von Qumran (Assen 1957); VanderKam, "Messianism," Puech, "Messianism, Ressurection" (above, n. 49).

from the Babylonian exile. The vision of Two Anointed, who together will govern Israel's restored polity, is derived from the teaching of the post-exilic prophet Zechariah, who presented to the returnees a blueprint for the organization of the province of Jahud as a *state in nuce* in the framework of the Persian Empire. The socio-religious structure which Zechariah proposed is quite distinct from that which obtained in the Judean body politic in the era of the monarchy. In those days, the king was in charge not only of the mundane affairs of the realm, but also wielded controlling power over the religious institutions, foremost over the temple in Jerusalem (2 Kgs 12:7-17 = 2 Chr 24:4-14; 2 Kgs 22-23 = 2 Chr 34-35; 2 Chr 17:7-9; 26:16-19; 29-31; 33:15-16). The high priest was considered a royal official (2 Sam 8:17 = 1 Chr 18:16; 2 Sam 20:25-26; 1 Kgs 4:2,4,5) whom the king could appoint or depose at will (1 Kgs 2:26-27,35; cp. 2 Chr 24:20–22). In the face of the profoundly changed internal and external political circumstances, Zechariah propagated a system of shared responsibilities (Zech. ch. 3): king and priest, the two anointed (Zech 4:11-14; 6:9-15), were to complement each other, guided by a "counsel of peace" (Zech 6:13).

The prophetically-apocalyptically motivated Covenanters embraced Zechariah's plan, and modelled upon it their perception of the future age. Identifying as the returnees from the exile, they accepted the embellished image of that period as the prototype of the future eon. An idealized biblical past was projected into the vision of the fervently awaited blissful age to come.

Concluding Remarks

Let me summarize my reflections on how Qumran studies should proceed so as to achieve an adequate picture of the 'Essential Community of the Renewed Covenant' and its conceptual universe?

The expectations that the scrolls would shed new light on historical events which affected Judaism as a whole at the turn of the era, did not materialize. And the various attempts to identify the *yahad* with a specific, Jewish faction of that dark age of first-hand documentation, previously known from retrospective reports of later historians and literary sources, has not produced satisfactory results. A shift of emphasis is needed.

Practically all theories put forward take their departure from the juncture in history when the Covenanters' community emerges as a fully organized socio-religious entity. In contrast, I suggest that in order to achieve a better comprehension of the *yahad*'s specifity, we should essay to uncover the roots of the 'Movement of the Renewed Covenant' and trace the early stages of its development, before it crystallized in the structured community whose members deposited the scrolls in the caves at Qumran. Efforts to elucidate the socio-religious profile of the essential 'Community of the Renewed Covenant' should be aimed at extracting pertinent information from the Covenanters' own literature, first and foremost from their Foundation Documents.

Instead of pursuing the so far fruitless search for a *historical identification* of the *yahad* and of the main antagonists in the drama portrayed in the scrolls with groups and historical figures known from ancient sources, research should concentrate on the attempt to gauge the quintessence of that community's *socio-religious identity*. The more transparent this identity will become, the better we shall be able to define the place of the Community of the Renewed Covenant in the panorama of socio-religious entities which together constituted Judaism on the threshold of the Christian era.

The Socio-Religious Background of the Paleo-Hebrew Biblical Texts Found at Qumran[1]

by

EMANUEL TOV

The Qumran finds include several forms of writing in paleo-Hebrew characters. Starting with the texts which use the smallest number of paleo-Hebrew letters, the following three types of use of paleo-Hebrew are recognized:

1. Individual paleo-Hebrew letters used as scribal markings in the margins of texts written in square characters.
2. Divine names written in paleo-Hebrew characters in texts written in square characters.
3. Texts written completely in paleo-Hebrew characters.

This discussion is concerned with the background of the different uses of the paleo-Hebrew characters in the Qumran texts. Each of the three groups of documents may have a different background, since the texts are of a different nature. At the same time, our analysis attempts to establish that the use of paleo-Hebrew characters in the Qumran scrolls is closely connected with the ideology of the Qumran scribes.

1. Individual paleo-Hebrew letters used as scribal markings in the margins of texts written in square characters

Several individual paleo-Hebrew letters written in the margins of some manuscripts penned in the square script (1QIsa[a], 1QS, 4QpIsa[c], and 5QLam[a]) and at the ends of lines in 4QCant[b] probably draw attention to certain matters or passages of special interest. These signs, like most other scribal signs in the

[1] For bibliographical references relating to the published and unpublished documents the reader is referred to E. Tov with the collaboration of S.J. PFANN, Companion Volume to the Dead Sea Scrolls Microfiche Edition (Second Revised Edition; Leiden, 1995). Thanks are due to Prof. Stegemann for commenting on an earlier version of this article and for providing me with a copy of his Habilitationsschrift (see n. 5).

Qumran manuscripts, were probably inserted in the text after the writing was completed.[2]

The decision as to whether a certain letter belongs to either the Cryptic A script (as reflected by 4Q186, 4Q249, 4Q298, 4Q317, and in a few fragmentary texts – 4Q250, 4QCal. Document C^{f} [4Q324c], 4Q313 [unclassified frgs.]) – or the paleo-Hebrew script is sometimes difficult, especially as some of the letters were ornamented or stylized. Nevertheless, for the sake of the description, a distinction between these two scripts is made here, although letters of both types were used together in the text of 4QHoroscope and in the margin of 1QIsa^{a}. The use of the paleo-Hebrew letters, with the exception of the use of the paleo-Hebrew *waw* as a paragraph sign, probably reflects the same background as the use of letters of the Cryptic A script.

Although the scribal marks written in the margins of some manuscripts have been known for some time, no satisfactory explanation for their occurrence has been suggested so far, and still today some of them remain enigmatic. They probably direct attention to certain details in the text or to certain pericopes, but they may also refer to the reading by the Qumran covenanters of certain passages. The function of the letters in 4QCant^{b} probably differs from that in the other texts, as they probably served as a special type of line-filler.[3]
The presence of individual letters in the Cryptic A script in the margins of manuscripts has been explained as pointing to a Qumran sectarian background.[4] It is suggested here that the similar appearance of individual paleo-Hebrew letters probably points in the same direction, although there is no direct proof for this argument. This assumption is supported mainly by the argumentation concerning the use of paleo-Hebrew letters for the tetragrammaton, as discussed in the next section.

2. Divine names written in paleo-Hebrew characters in texts written in square characters

a) Introduction

In several Qumran texts, mainly those of a nonbiblical sectarian nature, a special approach towards the writing of the divine names, especially the tetragrammaton, is evident. As in the rabbinic literature, most sectarian texts avoided the mentioning of the tetragrammaton and אלהים as much as possible,

[2] For details, see E. Tov, "Letters of the Cryptic A Script and Paleo-Hebrew Letters Used as Scribal Marks in Some Qumran Scrolls," DSD 2 (1995).

[3] See E. Tov, "Three Manuscripts (Abbreviated Texts?) of Canticles from Cave 4," in: JJS 46 (1995) 88–111.

[4] See the article mentioned in n. 2.

finding alternative ways of expression. This avoidance was described in detail by Stegemann[5] on the basis of the evidence available in 1978 and the assumption of this avoidance is still true for most of the texts known today. Note for example the circumlocution of the divine name as השם הנכבד in 1QS VI,27. Special cases are the replacement of the tetragrammaton with הואהא in 1QS VIII,13 (= Isa 40:3) and יוד (representing an abbreviation י) in 4Q511, frg. 10, line 12 (= Ps 19:10). Reflecting a similar approach to the divine names, other scribal solutions were also invoked, not for the avoidance of these names, but for their safeguarding when they were included in the text, especially in biblical quotations. Thus, in addition to the writing of the tetragrammaton in square characters, which occurs relatively infrequently in the Qumran texts, three special scribal systems were employed for the writing of the divine names, esp. the tetragrammaton. The first system, described in paragraphs (b)–(c), probably ensured the non-erasure of the divine names, while the two other systems, described in paragraph (d), indicate a special approach to the tetragrammaton, possibly regarding its pronunciation.

b) Data

The representation of the divine names (mainly the tetragrammaton) in paleo-Hebrew characters in several of the Qumran manuscripts has been noticed from the earliest days of the Qumran discoveries, since it is found in several texts from cave 1. Especially the occurrence of the tetragrammaton in paleo-Hebrew characters in 1QpHab has drawn much attention. Very valuable is the detailed description of the data and analysis by Stegemann, ΚΥΡΙΟΣ. Some aspects of this scribal practice could not be tackled in the past since not all the texts were known, and even today we are not certain that all occurrences of the writing in paleo-Hebrew characters are known to us. In any event it seems that sufficient information is known today in order to address the question of the distribution of the special writing of the tetragrammaton. For an analysis of the evidence

[5] H. Stegemann, ΚΥΡΙΟΣ Ο ΘΕΟΣ ΚΥΡΙΟΣ ΙΗΣΟΥΣ – Aufkommen und Ausbreitung des religiösen Gebrauchs von ΚΥΡΙΟΣ und seine Verwendung im Neuen Testament (Habilitationsschrift, Bonn 1969), idem, "Religionsgeschichtliche Erwägungen zu den Gottesbezeichnungen in den Qumran-texten," in: M. Delcor, ed., Qumrân: sa piété, sa théologie et son milieu (BETL 46; Paris-Leuven, 1978) 195–217. For a detailed analysis, see also E. Schuller, Non-Canonical Psalms from Qumran – A Pseudepigraphic Collection (HSS 28; Atlanta, GA 1986) 40–41. C. Newsom went even one step further when claiming that "any text containing the tetragrammaton in free and original composition can be presumed to be of no-Qumran authorship." See her article "'Sectually Explicit' Literature from Qumran," in: W. H. Propp and others, eds., The Hebrew Bible and Its Interpreters (Winona Lake, IN 1990) 167–187. The quotation is from p. 177. Newsom's claim is probably correct, but must still be tested for the whole corpus.

known until 1980, see Skehan[6] and for an earlier, more detailed, analysis, see Stegemann, ΚΥΡΙΟΣ, 149–151. A full list of the evidence known in 1983 was provided by Mathews,[7] and three further texts are mentioned below: 4QExod^{j}, 4QLev^{g}, 4QS^{d}. In one instance (4QpPs^{b}) the divine name is written in what looks like mirror writing of Greek letters with Hebrew meanings. The divine name was also written in paleo-Hebrew characters in one Aramaic text, 4QpsDan^{a} frg. 1,2 אלהכה (all letters except the *kaph* are written in paleo-Hebrew characters).

It is unclear why certain documents use paleo-Hebrew characters for the tetragrammaton, while others wrote the tetragrammaton in square characters. The two different systems are visible in the *pesharim*, since in 4QpIsa^{b,c}, 4QpMic, 4QpNah, 4QpZeph, and 4QpPs^{b} the tetragrammaton is written in square characters, while in other *pesharim* it was written in paleo-Hebrew characters (see below). A similar list can be drawn for liturgical Psalm collections and also for the biblical texts. Some of these texts were written at the same time, so that different scribal habits rather than a different chronological background must be assumed. The latter assumption was espoused by P.W. Skehan who ascribed the writing of the tetragrammaton in paleo-Hebrew characters to a late stage of the writing of the Qumran scrolls.[8]

It is not impossible that in some manuscripts spaces were left for the paleo-Hebrew words to be filled in later either by the scribe himself or by a different one. Thus in 4QpIsa^{e}, for which the use of the tetragrammaton is not evidenced in the text itself, a space was left open in frg. 6, line 4 where the MT contains the tetragrammaton. Possibly the space was intended to be filled in later (or was the tetragrammaton omitted intentionally, indicated by a space in the middle of the line?). On the other hand, the writing in 11QPs^{a} indicates that the same scribe wrote both the square characters and the paleo-Hebrew letters, as is evident from ligatures of the two types of characters in cols. IV,3,11 and XIII,12,14 which seem to have been performed in one stroke. On the other hand, according to Stegemann, ΚΥΡΙΟΣ, p. A 90, n. 501, the lack of space between the tetragrammaton and the surrounding words shows that the tetragrammaton had to be squeezed in an existing space (e.g., cols. IV,11; X,9; XIII,8.12; XVI,11).

The Qumran texts differ internally with regard to the details of the use of paleo-Hebrew characters. For example, 4QLev^{g}, 4QIsa^{c} , and 4QpPs^{b} wrote

---

[6] P.W. Skehan, "The Divine Name at Qumran, in the Masada Scroll, and in the Septuagint," Bulletin IOSCS 13 (1980) 16–44.

[7] K.A. Mathews, "The Background of the Paleo-Hebrew Texts at Qumran," in: C.L. Meyers and M. O'Connor, eds., The Word of the Lord Shall Go Forth, Essays in Honor of David Noel Freedman in Celebration of His Sixtieth Birthday (Winona Lake, IN 1983) 549–568.

[8] P.W. Skehan, "The Qumran Manuscripts and Textual Criticism," SVT 4 (1957) 151.

the prefixes to the divine names in paleo-Hebrew characters, while 11QPs[a] did not. That the scribe of 4QIsa[c] should not be considered as detached from the rules laid down in the Talmud is shown by the fact that only this text treated צבאות as a divine name, writing it with paleo-Hebrew characters, and in this regard it reflects the main view presented in *y. Meg.* 1.71d.

The following texts contain the paleo-Hebrew form of the *tetragrammaton* and/or of אל(הים) and צבאות (in the list "[Q]" *et sim* denotes the writing in the Qumran practice of orthography and morphology):

α. *Nonbiblical compositions, probably all sectarian*[9]

1QpMic [Q]
1QpHab [Q]
1QpZeph [Q]
1QMyst [Q]
1QH[a,b] [Q]
4QpPs[a] [Q]
4QpPs[b] [too fragmentary for orthographical analysis][10]
4QAges of Creation (4Q180) [Q]
4Q183 [not Q?], probably reflecting the same manuscript as 4QpPs[a][11]
4QpIsa[a] [Q]
4QS[d] [not Q]
6QD [Q?]
pap6QHymn (6Q18), possibly sectarian [Q]
11QPs[a] [Q]
As indicated above, possibly 4QpIsa[e] was meant to include also a paleo-Hebrew tetragrammaton.

---

[9] 4QPBless (= 4QpGen49), based on J. ALLEGRO, "Further Messianic References," JBL 75 (1956) 180 has to be deleted from the list of MATHEWS, "The Background," 561. The fragment published by ALLEGRO is actually 4QpIsa[a].

[10] Frg. 5 of this composition contains the word לאל written in unusual letters. ALLEGRO named them "some cryptic form" (DJD V, p. 53), while SKEHAN, "The Divine Name," 27 speaks of "distorted, unnatural paleohebrew lettering." The letters look like Greek and Latin letters in mirror writing with Hebrew values (α = א and L = ל), and therefore resemble the Cryptic A script of 4QHoroscope, which includes a few Greek letters.

[11] Thus J. STRUGNELL, RQ 7 (1970) 263. This composition is named 4QMidrEschat by A. STEUDEL, Der Midrasch zur Eschatologie aus der Qumrangemeinde (4QMidrEschat[a.b]) (Studies on the Texts of the Desert of Judah 13; Leiden/New York/Köln 1994).

β. *Biblical manuscripts*[12]

4QExod[j] in Exod 8:1 [too fragmentary for orthographical analysis]
4QLev[g] [too fragm.]
11QLev[b] [too fragm.]
4QDeut[k2] in Deut 26:3 [Q]
4QIsa[c] [Q]
1QPs[b], not necessarily a biblical text [too fragm.][13]
3QLam [too fragm.]

γ. *A rewritten Bible text (probably)*

2QExod[b] [too fragm.]

δ. *A manuscript which is too fragmentary for an identification of its nature*

3Q14 [too fragm.]

Altogether, twenty-three compositions use paleo-Hebrew characters for the divine names. Fifteen or sixteen (if 1QPs[b] is included) texts are nonbiblical. Fourteen nonbiblical texts reflect the views and/or terminology of the Qumran community, six or seven (if 1QPs[b] is included) are biblical manuscripts, one is probably a rewritten Bible manuscript, and the nature of one composition (3Q14) is unclear. If 4QpIsa[e] indeed intended to include a paleo-Hebrew tetragrammaton (see above), one text needs to be added to the statistics. On the whole, the percentage of sectarian manuscripts in this group is thus high in comparison with that of the overall percentage of the sectarian compositions among the texts found at Qumran. A special link between the writing of the divine names in paleo-Hebrew characters and the Qumran community is therefore a fact, especially since at least some of the biblical manuscripts could also have been copied by the Qumran scribal school.

---

[12] The following manuscripts of the revisions of the LXX similarly presented the tetragrammaton in paleo-Hebrew characters in the middle of the Greek text, probably reflecting a similar approach to the sacred character of the paleo-Hebrew letters: the Aquila fragments of Kings and Psalms of the 5th-6th cent. CE published by F.C. BURKITT (Cambridge 1897) and C. Taylor (Cambridge 1900), the Psalms fragments of Symmachus of the 3rd–4th cent. CE, Pap. Oxy. 1007 (third century CE; double yod) and 3522 of Job (first century CE), and both scribes of 8ḤevXIIgr (first century BCE). Scribe A of 8ḤevXIIgr probably wrote both the Greek text and the paleo-Hebrew tetragrammaton, since occasionally the tetragrammaton is written in almost one continuous movement together with the next letter (col. 28, line 37; col. 8, line 6). Also the scribe of Pap. Oxy. 3522 wrote the paleo-Hebrew characters himself.

[13] According to the editors of this text (D. BARTHÉLEMY and J.T. MILIK), 1QPs[b] does not necessarily reflect a scroll of all the Psalms, and it could have belonged to the same scroll as 1Q30 (liturgical text?), written in almost the same handwriting.

We now turn to the orthographical-morphological systems employed in these texts.

c) The relation between the use of the paleo-Hebrew characters for divine names and other scribal practices of these texts

It was suggested by the present author that the Qumran documents can be subdivided into texts reflecting a system of special orthographical-morphological-scribal features and those which do not.[14] The former group was named tentatively the "Qumran practice." When assessing the nature of the list of documents using the paleo-Hebrew characters for the divine names, we note that the greater part reflects the Qumran practice, while the evidence cannot be assessed well for the small fragments, especially of biblical texts.

d) Additional types of special treatment of the tetragrammaton in other manuscripts

Two additional scribal systems are used for the writing of the tetragrammaton in the Qumran manuscripts:

(α) Four dots (named *tetrapuncta* by Stegemann, ΚΥΡΙΟΣ, 152) represent the tetragrammaton in several sectarian nonbiblical texts. This practice undoubtedly reflects reverence for the tetragrammaton, considered so sacred that it should not be written with regular characters lest an error be made or lest it would be erased by mistake. It is not likely that these dots were intended to be replaced by the tetragrammaton in paleo-Hebrew characters, since the scribes simply did not leave sufficient space for this purpose. Besides, the custom of writing the dots simply was too wide-spread in order to assume anything else but the assumption of an intended use of these dots for representing the name of God.

The practice of writing four dots for the tetragrammaton is evidenced in three texts probably written by the same scribe, namely, 1QS, 4QSam^{c} (frg. 1, line 3; 3, line 7), and the supralinear corrections in 1QIsa^{a} col. XXXIII,7 (Isa 40:7) and XXXV,15 (Isa 42:6). The last mentioned instance seemingly presents five dots, but study of the manuscript shows that one of the spots of ink actually is a remnant of one of the four letters of the tetragrammaton in the square script

---

[14] "The Orthography and Language of the Hebrew Scrolls Found at Qumran and the Origin of These Scrolls," Textus 13 (1986) 31–57; "Hebrew Biblical Manuscripts from the Judaean Desert: Their Contribution to Textual Criticism," JJS 39 (1988) 5–37; "Scribal Practices Reflected in the Documents from the Judean Desert and in the Rabbinic Literature-A Comparative Study," in: M. Fox and others (eds.), Festschrift M. Haran (Winona Lake, IN, 1995), in press; "Tefillin of Different Origin from Qumran?" in: J. Licht Memorial Volume, in press.

which was at first written, and then erased, on the same spot.[15] The same dots also appear in other documents: 4QTest frg. 1, line 19, 4QTanḥ (two clusters of two dots; frgs. 1–2 i; lines 6, 7, etc.), 4Qpap paraKings et al. (4Q382; three times), 4Qpap psEzek[e]? (4Q391 frgs. 36, 55, 58, 65), 4QPrayer (4Q443), 4QNarrative C (4Q462), the last one using both four single dots (line 7) and two clusters of two dots (line 12), and an Aramaic document, 4QTob[a] ar.[16] All these texts, with the exception of 4Qpap psEzek[e]? and the Aramaic 4QTob[a] ar, are written in the Qumran practice of orthography and morphology.

(β) A colon, followed by one space, is systematically placed before the tetragrammaton (written in the square script) in 4QRP[b] (4Q364), written in the Qumran practice of orthography and morphology.

Both groups of texts (α, β) are written in the Qumran orthography and morphology, and this observation should be combined with the aforementioned evidence for the use of the paleo-Hebrew characters for the divine names (with the possible exception of 4QS[d]).

The picture which emerges from a study of the distribution of the three types of special writing systems for the divine names is that they are closely connected with the writing in the Qumran scribal practice. The evidence is not massive for all the texts, but it is clear-cut for the majority of the texts, while the other texts are too fragmentary for analysis. For one thing, the majority of the texts using the paleo-Hebrew characters, that is, 14 out of 22, are of a sectarian nonbiblical nature. At the same time, the negative evidence must also be taken into consideration: no text has been preserved which is either non-sectarian or clearly not written in the Qumran practice which contains any of the aforementioned scribal systems for the writing of the divine names.

This brings us to a discussion of the background of this custom.

e) The background of the writing of the divine names in paleo-Hebrew characters

The discussion of the background of the writing of divine names in paleo-Hebrew characters was introduced well by Siegel.[17] Siegel quoted extensively from *y. Meg.* 1.71d (parallels in *b. Shev.* 35b) providing the rules for the writing

---

15 The transcription with five dots in the edition of Burrows is therefore imprecise. As a result, the view of M. Delcor, RHR 147 (1955) 153 according to which these five dots represent the name אדוני is therefore without support.

16 Tob 4:21 (frg. 11,1 in DJD XIX), 12:22 (frg. 11,1), and 14,2 (frg. 18,11).

17 J.P. Siegel, "The Employment of Palaeo-Hebrew Characters for the Divine Names at Qumran in the Light of Tannaitic Sources," HUCA 42 (1971) 159–172; this discussion runs parallel with the author's doctoral dissertation, The Scribes of Qumran. Studies in the Early History of Jewish Scribal Customs, with Special Reference to the Qumran Biblical Scrolls and to the Tannaitic Traditions of Massekheth Soferim, Brandeis University 1971 (University Microfilms, 1972) 29–45.

of the divine names, in particular stipulating which divine names may not be erased. These sources also refer to the possible erasure or non-erasure of the prefixes and suffixes of the divine names. According to Siegel, this tannaitic text provides the background for the use of the paleo-Hebrew characters for the divine names in the Qumran texts. The scribes apparently devised a system using paleo-Hebrew characters for the divine names, in order that the writing in those ancient characters, whose sanctity gave the divine names a special status, would ensure that the divine names would not be erased. While Siegel's explanation is certainly acceptable, it provides only a partial answer to the use of paleo-Hebrew characters. The main difficulty is that the *halakhah* actually did not prescribe the writing of the divine names in paleo-Hebrew characters; the *halakhah* only prescribed which divine names may not be erased. Even if we assume some relationship between the Qumran custom of the use of paleo-Hebrew characters and the *halakhah*, we still do not know how other scribes related to the prescriptions of the rabbis. For example, what was the view of the scribes writing within the Masoretic tradition? Since the scribes writing within that tradition did not use paleo-Hebrew characters, how did they carry out the rabbinic prescription that the divine names should not be erased? There is no answer to this question, and probably the only possible reply is that these scribes took special care not to err in the writing of the divine names, so that they did not have to erase them.[18]

We cannot examine the question as to how the scribes of the texts usually identified with the Masoretic family, coped with the rabbinic rules, and the only practice which can be examined is the one visible system for insuring that the sacred names were not erased, namely their writing in paleo-Hebrew characters. The use of these characters gave these words a higher degree of sacredness, at least in the eyes of certain religious and/or scribal circles prohibiting their erasing. This assumption of a special status is supported by the practice of 11QPs[a], in which text 28 words were erased,[19] while the tetragrammaton, written in paleo-Hebrew characters, was not erased, as far as we can see. Instead of being erased, the tetragrammaton was twice marked with cancellation dots, above and below (col. XVI,7; XXI,2).

According to Siegel, the Qumran practice (if indeed it is a Qumran practice) of using paleo-Hebrew characters reflects the rabbinic regulations. However, some clarification is in order. We only know about the sensitivity of the

---

18 Possibly a partial answer to this question is provided by 4QIsa[d] which uses the cancellation dots only twice, namely in the case of an incorrectly written tetragrammaton: frg. 6, lines 7 and 10. Thanks are due to Prof. E. Ulrich for showing me his transcription of this text prior to its publication. Likewise, in 1QIsa[a] the cancellation dots are used rather infrequently, among other things three times for the tetragrammaton (col. III,24,25 = Isa 3:17,18; XLVI,21 = Isa 56:8).

19 For a list, see J. A. Sanders, The Psalms Scroll from Qumran Cave 11 (11QPs[a]) (DJD IV; Oxford 1965) 9.

halakhah regarding the erasing of divine names, but at the same time the *halakhah* did not actually prescribe the writing of the divine names in paleo-Hebrew characters. Nevertheless, it stands to reason that the scribes who used the paleo-Hebrew characters closely reflected the spirit of the mentioned *halakhah*, while finding a practical solution to the problem raised by it. In reaction to the prohibition of the erasures, some scribes apparently turned to paleo-Hebrew characters, which were considered so sacred that under no circumstances could they be erased. In this way, the scribes, when erring could never erase a divine name erroneously, for they knew that those words should not be erased. It should be pointed out that this description of the sanctity of the letters is hypothetical, but it is supported by the fact that according to tradition the Stone Tablets (see the view of R. Levi in *y. Meg.* 1.71c) and the Torah (see *b. Sanh.* 21b to be quoted below) were written in paleo-Hebrew characters.[20] Furthermore, it should be pointed out that manuscripts written completely in paleo-Hebrew characters reflect a different and far stricter approach to scribal precision than texts written in square characters (see section *d* below and the appendix) and it stands to reason that they reflect the same approach as the writing of single words in paleo-Hebrew.

The analysis so far was based on three assumptions to which we add a fourth one:

(α) The use of the paleo-Hebrew characters for divine names is almost exclusively linked to texts written by the Qumran scribes, certainly for the nonbiblical manuscripts, since they reflect the Qumran orthography and morphology as well as scribal practices.

(β) The use of paleo-Hebrew characters implies the view that these characters reflect a higher level of sanctity.

(γ) The use of the paleo-Hebrew characters for divine names reflects the spirit of the *halakhah,* although this particular solution is not mentioned in rabbinic sources.

(δ) The combination of these assumptions leads to an additional supposition, namely that (the) scribes belonging to the Qumran community ascribed a higher degree of sanctity to the use of paleo-Hebrew characters in general (that is, not only with regard to the writing of the divine names) than to the square script.

This assumption is discussed now. In principle the writing of the divine names in paleo-Hebrew script could somehow be connected with the writing of complete Bible texts in that script, but there is no indication for linking the two types of texts. In fact, from the outset there has been no indication that the Bible texts written in paleo-Hebrew characters were written at Qumran or by Qumran

[20] See the detailed discussion, especially on the later rabbinic interpretation, by S. Goren, "Haketav bo nitnah ha-Torah," Maḥanayim 106 (Tel Aviv 1967) 7–13; M.M. Kasher, The Script of the Torah and Its Characters (Torah Shelemah 29; Heb. Jerusalem 1978) 1–49.

scribes. Thus, while it does not necessarily follow that the scribes who wrote the divine names in paleo-Hebrew characters were the same scribes who wrote manuscripts which had been written as a whole in paleo-Hebrew characters,[21] the former could still have been influenced by the latter. What the writing of complete texts and of single words in paleo-Hebrew have in common is that both were rejected by the Rabbis (see below). No explicit remarks against the writing of the divine names in paleo-Hebrew characters are found in the rabbinic literature, but since the use of paleo-Hebrew script was forbidden for complete biblical texts, individual words written in that script would also have been prohibited.

This leads to an analysis of complete Bible texts written in paleo-Hebrew.

3. Texts written completely in paleo-Hebrew characters

At Qumran fragments of 11–14 biblical texts written in the paleo-Hebrew script have been found as well as a few paleo-Hebrew texts of uncertain nature:[22] 1QpaleoLev, 1QpaleoNum (same scroll as 1QpaleoLev?; frgs. 16–24 possibly reflect additional scrolls); 2QpaleoLev; 4QpaleoGen-Exod^{l}, 4QpaleoGen^{m}, 4QpaleoExod^{m}, 4Qpaleo-Deut^{r,s}, 4QpaleoJob^{c}; 6QpaleoGen, 6QpaleoLev; 11QpaleoLev^{a}. Two fragments (4Q124–125) are unidentified. 4QpaleoParaJosh, probably not a biblical text, contains parts of Joshua 21.

Beyond Qumran, also the two texts written on both sides of the enigmatic nonbiblical papyrus fragment found in Masada, pap paleoMas 1o (Mas1039–320) are written in paleo-Hebrew characters. The content of the two texts is described by S. Talmon.[23]

These texts, rather than preceding the use of the square script, were actually written at a relatively late period, possibly but not necessarily as a natural continuation of the earlier tradition of writing in the "early" Hebrew script. They were concurrent with the use of the square script, as can also be proved by a paleographical examination of the paleo-Hebrew script.[24] It is tacitly assumed

---

21 Thus SIEGEL, "The Employment," 170.

22 See M. D. MCLEAN, The Use and Development of Palaeo-Hebrew in the Hellenistic and Roman Periods, unpubl. diss., Harvard University, Cambridge, MA 1982, 41–47 (University Microfilms); P. W. SKEHAN, E. ULRICH, J. E. SANDERSON, Qumran Cave 4, IV-Palaeo-Hebrew and Greek Biblical Manuscripts (DJD IX; Oxford 1992).

23 "Fragments of Scrolls from Masada," Eretz-Israel 20 (1989) 1278–286.

24 See M. D. MCLEAN, loc. cit.; R. S. HANSON apud D. N. FREEDMAN and K. A. MATHEWS, The Paleo-Hebrew Leviticus Scroll (11QpaleoLev) (Winona Lake, IN 1985) 20–23; idem, "Paleo-Hebrew Scripts in the Hasmonean Age," BASOR 175 (1964) 26–42. For an earlier discussion, see L. BLAU, "Wie lange stand die althebräische Schrift bei den Juden im Gebrauch?" in: M. BRANN und F. ROSENTHAL, eds., Gedenkbuch zur Erinnerung an David Kaufmann (Breslau 1900) 44–57.

by most scholars that with the revival of the paleo-Hebrew script in the Hasmonean period, texts were transformed from the square to the paleo-Hebrew script,[25] and this is probably correct, although it is not impossible that the habit of writing in the paleo-Hebrew script had never ceased.

The fragments written in the paleo-Hebrew script contain only texts of the Torah and Job, both of which are traditionally ascribed to Moses (cf. manuscripts and editions of the Peshitta in which Job follows the Torah).[26] The longest preserved texts written in the paleo-Hebrew script are 4QpaleoExod[m] and 11QpaleoLev[a].

All texts written in the paleo-Hebrew script reflect a similar scribal approach, but the scribes often displayed their individuality in specific features:

(1) In only two paleo-Hebrew texts (4QpaleoExod[m] and 11QpaleoLev[a]) was a large paleo-Hebrew *waw* written in the spaces between the paragraphs, when the first word of the following paragraph would have started with this letter.

(2) 4QpaleoDeut[r] is the only text not using dots as word dividers (it uses spacing instead).

(3) In two texts little diagonal strokes (apostrophes) are written at the ends of sheets for the drawing of straight lines (2QpaleoExod and 4QpaleoExod[m]), and in two other texts they are not used (4QpaleoGen-Exod[l], 11QpaleoLev[a]). In a group of texts written in square characters guide dots are used for this purpose.

(4) The indication of paragraphs by systems of spacing differs in the various texts.

While the texts written in the paleo-Hebrew and square scripts share most of the components of a common scribal tradition, there are also differences between them. In the following three areas the manuscripts written in the paleo-Hebrew script differ from the manuscripts written in the square script in details which are inherent with the writing in the former script:

(1) the lack of distinction between final and nonfinal letters in the paleo-Hebrew script;

(2) the splitting up of words between lines in that script;[27]

(3) the use of dots as word dividers in that script, except for 4QpaleoDeut[r], as mentioned above.[28]

But there is also another major difference between the paleo-Hebrew texts and the ones written in the square script, which is not connected to the character of the scripts. Whereas all the texts written in the square script show scribal

---

25 Thus Mathews, "The Background."

26 One explanation for the writing of a text of Job in paleo-Hebrew would be to assume that Job was ascribed to patriarchal times. But it is probably more sound to assume that Mosaic authorship was ascribed to that text, cf. b. B. Bat. 14b–15a.

27 Cf. i.a., the Mesha inscription, the Lakhish ostraca and see M. Lidzbarski, Handbuch der Nordsemitischen Epigraphik nebst ausgewählten Inschriften (Weimar 1898) 126–127.

28 Except for 4QpaleoDeut[r].

intervention in different degrees,[29] including the carefully transmitted texts of the Masoretic family, the texts written in the paleo-Hebrew script show virtually no scribal intervention, neither by the original scribes nor by subsequent scribes or readers. It is not impossible that some elements in the text have been erased, but if that is the case, such erasures are no longer visible.[30] The only instances mentioned by the editors of the paleo-Hebrew texts are one erasure in 1QpaleoLev, two supralinear additions in 4QpaleoExod^{m} by a later hand (see *DJD* IX, p. 64), and one supralinear correction and one linear correction in 4QpaleoGen-Exod^{l} (see *DJD* IX, p. 25). This situation implies that the texts written in the paleo-Hebrew script reflect a more careful textual transmission than that of the manuscripts written in the square script, which must have been connected with the different milieus in which they were written. This fact is unrelated to the content of the paleo-Hebrew biblical manuscripts, since they reflect completely different textual traditions (see below).

We now turn to the background of the writing of the paleo-Hebrew texts. In fact, the only external information about the writing in paleo-Hebrew characters is of a negative nature. It is contained in the rabbinic traditions regarding the use of the paleo-Hebrew script for sacred texts. Various statements in the rabbinic literature, e.g., *m. Yadayim* 4.5 forbid use of this script for biblical texts:

"If an Aramaic ⟨portion of Scripture⟩ was written in Hebrew, or if ⟨Scripture that is in⟩ Hebrew was written in an ⟨Aramaic⟩ version, or in Hebrew script [וכתב עברי], it does not render the hands unclean. ⟨The Holy Scriptures⟩ render the hands unclean only when they are written in Assyrian characters [אשורית], on leather, and with ink." (cf. *b. Shabb.* 115b)

A similar statement in stronger terms: *b. Sanh.* 21b,

Mar Zuṭra; or, as some say, Mar ʿUkba; said: "Originally the Torah was given to Israel in Hebrew characters [בכתב עברי] and in the sacred ⟨Hebrew⟩ language [ולשון הקודש] later, in the time of Ezra, the Torah was given in the Assyrian script [כתב אשורית] and the Aramaic language. ⟨Finally,⟩ Israel selected the Assyrian script and the Hebrew language, leaving the Hebrew characters and Aramaic language for the ordinary people [להדיוטות]." (cf. *b. Meg.* 9a; *t. Sanh.* 5.7; *y. Meg.* 1.71b–c)

These statements were directed against those who used the paleo-Hebrew script in the time of the Talmud, that is, the Samaritans among others, but also the groups writing and using the paleo-Hebrew scrolls found in Qumran-note that the "ordinary people" [הדיוטות] in the dictum in *b. Sanh.* 21b is explained

[29] For an analysis, see E. Tov, "The Textual Base of the Corrections in the Biblical Texts Found in Qumran," in: D. Dimant and U. Rappaport (eds.), The Dead Sea Scrolls – Forty Years of Research (Leiden/Jerusalem 1992) 299–314. Our analysis is based on the texts from the Judean Desert analyzed until 1995, and there are probably no exceptions to this rule pertaining to texts written in the square script.

[30] See P. W. Skehan, E. Ulrich, and J. E. Sanderson, Qumran Cave 4.IV, 64.

as Samaritans by Rab Ḥisda in the continued discussion. Alongside the texts written in the square script, there were paleo-Hebrew texts, such as found at Qumran, and at a certain point also the Torah scrolls of the Samaritans, who claimed authenticity for their Torah as opposed to the scrolls written in the square script. It is thus understandable that the rabbis rejected the writing in the paleo-Hebrew script, not because of any intrinsic religious reason, but due to party politics,[31] since their opponents used biblical scrolls written in the paleo-Hebrew script. Hence, they had to formulate a strong counterclaim, which they found by ascribing the writing in the square script to no less an authority than Ezra (see above and IV Ezra 14.42).

During which period the negative attitude of the rabbis toward the old script developed is unclear.[32] Diringer suggested that the Hasmonean kings adopted the old script under the influence of priestly Sadducean families.[33]

Against this background it is now in order to turn to the background of the writing in paleo-Hebrew characters in the texts found at Qumran. The first issue to be addressed is the textual character of the biblical texts written in paleo-Hebrew characters. One of the texts is of an independent textual character (11QpaleoLev[a]), and another one pre-Samaritan, lacking the (later) Samaritan features (4QpaleoExod[m]), while the other texts seem to belong to the Masoretic family (1QpaleoLev, 1QpaleoNum, 4QpaleoGen-Exod[l], 4QpaleoDeut[r 34]).[35] While the classification of the Qumran texts will remain controversial, certain characteristics are beyond doubt. Thus, while the term "pre-Samaritan" such as used here may be right or wrong, the closeness of 4QpaleoExod[m] to the Sam. Pent. is evident, and that of other texts to the MT is equally clear. Because of the different textual nature of these texts, it would not be logical to assume that the common feature of their writing in paleo-Hebrew characters has anything to do with their textual character.[36]

---

31 Thus J. P. Siegel, The Scribes of Qumran. Studies in the Early History of Jewish Scribal Customs, with Special Reference to the Qumran Biblical Scrolls and to the Tannaitic Traditions of Massekheth Soferim, unpubl. diss. Brandeis University 1971, p. 181 (University Microfilms, 1972); M. Bar-Ilan, "Scribes and Books in the Late Second Commonwealth and Rabbinic Period," in: M. J. Mulder (ed.), Mikra, Compendia Rerum Iudaicarum ad Novum Testamentum, Section Two, I (Assen-Maastricht/Philadelphia 1988) 129.

32 According to Mathews, "The Background," 559 this approach should be traced back to the period of the "Hasmonean-Sadducean coalition which opposed the Pharisees."

33 D. Diringer, "Early Hebrew Script versus Square Script," in: D. W. Thomas (ed.), Essays and Studies Presented to Stanley Arthur Cook (London 1950) 35–49, esp. 48–49.

34 In the text covered by 4Qpaleo-Deut[r], the MT and the Sam. Pent. do not differ much from each other, so that this manuscript could also reflect the Sam. Pent.

35 The fragmentary texts (e.g., 4QpaleoGen[m], 4QpaleoDeut[s]), which are listed above and are not included in this list, also seem to be Masoretic.

36 See the summary statement of E. Ulrich, "The Palaeo-Hebrew Biblical Manuscripts from Qumran Cave 4," in: D. Dimant and L. H. Schiffman (eds.), A Time to Prepare the Way in the Wilderness. Papers on the Qumran Scrolls by Fellows of the Institute for Advanced Studies of the Hebrew University, Jerusalem, 1989–1990 (Studies on the Texts of the Desert

But there is one specific group of paleo-Hebrew texts which seems to defy any explanation. Against the background of the rabbinic prohibition of the use of the paleo-Hebrew script is it particularly puzzling to see among the Qumran texts several paleo-Hebrew manuscripts (probably the majority)[37] of proto-Masoretic character. After all, the connection between these proto-Masoretic texts and Pharisaic circles is evident. Some scholars even call the proto-Masoretic texts "proto-rabbinic," and to some extent this term is more precise than the term proto-Masoretic. When the biblical text is quoted in the Talmud and midrashim it is that of the MT, and when the rabbinic circles produce an Aramaic translation, it is again based on a text which is more or less identical with the MT. Is it therefore hardly understandable that the same circles who prohibited the use of paleo-Hebrew characters would have produced copies of the proto-Masoretic texts written in paleo-Hebrew characters. Because of this difficulty, one of the links in our argumentation is probably wrong, as will become clear from the analysis in the next paragraphs.

Within that analysis it is relevant to remember that the writing of individual words (divine names) in the paleo-Hebrew script in texts written in the square script was especially frequent in sectarian nonbiblical texts, as well as in several biblical texts of undetermined character.

How then should we describe the background of the writing of complete paleo-Hebrew texts or of individual words? If we follow our own view (see n. 14) on the Qumran scribal school (characterized by features of orthography, morphology and scribal practices), it should be noted that none of the paleo-Hebrew texts shares these characteristics. This situation may indicate that none of the paleo-Hebrew texts was written by the Qumran scribes. Reacting to this possibility we conclude that there is no major argument either in favor of or against the view that the biblical texts which are completely written in paleo-Hebrew characters were copied by the Qumran scribes.[38] It is also unlikely that the paleo-Hebrew texts came from Pharisaic circles, since the use of the paleo-Hebrew script was strictly forbidden in the Talmud (see above). We must therefore turn to a third possibility, based on criteria of script, textual character and scribal approach. We suggest here that the paleo-Hebrew texts found at Qumran came from the circles of the Sadducees who ascribed much importance to the authenticity of the ancient characters. This explanation should alleviate

of Judah 16; Leiden 1995) 129: "In sum, except for their script, the palaeo-Hebrew biblical manuscripts from Qumran cave 4 do not appear to form a group distinguishable from the other biblical scrolls in either physical features, date, orthography, or textual character."

[37] Thus ULRICH, "The Palaeo-Hebrew Biblical Manuscripts," 128.

[38] Our own view remains a mere theory, and we should be open to the possibility that all or some of the paleo-Hebrew texts were nevertheless written by the Qumran scribes. MATHEWS, "The Background," is not consistent in his approach to this issue. On the one hand he speaks about the Essene origin of the paleo-Hebrew texts (pp. 551, 558), but at the same time he also considers these texts as having been brought to Qumran (p. 557).

the difficulty of the apparent contradiction mentioned above. If this hypothesis holds ground, it is understandable that on the one hand the rabbis prohibited the use of paleo-Hebrew characters, while on the other hand such texts of proto-Masoretic content were written by others. These paleo-Hebrew texts of proto-Masoretic content, which in the past have been connected with the rabbis, should thus be ascribed to the Sadducees. Likewise, on the basis of Diringer's remarks (n. 33), Naveh hesitatingly ascribed the paleo-Hebrew texts from Qumran to the Sadducees, without any arguments.[39]

We suggest:

(1) The suggestion that the paleo-Hebrew biblical texts found at Qumran came from the circles of the Sadducees is reached by way of elimination, since they could not have come from the Pharisees, who forbode their use, nor from the Qumranites, whose characteristic features are not visible in the texts.

(2) There are positive arguments in favor of the view that the paleo-Hebrew texts came from the Sadducees. Several paleo-Hebrew texts are close to the Masoretic text, which must have had a central place in Israel. While the proto-Masoretic texts written in square characters are associated with the Pharisees, similar texts written in paleo-Hebrew characters cannot be associated with them because of the previously mentioned reasons. Therefore, since we cannot identify these paleo-Hebrew texts with the Pharisees, and since they must have originated from another major religious source in Israel, the only alternative seems to be that of the Sadducees. Proto-Masoretic texts written in the square script were undoubtedly connected with the Pharisees, and it is likely that Proto-Masoretic texts written in the paleo-Hebrew script were connected with the Sadducees. It has often been argued that the MT originated from the temple circles, where some textual activity on the Bible text took place-note that the temple employed professional *maggihim,* "correctors," or "revisers," whose task it was to safeguard precision in the writing and transmission of the text: "*Maggihim* of books in Jerusalem received their fees from the temple funds (*b. Ketub.* 19b)."[40] In the temple the proto-Masoretic text was presumably kept

[39] J. NAVEH, Early History of the Alphabet (Jerusalem 1982) 122.

[40] Furthermore, it is not impossible that an effort was made in temple circles to limit the range of differences between early texts, for a Talmudic tradition reports on the limiting of the differences between three specific texts by comparing their readings in each individual instance of disagreement. Apparently this was done in order to compose from them one single copy which would reflect the majority readings (the agreement of two sources against the third one). Although such a procedure seems to be the implication of the baraita to be quoted below, the procedures followed are not sufficiently clear.

> Three scrolls of the Law were found in the temple court. These were the maʿon ("dwelling") scroll, the zaʿaṭuṭê ("little ones") scroll, and the hy' scroll. In one of these scrolls they found written, "The eternal God is your dwelling place (מעון, maʿon)" (Deut 33:27 𝔐 מענה). And in two of the scrolls it was written, "The eternal God is your dwelling place (mʿonah ⟨that is, referring to מעונ⟩)." They adopted the reading found in the two and discarded the other. In one of them they found written, "He sent the little ones (zaʿaṭuṭê) of

intact, and this description suits the further assumption that the temple also kept the paleo-Hebrew Masoretic texts alive. The proto-Masoretic texts thus were embraced, in different scripts, by both the Pharisees and the Sadducees, both of whom were connected with the temple. If this description is correct, texts of proto-Masoretic content were central in Israel, with those of the Pharisees in the square script and those of the Sadducees in the paleo-Hebrew script. At the same time, it is not impossible that the Sadducees embraced proto-Masoretic texts both in the paleo-Hebrew and the square script.

(3) The scarcity of scribal intervention in the paleo-Hebrew texts as opposed to a large amount of scribal intervention in biblical and nonbiblical texts written in the square characters shows how careful the transmission of the paleo-Hebrew texts must have been. This feature could lead us to the Pharisees, but since they must be ruled out because of their prohibition of the paleo-Hebrew script, it leads again to the Sadducees. The Sadducees were more strict than the Pharisees with regard to the laws, so that the lack of scribal intervention in the paleo-Hebrew texts would suit them.

(4) Probably the priestly families of the Sadducees were instrumental in the preservation and revival of the paleo-Hebrew script, although this assumption cannot be documented by explicit statements to this affect. Diringer (see n. 33) suggested that the Sadducees were instrumental in influencing the Maccabees in reviving the ancient script, as reflected in the coins inscribed in that script, and possibly also reflected by the paleo-Hebrew biblical manuscripts. Also Siegel suggested that "the palaeo-Hebrew script was kept alive by the older, more conservative Priestly and Levitic families."[41] The main argument pointing to the Sadducees and Samaritans as using paleo-Hebrew characters is the abovementioned Talmudic reference to the "ordinary people" [הדיוטות] as using the paleo-Hebrew characters and the assumption that this is a polemical anti-Sadducean and anti-Samaritan statement.

(5) The evidence concerning the use of the paleo-Hebrew script for the divine names seems to point in the same direction. It was shown above that the writing of the divine names in the paleo-Hebrew script gave those words a greater sanctity, and that this approach is reflected especially in manuscripts of a Qumran sectarian background. If the writing of single words (the divine names) gave those words a greater sanctity, the writing of complete manuscripts in paleo-Hebrew characters would also give them greater sanctity, not in the eyes of the Pharisees, and apparently only in the eyes of the Sadducees and Samaritans. This assumption does not contradict the assumption that the use of the

---

the sons of Israel" (Exod 24:5). And in the two it was written, "He sent young men (naʿarê) of the sons of Israel." They adopted the two and discarded the other. In one of them they found written הוא, hw' nine times, and in two, they found it written היא, hy', eleven times. They adopted the reading found in the two and discarded the other (y. Taʿan. 4.68a).

[41] "The Employment," 171.

paleo-Hebrew script also conveyed nationalistic feelings, as it was used in the coins of the Hasmonean kings and of the leaders of the two revolts against the Romans.

The fact that the paleo-Hebrew texts reflect biblical texts of sundry textual character, while not necessarily strengthening the assumption that they are Sadducean, is easily explained by our assumption. For the situation that texts of a different textual background have something in common, viz., their script, can only mean that they came from a certain socio-religious background differing from that of the other circles in ancient Israel which diffused texts in the square script. The assumption that these were the Sadducees seems to be the most logical one. Our description refers to the proto-Masoretic texts written in the paleo-Hebrew script, and not necessarily to the other texts. It is not clear whether the Sadducees also produced 4QpaleoExod^{m} which has clear affinities to the Samaritan Pentateuch.[42]

When comparing the two assumptions relating to the writing in paleo-Hebrew characters of both individual words (the divine names) and complete texts, we note that they point in the same direction. We further note that the closeness between the Qumran sectarian views and those of the Sadducees has been stressed by several scholars, in different ways, especially in the wake of the *halakhot* listed in 4QMMT, the "Halakhic letter."[43] The *working hypothesis* suggested here is thus as follows. The Sadducees held on to certain views on the writing of the Bible manuscripts, believing in the sanctity of the writing in the paleo-Hebrew script as more authentic and hence more sacred than the writing in the square script. The Sadducees also believed in a rigid scribal transmission disallowing scribal intervention in the text. The texts written in the paleo-Hebrew script found at Qumran thus derived from Sadducean circles. At the same time, the Qumran scribes, or some Qumran scribes, while accepting the basic views of the Sadducees, did not continue these traditions strictly. They probably wrote mainly in the square script (although it is not impossible that they also wrote some of the paleo-Hebrew texts), but they accepted from the Sadducees the principle of the sanctity of the paleo-Hebrew script, and adher-

---

[42] There is no need to connect that scroll with the Samaritans since it does not contain the Samaritan sectarian readings. Besides, also a scroll written in the square script, 4QNum^{b}, is close to the Sam. Pent., so that affinity to the Sam. Pent. does not necessarily imply Samaritan authorship.

[43] See E. QIMRON and J. STRUGNELL, Qumran Cave 4.V. Miqṣat Ma^{c}ase ha-Torah (DJD X; Oxford 1994), especially the appendix to that volume by Y. SUSSMANN ("The History of the Halakha and the Dead Sea Scrolls," pp. 179–206). For further analyses, see L.H. SCHIFFMAN, "Qumran and Rabbinic Halakhah," in: S. TALMON, ed., Jewish Civilization in the Hellenistic-Roman Period (Philadelphia 1991) 138–146; J. BAUMGARTEN, "Recent Qumran Discoveries and Halakha in the Hellenistic-Roman Period," ibid., 147–158; L.H. SCHIFFMAN, "The Temple Scroll and the Systems of Jewish Law of the Second Temple Period," in: G.J. BROOKE (ed.), Temple Scroll Studies (Sheffield 1989) 143–155; IDEM, Reclaiming the Dead Sea Scrolls (Philadelphia-Jerusalem 1994) 83–89.

ing to the principle that divine names should not be erased, they used that script for writing the divine names, mainly in the nonbiblical texts. The above description does not pertain to all the texts which presumably were written by the Qumran scribal school. Some scribes used the square script for the divine names, although on the whole the Qumran scribes avoided using the divine names as much as possible.

The nature and status of the nonbiblical paleo-Hebrew fragments from Qumran and Masada remains unclear, and is not necessarily connected with the above discussion. The Masada fragment contains הרגרי[ז]י[ם] in the Samaritan spelling (as one word), and is therefore ascribed by Talmon to Samaritan circles.[44]

Appendix

Scribal Intervention in the Biblical Manuscripts[45]

Many of the texts from the Judean Desert contain a relatively large number of scribal interventions such as described below, some as many as an average of one scribal intervention in every four lines of text (thus 1QIsa[a]). On the other hand, according to Talmudic sources the sacred character of the text allows only for a minimal number of corrections. The opinions quoted in *b. Menah.* 29b mention either two or three corrections per column as the maximal number permitted, while the different opinions in *Sof.* 3.10 allow for either one or three corrections. Scrolls containing a greater number of corrections in a single column could not be used according to those texts. Most of the Qumran scrolls would thus not have passed the scrutiny of the rabbis.

A distinct difference between the texts written in the square script and those written in the paleo-Hebrew script is recognizable with regard to the amount of scribal intervention. We first turn to the texts written in the square script. The more precise and careful the scribal transmission of a certain text, the less mistakes will be made, hence less corrections are expected. However, only some scribal interventions refer to mistakes, while the other ones reflect other aspects of the scribe's willingness to intervene. In our view, these two issues are closely related. A scribe who wrote his text carefully and did not correct many scribal errors, usually did not allow for other types of scribal intervention. Apparently this also applies to the readers of such a scroll, although the approach of the *secunda manu* interventions could be different from that of the first scribe. The smallest amount of scribal intervention is found in some of the representatives of the proto-Masoretic text, usually reflecting a carefully trans-

---

[44] S. Talmon, "Fragments of Scrolls from Masada," Eretz Israel 20 (1989) 283.

[45] See the article quoted in n. 29.

mitted text. MurXII with 600 lines of preserved text, contains only eight scribal interventions, that is an average of one correction on every 75 lines. 1QIsa[b] contains an average of one correction on every 41 lines. On the other hand, 4QTest has an average of one correction for every four lines,[46] and this is also the average for the almost complete 1QIsa[a] with 250 supralinear additions of words or letters as well as 148 crossings out, erasures and dotted letters.[47] The differences between the various scrolls are thus manifest, and the principle seems to be that the more carefully transmitted texts contain a smaller number of mistakes and scribal interventions. But this does not hold for all carefully transmitted texts. Thus one of the proto-Masoretic texts, which are usually very careful, 4QJer[a], contains an average of one intervention in every three lines.

On the other hand, texts written in the paleo-Hebrew script display virtually no scribal intervention (see above).

Bibliography

J. ALLEGRO, "Further Messianic References," JBL 75 (1956) 174–87.

M. BAR-ILAN, "Scribes and Books in the Late Second Commonwealth and Rabbinic Period," in: M.J. MULDER (ed.), Mikra, Compendia Rerum Iudaicarum ad Novum Testamentum, Section Two, I (Assen-Maastricht/Philadelphia 1988) 21–38.

J. BAUMGARTEN, "Recent Qumran Discoveries and Halakha in the Hellenistic-Roman Period," in: S. TALMON (ed.), Jewish Civilization in the Hellenistic-Roman Period (Philadelphia 1991) 147–158.

L. BLAU, "Wie lange stand die althebräische Schrift bei den Juden im Gebrauch?" in: M. BRANN und F. ROSENTHAL (eds.), Gedenkbuch zur Erinnerung an David Kaufmann (Breslau 1900) 44–57.

D. DIRINGER, "Early Hebrew Script versus Square Script," in: D.W. THOMAS (ed.), Essays and Studies Presented to Stanley Arthur Cook (London 1950) 35–49.

S. GOREN, "Haketav bo nitnah ha-Torah," Maḥanayim 106 (Tel Aviv 1967) 7–13.

R.S. HANSON APUD D.N. FREEDMAN and K.A. MATHEWS, The Paleo-Hebrew Leviticus Scroll (11QpaleoLev) (Winona Lake, IN 1985) 20–23.

–, "Paleo-Hebrew Scripts in the Hasmonean Age," BASOR 175 (1964) 26–42.

M.M. KASHER, The Script of the Torah and Its Characters (Torah Shelemah 29; Heb. Jerusalem 1978) 1–49.

E.Y. KUTSCHER, The Language and Linguistic Background of the Isaiah Scroll (1 Q Is[a]) (Studies on the Texts of the Desert of Judah VI; Leiden 1974).

M. LIDZBARSKI, Handbuch der Nordsemitischen Epigraphik nebst ausgewählten Inschriften (Weimar 1898).

[46] The same scribe wrote also 1QS. This scroll contains an average of one correction per six lines.

[47] See the evidence listed by E.Y. KUTSCHER, The Language and Linguistic Background of the Isaiah Scroll (1QIs[a]) (Studies on the Texts of the Desert of Judah 6; Leiden 1974) 522–531, 555–558.

M. D. McLean, The Use and Development of Palaeo-Hebrew in the Hellenistic and Roman Periods, unpubl. diss., Harvard University, Cambridge, MA 1982.
K. A. Mathews, "The Background of the Paleo-Hebrew Texts at Qumran," in: C. L. Meyers and M. O'Connor (eds.), The Word of the Lord Shall Go Forth, Essays in Honor of David Noel Freedman in Celebration of His Sixtieth Birthday (Winona Lake, IN 1983) 549–568.
J. Naveh, Early History of the Alphabet (Jerusalem 1982).
C. Newson, "'Sectually Explicit' Literature from Qumran," in: W. H. Propp and others (eds.), The Hebrew Bible and Its Interpreters (Winona Lake, IN 1990) 167–187.
E. Qimrom and J. Strugnell, Qumran Cave 4.V. Miqṣat Maᶜase ha-Torah (DJD X; Oxford 1994).
J. A. Sanders, The Psalms Scroll from Qumran Cave 11 (11QPs[a]) (DJD IV; Oxford 1965).
L. H. Schiffman, "The Temple Scroll and the Systems of Jewish Law of the Second Temple Period," in: G. J. Brooke (ed.), Temple Scroll Studies (Sheffield 1989) 143–155.
–, "Qumran and Rabbinic Halakhah," in: S. Talmon (ed.), Jewish Civilization in the Hellenistic-Roman Period (Philadelphia 1991) 138–146.
–, Reclaiming the Dead Sea Scrolls (Philadelphia-Jerusalem 1994).
E. Schuller, Non-Canonical Psalms from Qumran – A Pseudepigraphic Collection (HSS 28; Atlanta, GA 1986) 40–41.
J. P. Siegel, "The Employment of Palaeo-Hebrew Characters for the Divine Names at Qumran in the Light of Tannaitic Sources," HUCA 42 (1971) 159–172.
–, The Scribes of Qumran. Studies in the Early History of Jewish Scribal Customs, with Special Reference to the Qumran Biblical Scrolls and to the Tannaitic Traditions of Massekheth Soferim, Brandeis University 1971 (University Microfilms, 1972).
P. W. Skehan, "The Qumran Manuscripts and Textual Criticism," SVT 4 (1957) 151.
–, "The Divine Name at Qumran, in the Masada Scroll, and in the Septuagint," Bulletin IOSCS 13 (1980) 16–44.
–, E. Ulrich, and J. E. Sanderson, Qumran Cave 4.IV, Palaeo-Hebrew and Greek Biblical Manuscripts (DJD IX; Oxford 1992).
H. Stegemann, ΚΥΡΙΟΣ Ο ΘΕΟΣ ΚΥΡΙΟΣ ΙΗΣΟΥΣ – Aufkommen und Ausbreitung des religiösen Gebrauchs von ΚΥΡΙΟΣ und seine Verwendung im Neuen Testament (Habilitationsschrift, Bonn 1969).
–, "Religionsgeschichtliche Erwägungen zu den Gottesbezeichnungen in den Qumrantexten," in: M. Delcor (ed.), Qumrân: sa piété, sa théologie et son milieu (BETL 46; Paris-Leuven, 1978) 195–217.
A. Steudel, Der Midrasch zur Eschatologie aus der Qumrangemeinde (4QMidrEschat[a.b]) (Studies on the Texts of the Desert of Judah 13; Leiden/New York/Köln 1994).
S. Talmon, "Fragments of Scrolls from Masada," Eretz Israel 20 (1989) 278–286.
E. Tov, The Orthography and Language of the Hebrew Scrolls Found at Qumran and the Origin of These Scrolls," Textus 13 (1986) 31–57.
–, "Hebrew Biblical Manuscripts from the Judaean Desert: Their Contribution to Textual Criticism," JJS 39 (1988) 5–37.
–, "The Textual Base of the Corrections in the Biblical Texts Found in Qumran," in: D. Dimant and U. Rappaport (eds.), The Dead Sea Scrolls – Forty Years of Research (Leiden/Jerusalem 1992) 299–314.

–, with the collaboration of S.J. PFANN, Companion Volume to the Dead Sea Scrolls Microfiche Edition (Second Revised Edition; Leiden 1995).

–, "Tefillin of Different Origin from Qumran?" in: J. Licht Memorial Volume, in press.

–, "Scribal Practices Reflected in the Documents from the Judean Desert and in the Rabbinic Literature – A Comparative Study," in: M. Fox and others (eds.), Festschrift M. Haran (Winona Lake, IN 1995), in press.

–, "Letters of the Cryptic A Script and Paleo-Hebrew Letters Used as Scribal Marks in Some Qumran Scrolls," DSD 2 (1995).

–, "Three Manuscripts (Abbreviated Texts?) of Canticles from Cave 4," in: JJS, 46 (1995), 88–111.

E. ULRICH, "The Palaeo-Hebrew Biblical Manuscripts from Qumran Cave 4," in: D. DIMANT and L.H. SCHIFFMAN (eds.), A Time to Prepare the Way in the Wilderness. Papers on the Qumran Scrolls by Fellows of the Institute for Advanced Studies of the Hebrew University, Jerusalem, 1989–1990 (Studies on the Texts of the Desert of Judah 16; Leiden 1995) 103–129.

W.G. WADDELL, "The Tetragrammaton in the LXX," JTS 45 (1944) 158–161.

The Leadership of the Qumran Community: Sons of Zadok – Priests – Congregation[1]

by

Geza Vermes

A study combining Qumran, Josephus and the Leontopolis episode of the history of the Jews in Egypt appears to be an apposite subject to be offered with warm wishes of friendship to honour the celebrated author of *Judentum und Hellenismus*.

Recognition that the sons of Zadok occupied a leading position in the hierarchically organized group now known as the Qumran Community long predates the discovery of the Dead Sea Scrolls. As far back as 1910, Solomon Schechter entitled his edition of the Damascus Document, Fragments *of a Zadokite Work*, because in his view the Sons of Zadok were „connected with the government of the Sect".[2]

The Damascus Document refers to „the Priests, sons of Zadok" twice in addition to their mention in a quotation of Ezekiel 44:15, on which the first allusion depends.[3]

CD 3:20-4:4

„Those who hold fast to it [the sure house in Israel] are destined to live for ever and all the glory of Adam shall be theirs, as God ordained for them by the hand of the prophet Ezekiel, saying, *The Priests, the Levites, and the sons of Zadok who kept the charge of my sanctuary when the children of Israel strayed from me, they shall offer me fat and blood* (Ezek. 44:15). *The Priests* are the converts of Israel who departed from the land of Judah, and those who joined them (pun on Levites). *The sons of Zadok* are the elect of Israel, the men called by name who shall stand at the end of days."

The context is clearly eschatological. This is evident from the introductory phrase and the citation of the eschatological section of Ezekiel. Obscure in

---

[1] The original version of this paper was read at a meeting of the Oxford Forum for Qumran Research held on 2 May 1994.

[2] Solomon Schechter, Documents of Jewish Sectaries, vol. I (Cambridge, 1910), p. xxi.

[3] Neither passage is attested in the Cave 4 fragments of D.

itself, the naming of the sons of Zadok implies that they were believed to have a leading role in the life of the elect in the last days.

The identity of the eponymous Zadok appears a little later in the same document.

CD 5:3-5

„But David had not read the sealed book of the Law which was in the ark (of the Covenant), for it was not opened in Israel from the death of Eleazar and Joshua, and the elders who worshipped Asthoreth. It was hidden and (was not) revealed until the coming of Zadok."

In sum, the establishment of an eschatological sect, linked to a „new Covenant in the land of Damascus", is credited to a priestly group designates as Zadokite.

The Zadokites

There is a distinction in Ezekiel between provincial Levites and the Jerusalem priesthood of the sons of Zadok = sons of Aaron. The latter alone were to perform priestly functions in the Temple.

According to biblical tradition, the priesthood was legitimately inherited through Eleazar and Ithamar, sons of Aaron. But the sons of Zadok descended from Eleazar through Phinehas, and later through Zadok, and their line continued with pre-exilic high priests.[4] Ezra himself was a descendant of Zadok (Ezr. 7: 1-5). Furthermore, Jesus ben Sira (Ecclus 45:23-4) connects the high priesthood to the covenant made with Phinehas and expressly declares in 50:24 (Hebr.) that the high priest Simeon, his contemporary, was of his lineage. Likewise in 51:12 (Hebr.), Ben Sira praises God for „choosing the sons of Zadok to be priests". So in the early second century BCE, being a Zadokite was synonymous with belonging to the family of high priests.[5] The Zadokite dynasty came to an end – unless we believe Josephus, or rather one of his accounts which contradicts another – with the appointment of Menelaus as high priest under Antiochus Epiphanes, a subject to be discussed below.

---

[4] Cf. 1 Chron 5:30-41//ET 6:2-15. The last high priest of the First Temple was Jehozadak (2 Kgs 25:18) and the first at the time of the return from the exile was his son, Jeshua (Hag. 1:12). So the dynasty continued. The last high priest mentioned in Neh. 12:22 is Jaddua. Another Jaddua (Iaddus), contemporary of Alexander the Great, was father of Onias I (Ant. xi. 347); Onias II, son of Simon the Righteous, functioned in the second half of the 3rd c. BCE (Ant. xii. 156–66), and Onias III (Ant. xii. 225) was deposed by Antiochus Epiphanes. CF. E. SCHÜRER, G. VERMES, F. MILLAR, History of the Jewish People in the Age of Jesus Christ, vol. II (Edinburgh, 1979), pp. 251–253.

[5] Cf. JACOB LIVER, „The ‚Sons of Zadok the Priests' in the Dead Sea Scrolls" *RQ* 6 (1967), p. 23.

The Dead Sea Scrolls

When 1QS was first published in 1951,[6] the kinship with CD was immediately noted and acknowledged. The position of the sons of Zadok was given prominence thanks to two passages figuring on col. 5.

1QS 5:1–3

„They shall separate from the congregation of the men of falsehood and shall unite, with respect to the Law and possessions, under the authority of *the sons of Zadok*, the Priests who keep the Covenant, and of the multitude of the men of the Community who hold fast to the Covenant."

1QS 5:8–10

„He (the person wishing to enter) shall undertake by a binding oath to return with all his heart and soul to every commandment of the Law of Moses in accordance with all that has been revealed of it to *the sons of Zadok*, the Priests, Keepers of the Covenant and seekers of His will, and to the multitude of the men of *their* Covenant who together have freely pledged themselves to His truth and to walking in the way of His delight."

Zadokite supremacy appears also in the Messianic Rule or 1QS[a] which opens with the clear statement that the sons of Zadok precede in every sense the men of *their* Covenant.

1QS[a] 1:1–3

„His is the Rule for all the congregation of Israel in the last days, when they shall join [the Community to wa]lk according to the law of *the sons of Zadok* the Priests and the men of *their* Covenant who have turned aside [from the] way of the people."

Later they appear as the superiors of the Levites.

1QS[a] 1:23–25

„They (the Levites) shall cause all the congregation to go and come, each man in his rank, under the direction of the heads of family of the congregation – the leaders, Judges, and officers, according to the number of all their hosts – under the authority of *the sons of Zadok*, the Priests [and of all the] heads of family of the congregation."

Finally, all the men of renown called to the council of the Community, including the Levites, will appear before *the sons of Zadok*.

---

[6] M. Burrows, J. C. Trever & W. H. Brownlee, The Dead Sea Scrolls of St. Mark's Monastery, vol. II, fasc. 2 (New Haven, 1951).

1QS^a 2:2–3

„These are the men of renown, the members of the assembly, summoned to the Council of the community in Israel before *the sons of Zadok*, the Priests."

The Rule of Benedictions or 1QS^b contains a particular blessing for „the sons of Zadok, the Priests", especially chosen by God to re-establish his covenant for ever.

1QS^b 3:22–25

„The M[aster shall bless] *the sons of Zadok*, the Priests, whom God has chosen to confirm His Covenant for [ever, and to inquire] into all His precepts in the midst of His people, and to instruct them as He commanded."

In all the foregoing passages, the sons of Zadok undoubtedly constitute the ultimate authority in matters of doctrine and sectarian discipline regarding property. Yet, as I have already noted in the new English Schürer,[7] there is equivocation in 1QS itself, and also in the Messianic Rule (1QS^a), when on the one hand these documents assert the supremacy of the Zadokite priests, and on the other, appear to attribute the same privileges to *the sons of Aaron* in general with no Zadokite connection. In the excerpts in question the rights first reserved to the sons of Zadok alone is now granted to all the priests, irrespective of their clan affiliation.

1QS 5:20–21

„They shall examine his spirit (the person's who has entered the Covenant) in community with respect to his understanding and practice of the Law, under the authority of *the sons of Aaron*, who have freely pledged themselves in the Community to restore His Covenant and to heed all the precepts commanded by Him, and of the multitude of Israel who have freely pledged themselves in the Community to return to His Covenant."

1QS 9:7

„*The sons of Aaron* alone shall command in matters of justice and property, and every rule concerning the men of the Community shall be determined according to their word."

Similarly, in the Messianic Rule, the sons of Aaron figure three times as representatives of the final authority, twice without mention of the sons of Zadok, and once as it were in competition with them.

---

[7] Cf. note 4 above, p. 253, n. 56.

1QS^a 13–16

„At the age of thirty years... he may take his place among the chiefs of the Thousands of Israel... [under the authori]ty of the sons of [Aar]on the Priests."

Moreover, the statement concerning the subjection of the Levites to the sons of Zadok (1QS^a 1:23-25), already quoted, is also preceded by the simple sentence:

1QS^a 1:22–23

„The sons of Levi shall hold office, each in his place, under the authority of *the sons of Aaron*."

1QSa 2:11–13

Finally, according to the Messianic Rule (1QS^a 2:13) the Priest-Messiah will enter at the head of the whole congregation of Israel and of

„all [his] b[rethren, the sons of] Aaron, the priests".

It should be noted in passing that the War Scroll, which makes no reference to Zadokite priests, explicitly acknowledges as legitimate not just the line of Eleazar (to which Zadok belonged) but also that of Ithamar.[8]

This terminological clash between sons of Zadok and sons of Aaron largely remained untouched for some four decades of Qumran research during which period most scholars, including myself, – notwithstanding the more inspired and perspicacious moment testified to by Schürer, vol. II – happily and simply maintained, without any proviso, that the sect was governed by the sons of Zadok the Priests, the Keepers of the Covenant.

However, when in the early summer of 1991 I was invited by Professor Emanuel Tov and the Israel Antiquities Authority to edit the unpublished fragments of the Community Rule from Cave 4, my first cursory perusal of the remains of 4QS^b (4Q256) and especially of the better preserved 4QS^d (4Q258) compelled me to approach the whole issue from a new perspective. Both these manuscripts contain the section corresponding to 1QS 5, in fact 4QS^d seems to start as a new composition at that point,[9] but neither allude to the sons of Zadok. Let us take for illustration the opening of the better preserved 4QS^d, set against 1QS 5:1-3.

---

[8] 1QM 17:3.

[9] The broad right-hand margin, twice the size of the margins separating the subsequent columns, suggests that we have here the beginning of the manuscript. Columns 1–4 of 1QS, the ceremony of the renewal of the Covenant and the instruction on the two spirits, are structurally distinct from 1QS 5ff to which they were prefixed. Cf. G. Vermes, „Qumran Forum Miscellanea I", *JJS* 43 (1992), pp. 300–301.

1QS	*4QS*
They shall separate from the congregation of the men of falsehood and shall unite with respect to the Torah and possessions and they shall be under the authority of the sons of Zadok the Priests, Keepers of the Covenant, and of the multitude of the men of the Community who hold fast to the Covenant.	And they shall separate from he congregation of the men of falsehood and shall unite with respect to the Torah and possessions and they shall be under the authority of the Congregation *(ha-rabbim)*.

The second passage, 1QS 5:7-9, dealing with new recruits to the sect, is no less significant.

1QS	*4QS*
He shall undertake by a binding oath to return with all his heart and soul to every commandment of the Law of Moses in accordance with all that has been revealed of it to *the sons of Zadok*, the Priests, the Keepers of the Covenant.	He shall undertake by a bond to [return] with all his heart and soul [t]o all that has been revealed of the L[aw].

In both passages 4QS^{d} is supported by 4QS^{b} in not mentioning the sons of Zadok. In the first case, sons of Zadok are replaced by the more general „Congregation" (literally „the Many"). In the second, the manuscripts fail to name them as the particular beneficiaries of revealed doctrine concerning the Law. No substitute is given, and the sect as a whole appears as the recipient of these revelations. It should also be stressed that the phrase *ha-rabbim* is not a special invention in the 4Q manuscripts, but is a common designation of the community in 1QS 6:1-9:2 where the term occurs no less than 34 times. It is used in this semi-technical sense in CD (13:7, 14:7, 12, 15:8) and elsewhere. Consequently, „the Congregation" must be seen as part of the general sectarian nomenclature, and „the sons of Zadok" as a less fundamental idiom.

It should further be borne in mind that the priestly privileges of the sons of Aaron concerning teaching and administration of property are formulated in 4QS^{d} in the same terms as they appear in 1QS. So the explicitly missing feature in 4QS^{b} and 4QS^{d} is the Zadokite character of the communal leadership.

This absence can be explained by one of the following alternatives.

(1) Reference to the sons of Zadok was deleted by the scribes of 4QS^{d} and 4QS^{b}.[10] But since respect for the priesthood is intact in these manuscripts of

[10] The absence of the phrase in 1QS 5:2 is attributed by J. H. Charlesworth to a scribal error: „This (the absence of the phrase) may be due to parablepsis when the eye of the scribe skipped from one *'l py* to the next *'l py* in this sentence." Cf. The Dead Sea Scrolls: Rule of the Community and Related Documents (Tübingen/Louisville, 1994), p. 19, n. 84. However, the loss of *sons of Zadok* in the passage corresponding to 1QS 5:9 cannot be accounted for by parablepsis, yet Charlesworth's only explanation consists in a reference to his comments in the note to line 2! (Ibid., p. 23, n. 100).

4QS, the removal of the Zadokite leadership remains unjustified and unjustifiable. For although in the Florilegium from Cave 4 (4Q174, col. 1, 1. 17), Ezekiel 44:10 is applied to unworthy and self-seeking sons of Zadok: – „The Levites [strayed far from me following] their idols (Ezek 37:23). They are the sons of Zadok who [seek their own] counsel and follow [their own inclination] apart from the Council of the Community“[11] – there is nowhere in the Scrolls any hint at an anti-Zadokite revolt.

(2) The earlier, no doubt original, version of the Rule had no mention of the sons of Zadok. Final authority in all matters lay with the Congregation, but this was reconcilable with the acceptance of the doctrinal and legal expertise of the priest, i.e. the sons of Aaron. This democratically organized primitive community, alluded to also in CD 1:7 (a plant root sprung from Israel and Aaron), was subsequently joined by a group of Ẓadokite priests, i.e. those associated with the party of the reigning high priests, who achieved a successful „take-over“ thanks to their doctrinal expertise and social status.

A careful investigation of Qumran literature and of second century BCE Jewish history provides in my view a suitable setting for this momentous event.

Josephus repeatedly describes the great crisis in the Jerusalem priesthood between the accession of Antiochus Epiphanes in 175 BCE and the death of the third Hellenizing high priest Alcimus around 161 BCE. His various reports are confused and self-contradictory, but the features which concern our story are reasonably clear. To unravel the obscurities, it is best to turn first to the first and second books of the Maccabees which, apart from one serious problem, seem to provide a fairly clear picture of the sequence of events.

The account of 1 & 2 Maccabees

Antiochus Epiphanes was bribed to depose the high priest Onias (III), a zealot for the Law (2 Macc 4:2), in favour of his Hellenist brother Jason (Yakim). Three years later (c. 172 BCE), having paid another bribe to Antiochus, Menelaus obtained Jason's deposition and arranged also the murder of Onias III (171 BCE). According to the Greek manuscripts of 2 Maccabees, this Menelaus was of the (non-priestly) tribe of Benjamin, but according to the Vetus Latina and the Armenian version, he belonged to the priestly clan of Bilgah. In 162 BCE, Menelaus was executed by the Syrians who appointed Alcimus to succeed him (1 Mac 7:9). A group of formerly pro-Maccabaean Hasidim were ready to accept him as high priest as he was of the „seed of Aaron“ (1 Mac 7:13) only to pay with their lives for their credulity (1 Mac

[11] DJD V (Oxford, 1968), p. 53.

7:16).[12] Neither the first nor the second book of the Maccabees alludes to the foundation of a Jewish Temple in Leontopolis by Onias IV, the son of the last legitimate high priest. For this we have to turn now to Josephus.

Josephus

Josephus offers two notices on the Temple of Onias in *Bellum*, and three in *Antiquities*.[13] They contain internal contradictions in addition to disagreements between the two works.

Bellum

In *War* i.33 we learn that the high priest Onias (III) fled to Egypt where King Ptolemy (Philometor) gave him permission to build a small town and a temple, both similar to Jerusalem, in the nome of Heliopolis.

Recording the destruction of this temple in 73 CE, shortly after that of Jerusalem in 70 CE, *War* vii. 423–32 supplies more detail. The high priest is once more (erroneously) identified as Onias son of Simon, i. e. Onias III. The temple built by him had the shape of a tower, unlike that of Jerusalem, and was furnished, not with a seven-branched lampstand, but with a hanging gold lamp. However, the altar resembled that of Jerusalem. Onias is said to have been motivated by *rivalry with the Jerusalem priests* (431), and his move was justified by the prophecy of Isaiah 18:18-19, referring to *this* temple.

Antiquities

The first version of the Onias story appears in Book xii. 237. Here the founder of the Egyptian temple is definitely *not* Onias son of Simon (III). Not only is his death (not murder) noted, but Josephus includes the additional remark that he left an infant son (νήπιος). Onias was succeeded first by his brother Jason (238), and later by another brother, Menelaus, who apparently was also called Onias. Ten years later Menelaus died and Alcimus was appointed high priest (386). Then Onias son of Onias (i. e. Onias IV), who was a child (παῖς), not a νήπιος, when his father died, fled to Egypt because Alcimus „*was not of the*

[12] If, as the Greek manuscripts of 1 Mac state, Menelaus was of the tribe of Benjamin, hence not a priest, the willingness of the Hasidim to give their allegiance to Alcimus who was of the seed of Aaron, makes good sense.

[13] On the Temple of Onias see M. DELCOR, ‚Le Temple d'Onias en Egypte', RB 75 (1968), pp. 188–203; M. HENGEL, Judaism and Hellenism (London, 1974), pp. 224–227; R. HAYWARD, ‚The Jewish Temple at Leontopolis: A Reconsideration'. JJS 33 (1982), pp. 329–343; A. WASSERSTEIN, ‚Notes on the Temple of Onias at Leontopolis', Illinois Classical Studies 18 (1993), pp. 119–129.

family of high priests" (387). With royal authorization, he built a temple in Egypt similar to that of Jerusalem.

The second version comes in Book xiii. The same Onias son of Onias sought permission to build a temple similar to that of Jerusalem and instal priests and Levites, prompted by Isaiah „who had lived six hundred years before and had foretold that a temple to the Most High God was surely to be built in Egypt by a Jew" (63). The request was conveyed in a letter to Ptolemy and Cleopatra. It was to be erected in Leontopolis, having the same dimensions as the temple in Jerusalem (65-7). The quotation of Isaiah is adduced in support of the plea (68). Permission half-heartedly granted by the king and the queen „since you say that the prophet Isaiah foretold this long ago" (69–71). The temple and the altar were modelled on those of Jerusalem but were smaller and less lavish. Onias found *some* like-minded Jews 'Ιουδαίους τινὰς, priests and Levites, to serve in this new sanctuary (73).

The third version is included in Book xx in a list of high priests.

Antiochus deposed Onias surnamed Menelaus and appointed Alcimus: of the line of Aaron, but not of Onias' family (235). His *nephew*, Onias, fled to Egypt where he built a temple and was appointed high priest (236).

I would like to end this presentation of the Josephus accounts by stressing three important features, one of them figuring also in 2 Maccabees, which may assist in interpreting the sons of Zadok question in the Qumran texts.

1. Josephus makes a clear distinctions between those who belong to the seed of Aaron and those who are members of the family of the high priest (*Ant.* xii.387; xx.235; 1 Mac 7:13). The latter are considered as having a quasi natural claim to leadership over the lower ranks of priesthood.

2. The secession of Onias IV is explained as the result of priestly rivalry (*War* vii.431) and the impression is given that the Egyptian venture was a small-scale operation by *some* Jews (*Ant.* xiii. 75).

3. Josephus offers an exegetical inspiration for, or justification of, the building of the temple of Leontopolis (*Ant.* xiii. 64 – *War* vii. 432; *Ant.* xiii. 68).

Let me now compare the result of the survey of Josephus' treatment of the Onias episode with the second alternative of the conclusion arrived at following the discussion of the Qumran evidence:

„The earlier, no doubt original, version of the Rule had no mention of the sons of Zadok. Final authority in all matters lay with the Congregation, consisting of priests and lay Israelites, but this was reconcilable with the acceptance of the doctrinal and legal expertise of the sons of Aaron. This democratically organized primitive community was subsequently joined by a group of Zadokite priests, who achieved a successful ‚take-over' and became paramount leaders thanks to their social status and doctrinal expertise."

The last statement fits exactly the attitude of the Onias group of „Zadokite“ priests regarding the hierarchical order in the priesthood. Furthermore, the small-scale character of the Leontopolis adventure would imply that part, probably the majority, of the Jerusalem Zadokite failed to follow Onias to Egypt and probably sought allies among the religiously conservative parties in Judaea. Hence a possible association with the original nucleus of the Qumran community, leading to a Zadokite predominance. Finally, the *pesher*-type interpretation of Isaiah 18:18-19, justifying the erection of a temple and an altar and sacrificial worship on Egyptian soil may point to a Zadokite priestly origin of one of the most typical features of Qumran theology.

Bibliography

BURROWS, M., TREVER, J. C., BROWNLEE, W. H., The Dead Sea Scrolls of St. Mark's Monastery, vol. II, Fasc. 2 (New Haven, 1951).

CHARLESWORTH, JAMES, H., The Dead Sea Scrolls, vol. I. Rule of the Community and Related Documents (Tübingen/Louisville, 1994).

DELCOR, M., ‚Le Temple d'Onias en Egypte‘, RB 75 (1967), pp. 188–203.

HAYWARD, ROBERT, The Jewish Temple at Leontopolis: A Reconsideration‘, JJS 33 (1982), 429–443.

HENGEL, M., Judaism and Hellenism (London, 1974), pp. 224–227.

LIVER, JACOB, ‚The „Sons of Zadok the Priests“ in the Dead Sea Scrolls‘, RQ 6 (1967), pp. 3–30.

SCHECHTER, SOLOMON, Documents of Jewish Sectaries, vol. I. Fragments of a Zadokite Work (Cambridge, 1910).

SCHÜRER, E., VERMES, G., MILLAR, F., History of the Jewish People in the Age of Jesus Christ, Vol. II. (Edinburgh, 1979).

VERMES, G., ‚Qumran Forum Miscellanea‘, JJS 43 (1992), pp. 299–305.

WASSERSTEIN, A., ‚Notes on the Temple of Onias at Leontopolis‘, Illinois Classical Studies (1993), 119–129.

Physiognonomy, Initiation, and Rank in the Qumran Community

by

PHILIP S. ALEXANDER

4Q186 (formerly known as 4QCryptic, now as 4QHoroscopes) is one of the most intriguing texts from Qumran. At first regarded by scholars as something of a curiosity and an aberration, it is at last beginning to be treated with the seriousness that it deserves. The text is not, as has been widely supposed, a horoscope but a physiognomy.[1] Physiognomy, a respected scientific discipline in the ancient world, is based on the premiss that human psychology and physiology are intimately linked. As Pseudo-Aristotle argues, in one of the most influential texts on the subject to survive from antiquity, this is a reasonable deduction from everyday experience: "Mental character is not independent of and unaffected by bodily processes, but is conditioned by the state of the body; this is well exemplified by drunkenness and sickness, where altered bodily conditions produce obvious mental modifications. And contrariwise the body is evidently influenced by the affections of the soul – by the emotions of love and fear, and by states of pleasure and pain."[2] Obviously strong emotions

---

[1] J. M. ALLEGRO seems to have started the mis-classification in his preliminary edition of the text, "An Astrological Cryptic Document from Qumran", Journal of Semitic Studies 9 (1964), pp. 291–94. See further his edition in Discoveries in the Judaean Desert, vol. 5 (Oxford 1968), pp. 88–91 + pl. XXXI, together with J. STRUGNELL's, "Notes en marge du volume V des 'Discoveries in the Judaean Desert of Jordan'," Revue de Qumran 7 (1967–71), pp. 274–76. Translations: G. VERMES, The Dead Sea Scrolls in English, 4th ed. (Harmondsworth, 1995), p. 368; F. GARCÍA MARTÍNEZ, The Dead Sea Scrolls Translated (Leiden 1994), p. 456. L. H. SCHIFFMANN, Reclaiming the Dead Sea Scrolls (Philadelphia and Jerusalem, 5775/1994) pp. 318f, persists in referring to 4Q186 as a "Horoscope", despite the fact that he correctly describes the content of the text as physiognomic. To avoid confusion "horoscope" should be used only in its strict sense to denote a natal chart. 4Q186 should be renamed "4Q Astrological Physiognomy". Schiffmann, however, displays the new respect for the text when he concludes that "physiognomy and chiromancy played an important role in the sect's thought and practice." In this essay I develop ideas which I adumbrated in E. SCHÜRER, The History of the Jewish People in the Age of Jesus Christ, revised G. VERMES, F. MILLAR and M. GOODMAN, vol. III.1 (Edingburgh, 1986), pp. 364–69.

[2] Pseudo-Aristotle, Physiognomonics 805a, ed. R. FOERSTER, Scriptores Physiognomonici Graeci et Latini (Leipzig 1893), vol. I, p. 4. The translation is by T. LOVEDAY and E. S.

produce bodily effects, but these are normally transient events. Physiognomy makes the more radical claim that the dominant characteristics of the inner person – the mental, spiritual and moral qualities of the soul – are permanently registered on the physical body. It is possible, therefore, for the trained observer to deduce a person's character from his or her outward appearance. Physiognomy is first and foremost a divinatory science. It marks one of the earliest attempts to create a scientific psychology based on observation.

In 4Q186 physiognomy is linked with astrology. In antiquity astrology was regarded by some as "the queen of the sciences".[3] It was an old-established, well-systematized and, on the whole, prestigious body of knowledge, and attempts were sometimes made to give other doctrines and ideas precision and respectability by linking them to it. In the case of physiognomy the connection is natural and logical, for according to astrology, or, to be more precise, to one branch of astrology, a person's character, as well as his destiny, is determined by the configuration of the heavens at the time of his birth, and in particular by the sign of the zodiac under which he was born. Consequently, one's astrological sign, psychological make-up and bodily form can all be seen as inter-related. The object of 4Q186 is to discover the psychology, and, theoretically speaking, one could achieve this just as satisfactorily by working from the nativity as from the physiognomy. But the astrological approach presented certain practical problems. In the ancient world few commoners birth times were recorded with sufficient precision to cast a meaningful nativity, and in any case the sophisticated calculations needed would have been beyond all but the most expert. It was easier to work from the directly observable physiognomy to the psychology and from that to deduce something about the nativity.

At Qumran there was a strong interest in astrology and astronomy (the two subjects, of course, cannot be sharply dinstinguished in the ancient world). This interest is evidenced in the numerous calendrical texts (in which astronomy has a practical, liturgical function) and in the Enochic literature, which, to judge by the number of extant fragments, was avidly studied by the Qumran community. It is not surprising, therefore, to find in 4Q186 a piece of astrological physiognomy. It should be noted, however, that the link between physiognomy and astrology, though natural and well attested in other ancient physiognomies, was not inevitable. By introducing astrology the no-

FORSTER, in: J. BARNES (ed.); The Complete Works of Aristotle: The Revised Oxford Translation, vol. I (Princeton, 1991), p. 1237.

[3] See the classic statement of the pervasive influence of astrology by FRANZ CUMONT in his Astrology and Religion among the Greeks and the Romans (New York 1961). TAMSYN S. BARTON, Power and Knowledge: Astrology, Physiognomics and Medicine under the Roman Empire (Ann Arbor, 1994), pp. 97-100, has some useful comments on the attempts by physiognomists to organize their subject as a τέχνη by linking it to other sciences. See also the same author's Ancient Astrology (London and New York 1994), pp. 179–91.

tion of determinism is brought in and stressed: one's character, manifested in one's physical form, is fore-ordained.

Physiognomy strictly speaking is not found in the Hebrew Bible, though later Jewish physiognomists ingeniously found "pegs" in Scripture on which to hang physiognomic ideas. It is an import into Second Temple Judaism – part of a body of "alien wisdom", scientific ideas apparently largely of Babylonian origin, which was domesticated within Judaism by being associated with the ante-deluvian figure of Enoch. 4Q186 can only be properly understood when read against the extensive tradition of physiognomic speculation starting with Babylonian texts and extending through Greek and Latin sources down to the Jewish, Christian and Islamic middle ages and beyond.[4] Seen against this backdrop a number of features of 4Q186 stand out as particularly significant.

(1) The physiognomy of 4Q186 appears to be based on the whole body from head to toe. Many physiognomic systems concentrate on a specific part of the body: chiromancy (or palmistry, as it is commonly called) looks at the palm of the hand, and in particular at the lines on the palm; metoposcopy focuses on the lines on the forehead; phrenology observes the shape of the cranium. There was even a type of physiognomy based on the shape of the male genitalia. 4Q186, however, covers the whole body. In particular it involves observation of physical features which can be clearly seen. In other words its physiognomy can be applied simply by looking at the person. It does not require his co-operation: he does not have to be touched or examined intimately. We shall return in due course to the possible significance of this fact.

(2) The purpose of the 4Q186 physiognomy is to determine the character of a man's "spirit" *(ruaḥ)*. This is measured on a nine-point scale running from eight parts in the "house of light" *'bet ha-'or)* and one part in the "pit of darkness" *(bor ha-ḥosheq)* to eight parts in the "pit of darkness" and one part in the "house of light". (I assume, by the way, that the scale did not include zero, and that, consequently, no-one could be totally good or totally bad.) The term "house of light" here does not appear to have astrological reference.[5] Rather it is clearly contrasted with "pit of darkness" and has a strongly sectarian mean-

---

[4] FOERSTER, Scriptores Physiognomonici Graeci et Latini, I, p. VII asserts: "Fundamenta scientiae physiognomonicae... a Graecis iacta sunt". As JACQUES ANDRÉ (Anonyme Latin: Traité de Physiognomie [Paris, 1981], p. 9f) rightly remarks this underestimates the contribution of the Babylonians, who already in the second millenium B.C.E. were beginning to develop physiognomic ideas. He points particularly to the work of F. R. KRAUS, Die physiognomischen Omina der Babylonier (Leipzig, 1935), and Texte zur babylonischen Physiognomantik (Berlin 1939). Barton's chapter on "Physiognomics" in her Power and Knowledge, pp. 95–131, provides a useful up-to-date survey of the subject, with bibliography.

[5] The "houses" of modern astrology were called "places" by the ancient astrologers. In ancient astrology the zodiacal sign or signs ruled by a heavenly body were known as its "house", but this use of the term does not seem to be relevant here: see BARTON, Ancient Astrology, pp. 96–98.

ing, which is related, as I shall argue presently, to some of the central theological ideas of the Qumran community.

(3) The use of the nine-point scale is curious. Numerologically nine is not a particularly significant number. Why not ten or seven or twelve? One corollary of the choice of nine is clear: non-one can have light and darkness in equal proportions. One is either predominantly good or predominantly bad: the Rabbinic category of the morally intermediate *(beinoniyyim)* is ruled out.[6] Thus mankind is divided starkly into two categories.

(4) This ties in directly with the the two references in 4Q 186 to the predominantly good being "of the second column" *(ha-'ammud ha-sheni)*. This expression cannot be given a convincing astrological or physiognomic sense. Its proper context probably lies in the early Jewish tradition of the heavenly books in which the history of the world is recorded and in which the names of humanity are inscribed. *'Ammud* is used here in the sense of a "column" or "list" in a scroll.[7] Only two such lists are envisaged: one for the righteous, the other for the wicked, though somewhat surprisingly the list of the righteous appears to be the *second* list. The concept of the heavenly books is used to express a number of ideas in early Judaism. Commonly they appear in the context of divine judgement: they contain the record of everyone's deeds, which is consulted by the divine tribunal to determine what rewards and punishments should be meted out on the last day. Sometimes, however, we find the idea that the whole history of the world, and the deeds of each individual, are pre-inscribed in the heavenly books, and that the history of the world consists of the unrolling, or playing out, of a predetermined scenario.[8] 4Q 186 reflects the latter view. As we have noted it is strongly marked by a doctrine of

---

[6] See Tosefta Sanhedrin 13:3; Avot de-Rabbi Natan A41 (ed. Schechter 67a); Bavli Berakhot 61b; Bavli Rosh Ha-Shanah 16b; Bavli Yoma 75a. Maimonides, Yad: Hilkhot Teshuvah 3:1 neatly sums up the Rabbinic view: "Every human being has both merits and iniquities. He whose merits are greater than his iniquities is righteous; he whose iniquities are greater than his merits is wicked; he in whom merits and iniquities are evenly balanced is intermediate."

[7] I recognize the problem that this would be a very early use of 'ammud in this sense. I can only appeal to the intrinsic probability of my explanation and to the ease with which 'ammud can be metaphorically transferred to denote a list or "column" of writing. The Greek term for a "column" of writing on a page is σελίς (literally, "a cross-beam"): see F. G. KENYON, Books and Readers in Ancient Greece and Rome, 2nd ed. (Oxford, 1951), p. 55; E. G. TURNER, Greek Papyri: an Introduction (Oxford, 1968), p. 5. ALLEGRO, DJD V, p. 90, translates 'ammud as "vault", comparing "'ammudei shamayim of Jb 26[11], explained as 'vaults' in Enoch 18[3]." The basis for Vermes's claim that "in the astrological terminology of the document, the 'second Column' doubtless means the 'second House'" (Dead Sea Scrolls in English, p. 367) is unclear.

[8] For the former idea see Daniel 7:10; Revelation 20:12; for the latter, Revelation 5:1. Further my note to 3 Enoch 45:1, in: J.H. CHARLESWORTH (ed.), The Old Testament Pseudepigrapha, vol. I (New York, 1983), p. 296, where the heavenly curtain (pargod) takes the place of the heavenly book.

election or predestination. Whether one is good or bad has been foreordained and depends on the column in which one's name is inscribed in the heavenly record. Physiognomy can be a way of discovering to which column a man belongs.

(5) 4Q 186 appears to have linked certain human types with certain animals: note "his animal is the bull". One type of physiognomy in antiquity argued from analogy to animals. "The first method (of physiognomy)," writes Pseudo-Aristotle, "took as a basis for physiognomic inferences the various genera of animals, positing for each genus a peculiar animal form, and a peculiar mental character appropriate to such a body, and then assuming that if a man resembles such and such a genus in body he will resemble it also in soul."[9] In 4Q 186 this doctrine seems to have been linked somehow with astrology: the bull-like person is said to have been born "in the foot of the bull", that is to say, presumably, when the sun was in Taurus. Because the text is fragmentary we cannot tell now how this schema was carried through: some of the zodiacal signs are not, of course, animals. It is impossible to guess what happened under the non-zoological signs, or how an appropriate animal was assigned. However, the clear link between physiognomy and astrology in the text makes it very likely that the complete text of 4Q 186 differentiated only twelve human types – one for each sign of the zodiac.

It is too easy for us today to dismiss a document such as 4Q 186 as peripheral, even within the literature of Qumran, but such a reaction may be a mistake. With its blend of physiognomy and astrology it is, for its time, quite a sophisticated and "scientific" text. As I noted earlier physiognomy is not found in the Hebrew Bible, so knowledge of this sort of teaching points to contacts with a wider intellectual world.

What function could such a text have performed at Qumran? It might simply be an example of the general learning – the *doctrina* – of the Qumran scholars. Their preservation and study of the Enochic literature and related materials bears witness to their interest in "science" and in the secrets of the physical world. 4Q 186 may be an aspect of that interest, for physiognomy, as we have already remarked, was a part of ancient "science".[10]

Physiognomy may even have been a part specifically of priestly lore. In virtue of their functions the priests had an interest in anatomy and physiology. They were involved regularly in the dissection of animals while preparing them for sacrifice. From time immemorial they had been called upon to pronounce on physical symptoms related to disease and to ritual impurity. They were expected to decide whether certain physical blemishes *(mumim)* disqualified priests from serving at the altar, or rendered animals unfit for sacrifice. The link

---

9 Physiognomonics 805 a, ed. FOERSTER pp. 6f; trans. LOVEDAY and FORSTER p. 1237.

10 The importance of the Scrolls for documenting the beginnings of Jewish interest in science has been largely ignored.

between the priests and physiognomic doctrine may go back to the beginnings of the tradition in Babylonia. The priestly classes appear to have dominated the Qumran community. Physiognomy may have been brought by them to Qumran and studied there as part of their distinctive teachings.

There are grounds, however, for thinking that physiognomy played a more central role at Qumran. I observed earlier that the two key terms in 4Q186, "the house of light" and "the pit of darkness" have no obvious meaning in either physiognomy or astrology. Rather, they recall the distinctive theology of the sect, particularly the so-called Sermon on the Two Spirits in *Serekh ha-Yaḥad* (1QS), column 3, the express purpose of which is "to instruct all the sons of light and teach them the nature of all the children of men according to the kind of spirit which they possess, the signs identifying their works during their lifetime, their visitation for chastisement, and the time of their reward." The sermon asserts that "those born of truth spring from a fountain of light [*ma'yan 'or* = 'the house of light', *bet 'or*, in 4Q186], but those born of falsehood spring from a source of darkness [*meqor ḥoshekh* = 'the pit of darkness', *bor ha-ḥoshekh*, in 4Q186]." The Qumran doctrine of the two spirits is quite different from the Rabbinic doctrine of the *yeṣer ha-ra'* and the *yeṣer ha-ṭov*. The two *yeṣarim* are essentially psychological in character: they inhere in the human spirit and are ultimately under the control of, or can be influenced by, the human will.[11] The two spirits, by way of contrast, are objective cosmic forces. The degree to which one is ruled by them appears to be totally predestined and beyond one's control. It is one's fate or destiny. This is fully consonant with the physiognomic perspective of 4Q186 and would reinforce our interpretation of the problematic term *'ammud* in that document.

The declared purpose of the Sermon on the Two Spirits is to enable the instructed to discern the "spirit" of a man, but it is vague as to how exactly that discernment is to be achieved. The "signs" *('otot)* actually mentioned in the sermon as evidence of a person's participation in light and darkness are virtues and vices, such as humility, charity, greed and deceit. The declared principle seems to be, "by their fruits shall you know them." But the language is highly suggestive and the possibility cannot be ruled out that those signs may have been extended to include physiognomic criteria. It is perhaps no accident that the preamble of the Sermon on the Two Spirits uses the phrase, "the nature of the children of men" *(toledot kol benei 'ish)*, which contains a clear echo of Genesis 5:1, "This is the book of the generations of man *(zeh sefer toledot 'adam)*...", a verse later used by the Merkavah mystics to link physiognomy to Scripture. Thus the early mediaeval treatise known as *The Physiognomy of Rabbi Ishmael (Hakkarat panim le-Rabbi Yishmael)* opens with the words:

---

[11] For a useful survey of the evidence see G. H. COHEN STUART, The Struggle in Man between Good and Evil: An inquiry into the origin of the Rabbinic concept of Yeṣer Hara' (Kampen, 1984).

"This is the book of the generations of men *(toledot 'adam)*, to distinguish between the righteous and the wicked."[12]

If physiognomic criteria were applied at Qumran, who would have applied them, and when? It may be significant that 4Q186 is in code. In fact, it is doubly encoded: it employs the cryptographic device of mirror-writing (i.e. in this case it runs from left to right) and it is written in an arbitrary mixture of alphabets – Greek, palaeo-Hebrew and the standard square Hebrew script. Clearly its contents were not intended to be read easily by members of the group. It contained esoteric teaching which may have belonged exclusively to the province of the *maskil*. Another physiognomic text from Qumran, 4Q561, explicitly assigns the secret wisdom of physiognomy to the competence of the *maskil*. The duty of instructing the sons of light regarding the two spirits also falls, according to 1QS 3:13, within the province of the *maskil*. A point made earlier should be recalled, namely that the physiognomic criteria found in 4Q186 can be applied by simple observation, without the consent, or even the knowledge, of the person being observed. The priestly leadership of the Qumran community may have attempted to use physiognomy without the knowledge of the lay membership.

The most obvious point at which to apply a physiognomic test would have been when someone applied to join the community. This suggestion finds some support in the Damascus Document (CD 13:12), where the Guardian *(mevaqqer)* is given the role of examining "every man entering the congregation with regard to his deeds, understanding, strength, ability and possessions, and (he) shall inscribe him in his place according to his rank in the lot of light *(ke-fi heyoto be-goral ha-'or)*." The implication of this statement appears to be that whether or not one belongs to the "Sons of Light", and, indeed, one's position within that group, is foreordained. But how in practice the Guardian managed to distinguish the elect from the non-elect is not revealed. Comparison with the later Merkavah mystics is instructive. They too were interested in physiognomy, and a number of texts emanating from their circles have survived. Some mediaeval physiognomic works and fragments from the Genizah are also extant, which may, or may not, have Merkavah links.[13] There are significant parallels between the terminology of these later texts and Qumran.[14] One fragment in particular (T-S K21.88) shows a general combination of physiog-

---

12 For this text see my note in SCHÜRER, History of the Jewish People, III.1, p. 367. The early Jewish physiognomists found justification for their views not only in the expression toledot 'adam in Genesis 5:1 but also in the expression hakkarat panim in Isaiah 3:9, "The look on their faces (hakkarat peneihem) witnesses against them."

13 I discuss these texts and provide bibliography in SCHÜRER, History of the Jewish People, III.1, pp. 366–69.

14 See SCHÜRER, History of the Jewish People, III.1, p. 365. It is a moot point whether or not the Qumran physiognomies and the later Jewish texts form a continuous tradition. Schiffman, Reclaiming the Deads Sea Scrolls, p. 319, thinks that they do: "From the Dead Sea sect and

nomy and astrology reminiscent of 4Q186. Sherira Gaon asserts that the *yoredei merkavah* applied physiognomy and chiromancy *(hakkarat panim ve-sidrei sirṭuṭin)* to determine who was or was not fit to receive the mystical lore of the Chariot.[15] Also noteworthy is the physiognomic fragment embedded in *Seder Eliyyahu Rabba* chap. 29: "The Sages taught: If you see a man whose eyelids are fair and whose eyes are light, know that he is wicked before God." In context the implication appears to be that he is unfit specifically to receive the Account of the Chariot.

Outside Jewish circles the Pythagoreans appear to have used physiognomy as a means of controlling admission to their conventicles. Aulus Gellius reports a tradition that "first of all he [Pythagoras] studied by 'physiognomy' the young people who presented themselves to him to follow his teaching. This word means, to inform oneself of the nature and character of a person by certain deductions drawn from the qualities of his mouth and face, and from the lines and build of his whole body."[16] The Pythagoreans provide one of the best parallels in the Graeco-Roman world to the Dead Sea Sect – a similarity noticed by Josephus when he compared the Essenes and the Pythagoreans.[17] The use of physiognomy as a test of admission also at Qumran is perfectly plausible. The social profile of the Dead Sea group favours such a view. The sect set itself off against the rest of society and saw itself as the bearer of the true doctrine. There is a whiff of paranoia at Qumran. Physiognomy may have been resorted to in an attempt to preserve the purity of the community and to prevent its teaching falling into the wrong hands. The Sermon on the Two Spirits falls just short of physiognomy, but its language is highly suggestive. Physiognomic criteria may not have been applied constantly or systematically. Indeed, it is just possible that the introduction of physiognomy may have been based on a *secondary* interpretation of the Sermon on the Two Spirits. But there is good reason to believe that it *was* applied by some people some of the time.

The Qumran community was intensely hierarchical, each member apparent-

similar groups, the notions [of physiognomy and chiromancy] then passed into the hands of circles that eventually contributed these ideas to the Jewish esoteric tradition."

15 G. G. Scholem, Kabbalah (Jerusalem, 1974), p. 14.

16 Noctes Atticae I, 2. See also Jamblichus, De vit. Phyth. XVII, 71, 74 (Alexander, JJS 28 [1977], p. 168). Barton, Power and Knowledge, p. 96, discusses the sociology of physiognomics and notes its "more sinister uses ... for social control."

17 Josephus, Ant. 15.371: "... those we call Essenes, a group which employs the same daily regime as was revealed to the Greeks by Pythagoras." Cf. Hippolytus, Ref. 9.27. I accept the identification of the sect of the Dead Sea Scrolls and the Essenes. It is strange how dismissive modern scholarship is of the parallel between the Essenes and the Pythagoreans. The assumption is that, of course, Josephus is assimilating the Jewish group to the non-Jewish to help his non-Jewish readers, and in so doing he is guilty to greater or lesser degree of distortion. In fact the parallelism is highly perceptive – the very stuff of good historiography. Shrewdly Josephus confines the comparison to the social organization of the two groups. Hippolytus, more questionably, brings in similarity of doctrine.

ly being assigned a precise rank within it. In principle physiognomy could have been used to determine not only who entered the group, but the place and standing which he held within it. Someone with five parts in the house of light is just as much one of the Sons of Light as someone with eight parts, but it would be odd if the former had held a higher position within the "lot of light" than the matter. 1QS 5.23f envisages an annual, democratic examination of a man's "spirit and deeds" in full council, so that "each man may be advanced in accordance with his understanding and the perfection of his way, or moved down in accordance with the offences committed by him." It is hard to see how this could be reconciled with a view that each person's rank is pre-determined by the immutable proportions of light and darkness within him. It is possible that different views prevailed at different times at Qumran, or that 1QS 5:23f represents the exoteric, official position, whereas the priestly elite actually attempted clandestinely to apply physiognomy in accordance with the teaching of texts such as 4Q186.

4Q186 is not the only physiognomic text to survive from Qumran. I have already mentioned 4Q561 in passing.[18] This again involves the whole body, and evinces concern about the proportions of light and darkness. Unlike 4Q186, 4Q561 does not marry physiognomy with astrology. Nor should we forget 4Q534 (the so-called "Elect of God" text).[19] There has been much dispute over the identification of the figure referred to in this fragment as the "Elect of God". Some have argued that he is the Messiah, others that the text is speaking of the birth of Noah. The two positions are not as far apart as might seem at first sight. We are clearly dealing with the birth of a "Wunderkind", whose special qualities and destiny are marked by certain physiognomic features. The Wunderkind may well be an important figure from the past, but he might equally be an important figure from the future. In certain apocalyptic traditions, in the context of "signs of the end," physiognomy was applied to the identification of the Messiah, and, indeed, of the "anti-Christ" as well.[20] It is a

---

18 Preliminary edition: R.H. Eisenman and M. Wise, The Dead Sea Scrolls Uncovered (Dorset, 1992), pp. 263–5. Translation: Florentino García Martínez, The Dead Sea Scrolls Translated, p. 456. There is even less justification for calling this text a "horoscope". It should be renamed "4Q Aramaic Physiognomy". Moreover, the claim that 4Q561 is an Aramaic copy of 4Q186 (Florentino García Martínez, p. 508) is far from obvious to me.

19 Editions: J. Starcky, "Un texte messianique araméen de la grotte 4 de Qumran", in: École des langues orientales anciennes de l'Institut Catholique de Paris. Mémorial du cinquantenaire 1914–1964 (Paris, 1964), pp. 51–66; further: J. A. Fitzmyer, "The Aramaic 'Elect of God' Text from Qumrân Cave IV," Catholic Biblical Quarterly 27 (1965), pp. 348–72; reprinted in Fitzmyer, Essays on the Semitic Background of the New Testament (London, 1971), pp. 127–60; Florentino García Martínez, "4Q Mes Ar y el libro de Noé," Escritos de Biblia y Oriente, Bibliotheca Salmanticensis 38 (1981), pp. 195–232. Translations: Vermes, Dead Sea Scrolls in English, 4th edition, p. 369; Florentino García Martínez, The Dead Sea Scrolls Translated, p. 263.

20 These traditions are, on the whole, late: see, e.g. Sefer Zerubbabel: "This is the sign of

commonplace of folklore that any child born to affect history in a dramatic way will bear in his body the marks of his peculiar destiny. Two of the signs mentioned in 4Q534, viz., "lentils" (= freckles) and "moles", figure in the mediaeval Jewish physiognomies.[21] The text is not, of course, strictly speaking a physiognomy, nor does it involve astrology. But it presupposes physiognomy and uses physiognomy for literary ends. It provides further evidence for interest in physiognomy at Qumran.[22] The possibility cannot be ruled out that some members of the Qumran set would have seen physiognomy as playing a role not only in admitting members to the community, and, possibly, in determining rank within it, but also in helping to identify at the end of history the Sons of Light in general and the Messiah in particular.

Armilos: the hair on his head is coloured like gold. He is green to the soles of his feet. The width of his face is a span. His eyes are deep. He has two heads" (trans. MARTHA HIMMELFARB, in: D. STERN and M.J. MIRSKY, Rabbinic Fantasies [Philadelphia/New York 5750/1990], p. 81f). With such characteristics he would certainly stand out from the crowd! Further, I. LÉVI, "L'apocalypse de Zorobabel", Revue des Études Juives 68 (1914), p. 159 note 10; W. BOUSSET, The Anti-Christ Legend: A Chapter in Christian and Jewish Folklore (London, 1986), p. 156f. For possible earlier evidence of physiognomy in the context of eschatology see Revelation 9:7-11.

21 SCHÜRER, History of the Jewish People, III.1, p. 365.

22 The description of Sarah's physical charms in 1QGenAp 20:1-8 may owe something to physiognomy. Physiognomy probably influenced literary texts in antiquity, as well as in modern times (BARTON, Power and Knowledge, p. 95f).

Die Gesetzeswerke in Qumran und bei Paulus

von

David Flusser

Es ist allgemein bekannt, daß die Quellen des antiken Judentums für die Exegese des Neuen Testaments wichtig sind. Es ist auch nicht unbekannt, daß ein Vergleich zwischen diesen beiden Zweigen gerade der judaistischen Forschung zugute kommt, allein schon aus dem Grund, daß das Neue Testament einen großen Wert für die Judaistik besitzt. Rabbinische Quellen fließen nämlich viel reicher erst seit der Generation von Jabne, und für die frühere Zeit füllen die neutestamentlichen Schriften wenigstens teilweise beträchtliche Lükken aus. Das jüdische wie auch das urchristliche Material ist also begrenzt, und daher tappen wir bei manchen Problemen im Dunkeln. Weitere Arbeit und epochale Entdeckungen, wie die Schriftrollen vom Toten Meer, helfen uns dann weiter, aber bei diesem Fortschritt werden oft neue Probleme sichtbar, deren Existenz wir früher nicht einmal vermutet hätten. Dadurch wird unsere Neugierde gesteigert, und wir merken, daß wir bei der wissenschaftlichen Arbeit ein Stück vorangekommen sind. Ein gutes Beispiel für dies alles ist die jüdische Vorgeschichte der paulinischen „Werke" und „Gesetzeswerke". Anders gesagt: Wo kommen diese beiden Begriffe in den jüdischen Quellen vor und was bedeuten sie in ihrem jeweiligen Kontext[1]? Im Neuen Testament findet man diese zwei Wendungen nur bei Paulus und auch dort nur im Römerbrief und in der Epistel an die Galater[2].

Der Begriff „Die Werke" war damals allgemein jüdisch. Er kommt auch in den Schriftrollen von Qumran vor[3]. Die meisten Erwähnungen der „Werke" in den Schriftrollen sind nicht sehr ergiebig: Es handelt sich dabei fast immer um die Einschätzung der Leistungen eines jeden Mitgliedes der Sekte auf dem Gebiet der Gesetzespraxis. In den Schriften von Qumran kommen die

---

[1] Dazu siehe D. Flusser, Die rabbinischen Gleichnisse, Bern 1981, S. 100–103, 115, Anm. 110–124, und DJD, Qumran Cave 4. V, Oxford 1994, S. 139.

[2] Weitere Belege: Eph. 2,8–10; 2 Tim. 1,9 und Tit. 3,5 (deuteropaulinisch); Jak. 2,14–26 (polemisch).

[3] Siehe DJD, Qumran Cave 4. V, S. 139, Anm. 43. Zu der Stelle im „Florilegium" siehe weiter unten. Die Stellen in den Schriftrollen in: J. Licht, The Rule Scroll, Jerusalem, 1965, S. 135 (hebräisch).

„Werke“ immer in der Mehrzahl vor, dagegen spricht man in der rabbinischen Welt gewöhnlich von dem „Werk“ (in der Bedeutung von der gesetzlichen Tat, dem aktiven Tun oder Handeln) in der Einzahl. Paulus hingegen spricht im Griechischen immer von den „Werken“; anders kann er es ja in der griechischen Sprache nicht sagen. Auch in der griechischen Bibel wird oft das hebräische מעשה in der Mehrzahl übersetzt.

Vielleicht ist die rabbinische Einzahl auch durch Ex. 18,20 mitbestimmt: „Zeige (Mose) ihnen (Israel) den Weg, auf dem sie wandeln, und *das Werk*, das sie tun sollen.“ Übrigens ist die hebräische Einzahl für andere Sprachen unmöglich, und darum stehen auch hier schon in der griechischen Bibel *Werke*. Die ganze Beschaffenheit des Bibelverses lädt unwillkürlich ein, die Begriffe in ihm typologisch zu verstehen[4]. Den letzten Begriff („Werk“) pflegt man entweder als „Rechtssprüche“[5] oder als „gute Werke“ zu verstehen. Die zweite Scheinlösung wiederholt sich in den rabbinischen Quellen sehr oft, weil man den ursprünglichen Sinn des Begriffes „Werke“ nicht mehr verstanden hat[6].

Es war damals die vorherrschende Meinung im Rabbinismus, daß „nicht die Hörer des Gesetzes gerecht vor Gott sind, sondern die Täter des Gesetzes gerecht gesprochen werden“ (Röm. 2, 13). Im zweiten Buch Moses (24, 7) lesen wir, daß das Volk damals sprach: „Alles, was der Herr geboten hat, wollen wir tun und (darauf) hören.“ Sie setzen also das Tun vor das Hören[7]. Die Hauptsache ist das Tun. Nicht nur Paulus, wie wir gesehen haben, hat sich in diesem Sinne ausgesprochen, sondern so hat auch immer Jesus gedacht. Er hat mit dem damaligen Rabbinismus die Ansicht geteilt, man solle die Gebote des Gesetzes nicht nur hören, sondern man soll das Gehörte auch tun und es anderen lehren. Diesen Standpunkt haben die Kreise der jüdischen „Pietisten“ mit Nachdruck hervorgehoben. Darum wurden sie als „Fromme und Männer der Tat“ bezeichnet. Als man bei einem wichtigen Treffen rabbinistischer Gelehrter um 120 n. Chr. schließlich die Frage, ob das Lernen oder die Tat wichtiger sei, zur Entscheidung bringen wollte, fand man einen Kompromiß: „Das Lernen ist wichtiger, *weil es zur Tat führt*.“ Und Rabban Schimon ben Gamaliel, der Sohn des Gamaliel, der auch aus dem Neuen Testament bekannt ist, hat gesagt: „Alle meine Tage bin ich unter den Weisen aufgewachsen, und

---

[4] Z. B. *Mechilta d'Rabbi Jishmael*, ed. H. S. Horovitz et I. A. Rabin, Jerusalem 1960, S. 189–199, und zusätzliches Material in: Prolegomena ad litteras Tannaiticas, scripsit J. N. Epstein - E. Z. Melamed, Jerusalem 1957, S. 502 (hebräisch). Siehe auch Targum Pseudo-Jonathan zu Ex. 18,20.

[5] Siehe bBQ 100a und bBMez. 30b.

[6] Zum weiteren siehe D. Flusser in Anm. 1. Zu dem prinzipiellen Wert der „Werke“ und der verwandten „Gesetzeswerke“ (מעשה תורה) im Rabbinismus siehe noch D. Flusser, Paul's Jewish-Christian Opponents in the Didache, Gilgul, Leiden 1987, S. 82, Anm. 20, und A. Büchler, Types of Jewish-Palestinian Piety, New York 1968, S. 81–91, und Sh. Safrai, Teaching of Pietists in Mishnaic Literature, in: JJS XVI (1965), S. 15–33.

[7] Flusser, Gleichnisse, S. 101.

habe nichts Besseres für den Menschen gefunden als Schweigen. Nicht die Erforschung der Lehre *(midrasch)* ist wichtig, sondern die Tat, und wer viele Worte macht, bringt Sünden" (Av. 1,17).

Wir können also festhalten, daß der Begriff der „Werke" in den Schriftrollen aus Qumran vorkommt und wollen zugleich die große Bedeutung des „Werkes" (oder der religiösen Tat) im Rabbinismus hervorheben. Nun werden wir prüfen, was man heute über die Wendung „Gesetzeswerke" im alten Judentum weiß. Leider ist dieser für Paulus so wichtige Ausdruck im Judentum nur an zwei Stellen belegt, und zwar in den Schriftrollen vom Toten Meer. Wir werden diese zwei Stellen im Folgenden noch besprechen. Vorläufig möchten wir die Überzeugung aussprechen, daß dieser Begriff, der ausschließlich im Schrifttum von Qumran und auch dort nur an zwei Stellen belegt ist, während er in der rabbinischen Literatur überhaupt nicht auftaucht, nicht aus dem Essenismus zu Paulus gelangt sein kann, als ob Paulus hier gegen eine ursprünglich essenische Hochschätzung der Gesetzeswerke polemisiere. Eine solche Hypothese ist zwar für manche Ohren verlockend, aber sie kann kaum richtig sein.

Paulus hat sicher gemeint, daß der Ausdruck „die Werke" eine Kurzform der Wendung „die Werke des Gesetzes" sei, aber so einfach ist die Sache nun doch nicht. Die Gesetzeswerke sind nämlich von der allgemein jüdischen Wendung „das Gesetz tun" abgeleitet, welche schon längst vor Paulus im Judentum üblich gewesen ist[8]. Der älteste Beleg dafür ist Sir. 19,20, und dann 1 Makk. 2,67; 13, 48. Die Wendung befindet sich auch im Rabbinismus und in den Schriftrollen von Qumran und im Neuen Testament, unter anderem auch bei Paulus selbst (Röm. 2,13). Die Wendung „das Gesetz tun" bedeutet seine Gebote erfüllen, und aus dieser Wendung sind die „Werke des Gesetzes" entstanden. Aus dem Gesagten folgt, daß der Terminus „Werke des Gesetzes" außer bei Paulus nur eher zufällig an zwei Stellen im Schrifttum von Qumran belegt werden kann. Er ist aus dem allgemein jüdischen „das Gesetz tun" abgeleitet und hat somit nichts spezifisch Essenisches an sich. Auch der Umstand, daß die „Werke des Gesetzes" ja überhaupt nur an zwei Stellen in den Qumranschriften vorkommen, läßt darauf schließen, daß diese Wendung nicht gerade typisch essenisch ist. Zu einem Schlagwort wurde sie wahrscheinlich erst durch Paulus.

Die beiden Belegstellen, die von den Gesetzeswerken sprechen, sind: DJD X, Qumran Cave 4. V (MMT) C, Zeile 27[9] und 4Q 174 1–2, Col. III, Zeile 6f. (Florilegium)[10]. Wir werden mit der zweiten Stelle beginnen. Dieses Fragment beinhaltet zwei Midraschim der Sekte: Der erste, bis Zeile 13, ist zu

---

[8] Siehe darüber bei S. Abramsson, in: Leschonenu 13 (1954), S. 61–66 (hebr.).

[9] Siehe Qumran Cave 4. V, ed. E. Qimron and J. Strugnell, S. 62.

[10] DJD. Qumran Cave 4, ed. J. M. Allegro, S. 53. Text (mit deutscher Übersetzung) auch E. Lohse, Qumran, Darmstadt 1964, S. 256–7.

2 Sam. 7,10–13 (die Weissagung des Propheten Nathan)[11] und von der Zeile 14 folgt ein Midrasch zum ersten Psalm. Die Erwähnung der „Werke des Gesetzes“ befindet sich in Zeile 7 des Midraschs zu der Weissagung Nathans. Wahrscheinlich hat Devorah Dimant[12] Recht, wenn sie in dem essenischen Text Hinweise auf drei verschiedene Heiligtümer findet: das Heiligtum, das Gott selbst am Ende der Tage errichten wird (bis Zeile 5), das gegenwärtige Heiligtum Israels (Ende Zeile 5 bis Anfang Zeile 6)[13] und die essenische Einung als eine Art von „Mensch-Heiligtum“ (מקדש אדם)[14] (Zeilen 6b–7a). Uns geht hier nur das dritte, symbolische Heiligtum an.

„Und Er sagte, man solle Ihm ein ‚Mensch-Heiligtum‘ (also ein Heiligtum aus Menschen) bauen, damit man in ihm vor ihm als Rauchopfer Taten des Gesetzes darbringe.“[15] Über die symbolische Selbstdarstellung der Sekte als Tempelbau haben viele geschrieben, unter ihnen, vor grauen Jahren, auch ich[16]. Wenn wir die diesbezüglichen Stellen genauer durchlesen, werden wir hoffentlich mehr darüber erfahren, was die Taten (oder Werke) des Gestzes sind, welche die Essener als Rauchopfer vor Gott dargebracht haben.

Josephus (A. J. 18,19)[17] berichtet: Die Essener „senden in den Tempel fromme Gaben, aber sie führen ihren Opferdienst durch verschiedenartige Reinigungen[18] durch, welche sie für richtig halten. Deshalb schließen sie sich[19] von dem gemeinsamen Tempelbezirk aus und vollbringen selbst ihren Opferdienst.“ Leider ist die Stelle ungeschickt stilisiert, eine Eigenschaft, welche sie mit den letzten Büchern der Altertümer gemeinsam hat[20]. Vielleicht ist die ungeschickte Ausdrucksweise unserer Stelle auch dadurch verursacht worden, daß Josephus von seinen essenischen Berichterstattern den Standpunkt hebrä-

---

[11] Siehe darüber: D. Flusser, Two notes on the Midrash to 2 Sam VII, in: ders., Judaism and the Origins of Christianity, Jerusalem 1988, S. 88–98. Siehe auch: B. Gärtner, The Temple and the Community in Qumran, Cambridge 1965.

[12] D. Dimant in: Messiah and Christos, Tübingen 1992, S. 38. Siehe auch B. Gärtner, S. 30–35.

[13] Meint der Verfasser ausschließlich den Ersten Tempel?

[14] Diese seltsame Wendung ist aller Wahrscheinlichkeit nach durch das folgende (2 Sam 7,19) זאת תורת האדם אדני verursacht. Der Sinn dieser Worte ist unklar, aber das hat schon der griechische Übersetzer gesehen. Wie es in der biblischen Vorlage der Verfasser stand, können wir nicht wissen, aber das Wort האדם war dort mit Sicherheit belegt.

[15] Deutsche Übersetzung auch in J. Maier, Die Qumran-Essener: Die Texte vom Toten Meer, Bd. II, München 1995, S. 104.

[16] D. Flusser, The Dead Sea Sect and Pre-Pauline Christianity, in: Judaism and the Origins of Christianity, Jerusalem, 1988, S. 35–44. Die Studie wurde zum ersten Mal im Jahre 1958 in Scripta Hierosolymitana, IV (1958), Jerusalem (S. 227–236) veröffentlicht.

[17] Über die Stelle siehe meine Studie in Anm. 16, S. 270 und siehe besonders L. H. Feldmans Ausgabe der Altertümer: Josephus, Loeb Classical Library, Bd. IX (1965), S. 16, und Feldmans Anmerkungen dort.

[18] Ein sehr ähnlicher Ausdruck findet sich in bJ 2, 159.

[19] Nicht als Passivum, sondern als Medium zu verstehen (pace Feldman, S. 18, Anm.).

[20] An demselben Mangel leidet z. B. auch der Abschnitt über Johannes den Täufer (A. J. 18,116–118).

isch (oder aramäisch) gehört hat. Diese haben ihm berichtet, daß sie anstatt des Opferdienstes in Jerusalem ihren Opferdienst durch die Werke des Gesetzes (hier: durch ihre verschiedenartigen Reinigungen) vollbringen[21]. Das haben wir auch aus dem Florilegium von Qumran gelernt. Es gibt aber noch andere Stellen in den Schriftrollen, die von dem geistigen Opferdienst der Sektenmitglieder von Qumran reden. Wir werden hier nur eine solche Stelle erwähnen, die das Wesen der Werke des Gesetzes beleuchten kann.

Nach 1QS 9,3–5 ist die essenische Einung „eine Gründung des heiligen Geistes zur ewigen Wahrheit, um zu entsühnen die Schuld der Übertretung und das Verbrechen der Sünde, zum (göttlichen) Wohlgefallen der Erde (gegenüber), mehr als Fleisch von Brandopfern und Fett von Schlachtopfern: das Hebopfer der Lippen zum Gericht ist wie Opferduft der Gerechtigkeit und vollkommener Wandel wie ein wohlgefälliges freiwilliges Opfer." Die hier gebrachte Übersetzung von E. Lohse kann die überladene Ausdrucksweise der Stelle nicht genau wiedergeben. Sicher ist, daß der essenische Dichter sagen wollte, daß der vollkommene Lebenswandel der Gemeinde auf Erden sühnend wirkt, sogar mehr als der Opferdienst im Tempel. In der Ideologie der Sekte vom Toten Meer ist dieses Motiv mit der Auffassung verbunden, daß die Gemeinde eigentlich der Tempel Gottes sei (obzwar die Sekte hofft, daß einst der bestehende Tempel in Jerusalem gereinigt werden wird). Doch gleichzeitig ist das Motiv selbst, daß das geheiligte Leben der Gemeinschaft eine (fast gleichwertige) Aufgabe habe wie der Tempeldienst, selbständig, und ist sogar noch älter als die Tempelallegorie der Essener selbst, es hat schließlich die Essener bis heute überlebt, sowohl im Judentum als auch im Christentum. Man liest schon im Ps. 51,19: „Das Opfer, das Gott gefällt, ist ein zerbrochener Geist, ein zerschlagenes Herz wirst Du, O Gott, nicht verachten." Noch näher stehen 1QS 9,4–5 die Worte der apokryphen Psalmen aus Qumran (11QPs^a 154, Col. XVIII, Zeile 10–11)[22] und Ben Sira 32 (35), 1–5[23].

Bisher konnten wir feststellen, daß die „Gesetzeswerke" – wie auch die „Werke" – im damaligen Judentum genau das bedeuten, was man schon vermuten konnte, nämlich die Gesetzespraxis. Dies wird bestätigt durch die zweite Stelle in den Schriftrollen[24]. Das Werk, das teilweise aus Fragmenten rekonstruiert werden konnte, nannten die Herausgeber bezeichnend in hebrä-

---

[21] Das ist auch die Meinung von J. M. Baumgarten, Sacrifices and Worship among the Jewish Sectarians of the Dead Sea (Qumran) Scrolls, in: Harvard Theological Review 46 (1953), S. 155.

[22] DJD IV, (11QPs^a) ed. J. A. Sanders, Oxford 1965, S. 94.

[23] Wir bringen die Stelle in der Übersetzung von R. Smend: „Wer das Gesetz hält, bringt ein reichliches Opfer, ein Friedensopfer bringt der, wer das Gebot beobachtet. Wer sich gütig beweist, bringt ein Speisopfer, und wer Mildtätigkeit übt, bringt ein Lobopfer dar. Dem Herrn wohlgefällige Gabe ist es, das Böse zu meiden, und Versöhnung, vom Unrecht abzustehen." Vgl. auch 1 Sam. 15,22–23.

[24] DJD, Qumran Cave 4. V (MMT), ed. Elisha Qimron and John Strugnell, Oxford 1994,

isch „etwas von den Gesetzeswerken“, weil der Ausdruck selbst in dem Werk vorkommt, nämlich in dem dritten Teil (C), Zeile 27. Die Schrift war anscheinend ein Sendschreiben eines führenden Esseners an einen (pharisäischen) Herrscher[25]. Der Verfasser zählt dort Fälle aus der Gesetzespraxis der Essener auf, die sich von der Gesetzespraxis der Pharisäer unterscheiden. Er faßt dies folgendermaßen zusammen: „Wir haben an dich etwas von den Gesetzeswerken geschrieben, welche wir als gut für dich und dein Volk gehalten haben.“ Aus dem Zusammenhang kann man erkennen, daß hier die „Gesetzeswerke“ die Gesetzespraxis der Sekte bedeuten. Und in bezug auf den Sinn dieser Wendung ist zu beachten, daß in der Gemeinderegel (1QS) anstatt der Gesetzeswerke die Wendung „die Werke im Gesetz“ erscheint (1Qs 5,21; 6,18)[26]. Sonst spricht man in 1QS nur von den „Werken“. Daraus folgt, daß – wie bei Paulus – die Werke und die Gesetzeswerke dieselbe Bedeutung besitzen.

Für den jüdischen Hintergrund der „Werke“ und der „Gesetzeswerke“ wäre es nicht ohne Bedeutung, wenn es wirklich in den Schriftrollen (und im Rabbinismus) keinen Unterschied zwischen den Werken und den Geboten geben würde, denn für Paulus ist der Unterschied zwischen diesen beiden Begriffen nicht sichtbar. Daß die Werke und die Gebote im Rabbinismus nicht dasselbe sind, werden wir gleich zeigen. Was die Schriftrollen aus Qumran anbelangt, kann man aufgrund des erhaltenen Materials kaum etwas Genaueres sagen. Es ist zwar wahr, daß in den beiden Texten, in denen die „Gesetzeswerke“ vorkommen (MMT und das Florilegium), die Erwähnung der Gebote nicht vorhanden ist, aber daraus sollte man nun nicht schließen, daß die Werke und Gesetzeswerke in den Schriften von Qumran gleichbedeutend mit den Geboten seien, schon deshalb nicht, weil die beiden Texte äußerst fragmentarisch erhalten sind. In 1QS kommen sowohl die Werke als auch die Gebote vor; auch das weist darauf hin, daß diese zwei Worte nicht gleichbedeutend sind. Übrigens scheint es, daß auch in 1QS Werke und Gebote verschiedenen Inhalt haben. Wenn das stimmt, würde anscheinend der Unterschied zwischen den beiden Begriffen in den Schriften von Qumran derselbe sein wie im Rabbinismus, in dem die beiden Begriffe existieren.

Wenn man aber den Unterschied zwischen den Begriffen „Werke“ (und „Gesetzeswerke“) und dem Begriff „die Gebote“ genauer aufzeigen will, entstehen, sowohl äußere als auch innere Schwierigkeiten. Um die inneren Schwierigkeiten wenigstens teilweise zu überwinden, wird uns der Befund bei Paulus helfen können, wenn wir nämlich von dem Unterschied zwischen den Werken und dem Gebot bei ihm ausgehen, um von dort nach der früheren

---

C, Zeile 27 (S. 921) und S. 139 (5.3.2.2.). Vgl. auch M. Abegg, Paul ‚Works of the Law‘ and MMT, BAR 20 (1994), S. 52–55 und 82.

25 E. Qimron and J. Strugnell, „An Unpublished Halachic Letter from Qumran“, in: The Israel Museum Journal 4 (1985), S. 9–12.

26 Siehe dazu MMT, S. 139.

jüdischen Wurzel für diesen unterschiedlichen Sprachgebrauch zu fragen. Die äußere Schwierigkeit besteht darin, daß – im Gegensatz zu dem zentralen Begriff der „Gebote" – der Ausdruck „Werke" (oder, in der kollektiven Einzahl, „das Werk") seit der späteren talmudischen Zeit eigentlich vergessen wurde, und das, obzwar noch aus der nachtalmudischen Zeit Reste eines Buches auf uns gekommen sind, das „Sefer hamaasim" (das „Buch der Werke") hieß, dessen Inhalt eine Sammlung halachischer Entscheidungen gewesen ist[27]. Weil also der Ausdruck „Werke" schon früh obsolet geworden ist, während der Begriff der Gebote im Judentum sehr lebendig blieb, läßt sich bei diesem ungleichen Quellenzustand nur schwer etwas Eindeutiges über die Unterschiede zwischen diesen beiden Begriffen sagen.

Wenn man zu dem Kern des Problems möglichst nahe vorzudringen versucht, sollte man bedenken, daß, obzwar die beiden Begriffe verwandt sind, es viele Fälle gibt, bei denen man im Judentum ausschließlich nur von den Geboten oder von den Werken reden kann, und nicht umgekehrt. So z.B. Rabban Schimon, der Sohn des Gamliel, konnte sagen (Av. 1,17): „Nicht die Erforschung der Lehre ist wichtig, sondern die Tat" – da wären „die Gebote" unangebracht. Und nach der essenischen Gemeinderegel (1QS 5,23–24) soll man jedes Mitglied der Gemeinschaft in eine Rangordnung einstufen „entsprechend seinem Verständnis und seiner Werke", und das soll man Jahr um Jahr wiederholen: man soll erneut ihren Geist und ihre Werke prüfen, um entsprechend dem Verhalten der einzelnen Mitglieder die Liste zu korrigieren. In diesem Fall wäre es absurd, hier von den Geboten, und nicht von den Werken zu sprechen, schon deshalb nicht, weil man ja nur die Menge der Werke prüfen kann, und nicht die Menge der Gebote, da es doch eine Pflicht gibt, alle Gebote zu erfüllen. Es scheint, daß im Judentum bei den Werken ein Element von Freiwilligkeit besteht.

Andererseits gibt es im antiken Judentum Fälle, in denen man nur von den Geboten und nicht von den Werken sprechen kann. Es wäre abwegig von den von Gott befohlenen Werken zu sprechen, wo es um die Gebote Gottes geht. Nach der jüdischen Auffassung hat Gott Israel durch seine Gebote geheiligt und man erfüllt ein Gebot und nicht ein Werk. Nicht nur auf deutsch, sondern schon in der griechischen und in der hebräischen Sprache ist das Hauptwort „Gebot" von dem Zeitwort „gebieten" abgeleitet: das Gebot ist von Gott geboten, während die Tat (d.h. das Werk) Gott wohlgefällig ist. Also sind im Judentum die Werke und die Gebote eng verwandt, obzwar, wie wir gesehen haben, die Gebote von Gott ausgehen und die Werke vom Menschen. Daher kann man mit Recht von den Werken des Gesetzes sprechen, und dies ist zwar von der Wendung „das Gesetz tun" abgeleitet, aber gleichzeitig kann man (so

27 Über diese Sammlung siehe Z. Safrai, The Literature of the Sages, in: Compendia Rerum Judaicarum, Van Gorcum 1987, S. 405–7.

1QS) von den Werken *im* Gesetz sprechen. Und noch etwas: wir haben auch gesehen, daß es im rabbinischen Judentum eine wichtige dialektische Spannung zwischen dem Tun (also: den Werken) und dem Lernen des Gesetzes gegeben hat.

Obzwar gewisse Teilaspekte aufgrund des Mangels an Belegen unklar bleiben müssen, ist das Gesamtbild des jüdischen Hintergrundes der paulinischen Lehre in bezug auf die Gebote und die Werke durch die Untersuchung des damaligen Judentums, wie ich hoffe, greifbarer geworden. Paulus (Röm. 2,13) war der Meinung, daß das Hören des Gesetzes nicht genügt, sondern daß man das Gesetz auch tun muß. So dachte man damals im Judentum allgemein, und das war auch die Meinung von Jesus. Doch in seiner persönlichen Theologie erweiterte Paulus den Graben zwischen dem positiv gewerteten Gesetz und seinen Geboten, und den Gesetzeswerken, die er durchaus nicht als positiv wertet – eine Ausnahme ist Röm. 2,15. Diese extreme Spannung zwischen den zwei Begriffen bei Paulus wurde durch zwei Tatsachen gefördert. Es ist bekannt, daß im ganzen Neuen Testament der Begriff „Gebote" ein durchaus positiver Begriff ist. Paulus wollte daran nichts ändern (für ihn war ja auch das Gesetz immer heilig gewesen)[28], und da auch er den positiven Gehalt der Gebote behalten wollte, standen ihm sozusagen die Werke frei. Der zweite Anstoß für die fruchtbare Umdeutung der „Werke" bei Paulus war die Tatsache, daß schon vor Paulus die Begriffe „Werke" und Gebote nicht identisch gewesen sind; die Gebote hängen direkt von Gott ab, während die Werke von der Initiative des Menschen ausgehen.

Da wird schon die paulinische Theologie des Judentums anderswo[29] behandelt haben, wollen wir hier nur kurz die Überlegungen des Paulus in bezug auf die Werke erwähnen. Wie wir schon gesagt haben, sind die Gebote für Paulus an sich heilig, wogegen die Werke (oder: die Gesetzeswerke) bei Paulus eine nicht sehr rühmliche Rolle spielen. Das ergibt sich aus der Gnadenlehre des Paulus – zur Klärung der Sachlage sollten wir zunächst Röm. 7,12–13 anführen, als Ausdruck der schöpferischen Dialektik des Paulus auf diesem Gebiet. „Das Gesetz ist heilig, gerecht und gut. Ist dann, was doch gut ist, mir zum Tod geworden? Das sei ferne! Sondern die Sünde, damit sie als Sünde sichtbar werde, hat mir durch das Gesetz den Tod gebracht, damit die Sünde überaus sichtbar werde durchs Gebot." So wurde das an sich heilige Gesetz und das zu ihm gehörende Gebot zu einem geeigneten Durchgang für die Sünde. Allerdings kommen in diesem Ideenkreis des Paulus die Begriffe „Werke" und „Gesetzeswerke" nicht vor. Sie gehören zu einem anderen Aspekt der paulinischen Lehre von dem Gesetz, nämlich zu dem Gebiet der Gesetzeswerke dem

---

[28] Siehe D. Flusser, Durch das Gesetz dem Gesetz gestorben (Gal. 2,19), in: Judaica 43 (1987), S. 30–46.

[29] In der Abhandlung über das Judentum des Paulus in: TRE, die noch nicht veröffentlicht wurde.

Glauben gegenüber. Paulus meint, daß man durch die Gesetzeswerke vor Gott nicht gerecht werden kann. Und der Glaube, der den Menschen vor Gott gerecht machen kann, ist nach Paulus der Glaube an Jesus. „Israel aber, das nach dem Gesetz der Gerechtigkeit strebt, hat das Gesetz verfehlt. Warum? Weil es ihnen nicht um die Gerechtigkeit aus Glauben, sondern um die Gerechtigkeit aus Werken ging." (Röm. 9,31–32) Ist es Zufall, daß es bei Paulus kein Verbindungsglied gibt zwischen dem Komplex der Besudelung des Gesetzes und des Gebots durch die Sünde und dem Komplex der Gesetzeswerke und des Glaubens[30]? Wenn es ein Zufall ist, dann könnte man vielleicht annehmen, daß Paulus sich vorgestellt hat, daß das Gesetz und sein Gebot durch die Sünde praktisch entwertet worden sind, und dadurch der Mensch nicht durch die Gesetzeswerke gerecht werden kann – das kann er nur noch durch den Glauben. Doch die vorgeschlagene hypothetische Rekonstruktion befriedigt nicht. Vielleicht hat Paulus sich gar keine Gedanken über den Zusammenhang der beiden Systeme, des vom Gesetz und der Sünde und von der Gerechtigkeit aus Glauben und aus Werken gemacht. Es kann sein, daß es sich bei ihm um zwei voneinander unabhängige geniale Einfälle handelt[31].

---

[30] 1Klem. 32,4 hängt von Paulus ab. Klemens folgt dem charakteristischen Zug der paulinischen ‚Rechtfertigung' durch den Glauben, aber er mildert auch hier ab. Dazu siehe besonders: Clemens de Rome, ‚Epitre aux Corinthiens', ed. Annie Jaubert, SC No 167, Paris 1971, S. 64–5.

[31] Dagegen ist das Johannesevangelium sicher nicht ‚paulinisch' wie jetzt G. Röhser, Prädestination und Verstockung, TANZ 14, Tübingen 1994, erkannt hat, siehe dort besonders S. 204–6 und 253–4. Bei Johannes ist der Begriff der Werke nicht so prägnant gefaßt, wie im Rabbinismus und – mit einer anderen Sinngebung – bei Paulus, und ist durchaus positiv gewertet. Dabei ist dort die Grenze zwischen dem prägnanten Begriff der Werke und dem moralischen Handeln verwischt, wobei bei Johannes die (moralischen) Werke natürlich mit der jüdischen Lebensweise nichts zu tun haben.

Apocalyptic, Mysticism, and the New Testament

by

Christopher Rowland

As a young graduate student I vividly remember reading with a profound sense of gratitude Martin Hengel's statement of the importance for New Testament studies of the emerging mystical tradition of Judaism: 'Investigation of the Jewish Hekalot and Merkabah literature for early Christian christology has still a wide field to explore ...'[1]. I am glad to have this opportunity to explore aspects of that, still wide, field here.

Jewish mysticism[2] in all its various manifestations has had a long history from the very earliest times after the return from exile in Babylon by way of the mystics among the tannaim and amoraim through the kabbalah down to the Hasidic movements nearer our own day. According to M. Hagigah 2,1 Jewish mysticism is divided into two main branches, that concerned with cosmogony and cosmology based on Genesis 1 (*ma'aseh bereshith*) and that based on Ezekiel 1 and the throne-chariot of God (*ma'aseh merkabah*). The latter is

---

[1] M. Hengel, Son of God, English Translation, London 1974, p. 89. In addition to the New Testament documents considered here Ephesians and Hebrews would need to be included in a complete survey of the links between the New Testament and early Jewish mysticism (see briefly A. T. Lincoln, Paradise Now and Not Yet, Cambridge 1981; L. W. Hurst, The Epistle to the Hebrews, Cambridge 1992; O. Hofius, Der Vorhang vor dem Thron Gottes, Tübingen 1972; H. Odeberg, 'The View of the Universe in the Epistle to the Ephesians', Lund Universitets Årsskrift, 29).

[2] G. Scholem, Major Trends in Jewish Mysticism, London 1955; Jewish Gnosticism, Merkabah Mysticism and Talmudic Tradition, New York 1965; also I. Gruenwald, Apocalyptic and Merkavah Mysticism, Leiden 1978); idem, From Apocalyptic to Gnosticism: Studies in Apocalypticism, Merkavah Mysticism and Gnosticism, Frankfurt 1988; N. Deutsch, The Gnostic Imagination. Gnosticisn, Mandaeisn and Merkabah Mysticisn, Leiden 1995; D. Halperin, The Merkabah in Rabbinic Literature, New Haven 1980; idem, The Faces of the Chariot, Tübingen 1988, especially chapter 3 (see C. Morray-Jones' forthcoming monograph based on his dissertation, Merkabah Mysticism and Talmudic tradition, Diss. Cambridge 1988 and his review of Halperin's, Faces, in: JTS, 41 (1990); C. Rowland, The Open Heaven, London 1982; D. Hellholm, Apocalypticsm in the Mediterranean World, Tübingen (second edition with additional bibliography 1989); J. J. Collins and J. H. Charlesworth, Mysteries and Revelations, Sheffield 1991; P. Schäfer, The Hidden and Manifest God, New York 1992; J. Dan and F. Talmage, Studies in Jewish Mysticism, Cambridge/Mass. 1982, and G. A. Wewers, Geheimnis und Geheimhaltung im rabbinischen Judentum, Berlin 1975.

much more theologically orientated in so far as it deals specifically with the nature of God and the deity's immediate environment in heaven. What we have here is not a mystical communion of the saint with God as in Christian mysticism, but the participation in and knowledge of events which are unseen to the human eye. Jewish mysticism is much more a case of knowledge or enlightenment about things which remained hidden in heaven, whether cosmological, astronomical, eschatological or theological.

It seems probable that esoteric traditions associated with Ez. 1 and similar passages were inherited by (some) of the early tannaim from the apocalyptic milieu of Second Temple Judaism, though the precise relationship remains obscure. These traditions (as in apocalyptic) probably had both an exegetical and a 'practical' (i.e. visionary-mystical) aspect. The tradition was linked with authorities like Yohanan ben Zakkai and Rabbi Akiba though some disapproved of it. This hostility probably never died out and certainly extended down to the time of the redaction of the Mishnah (it seems likely that Rabbi disapproved of the tradition – j. Hagigah 2.1). By the early second century the practices of the esoteric tradition appears to have been engaged in by leading rabbis such as Akiba. Controversy concerning the status and legitimacy of the tradition is likely to have occurred during the first century, probably because of the way in which such traditions were developed in extra-rabbinic circles, not least Christianity.

The publication of the material from Caves 4 and 11 known as the Songs of the Sabbath sacrifice[3] has given support to the view that the origin of the idea of the Hekalot (heavenly Temple), liturgy and the existence of a complex angelology is linked with speculation about God's dwelling in the Second Temple period. These fragmentary texts offer us tantalising glimpses of a (speculative?) interest which need not necessarily be the property of a marginal group within Judaism. In them we find angelic beings described as 'gods' having a priestly function in a heavenly liturgy within the innermost sanctum of heaven (4Q405 23 ii). These divine beings have intimate knowledge of the divine secrets engraved in the heavens (e.g. 4Q402 4). The repetitive style is typical not only of the later Hekaloth material but also of the letter to the Ephesians. The mention of the different heavenly languages (4Q403 1 i 1–29) suggests a peculiar language for different parts of heaven that may be akin to the glossolalia mentioned in the New Testament and alluded to in works like the Testament of Job 48. The various parts of the structure of the heavenly Temple are themselves the object of praise (4Q403 i 1) and are made up of numerous

[3] See C. Newsom, The Songs of the Sabbath Sacrifice, Atlanta 1985 and on the expositions of the chapter in the apocalyptic tradition see C. Rowland, 'The Visions of God in Apocalyptic Literature', in: JSJ 10 (1979), pp. 138ff; C. Newsom, 'Merkabah Exegesis in the Qumran Community', JJS, 38 (1987); I. Chernus, 'Visions of God in Merkabah Judaism', JSJ 13 (1982), pp. 123ff and Gruenwald, Apocalyptic.

divine *merkaboth* whose parts themselves have become angelic beings (4Q403 1 ii cf. 11Q Shir Shabb f-c-k where a number of thrones are mentioned). The angelic host is divided into different groups each with their own leader and is so reminiscent of the complex angelology of a later text like 3 Enoch. (e.g. 4Q403 1 ii). The carefully defined order of the liturgy and the deferential nature of the worship of the different grades of angels to the group of higher status may illuminate the enigmatic reference to the 'humility and worship of angels' of Col. 2.18 (4Q403 1 ii). In heaven there is a variety of entrances (similar to the earthly Temple) in and out of which run the angelic host (4Q405 14–150) destined for the divine service (4Q405 23 i). In addition to the merkabah fragment published many years ago[4] (4Q405 20 ii-20–22) in which the movement of the divine *merkabah* is described, another text (4Q405 20 ii-21–22) speaks of the glorious chariots (*merkaboth*). They are a testimony to an extensive interest in the heavenly world which exceeds the detail of all the extant apocalyptic texts. The fragments provide an insight into the existence of speculations in the Second Temple period which give the lie to the notion that such interests were merely the creation of the early Christian era. We cannot, however, conclude that they originated in visionary experience, were part of a report of heavenly ascents or some other genre from the fragmentary evidence now extant.

The descriptions of the divine throne in the Jewish apocalypses owe their inspiration principally to the first chapter of Ezekiel, though it is apparent that Isaiah 6 has also been incorporated (e.g. 1 Enoch 14; Daniel 7,9; Apocalypse of Abraham 17; the Testament of Abraham 11; Revelation 4; Slavonic Enoch 22). There has been much debate about the character of that tradition. On the one hand there are those who consider that the evidence indicates that the study of Ezekiel involved a seeing again of Ezekiel's vision by the apocalyptists and rabbinic mystics. On the other hand there are those who argue that the material (particularly the rabbinic sources) will not bear the weight of such an interpretation and prefer to see the references as indicating a midrashic activity connected with these chapters which did not differ substantially in the earliest period from that connected with other parts of Scripture.

In apocalyptic texts the vision of the merkabah is often preceded by an ascent to heaven, though there is nothing in the Qumran material explicitly to suggest that humans ascend to heaven to witness these heavenly events[5]. This is a noteworthy development as compared with the biblical exemplars. Although Isaiah believes that he can be part of the heavenly court during the course of his

---

[4] Ed. J. Strugnell, in: Supplements to Vetus Testamentum vol. 7, Leiden 1960.

[5] This has been the subject of detailed study of late and the importance of this phenomenon writing emerging Judaism and Christianity cannot be underestimated see M. Dean-Otting, Heavenly Journeys: A Study of the Motif in Hellenistic Jewish Literature, Frankfurt 1984 and M. Himmelfarb, Ascent to Heaven in Jewish and Christian Apocalypses, Oxford 1993.

call-vision in the Temple (Isaiah 6 cf. 1 Kings 22.16), there is no suggestion that this involves an ascent to the heavenly world.

The most remarkable passage of this kind in the Jewish apocalypses, and which offers early testimony of interest in the divine merkabah, is 1 Enoch 14.8ff[6]. It is found in the context of Enoch's intercession for the doomed Watchers and is in some ways and extraordinarily long digression from the main point of the saga. Enoch is commissioned to announce judgement on the watchers and Azazel (13.1) and to convey their request that Enoch should intercede with God on their behalf (13.4ff). The watchers' petition is rejected (14.1ff) and Enoch recounts his experience in 14.2ff which leads to the heavenly ascent and another account of the divine rejection of the petition. Here we have an account of a mortal taken into the divine presence (parallel to other early Enoch traditions such as Jubilees 4.20ff, which may be dependent on 1 Enoch 14), the latter confirming the view that the former may present Enoch as a celestial high priest entering the heavenly Holy of Holies[7].

We probably have no way of knowing if the descriptions of God's throne in the apocalypses, with their amalgam of various biblical passages, are the product of conventional exegetical activity carried on in the confines of scribal activity. But the possibility should not be ignored that in the study of Scripture creative imagination could have been a potent means of encouraging the belief that the biblical passages were not merely written records of past events but vehicles of contemporary manifestations of the divine . That, of course, is precisely what the writer of the New Testament Apocalypse asserts in speaking about being 'in the spirit' (4.2 cf. 1.9). Such indications, when taken together with the obvious absence of the kind of orderly exegetical activity which we find in contemporary biblical commentaries, should make us wary of ruling out the possibility of the biblical text being, in the minds of the apocalyptic visionaries, a door of perception in which the text could become the means of opening up a living reality as its details merged with parallel scriptural passages to form the distinctive visions of heaven now found in some of the apocalypses[8].

---

[6] HALPERIN, Faces, pp. 78ff.

[7] HALPERIN, Faces, pp. 80ff.

[8] Or as HALPERIN, Faces, p. 71, has put it: 'When the apocalyptic visionary "sees" something that looks like Ezekiel's merkabah, we may assume that he is seeing the merkabah vision as he has persuaded himself it really was, as Ezekiel would have seen it had he been inspired wholly and not in part.' John of Patmos exemplifies Halperin's point: John follows Ezekiel's example in seeing the heavens opened (Rev. 4.1 cf. Ez. 1.1) and eating the scroll (Rev. 10.9 cf. Ez. 3.1ff) and, what is more, like Daniel, sees a divine figure who is the author of the revelations of what is to come (Rev. 1.13ff cf. Dan. 10.5f).

II

Mysteries are mentioned from time to time in the New Testament; revelations are reported, and the future can be predicted in the darkest of hues. But in the Apocalypse the whole panoply of apocalyptic is set before us. The panorama of divine wrath and restoration vividly portrayed in the visionary imagination seems to belong to a different world to much of the rest of the New Testament. Revelation is a continuation of much of what has gone before, however, certainly as far as the debts to the emerging mystical tradition are concerned[9]. The books of Ezekiel and Daniel have influenced the form and content of the book of Revelation. From the christophany at its opening via the visions of heaven, the dirge over Babylon, the war against Gog and Magog and finally the vision of the new Jerusalem all bear the marks of influence on the prophetic imagination of John of Patmos. Daniel's beasts from the sea become in John's vision a terrible epitome of all that is most oppressive and uncannily akin to the way of perfection symbolised by the Lamb that was slain[10].

This unique example in the early Christian literature of the apocalyptic genre is profoundly indebted to Jewish apocalyptic ideas. In Revelation the first chapter of Ezekiel, the *merkabah* chapter, has not only contributed to the visionary vocabulary of John but the initiatory visions (namely 1.13ff and 4.1ff) are dominated by it. While it may be supposed that the resources which John could call on to express the divine glory that confronted him were indeed limited (at least as far as scriptural exemplars were concerned), the extent of the indebtedness to Ezekiel points in the direction of more than a chance reference . When taken alongside those other descriptions of the divinity which are now extant from the Second Temple period, we may suppose that we have in Revelation a glimpse of the tip of a mystical iceberg now largely lost from our view. What is visible points to a distinctive use of the prophecy parallel to, but in significant respects different from, other apocalyptic texts.

Although the secrets which are revealed in Rev(elation) are largely concerned with the future hope, its outlook is at one with the mystical literature of Judaism. Its angelology, heavenly voices and preoccupation with the hidden is precisely what we find in the mystical literature. Revelation is not concerned with the minute detail of the heavenly ascent (indeed there is a minimum of interest in the paraphernalia of the apocalyptic ascent) nor does it offer details of what is required of the mystic to make a successful entry into the heavenly palaces. We cannot know what led to John's dramatic meeting with the heavenly son of man on the isle of Patmos, even if conjectures may be made about the

[9] In addition to C. Rowland, in: JSJ 10 (1979), and Gruenwald, Apocalyptic, see Halperin, Faces, pp. 87ff.

[10] On the connections of Daniel and Revelation with Ezekiel's, *hayyot*, see the suggestive comments of Halperin, Faces, pp. 76ff.

significance of the time (the Lord's Day) and the place (in exile as was the prophet Ezekiel).

The opening of the book describes a christophany with few parallels in the New Testament (the Transfiguration being a notable exception)[11]. There are some similarities with various christophanies and angelophanies from both Jewish and Christian texts. The elements of this chapter are inspired by several Old Testament passages, one of which is the first chapter of Ezekiel[12], particularly that at the climax of his call-vision where the prophet catches a glimpse of the form of God on the throne of glory in the dazzling gleam of bronze and Dan. 10.5f where we find a vision of a heavenly being broadly-based on Ezekiel and especially on the first chapter .

There are hints of a tradition of interpretation of Ez. 1[13], particularly in visionary contexts, in which the glorious figure on the throne acts in a quasi-angelic role. This is evident when we compare Revelation with the contemporary Apocalypse of Abraham, where there is a remarkably similar vision[14]:

Rev. 1.13–17...	*Apocalypse of Abraham 10f...*
and in the midst of the lamp stands one like a son of man, clothed with a long robe and with a golden girdle round his breast; his head and his hair were white as wool, white as snow; his eyes were like a flame of fire, his feet were like burnished bronze, refined as in a furnace, and his voice was like the sound of many waters; in his right hand he held seven stars,	... and the appearance of his body was like sapphire, and the look of his like chrysolite, and the hair of his head like snow, and the turban upon his head like the appearance of a rainbow (cf. Rev. 4.3) and the clothing of his garments like purple,

---

[11] Thoroughly explored in L. STUCKENBRUCK, Angel Veneration and Christology, Tübingen 1995.

[12] The vision of God's glory in human form was the basis of the shi'ur qomah speculation which may go back to the second temple period. See M.S. COHEN, The Shiʿur Qomah : the Liturgy and Theurgy in Pre-Kabbalistic Jewish Mysticism New York 1983; J.M. BAUMGARTEN, 'The Book of Elchesai and Merkabah Mysticism', JSJ, 17 (1986), pp. 212ff.

[13] Most recently discussed in L. STUCKENBRUCK, Angel Veneration and Christology, pp. 211f.

[14] A detailed comparison is offered in ROWLAND 'A Man Clothed in White Linen', JSNT, 24 (1985), pp. 99ff. It has been suggested that the angel Jaoel is conceived as the figure on the throne who moves from the throne, now covered with fire and with no reference to a human figure upon it, to act as Abraham's guide (J. FOSSUM, The Name of God and the Angel of the Lord, Tübingen 1985; C. ROWLAND, The Open Heaven especially pp. 94ff), but the evidence does not permit any certainty in this matter (see L.W. HURTADO, One God, One Lord, London 1990, p. 88f). At the very least this angel seems ontologically to be linked with God.

from his mouth issued a
sharp two-edged sword, and his face
was like the sun shining in full strength . . .

and a golden sceptre was
in his right hand . . .

The vision of Christ marks the very start of John's revelation, and although there are similar 'angelophanies' in Rev. 10.1ff and 14.6ff, this inaugural vision is not typical of the christoogy of the rest of the Apocalypse[15]. After the instruction to write the letters to the seven churches (a scribal role which resembles that of Enoch in 1 Enoch 12–14), John is called to heaven 'in the spirit' and is granted a vision of the divine throne with one seated upon it. There is no mention of a heavenly journey in this text preceding the granting of the vision of God. Indeed, Revelation is singularly lacking in the complex uranology which is typical of later Jewish apocalyptic texts and is sparse in the details communicated about the heavenly world. Nevertheless there is at the start of this new dimension of John's vision a vision of the throne which owes some of its details to Ez. 1 and to the related passage in Is. 6. Revelation 4 offers a heavenly throne scene which could easily have been written by any Jew, though some have found evidence of particular Christian influence in the reference to the twenty-four elders[16]. God sits in heaven surrounded by the celestial retinue, praised by the heavenly host. It is a reality which is cut off from normal human gaze and opened up only to the privileged seer.

The scene in heaven is transformed in chapter 5. John sees the scroll with seven seals, which contains the divine will for the inauguration of the eschatological process. The means of the initiation of that process turns out to be the coming of the messiah, the Lion of Judah. The paradox is that this messianic Lion turns out to be a Lamb with the marks of death. Superficially, the scene is similar to that described in Dan. 7.9, where there is also a heavenly court. Whereas in the latter a human figure comes to take divine authority, here it is a an animal. This parallels the way in which in 1 Enoch 89–90 animals represent men. Clearly, it was the fact that the Lamb's marks of slaughter qualified it to have this supreme eschatological role and to share the divine throne (7.17). At first the Lamb stands as one of the heavenly throng, but wins the right to superiority and the privilege of divine power, as the result of the conquest wrought through death .

There is in the imagery of this chapter an unusual development of the apocalyptic tradition. We are familiar with animals in dream visions from 1 Enoch 89ff (the so called Animal Apocalypse). These almost always are given symbolic significance as representing persons or nations (as the beasts represent kings in Dan. 7). In 1 Enoch, for example, animals represent humans, and

[15] Discussed in L. Stuckenbruck, Angel Veneration and Christology, pp. 205ff.

[16] C. Rowland, 'The Visions of God in Apocalyptic Literature', in: JSJ 10 (1979), pp. 138ff cf. L. Hurtado, 'Revelation 4–5 in the Light of Jewish Apocalyptic Analogies', JSNT, 25 (1985), pp. 105ff.

men (or shepherds) angels. What we have in Rev. rather is a picture of the heavenly world. Rev. 5 offers an unusual, perhaps unique juxtaposition of the throne theophany vision with the dream vision. We might have expected the angelic figure of chapter 1 to have been the suppliant before the divine throne. Instead there is resort to the animal symbolism of the dream vision in which the Christ is represented by a Lamb. And it is this symbol which is maintained throughout the apocalypse[17]. The use of that animal symbolism, when viewed in the light of the 1 Enoch material, suggests a determined attempt to stress the humanity of the messianic agent (humans are invariably animals and only become angelic proleptically in the case of Noah in 1 Enoch 89.1).

We may even speak of a mixing of genres here, all the more apposite when the message which the text seeks to convey is of the cosmos-shattering effects of the triumph of Christ. If we examine the Jewish apocalypses, it is apparent that there are several types of vision[18]. There is the report by the seer of what he has seen in heaven, usually after a mystical ascent. Then there is the communication to the seer of divine secrets by an angel in which heavenly visions play no part. Finally there is the dream vision in which the seer sees in a dream various objects (often animals) which afterwards by means of an angelic interpretation are explained. These have no independent existence except as part of the dream-vision and are merely symbols of persons and events which take place on earth.

There is usually a fairly clear distinction in the apocalypses between visions of the first type and visions of the third type. In type 1 we have attempts to describe the environs of God using the terminology of Ezekiel and Isaiah. These are no symbols but a report of what is actually believed to be the case in the world above. The dream vision with its extravagant symbols and interpretation are not usually mingled in the Jewish apocalypses as they are in Rev. 4–5. The vision in Rev. 4 is a good example of the first type of vision. John glimpses the activities in heaven normally hidden from human perception. If John had followed the conventions of apocalyptic set out in ch. 4 he might have been expected to have described Christ in language similar to that in 1.13ff. Instead we have the introduction of the language of the symbolic vision – ἀϱνίον ἑστηκὸς ὡς ἐσφαγμένον. The juxtaposition of visionary types has few parallels. The awkwardness of the juxtaposition reflected also in the oxymoron in 5.4f ἰδοὺ ένίκησεν ὁ ἐκ τῆς φυλῆς Ἰύδα, ἡ ῥίζα Δαυίδ, … ἀϱνίον ἐστηκός ὡς ἐσφαγμένον could reflect at the formal level the jarring nature of the eschatological reality to which John seeks to bear witness. The Lamb had affected the normal apocalyptic conventions and hitherto accepted patterns of discourse is shattered as well as the understanding and course of history.

---

[17] See L. Stuckenbruck, Angel Veneration and Christology, pp. 267ff.

[18] See the survey in J.J. Collins, Apocalypse. Morphology of a Genre (Semeia 14), Missoula 1979.

With the book of Revelation we are in the midst of the world of apocalyptic mystery. Despite attempts over the years to play down the importance of this book, the indications suggest that its thought-forms and outlook were more typical of early Christianity than is often allowed. The fact that we possess no visionary material elsewhere in the New Testament accounts for some of the differences, but they are superficial. Beneath the surface we have here convictions about God, Christ and the world which are not far removed from the so-called 'mainstream' Christianity of the rest of the New Testament. The synoptic eschatological discourses are an obvious example of a similar outlook but they are by no means alone. Revelation, with its indebtedness to a shadowy, perhaps embryonic, mysticism of the Second Temple period, prompts us to look closer at the other New Testament texts to see whether they too exhibit some of the tell-tale marks of mysticism which may enable us to pursue the mystical evidence further in less overtly apocalyptic texts.

III

We know Paul was influenced by apocalyptic ascent ideas (2 Cor. 12.2ff), and he emphasises the importance of this visionary element as the basis of his practice (Gal. 1.12 and 1.16 cf. Acts 22.17). His apocalyptic outlook enabled him to act on his eschatological convictions, so that his apocalypse of Jesus Christ became the basis for his practice of admitting Gentiles to the messianic age without the Law of Moses. His relegation of the Sinai covenant to a subordinate position to the new covenant in the Messiah contrasts with the firm subordination of the apocalyptic spirit of Ezekiel 1 to the Sinai theophany in the rabbinic traditions.

The mystical component in Paul's life stands like a central pillar fundamental for his whole career[19]. At the very start of that phase of his life he considered himself called to be an apostle of Jesus Christ. We are no longer in a position to know exactly whether Paul as a Pharisee may have been introduced to the arcane mysteries of apocalyptic. The so-called conversion (so called because, as many have pointed out, this was not the change from one religion to another but from one sect within Judaism to another) is shrouded behind the matter-of-fact accounts of the Acts of Apostles and the suggestive glimpses behind the veil in

[19] See A. SEGAL, Two Powers in Heaven, Leiden 1978; J. FOSSUM, The Name of God and the Angel of the Lord, Tübingen 1985; IDEM, 'Jewish Christian Christology and Jewish Mysticism', Vigiliae Christianae, 37 (1983), pp. 260ff; C. ROWLAND, The Open Heaven, especially pp. 94ff; 'The Vision of the Risen Christ', JTS, 31 (1980), pp. 1ff; J. ASHTON, Studying John, Oxford 1994; J. FOSSUM, The Image of the Invisible God. Essays on the Influence of Jewish Mysticism on Early Chrisology, 1995; L.W. HURTADO, One God, One Lord London 1990; and M. MACH, Die Entstehung des jüdischen Engelglaubens. Entwicklungsphasen des jüdischen Engelglaubens in vorrabinischer Zeit, Tübingen 1992.

Galatians. Yet, for all that, it is the mysterious world of apocalyptic vision which best explains that shattering moment in Paul's life. According to Acts 26.19 Paul describes what he has seen as an ὀπτασία[20]. In Galatians Paul speaks of the moment of disclosure as an ἀποκάλυψις (Gal. 1.12) and 1.16 of 'God being pleased to reveal his son to me'. In Gal. Paul affirms that he did not receive his commission by any human agency but διὰ ἀποκαλύψεως Ιησοῦ Χριστοῦ. His gospel is just as much the result of a direct confrontation with Jesus Christ as any that had been received by the 'pillar' apostles. Jesus of Nazareth, seated at the right hand of God but to be manifested in glory at the close of the age (1 Cor. 1.7), had proleptically revealed himself to the Pharisee Saul of Tarsus. In line with the Jewish apocalyptic tradition Paul thinks of another dimension to human existence normally hidden from sight but revealed to the favoured few. When Paul sees the risen lord, he sees a being in heaven.

It was an experience of a similar kind, as far as we are able to judge, to that recorded in 2 Cor. 12.2[21]. Here in a confession which events have squeezed out of him, the apostle speaks in oblique fashion about an experience fourteen years before when 'a man in Christ' was snatched up into paradise or the third heaven. Although there are those who contend that Paul chooses to boast about a third person here, the reference to the abundance of revelations in 12.6 suggests that Paul has himself in mind, or perhaps that 'apocalyptic self' which experiences such awesome things. While Paul speaks of the ineffable words he heard on that occasion, it appears to differ from the Damascus Road experience in not having that life-changing quality about it. According to Acts (22.17 and 27.23) the visions and revelations mentioned in 2 Cor. 12.2 were not Paul's only experiences.

The nature of the experience related in 2 Cor. has been much discussed. In a highly stylised account there is a case for supposing that Paul speaks in two different ways about the same experience. Others have argued for a two stage experience, with Paradise and the third heaven being successive stages on the mystical ascent. It is not impossible that the experience which is wrung out of him here has a particular relevance to his weaknesses because he nowhere *describes* a vision of God[22]. It may only be implied in the 'unutterable words'. Such a failure to reach the climax of the mystical ascent would indeed have been an admission of weakness which a mystic might have wished to conceal, though

---

[20] This is a term which is used in Dan. 10.16 (Theod.) of Daniel's vision of the exalted heavenly being (cf. Lk. 1.22 and 24.23). On Acts 26.19 see O. BETZ, 'Die Vision des Paulus im Tempel von Jerusalem' in BETZ et al., Abraham unser Vater, Wuppertal 1970, pp. 113ff. On Paul's glory christology C. NEWMAN, Paul's Glory-Christology: Tradition and Rhetoric, Leiden 1992, and S. KIM, The Origin of Paul's Gospel, Tübingen 1981.

[21] See the discussion in J. T. TABOR, Things Unutterable, University Press of America 1986. M. GOULDER, 'The Visionaries of Laodicea', ISNT 43 (1991) pp. 15ff.

[22] See P. SCHÄFER, 'New Testament and the Hekhalot Literature: The Journey into Heaven in Paul and in Merkavah Mysticism', Journal of Jewish Studies 35 (1984), pp. 19ff.

it would have suited Paul's argument in this section where weakness and failure are the marks of a true apostle[23].

That Paul is using traditional language and style of Jewish apocalyptic is apparent from the cosmological framework and language. His use of the Greek ἁρπάζω is particularly pertinent to our theme. It is a word used elsewhere in the New Testament to speak of the mysterious rapture of individuals, whether to heaven (1 Thess. 4.17; Rev. 12.5) or as the result of divine intervention (Acts 8.39[24]). The word is used of Enoch's translation in Wisdom 4.11 (cf. LXX Gen. 5.24 and Sirach 44.16 where μετατίθημι is used).

The 'things that cannot be uttered' have their parallels elsewhere in the Pauline corpus. Paul seems to have had recourse to a number of divine secrets which were of fundamental importance for his theology. In 1 Cor. 15.51, for example, he illuminates the problem of the relationship between mundane existence and the resurrection life by resort to a mystery about eschatological transformation. Also, in the doxology at the end of Romans, whose authenticity is often disputed, there is reference to revelation of the divine mystery in an unusual formulation reminiscent of the language of Ephesians[25]. Elsewhere he lets the Roman readers into the eschatological mystery of Israel's destiny in Ro. 11.25.

In 2 Cor. 3 Paul contrasts his apostolic ministry with the ministrations of Moses. The extent and apparent arrogance of the claims are at once apparent. Here is Paul not only placing his activity on a superior plane to that of Moses but subordinating the latter's pivotal role in the divine economy to himself and asserting the temporary nature of it. What starts off as a contrast ends up as an assertion about the present transformative glory which belongs to those who are ministers of the new covenant. These ministers do not need their faces veiled. The apostolic ministers reflect the divine glory. Such reflection of divine glory is apparent in 2 Enoch 22.8. Here the seer beholds the glory of God, and this results in his transformation so that he reflects the glory which he had been privileged to see[26]. In 2 Cor. 3 it is not merely a future phenomenon as elsewhere but something which begins in the present age.

---

23 I am much indebted in the discussion of this passage and what follows on the Pauline material to the work of my colleague Paula Gooder in Oxford.

24 There are other echoes of the [Enoch] tradition in this verse after πνεῦμα κυρίου ἥρπασεν τὸν Φίλιππον. The disappearance of Philipp is similar to that of Enoch attested in the Targumim (καὶ οὐκ εἶδεν ἀτὸν οὐκέτι ὁ ευνοῦχος cf. Fragment Targum לית אנן ידעין מא הוה בסופיה). Philipp's reappearance echoes LXX of Gen. 5.24 (Φίλιππος δε εὑρέθη εἰς Ἄζωτον cf. LXX καὶ οὐχ εὑρίσκετο, ὅτι μετέθηκεν ὁ Θεός).

25 On all this material see the survey in M. BOCKMUEHL, Revelation and Mystery, Tübingen 1990, and J.J. COLLINS and J.H. CHARLESWORTH, Mysteries and Revelations, Sheffield 1991.

26 C.R.A. MORRAY-JONES, 'Transformational Mysticism in the Apocalyptic-Merkabah Tradition', JJS, 43 (1992), and W.F. SMELIK, 'On Mystical Transformation of the Righteous into Light in Judaism', JSJ, 26 (1995).

The model of transformation of which Paul speaks in 2 Cor. 3 is nothing less than the divine image which believers share . The phrase 'from glory to glory' suggests a progressive transformation, similar to that in some of the apocalypses. In Asc. Is. 8.14; 11.22 for example the descent of Christ through the heavens leads to a progressive diminution of the glory he had possessed in the highest heavens. This enabled him to mislead the heavenly powers at his descent. Similarly Isaiah's ascent to the heavenly world brings about a transformation of his own body as he approaches the seventh heaven. In 2 Cor 4.1ff Paul indicates that there is a present possession of this heavenly glory in the ordinary ministrations of the apostle. Earth-bound witnesses should not be deceived, therefore, by the apparent humble persona into thinking that there is little of the glory of the highest heaven. This is nothing other than the knowledge of God's glory, the highest privilege granted to the apocalyptic visionary, but now located in the face of Jesus Christ and reflected in the suffering Apostle.

Paul sees himself and his intimate companions to be mystagogues who are like stewards in the divine palace with the privilege of administering the divine secrets (1 Cor. 4.1). Access to divine secrets is typical of the apocalypses and forms a central feature of the authority granted to the Teacher of Righteousness at Qumran (cf. 1 QpHab 7). Such mysteries do not only relate to the details of eschatological salvation and the reordering of conventional wisdom about its fulfilment but also about the central item of the gospel. This is most apparent in 1 Cor. 2.6f, where Paul talks of the content of the gospel itself as a mystery hidden from the rulers of the present age. It is this which is the essence of divine wisdom, perceived as foolishness to those who cannot understand the secret of the divine purpose. Here, in an argument reminiscent of the opening chapters of the Wisdom of Solomon, Paul contrasts the divine with the human wisdom and suggests that the clue to salvation is based upon the inability of those dominated by the epistemology of the present age to see the significance of what they were doing in crucifying the lord of glory (1 Cor. 2.9). This turns out to be the very heart of the divine mystery for the salvation of the world.

So the Christ event itself is an apocalyptic mystery hidden before all ages but only revealed in the last days (cf. 1 Peter 1.11f; Lk. 10.23f). This terminology is taken up in the (deutero –?) Pauline Colossians and Ephesians. In Col. 1.26 (cf. Ro. 16.27 and Eph. 3.3), for example, God's plan for the salvation of the gentiles is portrayed as a great apocalyptic mystery which Paul has been privileged to receive and which forms the basis for the apostolic ministry in which he is engaged. So the apostolic task is not a parochial affair, for the apostles themselves are engaged in an enterprise on a truly cosmic scale (1 Cor. 4.10) as God's fellow workers (3.9). Paul sees himself as an architect working according to a divine master-plan, parallel to Moses himself (Ex. 25.9 and 40: 'According to all that I show you concerning the tabernacle, and of its furniture, so you shall make it... And see that you make them after the pattern of them, which is being shown you on the mountain' cf. 1 Chron. 28.18 and 2 Cor. 3.16f). Indeed, that to which the apostles are bearing witness is itself an apocalyptic event.

In Ro. 1.17f Paul can speak of the gospel and its content as that which is revealed from heaven, and in Ro. 3.22, using slightly different terminology, he summarises the saving event of Christ as something which was heralded by the law and the prophets but is essentially a fresh and definitive revelation from God. That divine wisdom to which the true apostle has access is a mystery taught by the Spirit and which can only be understood by others who themselves have the Spirit. Indeed, in 1 Cor. 2.10 Paul sets out most explicitly his claim that the truth to which he has access is one that is a divine secret understandable only by those who are themselves inspired by the same spirit. Moreover, there is an intimate link between the medium and the message. By virtue of his own knowledge and practice the gospel can be observed in his own person and conduct : Paul has the mind of Christ himself (1 Cor. 2.16) and speaks words which are not taught by humans but by God (2.13 cf. Gal. 1.1). Those who regard themselves as wise according to the wisdom of the present age, and are unaware of the content of the divine mystery, turn out to be babes. Those who are truly mature are the ones who, according to the criteria of the age which is passing away, seem to be fools (3.18f). Understanding comes through the Spirit, and it is the Spirit which enables those who truly understand to have access to the most profound truths about God (1 Cor. 2.10), the very heart of the mystical ascent. The material in 1 Cor. 2 is a reminder that discussion of Paul's mysticism should not focus only in 2 Cor. 12.2ff, where Paul's ambivalence is everywhere apparent. Such ambivalence is comprehensible if we recognise that for Paul the central mystery is the cross of Christ. That is the wisdom of which he speaks, not the exclusive mystery which comes only via the heavenly ascent.

Possible cultic background for the accounts of mystical ascent[27] (most evident in 1 Enoch 14), as well as the explicit reference to impurity caused by menstrual blood in Hekaloth Rabbati 18[28], reminds us that access to holy places was limited to men. This was certainly true in the Temple. We *presume* that Paul's communities consisted of women as well as men, in the light of the occasional reference to women such as Chloe in 1 Cor. 1.11 and the significant role given to Phoebe in Ro. 16. That being the case, the transfer of cultic

[27] See HIMMELFARB, op. cit., and on the social background of apocalyptic see P. R. DAVIES, 'The social world of the apocalyptic writings', in: R. E. CLEMENTS, The World of Ancient Israel, Cambridge 1989 and the final chapters of P. L. ESLER, The First Christians in their Social Worlds, London 1994.

[28] Disucssed in G. SCHOLEM, Jewish Gnosticism, Merkabah Mysticism and Talmudic Tradition, New York 1965, p. 19ff.

imagery to a community which was of both sexes is a reminder that ritual impurity does not seem to have been a disqualification from access to the nascent Christian communities[29].

Paul's argument in 1 Cor. is that the supreme manifestation of divine wisdom is to be found in the crucified Christ, in complete contrast to what the wisdom of the world might have expected. It is a wisdom of which Paul claims to speak, but it is a wisdom which is such only among the τέλειοι and it is not clear that the Corinthians have demonstrated that they have reached that stage. The strife that exists among them means that they are still σαρκικοί and not πνευματικοί; still babes who need the milk rather than the stronger food more appropriate for those adult in the faith. What is perceived as folly escapes the attention of those who think merely according to this age's categories. Thus the rulers of this world would not have crucified the lord of glory if they had perceived his identity. It is that wisdom which Paul speaks ἐν μυστηρίῳ. It has to be spoken in this way because the fact that it is wisdom remains a mystery, hidden before all ages with God and remaining unrecognised. It would not be a mystery if it were evident, and yet in another sense, of course, it is a very accessible secret because it concerns an event in history rather than something hidden in heaven still waiting to be revealed (like the Parousia in 1 Cor. 1.7). The historical character of the mystery is paralleled in the Wisdom of Solomon. Here too the identity of the significant object is apparent to all, though the precise significance is what is missed by the majority. In contrast with the exclusive character of the heavenly ascent texts Paul offers a mystery which is open and accessible even if its significance is hidden from the majority because of the darkened minds of those who persist in living according to an age which is perishing (1 Cor. 2.6; 1.18).

IV

As with many other New Testament books, there is an apocalyptic and mystical thread running through Matthew's narrative. From the dreams of Joseph and the Magi, which protect the infant son of God, to the dream of Pilate's wife before the crucifixion, which serves to comment on the miscarriage of justice taking place, knowledge through dreams and revelations, of a kind familiar to us from the apocalyptic tradition, are a significant element in this gospel, notwithstanding that several of such accounts are held in common with the other two synoptics. Of these the first is the account of the Baptism, in which there is a clear allusion to Ezekiel 1.1 in all three gospels. The heavens are opened, just as they were to the prophet Ezekiel by the river Chebar, thus

[29] Though from later source we know that menstruation could be a bar on women being baptised. See the Hippolytus' Apostolic Tradition 20.6 (G. Dix ed., The Apostolic Tradition, London 1968, p. 32).

fulfilling the prophetic longing for God to rend the heavens and reveal the divine purposes (cf. Isaiah 64.1)[30].

And there are other links between the Baptism and the Jewish mystical tradition. The descent of the Spirit on Jesus is compared with that of a dove, and it may be possible to see hints of *ma'aseh bereshith* here, by linking the baptismal accounts with a rabbinic story concerning the early second-century teacher, Simeon ben Zoma[31]. In this story ben Zoma meditates on the first chapter of Genesis and in particular on the words at 1.6, and he sees a small gap separating the upper and lower celestial waters which he connects with the Spirit of God hovering on the face of the waters four verses earlier[32]. This small gap he compares to the small gap which exists when a bird hovers over its nest, and in the version of the story in the Babylonian Talmud the hovering of the Spirit of God is compared to a dove hovering over its young.

In the Beatitudes at the beginning of the Sermon on the Mount, Jesus declares that the pure in heart will see God. Once again we have terminology familiar from the mystical tradition in which the seer is vouchsafed a glimpse of the divine *kabod*, glory, after the heavenly ascent. Just as in the Jewish mystical tradition such a privilege comes only after a thorough grounding in Torah, Mishnah and Talmud, so here too in Matthew an ethical dimension is similarly stressed.

Less obviously connected with the apocalyptic and mystical tradition is Jesus' exposition of the significance of John the Baptist's person and activity in Matthew 11. All the synoptic gospels link John with the messenger who is to precede the great and terrible day of the Lord, 'Behold, I send my messenger to prepare the way before me' (Malachi 3.1). John's position is indeed exalted, in so far as the marginal figure baptising at the Jordan is identified with Elijah returned from heaven to announce the imminence of that great and terrible day. The significance of the allusion to the verses in Malachi, lost in our English translations, is the occurrence of the word ἄγγελος, usually translated 'messenger'. Even allowing for some flexibility of usage, due account needs to be taken of the fact that elsewhere in Matthew ἄγγελος refers to a heavenly emissary from God (e.g. 1.20; 28.5). Moreover, the verse from Malachi applied to John is an allusion to Exodus 23.30 which speaks of God's angel going before the people as they journey out of Egypt.

---

30 See further C. ROWLAND, The Open Heaven, pp. 358ff.

31 C. ROWLAND, op. cit., pp. 323 and 361.

32 Tosefta Hagigah 2.5; jHag. 77ab; bHag. 15a and Ber. R. 2.4. This was considered by I. ABRAHAMS, 'The Dove and the Voice', in: Studies in Pharisaism and the Gospels, Cambridge 1917, pp. 47ff. Such ideas could have arisen from a comparison of Gen. 1.2 with the only other occurrence of the verb רחף, 'to hover', at Deut. 32.11, where the bird hovers over her young. Whereas in the story of ben Zoma the meditation was a detached piece of cosmological speculation on the nature of the heavenly waters, in the story of the Baptism the creative Spirit hovers over the head of the Son of God.

Exodus 23.20 is a passage of some importance within Jewish mystical literature. It is used to support the belief in an exalted angel named Metatron whose greatness derives from the indwelling of the divine name in him (see b. San 38b). Although references to that angel who bears the divine name are found only in texts later than the New Testament, there is sufficient evidence to suggest that such beliefs were current at the end of the first century when early Christians were formulating their beliefs about Christ. One example of this comes in an apocalypse which is dated towards the end of the first century A.D. In it there appears an angel, the description of whom bears remarkable similarities with the vision of Christ in Revelation as well as with other Jewish texts (e.g. Apoc. Abr. 10f: 'I am called Jaoel by him who moves that which exists with me on the seventh expanse of the firmament, a power in virtue of the ineffable name that is dwelling in me').[33]

Though this material may not at first sight seem to be relevant for the interpretation of the reference to John the Baptist in Matthew 11, the identification of John with an angel belongs to an ancient tradition (and, in the Orthodox East, a continuing one). It is discussed by Origen who, in his commentary on the Gospel of John (ii.31 on 1.6), interprets 'there was a man sent from God whose name was John' with a quotation from the important Jewish pseudepigraphon The Prayer of Joseph.[34] He offers this as an example of the belief that a human being could be an incarnation of an angel.

'I Jacob who am speaking to you am also Israel an angel of God and a ruling spirit. Abraham and Isaac were created before any work. But I Jacob ... whose name is Israel ... am he who in God called Israel, which means a man seeing God, because I am the first-born of every living thing to which God gives life ... I descended to earth and tabernacled among humanity, and I was called Jacob.'

The importance of this Jewish work, which is quoted only partially by Origen, is that in it we learn that the patriarch Jacob is the incarnation of the exalted angel Israel. The terminology used here is reminiscent of that used of the incarnation of the Logos in John 1.14 and (if authentically Jewish) is testimony to a Jewish writing envisaging the possibility of a heavenly being becoming incarnate in human form. After the quotation there is a lengthy digression in which Origen argues for the belief that John the Baptist was an angel and took human form in order to bear witness to the light of the divine Logos.

---

[33] See C. ROWLAND, 'A Man Clothed in White Linen', JSNT, 24 (1985), pp. 99ff; see now the discission of this material by L. STUCKENBRUCK, Angel Veneration and Christology, p. 211f.

[34] The authenticity and theological provenance is discussed by J. Z. SMITH, 'The Prayer of Joseph', in: Religions in Antiquity, Supplements to Numen ed. J. NEUSNER, Leiden 1968. See also A. BÖHLIG, 'Jakob als Engel in Gnostizismus und Manichäismus', in: G. WIESSNER, Erkenntnisse und Meinungen, Wiesbaden 1978, pp. 1ff

The Transfiguration[35], particularly in its Matthaean version, has several points of contact with ancient Jewish theophanies and the traditions which developed from them. It especially resembles the Christophany of Rev. 1.13ff where the risen Christ appears to the exiled seer on Patmos, and where the links with the throne-theophany tradition based on Ezekiel are widely acknowledged. In the Transfiguration, alone of all the synoptic texts (and surprisingly so given the nature of the post-resurrection appearances), we come closest to the heavenly appearance of an exalted angelic figure[36].

Matthew 18.10 presupposes some kind of link between the little ones and their angels.[37] There is something special about the child. Once again, echoing the language of the apocalyptic tradition, we are told their angels have the privilege of beholding God's face, the highest of all privileges. The climax of the heavenly ascent is the vision of God enthroned in glory, something normally denied not only to mortals but also to angels. Indeed, I Enoch (14.21) explicitly states that the angels are unable to look upon the face of God. The angels of Matthew's little ones stand in close proximity to the throne of glory and share in that destiny which is vouchsafed to the elect in the New Jerusalem, described in Revelation 22.4, of seeing God face to face: 'His servants shall worship him, and they shall see his face, and his name shall be on their foreheads.' The little ones in Matt. 18.10, have a particular privilege just as in Matt. 11.25 it is 'the babes' to whom the significance of Jesus' ministry is revealed while it is hidden from the wise.

At the conclusion of the eschatological discourse (25.31–46) where we find a judgement scene, commonly called the Parable of the Sheep and the Goats, with a parallel not in the other synoptics but in a Jewish text, 'The Similitudes of Enoch' (I Enoch 37–71), where the heavenly son of man sits on God's throne of

---

[35] See W. Gerber, 'Die Metamorphose Jesu, Mk 9,2f par', ThZ 23 (1967), pp. 385ff; M. Mach 'Christus Mutans. Zur Bedeutung der Verklärung Jesu im Wechsel von jüdischer Messianität zur neutestamentlichen Christologie', in: I. Gruenwald ed., Messiah and Christ, Tübingen 1993; J. Fossum, 'Ascension, Metamorphosis. The Transfiguration of Jesus in the Synoptic Gospels', in: The Image of the Invisible God. Essays on the Influence of Jewish Mysticism on Early Chrisology, 1995; M. Sabbe, 'La rédaction du récit de la transfiguration', in, La venue du Messie, Bruges 1962, and J. A. McGuckin, The Transfiguration of Christ in Scripture and Tradition, Lewiston 1986.

[36] C. Rowland, 'Apocalyptic, the Poor and the Gospel of Matthew', JTS 45 (1994), pp. 504ff.

[37] Such a connection is found in the Jewish haggadah where the ancestors are regarded as the embodiment of the mysteries of God's throne and person. So one source says: 'The patriarchs are the merkabah, the throne-chariot ' (e.g. Bereshith Rabbah 47.6 and 69.3). Perhaps it is something similar which lies behind Paul's assertion in II Corinthians 3.18 that life under the new covenant means that 'we all, with unveiled face, are beholding the glory of the Lord and being changed from glory to glory.' In Targum Neofiti on Genesis 22 angels compete with one another to catch a glimpse of Abraham and Isaac whose features are engraved on the throne of glory.

glory, exercising judgement and vindicating the elect. A new element in the Matthaean scene, however, is the astonishment with which the righteous learn that they have in fact ministered to this glorious son of man in the persons of the naked, the poor, the hungry, the sick, the stranger, and those in prison. Their destiny, they discover, was determined at the moment of responding to the needs of those who appeared to be nonentities, to those who were apparently the farthest removed in every respect from this heavenly judge who now claims that what the righteous had done to them they had done to him. There are parallels to all this in the Jewish tradition, where respect for the human person created in God's image, irrespective of nation or religious affiliation, is to be found. Most akin to Matthew's sheep and goats is II Enoch, 42.8ff, where clothing the naked, feeding the hungry, looking after widows and orphans, and coming to the aid of those who have suffered injustice, are criteria for blessedness.

V

What is apparently the least apocalyptic document in the New Testament must now be considered[38]. The link between the Gospel and the Jewish mystical tradition has had its proponents in the past, for example Hugo Odeberg's commentary on the gospel[39]. He used later the Jewish mystical traditions as well as the Mandean texts to cast light on the first twelve chapters of the gospel. But until recently the voices raised in support of a connection between the gospel and the mystical and apocalyptic tradition of Judaism have been few and far between. The Gospel of John has frequently been regarded as an example of a type of Christianity which firmly rejected apocalyptic. What is meant is that there is no imminent expectation of the end. While few would want to dissent from that particular interpretation, one must question whether this means a wholesale rejection of John's indebtedness to apocalyptic. It must now be asked whether we can see the relationship between the Gospel of John and apocalyptic in a new light if we approach it in the way suggested already: how does the Gospel of John fit in with the quest for 'higher wisdom through revelation' to quote Martin Hengel's very apt characterisation of apocalyptic[40]? We should

---

[38] On this theme see N. Dahl, 'The Johannine Church and History', in: W. Klassen and G.F. Snyder, Current Issues in New Testament Interpretation, New York 1962 p. 131, P. Borgen, 'God's Agent in the Fourth Gospel' in ed. J. Ashton, The Interpretation of the Fourth Gospel, A. Segal, Two Powers in Heaven, Leiden 1978 and J. J. Kanagaraj, Mysticism in the Gospel of John, Diss. Durham 1995.

[39] H. Odeberg, The Fourth Gospel, Lund 1929.

[40] M. Hengel, Judaism and Hellenism, vol. 1. p. 210, English Translation London 1974.

not be put off by the lack of apocalyptic terminology in the gospel, for it *is* concerned with the revelation of divine mysteries even if there is an almost complete dearth of typical apocalyptic terms (1.51 and 12.32ff are exceptions). The mystery of the apocalypse is told in narrative form but that has the same ultimate and all-embracing concern.

When viewed from this perspective, the main thrust of its message appears to have a remarkable affinity with apocalyptic, even if we have to admit that the mode of revelation stressed in the Gospel differs radically from that outlined in the apocalypses. That is, the gospel does not offer visions and revelations through the conventional medium typical of the apocalypses, in particular by means of an ascent to heaven. If we are right to assume that the goal of apocalyptic is the attainment of knowledge of the divine mysteries, and in particular the mysteries of God, then it can be seen that much of what the Fourth Gospel says, relates to this theme. Jesus proclaims himself as the revelation of the hidden God. He tells Philipp 'He who has seen me has seen the Father' (14:8) and at the conclusion of the Prologue, the Evangelist speaks of the Son in the following way: 'No one has ever seen God; the only Son, who is in the bosom of the Father, he has made him known' (1:18). The vision of God, the heart of the call-experiences of Isaiah and Ezekiel and the goal of the heavenly ascents of the apocalyptic seers and rabbinic mystics, is related in the Fourth Gospel to the revelation of God in Jesus. All claims to have seen God in the past are repudiated; the Jews have 'neither heard God's voice nor seen his form' (5.37). Even when, as in Isaiah's case, Scripture teaches that a prophet glimpsed God enthroned in glory, this vision is interpreted in the Gospel as a vision of the pre-existent Christ (12:41). No one has seen God except the one who is from God; he has seen the Father (6:46). The vision of God reserved in the Book of Revelation for the fortunate seer (4.1) and for the inhabitants of the 'new Jerusalem' who will see God face to face (22.4) is found, according to the Fourth Evangelist, in the person of Jesus of Nazareth.

For the Fourth Evangelist, the quest for the highest wisdom of all, the knowledge of God, comes not through the information disclosed in visions and revelations but through the Word become flesh, Jesus of Nazareth and through the activity of the Spirit/Paraclete who is ultimately dependent on the Son. Thus while the Fourth Evangelist sets himself resolutely against any claim to revelation except through Christ, he presupposes and uses the basic framework of apocalyptic for his own christological ends in order to affirm the uniqueness of the disclosure in Christ and the inferiority of all earlier claims to divine knowledge. A very important feature of the gospel, long ago noted by Bultmann, is that the gospel of John is permeated with a major theme of the apocalypses: revelation. This has been thoroughly investigated now by John Ashton in a study which draws together several important contributions to the understanding of the gospel which take seriously the apocalyptic and mystical background of the text[41].

For John of Patmos it is the coming of the new Jerusalem from heaven which heralds an era when the dwelling of God is with humanity (Rev. 21.3). The verb (σκηνόω) is that used in Jn. 1.14 of the dwelling of the divine Logos among humankind. The major difference between these two verses is that Rev. still thinks of that presence of God as part of a future eschatological bliss, whereas the author of the Fourth Gospel considers that this is an event which has already taken place at the incarnation. This suggests that the life of Jesus of Nazareth is already in some sense at least an anticipation of that eschatological glory which is to be revealed at the end of the age. The climax of Rev. is the description of the new Jerusalem where the throne of God is set and the elect are granted the privilege of seeing God face to face (Rev. 22.4). In Rev. and the rest of the apocalypses the vision of God is a glimpse of the divine glory which is hidden in heaven, for God's 'glory is inconceivable' (indeed the form of God's glory on the throne is not described by John cf. Col. 1.15). The Fourth Evangelist agrees in insisting that God cannot be glimpsed through a door open into the heavenly court. Rather for him God has been revealed in a human person, Jesus, who is repeatedly described as the unique agent of the Father. No one else can see the things of God. The statement of Ex. 3.1 'no one can see me and live' is hinted at in 1.18 and is used as the basis of the new possibility which is offered in Christ alone to see definitively what Jews had claimed to see in an unmediated way in the past (5.39).

The unveiling of the things of God comes authoritatively only through the one who has seen God (1.18 and 6.46). Christ is the revealer *and* the content of the revelation. He makes known the divine will (7.16) and is the embodiment of God (14.9). Jesus not only speaks the truth; he is the truth. He is both intermediary who acts as go-between (hence the central importance of the agency motif in the gospel) and the intermediary who embodies the divine glory. The Fourth Gospel is at one with a trend in some apocalypses where there is a denial of heavenly ascent (at least of a conventional kind) to view the divine glory (4 Ezra 8.21). There is no vision of God unless it be a vision of Christ whether in his pre-existent or incarnate state (so 12.41). All those visions to prophets of old cannot be understood without reference to Christ, therefore. Unlike Jesus, the Jews have never in fact seen God's form or heard his voice (5.37 cf. Deut. 4.12). The goal of the heavenly ascent, to see the throne of God and the glory of God upon it, is located in Christ. Thus the means of gaining knowledge of God comes not through preparations for heavenly ascent but through recognition of the nature of Christ as the one sent from God who embodies the divine glory.

---

[41] J. ASHTON, Understanding the Fourth Gospel, especially pp. 381 ff.

One of the most unusual verses in the gospel is 1.51[42] – not least because here we have one of the two clear indications of use of the conventional language of the apocalypse. It comes at the climax of the first chapter, dominated as it is by christological themes (e.g. 1.1–18; 1.28; 1.37; 1,41; 1.45; and 1.49). It recalls other New Testament passages like Acts 7.56 and 10.11. The verse opens with an 'Amen', and a promise is granted to a group of people as the verb is plural (despite the fact that Jesus had been addressing Nathanael). The order of ascent followed by descent (similar to 3.13) suggests a link with Gen. 28.12. Whether the Son of Man is the means of the angels' ascent and descent or the goal of that action is debated. Most commentators favour the former, seeing the son of man as the intermediary between heaven and earth. The precise significance of the link with Gen. 28.12 has been variously explained, but possible links with the mystical tradition have been accepted as the result of the recognition that it is an interpreted Bible that we should be attending to in exploring the links with Genesis.

Ber. R. 68.12, although much later than the Fourth Gospel, indicates an earthly and heavenly dimension of humanity. What is important about the patriarch is that his features are those which are part of the divine merkabah and as such looking at Jacob would enable any one who was aware of this to know something of the secret of the merkabah. This is made evident in the targumim on Gen. 28.12 where it is stated explicitly that Jacob's features are those which are engraved on the throne of glory. There are four versions of this legend, three of which (Ps. Jonathan, the fragmentary Targum and Neofiti) are substantially the same . The version in Ps. Jonathan is reproduced here :

'And he dreamed and behold a ladder was fixed on earth and its top stretched to the height of heaven. And behold angels who went to Sodom and who had been banished from them because they revealed the secrets of the lord of the world. And they went until the time that Jacob left the house of his father. And they escorted hum in kindness to Bethel. And on that day they went up to the high heavens, spoke and said, Come see Jacob the pious whose features (איקונין) are fixed on the throne of glory which you desire to look on. So the rest of the holy angels of the LORD descended to look on him.'

The significance of this passage is that it reflects the belief that the secret things of God hidden even from the angels (1 Enoch 14.21 cf. 1 Peter 1.12) were now public in the features of the patriarch. It is a view we meet elsewhere in the rabbinic tradition where all the patriarchs are identified with the chariot (see

[42] On this verse and its mystical connections see C. ROWLAND, 'John 1.51 and the Targumic Tradition', NTS, 30 (1984), pp. 498ff, and on the link with the targumim J. FOSSUM, 'The Son of Man's Alter Ego' in, The Image of the Invisible God. Essays on the Influence of Jewish Mysticism on Early Christology, 1995; M. MCNAMARA, Targum and Testament, p. 146f; J. JERVELL, Imago Dei, pp. 96ff and p. 116; cf. M. SMITH, in: 'The Shape of God and the Humanity of the Gentiles', in: RELIGIONS IN ANTIQUITY, ed. J. NEUSNER, Leiden 1968.

also b. Hullin 91b).[43] In addition, we may recall that in the Prayer of Joseph Jacob and other patriarchs are said to be incarnations of exalted angels. In the targumic passage it is possible that either Jacob was identified with the face of the man on the chariot or even possibly with that of the form of God seated upon it. However we interpret that, what we find in the targumim on Gen. 28.12 is a development of the original verse where Jacob is merely a passive recipient of a vision of angels . Thus the patriarch becomes an important figure in the story, the object of concern for the angels.

If we compare this story with John 1 and transfer this understanding to the interpretation of the Fourth Gospel, we can see that it is the evangelist's intention to stress that Jesus is the embodiment of divine secrets[44], and the testimony to his importance is to be found in the fact that angels should want to descend to look upon him, thereby witnessing (as John the Baptist had done) to his importance. The targumic tradition in which a human figure is the embodiment of apocalyptic secrets is a particularly apposite one for a text which is intent on the demonstration that humanity is the unique bearer and evidence of the divine glory. As the person in whom the secrets of God and his throne are to be found, Jesus is seen as the goal of the heavenly ascent and the quest for knowledge of God. The apocalypse is not to be found in the visions of the mystics and in the disclosures which they offer of the world beyond, but in the earthly life of Jesus Christ. There is in the gospel narrative and its incarnational direction a definite attempt to stress that revelation is found in this human story. There is thus an implicit challenge to the whole of the apocalyptic tradition, based as it is on the communication of heavenly secrets by visions and related revelations, in so far as those revelations are unrelated to the definitive revelation in Christ. The unequivocal emphasis on Jesus as the focal point of revelation make the heavenly ascent and the heavenly secrets superfluous. To know Jesus and to hear his words is to be in direct contact with God. 1.51 indicates that the concern for the true visionary is not to raise eyes to heaven but to see revelation in the story that the evangelist is telling because they are testimony to the supreme manifestation of the invisible God. Nathanael is promised a vision of greater things climaxing in the prediction that he will see angels ascending and descending. Nothing further is said about such an angelophany elsewhere in the text. Indeed, John's gospel notoriously excludes references to 'supernatural' events like the Transfiguration, the angelic ap-

[43] The significance of the form of the ancestors for understanding the likeness of God is stressed also in bBB 58a: 'R. Ba'anah used to mark out caves . . . When he came to the cave of Adam, a voice came from heaven saying, Thou hast seen the likeness of my likeness (i.e. Abraham), my likeness itself (i.e. Adam) thou shalt not behold'.

[44] Whether the Son of Man is the goal of the angels' journey or the means of their ascent and descent will depend on how we translate ἐπὶ τὸν υἱὸν τοῦ ἀνθρώπου. Much will depend on how we construe passages like 1.33 and 6.16 (see further ROWLAND, op. cit above n. 39).

pearances at the Temptation or the empty tomb. When they are referred to it is in the context of a mistaken perception on the part of the crowd about the significance of a *bath qol* (Jn. 12.29). The gospel does not allow the reader to contemplate heavenly reality in any other place than Christ. 'Greater things than these' can be seen only in him.

Or perhaps it is only once they have been found in him that the entrance to the heavenly mysteries can be ascertained. So in Jn. 3 Jesus confronts Nicodemus with the uncompromising statement that he needs to be born again. It is a strange response which hardly begins to engage with the substance of Nicodemus' concerns. But then Jesus cannot merely engage with the discourse of this world for he has come to bear witness to truth (18.37) not to engage with the wisdom of the world. For Nicodemus to see the mystery of the Kingdom of God, focused as it is in Christ, there is need for a complete transformation which can only be likened to a birth. There is required an epistemological change involving an ethical as well as intellectual conversion[45]. Nothing less can allow the possibility of mystical enlightenment. But then seeing the angels will be to see them converging on the Son of Man. Recognition of his true identity is the prerequisite to the ultimate divine mystery. Rightly has John Ashton maintained that the Gospel of John is 'an apocalypse in reverse'[46].

Thus the Fourth Evangelist reiterates within his own distinctive theological language the theme we have found elsewhere in the New Testament. The divine mystery is located in the humiliation of the cross or the life of the one who humbled himself and was in solidarity with the meek of the earth, and yet the manifestation of the divine glory would be apparent to all on the last day (1 Cor. 1.7). The hidden lord, like the children of God, the identity of whom is only revealed in the messianic age (Romans 8.19), will as the result of an apocalypse be unveiled. The righteous in Matthew 25.31 ff are only apparent at the very moment when it is pointed out to them by the eschatological judge that their ministrations to the hungry, thirsty, the naked and the imprisoned has been service to the heavenly Son of Man, though he had been seen, albeit incognito, in the persons of the outcast of the world[47]. In the Gospel of John there is no apocalyptic denouement resembling that described in 1 Cor. 1.7 or Mark 14.62. The vision of the glory of the Son of Man is reserved for those with eyes to see (John 17.25) leaving the world, which refuses to see, still in darkness, without

---

[45] J. L. MARTYN, 'Epistemology at the Turn of the Ages: 2 Corinthians 5.16', in: Christian History and Interpretation: Studies Presented to John Knox, ed. W. R. FARMER et al., Cambridge 1967.

[46] J. ASHTON, Understanding the Fourth Gospel, Oxford 1991, pp. 337 ff and 381 ff.

[47] C. ROWLAND, 'Apocalyptic, the Poor and the Gospel of Matthew', JTS 45 (1994), pp. 504 ff.

the eschatological opportunity *in the future* to be bathed in the illumination of what Adorno has called 'the messianic light'[48].

Bibliography

ABRAHAMS, I., 'The Dove and the Voice', in Studies in Pharisaism and the Gospels, Cambridge 1917, pp. 47ff.

ADORNO, T., Minima Moralia, English Translation London 1974.

ASHTON, J. (ed.), The Interpretation of the Fourth Gospel, London 1986.

–, Understanding the Fourth Gospel, Oxford 1991.

–, Studying John, Oxford 1994.

BAUMGARTEN, J. M., 'The Book of Elchesai and Merkabah Mysticism', JSJ 17 (1986), pp. 212ff.

BETZ, O., 'Die Vision des Paulus im Tempel von Jerusalem', in: BETZ et al., Abraham unser Vater, Wuppertal 1970, pp. 113ff.

BORGEN, P., 'God's Agent in the Fourth Gospel', in: ed. J. ASHTON, The Interpretation of the Fourth Gospel, pp. 67ff.

BOCKMUEHL, M., Revelation and Mystery, Tübingen 1990.

CHERNUS, I., 'Visions of God in Merkabah Judaism', JSJ 13 (1982), pp. 123ff.

COHEN, M. S., The Shi'ur Qomah: the Liturgy and Theurgy in Pre-Kabbalistic Jewish Mysticism, New York 1983.

COLLINS, J. J., Apocalypse, Morphology of a Genre (Semeia 14), Missoula 1979.

COLLINS, J. J. and J. H. CHARLESWORTH, Mysteries and Revelations, Sheffield 1991.

DAHL, N., 'The Johannine Church and History', in: W. KLASSEN and G. F. SNYDER, Current Issues in New Testament Interpretation, New York 1962 (reprinted in J. ASHTON, The Interpretation of the Fourth Gospel, pp. 122ff.).

DAN, J. and F. TALMAGE, Studies in Jewish Mysticism, Cambridge/Mass. 1982.

DAVIES, P. R., 'The social world of apocalyptic, in: R. E. CLEMENTS, The World of Ancient Israel, Cambridge 1989.

DEAN-OTTING, M., Heavenly Journeys: A Study of the Motif in Hellenistic Jewish Literature, Frankfurt 1984.

DEUTSCH, N., The Gnostic Imagination. Gnosticisn, Mandaeisn and Merkabah Mysticisn, Leiden 1995.

ESLER, P. L., The First Christians in their Social World, London 1994.

FOSSUM, J., The Image of the Invisible God. Essays on the Influence of Jewish Mysticism on Early Christology, 1995.

–, The Name of God and the Angel of the Lord, Tübingen 1985.

–, 'Jewish Christian Christology and Jewish Mysticism', Vigiliae Christianae 37 (1983), pp. 260ff.

GEBER, W., 'Die Metamorphose Jesu, Mk 9,2f par', ThZ 23 (1967), pp. 385ff.

GRUENWALD, I., Apocalyptic and Merkavah Mysticism, Leiden 1978.

–, From Apocalyptic to Gnosticism: Studies in Apocalpticism, Markavah Mysticism and Gnosticism, Frankfurt 1988.

HALPERIN, DAVID, The Merkabah in Rabbinic Literature, New Haven 1980.

[48] T. ADORNO, Minima Moralia, English Translation London 1974, p. 247.

–, The Faces of Chariot, Tübingen 1988.
HELLHOLM, D., Apocalypticism in the Mediterranean World, Tübingen (second edition with additional bibliography) 1989.
HENGEL, M., Son of God, English Translation London 1974.
–, Judaism and Hellenism, English Translation London 1974.
HIMMELFARB, M., Ascent into Heaven in Jewish and Christian Apocalypses, Oxford 1993.
HOFIUS, O., Der Vorhang vor dem Thron Gottes, Tübingen 1972.
HURST, L. W., The Epistle to the Hebrews, Cambridge 1992.
HURTADO, L., 'Revelation 4–5 in the Light of Jewish Apocalyptic Analogies', JSNT 25 (1985), pp. 105.
HURTADO, L. W., One God, One Lord, London 1990.
JERVELL, J., Imago Dei, Göttingen 1960.
KANAGARAJ, J. J., Mysticisn in the Gospel of John, Diss. Durham 1995.
KIM, S., The Origin of Paul's Gospel, Tübingen 1981.
LINCOLN, A. T., Paradise Now and Not Yet, Cambridge 1981.
MCGUCKIN, J. A., The Transfiguration of Christ in Scripture and Tadition, Lewiston 1986.
MCNAMARA, M., Targum and Testament, Shannon 1972.
MACH, M., 'Christus Mutans. Zur Bedeutung der Verklärung Jesu im Wechsel von jüdischer Messianität zur neutestamentlichen Christologie', in: I. GRUENWALD ed., Messiah and Christ, Tübingen 1993, pp. 177 ff.
MACH, M., Die Entstehung des jüdischen Engelglaubens. Entwicklungsphasen des jüdischen Engelglaubens in vorrabbinischer Zeit, Tübingen 1992.
MARTYN, J. L., 'Epistemology at the Turn of Ages: 2 Corinthians 5.16', in: Christian History and Interpretation: Studies Presented to John Knox ed., W. R. FARMER et al., Cambridge 1967, pp. 269 ff.
MORRAY-JONES, C., Merkabah Mysticism and Talmudic Tradition, Diss. Cambridge 1988.
C. R. A. MORRAY-JONES, 'Transformational Mysticism in the Apocalyptic-Merkabah Tradition', JJS 43 (1992), pp. 1 ff.
MORRAY-JONES, C. R. A., 'Paradise Revisited (2 Cor. 12: 1–12): the Jewish Mystical Background of Paul's Apostolate', Harvard Theological Review 86 (1993), pp. 177 ff. and 265 ff.
NEWMAN, C., Paul's Glory-Christology: Tradition and Rhetoric, Leiden 1992.
NEWSOM, C., The Songs of the Sabbath Sacrifice, Atlanta 1985.
–, 'Merkabah Exegesis in the Qumran Community', JJS 38 (1987), pp. 11 ff.
ODEBERG, H., The Fourth Gospel, Lund 1929.
–, 'The View of the Universe in the Epistle to the Ephesians', Lund Universitets Årsskrift 29 (1933).
ROWLAND, C., 'The Vision of God in Apocalyptic Literature', in: JSJ 10 (1979), pp. 138 ff.
–, 'The Vision of the Risen Christ', JTS 31 (1980), pp. 1 ff.
–, The Open Heaven, London 1982.
–, 'A Man Clothed in White Linen', JSNT 24 (1985), pp. 99 ff.
–, 'John 1.51 and the Targumic Tradition', NTS 30 (1984), pp. 498 ff.
–, 'Apocalyptic, the Poor and the Gospel of Matthew, JTS 45 (1994), pp. 504 ff.
SABBE, M., 'La rédaction du récit de la transfiguration', in: La venue du Messie, Bruges 1962.

SCHÄFER, P., The Hidden and Manifest God, New York 1992.

–, 'New Testament and the Hekhalot Literature: The Journey into Heaven in Paul and in Merkavah Mysticism', Journal of Jewish Studies 35 (1984), pp. 19ff.

SCHOLEM, G., Major Trends in Jewish Mysticism, London 1955.

–, Jewish Gnosticism, Merkabah Mysticism and Talmudic Tradition, New York 1965.

SEGAL, A., Two Powers in Heaven, Leiden 1978.

SMELIK, W. F., 'On Mystical Transformation of the Righteous into Light in Judaism', JSJ 26 (1995).

SMITH, J. Z., 'The Prayer of Joseph', in: Religions in Antiquity, Supplements to Numen, ed. J. NEUSNER, Leiden 1968, pp. 27ff. (reprinted in Map is not Territory, Leiden 1978, pp. 24ff.).

SMITH, M., 'On the History of ἀποκαλύπτω / ἀποκάλυψις, in: D. HELLHOLM, Apocalyticism in the Mediterranean World.

–, 'The Shape of God and the Humanity of the Gentiles', in: Religions in Antiquity, ed. J. NEUSNER, Leiden 1968.

STUCKENBRUCK, L., Angel Veneration and Christology, Tübingen 1995.

TABOR, J. T., Things Unutterable, University Press of America, 1986.

WEWERS, G. A., Geheimnis und Geheimhaltung im rabbinischen Judentum, Berlin 1975.

1975.

Pagan or Jewish? The Presentation of Paul's Mission in the Book of Acts

by

DORON MENDELS*

In recent years a lively discussion about the origin of mission has reemerged. There are scholars who argue that Christian mission derived from Judaism, whereas others argue that it was not. Recently L. H. Feldman claimed that elements of mission can be detected in pre-Christian Judaism. This, however, cannot always be proven in a decisive manner, as Scot McKnight attempted to show.[1] As this problem is crucial for the understanding of pre-Christian Judaism and its relation to Christianity, I would like to address here one aspect of it.

In the past scholars who dealt with the problem of mission and conversion, have not drawn enough attention to the distinction between the ideas of mission, and its methods as presented by hellenistic texts. In this article, in honour of a scholar who dedicated his life to the study of Hellenism, Judaism and Christianity, I will try to detect the techniques and methods of mission as they appear in Christianity of the first century C.E., thus showing that they derive from the hellenistic, rather than from the Jewish, world of the time.

* I grateful to H. W. Attridge, Dvora Gera, J. Marcus, and D. Moody Smith who read earlier drafts of this article. Their comments were extremely helpful during the process of writing this final version.

[1] Cf. recently L. H. FELDMAN, Jew and Gentile in the Ancient World (Princeton, 1993), esp. chapter 9.4. Cf. in general A. VON HARNACK, Die Mission und Ausbreitung des Christentums, vol. I (Leipzig, 1924); JOACHIM JEREMIAS says of Jesus that he "came upon the scene in the midst of what was *par excellence* the missionary age of Jewish history" (in his Jesus' Promise to the Nations [London, 1958], p. 12). F. M. DERWACTER, Preparing the Way for Paul. The Proselyte Movement in Later Judaism (NY, 1930), p. 94 is more moderate saying that "the method of itinerant teaching and preaching was a common phenomenon of the time, and that the Jews of propagandist spirit followed it, as did the Christians and pagans". Recently S. MCKNIGHT dedicated a whole study to this problem claiming that Second Temple Judaism was largely unconcerned with missionary activity and that it was not a missionary religion (A Light Among the Gentiles. Jewish Missionary Activity in the Second Temple Period (Min, 1991). Basically I agree with this thesis (Mt 23:15 perhaps indicates that there were exceptions to the rule). However, MCKNIGHT does not offer an alternative explanation as to what was the origin of missionary activity.

Two sources of different nature can be used for our comparison, both of which contain a *comprehensive* description of mission in its different variations:

The Book of Acts, where Luke presents us with the most complete picture of the work of a great missionary. It must be noted that whether Luke's picture reflects reality remains a question which should not trouble us here. Furthermore, the problem of the "real" Paul who emerges from his letters, and its relation to Acts, is outside the scope of this study.[2]

The question that does arise is whether there exists in Jewish literature before Acts any text which contains such a comprehensive description of a missionary at work. The answer is no. We do have some sporadic descriptions of mission in Jewish and Samaritan texts, e.g. Abraham who teaches Chaldaic wisdom (Pseudo-Eupolemus, in Praeparatio Evangelica 9.17.2–9), but no description comparable to the one we find in Acts can be detected. Thus we turn to hellenistic literature.

The main source for missionary heroes is Diodorus Siculus whose *Floruit* occurred a century before Luke wrote the book of Acts. Diodorus wrote a world history, the *Bibliotheke*, which was reflective of the concepts, ideologies, and wishes of his era.[3] The *Bibliotheke*, in its socio-cultural setting, provides an excellent background for the discussion of Paul's activities as presented by Luke.

Diodorus was influenced by the middle Stoa, which included personalities such as Poseidonius (who came from Asia Minor and had the same cultural background as Paul[4]). Diodorus collected the stories concerning the culture-heroes, and their stories are well represented in the first five books of the *Bibliotheke* which deal with the mythologies of the ancient Near East. From a careful reading of Diodorus Siculus' *Bibliotheke* (Books I–V), it becomes clear that the stories concerning the culture-heroes and gods are not of the

---

[2] The literary problems of Acts are not discussed here. Cf. for those C. J. Hemer, The Book of Acts in the Setting of Hellenistic History (Tübingen, 1989), and C. J. Thornton, Der Zeuge des Zeugen: Lukas als Historiker der Paulusreisen (Tübingen, 1991); also G. E. Sterling, Historiography and Self-Definition (Leiden, 1992), pp. 311–389. Some scholars thought of the Book of Acts in terms of a traveller's tale (W. L. Knox, The Acts of the Apostles [1948], p. 55 and cf. also Hemer, Acts), or a romance (M. J. Schierling, "The Influence of the Ancient Romances on the Acts of the Apostles, Classical Bulletin 54 [1977–78], pp. 81–88). Some were more grounded and said that chapters 16–28 are an itinerary diary (E. Trocme, Le "Livre des Actes" et l'histoire [1957] pp. 128–138; G. Schille, "Die Fragwürdigkeit eines Itinerars der Paulusreisen", ThLZ 84 (1985) cols. 165–174, and A. D. Nock, Essays in Religion and the Ancient World (Cambridge, Mass. 1972), vol. 2, p. 824–825, and H. Conzelmann, Acts of the Apostles (Philadelphia, 1987), p. XXXIX. Cf. also E. Plümacher, "Eine Thukydidesreminiszenz in der Apostelgeschichte (Act 20,33-35 – Thuk II 97,3f)", ZNW 83 (1992), pp. 270–275.

[3] K. S. Sacks, Diodorus Siculus (Princeton, 1990).

[4] For the pre-Christian Paul cf. M. Hengel, The Pre-Christian Paul (Philadelphia, 1991).

author's invention. He must have found them in various sources, reworked them and given them a hellenistic interpretation, the extent or degree of which is at times hard to ascertain. The *Quellenforschung* of Diodorus Siculus' *Bibliotheke* is a very complicated matter in itself and will not be discussed here.[5]

Diodorus' motivation for introducing his stories about the wandering gods is mentioned in his illuminating introduction to book IV. Diodorus says that he is about to recount the deeds of those "most renowned heroes and demigods and, in general, about all who have performed any notable exploit in war, and likewise about such also as in time of peace have made useful discovery or enacted some good law contributing to man's social life" (4.1.5). He refers here not only to the culture-heroes and gods of Greek origin, but to those from "other nations" as well (4.1.5).

The culture-heroes, popular in hellenistic thought, were in fact primitive missionaries. Primitive mission in hellenistic thought before Paul is here understood as any action taken by individuals to convey a message, or to bring some sort of progress, to a population in and/or outside the political/religious and/or geographical sphere from which the mission/ary originates. The methods used to convey the message can be peaceful or warlike. Examples of such culture-heroes are Osiris, Dionysus, Semiramis and Myrina.

It will be argued here that the various methods of mission which are to be found in hellenistic culture-heroes, can be traced in Christian missionary activities as described by Luke. These similarities become more significant if one takes into account the differences in the *nature* of the sources involved, and the different filters the original aspects of mission passed through. Diodorus Siculus was a pagan author interested in mythology and the history of humankind, whereas Luke, the author of Acts, was a Christian who was very well aware of the position of Christianity versus Judaism and paganism, but who mainly focused on the history of Paul's mission (Acts 13ff). The Book of Acts, as well as Paul's letters, were the result of the great polemics of the first century C.E. between Judaism, Christianity and paganism. Diodorus Siculus' writing is, of course, free of this influence.

In spite of these and other differences, it is striking how similar the missionary techniques and methods of the hellenistic culture-heroes and Paul as described by Luke in Acts are. We should not be troubled by the fact that in Acts we do not find the exact wording which is found in Diodorus' *Bibliotheke*, since we do not claim that Luke used Diodorus directly. Luke was apparently familiar with hellenistic literary *topoi* concerning the culture-hero. In other words, the patterns of missionary activity embedded in tales of culture-heroes in antiquity penetrated the depiction of the missionary activities of Paul by Luke. As a result, his movements according to the book of Acts are much more

[5] Cf. Diodorus Siculus, in RE 9 (1903), cols. 663–704 (E. Schwarz); Sacks, Diodorus.

understandable when read against the background of certain acts of mission which we find in texts of the hellenistic world.

The aspects that can be discerned in hellenistic missionary heroes when comparing them to Paul's mission are the following:[6]

A. Holy people and gods

All missionaries in the sense mentioned above become holy people as a result of their mission.

Let us start with some examples from Diodorus. Drawing on Hecataeus of Abdera's *Aegyptiaca*, Diodorus says about Osiris that the motivation for his mission to other peoples was that "if he made men give up their savagery and adopt a gentle manner of life, he would receive immortal honours because of the magnitude of his benefactions" (*dia to megethos tes euergesias*, DS 1.17.2).[7] The Indians, Diodorus says, claimed that Osiris was a god because of the many deeds he performed there for the population (DS 1.19.8). Osiris achieved his goal of becoming immortal as "every people received him as a god because of his benefactions" (DS 1.18.5). On his return to Egypt he received "by reason of the magnitude of his benefactions... the gift of immortality with the approval of all men and honour equal to that offered to the gods of heaven. After this he passed from the midst of men into the company of the gods..." (DS 1,20.5-6).

The Sesostris myth somewhat duplicates the Osiris myth, but with some major changes.[8] Sesostris also left Egypt as a king, and it was predicted by the gods that Sesostris will become the ruler of the whole civilized world (a familiar theme in hellenistic literature). Indeed, Sesostris set up inscriptions all over the conquered territories which stated: "Sacred; this land the King of Kings and

[6] As far as I know this comparison has not been done. Heracles, for instance, was often equated in scholarly works with Jesus, but not with Paul. (Cf. M. Simon, Hercule et le Christianisme [Paris, 1955], and A. J. Malherbe, "Herakles," in Reallexikon für Antike und Christentum 14 (1988), cols. 569ff). Paul may have known of the Heraclean cycle because in Tarsus, his birthplace, one of the most important deities was Sandon, who is the Tarsian Heracles.

2 Cor 11:23-29 has been compared to the tribulations of Heracles, but this is very different from the subject under survey here. Cf. R. Hodgson, "Paul the Apostle and First Century Tribulation Lists", ZNW 74 (1983), pp. 59–80. The question of Paul as a wandering sophist is not discussed here: cf. about this aspect A. D. Nock, Conversion. The Old and the New in Religion from Alexander the Great to Augustine of Hippo (Oxford, 1933), pp. 191ff.

[7] For Hecataeus in DS I, see W. Spoerri, Späthellenistische Berichte über Welt, Kultur und Götter (Basle, 1959). For Osiris, cf. J. G. Griffiths, The Origins of Osiris and his Cult (Leiden, 1980). For *euergesia* cf. F. W. Danker, "Benefactor", The Anchor Bible Dictionary, vol. I, cols. 669–671; recently for its political meaning, A. Erskine, "The Romans as common Benefactors", Historia XLIII (1994), pp. 70–87.

[8] For the Sesostris myth cf. A. B. Lloyd, "Nationalist Propaganda in Ptolemaic Egypt", Historia 31 (1982), pp. 33–56.

Lord of Lords, Sesoosis [Sesostris], subdued with his own arms" (DS 1.55.7). It is only after his beneficial acts for the welfare of Egypt that he won "immortal glory for himself" (DS 1.56.1).

Semiramis, who became queen of vast parts of Asia and performed numerous benefactionary acts, disappeared and "some, making a myth of it, say that she turned into a dove and flew off in the company of many birds... and this, they say, is the reason why the Assyrians worship the dove as a god, thus deifying Semiramis" (DS 2.20.1-2).[9] These examples of deifications are in line with the Euhemeristic tradition, where heroes became gods after performing some important deeds.

Diodorus Siculus, drawing on Matris of Thebes, says that Heracles by his own labours brought under cultivation the inhabited world, thus receiving the gift of immortality (DS 4.8).[10] When Heracles arrived in Spain, he fought the army of king Chrysaor, and after "subduing" Iberia took the herds of cattle and left, but not before he had acted in a way similar to Abraham in relation to Melchizedek (Gen 14). Diodorus states that since Heracles "had received honours at the hands of a certain king of the natives, a man who excelled in piety and justice *(andros eusebeia kai dikaiosune diapherontos)*, he left with the king a portion of the cattle as a present. The king accepted them, but dedicated them all to Heracles..." (DS 4.18.3). The reason for this was Heracles' apparent godly nature. Arriving at the banks of the river Tiber where Rome was later founded by Romulus (DS 4.21.1), Heracles "received with favour the good-will *(eunoia)* shown him by the dwellers on the Palatine and foretold them that, after he had passed into the circle of the gods, it would come to pass that whatever men should make a vow to dedicate to Heracles a tithe of their goods would lead a more happy and prosperous life" (DS 4.21.3). While in Sicily, Heracles left behind him "imperishable memorials of his presence *(parousia)*". Near Agyrium he "was honoured on equal terms with the Olympian gods by festivals and splendid sacrifices, and though before this time he had accepted no sacrifice, he then gave consent for the first time, since the deity was giving

---

[9] Taken probably from Ctesias. Cf. for Ctesias K. MEISTER, Die griechische Geschichtsschreibung (Stuttgart, Berlin, Köln, 1990), pp. 62–64.

[10] For Matris of Thebes, cf. "Matris", RE 14.2 (1930), cols. 2287–2298 (HOBEIN). The secondary literature on Heracles abounds: cf. for instance, some of the most recent items: CORINNE BONNET, Melqart. Cultes et mythes de l'Héraklès tyrien en Méditerranée (Studia Phoenicia VIII, 1988); R. VOLLKOMER, Herakles in the Art of Classical Greece (Oxford, 1988); COLETTE JOURDAIN-ANNEQUIN, Héraclès aux portes du Soir. Mythe et histoire (Paris, 1989).

Cf. for the various literary sources for Heracles: GRUPPE in RE Supp. 3 (1918) cols. 1021 ff. For Heracles in general C. K. GALINSKI, The Herakles Theme (Oxford, 1972). For Herakles in art, cf. F. BOMMER, Herakles: Die Zwölf Taten des Helden in antiker Kunst und Literatur (Münster and Cologne, 1953); F. BOMMER, Herakles (Darmstadt, 1972 second ed.)

A comparison has been drawn between Heracles and Jesus. Cf. M. SIMON, Hercule, and an excellent survey of scholarship on this issue by MALHERBE, "Herakles", cols. 569–573.

intimations to him of his coming immortality" (DS 4.24.1). It now becomes quite clear that according to certain hellenistic writers immortality, the godly nature, is given to heroes as a consequence of their missionary activity.

It is interesting to note that not only does the hero become immortal, but at times his companions as well. For instance, before leaving Sicily Heracles dedicated a notable sacred precinct to Iolaus who was his companion on the campaign, and ordained that annual honours and sacrifices should be offered to him.

Luke could not depict Paul as a god, but he gives the impression that the apostle is a holy man *(theios aner)*, who at times has supernatural powers. For instance, in Ats 14:8-10: "Now at Lystra there was a man sitting, who could not use his feet; he was a cripple from birth, who had never walked. He listened to Paul speaking; and Paul, looking intently at him and seeing that he had faith to be made well, said in a loud voice, "Stand upright on your feet", and he sprang up and walked" (See also Acts 13:9-11; [14:12-18]; 15:12; 16:9; 16:25-34; 18:9; 19:6; 19:11-12; 20:9-12; 22:6ff; 23:11; 26:12ff; 28:3-6).

B. The wandering missionary

All hellenistic heroes mentioned by Diodorus and his sources travel from one place to another in order to convey some sort of message, or to perform some deed of a civilizatory nature. This description of movement is a common literary device used by authors in antiquity (Aeneas in Vergil, Anabasis by Xenophon, etc.). The real world of antiquity does, however, emerge from the texts if one examines the actual routes the cultural-heroes usually follow in their journeys. It would be sufficient to examine the set of maps of the ancient world published by the *TAVO* (Tübingen University) to realize that many of the courses the holy people followed according to Diodorus were in fact common commercial routes. It is possible that various authors whose works Diodorus Siculus used, such as Megasthenes, Hecataeus of Abdera and Dionysius Scytobrachion, who themselves reflect the Indian, Egyptian and Libyan "national" traits, wanted to "nationalize" certain of the international routes by taking their heroes through them.[11] Furthermore, the recording of specific geographical names by the sources (themselves not legendary, although the journeys are), gives a well-defined territorial framework to the act of mission. Let us now be more specific concerning the geographical aspect, and give some examples to

---

[11] Cf. D. Mendels, The Rise and Fall of Jewish Nationalism (NY, 1992), chapter 4. For holy men on the move see G. Anderson, Sage, Saint and Sophist (London and NY, 1994), pp. 167–187.

demonstrate the importance of creating a perimeter for the spread of civilization by its missionaries.

Osiris, who gathered "a great army, with the intention of visiting all the inhabited earth..." (DS 1.17.1), made his arrangements in Egypt and left on his missionary campaign. His first stop was Ethiopia. From there he went through Arabia, the Persian Gulf and the Indian Ocean, and reached India and "the limits of the inhabited world" *(kai tou peratos tes oikoumenes)*. In India he left "many other signs of his stay" (DS 1.19.8). He "visited" all the other nations of Asia *(epelthein de kai talla ta kata ten Asian ethne)*, and crossed into Europe and the Hellespont (DS 1.20.1). It should be noted that Osiris ignored all political and ethnical boundaries, and travelled from country to country, without the use of force. However, when he reached Thrace he encountered opposition to his acts from Lycurgus, the king of the Barbarians. Consequently, he slew Lycurgus and left Macedon, his son, as king of Macedonia. He left Triptolemus to care for Attica's agriculture, and he left Maron in Thrace "to supervise the culture of the plants which he introduced into that land and caused him to found a city to bear his name, which he called Maroneia" (DS 1.20.2-3). This statement, probably taken by Diodorus from the *Aegyptiaca* of Hecataeus of Abdera, shows Ptolemaic eagerness to claim Greece, Macedonia and Thrace in the third century B.C.E. from a civilizatory stand-point. "Finally, Osiris visited all the inhabited world in this way and advanced community life *(epelthonta ton koinon bion)*..." (DS 1.20.3). Osiris made a circuit around all of the eastern part of the world, a matter which will be discussed later on.

Semiramis wanted to surpass her husband Ninus' achievements of conquering many regions of Asia after succeeding him to the Assyrian throne. She was a cultivating queen and completed many enterprises of various natures, starting in Babylon and going through Media. Diodorus tells us that she advanced towards Ecbatana, being "ambitious both to leave an immortal monument of herself and at the same time to shorten her way", and that she cut a road through the cliffs "which to this day is called the road of Semiramis" (DS 2.13.5). Diodorus gives some details about her civilizatory enterprises in Ecbatana and the other regions through which she passed. She also visited *(epelthe)* Persis and many other countries "over which she ruled *(eperche)* throughout Asia" (DS 2.14.1), went through all of Egypt and subdued *(katastrepsamene)* most of Lybia. In addition she visited most of Ethiopia, and "after Semiramis had put in order *(katastesasa)* the affairs of Ethiopia and Egypt she returned with her force to Bactra in Asia" (DS 2.16.1). A futile attack on India which is recorded at length by Diodorus ended her stormy reign (DS 2.16-19). Semiramis, like Osiris, Sesostris, Dionysus and others, travelled a complete circle in carrying out her mission to civilize the world, and show her presence in it (*parousia*, DS 3.66.3).

Diodorus, drawing on Dionysius Scytobrachion's *Lybiaca*, provides details concerning the itinerary of Myrina and the Amazons.[12] He tells that when they arrived at the Caicus river Myrina "fixed the bounds of her campaign" *(orous thesthai tes strateias ton Kaikon potamon)* (DS 3.55.5). A similar thing is said about Sesostris who "fixed the limits of his expedition" while visiting Thrace (DS 1.55.6). This is of special interest as it shows that a limit to the crossing of boundaries and annexation of lands was a familiar theme in ancient thought.[13]

Elsewhere Diodorus tells us that Heracles wandered a great deal in the *oecumene* in order to perform his tasks,[14] and by this act of wandering he creates a perimeter which corresponds roughly to the "borders" of the Roman Empire during the time of Caesar. First he travelled in Greece (Peoloponnesus, Crete, and Thrace), and then sailed with the Argonauts to the Colchi. After bringing back the girdle of Hippolyte, he went on his tenth task which is of special interest here. Heracles left Greece, and made a round tour in the mediterranean basin, returning to Greece upon the termination of his task. The journey's actual aim was to "bring back" the cattle of Geryones "which pastured in the parts of Iberia which slope towards the ocean" (DS 4.17.1), but in fact Heracles performs civilizatory acts in many places where he passes. He goes to Crete, and from there he goes to Libya and large parts of the adjoining desert (DS 4.17.3-4). On his mission he visited both the land *(chora)* and the cities *(poleis)*. He then continued on his journey, going to Egypt and then back to Libya; "after Heracles had visited *(epelthon)* a large part of Libya he arrived at the ocean near Gadeira where he set up pillars on each of the two continents" (DS 4.18.2). Heracles then crossed into Spain, "subduing" Iberia, and handed the kingdom of Iberia over to "the noblest men among the natives". In Gallia he traversed the length and breath of it; "his success in these regions can be deduced from the many natives who joined his army of their own free will. He then, like Semiramis in Asia, built a route through the Alps to Italy (DS 4.19.3). Again, as in other places which he cultivated, he subdued the barbarians who used to plunder and hinder any army that crossed the Alps, and "those that were the leaders in lawlessness of this kind he slew, and made the journey safe for succeeding generations" (DS 4.19.4).

Diodorus, probably following Matris of Thebes' *"enkomion Heracleous"*, further tells us that Heracles crossed into Liguria, and arrived at the banks of the river Tiber at the future site of Rome (DS 4.21.1). Then he went down to the Cumaean Plain, and near the sea he carried out some construction work on the lake of Avernus. He also went down to Sicily with the cattle. "Upon his arrival in Sicily, Heracles desired to make a circle of the entire island *(boulomenos*

12 For Myrina and the Amazons, cf. J. C. RUSTEN, Dionysius Scytobrachion (Cologne, 1980).

13 Cf. in general J. S. ROMM, The Edges of the Earth in Ancient Thought (Princeton, 1992).

14 Cf. for this COLETTE JOURDAIN-ANNEQUIN, Héraclès, pp. 301 ff, and L. DACROIX, "Héraclès heros, voyageur et civilisateur", Bull Acad Belge 60 (1974) pp. 34–60.

egkuklothenai pasan Sikelian), and to set out from Pelorias in the direction of Eryx" (DS 4.23.1). He made the circuit of Sicily, and then he crossed Italy, went up the coast, made a circle *(egkuklotheis)* of the Adriatic and reached Greece. There is a lot more written about Heracles in Greece, and about his later journey with the Argonauts (DS 4.40.1f), but what has been mentioned so far is sufficient to illustrate the argument presented here. The story emphasized his circular movement, and his courageous deeds to defend civilization and its progress.

Within this context one can also mention a Jewish wanderer. According to the Gen. Apoc. (a Hebrew/Aramaic document from the early hellenistic period), Abraham wandered through the eastern *oecumene*, drew a perimeter, and arrived at the point of his original departure, in Palestine.[15] There is, however, a significant difference from other hellenistic heroes in that Abraham is not a civilizatory figure at all; he simply moves from place to place. Does this indicate the attitude of Judaism towards mission? In this context it strengthens the argument that Jewish literature of the hellenistic period was not the source for Luke in his description of Paul's mission.

This particular aspect of travelling from one destination to another is of great importance in Paul's mission. What Jesus did in a very limited region, namely moving from place to place in the Land of Israel, Paul does (like the culture-heroes) in the *oecumene*. In Acts, chapters 13ff, the loci where Paul preaches are briefly mentioned. At times Luke only recounts the names of places without providing any further information. Furthermore, the acts of "going", "sailing" and "visiting", i.e. the physical acts of moving, are emphasized throughout Paul's itinerary in the *oecumene*, which are reminiscent of the descriptions of the itineraries of the above mentioned culture-heroes. The emphasis in the hellenistic texts is on crossing boundaries, namely moving from one region to another with some obstacles being put in the hero's way. In most cases at a certain point a limit is put in geographical terms.

Culture-heroes are at times accompanied by famous assistants. For example, Osiris was assisted in his journey by Apollo and by his "sons" Anubis and Macedon; he also had Pan in his company, and Maron and Triptolemus who were experts in certain fields of agriculture. These famous mythological figures played a very important role in the act of mission. Paul also had assistants, who had important roles in the story of his mission (Barnabas, John, etc.).[16]

---

[15] For Abraham in the Gen Ap. cf. J. A. FITZMYER, The Genesis Apocryphon (Rome, 1971).

[16] Acts 13:13; 17:15-16; 18:5; 19:22; 19:29 (distinction between assistants and companions). For his missionary methods cf. D. SENIOR, C. STUHMUELLER, The Biblical Foundation of Mission (NY, 1983), part II. For Paul and his assistants being "envoys", "messengers", and the cynic thought which may have been behind it, cf. D. GEORGI, The Opponents of Paul in Second Corinthians (Edinburgh, 1986), pp. 2ff (dealing with the concept of *diakonos theou*). Missionary after Paul is defined by K. S. LATOURETTE: "Individuals or organized groups engaged in

C. Means of conveying the message

1) According to hellenistic concepts one could conquer territory "either by force or by persuasion" (cf. DS 19.85.5). The use of force was an efficient device for spreading an idea in pagan societies, as we can learn from the conquests of Osiris and Heracles. Their conquests, however, were imaginary, and in the real world of antiquity there were great variations in the degree of force used in spreading an idea. However, cultural, political and religious missions were seldom carried out by force in the Hellenistic world.[17] In fact, the spread of cults, a subject that was tackled many years ago by A. D. Nock, occurred as a natural progression and it is doubtful whether any force or even active mission was used.[18]

Returning to the subject of the culture-heroes, we have seen already that they were at times confronted with opposition, which was overcome by the use of force. Although Paul in Acts is depicted as a warlike man when opposition occurs, like the culture-heroes who seldom use war for spreading their mission, he himself does not initiate any war for spreading his ideas. Yet it is interesting to note that it has been shown convincingly by A. Malherbe that Paul's imagery of war comes from pagan sources rather than from Jewish ones (2 Corinth. 10:3-6; 12:12).[19]

2) More moderate methods were also used by culture-heroes in order to convince the recipients. For instance, their teaching *(didaskein)* some aspects of "progress" which according to our literary sources are known only to the culture-heroes. This applies mainly, as we will see later, to the technological sphere. One can find examples of the building of new roads, agricultural innovations, revealing of new languages, as well as various other inventions. These innovations were accepted willfully by the "just" and the "pious" because

---

religious proselytism as a vocation represent a phenomenon which has been confined largely but by no means entirely, to Christianity, Buddhism and Islam" (in Enc. of the Social Sciences X, p. 536).

[17] Some exceptions that can be given are, on the one hand the attempts made by Antiochus IV to hellenize the Jews in his realm (and repeated later by the emperor Hadrian), the social revolution of Aristonicus in 133 B.C.E., and on the other hand the judaizing of the Edomites by John Hyrcanus, and presumably also the judaizing of the Itureans by Aristobulus I. However, these latter missionary acts of the Jewish rulers may have derived from the idea of Holy War found in the Hebrew Bible, and not from pagan precedents or ideas.

[18] Cf. examples in M. Goodman, Mission and Conversion. Proselytizing in the Religious History of the Roman Empire (Oxford, 1994), chapter 2, and in general A. D. Nock, Conversion. For the missionary propaganda of the Indian king Asoka, cf. Nock, Conversion, pp. 45–47. For the comparison of the spread of Christianity with other religions, cf. H. D. Betz, "Hellenism" in The Anchor Bible Dictionary, vol. III, cols. 130ff.

[19] A. J. Malherbe, "Antisthenes and Odysseus, and Paul at War", HTR 76:2 (1983), pp. 143–173. It is interesting to note that Epictetus, Discours 3.26.29 describes the relationship with God as one between commander and soldier. The road from persuasion by words to persuasion by force can be very short indeed.

they were convinced that they would benefit from progress in their daily lives. But in certain cases they were forced to accept the innovations since it was brought to bear on them from above. It should be noted that technological innovations served as a symbol of progress in contrast to the claim that technological inventions were unimportant for the understanding of progress in antiquity.[20]

Paul was definitely not a technological culture-hero, but his methods of persuation were not too far removed from the ones used by culture heroes. He very wisely communicated with his gentile (and Jewish) audiences by presenting them with the socio-economic, religious, and even political reforms associated with his mission.[21] Unlike the culture-heroes, Luke presents him as one who did not focus on the enforcement of any material benefits. Paul, rather, conveyed his message by the act of discourse. In fact, he displaced "one universe of discourse by another", and this was his main goal. W. Meeks has shown that Paul aimed his address at the urban populations, in particular the middle class,[22] and it was among this class that there was some opposition to him, comparable to that encountered by hellenistic missionary heroes. The case of the silversmiths guild and other craftsmen in Ephesus is a good example of such an opposition (Acts 19). Unlike Heracles or Osiris, however, Paul was not capable of suppressing this resistance by force; at least so according to Luke. Thus the novel content of the message, the new universe of discourse, itself became a tool of persuasion during the encounter between the missionary and his recipient.[23]

---

20 Sue Blundell, The Origins of Civilization in Greek and Roman Thought (London and Sydney, 1986).

21 There exists an interesting illustration to this. R. M. Eaton says about Christian mission among the Nagas in India that among the factors that brought about the mass conversion of the Naga to Christianity were "the perception of Christianity as a new *technique*, a new way of tapping a source of power that could alleviate everyday problems" and "the experience of a wider social world resulting from imperial integration and modern warfare..." ("Conversion to Christianity among the Nagas, 1876–1971", The Indian Economic and Social History Review, vol. XXI, 1 (1984), p. 43) (I owe thanks to Professor D. Shulman for this reference).

22 W. A. Meeks, The First Urban Christians (New Haven, 1983). Perhaps his success among the gentiles brought about this opposition from the Jews; cf. P. R. Trebilco, Jewish Communities in Asia Minor (Cambridge, 1991), p. 26.

23 An interesting example of this latter point can be drawn from the presentation of the hellenistic historian Phylarchus of the socio-economic message of Cleomenes III, king of Sparta (in Plutarch, *Cleomenes*). Cleomenes came forward in 227 B. C. E. with an attractive "communist" message for the poor all over Greece. The latter became acquainted with this ideal of socio-economic equality through the communist Lycurgan regime which Cleomenes implemented on his own city, Sparta. At a certain juncture all of the poor, and some of the aristocrats in the Peloponnesus who were interested in social change, eagerly waited for Cleomenes to implement his communist ideas in their cities in a similar manner to his revolution which took place in Sparta. In other words, the poor outside Sparta became recipients of the innovations since the slogan of equality itself caused the spread of this particular mission. Surprisingly enough, Cleomenes III did not want to enforce his new ideas,

3) The use of showing wonders, miracles and other devices as a means of persuation. Paul does not use this method very often, but it does occur, according to Luke in Acts.[24]

D. Nature of message

As has already been seen, the idea of mission in hellenistic literature is not limited to the religious sphere. The nature of mission will now be addressed:

1. Cultural

In the hellenistic sources the cultural message is portrayed in simplistic terms, but behind this stands an elevated perception of the development of humankind, and its progress. The hero either cleanses a region of wild beasts or destroys other enemies which bother the native population. In other instances, the hero brings agricultural innovations, and plants new species of plants (usually, it seems, outside the sphere of his own "national" domain). Hellenistic civilizators also initiate urbanization in the *oecumene*. In all cases the texts emphasize that the acts performed by the heroes bring progress to the population (not necessarily using the standard term "progress", *prokope*). The following are examples of this.

Osiris had "the intention of visiting all the inhabited earth and teaching the race of men *(kai didaksai to genos ton anthropon)* how to cultivate the vine and sow wheat and barley". He hoped, according to Diodorus, that men would give up their savagery and adopt a gentle manner of life (*kai diaites hemerou metalabein*, DS 1.17.1-2). Osiris took with him "men who were experienced in agriculture, such as Maron in the cultivation of vine, and Triptolemus in the sowing of grain and in every step in the harvesting of it" (DS 1.18.2-3). Later it is stated that Osiris cared for the rural regions "teaching the inhabitants agriculture" (*didaksanta tous anthropous ta peri ten georgian*, DS 1.18.6). In India, it is said, Osiris introduced the ivy plants, and left "many other signs of his stay". In Thrace Osiris left Maron "to supervise the culture of the plants which he introduced into that land", and Triptolemus was designated to care for Attica's agriculture (DS 1.20.2-3). "Finally, Osiris in this way visited all the

---

which therefore did not take hold. At this point the recipients of his message turned their backs on him, and this was one of the reasons for his final downfall. Cf. D. Mendels, "Polybius and the Socio-Economic Reforms of Cleomenes III, Reexamined", Grazer Beiträge 10 (1981), pp. 95–104.

[24] Acts 13:9-11; 14:8-11. See also II Cor 12:11-12. Cf. the survey by A. von Harnack, The Acts of the Apostles (London, 1909), pp. 133–161. For this device in missionary gods in general, cf. Nock, Conversion, pp. 83–92.

inhabited world and advanced community life *(epelthonta ton koinon bion)* by the introduction of the fruits which are most easily cultivated" (DS 1.20.3). The "Indian" Dionysus,[25] Diodorus says, alongside his sharing with the knowledge of storing of the fruits with the Indians, he "allowed all people to share in his other discoveries" (DS 3.63.4; 3.70.7-8).

Heracles "by his own labours brought under cultivation the inhabited world" *(tois idiois ponois eksemerosai ten oikoumenen).*[26] He succeeded in relieving the region between Mycenae and Nemea in the Peloponnes of some terrible menace (DS 4.11.3-4). He also freed the Stymphalian lake of the multitude of birds which destroyed the fruits of the country (reminiscent of Abraham's invention of the plough which frightened the ravens, Jubilees 11:23-24). Heracles cleansed Crete of wild animals, and in Libya he cultivated "large parts of the adjoining desert", so that "Libya, which before that time had been uninhabitable because of the multitude of wild beasts... was brought under cultivation *(eksemerosas epoiese)* by him and made inferior to no other country in point of prosperity *(eudaimonia)*" (DS 4.17.4).

Another aspect of technological progress is the building of dikes, cities, roads, and water reservoirs. It should be emphasized here that in spite of the fact that the Greeks and Romans had cyclical views of the world, they considered progress *(prokope)* to be an important factor in their social lives provided that progress occurs *within* the scope of this cycle.[27]

Osiris founded some notable cities in Ethiopia *(poleis aksiologous ktisanta)*, and built dikes on the Nile so that at times of flood the water "might be let upon the countryside in a gentle flow as it might be needed, through gates which he had built" (DS 1.19.5). Osiris also founded many cities in India, and in Thrace he encouraged Maron to found a city "to bear his name which he called Maroneia" (DS 1.20.2-3). Ninus was the one who founded Nineveh, and Semiramis founded Babylon, and "amongst her other enterprises she built a temple to Bel, and other magnificent buildings in Babylon" (DS 2.7.2-12.3). She also founded other cities along the Euphrates and the Tigris rivers, in which she established trading-places for the merchants who brought goods from

---

[25] For Dionysus, cf. in general in Mythologies (Chicago, London, 1991) vol. I (YVES BONNEFOY), cols. 456–463.

[26] Y. BONNEFOY's Mythologies vol. I, p. 484 rightly states that already "in the fourth century a subtle shift made the warrior hero into a universal helper... Heracles is still the protector, but the warrior has softened into a benefactor (he is already *euergetes* in EURIPIDES: Heracles 1252)... The Hellenistic era will even establish him – a surprise – as a legislator and will make him a model of *philanthropia*..." Cf. also L. LACROIX, "Héraclès, héro voyageur et civilisateur", Bulletin de la Classe des lettres de l'Academie Royale de Belgique 60 (1974), pp. 34–59; M. DETIENNE, "Héraclès héros pythagoricien", Revue de l'Histoire des Religions 158 (1960), pp. 19–53.

[27] Cf. still the best study on progress in antiquity E. R. DODDS, The Ancient Concept of Progress (Oxford, 1973); cf. also SUE BLUNDELL, The Origins of Civilization.

Media, Paraetacene, and all the neighbouring region (DS 2.11.1). She built a park in Behistun (*kateskeuase paradeison*, DS 2.13.1-2), and she created another one in Chauon in Media. Diodorus emphasizes that the purpose of building these parks was the enjoyment of "luxury" (*truphe*, DS 2.13.3-4). In Ecbatana, she cut a road through the cliffs "which to this day is called the road of Semiramis" (DS 2.13.5). Many more details are given of her enterprises in Ecbatana and other regions which she passed through. These were mainly undertakings which brought technological progress to the region such as building roads through rough places, founding cities and exploiting the natural water resources for the welfare of the peoples.

It is said that Heracles founded the Libyan city of Hecatompylon, the City of the multitude of gates, and that it became very prosperous *(eudaimon)*. "And after Heracles had visited *(epelthon)* a large part of Libya he arrived at the ocean near Gadeira where he set up pillars on each of the two continents" (DS 4.18.2). By this act he made the straight of Gibraltar narrow in order that the great sea-monsters would not "pass out of the ocean into the inner sea". Others say that "the two continents are originally joined and that he cut a passage between them" (DS 4.18.4-5). In Gallia he founded the city of Alesia, which became famous in later years. "The Celts up to the present time hold this city in honour, looking upon it as the heart and mother city of all Celtica" (DS 4.19.2). Heracles also built a route through the Alps to Italy "with the result that it can now be crossed by armies and baggage-trains" (DS 4.19.3). In the Cumean plain "Heracles is said to have filled up the outlet and constructed the road which runs at this time along the sea and is called after him the "Way of Heracles" (DS 4.22.2). Heracles also built a lake at Agyrium in Sicily "as a mark of his gratitude to the people who had found favour with him" (DS 4.24.3). In addition Heracles sent out a colony *(apoikia)* to Sardinia.

Be that as it may, technological innovations served as the symbol of progress in hellenistic thought. Paul, as portrayed by Luke, definitely did not have this physical element in his mission (although the creation of communities within the boundaries of the Roman empire in the first century C.E. can be seen as analogous to the establishment of cities by the hero-cults). But does Paul emerge from the Book of Acts as one who had a more elevated idea of "progress" in mind when he went on his mission? Perhaps this aspect is to be read in between the lines of Acts. The gentiles who accepted his new message received it as a consequence of the enormous change it presented to them. As a result, they had to switch from their cyclical views (socio-economic, political and religious) to a linear approach to the world (cf. for instance the epitome of Jewish history in Stephen linked to the notion of *basileia tou theou)*. This view of development towards an *eschaton* (end) after which comes something new and unknown, contains the concept of moving forward. Progress was understood by the first Christians as a movement towards a completely different, yet more elevated, socio-economic and cultural life. For them the limit was not even the sky, but rather, the *"basileia tou theou"*.

2. *Religious*

Cultural and religious aspects cannot be distinguished easily from each other, but there are some instances where the religious aspect is specifically referred to. For instance, Heracles' wanderings contain a religious purpose, namely to spread his fame, and therefore his cult throughout the places in which he travels. We are in fact told that Heracles left traces of his cult in many of the places which he visited during his journey. It seems likely that it was Matris of Thebes and Apollodorus, or even the sources that they themselves used, who drew lines between the various spots where a Heraclean cult was found or was known to exist in their own time, thus connecting the loci and presenting them as one long course of Heracles' journey. But the presentation of a motivated journey to spread one's cult is what matters when one speaks of Hellenistic missionary thought predating Paul's mission. Some examples are:

Osiris did not organize pitched battles "since every people received him as a god because of his benefactions *(euergesias)*" (DS 1.18.5). The Boeotian Dionysus was said to have made a campaign throughout all the inhabited world and "instructed all men who were pious *(tois eusebesi ton antrhopon)* and cultivated a life of justice in the knowledge of his rites" (DS 3.64.7). Also "since the presence *(parousia)* of the god... became noised abroad in every region, and the report spread that he was treating all men honourably *(epieikos)* and contributing greatly to the refinement of man's social life, the whole populace everywhere thronged to meet him and welcomed him with great joy" (DS 3.65.1). Myrina was more active, and during a storm when she was carried away to an island (a well known motif in this kind of literature; see Acts 27:13ff), she "in obedience to a vision which she beheld in her dreams," sanctified the island to Cybele. The island was Samothrace, and the goddess "established the mysteries which are now celebrated on the island and ordained by law that the sacred area would enjoy the right sanctuary" (DS 3.55.9).

In the story of Heracles' journey there is much more about this aspect of "active" religious mission. During his travels Heracles arrived at the banks of the river Tiber at the future site of Rome (DS 4.21.1). He "received with favour the good-will *(eunoia)* shown him by the dwellers on the Palatine and foretold to them that, after he had passed into the circles of the gods, it would come to pass that whatever men should make a vow to dedicate to Heracles a tithe of their goods would lead a more happy and prosperous life" (DS 4.21.3). Henceforward, the source adds, many Romans gave a tithe of their wealth to Heracles. In other words, it seems that Heracles was trying to "convert" the people to adhere to his own cult instead of whatever religious course they were following.

In Syracuse, however, Heracles sacrificed to the goddesses Core and Demeter, and "commanded the natives to sacrifice each year to Core" (DS 4.23.4). In Sicily he dedicated a "notable sacred precinct" to Iolaus who was his companion on the campaign, and ordained that annual honours and sacrifices should be offered to him. In this case Heracles carried out some missionary work for another figure.

All of the above descriptions are, of course, put in simplistic terms in accordance with the mythographic literature fashionable in the hellenistic era. The Book of Acts is very different in its presentation of mission. However, the similarities cannot be overlooked. In Paul's case we understand, both from the Book of Acts and his own letters, that he indeed went from one place to another in order to get adherents to his new faith and to strengthen the Christian communities which already existed in the cities outside Palestine (according to Eusebius there were many other missionaries at the time, HE 3.4). He also set up new Christian centres all over the ancient near East. We should note here that Luke, who knew these centres, may have drawn lines in order to connect the various places which would then form one coherent entity (as was probably done by hellenistic authors in Heracles' case). By doing this, he described Paul's visit to different places as being several journeys with well-planned itineraries.

3. *Political*

In hellenistic literature the notion of a wandering god with a political message was very important in that the imperialistic claims were based on the belief that a certain national god visited the populations who were to be "annexed" to the ideal (or even more real) empire. Thus hero-gods such as Myrina and Sesostris went from one place to another in order to "convey" to the many peoples they visited that they were part of a new empire with an exact perimeter. Myrina even brought political change, i.e. "freedom" *(eleutheria)*, to some of the territories she conquered. Hence, the idea of political mission was used to validate any visionary empires which might materialize at any time in the future.[28]

This concept of an imaginary empire included the notion that a certain political rule brings freedom into a region in terms of justice and law, and it is implicit through all the descriptions discussed here. There are also some specific references: Semiramis "had put in order *(katastesasa)* the affairs of Ethiopia and Egypt" (DS 2.16.1); the Indian Dionysus "became the founder of notable cities ... and he both taught them (the Indians) to honour the deity, and

[28] Cf. MENDELS, Rise and Fall, chapters 4, 9. For the motif of adding territory in Paul's mission: P. BOWERS, "Paul and Religious Propaganda in the First Century," NT XXII, 4 (1980), pp. 316–323.

introduced laws and courts" (*kai nomous eisegesasthai kai dikasteria*, DS 2.38.5); the Boeotian Dionysus, however, "composed the quarrels between the nations and cities and created concord and deep peace where there had existed civil strifes and wars" (*kai ton polemon omonoian kai pollen eirenen kataskeuazein*, DS 3.64.7). Myrina could not really become a missionary of law and order, because – according to classical tradition – she was a woman, and Diodorus says that Heracles destroyed the Amazons in the regions where they ruled, "because he felt that it would ill accord with his resolve to be the benefactor of the whole race of mankind if he should suffer any nations to be under the rule of women" (DS 3.55.3). Hence Heracles brought prosperity to the cities in Libya inter alia by punishing "with death such men as defied the law or arrogant rulers" *(tous paranomountas anthropous e dunastas uperephanous apokteinas)*. He killed Busiris in Egypt, "the king of the land, who made it his practice to kill the stranges who visited the country" and in Gallia he put an end to the lawlessness and murdering of strangers to which the people had become addicted. In the Alps Heracles subdued the barbarians who used to plunder and hinder any army that crossed the Alps, and "those that were the leaders in lawlessness of this kind he slew" *(kai tous hegemonas tes paranomias anelon)*, and "made the journey safe for succeeding generations" (DS 4.19.4). Heracles thus became a heroe in the fight against pirates who posed a menace to civilization in the hellenistic period.

Paul, as described by Luke, "conquered" more and more territory in the *oecumene*; his message included a new system of law and social order (for instance Acts 24:25; mentioning justice, self-control and judgment). He did not go on a mission to eastern parts, namely to the east of the line drawn from Jerusalem to Damascus, but only into the Roman *oecumene*, and there he preached for a new order, which in fact presented an alternative to the Roman one in many of its aspects. It is therefore not accidental that he used a great deal of the political rhetoric fashionable at the time.[29] As he himself says at one point in Acts, he also wished to go to Rome, to the capital of the empire (19:21). He actually was the first to lay the foundation of the new idea of a Christian empire overlapping parts of the real Roman one. But this cannot altogether be divorced from the political concepts associated with borders and boundaries. By his *parousia* (presence) in the various regions, Paul did not dissociate

[29] For the use of rhetoric of empire in later Christian sources cf. AVERIL CAMERON, Christianity and the Rhetoric of Empire. The Development of Christian Discourse (Berkeley, LA, Oxford, 1991). I hope to deal with this aspect in the future.

Here it should be mentioned that scholars have associated the universalistic concept in Judaism (especially from the Hebrew Bible) with Paul's mission (cf. in particular GEORGI, Opponents, pp. 148ff). However, ideas that we find in ISAIAH 2 and elsewhere never speak of Jews who will *go* to the nations, thus being active in spreading their religion. In Paul's case as in the hellenistic culture-heroes, the apostle is *active* in walking from one place to another, spreading his mission.

himself from the notion of sovereignty in the hellenistic sense of the word. Thus Luke gives the impression that his movement and actual stay in cities and regions in itself constituted a message which had political overtones. Like the culture-heroes he crossed borders, within the boundaries of the Roman empire in which he travelled freely. In fact, we rarely hear of any limit made to a mission, unless this is done by a call of God (as in the case of Provincia Asia and Bithynia, Acts 16:6–9).

E. Cycle (Kuklos, anakuklos)

It is not accidental, we believe, that all culture-heroes walk in a circle, or circles, to form an enclosed territory with well-defined "borders" against the outside world. Osiris, Dionysus, Heracles, Sesostris, Myrina (and Abraham), all took a circular route in the regions we have described above, and returned at the end of their mission to their home base (unlike, for instance, Aeneas who travels from Ilium to Rome). In some cases the circular movement is even stated specifically (DS 4.23.1: "Heracles desired to make the circuit of the entire Sicily", *boulomenos egkuklothenai pasan Sikelian*, and 23.3; 25.1). Although the term *kuklos* or *anakuklosis* is not always used in the sources when gods and culture-heroes are referred to, the concept of cycle is what matters in Greek (and Roman) thought.[30] Moreover, the geographical background to the movements of the culture-heroes and gods should also be understood in terms of time. They move from one place to another, and naturally this takes time. At a certain period after their journey is completed they return to the point of departure, but of course later in time than when they had left. In fact, this concept of time is in line with the cyclical concepts to be found in Greek political thought (and somewhat differently in the mythologies of the ancient Near East). There are interesting variants on the cyclic concept ranging from the one of the Golden Age (Hesiod) to the political *metabole* of Plato's *Politeia*.[31] The case of culture-heroes provides yet another variant which has seemingly been overlooked by scholars within this context.

A close examination of the cyclical movements of our culture-heroes shows that mission is completed only after their return to the original base. It seems that none of the heroes cares to visit the same places he has visited beforehand,

---

30 *Kuklos* and its variants are generally used in the simple manner of "surrounding" a city, or a person, etc. In the New Testament one finds this use of *kuklos* only in Lk 19:43 (the enemies will "surround you"); Jn 10:24 (the Jews gathered "round" him); Acts 14:20 (the disciples gathered "round" him). In Polybius' Histories it is found in 1.17.13 (and elsewhere); the more spiritual meaning will be found in Polybius with the prefix *ana*. In Book 6.9.10 he says that "such is the cycle of constitutions, the course appointed by nature in which constitutions change, disappear, and finally return to the point from which they started".

31 Cf. recently the discussion of Blundell, The Origins of Civilization.

but more importantly, no hero repeats the cycle he has already concluded. As in other cycles found in the literature of antiquity (political and cultural), there are obstacles which occur during the movement within the cycle (in the political *metabole*, for instance, there are revolutions as well as other problems; Plato, *Politeia*, 7–9; Polyb 6.10). The obstacles which arise en route are of various types: wars, dangerous animals, notorious mythological figures who are intent on destruction, as well as bandits and robbers. Yet, in spite of all of this, the cycle is successfully completed in all cases.

According to the book of Acts, until his last journey to Rome, Paul travelled in circular routes, making great efforts each time to return to his spiritual base Jerusalem.[32] Paul even uses this concept in Romans 15:19 where he says: "By the power of signs and wonders, by the power of the Holy Spirit, so that from Jerusalem and as far round as Illyricum I have fully preached the gospel of Christ" *(oste me apo Ierousalem kai kuklo mechri tou Illurikou peplerokenai to euaggelion tou christou)*.[33] The cyclical journeys of Paul can be viewed as a common hellenistic literary device which has been used by Luke. Such literary devices served to express ideas. Thus Paul wanders in cycles throughout his mission, and he returns to his theological base Jerusalem (and not to Tarsus, which has no significance for his mission). Like Osiris (DS 1.18.3), Paul cuts his hair before his return to Palestine, in keeping with a vow he made prior to his return (Acts 18:18, and see also 21:23-24). This is one of the most striking similarities to be found. Also, like Sesostris and Osiris, Paul faces fierce and violent opposition on his return to his original base, Jerusalem.

At this point one can find a major difference between the cyclical heroes and Paul which has a bearing on our theme. Paul, according to Luke, is taken to Rome after completing various cycles. Unlike the culture-heroes he does not stay in the final base, Jerusalem, but is sent to Rome (where he had planned to go in any case). Rome lies outside the sphere of cycles the Book of Acts has drawn, and that the story ends in Rome is not accidental. Scholars have pointed out that Paul landed there because the story had to finish in the capital of the Empire,[34] and this is probably true. Yet why does the climax of his mission take place outside the cycles he himself has drawn? One could suggest that the fact that Paul was taken outside the sphere of his cyclical missions points to a divergence from the cyclical scheme so well-known in pagan culture. Luke presented Paul as breaking from the cycle, which in geographical terms implied a break in the cyclical Greek concept. Luke did not believe that history is

32 Cf. for the historicity of Acts H. Koester, History and Literature of Early Christianity (NY, Berlin, 1982), vol. II, pp. 49–52.

33 Cf. in general for the passage: J. Knox, "Romans 15:14-33 and Paul's Conception of his Apostolic Mission", JBL 83 (1964), pp. 1–11. Eusebius of Caesarea stressed this point many years later (EH 3.4.1).

34 For instance, N. A. Dahl, Das Volk Gottes... (Darmstadt, 1941, rep. 1963), p. 241.

cyclical, thus directs it towards a goal. Paul symbolizes the start of a linear process in his mission, which is divergent from the cycle. The mission is no longer progressing within a cycle, but going far beyond it. Since the graphical or geographical is very important in general for the presentation of ideas in Greek and Roman thought (Anabasis, Aeneas), one may speculate that Paul's movement to Rome is a graphical expression of a linear progress which becomes much more important in early Christianity than the cyclical one.

Other elements to be considered are the concepts of limit, border, and boundary. A cycle draws a specific perimeter, thus missions are limited in their scope, a matter which can be described in geographical terms. Hence Sesostris, when in Thrace, "fixed the limits of his expedition" *(dioper oria tes strateias poiesamenon*, DS 1.55.6), and Myrina "fixed the bounds of her campaign at the Caicus river" (*orous thesthai tes strateias ton kaikon potamon*, DS 3.55.5). Luke presents this popular hellenistic thought as a religious sanction. According to Acts 16:6-9, the Holy Spirit forbade Paul to go to certain regions, to Provincia Asia and to Bithynia, but instead ordered him to go forth to Macedonia. This accords with the literary presentation we have found in hellenistic literature.

F. The Recipients

We have already mentioned above that hellenistic missionary literature used a common definition of the true recipients of mission on the one hand, and its opponents on the other.[35] Here one arrives at the difference between *asebeis*

[35] Can we speak of conversion in pagan societies? Conversion has become an important issue in recent scholarship that examines conversions from paganism to Judaism and Christianity, and from the latter to the former. Cf. McKnight, A Light, and M. Goodman, Mission. See also E. Will, C. Orrieux, Proselytisme juif? histoire d'une erreur (Paris, 1992). An interesting description of conversion from a sociological point of view, unrelated to antiquity, can be found in the article by D. A. Snow and R. Machalek. Amongst other things they say that "... conversion concerns not only a change in values, beliefs, and identities, but more fundamentally and significantly, it entails the displacement of one universe of discourse by another or the ascendance of a formerly peripheral universe of discourse to the status of primary authority. Such a conception does not restrict conversion only to changes from one religion to another or to the adoption of a religious world view where one was previously absent..." (p. 170 in "The Sociology of Conversion", in Ann. Rev. of Sociol. 10 (1984), pp. 167–190 with extensive bibliography).

This article, and other studies quoted by the above mentioned authors, tend to ignore the process of pre-Christian conversion. According to my own definition (see above), a pagan can also undergo conversion. If a pagan starts to prefer the worship of one god to another (thus changing his social affiliations), he can be seen as a convert. What Celsus says many years later concerning the "monotheism" of pagans strengthens the point (cf. Origines, Contra Celsum 5.34). This is true in particular when a pagan becomes a member of a religious association which worships one specific god. Thus people in the hellenistic era who accepted Osiris, or worshiped Heracles because of his "benefits to humankind" (when they had not done so previously), were the recipients of the so-called "primitive" mission, and may be considered as and *eusebeis*.[36] In the case of the hellenistic culture-heroes we can also find this distinction. For instance, it is said that the Boeotian Dionysus "instructed all men who were pious and cultivated a life of justice in the knowledge of his rites..." (DS 3.64.7). The *eusebeis* and *dikaioi* were the recepients of Dionysus' mission. It has already been seen that when the report spread that Dionysus was "treating all men honorably *(epieikos)* and contributing greatly to the refinement of man's social life, the entire populace thronged to meet him and welcomed him everywhere with great joy". Diodorus adds that there were "a few, however, who, out of disdain and impiety, looked down upon him *(oligon d' onton ton di' uperephanian kai asebeian kataphronounton)*... but such persons were punished by him right speedily" (DS 3.65.1-2). Diodorus specifies how Dionysus punished the impious: "In some cases he made use of the superior power which attended his divine nature and punished the impious *(asebeis)*, either striking them with madness or causing them while still living to be torn limb from limb by the hands of women; in other cases he destroyed such as opposed him by a military device" (DS 3.65.3). Thus "Dionysus punished the impious *(asebeis)* but treated all other men honorably *(epieikos)*" (3.65.7). Yet in another version of the Dionysus story it is said that Dionysus' campaign against the Titans was for the "purpose of punishing the impious and conferring benefits upon the entire human race" (*epi kolasei men ton asebon, euergesia de tou koinou genous ton anthropon*, 3.72.4, cf. also 4.2.6 and 4.2ff). It was Heracles who handed over the kingdom of Iberia to the noblest men from among the natives.

Turning now to the Book of Acts it can be seen that Luke also drew the above definition between the god fearers and the impious (Acts 13:43; 13:49; 14:2; 17:4; 17:17; 24:15). Luke's use of this terminology, like his use of the above hellenistic literary devices, may indicate that Luke wished to describe Paul's missionary acts in a manner that would be familiar to the pagans among his audience.[37]

---

some kind of converts. However, people who believed that they were in the remote past subjugated by a missionary god, or used the new technological devices which were associated with one or another cultural-hero, can also be considered as the recipients of some kind of mission without necessarily having become converts.

[36] Cf. on this issue E. Schürer (ed. G. Vermes et al.), The History of the Jewish People in the Age of Jesus Christ (175 B.C. – 135 A.D.), vol. 3,1 (1986), pp. 150f, and in particular Joyce Reynolds and R. Tannenbaum, "Jews and God-Fearers at Aphrodisias" in The Cambridge Philological Society 12 (1987), pp. 48ff, and also McKnight, A Light, pp. 110–114. *Theosebeis* was used as a technical term for gentiles within the Jewish diaspora (Reynolds and Tannenbaum, *ibid.*, pp. 53ff). *Eusebeis* is a more general term used in the pagan world, and is not found in a Jewish context. Cf. also Claudius to the people of Alexandria; he uses *sebeia* for those who are faithful to the Augusti (for the English text cf. R. K. Sherk, The Roman Empire: Augustus to Hadrian [Cambridge, 1988], no. 44, line 24).

[37] For Luke's larger Greco-Roman audience, see J. C. Lentz, Luke's Portrait of Paul (Cambridge, 1993) with the older literature.

In conclusion, it can be argued that the framework and techniques of Paul's mission, according to the Book of Acts, have many aspects in common with pagan sources from the hellenistic era dealing with missionary hero-gods. The similarities concerning the methods of mission are too obvious to ignore their common origin.

Ibn Kammûnas Verteidigung des historischen Jesus gegen den paulinischen Christus

von

STEFAN SCHREINER

Wenn es auch zutrifft, daß Ibn Kammûnas *„Buch der Kritik der Untersuchungen der drei Religionen [kitâb tanqîḥ al-abḥâṯ lil-milal aṯ-ṯalâṯ]"*, von dem hier die Rede sein wird, des öfteren bereits einiges Interesse auf sich gezogen hat,[1] so ist ihm – aufs ganze gesehen – die Aufmerksamkeit, die es ohne Zweifel verdient, bislang jedoch nicht geschenkt worden. Eingereiht wird es üblicherweise unter die Werke der polemischen Literatur,[2] obwohl es doch sowohl seinem Inhalt als auch seiner Form nach dort so recht nicht hineingehört. Polemiken pflegen anders auszusehen.

Hier freilich interessiert nicht Ibn Kammûnas gesamtes Werk, sondern nur ein Kapitel daraus, nämlich seine Auseinandersetzung mit dem Christentum und damit zugleich auch sein Beitrag zur historisch-kritischen Bibelwissenschaft. Letzteres mag sich vielleicht merkwürdig anhören, wird aber sogleich plausibel, wenn wir uns Ibn Kammûnas Sicht des historischen Jesus zuwenden. Zunächst jedoch einige Anmerkungen zur Person der Autors, seinem Leben und Wirken sowie insbesondere zu den Umständen der Entstehung seines uns

---

1 Zuletzt von S. ROSENKRANZ, „Judentum, Christentum und Islam in der Sicht des Ibn Kammuna", in: Jud 52 (1996), S. 4–22.

2 Auf die Bedeutung dieses Werkes hat bereits M. STEINSCHNEIDER, Polemische und apologetische Literatur in arabischer Sprache zwischen Muslimen, Christen und Juden nebst Anhängen verwandten Inhalts, Leipzig 1877 (= Abh. z. Kunde des Morgenlandes VI,3) [= Neudruck Hildesheim 1966], S. 37–41 § 19, hingewiesen (ferner zitiert als: M. STEINSCHNEIDER [1]). Vgl. DERS., Die arabische Literatur der Juden. Ein Beitrag zur Literaturgeschichte der Araber, großenteils aus handschriftlichen Quellen, Frankfurt a. M. 1902 [= repr. Hildesheim [2]1986], S. 239–240 § 178 (ferner zitiert als: M. STEINSCHNEIDER [2]). Mit Recht nannte M. Steinschneider Ibn Kammûnas Buch „vielleicht die interessanteste unter den arab. Streitschriften zwischen den Religionen" (S. 240). S. dazu auch M. PERLMANN, „The Medieval Polemics between Islam and Judaism", in: S. D. Goitein (Hg.), Religion in a Religious Age, Cambridge, Mass. 1974, S. 103–138, dort S. 122–126; ferner H. SCHRECKENBERG, Die christlichen Adversus-Judaeos-Texte und ihr literarisches und historisches Umfeld (13.–20. Jh.), Frankfurt/M. - Berlin - Bern - New York - Paris - Wien 1994 (= Europäische Hochschulschriften XXIII, Bd. 497), S. 310–311.

hier interessierenden Buches, soweit sie im vorliegenden Kontext für dessen Verständnis von Wichtigkeit sind.

1. Der Autor und sein Werk

1.1 Der Autor

Von Ibn Kammûna selbst wissen wir nicht sehr viel. L. Nemoy sagte von ihm, er sei „by vocation an ophthalmologist with a clientele of patients among the upper echelons of the imperial capital of Baghdad, by avocation a keen and original student of philosophy and theology" gewesen,[3] und hat damit Ibn Kammûna ganz sicher treffend charakterisiert. Was von Ibn Kammûnas Leben und Werk bekannt ist, und das ist insgesamt, wie schon angedeutet, wenig genug, hat bereits M. Perlmann in den Einleitungen zu seiner Edition des arabischen Textes[4] sowie seiner englischen Übersetzung des *„Buches der Kritik der Untersuchungen der drei Religionen"*[5] zusammengetragen.[6] Dabei stützte er sich im wesentlichen auf die entsprechenden Angaben in dem biographischen Wörterbuch des Chronisten Kamâl ad-Dîn ʿAbd ar-Razzâq b. al-Fuwaṭî [al-Fûṭî] (1244–1323), da es „the only substantial source of biographical data about our author" darstellt.[7]

Demnach lebte Ibn Kammûna – mit seinem vollen Namen hieß er *Saʿd b. Manṣûr b. al-Ḥasan Ḥibbat Allâh Ibn Kammûna* und trug den Beinamen *ʿIzz ad-daula wad-dîn* (*die Stärke des Staates und der Religion*)[8] – von ungefähr 1215 bis ungefähr 1285 und bis zu seinem letzten Lebensjahr wohl fast ausschließlich in Baghdad. Die genauen Lebensdaten sind ebenso wenig überliefert wie alle näheren Einzelheiten aus seinem Leben. Überliefert ist nur, daß er sein uns hier interessierendes Buch[9] aller Wahrscheinlichkeit nach im Jahre 1280/81

---

[3] L. NEMOY, „Ibn Kammûnah's Treatise on the Differences between the Rabbanites and the Karaites", in: JQR 63 (1972–73), S. 97–135. 222–246, dort S. 97.

[4] Saʿd b. Mansûr Ibn Kammûna's Examination of the Inquiries into the Three Faiths. A Thirteenth-Century Essay in Comparative Religion, ed. M. PERLMANN, Berkeley-Los Angeles 1967 (= Univ. of California Publ., Near Eastern Studies no. 6), S. IX–XII (ferner zitiert als: M. PERLMANN [1]). Zur Person des Autors auch L. NEMOY, S. 97–102.

[5] M. PERLMANN, Ibn Kammûna's Examination of the Three Faiths. A thirteenth-century essay in the comparative study of religion, Berkeley-Los Angeles-London 1971, S. 1–9 (ferner zitiert als: M. PERLMANN [2]). – Bei Zitaten aus Ibn Kammûnas Buch weist die erste Seitenangabe jeweils auf die Edition des arabischen Textes, die zweite auf die englische Übersetzung. Die Übersetzungen der Zitate stammen, sofern nicht anders angegeben, von mir.

[6] Die beste Gesamtdarstellung ist noch immer: D. H. BANETH, „Ibn Kammûna", in: MGWJ 69 (1925), S. 295–311.

[7] M. PERLMANN [2], S. 1.

[8] So nach dem Text bei L. NEMOY, S. 103.

[9] Bekannt sind von Ibn Kammûna darüber hinaus ein „Traktat über die Unsterblichkeit der

geschrieben, und daß dieses Buch nur wenige Jahre später, nämlich 1284, einen Anschlag seitens – heute würden wir sagen – islamischer Fundamentalisten auf den Autor wegen Herabwürdigung des Islams ausgelöst hat, dem er tatsächlich auch beinahe zum Opfer gefallen wäre, wenn ihm nicht noch in letzter Minute die Flucht zu seinem Sohn, der in Ḥilla ein öffentliches Amt bekleidete, gelungen wäre. Dort in Ḥilla scheint Ibn Kammûna bald danach wohl auch gestorben zu sein.[10]

Den Lebensdaten zufolge gehört Ibn Kammûna also zu den Augenzeugen und Überlebenden der Ereignisse vom 10. Februar 1258, d.i. des Tages der Eroberung Baghdads durch Dschingis Khans Enkel Hülägü und der Gemetzel, die diesem Tage folgten.[11] Er erlebte und überlebte den Zusammenbruch des Kalifats und damit die schwerste Erschütterung der islamischen Welt.[12] Doch nicht allein dies ist von Wichtigkeit, so entsetzlich diese Ereignisse für die Bewohner Baghdads und Umgebung im einzelnen auch waren. Mit al-Muʿtaṣims, des letzten Abbasidenkalifen, Ermordung hörte zugleich auch der Islam auf, Staatsreligion zu sein. Fortan, bis zum Übertritt der Mongolen zum Islam (1298), lebten die überlebenden Muslime, Christen und Juden gleichermaßen unter der Herrschaft der Bekenner einer anderen Religion.[13]

Der Eroberer Baghdads, Hülägü selbst, war zunächst Anhänger des Schamanismus gewesen, bevor er sich dem Buddhismus zuwandte; seine Frau Doquz hingegen war eine nestorianische Christin. Und dies sollte für die in Baghdad am Leben gebliebenen Christen und Juden nicht ohne Folgen bleiben. Zwar hatte man Juden und Christen bereits während der Eroberung von den Metzeleien zu verschonen versucht, vielleicht sogar als Dank für die bei der

---

Seele" (arab. ed. L. Nemoy, New Haven 1944; engl. L. Nemoy, in: Ignace Goldziher Memorial Volume, 2 Bde, Budapest-Jerusalem 1948–58, Bd.II, S. 83–99 [Nachdruck beider Ausgaben in: *Ha-Rofê ha-ʿIvrî* – The Hebrew Medical Journal 35 (1962), S. 131–136.213–239], sowie ein „Traktat über die Differenzen zwischen Rabbaniten und Karaiten" (arab. ed. L. Nemoy, in: PAAJR 36 (1968), S. 107–165; engl. L. Nemoy, in: JQR 63 (1972–73), S. 97–135. 222–246).

10 M. Perlmann [1], S.IX; [2] S. 3 mit A. 5 (dort die engl. Übers. des entsprechenden Berichtes). Dasselbe nach W. Fischels dt. Übers. (in: ders., „Arabische Quellen zur Geschichte der babylonischen Judenheit im 13. Jahrhundert", in: MGWJ 79 (1935), S. 302–322, dort S. 319f), bei F. Niewöhner, *Veritas sive Varietas*. Lessings Toleranzparabel und das Buch von den drei Betrügern, Heidelberg 1988 (= Bibl. d. Aufklärung, Bd. 5), S. 230f (ferner zitiert als: F. Niewöhner [1]).

11 S. die Darstellung dieser Ereignisse mit Zusammenstellung aller relevanten Quellen bei B. Spuler, Die Mongolen in Iran, Berlin [4]1985, S. 46–53. Vgl. auch F. Niewöhner [1] S. 222–232.

12 M. Perlmann [1], S. X A. 2, verweist in diesem Zusammenhang auf ein von I. Goldziher mitgeteiltes Zitat Ibn Taimijjas: „Hülägü ist für die Muslime das, was Nebukadnezzar für die Kinder Israel war".

13 Zur Lage der Muslime, Christen und Juden unter den Mongolen s. B. Spuler, S. 165–195 (zum Christentum), S. 195–203 (zum Islam) und S. 204–208 (zum Judentum) (Lit.!).

Eroberung Baghdads erwiesene Hilfe, wie A. Ben-Ya'aqov vermutet hat.[14] Nun jedoch, nach der Eroberung, wird die Stadt von einem Buddhisten beherrscht; zum Buddhismus übergetreten war unterdessen auch Hülägüs Bruder Qubilai, der Groß-Khan der Mongolen (1260–1294), wobei von Qubilai selber angenommen wird, er habe sowohl Buddha als auch Moses, Jesus und Muhammad gleichermaßen verehrt, wenngleich sich der entsprechende Passus in Marco Polos Reisebericht, auf den sich diese Annahme stützt,[15] in dessen beiden ältesten greifbaren Versionen allerdings nicht findet.[16]

Gleichviel ob man diese Einstellung, sofern sie überhaupt der geschichtlichen Wirklichkeit entspricht, politisches Kalkül oder Pragmatismus nennen sollte oder aber als Ausdruck einer religiösen Toleranz ansehen darf – für das Leben der Untertanen im Rest des Abbasidenreiches, insbesondere für das Zusammenleben der Bekenner unterschiedlicher Religionen sollte dies schon von Bedeutung sein. Und wie wir aus anderen Quellen wissen, gab diese veränderte äußere Situation vor allem in den achtziger Jahren des 13. Jh. zu einer Reihe von Religionsgesprächen Anlaß, die von den Beteiligten allerdings durchaus nicht immer freiwillig geführt worden sind.[17] An solchen Religionsgesprächen hat auch Ibn Kammûna teilgenommen. Jedenfalls sind eben jene Religionsgespräche nach seinem eigenem Bekunden auch für ihn nicht nur eine unmittelbare Erfahrung gewesen, sondern haben ihm den Anstoß zur Abfassung seines Buches gegeben. In der Einleitung dazu berichtet er nämlich *expressis verbis*:

„Es waren Disputationen (*mufâwaḍât*), die mich veranlaßt haben, diesen Traktat zur Prüfung der Untersuchungen der drei Religionen, d.i. der Religion der Juden, der Religion der Christen und der Religion der Muslime zu schreiben" (S. 1/S. 11).

---

[14] A. Ben-Ja'aqov, *Yehûdê Bâvel – mi-sôf teqûfat ha-ge'ônîm 'ad yâmênû*, Jerusalem 1965, bes. S. 67ff. – Zum Schicksal der Juden im Jahre 1258 s. auch J. Mann, „Une source de l'histoire des Juifs au XIIIe siècle. La lettre polémique de Jacob b. Elie Pablo Christiani" in: REJ 82 (1926), S. 363–377, bes. S. 373f.

[15] Nach TH. A. Knust (Hg.), Marco Polo: Von Venedig nach China, Tübingen [4]1976, S. 134f, zitiert bei F. Niewöhner, „Die Wahrheit ist eine Tochter der Zeit. Ibn Kammûnas historisch-kritischer Religionsvergleich aus dem Jahre 1280", in: B. Lewis und F. Niewöhner (Hg.), Religionsgespräche im Mittelalter, Wiesbaden 1992 (= Wolfenbütteler Mittelalter-Studien, Bd. 4), S. 357–369, dort S. 358 (ferner zitiert als: F. Niewöhner [2]).

[16] Vgl. Marco Polo, Il Milione – Die Wunder der Welt, übers. von E. Guignard, Zürich [5]1989, S. 124f.

[17] S. dazu B. Spuler, S. 199. Daß offenbar die Jahre zwischen der mongolischen Eroberung Baghdads und der Konversion der Mongolen zum Islam (1298) eine für das Gespräch zwischen den Religionen günstige Zeit war, bestätigt neuerdings auch L. S. Northrup, „Muslim Christian Relations During the Reign of the Mamlûk Sultân al-Mansûr Qalawun A.D. 1278–1290", in: M. Gervers und R. J. Bikhazi (Hg.), Conversion and Continuity in Islamic Lands, Eighth to Eighteenth Century, Toronto 1990, S. 253–261. Den Hinweis auf diesen Aufsatz verdanke ich Frau Prof. H. Lazarus-Yafeh/Jerusalem.

Wenn auch die Baghdader Religionsgespräche der zweiten Hälfte des 13. Jh. Ibn Kammûnas Buch veranlaßt haben, das Buch selber ist dennoch kein Religionsgespräch im herkömmlichen Sinne, schon gar kein Protokoll eines solchen, weder nach seiner Form, noch nach seinem Inhalt. Auch ist es nicht, wie viele seiner Vorgänger, in Gestalt eines fiktiven Dialoges von Vertretern unterschiedlicher Religionen abgefaßt, die über den Wahrheitsgehalt und Wahrheitsanspruch ihrer jeweiligen Religion streiten. Vielmehr befleißigt sich der Autor in seiner eher monographischen Darstellung der drei Religionen einer erstaunlichen Neutralität, die geradezu Objektivität zu nennen ist. Jedenfalls ist seine Darstellung so „objektiv" gehalten, daß sie die Religionszugehörigkeit ihres Autors *explicite* nicht zu erkennen gibt. Und der Autor selbst verrät sie uns auch nicht, was immer wieder entsprechenden Spekulationen Vorschub geleistet hat.[18] Nur aus anderen Quellen wissen wir, daß Ibn Kammûna ein *failasûf al-yahûd*, ein *Philosoph der Juden* resp. *jüdischer Philosoph* gewesen ist,[19] wenn auch sein Judentum gelegentlich angezweifelt worden ist, und man sogar lesen kann, er sei zum Islam übergetreten.[20] Doch selbst wenn es so wäre, Ibn Kammûna hätte dafür eine plausible, pragmatische Erklärung, die zugleich einiges Licht auf seine Einstellung dem Islam gegenüber (und indirekt auf seine Religionszugehörigkeit) wirft:

„Daher finden wir bis auf den heutigen Tag nicht, daß irgend jemand zum Islam überträte, ohne daß er entweder von Furcht getrieben wäre oder nach einer angesehenen sozialen Stellung strebte oder von einer schweren Steuer betroffen würde (?) oder sich aus verachteter sozialer Stellung zu befreien suchte oder von Gefangenschaft (? evtl.: von einer Denunziation) betroffen würde (?) oder eine Mohammedanerin liebte, oder etwas ähnliches vorläge; niemals aber haben wir gefunden, daß ein Mann, der in seiner Religion und der des Islam bewandert und dabei in geachteter sozialer Stellung, wohlhabend und gottesfürchtig war, zum Islam übertrat, ohne daß eine von den genannten Ursachen oder etwas ähnliches vorlag" (S. 102/S. 149).[21]

---

18 Daß er seinen Traktat mit der *Basmala*, d. i. der Formel *Im Namen Gottes, des barmherzigen Erbarmers*, eröffnet (S. 1/S. 11), besagt freilich nicht mehr, als daß er sich an die Konventionen seiner Zeit hält.

19 M. Steinschneider [1], S. 39 § 19,5 und S. 47f § 30; C. Sirat, A History of Jewish Philosophy in the Middle Ages, Cambridge-Paris ²1990, S. 208f.

20 M. Steinschneider war der Ansicht, Ibn Kammûna sei „sicher als Jude geboren [...], aber gerirt sich als Muhammedaner" ([1], S. 39 § 19,5). Ibn Kammûnas Judentum ist hinlänglich bewiesen bereits von D. H. Baneth, S. 296f. 304ff. Zur Diskussion um diese Frage s. auch S. W. Baron, Social and Religious History of the Jews, Bd. V, S. 102; Bd. XVII, S. 181 mit 380f; B. Lewis, Die Juden in der islamischen Welt, München 1987, S. 91f; N. Stillman, The Jews of Arab Lands. A History and a Source Book, Philadelphia 5739/1979, S. 261. Zum grundsätzlichen Problem der Konversionen s. S. D. Goitein, A Mediterranian Society. The Jewish Communities in the Arab World as portrayed in the Documents of the Cairo Genizah, Bd. II, Berkeley-Los Angeles-London 1971, S. 299–311 mit 591–594.

21 Hier zitiert nach der Übers. D. H. Baneths, S. 305.

1.2 Ibn Kammûnas „Buch der Kritik der Untersuchungen der drei Religionen"

Ibn Kammûnas *„Buch der Kritik der Untersuchungen der drei Religionen"* selber besteht aus insgesamt vier Teilen, wobei allein schon die Gliederung ebenso wie der Umfang der einzelnen Teile höchst aufschlußreich ist. Ohne das Buch jetzt im einzelnen vorstellen oder gar rekapitulieren zu wollen,[22] sei gleichwohl ein kurzer Überblick über dessen Aufbau gegeben. Da Ibn Kammûna die drei von ihm untersuchten Religionen als prophetische Religionen, d.h. als jeweils auf einen prophetischen Stifter zurückgehende Religionen versteht, beginnt er seine Abhandlung mit einer grundlegenden Erörterung dessen, was Prophetie bedeutet und wodurch sich Propheten auszeichnen:

I. Teil (20 Kapitel) „Über den Beweis der Wahrheit des Prophetentums, seine verschiedenen Erscheinungsweisen, den Beweis seiner Existenz, seine Vorzüge und andere damit in Zusammenhang stehende Dinge" (S. 12–23/ S. 13–39).

Dabei folgt Ibn Kammûna weitgehend Mose b. Maimons (1135/8–1204) *Moreh Nevûkhîm* (Buch II §§ 41 ff. 45),[23] wie bereits D. H. Baneth gezeigt hat.

In historischer Reihenfolge vorgehend, schließt Ibn Kammûna im II. Teil (29 Kapitel) eine Darstellung des Judentums an:[24] „Über die Beweise der Juden für das Prophetentum des Mose, das schönste Gebet und Friede über ihn, und die Prinzipien der Gesetze, die er ihnen übermittelt hat, wie sie sie überliefert haben, sowie Fragen und Antworten dazu in aller Kürze" (S. 22–50/S. 40–77).

Hierin dienen ihm Jehuda ha-Lewi (1075–1141) und wiederum Mose b. Maimon als Gewährsleute, während er die kritischen Einwendungen gegen das Judentum vor allem der Polemik des zum Islam übergetretenen Samau'al al-Maghribi (um 1125–1175), Autor des polemischen Werkes *„Ifḥâm al-Yahûd [Die Juden zum Verstummen bringen]"*[25] entnommen hat, wie M. Perlmann bereits nachgewiesen hat.

Der Darstellung des Christentums ist der III. Teil (16 Kapitel) gewidmet: „Vom Glaubensbekenntnis (*muʿtaqad*) der Christen an den Herrn Jesus Christus (*as-sayyid Yašûʾ al-masîḥ*),[26] das ist ʿIsâ ibn Maryam,[27] Friede über sie beide; seine Botschaft; in welcher Weise er ihrer Meinung nach Prophet und Gott ist; Ansichten und Gegenansichten dazu" (S. 51–66/S. 78–99).

---

[22] S. dazu D. H. Baneth, S. 297–303; M. Perlmann [2], S. 4–7.

[23] Ed. [arab. und hebr.] Y. Qafiḥ, 3 Bde, Jerusalem 1972, Bd. II, S. 419 ff. 429–437.

[24] Dieses Kapitel edierte arab. und dt. bereits L. Hirschfeld, Saʿd b. Mansûr ibn Kammûnah und seine polemische Schrift *Tanqîḥ al-abḥâṯ limilal aṯ-ṯalâṯ*, (Diss. Heidelberg), Berlin 1893.

[25] Ed. et. transl. M. Perlmann, New York 1964 (= PAAJR 32); vgl. dazu auch F. Niewöhner [1], S. 198–204.

[26] Für Christus sagt Ibn Kammûna allenthalben *al-masiḥ* (= *ho christos*); den Namen Jesus schreibt er manchmal *Yašûʿ*, manchmal *ʿIsûʿ*.

[27] Dies ist die übliche (koranisch-)islamische Namensform.

Mit dem Islam schließlich befaßt sich Ibn Kammûna im IV. (dem mit Abstand umfangreichsten) Teil (42 Kapitel): „über den Glauben der Muslime (*ʿaqîdat ahl al-islâm*) an das Prophetentum Muhammads, Gott segne ihn und schenke ihm Heil, seine (Beglaubigungs-)Wunder (*muʿǧizâtihi*) und die Prinzipien seiner Religion; über die kritischen Einwände seitens ihrer Opponenten und eine richtige Weise der Antwort auf sie“ (S. 67–108/S. 100–157).

Soweit der Überblick über die vier Teile des Buches.

Wie oben schon angedeutet, ist Ibn Kammûnas Buch im eigentlichen Sinne kein polemischer Traktat. Es ist vielmehr eine allenthalben um Objektivität bemühte, sachlich-nüchtern abwägende Darstellung – M. Perlmann spricht von „studied aloofness and objectivity“[28] –, bei der das Ich des Autors geradezu auffällig hinter sein Werk zurücktritt, wie sich insbesondere in der Darstellung der Positionen anderer zeigt, auf die er verweist oder die er zitiert, oder mit denen er sich auseinandersetzt. Darin zeigt er sich als ein Autor, der nicht sogleich wertet oder werten will, sondern dem es zunächst einmal darum zu tun ist, fair darzustellen; und dies ganz bewußt.[29] Daß er am Ende mit seiner eigenen Ansicht zu den verhandelten Themen gleichwohl nicht hinterm Berg hält, ist natürlich sein gutes Recht und spricht nicht gegen, sondern vielmehr für ihn. Objektivität und Sachlichkeit, um die sich der Autor in seiner Darstellung durchweg bemüht, erweisen sich nicht zuletzt in seiner Vorgehensweise, seiner Methodologie, auch wenn sie nicht in allen Teilen formal dem gleichen Muster folgt.

2. Ibn Kammûnas Kapitel über das Christentum

In seinem Kapitel über das Christentum geht Ibn Kammûna gleichsam in sechs Schritten bzw. Abschnitten vor, ohne daß diese jedoch in jedem Falle vom Autor eigens als solche kenntlich gemacht worden sind.[30] Am Anfang des Kapitels steht:

2.1 Ein Resümee der christlichen Glaubenslehre

Seine Abhandlung über das Christentum beginnt Ibn Kammûna mit einem kurzen kommentarlosen Resümee dessen, was seiner Kenntnis nach den Hauptinhalt des christlichen Bekenntnisses und damit zugleich den Kern der

---

28 [2], S. 2f.

29 In seiner Einleitung schreibt er expressis verbis: „Ich habe keiner Religion einen Vorzug vor der anderen gegeben, sondern habe die Untersuchung einer jeden Religion in ihrem größtmöglichen Umfang vorgenommen“ (S. 1/S. 11).

30 Eine Zusammenfassung dieser Methodologie findet sich auch bei F. Niewöhner [2], S. 361.

christlichen Lehre ausmacht. Wie im Kap. 2, in seiner Abhandlung über das Judentum, bezieht er sich dabei interessanterweise auch im Blick auf das Christentum zunächst wiederum auf Jehuda ha-Lewi und dessen *Kitâb al-Khazarî [Sefer ha-Kûzarî]* (Buch I § 4), und zwar auf das Bekenntnis, das dieser dem christlichen Gelehrten, der den Chasarenfürsten zum Christentum zu bekehren versucht, in den Mund gelegt hat. Jehuda ha-Lewis Text fast wörtlich zitierend,[31] schreibt Ibn Kammûna unter der Überschrift: *Sie* [= die Christen] *lehren folgendes*:

„Wir glauben an alles, was in der Tora und den Überlieferungen (*âṯâr*) der Kinder Israel enthalten ist, die in ihrer Glaubwürdigkeit (*ṣidq*) unwiderlegbar sind, weil sie allgemein verbreitet, fortdauernd und vor einer großen Menge geoffenbart worden sind.[32] Und wir glauben daran, daß in der Spätzeit der Juden und in deren Folge sich das Göttliche verkörperlicht hat (*taǧassamat al-ilâhûtiyya*) und ein Embryo im Leib einer Jungfrau von den edelsten Frauen der Kinder Israel, vom Stamm Davids, geworden ist. Sie gebar ihn äußerlich als Menschen (*nâsûtiyyu ẓ-ẓâhir*), innerlich als Gott (*lâhûtiyyu l-bâṭin*), [ebenso] war er äußerlich als ein Prophet, innerlich als Gott gesandt. Er war vollkommener Mensch und vollkommener Gott (*insân tâmm wa-ilâh tâmm*). Er ist der Christus, der bei ihnen der Sohn Gottes genannt wird. Gott ist der Vater, der Sohn und der Heilige Geist" (S. 51/S. 78).

Dieses eben zitierte Summarium der christlichen Lehre, auf das im vorliegenden Zusammenhang nicht weiter einzugehen ist, wird sodann unter der Überschrift „Sie sagen" in einigen Teilen näher spezifiziert. Wiederum Jehuda ha-Lewi (*Kitâb al-Khazarî [Sefer ha-Kûzarî]* Buch I § 4) fast wörtlich zitierend, heißt es:

„Wir sind in Wahrheit Bekenner der Einheit [Gottes] (*naḥnu muwaḥḥidûna bil-ḥaqîqa*), auch wenn unsere Zungen von Dreiheit (*at-taṯlîṯ*) sprechen. Wir glauben an Ihn und an Seine Einwohnung (*bi-ḥulûlihi*) unter den Kindern Israel, ihnen zur Ehre, denn der göttliche Logos (*al-amr al-ilâhî*) hörte nicht auf, mit ihnen in Verbindung zu sein, bis sich ihr Volk (*ǧumhûruhum*) diesem Christus widersetzte und ihn kreuzigte. Da kam beständiger (göttlicher) Zorn über ihr Volk, und das (göttliche) Wohlgefallen wurde denjenigen einzelnen zuteil, die dem Christus folgten, von denen er zwölf Männer entsprechend der Zahl der Stämme Israels auswählte –, später dann den Völkern (*al-umam*), die jenen einzelnen (nach)folgten. Wir sind von den Kindern Israel, auch wenn wir nicht von ihrer leiblichen Nachkommenschaft (*min ḏurriyyatihim*) sind. Wir sind um so würdiger, Kinder Israels genannt zu werden, als wir dem Christus und seinen Gefährten folgen.

---

[31] Darauf verweist auch M. Perlmann [1], S. 51 A. 1; [2], S. 79 A. 1). Vgl. Abu l-Hasan Jehuda Halewi, Das Buch Al-Chazari, ed. [arab. mit hebr. Übers. des Jehuda ibn Tibbon] H. Hirschfeld, Leipzig 1887 [Neudruck Jerusalem 1970], S. 8f (dt. Übers. des arab. Textes: H. Hirschfeld, Das Buch al-Chazarî. Aus dem Arab. des Abu-l-Hasan Jehuda Hallewi, Breslau 1885, S. 7f.; des hebr. Textes: D. Cassel, Der Kusari, Neudruck Zürich 1990, S. 36–39.

[32] NB: Mit dieser dreifachen Ausage soll übrigens angezeigt werden, daß diese Überlieferungen die Bedingungen dessen erfüllen, was eine „verläßliche Überlieferung" genannt wird, ein Problem, auf das unten noch zurückzukommen sein wird.

Jenen

einzelnen, die gleichsam den Sauerteig für das Volk der Christen bilden, folgten viele, und sie verdienten den Status der Kinder Israels. Und sie waren erfolgreich und breiteten sich über viele Länder und Völker aus, indem sie die Leute zum christlichen Glauben riefen und ihnen auftrugen, den Christus und sein Kreuz zu verherrlichen, seinen Gesetzen (*aḥkâmahu*) und den Geboten der Jünger, seiner Gefährten (*waṣâyâ l-ḥawâriyyîna aṣḥâbihi*) zu folgen ebenso wie den Satzungen, die aus der Tora genommen sind (*qawânîn ma'ẖûḏatin mina t-taurât*), die wir lesen und deren Wahrheit unwiderlegbar ist, denn sie ist von Gott. Diejenigen, die diesem Ruf glauben, folgen ihm im Gehorsam, freiwillig und willentlich, ohne durch Schwert oder Zwang dazu genötigt zu sein" (S. 51/S. 78).

Ergänzend und gleichsam zusammenfassend zitiert Ibn Kammûna zum Abschluß dieses ersten Abschnittes das Nicänische Bekenntnis in einer (eigenen [?]) arabischen Übersetzung (S. 52/S. 79f). Probleme dieser Übersetzung sowie Ibn Kammûnas Quellen betreffende Fragen sollen uns hier allerdings nicht weiter beschäftigen.

2.2 *Meinungsverschiedenheiten unter den Christen*

In einem zweiten Schritt, auf den hier gleichfalls nicht näher einzugehen ist, verweist Ibn Kammûna auf Unterschiede und Gegensätze zwischen den Ansichten der Jakobiten, Nestorianer und Melkiten[33] hinsichtlich des Glaubensbekenntnisses, einzelner seiner Formulierungen und deren Interpretation (S. 52–54/S. 80–83). Auch hier ist er ganz der Berichterstatter; denn im Blick auf das, was er dazu zu schreiben hat, gilt: „All dies ist bekannt aus ihren eigenen Geschichtsbüchern" (S. 54/S. 82).

2.3 *Die Schriftwidrigkeit der christlichen Lehre*

Daß das Proprium des Christentums das trinitarische Dogma und das zentrale Problem darin die Christologie ist, oder anders gesagt: daß es das eigentliche Problem der christlichen Lehre ist, das trinitarische Dogma als ein monotheistisches Bekenntnis zu erweisen und plausibel zu machen, hat Ibn Kammûna dabei sehr deutlich gesehen. Unter dem Stichwort *Ansichten der Opponenten des Christentums*, zu denen er im letzten selber zählt, referiert er daher in (s)einem dritten Abschnitt zunächst solche Stimmen, die das christliche Bekenntnis, die Lehre von der Trinität mit der Idee des Monotheismus für unvereinbar und den Glauben an die Gottheit Christi zudem für schriftwidrig halten (S. 54–57/S. 83–86), um sodann selber in die Diskussion einzugreifen und sich diesmal am Ende des eigenen, wertenden Urteils nicht zu enthalten:

[33] In diesen drei Richtungen sieht Ibn Kammûna ebenso wie vor ihm Abu l-Fatḥ Muḥammad b. ʿAbd al-Karim aš-Šahrastani (gest. 1153) das Christentum hauptsächlich repräsentiert. Vgl. dessen *„Kitâb al-milal wan-niḥal"* ed. A. A. Manha & A. H. Faʿur, 2 Bde, Beirut 1414/1993, Bd. I, S. 262–272.

Denn was die Christen da lehren, „ist alles absurd (*muḥâl*)" (S. 56/S. 85) und „alle eure [= der Christen] Denominationen (*ǧamîʿu maḏâhibikum*) sind falsch (*bâṭila*)" (S. 57/S. 86); und dies zunächst deshalb, weil nach Ibn Kammûna weder die Lehre von den zwei Naturen Christi, noch die Vereinbarkeit von trinitarischem Dogma und monotheistischem Bekenntnis plausibel zu machen bzw. mit den Mitteln logischer Argumentation zu erklären sind (S. 54/S. 83), wobei er sich mit seiner Kritik der Reihe nach wiederum an die Adresse der Jakobiten (S. 56/S. 85f),[34] der Nestorianer (S. 56f /S. 86) und der Melkiten (S. 57/S. 86) wendet. Doch es geht dabei gar nicht nur um tiefgründige theologische Sätze, die problematisch und mit Entschiedenheit zurückzuweisen sind; allein schon die Anerkennung der Gottheit Gottes und die Ehrfurcht vor Ihm verbieten es, über Ihn etwas auszusagen, gleichviel in welcher Weise es geschieht, was ausschließlich in den rein menschlichen Bereich gehört, wie beispielsweise dies, daß Er im Bauch einer Frau gewohnt habe und dgl. mehr (S. 57f/S. 86f).

Gravierender jedoch als derlei problematische theologische Einzelsätze ist ihm ein grundsätzliches Problem, nämlich die Tatsache, daß das christliche Dogma von Grund auf schriftwidrig ist. Denn die Behauptung der Christen, Jesus sei Gott oder eins mit Gott (gewesen), hat – so Ibn Kammûna – das ebenso eindeutige wie einmütige Zeugnis der Evangelien gegen sich, oder anders formuliert, die Vorstellung von den zwei Naturen, der angenommenen Göttlichkeit und Menschlichkeit in der Person Jesu, ist aus den Evangelien nicht herleitbar, also nicht einmal aus der Heiligen Schrift der Christen selber zu begründen.

Unter der Behutsamkeit anzeigenden Überschrift *Gegen sie* [= die Christen] *mag man einwenden* (S. 57–62/S. 87–93) meldet sich daher Ibn Kammûna selber zu Wort und zitiert mit einer beeindruckenden Souveränität aus den Evangelien alle nur denkbaren Verse, die sich nicht nur gegeneinander ausspielen, sondern vor allem als Einwand gegen die Richtigkeit und Glaubwürdigkeit der christlichen Lehre heranziehen lassen. Bemerkenswert und auffallend sind dabei ebenso das Interesse, das Ibn Kammûna an der Person des historischen Jesus zeigt, wie die Entschiedenheit, mit der er aus den Evangelien aufzuzeigen versucht und für seinen Teil auch aufzuzeigen vermocht hat, daß der Jesus der Evangelien „nach seinen eigenen Worten und dem Zeugnis der Evangelisten" nichts anderes als ein Mensch gewesen ist und sich niemals als Gott oder ein göttliches Wesen, ja nicht einmal als Messias betrachtet oder je so tituliert hat. Erst später ist aus diesem Jesus der Christus „gemacht" worden, und Ibn

---

[34] *Expressis verbis* nennt Ibn Kammûna in diesem Zusammenhang den jakobitischen Theologen Yaḥyâ b. ʿAdî (S. 56/S. 85). Vgl. dazu die Fußnote von M. PERLMANN [2], S. 85 A. 10. Zu Person und Werk s. E. PLATTI, Yaḥyâ b. ʿAdî Théologien chrétien et philosophe arabe, Leuven/Louvain 1983 (= Orientalia Lovaniensia Analecta, vol. 14), sowie G. ENDRESS, The Works of Yaḥyâ b. ʿAdî. An Analytical Inventory, Wiesbaden 1977.

Kammûna weiß nicht nur, wie wir später noch sehen werden, wer dies getan hat, sondern bemüht sich zudem, den irdischen Jesus gegen eine solche „Vergottung" in Schutz zu nehmen, also den historischen Jesus gegen den christlichen Christus zu verteidigen.

Die von Ibn Kammûna gegen die Göttlichkeit Jesu beigebrachten und von seiner profunden Kenntnis des Neuen Testaments zeugenden Evangelienzitate lassen sich dabei in folgende sieben Argumente zusammenfassen:[35]

[1] Erstens fehlt jeglicher Beleg dafür, daß sich Jesus selber Gott genannt hätte; ganz im Gegenteil: „Des Menschen Sohn ist nicht gekommen, daß er sich dienen lasse, sondern daß er diene" (Mt 20,28; Joh 13,(5.)16; S. 59/S. 89).

[2] Zweitens sprechen gegen eine Göttlichkeit Jesu all jene Texte, die von seiner rein menschlichen Herkunft und Geburt (Mt 1,18–21 [vgl. dazu Lk 1,26–33]; Lk 2,48; Mt 13,55f; Mk 6,3) sowie von seinen spezifisch menschli chen Bedürfnissen und Regungen erzählen (Mt 11,18f; Lk 22,44; Mt 8,23–25). In diesem Zusammenhang verweist Ibn Kammûna auch auf die unterschiedlichen Stammbäume Jesu in Lk 3 und Mt 1, sowie auf die „Taufe durch Johannes zur Vergebung der Sünden" (Mt 3,13–17; Mk 1,9–11; Lk 3,21f), die, würde man sie von Gott aussagen, vollkommene Blasphemie wäre!

[3] Ein drittes Argument gegen die Göttlichkeit Jesu liefern jene Sätze, die von einer Unvollkommenheit seines Wissens (Mk 13,32) und seinem Mangel an Kompetenz (Mt 8,2–4; Mk 1,40–45; Lk 5,12–16) zeugen.

[4] Viertens, zu wem sollte Jesus gebetet haben (Mt 26,36–46; Mk 14,41), wenn er selber Gott gewesen ist? Und wie kann Gott überhaupt vom Teufel versucht werden (Mt 4,1–11)?[36]

[5] Fünftens, fragt Ibn Kammûna, hätte Judas Jesus für „eine so bescheidene Summe verraten, wenn er gewußt hätte, daß Jesus ein Prophet, geschweige denn Gott, (gewesen) ist?" (S. 60/S. 91).

[6] Sechstens, wie kann jemand Gott sein, wenn man ihm ins Gesicht schlagen und ihn bespeien kann (Mt 26,67f; Joh 18,22), wo es doch selbst einem Mose schon unmißverständlich verwehrt wurde, Gott auch nur ansehen zu dürfen, wie es heißt: „Nicht kann mich der Mensch sehen und lebendig bleiben" (Ex 33,20), und die Israeliten nicht einmal die Stimme Gottes verkraften konnten, sondern Mose baten: „Rede du mit uns [...], aber laß nicht Gott mit uns reden, damit wir nicht sterben" (Ex 20,19)?

---

[35] Frau Prof. H. Lazarus-Yafeh/Jerusalem macht mich freundlicherweise darauf aufmerksam, daß es sich bei den im folgenden vorgetragenen Argumenten um in der muslimischen antichristlichen polemischen Literatur auch sonst üblichen und verbreiteten Vorhaltungen handelt, und verweist mich auf das polemische Kompendium des Aḥmad b. Idris as-Sinhaǧi al-Qarâfî (gest. 1285), *Al-aǧwiba al-fâẖira ʿan al-asʾila al-fâǧira* [*Vorzügliche Antworten auf sündhafte Fragen*], ed. B. Z. ʿAwad, Kairo 1986. Vgl. dazu auch das Material in D. Sourdel, „Un Pamphlet musulman anonyme d'époche ʿAbbaside contre les chrétiens", in: REI 34 (1966), S. 1–33.

[36] NB: Die Perikope Mt 4,1–11 wird übrigens im vollen Wortlaut zitiert (S. 59f/S. 90f).

[7] Und siebentens, wie ist es zu erklären, daß Gott mit Mose, der nur sein Diener war, unzählige Male, mit seinem „Sohn“ Jesus hingegen nur ein einziges Mal in direkter Rede (Joh 12,28) gesprochen haben sollte (S. 61/S. 92)?

Ist Jesus nach dem eindeutigen Zeugnis der Heiligen Schrift der Christen selber also nicht nur nicht Gott, so war und ist er auch nicht einmal der Messias; denn – so lautet Ibn Kammûnas Argument – was in der [hebräischen] Bibel vom Messias und insbesondere von der messianischen Zeit gesagt ist – hier verweist er *expressis verbis* auf Jes 2,4; 11,4; 9,6 und 11,6 –,

„ist, wenn wörtlich genommen (*in kâna ʿalâ ẓâhirihi*), weder in der Zeit Jesu noch nach ihm je Wirklichkeit geworden. Ja, [von Verwirklichung der messianischen Hoffnung in Jesus kann man] nicht einmal dann [reden], wenn man darin [= den zitierten Bibelversen] nur ein Gleichnis sieht (*wa-in kâna maṯalan*), was wahrscheinlicher ist, für die Beseitigung des Bösen aus der Welt und das Verschwinden der Gegensätze zwischen den Geschöpfen“ (S. 61/S. 92).

In summa, „dies ist es, was ich [= Ibn Kammûna] für angebracht halte an Einwänden gegen sie [= die Christen]“ (S. 62/93).

2.4 Ibn Kammûnas Verteidigung der christlichen Lehre

Diese eben vorgebrachten Einwände mögen nun die Christen, wie sich Ibn Kammûna vorstellen kann, wiederum zu einer Gegenrede veranlassen, die er diesmal selber formuliert und ihnen in den Mund gelegt hat (S. 62–63/ S. 93–96), wie er ganz am Schluß seines Kapitels über das Christentum auch ausdrücklich bestätigt: „Die meisten dieser Erwiderungen habe ich nicht in den Diskursen der Christen (*fî kalâmi n-naṣârâ*) gefunden, sondern ich habe sie stellvertretend für sie (*niyâbatan ʿanhum*) und in Ergänzung zur Betrachtung ihres Glaubensbekenntnisses (*tatmîman lin-naẓari fî muʿtaqadihim*) angefügt“ (S. 66/S. 99), um ihnen gleichsam noch Argumentationshilfen zu ihrer eigenen Verteidigung an die Hand zu geben.

Unter der Überschrift *Das Beste, was sie darauf antworten können* (S. 62/ S. 93), stellt er acht Punkte zusammen, in denen er den Christen anbietet, was „sie vortragen können“, um seine Einwände zu entkräften. Und diese Sätze belegen nicht nur ein weiteres Mal, wie gut sich Ibn Kammûna in Fragen der christlichen Theologie und ihrer biblischen Bezüge auskannte, sondern zeugen zugleich auf eindrückliche Weise davon, darauf hat bereits H.D. Baneth aufmerksam gemacht, wie fair er „eine ihm unstreitig fremde Religion“ verteidigen kann.[37]

Die zugunsten der Christen zusammengestellten Argumente lauten:

---

[37] S. dazu H.D. Baneth, S. 300f, der die ersten sechs Punkte in dt. Übers. bietet, die hier zitiert werden. Die Übers. der letzten beiden stammt von mir.

„[1] Was die [göttlichen] Personen anbetrifft und die Beschränkung ihrer Zahl auf drei, so folgen wir in dieser Lehre dem geoffenbarten Wort, wissen aber nicht, was der Sinn der Beschränkung ihrer Zahl auf drei ist.

[2] Das Wie der Dreieinigkeit ist uns auf dieser Welt unbekannt; vielleicht enthüllt sich uns ihr Wesen in der kommenden Welt; unser Glaube daran beruht auf dem Evangelium, den Ueberlieferungen der Apostel und den Zeugnissen der Propheten [...].

[3] Die Aussagen und Erzählungen von Christus, die zu seiner Göttlichkeit im Widerspruch stehen, wie daß er geschlafen, gegessen, Schmerz empfunden habe, betreffen nur das Menschheitliche, das in ihm war (*huwa bi-ʿtibâri mâ fîhi mina n-nâsût*), nicht die Gottheit (*lâ bi-'tibâri l-ilâhût*) [...].

[4] Wenn ihr fragt, warum er nicht imstande gewesen sei, seinen Willen zu vollziehen, ohne auf die Erde hinabzusteigen, so entspricht eine solche Behauptung nicht unserer Lehre; vielmehr ist Gott allmächtig (*qâdir ʿalâ kulli šai'*)[38] und hat dies nach seinem Willen getan [...]; wir aber haben keinen Einblick in die tiefen Gründe seiner Weisheit; ferner läßt sich das gleiche gegen die Wunder aller Propheten einwenden [...]; ja gegen jede Handlung Gottes zum Nutzen der Menschen; denn er wäre imstande, ihnen jenen Nutzen ohne Vermittlung jener Handlung zukommen zu lassen.

[5] Was den Einwand betrifft, daß durch das Erscheinen Christi die Sünden nicht aus der Welt geschafft wurden, so haben wir gar nicht behauptet, daß sie ganz aufhören würden, [...] sondern nur, daß viel Unglaube und Unrecht aufhören würde; daß dies aber eingetreten ist, unterliegt keinem Zweifel; denn infolge seines Auftretens haben sich Glaube und Gerechtigkeit (*al-îmân wal-ʿadl*) in vielen Teilen der Erde verbreitet [...].

[6] Die Behauptung seiner Gottheit (*iddiʿâ' ilâhiyyatihi*) beruht nicht auf einem oder zwei oder mehr von seinen Lebensumständen, so daß ihm andere Propheten oder andere Menschen gleichgestellt werden könnten, sondern auf der Gesamtheit seiner Lebensumstände [...].

[7] Wenn von jemand anderem gesagt ist, er sei der Sohn Gottes (*ibn allâh*), so ist das eine Metapher (*maǧâz*), worin der Befürworter und der Opponent übereinstimmen, aber in bezug auf ihn [= Jesus] ist es Wahrheit, wegen der Verläßlichkeit der Überlieferung (*li-tawâtur*) der Apostel, in deren Autorität das Bekenntnis der christlichen Religion überliefert worden ist.

[8] Was seine [= Jesu] Worte anbetrifft ‚Ich bin nicht gekommen, die Tora zu zerstören, sondern ich bin gekommen, sie zu erfüllen' (Mt 5,17), so bedeuten sie, daß in der Tora die Ankunft des Christus verheißen ist, folglich für die Gesetze (*aš-šarâ'iʿ*), die in ihr enthalten sind, [gilt,] daß sie alle zu tun verpflichtend ist bis zu seinem Erscheinen (*ilâ ḥîni ẓuhûrihi*), nicht aber für immer oder bis zum Tag der Auferstehung (*lâ ilâ l-abad au ilâ yaumi l-qiyâma*). Denn seit er erschienen ist, ist sie zum Ende gekommen (*qad kamilat*), erstens durch Erfüllung seiner Verheißung (*bi-naǧâzi l-waʿdi bihi awwalan*), und zweitens durch Vollendung ihrer Verbindlichkeit (*bi-kamâli t-taklîfi bihâ ṯâniyan*)" (S. 62f/93–95).

Soweit die Argumente der Christen gegen Ibn Kammûnas Einwände, jedenfalls wie er sie sich vorstellt bzw. vorstellen kann. Bei einigen der Argumente

[38] Dies ist natürlich die übliche koranische Formulierung zur Bezeichnung der Allmacht Gottes; s. dazu J. Nosowski, Teologia Koranu. Wyklad systematyczny, Warszawa 1970, S. 63f.

wird anschließend das Für und Wider noch näher erwogen, so das Problem der Verläßlichkeit der Überlieferung, insbesondere bezüglich der Wunder(berichte), auf das unten noch zurückzukommen sein wird, und die Frage nach dem sogenannten „Christuszeugnis des Alten Testaments".

2.5 Das Problem der christologischen Interpretation des Alten Testaments

Das Problem der christologischen Interpretation alttestamentlicher Texte bzw. die Frage nach einem „Christuszeugnis des Alten Testaments" erscheint bei Ibn Kammûna unter den Einwänden der Opponenten des Christentums (zu denen er in gewissem Sinne schließlich selber gehört). Wenn Ibn Kammûna auch weiß, daß es

> viele Stellen in den Propheten gibt, die ihre [= der Christen] Gelehrten so gedeutet haben (*ta'auwwalû*),[39] daß sie beweisen (*yadillu*), daß der Herr Jesus Christus der in den prophetischen Büchern Verheißene (*huwa l-mauʿûd bihi fî kutubi n-nubuwwât*) ist" (S. 65/S. 98),

so hält er es mit den Opponenten, die da sagen: daß „wir nicht zugestehen (*innâ lâ nusallimu*), daß Er in der Tora die Ankunft des Christus verheißen (*waʿada*) hat" (S. 63/S. 95). Dennoch läßt er die Christen, um diesen Einwand zu entkräften, als Erwiderung darauf – gleichsam *pars pro toto* – Gen 49,10 und Dtn 18,15(–18) zitieren, letztere Perikope in Gestalt der Auslegung, die sie in der Rede des Simon Petrus in Apg 3,22–26 bekommen hat. Daß Ibn Kammûna gerade auf diese beiden Stellen zurückgreift, beweist einmal mehr seine profunde Sachkenntnis, denn beide Perikopen, Gen 49,10 ebenso wie Dtn 18,15(–18), gehören bekanntlich nicht nur zu den *loci classici* der christologischen Interpretation des Alten Testaments, sondern ebenso zu den loci classici in der jüdisch-islamischen Auseinandersetzung um die Ankündigung des arabischen Propheten in der Tora[40] und haben dort eine nicht minder lange Wirkungsgeschichte gehabt, wie H. Lazarus-Yafeh bereits hinlänglich belegt hat.[41]

Von dieser Einbettung in den Kontext der Polemik her verstehen sich auch die Unterschiede zwischen den Zitaten und dem überlieferten Bibeltext der zitierten Verse. Bei Ibn Kammûna nämlich lautet Gen 49,10: „Weder wird das Zepter von Juda, noch der Gesetzgeber[42] von zwischen seinen Füßen weichen,

---

[39] Gewiß nicht ohne Absicht benutzt Ibn Kammûna hier zur Qualifizierung der christlichen Exegese den Begriff, der die allegorische Auslegung (*ta'wîl*) bezeichnet (S. dazu H. Gätje, Koran und Koranexegese, Zürich-Stuttgart 1971, S. 51). Im Munde der Christen erscheint dagegen für ihre Bibelinterpretation der Begriff *tafsîr*.

[40] Darauf verweist auch M. Perlmann [2], S. 96 A. 60.

[41] H. Lazarus-Yafeh, Intertwined Worlds. Medieval Islam and Bible Criticism, Princeton, N.J. 1992, S. 75–110.150f.

[42] Die Deutung von *mehôqêq* als *ar-râsim* (Saadja: *al-murassim*) stützt sich auf Dtn 33,21.

bis kommt, dem die Befehlsgewalt (*al-amr*)[43] gehört und zu dem sich die Völker versammeln";[44] und Dtn 18,15: „Einen Propheten werde ich ihnen aufrichten aus der Mitte ihrer Brüder gleich dir, an den sollen sie glauben (*bihi fal-yu'minû*)".[45]

Nachdem Ibn Kammûna nun seinerseits die zitierte christliche Interpretation beider Perikopen eingehend diskutiert und mit (den üblichen) historisch-kritischen Argumenten zurückgewiesen hat (S. 64f/S. 96–98),[46] läßt er nun die Christen noch einmal gegen seine Kritik Stellung nehmen und den folgenden methodologisch wichtigen und gleichermaßen aufschlußreichen Satz vortragen:

„Simons Interpretation (*tafsîr*) ist für uns [= Christen] ein überzeugender Beweis (*ḥuǧǧa qâṭiʿa*), und darauf stützen wir uns, nicht auf den Literalsinn [des Textes] (*lâ ʿalâ mafhûmi l-lafẓi haḏâ*)" (S. 64/S. 97).

Denselben Grundsatz, daß nicht der Literalsinn eines Textes, sondern allein die überlieferte Auslegung maßgebend ist, läßt Ibn Kammûna die Christen dann auch gegen seine übrigen Einwände vertreten.

Am Ende freilich hält er fest:

„Die Kommentare[47] der Juden dazu schließen dies [= die Auslegung der Christen] aus. Viele Prophetenworte haben die Christen erheblich verfälscht (*ḥarrafa ... taḥrîfan*),[48] als sie sie aus dem Hebräischen ins Griechische und Syrische und dann ins Arabische übersetzten, eine Verfälschung, durch die deren Sinn völlig verfehlt ist (*yatafâwatû ... tafâwutan kaṯîran*), allerdings nur hinsichtlich weniger Worte. Die Christen wissen um diese Sinnverfehlung, zum Teil jedenfalls. Es ist möglich, daß diese Schrift(ver)fälschung (*at-taḥrîf*) aus Absicht (*ʿan qaṣadin*), aus Nachlässigkeit (*ihmâlin*) oder aus Mangel an Kenntnis der Sprache (*au qillati maʿrifatin bil-luġa*) geschehen ist, aus der übersetzt worden ist."

Und um sich für das Zitieren dieser unsachgemäßen, da von methodisch falschem Ansatz ausgehenden christlichen Interpretation der entsprechenden Schriftverse gleichsam zu entschuldigen, fügt er gleich noch hinzu:

---

[43] *al-amr* meint zugleich *ho logos*.

[44] S. dazu H. Lazarus-Yafeh, S. 98f.

[45] Ibn Kammûna zitiert hier jene Version, in der dieser Vers in der islamisch-jüdischen Polemik (s)eine Rolle gespielt hat. S. dazu H. Lazarus-Yafeh, S. 104–106.

[46] Das Königtum „ist mehr als 4 Jahrhunderte vor Jesus bereits von Juda gewichen", denn die Hasmonäer waren nicht vom Stamme Juda, sondern sie waren Aaroniden, also aus dem Stamme Lewi etc. (S. 64/S. 96f). Die kontroverse Auslegungsgeschichte dieses Verses dokumentierte in aller Ausführlichkeit schon A. Posnanski, Schiloh, Leipzig 1904.

[47] Hier spricht Ibn Kammûna mit Bedacht von *tafâsîr*. Vgl. o. A. 38.

[48] Auch hier ist die Wortwahl mit Bedacht vorgenommen: *taḥrîf* ist – neben *tabdîl* (zum Unterschied zwischen beiden Begriffen s. bereits M. Steinschneider [1], S. 322) – bekanntlich terminus technicus für den aus der islamischen Polemik stammenden gegen Juden und Christen gerichteten Vorwurf der „Schrift(ver)fälschung". Dazu H. Lazarus-Yafeh, S. 19–35; W. M. Watt & A. T. Welch, Der Islam, I, Stuttgart-Berlin-Köln-Mainz 1980, S. 118–130.

„Was ich zitiert habe, sind die von ihnen aus den prophetischen Büchern beigebrachten Belege, und ich habe sie in der Weise zitiert, in der sie die Christen übersetzt haben, nicht jedoch so, wie sie bei den Juden in Hebräisch lauten" (S. 65/S. 98).

2.6 Die Frage nach der Verläßlichkeit der Überlieferung

Das eigentliche Problem freilich, das nach Ibn Kammûna christliche Tradition und Lehre bereiten und das vor allem anderen der Klärung bedarf, ist nun nicht die Auslegung einzelner Bibeltexte, gleichviel ob sie der hebräischen Bibel oder dem griechischen Neuen Testament entnommen sind. Das eigentliche Problem ist vielmehr ein grundsätzliches, nämlich die Frage nach dem, was mit dem arabischen Begriff *tawâtur* (*verläßliche Überlieferung*) genannt wird. Dabei meint *tawâtur* eine „ungebrochene, zuverlässige, in der Öffentlichkeit geschehene und somit nachvollziehbare Überlieferung".[49]

Daß Ibn Kammûna dieses Problem der „verläßlichen Überlieferung" aufwirft, entspringt durchaus nicht nur seiner eigenen persönlichen Neigung, sondern gehört vielmehr seit der Antike bereits zu den Grundfragen aller Auseinandersetzung und Polemik zwischen den Religionen, die sich auf eine schriftlich überlieferte Offenbarungsurkunde berufen.[50] Wenn auch erst muslimische Gelehrte die Wissenschaft von der Prüfung der Verläßlichkeit einer Überlieferung zur Perfektion gebracht haben,[51] so begegnet uns die Diskussion um das Problem der Verläßlichkeit der Überlieferung gleichwohl nicht nur und nicht erst im Kontext muslimischer Auseinandersetzung mit Juden und Christen, sondern ebenso bereits in der antiken und mittelalterlichen Polemik zwischen Juden und Christen (*et vice versa*)[52] sowie später zwischen rabbanitischen Juden und Karäern – so beispielsweise in Jehuda ha-Lewis Verteidigung der Verläßlichkeit der rabbinischen mündlichen Tradition gegen die Einwürfe der Karäer (*Kitâb al-Khazarî [Sefer ha-Kûzarî]*, Buch III, bes. §§ 53 ff),[53] auf

---

49 Zur Sache s. H. LAZARUS-YAFEH, S. 41–47.

50 S. dazu die grundlegenden Erörterungen von H. A. WOLFSON, „The Veracity of Scripture in Philo, Halevi, Maimonides, and Spinoza", in: Alexander Marx Jubilee Volume (engl. section), New York 1950, S. 603–630, bes. S. 603–609 [= in: DERS., Religious Philosophy. A Group of Essays, New York 1965, S. 217–233, bes. S. 217–223].

51 H. LAZARUS-YAFEH, S. 41–43 mit Literaturhinweisen in A. 610. 63–64.

52 S. dazu die Beispiele bei H. A. WOLFSON, S. 609 ff, und H. LAZARUS-YAFEH, S. 43 f mit Literaturhinweisen in A. 65–70.

53 Am Ende von § 53 sagt Jehuda ha-Lewi, unausgesprochen anknüpfend an mAv I,1, ausdrücklich: „Zwischen uns aber und diesen Geboten [= aus dem Pentateuch, die er zuvor zitiert hat] gibt es keine andere Verbindung als die der wahrhaften Überlieferung, und diejenigen, welche uns die Gesetze überliefert haben, waren nicht einzelne, sondern viele, gelehrte und große Männer, die sich an die Propheten anreihten. Wären es aber auch nur die Priester, Leviten und siebzig Ältesten gewesen, welche die Vermittler der Tora gebildet haben, so wäre die Verbindung bis Mose hinauf doch niemals unterbrochen gewesen" (ABU L-HASAN JEHUDA HALEWI, Das Buch Al-Chazari, ed. [arab. mit hebr. Übers. des Jehuda ibn

die sich wiederum Ibn Kammûna im Kap. 2 seines uns hier beschäftigenden Werkes stützt (S. 27ff/S. 46ff).[54]

Hier, bei Ibn Kammûna also, steht die Verläßlichkeit derjenigen Überlieferung auf dem Prüfstand, auf die sich christliche Lehre be ruft. Es geht damit um eine Frage, deren Beantwortung uns zugleich zum methodologischen Kern in Ibn Kammûnas Argumentation führt.

Hat sich Ibn Kammûna, wie bereits mehrfach festgestellt worden ist, allenthalben befleißigt, eine möglichst objektive Darstellung der Ansichten der anderen zu liefern, so behält er sich das letzte Wort – und damit zugleich das abschließende Urteil – dennoch selber vor:

„Dann würde ich sagen ...“ (S. 63–65/S. 96–98),

und zwar zum Thema der ausführlich verhandelten Frage der Messianität Jesu ebenso wie zum grundsätzlichen Problem der Verläßlichkeit derjenigen Überlieferung, die die Grundlage der Formulierung christlicher Lehre (S. 65–66/S. 98–99) bildet. Und was er dazu zu sagen hat, ist in der Tat mehr als erstaunlich und verdient, genau gehört zu werden.

Denn im Hinblick auf die Berichte, die nach der Meinung der Christen die Göttlichkeit Jesu oder auch nur seine Messianität bezeugen (sollen), zu denen neben den oben zitierten Perikopen insbesondere die Wunder(berichte) der Evangelien[55] gehören (S. 65/S. 98), kommt Ibn Kammûna zu dem Schluß, daß all dies „nicht verläßlich überliefert“ (*ġairu mutawâtir*) und „nicht [glaubwürdig] bestätigt ist (*walâ mauṯûq ilaihi*)“, auch wenn die Christen natürlich dagegen halten und sagen, „daß alles, was von ihm [= Jesus] überliefert ist, [...] einwandfrei überliefert und wahr (*ṣaḥîḥ*)[56] ist“, woraus sie folgern, daß „die Wahrheit ihrer Religion nicht abrogiert wird (*ṣiḥḥatu šarîʿatihim lâ tunsaḫu*)“ (S. 65/S. 98).

Dies ändert jedoch nichts an Ibn Kammûnas Urteil:

Tibbon] H. Hirschfeld, S. 202ff.206f [Zitat]; dt. Übers. des arab. Textes: H. Hirschfeld, Das Buch al-Chazarî, S. 166f.; des hebr. Textes: D. Cassel, Der Kusari, S. 290ff.296f [Zitat]).

[54] Vgl. dazu auch L. Nemoys o. A. 3 genannten Aufsatz.

[55] Daß Ibn Kammûna – wie übrigens vor ihm auch Mose b. Maimon in seinem Iggeret Teman, S. 92f (Text), S. xvii (engl. Übers.) – in diesem Zusammenhang auf die Wunderberichte besonders rekurriert, hängt natürlich damit zusammen, daß gerade sie den Prüfstein in der Auseinandersetzung zwischen den Religionen um die jeweilige Verläßlichkeit ihrer Tradition bildeten. Vgl. dazu H. A. Wolfson, S. 604ff. Zum Problem der *Wunder(berichte)* im Zusammenhang interreligiöser Polemik vgl. auch das Material und dessen Diskussion in H. Lazarus-Yafeh, „Some Neglected Aspects of Medieval Muslim Polemics Against Christianity“ (wird in HThR erscheinen), die mir ihr noch unveröffentlichtes Manuskript dankenswerterweise zur Einsicht gegeben hat.

[56] Mit dem aus dem Hadîth stammenden Begriff *ṣaḥîḥ* [*einwandfrei überliefert*] wird eine Überlieferung dann bezeichnet, „wenn jeder der Überlieferer in einer Tradentenkette als zuverlässige Person bekannt war und die Gelegenheit gehabt hatte, die nächste Person in der (Tradenten-)Kette zu treffen, um die Geschichte von ihr zu hören“ (W. M. Watt & A. T. Welch, S. 235f).

„In der Tat, was die Berichte (*naql*) der Gefährten des Herrn Christus (*aṣḥâbu s-sayyidi l-masîḥ*) hinsichtlich der Wunder anbetrifft, so gestehen wir nicht zu (*lâ nusallimu*), daß sie auf einer verläßlichen Überlieferung beruhen, die Grund für die Gewißheit ist (*ʿalâ waǧhi t-tawâturi llatî huwa mûǧibun lil-yaqîn*), wie die verläßliche Überlieferung von ihrer Existenz und von der Existenz des Christus und seines Kreuzes. Vielmehr sind sie wie etwas, das sich verbreitet und in Umlauf kommt, und mit verläßlichen Überlieferungen vergleichbar scheint (*fa-yaštabihu bil-mutawâtirât*), in Wirklichkeit aber nicht verläßlich überliefert ist" (S. 65/S. 98).

Mit diesem Satz hat Ibn Kammûna eine in methodologischer Hinsicht in der Tat höchst bemerkenswerte Feststellung getroffen: Denn indem er von den Berichten der Jünger Jesu über dessen Wunder sagt, daß sie im Gegensatz zu der verläßlichen Überlieferung von der Existenz Jesu und dessen Leben und Sterben nicht auf einer vergleichbaren verläßlichen Überlieferung beruhten, die eine Gewißheit gewährleisten würde,[57] führt er ein Kriterium ein, das zu einer wichtigen Unterscheidung im Blick auf die Jesusüberlieferung zwingt, die diese Überlieferung am Ende in zwei Teile teilt. Denn er trennt damit gewissermaßen – wie es andeutungsweise bereits bei Saadja b. Joseph al-Fajjumi (882–942) geschehen ist,[58] und auch Mose b.Maimon in seinem *Iggeret Teman* getan hat[59] – die Berichte über den historischen Jesus von denjenigen, die sein Christussein und seine christologisch begründete Göttlichkeit beweisen sollen.

Doch damit nicht genug. Denn was den zweiten Teil der Berichte anbetrifft, also die Wunderberichte sowie jene, die die Göttlichkeit Jesu beweisen sollen, so erfüllen sie für Ibn Kammûna nicht nur nicht die Bedingungen einer verläßlichen Überlieferung, auch wenn die Christen natürlich das Gegenteil behaupten, sondern sie sind auch nur „das Argument von Überzeugten, das nicht zur Gewißheit führt, sondern vielleicht eine vorgefaßte Ansicht bestätigt, nachdem die Verläßlichkeit ihrer Überlieferung vorausgesetzt ist (*haḏâ iqnâʿiyyun ġairu mufîd lil-yaqîn bal ʿasâ an yufîda ẓannan ġâliban baʿda taslîmi tawâturi naqlihim*)" (S. 66/S. 99).

Zu „Überzeugten" aber sind die Jünger als Träger der Überlieferung von den Wundern, wie Ibn Kammûna weiß, durch das Ostererlebnis geworden, wie denn auch alle ihre „Berichte" über die Wunder Jesu aus eben jener nachösterlichen Perspektive geschrieben worden sind. So lesen wir bei Ibn Kammûna:

„Es heißt, daß die Jünger die wahre Natur des Herrn Christus nicht begriffen hatten (*lam yaʿrifû ḥaqîqata s-sayyidi l-masîḥ*) und nicht viel von dem wußten, was es um ihn ist, bis der Heilige Geist über sie gekommen ist (*illâ ʿinda ḥulûli rûḥi l-qudsi ʿalaihim*), und das

---

57 Zum Problem vgl. auch die Begriffsanalyse von Ch. H. Manekin, „*Belief, Certainty, and Divine Attributes* in the *Guide of the Perplexed*", in: Maimonidean Studies 1 (1990), S. 117–141, bes. S. 126ff.

58 S. dazu bereits H. Hailperin, „Saadia's Relation to Islamic and Christian Thought", in: Historia Judaica 4 (1942), S. 1–15.

59 AaO. S. 92f (Text), S. xvii (engl. Übers.).

war nach seiner Auferstehung aus dem Grabe und nach seinem Aufstieg in den Himmel" (S. 64/S. 97).

Mit dieser Unterscheidung trennt Ibn Kammûna indessen nicht nur die Berichte voneinander. Vielmehr unterscheidet, ja trennt er damit zugleich auch gleichsam prinzipiell zwischen dem *historischen Jesus* und dem *kerygmatischen Christus*, und dies ist bemerkenswert. Hat er doch damit mindestens im Ansatz nicht allein methodisch, sondern ebenso inhaltlich, auf seine Weise jene Diskussion vorweggenommen, die in unserem Jahrhundert erst geführt worden ist.[60]

3. Ibn Kammûnas Plädoyer für den historischen Jesus

Ist alles Gespräch um den *kerygmatischen Christus* – so die Konsequenz aus der e.e. Unterscheidung – letztlich immer nur ein Gespräch unter bereits „Überzeugten", das sich einer auf rationaler Plausibilität beruhenden Argumentation entzieht, so ist damit die Frage nach dem *historischen Jesus* für Ibn Kammûna keineswegs erledigt. Ganz im Gegenteil, denn von diesem historischen Jesus haben wir ja eine *verläßliche Überlieferung*, und diese besagt seiner Meinung nach unzweifelhaft, daß dieser Jesus sein ganzes Leben lang der fromme Jude war und blieb, der der Tora die Treue gehalten und niemals auch nur den Versuch gemacht hat, sie zu entwerten oder ganz und gar abzuschaffen.

Inbegriff des Judeseins Jesu ist für Ibn Kammûna der Satz aus Mt 5,17: „Ich bin nicht gekommen, sie [= die Tora] zu zerstören, sondern zu erfüllen" (S. 54/S. 83; S. 58/S. 88; S. 63/S.95), den er denn auch gleich mehrmals zitiert, als handele es sich dabei um den Schlüsselsatz zum Verstehen Jesu und seiner Sendung. Selbst dort, wo in den Evangelien von einem vermeintlichen Verstoß Jesu gegen ein Gebot der Tora erzählt wird, geht es, wie Ibn Kammûna zu erklären weiß, im Grunde um nichts anderes als um *Halacha*, um legitime Auslegung und Anwendung des Gebotes unter veränderten Bedingungen. So schreibt er:

„Als sie [= die Juden] ihm, wie es ihnen schien, Mißachtung einiger ihrer [= der Tora] Gesetze vorwarfen (*ankarû ʿalaihi mâ tawahhamûhu tafrîṭan fî baʿḏi aḥkāmihâ*), erklärte er ihnen, daß es nicht Mißachtung ist, und erläuterte ihnen dies entsprechend dem, was ihre Rechtsauslegung und ihr Gesetz verlangen (*wa-auḍaḥa lahum ḏalika mimmâ yaqtaḍîhi fiqhuhum wa-šarʿuhum*), wie es im Evangelium erwähnt ist" (S. 54/S. 83).

In dieser Hinsicht freilich unterscheidet sich Ibn Kammûna nur allzu deutlich von Mose b. Maimon. Hatte auch Mose b. Maimon in seinem *„Iggeret Teman* [*Brief an die Juden Jemens*]"[61] mit Hinweis auf bYev 45a noch zugestehen kön-

[60] Wie F. NIEWÖHNER [2], S. 361, durchaus richtig gesehen hat.

[61] Ed. A. S. HALKIN & B. COHEN, S. 12f (Text), S. iii (engl. Übers.)

nen, daß Jesus als ein „legitimer Jude geboren worden ist" (*hûlad kašer*), so fügte er doch gleich hinzu, daß dessen Auslegung der Tora und seine Lebenspraxis nicht nur den Rahmen des Judentums überschritten, sondern „zur Annullierung aller ihrer [= der Tora] Gesetze, zur Abschaffung aller ihrer Satzungen und zur Mißachtung aller ihrer Verbote" geführt haben.[62]

Im Gegensatz dazu hält Ibn Kammûna in seinem Schlußplädoyer für den historischen Jesus fest:

„Der Herr Christus hat keines der Gesetze der Tora verletzt (*lam yanquḍ šai'an min aḥkâmi t-taurāt*), sondern er hat nach allen ihren Geboten gehandelt bis zum letzten Ende (*bal ʿamala bi-ǧamîʿi farâʾidihâ ilâ âḫiri waqtin*), wie wir erläutert haben, und in diesem Sinne ist er auch ihr Vollender (*fa-huwa mutammim lahâ min haḏâ l-waǧhi aiḍan*)" (S. 63/S. 95).

Es ist dies übrigens zugleich auch Ibn Kammûnas Antwort an alle diejenigen-Christen, die der Ansicht sind, der Vers Mt 5,17 sei von Röm 10,4 her in dem Sinne zu interpretieren,

„daß in der Tora die Ankunft des Christus verheißen ist, für die Gesetze, die in ihr enthalten sind (*aš-šarâʾiʿu llatî fîhâ*), folglich [gilt], daß sie alle zu tun verpflichtend ist bis zu seinem Erscheinen (*innamâ yalzimu l-ʿamalu bi-ǧamîʿihâ ilâ ḥîni ẓuhûrihi*), nicht aber für immer oder bis zum Tag der Auferstehung (*lâ ilâ l-abad au ilâ yaumi l-qiyâma*). Denn seit er [= Jesus] erschienen ist, ist sie zum Ende gekommen (*fa-qad kamilat*), erstens durch Erfüllung seiner Verheißung (*bi-naǧâzi l-waʿdi bihi awwalan*), und zweitens durch Vollendung ihrer Verbindlichkeit (*bi-kamâli t-taklîfi bihâ ṯâniyan*)" (S. 63/S. 95).

Doch nicht nur Jesus selber ist der jüdischen Tradition, der Tora, treu gewesen und geblieben, auch seine Jünger waren es, jedenfalls bis zu einem gewissen Zeitpunkt. Denn erst im Laufe der Zeit haben – so Ibn Kammûna – spätere Anhänger der Lehre Jesu die Gebote der Tora nicht mehr befolgt und dies damit begründet, daß diese ihrer eben zitierten Meinung nach nur bis zur Ankunft, bis zum Auftreten des Christus Gültigkeit gehabt hätten, nicht aber über diesen Zeitpunkt hinaus. Den entscheidenden Anteil an dieser Veränderung – und damit an der Begründung des Christentums – hatte dabei Paulus:

„Veränderungen der Gesetze der Tora (*taġyîr aḥkâmi t-taurât*), wie die Erlaubnis [zum Genuß] des Schweinefleisches und das Unterlassen der Beschneidung und der [rituellen] Waschungen, sind von den Jüngern berichtet, nicht aber von dem Herrn Christus; denn

[62] Nicht ohne Grund sagt Mose b. Maimon in bezug auf Jesu Toraauslegung *ta'awwala ... ta'wîlan*. Zu Mose b. Maimons Auffassung von Jesus und dessen Toraauslegung vgl. auch die Erläuterungen A. S. HALKINS in der Einleitung zum *Iggeret Teman*, S. XIV mit A. 90–92. Von einer geradezu destruktiven Rolle Jesu in der jüdischen Geschichte spricht Mose b. Maimon trotz seiner insgesamt positiven Sicht des Christentums übrigens auch in (der unzensierten Version seines) *Mischneh Tora, Sefer Schoftim, Hil. Melakhim Kap. XI § 4*. S. dazu die Analyse von A. RAVITZKY, „*,To the Utmost Human Capacity': Maimonides on the Days of the Messiah*", in: J. L. KRAEMER (Hg.), Perspectives on Maimonides. Philosophical and Historical Studies, Oxford 1991, S. 221–256, bes. S. 227 ff. 245 f.

er hat an ihren [= der Tora] Gesetzen festgehalten (*fa-innahu lam yazul mutamassikan bi-aḥkâmihâ*), bis die Juden ihn gefangen genommen haben. [...] Seine [= Jesu] Gefährten[63] hielten lange Zeit an der Treue zu ihr [= der Tora] fest, bevor sie gegen sie zu verstoßen begannen und ihre Abrogierung verkündeten, [indem sie sagten,] daß sie zu befolgen nur bis zur Erscheinung des Herrn Christus verbindlich gewesen war, nicht länger. Das meiste davon geht auf die Meinung des Gesandten[64] Paulus zurück (*akṯaru ḏalika ʿan raʾyi Fûlûs ar-rasûl*)" (S. 54/S. 82f).

4. Ibn Kammûna und die historisch-kritische Bibelauslegung

Nun ist das, was wir in den gerade zuletzt zitierten Sätzen Ibn Kammûnas lesen können, durchaus nicht in allen Punkten etwas völlig Neues, und vielleicht auch nicht einmal Ergebnis seiner eigenen Studien und Entdeckungen. Das gilt für seine Sicht des historischen Jesus und seine Verteidigung von Jesu Judesein nicht anders als für seine Trennung des historischen Jesus vom kerygmatischen Christus; das gilt in gleicher Weise aber auch für seine Beurteilung der späteren christlichen Tradition, vor allem aber hinsichtlich der Rolle, die er bei deren Herausbildung Paulus zuweist, nämlich der eigentliche Begründer des Christentums (gewesen) zu sein, dessen Christentum freilich gleichsam eine Entstellung und Verfälschung des wahren, „jesuanischen Christentums" darstellt.

Daß nicht Jesus der Stifter des Christentums gewesen ist, sondern zwischen seinem Auftreten und dem Entstehen des Christentums vielmehr ein gewisser, vielleicht sogar längerer (?) Zeitraum anzunehmen ist, ist übrigens auch die Ansicht Mose b. Maimons gewesen. Zwar erwähnt er, anders als Ibn Kammûna, den Namen des seiner Meinung nach eigentlichen Be gründers des Christentums nicht, an der zeitlichen und sachlichen Differenz zwischen Jesus und dem (späteren) Christentum hält er gleichwohl fest. So schreibt er in seinem *Iggeret Teman*:

„Eine lange Zeit nach ihm (*wa-min baʿdihi bi-muddatin tawîlatin*) ist eine Religion entstanden, die die Kinder Esau [= die Christen] auf ihn [= Jesus] zurückführen, obwohl so etwas zu tun, nicht seine Absicht gewesen ist".[65]

---

63 Auffällig ist an dieser Stelle wiederum Ibn Kammûnas Wortwahl: Wenn er von Jesu Jüngern als toratreuen Juden spricht, nennt er sie *aṣḥabuhu* [*seine Gefährten*], dabei den Begriff benutzend, der im Arabischen zur Bezeichnung von Muhammads ersten Getreuen gebraucht wird. Die „nachösterlichen Jünger" hingegen, die in Jesus den „Christus" und „(Sohn) Gott(es)" er- und bekannt haben, nennt er mit dem christlich-arabischen Begriff *al-ḥawâriyyûn* [*die Jünger*].

64 Den Ibn Kammûna hier gleich Mose und Muhammad mit dem islamischen Begriff *ar-rasûl* nennt.

65 *Iggeret Teman,* S. 14f (Text), S. iv (engl. Übers.).

Ansichten von noch größerer Ähnlichkeit zu Ibn Kammûna sind darüber hinaus vor allem im frühen karäischen Schrifttum,[66] ebenso aber auch in der islamischen (antichristlichen) Polemik[67] nachweisbar. Hier finden sich sogar beinahe gleichlautende Sätze, was freilich nicht besagen soll, Ibn Kammûna sei von ihnen beeinflußt oder gar abhängig (gewesen), wenn dies allerdings auch nicht ausgeschlossen werden kann.

Pars pro toto sei hier nur auf den Karäer Ja'qûb al-Qirqisânî (10. Jh.) hingewiesen,[68] der sich in seinem *opus magnum*, seinem *Kitâb al-anwâr wal-marâqib [Buch der Lichter und Leuchttürme]*[69] ausführlich auch mit Jesus und den Anfängen des Christentum befaßt hat. Für unseren Zusammenhang von Interesse und Wichtigkeit ist daraus insbesondere das Buch I, Kap. 8.[70] In seinen Erörterungen über die Anfänge des Christentums stützte sich Ja'qûb al-Qirqisânî übrigens nicht nur auf karäische Gelehrte, darunter Benjamin b. Mûsâ an-Nihâwandî (1. Hälfte 9. Jh.) und andere.[71] *Die* Autorität in Fragen des Christentums war für ihn vielmehr Dâ'ûd [Dawid] b. Marwan ar-Raqqî (um 820 – um 890), mit dem Beinamen *al-Muqammiṣ*,[72] den er sogar ausführlich zitiert hat (Buch I, Kap. 8 §§ 5–7).[73]

Ohne hier *in extenso* auf diese karäischen Positionen einzugehen[74] - bemerkenswert ist tatsächlich deren, wenn auch nicht im strengen Sinne wörtliche, so doch immerhin sachliche Übereinstimmung insbesondere in der Beurteilung des Paulus und seiner Rolle bei der Herausbildung des Christentums mit der

66 S. dazu L. NEMOY, „The Attitude of the Early Karaites Towards Christianity", in: Salo W. Baron Jubilee Volume, New York-London 1975, II, S. 697–715 (= ferner zitiert als: L. NEMOY [3]); D. LASKER, Jewish Philosophical Polemics Against Christianity in the Middle Ages, New York 1977, S. 520. 57–61. 191–192. 1940. 196–200. 210.

67 S. dazu u.a. das in S.M. STERNS „Quotations from Apocryphal Gospels in 'Abd al-Jabbâr" , in: JThS NS 18 (1967), S. 34–57, und insbesondere in DERS., „'Abd al-Jabbâr's Account of How Christian Religion was Falsified by the Adoption of Roman Customs", in: JThS 19 (1968), S. 128–185, ausgebreitete umfangreiche Material.

68 Zur Person s. L. NEMOY, Karaite Anthology, New Haven 1952, S. 42ff (= ferner zitiert als: L. NEMOY [1]); C. SIRAT, S. 37–54 (Lit. S. 419f. 459); N. SCHUR, The Karaite Encyclopedia, Frankfurt/M.-Berlin-Bern-New York-Paris-Wien 1995 (= BEATAJ, Bd. 38), S. 174–176; zum Werk s. B. CHIESAS Einleitung in: B. CCHIESA & W. LOCKWOOD, Ja'qub al-Qirqisani on Jewish Sects and Christianity. A Translation of „Kitâb al-anwâr" Book I, with two introductory essays, Frankfurt/M.-Bern-New York-Nancy 1984 (= Judentum und Umwelt, Bd. 10), S. 15–47.

69 5 Bde, ed. L. NEMOY, New York 1939–1945.

70 Bd.I, S. 42–45; s. dazu [B. CHIESA &] W. LOCKWOOD, S. 60–64 (= Einleitung), S. 135–139 mit 178–180 (= engl. Übers.), sowie F. ASTREN, „History or Philosophy? The Construction of the Past in Medieval Karaite Judaism", in: Medieval Encounters 1 (1995), S. 114–143, bes. S. 133ff. 138ff.

71 Zur Person s. L. NEMOY [1], S. 21ff.; N. SCHUR, S. 211–213.

72 Zur Person s. L. NEMOY [3], S. 702–704; C. SIRAT, S. 17f. Seinen Beinamen *der Springer* soll er erhalten haben, weil er, als Jude geboren, später zum Christentum übergetreten, aber nach einiger Zeit wieder zum Judentum zurückgekehrt ist. S. dazu L. NEMOY [3], S. 703.

73 Bd. I, S. 43–45 (engl. Übers. S. 137–139).

74 Vgl. dazu A. 66.

Ibn Kammûnas. So schreibt Jaʿqûb al-Qirqisânî (zitiert nach W. Lockwoods Übersetzung):

„The Christian religion as practiced now was invented and proclaimed by Pûlus[75]: it was he who ascribed divinity to Jesus and claimed to be himself the prophet of Jesus his Lord. He introduced no duties and imposed nothing at all. He asserted that religion is nothing but humility. They say that the fasting and prayers which they observe are not compulsory duties but purely voluntary. They forbid no form of food but allow all animals, from the gnat to the elephant" (Buch I, Kap. 8 § 2).[76]

5. Ibn Kammûnas Fazit

Angesichts von so viel Übereinstimmung und Gemeinsamkeit mit anderen – und die Reihe der Parallelen, auf die in diesem Zusammenhang verwiesen werden könnte, ließe sich ohne größere Mühe verlängern – bleibt am Ende natürlich zu fragen, worin nun das Besondere und Eigene in Ibn Kammûnas hier betrachtetem Kapitel über das Christentum und den historischen Jesus zu sehen ist. Dies scheint mir in zweierlei zu liegen. Zu erinnern ist dazu zunächst noch einmal an Ibn Kammûnas Methodologie und vor allem an das durch ihre Anwendung erzielte Ergebnis, das Ibn Kammûna trotz aller Gemeinsamkeiten und Übereinstimmungen von seinen Vorgängern und möglichen Vorbildern unterscheidet. War auch sein Argument selber, wie zu sehen war, nicht neu, so doch dessen in seiner Darlegung verfolgter methodischer Ansatz, seine Einführung einer prinzipiellen Unterscheidung von Glaubenszeugnis und historischem, aus und auf Grund der *Verläßlichkeit der Überlieferung* gewonnenem Beweis und damit zugleich die Entdeckung der Bibel, in diesem Falle des Neuen Testaments, als Urkunde des Glaubens. In dieser Hinsicht hat F. Niewöhner durchaus recht, wenn er feststellt: „Nimmt man beide Aussagen zusammen – die Trennung zwischen dem historischen Jesus und dem geglaubten Christus sowie die Funktion des Paulus für die Ausformung des Christentums zu einer Religion – dann muß gesagt werden, daß Ibn Kammûna als Vorläufer der historisch-kritischen Bibelwissenschaft zu gelten hat. Und er argumentiert in der Tat kritisch wie historisch."[77] Doch damit nicht genug:

Erstaunlicherweise nämlich – und dies ist der zweite Punkt, in dem sich Ibn Kammûna gegenüber seinen Vorgängern und möglichen Vorbildern auszeichnet – zwingt solche Art historisch-kritischer Betrachtung der christlichen Religion und ihrer Grundlagen trotz aller daraus resultierenden Religionskritik Ibn Kammûna am Ende aber gerade nicht zu deren völliger Entwertung, wie sie in der zeitgenössischen Religionspolemik immer wieder begegnet. Im Gegen-

---

[75] Während der Name bei Ibn Kammûna *fûlûs* lautet, schreibt ihn Jaʿqub al-Qirqisani *fûlûṣ*.

[76] Bd. I, S. 43 (engl. Übers. S. 135 f.); vgl. dazu auch L. Nemoy [3], S. 705.

[77] AaO. [2], S. 362.

teil, vielmehr bewahrt sich Ibn Kammûna auch in seinem abschließenden Urteil über das Christentum noch jene allenthalben zu beobachten gewesene Fairness, mit der er seine *„Kritik der Untersuchungen der drei Religionen“* begonnen hatte:[78]

„[Die Überlieferungen der Christen sind ein Argument] von Überzeugten, das keine Gewißheit gewährt, sondern bestenfalls eine vorgefaßte Ansicht bestätigt, wenn zuvor die Verläßlichkeit ihrer Überlieferung zugestanden ist (*hadâ iqnâʿiyyù gairu mufîd lil-yaqîn bal ʿasâ an yufîda ẓannan ġâliban baʿda taslîmi tawâturi naqlihim*). Wenn man jedoch [dieses Argument] um eine Betrachtung aller Lebensumstände des Herrn Christus und der Lebensumstände seiner Gefährten ergänzt – hinsichtlich ihrer asketischen Lebensweise, ihrer Frömmigkeit und ihres Ertragens großer Leiden, während sie ihre Berufung erfüllten und die Grundlagen ihrer Religion bis zum Letzten ordneten (*fî zuhdihim wa-waraʿihim wa-taḥammulihimi l-mašâqqa l-ʿaẓîmata fî iqâmati haḏihi d-daʿwati wa-ntiẓâmi umûri haḏâ d-dîni ilâ haḏihi l-ġâya*) – dann wird aus der Summe aller dieser Faktoren klar, daß ihre Sache von göttlicher Unterstützung und allmächtiger Fürsorge getragen worden ist“ (S. 66/S. 99).

In diesem, zugleich seinem abschließenden Urteil über das Christentum weiß sich Ibn Kammûna offenbar unausgesprochen einig mit jener Empfehlung, die einst Rabban Gamliel gegeben und damit der urchristlichen Gemeinde gleichsam zu überleben ermöglicht hatte (Apg 5,58f); jedenfalls klingt Ibn Kammûnas Urteil unüberhörbar wie deren spätes Echo.

Bibliographie

Astren, F., „History or Philosophy? The Construction of the Past in Medieval Karaite Judaism“, in: Medieval Encounters 1 (1995), S. 114–143.

Baneth, D. H., „Ibn Kammûna“, in: MGWJ 69 (1925), S. 295–311.

Baron, S. W., A Social and Religious History of the Jews, 18 Bde, Philadelphia-London-New York ²1952/5712–1983/5743, Bd. V (4. Neudruck 1971); Bd. XVII (²1980/5740).

ben-Jaʿaqov, A., *Yehûdê Bâvel – mi-sôf teqûfat ha-geʾônîm ʿad yâmênû*, Jerusalem 1965.

Chiesa, B. & W. Lockwood, Jaʿqub al-Qirqisani on Jewish Sects and Christianity. A Translation of „Kitâb al-anwâr“ Book I, With Two Introductory Essays, Frankfurt/M.-Bern-New York-Nancy 1984 (= Judentum und Umwelt, Bd. 10).

Cunz, M., „Maimonides über den König Messias und das messianische Zeitalter“, in: Jud 42 (1986), S. 74–79

Endress, G., The Works of Yaḥyâ b. ʿAdî. An Analytical Inventory, Wiesbaden 1977.

[78] Nur spekulieren kann man freilich darüber, ob er sich dabei auch die Sicht des Christentums (und des Islams) zu eigen gemacht hätte, die Mose b. Maimon in seinem *Mischneh Tora, Sefer Schoftim, Hil. Melakhim* Kap. XI § 4 (Anhang nach der unzensierten Ausgabe) geäußert hat (dt. von M. Cunz, „Maimonides über den König Messias und das messianische Zeitalter“, in: Jud 42 [1986], S. 74–79, dort S. 75f). Zur Sache s. A. S. Halkin, S. XIV mit A. 90–91, I. Twersky, Introduction to the Code of Maimonides (*Mishneh Torah*), New Haven-London 1980, S. 452f, und J. Posen, „Die Einstellung des Maimonides zum Islam und zum Christentum“, in: Jud 42 (1986), S. 66–73.

FISCHEL, W., „Arabische Quellen zur Geschichte der babylonischen Judenheit im 13. Jahrhundert", in: MGWJ 79 (1935), S. 302–322.

GÄTJE, H., Koran und Koranexegese, Zürich-Stuttgart 1971.

GOITEIN, S. D., A Mediterranian Society. The Jewish Communities in the Arab World as Portrayed in the Documents of the Cairo Genizah, Bd. II, Berkeley-Los Angeles-London 1971.

HAILPERIN, H., „Saadia's Relation to Islamic and Christian Thought", in: Historia Judaica 4 (1942), S. 1–15.

HIRSCHFELD, L., Saʿd b. Mansûr ibn Kammûnah und seine polemische Schrift *Tanqîḥ al-abḥâṯ limilal aṯ-ṯalâṯ*, (Diss. Heidelberg), Berlin 1893.

[IBN KAMMÛNA] Saʿd b. Mansûr Ibn Kammûna's Examination of the Inquiries into Three Faiths. A Thirteenth-Century Essay in Comparative Religion, ed. M. PERLMANN, Berkeley-Los Angeles 1967 (= Univ. of California Publ., Near Eastern Studies no. 6); engl. Übers.: M. PERLMANN, Ibn Kammûna's Examination of the Three Faiths. A Thirteenth-Century Essay in the Comparative Study of Religion, Berkeley-Los Angeles-London 1971.

–, „Ibn Kammûnah's Treatise on the Differences Between the Rabbanites and the Karaites", ed. arab. L. NEMOY, in: PAAJR 36 (1968), S. 107–165; engl. Übers.: L. NEMOY, in: JQR 63 (1972–73), S. 97–135. 222–246.

–, „The Arabic Treatise on the Immortality of the Soul, by [...] Ibn Kammûnah", ed. arab. L. NEMOY, New Haven 1944; engl. Übers.: L. NEMOY, in: Ignace Goldziher Memorial Volume, 2 Bde, Budapest-Jerusalem 1948–58, Bd. II, S. 83–99 [Nachdruck beider Ausgaben in: *Ha-Rofê ha-ʿIvrî* – The Hebrew Medical Journal 35 (1962), S. 131–136. 213–239].

[JEHUDA HA-LEWI] Abu l-Hasan Jehuda Halewi, Das Buch Al-Chazari, ed. [arab. mit hebr. Übers. des Jehuda ibn Tibbon] H. HIRSCHFELD, Leipzig 1887 [Neudruck Jerusalem 1970]; dt. Übers. des arab. Textes: H. HIRSCHFELD, Das Buch al-Chazarî. Aus dem Arab. des Abu-l-Hasan Jehuda Hallewi, Breslau 1885; des hebr. Textes: D. Cassel, Der Kusari, Neudruck Zürich 1990.

KNUST, Th. A. (Hg.), Marco Polo: Von Venedig nach China, Tübingen ^{4}1976.

LASKER, D., Jewish Philosophical Polemics Against Christianity in the Middle Ages, New York 1977.

LAZARUS-YAFEH, H., Intertwined Worlds. Medieval Islam and Bible Criticism, Princeton, N. J. 1992.

–, „Some Neglected Aspects of Medieval Muslim Polemics Against Christianity", in: HThR 1996 (im Druck).

LEWIS, B., Die Juden in der islamischen Welt, München 1987.

MANEKIN, CH. H., „Belief, Certainty, and Divine Attributes in the Guide of the Perplexed", in: Maimonidean Studies 1 (1990), S. 117–141.

MANN, J., „Une source de l'histoire des Juifs au XIIIe siècle. La lettre polémique de Jacob b. Elie à Pablo Christiani" in: REJ 82 (1926), S. 363–377.

MARCO POLO, Il Milione – Die Wunder der Welt, übers. von E. GUIGNARD, Zürich ^{5}1989.

[MOSE B. MAIMON] *Iggeret Teman le-Rabbênû Mosheh ben Maimon*, ed. arab. et hebr. A. S. HALKIN, engl. Übers. B. COHEN, New York 1952.

–, *Rabbênû Mosheh b. Maimon, Moreh ha-Nevûkhîm (dalâlat al-hâʾirîn)*, ed. [arab. und hebr.] Y. Qafiḥ, 3 Bde, Jerusalem 1972.

NEMOY, L., Karaite Anthology, New Haven 1952 (= L. NEMOY [1]).

–, „Ibn Kammûnah's Treatise on the Differences Between the Rabbanites and the Karaites“, in: JQR 63 (1972–73), S. 97–135. 222–246 (= L. NEMOY [2]).

–, „The Attitude of the Early Karaites Towards Christianity“ in: Salo W. Baron Jubilee Volume, New York-London 1975, Bd. II, S. 697–715 (= L.NEMOY [3]).

NIEWÖHNER, F., *Veritas sive Varietas*. Lessings Toleranzparabel und das Buch von den drei Betrügern, Heidelberg 1988 (= Bibl. d. Aufklärung, Bd. 5) (= F. NIEWÖHNER [1]).

–, „Die Wahrheit ist eine Tochter der Zeit. Ibn Kammûnas historisch-kritischer Religionsvergleich aus dem Jahre 1280“, in: B. LEWIS und F. NIEWÖHNER (Hg.), Religionsgespräche im Mittelalter, Wiesbaden 1992 (= Wolfenbütteler Mittelalter-Studien, Bd. 4), S. 357–369 (= F. NIEWÖHNER [2]).

L. S. NORTHRUP, „Muslim Christian Relations During the Reign of the Mamlûk Sultân al-Mansûr Qalawun A. D. 1278–1290, in: M. GERVERS und R. J. BIKHAZI (Hg.), Conversion and Continuity in Islamic Lands, Eighth to Eighteenth Century, Toronto 1990, S. 253–261.

NOSOWSKI, J., Teologia Koranu. Wyklad systematyczny, Warszawa 1970.

PERLMANN, M., Sa'd b. Mansûr Ibn Kammûna's Examination of the Inquiries into Three Faiths. A Thirteenth-Century Essay in Comparative Religion, ed. M. PERLMANN, Berkeley-Los Angeles 1967 (= Univ. of California Publ., Near Eastern Stud. no. 6) (= M. PERLMANN [1]).

–, Ibn Kammûna's Examination of the Three Faiths. A Thirteenth-Century Essay in the Comparative Study of Religion, Berkeley-Los Angeles-London 1971 (= M. PERLMANN [2]).

PLATTI, E., Yaḥyâ b. 'Adî Théologien chrétien et philosophe arabe, Leuven/Louvain 1983 (= Orientalia Lovaniensia Analecta, vol. 14).

POSEN, J., „Die Einstellung des Maimonides zum Islam und zum Christentum“, in: Jud 42 (1986), S. 66–73.

POSNANSKI, A., Schiloh, Leipzig 1904.

RAVITZKI, A., „‚*To the Utmost Human Capacity*‘: Maimonides on the Days of the Messiah“, in: J. L. KRAEMER (Hg.), Perspectives on Maimonides. Philosophical and Historical Studies, Oxford 1991, S. 221–256.

ROSENKRANZ, S., „Judentum, Christentum und Islam in der Sicht des Ibn Kammuna“, in: Jud 52 (1996), S. 4–22.

SAMAU'AL AL-MAGHRIBI, *Ifḥâm al-Yahûd* – Silencing the Jews, ed. et. transl. M. PERLMANN, in: PAAJR 32 (1964), S. 5–31 (Text). S. 33–104 (engl. Übers.).

SCHUR, N., The Karaite Encyclopedia, Frankfurt/M.-Berlin-Bern-New York-Paris-Wien 1995 (= BEATAJ, Bd. 38).

SIRAT, C., A History of Jewish Philosophy in the Middle Ages, Cambridge-Paris ²1990.

SPULER, B., Die Mongolen in Iran, Berlin ⁴1985.

STEINSCHNEIDER, M., Die arabische Literatur der Juden. Ein Beitrag zur Literaturgeschichte der Araber, großenteils aus handschriftlichen Quellen, Frankfurt a. M. 1902 [= repr. Hildesheim ²1986].

–, Polemische und apologetische Literatur in arabischer Sprache zwischen Muslimen, Christen und Juden nebst Anhängen verwandten Inhalts, Leipzig 1877 (= Abh. z. Kunde des Morgenlandes VI,3) [= Neudruck Hildesheim 1966].

STERN, S. M., „Quotations from Apocryphal Gospels in 'Abd al-Jabbâr“ , in: JThS NS 18 (1967), S. 34–57.

–, „ʿAbd al-Jabbâr's Account of How Christian Religion was Falsified by the Adoption of Roman Customs", in: JThS 19 (1968), S. 128–185.

STILLMAN, N., The Jews of Arab Lands. A History and a Source Book, Philadelphia 5739/1979

AŠ-ŠAHRASTANI, Abu l-Fatḥ Muḥammad b. ʿAbd al-Karîm, *Kitâb al-milal wan-niḥal*, ed. A. A. MAHNA & A. H. FAʿUR, 2 Bde, Beirut 1414/1993.

SCHRECKENBERG, H., Die christlichen Adversus-Judaeos-Texte und ihr literarisches und historisches Umfeld (13.–20. Jh.), Frankfurt/M.-Berlin-Bern-New York-Paris-Wien 1994 (= Europäische Hochschulschriften XXIII, Bd. 497).

SOURDEL, D., „Un Pamphlet musulman anonyme d'époche ʿAbbaside contre les chrétiens", in: REI 34 (1966), S. 1–33.

TWERSKY, I., Introduction to the Code of Maimonides (*Mishneh Torah)*, New Haven-London 1980.

WATT, W. M. & A. T. WELCH, Der Islam, I, Stuttgart-Berlin-Köln-Mainz 1980.

WOLFSON, H. A., „The Veracity of Scripture in Philo, Halevi, Maimonides, and Spinoza", in: Alexander Marx Jubilee Volume (engl. section), New York 1950, S. 603–630, bes. S. 603–609 [= in: DERS., Religious Philosophy. A Group of Essays, New York 1965, S. 217–233].

IV. Rabbinic Judaism, Early Jewish Mysticism and Gnosticism

Tannaitic Benei Beraq: A Peripheral Centre of Learning

by

Aharon Oppenheimer

The Destruction of the Second Temple led to considerable changes in Judaism. Study of the *Torah* became the highest value and the Sages became the leaders of the people. Together with this a new phenomenon arose, local *batei midrashot* (study houses) which worked in parallel to the central leadership institution, and were usually set up around the figure of an important Sage in his home town. This *baraita* is an expression of the process:

The Rabbis taught: 'Justice, justice shalt thou pursue' (Deuteronomy 16:20). Follow the Sages to the *yeshiva*, follow R. Eliezer to Lod, Rabban Yohanan b. Zakkai to Beror Hayil, R. Joshua to Peqi'in, Rabban Gamaliel to Yavneh, R. Aqiva to Benei Beraq, R. Mattiya [b. Harash] to Rome, R. Hanania b. Teradyon to Sikhne, R. Yose to Sepphoris, R. Judah b. Betera to Nisibis, R. [Hananiah, nephew of R.] Joshua to the Diaspora, and follow Rabbi to Beth She'arim ...[1]

This *baraita* lists in chronological order the leading Sages from the periods of Yavneh, Ushah, and the time of R. Judah ha-Nasi, together with their *batei midrashot*, as well as Sages from the diaspora.[2] The list begins with a number of *batei midrashot* from the period of Yavneh, most of them in Judaea – Lod, Beror Hayil,[3] Peqi'in,[4] Yavneh and Benei Beraq. The source then adds Sikhne

---

[1] BT Sanhedrin 32b. The additions in square brackets are from the MSS from Munich, Florence, and Karlsruhe. And see The Babylonian Talmud with Variant Readings (Diqduqei Sopherim), ad loc; Yalqut Shimoni, Leviticus 611, ed. Hyman-Shiloni, p. 594.

[2] For the identification of Nisibis, and the site of the *bet midrash* of Hananiah, son of R. Joshua's brother, see: A. Oppenheimer, 'The Centre in Nisibis in the Mishnaic Period', Nation and History, I, ed. M. Stern, Jerusalem 1983, pp. 141–150 (Heb.).

[3] On Rabban Yohanan b. Zakkai's presence at Beror Hayil, rather than at Yavneh as we might have expected, see G. Alon, The Jews in their Land in the Talmudic Age, I, Jerusalem 1980, pp. 106–107.

[4] Peqi'in was situated between Yavneh and Lod. This is clear from the following source: 'It happened that R. Yohanan b. Baroqa and R. Elazar Hisma who came from Yavneh to Lod and welcomed R. Joshua in Peqi'in' (Tosephta Sotah vii, 9, ed. Lieberman, p. 193; JT Sotah iii, 18d; *ib*. Hagigah i, 75d; BT *ib*. 3a; Numbers Rabbah xiv, 4). See also Kaphtor va-Pherah, ed. Luncz, pp. 128, 302 (esp. n. 3), 328. In the parallels in the Jerusalem Talmud the name is

in Galilee, the home of R. Hananiah b. Teradyon who was active at the end of the Yavneh period, and was accounted one of the martyrs killed after the Bar Kokhva revolt. The *bet midrash* of R. Mattiya b. Harash in Rome also belongs to this period. Thus Benei Beraq is one of a number of settlements with a local *bet midrash,* which worked in parallel to the central authority at Yavneh, headed first by Rabban Yohanan b. Zakkai and later by Rabban Gamaliel.[5] Of course it is possible that the list in this *baraita* is incomplete, and that there were other *batei midrashot* at this time which grew up around other leading Sages in different towns and villages.

In Benei Beraq, then, there was a local *bet midrash* headed by R. Aqiva – one of the most outstanding figures, if not the most dominant figure, of the second half of the Yavneh period, and at the time of the Bar Kokhva revolt. Benei Beraq dates back to Biblical times, when it is described as being situated between Yehud and Gath-Rimmon in the territory of the tribe of Dan.[6] The *Annals of Sennacherib* relate that in 701 BCE the king of Assyria took Banay(a) Bar(a)qa together with Jaffa, Bit-Dagan and Asuru from the king of Ashqelon.[7] This evidence, together with the resemblance of the names, allows us to identify biblical and talmudic Benei Beraq with the Arab village of Ibn-Ibraq, also known as Hiriya. All the places mentioned in the Bible and the *Annals of Sennacherib* are to be found around this site. Pottery from the Israelite period found on the site supports its identification as ancient Benei Beraq.[8] The crossroads near the site is called 'Mesubbim crossroads' after the Sages who reclined (מסובים) on the night of the *Seder* in Benei Beraq with R. Aqiva (see below). The modern town of Benei Beraq, however, is situated some four km. north of the ancient site.

A tradition about the foundation of R. Aqiva's *bet midrash* in Benei Beraq is to be found in one of the versions of *Avot de- Rabbi Nathan.* This source tells of R. Aqiva, who reached the age of forty without having studied *Torah*, and as the shepherd of the flocks of Ben Kalba Savua married his daughter and was

given as Beqi'in (בקיעין), and it is possible that this is the correct version, from *Biq'ah* (בקעה), a valley.

5 It is possible that after the death of Rabban Gamaliel, and maybe even during his lifetime, the leadership institutions moved from Yavneh to Lod, and perhaps even worked for some time in both places. During the Bar Kokhva revolt and perhaps even in preparation for it, we can assume that the leadership institutions worked in some fashion at Betar. See for this ALON (*supra* n. 3), II, Jerusalem 1984, pp. 464–466; 625–627; A. OPPENHEIMER, 'Jewish Lydda in the Roman Era', HUCA, 69 (1988), pp. 115–129; J.J. SCHWARTZ, Lod (Lydda) Israel, From its Origins through the Byzantine Period, BAR International Series 571, Oxford 1991, pp. 79–100. On the status of Lod see also below.

6 Joshua 19:45.

7 D.D. LUCKENBILL, The Annals of Sennacherib, Chicago 1924, p. 31.

8 See I. FINKELSTEIN, 'An Exploratory Excavation of the Tel Next to the Mesubbim Crossroads (Ancient Benei Beraq', 'Atiqot 10 (1990), pp. 29–40 and bibliography *ad loc.* (Heb.).

encouraged by her to go and study. Following this we find a description of R. Aqiva's arrival in Benei Beraq, after studying with R. Eliezer and R. Joshua, and being joined by twenty four thousand pairs of pupils:

R. Aqiva came to Benei Beraq and was forced to teach *Torah* in public out of dire economic straits. Ben Kalba Savua heard that a great man had arrived in Benei Beraq and said: I will go to him and cancel my vow. He went and stood before him and said: Rabbi, I had a daughter who married a certain shepherd ... and I took all my property away from her ... Then he immediately gave him, R. Aqiva, all his property.[9]

The details of this incident would seem to be at least in part legendary. It is difficult to accept chronologically that R. Aqiva, who was put to death in the persecutions following the Bar Kokhva revolt (135–138 CE), could have been an adult while the Temple still stood, and the shepherd of Ben Kalba Savua, one of the Jerusalem nobility, until he married his daughter against her father's will.[10] It is true that there is a tradition that he lived for a hundred and twenty years,[11] but this is only to put his lifespan on a par with other great Jewish figures – Moses, Hillel the Elder, and Rabban Yohanan b. Zakkai. Thus it is likely that the tradition about him that he was the shepherd of Kalba Savua, one of the Jerusalem nobility, until he married his daughter against her father's will is also legendary. The parallel sources in *Avot de-Rabbi Nathan* tell us that he was motivated to go and study *Torah* while he was over the mouth of a well, when he was impressed by the power of the water and the rope to wear away the sides of the cistern.[12] However, we should note that the picture of R. Aqiva's ignorance in his youth, his humble origins, and the encouragement to study which he received from his wife is stressed time and again in other sources as well, and would appear to be based on reality.[13] In this context it is totally

---

9 Avot de-Rabbi Nathan, Addition B to version A, viii (after MS Vatican 44), ed. Schechter, p. 163. For the importance of this MS as part of the main evidence for version A, see M. Kister, Avot de-Rabbi Nathan: Studies in Text, Redaction and Interpretation (unpublished thesis, Jerusalem 1993), pp. 238–239 (Heb.) and cf. BT Ketubot 62b–63a; BT Nedarim 50a.

10 For the authenticity of the deeds attributed to R. Aqiva, see S. Safrai, Rabbi Aqiva b. Joseph, his Life and Teachings, Jerusalem 1971, pp. 10–30 (Heb.). Safrai contrasts the Babylonian tradition (qv. end of n. 9 above) with the traditions in the Avot de-Rabbi Nathan (qv. n. 12 below), and claims that in the Palestinian tannaitic tradition there is no mention of R. Aqiva's having been a shepherd, but he appears to have been a common workman with a small income. However we would point out that, firstly, not all scholars agree that the historicity of the sources in Avot de-Rabbi Nathan is equal to that of the Mishnah or the tannaitic *midreshei halakhah*; secondly, Safrai did not take in to account the Vatican MS of the Avot de-Rabbi Nathan cited above, which presents R. Aqiva as a shepherd, with similar details to those found in the Babylonian traditions.

11 Avot de-Rabbi Nathan version B, xii, ed. Schechter, p. 29; Genesis Rabbah c, 10, ed. Theodor-Albeck, p. 1295.

12 Avot de-Rabbi Nathan, version A, vi; version B, xii, ed. Schechter, pp. 28–30.

13 With regard to R. Aqiva's ignorance in his youth, he himself mentions the time when he was an *'Am ha-Aretz* (BT Pesahim 49b); cf. also his evidence of how he began to serve the Sages, after he had not followed the requirements of *halakhah* in dealing with a *met mitzvah*

reasonable that he should set up his *bet midrash* in Benei Beraq, after he had studied for a long time with the pupils of Rabban Yohanan b. Zakkai – R. Eliezer b. Hyrcanus at Lod and R. Joshua b. Hananiah at Peqi'in.

R. Aqiva headed a *bet midrash* at Benei Beraq where there were adult students who were preparing themselves for ordination as rabbis. The principle 'Go far to [find] a place of *Torah'*,[14] was an accepted one in the world of the Sages and their pupils, and shown by the fact that youths and even married men left their homes and families for prolonged periods in order to study *Torah* in one of the *batei midrashot* of the leading Sages. R. Aqiva himself had done this when, as we are told, he studied for two periods of twelve years with R. Eliezer and R. Joshua, with the support of his wife, who is described as a grass widow.[15] A similar tradition is related about R. Aqiva's pupils, R. Hananiah b. Hakhinai and R. Shimon bar Yohai, who studied for twelve or thirteen years without a break with their teacher in his *bet midrash* in Benei Beraq:

> It happened that R. Hananiah b. Hakhinai and R. Shimon bar Yohai went to study *Torah* with R. Aqiva in Benei Beraq. They stayed there thirteen years. R. Shimon bar Yohai sent to find out how (things were) back at his home, but R. Hananiah b. Hakhinai did not send to find out how (things were) back at his home. His wife sent to say 'Your daughter has grown up, come and (find someone to) marry her', but in spite of this he did not go. R. Aqiva was prophetically inspired and said to them 'Every one who has a grown up daughter should go and (find her someone to) marry ...'.[16]

This kind of studying, total immersion for many long years, produced the phenomenon of 'attendance on the Sages', where pupils took turns to wait on their fellow students in general and on their rabbis in particular. It would seem that this concept was developed and extended in R. Aqiva's *bet midrash* in Benei Beraq. To R. Aqiva himself the saying is attributed: 'Whoever did not wait on the Sages deserves the death penalty'.[17] R. Yohanan relates the following decision in the name of R. Shimon bar Yohai, R. Aqiva's pupil in

---

(JT Nazir vii, 56a; Masekhet Semahot iv, 12, ed. Higger, p. 125). He himself gives evidence of his lowly origins at the time when R. Elazar b. Azariah was appointed instead of Rabban Gamaliel who was temporarily displaced as head of the *Bet ha- Va'ad:* Not that he is more learned in *Torah* than I, but he comes from a better family than I. Happy is the man whose family entitles him to such things, happy is the man who has such backing (JT Berakhot iv, 7d). The support R. Aqiva had from his wife in going to study *Torah* is noted by Rabban Gamaliel when speaking to his wife, who was jealous of the jewellery which R. Aqiva's wife had been given by her husband: And did you do for me what she used to do for him, when she sold the very hair from her head and gave him the money so he could study *Torah*? (JT Shabbat vi, 7d).

14 Mishnah, Avot iv, 14; cf. 'pupils of the Sages who go from town to town and city to city to learn *Torah'* (BT Berakhot 63b).

15 BT Ketubot 62b–63a, and cf. the sources cited in nn. 9 and 12.

16 Leviticus Rabbah xxi, 8, ed. Margulies, pp. 384–387; Genesis Rabbah xcv [Vatican MS 30], ed. Theodor-Albeck, p. 1232; Pesikta deRav Kahana 27, ed. Buber 176b.

17 JT Nazir vii, 56b. For attendance on Sages see ALON (n. 3 above), II, Jerusalem 1984, pp. 476–478.

Benei Beraq: One who serves [those who study] *Torah* is greater that one who studies it.[18]

There is a certain discrepancy between the tradition of the twenty four thousand students who studied with R. Aqiva in Benei Beraq, and the following tradition of the close personal relationships between R. Aqiva and the pupils who studied with him for many years. This discrepancy is even greater in the parallels which do not actually mention Benei Beraq, and which compare the huge number of R. Aqiva's first disciples, all of whom died within a very short period of time, with his second group of disciples who later headed the leadership institutions during the Ushah period after the Bar Kokhva revolt:

R. Aqiva had twelve thousand pairs of pupils from Gevat to Antipatris, and all of them died at the same time. Why? Because they were jealous of one another, and in the end he ordained seven: R. Meir, R. Judah, R. Yose, R. Shimon, R. Elazar b. Shamu'a, R. Yohanan ha-Sandlar, and R. Eliezer b. Jacob; and others say: R. Judah, R. Nehemiah, R. Meir, R. Yose, R. Shimon bar Yohai, R. Hananiah b. Hakhinai and R. Yohanan ha-Sandlar ...[19]

The second group of R. Aqiva's disciples included R. Shimon bar Yohai, and in some sources also R. Hananiah b. Hakhinai, who lived and studied with him for many years in Benei Beraq. In other words, these are not disciples who were with him only for the short time before he was put to death by the Romans. Even if the number of twelve thousand pairs of pupils seems legendary, especially since one of the parallels mentions three hundred pupils (see n. 19), we still cannot reconcile the enormous difference in numbers between the first and second group of pupils. Obviously the size of the second group of seven pupils looks authentic, for throughout the history of the *tana'im* and *amora'im* the *batei midrashot* usually prepared only a very small number of adult pupils for ordination as rabbis. The solution to this crux comes from the geographical note, which mentions R. Aqiva's pupils, not in Benei Beraq this time, but from Gevat to Antipatris. Antipatris was the town founded by Herod and called after his father on the site of biblical Afeq, next to the sources of the River Yarqon, on the northern border of Judah. Gevat was Gabata, mentioned by Eusebius, sited to the east of the area he calls Daroma, on the southern border of Judah.[20]

---

[18] BT Berakhot 7b.

[19] Genesis Rabbah lxi, 3, ed. Theodor-Albeck, p. 660; Ecclesiastes Rabbah xi, 6; BT Yevamot 62b. In one of the parallels in the *midrash* there are numbers which look more likely, but there too the comparison is between the first three hundred pupils and the second seven pupils (Midrash Tanhuma *Hayyei-Sara* vi; cf. Tanhuma Buber, *Hayyei Sara* viii, pp. 122–123). The list of the names of the second group of R. Aqiva's pupils is repeated almost word for word in all the sources which deal with the renewal of the leadership institutions in Galilee after the Bar Kokhva revolt (Canticles Rabbah ii, 5; BT Sanhedrin 13b-14a; JT Hagigah iii, 78d. On these sources see A. Oppenheimer, Galilee in the Mishnaic Period, Jerusalem 1991, pp. 45–48 (Heb.).

[20] For Antipatris, see Josephus, *Ant.* xvi 142–143. For Gabata see Eusebius, *Onomasti-*

The expression 'from Antipatris to Gevat' in relation to Judah, is equivalent to the expression 'from Dan to Be'er- Sheva' in relation to all the Land of Israel.[21] Thus it would appear that the twenty four thousand pupils were spread all over the territory of Judah, which was the main area (and perhaps the only area) of the Bar Kokhva Revolt. We may add to this the evidence of Rav Sherira Ga'on:

And R. Aqiva had many pupils and these pupils of R. Aqiva were persecuted, but the jewish people relied on the second group of R. Aqiva's pupils ...[22]

From this it is clear that R. Aqiva's pupils did not die as the result of a plague, but as the result of persecution i.e. they were put to death by the Roman authorities. Thus it is clear that the reference here to the first pupils is not to pupils preparing for ordination as rabbis and leaders of the people, but to political followers who took some sort of part in the Bar Kokhva revolt. It must be remembered that it was R. Aqiva who said of Bar Kokhva 'This is the King Messiah', while Maimonides said of R. Aqiva, (perhaps quoting a source that is no longer extant) that he was 'the arms bearer of Ben Koseva the King'.[23] The talmudic literature tends to see the failure of the Bar Kokhva revolt and the deaths of its leaders and fighters as divine retribution for sin, and this is certainly the case with the sources discussed here. In other words, the sources which mention enormous numbers of pupils are not dealing with the pupils who studied *Torah* with R. Aqiva in his *bet midrash* in Benei Beraq, but with the followers of his political ideology, who were fighters in the forces of Bar Kokhva.[24]

Benei Beraq also received visits from other leading Sages of Yavneh, R. Aqiva's teachers and contemporaries, but there is no mention of a visit by

kon, ed. Klostermann, p. 70, 10–11; S. Klein, The Land of Judah, Tel Aviv 1939, p. 84 (Heb.); P. Schäfer, Der Bar Kokhba-Aufstand, Tübingen 1981, p. 18. For a discussion of 'Daroma' see J. Schwartz, Jewish Settlement in Judaea, Jerusalem 1986, pp. 33–41 (Heb.).

21 Cf. BT Sanhedrin 94b, where the two expressions appear together.

22 Iggeret Rav Sherira Gaon (Spanish version), ed. Lewin, p. 13.

23 For R. Aqiva's words see JT Ta'aniot iv, 68d; Lamentations Rabbah ii, 4; *ib.*, ed. Buber, ii, 16, p. 101. For the tradition cited by Maimonides see Mishneh Torah , Sepher Shophetim, Hilekhot Melakhim 11, 3.

24 Alon, after a discussion of the possibility that the first pupils were fighters who were put to death by the authorities –, rejects this theory, on the grounds that these sources appear to show that R. Aqiva taught his second group of pupils after the deaths of the first. This is unlikely, as it would not have left him long enough in the short time that remained between the end of the revolt and his own death (Alon [above n. 3], II, Jerusalem 1984, pp. 631–632). However it would seem reasonable that, having distinguished between the first group of pupils, and identified them as fighters in Bar Kokhva's army, and the second group, who were studying for ordination as rabbis in R. Aqiva's *bet midrash* in Bnei Braq, there is no further need to relate in detail to the legendary layer, such as when the second group studied. Another hint that the first group were followers of R. Aqiva's political ideology can be found in the incident which notes the good treatment afforded to the pupils of R. Aqiva by bandits (BT 'Avodah Zarah 25b: on this source see A. Oppenheimer 'The Jewish Community in Galilee during the Period of Yavneh and the Bar Kokhva Revolt', Cathedra 4 [1978] p. 61 [Heb.]).

Rabban Gamaliel although there is much evidence of his visits to other places (see below). A well known source found in the Passover *Haggadah* but not in the talmudic literature tells of a group of Sages seated on the night of the *Seder* in Benei Beraq. However, in the *Tosephta* there is a parallel source which tells of Rabban Gamaliel and the Sages seated at the *Seder* in Lod:

Tosephta Pesahim x, 12, ed. Lieberman, pp. 198–199	Passover *Haggadah*
It happened that Rabban Gamaliel and the Elders	It happened that R. Eliezer and R. Joshua and R. Elazar b. Azariah and R. Akqiva and R. Tarphon
were reclining [מסובים] in the house of Boethus b. Zonin at Lod and discussing the *halakhot* of Passover all night	were reclining [מסובים] in Benei Beraq and telling about the Exodus from Egypt all night long
until cock-crow	until their pupils came to them and said:
they removed the tables and they decided together to go to the *bet midrash*.	Rabbis, the time has come to say the morning *Shema*.

The most important difference between these two sources is undoubtedly the way in which the *Seder* is conducted. In Temple times the central event of the Passover festival was the pilgrimage to Jerusalem and the Passover offering. In the Yavneh period observance of the festival moved from attendance at public rituals in the Temple and in Jerusalem to the celebration of the *Seder* night in the home of every Jew. The difference between these two sources is in the content of the *Seder* night, or to be more exact, in the content of the Passover *Haggadah*. Rabban Gamaliel and the elders who were with him at Lod spent the *Seder* night discussing the *halakhot* related to the Passover offering. The rationale behind this is two-fold. First of all, while in the time of the Second Temple the Temple ritual and the *mitzvot* connected with the Temple, such as ritual purity and tithes, were at the top of the value-scale of the Jewish people, after the destruction of the Temple study of the *Torah* took their place. Hence the rule was laid down that 'Study of the *Torah* outweighs everything else'.[25] There were of course social implications to this: in Temple times the *Haver* who meticulously observed the laws of ritual purity and tithes stood at the top of the scale, while the *'Am ha-Aretz* who paid little attention to such laws was at the bottom. After the destruction the Sage took the place of the *Haver* – indeed he is often called *Haver* – and the term *'Am ha-Aretz* came to be used to signify someone ignorant of *Torah*.[26] It is in this context that we should understand the behaviour of Rabban Gamaliel and his colleagues, who focus on study and questions of *halakhah* in their observance of the most important festival of the

25 Mishnah, Peah i, 1.

26 See A. Oppenheimer, The 'Am ha-Aretz, A Study in the Social History of the Jewish People in the Hellenistic-Roman Period, Leiden 1977, pp. 67–117.

Jewish calendar. Secondly, the hope of the Sages of Yavneh that 'The Temple be rebuilt speedily', was the basis of many of their decisions, and even the first psalms of the *Hallel,* which form the core of the Passover *Haggadah*, end, according to R. Aqiva's opinion, with the blessing of Redemption, which includes the hope for the rebuilding of the Temple, the restoration of the ritual and the re-institution of the sacrifices and Passover offerings.[27] Not only this, but Rabban Gamaliel was of the opinion that although there was a total ban on sacrifice in the absence of the Temple, the Passover offering was an exception, and some form of it was obligatory even after the destruction: 'Moreover he [Rabban Gamaliel] gave three opinions applying the more lenient ruling. They may ... prepare a kid roasted whole on Passover night'.[28] This opinion was rejected by the Sages. Thus we can readily understand why Rabban Gamaliel, whether he still ate kid roasted whole or whether it was already forbidden by the rest of the Sages, should choose to discuss the *halakhot* dealing with the Passover offering.

Against this, the central focus of the *Seder* night in Benei Beraq was the narration of the Exodus from Egypt, in other words, the focus was on *midrash.* It may be presumed that the driving force behind this tendency was the local sage, R. Aqiva, who was responsible for the considerable development of the interest in *midrash.* This reaches such a peak that eventually the *aggadah* shows us God Himself sitting and adding crowns to the letters of the *Torah*, so that in generations to come the man named Aqiva b. Joseph can come and expound every jot and tittle.[29] Although R. Aqiva was also an authority in matters of *halakhah*, he preferred to base his *Seder* night on *midrash,* since whereas the *halakhah* was something with which a few individuals could fence themselves in, the *midrash* gave enlightenment to many. The *Seder* night was intended to be a popular festival, which it was possible for every Jew to celebrate in his own home, and for this reason *midrash* was preferred over *halakhah.* Evidence for

27 Mishnah, Pesahim x, 6. Note that the copiers of the Mishnah did not bother to include the words of R. Aqiva in their entirety, as they were well known to everyone from the Passover *Haggadah*.

28 Mishnah, Betzah ii, 7; ib. 'Eduyot iii, 11. It would appear that Rabban Gamaliel actually did this himself, for he instructed his slave Tavi: 'Go and roast the Passover offering for us on the grill' (Mishnah, Pesahim vii, 2. Here there is, after all, some difference from the sacrifice in front of the Temple, which was forbidden to be roasted on the grill, so that it could be roasted by the heat of the fire, and not by the heat of the grill which is hot from the fire [*loc. cit.*, beginning of the Mishnah]). Todos, one of the leaders of the Jewish community in Rome in the Yavneh Period, followed Rabban Gamaliel and 'made it custom among the people in Rome, to sit and eat kids roasted on the grill on Passover night. The Sages sent to him and said: "If you were not Todos, would we not have excommunicated you?" (JT Pesahim vii, 34a). It would seem that this custom, or at least the eating of roasted meat on the *Seder* night, is the basis for the alternative question found in the Mishnah, 'On other nights we eat flesh roast, stewed or cooked, but this night all is roast' (Mishnah, Pesahim x, 4), which in time was changed for the question about reclining (מסובין), which is found in the Passover *Haggadah* of today.

29 BT Menahot 29b.

this is to be found in the fact that the verses chosen to be expounded by *midrash* in the *haggada* are not, as we might expect, a passage from the book of Exodus telling directly of the details of the departure from Egypt. Instead, a passage is taken from the book of Deuteronomy [26:5–8] which includes the 'declaration of the first-fruits', with a reminiscence of the history of the Jewish people, ending with the exodus from Egypt. This passage was an integral part of the ceremony of bringing first-fruits when the Temple still stood. Everyone was obliged to recite it, or have it read for him, so that it was better known than other passages from the *Torah*, which is presumably why it was the passage chosen to be expounded in the Passover *Haggadah,* in order to fulfil the obligation to tell of the departure from Egypt.

The disagreements between Rabban Gamaliel and his companions and between R. Aqiva and his colleagues are also expressed, in literary form at least, at the end of each passage which tells of the actions of the celebrants after dawn breaks. R. Aqiva and his colleagues, who dealt with the narrative of the exodus from Egypt, turn to read the morning *Shema*, in other words, to prayer. Rabban Gamaliel and the Sages with him, who discussed the *halakhot* of Passover, go to the *bet midrash*, in other words to study *Torah*. The stress put on the fact that the *Seder* lasted all night long, but ended when day began, not only acts as a restraint on the precept 'the more one continues to discuss the Exodus, the more he is to be praised', but also establishes that the time appointed for prayer or study limits the length of the *Seder*. This is clear from the *Tosephta,* where the preceding *halakhah* states: 'A man is obliged to discuss the *halakhot* of Passover all night long'[30]. It is clear that this is connected with the time of eating the Passover offering 'until dawn breaks'. There is evidence for this in that R. Eliezer, who differs over the time for eating the Passover offering and lays down that it is only allowed up to midnight, is also of the opinion that the discussion of the *halakhot* of Passover on *Seder* night should only carry on until midnight: 'R. Eliezer said: How do you know that if there was a *havurah* of Sages or their pupils who were obliged to discuss the *halakhot* of Passover until midnight ...'.[31] Eventually R. Eliezer turned from discussion of the *halakhot* of Passover to the relation of the departure from Egypt, and even took part in the *Seder* at Benei Beraq which lasted until the time came for saying the morning *Shema*. Thus it is clear that the type of *Seder* conducted by R. Aqiva and his colleagues at Benei Beraq took the place of the type conducted by Rabban Gamaliel and the Sages who were with him at Lod.[32]

---

[30] Tosephta Pesahim x, 11, ed. Lieberman, p. 198.

[31] For the length of time during which the Passover offering could be eaten, see Mekhilta de-Rabbi Ishmael, Masekhta de-Pisha vi, (ed. Horowitz-Rabin), p. 19; for the opinion of R. Eliezer on the length of time for discussion of the *halakhot* of Passover on the *Seder* night, ib. xviii, (ed. Horowitz-Rabin), p. 74.

[32] This is not the only case where R. Aqiva succeeded in having his opinion preferred over

The sites of these two *Seder* nights in the sources under discussion – in Lod and in Benei Beraq – are also to be noted. It might have been expected that the Sages mentioned in the two episodes, especially Rabban Gamaliel, would have celebrated *Seder* night at Yavneh, where the leadership institutions were sited. This expectation is strengthened by the fact that the leadership institutions of the time used to assemble at Yavneh especially on the three pilgrim festivals, so that we find for example: '(With respect to) this *halakhah*: people from Asia went on pilgrimage on three pilgrim festivals to Yavneh ...'.[33] However, the very fact that Rabban Gamaliel of Yavneh was to be found in places outside the centre is not especially remarkable, for he frequently travelled to different towns and villages to supervise them, and even travelled in the Diaspora. It is probable that these journeys were modelled on the governmental progressions of the Roman Emperor and his governors, who travelled in order to consolidate their authority in the cities of the provinces.[34] On the other hand, we get the impression that Rabban Gamaliel's presence at Lod is not merely a supervisory visit, for not only was he there on *Seder* night, but he was also the owner of a house in Lod.[35] In *Tosephta Pesahim* there is further evidence which may even be connected with the preparations for this very Passover we are discussing (although it could also refer to another occasion):

R. Elazar *be* R. Zadoq said: Once we were sitting before Rabban Gamaliel in the *bet midrash* at Lod, and Zonin his deputy came and said: The time has come to remove the leaven. I went with my father to the house of Rabban Gamaliel and we removed the leaven.[36]

The simple meaning of this incident, which from the context must have happened on a Passover eve which fell on the Sabbath, is that Rabban Gamaliel's house was in Lod, for it is unthinkable that R. Elazar and his father would

---

that of Rabban Gamaliel. It was the same in the case of the Grace after meals (Tosephta Berakhot iv, 15, ed. Lieberman, pp. 21–22; BT Berakhot 37a; cf. JT Berakhot vi, 10b); the setting up of a lamp on a festival (Tosephta Betzah ii, 12, ed. Lieberman, pp. 289–290; and the setting apart of tithes from Samaritan produce (Tosephta Demai v, 24, ed. Lieberman, p. 93).

33 Tosephta Hullin iii, 10; ib. Parah vii, 4; ib. Miqva'ot iv 6.

34 See A. Oppenheimer, 'Rabban Gamaliel of Yavneh and his Travels in the Land of Israel', Sefer Perlman (ed. Z. Rubinsohn), Tel Aviv 1989, pp. 8–18 (Heb.); S. Safrai, 'Visits to Rome by the Sages of Yavneh', Sefer Zikaron le-S. U. Nahon (ed. R. Bonfil *et al.*), Jerusalem 1978, pp. 151–167 (= id. In Times of Temple and Mishnah, II, Jerusalem 1994, pp. 365- 381 [Heb.]); F. Millar, The Emperor in the Roman World, London 1977, pp. 28–40; A.J. Marshall, 'Governors on the Move', Phoenix 20 (1966), pp. 231–246; G.P. Burton, 'Proconsuls, Assizes and the Administration of Justice under the Empire', JRS 65 (1975), pp. 92–106.

35 It is possible that this house was in addition to a house in Yavneh. Similarly Roman governors are known to have had official residences in different cities of a province (see, B. Isaac, The Limits of Empire: The Roman Army in the East, Oxford 1990, pp. 172–173).

36 Tosephta Pesahim iii, 11, ed. Lieberman, p. 154. The parallel source in BT Pesahim 49a has Yavneh instead of Lod, but it is reasonable to assume that the more usual venue was cited here by mistake out of habit.

transgress the laws of the Sabbath in order to go to Yavneh. It is of course possible that Rabban Gamaliel of Yavneh had houses in various places. However, while his home was not necessarily in the settlement where the centre of leadership was sited, it is certain that he owned a house in Lod, which gives greater meaning to his connections there. This fact, and his conducting a *Seder* there, can be added to the series of sources which give evidence of the connections of the leadership institutions with Lod. From these sources it looks as if the leadership institutions were already working alternately in Yavneh and in Lod from the time of Rabban Gamaliel. They certainly moved to Lod in one form or another after his death and after the 'Quietus Uprising' (115–117 CE).[37]

The assembly of Sages at Benei Beraq also tells us of the important status of this settlement, and of the centrality of R. Aqiva who headed the local *bet midrash*. Whereas at Lod there is no mention of the names of the Sages present save for Rabban Gamaliel himself, clearly because of the difference in status between the head of the *Bet ha-Va'ad* and his colleagues, at the *Seder* at Benei Beraq the names of all the participants are noted, all of them well-known Sages of the Yavneh Period. R. Joshua b. Hananiah was R. Aqiva's teacher and headed the local *bet midrash* at Peqi'in, and it was he who gave him ordination as rabbi.[38] R. Eliezer b. Hyrcanus and R. Tarphon both headed the local *bet midrash* at Lod in turn, first R. Eliezer b. Hyrcanus and later R. Tarphon.[39] R. Elazar b. Azaria is mentioned in the middle of the list, and it may well be that he is placed in the centre of his colleagues on purpose, to show that he was the senior among them. This would be the case if this *Seder* night had taken place during the period when Rabban Gamaliel was temporarily displaced as Patriarch, and R. Elazar b. Azariah took his place.[40] These four Sages joined R. Aqiva in Benei Beraq, and there can be no doubt that this is evidence of R. Aqiva's central importance and the status of the institution which he headed and where he taught[41]. The Passover festival as celebrated by these five Sages at

---

[37] For full discussions of the whole subject of the position of Lod, with bibliography, see Oppenheimer's article and Schwartz' book (both in n. 5).

[38] See JT Sanhedrin i, 19a.

[39] Alon has suggested that R. Tarphon even had some sort of position similar to that of the Patriarch during the period between the 'Quietus Uprising' and the Bar Kokhva revolt (117–132CE). At that time the centre appears to have been at Lod, which may have been the reason for the move to Lod (ALON [*supra* n. 3], II, Jerusalem 1984, pp. 465–466; IDEM, 'The Patriarchate of Rabban Jochanan b. Zakkai', Jews and Judaism in the Classical World, Jerusalem 1977, pp. 321–323.

[40] See the Passover *Haggadah,* ed. M. Friedmann, Vienna 1895, pp. 84–85; ib., ed. R. Margulies, Tel Aviv 1946, pp. 24–25.

[41] It is interesting to note that Abarbanel, in his commentary on the *haggadah*, *Zevah Pesah* (Cremona 1557, photo. repr. Benei Beraq 1962), p. 42, objected to the identification of Benei Beraq with the name of a place, and interpreted the expression as meaning that the Sages reclined on glossy silk, *benei* taken as meaning 'articles made of [a certain material]', and *beraq*

Benei Beraq, dominated by the figure of R. Aqiva, was a landmark in the process of creation of the Passover *Haggadah* and the establishment of the widespread popularity of the *Seder* night, then as now.

Various sources give evidence of visits by Sages to Benei Beraq. In the context of a discussion on the permissibility of using the bath house on a sabbath or festival, an incident is related which happened when R. Elazar b. Azariah visited Benei Beraq:

R. Judah said: An incident took place in the bath house of Benei Beraq, when the pipes got blocked on the eve of a festival. R. Aqiva and R. Elazar b. Azariah entered, and used the sweat bath inside, and then bathed in cold water, for the hot water was covered with sawdust. Because many people transgressed the precept, they went back [on their ruling] and forbade it again.[42]

R. Aqiva and R. Elazar b. Azariah thus entered the bath house in Benei Beraq on a festival and used it as a sweat bath. The source notes that before the beginning of the sabbath (or festival) the furnace pipes in the bath house were blocked in such a way as to prevent their heating the water going into the bath house, so that they would not transgress the ban on cooking on the sabbath. The *halakhot* concerning bathing on the sabbath found in the Jerusalem Talmud (n. 42 above] became more and more strict: in the first stage, they even permitted bathing on the sabbath in this sort of situation, but when this permission led to transgression of the sabbath laws there was a second stage, when they permitted the use of the sweat bath only on the sabbath, with bathing in cold water afterwards outside. This is what R. Aqiva and R. Elazar b. Azariah did. In this case there were two further reasons for leniency – firstly, the incident in Benei Beraq happened on a festival, and not on the sabbath, and secondly, the hot water was covered with sawdust. However, in the third stage, as we see from the Jerusalem Talmud (*loc. cit.*) as well as the source under discussion here, going

from *mavriq*, meaning 'shiny or glossy'. There is also an opinion that the *Seder* night at Benei Beraq was a conspiratorial gathering of an underground group at the time of the Roman persecution, in order to plan the Bar Kokhva revolt. This is more or less the approach of I. A. Halevi, who claims in various places in his book *Dorot ha-Rishonim (*part I vol. 5, Frankfurt 1918; photo repr. [vol 3] Jerusalem 1967 [Heb.]) about every source where Sages from the Yavneh period are to be found outside Yavneh, that this was the result of persecution by the Romans. This is claimed to explain why there were no pupils present at the *Seder* night, and why the rabbis (who were in a sort of underground hideout) did not notice the dawn. (See for example Y. L. Hacohen [Fishman] Maimon, 'The Dinner Party at Benei Beraq', *Hagim u-Mo'adim,* Jerusalem 1950, pp. 207–216 [Heb.]). There is also a suggestion by Hershcovitz that the meeting of the rabbis was an anti-Christian trend ('The Meeting at Benei Beraq', *Or ha-Mizrah* 26 [1978], pp. 71–91 [Heb.]; see also ibid, pp. 229–246; 27 [1979], pp. 62–78; 28 [1980], pp. 62–78; 193–205; 332–349; 29 [1981], pp. 404–414; 30 [1982], pp. 75–89 [Heb.]). These explanations have no basis in critical research and are no more than unfounded exegesis.

42 Tosephta Shabbat iii, 3, ed. Lieberman, pp. 11–12; BT Shabbat 40a; cf. JT Shabbat iii, 6a.

into the bath house even just to use the sweat bath was forbidden on both sabbath and festival.[43]

The mark made by R. Aqiva on Benei Beraq is evident not only from the *bet midrash* which he headed, but also from his status as a local leader, in the way in which people turned to him, as to all the leading Sages when they lived in, or simply visited, a particular town or village.[44] In one case which took place in Benei Beraq and is cited in a *baraita* in the Babylonian Talmud, the matter which is brought to R. Aqiva includes the question of decisive evidence in a legal and financial matter, as well as respect for the dead:

An incident which happened at Benei Beraq: A certain man sold his father's property and then died. His family came and raised a query about this, saying: He was a minor when he died. They came and asked R. Aqiva: Is it possible to check him [for signs of maturity]? He said to them: You are not allowed to profane [the dead], and anyway, signs [of maturity] can change after death.[45]

The family of the dead man claimed that he had sold property even though he still had not developed the physical signs of maturity (at least two pubic hairs), so that his action was not valid. Thus they asked permission from R. Aqiva to check his hairs to see if he had attained maturity or not. R. Aqiva rejected the request of the family, who wanted to hold on to the property which had been sold, for two reasons: Firstly the matter did not justify the disgrace to the dead which would be involved; secondly, even after such an examination there would still remain some doubt, as hairs can grow after death.

In another situation R. Aqiva ruled for the local population as to whether to implement the *halakhah* regarding the burial of a child from Benei Beraq who appeared to have committed suicide:

And another incident about a child from Benei Beraq who broke a dish. His father threatened him, and the child was frightened by him and went and committed suicide in a pit. They came to ask R. Aqiva, who said: He should not be deprived of any [burial rites]. From this the Sages stated: A man should not threaten a child but should strike him immediately, or he should keep quiet and not say anything at all to him. R. Shimon b. Elazar says: [In the case of] one's inclination, a child or a woman – let your left hand push them away and your right hand bring them back.[46]

---

43 See Y. Eliav, '*Pyle – Puma – Sefat Medinah*, and a Halacha concerning Bath-houses', Sidra 11 [Heb. Forthcoming].

44 Thus, for example, R. Eliezer b. Hyrcanus and R. Tarphon, who had a *bet midrash* in Lod, lay down *halakhah* on local matters (see for example Tosephta, Ta'anit ii, 5 and parallels; Mishnah, Bava Metzi'a iv, 3). R. Aqiva, who headed the *bet midrash* at Benei Beraq also visited Lod sometimes, and it is possible that he ruled on *halakhah* on one or two local matters that arose there (e.g. Tosephta, Ahilot iv, 2 and parallels).

45 BT Bava Batra 154a; ib. 155a. It is interesting to note that most rabbinical decisions whether of *rishonim* or *aharonim* which deal with the subject of respect for the dead and the ban on profaning them are based on this decision of R. Aqiva's in this source.

46 Masekhet Semahot ii, 5, ed. Higger, pp. 103–104.

The general *halakhah* lays down that 'For a suicide one does not have any [burial rites]'.[47] R. Aqiva tended to leniency in implementing this even for ordinary suicides – as he says about R. Ishmael, who was convinced that it was right to curse a suicide : 'Leave him alone – don't praise him and don't curse him'.[48] In the incident we are looking at, he rules that in this case of a minor who committed suicide he must be treated like someone who died a natural death. The Sages certainly understood that in this specific case there is a form of contributory child-abuse implicit in the father's educational methods. In a similar incident which took place at Lod, R. Tarphon, the head of the local *bet midrash*, ruled the same way for Gorgius who ran away from school and committed suicide in a pit after his father threatened him.[49]

R. Aqiva's *bet midrash* is also mentioned in an incident which took place at the time of the persecutions which followed the Bar Kokhva revolt. It is true that Benei Beraq is not mentioned here by name, but it is most probable that this was in fact the site in question:

R. Meir said: Once we were sitting in the *bet midrash* in front of R. Aqiva and we were reading the *Shema,* but we did not read it aloud because of the *qasdor* who was stationed at the door. They said to him: A time of danger cannot [be used for] evidence.[50]

It would appear that the Romans accepted the fact of Sages meeting in the *bet midrash*, but regarded the reading of the *Shema* as subversive. Lieberman has suggested that the Roman persecutory measures were gradually increased, and from this source we can deduce that the ban on the reading of the *Shema* preceded the ban on meeting to study *Torah.*[51] This source is evidence that R. Aqiva did not always expose himself to danger, even with regard to reading the *Shema,* for which he subsequently died a martyr's death.[52] In this case R. Aqiva and his colleagues were prepared to deviate from the accepted custom of reading the *Shema* aloud, in order not to be arrested by the authorities.[53]

---

47 *Loc. cit.* i, p. 101.

48 *Loc. cit.* p. 102.

49 Ib. iv, p. 103.

50 Tosephta, Berakhot ii, 13, ed. Lieberman, pp. 8–9. In the Erfurt MS the words 'in the *bet midrash*' are missing. Lieberman and the talmudic dictionaries identify *qasdor* as *quaestor,* but in spite of the linguistic similarity it is difficult to accept this identification, for in the period in question the *quaestor* was a highly placed Roman functionary who was responsible for the governor's financial affairs, and there was only one for each province. Moreover, there was no quaestor at Judaea at this period.

51 See S. Lieberman, 'Persecution of the Jewish Religion', S. Baron Jubilee Volume (Hebrew section), Jerusalem 1975, p. 227.

52 JT Sotah v, 20c; ib. Berakhot ix, 14b; cf. BT Berakhot 61b.

53 Even when R. Aqiva was held prisoner in jail, his pupils asked him about matters of *halakhah* in indirect ways through questions with hidden meanings, and his rulings lay down that it is sometimes permissable to deviate from accepted *halakhah* in circumstances of persecutory legislation. Thus, for example, in connection with the leap year (see Tosephta, Sanhedrin ii, 8) or in connection with *halitzah* (JT Yevamot ii, 12d). See A. Oppenheimer,

After the imprisonment and death of R. Aqiva, the *bet midrash* in Benei Beraq ceased to function, but R. Aqiva's status and influence were so great that although the *bet midrash* which he headed was only active for one generation, Benei Beraq became the symbol of a place for studying *Torah*:

The rabbis taught ... The descendants of Sisera studied *Torah* in Jerusalem, the descendants of Sennacherib taught *Torah* in public. Who were these? Shema'iah and Avtalyon. The descendants of Haman studied *Torah* in Benei Beraq.[54]

The context in which the words quoted in this *baraita* were said, shows us that in all cases the intention is to show that at least some of the children of the greatest villains eventually converted to Judaism in the course of time. This much is clear from the descendants of Sennacherib, Shema'iah and Avtalyon. Later versions make R. Aqiva the descendant of Sennacherib who studied *Torah* in Jerusalem with Rav Shmuel bar Shilo (or Shilat) the descendant of Haman who studied *Torah* in Benei Beraq.[55] At any rate, in this legendary source two places which undoubtedly took precedence as places for studying *Torah* are mentioned in one breath with Benei Beraq – Yavneh and Jerusalem.

Benei Beraq continues to be mentioned in talmudic sources which relate to the period after the Bar Kokhva revolt, right up to the end of the tannaitic period. It continues to be a Jewish settlement and it even looks as if there were Sages who lived there, but it is mostly mentioned in connection with the fertility of its soil.

R. Judah ha-Nasi had less need for tours of inspection than his grandfather, Rabban Gamaliel, but even so there are some traditions which connect him with visits to the south, including Lod, which at that time was the only place that could compete to any degree with the centre in Galilee.[56] R. Judah ha-Nasi marvels at the agricultural produce of Benei Beraq when he arrives there on one of his visits: 'Once Rabbi entered Benei Beraq and found a bunch [of

---

'Sanctity of Life and Martyrdom after the Bar-Kokhva Revolt', Sanctity of Life and Martyrdom, eds. I. Gafni and A. Ravitzky, Jerusalem 1992, pp. 85–97.

[54] BT Sanhedrin 96b.

[55] See The Babylonian Talmud with Variant Readings on BT Sanhedrin 96b, s.v. ק, ר, p. 283. Rav Shmuel bar Shilat was a Babylonian *amora* of the first generation (the first half of the third century), and he is mentioned in particular in connection with Rav, the founder of the Academy at Sura. It is of course possible that, like Rav himself, he studied *Torah* in the Land of Israel.

[56] For sources where R. Judah ha-Nasi enacted *halakhah* in Lod see Tosephta, Niddah vi, 3; BT Niddah 47b (there are those who identify 'Diospera', where Rabbi made his ruling, with Diospolis, i.e. Lod [BT Shabbat 46a]). For R. Judah ha-Nasi as present in Lod at the head of a group of Sages and including Ashqelon within the borders of the Land of Israel (which necessitated freeing the city from its impurity as gentile territory, according to R. Pinhas b. Yair), and removing the obligation for tithes, see Tosephta, Ahilot xviii, 18; JT Shevi'it vi, 36c; *op.cit.* Yevamot vii, 8a.

grapes] lying there as big as a three year old calf'.[57] It is likely that this incident from the Jerusalem Talmud is a parallel to the midrashic source, although Benei Beraq is not actually mentioned in it by name:[58]

Rabbi said to R. Periri : Are you not going to show me that bunch [of grapes] in your vineyard? He went out to show it to him, until he thought he could see an ox far away. He said to him: Won't that ox damage your vineyard? He said to him: That ox you think you can see, that is the bunch [of grapes]. And he complained about him [R. Judah ha-Nasi]: 'While the king sitteth at his table, my spikenard sendeth the smell thereof' (Song of Solomon 1:12) – the Temple has been destroyed and do you still persist in your recalcitrance [producing such large and beautiful fruit]? He looked for it at once and could not find it. [R. Periri and his people] brought two radishes to Rabbi between New Year and the Day of Atonement, and it was straight after the Sabbatical Year, and they were the size of a camel's load. He said to him: Aren't these forbidden? Aren't they spontaneous growths? [R. Periri] said to [Rabbi]: They were sown after New Year. Then Rabbi allowed [people] to take greens immediately after the sabbatical year ended.[59]

We should note R. Judah ha-Nasi's ambivalent attitude to the huge bunches of grapes at Benei Beraq, for together with his wonder at the enormous size of the fruit, he shows a tendency to feel that it is not fitting to preen oneself on such magnificent produce as long as the Temple remains in ruins. On the other hand, the huge radishes which sprouted almost overnight serve Rabbi as a sort of catalist for more leniency in the list of rulings which eat into the Sabbatical year, through which he allowed trade in vegetables from the beginning of the eighth year, without their being suspect as spontaneous growths of the sabbatical year.[60]

Behind the legendary layers here there may be a real event which took place. If so, and if it is possible to site it in Benei Beraq, then even in the times of R. Judah ha-Nasi there was an active Sage in Benei Beraq, R. Periri. In the parallel source in JT Bava Batra and in some of the versions in JT Peah, the name is given as R. Perida. A Sage of this name appears together with R. Ammi, in the third generation of *amoraim* in the Land of Israel, in other words three generations after R. Judah ha-Nasi. It is possible that these were two different Sages, one a *tanna* who was active in Benei Beraq in the time of R. Judah ha-Nasi, and the second an *amora* from the third generation of *amoraim* in the

---

[57] Midrash Tannaim on Deuteronomy 26:9, pp. 173–174; Midrash ha-Gadol on Deuteronomy, *loc. cit.*, ed. Fisch p. 589.

[58] See S. KLEIN, 'In search of the large land-tenancy near Lod', S. Krauss Jubilee Volume, Jerusalem 1936, pp. 72–73 (Heb.).

[59] JT Peah vii, 20a–b. For the second incident cf. JT Bava Batra ix, 17a, where it is explicitly stated that R. Periri (or Perida) brought the radishes to Rabbi.

[60] On this subject cf. Mishnah, Shevi'it vi, 4; Tosephta, Shevi'it iv, 17, ed. Lieberman, p. 183. For the whole subject of R. Judah ha-Nasi's rulings relating to the Sabbatical year, see S. SAFRAI, 'The Observances Related to the Sabbatical Year and the Situation after the Destruction of the Second Temple [II]', Tarbiz 36 (1963), pp. 26–37 (Heb.), (= ID., In Times of Temple and Mishnah), II, Jerusalem 1994, pp. 446–457.

Land of Israel. However, since the Talmud itself actually stresses that R. Perida lived to a ripe old age, it is just about possible that this was the same Sage.[61]

Benei Beraq is mentioned once in the days of the *amoraim*, and in this context also in connection with the blessing placed on the agricultural produce of the settlement. Rami bar Yehezkel, a Babylonian *amora* of the second generation of Babylonian *amoraim*, in the second half of the third century, the brother of Rav Judah who founded the academy at Pumbedita, came to Benei Beraq, and gives this pastoral description of the plentiful produce he found there:

> Rami bar Yehezkel happened to come to Benei Beraq, and saw the goats eating under fig [trees]. Honey dropped from the figs and milk dripped from [the goats] and both were mixed together. He said: This is [what was meant by the biblical expression]: 'flowing with milk and honey' (Exodus 3:8 and *passim).*[62]

Since Rami bar Yehezkel visited the Land of Israel, and even stayed there for some time, we can deduce that in various places in the Babylonian Talmud where it says 'And Rami bar Yehezkel arrived',[63] this is a technical term to say that he came from the Land of Israel to Babylonia.

The archaeological investigations at the site of historical Benei Beraq show that settlement there continued during the Byzantine, Early Arab, and Crusader periods, and apparently ceased in the Mameluke period.[64] This paper has not attempted to deal with the population of Benei Beraq and the material aspects of the town, but to concentrate on the teaching centre which existed there in the Yavneh period. It is clear that the *bet midrash* at Benei Beraq was only active for one generation and was centred around the dominant personality of R. Aqiva. At that time some of rulings made there had merely local import, but there were also *halakhot* laid down with wider religious and national implications, such as the structure of the *Seder* night. The general conclusion which we can draw from all this is that even in the days of national leaders as widely influential as Rabban Gamaliel of Yavneh, there was also no small power wielded by the local *batei midrashot* which worked side by side with, and in parallel to the centre.

---

61 For R. Perida's exceptionally long life, see BT Megillah 27b–28a, and q.v. The Babylonian Talmud with Variant Readings, ad loc. for different versions of his name (see too BT 'Eruvin 54b). On the question of whether there are two Sages here or only one, scholarly opinion is divided. There are those who are sure there are two Sages here – see for example Ch. Albeck, Introduction to the Talmud, Jerusalem 1969, p. 262. Others think there is only one Sage – see A. Hyman, Toldot Tannaim ve-Amoraim, III, Jerusalem 1964, pp. 1032–1033.

62 BT Bava Batra 111b; Midrash ha-Gadol on Deuteronomy, vaethanan 6:3, ed. Fisch, p. 125.

63 E.g. BT Ketubot 21b; *ib.* Hullin 44a.

64 Finkelstein (*op. cit.* n. 8), p. 40.

The Function of Minim in Early Rabbinic Judaism

by

Martin Goodman

In the fateful years after 70 C.E. when Yohanan ben Zakkai and a small group of rabbinic sages in Yavneh began to formulate a new theology in reaction to the destruction of the Temple, another pious Jew of similar background, Flavius Josephus, composed a passionate tract in which he tried to define the essential character of Judaism.[1] Among the prime characteristics singled out by Josephus for praise in the *Contra Apionem* was the remarkable unanimity of Jews in their ideas about the nature of God and the correct way to worship him (*C.Ap.* 2. 179–81):

> To this cause above all we owe our admirable harmony. Unity and identity of religious belief, perfect uniformity in habits and customs, produce a very beautiful concord in human character. Among us alone will be heard no contradictory statements about God, such as are common among other nations, not only on the lips of ordinary individuals under the impulse of some passing mood, but even boldly propounded by philosophers; some putting forward crushing arguments against the very existence of God, others depriving Him of His providential care for mankind. Among us alone will be seen no difference in the conduct of our lives. With us all act alike, all profess the same doctrine about God, one which is in harmony with our Law and affirms that all things are under His eye. Even our womenfolk and dependants would tell you that piety must be the motive of all our occupations in life. (Loeb translation).

Doubtless Josephus exaggerated for the sake of his argument, for he asserted in *C.Ap.* that one of the signs that Jewish religious traditions were superior to Greek was the confusing variety of the latter,[2] and he could afford to idealise Judaism because he does not seem to have envisaged any Jewish readers of this work who might have contradicted him.[3] But precisely the importance of this claim in Josephus' apologetic makes implausible any suggestion that it lacked foundation altogether.

---

[1] For studies on Josephus, Contra Apionem, see J.G. Mueller, Des Flavius Josephus Schrift gegen des Apion (1877); L. Troiani, Commento Storico al "Contra Apione" di Giuseppe (1977); K. Keeble, A Critical Study of Flavius Josephus' Contra Apionem (1991).

[2] C.Ap. 2. 164, 172, 250–4.

[3] On the readers at whom C.Apionem was aimed, see P. Bilde, Flavius Josephus (1988), pp. 120–1.

Josephus' assertion of the theological unanimity of the Jews is all the more striking because of his willing confession in each of his three other published works (the *War*, the *Antiquities* and the *Life*) that Judaism embraced at least three distinctive philosophies or tendencies (Pharisaism, Sadduceeism and Essenism), which differed both with regard to practice (i.e. *halakha*) and belief (e.g. about divine intervention in human affairs and life after death).[4] Josephus referred to two of these earlier writings in a number of places in *Contra Apionem*, so he was presumably prepared for his readers to compare his apparently contradictory evaluations of variety within Judaism.[5] It is thus reasonable to assume that he did not himself see his different accounts as contradictory: in some sense, the Jews of these different *haireseis* all agreed on the theological principles fundamental to Judaism. Thus Josephus himself, despite his profession of adherence to the views of the Pharisees in his public life, could write with admiration about other types of Judaism, most notably the Essenes.[6]

Josephus' tolerance of variety within Judaism left only a little space for the concept of heresy. In his eyes there might be bad Jews, like Tiberius Julius Alexander, who lacked piety towards God in so far as he did not stand by ancestral customs,[7] and there might be odd Jews, like Bannus, who espoused distinctive views,[8] but although he wrote critically about the harshness of the Sadducees in their interpretation of the law,[9] he did not condemn them altogether, and although he criticised false prophets for their misleading messages, he did not suggest that their theology of prophecy was itself at fault.[10] The closest he came to condemning one type of Judaism as heresy was in his description of the so-called 'Fourth Philosophy', known only from Josephus' writings and condemned by him as responsible for the outbreak of the disastrous revolt of 66–70.[11]

The question I want to tackle in this paper is why some of Josephus' contemporaries in the nascent rabbinic schools of the land of Israel failed to take the same liberal stance as, in general, he did. I shall try to show that the concept of heresy was assumed by tannaitic rabbis. I shall then discuss the function of this concept in the construction of rabbinic self-identity in this crucial period. Finally I shall suggest possible explanations of the rabbis' attitudes.

---

[4] B.J. 2. 119–66; A.J. 18. 11–22; Vita 10–12.

[5] Cf. C.Ap. 1.1, 47–56.

[6] See G. Vermes and M. Goodman, The Essenes according to the Classical Sources (1989), pp. 34–59.

[7] A.J. 20. 100

[8] Vita 11.

[9] A.J. 20. 199.

[10] See, e.g., R. Gray, Prophetic Figures (1993).

[11] B.J. 2. 118; A.J. 18. 4–10. Cf. M. Hengel, Die Zeloten, 2nd ed., 1976, still the most influential study of this subject since its first publication in 1961.

It will be best to start by saying what I mean by a concept of heresy. The paradigm is the use of the term by Christians from early patristic times to refer to a theological opinion held in opposition to what those Christians considered to be the mainstream Church. Adoption of the concept presupposes both that a mainstream exists and that separation from the mainstream in certain ways is inherently wicked. A heretic is differentiated from an apostate by his claim to present another, better version of a theological system than that found in the mainstream. By contrast, an apostate may simply reject the system, offering nothing else in its place. If Judaism is categorised as a system of covenantal nomism, the distinction between types of sinner should be clear.[12] All Jews are bound by the covenant between God and Israel. Ordinary sinners are those who try to observe the covenant but do so badly; apostates are those who deny the covenant explicitly; heretics are those who (in the eyes of others) break the covenant by wilful misinterpretation of its meaning.

The need to establish that the tannaim had a notion of heresy arises particularly in the light of an influential and important article published by Shaye Cohen rather more than ten years ago.[13] Cohen argued there that the tolerance of variety which I have ascribed to Josephus was in fact found first among rabbis in Yavneh. The "significance of Yavneh", according to this eirenic view, lay in the non-partisan stance of the tannaim, who did not portray themselves as one party (the Pharisees) triumphant over others but rather subsumed variety within one united movement, tolerantly permitting differences on matters of halakha to remain unresolved in the open-ended discussions characteristic of the Mishnah. It will become apparent in the rest of this article that it seems to me that Cohen was right to assert the significance of the non-polemical style of early rabbinic literature, but wrong to suggest that it precluded a rabbinic notion of heresy which must be excluded from their generally welcoming embrace.

The evidence for a rabbinic notion of heresy lies primarily in references to *minim* and *minuth* in tannaitic texts.[14] The term *min* in reference to a deviant Jew is not found often in tannaitic writings, but the contexts in which it is found are sufficiently dissimilar and integral to the argument in each place to make it very unlikely that all such uses are later interpolations.[15] That the terms were

12 On Judaism as a system of covenantal nomism, see E. P. Sanders, Paul and Palestinian Judaism (1977).

13 S. J. D. Cohen, 'The significance of Yavneh', Hebrew Union College Annual 55 (1984), pp. 28–36.

14 Scholarly discussion of these terms has mostly concerned the birkat haminim. On the terms themselves surprisingly little has been written. Cf. D. Sperber, in Encylopaedia Judaica, vol. 12, pp. 1–3; F. Dexinger, 'Die Sektenproblematik in Judentum', Kairos 21 (1979), pp. 273–87.

15 The term min with this meaning is found in the following tannaitic texts: m. Ber. 9:5; m. R. Sh. 2:1; m. Sanh. 4:5; m. Hull. 2:9; t. Ber. 3:25; 6 (7):21 (Lieb.); t. Shab. 13 (14):5 (Lieb.);

significant to the tannaim seems fairly certain. Thus, the fact that the tannaim chose to use a new word of any kind to describe deviants, since the Bible has plenty of Hebrew words for wicked Jews, as did the sectarians at Qumran, demands explanation. Even more striking is the coinage of the term *minuth*, "heresy",[16] since the creation of an abstract noun to denote a religious tendency was not otherwise common in tannaitic texts (for example, there was no abstract noun in Hebrew for Pharisaism or Sadducaism).

That these *minim* were reckoned by the tannaim to be wicked is clear enough from every reference to them, like the chilling remark of R. Shimon b. Eliezer that "one must not repent of a curse, since it was from the repentance of Aaron and Moses that the *minim* separated" (*t. Meg*. 3 (4): 37 (Lieb.). However, it must be admitted that the precise meaning of the word *min* is far from sure. The derivation of the term is uncertain,[17] and the most plausible derivation (from the identical word meaning "kind" or "species") is unhelpful. As with all words, meaning must be deduced from context. In this case the examples to be considered will show that more than one variety of wicked Jew can come within the category of *min*.

The contexts in which references to *minim* are found in tannaitic compilations are rather limited. This is so even when the net is widened from examination solely of *minim* to include those passages in which the manuscripts now have terms other than *min* to denote a religious deviant. It is desirable to allow for terminological variety mainly because many variant readings can be found both in the manuscripts and in printed editions, often because of self-censorship by the editors, with the term *cuthi* (Samaritan) or *saddouki* (Sadducee) or *apikoros* (Epicurean) sometimes substituted for *min*.[18]

What, then, were *minim* said by the *tannaim* to do and say? They were portrayed as healers and miracle workers, as in the story in *t. Hullin* 2: 22–3 of the attempt by Jacob of Cfar Sima to cure R. Eleazar b. Dima of snake bite in the name of Yeshua ben Pantera.[19] They were said to follow a liturgy close to that of the rabbis but different from it in crucial respects, wearing *tefillin* and blessing the Jewish God, but doing both in the wrong way, for example, with the *tefillin* on the palm of the hand, not the forearm (*m. Meg*. 4: 8–9). They have books which look like kosher books and include the divine name (*t. Shabb*. 13 (14):5 (Lieb.)), and they produce meat by a process similar enough to

---

t. Meg. 3 (4):37 (Lieb.); t. B.M. 2:33 (Zuck.); t. Sanh. 8:7; 13:5 (Zuck.); t. Hull. 1:1; 2:20, 24 (in one ms.) (Zuck.); t. Parah 3:3 (Zuck.).

[16] The term minuth is used in m. Meg. 4:8–9; m. Sot. 9:15 (a post-tannaitic interpolation (see below)); t. Hull. 2:24.

[17] On possible derivations of the word min, see R.T. Herford, Christianity in the Talmud and Midrash (1903), pp. 362–5; G.F. Moore, Judaism in the First Centuries, Vol. 3 (1930), pp. 68–9.

[18] Cf. Sperber, in Encyclopaedia Judaica, vol. 12, p. 1.

[19] For the reference here to minuth, see t. Hull. 2:24?

rabbinic *shechita* to risk confusion (t. *Hull*. 1: 1; one of their more suspect habits was the collection of the blood of a slaughtered animal in a hole in the ground (*m. Hull* 2:9)). Finally, they might espouse deviant theological views in various unconnected areas: they might imply that there are two powers in heaven (m. *Meg*. 4:9), by saying "we give thanks" twice in prayer, or that there is no world to come (*m.Ber*. 9: 5; *t. Ber*. 6 (7):21 (Lieb.), or that man had some part in the creation of the world alongside God (t. *Sanh*. 8:7).

The method proposed by tannaitic rabbis to deal with *minuth* was essentially avoidance of contact.[20] Stories about contacts between tannaim and heretics presuppose that heresy might be attractive to rabbis, as in the story about R. Eliezer, who was arrested by a Roman governor on a charge of *minuth* and concluded after heartsearching that he must have suffered because "in Sepphoris I once found Jacob, a man of Cfar Sakhnin, and he said a word of *minuth* in the name of Yeshua ben Pantiri and it pleased me"(t. *Hullin* 2:24). Hence rabbis urged Jews to avoid the books, food and houses of the *minim* (t. *Hullin* 2:20).

Now, if such avoidance was wholly successful, one would expect heresies to have had no effect on the tannaim at all. But injunctions to avoid contact are only needed when contact would otherwise be probable, and we have no evidence that rabbis in the Yavnean period had the power to prevent such contacts, or, indeed, to impose any of their views outside their immediate circle.[21] Thus the tannaitic texts do record a few changes to rabbinic behaviour in reaction to heresy. According to *m. Megillah* 4: 8 there were a few areas of liturgy in which rabbinic Jews were urged to change, or at least control, the precise words used in prayer to avoid the danger of heresy:

"If one say (presumably, from the context, in prayer), "The good (pl.) will bless you", behold, this is the way of *minuth* . . . (if he said) "Thy mercies reach to the nest of a bird" or "May your name be remembered for the good" or "We thank, we thank", they put him to silence" (*m. Megillah* 4:9).

The last of these prohibitions is probably related to the heretical belief found elsewhere in the presence of more than one divine power in heaven,[22] but the reason for the other prohibitions is unclear. According to *m. R.Sh.* 2:1, the rules about taking evidence from witnesses of the appearance of the new moon, an essential element in the fixing of the calendar, were changed "since the *minim* acted perversely", so that "they should not receive evidence except from such as are known". This last reaction to the fear of heresy makes explicit what

---

20 I owe this point to Richard Kalmin, to whom I am grateful for sending me a copy of his study before publication.

21 For my view on these matters, see M. D. Goodman, State and Society in Roman Galilee, A. D. 132–212 (1983), pp. 93–118.

22 See especially A. F. Segal, Two Powers in Heaven (1977).

elsewhere is left implicit. The assumption which lies behind the prohibition in *t. Hullin 2:20* of the meat, wine and sacred books of the *minim* is that conscientious rabbinic Jews would check not just the actions but also the theological views of the butcher and grocer from whom they purchased foodstuffs and the scribe from whom they purchased scrolls of the Torah: in other words, no such purchases should be made except from "such as are known". It may be worth wondering what attitude tannaitic rabbis would have taken to the biblical scrolls in Qumran.

I can see no evidence that in the tannaitic period (i.e. before c. 200 C. E.) the rabbinic reaction to heresy went beyond such attempts by rabbis to protect themselves from quasi-infection. If this is so, and the effect on rabbis of their belief that they were confronted by heretics in the tannaitic period was therefore limited, it is worth asking why this was so. In the history of early Christianity, theology and practice both developed to a large extent through polemic against deviants.[23] St. Paul and heresiologists like Irenaeus advised their flocks on correct action and belief through highly effective rhetoric against specific heresies. Similarly specific polemic can be found among some Jewish sectarians in the Second Temple period, most obviously in the recently published *Miqsat Maasei haTorah* from Qumran, in which is recorded the views of one side in a dispute of two unnamed groups over the correct procedures to be followed by the priests in the Jerusalem temple.[24] In the accounts in tannaitic texts of the clashes between Pharisees and Sadducees before 70, the motivation for action by the Pharisees is specifically stated on occasion to have been the desire to confound the other side: for instance, during the red heifer ceremony, the priest was rendered unclean so that the Sadducees should not be able to claim that the ceremony must be carried out only by "those on whom the sun has set", i.e. the ritually pure (*m. Parah* 3: 7).[25]

By contrast, tannaitic rabbis do not seem to have been concerned much of the time either to analyse the precise constituents of *minuth* or to define their own views in contrast to heresies. It is notorious that in the Babylonian Talmud the *minim* disparaged by rabbis seem *sometimes* to have been gentiles, and specifically gentile Christians, rather than deviant Jews.[26] The same is also true of the assertion in *m. Sotah* 9:15 that "when the Messiah comes ... the empire will fall into *minuth*", which seems so transparent a reference to the Roman empire

---

[23] See, for example, E. P. SANDERS et al., Jewish and Christian Self-Definition (1980–82). One of the corollaries of the present study is that transfer of the same assumptions to self-definition by rabbinic Jews may be mistaken.

[24] E. Qimron and J. STRUGNELL, Discoveries in the Judaean Desert, vol. 10 (1994).

[25] For a discussion of the possible motivation behind these actions by the Pharisees, see M. D. GOODMAN, Mission and Conversion: Proselytizing in the religious history of the Roman Empire (1994), pp. 171–2.

[26] Cf. b. Pesahim 87b. See J. NEUSNER, Judaism and Christianity in the Age of Constantine (1987).

after Constantine that it must surely be a post-tannaitic interpolation. It is probably a mistake to indulge with the many ingenious scholars who have hunted for a precise referent for each rabbinic text in which heretics were attacked: the very fact that *minim* have been identified, in different passages, with Jewish Christians, Gnostics, Hellenistic Jews, Sadducees and others constitutes evidence that the rabbis who compiled these rabbinic documents used the term in a vague way.[27] The contrast to the prurient details in the writings of Christian heresiologists is striking. Despite their general interest in the classification of phenomena in the world about them the rabbis do not seem from the extant evidence to have been concerned to define *minim* or *minuth*; it was enough that the general category existed.

It should be clear that I do not believe that the attitudes of the rabbis can be explained, as it was by Shaye Cohen, in terms of the liberal outlook of the tannaim, because the rabbis were not liberal (unlike Josephus), just *vague* about the content of the heresies they condemned. Rabbis could be horrible to each other (as in disputes over the calendar, in which opposition might be publicly crushed by, for instance, R. Joshua ben Hananiah being made to appear before Rabban Gamaliel carrying his staff and purse on what he (Joshua) believed to be the Day of Atonement).[28] What looks like a liberal attitude by the rabbis of the Mishnah in apparently leaving halakhic disputes open may simply reflect the genesis of the Mishnah as a compilation of the views of jurists rather than a law code.[29]

It may be that a better explanation for the tannaitic attitude to *minim* lies in what Sacha Stern has described, perhaps unfairly, as the solipsism of the rabbis, the tendency to think about their Jewishness almost entirely in terms of the life of an adult male rabbinic Jew.[30] Rather than attack heretical Jews, the tannaim preached that heretics should be ignored. It may simply be that to a considerable extent they practised what they preached. Thus I have argued elsewhere that, for all we know, Sadducees and Essenes may have flourished long into the amoraic period; the fact that rabbis hardly talked about them does not imply their non-existence.[31] An examination of the nonsense enshrined in the comments of early rabbis about contemporary pagan cultic practices will show how little attention they paid to the world around them: the flourishing paganism revealed by inscriptions and archaeological excavation in the Decapolis and coastal cities apparently hardly impinged on the rabbis who produced the

[27] See. for example, R.T. Herford, Christianity in Talmud and Midrash, pp. 365–8; W. Horbury, 'The Benediction of the Minim', Journal of Theological Studies (1982), pp. 19–61.

[28] m. R. Sh. 2:8–9. Cf. also the excommunication of R. Eliezer b. Hyrcanus.

[29] On different theories about the purpose of the Mishnah, see now G. Stemberger, Einleitung in Talmud und Midrasch, 8th ed. (1992), pp. 113–52.

[30] S. Stern, Jewish Identity in Early Rabbinic Writings (1994), pp. 215–23.

[31] M.D. Goodman, 'Sadducees and Essenes after 70 C.E.', in S.E. Porter, P. Joyce and D.E. Orton, eds., Crossing the Boundaries. Festschrift Goulder (1994), pp. 347–56.

Mishnah and Tosefta in neighbouring Galilee in the second and third centuries.[32]

What, then, was the function of the concept of *minuth* in early rabbinic Judaism? There is no evidence that it served to hound out of the fold particular deviants whose continued presence was believed to threaten the health of the body politic of Judaism. Nor is there evidence that it served to define correct behaviour for rabbinic Jews by clarifying what was forbidden in thought or deed. The categories of Israel excluded from a share in the life to come according to *m. Sanhedrin* 10:1–3 (where *minim* are not mentioned) were impracticably vague: one category, for instance, was of those who read the "outside books", but the Mishnah neither defines such books nor states how much they must be perused for an otherwise good Jew to forfeit the world to come.

It is hardly likely that a solution to the problem will easily emerge; it may be enough simply to have shown that the problem exists. It may be that the vagueness of rabbinic references to *minim* results simply from the loss of much of the tannaitic tradition. It is entirely possible, for example, but unprovable, that a tannaitic tractate entitled *Minim* once existed within a much wider literature but failed to be preserved. In that case, vague allusions elsewhere in tannaitic texts will once have been clarified in the tractate dedicated to the subject. Alternatively, the vagueness of terminology may show not a lack of rabbinic interest in *minim* but simply the scarcity of rabbinic comment: the rabbis may have known exactly what they meant but just happened not to tell us.

Hence my own preferred explanation of the vagueness of the rabbinic conception of heresy is only a possibility: I do not know that it can be shown to be more plausible than other explanations, but it is, I think, no less possible, and it has the advantage that it coincides with the standard concerns of rabbinic discourse.

I suggest that the concept of *minuth* may have stemmed originally not from the practical need to deal with heretics but from a theoretical consideration of the impact on rabbinic thought of a category of Jews whose theology or behaviour placed them outside the covenant between God and Israel. For the rabbis, the *minim* will therefore have been an intellectual counterpart to the *tumtum* or *androgynos*.[33] What interested the rabbis was the way that contact between such *minim* and rabbinic Jews might affect the lives of rabbinic Jews. In this respect, rabbinic concerns about the *minim* ran parallel to their explora-

---

32 For a compilation of their statements, see M. HADAS-LEBEL, 'Le paganisme à travers les sources rabbiniques des IIe et IIIe siècles: contribution à l'étude de syncrétisme dans l'empire romain', ANRW II. 19.2 (1979), pp. 397–485.

33 On the tumtum, see Encylopaedia Judaica, vol. 2, p. 949 (s.v. 'androgynos'). It is characteristic of rabbinic discourse that all minim were treated by the tannaim as male.

tion of the impact of women of different statuses on the adult male rabbinic Jew.[34] The main difference was that the rabbis could not avoid contact with women, and the result was the whole order *Nashim* of the Mishnah, Tosefta and Talmuds. It was much easier in practice to avoid heretics, and that is precisely what the tannaim tried to do. That, I suggest, may be sufficient to explain the minimal *halacha* about *minim* in the rabbinic texts which survive. The best way to deal with a potential problem is often simply to ignore it.

Bibliography

BILDE, P., Flavius Josephus between Jerusalem and Rome: his life, his works, and their importance. Journal for the Study of the Pseudepigrapha Supp. Ser. 2). Sheffield. 1988.

COHEN S. J. D., 'The significance of Yavneh', HUCA 55 (1984), pp. 28–36.

DEXINGER, F., 'Die Sektenproblematik im Judentum', Kairos 21 (1979), pp. 273–87.

GOODMAN, M. D., State and Society in Roman Galilee, A. D. 132–212. (Totowa, N. J. 1983).

–, 'Sadducees and Essenes after 70 C. E.', in S. E. PORTER, P. JOYCE and D. E. ORTON, eds., Crossing the Boundaries: Essays in Biblical Interpretation in Honour of Michael D. Goulder (Leiden, 1994), pp. 347–56.

–, Mission and Conversion: Proselytizing in the religious history of the Roman Empire. Oxford, 1994.

GRAY, R. Prophetic Figures in Late Second Temple Jewish Palestine: the evidence from Josephus. New York and Oxford, 1993.

HADAS-LEBEL, M., 'Le paganisme à travers les sources rabbiniques des IIe et IIIe siècles: contribution à l'étude de syncrétisme dans l'empire romain', ANRW II.19.2 (1979), pp. 397–485.

HENGEL, M., Die Zeloten. Untersuchungen zur jüdischen Freiheitsbewegung in der Zeit von Herodes I. bis 70 n. Chr. 2nd ed., Leiden, 1976.

HERFORD, R. T., Christianity in Talmud and Midrash, London, 1903.

HORBURY, W., 'The Benediction of the Minim', Journal of Theological Studies, 33(1982), pp. 19–61.

KEEBLE, K., A Critical Study of Flavius Josephus' Contra Apionem. Oxford, M. Phil. thesis, 1991.

MOORE, G. F., Judaism in the First Centuries of the Christian Era: the age of theTannaim. 3 vols. Cambridge, Mass., 1927–30.

MUELLER, J. G., Des Flavius Josephus Schrift gegen des Apion. *Text und Erklärung*. Ed. C. J. Riggenbach and C. von Orelli. Basel, 1877.

NEUSNER, J., Judaism and Christianity in the Age of Constantine: History, Messiah, Israel, and the initial confrontation. Chicago, 1987.

QIMRON, E. and STRUGNELL, J., Discoveries in the Judaean Desert. Vol. 10: Qumran Cave 4: V Miqsat Maʿase ha-Torah. Oxford, 1994.

SANDERS, E. P., Paul and Palestinian Judaism: a comparison of patterns of religion. Philadelphia, 1977.

[34] See J. R. WEGNER, Chattel or Person? The status of women in the Mishnah (1988).

SANDERS, E. P. et al., Jewish and Christian Self-Definition. 3 vols. London, 1980–82.

SEGAL, A. F., Two Powers in Heaven: Early rabbinic reports about Christianity and Gnosticism. Leiden, 1977.

SPERBER, D., 'Min' in Encylopaedia Judaica, vol. 12 (Jerusalem, 1971), pp. 1–3.

STEMBERGER, G., Einleitung in Talmud und Midrasch. 8th ed., Tübingen, 1992.

STERN, S., Jewish Identity in Early Rabbinic Writings. Leiden, 1994.

TROIANI, L., Commento Storico al "Contra Apione" di Giuseppe. Pisa, 1977.

VERMES, G. and GOODMAN, M., The Essenes according to the Classical Sources. Sheffield, 1989.

WEGNER, J. R., Chattel or Person? The Status of Women in the Mishnah. New York and Oxford, 1988.

Die innerrabbinische Überlieferung von Mischna Abot[1]

von

Günter Stemberger

Spätestens seit dem Mittelalter ist Abot der populärste Traktat der Mischna und ist dies bis heute geblieben[2]. Die Aufnahme ins Gebetbuch hat dazu besonders beigetragen, zugleich auch die Textgestalt des Traktats – nicht nur durch Hinzufügung eines sechsten Kapitels – stark beeinflußt[3]. Innerhalb der Mischna ist der Traktat einzigartig, allein nicht gesetzlich orientiert, sondern der Tradition der Spruchweisheit verbunden. Oft gilt dies als Hinweis auf frühe Entstehung zumindest eines Kerns des Traktates[4], der dann auch gerne als Dokument des Pharisaismus betrachtet wird[5]. Die Traditionskette von Abot und die Brüche ihrer chronologischen Abfolge dienen oft als Kriterium der Quellenscheidung[6], ebenso der Vergleich mit dem Basistext der beiden Fassungen von Abot deRabbi Natan[7]. Andererseits wird oft die These vertreten, daß Abot erst etwa hundert Jahre nach der Mischna als Apologetik für deren

---

[1] Der Beitrag entstand im Rahmen des Forschungsprojekts Lengua y Literatura del Judaísmo Clásico der Universität Granada unter Leitung von Prof. M. Pérez-Fernández. Eine erste Fassung wurde am 28. 4. 1995 in Granada vorgetragen.

[2] Siehe M.B. Lerner, The Tractate Avot, in: S. Safrai, Hg., The Literature of the Sages (CRINT II/3) I, Assen/Maastricht 1987, 263–276; S. Sharvit, The Textual Criticism of Tractate Avot, ibid. 277–281.

[3] S. Sharvit, The Custom of Reading Abot on the Sabbath and the History of the Baraitot Associated Therewith (hebr.), Bar-Ilan 13 (1976) 169–187.

[4] I.B. Gottlieb, Pirqe Abot and Biblical Wisdom, VT 40 (1990) 152–164, p. 162: „the earliest of the sayings in Abot may not have been far removed in time from Ben Sira or even from parts of biblical Wisdom". Zur Verbindung mit der Weisheitstradition siehe auch M. Küchler, Frühjüdische Weisheitstraditionen (OBO 26), Freiburg-Göttingen 1979, 176–198; K. Berger, Neutestamentliche Texte im Lichte der Weisheitsschrift aus der Geniza von Alt-Kairo, ANRW 26,1, Berlin-New York 1992, 412–428.

[5] So z.B. R. Travers Herford, The Ethics of the Talmud: Sayings of the Fathers, New York 1962 (= ^{3}1945), 14: „Aboth as a document of Pharisaism".

[6] A.J. Saldarini, The End of the Rabbinic Chain of Tradition, JBL 93 (1974) 97–106; M.D. Herr, Continuum in the Chain of Torah Transmission (hebr.), Yitzhak F. Baer Memorial Volume (Zion 44), Jerusalem 1980, 43–56.

[7] L. Finkelstein, Introductory Study to Pirke Aboth, JBL 57 (1938) 13–50; ders., Mabo le-Massekhtot Abot we-Abot de-Rabbi Natan, New York 1950.

Autoritätsanspruch entstand und an Neziqin als die letzte in Palästina regulär studierte Ordnung angeschlossen wurde. Diese These geht i.w. auf einen Aufsatz von A. Guttmann[8] zurück, dessen Rezeption allerdings fast nur auf diesen Punkt – die Verbindung von Abot mit der Mischna um 300 – beschränkt blieb; seine Spätdatierung der Traditionskette als späterer Zusatz zur Mischna wurde dagegen m.W. kaum diskutiert, noch weniger die Grundlage seiner Argumentation, nämlich die Verwendung von Abot in beiden Talmudim.

Ein Weg, die Stellung von Abot innerhalb der Mischna bzw. das Verhältnis zu dieser genauer zu bestimmen, wäre eine sprachliche Analyse des Traktats im Vergleich mit der übrigen Mischna, die trotz der Arbeiten von E.Z. Melammed[9] noch nicht allzu weit gekommen ist; ein anderer ist die systematische Weiterführung der Fragestellung Guttmanns, wieweit der Traktat in der rabbinischen Tradition bekannt war und verwendet wurde; über explizite Zitate hinaus sind dabei auch Redewendungen und Phrasen von Abot zu beachten. Darum geht es im folgenden Beitrag[10].

1. Parallelen in der Mischna

Echte *Parallelen* zu Sätzen und Phrasen von Abot gibt es in der Mischna fast nur in Abot selbst. Das ist auffällig; denn andere Traktate sind durch zahlreiche Parallelen mit dem Gesamtwerk verbunden. Abot berührt sich mit der übrigen Mischna inhaltlich und in Redewendungen nur selten. Am ehesten können drei Texte als Parallelen gelten:

1,4–12: Zehn Namen der Traditionskette von Abot (von Jose ben Joezer bis Schammai) begegnen in derselben Reihenfolge in Chag 2,2 (Diskussion um die Erlaubtheit eines Opferritus am Feiertag); Chag kommentiert: „die ersten waren Patriarchen, die zweiten Vorsitzende des Gerichts". Diese Bemerkung hat keine Basis in Abot; Abhängigkeit einer Stelle von der andern, ganz gleich in welcher Richtung, ist nicht belegbar.

---

[8] A. Guttmann, Tractate Abot – Its Place in Rabbinic Literature, JQR 41 (1950f) 181–193 (= ders., Studies in Rabbinic Judaism, New York 1976, 102–114).

[9] E.Z. Melammed, Essays in Talmudic Literature (hebr.), Jerusalem 1986, 212–252.

[10] Aus methodischen Gründen müssen die beiden Fassungen von Abot de-Rabbi Natan beiseite bleiben. Siehe dazu M. Kister, Avot de-Rabbi Nathan. Studies in Text, Redaction and Interpretation (hebr.), Diss. Jerusalem 1993. Wie andere vor ihm betont er, daß Arn (in beiden Fassungen) einen früheren Text von Abot als den unserer Mischna voraussetzt. Er rechnet mit Anfängen von ARN in tannaitischer Tradition, die jetzige Form beider Fassungen sei aber irgendwo in der Mitte zwischen 5. und 9. Jh. anzusetzen (p. 217). Nicht systematisch ausgewertet wurden die fragmentarischen halakhischen Midraschim (Mekhilta de R. Simeon ben Jochai; Sifre Zutta; Midrasch Tannaim); Belege aus den kleinen Traktaten und späten Midraschim sind so häufig, daß eine volle Darbietung nicht mehr sinnvoll ist.

2,13: „R.Simeon sagt ... Und wenn du betest, mach dein Gebet nicht wie Festgesetztes, sondern Bittflehen vor dem Ort, gepriesen sei er“; in Ber 4,4 sagt R. Eliezer: „Wer sein Gebet wie Festgesetztes macht, dessen Gebet ist nicht Bittflehen“. Die Talmudim kommentieren nur die Fassung von Ber 4,4.

5,4 spricht von „unseren Vätern in der Wüste“ und zitiert dazu Num 14,22; ebenso Ar 3,5; doch unterscheidet sich die Art der Anwendung.

Mit der übrigen Mischna *gemeinsame Redewendungen* sind selten: „schlechtes Wasser“ (1,11; Chul 3,5); „und es ergibt sich, daß der Name des Himmels entweiht wird“ (1,11; Sanh 6,4); „leichtes Gebot“ (2,1; 4,2; Chul 12,5); *talmud tora* (2,2; Pea 1,1 u.ö.); „verwirkt sein Leben“ (3,4.7.8.10; BQ 3,10); „sie haben etwas, worauf sie sich stützen können“ (3,16, fehlt aber in MS Kaufmann; Chag 1,8); „in vier Zeitabschnitten“ (5,9; RH 1,2). Der übliche Text von 5,7 „Größer als er an Weisheit und Zahl“ findet sich auch in Ed 1,5, doch ist hier der Text von Abot sekundär angepaßt; in MS Kaufmann fehlt „an Weisheit und Zahl“, in anderen Textzeugen „an Zahl“. Mit 5,8 „Todesstrafen ... die nicht dem Gericht übergeben wurden“ vgl. Sanh 7,1 „Vier Todesstrafen wurden dem Gericht übergeben“.

Nicht einmal die populärsten Redewendungen von Abot (wie z.B. „Zaun um die Tora“, „die Tora empfangen“, „Joch der Tora“, „Verdienst der Väter“) begegnen in der übrigen Mischna (auch *derekh erets*, fünfmal in Abot, findet sich sonst nur in Qid 1,10 zweimal). Alle Wörter aufzulisten, die in der Mischna nur in Abot vorkommen, würde zu weit führen; da es sich nicht um technisches Vokabular wie bei einzelnen Sachkomplexen der Halakha handelt, ist die Tatsache sicher bemerkenswert. Verglichen mit dem Rest der Mischna macht Abot den Eindruck, eine Welt für sich zu sein.

2. Parallelen in der Tosefta

Ein wenig, doch nicht viel mehr erbringt ein Vergleich von Abot mit der Tosefta. Die längste wörtliche Parallele haben Ab 3,10 und tBer 3,3 (L. 12, R. 17) gemeinsam: „Er pflegte zu sagen: Jeder, an dem die Geschöpfe Wohlgefallen haben, an dem hat auch Gott Wohlgefallen. Und jeder, an dem die Geschöpfe kein Wohlgefallen haben, an dem hat auch Gott kein Wohlgefallen“. Doch ist nach dem Kontext der Tosefta R. Aqiba und nicht R. Chanina ben Dosa der Sprecher.

Kürzere Parallelen sind:

2,5 „Ein Ungebildeter ist nicht sündenscheu“; tBer 6,18 (L. 38, R. 52) nennt das als Begründung dafür, daß man im Morgengebet dankt, kein Ungebildeter zu sein. Der Erstdruck führt die Parallele fort: „und ein Am ha-arets nicht fromm“, offensichtlich aus Abot übernommen.

3,11 „... wer den Bund rückgängig macht und wer sich gegen die Tora frech verhält ... keinen Anteil an der kommenden Welt“. Was hier Teil einer längeren Aussage des R. Eleazar von Modiin ist, findet sich in tSanh 12,9 (Z. 433) als anonyme Ergänzung von Sanh 10, wer keinen Anteil an der kommenden Welt hat. In den anderen Teilaussagen gibt es keine Entsprechung.

4,16 „Diese Welt gleicht einem Vorraum vor der kommenden Welt ... in den Speisesaal“; tBer 6,21 (L. 39; R. 54) begründet eine Gebetsformel damit, daß „diese Welt vor der kommenden Welt wie ein Vorraum vor dem Speisesaal ist“. R. Jakob, in Abot der Sprecher, kommt hier nicht vor.

5,6 „Auch die Zange wird mit einer Zange gemacht“; der hier anonyme Satz kommt tEr 8,23 (L. 138) und tChag 1,9 (L. 379) im Namen des R.Jehoschua in Aramäisch (ebenso MekS zu 16,32, E.-M. 115 im Namen R. Jehudas)!

5,7 „Sieben Dinge sind am Ungebildeten (*golem*) und sieben am Weisen“. Laut tSanh 7,10 (Z. 427) soll man an einer Diskussion erst teilnehmen, wenn man weiß, worum es geht. „Darüber ist gesagt: Sieben Dinge sind am Ungebildeten“. Allein MS Erfurt ergänzt, wohl aus Abot: „und sieben am Weisen“. Es folgen keine Details, die Fortsetzung gilt wohl als bekannt. Doch die Phrase „fragt sachlich“ (*scho'el ke-ᶜinjan*) findet man auch in tSanh 7,7 (Z. 426) und die Wendung „sagt zum Ersten Erstes und zum Letzten Letztes“ in tSota 6,11 (L. 190), hier in der 1. Person. Direkte Abhängigkeit von Abot ist kaum anzunehmen.

5,18 „Jeder, der die Allgemeinheit zu Verdiensten führt, fällt nicht in Sünde. Und jeder, der die Allgemeinheit zur Sünde verführt, dem gibt man keine Gelegenheit, Buße zu tun“. In tJoma 4,10f (L. 253) findet sich der Text wörtlich; nur statt „fällt nicht in Sünde“ steht „dem gibt man keine Gelegenheit zur Übertretung“, formuliert also parallel zum zweiten Satz; auch fügt die Tosefta eine Begründung an, gestützt auf einen Bibelvers, wie dann auch nach dem zweiten Teil.

Außerdem findet man einige wenige *gemeinsame Redewendungen*: „nach der guten Seite“ (*le-khaf zekhut*: 1,5; tQid 1,13, L. 281); „und es ergibt sich, daß der Name des Himmels entheiligt wird“ (1,11; tSota 5,12, L. 180f); „freundlich empfangen“ (*meqabbel be-seber panim jafot*: 1,15; tSanh 9,3, Z. 428f); *talmud tora* (2,2; tPea 1,1, L.41, u. ö.); *derekh erets* (2,2 u. ö.; tSchebi 4,2, L. 179; tQid 1,17, L. 281; tSota 7,20, L. 199); „Verdienst der Väter“ (2,2; tBB 7,9, L. 154); „verwirkt sein Leben“ (3,4.7f.10; tAZ 6,17, Z. 471 zweimal); „sie haben etwas, worauf sie sich stützen können“ (3,16, nicht in MS Kaufmann; tEr 8,24, L.139); „die wesentlichen Halakhot“ (*gufe halakhot*: 3,18; tEr 8,24, L. 139; tChag 1,9, L. 379); „zu lernen, zu lehren, zu beachten und zu tun“ (4,5; tSota 8,10, L. 207f; ebenso SNum § 115, H. 126).

A. Guttmann schloß aus dem Fehlen einer Tosefta zu Abot, daß die Tosefta vor Aufnahme des Traktats in die Mischna, also vor 300, redigiert worden sein muß[11]. Das vereinfacht das Problem zu sehr (sollte das etwa für Tamid, Middot und Qinnim gelten, die auch keine Tosefta haben?); doch dürfte die geringe Zahl von Berührungen zwischen den beiden Werken, und das trotz der im Vergleich zur Mischna viel größeren Offenheit der Tosefta für haggadische Themen, es sehr wahrscheinlich machen, daß der Redaktor der Tosefta Abot nicht gekannt hat.

3. Halakhische Midraschim

Folgende *Parallelen* größeren oder kleineren Umfangs lassen sich feststellen:

1,1 „... den Männern der Großen Versammlung. Sie sagten drei Dinge: Seid zurückhaltend im Gericht; und stellt viele Schüler auf; und macht einen Zaun um die Tora". Die drei Sätze finden sich mit der Einleitung „und so pflegten die Männer der Großen Versammlung zu sagen" wörtlich in SDtn § 16 (F. 25), ebenso in Mek Pischa 6 (H.-R. 19), hier eingeleitet „um die Worte der Männer der Großen Versammlung zu erfüllen, die zu sagen pflegten".

1,6 „Beurteile jeden Menschen nach der guten Seite". Der hier R. Jehoschua ben Perachja zugeschriebene Satz ist in Sifra Qedoschim 4 (W. 89a) anonymer Kommentar zu Lev 19,15.

3,6 spricht R.Chalafta ben Dosa von der Gegenwart der Schekhina bei zehn Leuten, die sich mit der Tora befassen, bei fünf, drei, zwei und einem. Mek Bachodesch 11 (H.-R. 243) bringt anonym einen fast identischen Text: „Von daher sagten sie: Wenn immer zehn Menschen in die Synagoge kommen, ist die Schekhina mit ihnen, denn es heißt: ‚Gott steht in der Versammlung der Götter' (Ps 82,1)"; daß in Abot nicht von der Synagoge, sondern vom Studium der Tora die Rede ist, entspricht der allgemeinen Tendenz des Traktats. Auch die Fortsetzung folgt fast wörtlich und mit denselben Belegtexten; nur der Abschnitt über fünf fehlt.

3,11, wovon ein kleines Stück schon anonym in tSanh 12,9 vorkam, findet sich weitgehend in SNum § 112 (H. 121) als Kommentar zu Num 15,31: „‚Das Wort des Herrn hat er verachtet', das ist, wer sich gegen die Tora frech verhält; ‚und sein Gesetz gebrochen', das ist, wer den Bund des Fleisches rückgängig macht. Von daher sagte R. Eleazar von Modiin: Wer das Heilige entweiht und die Festzeiten verachtet und wer den Bund unseres Vaters Abraham rückgängig macht, auch wenn in seiner Hand viele Gebote sind, verdient er es, daß man ihn aus der Welt verstößt". Bis einschließlich „Hand" ist der Text wörtlich gleich Abot, das mit anderen Worten dasselbe sagt; einzig die schon zuvor gebrachte Wendung *ha-megalle panim ba-Tora* kommt an ihrer Stelle nicht mehr (wohl aber in MS Vat. 32) und die Klausel „wer seinen Nächsten öffent-

---

[11] A. Guttmann, Tractate Abot 188.

lich beschämt“ (die aber auch in Abot-MSS textlich variiert) fehlt. Aus der Zitatformel *mikan amar* ist klar, daß man auf einen festen Text zurückgreift, doch muß das nicht unbedingt Abot sein[12]. Eine kleinere Teilparallele findet sich auch in SNum § 111 (H. 116): Wie jemand, der alle Gebote übertritt, das Joch abwirft „und den Bund rückgängig macht und sich gegen die Tora frech verhält“, so auch, wer nur ein Gebot übertritt (ebenso Mek Pischa 5, H.-R. 15).

4,13 „R.Simeon sagt: Es gibt drei Kronen, die Krone der Tora und die Krone des Priestertums und die Krone des Königtums“. Der Satz findet sich anonym, eingeleitet mit „So kannst du sagen“ (*nimtseta omer*), in SNum § 119 (H. 144).

4,17 Der Satz R.Jakobs „Schöner ist eine Stunde in Buße und guten Werken in dieser Welt als das ganze Leben der kommenden Welt“ hat zwar keine direkte Parallele, doch eine gewisse Ähnlichkeit in SDtn § 29 (F. 47): „Von da pflegte R. Eliezer ben Jakob zu sagen: Schöner ist ein(e Stunde im) Gebet als hundert gute Werke“.

5,4 „Zehn Wunder geschahen unseren Vätern in Ägypten und zehn am Meer“ ist parallel zu Mek Beschallach 4 (H.-R. 100): „Zehn Wunder geschahen Israel am Meer“.

5,6 „Zehn Dinge wurden (am Vorabend des Sabbat) in der Dämmerung geschaffen“[13]. Der Satz ist ein Theologumenon, auf das die halakhischen Midraschim mehrfach verweisen: „Das ist eines von den zehn Dingen, (die am Vorabend des Sabbat) in der Dämmerung geschaffen wurden. Das sind sie ...“ (Mek Wajassa 5, H.-R. 171; MekS zu 16,32, E.-M. 115; SDtn § 355, F. 418; MTann zu 33,21, H. 219 aus MHG Dtn F. 772). Die Liste ist nicht einheitlich, beginnt jedoch in den Midraschim immer mit dem Regenbogen, nicht mit dem Mund der Erde wie in Abot. Auch noch die Parallele bPes 54a weicht von Abot stark ab, dessen Reihe erst in PRE 18,1 (fast) erreicht wird[14].

5,9 spricht von vier Zeitabschnitten, in denen sich die Pest ausbreitet; die dabei genannte Sequenz „im vierten (Jahr) wegen des Armenzehnten im dritten, im siebten wegen des Armenzehnten im sechsten“ findet sich wörtlich in SDtn § 109 (F. 169; ebenso MTann H. 174) in einer Kommentierung von MaasSch 5,6 (Fortschaffen der Feldfrüchte), eingeführt mit „von daher sagen sie“.

5,15 über verschiedene Schüler hat eine gewisse Parallele in SDtn § 48 (F. 110); der Vergleich mit einem „Schwamm, der alles aufsaugt“ kehrt hier wörtlich wieder.

Damit ist der Durchgang auch durch diese Schriftengruppe abgeschlossen.

---

[12] K.G. Kuhn, Der tannaitische Midrasch Sifre zu Numeri (Rabbinische Texte II/3), Stuttgart 1959, 793–810, plädiert für die SNum-Fassung als älteste und beste.

[13] Im von A. Katsh, Ginze Mishna, Jerusalem 1970, 119 veröffentlichten Geniza-Text fehlt Ab 5,6 völlig; „am Vorabend des Sabbat“ fehlt in MSS Kaufmann, Parma, Cambridge.

[14] Zur Zehnerreihe siehe F. Böhl, Das Wunder als Bedingung und die Schöpfung in der Abenddämmerung, WO 8 (1975), 77–90.

Der Wert der Parallelen ist unterschiedlich; eine wörtliche Parallele mit gleichem Autor ist die Ausnahme (1,1; 3,11 annähernd wörtlich); wörtliche Parallelen ohne Autor sind zu 1,6 und 4,13 zu finden; eine breite Parallele in Thema und Aufbau gibt es zu 3,6. Auch 5,6 über die zehn in der Dämmerung geschaffenen Dinge findet breite Entsprechung. Es ist hier nicht der Platz, die Parallelen traditionsgeschichtlich zu untersuchen. Doch dürfte klar sein, daß man an keiner einzigen Stelle annehmen muß, daß die halakhischen Midraschim von Abot und nicht von einer gemeinsamen Tradition abhängen.

Die Umschau in der gesamten frühen rabbinischen Literatur[15] (wobei bekanntlich die Datierung von Tosefta und halakhischen Midraschim noch immer umstritten ist) ergibt somit, daß nur ein kleiner Teil von Abot Parallelen in der in weitestem Sinn gleichzeitigen rabbinischen Literatur hat. Auch die typischen Redewendungen von Abot, die in späterer Literatur oft sehr beliebt werden, sind sehr dürftig belegt. Bedenkt man die enge Verflechtung dieser ganzen Literatur in ihren einzelnen Teilen, so ist das gewiß auffällig. Direkte Abhängigkeit von Abot ist nirgends belegbar. Wenn der Traktat den Rabbinen dieser Zeit zur Verfügung stand, muß er, verglichen mit anderen Texten der Zeit, ein Schattendasein geführt haben.

4. Palästinischer Talmud

Im palästinischen Talmud begegnen wir erstmals *expliziten Zitaten mit Einleitungsformeln*, die hier vor den Parallelen ohne Zitatformel gebracht werden sollen[16].

1,2 Mit der üblichen Einleitung von Mischna-Zitaten *taman teninan* bringt yTaan 4,2,68a (= yMeg 3,7,74b) wörtlich den ganzen Abschnitt über Simeon den Gerechten und fügt ohne Übergang an: „Und die drei sind in einem einzigen Bibelvers" (Jes 51,16).

1,18, wo Simeon ben Gamaliel ebenfalls drei Dinge nennt, auf denen die Welt steht, folgt an beiden Stellen wenige Zeilen später, wiederum eingeleitet mit *taman teninan*. Der Talmud führt das Zitat fort: „Und die drei sind eins: Wurde Recht getan, wurde Wahrheit getan; wurde Wahrheit getan, wurde Friede bewirkt. Es sagte R.Mana: Und die drei sind in einem einzigen Bibelvers" (Sach 8,16).

---

[15] Der Vollständigkeit halber füge ich noch eine Stelle aus dem Seder Olam 30 (Milikowski 445) an, die wörtlich den Abschluß von Ab 2,16 enthält: „Die Belohnung der Gerechten erfolgt in der kommenden Zeit".

[16] Schon A. Guttmann, Tractate Abot 187f bietet eine fast vollständige Liste, in deren Wertung ich jedoch zuweilen abweiche. Seine Liste der Babli-Parallelen 186f umfaßt nur die zehn mit „wir haben gelernt" eingeleiteten Texte, nicht die für die Fragestellung ebenso wichtigen Stellen ohne Zitatformel.

1,8 Der hier Jehuda ben Tabbai zugeschriebene Satz: „Verhalte dich nicht wie ein Oberrichter“[17] findet sich anonym in yBB 9,6,17a: „Und haben wir nicht so gelernt (*teninan*): Verhalte dich nicht wie Oberrichter“. Der Text fährt fort: „Und gemäß R. Chaggai im Namen des R. Jehoschua ben Levi ist es verboten, einem einzelnen sein Urteil zu offenbaren“. Die Parallele yKet 4,11,29a liest: „Hat nicht so R. Chaggai im Namen des R. Jehoschua ben Levi gesagt: Verhalte dich nicht wie Oberrichter, um nicht einem einzelnen sein Urteil zu offenbaren“. So wäre hier kein Mischnazitat gegeben; doch ist wohl anzunehmen, daß der Text in yKet irrtümlich verkürzt wurde und wie yBB zu lesen ist[18].

2,4 Der Hillel zugeschriebene Satz „Glaube nicht an dich selbst bis zum Tag deines Todes“ wird ySchab 1,3,3b anonym mit *taman teninan* eingeführt. Daran schließt eine „Begebenheit mit einem Chasid, der dasaß und lernte (*schone*): Glaub nicht an dich selbst bis an den Tag deines Alters“; von einem Geist verführt, wird er dann aufgefordert, sich der Fassung seiner Kollegen anzuschließen, wieder ohne Hinweis auf Hillel.

3,1 „Betrachte drei Dinge und du wirst in keine Sünde fallen“. Dieser Ausspruch des Aqabia ben Mahalalel kommt, ebenfalls in seinem Namen, in ySota 2,2,18a, eingeleitet mit *taman teninan*. Die folgende Ableitung aller drei Dinge von einem Vers (Koh 12,1 „Denk an deinen Schöpfer“; ein Wortspiel mit *borekha*) im Namen dreier Rabbinen schließt auch die drei Dinge selbst ein: woher du kommst, wohin du gehst, vor wem du Rechenschaft geben wirst. Der Text ist somit eindeutig im größeren Umfang bekannt.

3,11, teilweise schon in tSanh 12,9 belegt, in größerem Umfang in SNum § 112, wird in yPes 6,2,33b mit *lo ken teninan* eingeleitet. R.Eleazar von Modiin wird nicht genannt, doch der Text selbst ist wörtlich und vollständig, allein das Glied „und wer seinen Nächsten öffentlich beschämt“ fehlt (wie schon in SNum), ebenso das sekundär eingefügte „nicht wie die Halakha“. Die Stücke „wer den Bund rückgängig macht und wer sich gegen die Tora frech verhält“ in ySanh 10,1,27c sind Teil des Zitats von tSanh 12,9 (siehe oben).

4,8 zitiert als Satz des R.Jischmael, Sohn des R.Jose: „Richte nicht als einzelner; denn einzeln richtet nur der Einzige“. Anonym steht der Satz in ySanh 1,1,18a, eingeleitet mit *de-tninan*, somit als Mischna.

4,12 „Die Ehrfurcht vor deinem Meister sei wie die Ehrfurcht vor dem Himmel“. Der Satz Eleazars ben Schammua kommt anonym, mit *de-tninan* eingeleitet, in yNed 9,1,41b.

---

[17] So wohl statt *ᶜorkhe ha-dinim* bzw. *dajjanim „Rechtsanwälte“* mit dem Genizatext von KATSH zu lesen: *'arkhe* mit alef.

[18] Siehe die Synopse des größeren Zusammenhangs bei G. A. WEWERS, Probleme der Bavot-Traktate (TSAJ 5), Tübingen 1984, 255f, und C. HEZSER, Form, Function, and Historical Significance of the Rabbinic Story in Yerushalmi Neziqin (TSAJ 37), Tübingen 1993, 207. WEWERS 257 meint, die Einleitung des Abschnitts in Ket sei „textlich nicht korrekt überliefert“, HEZSER 208 stellt einfach das Faktum fest, daß das Zitat von Abot hier Teil der Aussage R. Chaggais ist. Doch wie wüßte man dann überhaupt, daß es ein Zitat im Zitat ist?

4,15 „Sei Schwanz den Löwen und nicht Haupt den Füchsen". Dieser Teil eines Mattia ben Cheresch zugeschriebenen Satzes wird in ySanh 4,11,22b von Rab zitiert: „Rab belegt es aus der Mischna; die Mischna sagt (*matnita amra*): Sei Schwanz ..."; dann führt er ein gegenteiliges Sprichwort an. Es ist fraglich, ob die Wendung *matnita amra* mit *teninan* gleichwertig ist; sie kann auch eine Baraita einführen[19].

Parallelen ohne Zitatformel:

1,1 Die Traditionskette findet sich wörtlich, doch in keiner Weise als Zitat markiert, in ySanh 10,1,28a. Die Mischna über die „außenstehenden Bücher" kommentierend, zitiert der Text Koh 12,12 („Es nimmt kein Ende mit dem vielen Bücherschreiben"); es folgen Auslegungen von 12,11: „Worte der Weisen sind wie Ochsenstecken" (*ke-darbonot*), darunter als zweite: „*Ke-darbonot*: Wie dieser Ball (*kaddur*) zwischen den Mädchen (*ha-banot*) – wie dieser Ball von Hand zu Hand übernommen wird, um schließlich in einer Hand zu bleiben, so empfing Mose Tora vom Sinai und übergab sie Josua und Josua den Ältesten und die Ältesten den Propheten und die Propheten übergaben sie den Männern der Großen Synode" (die Parallele KohR 12,10 deutet wenigstens durch den Schluß „usw." ein Zitat an). Die Wendung „Mose empfing Tora vom Sinai"[20], hier außerhalb von Abot erstmals belegt, findet sich auch in der Folgezeit erst wieder KohR, ist also durchaus nicht verbreitet.

2,5 „Ein Ungebildeter ist nicht sündenscheu" findet sich in yBer 9,1,13b, ist jedoch kaum von hier, sondern von tBer 6,18 (siehe oben) übernommen, wo es im selben Kontext steht.

5,19 führt drei Dinge an, die einen Schüler Abrahams auszeichnen: „ein gutes Auge, ein bescheidener Geist und ein demütiger Sinn". In ySanh 1,7,19c sind diese drei Eigenschaften für einen Platz im Sanhedrin gefordert; in yBer 4,2,7d bittet man darum im Morgengebet (MS Vatikan; MS Leiden fügt *nefesch tob* dazwischen). Eine direkte Beeinflussung läßt sich bei einer so kurzen Wortfolge natürlich nicht nachweisen; allerdings ist sie sonst in der klassischen rabbinischen Literatur nicht belegt.

5,20 „Und gib unseren Anteil an deiner Tora". Der Satz ist sonst nur in yBer 4,2,7d belegt, wieder als Teil des Morgengebets; es folgt die Bitte um den Aufbau des Tempels und Jerusalems, „schnell in unseren Tagen", sehr ähnlich wie in Abot direkt vor dem Zitat. Das Ganze gehört zur Gebetssprache; ob direkte Beziehungen zwischen den beiden Texten bestehen, läßt sich kaum beantworten.

Somit sind drei Stellen mit Autornamen durch für die Mischna übliche Zitatformel eingeleitet, ebenso fünf ohne Autor, mit Ausnahme von 3,11 kurze sittliche Maximen; dazu kommt 4,15, wo die Zitatformel nicht eindeutig ist.

---

19 J.N. Epstein, Introduction to the Text of the Mishnah (hebr.), Jerusalem 1948, 813.

20 Auch *qibbel tora* gibt es im pal. Talmud nur hier, dazu noch einmal *qibbelu et ha-tora* in ySchab 9,3,12a.

Von den Stellen ohne Zitatformel ist allein die Parallele zu 1,1 sicher. Daß sie nicht als Zitat eingeführt wird, ist angesichts ihrer Bedeutung in der späteren rabbinischen Tradition bedeutsam und bedarf der Erklärung.

5. GenR, LevR und PRK

Hier werden die wenigen Zitate aus den i. a. ins 5. Jh. datierten, d. h. in etwa mit dem palästinischen Talmud zeitgleichen Midraschim zusammengestellt. *Durch eine Zitatformel sind als Mischna-Text markiert:*

1,2 „Simeon der Gerechte gehörte zu den Resten ..." wird in PRK 19,6 (M.308) mit „dort haben wir gelernt" eingeleitet; mit den Worten „ganze Halakha" wird der Satz abgebrochen.

1,17 Der Simeon ben Gamaliel zugeschriebene Satz „All meine Tage bin ich großgeworden unter den Weisen ..." findet sich mit Autorenangabe, eingeleitet durch *di-tenan*, wörtlich in LevR 16,5 (M.360), in einigen MSS bis „Schweigen", in anderen bis zum Ende („Sünde").

1,18 „Rabban Simeon ben Gamaliel sagt: auf drei Dingen besteht die Welt" wird in PRK 19,6 (M.309) mit „dort haben wir gelernt" eingeleitet. Was die drei Dinge sind, erfährt man aus der folgenden Auslegung (cf. die Parallele in yTaan 4,2).

3,1 Die Aussage des Aqabia ben Mahalalel, deren erster Satz schon in ySota zitiert wurde, wird in LevR 18,1 (M. 389f) mit *(taman) ten(in)an* eingeleitet. Abot nennt die drei Fragen und wiederholt dann jede mit der zugehörigen Antwort; LevR läßt die erste Nennung der Fragen aus[21], gibt also zu jeder Frage gleich die Antwort (so dann auch TanB Chajje 7). Ist es denkbar, daß LevR die ältere Textform belegt? Die Fassung von Abot findet sich ja erst wieder in KohR 12,1!

4,17 setzt Aussagen R. Jakobs fort: „Er pflegte zu sagen: Schöner ist eine Stunde in Umkehr ... als das ganze Leben dieser Welt". Der Abschnitt kommt vollständig in LevR 3,1 (M. 58), mit *ke-di-tenan* eingeleitet. Direkt zuvor ist Jakob ben Korschai genannt, der wohl auch hier als Sprecher vorausgesetzt ist.

5,1 „Durch zehn Aussprüche wurde die Welt erschaffen" wird in GenR 17,1 (Th-A 151) mit *teninan* eingeführt; es folgt sofort die Liste der Bibelbelege. In Abot folgt die Frage, ob das nicht mit einem Ausspruch möglich gewesen wäre, und die Antwort, es sei mit zehn erfolgt „um die Bösen zu bestrafen, die die Welt vernichten ... und guten Lohn zu geben den Gerechten, die die Welt aufrecht erhalten"; dieselbe Begründung kommt wörtlich in GenR 10,9 (Th-A 86) zu Gen 2,1 („Gott ruhte von seinem Werk").

---

[21] Doch der Geniza-Text in Margulies V 68 bringt die drei Fragen wie in Abot und endet mit „usw.".

5,5 Unter den zehn Wundern im Tempel heißt es, daß „sie gedrängt stehen und sich bequem niederwerfen". Die Wendung kommt in GenR 5,7 (Th-A 37), von einem Teil der Textzeugen mit *di-tenan* oder *ke-di-tenan* eingeleitet; so auch LevR 10,9 (M. 218).

Dazu kommt eine Parallele mit *nicht eindeutiger Zitatformel*:

2,10 Den R. Eliezer zugeschriebene Satz „Hüte dich vor ihrer Kohle, damit du dich nicht verbrennst; denn ihr Biß ist der Biß eines Fuchses" zitiert in GenR 52,4 (Th-A 543f) R. Chijja bar Abba mit der Einleitung: „Ich sagte, groß sind die Worte der Weisen, die sagten: Hüte dich ...". Das Zitat reicht je nach Textzeugen bis „verbrennst", „Fuchs" oder bis zum Ende („Feuerkohlen").

Die Texte bestätigen das aus dem palästinischen Talmud gewonnene Bild, daß (relativ wenige) Abot-Texte als Mischna bekannt sind und so zitiert werden, andere klare Parallelen aber nicht so eindeutig darauf zurückgeführt werden.

6. Babylonischer Talmud

Im babylonischen Talmud gibt es eine Reihe von Texten, die Stellen von Abot explizit als Mischna bzw. Baraita zitieren oder sonst Abot sehr gleichen. Auch hier beginnen wir mit den *durch Zitatformel (ten[in]an) als Mischnatext ausgewiesenen Stellen:*

1,3 „Er pflegte zu sagen: Seid nicht wie Knechte ... nicht um den Lohn zu empfangen" wird in AZ 19a zitiert; daß Antigonos von Sokho der Sprecher ist, geht nicht hervor.

1,13 Hillels aramäischer Satz „Wer sich der Krone bedient, vergeht" (auch in 4,5) findet sich in Meg 28b ohne Autor.

2,1 „Achte auf ein leichtes Gebot wie auf ein schweres, denn du kennst nicht die Belohnung der Gebote" wird in Ned 39b zitiert (nur bis „schweres" auch in Tan und TanB Eqeb 1 ohne Einleitung und mit anderer Fortsetzung!); das vorausgehende und das folgende Stück dieses Abschnitts werden im Babli wie eine Baraita zitiert bzw. ohne Zitatformel gebracht!

2,4 Hillels Satz „Glaube nicht an dich bis zum Tag deines Todes" steht in Ber 29a anonym als Einwand gegen Abaje.

2,10 „Kehre um einen Tag vor deinem Tod". Diesen Satz R.Eliezers zitiert Schab 153a mit Autorennamen.

2,14 „R. Eleazar sagt: Sei eifrig, zu lernen (Tora und wisse)[22], was du einem Epikuräer antworten sollst" wird Sanh 38b zitiert.

3,2 Der erste Satz „R. Chanina ... würde jeder seinen Nächsten lebend verschlingen" wird in AZ 4a zitiert.

---

[22] Fehlt in MS Kaufmann.

4,13 „R. Jehuda sagt: Sei vorsichtig in der Lehre, denn ein Versehen in der Lehre gilt als vorsätzlich“. In BM 33b kommt der Satz mit Autorennamen.

4,14 „R. Nehorai sagt: Gehe ins Exil ... und stütze dich nicht auf deine Einsicht“ wird vollständig in Schab 147b zitiert; es folgt eine Baraita, ob er wirklich Nehorai geheißen habe.

5,5 „Zehn Wunder geschahen (unseren Vätern)[23] im Tempel...“. Joma 21a bringt den Text mit kleinen Auslassungen bis zum Ende („daß ich in Jerusalem übernachte“). Anlaß des Zitats ist die Diskussion um die Aussage Rabs: „Wenn Israel zum Wallfahrtsfest hinaufzieht, stehen sie gedrängt und werfen sich bequem nieder“[24].

Parallelen mit nicht eindeutiger Zitatformel:

1,5 „Und rede nicht viel mit der Frau“. Beruria bringt diesen Satz in Er 53b mit der Einleitung „Haben nicht so die Weisen gesagt?“; in Ned 20a ist er Teil einer Reihe von Verboten, eingeleitet mit *tana* und damit begründet, das führe zu Unzucht.

2,1 „Rabbi sagt: Welches ist der rechte Weg, den sich der Mensch wählen soll?“. In Tam 28a wird der Satz wie eine Baraita mit *tania* eingeleitet und anders als in Abot fortgeführt: „Er liebe die Zurechtweisungen“ (genauso in Tan Mischpatim 7 mit *teni*). In bNed 22b kommt der Text ohne direkte Zitatformel: „Rab Sechora fand sich einen Ausweg: (Rabbi sagt)[25] Welches ist ... wählen soll? Jeder, der dem, der ihm folgt, eine Ehre ist und ihm Ehre vor den Menschen bringt“. Das Zitat ist hier somit länger. Doch sind beide Texte kein sicheres Zitat von Abot, sondern belegen nur die Existenz analoger Traditionen. Erst die Fortsetzung wird direkt als Mischna zitiert (siehe oben).

3,11 Sanh 99a zitiert: „Von daher sagte R. Eliezer von Modiin ...“ Der Text geht bis zum Ende („kommende Welt“) mit kleinen Unterschieden (wie auch zwischen den einzelnen Textzeugen von Abot). Ein Hinweis auf die Mischna fehlt.

3,17 Das Gleichnis vom Baum im Sturm hat eine nahe Parallele in Taan 20a.

5,4 „Mit zehn Versuchungen versuchten unsere Väter den Heiligen, gepriesen sei er“. Der anonyme Satz von Abot kommt Ar 15a als Baraita (*tania*) im Namen des R.Jehuda!

5,6 „Zehn Dinge wurden in der Dämmerung erschaffen“. Diese auch in den halakhischen Midraschim breit belegte Tradition (siehe oben) kommt in Pes

---

23 „Unseren Vätern“ fehlt in MSS Kaufmann, Parma, Cambridge und dem Geniza-Text von Katsh. Ebenso im Talmud.

24 A. Guttmann, Tractate Abot 187, hält die Aussage Rabs, der sich auf eine Baraita stütze, für älter; die Mischna vertrete eine spätere Schicht; zudem sei der Text unserer Mischna schon die vom Babli korrigierte Fassung. D. Halivni, Sources and Traditions. A Source Critical Commentary on the Talmud. Seder Moed from Yoma to Hagiga (hebr.), Jerusalem 1975, 38–40, glaubt, in der Mischna habe nur gestanden: „Zehn Wunder geschahen im Tempel“; erst Rab habe sie, auf Quellen gestützt, detailliert.

25 „Rabbi sagt“ fehlt in MSS München und Vatikan 110.

54a zweimal, zuerst eingeleitet mit *tania*, dann mit *tanu rabbanan*, d.h. beide Male als Baraita. Die Listen stimmen weder untereinander noch mit Abot voll überein.

Parallelen ohne Zitatformel:

1,5 „Und die Armen seien Söhne deines Hauses" sagt Raba in BM 60b.

1,13 „Wer nicht zufügt, nimmt ab". Diese Hillel zugeschriebenen aramäischen Worte haben eine engste Parallele in BB 121b (cf. Taan 31a), wonach man ab dem 15. Ab fürs Studium Stunden der Nacht dazu nehmen soll: *de-mosif, josif, sche-eino mosif, jasef.*

2,1 Von diesem zum Teil als Mischna, zum Teil als Baraita zitierten Abschnitt kommt der Satz: „Und berechne den Verlust des Gebots gegen seinen Lohn und den Lohn der Übertretung gegen ihren Verlust" in BB 78b ohne jede Einleitung, doch mit etwas anderem Anfang als Auslegung zu Num 21,27 (*cheschbon*): „Rechnen wir die Rechnung der Welt: der Verlust ..." (cf. NumR 14,6). Der Satz scheint sprichwörtlich zu sein. Der Redaktor des Textes kennt entweder nicht die Stelle in der Mischna oder findet es nicht nötig, das anzugeben.

2,5 Der Hillel zugeschriebene Satz „Und wo es keine Männer gibt, bemühe dich, ein Mann zu sein" wird Ber 63a Bar Qappara zugeschrieben und aramäisch zitiert! Es ist kaum Übersetzung von Abot, sondern ein gängiges Sprichwort, als solches gewöhnlich in Aramäisch.

2,6 „Auch sah er einen Schädel, der auf dem Wasser schwamm. Er sagte dazu: Weil du ertränkt hast, hat man dich ertränkt, und schließlich werden auch die, die dich ertränkt haben, ertrinken". In Suk 53a stehen, eingeleitet mit *tania*, mehrere Aussagen Hillels: die erste („wenn ich da bin, sind alle da, und wenn ich nicht da bin, wer ist da?") ist vergleichbar dem Satz Hillels in Abot 1,14 „Wenn nicht ich für mich bin ..."; es folgt ein in tSuk 4,3 belegter Satz, dann nahtlos angefügt der Satz von Abot 2,6; eine Abhängigkeit von Abot ist nicht erkennbar.

2,8 Zu diesem langen Abschnitt gibt es eine einzige sachliche (nicht wörtliche) Parallele: „Wenn alle Weisen Israels in einer Waagschale sind und Eliezer ben Hyrkanos in der zweiten, wiegt er sie alle auf" wird in Joma 16a auf alle Weisen der Weltvölker und Daniel bezogen.

2,16 „Die Belohnung der Gerechten erfolgt in der kommenden Zeit", schon in Seder Olam 30 begegnet, findet sich in Er 21a in einer längeren Auslegung des R. Chisda. Es ist eine sprichwörtliche Wendung und kein Mischna-Zitat.

3,2 „Zwei, die sitzen, und Worte der Tora sind zwischen ihnen: die Schekhina weilt zwischen ihnen ... woher, daß sogar einer ..."? Ber 6a bietet eine enge sachliche und fast wörtliche Parallele. Thema und Schriftbelege sind gleich, ohne daß eine literarische Verbindung nachweisbar wäre. Dasselbe gilt für

3,6. Möglich ist, daß beide Texte auf Mek Bachodesch 11 (siehe oben) aufbauen oder auf eine gemeinsame Tradition zurückgehen. Warum zitiert man nicht Abot, wenn der Text als Mischna vorliegt?

3,8 Eine enge sachliche Parallele zum Vergessen der Lehre findet sich in Men

99b in einer Diskussion über Dtn 4, das auch in Abot der Belegtext ist; R. Dostai[26] wird wörtlich mit der Frage zitiert, ob das auch gilt, wenn einem die Lehre zu schwer geworden ist[27]. Alle Elemente von 3,8 sind vorhanden, ohne daß man von einem wirklichen Zitat sprechen könnte.

4,1 Die Fragenreihe Ben Zomas: „Wer ist weise, wer ist ein Held, wer ist reich" begegnet in Tam 32a. Alexander stellt die Fragen den Weisen des Südens in Aramäisch; sie wiederholen jeweils auf Hebräisch die Frage und antworten wie in Abot, doch ohne Bibelbeleg. Nach der Frage, was man tun soll, um zu leben bzw. zu sterben, die in Abot keine Parallele hat, fragt Alexander, was einer tun muß, um bei den Geschöpfen angenommen zu sein, was der vierten Frage in Abot („geehrt") entspricht. Die hebräische Wiederholung der Fragen könnte auf eine Art geprägter Vorlage schließen lassen. Ist aber eine so freie Wiederverwertung von Abot denkbar? Eher ist an ein gemeinsames Modell zu denken.

4,5 „R. Zadoq sagt: Mache sie [die Worte der Tora] nicht eine Krone, um dich durch sie zu vergrößeren und nicht einen Spaten, um damit zu graben". In Ned 62a ist das Teil eines Ausspruchs des R. Eliezer beR. Zadoq, kombiniert mit seiner Aussage SDtn § 48 (F. 114), von wo auch der Vergleich mit Nebukadnezzar übernommen wird, der sich der Tempelgeräte bediente. Der in Abot folgende aramäische Satz Hillels „und wer sich der Krone bedient, vergeht" (ein Selbstzitat aus Abot 1,13), kommt Ned 62a kurz zuvor fast gleich in Hebräisch als Aussage des R. Jochanan: „Jeder, der sich der Krone der Tora bedient, wird aus der Welt entwurzelt".

4,12 „Die Ehrfurcht vor deinem Lehrer (sei dir) wie die Ehrfurcht vor Gott". Diesen Eleazar zugeschriebenen Satz sagt Pes 108a R. Josef.

4,15 Der Mattja ben Cheresch zugeschriebene Satz „Sei Schwanz den Löwen und nicht Haupt den Füchsen", in ySanh 4,11 als Mischna zitiert, kommt in Sanh 37a als Aussage Abajes: „Sie können ihm sagen: Sei Schwanz ...". Das wirkt zwar wie der Hinweis auf einen bekannten Spruch, doch nicht auf Mischna.

4,18 „Besänftige nicht deinen Nächsten in der Stunde seines Zornes". Den R. Simeon (ben Eleazar)[28] zugeschriebenen Satz bringt Ber 7b leicht abgewandelt: „Und es sagte R. Jochanan im Namen des R. Simeon ben Jochai: Woher (weiß man), daß man einen Menschen in der Stunde seines Zornes nicht besänftigt?" (vgl. 7a).

5,1 RH 32a setzt die Aussage von den zehn Aussprüchen voraus, ohne direkt zu zitieren: R. Jochanan erklärt, die 10 Malkhijjot entsprechen den „zehn

[26] In MS München 95 fehlt der Name.

[27] Die Einleitung der Frage mit *jakhol* ist für die Mischna unüblich und für halakhische Midraschim charakteristisch!

[28] Das Patronym fehlt in MS Kaufmann.

Aussprüchen, mit denen die Welt erschaffen wurde". So auch oft in Midraschim.

5,18 Der Satz, der auch schon in tJoma 4,10f eine enge Parallele hat, findet sich ohne Einleitung im üblichen Text von Joma 87a in der genauen Formulierung von Abot, nur durch ein Wort abgeschwächt: „dem gibt man *fast* keine Gelegenheit, Buße zu tun". In Sota 47a und Sanh 47b beginnt der Satz: „Wer sündigt und die Allgemeinheit zur Sünde verführt"; das „fast" fehlt hier wie in Abot. In den Handschriften[29] fehlt „fast"; auch sind die Abschnitte zu Verdienst und Sünde durch einen Kommentar ähnlich tJoma 4,10f getrennt.

Anstelle einer genaueren Auswertung nur einige Hinweise. Die zehn mit Mischna-Zitatformel eingeführten Texte scheinen kein Problem zu bieten, wäre nicht die Herkunft der Liste der zehn Wunder im Tempel (5,5; Joma 21a) umstritten. Auffällig und näherer Untersuchung wert ist das Faktum, daß mit Ausnahme von 2,4 (ySchab 1,3; Ber 29a) kein direktes Zitat im Babli anderswo außer Abot in der klassischen rabbinischen Literatur zu finden ist. Beachtlich ist aber auch die lange Liste von Parallelen, die nicht als Mischna, sondern als Baraita zitiert werden, einem Amoräer zugeschrieben oder ohne jeden Hinweis auf eine Vorlage verwendet werden.

7. Späte Midraschim

Die Darbietung des reichen Materials muß aus Raumgründen unterbleiben. Relativ häufig sind Zitate in der *Tanchuma-Literatur*; die Zitatformeln trennen nicht klar Mischna und Baraita; eine Reihe von Parallelen sind auch hier noch ohne Hinweis auf ein Zitat. *Pirqe deR. Eliezer* verwendet neben Bibelversen und Zitaten tannaitischer Lehrer auch Sätze aus Abot ohne jeden Quellenhinweis gerne als Kapitelanfang[30], verleiht ihnen damit entsprechendes Gewicht. Der *Seder Elijahu* fällt durch die oft, doch nicht immer verwendete Zitatformel auf: „Es lehrten die Weisen in der Mischna"[31]. Sehr zahlreich sind die Zitate in *Midrasch Mischle*, i. a. als Mischna mit der Einleitung „dort haben wir gelernt" gekennzeichnet[32], aber auch allgemeiner eingeleitet mit „Von daher sagten die Weisen" (5, V. 39) oder ohne Hinweis auf ein Zitat. *Kohelet Rabba* leitet zweimal mit der Formel ein: „wir haben dort in Abot gelernt" (KohR 5,3: 1,17; 7,19: 2,2), zweimal mit „wir haben gelernt" (KohR 1,20: 5,5; 12,1: 3,1), aber

---

[29] München 95 und die beiden anderen (London, New York) schon in der Talmud Text Databank des S. Lieberman Institute des Jewish Theological Seminary, New York, aufgenommenen MSS. Alle Babli-Texte wurden in dieser Datenbank kontrolliert.

[30] PRE 13: 4,21; 16: 1,2; 18: 5,6; 26: 5,3; 43: 4,11.

[31] SER 12, F. 56; 14, F.67.68; 18, F. 103; 19, F. 112.116; 26, F.141. Auf die Zitierung eines Satzes von 4,2 in SER 16 (F. 76) als Tora wurde schon hingewiesen.

[32] Midr Mischle 1, V. 1.12; 2, V. 30; 9, V. 72.74; 15, V. 124; 22, V. 152f; 28, V. 178.

auch zweimal mit dem Kennwort einer Baraita, *teni* (KohR 7,3: 4,13; 9,8: 2,10), und bringt, was besonders verwundert, in KohR 12,10 den Anfangssatz des Traktates „Mose empfing Tora ...", wie schon ySanh 10,1 ohne jeden Hinweis auf ein Zitat! Aus den Zitaten im *Midrasch Psalmen* sei abschließend nur ein Beispiel genannt. Ein Zitat aus 2,1 wird in MidrPs 9,3 (B.41a) eingeleitet: „So haben die Weisen gelehrt in der Sprache der Mischna" (*bilschon hamischna*)! Bedeutet das, daß der Redaktor den Text nur als der Mischna ähnlich, aber nicht als direkten Bestand der Mischna kennt?

8. Einige Schlußbemerkungen

Die notgedrungen trockene Auflistung von Zitaten aus Abot bzw. Parallelen dazu hat weitreichende Folgen. Die Tatsache, daß Abot nur in relativ geringem Umfang direkt als Mischna zitiert wird, viele Zitate erst spät erstmals aufscheinen, aber auch oft als Baraita oder im Namen eines späteren Rabbi genannt werden, weckt Argwohn. A. Guttmann hat das Problem richtig gesehen; indem er sich auf die Parallelen in den Talmudim (im Babli jedoch nur auf die direkten Zitate) beschränkte und dabei die im Zusammenhang erwähnten Rabbinen als Datierungshilfe heranzog, schloß er auf die Aufnahme der ursprünglichen Schicht von Abot in die Mischna um 300 und vermutete vorsichtig „an apologetic move against Christian attacks on Pharisaic Nomism as being the essence of Judaism" als Grund dafür[33].

Etwas zurückhaltender kann man sagen: der Redaktion des palästinischen Talmud lag ein Kerntext von Abot schon als Teil ihrer Mischna vor; doch scheint die kleine Schrift noch lange eine Randexistenz geführt zu haben, vielleicht (auch) getrennt von der Mischna überliefert und so als Baraita zitiert worden zu sein. Besonders die Überlieferung des Textes in Babylonien ist dabei von Interesse, v. a. auch die Frage, was erst aus babylonischer Tradition in den Traktat gelangt ist. Wollte man die in der Toseftaforschung verbreiteten Kriterien auf Abot übertragen[34], müßte man schließen, daß Abot als redigierter Traktat in Babylonien (und auch in manchen anderen rabbinischen Kreisen) nicht oder kaum bekannt war, jedenfalls keine große Autorität hatte.

Daß Abot auch zur Zeit der Jeruschalmi-Redaktion noch nicht den Umfang der jetzigen fünf Kapitel hatte, scheint klar. Für eine erst zu leistende Quellenscheidung (die meisten bisherigen Arbeiten haben sich auf die Frage vormischnaischer Quellen konzentriert) könnten die Zitate und Parallelen eine wichtige Hilfe sein. Hier nur ein Punkt: Guttmann hat richtig bemerkt, daß die Traditionskette kaum zum ursprünglichen Bestand gehört. Er denkt an eine

---

[33] A. GUTTMANN, Tractate Abot 189.

[34] Siehe besonders Y. ELMAN, Authority and Tradition: Toseftan Baraitot in Talmudic Babylonia, Hoboken 1994.

Ergänzung in nachtalmudischer Zeit und sieht als Grund die Auseinandersetzung mit dem Islam[35]. Daß der Anfang von Abot erstmals im palästinischen Talmud zu finden ist, dort aber nicht als Zitat, dann erst wieder in KohR, und wieder nicht als Mischnazitat gekennzeichnet, ist ein gewichtiges Argument für eine späte Anfügung dieses Teils an Abot, was immer die Gründe dafür waren. Daß der Traktat eine so zentrale Stellung im Judentum bekommen hat, ist dagegen leicht zu begründen. Es ist nicht die Auseinandersetzung mit dem Islam, sondern der Kampf gegen die traditionskritischen Karäer, in deren früher Blütezeit Schriften wie Pirqe R. Eliezer, Seder Elijahu, Midrasch Mischle und Kohelet Rabba entstanden, die Abot auf einmal so ausführlich zitieren. Die Aufnahme in die Liturgie hat denselben Grund. Die Geschichte des Traktats bis zu dieser Zeit ist dagegen weithin erst zu klären.

---

[35] A. GUTTMANN, Tractate Abot 190.

The Adorable Adam of the Mystics and the Rebuttals of the Rabbis

by

JARL FOSSUM

In 1945 A. Altmann published an article in which he adapted the faulty theory of the religionsgeschichtliche Schule that there had existed a pre-Christian Gnostic concept of a heavenly Man with Iranian roots.[1] Altmann dealt with three motifs: (i) the angels oppose the creation of Adam; (ii) the angels adore Adam; (iii) God lets sleep fall upon Adam. The first motif, 'invariably expressed in the words, "What is man that Thou art mindful of him, and the son of man that Thou thinkest of him?" (Ps. 8.5),'[2] has recently been discussed in a Doctoral Dissertation by M. S. Kinzer.[3] The present article purposes to deal with the second theme. As for the third motif, I refer to the last chapter in my book, The Image of the Invisible God (NTOA 30; Freiburg & Göttingen, 1995)[4].

(1) 'The motif of the adoration of Adam by the angels appears in three different forms and sources in rabbinic literature.'[5] (i) The angels mistake Adam for God and want to exclaim 'Holy' before him, whereupon God lets sleep fall upon Adam so it becomes clear that the latter is human[6]. (ii) All creatures mistake Adam for their creator and wish to bow before him, but Adam teaches them to render all honour to God as their true creator[7]. (iii) The

---

[1] ,The Gnostic Background of the Rabbinic Adam Legends', JQR 35 (1945) pp. 371–91. Although the theory of the History of Religions School has now been discarded, ALTMANN's article never appears to have been discussed.

[2] Ibid. p. 371.

[3] ,All Things Beneath His Feet': The Influence of Psalm 8 on Early Jewish and Christian Literature (Diss.; University of Michigan 1995).

[4] To be true, the chapter does not deal with the Adam myth, but with the dream of Jacob (Gen 28.12) as interpreted in Jewish tradition: Jacob could be seen to have a heavenly counterpart, i.e. the divine Glory, the ,likeness as the appearance of Adam' (Ezek 1.26). ALTMANN, ,Background', is on the right track when saying that ,Jacob represents here the figure of Adam, the primordial Man' (p. 390), but he is wrong to assume the simple ,identity Jacob (Israel) and *Adam Kadmon*' (n. 15).

[5] ALTMANN, ,Background', p. 379.

[6] *Gen R.* 8.10 (parallel in *Yalqut* I § 23). Cf. STRACK & BILLERBECK, Vol. IV, p. 1127, n. 1.

[7] *Pirke de R. Eliezer* ch. 11 (cf. *Tanḥ* פקודי § 3, end: *Midrash Hagadol* I.56).

angels mistake Adam for God and wish to exclaim 'Holy' before him, whereupon God reduces Adam's size[8].

As Altmann notes, although the sources differ with regard to the remedy of the angels' mistake, they must 'have drawn from an older common source which spoke of the adoration of Adam by the angels.'[9] Although the Prague MS of the late Bereshit Rabbati, fathered upon R. Moses ha-Darshan (first half of the 11th cent.), 'distinctly contains a passage in which God commands the angels to adore Adam,'[10] Altmann does not believe that this theme could have originated with Jews on account of the fact that there is no Biblical warrant for it. However, the motif is prevalent in the Christian Adamic literature[11], which, according to Altmann, is 'decisively formed by Gnostic influences.'[12] By way of evidence, Altmann cites a couple of texts in the Mandean corpus where the angels are commanded to pay homage to Adam and Eve. He concludes that 'the adoration motif goes back to the Adam literature and is used by the above quoted Midrashim as a weapon against the Gnostic implications of the Adam-conception as set out in the Adam Books.'[13]

Why does the motif crop up again without a polemical gist in Bereshit Rabbati? Altmann avers that it was conveyed through the late 'influence of the Koran'.[14]

(2) Now the two Mandean texts cited by Altmann contain some notable differences. The version in Right Ginza X relates that the demiurge Ptahil, after having created the world, formed Adam and Eve, and commanded the 'angels of the house' to worship the first human couple in his 'world of darkness'. Ptahil and the planets are unable to make Adam and Eve stand on their feet; it is not until Ptahil goes to his father, Abatur, and obtains the 'secret mana', which he 'throws' into the first human couple, that they can stand erect[15].

Apart from the fact that Mandeism cannot be proven to antedate the earliest Adamic books, the Mandean myth summarized above does not throw any light on the Adam myth in the Adamic literature. In the Adam books, the first man is a heavenly being, even the divine 'Image', created by God himself. The angels

---

8 *Sefer Ḥasidim*, Wistinetzki p. 290.

9 Altmann, ‚Background', p. 382.

10 Ibid. p. 383.

11 Already J. W. Hirschberg, Jüdische und christliche Lehren im vor- und frühislamischen Arabien (Mémoires de la commission orientaliste 32, Polska Akademia; Kraków 1939) pp. 50ff., denied the Jewish origin of the myth and argued for the existence of Jewish polemics against the Christian Adamic literature. Altmann does not appear to have known Hirschberg's work.

12 Altmann, ‚Background', p. 385. Cf. already W. Staerk, Die Erlösererwartung in den östlichen Religionen (Stuttgart 1938) pp. 13–14, 186ff.

13 Altmann, ‚Background', p. 387.

14 Ibid. p. 383.

15 Petermann p. 240.23–p. 241.16; Lidzbarski p. 242.12–38. The ‚angels of the house' apparently are identical with the planets.

are commanded by God or Michael to worship the divine 'Image'. Satan, however, refuses to do so and is therefore thrown down from heaven[16]. Satan does not appear in the Mandean anthropogony cited above.

The other Mandean version, which is found in two recensions (Right Ginza I and II.1), relates that the 'Lord of Greatness' or 'King of Light' commissioned Hibil-Gabriel to create Adam and Eve as well as the world, and announced that some of the 'angels of fire' should be submissive to Adam. The 'Evil One', however, would not submit himself and was thus laid in bondage[17].

In his literary- and tradition-critical study of Mandean anthropogony, K. Rudolph argues confidently that the latter version, representing the 'monistic conception of the anthropogony', is secondary and shows influence from Islam[18]. Yet, as Rudolph himself correctly notes, it is undeniable that the 'monistic' version of the Mandean anthropogony as well as cosmogony has 'ältere Vorbilder' in Judaism and Christianity.

Although the 'monistic' anthropogony manifestly shows similarities with the Adam myth in the Adamic literature, the differences must not be overlooked. In the Adamic books, Adam is not the creation of Michael, Gabriel or any other angel, and in the Mandean anthropogony the reason for the angels' submission to Adam is not that he is the image of God. Mandeism cannot help us to explain the Adam myth in the Adamic writings.

(3) Are the rabbinic texts to be seen simply as polemics against the portrayal of Adam in the Adamic literature? To be true, the Adamic books go beyond the Bible where it is only said that Adam was created in or after God's image, and although 'crowned with honour and glory', still a 'little lower than the angels[19]. On the other hand, we should bear in mind that the early Christians had the same Bible as the Jews, and we should not accept too readily the view that the Christians were more prone to mythological speculation than each and every Jewish group[20]. As a matter of act, there are a large number of so-called apocryphal and pseudepigraphical Jewish texts (not to mention Philo's works) in which Adam is glorified far beyond what is imaginable on the basis of the Bible. The scholars of the religionsgeschichtliche Schule endeavoured to explain this new development in Israelite-Jewish religion by drawing on the religions of Iran and/or Babylonia[21]. However, it appears impossible to find an

---

[16] E.g., *Life of Adam and Eve* chs. 13ff.; *Gospel of Bartholomew* IV.53ff.; *Cave of Treasure*, Bezold p. 5; *Apoc Sedrach* 5.2f.; *Discourse on Abbaton*, Budge 13a–14a. Cf. Hirschberg, Lehren pp. 50ff.

[17] Petermann p. 12.21–p.13.12; Lidzbarski p. 15.9–26; and cf. Petermann p. 34.5–9; Lidzbarski p. 34.10–15. For the term ‚angels of fire', see below, n. 45.

[18] Theogonie, Kosmogonie und Anthropogonie in den mandäischen Schriften (FRLANT 58; Göttingen 1965) p. 308.

[19] Ps 8.5. The Hebrew text reads ‚Elohim', but all the ancient versions translate ‚angels'.

[20] The New Testament cannot be said to foster a lofty view of Adam.

[21] C. H. Kraeling, Anthropos and Son of Man (CUOS 25; New York 1927, reprinted 1966)

Iranian or Babylonian heavenly Man figure who is the image of the highest God and is deemed worthy of worship by the other heavenly beings.

Finally, the consensus among the scholars now seems to be that the Adamic literature is basically Jewish[22]. The motif of the adoration of Adam may thus have been Jewish to begin with. The polemical rabbinic texts may have a wider address than that of the Adam myth in the Adamic literature; they may have in view Jewish as well as Christian conceptions.

(4) In might be helpful to look at the reasons *why* Adam was confused with God. In Gen R. 8.10 R. Hoshayah (c. 225 C. E.) supplies a simile throwing light on the confusion of the angels:

What does this resemble? A king and a governor sat in a chariot, and his subjects wished to say to the king, 'Domine!', but they did not know which it was. What did the king do? He pushed the governor out of the chariot, and so they knew who was the king.

Adam originally had a physical appearance which was indistinguishable from that of God. By being pushed out of the chariot, he is to be understood to assume earthly human nature, for this act must have a meaning similar to that of God letting sleep fall upon Adam (sleep being a sign of mortality and death)[23].

Altmann says that the 'Midrash refers to Adam after his sin.'[24] Now Adam's transgression is not mentioned; the mistake is that of the angels and not Adam's. Moreover, the angels' mistake is quite understandable even according to R. Hoshayah's simile, which grants Adam's original closeness to God and his divine resemblance. The whole passage does not have the appearance of being a corrective to the Adam myth as found in the Adamic literature, where the angels are not confused as to the identity of God and where the veneration of the angels and Adam's fall are not associated acts. The point of the rabbinic text would seem to be that the idea of the close resemblance of God and Adam leads to dangerous ground and has to be checked. R. Hoshayah may have taken recourse to the traditional myth of the fall of Adam, but we really have a quite different myth before us.

However plausible this argument is found, the other two texts do appear to have another target than the Adamic literature. In Pirke de R. Eliezer ch. 11,

---

pp. 158ff., would seem to represent the latest of these attempts. Instead of looking to Iran, a more fruitful avenue to explore would seem to be the Near Eastern royal ideology. There is some evidence to the effect that the king was seen as the incarnation of the primal man; cf. below, n. 27, and n. 44. The later Adam mythology may be seen in part as a revival of this ideology. Cf. e. g. STAERK, Erlösererwartung pp. 135–36, 471–76.

22 J. R. LEVINSON, Portraits of Adam in Early Judaism (JSPSup 1; Sheffield 1988), includes the *Life of Adam and Eve*. See also M. STONE, The History of the Literature of Adam and Eve (SBLEJL 3; Atlanta 1992). While LEVINSON does not think that there ever was a single Adam myth or a Semitic *Vorlage* for the Adam books, STONE (p. 64) is more willing to see an ancient unity behind the various later versions.

23 On sleep, see GINZBERG, Vol. V, p. 80, n. 25, and p. 86, n. 37.

24 ‚Background', p. 388.

all creatures, overwhelmed by the impression of the God-like Adam, think that he is their creator. Here the heretical mistake apparently involves the idea that Adam is the demiurge. This notion is not found in the Adamic writings.

In Sefer Hasidim the angels apparently mistake Adam for God because of the former's huge proportions[25], for God has to reduce Adam's size. Now this story would seem to go back to Alphabet of R. Aqiba 59, where the angels do not mistake Adam for God, but – upon noting his diving resemblance – cry, 'Are there two powers in the world?!' In this version the size of Adam is said to have filled the entire world. Again, the Adamic literature contains nothing similar to these two versions.

There are many rabbinic passages in which Adam is described as an originally enormous being[26]. In some texts, God is said to have diminished Adam's size because of his transgression, in which case the huge size of the first man can be seen as part of the divine image (although this is not always made explicit). These passages, however, throw no immediate light on our texts, where the reduction of Adam's size is said to be a response to angels' mistake of regarding Adam as God or viewing him as God's partner. Our texts apparently combat the heretical notion of a cosmic Man figure infringing upon the monotheistic dogma.

Although the Adamic literature portrays Adam as a heavenly being and the very 'Image' of God worthy of angelic adoration, it is clearly not the target of the rabbinic polemics. The surmise that the rabbinic polemics have a broader address now has to be taken up.

(5) Whereas the idea in the Adamic books that Adam, the first human being, is the divine ‚Image' and even is enthroned in heaven cannot find a Biblical foundation[27], it has a curious similarity in the Kabbalistic conception of Adam Kadmon. The difference is that Adam Kadmon is the model of the earthly man: ‚The Godhead thus had [...] a mystical form of manifestation, [...] the form of Man upon the throne which represents that highest Urbild, in whose Ebenbild man was created.'[28] This refers to the vision of the prophet Ezekiel of a throne

---

[25] For the giant Body of God, see below.

[26] Strack & Billerbeck, Vol. IV, pp. 946–47. B. Barc, ‚La taille cosmique d'Adam dans la littérature juive rabbinique des trois premiers siècles apres J.-C.', RSR 49 (1975) pp. 173–85, has attempted a tradition-critical classification of the various texts.

[27] *Life of Adam and Eve* ch. 47 and *Apoc Mos* 39.3 ff. teach that Adam will be placed upon the throne of Satan at the end of times. In the *Armenian Death of Adam*, Lipscomb 16–20, Adam is placed upon the divine throne after his death. In the *Discourse on Abbaton*, Budge 13a, Adam is seated upon a throne of his own from the beginning.

In Ezek 28.2 the king of Tyre – the description of whom is modelled upon a variant myth of the first man – says: ‚I am a god (el); I sit upon the seat of Elohim.' The rabbis could take Ezek ch. 28 to describe Adam; see e. g. *Pesiq Rav Kah* 26.3.2. The 'holy mountain' on which 'Eden, God's Garden', is to be found and from which the king is thrown down is heaven; cf. Isa 14.12–13. See further below, n. 44.

[28] G. Scholem, Von der mystischen Gestalt der Gottheit (Zürich 1962) p. 21. Cf. already L.

with a ‚likeness as the appearance of אדם upon it above.'[29] This ‚likeness as the appearance of a man' is identified by the prophet two verses below: ‚This was the appearance of the likeness of the Glory of the Lord.'

Are the rabbinic polemics directed against early Jewish mystical teachings about the divine Glory, the heavenly Man, or against notions showing a rapprochement, even a confusion, between the heavenly Man and the earthly Adam? It would also be perfectly reasonable that the rabbis shared any confusion that existed on this subject[30].

(a) We shall first turn to the heretical idea that Adam was the demiurge. The rabbis had to combat certain Minim who asserted that an Adam figure had helped God in his work of creation: ‚Our rabbis taught: „Adam was created on the eve of the Sabbath." And why? Lest the Minim should say: „The Holy One, blessed be He, had an associate in the work of creation."'[31] This Adam figure must have been pre-existent[32]. The rabbis, however, maintained that there was only one Adam, the one created on the sixth day, the ‚eve of the Sabbath'.

Still, the idea of a demiurgic Man figure crops up even in rabbinic sources, for in Aboth de R. Nathan ch. 39 we read that heaven and earth were created by a ‚Likeness (דמות) on high'.[33] This divine ‚Likeness' is of course the same as the ‚Image' (צלם) of God, both terms being used synonymously in Gen 1.26-27. The image/likeness after which Adam was created has here been hypostasized as a heavenly Man responsible even for the creation of the world[34].

The concept of the demiurgic Adam would seem to appear as early as in the Book of Wisdom, for here we read: ‚Sophia guarded to the end the Firstformed Father of the World (πρωτόπλαστον πατέρα κόσμου) who was created alone, and delivered him out of his transgression and gave him power

---

GINZBERG, ‚Adam Kadmon', Jewish Encyclopedia (New York & London 1901), Vol. I, p. 183, col. a. For early evidence for the creation of man after the model of the Glory, see J. E. FOSSUM, Image p. 20, n. 30.

29 Ezek 1.26.

30 Cf. below n. 50. In Mandeism the heavenly Adam, Adakas = Adam Kasia (the 'Hidden Adam'), and the earthly Adam are not always clearly distinguished; see V. SCHOU PEDERSEN, Bidrag til en Analyse af de mandaeiske Skrifter (Aarhus 1940) pp. 189ff.; RUDOLPH, Theogonie pp. 273ff., 296ff., 338, n. 1.

31 *t Sanh* 8.7; *b Sanh* 38a.

32 Or brought into being on the first day. For the notion of the heavenly Man as identical with the primoridal light (φῶς; cf. φώς, ‚man'!) in Judaism and Gnosticism, see FOSSUM, Image pp. 16–17, 20ff.

33 SCHECHTER p. 111. The rabbis must not be seen as forming a unified body of scholars agreeing on every issue. ALTMANN, ‚Background', pp. 385–86, admits that some of the rabbis came to conceive of ‚Adam as being of almost divine character'. Of course he is wrong that this was due to ‚Gnostic influence'.

34 For the bodily connotations of the Biblical terms ‚image' and ‚likeness', see FOSSUM, Image p. 29, n. 65, and p. 35, n. 83.

to get dominion over all things.'[35] The title ‚Firstformed Father of the World' could be used as a name of the creator in the Hellenistic age, as is evidenced by Philo's works and Corpus Hermeticum[36].

Wis 10.1 says that Adam was ‚created alone', which may be taken to imply that it is not the man who was created together with Eve who is described. The ‚Firstformed Father' who has created the world naturally was brought into being before the first human couple.

Now our text also speaks about Adam's ‚transgression' and thus presupposes the Biblical myth of the fall of the first man. This is clearly an instance of the rapprochement between the heavenly Man and the earthly Adam mentioned above. This reconcilement caused a restitution and glorification of the latter, as is evidenced by several texts[37]. Similarly, Wis 10.2 says that Adam was delivered out of his transgression and given dominion over everything. Something new has clearly been added to the Biblical myth.

The restitution of Adam is also found in a basically Jewish prayer existing in two recensions in the Greek magical papyri[38]. Here, too, the προπάτωρ Adam (I. 199) is called πατὴρ κόσμου (IV.1170, 1182), as well as the ‚Firstmanifested and Firstborn Deity' (πρωτοφυής καὶ πρωτογενὴς θεός [I. 195–6]). He is not only portrayed as having been raised to heaven and become the ‚Eternal Aion' and ‚Eternal Lord of the Pole' (αἰωνοπολοκράτωρ [I.200–201])[39]; in accordance with the title ‚Father of the World', he is even ascribed with demiurgic

---

35 10.1–2.

36 A. Dupont-Sommer, ‚Adam. „Père du Monde" dans la Sagesse de Solomon (10,1.2)', RHR 119 (1939) pp. 182–91.

37 *Epist Apost* ch. 39; Tertullian, *De Paen* 12.9 (apparently quoting from a lost work). See further the magical prayers discussed below. In the *Pseudo-Clementines* it is even denied that Adam sinned; see *Hom* III.17; 21; cf. II.52.

38 Preisendanz I.195 ff.; IV.1167 ff. See E. Peterson, ‚Die Befreiung Adams aus der 'Ανάγκη', in his Frühkirche, Judentum und Gnosis (Rome, Freiburg & Vienna 1959) pp. 107–128.

39 The heavenly Adam is further said to ‚rest upon the ἑπταμέριον' (I.201), which Peterson, ‚Befreiung', p. 114, takes to be the constellation of the chariot and an allusion to the chariot throne in Jewish tradition.

Peterson, 'Befreiung', n. 27, further notes that the qibla apparently is the North (Pole), but he is at a loss as to any explanation. Now the mountain of God, on which the Garden of Eden was located, is called *Zaphon*, 'North', in Isa 14.13. Cf. above, n. 27, and see further below, n. 44.

In 2 *Enoch* 30.11–14 Adam, described as the king of earth endowed with God's wisdom, is assigned ‚four special stars'. Are they angels and do they surround Adam's Merkabah throne? Adam is here said to be a ‚second angel', but if the lost original was in Hebrew, Adam may have been characterized as a ‚second Elohim' in the sense ‚second god'. This is a title given to the Logos in Philo, *Quaest in Gen* II.62. The context is an interpretation of Gen 1.26-27 where the divine image/likeness is taken to refer to the Logos. The discussion may presuppose the Jewish mystical idea that the divine image is a heavenly Man, even the Glory. Cf. above, n. 28. 2 *Enoch* ch. 30 may witness an amalgamation of the heavenly Man and Adam. See further next note.

functions: ‚[...] you who breathed animation into the whole world, you who put the fire on the ocean of heaven and separated the earth from the water' (IV.1171–2), ‚[...] creator of the world, creator of all' (IV.1195).

(b) Furthermore, standing amidst ‚innumerable myriads of angels', whom he has created (I.207–8), the heavenly Adam is even the ‚Holy and Powerful Name which is adored by all the angels' (τὸ ὄνομα τὸ ἅγιον καὶ τὸ ἰσχυρόν, τὸ καθηγιασμένον ὑπὸ τῶν ἀγγέλων πάντων [IV.1183–4])[40]. Here we find the motif which is shared by all three polemical texts: the adoration by the angels.

The same motif is also found in a quite early text, where, however, the hero who ascends to heaven and takes the place of the heavenly Man is not identified as Adam. In the Exagoge by the Alexandrian Jewish playwright Ezekiel (2nd cent. B.C.E), Moses in a dream ascends Mt. Sinai, on the summit of which ‚stood a great throne reaching to the corners of heaven. On it was seated a noble Man (φώς)[41], with a diadem on his head and holding a sceptre in his left hand.'[42] With his right hand, the Man on the throne beckoned Moses to approach, seated him on the throne, and handed him the diadem and the sceptre[43]. Moses is thus enthroned as the Man in heaven.

The text goes on to say that a ‚multitude of heavenly bodies fell on their knees' before the enthroned Moses[44]. The stars in Israelite-Jewish tradition are

---

40 In I.206 it is said that Adam *possesses* ‚the Powerful Name which is adored by all the angels.' This Name is of course the Name of God: it is ‚the Hidden Name (τὸ κρυπτὸν ὄνομα) which reaches from the firmament to the earth' (I.217–19). For the cosmological function of the divine Name, holding the universe together as it were, see J. E. FOSSUM, The Name of God and the Angel of the Lord (WUNT 36; Tübingen 1985) pp. 81, 248 ff., 257–58. Since Adam could be regarded as the possessor or even the personification of the divine Name, his *own* name came to be seen as vested with similar significance and power. In 2 *Enoch* 30.14 Adam is said to have been ‚assigned a name from the four components', i. e. from east (A), west (D), north (A), and south (M). Cf. *De Montibus Sina et Sion* 4. In *Sib Or* III.28 he is called ‚Adam Tetragrammaton' with a term used for God's four-lettered Name.

Speculations on the name of Adam also went on among the rabbis. R. Judah ben Simon took the name ‚Adam' in Eccl 2.21 (‚For אדם may do his work with wisdom [...]') as a name of God, the proof being found in Ezek 1.26; see *Gen R.* 27.1; etc. See further P. B. MUNOA, Four Powers in Heaven: The Interpretation of Daniel 7 in the Testament of Abraham (Diss.; University of Michigan 1993) p. 222.

41 Cf. above, n. 32.

42 Apud Eusebius, *Praep ev* 9.28.2.

43 In the *Discourse on Abbaton*, God places Adam upon a ‚great throne' in heaven and gives him a ‚crown of glory' and a ‚royal sceptre'.

44 The king, believed to be seated on the divine throne, was to be accorded worship; see 1 Chron 29.20, 23–24. The divine throne, on which the king was sitting, was in the Jerusalem sanctuary; see 1 Chron 28.5; 2 Chron 9.8. The royal throne on Mt. Zion was an image of the cosmic mountain on which the paradisiac Garden was to be found; see 1 Kings 10.18–20; 2 Chron 9.18–19. See G. WIDENGREN, 'Psalm 110 und das sakrale Königtum in Israel', in P.H.A. NEUMANN (ed.), Zur neueren Psalmenforschung (WF 192; Darmstadt 1976) pp. 188–89, 191. Cf. above, n. 27. According to Ps 48.2, 'Mt. Zion is in the far north', the mythical location of Paradise. Cf. above, n. 39. See also below. n. 47.

1 *Enoch* ch. 25 says that God's throne is found on the 'mountain' with the Tree of Life, i. e. in

identified as angels[45], so Ezekiel the Tragedian provides early evidence for the idea of the angels' adoration of the heavenly Man.

(c) Since the throne of the Phōs is said to reach to the ‚corners of heaven', it must have cosmic proportions. Accordingly, the Man who occupies the heavenly throne must be understood to be of enormous size[46]. This brings us to the concept of the image of God found in the last polemical text(s). That God was thought to have a body of cosmic proportions is stated implicitly in Isa 66.1, ‚The heavens are My seat and the earth My footstool.'[47] The Isaiahnic passage is often quoted in the Shi^cur Qomah, the ‚Measure of the [divine] Body'. A typical excerpt from this mystical work, put into the mouth of R. Ishmael, a pillar of orthodoxy, runs as follows:

I have seen the King of kings over kings, the Holy One, sitting upon a high and elevated throne [...]. What is the measure of the Body of the Holy One, blessed be He, which is hidden from all men? The soles of His feet fill the entire universe, as it is said, ‚The heavens are My seat and the earth My footstool.' The height of His soles is 30000000 parasangs [...][48].

The text goes on to list the fantastic measurements of each and every part of the divine body, which is of cosmic proportions, as implied by the quotation of the Scriptural passage: seated in heaven, God rests his feet upon the earth.

Although Isa 66.1 speaks straightforwardly about God, the Shi^{c}ur Qomah is more subtle. G. Scholem correctly observes

[...] that the Shiur Komah referred no to the ‚dimensions' of the divinity, but to those of its corporeal appearance. This is clearly the interpretation of the original texts. Already the ‚Lesser Hekhaloth' interpret the anthropomorphosis of the Shiur Komah as a representation of the ‚hidden glory'. Thus, for example, Rabbi Akiba says: ‚He is like us, as it were, but greater than everything, and that is His glory which is hidden from us (כבודו שנסתר מפנינו).'[49]

Paradise. Enoch, the seventh and thus the perfect son of Adam, ascends to heaven and is identified as the '(Son of) Man'; see 71.14ff. He is seated on the 'Throne of Glory'; see 45.3; 55.4; 61.8; 62.2 (?); 69.29. He is accorded worship along with God by the earthly powers; see 46.5–6; 48.5, 10; 62.6, 9. According to 51.3, it appears that God himself will glorify the Son of Man, so it does not seem unreasonable that the heavenly powers as well will worship the Son of Man along with God; see 61,7ff.; 69. 27. See E. Sjöberg, Der Menschensohn im Äthiopischen Henochbuch (SHVL 41; Lund 1946) p. 68, n. 32.

[45] E.g., Job 38.7; Isa 14.12-13; Ezek 28.14. The ‚angels of of fire' in the ‚monistic' version of the Mandean anthropogony are identical with the stars, as can be seen from *Right Ginza* II.1, Petermann p. 32.24.

[46] When Enoch ascended to heaven in order to be enthroned, he was ‚enlarged to the size of the length and width of the world' (3 *Enoch* 9.2). See further Fossum, Image pp. 106–107.

[47] For the idea that it is the sanctuary in particular which is God's footstool, see 1 Chron 28.2; Ps 99.5; 137.7; Eccl. 2.1. Cf. above, n. 44, and further below, n. 49, end.

[48] Cohen p. 87.94–96 and 98–102. A parasang is a Persian mile, c. 3/4 of an English mile. Already Origen, *Hom in Gen* I.13, says that some Jews in substantiation of their belief that God has a body cite Isa 66.1.

[49] Major Trends in Jewish Mysticism (3rd ed.; New York 1954 and reprints) p. 66. For the

While the mystics referred Isa 66.1 to divine Man in heaven, the rabbis responded with the statement that God had diminished the original size of Adam. However, the latter were (deliberately?) misinterpreting the identity of their opponents' Man figure, for the mystics did not speak about the first human being, but about the Glory.

Targum Ezek 1.26 reads, ‚likeness as the appearance of Adam'. Since ‚Adam' in Aramaic does not mean ‚man' but is a proper name, the Targum provides evidence to the effect that ‚Adam' actually could be seen as a name of the Glory[50]. This certainly must have contributed to the misinterpretation and/or confusion of the rabbis.

(6) The version in Bereshit Rabbati cannot be said to represent the original form of the myth of the angels' adoration, because God commands them to worship the first man. Still, it must be deemed closer to the original than the older texts discussed by Altmann, for it has retained the non-polemical form of the story. Influence from the Qur'ān can be ruled out, for the rebellious Satan figure, so prominent in the Muslim sources[51], is absent in Bereshit Rabbati. In this Jewish text we have an example of the fact that a late writing may preserve ancient notions.

Bibliography

The abbreviations follow the style manual of *Journal of Biblical Literature*. Editions/translations are cited for only the more unfamiliar and/or inaccessible primary sources.

ALTMANN, A., ‚The Gnostic Background of the Rabbinic Adam Legends', JQR 35 (1945) pp. 371–91.

BARC, B., ‚La taille cosmique d'Adam dans la littérature juive rabbinique des trois premiers siècles après J.-C.', RSR 49 (1975) pp. 173–85.

---

text from the *Lesser Hekhaloth*, see SCHÄFER p. 148, § 352. I. GRUENWALD, Apocalyptic and Merkavah Mysticism (AGAJU 14; Leiden 1980) p. 142, dates this work to the second or third century C. E. For the high age of the rudiments of the *Shi^cur Qomah*, see further FOSSUM, Image pp. 35–36. It could be said that the shrine was the place where the Glory was enthroned; see Ezek 9.3; 10.1,4. Cf. Jer 17.12. See further Targum 1 Chron 28.2. The earthly temple was of course modelled on the heavenly one.

[50] Moreover, the prophet Ezekiel is called the ‚son of Adam' throughout the Targumic version. S.H. LEVEY, The Targum to Ezekiel (The Aramaic Bible 13; Wilmington 1987) pp. 6–9, takes Ezekiel as a ‚counterpart of Adam', who had seen the Merkabah throne; see *Life of Adam and Eve* ch. 25.

In the Jewish prayers surveyed above, the supplicant clearly refers to himself as Adam *salvandus*, who thus cannot be entirely differentiated conceptually or substantially from Adam *salvator*: the latter has experienced the restoration which the former begs to obtain. See PETERSON, ‚Befreiung', pp. 109–113.

[51] Surah 2.27 ff.; 7.10 ff.; 15.26 ff.; 17.62 ff.; 20.114 ff.; 38.71 ff.

Bezold, C., Die Schatzhöhle (2 vols.; Leipzig 1883/88).
Budge, E. A. Wallis, Coptic Martyrdoms in the Dialect of Upper Egypt (London 1914), cited by folio.
Cohen, M. S., The Shi^cur Qomah. Texts and Recensions (TSAJ 9; Tübingen 1985).
Dupont-Sommer, A., ‚Adam. „Père du Monde“ dans la Sagesse de Solomon (10.1,2)‘, RHR 119 (1939) pp. 182–91.
Fossum, J. E., The Name of God and the Angel of the Lord (WUNT 36; Tübingen 1985).
–, The Image of the Invisible God (NTOA 30; Freiburg & Göttingen, 1995).
Ginzberg, L., ‚Adam Kadmon‘, Jewish Encyclopedia (10 vols.; New York & London, 1901), Vol. I, pp. 181–83.
–, The Legends of the Jews (6 vols.; Philadelphia 1909–28 and reprints).
Gruenwald, I., Apocalyptic and Merkavah Mysticism (AGAJU 14; Leiden 1980).
Hirschberg, J. W., Jüdische und christliche Lehren im vor- und frühislamischen Arabien (Mémoires de la commission orientaliste 32, Polska Akademia; Kraków 1939).
Kinzer, M. S., ‚All Things Beneath His Feet‘: The Influence of Psalm 8 on Early Jewish and Christian Literature (Diss.; University of Michigan 1995).
Kraeling, C. H., Anthropos and Son of Man (CUOS 25; New York 1927, reprinted 1966).
Levey, S. H., The Targum to Ezekiel (The Aramaic Bible 13; Wilmington 1987).
Levinson, J. R., Portraits of Adam in Early Judaism (JSPSup 1; Sheffield 1988).
Lidzbarski, M., Ginza (QRG 13/4; Göttingen, 1925).
Lipscomb, W., The Armenian Apocryphal Adam Literature (ATS 8; Philadelphia 1990).
Munoa, P. B., Four Powers in Heaven: The Interpretation of Daniel 7 in the Testament of Abraham (Diss.; University of Michigan 1993).
Pedersen, V. Schou, Bidrag til en Analyse af de mandaeiske Skrifter (Aarhus 1940).
Petermann, H., Thesaurus, sive Liber Magnus, vulgo „Liber Adami“ appellatus, opus Mandaeorum summi ponderis (2 vols.; Leipzig 1867).
Peterson, E., ‚Die Befreiung Adams aus der ᾿Ανάγκη‘, in his Frühkirche, Judentum und Gnosis (Rome, Freiburg & Vienna 1959).
Preisendanz, K., Papyri Graecae Magicae (new edition in 3 vols. by A. Henrichs, Stuttgart 1973/74), cited by No. and line(s).
Rudolph, K., Theogonie, Kosmogonie und Anthropogonie in den Mandäischen Schriften (FRLANT 58; Göttingen 1965).
Schäfer, P., Synopse zur Hekhalot-Literatur (TSAJ 2; Tübingen 1981).
Schechter, S., Masseketh Aboth de Rabbi Nathan (reprint New York 1945).
Scholem, G., Major Trends in Jewish Mysticism (3rd ed.; New York 1954 and reprints).
–, Von der mystischen Gestalt der Gottheit (Zürich 1962).
Sjöberg, E., Der Menschensohn im Äthiopischen Henochbuch (SHVL 41; Lund 1946)
Staerk, W., Die Erlösererwartung in den östlichen Religionen (Stuttgart 1938).
Stone, M., The History of the Literature of Adam and Eve (SBLEJL 3; Atlanta 1992).
Strack, H. L., & P. Billerbeck, Kommentar zum Neuen Testament aus Talmud und Midrasch (six parts in 7 vols.; Munich 1922–28).
Widengren, G. ‘Psalm 110 und das sakrale Königtum in Israel’, in P. H. A. Neumann, Zur neueren Psalmenforschung (WF 192; Darmstadt 1976) pp. 185–216.
Wistinetzki, J., Sefer Ḥasidim (Frankfurt a. M. 1925).

Jewish Liturgy and Magic[1]

by

Peter Schäfer

"Jewish liturgy and magic" seems to be a rather odd combination, at least at first sight. If we have in mind the traditional synagogue service from antiquity up to modern times, with its solemn prayers and benedictions, there is hardly anything in it we would associate with magic in particular. The enlightened 19th century Protestant Christian notion of a religion that becomes all the more "religious" the fewer rudiments of "primitive" magic are left in it,[2] has definitely influenced the way modern Judaism defines itself. But things are not that easy, neither for modern Judaism (one only needs to look at the Wailing Wall in Jerusalem with the notes attached to it) nor for late antiquity. The same is true with regard to the Jewish Temple ritual: one is not inclined to associate it with magical practices either, and yet nothing has evoked more curiosity than the mysterious custom of the High Priest uttering the ineffable and inexplicable name of God, the tetragrammaton, once a year (at the Day of Atonement) in the Temple.

I will deal in this article with both elements of Jewish liturgy, Temple ritual and prayer, and their relationship with magic. In doing so I will refer to Jewish magical texts of late antiquity or the early Middle Ages which have been published only recently or are still unpublished.

1. Ritual

One of the most "magical" Temple rituals is the so-called ordeal of jealousy inflicted on a woman who is suspected of adultery, described in the Book of Numbers 5:11–31: it consists mainly of drinking the so-called "water of bitterness", i.e., water mixed with dust from the floor of the Tabernacle (Temple)

---

[1] A slightly different version of this article was presented as a paper during the symposium on magic which was held on March 27–28, 1995, at the Institute for Advanced Study, Princeton. It is with pleasure and gratitude that I offer it as a token of my appreciation to a teacher, colleague, and friend.

[2] See, e.g., Frazer, Golden Bough, vol. 1, pp. 62–78.

into which "curses" or "spells" are dissolved (the curses are first written down on a "scroll" and the writing is then dissolved in water). The "curses", according to the plain meaning of the text, obviously consisted of this very sentence, uttered by the priest: "May the LORD make you a curse and an imprecation among your people, as the LORD causes your thigh to sag and your belly to distend; may this water that induces the spell enter your body, causing the belly to distend and the thigh to sag" (Num. 5:21 f.). It is this sentence, which the priest is then said to "put down in writing and rub it off into the water of bitterness" (ibid., v. 23).

Later Jewish traditions did not only pretend to have continued the ritual, despite the Mishnah's insistence on its abrogation,[3] they also transmit a much more elaborate curse formula including all the crucial names which alone guarantee the efficacy of the ritual. These are preserved in two Genizah fragments, now belonging to the Library of the Jewish Theological Seminary in New York (JTSL ENA 3635.17) and to the Cambridge University Library (K 1.56), first published by A. Marmorstein[4] and republished in the first volume of magical texts from the Cairo Genizah, edited by Shaul Shaked and myself.[5] They don't tell us when and where this ritual was performed. We only know that the fragments were most probably written in the 11th and 12th century in a script which is vaguely called "oriental": the former, of course, doesn't say anything about the dating of the actual performance of the ritual; the latter at least gives a clue as to its geographical location, namely, that it belongs to the Jews of the East (Egypt, Palestine, Babylon) and not to European or Ashkenazi Judaism.

The text[6] begins with the celebrated formula, originally recited after the holy name of God consisting of four letters (the tetragrammaton) was uttered in the Temple, and later during the synagogue service after the recitation of the first sentence of the *Shema*ᶜ: "Blessed be the *name* of the glory of his kingdom for ever and ever" (17a/1). This is taken literally: as we can see immediately, it is this name which is in the center of the text and the ritual. From lines 7 ff. we learn that "all the names by which the angels call him (i.e., God) ... have been written down from the mouth of R. Ishmael", who received them from the angel Meṭaṭron, "up until the time of Israel's Synhedrium (whose members) used to know the seventy names" (lines 15 f.). Hence, the name of God consists in the end of seventy names (a well-known tradition),[7] and these seventy names are transmitted by R. Ishmael, one of the heros of early Jewish mysticism (Hekhalot literature), who anachronistically is made a High Priest – of course in order to establish the connection with the Temple ritual.

From this it becomes clear that the hidden (seventy) names form the one

---

[3] m Sot 9:9.

[4] Beiträge, pp. 377–383.

[5] Magische Texte, vol. 1, pp. 17–45; see also Veltri, ᶜInyan Sota, pp. 23–48.

[6] For a full English translation of JTSL ENA 3635.17 see the appendix.

[7] See Synopse, §§ 4, 46, 71 ff.

ineffable name of God (17a/18f.) which the High Priest uttered during the Temple service (17b/3), and that it is this name, or rather these names, which the woman had to drink (17a/20). Our text knows very well, closely following the biblical original, that the water in itself is not bitter but is made bitter by the curses and, as it adds, by the names (17b/12). And then it fills, so to speak, the gap in the biblical *Vorlage* and conveys the names missing in Num. 5:23:

"(These) are the adjurations, the curses and the names that the High Priest used to write on a scroll (17b/13ff.)."

What follows is a re-telling of the biblical ritual into which the names are neatly implanted (17b/15–17c/16). They start with the common biblical phrase *YHWH* (the tetragrammaton), *elohe Jisra'el* (17b/15), and turn into the usual *nomina barbara*, i.e., permutations of letters which are all believed to be components of the *one* name of God. This part breaks off abruptly in 17c/16 with the quotation of Num. 5:28 ("But if the woman has not let herself become defiled and is pure" etc.) – the author does not seem to be particularly interested in a positive outcome of the ordeal.

Then the text proceeds to describe the "way we practice today, due to the fact that we no (longer) have a priest, no (longer) holy water, and no (longer) a Tabernacle" (17c/17–19). The author is very concerned to justify that the ritual can be performed even today and to specify by whom: a man (literally a man: *adam*) who is godfearing, has purified himself from sin, is completely pure, and preoccupies himself with these names (i.e., knows the proper use of the names) – such a man "resembles an angel and a High Priest" (17d/7), i.e., is able to perform the ritual.

Of course, this ritual has to be slightly different from the biblical one. Since we no longer have the "holy water" mentioned in the Bible, "running water" out of a spring must do (17d/11), and the vessel being used has to be new, like in many other magical texts (17d/11f.). The same is true for the dust: since we don't have the Tabernacle any more, dust from the synagogue must do, to be sure not any dust but dust taken from the four corners of the Torah shrine, which is not by coincidence called here in Hebrew *hekhal shel torah*, i.e., the same word used for the Temple hall in front of the Holy of Holies. Then one has to write down the names "that we wrote down above" (17d/17f.), to dissolve them in water, and to let the woman drink: "immediately you will see [the sign], ... and the wonders, and the power of his (i.e., God's) holy names" (17d/19). The appropriate benediction for this successfully performed ritual can only be: "Blessed be he, and blessed be his living and eternal *name* forever" (ibid.).

This is a stunning ritual, the more so as it is the only one I am aware of that so insolently maintains to continue a practice clearly connected with the Temple. The Rabbis of classical Judaism did everything to disconnect themselves from the Temple worship, to transform the ritual of the Temple into something new and different, and here we have a group (?) which claims to do the same thing as the priests and even the High Priest in the Temple did. Moreover, the group behind our text tells us quite self-confidently that they are the final recipients of the hidden magical names used by the priests in the Temple ritual but not disclosed in the biblical text. The chain of tradition inaugurated by Meṭraṭon, the Prince of the divine countenance (i.e., the highest angel), does not come to an end with the members of the Synhedrium: our group is the true heir of this tradition, is the successor of the holy Synhedrium.

This does allow us to speculate about the circles to which our text could be attributed. The self-assurance of our author or authors, the claim to be in possession of the secret tradition of the holy name or names of God, to use these names as part of a ritual which was believed to have come to an end with the destruction of the Temple, and not least the connection with R. Ishmael, the hero of Merkavah mysticism, all this makes it quite probable that our text originated in the same circles, or to be more cautious, in circles close to those which are responsible for the Hekhalot literature. We know from the Hekhalot texts that some of them indulged in Temple fantasies and were very concerned about locating their mystical and magical exercises in a Temple setting.[8] It therefore wouldn't come as a complete surprise if the circles behind these texts boasted of being able and privileged to perform the ritual of the ordeal of adultery, long after the Temple had been destroyed. In any case, the text shows how closely mysticism, magic, and, indeed, ritual were interwoven in late antiquity/early Middle Ages.

2. Prayer

Prayer constitutes an important component of any kind of Jewish mysticism. This is certainly true for its earliest stage, Merkavah mysticism, where prayer can be used as a tool for achieving the heavenly journey (the mystic has to say certain prayers in order to ascend to the throne of Glory)[9] and can serve, too, as the appropriate response to the successfully undertaken ascent: when the mystic has arrived at the goal of his desire, he bursts out into a solemn prayer or rather hymn, with which he joins in the heavenly liturgy of the celestial powers. For the latter I have coined the phrase *unio liturgica*, indicating that it is this liturgical communion with the angels which characterizes the climax of the heavenly journey rather than the vision of God upon his throne.[10]

Most prayers in the Hekhalot literature are permeated in one way or the other with magical elements, testifying again to the close relationship between

8 See, e.g., Synopse, §§ 202, 297ff., 309.

9 See Schäfer, Hidden and Manifest God, pp. 86ff.

10 Ibid., p. 165.

mysticism and magic. These prayers, which I call incantational prayers, are well-known and documented.[11] What is less well-known are prayers which combine in an unprecedented way the regular formula of the Jewish prayer with magical ingredients, or rather vice versa, combine clearly magical material with elements of the classical prayer, thus giving these texts a very distinctive flavor. The first example I would like to refer to are two fragments, again from the Cairo Genizah, which are not yet published but will appear in the second volume of our corpus of magical texts.[12] They belong together and are part of a codex, a magical manual. The script is again "oriental" and can be dated to the 11th century C. E.

Our text is a collection of magical recipes, dealing with all kinds of requests. Its respective units are organized according to the simple *im biqqashta* formula: "If you wish such and such ...", followed by a set of *nomina barbara*, which is well-known from many other instances. The various subjects are: prognoses (K 1.35, 1a/16: "if you wish [to know] everything that will be [in the future]"), resurrection (1a/21: "[if] you wish [to resurrect] someone who is dead from his grave"), angels (1a/26f.: "if you wish to see the angels and have them show you whatever you shall desire and ask them"), increase of something, probably knowledge (1b/5: "if you wish to increase [ ]"), request to a high- ranking person (1b/8: "if you wish to address a request to a [ruler]"), rescue from [death] (1b/11: "if you wish to rescue a person from death"), speaking with someone (1b/14 and 20: "if you wish to speak with [ ]"), knowledge of something (1b/17: "if you wish that they make known to you [ ]"), speaking with the Pleiades (1b/23: "if you wish to speak with the Pleiades"), speaking with the moon (1b/26f.: "if you wish to speak with the moon"), speaking with the sun (1b/29: "if you wish to speak with the sun"), speaking with the *ḥayyot*, the creatures who carry God's throne (K 1.48, 1a/2f.: "if you wish to speak with the four-faced [*ḥayyot*] that they make known to you what you wish to know"), Prince of the hosts of God (1a/5f.: "if you wish that the Prince of the hosts of God speaks with you and makes known to you what you wish to know"), vision (1a/8–10: "if you wish to see *the marvels of the omniscient God* [Job 37:16] and the throne of Glory and the ministering angels"), service of the harmful spirits (1a/13: "if you wish that the harmful spirits in the sea and on the mainland serve you"), and finally service of the wild animals (1a/15–17: "if you wish that the wild animals of the sea and of the mainland should come before you so that you shall send them in all your desires").

As far as the content of the requests is concerned, the text has a carefully arranged order: it begins with some matters of various concern which are all

[11] See SCHÄFER, Jewish Magic Literature, pp. 76ff.

[12] T.-S. K 1.35 and K 1.48. The concluding benediction in K 1.48 (see below) has already been published, together with a brief commentary, by ABRAMSON, Nusaḥ berakhah, pp. 163f.

connected, so to speak, with the earth, and then follows an ascending pattern: Pleiades, moon, sun, *ḥayyot*, angelic prince, and, the climax, the vision, to be sure not of God but of his wonders and throne of Glory. After this a descending pattern is adopted: with the service of the harmful spirits and the beasts, the requests of our adept come back to the earth again.

Now, what makes this text so peculiar is not the content of the magical recipes (we find very similar ones, e.g., in *Sefer ha-Razim*) but another pattern of its organization. In addition to the rather boring "if you wish" formula, there is another element which divides the various literary units and which can easily be overlooked because, for the most part, it consists of one word only and may be misunderstood as belonging to the mostly meaningless *nomina barbara* (and often it is missing altogether because our text is badly preserved). On closer inspection one realizes that these scattered words belong to the benedictions of the so-called *Eighteen-Benedictions* or ᶜ*Amidah* prayer, together with the *Shemaᶜ Israel* the most important daily prayer of the synagogue. They are:

K 1:35:

1a/15: *magen*, i.e. *magen Avraham* ("shield of Abraham"), which is the blessing (eulogy) of the first benediction;

1a/20: *meḥayyeh*, i.e. *meḥayyeh ha-metim* ("who resurrects the dead"), the eulogy of the second benediction;

1a/26: *ha-'el*, i.e. *ha-'el ha-qadosh* ("the holy God"), the eulogy of the third benediction;

The following eulogies are missing in the fragment but according to the structure of the text we may safely assume that 1b/4 included the fourth, 1b/7 the fifth, 1b/10 the sixth, 1b/13 the seventh, 1b/16 the eighth, 1b/19 the ninth, and 1b/22 the tenth eulogy. The following blessings are again preserved:

1b/26: *ohev ṣed'*, i.e. *ohev ṣedaqah* ("who loves righteousness"), the eulogy of the eleventh benediction;

1b/29: *makhniaᶜ*, i.e. *makhniaᶜ zedim* ("who humiliates the wicked"), the eulogy of the twelfth benediction;

K 1.48:

1a/1: *mivtaḥ*, i.e. *mivtaḥ la-ṣadiqim* ("support for the righteous"), the eulogy of the thirteenth benediction;

1a/5: *boneh*, i.e. *boneh Yerushalayim* ("who builds Jerusalem"), the eulogy of the fourteenth benediction;

1a/8: *shomeaᶜ*, i.e. *shomeaᶜ tefillah* ("who hearkens to [the] prayer"), the eulogy of the fifteenth benediction;

1a/12: *she-'otkha*, i.e. *she-'otkha be-yir'ah naᶜavod*, ("whom we worship in fear"), the eulogy of the sixteenth benediction;

1a/15: *ha-ṭov*, i.e. *ha-ṭov lekha lehodot* ("to whom it is good to give thanks"), the eulogy of the seventeenth benediction;

1a/20f.: ᶜ*ośeh ha-shalom* ("who brings about peace"), the eulogy of the eighteenth benediction.

From the wording and number of the benedictions something else, something very important (not for Jewish magic but for Jewish liturgy), becomes immediately clear: what we no doubt have here is the Eighteen Benedictions prayer in its ancient Palestinian form, not in its younger Babylonian version which has replaced the Palestinian and is still in use today. It (the Palestinian version) consists of eighteen benedictions proper, whereas the Babylonian has nineteen benedictions, and it differs in the formulation of the benedictions. Although in most cases it is impossible to decide whether the eulogies in our text belong to the Palestinian or the Babylonian version (because they quote one word only and the eulogies are often very similar), there is in a few instances clear evidence of a Palestinian wording: the twelfth,[13] the thirteenth,[14] the sixteenth,[15] and the eighteenth[16] benedictions are peculiar to the Palestinian form of the prayer, all the others could theoretically belong to both versions.[17] This, together with the number of eighteen benedictions, is a strong corroboration of the assumption that our text as a whole reflects indeed the Palestinian version of the Eighteen Benedictions prayer.

Why am I emphasizing this? Everyone familiar with the history of the text of the Eighteen Benedictions knows that we are not blessed with sumptuous textual evidence for the Palestinian version.[18] Hence, our fragment turns out to be not only important evidence for the interrelationship between magic and liturgy, but also an unexpected witness for the earliest form of one of the most classical (and non-magical) prayers in Judaism.

When we finally ask where to locate our magical prayer, the text itself may give a clue again. It begins with a confession of sins, which clearly belongs to the Day of Atonement, and concludes, immediately after having quoted the eighteenth benediction, with a eulogy of its own which reads as follows:

---

[13] The Babylonian version of the twelfth benediction has: *shover oyevim u-makhnia^c zedim*. That our text reads *makhnia^c* instead of *u-makhnia^c* points to the Palestinian version.

[14] Here again the Babylonian version has *mish^{c}an u-mivtaḥ la- ṣaddiqim*. The missing *waw* again points to the Palestinian version.

[15] *She-'otkha be-yir'ah na^{c}avod* is unmistakably Palestinian.

[16] The same is true for *^{c}ośeh ha-shalom*.

[17] The only exception is the eleventh benediction, *ohev ṣedaqah*, which seems to be Babylonian (*ohev ṣedaqah u-mishpat*) rather than Palestinian (*ohev ha-mishpat*). However, we may be dealing here with a textual witness which has preserved a different version of the eleventh Palestinian eulogy, or one which literally depicts the intrusion of the Babylonian into the Palestinian tradition.

[18] For the most comprehensive documentation so far of the relevant material see FLEISCHER, Eretz-Israel Prayers and Prayer Rituals.

"Blessed be you, God, our Lord, King of the universe, who sanctified his great name in his world, and who revealed it to the *bene meron*[19] in order that they serve with it in holiness and purity, and who commanded us to sanctify it, be it in script or in speech. Blessed be you, God, our Lord, King of the universe, who sanctified us with his commandments, and commanded us (to keep) the sanctity of the name."[20]

The term *bene meron* mentioned here is a further indication that the prayer belongs to the High Holidays. The expression is probably taken from the Latin *numerus* and alludes to the Mishnah (*Rosh ha-Shanah* 1:2): "At four times in the year is the world judged: ... on New Year's Day all that come into the world pass before him like *bene meron* (= 'legions of soldiers' or 'flocks of sheep'), for it is written (Ps. 33:15), *He that fashioneth the hearts of them all, that considereth all their works*."[21] What we have here, therefore, is a penitential ritual of the High Holidays in which magical formulas are implanted. An essential part of these formulas are the eighteen benedictions combined with *nomina barbara* which, of course, are again permutations of God's one name, the tetragrammaton. And it is certainly not by coincidence that the quoted benediction at the end of our prayer focusses precisely on this name: God has revealed it to the *bene meron*, i.e., to those who confess their sins on the High Holidays and ask for absolution. *They* obtain the required state of purity in order to be able "to serve with it", i.e., to use it in the proper way – which, of course, is the one demonstrated in the prayer.

Hence, the prayer communicates at the same time (and in a rather strange combination) a submissive and a self-assured or even coercive attitude. Its author or authors in the end know very well that the great and holy name of God has been revealed to them, and they praise God because they are chosen to keep or observe the sanctity of the name. The eulogy, "and commanded us (to keep) the sanctity of the name (*qedushat ha-shem*)", is very unusual. It refers to the third benediction in the Eighteen Benedictions prayer which begins, according to the Palestinian version, "You are holy, and your name is frightful",[22]

---

19 This reading (*bene meron*) has been suggested by SHAKED (Peace be Upon You, p. 204). It is, however, not unequivocal: possible is also the reading *bene ydyrwn (yediron)* which has been suggested by ABRAMSON (Nusaḥ berakhah, p. 164), and which may be a corruption of *'dyrywn (adiriron)*. The latter, a well-known name of God particularly in the Hekhalot literature (cf. Synopse, §§ 204, 220, 301, 411, 419, 516), enforces the connection of our prayer with Merkavah mysticism proposed below.

Most interesting in this context is the phrase in *Megillat Aḥimaaz* (ed. KLAR, p. 12, line 20) which says of the legendary Aaron of Baghdad (who seems especially to have transmitted to the West magical traditions; see DAN, Aaron of Baghdad, col. 21): "he is like the *bene meron* for the King *Adiriron*". This combination of *bene meron* (i.e. Israel on New Year's Day) and God (*Adiriron*) could explain the strange *bene yediron* (= *adiriron*) in our prayer, if this reading is correct.

20 T.-S. K 1.48, fol. 1a/21–26.

21 Translation DANBY, Mishnah, p. 188.

22 SCHECHTER, Genizah Specimens, p. 657.

and which is called in the Mishnah *qedushat ha- shem*,[23] but there is no eulogy in any of the known synagogue prayers which explicitly mentions, like our text, the "sanctity of the name". The only parallel I have come across so far is again, and not surprisingly, in the Hekhalot literature. There, in the so-called *Lesser Hekhalot*, the name of God plays a predominant role. It was revealed to R. Aqiva, the other hero of this literature, when he had a vision of the *Merkavah*, the divine throne. R. Aqiva, in turn, taught it to his students and admonished them that only one who uses it in "fear, terror, purity, sanctity, and humility ... will be successful in all his endeavors ...", and then the text concludes with our eulogy: "Blessed be you, God, who sanctified us with his commandments, and commanded us (to keep) the sanctity of the name".[24]

No doubt, therefore, that the author or authors of our magical prayer regarded themselves to be part of precisely this tradition: they are the true students of Aqiva who did purify themselves and are now able to use the name successfully as it is meant to be used, for magical purposes. Hence, we may conclude again that the circles behind our prayer are close to those who composed the Hekhalot literature. Whether this implies that they actually belonged to the initiates of Merkavah mysticism, or that they are rather a later echo of the practices exercised in Merkavah mysticism, is a different question. The latter probably is the easiest way out: one immediately thinks of the *ḥaside ashkenaz*, the German Pietists, who were very convinced of their own purity and piety; and as a matter of fact, there is a formula of a eulogy similar to the one quoted above which explicitly mentions the *ḥasidim*, the "pious".[25] I am inclined to believe, however, that the strong emphasis put on the name, together with the vision of the *ḥayyot*, of the "Prince of the hosts of God", and of the throne of Glory as the climax of the requests to be fulfilled by uttering the prayer, that this typical combination strongly points to the former possibility.[26]

My second example is a prayer of which I have edited most of the fragments known so far.[27] It is preserved in two versions, one of which bears the title *Sheva^c de-Eliyahu*, i.e., "The Seven [Benedictions] of Elijah",[28] and the other *Sheva^c Zuṭarti*, i.e., "The Lesser [Prayer of] Seven [Benedictions]".[29] Again, like the text we discussed just now, this prayer contains magical elements

[23] m RhSh 4:5.

[24] Synopse, § 337.

[25] T.-S. K 1.115, fol. 1b/1–5, to be published in Magische Texte aus der Kairoer Geniza, vol. 2. See also BAR-ILAN, Mysteries, p. 149.

[26] In addition, of course, to the chronological problem: whereas T.-S. K 1.115 is dated around 1200 and therefore could reflect *ḥaside ashkenaz* influence, T.-S. K 1.35 and K 1.48 most probably are earlier and belong to the 11th century.

[27] Geniza-Fragmente, pp. 140–158.

[28] MSS Cambridge T.-S. K 21.95.P, K 21.95.T, K 1.144, NS 322.21, NS 322.72, Oxford Heb. a.3.25a.

[29] MS Oxford Michael 9, fol. 115a/3–116a/27.

combined with classical benedictions. The latter, this time, are not the eighteen benedictions of the daily ᶜ*Amidah* prayer but the seven benedictions of the ᶜ*Amidah* to be used on Sabbath or Holidays – and again, the wording of the eulogies is of particular interest. The following eulogies are preserved:

First:
magen [*Avraham*] ("shield of Abraham") = Oxford, Michael 9, fol. 115a/22.

Second:
meḥayyeh [*ha-metim*] ("who resurrects the dead") = K 21.95.P, fol. 2a/1; Heb. a.3.25a/13; Michael 9, fol. 115b/6f.

Third:
ha-'el ha-qadosh ("the holy God") = K 21.95.P, fol. 2a/19; NS 322.72, fol. 1a/6f.; Heb. a.3.25a/31; Michael 9, fol. 115b/14 reads: *ha-'el ha-meqaddesh* ("the God who sanctifies").

Fourth:
This is the crucial benediction which determines whether the prayer belongs to the Sabbath or a Holiday liturgy: either *meqaddesh ha-shabbat* ("who sanctifies the Sabbath") or *meqaddesh Yisra'el* [*we- ha-zemanim*] ("who sanctifies Israel [and the festive seasons]"). K 21.95.P, fol. 2b/17, and Michael 9, fol. 115b/24f., read only *meqaddesh* and leave the application open. NS 322.72, fol. 1b/7f., clearly has [*meqaddesh*] *Yisra'el*, and Heb. a.3.25a/47f. reads *meqaddesh* and deletes the word *Yisra['el]*. Hence, with the exception of NS 322.72, the fragments obviously want to leave it open whether the prayer is to be used on a Sabbath or on a Holiday.

Fifth:
*she-'otkha levadkha be-yir'ah na*ᶜ*avod* ("whom alone we worship in fear") = K 21.95.T, fol. 1a/14f.; Heb. a.3.25a/67 (only *she-'otkha*); Michael 9, fol. 116a/3f. (only *she-'otkha*).

Sixth:
ha-ṭov lekha [*lehodot*] ("to whom it is good to give thanks") = K 21.95.T, fol. 1b/11; Michael 9, fol. 116a/15 (only *ha-ṭov*).

Seventh:
mevarekh ᶜ*amo Yisra'el we-*ᶜ*ośeh ha-shalom* ("who blesses his people Israel and brings about peace") = K 1.144, fol. 2a/18f.; Michael 9, fol. 116a/27 (only ᶜ*ośeh ha-shalom*).

Here, as in the previous prayer, the fifth and the sixth eulogies clearly point to a Palestinian origin of this Seven Benedictions prayer; the seventh seems to combine Babylonian (*mevarekh et* ᶜ*amo Yisra'el*) and Palestinian elements (*we-*ᶜ*ośeh ha-shalom* instead of *ba-shalom*).

As far as the magical component is concerned, the prayer does not follow the *im biqqashta* ("If you wish such and such") pattern but the adjuration formula: *mashbia*ᶜ *ani* ᶜ*alekha* ("I adjure you ..."). The means of the adjuration is always the holy name of God. This is already made clear in the benediction which opens the prayer:

"Blessed be you, God, King of the universe, who rules the spirit, with your eternal praises. Hearken, [my God,] to the utterance of my prayer. Holy [12 times], and I will sanctify[30] this your sanctified name within me ... And place within me the fear of your name ... Blessed be you, God, who hearkens to the prayer and to the entreaties, and blessed be his name, which our eyes long for. And with his name we[31] adjure, decree, and establish."[32]

This is a very self-assured benediction; the one who prays it communicates again a submissive and a coercive attitude towards God. He asks that his prayer be answered and yet, at the same time, he knows that he is in the possession of God's holy name ("your sanctified name within me"), the most potent means to accomplish an adjuration. Immediately after this introductory benediction he starts his adjurations, which all begin with the formula "I adjure you", and use different permutations of the tetragrammaton. The object of the adjurations is Metatron,[33] the highest angel, who is also called the Prince of the Divine Countenance,[34] but, as very often in this kind of literature, the borderline between God's angel and God himself is blurred: in the end it is God to whom the adjuration is directed. This becomes clear even from the first adjuration which quotes Elijah's encounter with God in a cave on Mount Horeb: God is not in the "great and strong wind", not in the earthquake, and not in the fire, but in the "faint murmuring sound" (*qol demamah daqqah*) which talks to Elijah (1 Kings 19:11ff.). The knowledge and the proper use of God's holy name puts not only the angels but God himself at the adept's disposal.

The request to be accomplished by the seven adjurations is always the same: "so that he brings about deliverance and rescue from distress [to the burdened, and so that he cures (me)] and drives away every spirit from my body and every demon from me. Amen, [Amen], Amen; Sela, [Sela, Sela; instantly,] instantly, instantly; three (times) swiftly. Three (times) easily; quickly, behold, quickly [and easily it will come to pass] (and then follow the respective eulogies of the Seven Benedictions prayer)".[35] This is a relatively open formula which obviously was intended to be used for all kinds of illnesses connected with evil spirits and demons.

But why Elijah? Why is Elijah the hero of our incantational prayer? The first reason, I believe, is because he is a second Moses:[36] Like Moses he went to Mount Horeb, the mount of God (the journey took him forty days and forty nights), like Moses he hears God speaking to him when he passes by (Elijah is

---

30 Following Michael 9, fol. 115a/4 (*aqqadesh*), instead of *qadosh*.

31 Following Michael 9, fol. 115a/8 (*anaḥnu*), instead of *ani*.

32 K 21.95.P, fol. 1a/4–10.

33 K 21.95.P, fol. 1a/16ff.; 1b/10ff.

34 T.-S. K 21.95.T, fol. 1a/16; Heb. a.3.25a/69 (here called *swryh mal'akh ha-panim* who is obviously identical with Metatron; for Suriah and Metatron see also Synopse, § 200).

35 K 21.95.P, fol. 1b/2–4. The formula varies slightly in the different cases.

36 1 Kings 19:8–14; Ex. 33:18–23.

hidden in a cave, Moses in a crevice of a rock). Moses hears God pronouncing his holy name, the tetragrammaton,[37] Elijah hears the "faint murmuring sound",[38] which in our prayer is understood, no doubt, as pronouncing the secret name.[39] The only difference is, that unlike Elijah, Moses is honored, in addition to hearing God's name, with seeing God's back.[40] This striking similarity between Elijah and Moses is emphasized also by our prayer when it explicitly says that the name of the "great, powerful, awesome, and bold God" was "written down for Moses, the prophet, who did not pass it on[41] (to) any other prophet except for Elijah the Tishbite".[42] Precisely this connection is made also in the first text we discussed, the ordeal of adultery, which mentions the names "that were revealed to Moses at Sinai and in the thorn-bush", as well as those "that were revealed to Elijah on Mount Carmel".[43]

This brings us to the second, even more important reason. What happened on Mount Carmel? Mount Carmel is the venue of Elijah's contest with the prophets of Baal. The contest consists in setting up a sacrifice for both parties, and the one who succeeds in setting fire to it miraculously, i.e., without natural means, has proven that its god is the true God. How does it work? Elijah gives the following instruction: "You invoke your god by name (lit. 'you call your god by name' or 'you utter the name of your god'), and I shall invoke the LORD by name (and here the tetragrammaton is used for 'LORD'); the god who answers by fire, he is God".[44] Of course, Elijah wins the contest because, in terms of magical performance, the name of his God is more potent than the name of Baal.

This, I think, is the main reason for connecting Elijah with magical practices. He knew, like Moses, the potent name of God, and he is, like Moses, an arch-magician who impressively proved its power (Moses did it in the contest with the Egyptian magicians).[45]

If we finally ask about the historical context of our prayer, we again have the choice between the German Pietists and the much earlier Merkavah mystics. The well-known adaptation of Hekhalot texts by the German Pietists, which makes it sometimes difficult even within the Hekhalot literature itself to distinguish between "original" Hekhalot texts and "later" adaptations, does not allow a definite answer. However, in view not only of the rather early date of the fragments (11th century?) but also of the strong Merkavah flavor of the

---

37 Ex. 33:19.

38 1 Kings 19:12.

39 After the quotation of this verse follow *nomina barbara* (K 21.95.P, fol. 1a/12ff.).

40 Ex. 33:23.

41 *hizkiro* (Michael 9, fol. 116a/18) instead of *hizhiro*.

42 K 21.95 T, fol. 1b/12–14.

43 JTSL ENA 3635.17, fol. 17a/11 f.

44 1 Kings 18:24.

45 Ex. 7:8ff. That the revelation of the name historically comes later, is not relevant here.

prayer[46] there is much to argue in favor of a close connection, in terms of contents and of time, to Merkavah mysticism. The Merkavah mystics, of course, were not the only ones in late antiquity who used magical practices, but they definitely had a marked interest in linking magical adjurations and recipes with the daily prayer. The point at which magic and liturgy converge is the name of God which plays an important role in the classical prayer, yet becomes the very center of every activity of the Merkavah mystics. They no doubt present the most productive attempt to amalgamate both and to create a religious system which integrates magic thoroughly – and deeply imbues Judaism for the following centuries.

Appendix

JTSL ENA 3635.17

17a

1 Concerning a woman suspected of adultery.
Blessed be the name of the glory of his kingdom for ever and ever.
2 He who created the world with the measure of mercy
3 and created the angels in heaven, class
4 upon class and host upon host, and who created
5 the spirits, the demons and the evil spirits,
6 a thousand years before he created Adam.
7 And all the names, by which the angels | who serve before him
8 call him, in [praise] and in song,
9 they have all been written down from the mouth of R. Yishma'el,
10 the High | Priest, and R. Yishma'el (received them) from the mouth of Meṭraṭron, the prince
11 of the countenance. Amongst them (are the names) that were revealed to Moses at Sinai
12 and in the thorn-bush, amongst them those that were revealed to Elijah on Mount Carmel,
13 and amongst them those that were revealed to each and every prophet from the mouth of
14 MSMRYH, who stands before the curtain, up until
15 the time of Israel's Synhedrium, (whose members) used to know the seventy
16 names, and the "name in purity" as well as the "name in impurity",
17 and every principle of practice, they used to know everything.
18 And know and understand that from amongst these hidden names,
19 that (constitute) the unutterable name, one used to give to
20 the woman suspected of adultery to drink. Through [the power] of these names shall her belly distend
21 and her thighs sag.

[46] See, e.g., K 21.95.P, fol. 1b/2.9; 2a/15f.; 2b/12; K 21.95.T, fol. 1a/16ff.; 1b/12; K 1.144, fol. 2a/6ff.; Heb. a.3.25a/27ff.69ff.

17b

1 And these sayings together with these names, one used to
2 write for her. And these (names) are the unutterable name
3 that the High Priest used to mention in holiness and purity.
4 The verse, that one (thereby) says (reads): *The priest shall put these curses down in writing*
5 *on a scroll and rub it off into the water of bitterness.*[1]
6 For these are the names with the curses, and these
7 are the sayings that we mentioned above.
8 But the bitter water was not (mentioned) above,
9 (but rather stems) from this verse which reads: *The priest shall take holy*
10 *water* etc.[2] (It) thus (concerns) holy (and) pure water
11 and dust. And there is nothing therein that is bitter, but
12 the water is bitter due to the curses and the names,
13 through which they died. [And these] are the adjurations,
14 the curses and the names, that the High Priest used to
15 write on a scroll: with the name of the LORD, God of Israel
16 YHWH 'H WHW MHW 'HW HWMH,
17 do I adjure you, N. N., with the name of
18 Y'YLNH YHW 'LWH BHW 'LWH WHW
19 'L ḤYNHW 'LDMN HW 'LŠTBHW
20 'L 'L BHH 'HW 'L 'DBTW HW

17c

1 'LLHBHW 'LNWDHW 'LHWDD HW
2 'LGRNYMHW 'LṢPŠGŠHW 'LYH WHHYHW
3 WBYṬHYWYHW WB'HYH HYH 'BHW
4 ṢYṢWṢYH RGMṬYH B'Ṣ'CṢYH
5 BHDRYH. Blessed be the name of the glory of his kingdom for ever and ever. I adjure
6 you with these names. And the LORD shall place these
7 names in my belly. Because (you shall be) *a curse and an imprecation*
8 *among your people, as the LORD causes your thigh*
9 *to sag and your belly to distend.*[3] ṢBH ṢBH
10 ṢB'WT RṢWṢWT ṢWṢWT ṢṢṢYṢWT
11 GWRWWṢWT WMRYRWT. And the curses (read):
12 *May the water enter* etc.[4] And you shall twice say "Amen".
13 You shall give her to drink, so that her belly immediately distends
14 and her thighs sag. And thus shall this woman
15 be a curse and an imprecation amongst her people. *But if*
16 *the women has not defiled herself and is pure* etc.[5]
17 This is the accepted way, that we
18 practice today, due to the fact that we no (longer) have a priest,

[1] Num. 5:23.
[2] Num. 5:17.
[3] Num. 5:21.
[4] Num. 5:21.
[5] Num. 5:28.

19 no (longer) holy water, and no (longer) a Tabernacle.

17d

1 Know and understand that if a man is god-
2 fearing in these times, and cleanses himself from
3 sins and from transgressions and wanders
4 upon the path of purity, and (if) purity is in his body
5 and purity in his flesh, (and if) he occupies himself with these
6 names (and) conducts himself [upon these] paths,
7 then he resembles an angel and a High Priest.
8 (In) everything that he does, he will not return empty-
9 handed. At the beginning of the procedure he shall take, instead of
10 what (scripture) says: *(The priest shall take) holy water*,[6] you should take
11 running water from a running spring in a new
12 vessel. And instead of the dust that (was) in the Tabernacle,
13 go to the synagogue and take dust
14 from the four corners of the Torah shrine,
15 from above and below, and throw
16 this dust into the spring water
17 that you gathered and write these (names) that we wrote down
18 above. Then rinse it with water
19 and give (it) to the woman. And immediately you will see [the sign] and the lofty mighty deeds of the [LORD], (his) wonders and the power of his holy names. Blessed be he and blessed be his living and eternal name for ever. Amen.

Bibliography

Abramson, S., "Nusaḥ berakhah ^{c}al 'qedushat ha-shem'", *Torah she-be^{c}al peh* 14, 1972, pp. 156–164.

Bar-Ilan, M., *The Mysteries of Jewish Prayer and Hekhalot*, Ramat-Gan 1987 (in Hebrew).

Dan, J., art. "Aaron of Baghdad", *EJ*, vol. 2, 1971, col. 21.

Danby, H., *The Mishnah*, Oxford 1933, ^{16}1987.

Fleischer, E., *Eretz-Israel Prayers and Prayer Rituals as Portrayed in the Geniza Documents*, Jerusalem 1988 (in Hebrew).

Frazer, J. G., *The Golden Bough*, vol. 1, 2nd ed., London 1900.

Klar, B., ed., *Megillat Ahimaaz*, Jerusalem 1974.

Marmorstein, A., "Beiträge zur Religionsgeschichte und Volkskunde", *JJVK* 25, 1924–25, pp. 377–383.

Schäfer, P. (in collaboration with M. Schlüter and H. G. von Mutius), *Synopse zur Hekhalot-Literatur*, Tübingen 1981.

–, *Geniza-Fragmente zur Hekhalot-Literatur*, Tübingen 1984.

–, "Jewish Magic Literature in Late Antiquity and Early Middle Ages", *JJS* 41, 1990, pp. 75–91.

6 Num. 5:17.

–, *The Hidden and Manifest God*, Albany, New York, 1992.

Schäfer, P., and Shaked, Sh., *Magische Texte aus der Kairoer Geniza*, vol. 1, Tübingen 1994.

Schechter, S., "Genizah Specimens", *JQR* (O. S.) 10, 1898, pp. 654–659.

Shaked, Sh., 'Peace be Upon You, Exalted Angels': on Hekhalot, Liturgy and Incantation Bowls", *JSQ* 2, 1995, pp. 197–219.

Veltri, G., "ᶜInyan Sota: Halakhische Voraussetzungen für einen magischen Akt nach einer theoretischen Abhandlung aus der Kairoer Geniza", *FJB* 20, 1993, pp. 23–48.

Yaldabaoth and the Language of the Gnostics

by

JOSEPH DAN

The Name of God is one of the most essential and indicative elements in the consciousness of a religion; so is the name of its Satan. It is no wonder that for over a century the name of one of the central divine-demonic figures in the gnostic pantheon interested and perplexed scholars. We need to understand the naming of this evil figure, responsible for creating and governing the universe, in order to have a more accurate picture of the gnostic world of images and myths. Despite intense efforts of past scholars, a new analysis of the problem still seems worth our while.

One of the last papers written by the late Prof. Gershom Scholem was dedicated to a detailed discussion of the origin of the gnostic name of the evil Yaldabaoth[1]. Unlike other powers which constitute the gnostic hierarchy of the evil, demiurgic powers, this name remained enigmatic, even though many attempts to explain it were offered by scholars. In this paper, Scholem reviewed and criticized two hundred years of scholarly attempts to interpret the strange name of this key figure in gnostic mythology, whose centrality increased especially after the publication of the Nag Hamadi texts. He expressed surprise that his suggestion in his 1960 book, "Jewish Gnosticism, Merkabah Mysticism and Talmudic Tradition"[2] had not led to a renewed discussion of the problem, and returned to a detailed exposition of the debate about the meaning of this name.

Scholem's analysis is divided into two parts, reflecting the two main elements which, according to him, constitute the name: First, he intended to disprove the commonly held view that the second syllable in the name Yaldabaoth originated from an Aramaic root, meaning, according to the preferred transcription of a Semitic alphabet, either "chaos" or "terror", and derived from the Semitic בהות or a variation thereof, which was regarded as the hypothetical plural form of בהו, therefore meaning, presumably, "chaos". Another attempt connected

[1] Jaldabaoth Reconsidered, Mélange d'Histoire des Religions offertes à Henri-Charles Puech (Paris 1974), pp. 405–421. The name is spelled in English either Yaldabaoth, Jaldabaoth or Ialdabaoth. I chose the spelling used in: J. M. ROBINSON, The Nag Hammadi Library in English, New York 1977.

[2] New York 1960 (revised edition, 1965), pp. 71–72.

the word with the Semitic בעות, presumably meaning "terror", though such a word does not exist in this form. Other interpretations included the attempt to see the name as constructed from three words, e.g. הי אל דאבהות the "Father God", and several other similar suggestions. Another very imaginative reading regarded the name as having been derived from אל תאבות, which was interpreted as "god of lust"[3]. Scholem objected to all these explanations on the grounds that they create non-existent words and meanings, without any firm foundation either in the gnostic context or in any parallel text in a Semitic language[4].

Scholem's second aim in writing the paper was, to suggest an alternative explanation of the term. Scholem proved, conclusively, I believe, that the second half of the name is an abbreviation of the Hebrew term "Sabaoth". He presented parallels from magical texts and other sources to show that the Hebrew appellation, describing divine strength, could be abbreviated at the end of a word, especially as in Hebrew the term צבאות usually appears at the end of a series of divine names[5].

As to the first half of the name Yaldabaoth, Scholem did follow several of his predecessors in understanding it as the Semitic ילד, which Scholem interpreted, because of the context, as meaning here: "father of", "the one who gave birth to", as Yaldabaoth is described sometimes as the father of Sabaoth[6]. The whole name, according to Scholem, thus fits the context perfectly, and was formed by the gnostic writers to describe the power from which the main demiurgical force, namely Sabaoth, sprang[7].

It seems that Scholem's view on two basic elements of this problem do not arouse any difficulty: That the name Yaldabaoth is based on Semitic roots, most probably Hebrew ones, and that the ending is derived from the ancient title of the God of the Old Testament – Sabaoth – who played such a central role

---

[3] See the detailed bibliography and list of suggestions in Scholem's paper, especially pp. 405–410.

[4] Since Scholem's paper was published, a monograph has at last been dedicated to the figure of Yaldabaoth: H. M. JACKSON, The Lion Becomes Man, The Gnostic Leontromorphic Creator and the Platonic Tradition, Atlanta 1985. Dr. Jackson analyzed in this book in great detail all the gnostic references to Yaldabaoth, and then held on only to one detail – the description of the demiurge in a semi-leonic form. He then proceeded to collect, in a most admirable fashion, all clear and possible references to lions in the Bible, in Greek and Hellenistic literature, in the traditions of the Middle East, and tied it all together with Platonic philosophy. The work does not, however, contribute in any way to an understanding of the name itself.

[5] See Scholem, pp. 418–419.

[6] Yaldabaoth is prominently described in the Apocryphon of John (Nag Hammadi II, 1, 23–24), sometimes called Aldabaoth, as the archon "full of ignorance" who fathered, by rape, "Yave" and "Eloim". In the Hypostasis of the Archons (NHL II, 4, 95–97) he is identified with Sakla, the Hebrew-Aramaic "fool", and is cast into the Abyss by Sophia; it seems that this text makes Yaldabaoth the father of Sabaoth (96, l. 15).

[7] Scholem, pp. 420–421.

in magical as well as gnostic texts[8]. I dare to return to this problem and suggest a different interpretation of this name only because one element was left unexplained in Scholem's structure: The term yalda- ילד as "father of" simply does not exist in Hebrew. "Father of" in Hebrew (as in other semitic languages) is "avi" (אבי) and not "yalda-". Why would the gnostics use such an usual form of a very common structure? If they had wanted to denote that Yaldabaoth was the father of Sabaoth, why not use the simple form "Avi Sabaoth"? It is not enough to suggest a possible derivation of a name; we should also try to explain why this form was selected and preferred over other possibilities, but it seems that such an explanation concerning the use of ילד instead of אבי is not plausible.

Another valid objection to Scholem's suggestion, based on the context, was raised by Simone Petrement: According to the text, Yaldabaoth was the father of several powers, usually six or seven, and not of Sabaoth alone; why should his name be derived from this offspring alone and the others disregarded?[9]

The importance of the understanding of this name is connected with the persistent efforts of scholars to describe definitively the relationship between gnosticism and Judaism. While there can be little doubt today about the existence of ties between Judaism in the period immediately before and immediately after the destruction of the second temple (70 C.E.) and the then emerging gnosticism, the exact nature of this connection is unclear, and conflicting views have been expressed trying to define it[10]. There is little doubt that the extent of creativeness revealed by gnostics in using Hebrew terminology can serve as one (of the many) indicators of the closeness of these gnostics to

---

8 See the analysis of the name by B. LAYTON, The Hypostasis of the Archons, HTR 69 (1976), pp. 73–74. An exception is the discussion of this problem by F. T. FALLON in: The Enthronement of Sabaoth, Leiden 1978, pp. 32–34, who seeks to re-affirm the validity of earlier interpretations, again evoking as sources ancient Cannanite and Phoenician myths. It seems strange in a detailed study in which Biblical names of God, especially Sabaoth and Adonaios play such a prominent role in the gnostic myths analyzed by Fallon. Reading Fallon's study one is much more inclined to look for a Hebrew source, one which denotes the God of the bible, for Yaldabaoth, than any other possibility. It should also be noted that other Hebrew or Aramaic terms which are used in gnostic mythology did not undergo any far-reaching change or linguistic transformation, like Samael, Sakla and Achamoth, and their sources in Hebrew and Aramaic are obvious. No creative treatment was given to these names and terms before their introduction into the gnostic systems.

9 S. PETREMENT, A Separate God: The Christian Origins of Gnosticism, Translated from the French by C. HARRISON, San Francisco 1990, pp. 43–44.

10 The literature concerning the relationship between Judaism and gnosticism has become a vast one. A survey of the main studies and suggestions up to 1973 can be found in: E. YAMAUCHI, Pre-Christian Gnosticism, A Survey of the Proposed Evidence, Michigan 1973, which also includes a detailed bibliography. See especially pp. 143–162. A more recent survey is presented in Fallon's work (above, note 7); B.A. PEARSON, Gnosticism, Judaism and Egyptian Christianity, Minneapolis 1990 (the various papers collected in this work include detailed references to previous studies on this relationship by the author and by other scholars).

Hebrew religious terminology. Thus, if Scholem's interpretation of Yaldabaoth is accepted, one has to assume that the gnostics who used it combined a Hebrew verb and a Hebrew divine title in an original manner, not found in their sources, indicating an attitude of creative innovation towards the Hebrew language and its terminology concerning divine powers[11]. Similarly, any other explanation of the name Yaldabaoth would necessarily include a statement on the attitude of the gnostics towards their Hebrew sources.

The main argument for the need to seek a better explanation for this name is the fact that it is so different from all the other divine names of Hebrew origin used in these gnostic texts. The centrality of the name Sabaoth in this context, the frequent use of terms derived from the tetragrammaton (Yao, Yave, etc.), and the names based on El, Elohim and Adonai, clearly denote that the gnostics used the common, frequent Jewish names of God, without changing them and without creating any new combinations. We do not find in these texts examples of complex names derived from a creative use of previously unrelated Semitic roots, to convey a hidden, mythological meaning. The context demands, I believe, a search for a simple Hebrew name of God, often used, lacking any specific mythological meaning, like all the other Biblical names of God used here. Therefore, the premise behind the following suggested explanation of the name Yaldabaoth is that the gnostics did not create that name; that like other Hebrew terms found in their writings, Sabbaoth, Achamoth, Adonayos, Yave, they took an existing name from Hebrew sacred texts and used it in their mythology concerning the evolvement of the divine pleroma and the archons. Yaldabaoth should be viewed as one more name of God in Hebrew. But where do we find in Hebrew texts such a name describing God?

Similar reasoning directed Grant[12] and Petrement[13] to seek explanations for the name Yaldabaoth based on usual Hebrew biblical names of God, combinations derived from Yao and El. This quest is supported by the fact that such names, first and foremost Sabaoth itself, are regarded as the offspring of Yaldabaoth; this should, therefore, be a more general combination, the source

---

[11] An attempt to follow Scholem's basic concept, but also to harmonize it with traditional interpretations which denote the mythical nature of the name, is presented by M. Black, An Aramaic Etymology for Jaldabaoth, in: A. H. B. Logan and A. J. M. Wedderburn (editors), The New Testament and Gnosis: Essays in Honor of Robert McL. Wilson, Edinburgh 1983, pp. 69–73; and compare: "Adam, Ist die Gnosis in aramäischen Weisheitschulen entstanden?" in: U. Bianchi (ed.), The Origins of Gnosticism, Colloqium of Messina 1966, Leiden 1967, pp. 291–301. Like Scholem, Black tried to read the first element in the name, but the second element he read – in a way mentioned, but rejected by Scholem – as the Aramaic for "shame", seeing in the whole name "Son of Shame". It is still an artificial construction, an appellation not found anywhere else.

[12] See his paper in Vigiliae Chirstianae, Amsterdam, vol. 11 (1957), pp. 148–149; Compare N. A. Dahl, in B. Layton (editor), The Rediscovery of Gnosticism, Proceedings of the Yale International Conference on Gnosticism, vol. II, Leiden 1981, pp. 705, 36.

[13] Petrement, ibid, pp. 44–46.

from which all the other names are mere derivations or details. The reasoning which directed Grant and Petrement seems to me to be completely valid; the only problem is that they tried to construct the name, rather than look whether it could be found in another Hebrew context. I believe that it can be proved that such a combination did exist in Late-Antiquity Judaism.

One of the most influential works in the history of Jewish mysticism, though in itself not necessarily mystical, is the Sefer Yezira, "The Book of Creation", which describes, in an enigmatic manner, the first stages of the emergence of existence from chaos. This work, which was probably written in Hebrew in the 3rd or 4th century C.E., opens with the words:

"With thirty-two esoteric paths of wisdom engraved Yah Adonai Zevaoth the God of Israel the living God El Shaddai ... and created His world with three books"[14]. The series of divine names in Hebrew is: .יה אדני צבאות אלהי ישראל אלהים חיים This is the description of God as the Creator, in the actual process of the beginning of any kind of existence. This series of names first suggested to me the possibility that the explanation to the name Yaldabaoth may be hidden here.

A similar series of names can be found in another early Hebrew text: In the first chapter of the tractat Berachot of the Babylonian Talmud we find a strange story, presented as a barayta, which was discussed by many scholars:

"We have learned: Said Rabbi Ishmael son of Elisha: Once I entered to present ... in the innermost chamber [of the temple] and I saw Akhatriel Ya Adonai Zevaot sitting on a lofty throne and He said to me, Ishmael my son, give me a blessing"[15].

This section is unique in the Talmud, or even in Talmudic-Midrashic literature as a whole, on several counts: Rabbi Ishmael ben Elisha is described as a high priest, a fact not mentioned in any other Talmudic source. He is described as entering the holy of holies of the temple, when according to Talmudic sources he was martyred by the Emperor Hadrian probably after the Bar-Kochba rebellion, about 135 C.E. Therefore, he could only have been a very young boy when the temple was destroyed in the year 70 C.E., and certainly could not have served as a High Priest in the temple. And thirdly, in no other Talmudic text is the archangel Akhatriel described as the divine power revealed in the holy of holies, and entitled by the divine names Ya Adonai Zevaot. There can be little doubt that this short section is an interpolation into the Talmud from a very different religious and intellectual context.

Such a context is easily found: All three elements, so out-of-place in the

---

14 Concerning the variations found in different versions of the Sefer Yezira, see: I. GRUENWALD, A Preliminary Critical Edition of the Sefer Yezira, Israel Oriental Studies vol. I, 1971, p. 140.

15 Bavli Berachot 7a. See G. SCHOLEM, Major Trends in Jewish Mysticism, 2nd. ed., New York 1954, p. 356 n. 3.

Talmudic tractat, are central to a very distinctive part of the ancient Hebrew mystical group of texts known as Hekhalot and Merkabah mysticism. In the most extensive text of this library, Hekhalot Rabbati, Rabbi Ishmael is consistently described as a high priest son of a high priest, and his group (which includes Rabbi Akivah and other sages who flourished two generations after the destruction of the temple) assembles in the temple to practice the mystical ascension to the divine palaces[16]. And Hekhalot Rabbati is one of the only four texts among the two dozen texts of Hekhalot and Merkabah literature which includes names of divine powers entitled by divine names, the usual formula being Adonai Elohey Yisrael (יהוה אלהי ישראל).

The other three texts which use the same formula are: Hekhalot Zutartey (probably the oldest of these texts), in which Rabbi Akibah is the hero and Rabbi Ishmael is not mentioned[17]; the anthology of hymns published by Scholem under the title "Ma'aseh Merkabah"[18], and, in the most detailed manner, Sefer Hekhalot, better known as the Third Book of Enoch or the Hebrew Book of Enoch, which was studied by Hugo Odeberg and Philip Alexander[19]. These four texts include a concept of divine pleroma, consisting of several powers which are differentiated from the angelic hosts crowding the pages of this literature by the divine title added to their names, each formula containing an element, at least, of the tetragrammaton. This specific group of ancient Jewish mystics, who developed the idea of the mystical ascension, the ירידה למרכבה, also developed the concept of the divine pleroma, consisting of powers which carry distinctive names, to which a formula of this sort is added.

The consistency of this concept of the pleroma is most clearly attested by the treatment of this subject in the Third Book of Enoch. In the first part of this work we find a description of the elevation of Metatron from a human being, Enoch son of Jared, to the greatest power in the divine pleroma, second only to God himself. In the description of one stage in this process of elevation, Metatron states that a decree from heaven appointed him ruler of all the princes of the divine kingdom, and of all the powers of heaven, except "eight great princes, honored and feared, who are called by the name of YHVH their king"[20]. In the second part of this work there is a detailed description, stage by

[16] See: J. Dan, Three Types of Ancient Jewish Mysticism, Cincinnati, 1985.

[17] Published in a critical edition by R. Elior, Supplement I (1972) to Jerusalem Studies in Jewish Thought, and compare Schäfer, Synopse (below, note 22), §§ 335–419.

[18] Printed as Appendix C in G. Scholem's Jewish Gnosticism (above, note 2), pp. 101–117.

[19] H. Odeberg, 3 Enoch or The Hebrew Book of Enoch, Cambridge University Press, 1928; reprinted with a prolegomenon by J. C. Greenfield, New York 1973. A new translation with an introduction and commentary by P. Alexander is included in: J. H. Charlesworth (editor), The Old Testament Pseudepigrapha, vol. I, New York 1983, pp. 223–315.

[20] Odeberg, Hebrew Enoch, pp. 15–16 of the Hebrew text: חוץ משמונה שרים גדולים הנכבדים והנוראים שנקראים בשם ה׳ מלכם מטטרון עבדי שמתיו לשר ולנגיד על כל שרי מלכותי ועל כל בני מרומים.

stage, of the heavenly realm, and the author makes a clear division between the lower parts of the divine worlds, governed by archangels, and the highest pleroma, governed by princes who include the title יהוה אלהי ישראל in their names[21]. In this text, therefore, we find a systematic statement of what is implied in the other three works in this group: Besides God, there is a divine pleroma, comprised of several supreme powers, which have an "angelic" name to which is added a title including the divine name, and which have functions usually attributed to God himself and are described in terms (e.g., "sitting on the throne of glory") usually reserved only for God himself.

The lists of the powers of the pleroma necessarily include the divine title as a repetitive element, when the same divine formula is added to each name in the same rhythm (and there is an element of rhythm and repetition in the style of Hekhalot writings as a whole, suggesting that many portions were recited orally; not only the hymns, but the descriptions and the holy names as well). Listeners of such a rhythmical recitation hear the divine title repeated constantly like a refrain. This is likely to be the most memorable element that would strike one's attention on first encountering Hekhalot mystical circles and their oral expressions.

In the Hebrew texts of Hekhalot literature which were preserved (and, undoubtedly, edited during the long period of transmission from their first appearance, probably in the third century to the first written texts that we have from the 9th and 10th centuries), the most frequent formula is The Lord God, God of Israel. But it can easily be proved that this was not the only formula, and probably not the oldest one. As mentioned above, the Talmud preserved a different one – Yah Adonai Zevaot (יה אדני צבאות). When checking such formulas in this literature one comes across another one, which seems to be the most prominent apart from the one mentioned above: the formula is יה אלהים אדני צבאות, in several small variations[22]. It seems to me that this formula is an old one, and that it had a much more central place in the older stratum of Hekhalot mysticism than in the later edited texts that have reached us.

It should also be noted that the difference between יהוה אלהי ישראל and the other one, יה אלהים אדני צבאות may not be completely accidental. The first one, so often used in our texts, emphasizes the specific Jewish character of the

---

21 ODEBERG, p. 47: "Those great princes who are called God in the name of the Holy One Blessed be He" השרים הגדולים שהן נקראים ה׳ בשמו של הקב״ה אין פתחון פה לכל שבעולם חוץ מאותם.

22 Some relevant examples are: Achatriel Yah Adonai Elokey Zevaoth (See P. SCHÄFER, Synopse zur Hekhalot-Literatur, Tübingen 1981, § 138); Achatriel Yah Adonai Zevaoth (§ 151); Yah Yah Ehyeh Yao Zevaoth Elokey Yisrael (§ 341, and compare §§ 597, 501 and many others. After publishing the Synopse (and the Genizah fragments of Hekhalot literature), Prof. Schäfer published a two-volume concordance: Konkordanz zur Hekhalot-Literatur I–II, Tübingen 1986, 1988. This last work considerably facilitated the preparation of this paper.

pleroma, and declares the centrality of the relationship between God and the people of Israel, whereas the older formula has a more universal character, which may be more attractive to someone whose religious outlook does not revolve around the national character of the God of the Bible.

On the basis of these considerations it is possible to suggest, that the gnostic Yaldabaoth is a combined form of the universalistic formula used by Hekhalot mystics to describe the powers of the divine pleroma, in addition to the specific name of each power, a formula frequently recited orally, and thus the only key letters preserved in the non-Hebrew form: From יה אלהים אדני צבאות the Greek and Coptic preserved the Yah, the L of "Elohim", the D of Adonay, and the ending, "baoth" of "Zevaoth", to create the combined name Yaldabaoth.

If this suggestion is correct, several conclusions may be drawn. It would indicate some familiarity of ancient gnostic sources with Hekhalot mysticism, but on a very superficial level. The connection between Yaldabaoth and the pleromatic formula of the Jewish mystics could not be accepted as proof that the gnostic sources were familiar with the mystical texts of Hekhalot literature; it proves only that they heard the frequently recited "refrain" which these mystics added to the lists of the powers of the pleroma. We cannot even be certain that the gnostics knew any Hebrew, in the same way that the use of the names Sabaoth or Adonaios in gnostic texts does not imply any knowledge of Hebrew.

The way the gnostics used the term Yaldabaoth is completely different from the way the Hekhalot mystical texts applied it. For the gnostics, this was a proper name of one power, whereas for the Jewish mystics it was a title denoting the difference between the angelic realm and the divine one, added to the proper names of the powers of the pleroma. Therefore, no direct, substantial influence of Hekhalot mysticism on gnosticism can be inferred.

The name Yaldabaoth, if this analysis is correct, is just one more example of the way gnostic texts (like magical texts) used the Hebrew names of divinity for their own, very different, purposes. The formula combining four central Biblical names of God into one unit appealed to their authors, when they heard the Hekhalot mystics using it as if it were one word, one name, in constant repetition. For them, Yaldabaoth was just one more sound denoting the Jewish God, the creator of heaven and earth, on an equal basis with Adonai, Yhaveh, Yao, Elohim and Shaddai, and they used it in the same contexts in which all those others were so frequently used. The further history of Yaldabaoth as a personal name for a mythical power needs to be studied in the context of the history of gnosticism by itself.

Leib und Leiblichkeit im Judentum

von

Schalom Ben-Chorin

Die Pflichtenlehre des Judentums umfaßt 613 Vorschriften, davon 248 Gebote und 365 Verbote.

Die Tradition bringt diese Zahlen mit dem menschlichen Körper und den Tagen des Jahres in Verbindung. Nach talmudischer Vorstellung hat der Körper des Menschen 248 Glieder und Sehnen. Dieser Zahl entsprechen nun die Gebote, denn der Körper des Menschen wird als Mikrokosmos gesehen, der, wie das Weltall, auf das Schöpferwort Gottes entstanden ist.

Die Zahl 365 der Verbote weist natürlich auf die Tage des Jahres hin, so daß Gott als der Schöpfer des Raumes und der Zeit gleichsam sichtbar wird.

Eine Leibfeindlichkeit, wie sie im Christentum bemerkbar ist, kennt das Judentum nicht, so daß auch das Zölibat im Judentum keinen Raum finden konnte.

Unter den Hunderten von Rabbinen, die im Talmud genannt werden, gibt es nur einen Weisen, der unverheiratet geblieben ist, Ben-Asai, ein Zeitgenosse des Rabbi Akiba im 2. Jahrhundert, der in den Sprüchen der Väter (IV, 2) genannt wird. Seine Genossen warfen ihm vor, daß er ein Mörder sei, denn wer das Menschengeschlecht nicht vermehrt, der vermindert es.

Ben-Asai entschuldigte sich damit, daß seine ganze Liebe der Thora, dem Gesetz Gottes, gilt, und er daher diese Gottesliebe nicht mit der Liebe zu einer Frau teilen könne.

Dies wurde aber nie zur Regel, ganz im Gegenteil gilt das Gebot Gottes an das erste Menschenpaar, Adam und Eva: „Seid fruchtbar und mehret euch, und füllet die Erde“ bis heute.

Die Tradition macht hier die Einschränkung, daß dieses Gebot nur für den Mann gilt, der seiner Pflicht erst genügt hat, wenn er einen Sohn und eine Tochter zeugt.

Die Frau darf sogar empfängnisverhütende Praktiken einhalten (wenn sie von vielen Geburten schon ermüdet oder gesundheitlich angegriffen ist), während dem Mann Kondome untersagt bleiben.

Der Geschlechtsverkehr dient aber nicht nur der Fortpflanzung, sondern darf auch als Freude am Körper empfunden werden, ja es gibt sogar die Pflicht des Mannes, seine Frau durch den ehelichen Verkehr zu erfreuen. Insbesondere am Sabbath gilt dies als Gebot, denn die Definition des Propheten Jesaja: „Du sollst den Sabbath eine Wonne nennen", weist auf die Freuden des Körpers hin.

Hierin unterscheidet sich das normative Judentum von der jüdischen Sekte der Karäer, die den Geschlechtsverkehr am Sabbath verboten, da es dem Pflügen und Säen gleichkäme.

Die Rabbinen aber haben jede Leibfeindlichkeit streng verbannt, allerdings unter Einhaltung der Reinheitsvorschriften, die dem Manne den Verkehr mit seiner Frau in der Zeit der Menstruation verbietet. Erst eine Woche nach der monatlichen Regel ist ihm seine Gattin wieder gestattet, was die Freude an der Leiblichkeit erhöhen soll.

Der menschliche Körper wird als ein Wunderwerk des Schöpfers gepriesen:

> „Gelobt seist du Ewiger, unser Gott, König der Welt, der den Menschen gebildet mit seiner Weisheit und an ihm erschaffen viele Öffnungen, viele Höhlungen. Offenbar und bekannt ist es, vor dem Throne deiner Herrlichkeit, daß, wenn eine von ihnen offen oder eine von ihnen verschlossen bliebe, es nicht möglich wäre zu bestehen und vor dich hinzutreten. Gelobt seist du, Ewiger, der da heilt alles Fleisch und wunderbar wirkt."

Besonders observante Juden sprechen dieses Gebet auch beim Waschen der Hände nach verrichteter Notdurft.

Aus diesem Gebet wird die volle Bejahung des Leibes als das Wunder des Körpers sichtbar.

Die Ehe ist im Judentum zwar kein Sakrament, aber die Braut gilt dem Manne als angeheiligt, und in den sieben Segenssprüchen unter dem Trauhimmel wird Gott als der Schöpfer der Freude gepriesen. Der letzte dieser Segenssprüche preist den Schöpfer, der den Bräutigam durch die Braut erfreut.

Die Freude bildet ein Grundmotiv im Judentum, wie es der Psalmist ausdrückt: „Dient dem Herrn in Freuden".

Die drei großen Wallfahrtsfeste, Passah, Wochenfest und Laubhüttenfest, stehen unter den Signum der Freude, und dabei ist nicht nur eine geistliche Freude gemeint, sondern auch die körperlichen Freuden, wie Essen und Trinken, und der Geschlechtsverkehr. Jede asketische Enthaltsamkeit liegt hier außerhalb solcher Bejahung des Leibes.

Ausnahme macht nur der Versöhnungstag, an welchem fünf Kasteiungen geboten sind, darunter die Enthaltsamkeit von Speise und Trank, und dem ehelichen Umgang.

Sofort nach der Beendigung des strengen Fasttages aber soll mit dem Bau der Laubhütte begonnen werden, dem Symbol des Freudenfestes der Laubhütten, das mit dem, in der Bibel noch nicht genannten, Thora-Freudenfest beendet wird.

Dieses Fest trägt gleichsam antipaulinische Züge. Während Paulus das Gesetz als Bürde und sogar als Fluch empfand, da der Mensch nicht in der Lage ist, dem Gesetz Gottes voll zu entsprechen, hat das normative Judentum die Thora als die Weisung Gottes in großer Freude empfangen.

In der hebräischen Antike schlossen sich Reigentänze der Jungfrauen in den Hügeln Jerusalems an den strengen Fasttag an, wobei die jungen Männer auf Brautschau gingen, so wiederum der kreatürlichen Freude Ausdruck gebend.

Die Freude an der Leiblichkeit fand in der hebräischen Bibel im Hohen Lied beredten Ausdruck. Hier wird die Leiblichkeit uneingeschränkt beschrieben, die Schönheit der Freundin und des Freundes, die einander zugetan sind, ohne daß von irgend einer gesetzlichen oder sakramentalen Ehe die Rede ist.

Ohne jede Zurückhaltung werden die Brüste der Geliebten und die starken Schenkel des Liebhabers geschildert, die Freuden der Leiblichkeit kommen hier unverhüllt zum Ausdruck.

Sowohl im späteren Judentum wie im Christentum wurde diese Freizügigkeit des Hohen Liedes durch Symbolisierungen abgeschwächt. Die Liebe zwischen zwei jungen Menschen wurde auf das Verhältnis von Gott und Israel schon durch Rabbi Akiba im zweiten Jahrhundert gedeutet, und von den Kirchenvätern auf das Verhältnis von Christus und der Kirche.

Diese gekünstelten Auslegungen sollten der erotischen Dichtung ihren Stachel nehmen, um sie in den Kanon der heiligen Schriften aufzunehmen.

Das Hohe Lied aber bleibt der Hochgesang einer bedingungslosen Erotik.

Die Frage: Liebeslied oder heiliges Lied? hat der Dichter Max Brod in gültiger Weise beantwortet: das Hohe Lied ist ein heiliges Lied, *weil* es ein Liebeslied ist, denn von allen Boten Gottes spricht Eros am eindringlichsten zu uns.

Das Hohe Lied selbst sagt es in wunderbarer Weise:

> Denn stark wie der Tod ist die Liebe
> Ihre Flammen Feuerflammen
> Eine Lohe Gottes.

Das Christentum unterscheidet in hellenistischer Weise die irdische und himmlische Liebe, Eros und Agape, im Hebräischen aber gibt es nur, wie im Deutschen, das eine Wort: Liebe (Ahava).

Die Kabbala, die jüdische Mystik, geht so weit, daß sie die Erotik im Wesen der Gottheit aufspürt. Als weiblicher Partner Gottes wird die Schechina beschrieben, die in etwa der Sophia entspricht, der Weisheit, die ebenfalls als weibliches Element, in der christlichen Mystik eine Rolle spielt.

Die Kabbala aber erkennt eine Paarung Gottes mit der Schechina als fortzeugendem Schöpfungsakt.

Die glühende Erotik in der Kabbala hat die Rabbinen dazu geführt, das Studium des Hauptwerkes der Kabbala, des Buches Sohar, erst Männern im

Alter von vierzig Jahren zu gestatten, damit Jünglinge nicht durch die erotischen Gleichnisse zu Ausschweifungen verführt werden.

Die wiegenden Körperhaltungen beim Gebet, die wohl ursprünglich auf das Psalmwort hinweisen: „Alle meine Gebeine sprechen, Herr, wer ist wie du?“, wurden vom Schöpfer des Chassidismus, einer ostjüdischen pietistischen Bewegung im 18. Jahrhundert, auf die Bewegungen beim Beischlaf gedeutet, so daß im Gebet eine Vereinigung mit der Schechina erzielt wird.

Der Chassidismus stellt eine Art Popularisierung der kabbalistischen Mystik dar, und hat zu besonderer Freude an der Leiblichkeit geführt. Wortloser Gesang und Tanz erheben das Gebet zur Ekstase, wobei sogar ein kräftiger Schluck Branntwein nicht nur gestattet, sondern empfohlen wurde.

Eine Depravation des Chassidismus stellte die pseudomessianische Bewegung des Jakob Frank im 18. Jahrhundert dar, dessen Tochter Eva in orgiastischen Kulten als Schechina verehrt wurde.

Die Frankisten ihrerseits schlossen wiederum an die pseudomessianische Bewegung des Sabbatai Zewi an, der ebenfalls die Leiblichkeit überbetonte, sich mit der Thora, der Weisung Gottes, vermählte und alle Ansätze zur Askese zugunsten einer mystischen Leiblichkeit verwarf.

Man kann also sehen, daß im Judentum von den biblischen Anfängen bis in späteste Epochen, Leib und Leiblichkeit als positive Größen erscheinen, ganz im Gegnteil zum Christentum, wo eine bis zum Masochismus gesteigerte Leibfeindlichkeit mehr und mehr um sich griff. Wenn etwa der heilige Dominikus darüber Buch führte, wie viele Geißelhiebe er sich pro Tag beibrachte, oder wenn die sogenannten Säulenheiligen als einsame Büßer auf hohen Säulen bis zu ihrem Tode verharrten, oder wenn Anachoreten in der Thebais jeden menschlichen Umgang mieden, so gibt es dafür keine Parallelen im Judentum, das immer ein Anwalt der Leiblichkeit geblieben ist.

Das antike Hebräertum war eine sakramentale Männergemeinschaft, gekennzeichnet durch die Beschneidung des männlichen Gliedes als Bundeszeichen, das bereits dem Stammvater Abraham offenbart wurde.

Es gibt kein vergleichsweises Sakrament für die neugeborenen Mädchen, was auf den patriarchalischen Grundcharakter des Judentums hinweist.

Die Beschneidung darf aber nicht im Sinne einer Leibfeindlichkeit gedeutet werden, wenngleich es Exegeten gab, die meinten, daß durch die Beschneidung der Vorhaut eine Minderung der Sexualität erzielt würde. Davon kann aber nicht die Rede sein, wohl aber will die Beschneidung einen Blutbund zwischen Gott und Israel symbolisieren. So spricht Zippora, die Frau des Mose, bei der Beschneidung ihres Sohnes in der Wüste: „Ein Blutsbräutigam bist du mir ...“.

Offenbar tritt die Beschneidung anstelle des Sohnesopfers, das bei der Bindung Isaaks auf dem Berge Moria überwunden wurde.

Das Sohnesopfer könnte im Sinne der Leibfeindlichkeit gedeutet werden, da die Frucht des Leibes geopfert werden mußte. Das Hebräertum aber trat von der frühesten Zeit an für die Erhaltung des Leibes ein, diesem Wunderwerk des Schöpfers.

Vorstellungen, wie sie im scholastischen Mittelalter bei Thomas von Aquin vertreten wurden, der in der Frau eigentlich eine Mißgeburt des Mannes sah, konnten im Judentum nie Fuß fassen.

Von der Schöpfungsgeschichte der Genesis ausgehend, hat das Judentum immer die Erkenntnis gewahrt, daß Mann und Frau gleichermaßen von Gott geschaffen wurden, ja die talmudische Legende spricht sogar davon, daß Mann und Frau ursprünglich eine Einheit bildeten, die erst getrennt werden mußte. Aber auch nach dieser Teilung der Geschlechter streben sie immer wieder zur Vereinigung, die sich im Liebesakt konkretisiert.

Bei alledem kann aber nicht von einer Verabsolutierung des Leibes gesprochen werden, der als das Gefäß der Seele erkannt wird. Der dreidimensionale Mensch, bestehend aus Körper, Geist und Seele, bleibt die von der Schöpfung intendierte Ganzheit.

Der Geschlechtsakt wird im biblischen Hebräisch als Erkennung bezeichnet, denn nur in der körperlichen Vereinigung findet die volle Erkenntnis von Ich und Du statt. Die Rolle des Leibes bleibt daher unabdingbar, so daß es nicht die Vorstellung einer höheren Stufe der Menschlichkeit durch eine Überwindung des Leibes geben kann.

Mit der leiblichen Vollendung des Menschen tritt auch seine religiöse Verantwortlichkeit ein. Bei den Mädchen wird das sehr früh angesetzt, mit zwölf Jahren, und bei den Knaben mit dreizehn Jahren und einem Tag.

Diese Vorstellung von körperlicher und geistiger Selbstverantwortlichkeit geht, was den Knaben anlangt, auf den Gesetzeslehrer Jehuda Ben-Thema zurück, der in den Sprüchen der Väter eine Art Lebensprogramm entwirft. Mit achtzehn Jahren sollte der Jüngling bereits unter den Trauhimmel treten, die Braut war noch jünger, damit der Mensch mit seiner Leiblichkeit zum Recht kommt, ohne aus den Begierden der Leiblichkeit auf Abwege zu geraten.

Als Vergeudung des männlichen Samens wird fälschlich der Begriff Onanie gebraucht, Masturbation oder Selbstbefriedigung, die religionsgesetzlich nicht gestattet ist. Von einer weiblichen Selbstbefriedigung ist nie die Rede, ebenso nicht von der lesbischen Liebe, während die männliche Homosexualität streng verpönt bleibt.

Der Grund für diese so verschiedenartige Bewertung liegt darin, daß nur die männliche Knabenliebe, aber auch die Masturbation bei Männern zur Verminderung der Nachkommenschaft führen kann, während die weiblichen Formen derselben Praktiken nicht unbedingt diese Folgen haben. Die Bezeichnung „Onanie" ist völlig abwegig, denn der biblische Onan (Gen 38, 6–10) erregt den Zorn Gottes dadurch, daß er die Schwagerehe mit Thamar, der Witwe seines kinderlosen Bruders, nicht vollzieht, sondern in Koitus interruptus seinen Samen zur Erde fallen ließ, um seinem Bruder keine Nachkommen zu zeugen.

Der Vollzug der sogenannten Leviratsehe besteht heute nur noch theoretisch, da durch die Einführung der Monogamie im Judentum in christlichen Ländern durch Rabbenu Gerschom ben Jehuda aus Mainz im 10. Jahrhundert eine Wiederverheiratung des Schwagers unmöglich gemacht wurde. Es muß also eine Art Schandritual, Chaliza genannt (Deut 25, 7ff.), durchgeführt werden, um den Schwager von der Pflicht zu entbinden, seinem kinderlos verstorbenen Bruder Nachkommen zu zeugen.

Man sieht aus allen diesen Vorschriften, daß die Erhaltung von Leib und Leben zu den Grundmotiven des Judentums gehört, das den Leib nie gering geschätzt hat, wie das im Christentum oft der Fall war.

So spricht Franziskus von Assisi vom Leib als dem „Bruder Esel", der sich störrisch der Askese widersetzt.

Eine solche Negation des Leibes und der Leiblichkeit konnte im Judentum nie Raum finden.

Noch bei Paulus, der ein Schüler des Rabban Gamaliel war, der für seine Bejahung von Leib und Leiblichkeit bekannt ist, findet sich der Gedanke der Heiligkeit des Leibes als Gefäß der Seele. Die totale Entwertung von Leib und Leiblichkeit im späteren Christentum, vor allem im Mittelalter, konnte, wie gesagt, in das Judentum nicht eindringen. Ganz im Gegenteil, wurden und werden der Leib und die Seele in ihrer unlösbaren Einheit in Lehre und Gebet verkündigt, wofür hier eine synagogale Dichtung aus der Liturgie des Versöhnungstages angeführt sein soll:

> Der Leib ist dein,
> Die Seele ist dein,
> erbarme dich deiner Schöpfung.

Aus dieser Gleichstellung von Leib und Seele werden auch die strengen Verbote jeder Verstümmelung des Leibes durch kultische Einschnitte im Körper, aber auch Tätowierung, verständlich.

Die Reinheit des Leibes gilt als göttliches Gebot, so daß Waschungen und Bäder in den Rang religiöser Pflichten erhoben wurden.

Während im christlichen Mittelalter hygienische Vorschriften oft in Vergessenheit gerieten, hatten die Juden ihre Ritualbäder, die jede Vernachlässigung des Leibes verboten. Das Händewaschen vor jeder Mahlzeit galt und gilt als göttliches Gebot, so daß die Pharisäer den Jüngern Jesu vorwerfen konnten, daß sie dieses Gebot nicht immer streng eingehalten haben.

Die Hochschätzung von Leib und Leiblichkeit im Judentum hat in den Jahren des Schwarzen Todes im Mittelater dazu geführt, daß die jüdische Gemeinden von der Pest weniger bedroht waren als ihre Umwelt, andererseits aber zum Verdacht der Brunnenvergiftung, die den Juden zur Last gelegt wurde.

Jede Vernachlässigung von Leib und Leiblichkeit wird im Judentum als Sünde gesehen, niemals zugunsten einer Askese als Tugend.

In der Hymne „Adon Olam“ (Herr der Welt), die zu den Kernstücken des jüdischen Gottesdienstes zählt, drückt die letzte Strophe den unlöslichen Zusammenhang von Leib und Seele aus:

> In seine Hand empfehle ich meinen Geist
> Zur Zeit, da ich schlafe und erwache,
> und mit meinem Geist auch meinen Leib,
> Gott ist mit mir, ich fürchte mich nicht.

Index of Sources

1. Bible

Gen

1 405
1:2 419
1:26–27 534 f
4:3–4 100
5:24 (LXX) 415
8:20 100
14 435
21:2 155
22 99–116, 102
22:4 106
25:21 106
27:3 155
28:12 425 f, 529
49:10 466

Ex

3:1 424
4:21–26 103
7:8 ff 552
12:21–23 103
18:20 396
20:3 (LXX) 175
20:19 463
22:28 101
23:20 419
23:30 419
24:7 396
25:9 416
25:40 416
30:12 201 f
32:2–9 303
33:18–23 551
33:18 ff 537
33:19 552
33:20 463
33:23 552
34:20 101

Lev

19:18 204
20:6 157

Num

5:11–31 541
5:17 554 f
5:21 554
5:21–22 542
5:23 542 f, 554
5:28 543, 554
8:18 101
14:22 ff 79
15:37–41 202
17:23 94
20:6 ff 157
23:7 (LXX) 300
23:23 157
24 299
24:7 (LXX) 296, 300
24:17 (LXX) 300
24:24 (LXX) 300
26:16–17 296

Deut

4:12 424
6:4 78
6:4–5 204
6:4–9 202
6:11–21 202
12:31 101
14:1–2 103
15:15–17 103
18:9–10 101
18:10–14 157
18:15 466 ff
21:7–8 206
21:23 109
25:7 ff 570
26:3 206

26:5–8 491
26:5–10 206
26:13–15 206
27–28 346
32:11 419
32:39 170
32:39 (LXX) 175
33:21 466

Josh

8:30–35 346
13:22 157
23:1–24:27 347

Judg

11 102

1 Sam

15:22–23 399
28:3 ff 157

2 Sam

7:10–13 398
7:19 398
8:17 351
20:25–26 351

1 Kgs

1:1–4 94
2:26–27 351
2:35 351
4:2 351
4:4–5 351
18:24 552
19:8–14 551
19:11 ff 551
19:12 552
22:16 408

2 Kgs

3:26–27 101
12:7–17 351
14:6–16 200
16:6 214
22:4 200
22:23 351
25:18 376
25:25 214

Isa

2:2–4 53
2:4 464
6 408, 411
6:11–13 342
9:4 464
11:4 464
11:6 464
11:10–16 296, 298
11:11 299
11:11–16 300
14:12–13 533, 537
18:18–19 384
19:13 300
19:18–21 193
19:19–23 (LXX) 299
19:20 (LXX) 300
19:25 (LXX) 300
27:13 299
40:3 344
40:6–8 52, 54
42:1–4 50
42:5–8 50
42:18–25 61
44:6 (LXX) 175
45:18 ff 54
48:17–19 46
49:1 50, 54
49:6 50 f, 54
49:7 57, 67
49:8–12 58, 61
49:22–23 56
50:4–9 60
50:8–9 46
51:1–8 47
51:4–8 48
51:12–16 54
53 105 f, 108 ff
54:1–10 66
54:11–17 59 ff
55:5–7 46
61 62 f
61:1 173
64:1 418
66:1 537

Jer

1:9 56
1:12 94
5:18 342
19:5 100
23:5–8 298

25:11–13	342
29:10	342
30:11	342
31:1–40	346
31:31–34	49
46:28	342

Ezek

1	405f
1:26	529, 534, 536
4:4–6	343
20:25–29	103
28:2	533
28:14	537
30:13–14	301
30:13–18	300
37:19–28	298
44:10	381
44:15	375

Hos

11:11	299
12:2b	183

Joel

3:9	301

Amos

9:11–12	193
9:11–15	298

Nah

3:8	301

Zech

1:12	342f
1:13–17	344
2:8	194
3	351
3:10	342
4:2	95
4:11–14	351
6:9–15	351
8:1–17	344
8:12	342
8:23	215
10:8–12	299
10:11	301

Mal

3:1	419

Ps

8:5	529, 531
17:21–46	298
33:15	548
46	53
51:19	399
87:7	95
106:47	298
139:15	95

Prov

1–9	85
15:8	78
16:10–15	86
21:3	78
27	78

Job

1:9	77
1:21	95
2:4–5	77
36:26ff	71
37:16	545
38:7	537
38:39–39:30	90

Qoh

2:21	536
36:11	298

Esth

2:5	215

Dan

4:19	186
5:18–23	186
7	411
7:9	407, 411
7:10	388
9:2	342
9:24–27	182
10:5–6	410
11:2–4	184
11:2–12:13	182
11:3	189
11:5–20	184
11:14	191, 194

11:16	183
11:16–17	189
11:17	191 f
11:18	190
11:19	195
11:20	183
11:21–45	182
11:22	194
11:24	189
11:30	190, 301
11:30–35	194
11:36	189
11:36–39	194
11:41	183
11:45	190

Ezra

1:1	342
7	198
7:1–5	376
9:2	342

Neh

3	200
9:2	342
9:31	342
10:1	345
10:32–33	200
10:34	200
11:23	345
12:22	376
13:6–31	200

1 Chr

5:30–41	376
18:16	351
28:5	536
28:18	417
29:20	536
29:23–24	536

2 Chr

3:16–17	417
17:7–9	351
24:4–14	351
24:6	201
24:20–22	351
26:16–19	351
29–31	351
33:15–16	351
34–35	351
36:21–22	342

Mt

1	463
1:18–21	463
3:2	46
3:13–17	463
4:1–11	463
4:17	46
5:17	465, 471 f
6:7–8	78
8:2–4	463
8:23–25	463
11	419 f
11:18–19	463
11:25	421
13:55–56	463
14:3–12	262
18:10	421
20:28	463
22:34–40	204
25:31 ff	427
26:36–46	463
26:67–68	463

Mk

1:9–11	463
1:40–45	463
6:3	463
6:17–28	262
6:34	296
12:28–34	204
13:1–2	11
13:22	463
14:41	463
14:62	427

Lk

1:9	264
1:22	414
1:26–33	463
2:21–22	278
2:22	264
2:38	299
2:42	264
2:48	463
3	463
3:6	278
3:21–22	463
5:12–16	463
5:14	264
9:31	303
10:23–24	416
10:25–28	204

15 272–280
19:43 448
22:44 463
24:23 414

Jn

1:14 420, 424
1:18 423
1:51 423, 425 f
2:1–11 29
2:6 28
3 427
3:8 71
3:16 104, 113
4:1 423
5:1–18 29
5:37 423
6:14–15 296
6:46 423
10:24 448
12:28 464
12:29 427
12:32 ff 423
12:41 423
14:8 423
17:25 427
18:22 463
18:37 427
22:4 423

Acts

3:22–26 466
4:19 86
5:29 86
5:36–37 275
5:58–59 476
6:11 264
6:13 273
6:14 264
7:35 299
7:56 425
8:39 415
10–11 278, 318
10:11 425
13:9–11 442
13:28 264
13:43 451
13:49 451
13 ff 439
14:2 451
14:8–10 436
14:8–11 442
14:20 448
15 263–265, 273, 277 f, 279
15:1 263, 264
16:6–9 448, 450
17:4 451
17:17 451
18:6–7 278
18:12 273
18:18 449
19 441
19:21 447
21:23–24 449
21:28 273
22:17 413 f
24:15 451
24:25 447
26:19 414
27:23 414
28:26–28 278

Rom

1:17–18 417
2:13 396 f, 402
2:15 402
2:28–29 220
3:22 417
7:12–13 402
8:19 427
8:32 109
9:31–32 403
10:4 472
11:25 415
12:3 306
15:19 449
16 417
16:27 416

1 Cor

1:7 414, 418, 427
1:11 417
1:18 418
2 417
2:6 418
2:6–7 416
2:9 416
2:10 417
2:13 417
2:16 417
3:9 416
3:18–19 417
4:10 416

15:3b 109
15:51 415

2 Cor

3 415
4:1ff 416
10:3–6 440
12:2 414
12:2ff 413, 417
12:6 414
12:11–12 442
12:12 440

Gal

1:1 417
1:12 413f
1:16 413f
3:13–14 109

Eph

2:8–10 395
3:3 416

Col

1:26 416

1 Thes

4:17 415

1 Tim

1:9 395

Tit

3:5 395

Heb

11:17–19 110
12:26–27 297

1 Pet

1:11–12 416
1:12 425

Jas

2:14–26 395
3:6 95

Rev

1:3ff 409
1:9 408
1:13–17 410
1:13ff 412, 421
1:18 424
4 407, 411
4–5 412
4:1ff 409
4:2 408
5 411
5:1 388
5:4–5 412
5:37 424
6:46 424
7:16 424
7:17 411
10:1ff 411
12:5 415
12:41 424
14:6ff 411
14:9 424
16:12 299
21:3 424
22:4 421, 424
25:31–46 421

2. Apocrypha and Pseudepigrapha

ApAb

10–11 410, 420
17 407

TAb

11 407

LAE

13ff 531
25 538
47 533

LetAris

160 205

2 Bar

40 294

Bel

28 219

1 En

12–14 411
13:1 408
13:4ff 408
14 407f, 417
14:2ff 408
14:18ff 408
14:21 421, 425
37–71 421
41:5–42:3 299
89:1 412
89ff 411

2 En

22 407
30:11–14 535
30:14 536
42:8ff 422

2 Ezra

1:38–39 303
9:3 297
11:45 294
12:34 294
13:45–46 299

4 Ezra

4:14–32 262
8:21 424
14:42 366

Jdt

8:25–27 106

Jub

4:20ff 408
11:23–24 443
17:15–18:19 106
20:2 204
36:4 204

1 Mac

1:11 215
1:43 215
1:60–61 235
2:6 215
2:15–25 214
2:37 235
2:67 397
4:2 214
5:13 235
6:43–47 236
7:13 383
8 213
10–15 213
10:73 155
10:80 155
11:47–51 214
13:16–20 235
13:28 235
13:48 397
14:33–37 214
14:40–47 214
14:41 201
16:11 235
16:16 235

2 Mac

1:27 298
2:14–15 326
2:21 219
3:32 215
4:2 381
4:10 219

4:11 215
4:13 219
4:15 219
4:35 215
5:22–23 216
6:1 217f
6:1–11 216
6:6 217–219
6:7–9 217
6:9 219
6:10 217
6:25 219
7 107
7:37 218f
8:1 219
9:13–16 218
9:17 218f
9:20 218
11:24 219
14:38 219

4 Mac

6:27–28 108

ApMos

39:3ff 533

AsMos

8:1 217

ApSedr

5:2–3 531

SibOr

3:28 536
3:46–60 301
3:49 296
4:138–39 299
5:137–49 299
5:403–33 294

Sir

5:3 75
7:17 77
19:20 397
32(35):1–5 399
44:16 (LXX) 415
44:19–21 106
45:23–24 376
50 203
50:24 198f
50:24 (hebr) 376
51:12 (hebr) 376

PssSol

17:41 296

WisSol

4:11 415
10:1–2 535
18:9 302

Sus

22–23 (LXX) 212
56–57 (LXX) 213

Tob

4:21 360
12:22 360
14:2 360

TestXII.Sim

6:4 301

3. Qumran

1QGenAp

ii 19–22 326
20:1–8 394

1QM

17:3 379
i 4 301
ii 13–14 301

1QpHab

7 416
ii 3 345

1QS

3:13 391
5:1–3 377, 379
5:2 380
5:7–9 380
5:8–10 377
5:20–21 378
5:21 400
5:23–24 393, 401
6:1–9:2 380
6:18 400
9:3–5 399
9:7 378
10:10 205
10:14 205
ix:10–11 350

1QSa

1:1–3 377
1:22–23 379
1:23–25 377
2:2–3 378
2:11–13 379
13–16 379

1QSb

3:22–25 378

4Q159

6–7 202

4Q174

1–2 iii 6–7 397 ff
i 1:17 381

4Q390

1 4 342 f

4Q402

4 406

4Q403

1 i 1–29 406
1 ii 407
1 ii 2:18 407
i 1 406

4Q405

14 ff 407
20 ii 20–22 407
23 i 407
23 ii 406

4QMMT

79–82 337, 342, 349 f
C 27 397 ff

4QSd

1:1–3 379

11QPsa

154 xviii 10–11 399

11QShirShabb

f c k 407

CD

1:2–8 342
1:2–11 342
1:5–11 345
1:7 381
1:9–10 343
1:11 343
1:12–13 344
2:11–12 346
2:14–3:20 346

3:20–4:4	375
5:3–5	376
6:19	345
6:20–21	204
8:29	345
8:35	345
12	380
13:7	380
13:12	391
14:7	380
15:8	380

4. Papyri

CPJ ii

157	293
157–58	284
229	285
435–50	284

CPJ iii

520	284

5. Rabbinic Literature

Mishna

Ber

4:4	513
9:5	505

Pea

1:1	489

Ter

4:7	154

Bik

1:4	279

Pes

7:2	490
10:4	490
10:5	296
10:6	490

Sheq

1:5	201
3:3	202

Bes

2:7	490

RHSh

1:2	548
2:1	505
4:5	549

Meg

4:8–9	504 f

Hag

1:2	342
1:12	376
2:1	405 f
2:2	512
2:6–7	57, 297
2:15–23	342
2:18–19	342
2:20–23	344
3:21–22	57

Sot

9:9	542
9:14	285
9:15	506

San

10:1–3 508

Ed

3:11 490

Av

1:1 468
1:17 397, 401
4:4 77
4:14 486

Hul

2:9 505

Tam

4:3 206

Kel

15:6 326

Par

3:7 506

Yad

4:5 365
4:6 339

Tosefta

Ber

2:13 496
3:3 513
6:18 513
6:21 505, 514

Dem

3:1 154

Shab

3:3 494
13:5 504

Er

8:23 514

Pes

3:11 492
10:11 491
10:12 489

Yom

4:10f 514

Meg

3:37 504

Hag

1:9 514
2:6 419

San

2:7 326
5:7 365
7:10 514
8:7 505, 534
12:9 514
13:3 388

Hul

1:1 505
2:20 505f
2:22–23 504
2:24 505
3:10 492

Talmud Yerushalmi

Ber

4:2 (7d) 519
9:1 (13b) 519

Pea

7 (20a–b) 498

Shab

1:3 (3b) 518

Pes

6:2 (33b) 518
7:34a 490

Suk

5:1 (55a–b) 286

Taan

4 (68a) 325
4:2 (68a) 517
4:8 (68d) 296

Meg

1 (71b–c) 365
1 (71c) 362
1 (71d) 357, 360

Hag

2:1 (77a) 406
2:1 (77b) 419

Sot

2:2 (18a) 518
5 (20c) 496

Ned

9:1 (41b) 518

Naz

7 (56a) 486
7 (56b) 486

BB

9:6 (17a) 518

San

1:1 (18a) 518
1:7 (19c) 519
4:11 (22b) 519, 524
10:1 (28a) 519

Talmud Bavli

Ber

6a 523
7a 561
7b 487, 524
29a 521
33a 203
61b 388
63a 523

Shab

115a–b 326
115b 365
147b 522
152a 94
153a 521

Er

21a 523
53b 522

Pes

54a 522 f
108a 524

Yom

16a 523
21a 522, 525
75a 388
87a 525

Suk

53a 523

RHSh

16b 388
32a 524

Taan

20a 522

Meg

9a 365
28b 521

Hag

15a 419

Yev

45a 471

Ket

19b 368
21b 499
62b–63a 486
100b 326

Ned

20a	522
22b	522
39b	521
62a	524

Sot

22b	239
47a	525
48b	341

BQ

100a	396

BM

30b	396
33b	522
60b	523

BB

14b–15a	364
14b	326
58a	426
78b	523
111b	499
154a	495
155a	495

San

11a	341
21b	362, 365
32b	483
37a	524
38a	534
38b	420, 521
47b	525
93b	296
94b	488
96b	497
97b	297
99a	522

Shevu

35b	360

AZ

4a	521
19a	521
58b	349

Men

29b	371, 490
65a	349
99b	523 f

Hul

91b	426

Ar

15a	522

Tam

28a	522
32a	524

ARN A

8	485
39	534
41	388

ARN B

7	485

Sof

3:10	371

Masekhet Semaḥot

1	496
2:5	495
4	496

MekhY

Pisha

6	515

Bo

7	105
11	105

Beshallaḥ

4	516

Yitro	396

Baḥodesh

11	515

Sifra

Qedoshim

4 515

Emor

9:5 294

SifBam

§ 111 516
§ 112 515
§ 119 516

SifDev

§ 16 515
§ 29 516
§ 33:27 325
§ 48 516
§ 53 202
§ 109 516

MTann

26:9 498

BerR

2:4 419
5:7 521
8:10 529, 532
10:9 520
17:1 520
28:12 425
52:4 521
61:3 487
68:12 425
95 486

ShemR

18:12 297

WaR

3:1 520
10:9 521
16:5 520
18:1 520
21:8 486

DevR

1:23 297

EkhaR

1:13 299

QohR

3:7 74
3:17 294
12:1 520
12:5 94
12:10 526

Tan

§ 3 529

PesK

26:3.2 533
27 486

SOR

6 341
30 285, 523

MTeh

9:3 526

PRE

11 529, 532
18:1 516

SER

29 392

YalqShim

§ 23 529

TFrag

on Ex

12:42 303

TPsJ

on Gen

28:12 425

on Deut

30:4 303

TJon

on Ezek

1:26 538

TO

on Num

24 301

Megillat Aḥima'az

(ed. Klar) p.12/20 548

ABdRA

III:59 533

Synopse zur Hekhalot-Literatur

§4 542
§46 542
§71ff 542
§200 551
§202 544
§204 548
§220 548
§297ff 544
§301 548
§309 544
§337 549
§411 548
§419 548
§516 548

Magische Texte aus der Kairoer Geniza I and II

JTSL ENA

3635.17

17a/1ff 542ff, 553
17a/11–12 552

MS Oxford Heb

a.3.25a

1a/69 551
1a/27ff 553
1a/69ff 553

T.-S. K

1.35
1a/16ff 545ff

1.48
1a/2ff 545ff
1a/21–26 548

1.115
1b/1–5 549
1.144
2a/6ff 553

21.95.P
1a/4–10 551
1a/12ff 552
1a/16ff 551
1b/2–4 551
1b/2.9 553
1b/10ff 551
2a/15–16 553
2b/12 553

21.95.T
1a/16 551
1a/16ff 553
1b/12–14 552
1b/12 553

MS Oxford Mich

9,115a/3–116a/27 549
9,115a/4 551
9,115a/8 551
9,116a/18 552

MHG

1:56 529

PRK

19:6 520

6. Antique Authors

Appian

Mithr.
106:498 302

Syr.
1:252 302

Arrian

3:3 157
4:4 152
7:3 158
7:18 158

Aulus Gellius

Noct. Att.
1:2 392

Cassius Dio

50:27.1 219
62:7 289
66:2 307
66:4–5 307
66:150.3–4 230
68:24–25 291
68:32 283, 288

Diodorus

1–5 432ff
28:3 185
29:15 185

Diogenes Laertius

6:24 158

Epictet

Disc.
3:26.29 440

Euripides

Alc.

393ff 71

Gilgamesh–Epic

table III 71

Hesiod

Erga
40 38

Hippolytus

Ref.
9:27 392

Historia Augusta

Hadr.
5:2 286

Homer

Il.
1:69–72 156
12:237–240 156f

Od.
2:146ff 156
2:157ff 157
12:201 157
12:218–219 157

Jamblichus

De vit. Pyth.
17:71.74 392

Josephus

Ant.
1:94 223
1:130.1–4 107
1:130.222–36 107
2:41–58 224
2:243–53 224
4:91–92 155
4:196 205
4:212 206, 298
6:185 155
6:189 155
7:101 223
11–20 235
11:133 299
11:347 376
12:75 383
12:119 154
12:135 193
12:138–44 186
12:156–66 376

12:225	376	15:222–26	247
12:237–38	382	15:223–24	250
12:386	382	15:227–28	242
12:387	383	15:229	247
12:387–88	199	15:231	242, 250
13:62 ff	199	15:232–35	249
13:63 ff	383	15:236–39	250
13:68	300, 383	15:240–46	250
13:69–71	383	15:247–45	249
13:73	383	15:247–51	244
13:75	154	15:251	249
13:81	252	15:253–66	252
13:230–35	236	15:254	253
13:250–51	223	15:256–58	253
13:284–87	293	15:258–59	253
13:302	237	15:260–66	253
13:308	237 f	15:371	392
13:318	208	16	253, 255
13:320	237	16:8–10	255
13:399–404	239	16:9–10	255
13:407	237 f, 239	16:31–57	260
13:408 ff	238	16:59–60	260
13:409	238	16:66	255
13:417	239	16:69	255
13:418 ff	238	16:73–74	255
13:422–27	238	16:183–86	223
13:430–32	239	16:183–87	242
13:432	241	16:193	256
14:9	223	16:201	255
14:78	240	16:205	255
14:456	242	16:220–26	252, 254
15	253	16:225	269, 280
15–17	260	16:227	252
15:23–24	248	16:256	256
15:41	248	16:275–85	254
15:44 ff	248	16:286–99	254
15:53–56	248	16:346–45	260
15:54–56	245	16:346–50	260
15:62 ff	248	16:352	260
15:65	252	17	253
15:65–70	244	17:9 f	252
15:71–73	249	17:10	255
15:80–87	244	17:23–27	155
15:81	249 f	17:32	258
15:87	249 f	17:36–40	256
15:97–99	250	17:44	256
15:166–68	249	17:54	260
15:169–73	249	17:54–57	254
15:174	245	17:63	254
15:206	251	17:81	260
15:213	250	17:93	256
15:218–19	242	17:100–05	260
15:219	248	17:106–21	256

17:110–20	260
17:134	235
17:137–41	256
17:147	252, 258
17:187	260
17:189	252, 258
17:193	258
17:220	253, 261
17:224	253, 261
17:230	253, 261
17:238	260
17:240–47	260
17:285	297, 302
17:299–314	260
17:317–20	261
17:321	252
17:339	258
17:344	261
17:350–56	260
18:4–10	502
18:19	398
18:31	258
18:133	252
18:143	253
18:240–46	261
18:250–53	261
19:276–77	231
19:277	229, 232
19:357	232
20	272–280
20:17–96	277
20:34–48	263, 265–272
20:75	271
20:97–99	296
20:97–102	275
20:100	502
20:104	232
20:143	232
20:145–46	232
20:145–56	230
20:169–72	296
20:199	502
20:235–36	383
20:236	199
68	223
104	223
108	223
159	223
186	227
354	232

Bell.	
1	255
1:5	299
1:13	234
1:33	382
1:42–44	236
1:57–60	236
1:71	237
1:76	237 f
1:85	237
1:107	237 f
1:107–08	239
1:109 ff	238
1:111	239
1:112–13	238 f
1:115	238
1:116	238
1:117	238
1:269–71	256
1:344	242
1:364	246
1:435	242
1:437	245
1:439	246
1:441	252
1:441–43	243
1:443–44	242
1:446	252
1:476	256
1:478–79	255
1:483	246
1:498	256
1:535	255
1:538	255
1:566	252, 255
1:574	260
1:574–77	254
1:583	254
1:605	260
1:630–35	260
1:637	260
1:641	235
1:641–44	256
1:646	252, 258
1:666	258
2:14	261
2:15	253
2:20	261
2:26	252 f, 261
2:31	260
2:34	260
2:93–95	261
2:98	252, 258

2:110 258
2:111 261
2:118 502
2:159 398
2:167 258
2:182–83 261
2:217 231
2:221 231
2:310–14 231
2:333 231
2:402–05 231
2:407 231
2:426 231
2:487–488 152
2:494–98 284
2:595 231
3:133 225
3:303–04 225
3:336 225
4:81 225
4:115 225
4:312–13 296
4:505 225
4:538–44 228
4:560 225
5:430 225
6:201 225
7:37–50 292
7:42ff 199
7:78 294
7:399 228
7:409–19 292
7:420–36 292
7:423–32 382
7:426 293
7:431–32 383
14 234
31–54 236
433 225
513 225

c. Ap.
1:18 234
1:200–204 147–158
1:259 157
2:74 306
2:84 223
2:179–181 501
2:205 306
2:217–18 305
66 234

Vita
4 235

11 502
48 232
119 232
177 227
180 232
186 226f
343 232
355 232
362–64 233
414–15 222
426–27 222

Juvenal

Sat.
6:155–58 232
14:96–106 265

Livius

33:40.1–3 185
37:25.5 190
37:36.7–8 191
37:37.1–45.21 185

Philo

Abr.
189 107

De decal.
1:4–7 305

Legat.
214–17 302

Mos.
2:273 303

Praem.
95 296

Prob.
92–96 158

Quaest. Gen.
2:62 535

Spec.
1:76–78 201

Plato

polit.
7–9 449

Plutarch

Alex.
27 157
33 157
45 152
64–65 158
69 158

Polybius

Hist.
1:17.13 448
5:86.9–10 192
5:87.3 184
6:9.10 448
6:10 449
11:34.16 190
15:37.2 190
16:39.1–5 185
16:39.1 193
20:6–7 310
21:16–17 185
28:1–4 185
28:20.9 185
38:22.1–3 187

Pseudo-Aristotle

Physiogno.
805a 385

Strabo

Geogr.
16:1.4 158
16:1.64 158
16:1.68 158

Suetonius

Titus
7:1 230

Tacitus

Hist.
2:2.1 230
2:81.2 231

7. Christian and Gnostic Writings

Clem

32:4 403

ActsApost.

11:19–20 293
13:1 293
13:4–6 293

Celsus

Aleth. log.
4:86.88 156

Clement

Ecl.
6:1–2 296

Prot.
5:78.4–5 161
7:74.4–5 161ff

Str.
5:12.78.4 164
5:14.123.1 161ff
5:14.123.1–2 164
5:14.123.2–124.1 161ff
5:14.126.5 164
5:78.4–5 161ff
124:1 164
126:5 161ff
127:2 161ff
133:2 161ff

EBar

4:3 294
12:9 294
16:4 294

Epist. Apost.

39 535

Eusebius

Chron. Trajan
17–19 287
17 297

H.e.
2:2.1–2 290
3:4 446
4:2.2 283, 287–89, 292
4:2.3 297
4:2.3–5 288f
4:2.5 290

P.e.
9:17.2–9 432
9:20.1 106
9:28.2 536
13:12.5 159

GBart

4:53ff 531

Origen

Cels.
5:34 450

Hom. in Gen.
1:13 537

Jo.
2:31 420

Orosius

Hist.
7:12.6 297

Pseudo-Clementines

Hom.
3:17 535
3:21 535
2:52 535

Tertullian

De paen.
12:9 535

Theophilus

Autol.
3:2 160

Apokryphon of John

NHL II:
1.23–24 558

Hypostasis of the Archons

NHL II:
4.95–97 558

Right Ginza

i 530
ii:1 531
ii:7 531
x 537

8. Islamic Writings

Kammûna

Kitâb tanqîḥ al abḥaṯ
(ed. Perlmann)
p.1/11 456
p.51/78 460f
p.54/83 471
p.62–63/93–95 465
p.63/95 472
p.64/97 467
p.65/98 466, 470
p.102/149 457

Koran

Sure
2:27ff 538
7:10ff 538
15:26ff 538
17:62ff 538
20:114ff 538
38:71ff 538

9. Medieval Authors

Moses ben Maimon

Mishne Tora
Melakhim 11:4 476
Teshuva 3:1 388

More Nevukhim
II §§ 41 ff 458
II §§ 45 458

Sefer Ḥasidim

§ 1145 530, 533

Yehuda ha–Levi

Sefer Kuzari
I § 4 460
III § 53 ff 468

Greek Terms

Ἄβραμος ὁ μακαριότατος 306
ἄγγελος 419
ἀγεραστος 306
ἀδελφή 226
ἀδελφός 226
ἅδης 77
αἰτία 181, 195
ἁπλότητα τῆς ἀνθρώπου 239

δῆμος 213

ἔθνος 211, 213
ἔθος 263f, 267, 270, 272f, 279f
ἔργον 79

θρησκεία 107

ἱερὸς λόγος 161, 175
Ἰουδαία 211
Ἰουδαίος 211–220

καλὸς καὶ ἀγαθὸς 313
κατέχων 187
κίνησις 290

λόγος 79

μεγαλοψυχία 308
μυστήριον 418

νήπιος 382
νόμος 263
νοῦς 169

οἶκος 315
οἰκουμένη 276

παῖς 382
πατὴρ κόσμου 534
πατρῶοι νόμοι 218
πλῆθος 213
πνευματικοί 418
πόλεμος 285, 290
πολιτεύεσθαι 217
πολίτευμα 313f
προεδρία 308
πρόφασις 181, 195

σαρκικοί 418
σελίς 388
στάσις 290, 293, 295
σωτηρία 317

τέλειοι 418
τιμή 305
τῦφος 305

ὕβρις 248

φιλανθροπία 308
φῶς 534ff

ψυχή 169

Hebrew Terms

אבי 559
אכלן 328
אל תאבות 558
ארץ הצבי 183, 185

בהו 557
בהות 557
בור החושך 387, 390
בינוניים 388
בני מרון 548
בעות 558
ברית 338, 345ff
בת האנר 387, 390

גאלה 296
גוי 58
גורל 391

הבל 70ff
הדיוטות 365, 369
הואה 328
הכרת פנים וסדרי סרטוטין 392
הכרת פנים לרבי ישמאל 390
הכשהן 126
הפחה 120, 126
השם הנכבד 355

זכות אבות 106
זרע הקדש 342
זרע ישראל 342

חיות 545
חרות 296

יה אדני צבאות אלהי ישראל אלהים חיים 561
יה אדני עבאות 563
יה אלהים אדני עבאות 563f
יהד 119
יהודה 211
יהודי 211f
יהוה אלהי ישראל 562f
יורדי מרכבה 392
יחד הברית החדשה 323–352

ילד 558f
יצר הטוב 390
יצר הרע 390
ירידה למרכבה 562
ירתא 120

כנגד מידה מידה 109
לנטוע 56
לנטת 56

מדינתא 120
מומים 389
מורה (ה)צדק 338, 341, 343, 345
מחשבי קצים 343
מעין אור 390
מעשה בראשית 405
מעשה מרכבה 405
מעשה 396
מקדש אדם 398
מקור החושך 390
משטמה 328
משיח 182
משכיל 391
משפט 52, 65

ספר המצשים 401
ספר העזרה 325
ספרי המירם 339
ספרים חיצונים 339

עבר הנהר 120
עמוד השני 388
עמוד 390
עקדת יצחק 99–116

פדיון הבן 101
פעיה 65
פשרים 66

צבאות 357, 558
צדיק 84
צדקה 53

קדשת השם 548f
קול דממה דקה 551
קץ 342
קרוב 46

רוח 387
רשע 85

שאול 77
שופר 113
שמרין 119f, 127f

תולדות קול בני איש 390
תורה שבכתב 339
תורה שבעל פה 339
תחת השמים 70ff
תחת השמש 70ff
תכנה 114

Index of Subjects

Aaron 376, 381
Aaron of Baghdad 548
Abatur 530
Abraham 21, 167, 171, 435
Achaemenid 119 ff
Achaemenides 120
Achamoth 560
Adam 529–538
– Kadmon 533
Adiabene 265 f, 274, 277
Adonayos 560
Agrippa I 229
Agrippa II 226, 229
Akhatriel 561
Akmonia 311, 314
Alcimus 381 ff
Alexander the Great 135, 147, 151, 153, 156
Alexander Yannaeus 235, 241
Alexandra 246
Alexandria 152, 289
Am ha–Areṣ 489
Amida 298, 546 ff
Palestinian form 547
Angelology 407 f
Antiochus II 190
Antiochus III 151, 184, 186, 189 f
Antiochus IV 181 f, 186, 189 f, 191, 193, 198 f, 217 f, 381 ff
Aphrodisiacum 94
Apocalypsis 406 ff
Apocalyptic 405–428
Apostate 503
Apostolic Council 263
Aqeda 99–116
Archaeology 3–33
Aristobulus 159 ff, 240
Aristobulus I 235
Aristobulus III 246
Artaxerxes II 132
Artaxerxes III 124, 131 f, 134
Ashdod 134
Askalon 134
Assyria 299
Astrology 386 ff
Astronomy 386
Atonement 106 ff
– Day of 547, 566
Aulus Gellius 392
Auspicium 156

Baal
– of Tarsos 129
Baal–Zeus 71
Babata 11
Babylon 48, 127
Babylonia 526
Baghdad 455 f
Bar Kokhba 488
– Revolt of 119, 288, 296 ff
Barbara superstitio 158
Beirut 310
Benediction(s)
– Seventh of the Amida 296
– Seven cf. Sheva‘ de–Eliyahu
– Tenth of the Amida 296
– the lesser Prayer of Seven cf. Sheva‘ Zuṭarti
Benefactors 305–319
Benei Beraq 483–499
Berenice 225, 229–233, 316
Bet Midrash 483 f, 486, 488, 491–493, 496–499
Beth She’an 317
Bethlehem 12 ff
Body 565–571

Caesarea 8, 17, 310
Calendar 348
Carmel 6
Celibacy 565
Chaos 557
Chassidism 568
Christian Society 319
Christology 30
Circumcision 104, 217, 219, 263, 265, 269 f, 272, 277 ff, 568

Citizenship 153
Clement 161 ff
Cleopatra 248
Coins
- Drachme 121 ff
- Images on 128
- Minting of 121
- of Juda and Samaria 119
- of the Bar Kokhba Revolt 119
- of the Persian Provinces 119
Commandment 401, 565
Composition 69–98
Congregation 375–384
Constantinus Porphyrogenitus 243
Conversion 218
- to Judaism 263
Corporealty 565
Covenant 345 ff
Crucifixion 114
Cyprus 283 ff, 289 f, 293 f, 302
Cyrenaica 313
Cyrene 283 ff, 289
Cyrill 160
Cyrus 44 ff, 48

Damascus Document 375
Darius III 124
David 58, 80
Death 106 ff
Decalogue 90
Decapolis 507
Demiurge 534
Diaspora 305–319
Diodorus Siculus 432
Dionysos 188, 433, 437
Disputations
- Religious 456
Doctrine of Trinity 461
Donors 315

Eagle
- of Zeus 129
Egypt 283 ff, 289, 299
- Ptolemaic 152
Elazar ben Yair's Wise Relative 228–229
Elija 303, 551 f
Elisa
- Student of 47
En Gedi 16 f
Enoch 387
Epicurean 504
Epigraphy 310 ff
Essenes 336 ff, 507

Euergetism 305–319, 308 ff
Eulogy 550
Eusebius 160 ff
Exile 45 ff, 53, 297
Ezekiel the Tragedian 536

Fayum 284
Festivals 217
Frank, Jakob 568

Gadara 310
Gate
- Cilician 134
Gaza 134
Gem 134
Geniza 324, 542
Gentiles 263–280
Gerizim (Mount) 216
Gesetzeswerke 395–403
Gnosticism 507, 557 ff
God 263–280
- Immanence 167
- Transcendent 167
God–Fearer 265 ff, 278
Gospel of John 403
Gottesknecht 43–68
Grandee
- Persian 120

Halakha 361 f, 471, 503, 509
Half Sheqel Temple Tax 198, 199–202
Halle 36
Ḥaside Ashkenaz 549, 552
Ḥasidim 549
Hasmoneans 10, 119 ff, 235 ff
Hecataeus of Abdera 147–158, 434
Heilsgeschichte 19
Hekhalot Literature 405 f, 549, 562 ff
Helene 265 ff, 269, 277
Hellenism 198, 305
Hellenistic Time 181–195
Hellenization 208
Heracles 435 f, 438 ff, 443 ff
Heraclit 28, 167
Herod 10, 14, 26, 246, 248
Herodian Dynasty 229 ff
Highpriest 376, 542
Hillel the Elder 485
Homosexuality 569
Hülägü 455 f
Hyrcanus 208, 240 f
Hyrcanus II 246

Ibn Kammûna 453–476
India 9
Initiation 385–394
– Hellenistic Mystery Rites 161
Inscription
– Aphrodisias 272, 311
– Greece 310 ff
– Theodotus 311
Ioudaia/Yehudah 211
Isaac 21
Islam 527
Israel 44 ff, 55
– status confessionis 181–195
Iudaeus 211
Izates 265–271, 274, 277, 279 f

Jacobites 461 f
JAHWE 44 ff
Jericho 4 ff, 21 f
Jerusalem 8, 11 f, 25, 28, 59 f, 302, 325 f, 449
– New 60, 421, 424
– Redemption of 299
Jesus 3 f, 6, 13, 27 f
Jews 211–220
– Christians 507
– Diaspora 310
– Hellenistic 507
– Soldier 147, 154
John the Baptist 420
Joseph 21 f
Josephus 147, 221–262, 224 ff, 375
Jubilees 111
Juda 119–135
Judaeans 211–220
Judas Maccabaeus 155
Judas the Galilean 277
Justus' of Tiberias Sister 226–228

Kabbala 567 f
Karaites 468, 474 f, 527, 566
Kyme 309

Land
– Conquest of the 21
Law
– Ancestral 217 f, 232 f
– Food 219
– Jewish 263–280
– Mosaic 169, 264
Leiden 36
Leontopolis 193, 199, 375
Light
– Sons of 391
Liturgy
– Jewish 541–553
Lod 483, 491–493, 496 f
Logos 79
Lydia 151

Maccabees 198 ff, 201, 381–382
– Dynasty 208
– Era 197–209
– Party 214
Macedonians 135
Magic 541–553
Magical Recipes 545
Mandeism 530 f
Marco Polo 456
Mariamme 222, 242–252
Marriage 566
Martyrdom 99, 105 ff
Masada 10 f, 26, 326 ff
Mattathias 214
Maussollos 132 f
Mazday 127
Megilla 97
Melchites 461 f
Melchizedek 435
Melitto of Sardis 110
Menelaus 381
Mesopotamia 283 ff
Messianic Age 413
Messianism 283 ff, 294–304, 350 f
– Zelotic 299
Messias 104, 110 ff
Meṭaṭron 544, 551
minim 501–510
Minting 126
Misogynism 223
Mithrapata 133
Monobazus 271
Monogamy 570
Moses 162, 171 ff, 303, 305, 485, 536, 551 f
Moses ben Maimon 458, 470 f, 473
Mosollamus 147–158, 153
mufāwaḍāt 456
Musaeus 161
Myrina 433
Mystic 529–538
– Merkava 391, 405 ff, 549, 552 f, 562 ff
Mysticism 405–428

Nablus 121
Nag Hammadi 557
Name(s)
– Divine 354–363

– of God 542f, 557
– Seventy 542f
Nazareth 12
Nehemia 199ff
Nicene Creed 461
Nicolaus of Damascus 221–262, 234

Obole 121ff
Octavian 246
Onias 182, 192, 193
Onias III 381
Orpheus 160ff
Osiris 433f, 437, 439, 442f, 445
Owl
– of Pallas Athene 129

Palestine 310
Paneas 193
Passover 106, 111, 114, 489–494, 566
Patriarch(s) 21
– Jacob 55
Paul 395–403, 413, 472ff, 567, 570
Pentateuch
– Samaritan 366
Perikles 133
Pharisaic 400
Pharisees 223, 239, 241, 264, 272, 368f, 400, 502f, 506
Philo the Elder 106
Philosophy
– Peripatetic 161, 234
– Platonic–Aristotelian 161
– Stoic 157f, 161, 167, 432
Phocaea 314
Phoenicia 134
Phrygia 151
Physiognomy 385–394
Pietists
– German cf. Ḥaside Ashkenaz
Pious cf. Ḥasidim
Politeuma 313f
Pompey 240
Pontius Pilate 14
Pottery 6, 8
Prayer 544–553
– of Joseph 420
Priesthood 376
Priests 375–384
Prohibition 565
Prostates 312
Pseudo–Aristotle 385, 389
Pseudo–Hecataeus 148
Pseudo–Justin 160
Pseudo–Orpheus 159–176
Ptahil 530
Ptolemaius I 129
Ptolemaius II 123, 190
Ptolemaius III 123
Ptolemaius IV 184, 186ff
Ptolemaius V 185
Ptolemies 135, 184
Pythagoreans 392

Qubilai 456
Quietus
– War of 285
Qumran 3f, 10, 15ff, 26ff, 47, 323–352, 353–372, 375–384, 385–394, 395–403, 506
– Community 209

R. Aqiva 406, 483–488, 490f, 493–497, 549, 562, 567
R. Elazar ben Azaria 493, 494
R. Eliezer 483, 485f, 493
R. Hoshaya 532
R. Moses ha–Darshan 530
R. Tarphon 496
R. Yehoshua 483
R. Yehuda ha–Nasi 497, 498
R. Yishmael 390, 542, 544
R. Yoshua 485f, 493
Rabban Gamaliel 476, 483, 489–492, 492, 499
Rabban Shimon ben Gamaliel 396, 401
Rabban Yoḥanan ben Zakkai 113, 406, 483, 485, 486, 501
Raphia 184, 188, 192
Redemption
– Messianic 303
– of the firstborn 101
Resurrection 99, 106ff
Revolt
– First against Rome 292, 296ff
– under Trajan 283–303
Rome 449
Rosh ha-Shana 113f

Saadja ben Joseph al Fajjumi 470
Sabbaoth 560
Sabbath 217, 219, 492, 566
Sacrifice
– of the Firstborn 99ff
Sadducees 367ff, 502, 504, 506f
ṣaḥīḥ 469
Sakla 558

Salome Alexandra 222, 235, 237–242
Salome, sister of Herod 222, 252–262
Salomo 72ff
Samaria 119–135, 121, 216
Samaritans 366, 369ff, 504
Samaual al–Maghribi 458
Samos 315
Sardis 317
Satan 531, 557
Scipio 185, 187
Script
– Paleo–Hebrew 120, 353–372
Scythopolis 317
Sea
– of Galilee 12
Sefer ha–Razim 546
Sefer Yezira 561
Seleucid state 217
Seleucids 184
Semiramis 433, 435, 437f
Sepphoris 12, 17
Serekh ha–Yaḥad 390
Servant of the Lord cf. Gottesknecht
Sesostris 434f, 437f
Sexual Intercourse 565f, 569
Shabbat 494
Shavu'ot 566
Shema' Yisra'el 198, 202–207, 491, 496f, 546f
Sherira Gaon 392
Sheva' de–Eliyahu 549
Sheva' Zuṭarti 549
Shi'ur Qoma 537
Sidon 127, 129
Simon bar Giora's Wife 228
Simon ben Zoma 419
Simon the Hasmonean 236
Sinai Covenant 413
Skopas 185, 193
Song of Songs 567
Sophia 558
Spirit 417f
Stamp Cut 125
Stobi 311, 316
Stoics 28
Sufferer
– innocent 108
Sukkot 313, 566
Susanna 212f
Syllaeus 269f, 280
Synagogue 4, 10f, 311f
Syria 71

tafsīr 466ff
Tannaim 503f, 507
Tarsos 127
tawātur 467
ta'wīl 466
Teacher
– of Righteousness 416
Tefillin 504
Temple 78, 217, 219, 376
– of God 399
– Ritual 541–544
– Service 399
Tetragrammaton 354–363, 543
Theodicy 97, 105
Theodoret 159ff
Theophilus 160
Theudas 277
Thomas von Aquin 569
Thucydides 234
Tiberias 17
Tobiades 192
Traditions
– Invented 197–209
Transfiguration 421
Tyre 129

Unio liturgica 544
Usha 483

Water
– of Bitterness 541
Women 221–262
Works 395

Ya'qûb al–Qirqisânî 474f
Yaldabaoth 557–564
Yason (Yakim) 381
Yavne 483f, 490, 492f, 501, 503
Yehuda ha–Levi 458f, 460f, 468

Zadokites 337f, 375–384, 376–384
Zeus 128, 175
Zion 44ff, 55, 80, 95
Zodiac 389
Zweinaturenlehre 462f
Zwi, Sabbatai 568

Modern Authors

Abel, E. 162
Abrahams, L. 419
Abramson, S. 397, 545, 548
Adcock, F. E. 292
Adorno, T. 428
Aharoni, Y. 7
Albeck, C. 499
Albright, W. F. 16, 18
Alexander, P. S. 385, 388, 391 f, 562
Allegro, J. M. 202, 357, 385, 388, 397
Alon, G. 230, 298, 484, 486, 488, 493
Altmann, A. 529, 530, 531
Anderson, B. W. 30
Applebaum, S. 155, 283, 286 f, 292, 297, 299, 301, 313
Ashton, J. 413, 424, 427
Assmann, J. 200
Astren, F. 475
Attridge, H. W. 274
Avigad, N. 30, 326
Avishur, Y. 156

Badian, E. 134
Báez-Camargo, G. 22
Bailey, J. L. 221, 224
Baillet, M. 348
Baldwin Bowsky, M. W. 313
Bammel, E. 253
Baneth, D. H. 454, 457 f, 464
Bar Adon, P. 15
Bar-Ilan, M. 366, 549
Bar-Kochva, B. 152, 155
Barag, D. 121, 123, 129
Barc, B. 533
Barnes, T. D. 283 ff, 286 f, 290, 297, 301 f
Baron, S. W. 457
Barrera, J. 201
Barthelemy, D. 358
Barton, T. S. 386 f, 392, 394
Bauer, W. 266
Bauernfeind, O. 223
Baumgarten, A. I. 200, 202, 208, 272
Baumgarten, J. 332 f, 337, 370, 399, 410
Baumgartner, W. 182
Begrich, J. 51
Behm, J. 345
Ben-Ya'aqov, A. 456
Benoit, P. 16, 296, 335
Bentwich, N. 236
Bentzen, A. 191
Berend, D. 133
Berger, K. 511
Bergmeier, R. 336
Betz, O. 27, 295, 335, 414
Beuken, W. M. A. 48, 51, 54, 57, 62 f, 67
Bevenot, H. 214
Bianchi, U. 560
Bickerman, E. 151, 199, 201, 205, 208, 218
Bilde, P. 501
Black, J. S. 37
Blau, L. 203, 206, 363
Blundell, S. 441, 443, 448
Boardman, J. 134
Bockmuehl, M. 415
Böhl, F. 516
Böhlig, A. 420
Bogaert, P. M. 301
Bommer, F. 435
Bonfil, R. 492
Bonnefoy, Y. 443
Bonnet, C. 435
Bousset, W. 148, 394
Bowman, J. 334
Braud, D. C. 230
Braun, M. 224
Bright, J. 16
Brod, M. 567
Broer, I. 280
Brooten, B. J. 253, 315
Broshi, M. 202, 324
Brown, C.-A. 221
Brueggemann, W. 23
Brunt, P. A. 298, 302
Büchler, A. 396
Bull, R. J. 9
Bultmann, R. 29
Burkert, W. 175
Burkitt, F. C. 358

Burns, J. E. 9
Burton, G. P. 492

Callaway, J. A. 16
Cameron, A. 447
Camp, C. V. 222
Carleton Paget, J. N. B. 295
Carradice, I. 132
Charlesworth, J. H. 25 f, 29, 161 ff, 335 f, 380, 405, 415
Charlesworth, M. P. 292
Chernus, I. 406
Childs, B. S. 19
Chilton, B. D. 105
Chrystal, G. 37
Clements, R. E. 417
Clementz, H. 269
Cohen Stuart, G. H. 390
Cohen, B. 471
Cohen, G. M. 155
Cohen, M. S. 410, 537
Cohen, S. J. D. 223 f, 227, 229, 259, 265 f, 269 f, 279, 503
Collins, J. J. 28, 150, 405, 412, 415
Collins, R. F. 345
Combe, T. 121
Conzelmann, H. 29, 189
Coogan, M. D. 25
Cook, S. A. 292
Corbo, V. C. 14
Coüasnon, C. 14
Crook, J. A. 230
Cross, F. M. 4, 31, 120, 325, 336 f
Cumont, F. 386
Cunz, M. 476

Dacroix, L. 438
Dahl, N. A. 109, 449, 560
Dalbert, P. 148
Dan, J. 227, 405, 548, 562
Danby, H. 548
Danker, F. W. 308, 434
Daumas, F. 188
Davies, P. R. 25, 105, 417
Davies, W. D. 284
Dayagi-Mendels, M. 9
De La Habba, L. 22
De Vaux, D. R. 15 f, 24, 296, 324
Dean-Otting, M. 407
Delcor, M. 360, 382
Denis, A.-M. 160 ff
Deppert-Lippitz, B. 133
Derwacter, F. M. 431
Desroches, H. 199
Detienne, M. 443
Dever, W. G. 24
Dexinger, F. 503
Dibelius, M. 275
DiLella, A. 199
Dimant, D. 342, 398
Dinur, B. 259
Diringer, D. 366, 368 f
Dittenberger, W. 230
Doante, T. W. 109
Dodds, E. R. 443
Dornseiff, F. 150
Dothan, M. 318
Douglas, M. 200
Driver, G. R. 335, 344
Duhm, B. 49, 62 f
Dunn, J. D. G. 292, 295
Dupont-Sommer, A. 535

Eaton, R. M. 441
Edwards, A.J. 9
Efron, J. 259
Eichrodt, W. 18, 30
Eisenman, R. 335, 344, 393
Elbogen, I. 203
Eliav, Y. 495
Elior, R. 562
Elliger, K. 49, 52
Elman, Y. 526
Elter, A. 150, 162
Endress, G. 462
Engel, H. 212 f
Engers, M. 150
Ephron, J. 148
Epstein, J. N. 519
Erhardt, A. 276
Erskine, A. 434
Eshel, E. 205
Eshel, E. and H. 201
Esler, P. L. 417

Fallon, F. T. 559
Farmer, W. R. 427
Feldman, L. H. 23, 148, 158, 221, 224, 229, 236, 265 f, 268, 270, 272, 274, 280, 398, 431
Fesi, J. 189
Finkelstein, I. 24, 484, 499
Finkelstein, L. 284, 294, 511
Finley, M. I. 298
Fischel, W. 455
Fischer-Bossert, W. 128
Fitzmyer, J. A. 27 f, 32, 276, 280, 393, 439

Fleischer, E. 202, 207, 547
Flusser, D. 29, 201, 395f, 398, 402
Foerster, G. 317
Fossum, J. 413, 421, 425, 534
Frankfurter, D. 284, 301
Fraser, P.M. 148
Frazer, J.G. 541
Freedman, D.N. 24, 363
Fuks, A. 257, 297

Gabra, E. 150
Gärtner, B. 398
Gätje, H. 466
Gafni, I. 265, 497
Gager, J.G. 150
Galinski, C.K. 435
García Martínez, F. 393
Gauger, J.-D. 150
Gauthier, H. 188
Gauthier, P. 308
Geffcken, J. 148
Geissen, A. 190
Georgi, D. 439, 447
Gerber, W. 421
Gese, H. 77, 80, 83, 90, 95
Giangrande, G. 234
Gil, M. 156
Gilbert, G. 265f, 268, 274
Ginzberg, L. 532, 534
Glueck, N. 16
Goethe, J.W.v. 91
Goitein, S.D. 457
Golb, N. 325, 335
Goldstein, J. 214f, 217f
Goodman, M. 268, 271f, 440, 450, 502, 505ff
Goppelt, L. 29
Goren, S. 362
Gottlieb, I.B. 511
Grabbe, L.L. 285
Graetz, H. 265
Grant, M. 244, 248, 252, 257
Grant, R.M. 287, 560
Graves, R. 110
Gray, R. 502
Greenberg, M. 206
Gressmann, H. 148
Griffiths, J.G. 434
Grimm, C.L.W. 217
Gross, M.D. 347
Gruen, E.S. 157
Gruenwald, I. 405f, 409, 421, 538, 561
Gunkel, H. 3, 40
Gutman, S. 10
Gutman, Y. 150, 156, 300
Guttmann, A. 512, 514f, 517, 522, 526f

Haacker, K. 295
Habicht, C. 215
Hacohen, Y.L. 494
Hadas-Lebel, M. 270, 508
Haenchen, E. 263, 266
Hailperin, H. 470
Halivni, D. 522
Halkin, A.S. 471, 476
Halperin, D. 405, 408, 409
Hands, A.R. 308, 310, 316
Hanfmann, G.M.A. 317
Hanhart, R. 187
Hansen, G.W. 278
Hanson, R.S. 363
Harnack, A.v. 110, 275, 286f, 431, 442
Harrelson, W. 24
Harrison, C. 559
Hasel, G. 30
Hayes, J.H. 18
Hayward, D. 382
Healy, J.F. 293
Hecht, D. 277
Heinemann, J. 202
Heller, D. 213
Hellholm, D. 405
Helm, R. 287
Hemer, C.J. 432
Hengel, M. 10f, 19, 33, 42, 99, 109, 113, 123, 132, 148, 150, 183, 186ff, 193, 195, 214, 272, 283, 285, 292, 295ff, 299ff, 305, 382, 405, 422, 432, 502
Hennessy, J.B. 7
Herford, R.T. 504, 507
Hermisson, H.-J. 44f
Herr, M.D. 294, 511
Hezser, C. 518
Hill, G.F. 121
Himmelfarb, M. 394, 407, 417
Hirschberg, J.W. 530, 531
Hirschfeld, L. 458ff
Hobsbawm, E. 197
Hodgson, R. 434
Hodot, R. 309
Hölscher, G. 223, 236, 259
Hofius, O. 405
Hohlfelder, R.L. 9
Holladay, C.R. 148f, 151
Holland, T.A. 4
Holum, K.G. 9

Homés-Fredericq, D. 7
Hooker, M. D. 106, 113
Horbury, W. 313, 507
Hornblower, S. 133
Hubbard, B. J. 275
Hüttenmeister, F. 317
Hurst, L. W. 405
Hurtado, L. W. 410f, 413
Hurter, S. 133
Hyman, A. 499

Ilan, T. 238, 242, 257, 259
Ilg, N. 345
Isaac, B. 492
Ivry, S. 338

Jackson, H. M. 558
Jacoby, F. 148, 276
James, E. O. 109
Jaubert, A. 345
Jeremias, J. 29, 431
Jervell, J. 425
Jeselsohn, D. 121
Jones, A. H. M. 248, 257
Jordan, R. 232
Jourdain-Annequin, C. 435, 438
Juel, D. 27

Kahana, A. 213, 215
Kapelrud, A.S. 345
Kasher, A. 151ff
Kasher, M. M. 362
Kasowski, C. J. 347
Kastner, J. M. 264
Katsh, A. 516
Kee, H. C. 338
Keeble, K. 501
Kenyon, F. G. 388
Kenyon, K. M. 16
Kern, O. 162
Kim, S. 414
Kimelman, R. 203
Kindler, A. 121, 318
Kinzer, M. S. 529
Kister, M. 512
Kitchen, K. A. 5, 21
Klassen, W. 422
Klausner, J. 241
Klein, S. 498
Knox, J. 449
Knox, W. L. 276, 432
Koch, H. 275
Koenen, K. 62
Koester, H. 280, 449
Kohler, K. 335
Kraabel, A. T. 317
Kraabel, T. 272
Kraeling, C. H. 531
Kraeling, E. G. 154
Kratz, R. G. 46, 48
Kraus, F. R. 387
Krauss, S. 285
Krenkel, M. 275
Kroll, W. 158
Küchler, M. 511
Kümmel, W. G. 29, 160ff, 276, 280
Kuenen, A. 36
Kuhn, K. G. 272, 516
Kutscher, E. Y. 372
Kutzmann, R. 301

Lacroix, L. 443
Lafargue, M. 161ff
Landsberger, B. 339
Laqueur, R. 240, 287
Lasker, D. 474
Latourette, K. S. 439
Layton, B. 559
Lazarus-Yafeh, H. 466f
Le Bohec, Y. 311
Leach, Edmond 102
Lentz, J. C. 451
Lepper, F. A. 285, 292
Lerch, D. 111
Lerner, M. B. 511
Lesquier, J. 152
Levenson, J. D. 103ff, 111f
Levey, S. H. 538
Lévi, I. 394
Levine, A.-J. 213, 221
Levine, L. I. 4, 9, 11, 203
Levinson, J. R. 532
Levy, J. H. 153, 156f
Lewis, B. 197, 457
Lewis, M. 307
Lewy, H. 150
Licht, J. 205
Lidzbarski, M. 364
Lieberman, S. 496
Liebmann-Frankfort, T. 286
Lightfoot, J. B. 291
Lincoln, A. T. 405
Liver, J. 201, 376
Lloyd, A. B. 434
Lobeck, C. A. 162
Loewe, R. 286

Loewenstamm, S. 273
Logan, A. H. B. 560
Lohfink, N. 28; 345 f
Lohse, E. 109; 397; 399
Lookwoods, W. 475
Louth, A. 287
Luckenbill, D.D. 484
Lüderitz, G. 313

Mach, M. 413; 421
Machalek, R. 450
Machinist, P. 120 f; 123 f
Mack, B. 198; 199
MacLennan, R. S. 295
MacMullen, R. 156
Macurdy, G. H. 230; 242; 262
Maier, J. 398
Maiuri, A. 9
Malherbe, A. J. 434 f; 440
Malinine, M. 188
Mandelkern, S. 153
Mandell, s. 201
Manekin, C. H. 470
Mann, J. 456
Marcovich, M. 160; 165
Marcus, R. 151; 245; 252
Marmorstein, A. 542
Marshall, A. J. 492
Martyn, J. L. 427
Mason, S. 239 f; 272; 274; 276
Mathews, K. A. 356 f; 363 ff
Mazar, A. 9
Mazar, B. 16
McCarter, P. K. 21 f
McEleney, N. J. 265 ff
McGuckin, J. A. 421
McKnight, S. 431; 450 f
McLean, M. D. 363
McMullen, R. 308
McNamara, M. 425
Meeks, W. A. 441
Meister, K. 434; 435
Melammed, E. Z. 512
Mélèze-Modrzejewski, J. 284 f; 289 f
Mendeles, D. 149; 151
Mendels, D. 436; 442; 446
Merivale, C. 292; 294
Merleau-Ponty, M. 20
Meshorer 119; 121 f
Meyer, E. A. 308
Michel, O. 223
Mildenberg, L. 119; 120 ff; 124; 127; 130; 132 f; 297
Milik, J. T. 296; 358
Milikowski, C. 517
Millar, F. 285; 376; 492
Miller, P. D. 23
Mireaux, E. 230
Momigliano, A. 188
Mommsen, T. 288; 292
Montaner, L. 201
Moore, C. A. 212 f
Moore, G. F. 331; 504
Mørkholm, O. 123
Morray-Jones, C. R. A. 405; 415
Mosshammer, A. A. 287
Motta, L. 287
Moysey, R. A. 133
Müller, J. G. 156; 501
Mulert, H. 40
Munoa, P. B. 536

Naor, M. 259
Naveh, J. 318; 368
Negev, A. 7
Nemoy, L. 454; 474 f
Netzer, E. 9; 11
Neusner, J. 267; 349; 420; 506
Newman, C. 414
Newsom, C. 327 f; 355; 406
Niebuhr, R. 30
Niehoff, M. 224
Niewöhner, F. 455 ff; 475
Nock, A. D. 434; 440; 442
Nöldecke, T. 41
Northrup, L. S. 456
Nosowski, J. 465
Noy, D. 307; 313 f

O'Fearghail, F. 203
Odeberg, H. 405; 562
Oderberg, H. 422
Oorschot, J. v. 45 f; 48
Oppenheimer, A. 484; 487 ff; 492 f; 496
Orrieux, C. 265
Otto, J. C. T. 110
Otto, W. 188; 244; 247 f; 254

Patai, R. 110
Pearson, B. A. 559
Pédech, P. 181
Perlmann, M. 454 f; 458
Perowne, S. 257
Petermann, H. 537
Peterson, E. 535; 538
Petrement, S. 559 f

Petrie, F. 18
Petuchowski, J. 202
Pfann, S. J. 15; 353
Platti, E. 462
Plümacher, E. 432
Polanyi, M. 20f
Posen, J. 476
Posnanski, A. 467
Preisendanz, I. 535
Price, J. J. 227; 295ff; 296
Prussner, F. C. 18
Pucci Ben-Ze'ev, M. 150
Pucci, M. 287
Puech, E. 335; 350

Qafiḥ, Y. 458
Qedar, S. 121
Qimron, E. 332; 337; 350; 370; 397; 400; 506
Quell, G. 345

Raban, A. 9
Rabello, A. M. 253
Rabin, C. 334; 342
Rad, G. v. 18
Rajak, T. 208; 224; 227; 229f; 254; 307; 314
Ramsay, W. M. 314
Ranger, T. 197
Rappaport, U. 149; 152; 158; 208
Ravitzky, A. 472; 497
Raviv, H. 155
Reeg, G. 317
Reimer, G. 36
Reynolds, J. 265; 278; 316; 451
Riedweg, C. 159–176
Riesner, R. 27; 335
Ringgren, H. 31
Roberts, J. J. M. 6
Robinson, J. M. 557
Röhser, G. 403
Rogers, G. M. 308
Rogers, P. M. 230
Rokeah, D. 294; 300
Romm, J. S. 438
Root, M. C. 135
Rosenkranz, S. 453
Roth, C. 334; 344
Roth-Gerson, Lea 317
Rouse, W. H. D. 317
Routh, M. J. 110
Rowland, C. 405f; 409ff; 413; 419ff; 425; 427
Rubinsohn, Z. 492
Rudolph, K. 531
Runnals, D. 225
Rusten, J. C. 438

Sabbe, M. 421
Sachhi, P. 335
Sacks, K. S. 432
Safrai, S. 4; 396; 401; 485; 492; 498; 511
Saldarini, A. J. 511
Sanders, E. P. 503; 506
Sanders, J. A. 4; 361
Sanderson, J. E. 363
Sandmel, S. 334
Sarna, N. 100f
Scanlin, H. 4
Schäfer, P. 405; 414; 488; 538; 542; 544f; 562; 563
Schalit, A. 152; 223; 234; 257
Schaller, B. 148
Schechter, S. 375; 534; 548
Scheiber, A. 315
Schierling, M. J. 432
Schiffman, L. 205
Schiffman, L. H. 265; 269; 271; 279; 337; 370; 385
Schille, G. 432
Schlatter, A. 150; 193
Schlosser, J. 301
Schmid, W. 149
Scholem, G. 392; 405; 417; 533; 537; 557ff
Schreckenberg, H. 274f; 276; 453
Schürer, E. 148; 202; 206; 214; 265; 269; 274ff; 285; 287; 290; 376; 385; 391; 394; 451
Schuler, E. 221
Schuller, E. 348; 355
Schur, N. 474
Schwartz, D. R. 221; 233; 240; 261; 263f; 275f; 278f; 349
Schwartz, J. 188; 285; 484; 488; 493
Schwartz, S. 215; 230; 231; 240; 243ff
Schweitzer, A. 27
Seeligmann, I. L. 300
Segal, A. F. 99; 264; 271; 347; 413; 505
Segal, M. 199; 326
Senior, D. 439
Seow, C. L. 20
Seyrig, H. 128
Shaked, S. 542; 548
Sharvit, S. 511
Sheppard, A. R. 314
Sherk, R. K. 451
Shinan, A. 224
Shutt, J. H. 268
Shutt, R. J. 205

Siegel, J.P. 360ff; 366
Siegert, F. 265; 268
Sievers, J. 214; 237; 240
Silber, M. 198
Simon, M. 434
Sirat, C. 207; 457; 474
Skehan, P. 199; 356f; 363
Sly, D. 222
Smallwood, E.M. 248; 251; 255; 257; 285ff; 289f; 315
Smelik, W.F. 415
Smend, R. 37; 399
Smith, A. 200
Smith, J.Z. 420
Smith, M. 425
Smith, W.R. 35ff; 37
Snow, D.A. 450
Snyder, G.F. 422
Sottas, H. 188
Spaer, A. 121; 124; 126f
Sperber, D. 503f
Spicq, C. 264; 266
Spiegel, N. 156
Spiegel, S. 105
Spoerri, W. 434
Spuler, B. 455f
St. John Thackery, H. 223; 234; 236; 244f
Stählin, O. 149
Staerk, W. 530
Starcky, J. 393
Starr, C.G. 132; 133ff
Steck, O.H. 49ff; 53; 55f; 62f
Stegemann, H. 272; 335f; 355f
Steinschneider, M. 453; 457; 467
Steinthal, H. 203
Stemberger, G. 285f; 507
Sterling, G.E. 150f; 432
Stern, M. 150f; 156; 215; 224; 228; 230; 235; 243ff; 257f; 260; 264; 270; 276; 280; 285; 289f; 483
Stern, S. 507
Steudel, A. 357
Stillman, N. 457
Stinespring, W.F. 12
Stone, M. 532
Stroumsa, G. 200
Strugnell, J. 328; 337; 350; 357; 370; 385; 397; 400; 407; 506
Stuckenbruck, L. 410ff; 420
Stuhmuller, C. 439
Sukenik, E.L. 10; 324
Sussmann, Y. 201; 337; 370
Swetnam, J. 105

Tabor, J.T. 414
Täubler, A. 280
Talmage, F. 405
Talmon, S. 323; 327ff; 337; 339ff; 348; 350; 363; 371
Talmon, T. 346
Tannenbaum, R. 265; 272; 278; 316; 451
Taylor, C. 358
Taylor, J. 7
Taylor, S. 42
Tcherikover, V. 150; 152f; 208; 257; 287; 289
Teicher, J. 335
Theissen, G. 272
Thiering, B. 27
Thierry, B. 335
Thissen, H.-J. 188
Thompson, D.J. 285; 293
Thornton, C.J. 432
Tov, E. 330; 340; 353; 354; 365
Travers Herford, B.R. 511
Trebilco, P. 314f
Trebilco, P.R. 441
Trenchard, C.W. 222
Trocme, E. 432
Troiani, L. 501
Tsafrir, Y. 4
Turner, C.H. 290
Turner, G. 388
Tushingham, A.D. 336
Twersky, I. 476

Ulrich, E. 4; 340; 363; 366f
Urbach, E.E. 341; 349

Valckenaer, L.C. 171; 174
Van Den Broek, R. 295
Van Seters, J. 21
VanderKam, J.C. 28; 335f; 350
Veltri, G. 542
Vermes, G. 105f; 207; 376; 379; 385; 388; 502
Vermeylen, J. 45; 62
Versnel, H.S. 309
Veyne, P. 308
Vielhauer, P. 280
Vollkomer, R. 435
Vriezen, T.C. 31

Wacholder, B.Z. 148f; 223; 225; 234; 235
Walter, N. 148; 160ff; 162f
Wasserstein, A. 382
Watt, W.M. 467

Weber, M. 341; 343
Weber, W. 286; 295; 300
Wedderburn, A. J. M. 560
Weinberg, J. J. 270f
Weinfeld, M. 18; 23f
Weiskopf, M. 133
Weiss-Rosemarine, T. 228
Welch, A. T. 467
Wellhausen, J. 3; 35–42
Wendland, P. 150
Wertheimer, J. 198
Wewers, G. A. 405; 518
White, M. L. 307
Wieder, N. 335
Wiesehofer, J. 133
Wiessner, G. 420
Wilk, R. 150
Will, E. 265
Willrich, H. 148
Wilshire, L. E. 57; 58
Wilson, S. G. 264; 276
Wintermute, O. 204
Wirth, G. 134
Wise, M. 335; 344
Wolfson, H. A. 468f
Woude, A. S. v. d. 350
Wright, G. E. 18f; 32

Yadin, Y. 7; 10; 16; 20; 24; 155; 228; 324; 326ff
Yamauchi, E. 559

Zangenmeister, C. 287
Zangger, W. 9
Zeitlin, S. 217; 223; 244; 247f; 251; 335
Zerubavel, Y. 198
Zias, J. 25
Ziegler, J. 189
Zunz, L. 203